The Dwight and Lucille Beeson Wedgwood Collection at the Birmingham Museum of Art

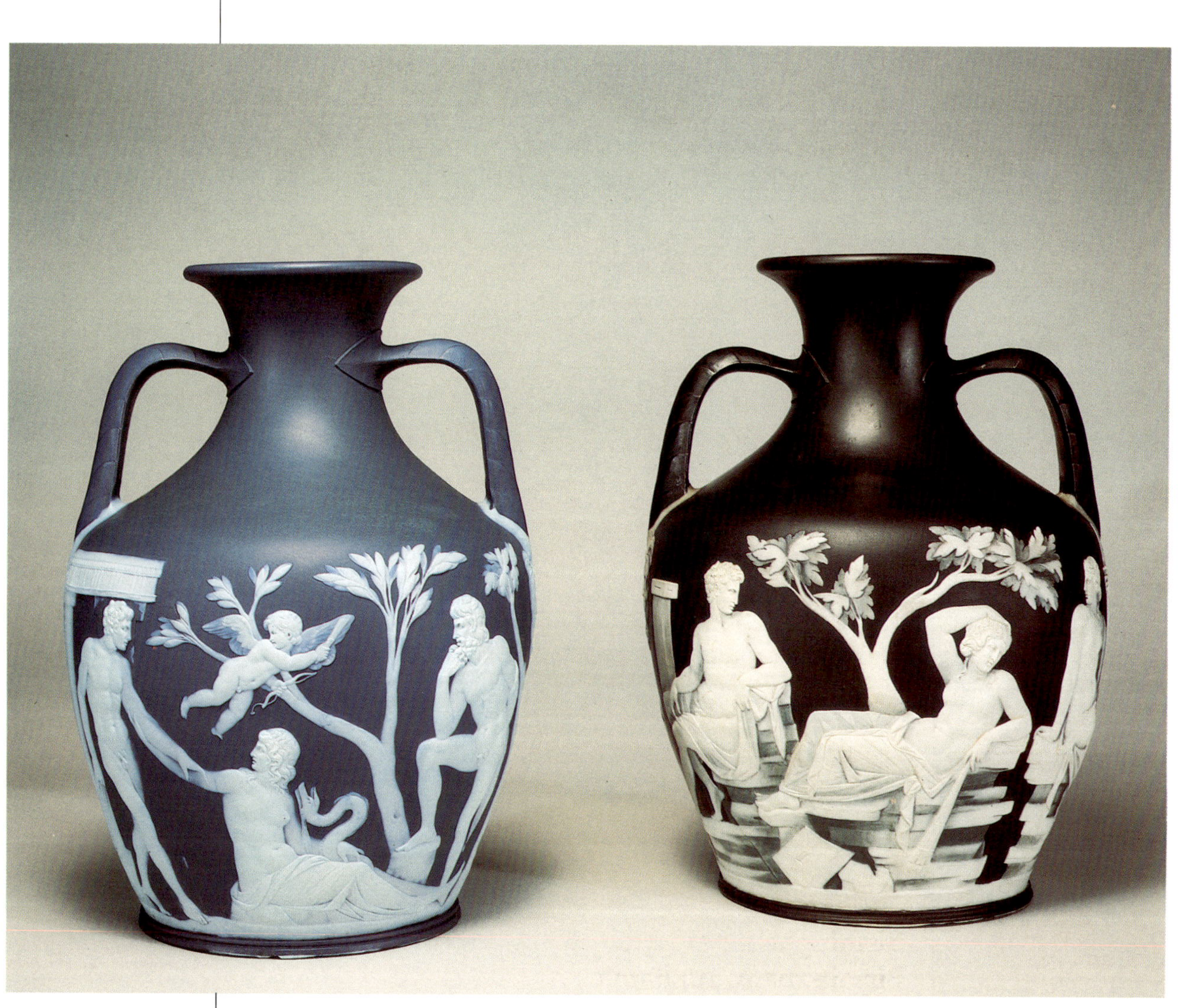

The Dwight and Lucille Beeson Wedgwood Collection at the Birmingham Museum of Art

Birmingham, Alabama

Elizabeth Bryding Adams

Birmingham Museum of Art
Birmingham, Alabama

Dedication

To Lucille Stewart Beeson
My Fairy Godmother
E. B. A.

(Cover) *Britannia Triumphant,* ca. 1798-1809, attributed to John Flaxman, Jr., modeler. Jasper, solid blue with blue wash, solid white ground with white wash and green relief; 13" x 11 7/16" (cat. 279).

(Frontispiece) Left, *Slate Blue Portland Vase Copy,* ca. 1791, jasper, solid slate blue ground with blue wash and white relief, 9 3/4" x 4 15/16" (cat. 292); right, *Darwin Portland Vase Copy,* 1790-92, jasper, solid black ground with black wash and white relief and addition of local color, 10" x 5 1/16" (cat. 291).

Library of Congress Cataloging-in-Publication Data

Birmingham Museum of Art (Birmingham, Ala.)
The Dwight and Lucille Beeson Wedgwood collection at the Birmingham Museum of Art, Birmingham, Alabama / Elizabeth Bryding Adams.
p. cm.
Includes bibliographical references and index.
ISBN 0-931394-32-5
1. Wedgwood ware--Catalogs. 2. Beeson, Dwight Moody, 1903–1985--Art collections--Catalogs. 3. Beeson, Lucille Stewart, 1905– --Art collections Catalogs. 4. Wedgwood ware--Private collections--Alabama--Birmingham--Catalogs. 5. Wedgwood--Alabama--Birmingham--Catalogs. 6. Birmingham Museum of Art (Birmingham, Ala.)--Catalogs. I. Beeson, Dwight Moody, 1903– 1985. II. Beeson, Lucille Stewart, 1905– . III. Adams, Elizabeth Bryding, 1953- . IV. Title.
NK4335.B62 1992
738.3 ' 09424 ' 63--dc20 92-4449
CIP

Notes

All references to Wedgwood manuscripts are to those on loan to Keele University, Stoke-on-Trent, England, or at the Wedgwood Museum at Barlaston, Stoke-on-Trent. These manuscripts are cited by kind permission of the trustees of the Wedgwood Museum. Spelling and punctuation have been left in the original form. The letters "W/M" before accession numbers indicate the Wedgwood/Moseley Collection; "LHP" designates the Leith Hill Place Collection; and "E" stands for manuscripts from Etruria, referring to specific letters from Josiah Wedgwood to Thomas Bentley. Catalog, oven books, pattern books, shape books, pottery memos, and commonplace books are primary documents also housed at the Wedgwood Museum.

This catalog was funded by a generous grant from the National Endowment for the Arts, a federal agency, and by Mrs. Lucille Stewart Beeson.

Photography

Color photographs are by Owen Murphy, Jr., and Harold Kilgore. Black-and-white photographs are by George Flemming, Robert Linthout, Owen Murphy, Jr., and Harold Kilgore.

This catalog was copy edited by Brenda Waldron Kolb, and was designed by Joan Kennedy. Typography was output by Compos-It, Inc., in Schneidler medium; color separations are by Capitol Engraving, Birmingham; printing is by EBSCO Media, Inc., on 80 lb. Signature dull, an acid free paper.

Contents

Preface

Today, the cataloging of any decorative arts collection is a task not speedily accomplished. The connoisseur and material culturalist cannot analyze an object simply by examining its outward appearance; he or she must now delve into the life of its maker and the history of its times to understand fully its use, construction, and decoration. For this book on the Dwight and Lucille Beeson Wedgwood Collection, each piece has been thoroughly researched, with the documentation coming from many primary and secondary sources. The Wedgwood archive, on loan to Keele University, Stoke-on-Trent, England, holds approximately seventy-five thousand documents that pertain to the life and business of Josiah Wedgwood—a remarkable number of documents on one man and his company, equaled in the twentieth century only by the papers in the depositories for United States presidents and other internationally significant public figures. Needless to say, with so massive an amount of material, the study of Josiah Wedgwood could fill a lifetime and, indeed, has done so for a number of British scholars. Fortunately for this author, much of the material has been read by others and a portion of it published, although the total is still being cataloged, with a completion date of roughly the year 2000. Thus this book is based on secondary sources that reprint primary material and on correspondence with researchers, archaeologists, and curators in this country and England. With the new research on early English pottery now coming to light, which has turned the whole field of English pottery upside down, axioms concerning Wedgwood are currently being reexamined and are particularly challenged in Robin Reilly's *Wedgwood*, published in 1989. Both enlightening and frustrating, the reanalysis has upset many of what Wedgwood scholars had previously held to be truths.

Excavation of 3 of the 130 to 150 pottery sites in the Staffordshire area reveals that most of the potters were producing tortoiseshell ware, salt glaze, blackware, red stoneware, and cream ware at the same time. Historians of ceramics hope that many more such sites will be excavated in the future, so that, by locating and reviewing primary documents about each pottery and by examining existing signed or marked pieces, we can be confident about what wares were made by which pottery. For now, origin can be determined only if the decoration and other physical evidence of a shard from one of the excavations match exactly the decoration and other physical characteristics of a particular piece preserved intact in another collection.

Thus, in hopes of challenging the reader to investigate the many recent and forthcoming monographs based on archaeological evidence and primary documents, the author has proceeded cautiously in providing information and has left out many of the dicta of past histories of ceramics. It is also hoped that the bibliography will aid and encourage the reader to research this new material and reanalyze his or her collection accordingly.

Acknowledgments

There are many people who have aided me in the four-year production of this book. First and foremost I would like to thank my dear friend Lucille Stewart Beeson for the gift of Wedgwood that she and her husband, Dwight, made to the Birmingham Museum of Art. She has waited patiently during the long road to publication. Without her wonderful resource library, previous research on catalog cards, and continual encouragement, this book would never have come to fruition. Indeed, it has been a pleasure and an honor to work with such a fine collection.

Second, I am grateful to the board of the Birmingham Museum of Art for allowing me the time to complete the work. Third, I wish to thank Frances Sommers, Katherine Estes, and Gail Trechsel, the former curator of decorative arts at the Birmingham Museum of Art, all of whom helped with the research and the cataloging of the fourteen hundred objects in the collection. Joan Kennedy was responsible for the beautiful layout of the book as well as moral support to the author; and Brenda Kolb patiently and efficiently took on the tremendous job of editing. I would like to thank other museum staff members: Lisa Stewart, Portia Stallworth, and Diann Walton.

I am most appreciative, for the use of the primary materials, to the trustees of the Wedgwood Museum, Barlaston, Stoke-on-Trent, and Keele University Library, where the Wedgwood manuscripts are deposited. Gaye Blake Roberts, curator of the Wedgwood Museum in Barlaston, England, kindly read the manuscript to check for the accuracy of its technical and documentary information. Several scholars in England have been of great assistance: David Barker, Aileen Dawson, Ann Eatwell, Pat Halfpenny, Terrence Lockett, Lynn Miller, Michael Raeburn, Robin Reilly, Hugh Tait, and Lorna Weatherill. American colleagues to whom I am indebted include John Austin, Carolyn Conley, Raymond Lane, Nancy Ramage, and the interlibrary loan department of the Birmingham Public Library.

I would like to thank my family for their help and understanding. I am grateful, also, to the National Endowment for the Arts for its funding of a professional development grant that allowed me to travel to England in 1988 to study English ceramics and for its partial funding of this book.

And, finally, I extend my thanks, again, to Dwight and Lucille Beeson, who provided the balance of the monies needed to publish this book, including its fine color illustrations.

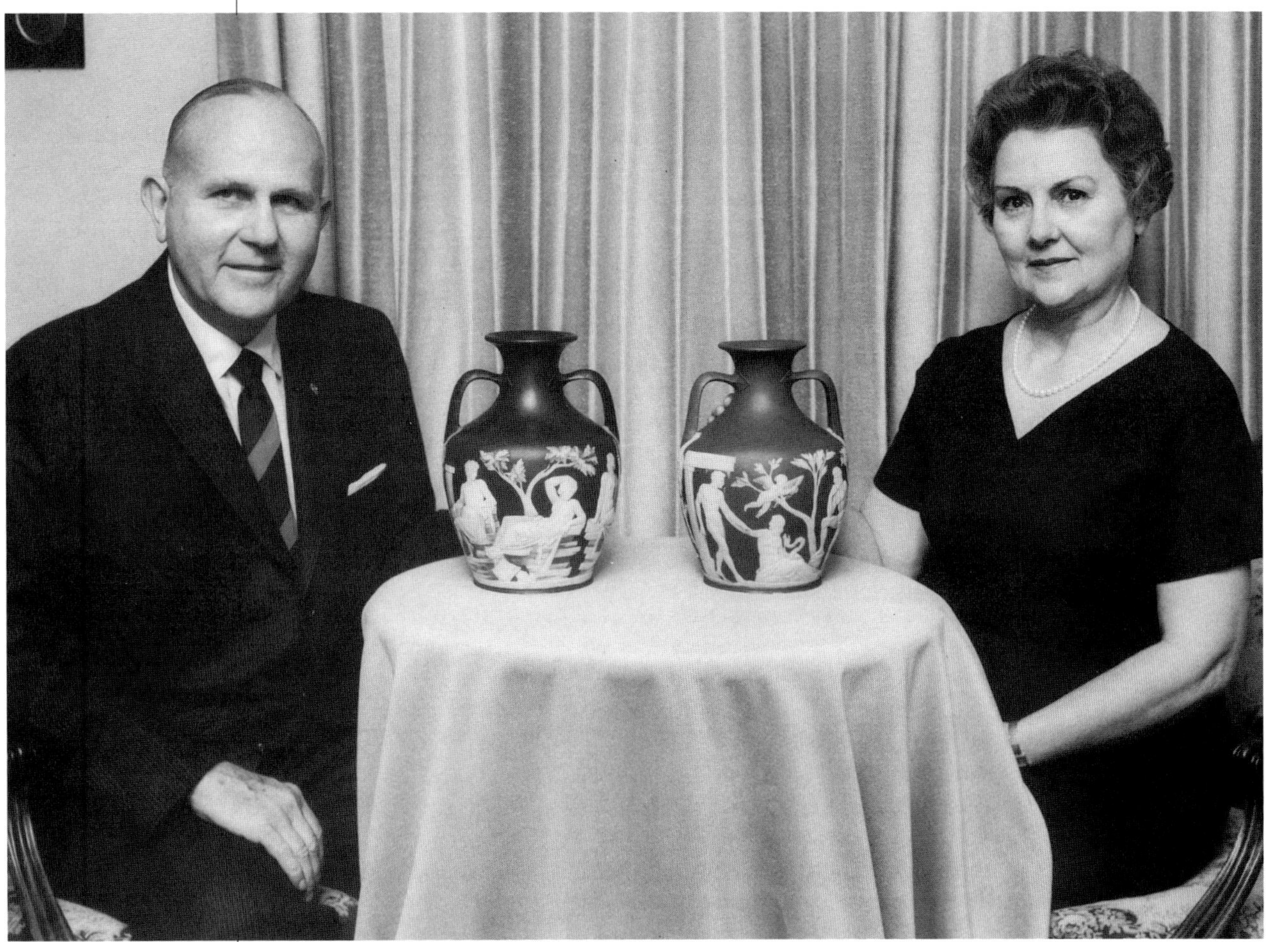

Fig. 1 *Dwight and Lucille Beeson with their eighteenth-century copies of the Portland vase.*

Introduction

Dwight and Lucille Beeson began collecting Wedgwood around 1946. The Beesons had traveled to New York, where Mrs. Beeson saw an exhibition of Wedgwood and other eighteenth-century pottery at the Metropolitan Museum of Art and was particularly fascinated with the delicacy of the bas-relief figures on Wedgwood's jasper ware and the process of its application. Not long afterward, Mrs. Beeson began buying a few pieces—first a pair of jasper-ware vases (ca. 1880) (cat. 382) and then a jasper portrait medallion of Lord Camden (ca. 1780) (cat. 699). Mr. Beeson had not yet been bitten by the collecting bug. But during an illness that confined him to bed, he asked his wife to read to him for entertainment, and she shared a biography of Josiah Wedgwood, thus beginning Mr. Beeson's interest in and knowledge of Wedgwood and his ware. Soon thereafter, on a trip to New Orleans, Mr. Beeson located, in a shop on Royal Street, eight more pieces of Wedgwood, which he purchased.

As they continued to collect Wedgwood, the Beesons also collected and studied books on the subject, eventually building an outstanding library of most of the publications about Wedgwood that had been published from the nineteenth century onward. In addition, Mrs. Beeson collected copies of many of the eighteenth-century books that Wedgwood had in his own library—books that had served as design sources, particularly for Wedgwood's jasper ware.

In 1965 Mrs. Beeson saw an exhibition of wares from the Wedgwood and Bentley period (1769-80). The quality of the pieces was most impressive, leading the Beesons to concentrate only on objects from this time. According to Mrs. Beeson, it took a long time to reach that point. "You have to buy a lot before you feel that you are expert enough to buy more expensive pieces. As you develop a sense about them, you want to discard some and then refine the collection."

Dwight Moody Beeson (1903-85) was a native of Mississippi. After graduating from Emory University, he began his lifelong association with Liberty National Life Insurance Company, now the Torchmark Corporation. Lucille Stewart Beeson was born in 1905 in Tennessee. One of the first women to receive a law degree from the Atlanta Law School, she later entered the field of accountancy for a number of years before marrying Mr. Beeson. The couple has contributed generously to the cultural life of the city of Birmingham, Alabama, to Samford University in Birmingham, and to Bob Jones University in Greenville, South Carolina. As was Josiah Wedgwood in the eighteenth century, Mr. and Mrs. Beeson were elected, in 1968, to the Royal Society for the Encouragement of Arts, Manufactures, and Commerce in England, founded in London in 1754. Both Beesons were also long-time members of the boards of the Birmingham Museum of Art and the Wedgwood International Seminar.

The Beeson collection of roughly fourteen hundred pieces was assembled through purchases at auction, from dealers, and from other collectors such as Ann Brodkiewicz, M. Mellanay Delhom, Fred and Mary Tongue, and Charles Smith. In addition, the Beesons purchased two major collections, one in 1965 from Dr. Harold L. Klawans of Chicago and the other in 1967 from the estate of Dr. Francis Jennings Vurpillat of South Bend, Indiana. Mrs. Beeson continues to add rare examples of Wedgwood to the collection even today.

Until 1975 the Beesons' Wedgwood graced their home in Birmingham. The pieces were used in an eighteenth-century manner, with busts on top of bookcases, plaques on walls, and garniture on mantels. The decision was then made to donate the collection to the Birmingham Museum of Art. Mrs. Beeson later wrote in the *American Wedgwoodian*: "Wedgwood has been my world for over thirty years! When one has had a long-time dream and has seen it realized, has personally placed each object in a beautiful new gallery—well, I do have a special pride."

The Dwight and Lucille Beeson Wedgwood Collection is permanently displayed in a 2,500-square-foot gallery at the Birmingham Museum of Art. The exhibition reveals the development of Wedgwood pottery from the red stoneware produced in the 1760s to the work of Émile-Aubert Lessore produced in the 1870s. While highlighting the major objects in the collection, the gallery also shows even the tiny intaglios in a historical context with visual clarity.

In addition, the Birmingham Museum of Art houses a portion of the archives of the Wedgwood International Seminar, which held meetings in Birmingham in 1978 and 1990, as well as the books from the Beeson library and the Elizabeth Chellis Wedgwood library, purchased by Lucille Stewart Beeson for the museum in 1992. The Chellis library contains over one thousand pieces, including books, letters, and catalogs, pertaining to life in the eighteenth century as well as English pottery and porcelain in general and that of Josiah Wedgwood in particular. Acclaimed in January of 1963 by *The American Wedgwoodian* as "America's largest Wedgwood library," the book collection marvelously complements the unsurpassed quality of the Beeson's Wedgwood and establishes the Birmingham Museum of Art as a center for research and study of eighteenth-century English ceramics.

1
The Pottery Industry in Eighteenth-Century England

In order to understand fully the history of Josiah Wedgwood and his success in the pottery industry, one must study the history of England in general and the Staffordshire area in particular. In 1603, with the succession of James I to the throne, England fell into a state of political and religious turmoil that did not subside until the reign of William and Mary and the establishment of the Bill of Rights in 1689. England was primarily a rural country of small hamlets and towns whose populations totaled five million people; there were, however, half of a million people already living in London. England was also on the way to becoming the world's greatest mercantile power, banking and credit capital, and naval force. These factors, together with revolutionary scientific developments, aided the new consumerism, then in its infancy, and its insatiable demand for new goods.

Potters had been functioning in the Staffordshire area from late medieval times, producing such items as butter pots, storage jars, salt kits, and cooking pots. The area was not agriculturally rich, but the natural resources of timber, coal, and fine clays promised longevity for the pottery industry. Dairy farming was important, but there was no other rival trade, so most of the province's capital and talent were directed toward pottery. Because five to twelve tons of coal were needed to process one ton of clay, most potteries were located near coal deposits. Advancing the mining of coal in the 1690s was a modest scientific invention by Thomas Newcomen (1663-1729) and Thomas Savery (ca. 1650-1715): "a machine for raising water by fire." It was used to pump water out of the coal mines, whose frequent flooding slowed the excavation process. With this flooding problem removed, the delivery and mining of coal became a national industry and created immense fortunes. Potters were among the many businessmen who contracted with mining firms for their fuel.

The first potworks were simply small outbuildings accessory to family cottages and farmhouses. But the expertise of a skilled and industrious work force, which was passed within families from one generation to the next, was Staffordshire's greatest asset, and in the eighteenth century it oversaw a great expansion in production and the number of factories, employees, and exported products. Improvements were made in factory buildings and their organization as well as division of labor, production techniques, and transportation. Wedgwood himself wrote that, by 1710, Burslem, home of Wedgwood's potworks, had become a prominent pottery center, probably the largest in Great Britain, and that it had already acquired a name for its skill and craftsmanship. In fact, between 1660 and 1710 and again between 1711 and 1750, the number of potters working in the Staffordshire area more than doubled. While traveling through the district in 1750, Richard Pococke described the wares of the potteries: "Stoke made white stoneware; Shelton was 'famous for the red china'; Hanley made 'all sorts of pottery'; Burslem produced 'the best white and many other sorts'; and Tunstall made 'all sorts' and was 'famous for the best bricks and tiles.'" He further listed "white stoneware glazed with salt, dry red china ware, glazed redware, coloured glaze stoneware, japanned ware, tortoise-shell, enamelled, and a variety of self-coloured wares, blue, yellow, brown, and dove-colour."[1] Recent archaeological excavations of the William Greatbatch dumping site in Lower Lane in Staffordshire confirm that this variety of wares was indeed produced. They show that the Staffordshire pottery industry comprised not only Wedgwoods, Spodes, and Turners but also many individuals whose names have not appeared in documents.

Continued research and archaeological investigation may someday reveal a more accurate picture.

In 1763 a petition concerning the improvement of the local roads was made to Parliament, and it gives a picture of what the potteries had become:

> In Burslem and its neighbourhood are near 150 separate Potteries for making various kinds of stone and earthenware, which, together find constant employment and support for near 7000 people. The ware of these Potteries is exported in vast quantities from London, Bristol, Liverpool, Hull, and other seaports to our several colonies in America and the West Indies, as well as to every port in Europe.[2]

The growth in Staffordshire is attributed to many factors. One was technical advancement in the coal-mining industry (as mentioned above). A second was the use of raw materials that were being imported for the first time, including white ball clays from the coastal areas of Devon and Dorset in southwestern England and flint (used to strengthen and lighten the color of the clay) from the coastal areas of eastern England. Ball clay began to be substituted for the brown, orange, and yellow local clays in about 1710. While it vitrified at relatively low temperatures, it could be used in mixtures of clay and siliceous materials for stoneware fired at higher temperatures. The major problems with ball clay and flint were the expense in transporting them from the coast and the fluctuations in their availability. By the end of the eighteenth century, from one-third to one-half of the product was flint, which prevented the glazes from crazing. Raw flint had to be broken down from a crystalline form into a powder by heating and grinding. Prior to 1719 the flint was ground with a mortar and pestle; later the grinding was accomplished in open stone mills. However, both methods proved to be hazardous, for the airborne particles of ground flint were ingested by workers and caused debilitating diseases. Waterpowered flint mills were developed by 1725, and the grinding became a wet process conducted in closed areas in order to contain the dust.

Within the Staffordshire area were six pottery towns—Burslem, Fenton, Hanley, Longton, Stoke-on-Trent, and Tunstall—known collectively as "the Potteries." They were located on an irregular line along deposits of clay and coal. The grinding and washing processes were aided by water, which was readily available. In the late seventeenth century, the working life of the people was rather modest, characterized by simple tools and raw materials. Yet, only a few decades later, these domestic enterprises were developing rapidly into small factories. This is evident by the number and size of the buildings needed to make pottery as well as the size of the surrounding land called into use; the increasing value and amount of the equipment, tools, and materials used; and the specialization of labor skills, with one factory employing as many as twenty to twenty-five employees. Arnold Bennett wrote of the people of the Staffordshire potteries: "The horse is less to the Arab than clay is to the Bursley [Burslem] man. He exists in it and by it: it fills his lungs and blanches his cheeks; it keeps him alive and it kills him. His fingers close round it as round the hand of a friend. He knows all its tricks and aptitudes; when to coax and when to force it, when to rely on it and when to distrust it."[3]

By 1760 the potteries in Staffordshire had reached industrial scale. Josiah Wedgwood was the first manufacturer to organize a labor force by skills, a method that proved to be most productive as well as a deterrent to disease caused by the ingestion of ground flint. The apprenticeship program, through which Wedgwood himself had learned his trade, had begun to decline in the late seventeenth century, and his establishment of factory discipline, his segregating workers by specific tasks, altered it still more.

By the end of the eighteenth century, a multitude of smoke-bellowing bottle kilns contaminated the air in Staffordshire. In addition to flint and lead poisoning from the glazing of pottery, the air pollution also caused the area to suffer a high mortality rate, a condition that was not improved until the middle of the twentieth century.

Consumerism

In the middle of the eighteenth century, the social structure of England was beginning to change. From medieval times there had been a great disparity between the nobility and the lower classes. However, in the eighteenth century, as the middle and lower classes began to increase in number, wealth, and stature, they sought to emulate the aristocracy by purchasing goods and luxuries previously enjoyed only by the upper classes, thus stimulating the dynamics of supply and demand. Luxuries came to be seen as mere decencies, and decencies came to be seen as necessities. Where material possessions were once valued according to their durability, they were now increasingly valued according to their fashionability. This desire to consume was not what was novel in the eighteenth century; rather, what was new was the ability to consume. Rich clothes, fine furs, and precious gems marked the divinity of a king and radiated the splendor and standing of his court. They could also underline the exclusive status of the nobility or the professional status of lawyers, doctors, and the educated elite.

The spending boom approached revolutionary proportions in the third quarter of the eighteenth century. With all classes enjoying what was called "universal luxury,"[4] men and, in particular, women purchased as never before, the rich leading the way. The construction of magnificent houses reached a crescendo in the 1760s and 1770s, when the Adam brothers designed or redesigned many neoclassical buildings. Sophisticated furniture was commissioned from the published directories of Chippendale, Hepplewhite, and Sheraton. High-quality porcelain and pottery appeared for the first time in English history, furnished by the Chelsea, Bow, Worcester, and Derby factories for the wealthy and by Wedgwood for those less privileged. Wonderful new gardens were created, and whole estates were replanted for posterity. The novelty of fashion became irresistible, with the masses insisting upon possessing good pottery, furniture, fabrics, cutlery, wallpaper, and even improved breeds of animals. In imitation of the rich, the middle ranks spent more, while, in imitation of the latter, the rest of society joined in as best they could. Whole newspapers were devoted to advertisements, engendering a rewarding market response for such prolific inventiveness. As long as the inventor could make his new product fashionable and accessible and could disperse it widely through commercial agents, it would sell. Temporary tangents from the prevailing "Greek" style allowed the market to be refreshed with such novelties as the sphinxes and crocodiles of the Egyptian style as well as variations on the Chinese and Gothic styles, but, in general, neoclassicism dominated the English market.

The intellectual origins of the consumption revolution can be traced to the 1690s. The rich were expected to buy the luxuries and the poor to have enough to subsist. That all levels of society might acquire what they coveted, generating new spending and producing habits capable of destroying all traditional limits to the wealth of nations, was unthinkable. It was not until the last decade of the seventeenth century that the idea of consumption lost its pejorative meaning. Through spending, self-improvement and genuine social mobility had gradually become possible and acceptable.

Such views were accompanied by changing attitudes toward labor wages. High wages were both socially and economically desirable, acting as an incentive for the work force and allowing workers to benefit from the growing output of consumer goods. Indeed, wages did gradually improve during the seventeenth and eighteenth centuries. Whole families were employed for long hours at these rising wage rates, thus increasing their overall earnings. Wives went to work, thereby increasing the demand for goods that had once been made at home. These women were often employed as domestic servants and therefore became another vital link to the spending habits and life-styles of the upper and middle classes. They also became a channel by which the latest styles were communicated and the desire for new commodities was spread. Increased consumption further boosted demand and thus the interests of the work force, the entrepreneurs, and the economy.

Another prime advantage for the creation of a consumer society in England lay in the size and character of its capital city. The remarkable growth of London—from some 200,000 inhabitants in 1600 to 900,000 in 1800—was unique in Europe. One in six of the total adult population of England had lived or was living in London and therefore had been exposed to the shops, the life-style, and the prevailing fashions in this vibrant city. London also had a long history of demand for pottery, including delftware, porcelain, and finer stoneware. By the 1750s Chelsea and Bow had factories and warehouses that produced and sold in London.

A considerable obstacle to this expansion of the pottery industry was the state of transportation. Because roads were barely passable by carts in summer and were altogether impassable in winter, pottery was often carried on the backs of workmen. The packhorse was also used to transport both raw materials and the finished product. Each packhorse could carry but two crates, making the development of a national market difficult. Thus, as early as 1760, Josiah Wedgwood joined Thomas Whieldon and eight other Burslem potters to begin constructing turnpikes (toll roads). In 1765 a scheme was devised to connect the rivers of Trent and Mersey by a canal, in effect linking the potteries with Liverpool and Hull. The River Weaver had been canalized in 1733, linking Staffordshire with London wholesalers and retailers. Wedgwood then produced a pamphlet, written by Thomas Bentley and corrected by Erasmus Darwin, setting out the advantages and savings of canals. Thus the packhorse took the pottery to the river; the pottery was then shipped down to the port; and then the pottery was transported along the coast to the larger markets. For Wedgwood's convenience the canal also passed alongside his factory, Etruria. The full canal system, completed in 1777, was estimated by Wedgwood to cost a total of three hundred thousand pounds.[5]

Wedgwood and Marketing

Josiah Wedgwood capitalized on the new societal demands in several ways. First, he improved or invented several ceramic bodies, the first being cream ware, which imitated porcelain in its lightness and beauty but was more durable and less expensive to produce. Second, he did not charge the amount his pottery was worth in terms of its production costs; he charged what the nobility would pay for it. Wedgwood wrote to Bentley on August 23, 1772, that "a great price was . . . at first necessary to make the Vases esteemed Ornaments for Palaces."[6] Third, he capitalized on the latest tastes, especially neoclassicism; his wares emulated the strengths of Greek and Roman art and society. He even went so far as to dictate what to call his wares. Wedgwood wrote to Bentley in February of 1769:

> Urns [are] a better name very true, call them so, I have consulted Mr. Chambers upon the difference between Urns & Vases, he says there is a real difference in the characters. . . . The Character of Urns is simplicity, to have covers, but no handles, nor spouts, they are Monumental, they may be either high or low, but

sho[d]. not seem to be Vessels for culinary, or Sacred uses,—Vases as such as might be used for libations, & other sacrificial, festive & culinary uses, such as Ewers, open vessels &c.[7]

Fourth, reacting to the needs of his time, Wedgwood produced a range of goods that accommodated every aspect of life, from kitchen to dining room, drawing room to garden, and conservatory to dairy. Other examples include bin labels for the cellar, bidets for the bathroom, and dog bowls for the kennels, objects that provided for all the daily needs from birth to death. Wedgwood gave his eighteenth-century customer—whether eating, drinking, cleaning, or entertaining—a remarkable range of household consumer goods.

Wedgwood realized that new materials alone were not enough. They had to be turned into articles reflecting the latest artistic taste, which would establish his reputation in fashionable society. With his partner, Thomas Bentley, Wedgwood sensed the lure of the neoclassical style and was able to give it expression in ceramics as no other European potter could. "Elegant simplicity" was the hallmark of neoclassicism, and Wedgwood's wares, both useful and ornamental, were its supreme manifestation in ceramics. Wedgwood was also fortunate to enjoy the encouragement and advice of one of the greatest advocates of the revived interest in the classical art: Sir William Hamilton, British ambassador to the court of Naples. Hamilton's four volumes on Etruscan, Greek, and Roman antiquities provided a rich source for Wedgwood's designs.[8] On May 23, 1786, in a letter from Naples, Hamilton paid Wedgwood a generous compliment:

> It is with infinite satisfaction that I reflect upon having been in some measure instrumental in introducing a purer taste of forms & ornaments by having placed my Collection of Antiquities in the British Museum, but a Wedgwood and Bentley were necessary to diffuse that taste so universally, and it is to their liberal way of thinking & industry that so good a taste prevails at present in Great Britain. I have always and will always do them that justice.[9]

Wedgwood made his wares popular by numerous marketing schemes. In 1767, through an order of a cream-ware tea set from Queen Charlotte, he was granted the title of "Potter to Her Majesty." If the queen desired Wedgwood's ware, so would the aristocracy; using the product meant having tastes and values similar to those of royalty. Wedgwood wrote on June 19, 1779, "Fashion is infinitely superior to merit in many respects; & it is plain from a thousand instances that if you have a favourite child you wish the public to fondle & take notice of, you have only to make choice of proper sponsers [*sic*]."[10] He then sent special pieces with foreign ambassadors as gifts to their respective sovereigns. This introduced Wedgwood's ware to the world and led to a commission by Catherine the Great of Russia for a dinner and dessert service consisting of 952 pieces.

Wedgwood backed his introductory approach with a score of marketing techniques, many of them used as well by Chelsea and Bow in the 1750s. Knowing that the landed gentry visited London for "the Season" and went to Bath for the health-restoring waters, he engaged in both places splendid showrooms to display his wares. Liverpool and Dublin were sites of later showrooms. As he wrote to Bentley on May 23, 1767, "We must have an Elegant, extensive, & Convent[t]. shew room, with store rooms, & some conveniences for two servants."[11] It would enable him "to shew various Table & desert services completely set out on two ranges of Tables, six or eight at least[;] such services are absolutely necessary to be shewn in order to do the needfull with the Ladys in the neatest, genteelest & best method. The same, or indeed a much greater variety of setts of Vases sho[d]. decorate the Walls, & both these articles may, every few days, be so alter'd, revers'd, & transform'd as to render the whole a new scene."[12] The accessibility of the showroom was limited to the middle to upper classes; as Wedgwood wrote to Bentley, "for you well know they [the gentry] will not mix with the rest of the World any farther than their amusements, or conveniencys make it necessary to do so."[13] Further, Wedgwood wrote suggesting that Bentley show the vases exclusively in order to emphasize their rarity and prevent others from copying as long as possible:

> I think you sho^{d}. make a point of shewing, & selling these yourself only. . . . They may without offence tell any customer that you take that branch of business upon yourself—They will think them the more precious—you can tell them the history of the piece & all about it, & let them know that we do not make good things by chance, or at randum [*sic*]—It will baulk the spies for some time at least who are daily haunting the rooms, & answer many other valuable purposes.[14]

Indeed, the showrooms were successful, for Wedgwood wrote on May 1, 1769, that there was "No geting [*sic*] to the door for Coaches, nor into the rooms for Ladies & Gentn."[15]

Wedgwood and Bentley also advertised in newspapers. A draft advertisement that Wedgwood sent for approval to Bentley on February 17, 1771, reads as follows:

> JOSIAH WEDGWOOD POTTER TO HER MAJESTY being honor'd with the continued patronage & support of the Nobility & Gentry of these Kingdoms, constantly endeavours to give to his manufacture all the variety & perfection he is able; & with this view he has lately model'd & finish'd. at very great expence, all the Articles necessary for a complete Table & Desert service of a new pattern, in which he has endeavour'd to unite beauty of form, with the greatest simplicity. . . . The Goods are deliver'd safe & carr^{e}. free to London, for ready money only.[16]

Wedgwood later related, in writing to his wife on March 2, 1769; "I have very little time to say farther at present, only I must acquaint you that customers come in apace in consequence of the advertisem^{ts}."[17]

Another opportunity for career advancement came in 1783, when Wedgwood was elected to the Royal Society, and he took full advantage of the honor. The Beeson collection contains two white jasper medallions with blue decoration impressed, on the front, "By J. Wedgwood F. R. S." and, on the back, "No. 10" and "No. 170," respectively (cats. 726, 727). They are thought to have been made to accompany pyrometer sets (see p. 31), again showing Wedgwood's great prominence and his success in the arts.[18]

But capturing the English market was not enough for Wedgwood. He wrote on August 6, 1770, "With respect to the sale of Vases, . . . if we cannot sell enough in London we must try elsewhere & I cannot think of any other places so proper as Dublin & Bath, unless we can make an inroad into China which I think we sho^{d}. endeavour to effect, but this last must be a work of time & I think we sho^{d}. try the other places in the interim."[19]

With great excitement, Wedgwood considered every country in the world a challenge to his marketing abilities. France, however, tempted him the most, to judge from the following pronouncement, which he made on September 13, 1769: "And do you really think we may make a complete conquest of France? Conquer France in Burslem?—My blood moves quicker, I feel my strength increase for the contest.—Assist me my friend, & the victorie is our own. . . . We will fash^{n}. our Porcelain after their own hearts, & captivate them with the Elegance & simplicity of the Ancients."[20]

2
Staffordshire Pottery

In the Beeson collection, there are numerous examples of early-eighteenth-century pottery made in the Staffordshire area prior to Wedgwood's production. As the pieces are not marked, their attribution to Staffordshire can be only tentative. The bodies include red stoneware, blackware, salt glaze, tortoiseshell, agate ware, and cream ware. In this grouping are pieces attributed directly to the Elers brothers, Thomas Whieldon, William Greatbatch, and Josiah Wedgwood.

The most common pottery in Staffordshire in the mid-eighteenth century was unglazed red stoneware, which was inspired by the Chinese Yixing ware made from the sixteenth century onward. Large deposits of this red clay in Staffordshire made it easily accessible to the potters. The ware was perfected by John Philip Elers and David Elers, the Dutch brothers whose refined work may be accounted for by the fact that they were originally silversmiths. They made "brown jugs" and "red teapots" at Vauxhall in London from about 1690 to 1693, then moved to Bradwell Wood in northern Staffordshire until sometime in 1698. As Wedgwood stated to Bentley on July 19, 1777, "The next improvement introduc'd by Mr. E. [John Philip Elers] was the refining of our common red clay, by sifting, & making it into Tea & Coffee Ware in imitation of the Chinese Red Porcelaine, by casting it in plaister moulds, & turning it on the outside upon Lathes, & ornamenting it with the Tea branch in relief, in imitation of the Chinese manner of ornamenting this ware."[1]

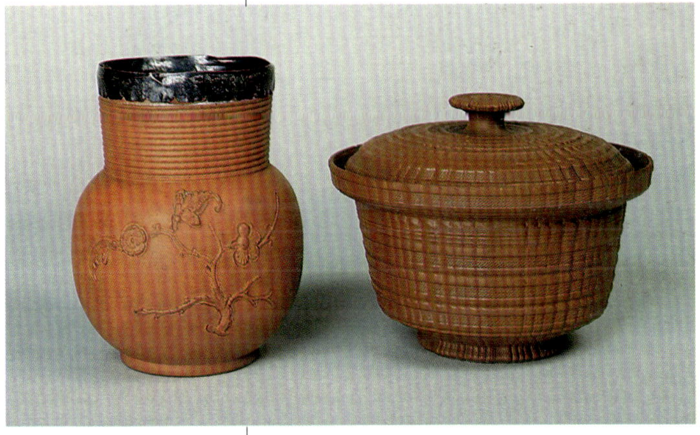

Color plate 1 Left, *Mug, ca. 1690, red stoneware with applied decoration with silver rim, 4 1/2" x 2" (cat. 12);* right, *Sugar Bowl, 1760-70, red stoneware with "rose" engine-turning, 3 5/8" x 3 3/16" (cat. 13).*

Wedgwood's reference to "casting it in plaister moulds" alludes to a process called slip casting, by which the red clay was mixed with water and poured into a plaster mold, the excess was poured off, and the remaining clay was allowed to dry, after which the mold was removed. A slip-cast mug in the Beeson collection is attributed to the Elerses, thus dating it to about 1695 (cat. 12, pl. 1). The piece has an unglazed, bulbous body with a lathe-turned, ribbed neck topped by a silver rim. Pseudo-Chinese plum blossoms in mold-applied relief decorate the side. No mark appears on the bottom.

Wedgwood made some pieces of red stoneware in his earliest years of production, although generally not by slip casting but by the potter's wheel. He is credited with the first use of "rosette" engine turning for decoration. Pieces of redware with this type of decoration and an imitation Chinese mark that includes a "W" (shards have been found at Wedgwood's factory site at Brick House) have been attributed to Wedgwood.[2] An unglazed, rosette-turned sugar bowl in the Beeson collection has five of these marks on the lid and one mark on the bottom of the bowl (cat. 13, pl. 1). With the rise of neoclassical taste, red stoneware became unfashionable until in 1776, when Wedgwood refined the body and christened it with a new name: rosso antico (see p. 155).

Another creamer and a teapot in the Beeson collection (cats. 18, 19, pl. 2) are in the so-called blackware, often given the generic name "Jackfield," referring to pottery produced at two sites, one in Shropshire and the other in Staffordshire. The body of the ware from Shropshire is made of red earthenware completely covered with a

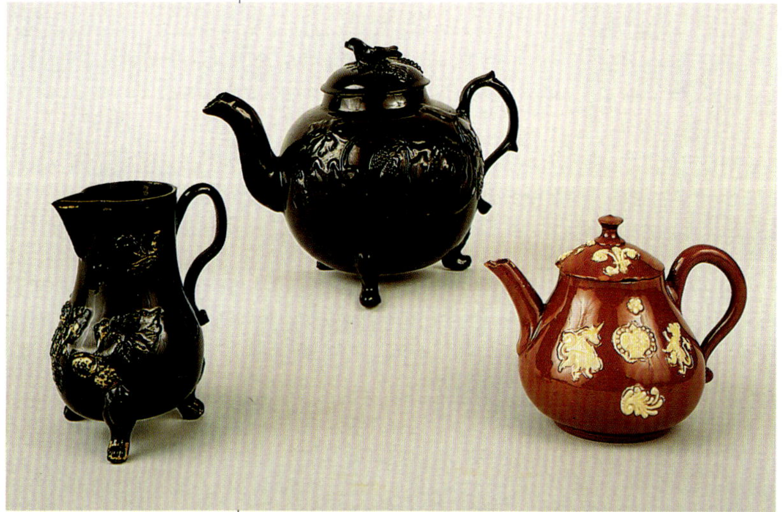

Color plate 2 Left, *Cream Pitcher,* Jackfield, *ca. 1755-60, red stoneware colored with manganese and iron oxides covered with clear glaze and applied decoration with gilding, 4 3/8" x 2 3/4" (cat. 18);* center, *Teapot,* Jackfield, *ca. 1755-60, red stoneware colored with manganese and iron oxides covered with clear glaze and applied decoration with gilding, 5 1/2" x 4 3/4" (cat. 19);* right, *Teapot,* Lion and Unicorn, *ca. 1780, red earthenware with interior and exterior glaze and applied cream-ware decoration, 5 1/4" x 2 1/4" (cat. 6).*

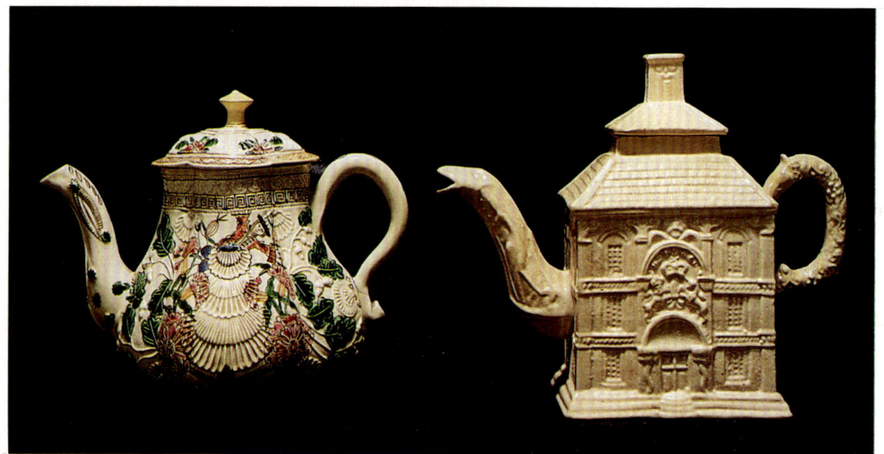

Color plate 3 Left, *Teapot,* Prince Charles Stuart, the Young Pretender, *ca. 1760, stoneware, salt-glazed with overglaze polychrome enamels, 4 3/4" x 2 3/4" (cat. 5);* right, *Teapot,* Lion and Unicorn, *ca. 1740-50, stoneware with salt glaze, 5 1/4" x 3 3/8" (cat 4).*

black glaze and is usually undecorated. The wares from the Staffordshire region, however, are made of cream ware—that is, white pipe clay with flint, which is colored with manganese and iron oxide and covered with a clear glaze. They frequently have raised, applied reliefs (like those on red stoneware), which were often gilded. Judging by these characteristics, the two examples in the Beeson collection, which also have traces of gilding remaining, are of Staffordshire origin. They are unmarked and date between 1755 and 1760.

John Astbury (1688-1745) was one of the first Staffordshire potters to coat earthenware with white slip made of flint, in the early eighteenth century.[3] He is also known to have been one of the first to use stamped decoration made from white Devon clay on red earthenware covered with a clear lead glaze. In the Beeson collection there is a fine teapot that fits this description and that depicts the royal crest of the lion and unicorn surrounding a crown (cat. 6, pl. 2). Stamped decoration is a type of ornamentation achieved by applying pads of clay in a metal mold directly to the body. The mold is then removed, often leaving a slightly rough edge around the addition. (For sprigged decoration, on the other hand, the clay pieces are made separately in plaster molds, removed when in a leather-dry state, and then applied to the body with a watered clay or slip as the adhesive.)

Salt-glazed stoneware was introduced to the Staffordshire potters sometime before 1719.[4] Composed of Devonshire clay and calcined flints with a salt glaze, the ware quickly became a standard of the district. A cheaper version of salt-glazed ware was developed from coarse local clays that were dipped in a Devonshire clay-and-flint slip and then salt-glazed. This second ware is distinguished from the first by the crazing in the glaze.[5]

Salt-glazed ware was molded into intricate forms and often decorated with overglaze enamels. The method of salt glazing is achieved by throwing salt into the kiln when it reaches its maximum temperature. The heat causes the salt to volatilize into a gas of sodium oxide and hydrochloric acid, which adheres to the hot ware and combines with the alumina and silica in the clay to form a hard glaze. This kind of ware is rarely attributed to a single potter, because all of the better-known potters are believed to have produced it. Wedgwood and others fashioned salt-glazed ware until the early 1770s, when it was superseded by cream ware.

Two teapots in the Beeson collection (cats. 4, 5, pl. 3) are made of salt-glazed stoneware. One dating from 1745-60 is in the form of a house with a serpent spout and handle. The British royal coat of arms is depicted above the door frame on one side, and the arms of Holland appear on the other. The second teapot, in a bombé shape, has molded shells decorated with carnations and leaves in red, green, and blue enamel. Depicted in almost cartoon form on both sides is a wonderful eighteenth-century-style figure of a man with arms and legs flailing, reputed to represent Prince Charles Edward Stuart (1720-88). Known as the Young Pretender, the prince was one of the most popular subjects of the mid-eighteenth-century decorator. The plain handle of the teapot has underglaze blue decoration in Chinese-like motifs.

A Staffordshire potter whose name is almost as familiar as Wedgwood's is Thomas Whieldon (1719-95). Because of this familiarity and Whieldon's relationships with the potters Josiah Spode, William Greatbatch, Aaron Wood, and Josiah Wedgwood, many Staffordshire wares are generically called Whieldon ware. Whieldon's pottery, located at Fenton Vivian (1750-61), was excavated in 1968 and revealed little stratification because of intrusions from nearby works. It is apparent from other recent excavations and documentary evidence, however, that Whieldon produced the same range of wares as did the 150 or so other potters of the Staffordshire area. Unfortunately, none of his pieces or those from his partnerships is marked, so exactly what he produced is a matter of speculation.

One red stoneware teapot in the Beeson collection has been attributed to Whieldon (cat. 22, pl. 4).[6] Dating from between 1760 and 1800, this octagonal, molded teapot is completely covered with decorative Chinese motifs which surround a seated Chinese man in the center.

The most common decorative device attributed to Whieldon is tortoiseshell mottling. Popular in England from about 1750 to 1785, tortoiseshell ware is a type of cream ware covered with a variety of metallic oxides—cobalt, manganese, antimony,

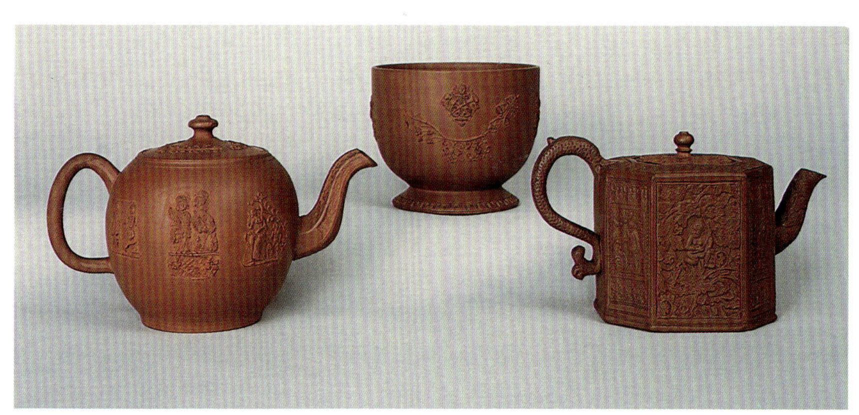

Color plate 4 Left, *Teapot,* Oriental Figures, *ca. 1780, red stoneware, applied decoration 4 1/4" x 3 3/4" (cat. 21);* center, *Sugar Bowl, 1770-80, red stoneware with applied decoration, 3 7/16" x 3 1/8" (cat. 8);* right, *Teapot,* Oriental Figures, *1760-70, red stoneware with applied decoration, 3 7/8" x 3 5/8" (cat. 22).*

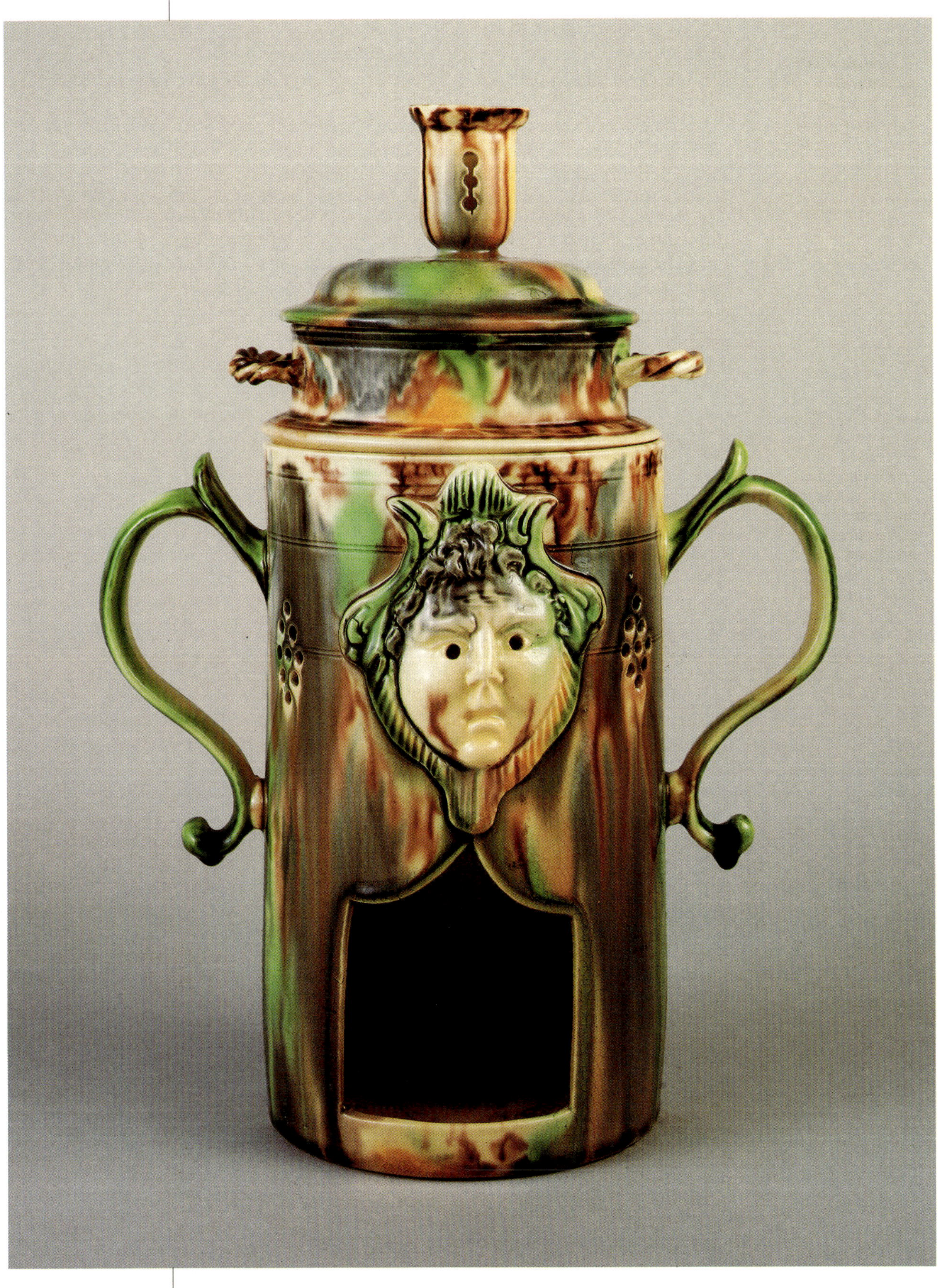

Color Plate 5
Veilleuse, ca. 1760, creamware with multicolored metallic oxides under a clear lead glaze, 11" x 4 1/2" (cat. 11).

and/or copper—which are melted into the lead glaze. After biscuit firing, the piece was splashed or sponged with these oxides and then a clear lead glaze. During the second firing, as the outer glaze formed its glassy surface, the oxides flowed and blended underneath, resulting in the mottled effect. Whieldon probably produced these wares before, during, and after his partnership with Wedgwood, and both continued production thereafter.

There are a number of tortoiseshell pieces in the Beeson collection, notably a food warmer (veilleuse) (cat. 11, pl. 5) and two teapots (cats. 2, 10, pl. 6). The food warmer, dating about 1760, has a cylindrical pedestal and two rococo-type handles. Above the pointed arch aperture on the front and repeated on the rear is a female-mask head with long braids wrapped around the chin. Small holes designating eyes serve as air vents in addition to the nine holes placed above in diamond-shaped groups. Atop the pedestal is a bowl with two interlaced loop handles and its cover with a tall candle socket. Over the entire piece is a clear lead glaze with mottled hues of gray, green, and brown. (See pp. 43–44 for a discussion of the history and use of the veilleuse.)

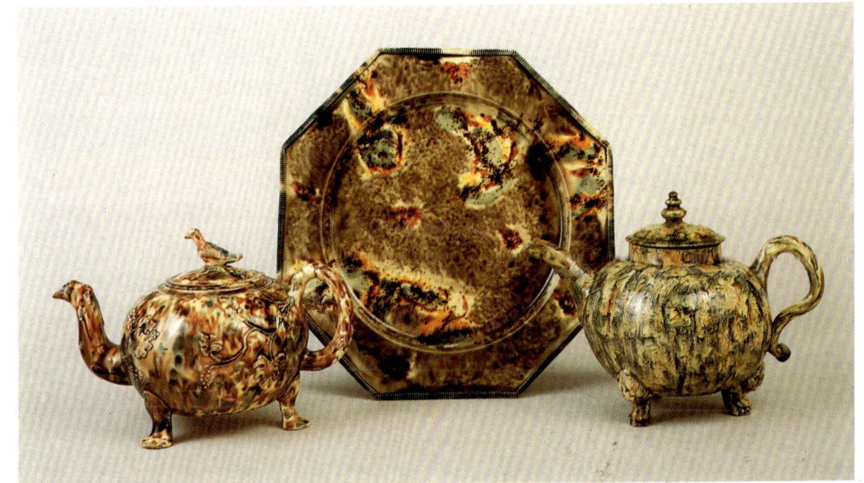

Color Plate 6
Left, *Teapot 1750-60, cream ware with multicolored metallic oxides under clear glaze and applied decoration, 4 5/8" x 4 1/4" (cat. 2);* center, *Plate,* Tortoiseshell, *ca. 1770, creamware with multi-colored metallic oxides under clear lead glaze, 8 3/4" (cat. 9);* right, *Teapot, ca. 1775, agate ware, 5 1/8" x 4 1/2" (cat. 1).*

The two tortoiseshell teapots have crabstock handles and spouts. The smaller example, colored in gray and brown, has a bird finial on the lid; the larger one has a light spattering of green, gray, and ocher mottling, the lid being a total replacement. Both bear sprigged decoration of the same type found on Wedgwood jasper ware, rosso antico, and caneware.

The Whieldon and Wedgwood partnership lasted from 1754 to 1759. Their products are thought to include tortoiseshell ware, agate ware, and possibly cauliflower and pineapple ware. Surviving documentary evidence does show that, during their partnership, Wedgwood frequently attempted to perfect colored glazes. Wedgwood anticipated the need for new materials to supplant the tortoiseshell ware, as he suggested in the preface to his experiment book:

> This suite of Experiments was begun at Fenton Hall, in the parish of Stoke upon Trent, about the beginning of the year 1759, in my partnership with Mr Whieldon, for the improvement of our manufacture of earthen ware, which at that time stood in great need of it, the demand for our goods decreasing daily, and the trade universally complained of as being bad & in a declining condition.
>
> White stone ware [salt glaze] was the principal article of manufacture; but this had been made a long time, and the prices were now reduced so low, that the potters could not afford to bestow much expence upon it, or make it so good in

any respect as the ware would otherwise admit of. And with regard to Elegance of form, that was an object very little attended to.

The article next in consequence to Stoneware was an imitation of Tortoise-shell. But as no improvement had been made in this branch for several years, the country was grown weary of it; and though the prices had been lowered from time to time, in order to increase the sale, the expedient did not answer, and something new was wanted, to give a little spirit to the business.

I had already made an imitation of Agate; which was esteemed beautiful & a considerable improvement; but people were surfeited with wares of these variegated colors. These considerations induced me to try for some more solid improvement, as well in the Body, as the Glazes, the Colours, & the Forms, of the articles of our manufacture.

I saw the field spacious, and the soil so good, as to promise an ample recompence to any one who should labour diligently in its cultivation.[7]

Wedgwood's first success was a new green lead glaze that could cover a cream-ware body. The formula in the experiment book is dated March 23, 1759, and is described as "a Green Glaze to be laid on Common for Creamcolor Biscuit ware. Very good. . . . N°. 7 This is the result of many experiments which I made in order to introduce a new species of color'd ware."[8] In an effort to copy the rococo ware made popular by European porcelain factories, Wedgwood utilized the green glaze for the leaves on fruit or vegetable ware. In the Beeson collection, three of the five pieces in imitation of cauliflowers may be examples of Wedgwood's early ware in cooperation with William Greatbatch (cats. 26, 29, pl. 7).

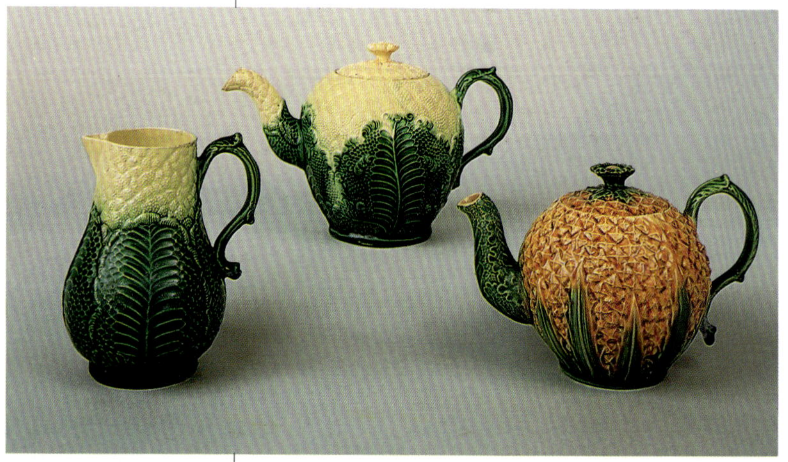

Color plate 7
Left, *Cream Pitcher,* Cauliflower, *1760-70, cream ware with green glaze, 4 1/2" x 2" (cat. 26);* center, *Teapot,* Cauliflower, *1760-70, cream ware with green glaze, 4 1/2" x 2 3/8" (cat. 29);* right, *Teapot,* Pineapple, *1760-70, cream ware with green and yellow-brown glaze, 4" x 2 1/8" (cat. 30).*

William Greatbatch (ca. 1735-1813), another early potter, modeler, and blockcutter in Staffordshire, was apprenticed to Thomas Whieldon at Fenton Vivian during the Whieldon-Wedgwood partnership from 1754 to 1759. By 1762 he had set up his own pottery at Lower Lane in Fenton, and he remained there until his bankruptcy was announced in the *London Gazette* in February of 1782. Documentary evidence suggests that from 1762 to 1765 he was supplying Wedgwood (although not exclusively) with a large amount and range of wares, both biscuit and glazed.[9] Archaeological evidence suggests that he was making wares similar to those of the other potteries.[10] In relationship to the Beeson collection, he supplied the rococo-style teapots, including those molded in cauliflower, pineapple, and cornucopia shapes. Of note is a teapot from Greatbatch's period of production, dating from about 1765 to 1770. A tea canister and cream pitcher that may also have been made by Greatbatch date from a later time, as the cream-ware body is lighter in color.

A letter of 1764 from Greatbatch to Wedgwood supports the idea that they were collaborating at this time: "There are ready two of the crates of Pine Apple ware and a large quantity of plates about a gross and 1-2 of light colour teapots."[11] Land-tax returns show that Greatbatch's independent tenancy at Fenton ceased between 1781 and 1783. He was probably taken on at Etruria soon thereafter, as there are letters written by him from Etruria in 1786. Greatbatch's extremely high wages of five shillings a day, "whether at work or play, and a house rent free,"[12] show that Wedgwood had high regard for his work. Greatbatch continued to receive a pension for life; the last letter he wrote from Etruria is dated 1804.

Two other teapots in the Beeson collection, each decorated with relief-molded fruit in baskets, are attributable to Greatbatch (cats. 15, 16, pl. 8). Both were made of cream ware: one is completely colored in the green glaze; the other has underglaze metallic oxides of green, blue, yellow, and purple.[13]

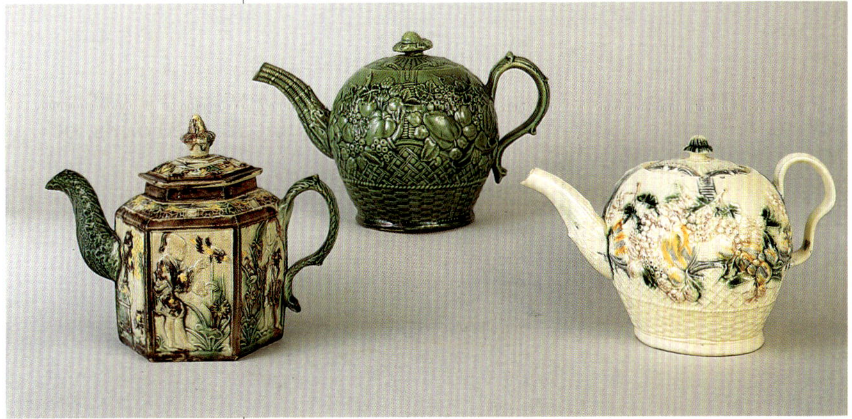

Color plate 8
Left, *Teapot,* Chinese, *1760-70, cream ware with multicolored oxides under clear glaze, 5 1/4" x 3 7/8" (cat. 14);* center, *Teapot, 1765-75, cream ware with green glaze, 5" x 3 5/16" (cat. 16);* right, *Teapot, 1770-80, cream ware with underglaze polychrome decoration and molded body, 4 1/2" x 3" (cat. 15).*

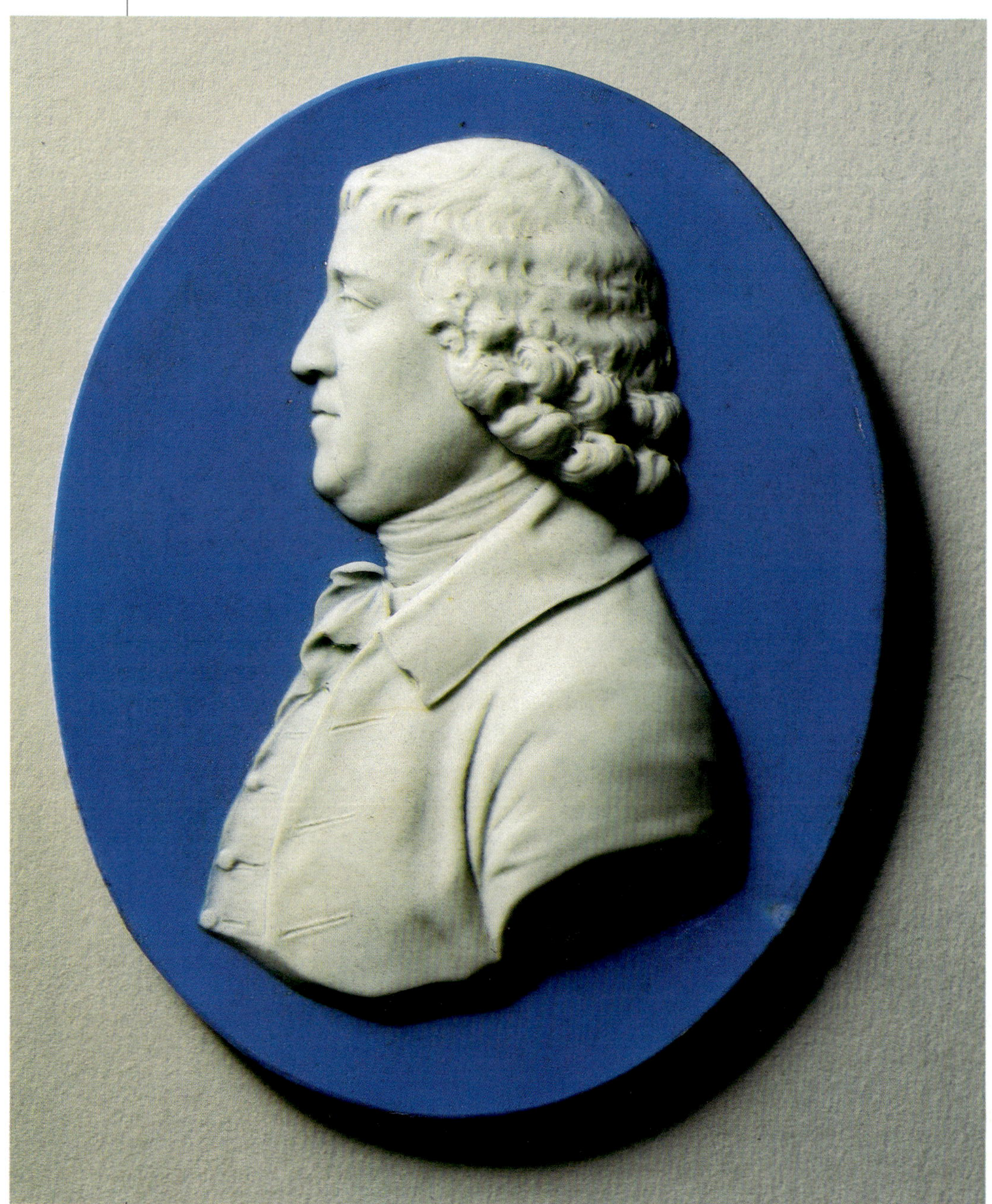

Color plate 9 *Portrait medallion,* Josiah Wedgwood, *ca. 1800, jasper, solid white ground with dark blue wash front and back and white relief, 4" x 3 3/16" (cat. 710).*

3
Josiah Wedgwood

For most people today, the term "Wedgwood" evokes an image of commemorative blue-and-white, jasper-ware plates and vases that can be found at department and jewelry stores. This book endeavors to dispel the image by portraying Josiah Wedgwood as a Renaissance man who made many different types of pottery as well as many contributions to the pottery industry and to English society, while rising from modest beginnings to become one of the wealthiest men in England. Born the twelfth child of a mediocre potter and endowed as a young man with the promise of only a twenty-pound inheritance, Wedgwood died, in 1795, worth five hundred thousand pounds and was the owner of one of the finest industrial concerns in England. His name was known throughout the world, and he had become a force in industry, commerce, science, and politics as well as the dominant figure in the potting industry.

Josiah Wedgwood, the youngest child of Thomas and Mary Wedgwood, was born in 1730 (the exact day is unknown), and he was baptized on July 12 of the same year at Saint John's Church in Burslem (pl. 9, cat. 710). From his family's fourth generation of potters, Wedgwood had his formal education ended with the early death of his father in 1739. From 1744 to 1749 he was apprenticed to his brother Thomas "to Learn his Art, Mistery, Occupation, or Imployment of Throwing and Handleing."[1] An injured knee resulting from an earlier attack of smallpox limited Wedgwood's ability to turn a foot-pedaled pottery wheel, yet he continued to pursue pottery. After his apprenticeship, Wedgwood remained with his brother for another three years and then became associated with the potters John Harrison and Thomas Alders at Cliff Bank near Stoke. In 1754, after two years at Cliff Bank, Wedgwood entered into his second partnership, this time with the famous and innovative Thomas Whieldon. Indeed, this partnership lasted five years, during which time Wedgwood and Whieldon manufactured mostly white stoneware and tortoiseshell ware. With the successful creation of a green glaze came the end of the Whieldon-Wedgwood partnership and the beginning of Wedgwood's setting up of his own business in Burslem. Throughout the 1760s, green-glazed pieces continued to be made, mostly from old salt-glazed patterns.

On May 1, 1759, Wedgwood started his own pottery, renting the Ivy House Pottery at Burslem (which consisted of two kilns, workshops, and cottages) from his cousins, Thomas and John Wedgwood, who were also the uncles of Josiah's future wife, Sarah. Another cousin, Thomas Wedgwood (1734-88), taken on as a journeyman for the next six years, became the works manager, enabling Josiah to pursue his experiments and other endeavors.[2] The two remained at Ivy House until 1763, when they moved into slightly larger premises at the Brick House and Works in Burslem (later known as the Bell Works, the workmen being summoned by a bell instead of the customary horn).

On January 25, 1764, Josiah married Sarah Wedgwood (1734-1815), his third cousin, and from this union came eight children, six of whom attained adulthood (pl. 10). Sarah's contribution to Josiah's

Color plate 10
George Stubbs (1724-1806), The Wedgwood Family in the Ground of Etruria Hall, *1780. Oil on wood panel, 47 3/4" x 72 1/2" (19 x 36.7 cm). Courtesy of the Trustees of the Wedgwood Museum, Barlaston, Stoke-on-Trent, England.*

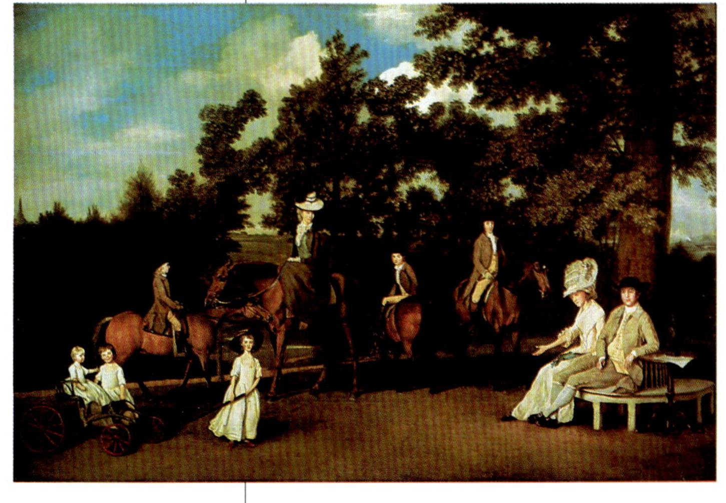

business pursuits is described in a letter of January 1768: "I speak from experience in Female taste, without which I should have made but a poor figure amongst my Potts, not one of which, of any consequence, is finished without the Approbation of my Sally."[3] She even participated in his experimentation, as he wrote to his brother John on March 6, 1765:

> I have just begun a Course of experiments for a white body & glaze which promiseth well hitherto.
>
> Sally is my chief help mate in this as well as other things, & that she may not be hurried by haveing too many Irons in the fire as the phrase is I have ord[d]. the spining [*sic*] wheel into the Lumber room.
>
> She hath learnt my characters, at least to write them, but can scarcely read them at present.—This business I often think if you could but once enter intwo the spirit of it, wo[d]. be the prettiest employm[t] for you imaginable.[4]

Being confined mainly to his business, located in isolated Burslem, Wedgwood missed the stimulation of others' company. He wrote on March 11, 1765:

> Your feast at Turnham Green (mental feast I mean) was just what I expected, from the meeting and collision of such Geniuses as were there assembled, & from your description with a little of the art of designing I could spread a yard of Canvas over with an excellent Group of figures.—How happy sho[d]. I have been in partakeing of so instructive, & elegant an Entertainm[t].!—but alass I must be content with fashioning my clay at an humble distance from such comp[y]. & live, breathe, & dye, amongst Animals but one remove above the Earth they are teazeing.[5]

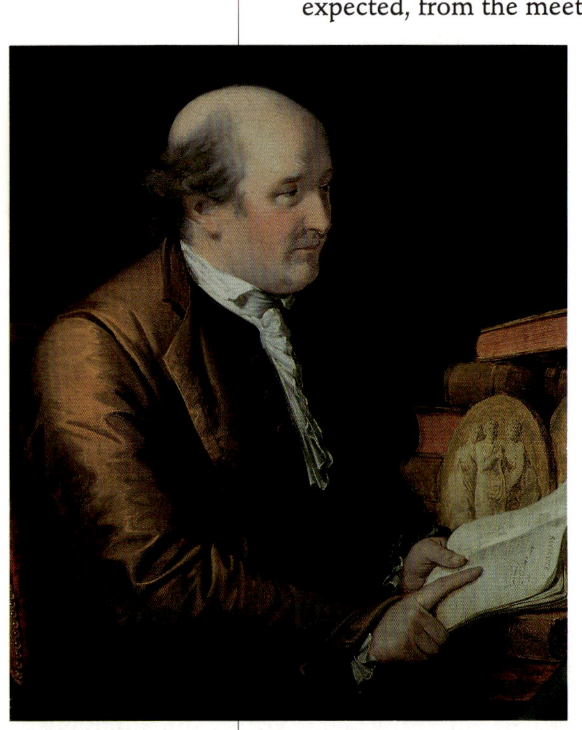

Color plate 11
Attributed to Joseph Wright (1734-97), Portrait of Thomas Bentley *(1730-80), 1769-80. Oil on canvas, 35 1/4" x 27 3/4" (89.7 x 70.5 cm). Courtesy of the Trustees of the Wedgwood Museum, Barlaston, Stoke-on-Trent, England.*

In 1766 Thomas Wedgwood and Josiah Wedgwood entered into a partnership for the manufacture of "useful" or domestic ware, with Thomas taking one-eighth of the profits of this part of the business. According to a letter of September 3, 1770, the collaboration involved "such vessels as are made use of at meals."[6] "Useful" wares were distinguished from the "ornamental" wares produced under the partnership formed by Wedgwood and Thomas Bentley (1730-80) in 1769 (pl. 11).

Bentley and Wedgwood had first met in 1762 in Liverpool through Wedgwood's physician, Dr. Matthew Turner (d. 1788?). Although Bentley had been a longtime confidant, it was not until Josiah's brother John slipped into the Thames River and drowned, that Josiah felt the need to confirm their mutal interest in a partnership. He then wrote to Bentley on June 14, 1767: "Let us now be dearer to each other if possible than ever, let me adopt you for my Bro[r].—& fill up the chasm this cruel accident has made in my afflicted heart."[7] Further, on August 5, 1767, Wedgwood wrote:

> I am going on with my experiments upon various Earths Clays, &c. for different bodys, & shall next go upon Glazes. Many of my experiments turn out to my wishes, & convince me more & more, of the extensive capability of our Manufacture for further improvements. . . . Such a revolution, I believe, is at hand, & you must assist in, proffitt by it.[8]

On November 15, 1767, a proposal was drawn up for a partnership that was consummated on August 10, 1769. The contract reads: "That W & B do enter into Partnership in making ornamental Earthenware or Porcelain viz Vases, Figures, Flowerpots, Toylet Furniture, and such other Articles as they shall from Time to Time agree upon. The partnership to continue for the space of 14 years. . . . J W shall advance the money necessary to carry out the sd business, for which he shall be paid 5 pr Ct by the Company."[9]

Thomas Bentley was the son of a wealthy Derbyshire country gentleman. He had had a classical education, spoke French and Italian, and had traveled in Europe. Having been for some twenty-three years a Liverpool merchant with seven years of training in accountancy, Bentley became Wedgwood's London agent. As the voluminous surviving correspondence between Wedgwood and Bentley relates, Bentley served as Wedgwood's confidant and adviser, particularly in matters of sales and marketing. In his first greeting of the new year of 1771, Wedgwood wrote to Bentley of his hopes for their business: "You will be so good to let us know what is going forw[d] in the Great World. How many Lords & Dukes visit your rooms, praise your beauties, thin your shelves, & fill your purses; & if you will take the trouble to acquaint us with the daily ravages made in your stores, we will endeavour to replenish them."[10]

As these quotations show, all manner of life in the eighteenth century is revealed in these letters; thus they are important to social, economic, political, and scientific history as well. Wedgwood wrote to Bentley on October 26, 1762:

> I will be quite honest & tell you what you have to expect from me—that I may as the Vicissitudes of life may furnish occasions, sometimes call upon you for advice,—at other times I may call upon you for assistance to settle an opinion—or to help me form a probable conjecture of things beyond our kenn & sometimes I may want that Valuable, & most difficult office of Friendship, reproof.[11]

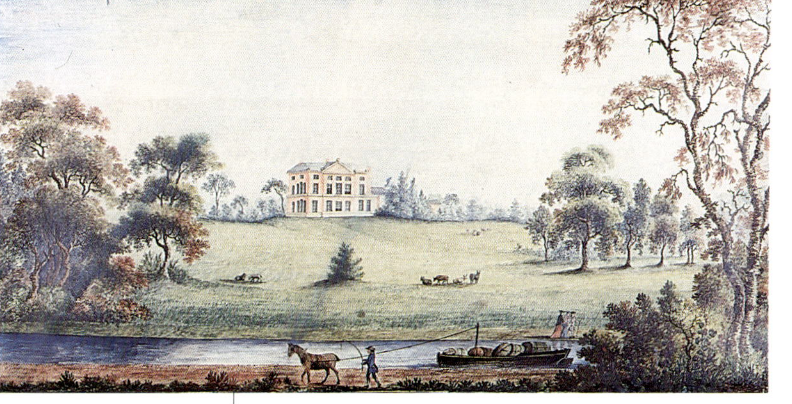

Color plate 12
Attributed to Edward Stringer (fl. 1770-83), Etruria Hall, *ca.1773. Enamel on Wedgwood earthenware, 7 1/2" x 14 1/2" (19 x 36.7 cm). Courtesy of the Trustees of the Wedgwood Museum, Barlaston, Stoke-on-Trent, England.*

Bentley courted aristocratic customers and advised Wedgwood on fashionable taste and trends. His influence encouraged Wedgwood to enlarge his line of ornamental wares and to discard the "French and Frippery" of the rococo for the classical revival.[12] Wedgwood stated on September 3, 1770: "Ornament is a field which notwithstand[g] you have bestowed one years close attention upon it, & I many, yet it appears to me that we are but just stepp'd or steping [*sic*] into it. . . . We shall reap, both Fame & Proffit."[13] On December 18, 1778, Bentley confirmed his affection in a rare surviving letter to Wedgwood: "I fancy I can do anything with your help, & I have been so much used to it, that when you are not with me, upon these occasions I seem to have lost my right Arm."[14] Their friendship was truly a solid one, lasting until Bentley's untimely death in 1780. During the eleven-year partnership, the pottery produced some of its finest works, particularly in the variegated and basalt wares, with outstanding examples of tablets, plaques, and medallions in jasper ware.

A site Wedgwood had purchased in 1766—the Ridge House Estate between Burslem and Stoke—became Wedgwood and Bentley's new factory (pl. 12). Opened on June 13, 1769, it was named Etruria to reflect the influence and popularity of recently excavated Greek and Italian red-figured vases and other ancient pottery. Etruria was a model industrial town housing 290 workers and producing chiefly ornamental ware; useful ware continued to be made at the Bell Works in Burslem until 1772 or 1773. Cousin Thomas Wedgwood then moved to the new factory, supervising cream ware until 1788.

Factory Discipline and Wedgwood

"I do strive to make things pass on with me as easy as possible, & hope to be makeing some progress in that very usefull Philosophy, but to keep 150 hands of various professions, & more various tempers & dispositions, in tolerable order is no easy task."[15] For this cumbersome but ever so important reason, Wedgwood divided his laborers into a crude assembly line and established factory discipline. With the tremendous demand and growth in the number of wares produced by potters in the eighteenth century, a new organization of labor was needed. His plans for Etruria revealed "the scheme of keeping each workshop separate, which I have much set my heart on," as he wrote to Bentley on July 26, 1769.[16] There were to be "five portions" by which the clay was moved in a logical fashion from shop to shop.[17] Each workman was trained in a particular skill and was not allowed to wander within the factory. "We are preparing some hands to work at red & black . . . constantly & then we shall make them good, there is no such thing as making now & then a few of any article to have them tolerable."[18] The division proceeded as follows:

> Each workshop had its specialist: in coloured ware, there were painters, grinders, printers, liners, borderers, burnishers and scourers; in jasper, there were ornamenters, turners, slip-makers, grinders, scourers, and mould-makers; in black ware, there were turners, throwers, handlers, seal-makers, mould-makers, and slip-makers; and in all there were modellers, firemen, overlookers, porters and packers. Other distinct professions included saggar-makers, lathe-turners, spout-makers, wedgers, engravers, polishers, dressers, sorters, dippers, brushers, stirrers, placers and coopers.[19]

Each shop had a supervisor to aid Wedgwood in the overall management of this large group of workers. "Out of the 278 men, women, and children that Wedgwood employed in June 1790, only five had no specified post."[20]

Wedgwood's commonplace book entitled "J. W. Experiments, Potters' Instructions, Etc., 1780," further detailed the workers' handling and attention to the pottery they were producing.[21] For example, the book notes the need to check everything, from the number of holes in the grate of a teapot spout to the finish of the surface, by the turners. Because of inspections such as these, the quantity of lost ware decreased and the standard of each pot improved.

The task of retraining workmen for a special purpose proved to be a further difficulty. Wedgwood wrote to Bentley on November 19, 1769:

> We have now got thirty hands here, but I have much ado to keep the new ones quiet. Some will not work in Black. Others say they shall never learn this new business, & want to be releas'd to make Terrines & sa:[uce] boats again. I do not know what I shall do with them, we have too many fresh hands to take in at once, though we have business enough for them, if they knew how, or wo[d] have the patience to learn to do it, but they do not seem to relish the thoughts of a second apprenticeship.[22]

Despite the grumbling, the one-task apprenticeships continued: "In 1790 nearly

25 percent of the workmen were apprentices, many of them girls."[23] Moreover, Wedgwood set up new standards of performance, though they were difficult for him to enforce with the independent potters: the hours of the workday were set and unvarying; standards of cleanliness and order were to be observed; and no drinking was allowed. Of particular interest is a scheme that can be compared with the present-day time clock: Wedgwood made a list of "all the [worker's] names in alphabetic order on a board hung up in the lodge," and the porter marked off with chalk the name of each worker as he arrived.[24]

Wedgwood and Cost Accounting

A system of cost accounting aided Wedgwood in wisely managing his various business concerns, particularly during lean and depressed years.[25] Information in the Wedgwood archives indicates that he was quite sophisticated in his business affairs and knowledgeable about accountancy. A falloff in trade during the months of August and September of 1772 spurred him to examine production costs and to guide his managerial decisions accordingly. He wrote to Bentley on August 5 of that year:

> It will deserve our serious discussion whether we shd not lower the prices of Pebble & Gilt Vases very considerably, for this purpose I am forming a price book of Workmanship &c which is to include every expense of Vase making as near as possible from the Crude materials, to your Counter in London upon each sort of Vases, of this we will send you a specimen & you will then be able to judge better what we can do in this respect, what will be most prudent is the next question for our Consideration.[26]

Shortly thereafter, on August 23, Wedgwood sent to Bentley his detailed analysis of production, which included the following categories: "Materials to the Wheel," "Throwing, Turning, finishing to the Oven," "Burning Bisket," "Burning Gloss with all Materials," "Modeling and Molds," "Coals for all the Workshops, exclusive of Ovens and Slip Kilns," "Wages to Boys, Odd Men, Warehouse and bookkeeping," "Rent, Wear and Tear, and incidental expenses," "Gilding," "Plinths, brasswork, and fastening," "Carriage to London and packages," "Add for Loss in breakage, Accidents and imperfect pieces," "Expence of Sale," "Interest on Capital in Trade," all of which equaled the "Total Expence of each piece."[27] In the final analysis, Wedgwood decided that he was achieving a considerable profit margin and therefore could afford to lower his prices and regularize them during the lean times, although he still raised them when the market was better, in anticipation of future depressed periods. By making his wares more affordable, Wedgwood could engage the favor of the middle classes. As he wrote in the same letter: "The Great People have had these Vases in their Palaces long enough for them to be seen & admired by the Middling Classes. . . . Their character is established, & the middling People would probably by quantitys of them at a reduced price."[28] That Wedgwood was aware of the economics of large-scale production is clear from his next remark: "As I have now got a book [on the costs of workmanship] for my own use & speculation, with the prices of workmanship of every article, I shall proceed in the same way where I think there is room for it . . . & the consequence of lowering the price of workmanship will be a proportional increase of quantity got up."[29] There is additional documentary evidence in the Wedgwood archives that Wedgwood kept this lesson in the forefront of his mind and that it subsequently affected what he produced, how much he produced, the wages he paid, the new techniques he adopted, and the pricing of each item.[30]

Wedgwood and Science

Before Wedgwood could implement any of his theories on cost accounting and so forth, it required the concerted effort of Wedgwood as artist and scientist to develop his wares. During his lifetime Wedgwood invented or improved numerous wares for the pottery industry. These improvements were copiously recorded in a series of experiment books, begun in 1759 and continued for the next thirty-five years, that detailed the results of over ten thousand trials. Of note were his improvements to cream ware and pearl ware and his invention of basalt and jasper ware.

Wedgwood's library was immense; among its volumes were not only books on antiquities but also the collected works of eminent scientists on chemistry and mineralogy. Fortunately, there exists a list of all the works in Wedgwood's library, books that helped to improve Wedgwood's overall education and also provided sources for the shape and design of many of his wares.[31] Indeed, Wedgwood wrote of his library on December 29, 1779: "My wife says I must buy no more books 'till I build another house and advises me to first read some of those I have already—What nonsense she talks sometimes!'"[32]

Josiah Wedgwood's belief in experiment, his adoption of scientific techniques, his extensive purchases of and familiarity with scientific literature, his friendship with other scientists, his membership in scientific societies, and his own published scientific work justify him as a true scientist of his age. By the 1780s he had established an international reputation among scientists, which was a great accomplishment for a man with so little formal education. In 1774, Wedgwood wrote to Bentley concerning his experiments:

> And the Fox-hunter does not enjoy more pleasure from the chace, than I do from the prosecution of my experiments when I am fairly enter'd into the field, & the farther I go, the wider this field extends to me. The Agate, The Green & other colour'd Glazes have had their day, & done pretty well. . . . The Cream-colour is of a superior Class, & I trust has not yet run 'its race by many degrees. . . . These are a few of the Roots . . . & I never look over my Books, but I find many more which I should very gladly bring into action.[33]

Long-term relationships with the great scientists of the day, including Matthew Turner, Erasmus Darwin, and Joseph Priestley, and with engineers such as Matthew Boulton and James Watt, all of whom were members of the Lunar Society, increased Wedgwood's understanding of chemistry and experimentation. In June of 1779, he formulated "a new excellent composition and cheap"[34] for a very hard stoneware body that withstood "the severest <u>necessary tests</u>" when used by chemists and apothecaries.[35] He then perfected a range of scientific products, including crucibles, distilling and melting pots, filter funnels, retorts, siphons, tubes, and mortars and pestles. The last-mentioned are described in his catalog of 1779: "The Mortar will be of great Use of Chymists, Experimental Philosophers and Apothecaries, as well as for culinary Purposes; not being liable, like Metals or Marble, to be corroded by Acids or any other chemical Menstrum." In the early 1780s, Wedgwood was prepared to provide such apparatus free of charge to chemists and scientists, in the interest of furthering research and information exchange. But when the demand increased dramatically, he was forced to charge customers for his superior products. "Mortars we find go every where," Wedgwood wrote to Bentley on June 13, 1780.[36] Three mortar-and-pestle sets of different sizes are in the Beeson collection (cats. 75, 76, 77). Of particular interest is one marked "Wedgwood and Bentley" and dated about 1779 and another impressed "Wedgwood / Best Composition" and produced between 1914 and 1918 (pl. 13).

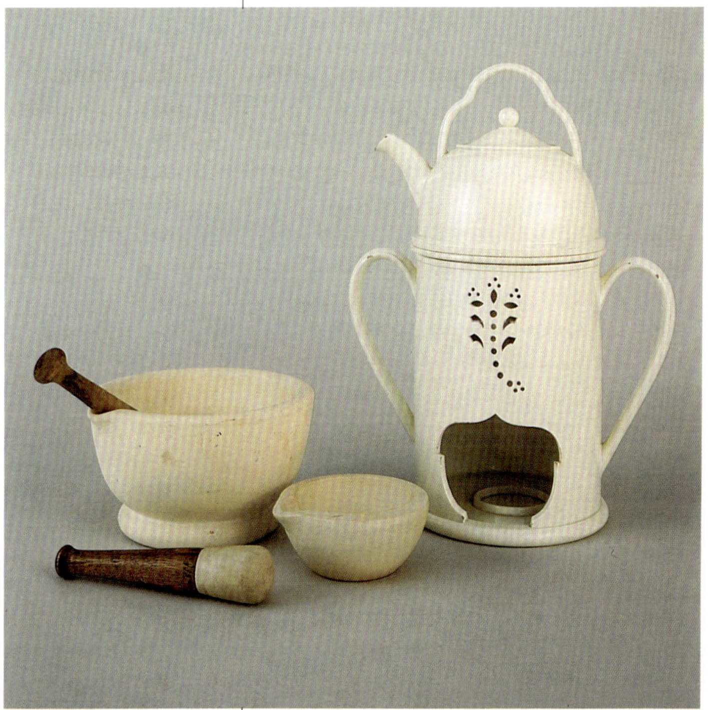

Color plate 13
Left, *Mortar and Pestle, 1914-18, stoneware, mortar: 3 15/16" x 4 3/4", pestle: 7 1/4" (cat. 77);* center, *Mortar and Pestle, ca. 1780, stoneware, mortar: 1 7/8" x 2 1/4", pestle: 6", (cat. 75);* right, *Veilleuse, ca. 1790, cream ware, 13 3/8" x 6 1/16" (cat. 74).*

Wedgwood's scientific experiments were directly related to the advancement of his business. One problem facing all potters and metallurgists of the eighteenth century involved the breakage of pottery in the kiln due to inconsistent heat or overheating. To remedy this loss, Wedgwood developed an instrument called the pyrometer to measure the degree of shrinkage of clay during firing and consequently the temperature inside the kiln. On May 9, 1782, he presented to the Royal Society a paper entitled "An Attempt to Make a Thermometer for Measuring the Higher Degrees of Heat." An entry in Wedgwood's first commonplace book, dated May 19, 1781, is the first record of his idea for making such a device. The instrument held a number of clay pieces that were placed in a kiln. As the kiln grew hotter, the pieces began to contract. At various intervals a piece was removed from the kiln and quickly cooled, thus showing the degree of shrinkage for that period of heat. Wedgwood then recorded temperature variations alongside these pieces. The flaw in his experiment was twofold: he was not able to maintain constant temperature in the kiln over a prolonged period of time, and the composition of the clay was not necessarily uniform. Had these two elements been consistent, he would have observed progressive shrinkage. The instrument gained approval from the scientific community, however, as evidenced by Wedgwood's election to the Royal Society in 1783. Upon his death, an obituary noted: "His communications to the Royal Society shew a mind enlightened by science, and contributed to procure him the esteem of scientific men at home and throughout Europe."[37]

Apart from his pottery experiments, Wedgwood pursued many other interests that also gained him membership in the Philosophical Society (1781), the Antiquarian Society (1786), and the Royal Society for the Encouragement of Arts, Manufactures, and Commerce (1786), and he was frequently an honored guest at the Lunar Society.[38] Humanitarian causes, such as the Antislavery Society, were given Wedgwood's active support. His political inclinations were liberal, which made him a sympathizer for the cause of independence during the American Revolution as well as the early stages of the French Revolution.

In 1790 Wedgwood retired, having taken into partnership his three sons, John, Josiah, and Tom, and his nephew Thomas Byerley. His working life had been a hectic and fruitful one: as he described it in a letter to Bentley of September 8, 1767, "Why you never knew so busy a Mortal as I am,—Highways—surveying R[idge] H[ouse] Estate—Experiments for Porcelain, or at least—a new Earthen ware, fill up every moment allmost of my time."[39] He continued to collect books, engravings, and objects of natural history, and he continued to look toward the future. "But oh! time—time—There is no time to bring to maturity a thousandth part of the possibilitys in our engaging and prolific business. I see, at a single glance, immensely farther than I shall ever be able to travel & whether any of my young men [will] have the perseverance sufficient to carry them to the heights from whence alone such prospects can be view'd I have much more doubt than expectation."[40]

Wedgwood died at his home, Etruria Hall, on January 3, 1795, after a short illness, at sixty-four years of age (pl. 14). He was buried in the churchyard at Stoke-on-Trent, where his epitaph states that he "converted a rude and inconsiderable Manufactory into an elegant art and an important part of national commerce." Wedgwood bequeathed to his heirs a fortune resulting from a lifetime of ceaseless discipline and an ingenious combination of the arts and sciences. No small part of Wedgwood's achievement was his tremendous influence on the decorative arts in England and elsewhere. As an admirer once stated the case, in an analogy that Wedgwood repeated to Bentley on August 24, 1770: "When Roman luxury increas'd, Etruscan ware gave place to Plate [silver]; but when English luxury seems at the height, [Wedgwood's] elegant taste has put to flight Gold & Silver vessels, & banished them from our Tables."[41]

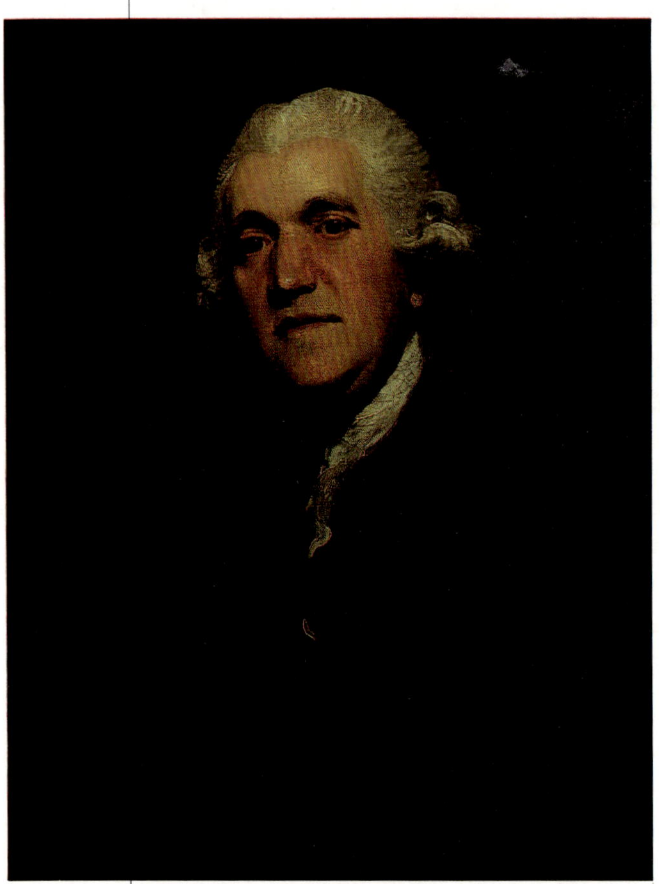

Color plate 14 *Sir Joshua Reynolds (1723-92),* Portrait of Josiah Wedgwood, *1782. Oil on canvas, 29 1/2" x 24 3/4" (75 x 63 cm). Courtesy of the Trustees of the Wedgwood Museum, Barlaston, Stoke-on-Trent, England.*

4
Cream Ware

The two great discoveries made in European ceramics in the eighteenth century were porcelain and cream ware. Exports from China had inspired popular demand for porcelain, leading to the establishment of the royal porcelain factories in Europe. Yet only the wealthy could afford the expensive porcelain for their tables, with the majority of the population serving food in crude crockery and wooden bowls. But with the economic growth of the middle class, a new market developed of those who desired pottery tableware for their homes. Cream ware fulfilled the need of this market and soon became the everyday dishes for all manner of people, from castle to cottage. Because it was affordable yet durable, it eventually replaced tin-glazed earthenware, which flaked and chipped easily.

Potters had traditionally whitened the crude clay bodies of their wares by adding tin oxides to a covering lead glaze, producing the white-coated ware called tin-glazed earthenware or, more commonly, delftware. The first cream ware was also a body of darker clay coated with a lead oxide mixed with a white clay slip. This cream-colored slip was made from clays imported from Devonshire, with calcined flint added to whiten the body. A number of potters contributed to the development of cream-colored ware. An early reference by Dr. Robert Plot in his *Natural History of Staffordshire* (1686) states that dusting the body with calcined lead before firing made a glaze that was almost colorless.[1] By the 1740s the method of production was changed by firing the ware twice, first to a biscuit stage and then a second time after glazing with a liquid of lead and flint in water.

Many Staffordshire potters, including Thomas Whieldon, John Astbury, and John Warburton, were working toward the improvement of cream ware. It was Wedgwood's numerous experiments to refine the body and glaze, however, that resulted in the new standard for earthenware. For the body Wedgwood added flint to the whitest clays of Staffordshire, Devon, and Cornwall. The same two ingredients, flint and clay, were used in the glaze, which was absorbed by water into the body, producing a yellowish-green color that may be seen in the ware's crevices, where the glaze is thicker. Wedgwood described his new product in 1763 as "a species of earthenware for the table, quite new in appearance, covered with rich and brilliant glaze, bearing sudden alterations of heat and cold, manufactured with ease and expedition, and consequently cheap."[2] On February 27, 1768, he wrote:

> With respect to the colour of my ware I endeavour to make it as pale as possible to continue its cream-colour & find my Customers in general, though not every individual of them, think the alteration I have made in that respect a great improvmt but it is impossible that any one colour, even though it were to come down from Heaven, shd please every taste, & I cannot regularly make two creamcolours, a deep & light shade without having two works for that purpose.[3]

His experiment book shows even further developments in 1776, with trials "2383 to 2410—To improve our creme colour Gloss."[4]

Wedgwood's experimentation with cream ware dates from 1760 or early 1761, yet it was not until 1766 that he seemed assured of its success. He wrote on August 1:

> Pray sell the Green & Gold for Pensacola, the new discover'd Island, or where you can, for I never will take it again, so make your best of it. I am quite clearing my Wareh°. of Colour'd ware, am heartily Sick of the commodity & have

> been so long but durst not venture to quit it 'till I had got something better in hand, which, thanks to my fair Customers, I now have & intend to make the most of it.[5]

Early cream ware is unmarked, giving rise to problems of attribution. In 1771, Wedgwood proposed to Bentley the marking of all their wares.[6] Factories such as Leeds, Liverpool, and Neale then followed Wedgwood's example and began to mark their pottery as well.

Cream ware was one of Wedgwood's most important products on two accounts. First, by virtue of its color and availability, cream ware brought Wedgwood's pottery to the forefront of the English and European markets. Second, in 1765, cream ware received the patronage of Queen Charlotte, launching Wedgwood's career as a potter and making his ware desired by all levels of society. The queen first submitted an order to Wedgwood for "a complete sett of tea things, with a gold ground & raised flowers upon it in green, in the same manner of the green flowers that are raised upon [melons]. . . . The articles are 12 Cups for Tea, & 12 Saucers, a slop bason, sugar dish wth. cover & stand, Teapot & stand, spoon [tray],—Coffeepot, 12 Coffee cups, 6 pr. of hand candlesticks & 6 Mellons with leaves, 6 green fruit baskets & stands edged with gold." She was so pleased with the ware that she permitted Josiah Wedgwood to style himself "Potter to Her Majesty."[7] On July 6, 1765, Josiah reported to his brother John: "I shall be very proud of the honour of sending a box of patterns to the Queen, amongst which I intend sending two setts of Vases, Creamcolour engine turn'd, & printed, for which purpose nothing could be more suitable than some copperplates I have by me."[8] Thus the name queen's ware became synonymous with cream ware.[9]

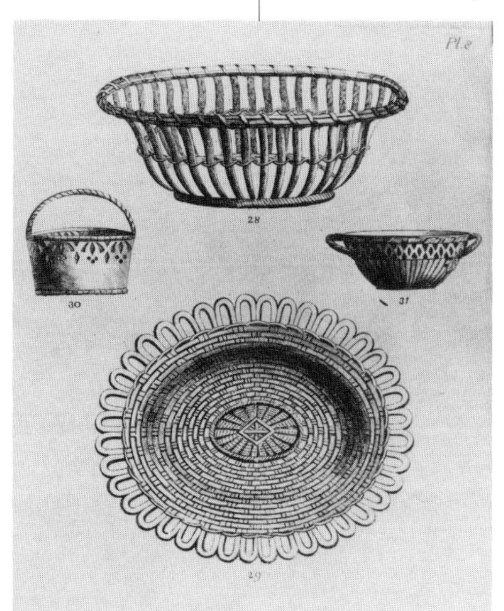

Fig. 2 *Plate 8 from Wedgwood's first* Queen's Ware Catalogue *of 1774, engraved by John Pye and available in both French and English. This plate shows Fruit Basket #28, Fruit Basket Stand #29, and two Sweetmeat Dishes, #30 and #31. Courtesy of the Trustees of the Wedgwood Museum, Barlaston, Stoke-on-Trent, England.*

The success of this new ware was great, surprising even Wedgwood. As he wrote to Bentley on September 8, 1767:

> The demand for this s^d. Creamcolour, Alias, Queens Ware, Alias, Ivory still increases.—It is really amazing how rapidly the use of it has spread allmost over the whole Globe, & how universally it is liked.—How much of this general use, & estimation, is owing to the mode of its introduction—& how much to its real utility & beauty ? are questions in which we may be a good deal interested, for the goverm^t. of our future Conduct. . . . Dont you think we shall have some Chinese Missionaries come here soon to learn the art of making Cream-colour? [10]

Wedgwood was not exaggerating the ware's popularity. In the 1760s, cream ware became the standard earthenware of the Staffordshire pottery industries and soon the standard tableware for the world.

The shapes for cream ware for the table were derived by Wedgwood and his contemporaries from European and oriental porcelain as well as silver forms of the period. But there was a great need for other items, and Wedgwood produced cream ware for every conceivable domestic, commercial, and industrial use. For the household he made cups, saucers, plates, tea services, tureens, pitchers, sauceboats, and products for feeding babies. For commercial use he made scales, measures, funnels, bowls, and mortars and pestles. For industrial use he made such items for the dairy as milking pails, strainers, ladles, churns, and tiles for the walls. Many of these are illustrated in nine plates depicting a total of thirty-five items in *The Queen's Ware Catalogue*, published by Josiah Wedgwood and Thomas Wedgwood in 1774 (fig. 2). The introduction states: "It being impossible to send specimens . . . and the Names conveying but a very imperfect Idea of the Forms, it has been thought proper to send a few Prints of the Pieces, which will explain the Uses, and show their Forms better than could be done by Words alone."[11]

Transfer Printing

The smooth, creamy surface of glazed cream ware provided an excellent surface for a type of decoration called transfer printing, or black printing. It is seen on a large group of items in the Beeson collection, including plates, cups and saucers, tea canisters, and a large pitcher. The invention of transfer printing was claimed by a number of entrepreneurs: John Brooks of Birmingham in 1752; Robert Hancock of London and Worcester; Jean Rouquet in 1755; Captain Henry Delamain between 1753 and 1756; and John Sadler and Guy Green of Liverpool in the summer of 1756.[12] John Brooks should probably receive the credit, yet Sadler and Green may have invented the method independently.

The transfer process was initially glue-bat printing and is now thought to be the earliest method of printing onto glazed cream ware.[13] In 1764 the two most popular ink colors were black and red; brown, purple, and green were in general use by 1770. In Wedgwood's commonplace book of 1786-94 there is a recipe for bats for on-glaze printing.[14] *The Official Descriptive and Illustrated Catalogue of the Great Exhibition of 1851* contains the following statement by Thomas Battam:

> The "Bat printing" is done upon the glaze, and the engravings are for this style exceedingly fine, and no greater depth is required than for ordinary book engravings. The copper plate is first charged with linseed oil, and cleaned off by hand, so that the engraved portion alone retains it. A preparation of glue being run upon flat dishes, about a quarter of an inch thick, is cut to the size required for the subject, and then pressed upon it, and being immediately removed, draws on its surface the oil with which the engraving was filled. The glue is then pressed upon the ware, with the oiled part next the glaze, and being again removed, the design remains, though, being in a pure oil, scarcely perceptible. Colour finely ground is then dusted upon it with cotton wool, and a sufficiency adhering to the oil leaves the impression perfect, and ready to be fired in the enamel kilns.[15]

This process of transfer could be used only on glazed pieces from which superfluous dust could be removed. Unglazed biscuit ware required another method, one called flat-press printing. A sheet of wet, soapy pottery tissue was laid on a heated, etched plate containing pigments mixed with a thick, boiled oil. The paper was then placed on the biscuit ware and rubbed with rolled flannel. Next, the piece was immersed in water to wash off the paper. Because the color was mixed with oil, it remained undisturbed. In order to prevent the print from rejecting the water-based glaze, the oil had to be removed from the colored ink, which was accomplished by baking in the hardening kiln.[16]

Wedgwood's first recorded account with the Liverpool printing firm of Sadler and Green was dated September 23, 1761, and their business association continued until possibly 1799, when Guy Green died.[17] It appears that Sadler and Green purchased glazed cream ware to decorate and then sell back to Wedgwood or to other customers.[18] Their designs came either from engravers whom they hired or from copper plates supplied by clients. In April of 1765, Wedgwood, who was constantly in search of new prints, wrote that a friend and promoter, Sir William Meredith, was sending them to him: "The last post bro^t^. me five pacquets from S^r^. W^m^. inclosing prints of different sorts which he is so Obliging to employ his good taste in picking up for me at Printshops."[19] On May 12, 1770, Wedgwood wrote to Bentley:

> I have had a good deal of talk with Mr Sadler, & find him very willing to do

> anything to improve his patterns. He has just completed a sett of Landskips for the inside of dishes &c. with childish, scrawling sprigs of flowers for the rims, all of which he thinks very clever, but they will not do for us. . . . I am afraid of trusting too much their taste, but they have promis'd to offtrace & coppy any prints I shall send them without attempting to mend or alter them. I have promis'd to send him the red chalk plates and a few prints of flowers immediately & beg you will send him the plates & pick out some prints of diff[t] size flowers to send along with them by the coach to Liverpool.[20]

Because Liverpool was a great center of commerce, Wedgwood used Sadler and Green for their ability to merchandise his ware as well as for their expertise in transfer printing. This trade between Burslem and Liverpool later inspired Wedgwood's interest in the development of the Trent and Mersey Canal and Turnpike.

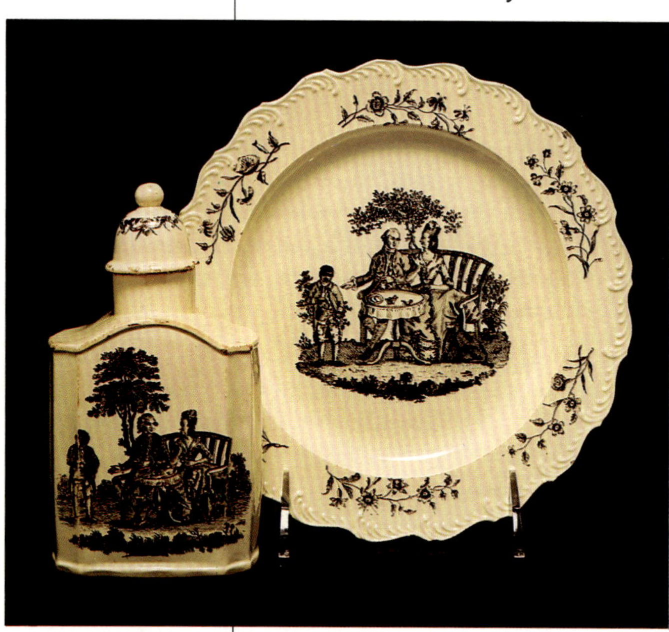

Color plate 15
Left, *Tea canister,* The Tea Party *and* The Good Shepherd, *ca. 1775, cream ware with transfer decoration, 5 9/16" x 3 1/2" (cat.63);* right, *plate,* The Tea Party, *ca. 1770, cream ware with transfer decoration, 7 5/8" (cat. 62).*

Sadler and Green also mass-produced tin-glazed tiles, which were used for architectural ornament in the seventeenth and eighteenth centuries and won the market of the popular tin-glazed tiles imported from Holland. Recognizing the selling opportunity here, Wedgwood seized on the plan for competing in this huge market and began making cream-ware tiles by 1767. On August 5 of that year he wrote to Bentley: "Creamcolour Tyle are much wanted, & the consumption will be great for Dairys, Baths, Summer houses, Temples, &c. &c."[21] There are three transfer-printed, tin-glazed earthenware tiles in the Beeson collection (cats. 66, 67, 68) that are thought to have been printed by Sadler and Green. One of them, called "The Tithe-Pig," shows a farmer's wife offering her baby, instead of the farmer's pig, as a tithe.[22] The tile is sometimes found signed "J. Sadler Liverpl." The second tile depicts Doctor Lubbert performing a tooth extraction (in essence, the sense of touch or feeling) from Dutch tiles of the Five Senses.[23] The third tile, possibly from a French source, depicts a lady and gentleman dancing to the tune of a fiddler and shows an obelisk in the background.[24]

One of the most popular transfer-printed designs was the tea party engraved by Robert Hancock (1730-1817). It was first published, on page 37 of an unidentified pattern book, by John Bowles and Son in London in 1756.[25] Hancock was one of the first English engravers to work with transfer printing on porcelain. Used primarily on cream-ware items concerned with tea drinking, this print appears in black on a plate and tea canister in the Beeson collection (cats. 62, 63, pl. 15). The subject was in use by Wedgwood by 1763, as recorded in a letter of July 8 sent to him by Sadler and Green: "The Tea Drinkers large teapot you'll see are very pale, tho' quite a new plate: but the Engraver sent it down not half finished—he left it just as it was etch'd, without ever touching it with the Graver . . . but we shall mend that Matter very soon I hope."[26]

A second popular print employed by Wedgwood on cream ware is the "disheveled" or "exotic" birds. Sadler and Green reproduced this print for Wedgwood as early as 1761 in various adaptations, which were used by porcelain factories such as those in Sèvres, Worcester, and Meissen. A platter, a cup and saucer, and a teapot in the Beeson collection display this print (cats. 71, 72, 73, pl. 16).

Enameling

Enameling was another form of decoration on cream ware. Again Sadler and Green worked with Wedgwood to enamel the edges of his cream ware as well as on top of transfer decoration. In the Beeson collection, a small dessert plate with dark brown, transfer-printed seashells enameled with a bright green wash exemplifies this technique (cat. 64). As Wedgwood wrote to Bentley on December 14, 1776:

> I had wrote to Mr Green upon the first sight of the Shell Patterns that they were color'd too high, & must be kept down, especially the Green, Shells & Weeds may be color'd as chaste as any subjects whatever, & I hope we shall get into the way of it in time. But this Pattern was intended chiefly for abroad, & Foreigners in general will bear higher colouring, & more forcible contrasts than the English.[27]

A bill to Wedgwood from Guy Green includes "12 3/4 Doz. small Plates green shell @ 4/6 L2.17 1/2."[28]

As discussed in chapter 2, enameled decoration was first successfully achieved on salt-glazed ware. With cream ware, the piece was fired twice, then decorated, and fired at least a third time at a lower temperature to stabilize the enamel. The final firing process could be lengthy, because the various colors required different firing temperatures in order not to burn off the enamel. Pigments for enameling were derived from various mineral oxides—copper for green, cobalt for blue, antimony for yellow, and manganese for brown—that were combined with glass before being ground into powder and then mixed with oil for painting. Early enameling was completed by specialized decorating shops, usually located in London.[29] For most potters enameling was executed in London rather than in Staffordshire because there were more craftsmen there, and the always-present risk of breakage made it advisable to transport wares before they were decorated.

Numerous accounts show that Wedgwood sent his pottery to various shops to be enameled. A note dated July 12, 1763, from William Greatbatch to Wedgwood refers to one enameler: "I shall send Mr. Courzen's ware to his painting shop to Night."[30] And a letter dated March 11, 1763, shows that Wedgwood was also engaged in business with the enamelers Robinson and Rhodes, later D. [David] Rhodes and Company of Leeds, and Rhodes and [William Hopkins] Craft (1735?-1811) at the Cheyne Row and Greek Street Studios in London.[31] On March 24, 1768, Wedgwood wrote to Bentley in praise of Rhodes's work: "I have already agreed with one very usefull Tennant, A Master Enameler, & China piecer. . . . I have long had connections with this Man, who is sober, & steady, he is just come out of yorkshire to settle here. . . . He paints flowers, & Landskips very prettily, prepares a pretty good powder gold, & has a tolerable notion of colours."[32] Rhodes was listed as one of the master decorators for the renowned Catherine the Great Frog Service (see chap. 5), and he enjoyed a long business relationship with Wedgwood that lasted until his death in 1777.

Two teapots in the Beeson collection have enameled decoration characteristic of Wedgwood's work. One is decorated on one side with a woman in a combination of oriental and European dress and on the other

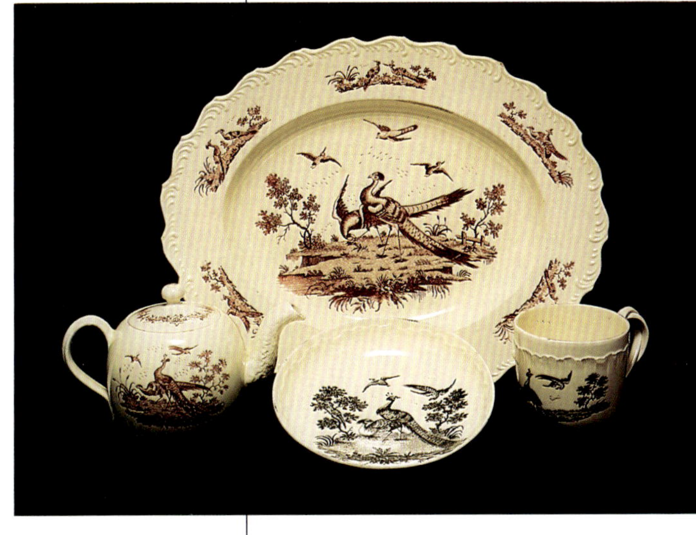

Color plate 16
Left, *Teapot,* Exotic Bird, *ca. 1780, cream ware with red transfer decoration, 3 7/8" x 3 3/8" (cat. 73);* center, *platter,* Exotic Birds, *ca. 1780, cream ware with red transfer decoration, 11 1/8" x 9" (cat. 71);* right, *cup and saucer,* Exotic Birds, *ca. 1780, cream ware with transfer decoration, cup: 2 7/8" x 1 3/8", saucer: 5 1/8" (cat. 72).*

side with a building in a landscape (cat. 55, pl. 17). Its colors—red, black, blue, green, rosy purple, and yellow—are typical, and it has the Wedgwood double-flower knob, cauliflower or cabbage spout, and double intertwined handle. The enameling technique is primitive in nature.

The second enameled teapot—a rare example of Wedgwood cream ware with classical decoration—bears a profile view of a Grecian woman on one side and a Grecian urn on the other (cat. 45). The lid has a small painted urn connected with scrolls to the decoration on the sides. Both the cauliflower spout and the strap handle with scales are characteristic of Wedgwood. The palette and application of the enamel are comparable with those on the first teapot.

In the Beeson collection are three jelly-mold cores painted with overglaze and underglaze enamel flowers and one very rare jelly-mold cover (cats. 56, 57, 54, pl. 18). Wedgwood made enameled jelly molds in both cream ware and pearl ware. The decorated core is designed to be fitted into an appropriately shaped cover filled with the gelatinous dessert. When the jelly sets, the outer cover is removed, leaving the decorated core to be seen through the clear jelly. The designs for the enameling on the two rectangular cream-ware molds, are found in color in Wedgwood's 1802 shape drawing book numbers 1 and 7 (fig. 3, in the Wedgwood archives). In his diary on March 28, 1782, Parson Woodforde wrote of the jelly mold as a table ornament: "And a very pretty pyramid of Jelly in the Centre, a Landscape appearing thro' the Jelly, a new device and brought from London."[33]

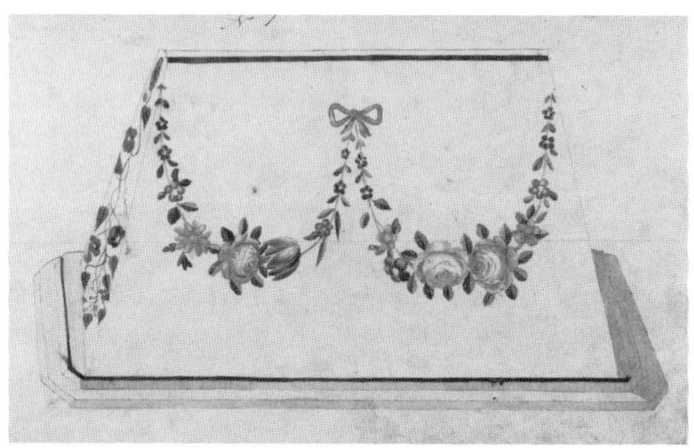

Fig. 3 *Jelly Mold Design from the 1802 shape drawing book, No. 1. Watercolor. Courtesy of the Trustees of the Wedgwood Museum, Barlaston, Stoke-on-Trent, England.*

Wedgwood's border patterns, which were often copied by other potteries, were another of his important contributions to English ceramics. The border patterns were gathered together in pattern books, which were used primarily by traveling salesmen to aid their customers in selecting their purchases. The first of Wedgwood's pattern books, containing border designs for use on dinner services, has a paper watermark of 1810 and was completed in 1814, according to an inscription on its final page (pl. 19). (The book is actually a copy of previous books, for Wedgwood had been producing patterns for tableware since at least 1769.) It includes 663 numbered patterns; each one is described on the facing page, and together they evolve from a restrained, classical-revival style to oriental motifs as the latter become fashionable in the early nineteenth century. There are seven other Wedgwood pattern books, dating approximately from 1800 to 1870. It is interesting to note that over 2,000 patterns were recorded by 1844 and another 8,000 were added in the next twenty years; the great number of patterns testify to the great demand for decorated services in the middle to late nineteenth century.

In the Beeson collection are two plates enameled in red and black with such border decorations; one has an anthemion border (no. 72 in Wedgwood's pattern book of 1770), and the second has a border of a Greek key and tongue with a female figure in the center (cats. 183, 197, pl. 20).[34] Cream-ware plates enameled with Etruscan decoration in imitation of the decorative motifs on Greek and Roman vessels were popular because of the recent excavations in Italy (see chap. 8). It is doubtful that these plates were used as tableware, as the hand-painted surfaces scarred easily.

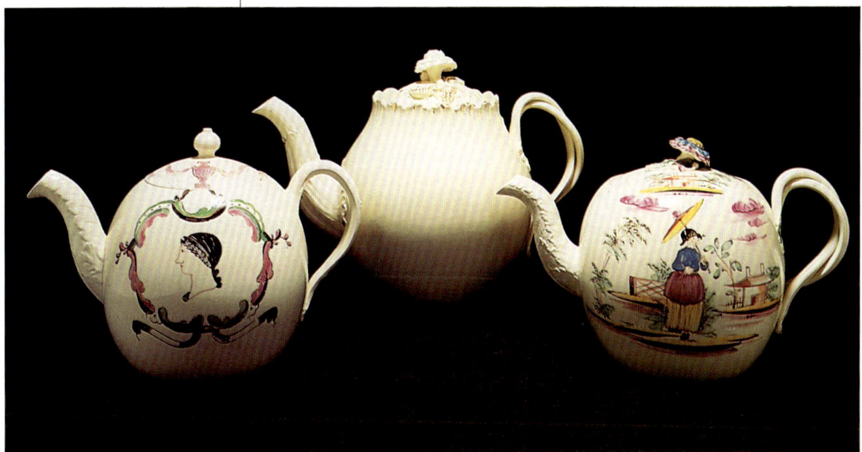

Color plate 17 Left, *Teapot,* Grecian Bust, *ca. 1775, cream ware with overglaze enamel decoration, 5 3/4" x 2 1/8" (cat. 58);* center, *Teapot, ca. 1780, cream ware with gilding, 6 1/2" x 3" (cat. 45);* right, *Teapot, ca. 1775, cream ware with overglaze enamel decoration, 5 5/16" x 3 3/8" (cat. 55).*

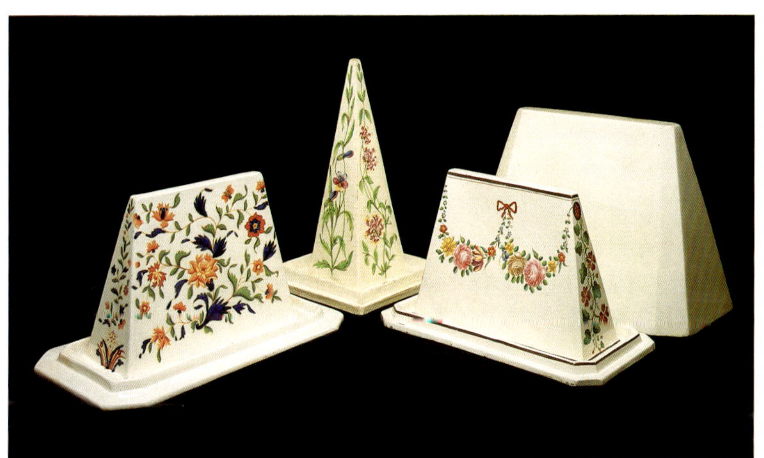

Color plate 18 Left and right, *Jelly Mold Core and undecorated cover, ca. 1790, cream ware with overglaze enamel decoration, mold: 6 1/2" x 9", core: 5 1/4" x 9 9/16" (cat. 54);* second from left, *Jelly Mold Core, ca. 1790, cream ware with overglaze enamel decoration, 4 7/8" x 8 1/2" (cat. 57);* second from right, *Jelly Mold Core, ca. 1790, cream ware with overglaze enamel decoration, 4 13/16" x 5 1/16" (cat. 56).*

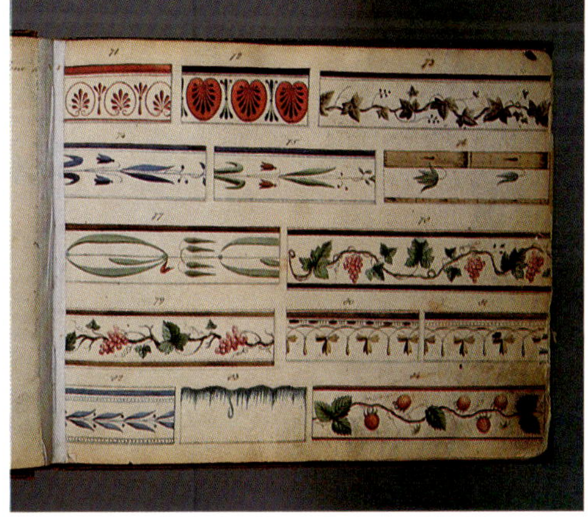

Color plate 19 *Page from Wedgwood's first pattern book, watercolor and ink on paper, ca. 1769-1814. Courtesy of the Trustees of the Wedgwood Museum, Barlaston, Stoke-on-Trent, England.*

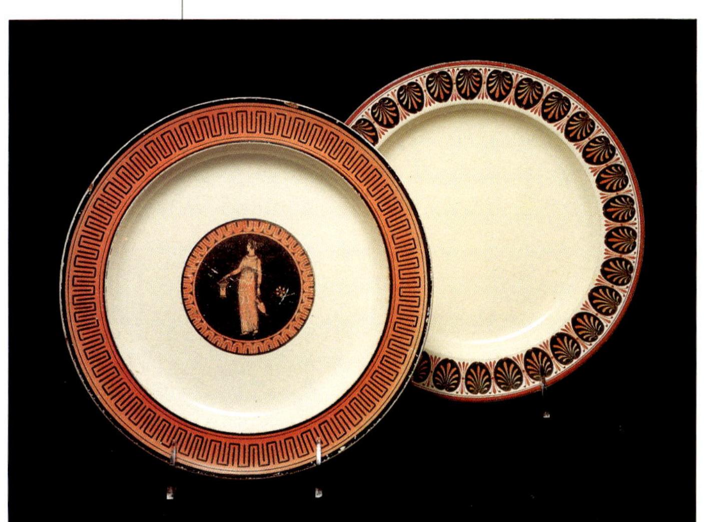

Color plate 20 Left, *Plate,* Etruscan, *ca. 1790, cream ware with red printed and black enamel decoration, 9 3/4" (cat. 183);* right, *Plate,* Etruscan, *ca. 1790, cream ware with red printed and black enamel decoration, 9 11/16" (cat. 197).*

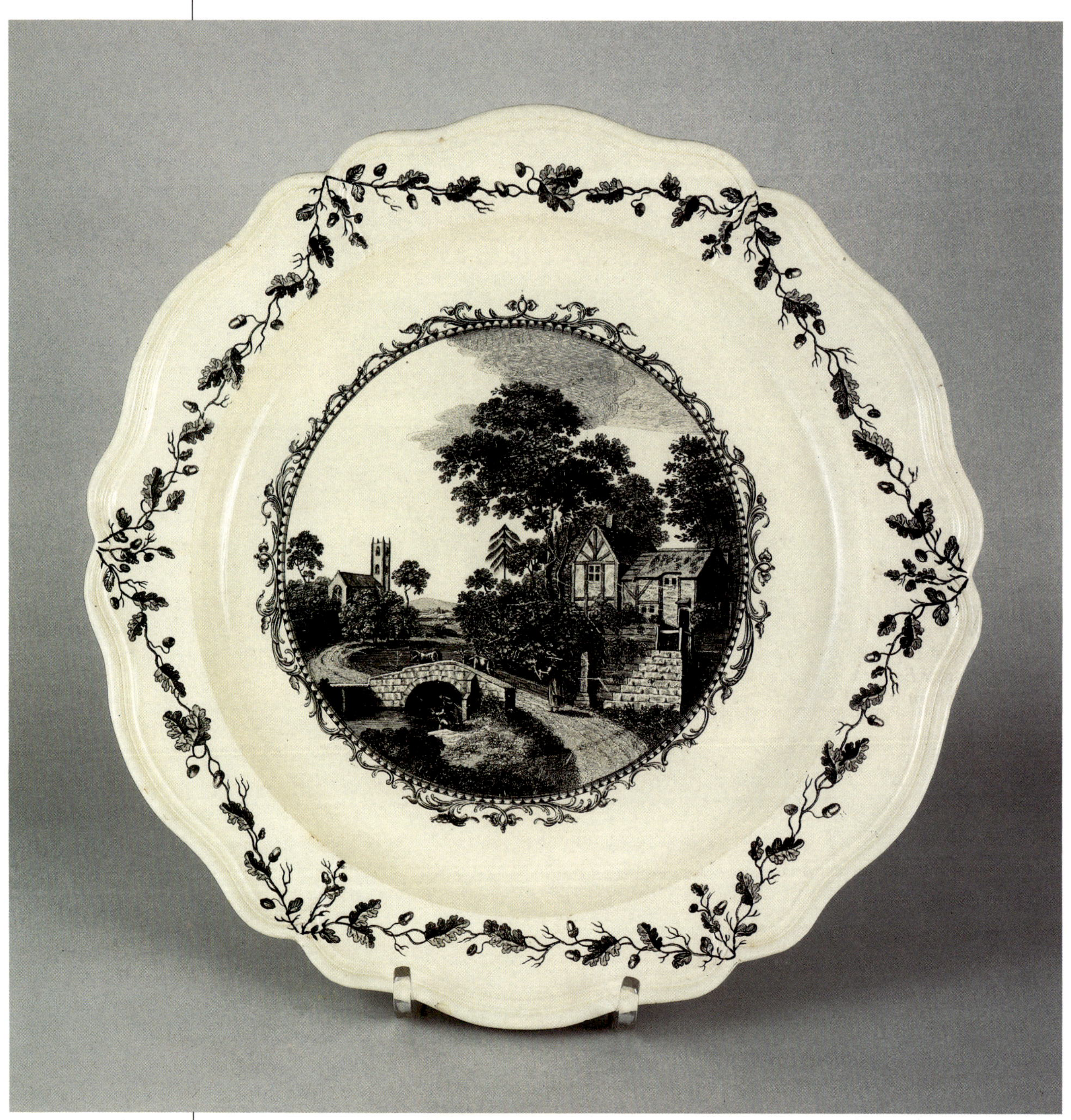

Color plate 21 *Platter,* English Landscape, *ca. 1790, cream ware with transfer decoration, 16" (cat. 65).*

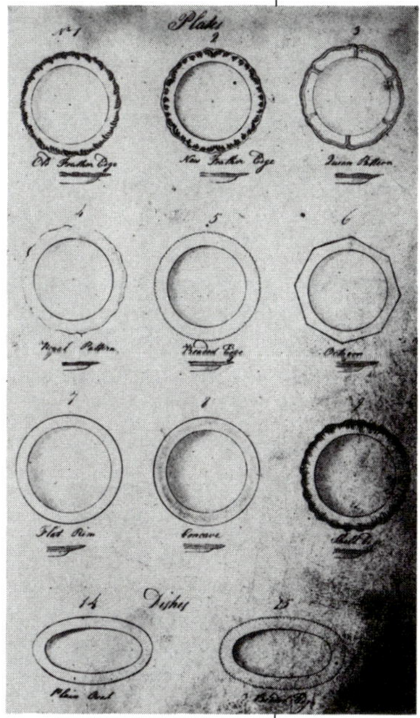

Fig. 4 *Plates and dishes from the 1802 shape drawing book. 1 Old Feather Edge, 2 New Feather Edge, 3 Queen Pattern, 4 Royal Pattern, 5 Beaded Edge, 6 Octagon, 7 Flat Rim, 8 Concave, 9 Shell Edge, 14 Plain Oval, 15 Beaded Edge. Courtesy of the Trustees of the Wedgwood Museum, Barlaston, Stoke-on-Trent, England.*

The Rococo Style

The rococo style is prominent in a number of Wedgwood's cream-ware dishes and plates with three distinct edges: the feather edge, the queen's edge, and the shell edge (fig. 4). The feather edge was popular in the late 1760s, as attested by Wedgwood in a letter of February 18, 1767: "I shall send too a service of feather edge & a service of plain, we shall have feather edged En^{o}. soon, as allmost all the best now ord^{d}. are of that pattern."[35] Characteristic of Wedgwood's feather edge—a molded border decoration of repeated feathery forms—are seven barbs with a small space between the third and fourth barb. This is seen also in Chelsea porcelain.[36]

The queen's edge refers to a shape used on the original service Wedgwood made for Queen Charlotte in 1765: each plate has six lobes around the rim. In an example in the Beeson collection, a large, transfer-decorated platter depicts the landscape of possibly southern England or the Isle of Wight surrounded by a running border of oak leaves and acorns (cat. 65, pl. 21).

The shell edge, as seen in a miniature set and a dessert plate (cat. 39, pl. 22, and cat. 44), was a duplication of the edge of the pecten shell. Wedgwood introduced this molded border in 1770, and it was especially popular from 1779 to 1830. The edge is decorated with either green, blue, or red enamel. "Toys," or miniature tableware services created in the eighteenth and nineteenth centuries, were sometimes used by ladies for miniature houses. In 1795 Queen Charlotte placed an order with Wedgwood for two toy tea sets.

Rococo cream-ware pieces often had gilt decoration. In a letter of August 2, 1765, to his brother John, Wedgwood wrote: "On second thought it may not be amiss to know all one can about this burning on gold polishing, & burnishing the same—burnishing is a different operation to polishing, & I sh^{d}. be glad to know w^{t}. instrument they make use of & be furnish'd with one of them."[37] Letters to Bentley indicate that Wedgwood was experimenting with gilding from at least 1765 through 1771. The method of application resulted in gilt that was impermanent and over time was subject to wear, as is evident in a fine cream-ware teapot with only a small amount of gilt decoration remaining on the spout, handle, rim, and lid (cat. 45, pl. 17, p. 39). The bulbous shape, with double-strap handles terminating in molded leaves, a shell spout,[38] and a floral knop twisted to one side, copies European

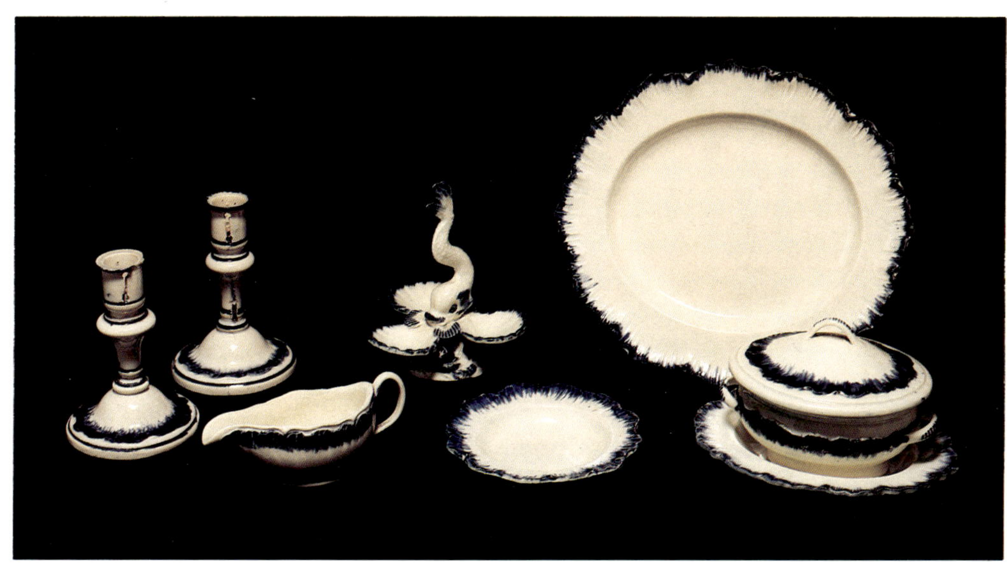

Color plate 22 *Sixty-one piece Miniature Dinner Set, ca. 1785, cream ware with blue underglaze decoration, largest piece: 5 1/4", smallest piece: 3" (cat. 39).*

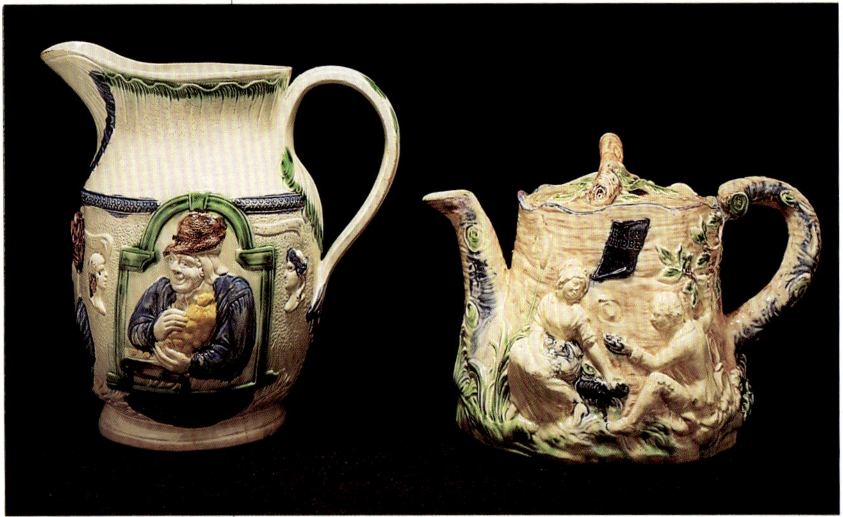

The teapot on the right, in the style of Ralph Wood, is unmarked. But based on its similarity to a pitcher of the same subject impressed "I. VOYEZ 1788", the teapot is attributed to John Voyez. Voyez apparently lent or made different molds for a number of potteries, including those of Robert Garner, Thomas Astbury, and Enoch Wood. One side depicts Hebe with her lover and the other shows cherubs beneath a portrait medallion with the word "Shenstone" inscribed above. William Shenstone (1714-63) wrote a poem titled "Absence", which formed the first part of A Pastoral Ballad in Four Parts *of 1743, beginning "When forc'd the fair nymph to forego, What anguish I felt at my heart!" The text was later adapted to a song, substituting for "the fair nymph" the words "fair Hebe". The portrait of Shenstone was either adapted from a portrait medallion of Frederick the Great or from an engraved portrait bust of Shenstone himself in the frontispieces of R. and J. Dodsley's original edition of the poet's works in* Verse and Prose *of 1764-69. An example similar to this one in the Mint Museum in Charlotte, North Carolina, has a stand for the teapot molded in the same rustic fashion.*

Color plate 23
Left, *Pitcher,* The Spendthrift, the Miser, and Shakespeare, *ca 1790, cream ware with polychrome underglaze decoration, 8 3/16" x 4 1/8" (cat. 31);* right, *Teapot,* Fair Hebe, *ca. 1790, cream ware with underglaze polychrome decoration and molded body, 6 1/4" x 6 1/4" (cat. 32).*

porcelain of the mid-eighteenth century and illustrates Wedgwood's rather retardataire use of rococo design.

Gilding as a decorative motif began to lose favor among Wedgwood's clients by 1772. On March 7 of that year, Wedgwood wrote: "The same noble contempt for Gold reigns, . . . at Dublin as in London—They cannot bear anything Gilt beyond a picture frame, & their stomachs are a little squeamish even about the frames! What will this world come to! Gold, the most precious of all metals, is absolutely kicked out of doors, & our poor Gilders I believe must follow it."[39]

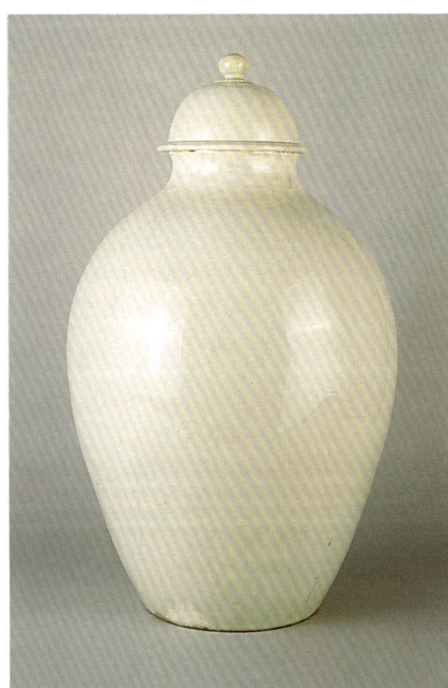

Color plate 24
Cream Cullier, ca. 1780, cream ware with pearl glaze, 21 1/4" x 7 1/4" (cat. 78).

Utilitarian Ware

Cream skimmers, cream culliers, ladles, milk pans, and settling pans were part of Wedgwood's large assortment of "useful wares," or dairy implements produced in cream ware and in pearl ware in the eighteenth and nineteenth centuries. Most of these useful pieces were undecorated unless they were made by special order; and then they were transfer-printed and/or hand-enameled to match the wall tiles on the interior of the dairy.

In the Beeson collection, a rare piece made of cream ware with a pearl glaze, is a large jar or cream cullier covered by a turned top with a knop (cat. 78, pl. 24); it resembles Chinese-decorated porcelain jars of the eighteenth century. An entry of August 1780 in Wedgwood's oven book records a drawing of a similar piece, listing "9 Cream Cullier large Jarrs." This is the only known example in existence and may have been created to be decorated by George Stubbs (1724-1806) in accordance with the following terms, which are set forth in a letter from Wedgwood to Bentley dated August 7, 1780, and which appear not to have been fulfilled:

> We have been considering, & reconsidering some subjects besides tablets for Mr. Stubs [*sic*] to paint in enamel, & are now making some large jarrs for that purpose. The present idea is to cover them over with painting, with ground—figures, trees & sky without any borders or divisions, in short to consider the whole surface as one piece of canvas & cover it accordingly, & under this idea we find a simple jarr form the best for our purpose, & they will come cheap enough which, as times are, may be something in their favor. . . . We are going for the second time to the works to see the jarrs turned & to prepare some clay tablets for modeling upon.[40]

In a letter of August 13, 1780, Wedgwood continued:

> I was telling Mr. Stubs that our vases would sell if they were painted with free masterly sketches . . . but that our stippleing method was tedious beyond all bearing. He was of the same opinion, & will try his hand upon half a doz^{n} jarrs we have made for that purpose, but these are only for himself & friends, & I have not made any other proposals to him—perhaps it will be best to defer it till he has tried his hand upon his jarrs.[41]

This jar is unfortunately unpainted, indicating that the experiment was probably unsuccessful.

Throughout his life, Josiah Wedgwood was always interested in new inventions and knew of the ever-strong market for tea products. His firm introduced the "Simple yet Perfect," or "syp," teapot (cat. 80) about 1905 and continued its production for nearly fifteen years. A separate compartment in the top held the tea leaves, which were brewed when the teapot was tilted on its short legs; after the tea was brewed, it was used in the normal fashion. Both decorated and undecorated versions were available in several different sizes.

The food warmer, or veilleuse, evolved from the simple night-light, which is referred to in Wedgwood's *Queen's Ware Catalogue* of 1774: "Night Lamps, to keep any Liquid warm all night." The name derives from the French verb *veiller*, meaning to keep a night vigil. The object was a hollow pedestal in pottery or porcelain on which sat a bowl for water to warm a covered bowl or teapot above. Inside the pedestal was a small, semiglobular cup called a godet, which held a flaming wick in oil to heat the contents above. In England tea and food warmers were first made in delftware, the earliest known example dating from about 1750, and they continued to be in vogue for the next hundred years. Food warmers were more prevalent in Great Britain than were tea warmers, as the British liked their tea fresh and used it sparingly.

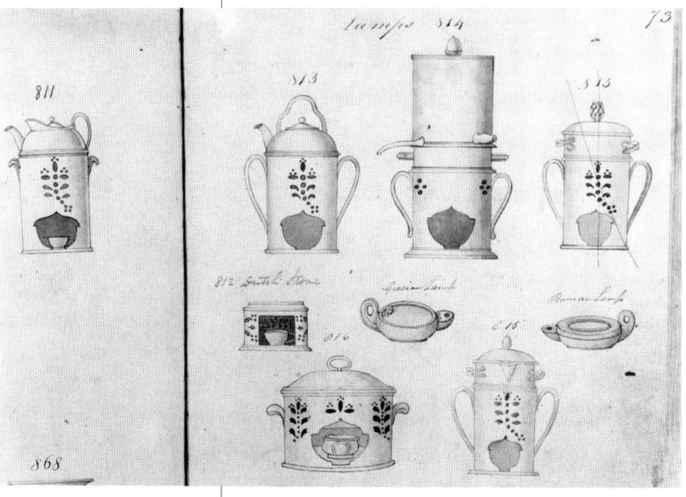

Fig. 5 *Lamps and Food Warmers from the 1802 shape drawing book. Courtesy of the Trustees of the Wedgwood Museum, Barlaston, Stoke-on-Trent, England.*

Early nineteenth-century catalogs quoted various prices for four different sizes of warmers, which varied in height from nine to twelve inches. In Wedgwood's 1802 shape drawing book (fig. 5) (p. 73) and *Queen's Ware Catalogue* of 1817 (p. 15) are pictures of "Lamps" showing the pierced leafage spray that appears on all known Wedgwood food and tea warmers. (This pierced decoration aided in the circulation of air.) A cream-ware tea warmer in the Beeson collection is identical to shape 813 in both books mentioned above (cat. 74, pl. 13, p. 31). Most of Wedgwood's veilleuses have no transfer-printed or enamel decoration.

Portrait Medallions

Cream-ware portrait medallions are rare, and most are thought to have been made by factory ornamenters for their reference.[42] There are four examples in the Beeson collection: Queen Charlotte, Prince Lambertini, Artemisia, and an unknown gentleman (cat. 748, pl. 81, p. 104; cat. 785; and cats. 698, 697, pl. 64, p. 89). Characteristic of these pieces is the word "WEDGWOOD," in uppercase letters, impressed on the back along with the name of the subject in script. Most of these portrait medallions have a small hole punched at the top for hanging, and sometimes the impression of burlap is seen on the back where the clay was pressed into the mold. Many are slightly warped from firing. There are sometimes numbers and letters on the back describing their location in Wedgwood's catalogs.[43]

5
The Frog Service of Catherine the Great of Russia

In 1773 and 1774 Wedgwood devoted himself to what was perhaps his most famous and ambitious endeavor: the creation, for Catherine the Great of Russia, of a dinner-and-dessert service for fifty people. Alexander Baxter, a merchant in Saint Petersburg who was also the Russian consul in London, received a 10-percent fee, according to Wedgwood's accounts, for prompting the commission of the service. It is not unlikely that Baxter saw Wedgwood's work at the residence of Lord Charles and Lady Jane Hamilton Cathcart, British ambassadors to Saint Petersburg from 1768 to 1776; the Cathcarts' residence often served as an informal showroom for new Wedgwood pieces.

The empress was entranced with the Western world and particularly with British life. She employed the Scottish architect Charles Cameron to build palaces and decorated them with English ceramics and paintings. She even had the palace grounds transformed into the kind of landscape favored by Capability Brown, miraculously forcing the lush greenery of England to survive in the cold climate of Russia.[1] Thus Josiah Wedgwood's proposal of views of England, Scotland, and Wales as the decoration for this service could not have suited Catherine's taste better.

This was not Catherine's first encounter with Wedgwood, as he had made a small cream-ware service for her in 1770. It was decorated in what is now called the "husk" pattern, with naturalistic flowers in mulberry pink. Her new service, also made of cream ware, was designed for Chesmenski Palace (*La Grenouillière*), named to honor the naval commander Alexei Orlov's victory over the Turks at the battle of Chesmen. Chesmenski Palace was built by the architect Yuri Velten near a frog swamp, in the environs of Saint Petersburg, so a small green frog was used as the crest on the top of each piece. In a letter dated March 23, 1773, Wedgwood speculated to Bentley: "I suppose it must be painted upon the Royal pattern & that there must be a border upon the rims of the dishes & plates &c of some kind, & the buildings &c in the middle only. . . . The Frog . . . may perhaps be printed."[2]

The architecture of the palace was Gothic revival in style, the earliest example in Russia. A letter written by Wedgwood to Bentley on March 29, 1773, implies that Catherine may have asked that all of the buildings pictured on the Frog Service be in the Gothic style: "As to our being confin'd to Gothique Buildings only, why there are not enough I am perswaded in Great Britain to furnish subjects for this service."[3] Yet Wedgwood attempted to comply with her wishes, as the inner border on the dessert service is somewhat Gothic in appearance.

On the title page of the original *Catalogue and General Description*, Wedgwood and Bentley described their work as "a Complete Service of Porcelain or Queen's China ornamented with various views of ruins in Great Britain, country seats of the nobility, gardens, landscapes, and other embellishments, all painted in enamel, and executed according to the orders and instructions of the most illustrious patroness of arts, the Empress of all the Russias."[4] The task was truly monumental: the service consisted of 952 pieces ornamented by hand in overglaze enamel with 1,222 different views. Depicted were gardens, ruins, bridges, palaces, castles, churches, and some of the great English mansions of the eighteenth century, including Hagley Hall, Castle Howard, Barlaston, Blenheim, and Wedgwood's own home, Etruria Hall. Nearly 100 views are of architectural landmarks of London and the picturesque banks of the Thames. Some of the landscapes were even drawn from nature, and a camera obscura was used to further the work. Today the service is an invaluable historical record of buildings and landscapes that have either disappeared or been drastically altered.

The major design sources were prints, both contemporary and older ones. The location of these prints of landscapes and architectural subjects proved to be Wedgwood's main problem. "I have no idea of this service being got up in less than two or three years if the Landskips & buildings are to be tolerably done, so as to do any credit to us, & to be copied from pictures of real buildings & situations. . . . Why all the Gardens in England will scarcely furnish subjects sufficient for this sett, every piece having a different subject."[5] Wedgwood borrowed books, prints, and drawings from various individuals to use as source material, including *Antiquities*, by Nathaniel Buck; *Journeys to the Hebrides*, by Thomas Pennant; *Views of the Gardens and Buildings at Kew in Surry* [sic], by William Chambers; and *Beauties of Stowe*, by George Bickham.[6]

The cream ware was potted at the Etruria factory in Staffordshire and was decorated at the Chelsea decorating studio. Painting began on April 3, 1773, with the work being done by approximately thirty-three decorators supervised by Thomas Bentley. Two different borders were used: the acorn and oak leaf for the dinner service and the ivy and berry for the dessert service. The ensemble was painted totally by hand in sepia, the only color being the green frog crest at the top. In an assembly-line fashion, the decorators divided up the borders, the frogs, and the central scenes. While they remained faithful to the original outlines of the engravings, they showed some artistic license in adapting a view to the shape of its vessel. On the back of each piece, under the glaze, was a number keyed to the *Catalogue of the Complete Service*, which provided the title and location of each view.

Before the work was completed in 1774, Wedgwood wrote to Bentley concerning an exhibition of the Frog Service before its departure for Russia:

> On one side, it [the exhibition] would bring an immense number of People of Fashion into our Rooms—wo^{d} fully complete our notoriety to the whole Island, & help us greatly, no doubt, in the sale of our goods, both usefull & ornamental. It wo^{d} confirm the consequence we have attain'd. . . . We should shew that we have paid many comp^{ts} to our Friends & Customers, & thereby rivet them more firmly to our interests, but . . . you see the danger. For suppose a Gent^{n} thinks himself neglected, either by the omission of his seat . . . or by puting it upon a small piece. . . . He then becomes our enemy. . . . I am not able to determine anything, but your opinion thrown into either scale will make the other kick the beam.[7]

Obviously Bentley supported the idea, for an exhibition of the entire service was held at the new Portland House showroom on Greek Street in Soho in June of 1774 and remained on view there for two months. An advertisement in the newspaper gave the location for the exhibition and stated that admission was by ticket only. The nobility visited the showroom in great and increasing numbers, and before the first week was over, the Russian service was one of the most popular sights in London; indeed, Queen Charlotte herself came to view it. The public showing of the service became an advertising scheme that successfully won the patronage of the court and its circles, the friendship of the artistic world, and the respect of the gentry and aristocracy.

By October of 1774, Wedgwood's cream ware had arrived in Russia and had been paid for, despite his earlier fears that he might never receive payment. The total cost to Wedgwood and Bentley was £2,290, excluding Baxter's 10-percent commission, and Catherine did indeed pay approximately £2,700, providing Wedgwood a small profit along with worldwide acclaim. Until 1830 the service was located in Chesmenski Palace and thereafter in the English Palace at Peterhof. Since 1912 a portion of the 770 pieces that survive have been on display at the Hermitage in Leningrad.

Wedgwood continued to exploit the success of this service by producing and displaying similar examples. They differed from the original set, however, in that they were painted in polychrome without the frog. After the completed service was sent to Russia, they were exhibited continuously at the Greek Street showroom. A letter dated June 20, 1774, and written by Wedgwood to Bentley states: "I should be glad to have a few duplicates of the Russian Service sent to Etruria next Monday. . . . I think the fine painted pieces condemn'd to be set aside, whether it be on account of their being blister'd, or duplicates, or any other fault, except poor & bad painting, should be divided between Mr. Baxter & Etruria, & we may paint more, without the Frog, to be shewn in Greek Street."[8] Sixteen of these polychrome examples exist. They are distinguished not only by their coloring and their place-name on the front but also by their 8 7/8-inch size, which is unlike any plate in the service sent to Russia. Also known to be outside of Russia are twenty-one monochrome examples. They are thought to be either rejects or duplicates of objects sent to Russia. Two of the monochrome pieces and one of the polychrome plates are in the Beeson collection.

The large monochrome serving platter depicts Ditchley Park in Oxfordshire (cat. 36, pl. 25). Its enameled number 434 in the original catalog does not correspond to that entry (which describes a view of Richmond, Surrey). The scene of Ditchley

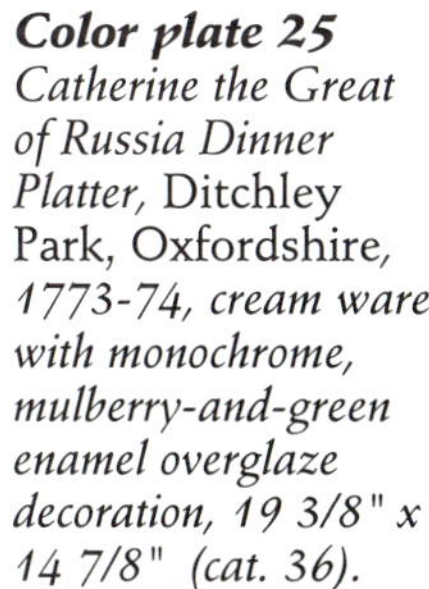

Color plate 25
Catherine the Great of Russia Dinner Platter, Ditchley Park, Oxfordshire, *1773-74, cream ware with monochrome, mulberry-and-green enamel overglaze decoration, 19 3/8" x 14 7/8" (cat. 36).*

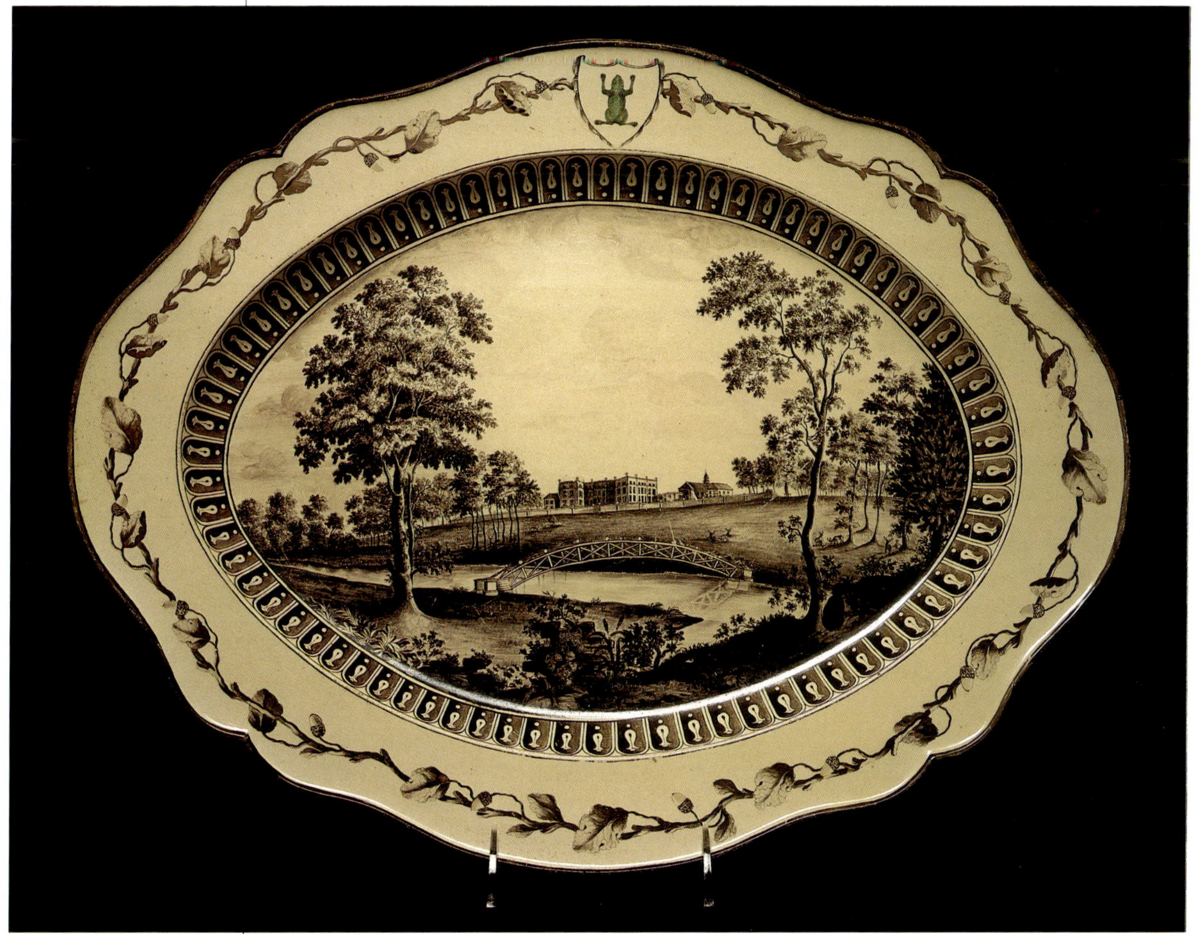

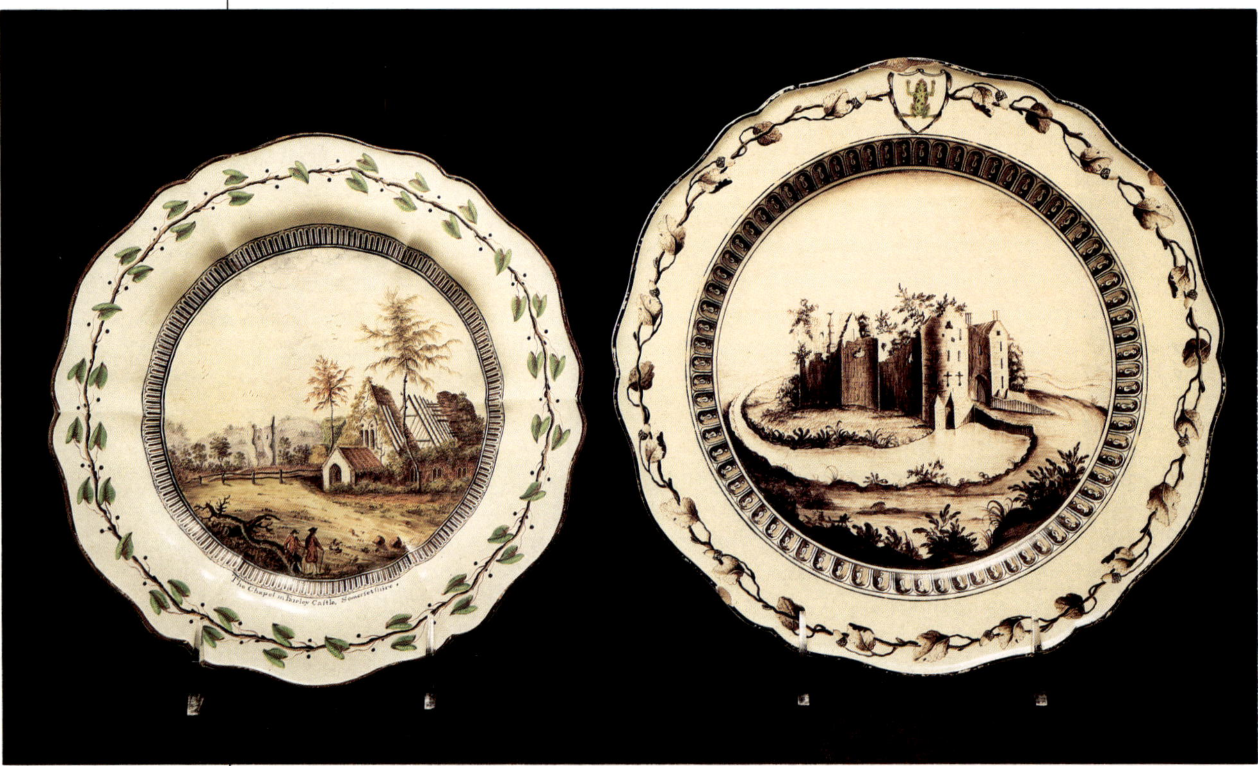

Color plate 26
Left, *Catherine the Great of Russia Dessert Plate,* The Chapel in Fairley Castle, Somersetshire, *1773-74, cream ware with polychrome enamel overglaze decoration, 8 15/16" (cat. 38);* right, *Catherine the Great of Russia Dinner Plate,* Saint Brivals Castle, Gloucestershire, *1773-74, cream ware with monochrome, mulberry, and green enamel overglaze decoration, 9 7/8" (cat. 37).*

Park that appears on a piece of the service that survives in Russia is Bentley catalog number 231. The printed source, by Luke Sullivan and published on March 1, 1759, is entitled *A View of Ditchley in Oxfordshire, the Seat of the Rt. Honble, the Earl of Litchfield.*[9] The house dates from 1722 and was built for the Lee family, from whom the Confederate general Robert E. Lee descended. James Gibbs was the architect, and the interior decorators were William Kent and Henry Flitcroft. Used as the weekend headquarters of Winston Churchill during World War II, the house is now an Anglo-American conference center and is open to the public by appointment.

A smaller plate with an acorn-and-oak-leaf border is marked number 30 and displays a view of Saint Brivals Castle in Gloucestershire (cat. 37, pl. 26). Wedgwood's printed source for the view was an engraving entitled *The East View of St. Bravels* [sic] *Castle, in the County of Gloucester.*[10] The origins of the castle are thought to date back to the twelfth century, but most of the structure dates from the thirteenth century. Located on the Welsh border, the castle has no military history but was used for royal hunting parties in the Forest of Dean. It is now a youth hostel and the property of the Crown.[11]

The polychrome plate depicts the chapel in Fairley Castle, Somersetshire, now known as Farleigh Hungerford Castle (cat. 38, pl. 26). It was built by Sir Thomas Hungerford in the middle to late fourteenth century.[12] The same scene was used on two cream-ware dishes in the Russian service (Bentley catalog nos. 637, 1102).

6
White Terra-cotta Stoneware

Crystalline Vases

In the mid-eighteenth century, ancient vases made of variegated stone were quite popular, although costly. Knowing the desirability of and the potential demand for these decorative pieces, architect Robert Adam, in collaboration with metalsmith Matthew Boulton, began producing vases of Derbyshire stone, called "blue john," with ormolu mounts. In about 1760, Wedgwood and Bentley accepted the challenge themselves and began producing cream-ware vases in imitation of stone, with gilded handles and edges creating the effect of metal fittings, or ormolu. Wedgwood's vases were so successful that, by November of 1768, Boulton proposed to make ormolu mounts for Wedgwood.[1] On December 1, 1769, Wedgwood wrote to Bentley: "We have some Medallion Vases in the Oven, & are making plenty of them which you shall see in due time, I now give my self up allmost entirely to Vasemaking & find myself to improve in that Art & Mysterie pretty fast."[2]

A second clay called white terra-cotta stoneware was also used for the body of the vases. Wedgwood first mentioned white terra-cotta stoneware in a letter of September 27, 1769.[3] White terra-cotta stoneware is a confusing term, as most people today think of terra-cotta as a red clay, but Wedgwood's use of the word "terra-cotta" refers to its actual meaning: baked earth. The ware was used first for making medallions, plaques, tablets, and, soon thereafter, vases.[4] White terra-cotta stoneware is described in a variety of ways in Wedgwood's catalogs: "fine white terra-cotta" (1774), "white waxen Biscuit Ware, or Terra Cotta" (1779), and "White porcelain biscuit with a smooth wax-like surface" (1787). Its composition, as found in Wedgwood's second experiment book, was "one part Purbeck clay and two parts Cornish Moorstone."[5] These elements are similar to those in cream ware, with the exception of a greater proportion of flint and the addition of Derbyshire chert. Frequently confused with cream ware, white terra-cotta stoneware has greater definition within the decorative elements of the piece and a less visual appearance of the puddled green cream-ware glaze at the crevices.[6]

"Crystalline," the name Wedgwood gave to this ware, is synonymous with variegated, marbled, porphyry, granite, agate ware, and Egyptian pebble glazing. Three different methods were used to achieve the desired effect. For variegated, marbled, porphyry, and granite, a mixing or dusting of metallic oxides of different colors was placed under a clear lead glaze. For agate ware, clays of different colors were wedged together into a body (solid agate), or colored slips were used; the colors could include brown, red, yellow, and white. Egyptian pebble, or speckled, ware was produced by spraying colored slips onto the surface. There are ten vases with crystalline decoration in the Beeson collection, all from the

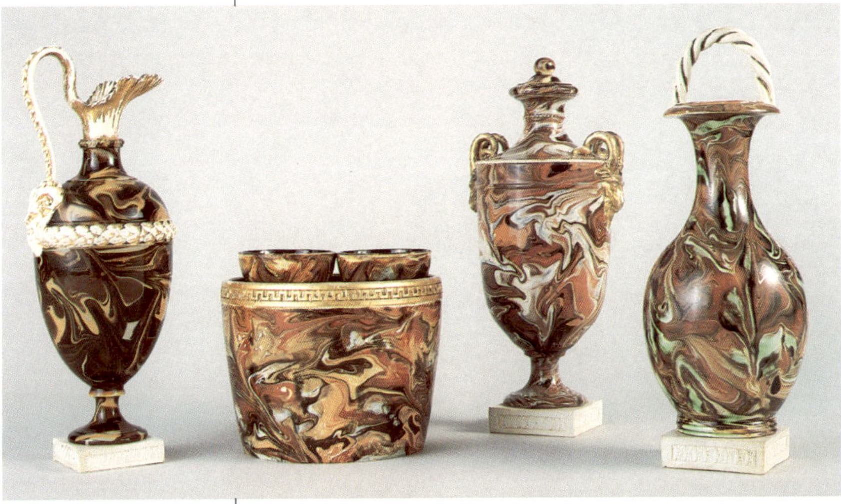

Color plate 27
Left, *Ewer, ca. 1770, white terra-cotta stoneware with agate slip underglaze, white terra-cotta base, and gilding, 8 15/16" x 1 7/8" (cat. 93);* second from left, *Pair of Bulb Pots, ca. 1770, cream ware with agate slip underglaze, gilded border, and glazed interior, 3 3/4" x 4 1/16" (cat. 91);* third from left, *Covered Vase, ca. 1770, white terra-cotta stoneware with agate slip underglaze, white terra-cotta stoneware base, and gliding, 8 3/4" x 2 1/4" (cat. 96);* right, *Vase, ca. 1775, white terra-cotta stoneware with agate slip underglaze, terra-cotta stoneware base, 8 7/8" x 2 3/16" (cat. 95).*

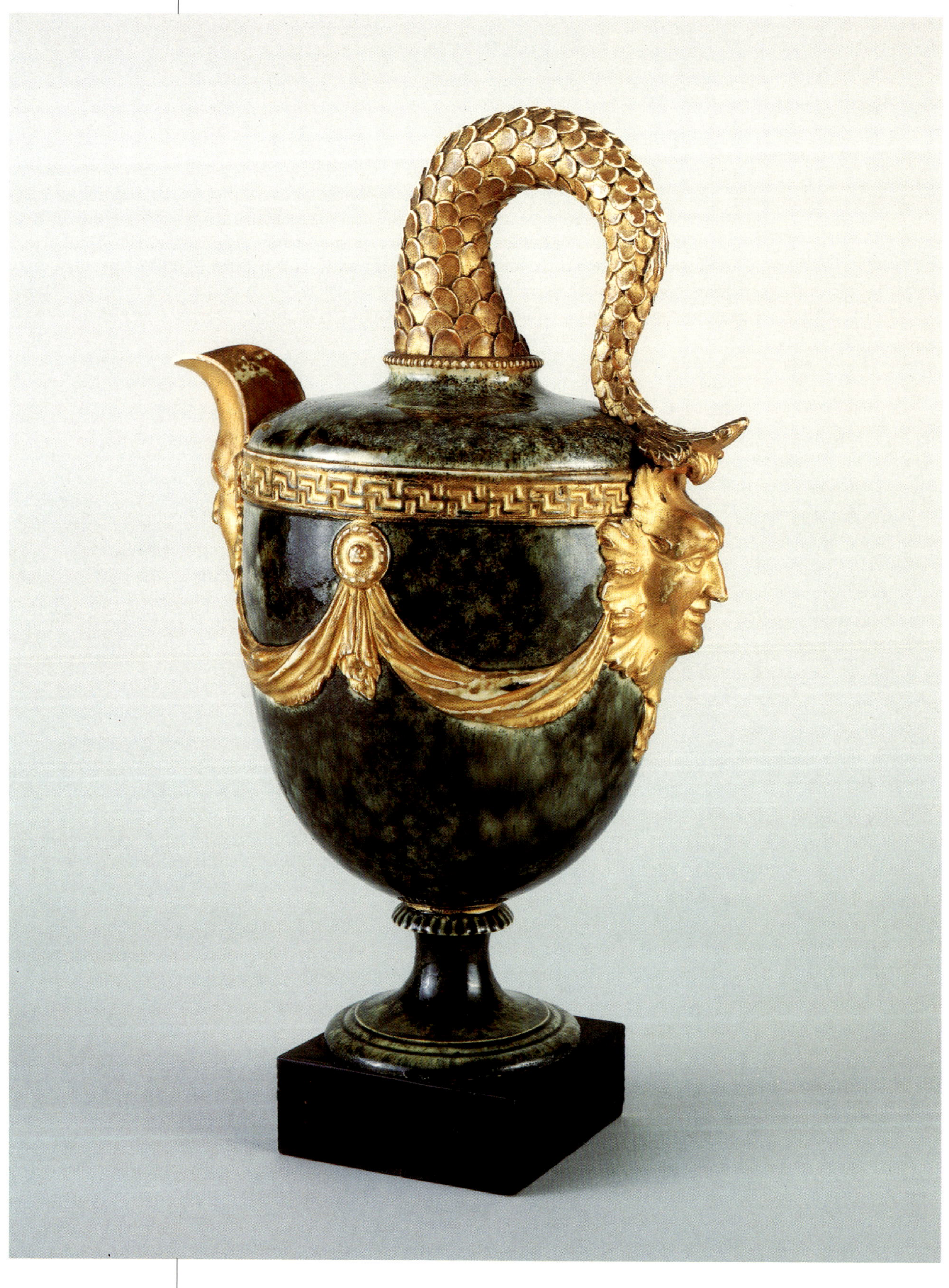

Color plate 28
Stella Ewer,
ca. 1775, white terra-cotta stoneware with sponged color underglaze, basalt base, and gilding, 12 1/8" x 3 1/8" (cat. 84).

Wedgwood and Bentley period of 1769-80 (cats. 84-88, 92-96, pl. 27).

Wedgwood wrote to Bentley on May 1, 1769: "Vases, . . . Vases are all the cry."[7] "I could sell £50 or £100 worth Per day if I had them!"[8] Their success even forced Wedgwood to say wearily: "Strange as it may sound I sho^{d}. be glad never to receive another order for any particular kind of Vases, & I sho^{d}. wish you to avoid taking such ord^{rs} as much as you decently can, at least 'till we are got into a more methodical way of making the same sorts over again, & there is no other way of doing this but by having models, & mould of every shape & size we make. This plan I have been pursueing some time, & have many models ready to fire this week."[9]

Wedgwood's vases were usually composed of three separate parts—the body, the foot, and the plinth. The body and foot were of the same medium and were glued together. The plinth, often impressed underneath around the hole with a wafer mark bearing the names of Wedgwood and Bentley, was made in both basalt and white terra-cotta stoneware and was affixed with a screw and nut that eliminated warpage of the heavy body on the small stem during the firing. Wedgwood was the first potter to use this method of constructing vases. On April 3, 1771, he wrote to Bentley: "There is a way in which I believe they may be made with slender & yet straight feet, & that is to make & fire them seperate, & afterwards fix the Vase, foot, & plinth together by a pin, screw & nut, & I believe in this way they may be made to hold water by putting a piece of leather betwixt the screw head & the bottom of the inside of the Vase."[10] This sectional sequence soon became the norm at Wedgwood and was used for many white terra-cotta stoneware, basalt, and jasper vases.

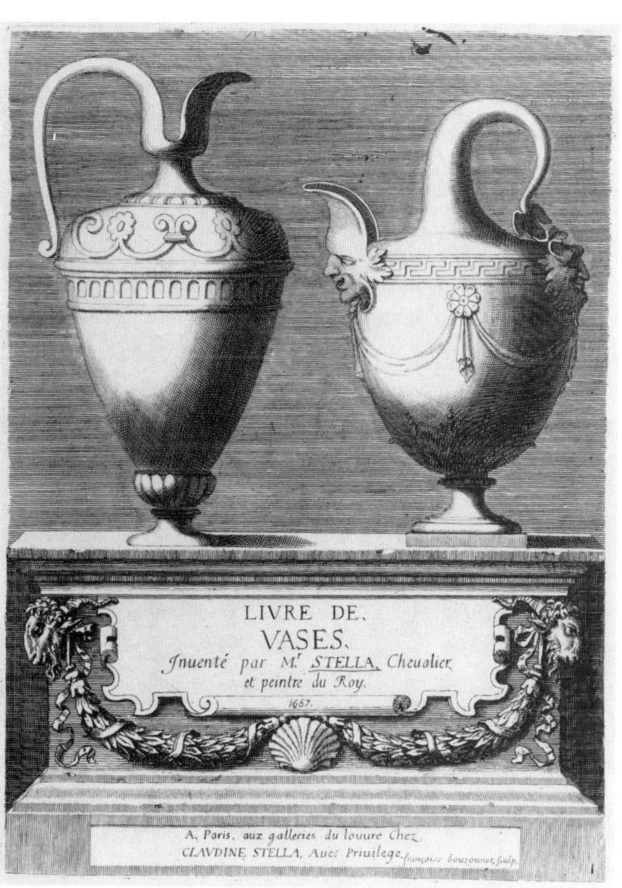

Fig. 6 *Title page to* Livre de vases *by Jacques de Stella, Paris, ca. 1667. Etched by Françoise Bouzonnet Stella, the author's niece. Courtesy of the Victoria and Albert Museum, London, England.*

The finest example in the Beeson collection is the crystalline ewer that Wedgwood commonly referred to as "Stellas Ewer," after the French painter and etcher, Jacques de Stella (1596-1657) (cat. 84, pl. 28).[11] The source for the design is the title page of *Livre de vases aux galeries de Louvre,* which contained illustrations of cases by de Stella in the Louvre (fig. 6). On August 22, 1770, Wedgwood wrote to Bentley: "I am glad you have met with such a Treasure in Stella, & shall be glad to have it here for our edifications—Cannot M^{r}. Coward offtrace the heads and handles & so we may have the book allmost immediately, for I long to see it."[12] On this ewer, the overall design, including the masks and fishtail, was taken from the book illustrated by de Stella.[13] Elements of other vases of this period were also copied from this book, which is known to have been in Wedgwood's library.[14]

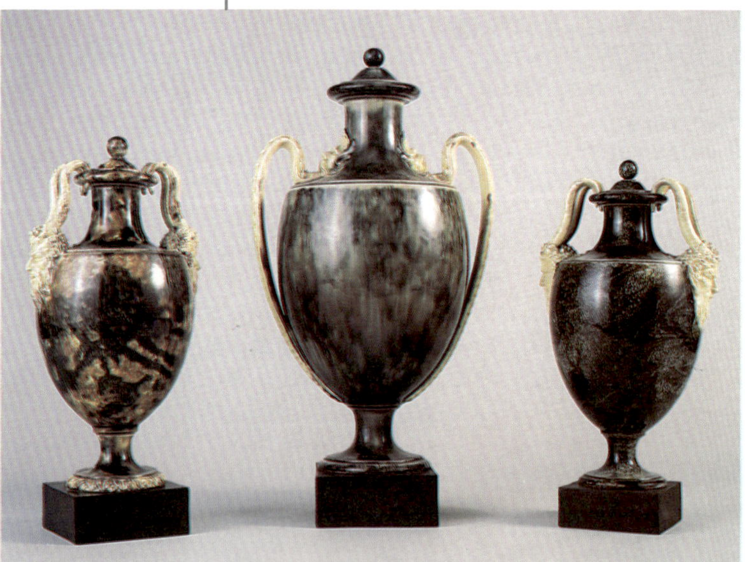

Color plate 29
Left, *Covered Vase, ca. 1770, white terra-cotta stoneware with sponged color underglaze and basalt base, 9 7/8" x 2 15/16" (cat. 88);* center, *Covered Vase, ca. 1770, white terra-cotta stoneware with sponged color underglaze and basalt base, 12 1/2" x 3 3/16" (cat. 92);* right, *Covered Vase, ca. 1770, white terra-cotta stoneware with sponged color underglaze and basalt base, 9 1/8" x 2 11/16" (cat. 87).*

There are in the Beeson collection several crystalline satyr-head vases that were later made in basalt and jasper ware (cats. 86-88, 92, pl. 29). The designer of the satyr-head vase was Joseph-Marie Vien (1716-1809), whose work was etched by his wife, Marie Thérèse Reboul Vien (1729-1805) in *Suite de vases composée dans le gout de l'antique*. Wedgwood and Bentley recorded this design as "Number I shape" in their ornamental shape book, and potteries such as Chelsea used the design as well.[15] An example in basalt appears on a table in George Stubbs's portrait, *The Wedgwood Family in the Grounds of Etruria Hall* (see pl. 10).

Although Wedgwood and Bentley continued to make crystalline vases into the 1780s, the popularity of these vases among the upper classes was short-lived, because by 1772 the preference for basalt was on the rise. Wedgwood wrote to Bentley on August 19, 1772: "What articles are likely to be benefitted by lowering the prices ? & what not,—Bough pots must be low or they will not sell at all, & I think more Pebble Vases wd be sold if they were lower'd within reach of those who prefer Pebble Gilt Vases to black ones. People of fine taste we know will not buy them at any price, & whether we have customers enough of the other sort to make it worth while to lower them much, you are the best judge."[16] The Wedgwood and Bentley *Ornamental Catalogue* of 1773 shows what the partners had decided: the vases were advertised and sold as mantel garniture in pairs and in sets of three, five, and even seven, and the prices were not lowered (pl. 30).

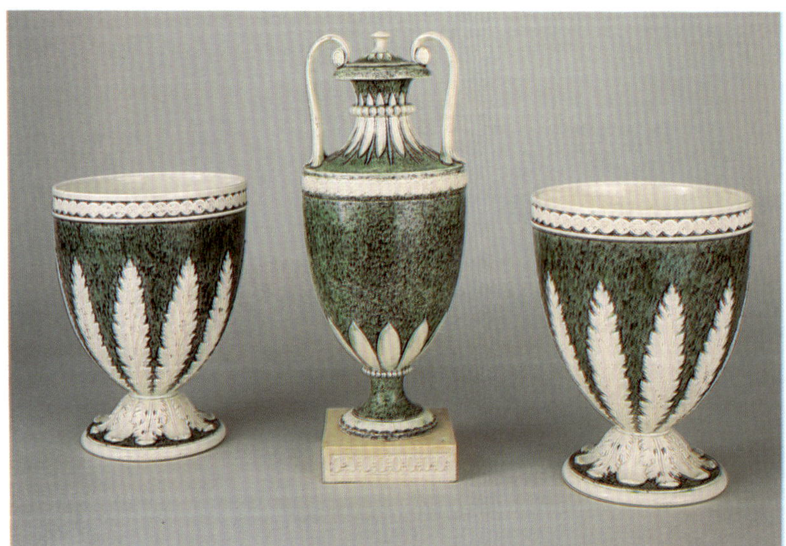

Color plate 30 Left and right, *Pair of Vases, ca. 1770, white terra-cotta stoneware with imitation porphyry under a pearl glaze, 6 13/16" x 4" (cat. 102);* center, *Covered Vase, ca. 1770, white terra-cotta stoneware with imitation porphyry under a pearl glaze, and white terra-cotta stoneware base, 10 7/8" x 3 3/8" (cat. 104).*

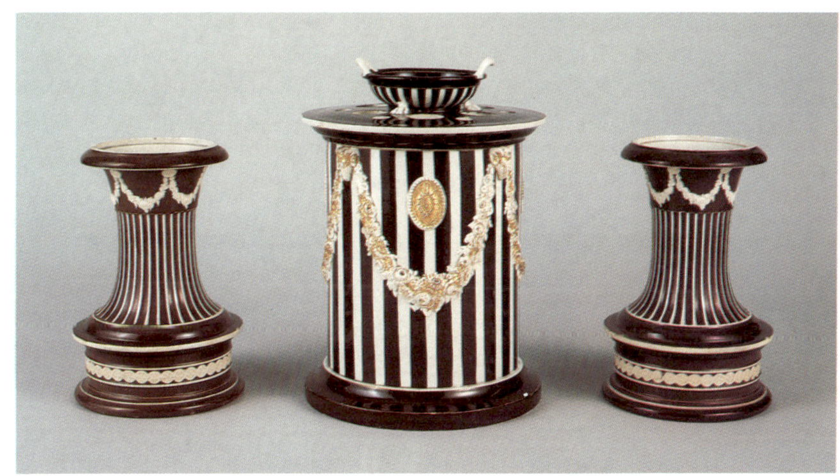

Color plate 31 Left and right, *Pair of Vases, ca. 1790, white terra-cotta stoneware with slip decoration under pearl glaze, 6 11/16" x 4 7/16" (cat. 97);* center, *Potpourri Vase, ca. 1790, white terra-cotta stoneware with slip decoration, pearl glaze, and gilt, 8 15/16" x 6 1/4" (cat. 106).*

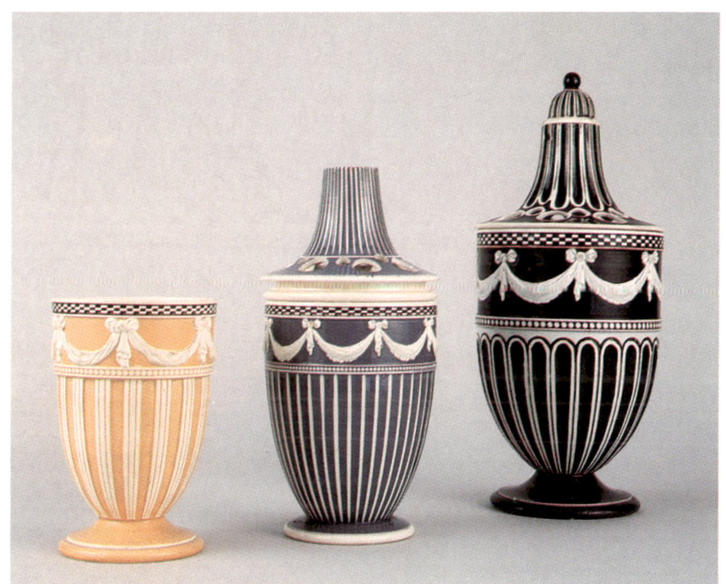

Color plate 32 Left, *Vase, ca. 1780, white terra-cotta stoneware with slip decoration and clear glaze, 5 7/16" x 3 3/8" (cat. 100);* center, *Bulb Pot, ca. 1785, cream ware or white terra-cotta stoneware with slip decoration and pearl glaze, 9 7/16" x 3 1/16" (cat. 101);* right, *One of a Pair of Potpourri Vases, ca. 1785, cream ware or white terra-cotta stoneware with slip decoration and pearl glaze, 10 15/16" x 3 7/8" (cat. 105).*

Slip-Decorated Vases

From 1773 to about 1790, slip-decorated vases and bough and bulb pots were made in cream ware and white terra-cotta stoneware; they were made later in pearl ware (cats. 97, 106, pl. 31). The objects were covered with clay slips of different colors—blue, brown, buff, peach, and white—often with engine-turning showing through the slip and the clear lead or pearl glaze. Pendant swags, beads, and leaves were often applied and frequently gilded, again in effect of ormolu.[17]

Bough and bulb pots with this slip decoration were extremely popular forms in the late eighteenth century and were among Wedgwood and Bentley's most successful items. In his first commonplace book, Wedgwood wrote of "Essential properties of Bow Pots": "To hold a good quantity of flowers, unless they are small ones for a choice flower or two out of the hot house;—therefore they should be kept as wide as the beauty of their shape will admit of in the neck & top—but so as Not to turn out at the top, for that spreads the flowers disagreeably. To be of a different earth, colour, or composition, from the common earthenware in use at the time being, and to come at a moderate price."[18] A variety of bough and bulb pots are included in the Beeson collection (cats. 100, 101, 105, pl. 32).

A large and rare bouquetière of about 1790, in oval form, shows another variation on the bulb pot (cat. 103, pl. 33). The body is white terra-cotta stoneware decorated with unglazed black slip. Molded in a basket-weave pattern, the pot is accented with hand-twisted white rope at the lip, ankle, and foot. This container was made to accommodate cut flowers through its pierced lid. The interior is lightly glazed for protection from floral stains.

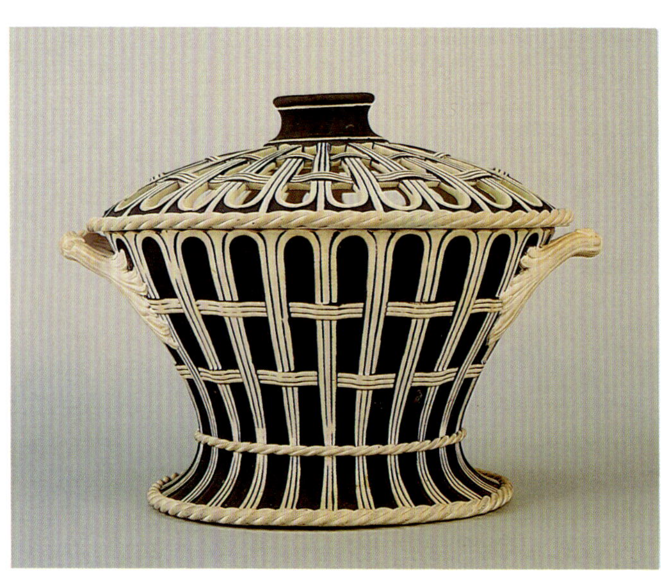

Color plate 33
Covered basket, ca. 1785, white terra-cotta stoneware with mat black slip decoration and glazed interior, 8 1/4" x 7 3/4" (cat. 103).

7
Basalt

The invention of basalt ware has been attributed to Staffordshire potters other than Wedgwood, yet no shards from archaeological excavations in the area have documented this fine-grained stoneware before his time.[1] Wedgwood created a completely black body by combining a refined car, an iron oxide that yielded a brown-black, and manganese, a dark purple.[2] Car was a sediment found in the drainage of neighboring coal deposits. The first documentary evidence of a black basalt vase is dated August 30, 1768, a letter in which Wedgwood mentions "a basket containing 2 Etruscan bronze Vases full of my best compliments to Miss Tarleton, . . . & [I] beg her acceptance of them as an offering of first fruits."[3] As Wedgwood wrote to Bentley on January 13, 1771: "Some of my present views are . . . to make a black body, that shall shrink little or none in burning. To make a black & a red body as light as can be consistent with other necessary qualitys. . . . The next to make Tablets & figures &c without cracking, & the third to make real Antiques you know."[4] The ware was not easily perfected: "It is impossible to make the surface [of the black vases] allways alike, the difference being made in the fire. . . . But I am trying another method to render the surface smoother in general."[5]

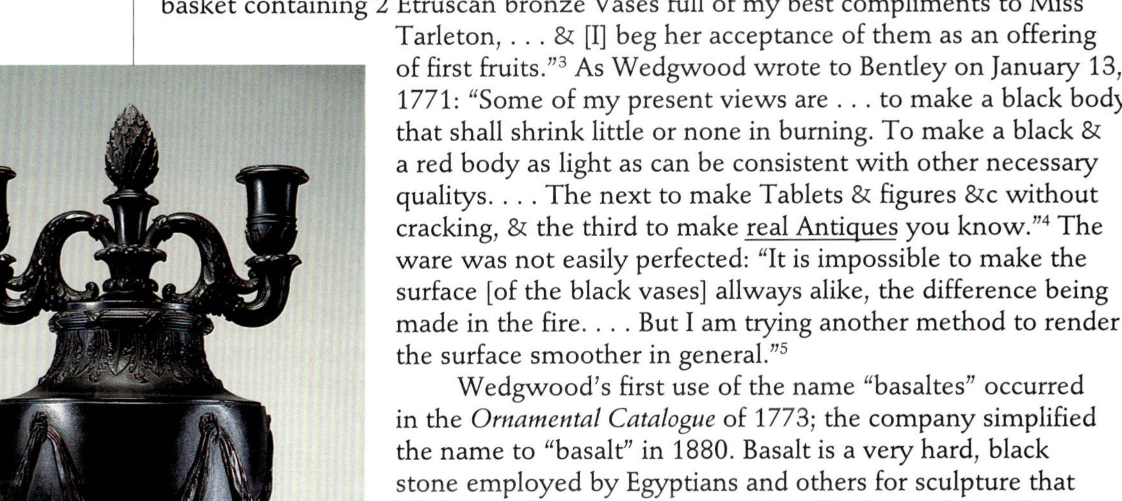

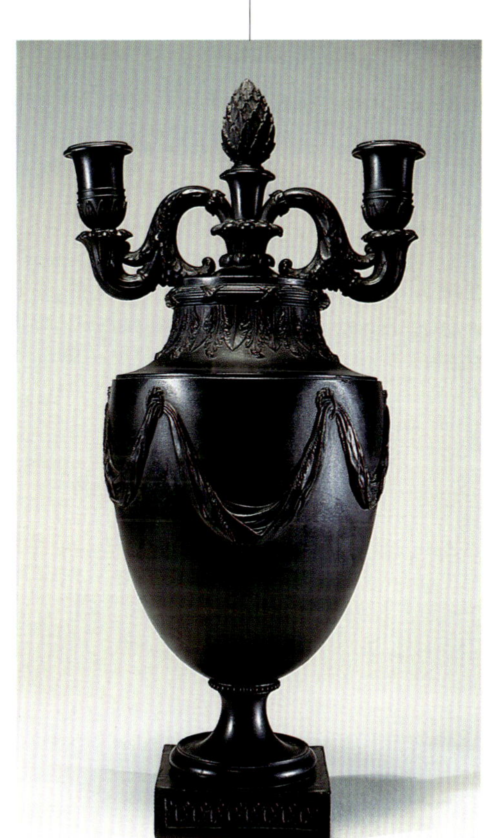

Color plate 34
Vase with Candelabra, ca. 1780, basal[illegible] 16 3/4" x 3[illegible] (cat. 121).

Wedgwood's first use of the name "basaltes" occurred in the *Ornamental Catalogue* of 1773; the company simplified the name to "basalt" in 1880. Basalt is a very hard, black stone employed by Egyptians and others for sculpture that Wedgwood's stoneware resembled. Wedgwood described the ware as "Antique Vases, Urns, etc. of a fine Black Porcelaine, having nearly the same Properties as the Basaltes, resisting the Attacks of Acids; being a Touch-stone to Copper, Silver and Gold; and equal in Hardness to Agate or Porphyry."[6] Here, for the first time, Wedgwood initiated the copying of ancient vases, thus creating his own market rather than competing with the production of semiprecious stone vases made by other designers of the time. Wedgwood is often quoted as saying, "The Black is Sterling and Will last forever."[7]

Due to the composition of the body, basalt ware had a naturally polished look. Of this polishing Wedgwood wrote on August 31, 1768: "NB the polish is natural to the Composition and is given in burning, they are never oil'd &c."[8] But two years later Wedgwood admited to polishing the ware while it was still in a biscuit state. In a letter to Bentley dated August 11, 1770, already quoted above, he wrote: "I am trying another method to render the surface [of the black vases] smoother in general when no accidents happen in the fireing, which is to burnish them when they are pretty hard, with steel burnishers, 'till they have the polish of a Mirror; but as this is done by hand it is very tedious work but they take an admirable polish if the fire does not destroy it which I can acquaint you of soon, having sent one of them to Burslem to be bisketed there."[9] But even if left unpolished, basalt still has a gloss, which is imparted to it during the firing.

Tablets and Medallions

In 1769 Wedgwood introduced a method of decoration for basalt called bronzing, which was achieved by lightly firing a film mixture of aqua regia and bronze filings onto the ware. Matthew Boulton is credited with being the first to treat vases to resemble antique bronze; Wedgwood may have secured this technique from Boulton and his partner, Dr. John Fothergill. In February 1769, Wedgwood described the method of "Bronzing" in a letter to Bentley:

> Lay Dr Turners brown Varnish on the same as for gilding, then mix some of y^{r} bronze powder in a saucer with a large proportion of Lampblack, both dry. W^{n} the size is of a proper dryness for gilding, lay this powd^{r} on plentifully wth a large camel hair, or soft pencil, . . . warm the vases, . . . when dry rub them well with a hard brush, dry them with a gentle warmth, & they are finish'd.[10]

Because the firing method was not permanent, pieces with even traces of this treatment are rare.

The Beeson collection is fortunate to have a bronzed basalt tablet: *The Apotheosis of Homer; or, Homer and Hesiod* (cat. 124, pl. 35). It portrays the deification of Homer for his writing of his epic poems the *Iliad* and the *Odyssey*. The design source is in Hamilton's *Antiquités*.[11] (While the tablet shows the figures in the same positions as on the ancient vase, Wedgwood's later jasper-ware vases with the same scene display it in reverse.) In a letter to Hamilton dated February 26, 1779, Bentley praised the tablet: "Having modelled a large Tablet from one of the unpublished Designs in your Excellency's Collection at the British Museum which we copied from a drawing lent us by Mr. D'Hancarville, and which we consider as one of the most perfect Specimens of the present State of our Ornamental Manufactory, we could not resist the desire of presenting you with a Coppy [*sic*] of this Work, which has come happily thro' the fiery Trial, and which we hope you will do us the Honour to place in your Cabinet, or in some of your Apartments."[12] On June 22, Hamilton wrote back to Wedgwood and Bentley, saying, "Your Delightfull Basrelief of the Apotheose [*sic*] of Homer, or some celebrated Poet indeed it is far superior to my most sanguine expectation."[13] In a subsequent letter, dated July 24, 1786, Hamilton referred to John Flaxman, Jr., as the modeler and stated: "I never saw a bas-relief executed in the true simple antique style half so well as that he did of the Apotheosis of Homer from one of my vases."[14] The letter does not say whether the tablet given to Hamilton was of jasper ware or basalt, but the reference to the "antique style" may mean that it was of bronzed basalt. The tablet in the Beeson collection has at least twenty firing holes on the back as well as remnants of plaster, indicating that it had been inserted in an architectural framework.

The earliest basalt medallions made by Wedgwood were self-framed, and in the Beeson collection is a self-framed portrait of Minerva, the Roman goddess of wisdom and patroness of the arts (cat. 112; pl. 36). A possible design source is in Montfaucon's *L'Antiquité expliquée* (fig. 7).[15] This bas-relief was modeled by John Flaxman, Jr., in 1775, and two block molds of the subject exist at the Wedgwood factory. Minerva is portrayed in profile and is dressed in the garb of a warrior. Her helmet displays the profile of a man's head with a laurel wreath, on top of which appears the mythological figure of a dragon. On the back are smoothing marks executed by hand. The frame is gilded and has an inner border of reeds with crossed straps within an outer frame of fluted cavettos. This medallion is unsigned but dates from the Wedgwood and Bentley period.

Also in the Beeson collection is one of the sixteen self-framed medallions by Wedgwood from Herculaneum wall paintings entitled *Letter to Polyphemus* (cat. 118, pl. 37). Wedgwood's medallions were modeled from the original bas-reliefs brought

Color plate 35
Tablet, Apotheosis of Homer, *1775-80, basalt, bronzing, 7 3/4" x 14 3/4" (cat. 124).*

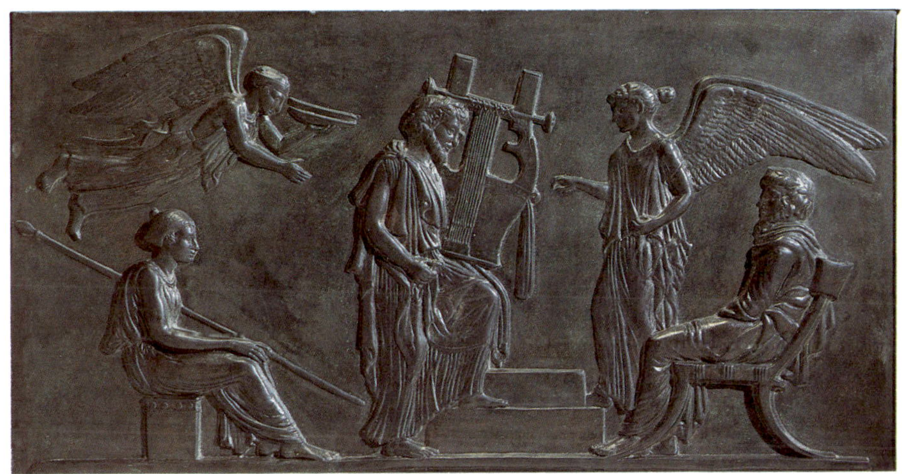

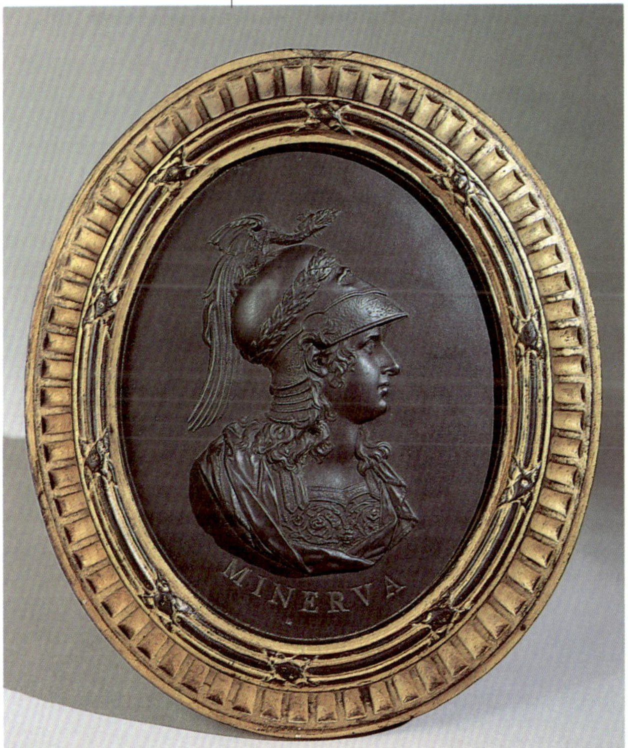

Color plate 36 *Roundel,* Minerva, *ca. 1780, basalt, gilt decoration, self-framed, 7 3/4" x 6 3/4" (cat. 112).*

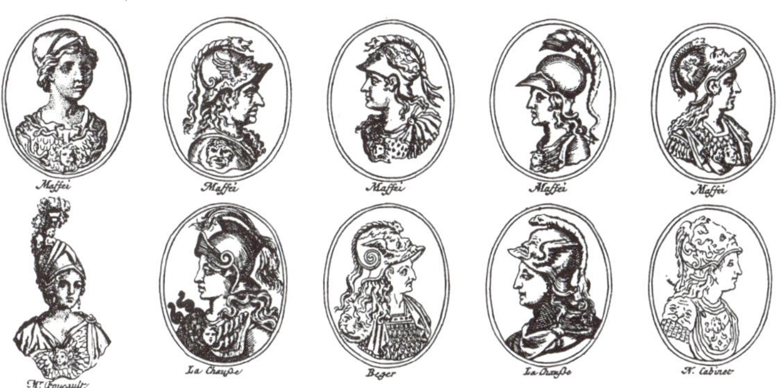

Fig. 7 *Montfaucon,* L'Antiquité expliquée, *vol. 1, pt. 1, p. 85, pl. 41, figs. 9-13.* Minerva.

to England from Italy by the marquis of Lansdowne. John Bacon, Sr., is said to have been the modeler,[16] and the plaster casting was by Hoskins and Oliver, whose invoice of December 31, 1770, states, "Making Molds on sixteen round Basso-relievos."[17] There also exist some examples of this series in white terra-cotta stoneware and basalt with encaustic decoration. This roundel is unmarked but was made in the eighteenth century.

Two small, oval, nineteenth-century basalt plaques in the Beeson collection represent scenes from the *Marriage Supper of Perseus and Andromeda* and the *Destruction of Niobe's Children* (cats. 168, 169). They are based on Renaissance bronzes by Jacob Cornelisz (1477-1533) after originals by Guglielmo della Porta and may depict stories from Ovid.[18] These self-framed plaques are two of a set of four that was listed in the first edition of Wedgwood's 1773 catalog. The catalog's preface suggests their use to have been "for inlaying, as Medallions in the Pannels of Rooms, as Tablets for Chimneypieces, or for hanging up as Ornaments in Libraries &c."

Another fine basalt tablet of the eighteenth century is entitled *Bacchanalian Sacrifice* (cat. 147). It was made by pressing clay into a mold, as evidenced by the eight shallow depressions on the back. The figures on the front were then carefully modeled and undercut. The design is attributed to the French sculptor Claude Michel Clodion (1738-1814).[19] Several of Wedgwood's bas-reliefs appear to have been copied or adapted from Clodion's work. In the Beeson collection is a sister tablet made of artificial stone and entitled *Bacchanalian Triumph* (see cat. 424, pl. 139, p. 149), and it was obviously designed by the same hand. Both subjects are listed in Wedgwood's catalogs (as nos. 70 and 71) from 1773 onward.

Another of Wedgwood's early basalt tablets, *Death of Meleager,* is listed in the 1773 catalog (cat. 140, pl. 38). (It is sometimes erroneously titled *Death of a Roman Warrior.*) The figures on the tablet are a composite of several sources. Wedgwood copied the central group from a Greek marble relief in the Capitoline Museum. The dead figure in the center of the tablet may have been copied from an engraving of a Roman marble in Montfaucon's *L'Antiquité expliquée* (fig. 8).[20] Large indentations on the back behind each figure show that the piece was mold-pressed.[21]

The *Procession of Senators* basalt tablet may have been modeled by either Camillo Pacetti or Angelo Dalmazzoni, who were employed by Wedgwood in Rome from 1787 (cat. 133, pl. 39). Most of the scene is copied from decoration on the Ara Pacis of Augustus, which commemorates the emperor's victory in Spain and Gaul.[22] The tablet was first listed in the French edition of Wedgwood's catalog of 1788. Eight of the thirteen figures were applied separately to the tablet and have small basalt buttons on the back for support.

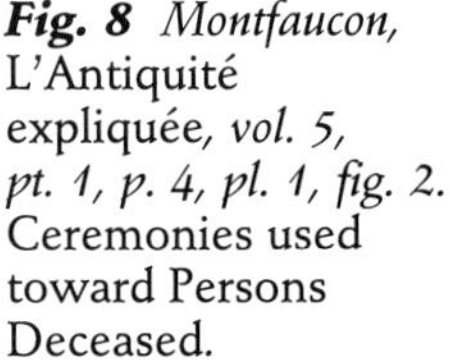

Fig. 8 *Montfaucon,* L'Antiquité expliquée, *vol. 5, pt. 1, p. 4, pl. 1, fig. 2.* Ceremonies used toward Persons Deceased.

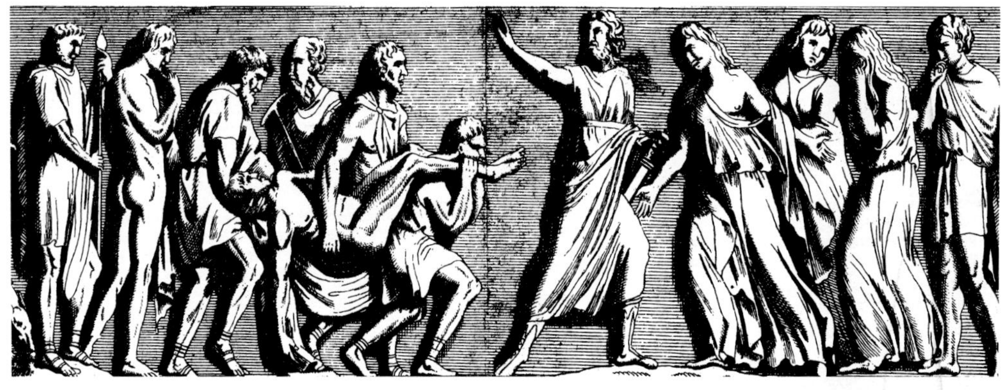

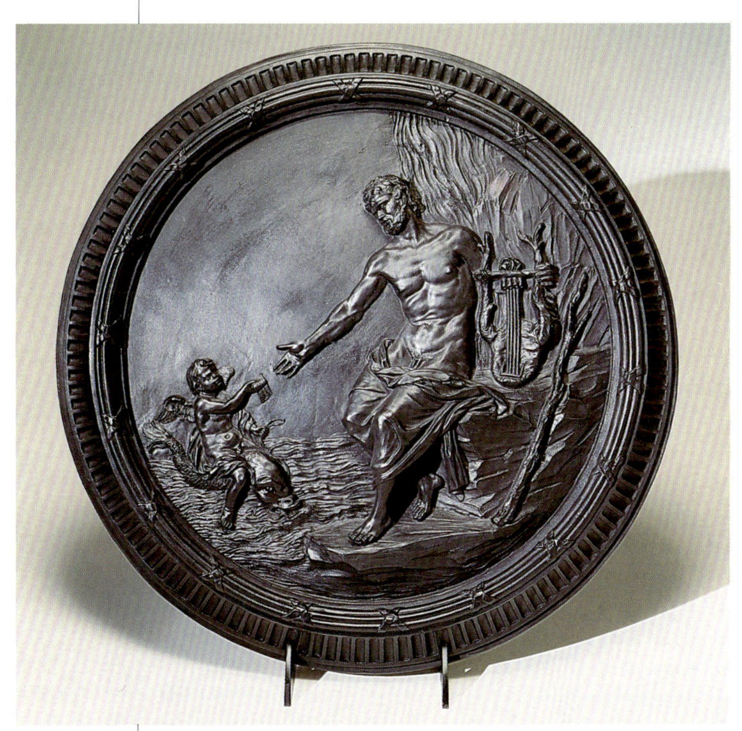

Color plate 37 *Roundel,* Letter to Polyphemus, *ca. 1775, basalt, self-framed, 15" (cat. 118).*

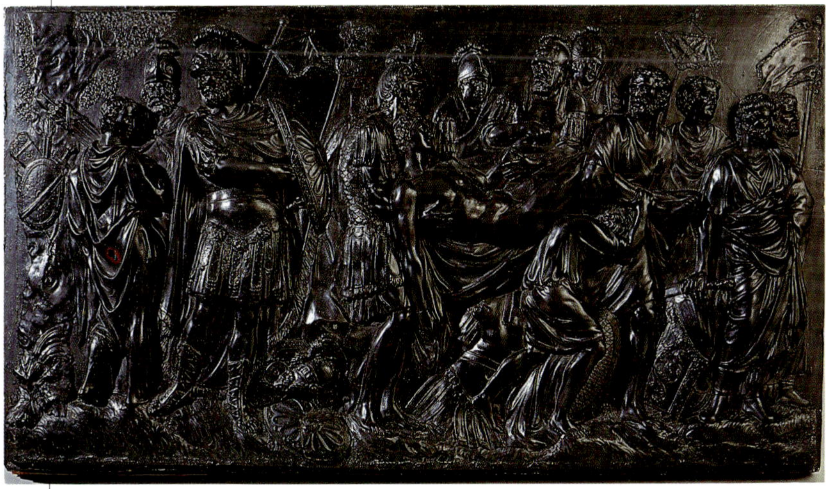

Color plate 38 *Tablet,* Death of Meleager, *ca. 1782, basalt, 19 3/4" x 11 1/8" (cat. 140).*

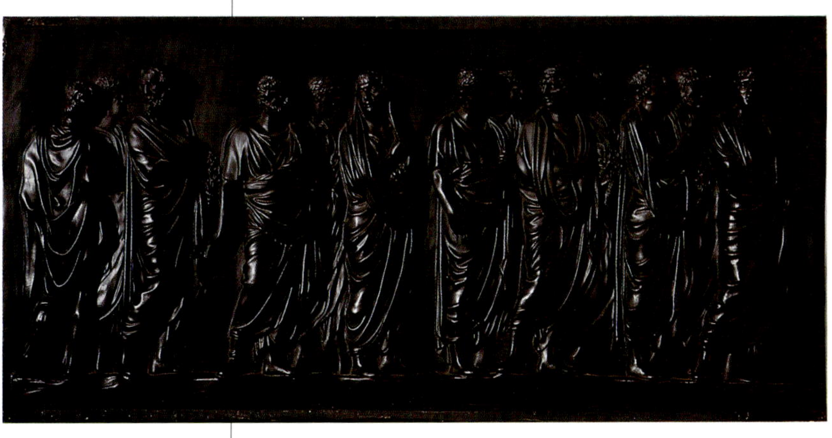

Color plate 39 *Tablet,* Roman Procession *or* Procession of Senators, *ca. 1790, basalt, 20 1/4" x 10" (cat. 133).*

Busts and Figures

During the age of neoclassicism in England, the acquisition of bronze portrait busts of ancient Romans was a popular pastime. In typical entrepreneurial fashion, Wedgwood began to copy these bronzes, stating in his *Ornamental Catalogue* of 1779:

> The black Composition having the Appearance of antique Bronze, and so nearly agreeing in Properties with the Basaltes of the Aegyptians, no Substance can be better than this for Busts, Sphinxes, small Statues, &c. and it seems to us to be a great Consequence to preserve as many fine Works of Antiquity and of the present Age as we can in this composition, for when all pictures are faded and rotten, when Bronzes are rusted away, and all the excellent works in Marble dissolved, then these copies like the antique Etruscan vases, will probably remain, and transmit the Works of Genius and the Portraits of illustrious Men, to the most distant Times.

Most of Wedgwood's busts were of Greek and Roman statesmen, but writers, mythological figures, and prominent men and women of literature and science, both historical and contemporary, were also portrayed. Wedgwood was at first hesitant about making basalt busts and figures, as he wrote to Bentley on October 1, 1769: "I believe Vases are much better articles, for us, than figures. . . . Figures, & other things may come in very well when we have no sale for all the Vases we can make,"[23] although he had urged Bentley on September 13, 1769, to get "some figures from the Cabinets of yr. Noble customers, which have not yet appeared in the shops . . . & I will endeavour to execute them in Terra Cotta."[24] But by August of 1774, Wedgwood wrote: "We are going on very fast now with the Busts, having four of our principal hands allmost constantly employ'd on them."[25]

Basalt busts and figures were made on a large scale in the 1770s, when they were in public demand for use, along with flanking vases, as mantel garniture in the libraries and galleries of large estates. Only rarely were busts and figures made in jasper ware and caneware. By the publication of the first *Ornamental Catalogue* (1773), there were twenty-three basalt figures of classical subjects and three busts. The sources on which they were based were either the antiques themselves or later reproductions in bronze or marble. From these originals were made plaster copies and molds to create the basalt figures. The artisans at the London firm of Hoskins and Oliver (later Hoskins and Grant), who were cast and mold makers, supplied Wedgwood with plaster copies and molds such as these from September of 1769 to 1779. Other casts came from the Royal Academy; as Wedgwood wrote to Bentley on February 16, 1771: "I wrote to you in my last concerning Busts. I suppose those at the Academy are less hackneyd & better in General than the Plaister shops can furnish us with; besides it will sound better to say—This is from the Academy, taken from an Original in the Gallery of &c. &c."[26] The molds were expensive but ready for immediate use: all that remained to be done was to press the clay into them. Because the quality of molds was often unsatisfactory, Wedgwood is known to have had modelers at Etruria improve the details of his clay pieces after molding. By 1774, he had begun to economize by ordering only plaster copies, from which he made his own molds. On September 11, 1774, Wedgwood wrote to Bentley: "The Busts will employ him [William Hackwood, one of Wedgwood's modelers] for a year or two before our collection is tolerably complete, & I am much set upon having it so, being fully perswaded they will be a capital article with us, & Hackwood finished them admirably. . . . I hope in time to send you a collection of the finest Heads in this World."[27] Soon the demand for Wedgwood's basalt busts and figures, which were cheaper and more durable, eclipsed the demand for plaster ones.[28]

Molds and casts were made by the following method. The original piece was copied in either clay or wax and then dissected into various parts. It was important that the modeler adapt the figure to have the smallest number of parts so that it could be easily reassembled. From each part was made a plaster mold, and the molds were then put back together with slip and fired.

Three of the first modelers at Etruria were Thomas Boot, William Hackwood, and Charles Denby. Thomas Boot modeled for Wedgwood from 1769 to 1773 and was responsible for some of the first basalt figures (such as the sphinxes, triton, and lions discussed on pp. 151–53). William Hackwood (ca. 1757-1839) is first mentioned in a letter from Wedgwood to Bentley dated September 20, 1769: "I hired an ingenious Boy last night for Etruria as a Modeler. He has modeled at night in his way for three years past, has never had the least instructions, which circumstance considered he does things amazingly & will be a valuable acquisition."[29] Hackwood became Wedgwood's chief modeler for ornamental work and was employed until 1832. The secret of Hackwood's proficiency was the hand-finishing and undercutting between the relief and the ground of the bas-relief, a technique that rendered a more precise image and accentuated the dimension; this process was executed immediately after the piece was removed from the mold and in a leather-hard state. Wedgwood was so pleased with Hackwood's work that on November 4, 1778, he wrote to Bentley: "Some of the tablets lately sent are finish'd very high by Hackwood at a considerable expence. . . . You will easily perceive the difference in the hair, faces, fingers &c., & more palpably by all the parts capable of it being undercut which gives them the appearance, & nearly the reality of models."[30] In addition to remodeling and finishing casts by Hoskins and Grant, Hackwood restored models of gems and figures that later became the foundation of the jasper portrait medallions. Although not considered an artist in his own right, Hackwood was unsurpassed by the other modelers who worked for Wedgwood.[31]

Charles Denby was a painter and modeler who had previously worked for the Derby factory. He began to work for Wedgwood in 1769 at Etruria but moved to the Chelsea Decorating Studio in London on May 28, 1770. Soon after hiring Denby, Wedgwood described his new employee: "He applys close to business, has a delicate modesty in his manners, and I think will be an agreeable & usefull assistant to us in a little time. . . . He is really learned in the Anatomy and the drawing of a Human figure."[32]

One of the finest basalt busts in the Beeson collection portrays Dr. John Fothergill (1712-86) (cat. 116, pl. 40), a Quaker physician from Edinburgh and member of the Royal Society. This magnificently carved bust was made in May 1781 by the modeler John Flaxman, Sr.[33] The stand is not original to the bust. In 1763, Fothergill entered into a partnership in the toy-making business with Matthew Boulton, a relationship that lasted until 1781. Fothergill brought his mercantile skills to the partnership and traveled abroad to establish agencies for the sale of their goods. Fothergill became acquainted with Wedgwood through the latter's pursuit of Cherokee kaolin clay in North Carolina and through the Royal Society, and Fothergill often helped Wedgwood with his experiments. On September 12, 1767, Wedgwood wrote of Fothergill: "I have had a letter from D^r. Fothergill not long since who tells me he has a fr^d. who has lately been at the place where the Cherokee Earth is got, that he could easily procure me a few hun^d. pounds of it for tryal, but it will unavoidably come so dear that unless the finest Porcel can made of it, it cannot answer. I have thanked the Good Doct^r. who indeed wrote me a very friendly letter."[34]

Wedgwood also made a jasper portrait medallion of Fothergill, which was designed after a medical-society medal made by Lewis Pingo and dated 1773. An

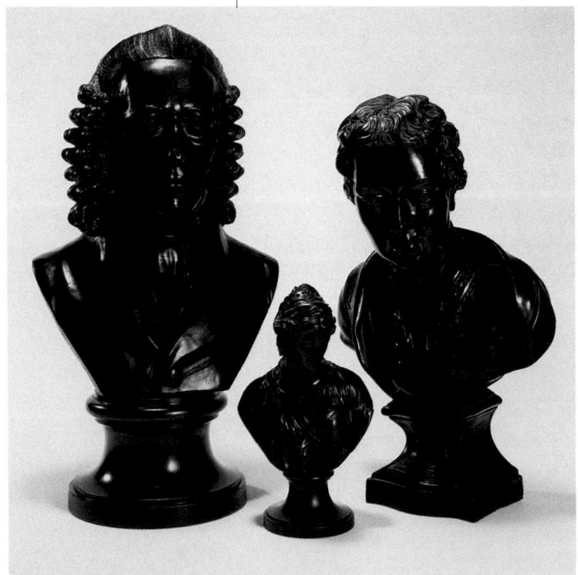

Color plate 40
Left, *Bust,* Dr. John Fothergill *(1712-86), ca. 1781, basalt, 16 3/4" (cat. 116);* center, *Bust,* Zingara, *ca. 1775, basalt, 8" (cat. 114);* right, *Bust,* Joseph Addison *(1672-1719), ca. 1780, basalt, 14 1/4" (cat. 113).*

early-nineteenth-century example of this medallion, first listed in Wedgwood's catalog of 1779, is catalog number 716 in this collection.

The second largest basalt bust in the Beeson collection is of the English writer Joseph Addison (1672-1719), whose well-known *Essays and Poems* was being reprinted during the second half of the eighteenth century (cat. 113, pl. 40). The figure, supplied in plaster by Hoskins and Grant in 1775, is dressed in contemporary garb with a hint of drapery around its shoulders. Made as an ornament for the top of a cabinet, the bust and stand are in one piece with a hollow "stovepipe" base. That it has no mold marks makes it distinctive of the eighteenth century.

Another eighteenth-century basalt bust in the collection is of Zingara, a word that means "gypsy girl" in Italian (cat. 114, pl. 40). The bust, bolted to its base, was supplied by the modeler Richard Parker in 1774 from a sculpture by Joseph Wilton.

Busts and figures continued to be made by the Wedgwood firm throughout its history. A nineteenth-century bust of Lord Nelson is discussed elsewhere on page 151; two nineteenth-century fictional figures include Poor Maria and Crouching Venus (cats. 155, 165). Poor Maria was a character in Laurence Sterne's novel *A Sentimental Journey*, published in 1768. The figure was modeled by William Hackwood in 1783 after designs by Lady Templetown. Crouching Venus was just one of many variations on the subject that were produced by the Wedgwood firm. The original model, known as *The Venus of Vienne*, may have been *Venus Bathing* by Daedalus of Bithynia (third century B.C.), as described by Pliny.[35] Wedgwood's figure shows distinct cast lines throughout and has a separate brass base, indicating its nineteenth-century origin.

The rest of the basalt figural forms in the Beeson collection are decorative elements on lamps, candlesticks, crocus-bulb pots, flower arrangers, ewers, and vases produced in the nineteenth century. The vestal reading lamps, as they are called, are a pair of lamps that incorporate female figures as the handles, one with a book and the other with a pitcher (cat. 185). The figures are thought to have been modeled by William Keeling (1763-90) and were popularly made in basalt until the 1930s A pair of female figures as candlesticks, also attributed to Keeling, are often entitled *Ceres and Cybele*, but they do not have the traditional symbols of the goddesses of the lion and cornstalk (cat. 164). Another candlestick depicts the figure of Diana, originally paired with Minerva (cat. 158). Listed as number 263 in Wedgwood's shape book of about 1785-90, the two have been attributed to the modeler Henry Webber. (See p. 130 for further information concerning this attribution.)

A figure of a griffin, a mythological animal having the head of an eagle and body of a lion, is also found in the candlestick form (cat. 166). A wooden block mold for the griffin in the Wedgwood Museum is thought to have been made in about 1768 by John Coward, a woodcarver working for Wedgwood from 1765 through 1770. Wedgwood may have designed the griffin from an engraving in the 1791 edition of *Treatise on Civil Architecture,* by Sir William Chambers.[36]

More unusual figural forms include a crocus pot in the shape of a porcupine, with an undertray dating from the nineteenth century, and an egret on a rock, a vase designed by Ernest W. Light in about 1918, with holes intended to be used for holding individual flowers (cats. 170, 172).

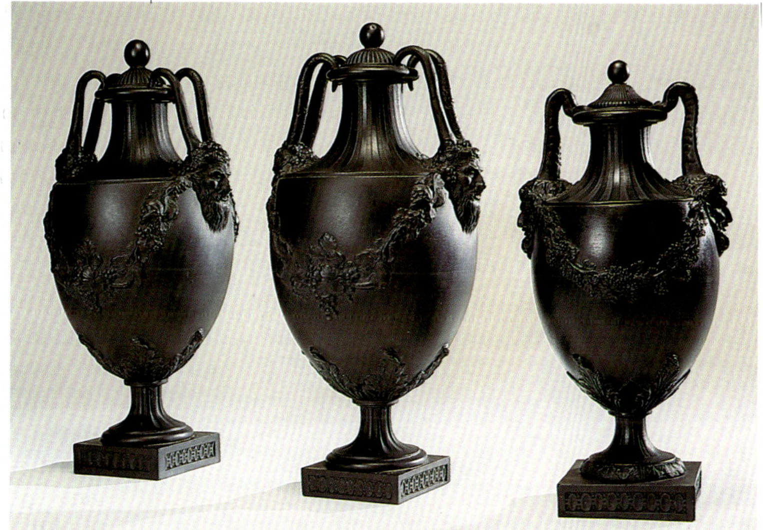

Color plate 41 Left, *Pair of Covered Vases, ca. 1775, basalt with engine-turning, 8 13/16" x 2 1/8" (cat. 119);* right, *Covered Vase, ca. 1775, basalt with engine-turning, 7 7/8" x 2 3/8" (cat. 120).*

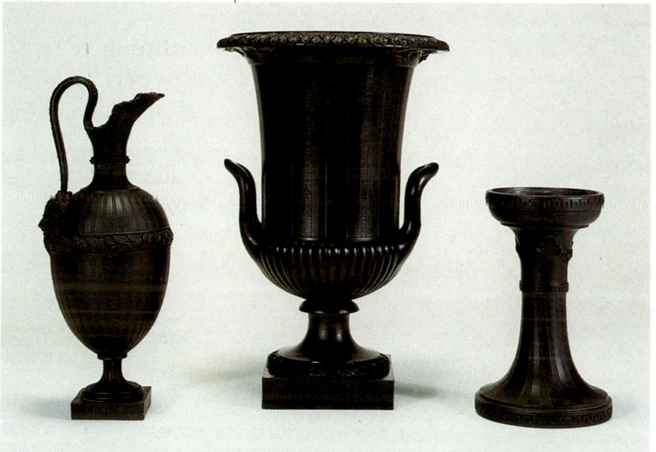

Color plate 42 Left, *Ewer, ca. 1778, basalt with engine-turning, 9 1/2" x 1 15/16" (cat. 128);* center, *Vase, ca. 1775, basalt with engine-turning, 10 1/2" x 3 11/16" (cat. 123);* right, *Vase, ca. 1775, basalt with engine-turning, 6" x 3 3/4" (cat. 129).*

Vases and Ewers

The *Ornamental Catalogue* of 1779 proudly describes the basalt vases that Wedgwood offered for sale: "Antique vases of Black Porcelain in Artificial Basaltes (highly finished with bas-relief ornaments). Of this Species of Vase we have a great variety of Forms, the sizes from three or four inches high to more than two feet. . . . The Sets of five pieces for chimney pieces sell from about two guineas to Six to Eight Guineas a Set. From all the specimens we have seen, and the observations of others, we have reason to conclude that there are not any vases of Porcelain, Marble, or Bronze, either ancient or modern, so highly finished and sharp in their Ornaments as these Black vases."

The Beeson collection boasts fourteen medium-sized basalt vases, all but one marked "Wedgwood and Bentley," impressed either on the bottom of the piece or within a wafer on the plinth. These elegant vases, often austerely decorated or with engine-turning, are some of the finest objects Wedgwood produced.

Wedgwood used three different types of decoration on the vases: bas-relief, engine-turning, and encaustic painting. The bas-relief decoration of swags, satyr heads, and mythological figures was molded in one with the piece until June 1776, when Wedgwood felt with confidence his success in sprigging the ornamentation (see pl. 41).[37] Sprigging allowed Wedgwood to achieve infinite combinations of decoration for his various shapes.

Engine-turned decoration was most widely employed for ornamentation on basalt ware, although it was also used on red stoneware, cream ware, and jasper ware (see pl. 42). Never copied successfully by Wedgwood's contemporaries, it is considered one of his finest ornamental details. The decoration was achieved by turning on a lathe unfired, leather-dried pottery. The lathe worked on the same principle as the wood-turning lathe, but with an eccentric motion in which the vase, at predetermined intervals, moved alternately toward and away from the hand-held cutting tool. Wedgwood learned of this kind of lathe from the metalsmith Matthew Boulton in 1763 and installed one in his own workplace the same year. This lathe is now in the Wedgwood Museum in Barlaston, and a similar lathe is still being used at the Wedgwood factory today.

Two spectacular basalt pieces in the Beeson collection are a bulb pot and a large vase entitled the *Procession of Little Boys; or, Cupids Carrying Garlands* and that are attributed to John Flaxman, Jr. (cats. 125, 126, pl. 43). Both are impressed with the names of Wedgwood and Bentley and date to about 1775. The bulb pot consists of a base and two bulb trays; the large vase has other decoration of applied oak leaves and is engine-turned.

A large, very rare Wedgwood vase in basalt depicts, in the center of the body, a design by Lady Diana Beauclerk (see p. 111) entitled *Bacchanalian Boys*; the design is surrounded by leafage and masks (cat. 109, pl. 44). The figure of a small child forms the knop, and unusual leopards' heads serve as handles. The design for the leopards' heads was from either Jacques de Stella, *Livre de vases* (1667), or Robert Adam and James Adam, *The Works in Architecture* (1778) (fig. 9).[38]

Another basalt vase that has hook handles, festoons, and a medallion, with figures—in this case, *The Three Graces* (cat. 115)— on the front, has a known design source of a suite of numbered plates etched and designed by Stefano della Bella (1610-64) in the book *Raccolta di vasi diversi.*[39] Similar silver vases are known to exist from the same time. As Matthias Darley wrote in the dedication to his *Book*

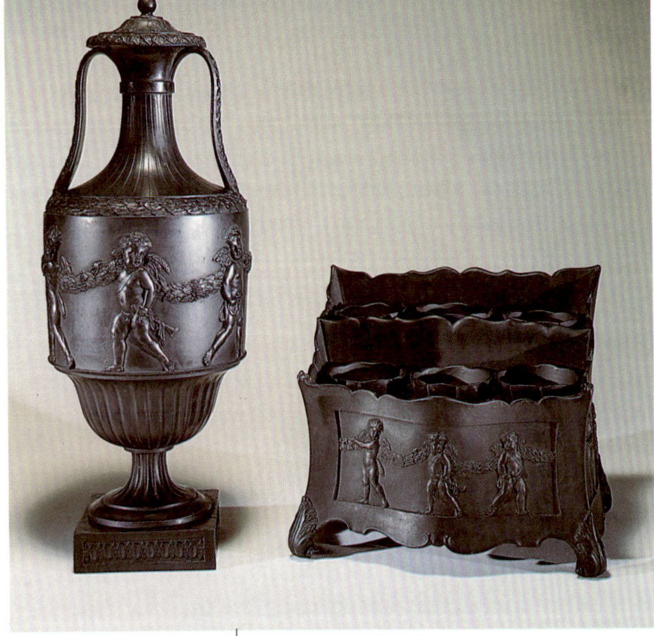

Color plate 43 Left, *Covered Vase,* Procession of Little Boys, *ca. 1775, basalt with engine-turning, 21 5/8" x 3 13/16" (cat. 126);* right, *Bulb Pot,* Procession of Little Boys, *ca. 1775, basalt with glazed interior, 7 1/8" x 7 15/16" x 8 5/8" (cat. 125).*

Color plate 44 *(p. 65) Covered Vase,* Bacchanalian Boys, *ca. 1790, basalt, 19 5/16" x 5 1/2" (cat. 109).*

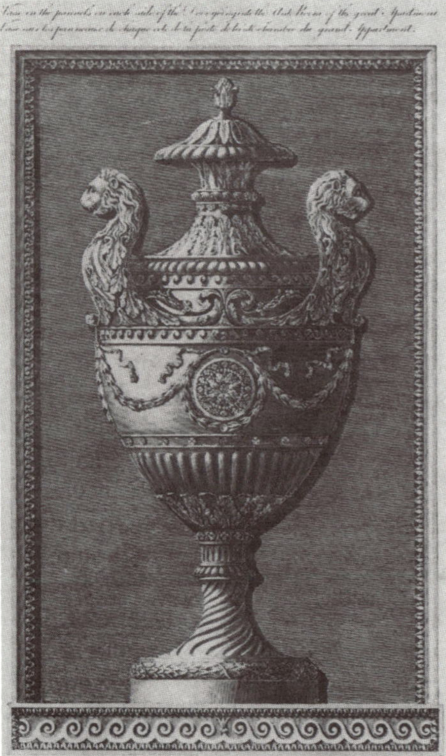

Fig. 9 The Works in Architecture, *by Robert Adam and James Adam, 1778. Courtesy of the Victoria and Albert Museum, London, England.*

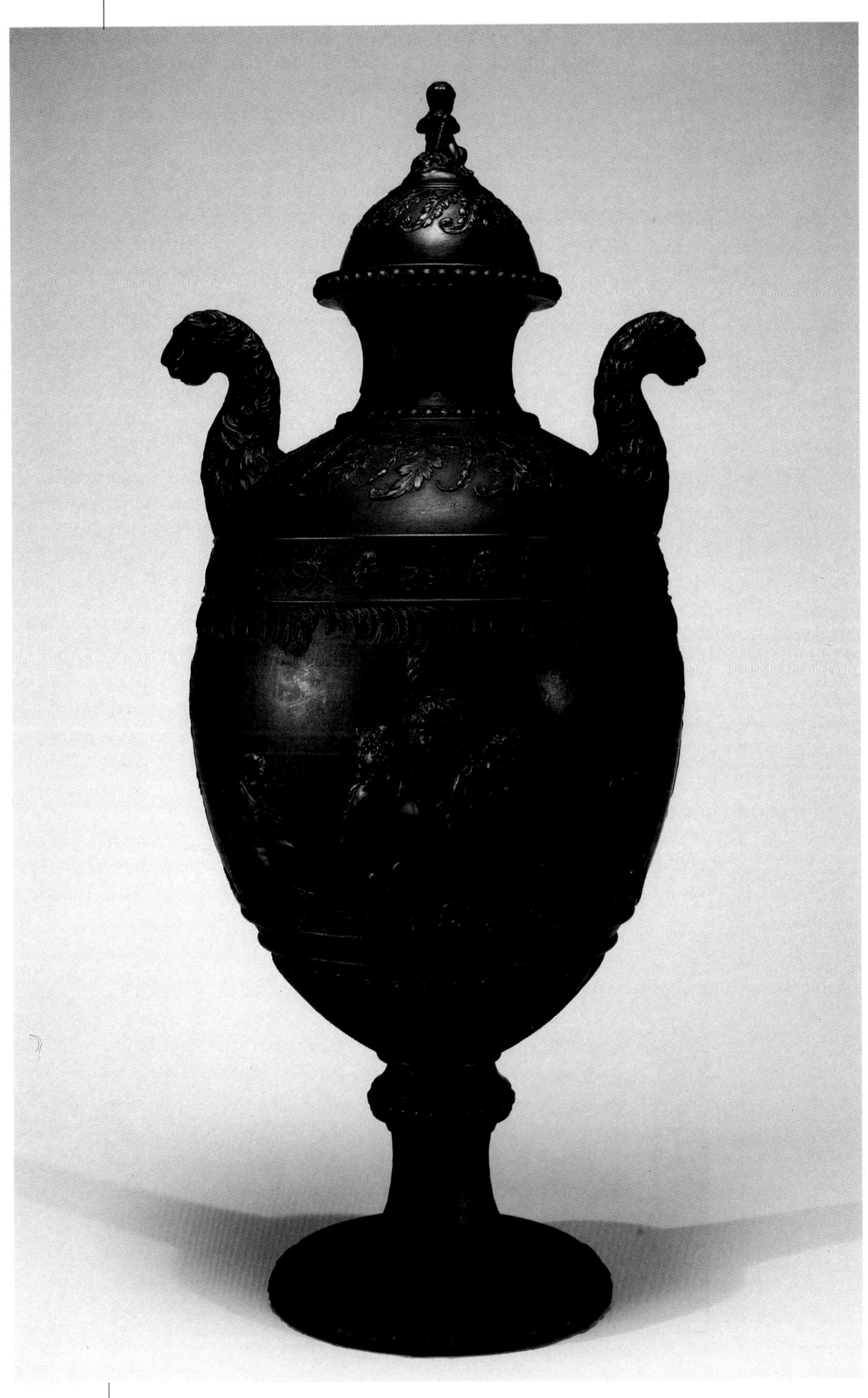

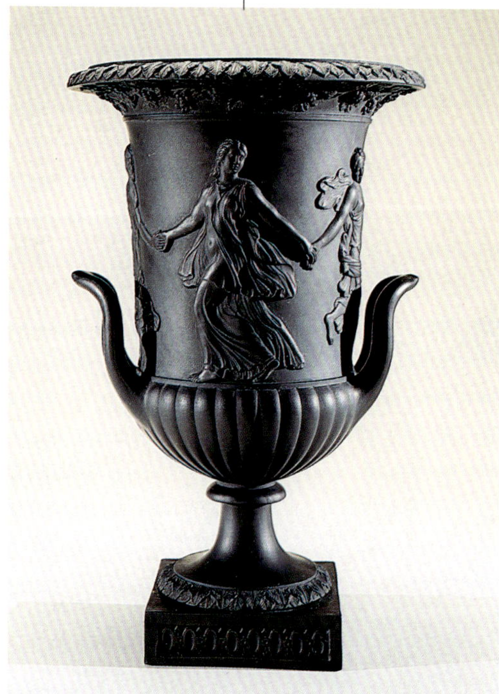

Color plate 45
Vase, Dancing Hours, *ca. 1780, basalt, 10 9/16" x 3 9/16" (cat.131).*

of Architecture (1773), "Witness the Pottery of this Kingdom, there is now performances in Clay which would make the heavy handed Silversmith blush."[40]

The beautifully detailed, classical figures of the Dancing Hours—personifying the hours of the day—appear on another basalt vase in the Beeson collection (cat. 131, pl. 45). Wedgwood favored this design particularly on his jasper ware. The source of most of the figures—believed to have been modeled by John Flaxman, Sr.[41]—is either a pair of engravings by Bartoli in *Admiranda Romanorum antiquitatum* (fig. 10) or a white marble and lapis-lazuli frieze from the Borghese Palace in Rome, now in the Lady Lever Art Gallery in Port Sunlight, England.[42] The frieze was based on a marble Greco-Roman relief, *Les Danseuses Borgheses,* of the first or second century B.C., now located in the Louvre.[43]

Popular in both the eighteenth and the nineteenth centuries were the figures of a triton and a satyr on a pair of basalt ewers intended to hold water and wine (cats. 130, 111, pl. 46). The triton, the son of Poseidon and Amphitrite, is half fish and half human; the satyr (also known as Silenus), who is half man and half goat, was schooled by Bacchus and is usually accompanied by him. The figures are part of the handles of the ewers; the water ewer is called *Sacred to Neptune,* and the wine ewer is called *Sacred to Bacchus.*[44] The first dates to between 1769 and 1780; the second is from the nineteenth century.

John Flaxman, Sr., is credited as the modeler because a pair of wine and water ewers is listed on an invoice sent to Wedgwood by John Flaxman on March 25, 1775. The receipt is signed, "John Flaxman, junr, for my father." The plaster molds for these ewers are still in the Wedgwood Museum today. Claude Michel Clodion is believed to have made the original water and wine ewers in metal, for they are listed in the sales of Clodion's work in 1780.

In addition to these basalt ewers, caneware and jasper-ware examples were produced in the eighteenth century as well as majolica and bone-china examples in the nineteenth century. In the Beeson collection is another set of triton ewers in

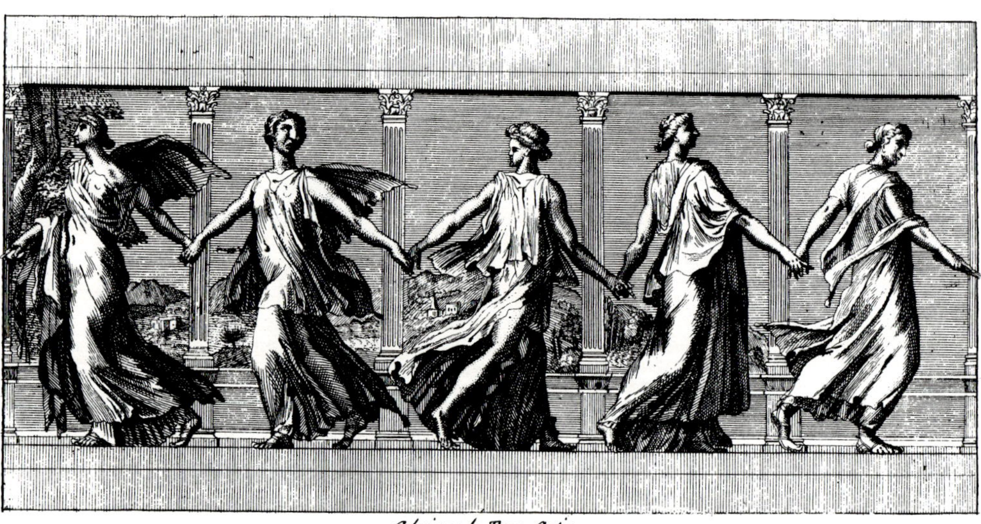

Fig. 10 *Montfaucon,* L'Antiquité expliquée, *vol. 3, pt. 2, p. 199, pl. 54, fig. 1.* Dancing Hours.

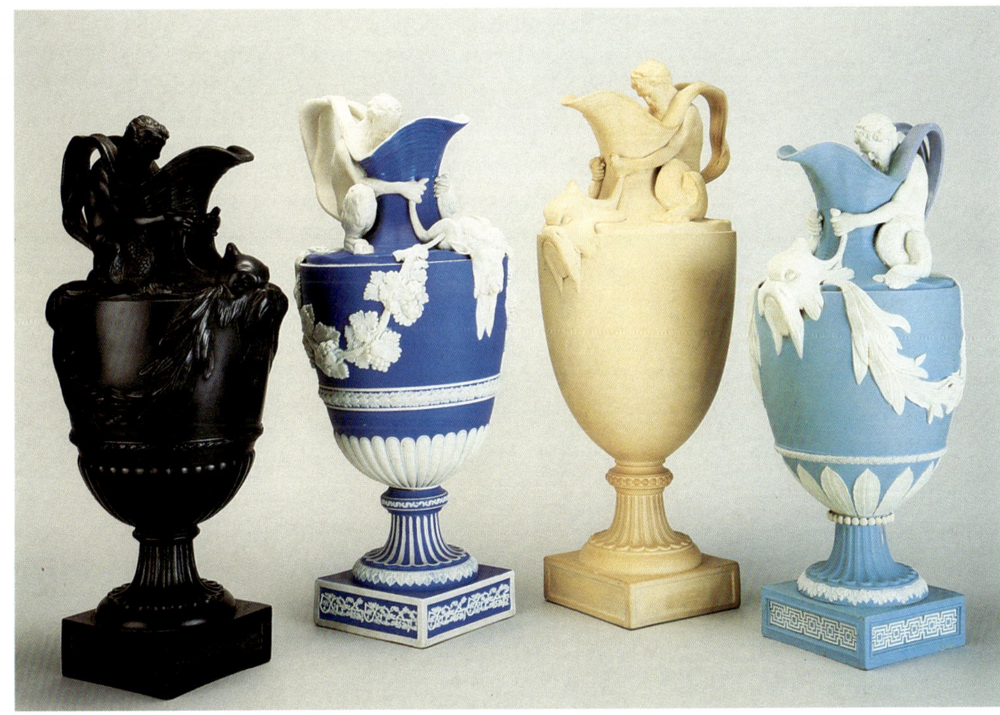

Color plate 46
Left, *Wine Ewer,* Sacred to Neptune, *ca. 1780, basalt, 15 1/4" x 4 (cat. 130);* second from left, *Wine Ewer,* Sacred to Bacchus, *ca. 1800, jasper, solid white ground with blue wash and white relief, 16 1/8" x 4 7/16" (cat. 280);* third from left, *Water Ewer,* Sacred to Neptune, *ca. 1800, caneware, tracings for exterior decoration, 17 1/4" x 4 1/2" (cat. 423);* right, *Pair of Water Ewers,* Sacred to Neptune, *ca. 1800, jasper, solid blue ground with white relief, 15 3/8" x 4 3/16" (cat. 298).*

light-blue-and-white jasper ware, one from the eighteenth and one from the nineteenth century; also from the nineteenth century are two examples, a satyr ewer in dark-blue-and-white jasper ware and a triton ewer with unfinished decoration in caneware (cats. 298, 280, 423, pl. 46).

Two potpourri vases in basalt exemplify the use of enamels in the Chinese *famille rose* decoration (cat. 175, pl. 47). Josiah Wedgwood II introduced this decorative ware with the "Peony pattern" in 1810, using opaque enamels ranging in color from pink to purple rose. Throughout the eighteenth century, French, German, and English porcelain factories had made copies of the Chinese products, which date from the early years of that century, but Wedgwood was the first to use the enamel on a black ware.

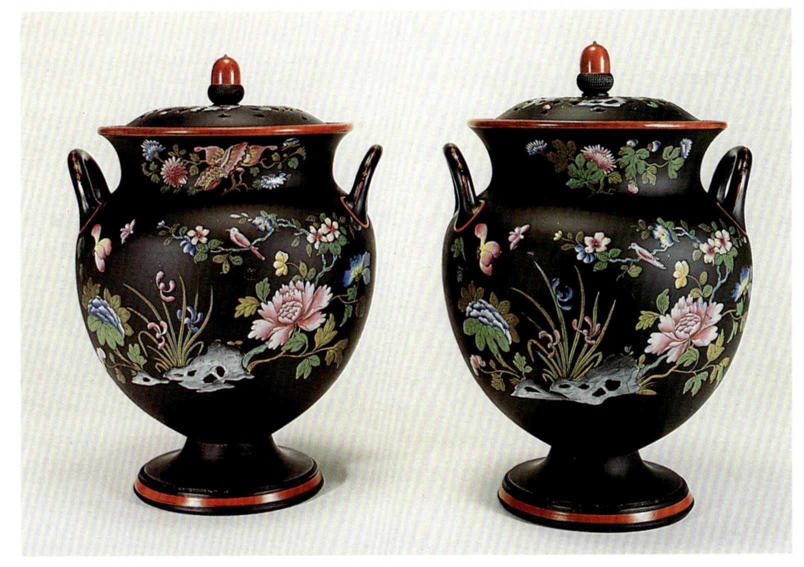

Color plate 47
Pair of Potpourri Vases, Peony Pattern, *ca. 1820, basalt with enamel decoration, 12 1/2" x 5 1/2" (cat. 175).*

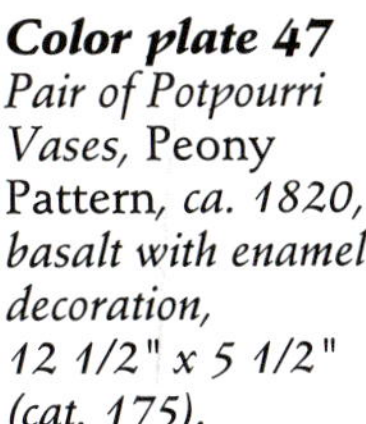

In the Beeson collection is one other large basalt vase (cat. 110; pl. 48); it is not by Wedgwood, but it is attributed to the modeler and potter John Voyez (1735-1800). Voyez was a French modeler whom Wedgwood hired in 1768, as he reported to Bentley on March 31:

I have hired a Modeler for three years, the best I am told in London, he serv'd his time with a silversmith, has work'd several years at a China Work, has been two or three years carving in wood & marble for Mr. Adams the famous Architect, is the perfect Master of the Antique stile in ornaments, Vases &c, & works with equal facility in Clay, wax, wood, Metal or stone.[45]

Color plate 48
Vase, Prometheus Bound, *1769, John Voyez (1735-1800) modeler, basalt, 20 1/4" x 4" (cat. 110).*

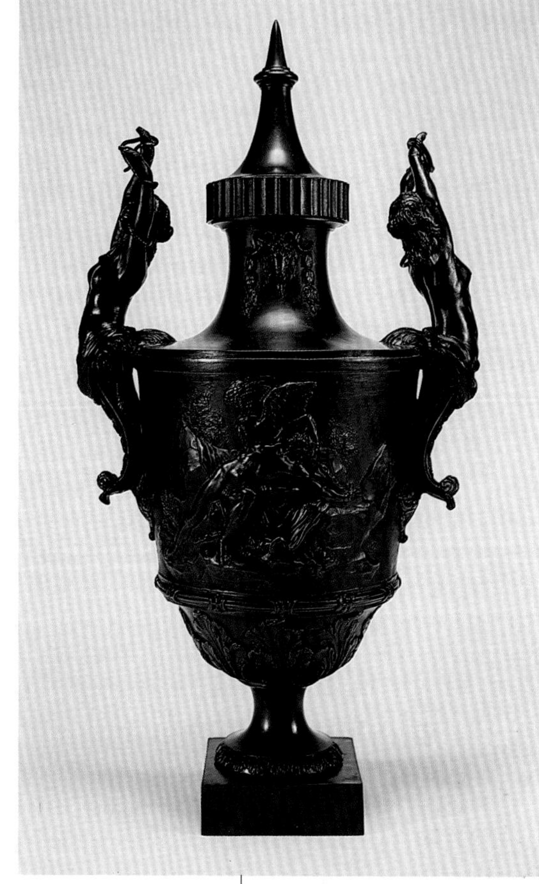

After working in London, Voyez moved to Staffordshire, where he could work directly with Wedgwood; yet, by January of 1769, the Crown Book of the Oxford Circuit stated that John Voyez was sentenced to seven years in prison "for stealing 11 Models of Clay val' 51s, 15 moulds of Clay val' 50s and 15 Moulds of Plaisster val' 50s. Goods of Josiah Wedgwood at the par' of Burslem on the 28th January 9 G. 3d." His sentence was apparently modified, for Wedgwood's letters indicate that he was incarcerated for only three to five months.

Despite these difficulties, Wedgwood still regarded Voyez as a talented modeler. Wedgwood wrote to Bentley on April 9, 1769: "What then do our competitors stand most in need of to enable them to rival us the most effectually—Some Person to instruct them to compose good forms, & to ornam[t] them with tolerable propriety. V [Voyez] can do this much more effectually than all the Potters in the country put together."[46] Wedgwood's concern about his competitors proved to be appropriate, for, upon Voyez's release from prison in the summer of 1769, Voyez went to work for Humphrey Palmer, owner of the Church Works pottery in Hanley, Staffordshire, and one of Wedgwood's keenest competitors. Voyez subsequently worked for a member of the Hales pottery, Ralph Wood of Burslem, and independently.

During the last few months of 1769, Voyez conceived of a design for a basalt vase entitled *Prometheus Bound.* The example in the Beeson collection is signed "J. Voyez Sculpt / 1769" beneath the center relief. There is on the piece no mark indicating a factory. A second Prometheus vase—in the Holburne of Menstrie Museum in Bath, England—has, in addition to the date and signature, the potter's mark "Made by H. Palmer / Hanley Staffords." The modeling is in the baroque manner, unlike the staid neoclassicism that predominated at the time.

Voyez's theme is well known in Renaissance art, and the design was derived from an as yet unknown ancient source. Prometheus, the son of Iapetus and Clymene and the brother of Atlas, stole fire from the heavens and gave it to mortals. To punish Prometheus, Zeus chained him to a rock on Mount Caucasus, and every day an eagle came and preyed on his liver, which regenerated that night. (It is this scene that is depicted on each side of the vase.) Prometheus was finally released by Hercules, who then killed the eagle. The bound female figures at the top of the vase function as handles.

Color plate 49
Center, Sacrifice to Peace, *ca. 1790, basalt, 2 1/2" x 2" (cat. 1013);* clockwise from top*:* Lord Camden*, ca. 1780, caneware, 15/16" x 11/16" (cat. 995);* Apollo*, ca. 1780, basalt with blue jasper wash front and back, 1" x 7/8" (cat. 1020);* Doctor Lucas*, ca. 1775, jasper, brown ground with white layer on front, 7/8" x 3/4" (cat. 993);* Male Classical Head*, ca. 1790, basalt, self-framed, 1" x 7/8" (cat. 1021);* Homer*, ca. 1790, basalt, self-framed, 1 1/4" x 1" (cat. 1018);* Bust of Pindar*, ca. 1790, basalt, 1" x 7/8" (cat. 1023);* Venus and Cupid with Dolphin*, ca. 1775, jasper, brown ground with white layer on front, 3/4" (cat. 1037);* Roman Head*, ca. 1775, basalt with gray jasper wash on front and back, 13/16" x 11/16" (cat. 1042).*

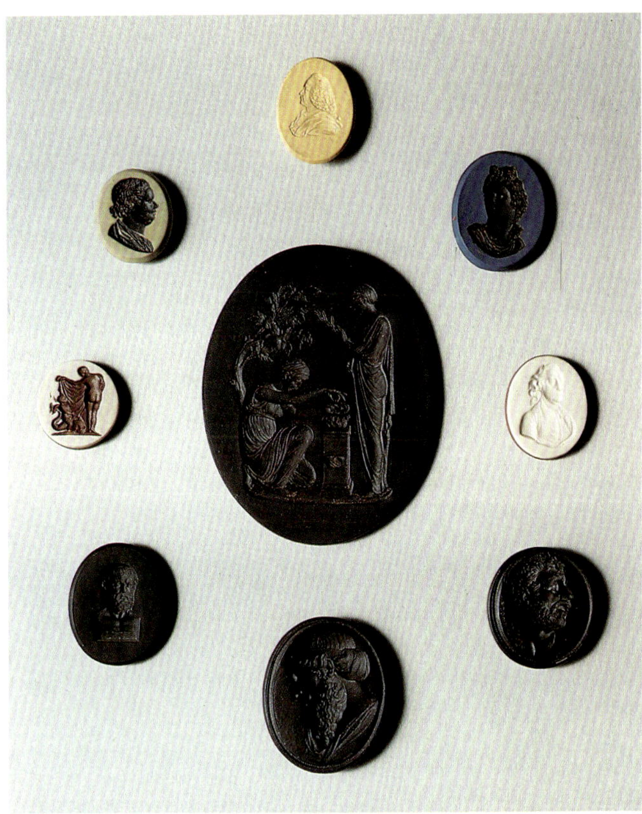

Intaglios

Cameos and intaglios were listed in Wedgwood's first *Ornamental Catalogue* (1773). Sources for these pieces were often Roman gems. On September 30, 1769, Wedgwood wrote to Bentley: "Though the Gems from Italy may be too small to apply to the Vases themselves, they will make very good Studys & we can have larger [ones] modeled by them much better than from prints, we can likewise paint after them—Gems are the fountain head of fine & beautiful composition, & we cannot you know employ ourselves too near the fountain head of taste."[47] Ten years later, he announced, "By Favour of the Nobility, &c. who are in Possession of original Gems, or fine Impressions of those in foreign Collections, we have been enabled to make our List pretty numerous."[48]

Most of the seals and intaglios in the Beeson collection are made of basalt (cats. 997, 999, 1014, 1019, 1021, 1022, 1024, 1037, 1042, pl. 49), a few examples being of jasper ware, caneware, redware, or a combination thereof. The Italian term "intaglio" means an incised design below the surface. Sometimes a lapidary wheel was used for polishing the surface, leaving a high gloss. Intaglios were intended for decorative elements in jewelry, furniture, and seals with shanks.

Wedgwood and Bentley marked most of their intaglios "W&B," with a number referenced to Wedgwood's or James Tassie's catalog. (For information on James Tassie see page 93). Wedgwood wrote to Bentley on June 21, 1773, "I have been buying some small Types, & ordering a still smaller stamp cut with Wedgwood & Bentley to mark our seals with."[49] Because each intaglio was relatively inexpensive, collections of intaglios were readily established in the eighteenth century. Wedgwood is known to have made about seventeen hundred different designs, most of which were also available in cameo form. The subject matter varies greatly, encompassing likenesses of famous classical figures, Wedgwood's contemporaries, mythological scenes, and letters of the alphabet.

Teaware

Despite the commitment of the Wedgwood and Bentley partnership to ornamental ware, their first production in basalt included teaware: cups and saucers, creamers, teapots, punch kettles, pitchers, ewers, and mugs. These pieces established a staple of sorts that was popular throughout the eighteenth century. Eighteenth-century women prided themselves upon their white hands, and the stark black of this teaware provided an attractive visual contrast. As Wedgwood wrote to Bentley

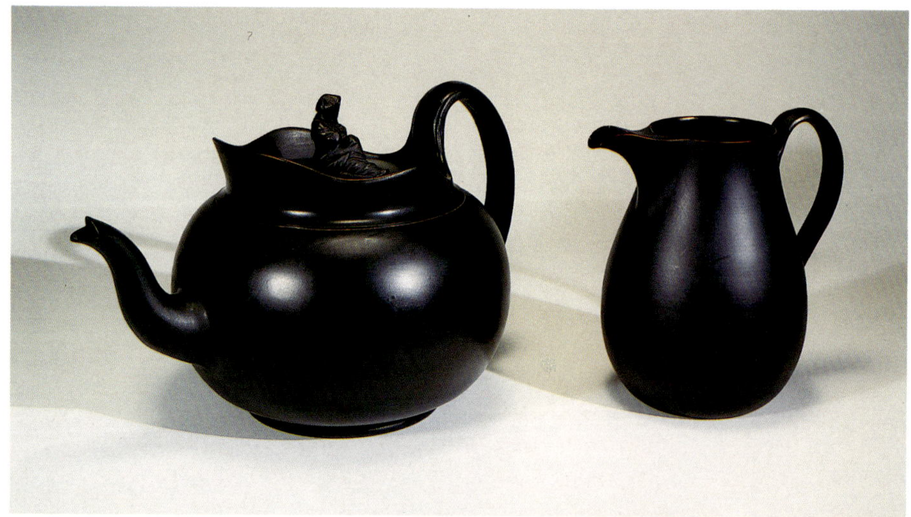

Color plate 50
Left, *Water Kettle, 1775-80, basalt, 7 1/4" x 4 3/4" (cat. 135);* right, *Pitcher, ca. 1775, basalt with glazed interior, 6 7/8" x 3" (cat. 136).*

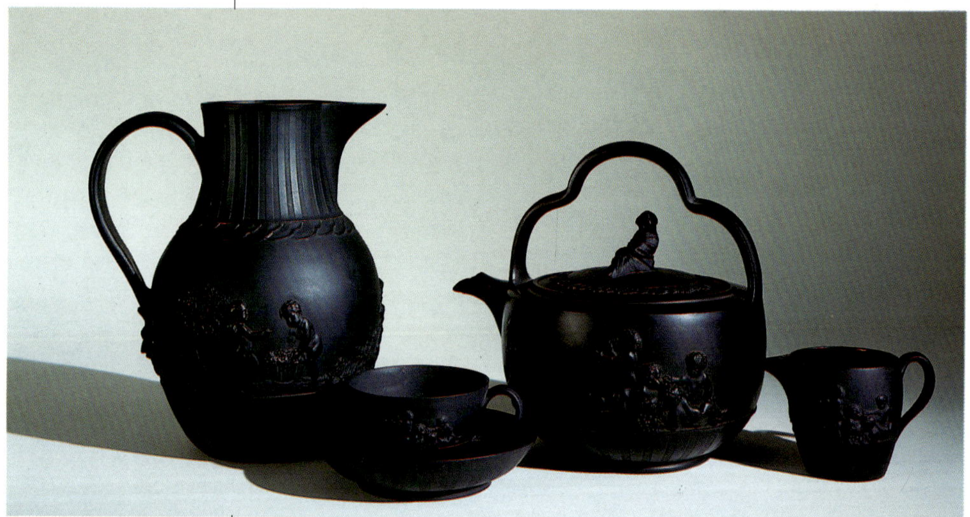

Color plate 51 Left, *Pitcher,* Bacchanalian Boys, *ca. 1785, basalt, engine-turning with glazed interior, 8 1/16" x 3 1/16" (cat. 141);* second from left, *Cup and Saucer,* Bacchanalian Boys, *ca. 1780, basalt, engine-turning with unglazed interior, cup: 1 7/8" x 1 3/8", saucer: 5 1/16" (cat. 142);* third from left, *Rum Kettle,* Boys at Play, *ca. 1775-80, basalt, engine-turning with glazed interior, 7 1/4" x 3 3/4" (cat. 149);* right, *Cream Pitcher,* Bacchanalian Boys, *ca. 1785, basalt, engine-turning with glazed interior, 2 9/16" x 1 1/2" (cat. 143).*

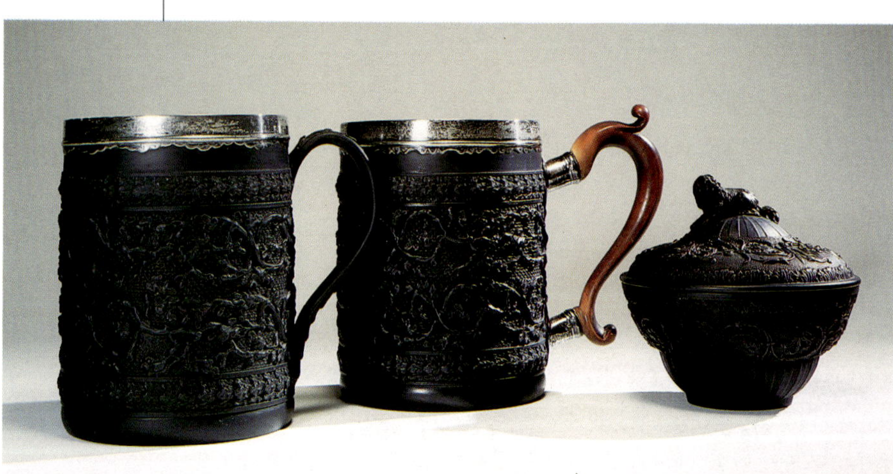

Color plate 52 Left, *Cider Mug, ca. 1778, basalt with glazed interior and silver rim, 5 13/16" x 4 5/16" (cat. 154);* second from left, *Cider Mug, ca. 1778, Peter Freeman, silversmith, basalt with glazed interior, silver rim, and fruitwood handle, 5 3/4" x 4 1/4" (cat. 153);* right, *Sugar Bowl, ca. 1777, basalt, engine-turning with spaniel finial and unglazed interior, 4 5/8" x 2 1/8" (cat. 151).*

on December 26, 1772: "Thanks for your discovery in favor of the black Teapots. I hope white hands will continue in fashion & then we may continue to make black teapots'till you can find us better employment."[50] On September 30, 1776, Wedgwood wrote: "Our Black Teapots sell very well at Dublin, & Bath, & a few at Liverpool, & will allways be the most salable part of our stock."[51] The earliest wares were either undecorated or simply engine-turned (pl. 50). Upon his perfection of the bas-relief on basalt, Wedgwood frequently used, in high relief, the decorative theme of the Bacchanalian boys at play (pl. 51). With the exception of a sugar bowl and a pair of cups and saucers, all of the basalt teaware in the Beeson collection is glazed on the inside, because the ware was intended for holding liquids; however, the glazing proved to be problematic for Wedgwood, because it often caused the teapots and kettles to crack when they were exposed to hot water. He abandoned the interior glazing for a period of time, but resumed it by January of 1776.[52]

In the Beeson collection, a sugar bowl with a spaniel finial and two mugs from the Wedgwood and Bentley period beautifully display the use of molded oak-leaf decoration over a textured or "dimpled" ground, as Wedgwood referred to it (cats. 151, 153, 154, pl. 52).[53] Wedgwood is known to have used the same motif on basalt desk sets. Both mugs, with silver mounts attached around the rims, originally had ceramic handles connected to their bodies. The handle on one mug must have broken or been flawed, however, as a handle made of fruitwood was attached with silver mounts in the eighteenth century. The new wooden handle may have been carved by John Coward, whom Wedgwood hired as a repairer in 1768; on February 23, 1769, Wedgwood wrote from London to his wife, Sarah: "I have settled a plan & method with Mr. Coward to Tinker all the black Vases that are crooked. . . . I wish you could send me a parc.l of these Invalids by Sundays Waggon."[54] One month later, he wrote to Bentley: "We have doctored, I wont say Tinkered, near 100 [pounds] worth of what we deem'd reprobates here, & by the next weeks end I believe shall not have a single waster left."[55]

Desk Sets

The Beeson collection contains two Wedgwood and Bentley basalt desk sets including an inkwell and sand box or sand shaker (cats. 197, 199, 200, 201; fig. 11).

Fig. 11 *Copier with Inkwell, ca. 1780, James Watt (1739-1819), Birmingham, England, mahogany and brass box, basalt inkwell, box: 6 7/8" x 17 3/4" x 11 1/2", Inkwell: 1 1/2" x 1 1/4" (cat. 182).*

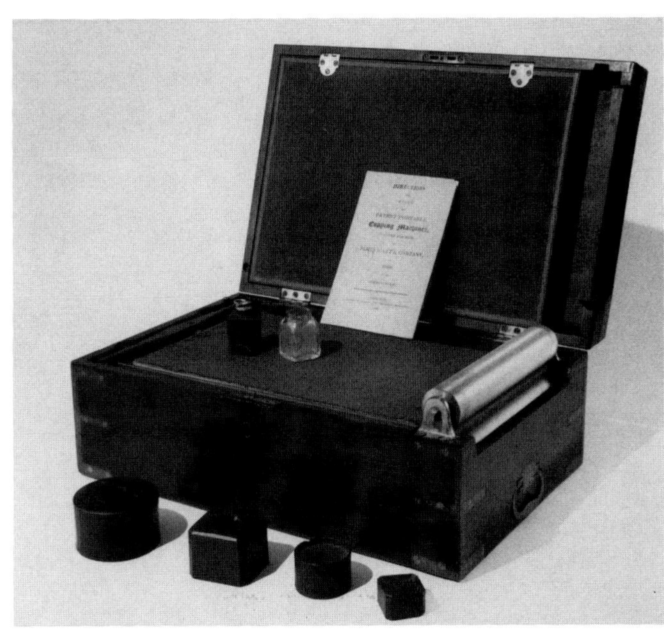

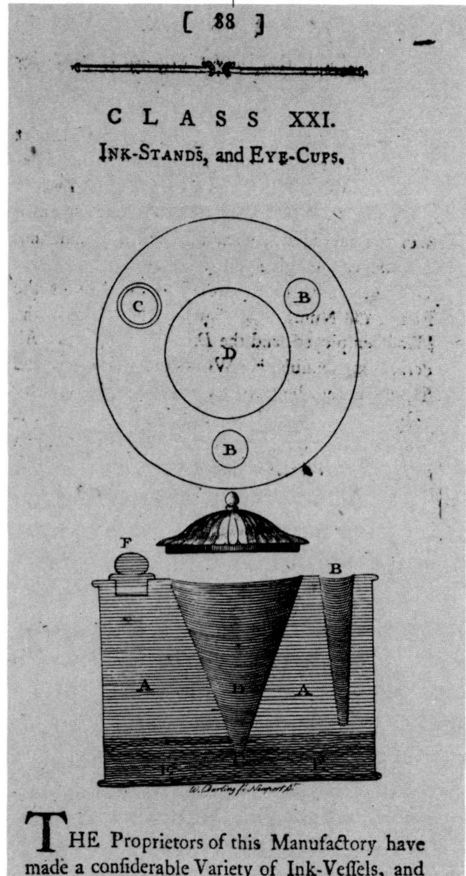
[88]

CLASS XXI.

INK-STANDS, and EYE-CUPS.

THE Proprietors of this Manufactory have made a considerable Variety of Ink-Veſſels, and Ink

Wedgwood's interest in improving the common inkwell is seen in these examples and his illustration and explanation in his *Ornamental Catalogue* (1777) (fig. 12). He made a wide variety of them, as he stated on October 22, 1777: "We have modeled 8 or 10 sizes of square ink-pots, some of them low ones that we may be able to fit all sizes & sorts of the wood stands in the shops, & private houses, for I hope we shall make ink-pots for all the world."[56] To the large opening in the center of the ink-well, where the pen was dipped into the ink, Wedgwood added smaller holes for filling the well and other holes that did not penetrate through to the ink to hold the quill pens; he also added a stopper to prevent the evaporation of the ink. The sander had the traditional surface, which was perforated like the top of a salt shaker, so that sand could be sprinkled onto the paper to blot the ink.

Fig. 12 *"Ink-stands and Eye-cups", Wedgwood Catalog of 1777, p. 88.*

"The proprietors of the Manufactory have made a considerable Variety of Ink Vessels and Ink-stands; but the best and most convenient that has ever been brought into Use, they apprehend, is one represented in the above Engraving, and which being new, will require some Explanation.
Explanation of the Plate.
A.A. The Ink Cistern filled with Ink up to F.
B. Pen Tubes which are closed at the Bottom, and therefore do not admit any Air into the Cistern.
C. An opening that communicates with the Cistern; and an Air-tight Plug.
D. A Cone through which the Vessel is filled; first taking out the Plug C, and then pouring in the Ink till the Cone is full; after which the Plug must be returned to its Place, and the Ink poured out of the Cone, or taken out with a Spunge, down to E. The Ink will then remain in the Cistern at F, and the Vessel act as a Fountain; the Pen taking up the Ink through the Cone D. at E.

Courtesy of the Trustees of the Wedgwood Museum, Barlaston, Stoke-on-Trent, England.

8
Etruscan Ware

In the continuing tradition of producing wares with historical antecedents, Wedgwood copied Greek vases in the red-figure style found in Etruscan tombs then being discovered. Excavated during the eighteenth century, the tombs yielded pottery that was primarily Greek, and Wedgwood acknowledged the fact in his *Ornamental Catalogue* (1773): "It is evident the finer Sort of Etruscan Vases, found in Magna Graecia, are truly Greek workmanship, and ornamented chiefly with Grecian Subjects, drawn from the purest Fountain of the Arts." Wedgwood was probably first made aware of these vases in *Receuil d'antiquités Egyptiennes, Etrusques, Grecques, Romaines, et Gauloises,* by Anne-Claude-Phillippe, Comte de Caylus, published between 1752 and 1767.

Vases excavated from Greek tombs in Nola and Capua, near Naples, were brought back to England by Sir William Hamilton, British ambassador to the court of Naples from 1764 to 1800. These Greek vases were of great interest to Wedgwood, as he indicates in a statement made to Bentley in January 1768:

> You will as easily imagine what may be of any use to me in the Antiquitys if you find time to dip into them. The colours of the Earthern [*sic*] Vases, the paintings, the substances used by the Ancient Potters, with their methods, of working, burning, &c. . . . Who knows what you may hit upon, or what we may strike out betwixt us you may depend on an ample share of the proffits arising from any such discoverys.[1]

Hamilton's collection comprised bronzes, gems, and other antiquities in addition to several hundred Greek vases, descriptions of which he published in *Antiquités Etrusques, Grecques, et Romaines: Tirees du cabinet de M.* [sic] *Hamilton.* He subsequently sold many of the vases to the British Museum in 1772 in order to defray the costs of his book.[2] Having been given a copy of this expensive set of books by Sir Watkin Williams Wynn, an admirer and patron of his work, on September 20, 1769, Wedgwood reported to Bentley: "May not you give Ld. Cathcart a hint that we are preparing to paint the Etruscan Vases after Mr. Hamilton's book?"[3]

The decoration on the original Greek wares was much more complicated than Wedgwood realized, and, in fact, it was not until the middle of the twentieth century that the original formula was deciphered. Classical ware was produced by using a red-burning clay for the body of the vase, reserving the area for the figures and covering the rest of the body with a black slip. The secret of the fluid slip—using urine or stale wine as the thinning agent—was unknown in the eighteenth century.[4]

Wedgwood achieved the same effect by reversing the technique, using a black body—basalt—and painting the surface. This decoration, part enamel and part slip, was his own invention and could be applied very thinly and accurately, resulting in a mat, rather than a glossy, finish.

In his commonplace book of August 1773, Wedgwood wrote: "Our encaustic colors differ essentially from common enamel colors, being hard and smooth, but not glossy." He referred to the ware as the "painted Etruscans" and described them as "vases and encaustic paintings where every succeeding Vase and every Picture is made, not in a mould, or by a stamp, but separately by the Hand, with the same attention and diligence [as the ancients had exercised]." The word "encaustic" is misleading, however, as, by definition, it is a method of decoration whereby colored clays are inlaid in a clay body; as he stated, Wedgwood painted his vases with a mat enamel.

Wedgwood knew his technique of painting with a mat enamel was different from the technique of the Greeks, but, for advertising purposes, he claimed in his ornamental catalogs:

> The Art of Painting Vases in the Manner of the Etruscans has been lost for Ages; and was supposed, by the ingenious Author of the Dissertation on Sir William Hamilton's Museum [collection], to have been lost in Pliny's Time. The Proprietors of this Manufactory have been so happy as to rediscover and revive this long lost Art so as to give Satisfaction to the most critical Judges; by inventing a Set of Encaustic Colours, essentially different from common Enamel Colours, both in Nature and Effects, . . . and by the Discovery of a Composition proper to receive them. . . . When the manufacturers had carefully examined the original Etruscan vases, they were convinced that the colours of the figures could not be successfully imitated with enamel, and that their success in attempting to revive this lost art would chiefly depend upon the discovery of a new kind of enamel colours. . . . By a great variety of experiments, this discovery has been made, and a set of encaustic colours invented.

Wedgwood's enameled ware was very difficult to produce, however, as he communicated to Bentley in December 1768: "I have been turning two or three sorts of faithfull copys from Etruscan Vases & am quite surpris'd both at the beauty of their forms, & the difficulty of making them, especially in pairs."[5] Wedgwood attempted to patent the Etruscan vases in November 1769, the patent reading, "Patent No. 939 for The purpose of ornamenting Earthen and Porcelain Ware with an Encaustic Gold Bronze, together with a peculiar Species of Encaustic Painting in various Colours in imitation of the Antient Etruscan and Roman Earthenware."[6] He met with opposition from the potter Humphrey Palmer, whom Wedgwood quoted as having said, "Our Patent is not founded upon a <u>new invention</u>, but upon an <u>improvement</u> only, & they do not fear, if this sho[d]. fail them, of proving that our Patent will be a <u>detriment to trade</u>."[7] Wedgwood refuted this point in a letter of March 3, 1771: "I sho[d]. imagine that Antiquaries, Connoisseurs & Artists are the only proper Persons to prove that no such Painting as ours has been done in Europe since the time of the Etruscans, & consequently that our Patent is founded upon a real invention."[8] The two potters finally agreed in June of that year to a compromise: that "each should pay their own costs, That Mr. P— sho[d]. be admitted to share in the P—t & that it sho[d]. be left to reference what he sho[d]. pay for his share of the P—t."[9] Wedgwood never attempted to patent any of his other inventions.

After beginning the production of his Etruscan vases in 1768, Wedgwood named his new factory Etruria. On the day the factory opened—June 13, 1769—Wedgwood threw six basalt vases, while his partner, Thomas Bentley, turned the potter's wheel.[10] Later that year, on November 19, Wedgwood wrote to Bentley of these vases: "The six Etruscan Vases three handled sent to you a fortnight since were those we threw & turn'd the first at Etruria, & sho[d]. be finish'd as high as you please, but not sold. they being <u>first fruits</u> of Etruria."[11] Today known as the First-Day Vases, they were painted with a red enamel by William Hopkins Craft in the London decorating studio. On the front were figures from Hamilton's *Antiquités*;[12] on the back was a painted inscription: "One of the first Days Productions at Etruria in Staffordshire, by Wedgwood and Bentley / Artes Etrurias Renascuntur" (the arts of Etruria reborn). Craft and his assistants appear to have been responsible for much of the painting on the Etruscan vases. David Rhodes is noted on extant bills for fourteen of them during September, October, and November of 1769, but these are now thought to be vases he purchased to be painted and sold for himself.[13]

Etruscan ware was costly, a fact that Wedgwood, in a letter to Bentley dated

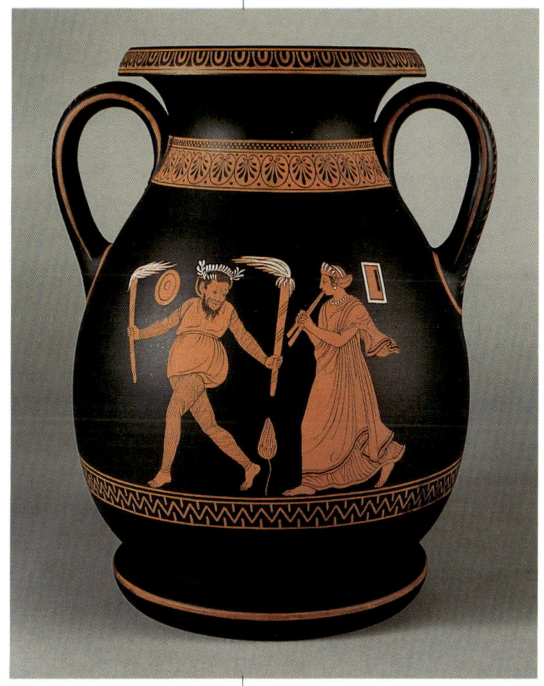

Color plate 53
Vase, Scene of a Theatre, *ca. 1815, basalt with encaustic decoration, 11 1/4" x 9" (cat. 184).*

December 3, 1772, lamented: "The Grecian vases we have are sadly too dear. . . . Whenever we tell the price . . . I am sure of a full stare . . . & either some note of admiration, or absolute silence."[14] In order to bring the price down, he attempted to introduce printing on the vases; the experiment was not successful, however, and Wedgwood continued with the hand-painting along with outlining and stenciling.[15] Among the fourteen pieces in the Beeson collection one finds two distinct decorative methods. The majority have a deep, muddy orange color, slightly watery-looking in the painting technique, with light black delineating lines and heavy, white-enamel accents. A smaller number, although generally carefully delineated, are painted with a brighter orange and seem to have a thinner layer of paint; they also have more border decoration. These distinctions indicate production of about 1790 for the early group and the nineteenth century for the later group.

As previously noted, Sir William Hamilton's collection of vases was published in the hand-colored, four-volume catalog entitled *Antiquités Etrusques, Grecques, et Romaines: Tirees du cabinet de M. Hamilton.* In Wedgwood's own ornamental catalogs between 1773 and 1787, he continually acknowledges his debt to Hamilton, stating, "The Vases of this Class . . . as well as the Paintings are copied from the antique with the utmost Exactness; as they are to be found in Dempster, Gorius, Count Caylus, Passerius, but more especially in the most choice and comprehensive Collection of Sir William Hamilton." The illustrations on ten of the fourteen Etruscan pieces in the Beeson collection were derived in part or wholly from examples published by Sir William Hamilton (see pls. 53, 54).

The text was written by the French art historian and book publisher Pierre François Hugues (ca. 1719-1805), known as Baron D'Hancarville. Hamilton supplied the vases and the money (eventually six thousand pounds), and left D'Hancarville to the rest. The four volumes are indeed among the most beautiful of works published

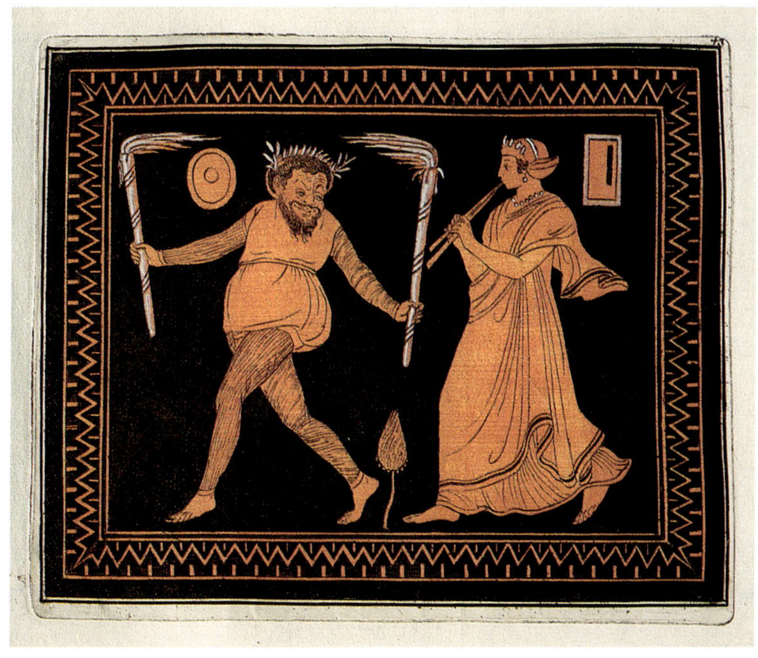

Color plate 54
Sir William Hamilton and P. H. d'Hancarville, Antiquités Etrusques, Grecques, et Romaines, *4 vols. Naples, 1766-77, vol. 1, pl. 43.*

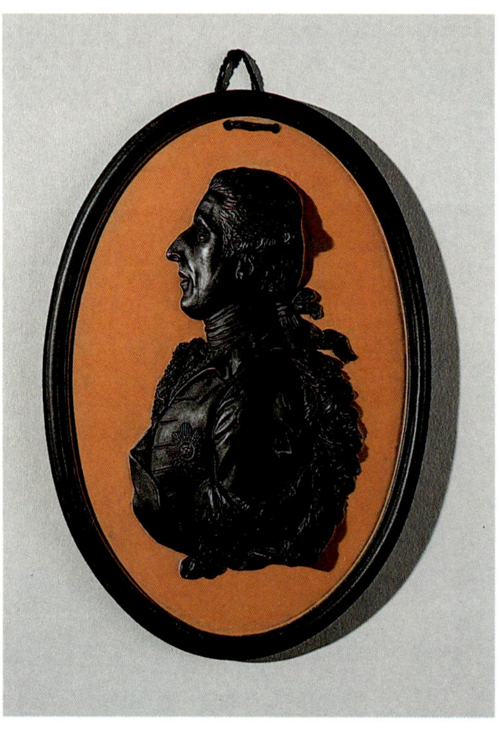

Color plate 55 *Portrait Medallion,* Sir William Hamilton, *1772, Joachim Smith, modeler, basalt with encaustic decoration on front and back, 6 3/16" x 4 7/16" (cat. 738).*

in the eighteenth century, fulfilling Hamilton's desire to improve English design by encouraging craftsmen to study the arts of the ancients. The text of the books deals very little with the vases themselves and mentions only briefly Hamilton's intentions that they encourage and refine craftsmanship. Instead, D'Hancarville's discourse focuses upon questions on the origins of art, Christianity, and ideal beauty.[16] Concerning the contemporary debate about which peoples had first cultivated the arts, he favors the Etruscans over the Greeks.

The Beeson collection is fortunate to include a first edition of Hamilton's four-volume work, which was published in Naples by Francesco Morelli. The dates given on the title pages are 1766 (vol. 1) and 1767 (vol. 2–4), but volume 1 did not actually appear until 1767, and volume 4 came out in 1776. Spectacular color plates accompany measured drawings of each vase. A number of artists were responsible for them, including the designers Giuseppe Bracci, Edmondo Beaulieu, and Giovanni Battista Tierce as well as the engravers and etchers Carmine Pignatari, Antoine Alexandre Joseph Cardon, Carlo Nolli, Filippo de Grado, Tommaso Piroli, and Aniello Lamberti.[17] (A publication of Hamilton's vases in three volumes, published by Wilhelm Tischbein between 1790 and 1794, is in cartoon and also in the Beeson collection.)

Sir William Hamilton was born into a wealthy family in Scotland in 1730, the grandson of the third duke of Hamilton. A British diplomat and an antiquary, he was the British ambassador at Naples from 1764 to 1800 and in 1772 was made a knight of Bath. Hamilton was married twice, the second time to Emma Hart, who was famous not only for her promiscuity but also for her confidence with Queen Maria Carolina of Naples. She became known publicly as Lord Nelson's mistress, an arrangement that Hamilton seems to have tolerated.

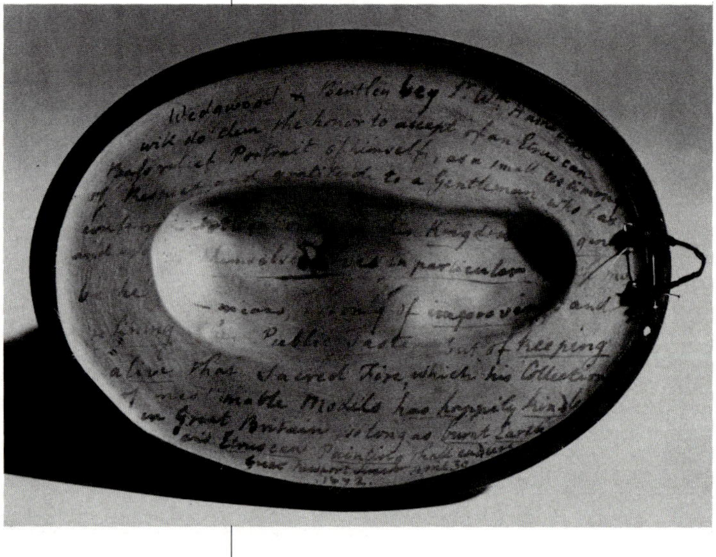

Fig. 13 *Portrait Medallion,* Sir William Hamilton, *reverse side of color plate 55 showing the inscription in Thomas Bentley's hand, and the thumbprint depression.*

As a result of his interest in and promotion of the neoclassic style, Hamilton was a well-known figure of his time, and Wedgwood listed his portrait in every edition of his catalog from 1773 to 1788. There is in the Beeson collection a rare and unusually large portrait medallion of Hamilton that is cast in the Etruscan style—black basalt, with the background around the bas-relief portrait painted in Etruscan orange (cat. 738, pl. 55). This is in all likelihood the first version of Hamilton's profile that Wedgwood issued. The modeler of the portrait was Joachim Smith. In a second issue found in jasper ware, the hair and cloak are truncated, and in a third issue Hamilton is portrayed in the garb of a Roman emperor. Of note on the back of the Beeson example is the following inscription in Thomas Bentley's hand (fig. 13):

> Wedgwood & Bentley beg Sir Wm. Hamilton will do them the honour to accept of an Etruscan Bas relief Portrait of himself, as a small testimony of Respect and gratitude to a Gentleman who has confirmed his obligations upon this Kingdom in-general and upon themselves in particular which may be the means, not only of improving and refining the Public Taste but of keeping alive that Sacred Fire, which his Collection of inestimable Models has happily kindled in Great Britain, so long as burnt Earth and Etruscan Painting shall endure.
> Great Newport Street, April 30, 1772.

The date probably commemorates Hamilton's sale of the first part of his collection to the British Museum on March 20, 1772.

One of the earliest Etruscan pieces in the Beeson collection is a ewer, the shape of which derives from the form of the Greek oinochoe (cat. 188, pl. 56). The piece has a shiny surface, with engine-turning at the neck and foot. For the design the enameler used an unusual amount of white paint as compared with other Etruscan vases by Wedgwood. This technique of painting is found on one other ewer in the British Museum and also on a vase inscribed "31 January 1774" in the Wedgwood Museum; thus this ewer possibly dates from around 1775.[18] The subject on the ewer is Dedalus building his wings. Wedgwood's source was most likely Montfaucon's *L'Antiquité expliquée* (fig. 14). The scene is described as follows: "Daedalus . . . made Waxen Wings for himself and his son Icarus. . . . Dedalus finished his Flight successfully, and arrived in Sicily. Dedalus is represented in a Gem making his Wings, and uses a Mallet, which is not a proper tool for making waxen Wings; but the Graver doth not always observe the strict Fable."[19]

Wedgwood also made "useful" ware with Etruscan decoration. Three pieces of teaware in the

Color plate 56
Left, *Pitcher,* Daedalus Building His Wings, *1775-80, basalt with encaustic decoration, engine-turning, 9 1/4" x 2 11/16" (cat. 188);* right, *Ewer,* Ceremony from a Wedding, *ca. 1780, basalt with encaustic decoration, 10 1/2" x 2 716" (cat. 187).*

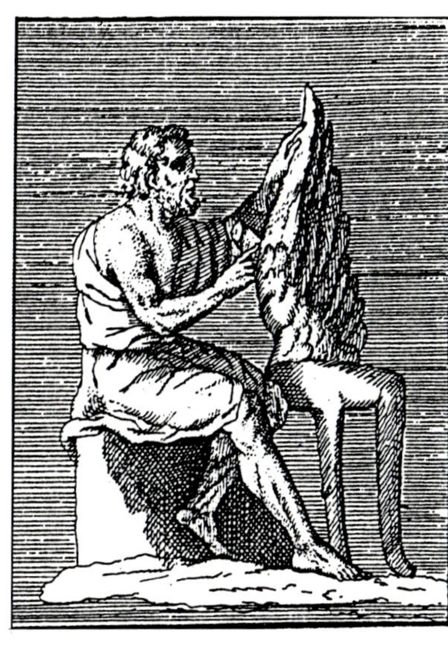

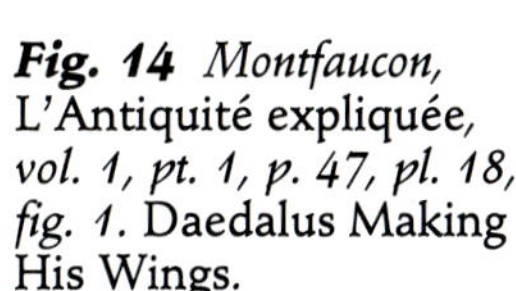

Fig. 14 *Montfaucon,* L'Antiquité expliquée, *vol. 1, pt. 1, p. 47, pl. 18, fig. 1.* Daedalus Making His Wings.

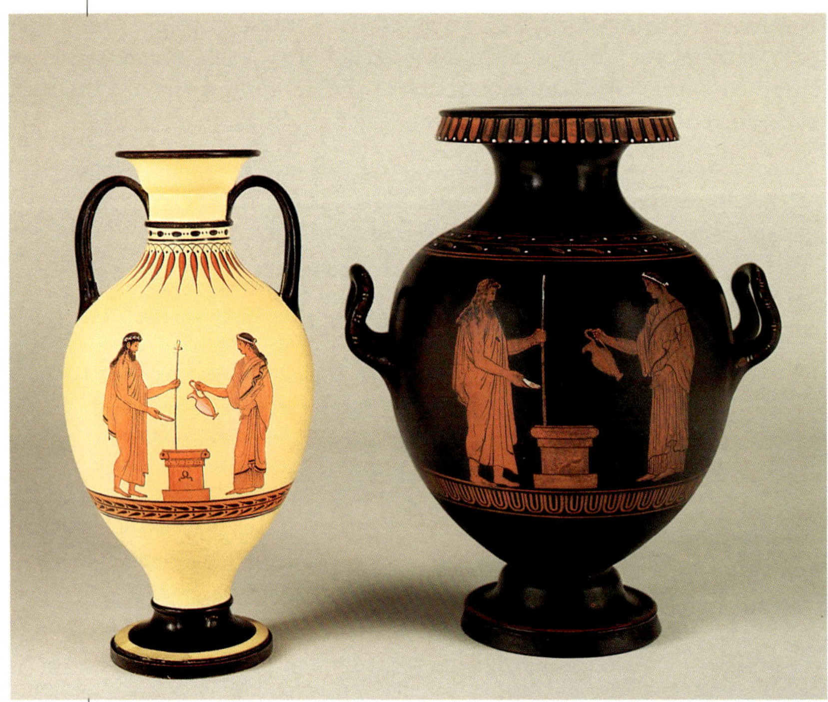

Color plate 57 Left, *Vase,* A Sacrifice, *ca. 1790, caneware with encaustic decortation, 8 3/4" x 2 3/4" (cat. 189);* right, *One of a Pair of Vases,* A Sacrifice, *ca. 1785, basalt with encaustic decoration, 9" x 3 1/2" (cat. 186).*

The two figures on vase A of the pair of basalt vases (ca. 186) and on a second example in caneware (cat. 189) show a design from Hamilton's Antiquités, *vol. 1, pl. 122, entitled* A Sacrifice. *Basalt vase B from the pair also has two figures, one of which is illustrated in vol. 1, pl. 109, of Hamilton's* Antiquités. *The source of the second figure is unknown.*

Color plate 58
Pair of Vases, The Race of Atalanta and Hippomenes *and* Diomedes Casting His Spear against Mars, *ca. 1790, basalt with encaustic decoration, 11 7/8" x 4 5/8" (cat.185).*

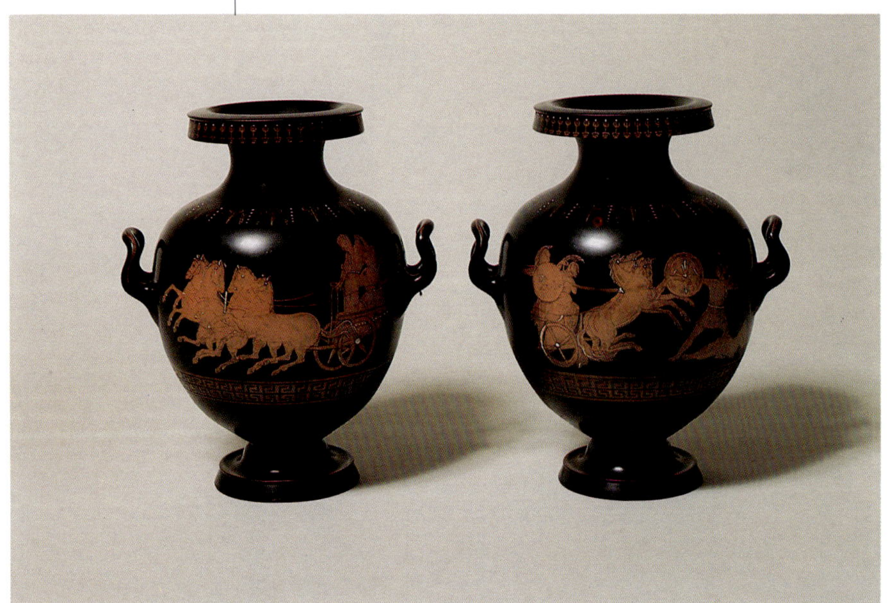

The printed source for this pair of vases is from two different books (cat. 185). The vase on the right depicts Diomedes casting his spear against Mars, taken from John Flaxman's illustration in the Iliad *of 1792. The vase on the left shows Castor and Pollux carrying off the daughters of Leucippus, or* The Race of Atalanta and Hippomenes, *taken from Hamilton's* Antiquités, *vol. 1, pl. 130, and vol. 2, pl. 22.*

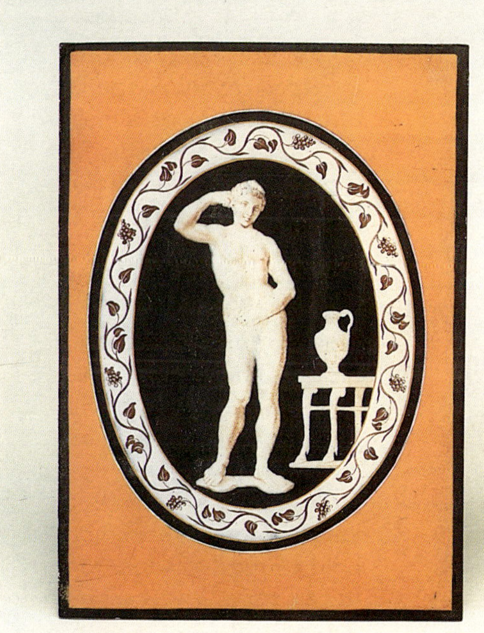

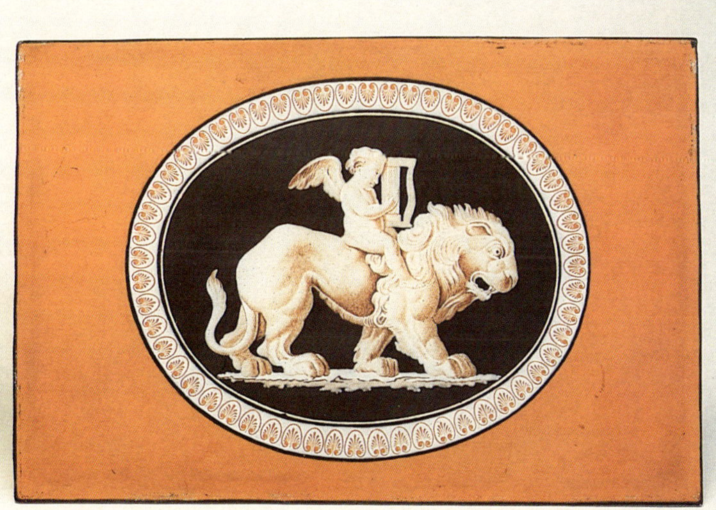

Color plate 59
Left, *Plaque,* Athlete Oiling Himself, *ca. 1770, basalt with encaustic decoration, 5 1/2" x 7 1/2" (cat. 194);* right, *Plaque,* Amore e Leone, *ca. 1770, basalt with encaustic decoration, 9 1/4" x 6 1/16" (cat. 193).*

These two unmarked basalt panels with Etruscan decoration are extremely rare and were probably made prior to 1780 (cats. 193, 194). The plaque on the right Wedgwood titled Amore e Leone, *depicting a cupid mounting a lion. The design source is in Stosch's* Pierres antiques gravees, *pl. 53, entitled* Amor Leonem domans. *A similar engraving is found in Hamilton's* Antiquités, *vol. 3, p. 211, and Montfaucon's* L'Antiquité expliquée, *vol. 1, p. 110, pl. 58, fig. 6, from the Maffei collection (fig. 15). Montfaucon describes the scene as follows: "The Little God rides up the Back of another Lion, and plays upon his Lyre at his Ease, while the Lion stalks along slowly. The Graver of this Piece is Plotarchus, as the Greek inscription shows."*

The source of the second plaque on the left was taken from a sardonyx gem entitled "Athlète versant de l'huile," after a Greek statue. It is seen in three early publications: Venuti, Collectanea Antique *(1736) pl. 75; Natter,* Methode, *(1754) pl. 25; and* Marlborough Gems *(ca. 1780), vol. 1, engraved by Bartolozzi after a design by Cipriani.*

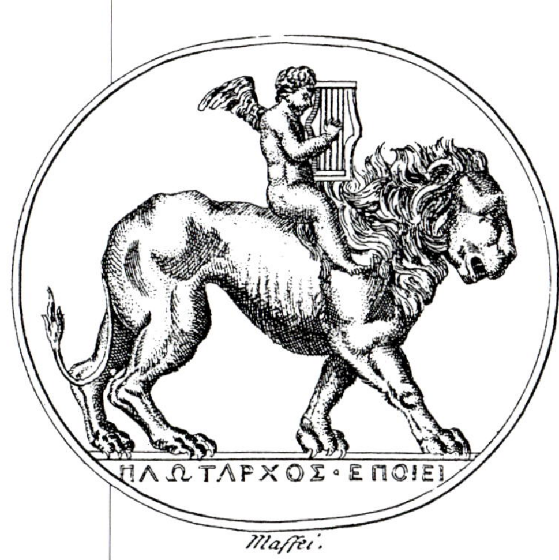

Fig. 15 *Montfaucon,* L'Antiquité expliquée, *vol. 1, pt. 1, pl. 58, fig. 6.* Amore e Leone.

collection, although not a set, have various "Greek patterns" and date from about 1770 to 1790 (see pl. 60). With the exception of the handleless cup and saucer (cat. 199), they are all glazed on the inside and are thus intended for actual use. The rare chocolate pot is marked "Wedgwood & Bentley" (cat. 200). The decorative border on the teapot is number 71 in Wedgwood's pattern book (cat. 198).

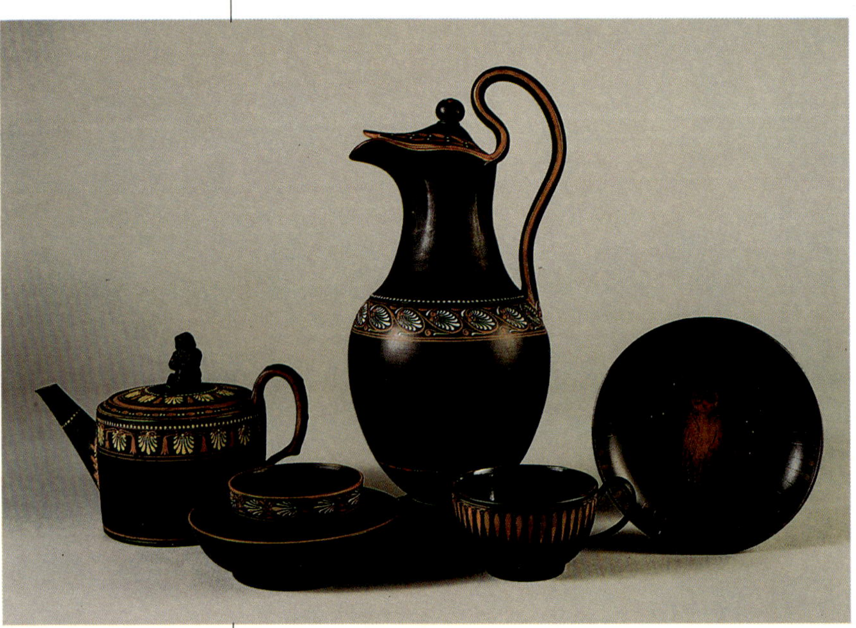

Color plate 60
Left, *Teapot, ca. 1780, basalt with encaustic decoration, 4 1/4" x 3 1/8" (cat. 198);* second from left, *Cup and Saucer, ca. 1785, basalt with encaustic decoration, cup: 1 11/16" x 1 3/8", saucer: 4 5/16" (cat. 199);* third from left, *Covered Chocolate Pot, ca. 1780, basalt with encaustic decoration, glazed interior, 10" x 3 1/2" (cat. 200);* right, *Cup and Saucer,* Owl, *ca.1772, basalt with encaustic decoration, cup has glazed interior, cup: 1 3/4" x 1 1/2", saucer: 5 3/16" (cat. 196). The saucer of this set shows an owl, "Symbol of Athens and Minerva," from Hamilton's* Antiquités, *vol.1, pl. 41 (cat. 196). The border design is from Wedgwood's pattern book of 1770, no. 58.*

In 1790, Josiah Wedgwood II wrote to his brother Tom of these pieces: "Your black tea ware with lively colors I dare say will please the foreigners, but the English I am afraid will not admire them. We are not bold enough to adopt at once anything that is new and beautiful but require the sanction of fashion to give it value."[20] Fortunately for Wedgwood, the sanction of fashion was not long in coming. There was soon considerable demand for Etruscan pieces by such patrons as George III, Queen Charlotte, Catherine II of Russia, and other kings, queens, dukes, princes, and barons throughout Europe, and before long numerous country houses had entire rooms dedicated to the Etruscan style, the most notable example surviving until today being Osterley Park House, with its Etruscan dressing room designed by Robert Adam between 1775 and 1779.

9
Neoclassicism

In eighteenth-century England the baroque style began to wane as the populace renewed their interest in classical architecture. The Venetian architect Andrea Palladio, who had been the first to articulate the new style, inspired a flood of architectural pattern books celebrating classical antiquity. For centuries, Englishmen traveling to Greece had avoided the Acropolis; in 1605 accoring to William Biddulph, an explorer and at the time a chaplin at Constantinople, "Athens is still inhabited. . . . This City was the mother and nurse of all liberal Arts and Sciences: but now there is nothing but Atheism and Barbarism there: for it is governed by Turks and inhabited by ignorant Greeks. None of the ancient buildings are yet to be seen."[1] By 1620, however, a new incentive arose: the quest for ancient artifacts. The Ottoman Empire began to fall in the second half of the seventeenth century, and the English began collect and fill their houses and gardens with marble statuary. By 1680, because of the significant number of Englishmen traveling to and living in Greece, Lancelot Hobson was appointed British consul to Athens, further opening avenues of exploration into the country.

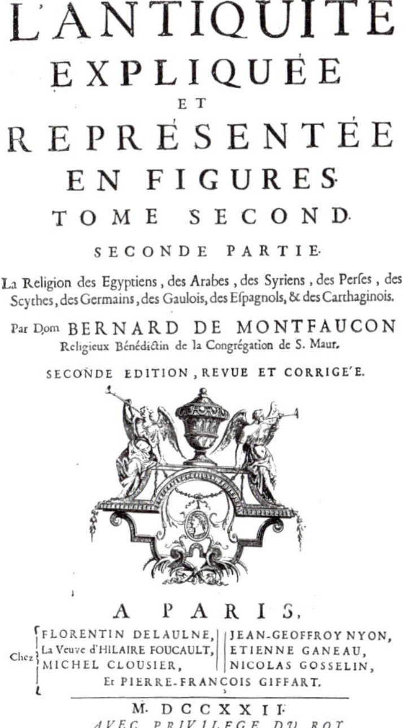
L'ANTIQUITÉ
EXPLIQUÉE
ET
REPRÉSENTÉE
EN FIGURES.
TOME SECOND.
SECONDE PARTIE.
La Religion des Egyptiens, des Arabes, des Syriens, des Perſes, des Scythes, des Germains, des Gaulois, des Eſpagnols, & des Carthaginois.
Par Dom BERNARD DE MONTFAUCON
Religieux Bénédictin de la Congrégation de S. Maur.
SECONDE EDITION, REVUE ET CORRIGE'E.

A PARIS,
Chez FLORENTIN DELAULNE, La Veuve d'HILAIRE FOUCAULT, MICHEL CLOUSIER, JEAN-GEOFFROY NYON, ETIENNE GANEAU, NICOLAS GOSSELIN, Et PIERRE-FRANÇOIS GIFFART.
M. DCCXXII.
AVEC PRIVILEGE DU ROY.

Fig. 16 *Title page of Bernard de Montfaucon,* L'Antiquité expliquée et représentée en figures, *1722.*

George Wheler was an early voyager who collected objects and produced one of the first detailed pictures of Greece. His journal, *Journey into Greece* (1682), was dedicated to Charles II, who rewarded the author with knighthood. Wheler later donated his valuable collection of marbles to Lincoln College at Oxford.

Another important and widely distributed work concerning the arts of the ancients was *L'Antiquité expliquée et représentée en figures,* published by Bernard de Montfaucon in five two-part volumes in 1719, followed by a five-volume supplement in 1724 (fig. 16). The text was a study of ancient history, culture, and myths, and it included illustrations of cameos, coins, furniture, gems, and statuettes that served as invaluable sources for architects and designers.

In 1734, the Society of Dilettanti was formed in England to foster and promote neoclassicism in English culture. The group of young men of wealth and aristocratic birth had originally banded together as a dining club. Most had taken the grand tour of the Continent, an experience that led them to cultivate a great enthusiasm for bringing the treasures of the ancient world to Britain. They sponsored excavations and the publication of a book entitled *The Antiquities of Athens, Measured and Delineated by James Stuart, F.R.S. and F.S.A., and Nicholas Revett, Painters and Architects.* First published in 1762, this volume and the four others that followed became the foundation of the modern study of Greek archaeology and the promotion of neoclassical decoration. Of the over five hundred subscribers to the first volume, only four were architects and three were builders.[2] (William Hogarth caricatured the volumes in the print entitled *The Five Orders of Perriwigs, . . . Measured Architectonically . . . from the*

Statues, Bustos, and Basso-Relievos of Athens, Palmira, Baalbec, and Rome.)

The principals of the Society of Dilettanti were Sir Francis Dashwood and Lord John Montagu Sandwich. Under their leadership, archaeology became a sport considered both fashionable and fun, an attitude that fostered many of the great collections accumulated by early members of the Dilettanti: the Lansdowne marbles, the Hamilton vases and manuscripts, the Worsley marbles, the Farnborough paintings, and the Hope vases.

In 1777, the year in which Sir William Hamilton was elected into the society, Sir Joshua Reynolds painted a formal portrait showing fourteen members relaxing after dinner. The painting shows Hamilton holding a vase and one of his manuscripts; the archmaster and secretary are in ceremonial dress; and the rest of the group are examining presumably obscene objects and making irreverent gestures. Despite this reputation for cultivating a certain lasciviousness, the society is credited with the establishment of neoclassicism in England; members such as James and George Gray played a prominent part in the discoveries at Herculaneum, and Sir William Hamilton for his Pompeian studies.

Hamilton's collection had a profound effect on a whole generation of tastemakers, particularly Robert Adam and Josiah Wedgwood. His wife, Emma Hamilton, should also be recognized as a promoter of neoclassicism. Popularly known today as the mistress of Lord Nelson, Emma performed a series of tableaux modeled on Pompeian frescoes and Greco-Roman statues. Imitating the sculptures of the ancients, she dressed in a white chemise gown with shawls and wore her hair loose and flowing; her props included one or two Etruscan vases. Antiquity had been brought into the drawing rooms of the most fashionable homes.

Johann Joachim Winckelmann should also be added to this list of advocates of the ancients. By day he was a poor schoolteacher; by night he read Plutarch or Sophocles. Patronized by Augustus the Strong, Elector of Saxony and King of Poland, Winckelmann soon found himself in Rome boasting the title of papal antiquary and proclaiming, "There is only one way for the moderns to become great and perhaps unequalled: by imitating the Ancients." He further stated that "good taste . . . was born under the sky of Greece" and managed to influence even such great writers of the time as Byron, Keats, Shelley, and Landor. Winckelmann's book *Reflections on the Imitation of Greek Works in Painting and Sculpture* (1755) was twice reprinted in England. But it was his *History of Ancient Art*, which traced the origin, growth, development, and decadence of art, that established him as the father of archaeology and the voice of neoclassicism.

By the turn of the nineteenth century, numerous volumes had been written. The ruins of Pompeii and Herculaneum in Italy, the two cities overwhelmed by the eruptions of Mount Vesuvius in A.D. 79, had been discovered during the first two decades of the eighteenth century, and excavation began at Herculaneum in 1738 and at Pompeii in 1748. The spectacular wall paintings uncovered there provided further design sources.[3]

In 1812 the Society of Dilettanti sponsored one final archaeological trip, with Sir William Gell in command. Five temples were excavated, examined, and recorded.[4] The society had intended "to engrave and offer them to the Public for the Improvement of National Taste," but because of the high cost of the expedition, the two-volume work did not appear until 1817 and 1840. These were the last published efforts of the Society of Dilettanti, and its role as England's coterie of tastemakers began to fade.

The Adam Brothers

The term "neoclassic" was first used in Europe in the 1880s to refer to the period, during the late eighteenth and early nineteenth centuries, when society turned from the interests of the Renaissance to a fascination with the antique. As England's reaction against the frivolity of the rococo, neoclassicism flourished in the atmosphere of national self-confidence that characterized the beginning of the reign of George III, which, it was hoped, would, in Robert Adam's words, "fix an Aera no less remarkable than that of Pericles, Augustus or the Medici."[5] Indeed, the neoclassic style dominated the work of architects Robert Adam and James Adam during the 1760s and 1770s. Their style was neither Palladian nor Grecian but a synthesis of their own creation—a combination of the Greek, Roman, Hellenistic, Etruscan, and Renaissance influences that reflected the spirit of classical art. In 1773 the Adam brothers' first volume, *Works in Architecture*, boasted of the defeat of Palladianism: "The massive entablature, the ponderous compartmented ceiling, the tabernacle frame, almost the only species of ornament formerly known in this country, are now universally exploded and in their places we have adopted a beautiful variety of light mouldings, gracefully formed and delicately enriched," that embody "the beautiful spirit of antiquity."[6]

The Adam style was an instant and widespread success. Architecture and interior design featured the new classical vocabulary, one that was familiar to all, due in large part to books on classical antiquities. By the 1780s, architects, sculptors, painters, and potters from England, Europe, and America were producing neo-classical works of remarkable homogeneity. Robert Adam's Edinburgh University, John Soane's Bank of England, Jean-Antoine Houdon's sculpture of George Washington, Antonio Canova's two papal monuments of Cupid and Psyche, Jacques-Louis David's great paintings, John Flaxman's illustrations of Homer, and Josiah Wedgwood's jasper ware were some of the artistic and political masterpieces of this time. Yet the artisans who were born during the last two decades of the eighteenth century grew up in a world in which the battle against the rococo had been won. They felt their predecessors had not paid enough attention to the antique. In 1772, James Wyatt took London by storm with the building of the Pantheon and became the successor to Robert Adam as England's preeminent architect. Here the spirit of neoclassicism began to die, and the force of the Greek Revival began.

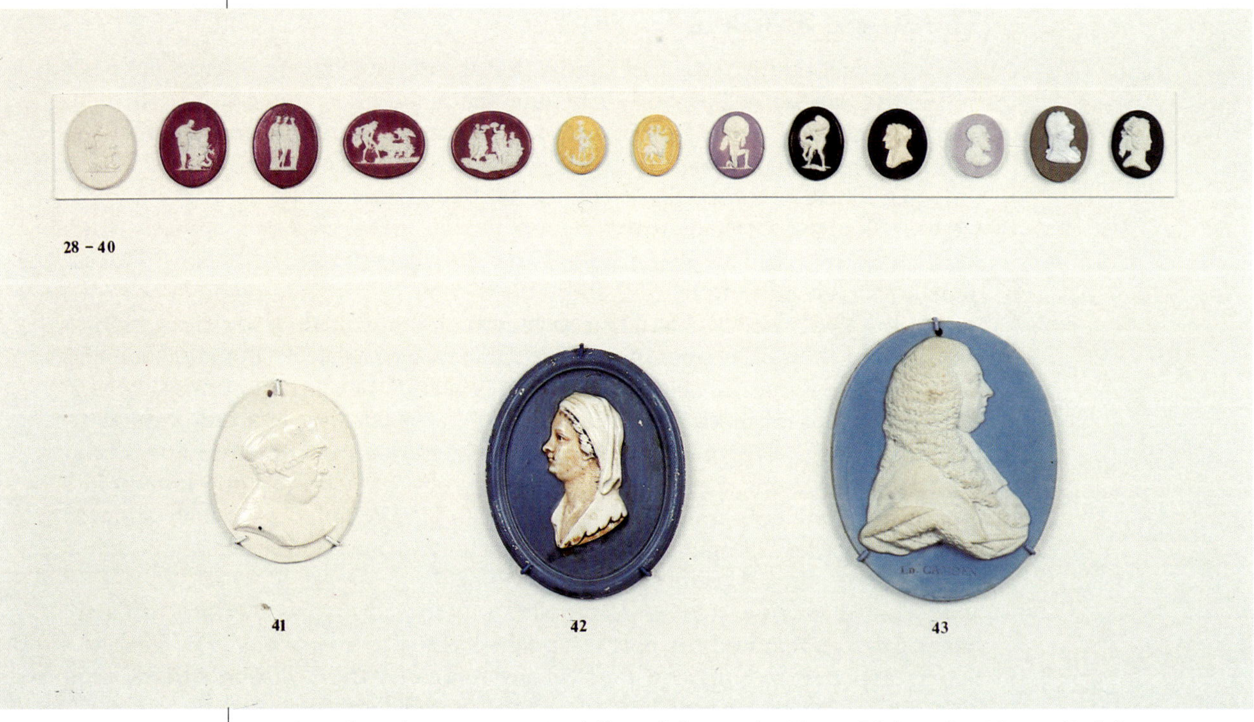

Color plate 61 Top row, *Medallions,* left to right*:* Venus Hiding Cupid on a Dolphin*, ca. 1775, jasper, solid white ground, 1" x 13/16" (cat. 684);* Venus Hiding Cupid on a Dolphin*, ca. 1775, jasper, solid white ground with lilac enamel on front and lilac wash on back, 1" x 13/16" (cat. 685);* Three Graces*, jasper, solid white ground with lilac enamel on front and lilac wash on back, 1" x 13/16" (cat. 686);* Achilles Staying the Chariot of Victory*, ca. 1775, jasper, solid white ground with lilac enamel on front and lilac wash on back, 13/16" x 1" (cat. 687);* Corybantes Striking Their Bucklers to Prevent the Cries of the Infant Jupiter from Being Heard by Saturn*, ca. 1775, jasper, solid white ground with lilac enamel on front and lilac wash on back, 13/16" x 1" (cat. 688);* Harpocrates*, ca. 1775, jasper, solid white ground with yellow enamel on front and black wash on back, 3/4" x 9/16" (cat. 689);* Bacchus and Ariadne Riding a Tiger*, ca. 1775, jasper, solid white ground with yellow enamel on front and black wash on back, 3/4" x 9/16" (cat. 690);* Hercules Holding the World*, ca. 1775, jasper, solid white ground with lilac enamel on front and black wash on back, 3/4" x 11/16" (cat. 691);* Hercules Binding Cerberus*, ca. 1775, jasper, solid white ground with gray enamel on front and black wash on back, 7/8" x 5/8" (cat. 692);* Head of a Woman*, ca. 1775, jasper, solid white ground with brown enamel on front and back, 13/16" x 3/4" (cat. 693);* Cato*; ca. 1780, jasper, solid white ground with lilac wash on front with white relief, 3/4" x 5/8" (cat. 694);* Male Head*, ca. 1795, jasper, solid light brown ground with white glass paste relief, 7/8" x 5/8" (cat. 695);* Female Head*, ca. 1790, jasper, solid brown ground with white relief, 3/4" x 9/16" (cat. 696);* bottom left, *Portrait Medallion,* Bust of Male Figure*, ca. 1780, white terra-cotta stoneware with clear glaze, 2 1/8" x 1 13/16" (cat. 697);* bottom center, *Portrait Medallion,* Artemisia*, 19th century, cream ware with enamel, 3" x 2 7/16" (cat. 698);* bottom right, *Portrait Medallion,* Lord Charles Pratt Camden*, ca. 1778, jasper, solid blue ground with light blue wash and white relief, 3 1/4" x 2 11/16" (cat. 699).*

10 Jasper Ware

In 1769, Wedgwood wrote to Bentley: "Elegant simplicity—[I] shall, more than Ever, make that idea a leading principle in my usefull, as well as our Ornamental works."[1] One of the many English artists who ushered in neoclassicism, Josiah Wedgwood created a new ware to capture the pastel colors being used by the architects Robert Adam and James Wyatt as well as the mythological figures revealed on recently excavated classical artifacts. His jasper ware was a deliberate invention of a fine clay body that could either remain white or accept color. Like porcelain, jasper ware is fired at a high temperature and, by virtue of its ingredients, becomes translucent when thinly potted.[2] Indeed, although he realized the difference between jasper ware and porcelain, Wedgwood described jasper as "my porcelain."[3]

The ware was the product of over five thousand exhaustive experiments that Wedgwood made between 1772 and 1776. On August 30, 1774, his frustration was evident: "If I had more time, more hands, & more heads I could do something. . . . A Man who is in the midst of a course of experim[ts]. sho[d]. not be at home to any thing or any body else but that cannot be my case. Farewell—I am almost Crazy."[4] Yet only four days later, on September 3, 1774, he wrote: "I believe I shall make an excellent white body, & with absolute certainty, without the fusible Sparr."[5] The formula Wedgwood ultimately settled upon was a body composed of 10 percent flint, 59 percent barium sulphate, 2 percent barium carbonate, and 29 percent clay (silica and alumina). The barium sulphate was the key ingredient: it supplied the fusible substance that could withstand high temperatures. Wedgwood encountered problems caused by inconsistencies in his materials and a confusion between sulphate of barium, or "cawk," and carbonate of barium, in the form of witherite. Once he solved the mystery, Wedgwood sent small medallions to Bentley in London so that they could be colored by enameling or staining. Yet this method of coloration proved unsuccessful, and Wedgwood soon wrote to Bentley of his dissatisfaction, saying that "preserving the outlines clean & sharp, & this in the small figures is not practicable."[6]

The Beeson collection contains a number of these experimental small medallions, which were molded in one complete piece, with the enamel or stain painted around the figures (cats. 684-96, pl. 61). A paper note glued to the back of their original frame states: "Specimens of very early Wedgwood [Wedgwood and Bentley period]. The five pink, two yellow, and two brown are specimens of Wedgwood's earliest attempts at colored grounds, the color being painted on previous to the firing." Indeed, these pieces must represent what Wedgwood described in a letter to Bentley dated September 5, 1774: "They are painted in a new species of Enamel, upon color'd grounds, from Gems &c—."[7] These medallions, as the figures reveal, are not pure white: they have small specks of black within them. On July 11, 1775, Wedgwood wrote of solving this problem: "I can make the blue grounds fine enough for any thing or any body & take away that freckled, Linsey Woolsey appearance."[8] The reverse of these gems was either painted or stained black; one example has a very light lilac stain on the back, and the enamel on the front has a polished or glazed finish.

Another small medallion from this group exhibits a soft, waxy, white composition throughout, with no color on the front and back. On August 6, 1775, Wedgwood wrote: "I shall send you some of the specimens from this substance with other things, particularly the chalky body made waxen & its whiteness preserv'd."[9] This waxen body is thought to be a further development of white terra-cotta stoneware, not jasper.

By December 12, 1774, Wedgwood had begun to color the clay itself.[10] Nearly three weeks later, on New Year's Day, having sent samples to Bentley, he wrote: "I am glad you think the white body of sufficient fineness & have no reason to doubt of being able to continue it so. The blue body I am likewise absolute in of almost any shade, & have likewise a beautifull Sea Green, and several other colours, for grounds to Cameo's, Intaglio's &c."[11] There continued to be problems with the coloring of the ground, as it often bled into the white relief. Perhaps Wedgwood was addressing this problem when he wrote to Bentley in 1775: "Those heads, and figures which can be made separately, undercut a little at the edges, then fixed to the ground, & fired bisket will be less liable to staining."[12] It was not until January 14, 1776, that he felt confident enough to claim success: "I believe I can now assure you of a conquest, & a very important one to us—No less than the firing of our fine Jasper & Onyx with as much certainty as our Basaltes."[13]

The word "jasper" first appears in Wedgwood's extant correspondence on November 27, 1775: "I am glad to hear our Jasper bears enameling as I much fear'd it would not. We shall make the Gems of it in future for Bracelets, Rings &c."[14] Wedgwood no doubt utilized the word "jasper" because it refers to a precious stone, such as a green quartz found in Greece. The term is defined in the sixth and final edition of the 1787 *Ornamental Catalogue*:

> Jasper: a white porcelain bisque, of exquisite beauty and delicacy, possessing the general properties of the basaltes, together with that of receiving colours through its whole substance, in a manner which no other body, ancient or modern, has been known to do. This renders it peculiarly fit for cameos, portraits, and all subjects in bas relief; as the ground may be made of any colour throughout, without paint or enamel, and the raised figures of a pure white.

The result was a dense, white stoneware that could be potted very thinly and stained with metallic oxides, resulting in colors of light and dark blue, gray, green, lilac, yellow, brown, and black. All were colors that conformed closely to those used by the Adam brothers in their classical interiors.

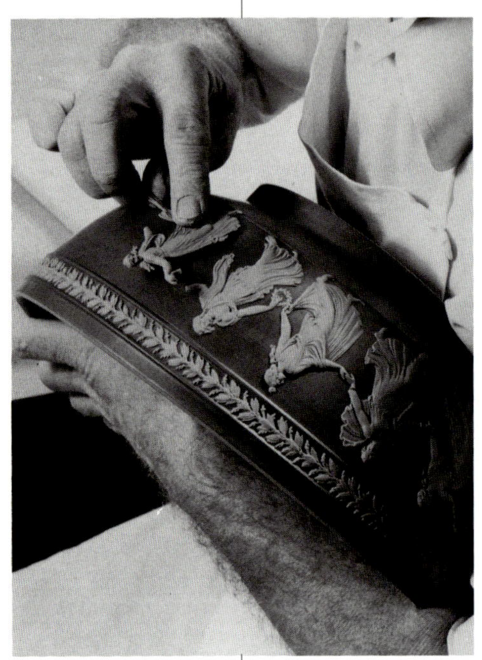

Fig. 17 *Contemporary factory worker ornamenting a vase with bas-relief which is applied to jasper ware by hand, a method that has continued since the eighteenth century. Courtesy of the Trustees of the Wedgwood Museum, Barlaston, Stoke-on-Trent, England.*

The white bas-relief figures on jasper ware are of the same stoneware material as the body, only uncolored. They were made in separate clay molds, then dampened and applied individually to the main body (fig. 17). In the eighteenth and early nineteenth centuries, the figures were then carefully touched up in detail and often undercut around the edges; when firing took place, the figures and the body became one. Wedgwood described the process to Sir William Hamilton in a letter of June 24, 1786: "They have been the object of very much labour and time, every ornament and leaf being made in a separate mould, and then laid upon the vase with great care and accuracy, and afterwards wrought over again on the vase itself by an artist equal to the work. . . . I spare neither time nor expense in the modelling and finishing of my ornaments."[15]

Before the latest research (and particularly Robin Reilly's), it was thought that most eighteenth-century jasper ware was colored throughout, but close examination of early medallions and plaques and a careful analysis of Wedgwood's letters and a document entitled "Memorandum Novr 23 1777 Jasper Composition"[16] reveal that much of what appears to be solidly colored jasper ware is a body of coarsely ground jasper with a dip or wash of a fine layer of jasper slip on top. This washing was done

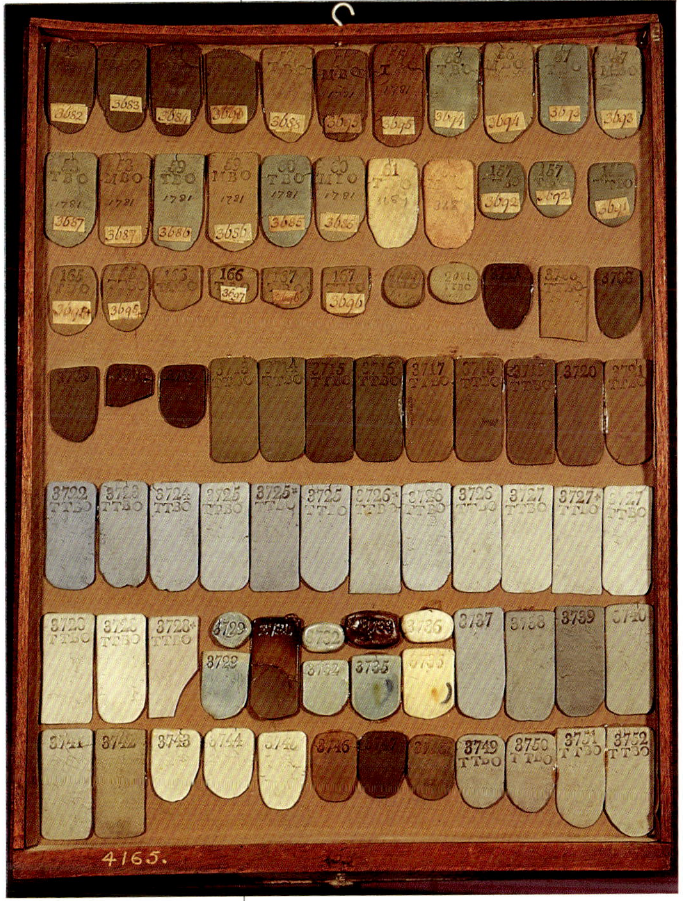

Color plate 62
Tray of jasper trials, each marked with an experiment number and some with coding as to firing, ca. 1773-76. ("TBO" means top of biscuit oven.) Courtesy of the Trustees of the Wedgwood Museum, Barlaston, Stoke-on-Trent, England.

for several reasons. At this period, cobalt was purchasable from Saxony only in small quantities and at great expense; however, sometime later, deposits were found in Cornwall, and the cost of cobalt was lowered substantially. On April 13, 1777, Wedgwood wrote to Bentley concerning the economy of the washing: "In the box are two heads with exquisite blue grounds. . . . I wish we may be able to make you some Tablets in this way. They are color'd with the Cobalt @ 36/- Per lb which being too dear to mix with clay of the whole grounds we have wash'd them over, & I think them by far the finest grounds we have ever made."[17] This washing also enabled Wedgwood to achieve subtler shades of color than a solid ground had previously afforded him and eventually led to engine-turning of the jasper—the cutting away of the outer color to the base color.

On November 3, 1777, Wedgwood further confirmed his success: "I have tried my new mixing of Jasper, & find it very good. Indeed I had not much fear of it, but it is a satisfaction to be certain, & I am now absolute in the precious article & can make it with as much facility, & certainty as black ware . . . We have only now to push it forward into the world—keep our secret, &c &c."[18] By mid-December of 1777, Wedgwood had perfected the colors of green, yellow, and lilac for shading jasper (pl. 62).

A portion of Wedgwood's "Memorandum Novr 23 1777 Jasper Composition" explains the necessity of washing the two slightly different compositions.

> The coarser the body is, the less subject it will be to warp and bend in burning, & vice versa. In order therefore to give the body the stability in burning required, the materials must be coarsely ground, but then the surface will be coarse likewise, and as the articles to be made of this beautiful composition are not to be glazed, a kind of semipolish is required upon the surface, that the biscuit may look fine, & wash perfectly clean.
>
> In order to produce this effect, take some of the composition, ground sufficiently to take the smoothness required, & make it into slip, in which dip your pieces, and when dry polish it. The slip may be thin to produce this effect, so thin perhaps as not to injure a figure.

This method could be used in either molding a piece or turning one. Molding required that the fine blue slip be poured first and allowed to dry, followed by the coarse white forming the interior of the piece; finally, the fine blue slip was poured and quickly removed. For a thrown piece the coarse composition was used first, then washed on the interior with the fine white and on the exterior with the fine blue. The memorandum also suggests that some of the surfaces thought to be lapidary-polished may indeed be a natural "semipolish in the burning" of the fine composition as it "nearly converts into glass."[19]

This final composition of the wash and the body resulted from grinding the clay in two different mills, the first a water mill and the second a windmill. On March 10, 1776, Wedgwood wrote to Bentley and explained the difference:

> When ground in our little Mill [wind], the particles are uniformly small, but when ground in a large Flint Mill [water] with Stones of near half a Ton weight, many of the particles in the composition are crush'd & divided infinitely smaller than we can make them in a Dish, or upon our small Mill & I have long known that the surface of our Jasper will be rough, & harsh, or smooth & polish'd in proportion to the fineness (smallness) of the particles in the composition.

Thus the water mill was used for grinding the fine jasper slip or wash and the windmill for the coarser clay body.[20] A letter from Wedgwood to Bentley dated May 20, 1776, reveals Wedgwood's experimentation with the clays: "The Boy with blue Drapery was made in haste & is much seam'd, & being made of two sorts of Clay, I mean Clay ground on two different Mills (Wind & Water), he is crack'd all over."[21] Less than a month later, in a letter dated June 6, 1776, Wedgwood says: "The Glossy composition is not so good as the opaque. The whole difference arises from one being ground upon the Wind, & the other upon a water Mill. It is very good with a certain degree of fire, but is much more delicate in that respect than the composition ground upon the Wind Mill."[22]

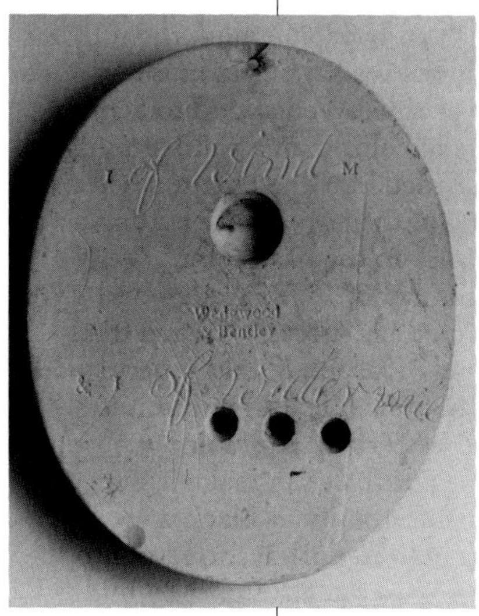

***Fig. 18** Back of Portrait Medallion,* Lord Charles Pratt Camden, *ca. 1778, jasper, solid blue ground with light blue wash and white relief, 3 1/4" x 2 11/16" (cat. 699).*

A blue-and-white, jasper-wash medallion of Lord Charles Pratt Camden (1714-94), in an inscription on the back, further relates the grinding and mill story: "1 of Wind M & 1 of Water mill" (cat. 699, fig. 18, pl. 63). This passage obviously refers to the clay of which the medallion is made, and thus the medallion further verifies Wedgwood's experimentation using both wind- and water mills. This was the first portrait medallion and also the first piece marked "Wedgwood & Bentley" that the Beesons purchased. The design source of the medallion is from a medal by Thomas Pingo of 1766; the medallion was first made by Wedgwood in November 1779.[23]

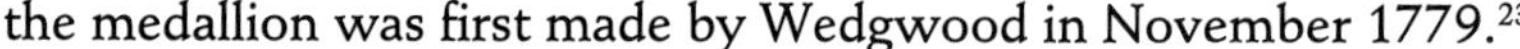

Wedgwood even explained the composition of the jasper in the introduction to the 1779 *Ornamental Catalogue*:

> It may be proper to observe here, that this artificial Jasper is made in two Colours; the Relief of one Colour and the Ground of another, which is not laid upon the Surface like Enamel, but goes thro' the whole Mass; and that the Grounds admit of a good polish; so that those who prefer a bright to a mat Surface, may have Pictures and Bas-reliefs from the Size of a Ring to that of a large Chimney-piece tablet or Cameo Picture.

With this description in mind, one can easily distinguish the early jasper medallions, plaques, and tablets from the nineteenth-century examples. The most obvious sign, of course, is the "Wedgwood and Bentley" mark. The second characteristic of the early jasper medallions is the use of large firing holes or combinations of large, medium, or small ones directly behind the applied figures (cat. 251, pls. 64, 65). These often appear to be gouged out in a rough manner, sometimes before and sometimes after the application of the figure. These holes also reveal that the earliest jasper ware generally is not solid in color but has a grayish blue, grainy ground washed over with the fine, darker blue slip on the front. Moreover, the edges of eighteenth-century medallions, plaques, and tablets are not rounded, as they are in the nineteenth-century examples, but are squared off and nearly flat and never have a concave back. Medallions, plaques, and tablets of solid jasper ware as well as jasper wash, however, were produced in the nineteenth century.

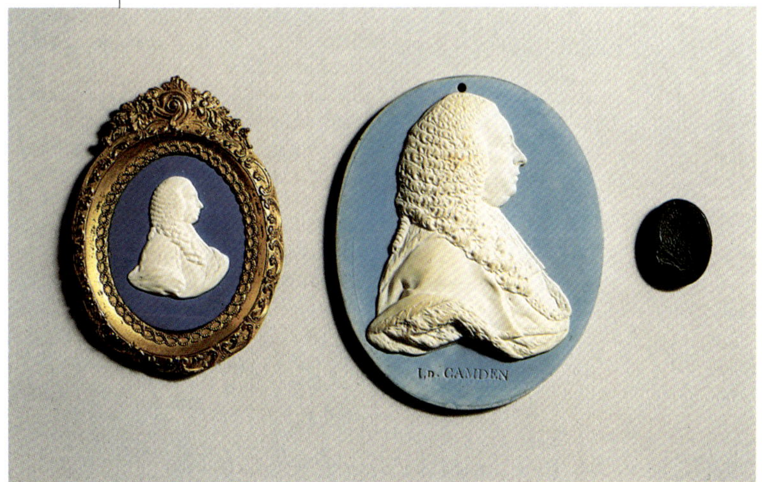

Color plate 63 Left, *Portrait Medallion,* Lord Camden *(*Charles Pratt Camden*), ca. 1778, jasper, solid blue ground with dark blue wash and white relief, ormolu frame, 1 11/16" x 1 7/16" (cat. 757);* center, *Portrait Medallion,* Lord Camden, *ca. 1778, jasper, solid blue ground with light blue wash and white relief, 3 1/4" x 2 11/16" (cat. 699);* right, *Intaglio,* Lord Camden, *ca. 1790, basalt, 7/8" x 5/8" (cat. 996).*

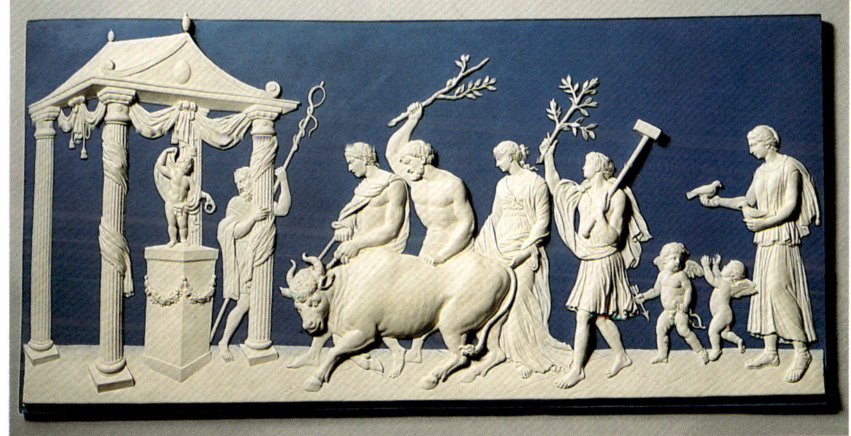

Color plate 64 *Tablet,* Sacrifice to Eros, *ca. 1780, jasper, solid blue ground with dark blue wash on front and white relief, 22 1/8" x 10 5/8" (cat. 251).*

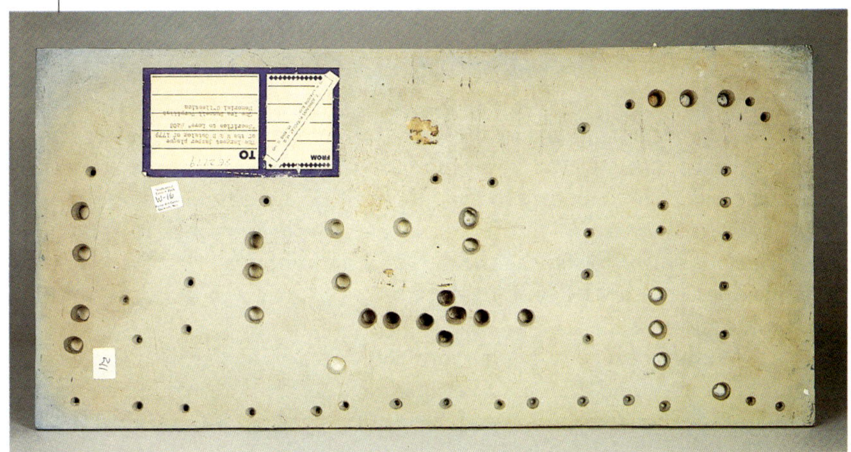

Color plate 65 *Back of Tablet above,* Sacrifice to Eros, *ca. 1780.*

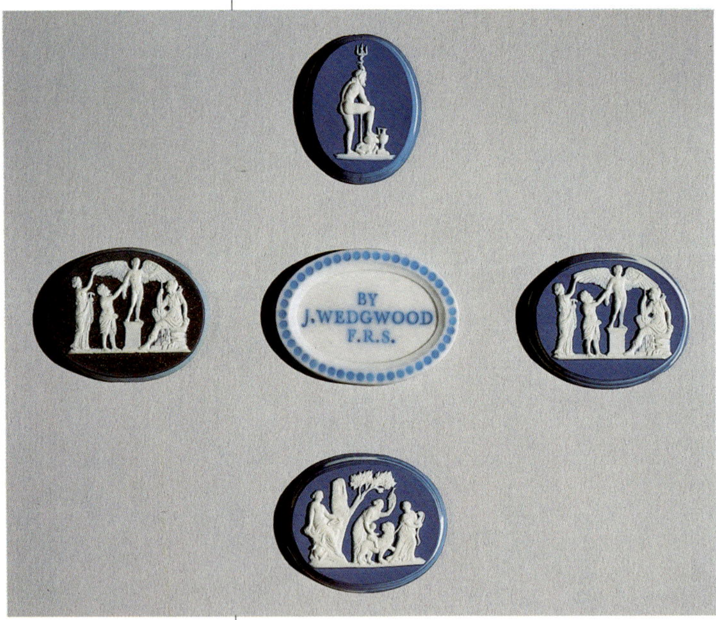

Color plate 66 *Medallions,* clockwise from top, Neptune, *ca. 1780, jasper, marbled blue-and-white ground with dark blue wash on front and white relief, 1 1/2" x 1 1/4" (cat 857);* Daedalus Fixing the Wings of Icarus, *ca. 1780, jasper, marbled blue-and-white ground with dark blue wash on front and white relief, 1 1/2" x 1 1/4" (cat. 703);* The Education of Bacchus, *ca. 1780, jasper, marbled blue-and-white ground with dark wash on front and white relief, 1 3/8" x 1 3/4" (cat. 858);* Daedalus Fixing the Wings of Icarus, *ca. 1780, jasper, solid blue ground with dark-blue-and-brown wash and white relief, 1 11/16" x 1 5/16" (cat. 702);* center, Wedgwood Insignia Medallion, *ca. 1784, jasper, solid white ground with blue stamped letters and dots, 1 7/8" x 1 3/8" (cat. 726).*

The four outer classical medallions seen above show the beveled edge which was often lapidary-polished on many of Wedgwood and Bentley's early medallions. The example to the far left has a dark bluish brown wash over the blue-gray ground. The other three show a solid blue ground with dark blue wash on the front and a variegated edge. This edge is produced either by combining two different colors of jasper clays, or by highlighting the beveled edge with a jasper slip. The center medallion is thought to be one that was included with Wedgwood's pyrometer kit celebrating his induction as a fellow of the Royal Society in 1783.

Intaglios and Medallions

The first items of production in jasper ware were intaglios and medallions in imitation of the popular Greco-Roman gemstones (pl. 66). Many of the subjects are well known to us today, including classical scenes, heads of Roman and Greek heroes, kings, popes, and emperors. Yet just as many represent people of the eighteenth century: poets, painters, and philosophers both famous and less well known.

Collectors of Wedgwood's classical medallions often kept them in small cabinet drawers or in boxes with legends underneath the tops. One such box from the nineteenth century exists in the Beeson collection (cat. 527). These circular jasper medallions, cast in solid blue with white relief, have concave bodies and "WEDGWOOD" impressed in uppercase letters on the back. The case itself is made of cardboard and covered in red leather. It is stamped "Josiah Wedgwood 1730-1795" in gold on the top.

As he stated in the 1779 *Ornamental Catalogue*, Wedgwood considered the small cameos and intaglios also "fit for Rings, Buttons, Lockets, and Bracelets" and the medallions "especially [fit] for inlaying in fine Cabinets, Writing-Tables, Bookcases, &c. . . . The Ladies may display their Taste a thousand Ways, in the Application of these Cameos." There were 440 cameos and 379 intaglios listed in this catalog, and these numbers grew rapidly to 1,764 cameos and 456 intaglios in the 1787 *Ornamental Catalogue*. Wedgwood explained in the latter that the "bas-reliefs, medallions, tablets &c . . . were made by some of the best artists in Europe. . . . These bas-reliefs, chiefly in the jasper of two colours, are applied as cabinet pictures, or for ornamenting cabinets, book cases, writing tables, in the composition of a great variety of chimneypieces, and other ornamental works. With what effect they are thus applied, may be seen in the houses of many of the first nobility and gentry in the kingdom."

Wedgwood soon began to bevel and lapidary-polish the edges of these small intaglios and medallions. On August 23, 1779, he wrote to Bentley: "The principal advantage in my opinion, polishing the edges, is' its shewing the fine texture of the composition, & giving it a stone like appearance. . . . If you approve of this idea I will endeavour to execute it in our next pieces."[24] More than two years earlier, on January 1, 1777, John Griffiths from Birmingham had begun a three-year contract as Wedgwood's lapidary.[25]

Classical Design

Like many of his professional contemporaries, Wedgwood found the sources for his classical designs in books, on gems, and on other vases. His sources were rich and varied, including the objects in the collections of his patrons, Sir William Hamilton and Sir Watkins Williams Wynn, as well as objects and books at the British Museum and books that he and Bentley owned jointly: according to a catalog Bentley prepared on August 10, 1770, the firm had thirty-one books, a princely number for a business at that time.[26]

Wedgwood often combined the motifs and designs from several of these various sources, so the exact origin of a design can sometimes be difficult to determine. The "improvements" Wedgwood made to the originals included draping nude figures, as he acknowledged to John Flaxman in 1790: "The nude is so general in the works of the ancients, that it is very difficult to avoid the introduction of naked figures. On the other hand, it is absolutely necessary to do so [clothe the figures] or to keep the piece for our own use."[27] As Wedgwood knew, these modifications made his ware more marketable to the English, and, as he wrote to Erasmus Darwin on June 28, 1789, he did not feel the need to apologize for these alterations:

> I only pretend to have attempted to copy the antique forms, but not with absolute servility. I have attempted to preserve the style and spirit or if you please the elegant simplicity of antique forms, and so doing to introduce all the variety I was able, and this Sir William Hamilton assures me I may venture to do and that is the true way of copying the antique.[28]

Classical Plaques and Medallions

Possibly the two earliest jasper-ware plaques in the Beeson collection are framed in mirrored sconces with two swinging arms designed to hold candles (cat. 630, pls. 67, 68). The medallions depict dancing nymphs copied from wall paintings.[29]

Color plates 67 & 68 *Pair of Sconces,* Herculaneum Figures, *1775-80, jasper, solid blue ground with blue wash on front and white relief, Florentine mirrored frame, plaques: 10 1/8" x 7" each (cat. 630).*

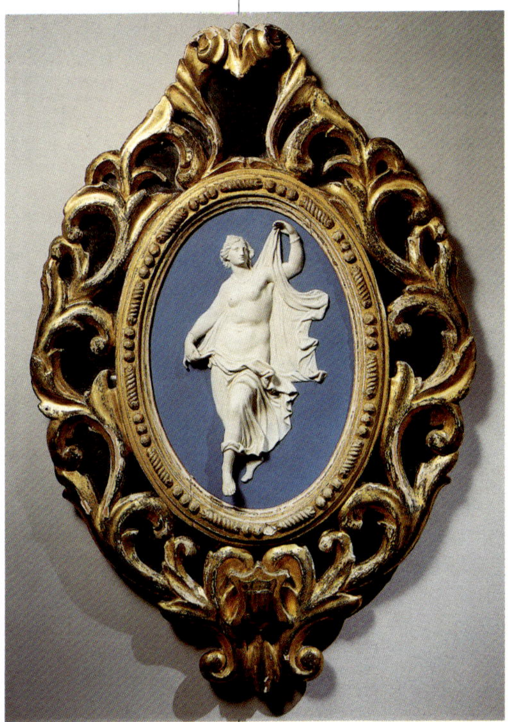

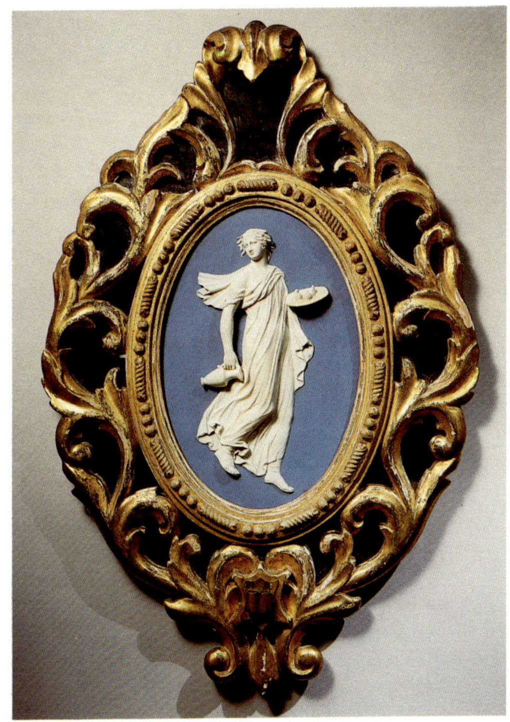

In 1772 Wedgwood made the molds for these nymphs from a set of plaster casts that were owned by the marquis of Lansdowne. In his *Ornamental Catalogue* of 1773, Wedgwood described the set as being from Herculaneum and as available in pale terra-cotta and basalt. Wedgwood first mentioned producing these figures in jasper ware in a letter to Bentley of January 1, 1775, and the first order of jasper ware was mentioned on March 28, 1778:

> Mr. Blythe orders amongst other things, Class 2 N°s. 51 to 56 which are Herculaneum Nymphs framed; & these to be made in blue and white Jasper!—They will come high though perhaps not higher than your enam^d grounds if we can make them at all. I understand the frames & grounds to be requir'd of blue & the figures white—you will correct me by return if I am wrong. I wo^d. much rather make them without frames, but will attempt them either way, though I think they would look infinitely better in carv'd & gilt frames than in any we can make, especially if they are the same color of the ground of the picture—Even black turn'd ones are much better, & lighter than ours, & either gilt or black will come cheaper.[30]

One figure carries a pitcher and tray of pears and is thought to be Hebe. On the second medallion is another woman; she is half nude, with a billowing garment over her shoulder. The medallions have a dark blue wash on the front over the light blue solid ground. One also sees on the back nineteen large to medium-size firing holes behind the area of the figure on the front. They are impressed "WEDGWOOD & BENTLEY" in uppercase letters and date to between 1775 and 1780.

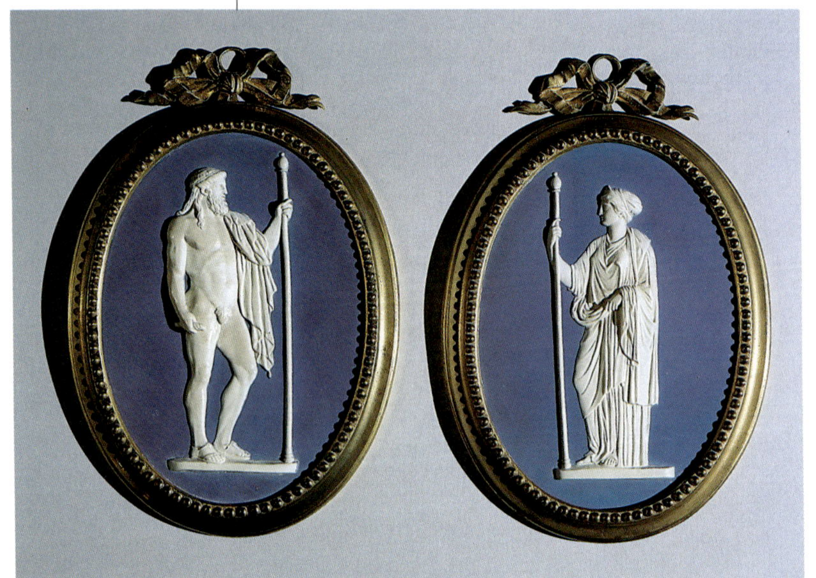

Color plate 69
Left, *Plaque,* Jupiter, *1775-80, jasper, solid blue ground with blue wash on front and white relief, 7 7/16" x 5 1/2" (cat. 244)*; right, *Plaque,* Juno, *1775-80, jasper, solid blue ground with blue wash on front and white relief, 7 3/8" x 5 1/2" (cat. 245).*

Two other very fine, large plaques are of the mythological figures of Jupiter and Juno (cats. 244, 245, pl. 69). They were modeled by John Flaxman, Sr., as evidenced by a bill of April 1775.[31] The relief is thought to have been cast from the base of a candelabrum originally found in the villa of Hadrian and now part of the Vatican collection.[32] They are listed in the French-language Wedgwood *Ornamental Catalogue* of 1788 (class 2, nos. 98, 99.) These plaques have the typical dark blue wash over a light blue solid ground, as found on the early Wedgwood and Bentley ware, as well as the numerous large and small firing holes.

A round plaque of the Gorgon Medusa is one of six different designs known to have been made by Wedgwood and Bentley (cat. 840, pl. 70). Recent scholarship has questioned the subject and suggested it may be Perseus.[33] Regardless, in the Wedgwood *Ornamental Catalogue* of 1787 (class 2, no. 94), in the bas-relief section, is listed a "large head of Medusa; from an exquisite marble in the possession of Sir W. Hamilton." Numerous heads with snakes and wings appear in Montfaucon and are entitled "Medusa" (fig. 19).[34] The plaque has very high relief and sixteen firing holes on the back. On the lapidary-polished front edge are three different shades of blue, which were produced by painting washes of different colors of jasper slip on the edge. This Medusa was modeled by John Flaxman in 1776.[35]

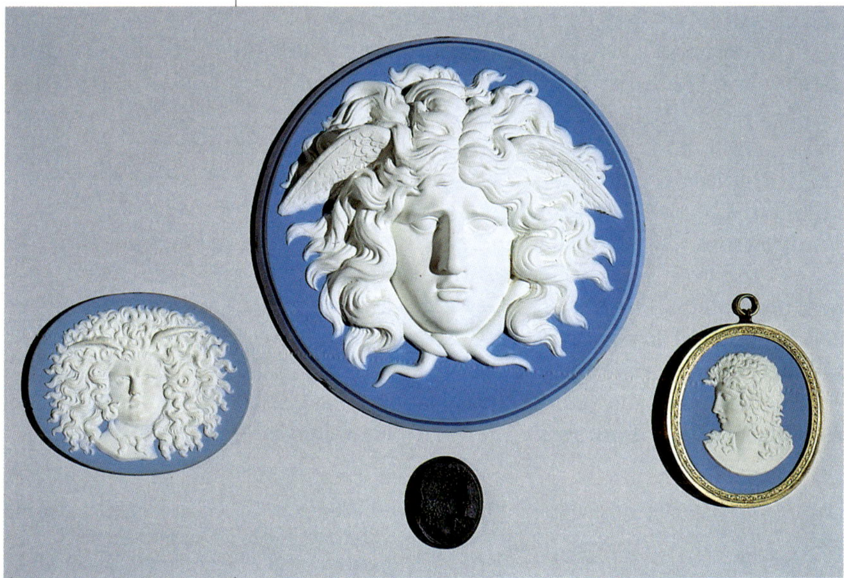

Another impressive, albeit smaller, medallion of Medusa is also in the collection and is marked "Wedgwood & Bentley" (cat. 839, pl. 70). This relief, which is in an oval format, is attributed to John Flaxman. Note that neither the previous example nor this one has hair of snakes, which, according to mythology, Medusa acquired as a punishment meted out by Athena after Medusa had defiled the temple of Athena. The source for this medallion is Montfaucon's *L'Antiquité expliquée.*[36] The piece has a medium-dark wash on the front over a light blue ground. A third version, also in blue-and-white jasper, is called the Strozzi Medusa (cat. 841, pl. 70); it is also in the collection and is marked "Wedgwood & Bentley" in upper- and lowercase letters. The original (ancient) Strozzi Medusa medallion was in the collection of the duke de Strozzi in Rome.[37] It shows Medusa in profile, as originally modeled by James Tassie (1735-99). Tassie, a Scotsman, was in competition with Wedgwood for the medallion and intaglio market, and he developed a glass paste with which he could reproduce the ancient gems. A portrait of Tassie by David Allen, which is now in the Scottish National Portrait Gallery in Edinburgh, depicts Tassie holding his glass-paste example of the Strozzi Medusa. The medallion is also pictured on the title page of Tassie's first catalog (1775). Wedgwood's relations with Tassie were amicable, and Tassie supplied Wedgwood with several molds for classical and portrait medallions, with the result that the two men produced at times the same subject. (For an additional representation of Medusa and her connection to Perseus and Andromeda, see the discussion of a Lessore charger on pp. 165-66.)

Color plate 70 Left, *Medallion,* Medusa, *1775-80, jasper, solid blue ground with blue wash on front and white relief, 2 7/8" x 2 3/8" (cat. 839);* center top, *Plaque,* Medusa, *1775-80, jasper, laminated in three layers: solid light blue, dark blue, and light blue with white relief, 5 1/8" (cat. 840);* center bottom, *Intaglio,* Strozzi Medusa in Profile, *ca. 1790, basalt, 1 1/8" x 15/16" (cat. 1031);* right, Strozzi Medusa in Profile, *1775-80, jasper, solid blue ground with darker blue wash on front and white relief, 2 1/8" x 1 13/16" (cat.841).*

In the Beeson collection, an oval plaque of Bacchus and the panther has special significance, for it is marked on the back "From the Collection of W. Erasmus Darwin, Esq." (cat. 257). (William Erasmus Darwin was the first son of naturalist Charles Darwin and great-grandson of Josiah Wedgwood.) In solid blue jasper with white relief, the plaque has as its design source a portion of a frieze from the tomb of Lysicrates in Athens.[38] The frieze shows Bacchus resting, for he has already transformed the Tyrrhenian pirates into dolphins. This medallion dates to around 1800, because it is solid jasper with no firing holes but has an unusual, very small, uppercase "WEDGWOOD" mark.

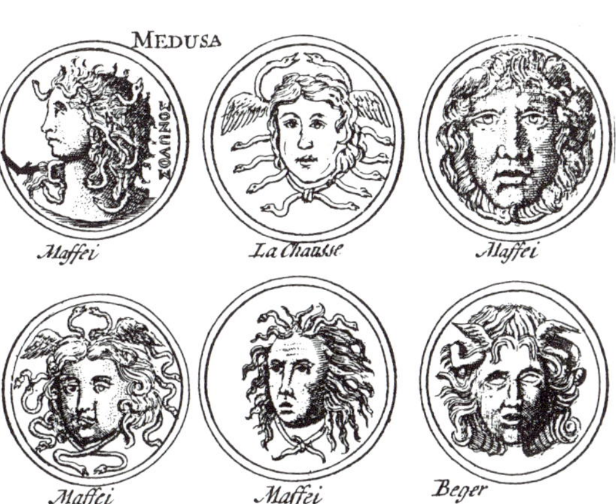

Fig. 19 *Montfaucon,* L'Antiquité expliquée, *vol. 1, pt. 1, p. 89, pl. 43, figs. 2-7.* Medusa.

Two plaques of the Bacchanalian boys, originally

from a set of six rectangular ones by François Duquesnoy (1594-1643), are extremely fine examples of Wedgwood's waxy, high-relief figures (cats. 247, 248). One is titled *The Drunken Silenus* and the other *Bacchanalian Boys at Play*. Mary Landré supplied casts of the six plaques to Wedgwood, as noted on an invoice of 1769.[39] These two are marked "WEDGWOOD & BENTLEY" in uppercase letters and are first listed (class 2, nos. 13, 14) in the *Ornamental Catalogue* of 1779. A later but similar example of the drunken Silenus has an additional tree added to the background, which enlarges the composition (cat. 249). This plaque is marked "WEDGWOOD" and has six firing holes, yet the ground color is the same throughout; it therefore possibly represents work produced soon after Bentley's death, as it is very well executed.

Wedgwood produced many different plaques that portrayed Hercules. Three in the Beeson collection are marked "WEDGWOOD & BENTLEY" (cats. 254, 255, 256, pl. 71). The subjects are the young Hercules, attributed to Flaxman, about 1777; the Farnese Hercules, by Flaxman, from 1776; and Hercules binding Cerberus, by

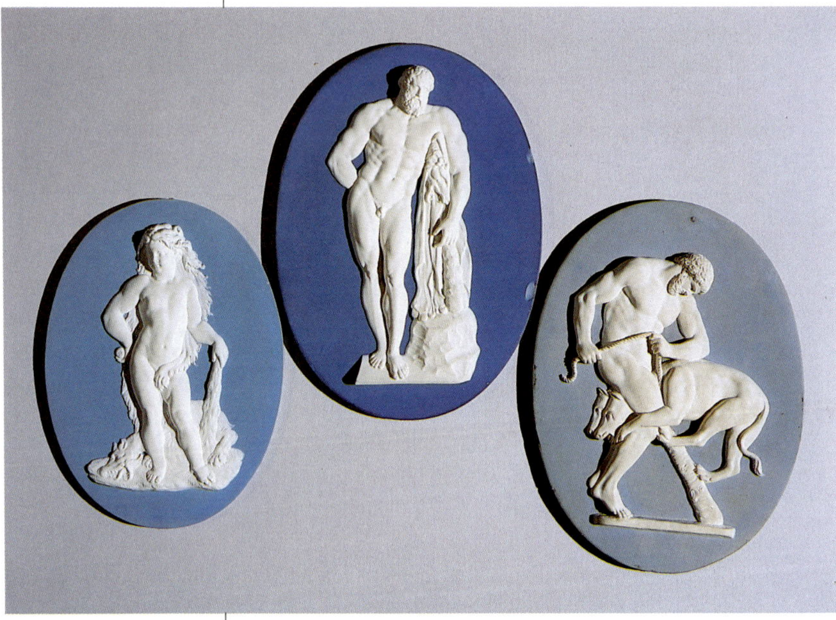

Color plate 71 Left, *Plaque,* Young Hercules, *1775-80, jasper, solid blue ground with blue wash on front and white relief, 6 1/4" x 5" (cat. 254);* center, *Plaque,* The Farnese Hercules, *1775-80, jasper, solid blue ground with dark blue wash on front and white relief, 7 1/2" x 5 1/2" (cat. 255);* right, *Plaque,* Hercules Binding Cerberus, *1775-80, jasper, solid blue ground with white relief, 7 3/8" x 5 9/16" (cat. 256).*

Fig. 21 *Montfaucon,* L'Antiquité expliquée, *vol. 1, pt. 2, p. 137, pl. 66, fig.* 3. Hercules.

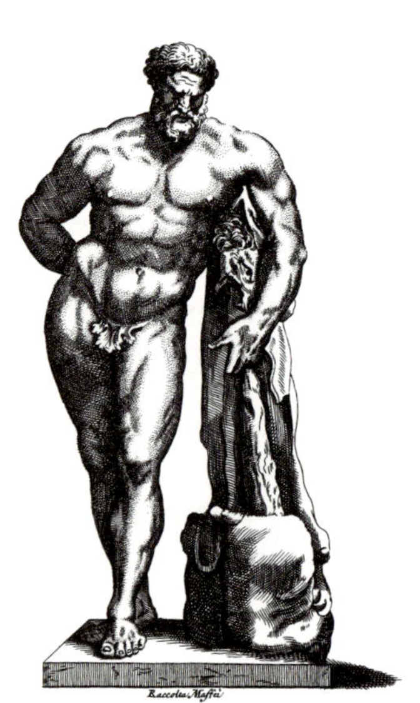

Fig. 20 *Montfaucon,* L'Antiquité expliquée, *vol. 1, pt. 2, p. 124, pl. 62, fig. 11.* Hercules.

Flaxman, from 1775. The second and third are derived from Montfaucon (figs. 20, 21). The Farnese Hercules is described as follows: "Hercules more commonly represented with a Beard. That of Farnese, the finest of all, is a Masterpiece of Art: It is the Performance of Glycon the Athenian, who has immortalized his Name, by putting it at the bottom of this admirable Statue. Hercules is here represented leaning on his Club, which is covered with the Lion's Skin."[40] The source of the design is a statue of Hercules by Lysippus, the illustrious sculptor from ancient Greece; the statue is now located at the Louvre. The plaque depicting Hercules binding Cerberus is also described in Montfaucon:

> Hercules is here in the Action of binding the Dog Cerberus. He has put between his Legs Cerberus's three Heads, whereof but two appear. The Infernal Dog struggles, but in vain. Hercules is naked here; he had laid down his Lion's Skin and his Club, which are on one side. The Sculptor Dioscorides is perhaps the same that is mentioned by Pliny and Suetonius, who place him in the Age of Augustus.[41]

All three plaques have multiple firing holes and are listed in the 1778 *Ornamental Catalogue*. Two have a dark wash over a light blue ground on the front, and one is a solid blue jasper.

The Triumph of Bacchus is another Wedgwood and Bentley plaque in the collection (cat. 250). In blue-and-white jasper, it is listed as number 53 in the 1779 *Ornamental Catalogue* and appears in both an oval format, as in the Beeson collection, and a rectangular form, as in the Wedgwood Museum in Barlaston, which also has two additional figures standing before the horses. The design was modeled by William Hackwood in 1776 and was made to be paired with *The Birth of Bacchus*. On January 6, 1776, Wedgwood wrote to Bentley of these tablets:

> Hackwood has nearly finish'd the two Tablets of the Birth & Triumph of Bacchus, but I am afraid we shall not be able to make either of them in one continued Tablet. . . . We could make them to fill a Frize [*sic*] very cleverly in seperate pieces, the grounds of the ovals blue, & the figures white, & all the pieces together making up one subject would be better to fill a frize with, than detached statues & figures, which have no connection one with another.[42]

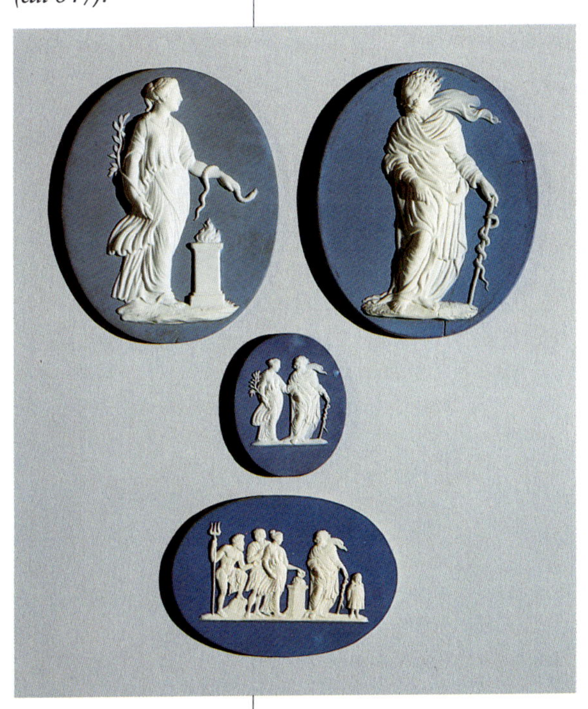

Color plate 72
Top left, *Medallion,* Hygeia, *1775-80, jasper, solid blue ground with white relief, 3 5/16" x 2 5/8" (cat. 813);* top right, *Medallion,* Aesculapius, *ca. 1780, jasper, solid blue ground with white relief, 3 1/4" x 2 9/16" (cat. 814);* center, *Medallion,* Aesculapius and Hygeia, *ca. 1780, jasper, marbled blue-and-white ground with dark blue wash on front and white relief, 1 3/4" x 1 3/8" (cat. 816);* bottom, *Medallion, A* Sacrifice to Aesculapius, *ca. 1780, jasper, solid white ground with dark wash on front and white relief, 1 7/8" x 2 3/4" (cat 817).*

The goddess Minerva is represented in the collection on a large, oval plaque/medallion that has a gray-blue ground and a blue wash (cat. 844). She is shown standing in her traditional helmet and dress, and holding in her right hand a small globe with a dove resting on top and in her left hand a spear. The back of the medallion is marked "WEDGWOOD & BENTLEY" with eight firing holes as well as a depression behind the relief, which is very high and has the waxy surface of early jasper ware. This example may be the one credited to John Flaxman, Jr., as modeler in 1775. A Minerva of similar size is listed among the bas-reliefs and medallions in the 1779 *Ornamental Catalogue* (class 2).

Four other Wedgwood and Bentley plaques and medallions represent the figures of Aesculapius and his daughter, Hygeia (cats. 813, 814, 816, 817, pl. 72). On October 27, 1777, Wedgwood wrote of the medallions, "We have 4 new subjects of a proper size for that purpose

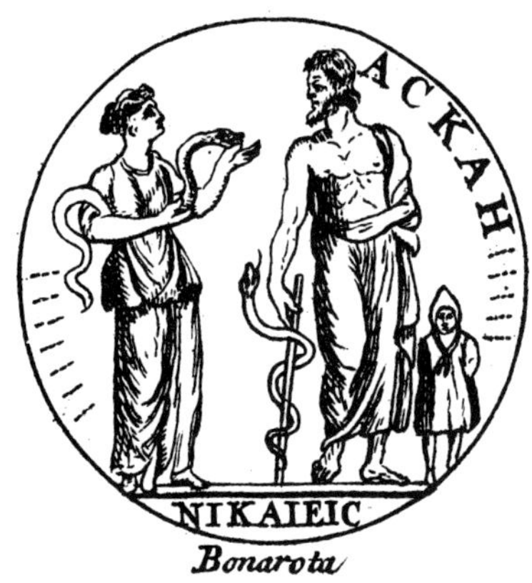

Fig. 22 *Montfaucon,* L'Antiquité expliquée, *vol. 1, pt. 2, p. 181, pl. 86, fig. 12.* Aesculapius and Hygeia.

& all decent & clever. They are Scevola—Curtius—A sacrifice with Esculapius, Hygeia & other figures, & another scrifice [*sic*] its companion."[43] A design source exists in Montfaucon (fig. 22).[44] The figure of Aesculapius can also be found on a Renaissance gem modeled by Valerio Vicentino.[45] Both figures are listed in class 1 of Wedgwood's 1779 *Ornamental Catalogue.* A different and larger, solid-jasper tablet of the two figures, taken from a marble bas-relief in the Capitoline Museum in Rome, is thought to date to about 1800 (cat. 266). It has the interesting feature of gray lines that were added to the two white bas-relief columns in the background to simulate marble.

One of Wedgwood's most successful mythological subjects was the marriage of Cupid and Psyche, along with its companion subject, the sacrifice to Hymen. There is a variety of sizes and dates in medallions of both of these subjects in the Beeson collection (cats. 910, 911, 912, 914, 915, pls. 73, 74). The two most important, however, are marked "Wedgwood & Bentley" in upper- and lowercase letters, with a solid blue ground and medium blue wash on the front; on the back of each are six firing holes (cats. 910, 911). The figures are very finely modeled and in high relief. On the basis of this quality, John Flaxman, Sr., is credited with their modeling.

The marriage of Cupid and Psyche, first represented by Wedgwood in 1771, is depicted and described by Montfaucon:

> The Marriage of Cupid and Psyche is differently represented in the following image. We may observe there the Ceremonies of the Wedding. Cupid's head is cover'd with a Veil, and he is holding a Pidgeon or Turtle-Dove. By his side is Psyche cover'd all over with a large Veil, so that nothing is to be seen but her Butterfly Wings. They walk on, side by side, chain'd together. Another, cupid, who holds them by the end of the Chain, carries a Torch to celebrate the Marriage. Another, who walks behind Cupid and Psyche, holds over both their Heads a sort of a Basket full of Fruits. Another at the opposite End seems to be preparing the Wedding Feast (fig. 23).[46]

Montfaucon was copying the Marlborough gem taken from a sardonyx cameo wrought by Tryphon in the first century A.D.; the gem was originally in the collection of the earl of Arundel and, from 1780 to 1875, in that of the third duke of Marlborough (thus its name). The gem is now in the collection of the Museum of Fine Arts in Boston.[47]

In addition to Montfaucon, several other design sources were evidently available and adapted by Wedgwood when he formulated other versions of the two scenes. A second source was an engraving by Theodorus Netscher in the book *Pierres antiques gravées,* which was in Wedgwood's library.[48] And Wedgwood may have copied Tassie's version of the subject, yet another alteration of the Marlborough gem.

The modelers Hackwood, Lochée, Webber, and John Flaxman, Jr., are known to have remodeled Wedgwood's first Cupid and Psyche medallion between 1774 and 1788.[49] The companion piece was originally called *Cupids with Goat* in a small version and *A Sacrifice to Hymen* in a larger. The design source for the companion piece is an engraving by Francesco Bartolozzi after Giovanni Cipriani.[50]

Other outstanding jasper plaque/medallions of Cupid in the Beeson collection

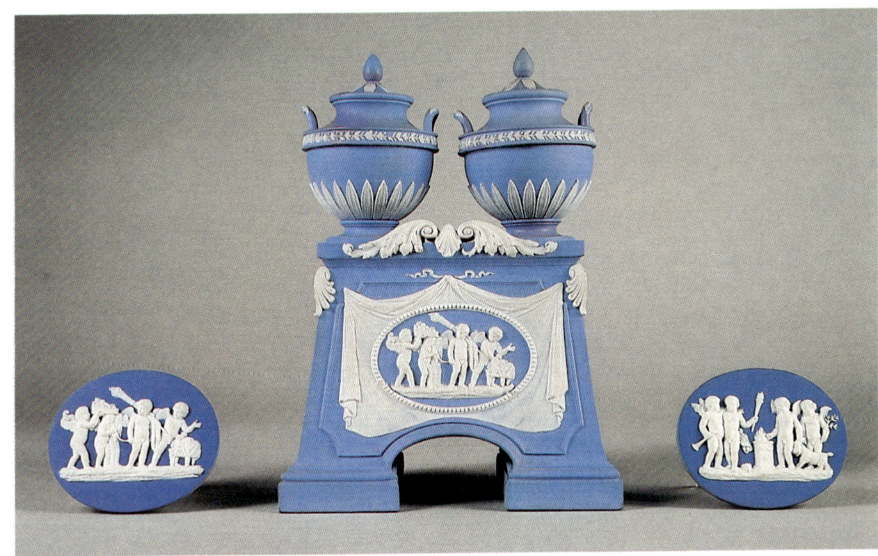

Color plate 73
Left, *Medallion,* Marriage of Cupid and Psyche, *1775-80, jasper, solid blue ground with dark blue wash on front and white relief, 3 3/8" x 2 11/16" (cat. 910);* center, *Inkstand,* Marriage of Cupid and Psyche *and* Trophies of Love and Harmony, *ca. 1795, jasper, solid blue ground with white relief, 8 3/4" x 6 1/2" (cat. 627);* right, *Medallion,* Sacrifice to Hymen, *1775-80, jasper, solid blue ground with dark blue wash on front and white relief, 3 1/2" x 2 7/8" (cat. 911).*

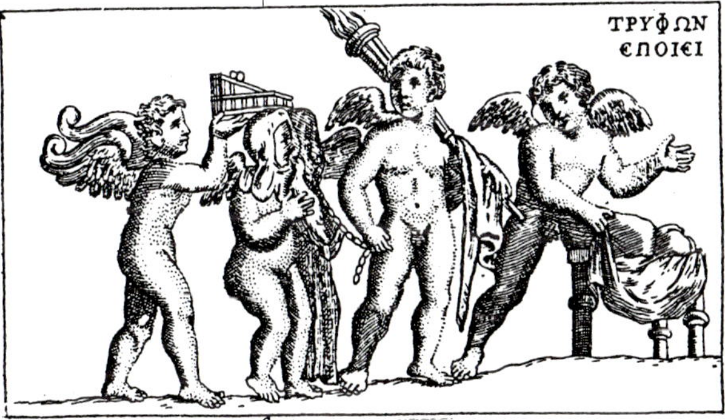

Fig. 23 *Montfaucon,* L'Antiquité expliquée, *vol. 1, pt. 1, p. 117, pl. 61, fig.* 3. Marriage of Cupid and Psyche.

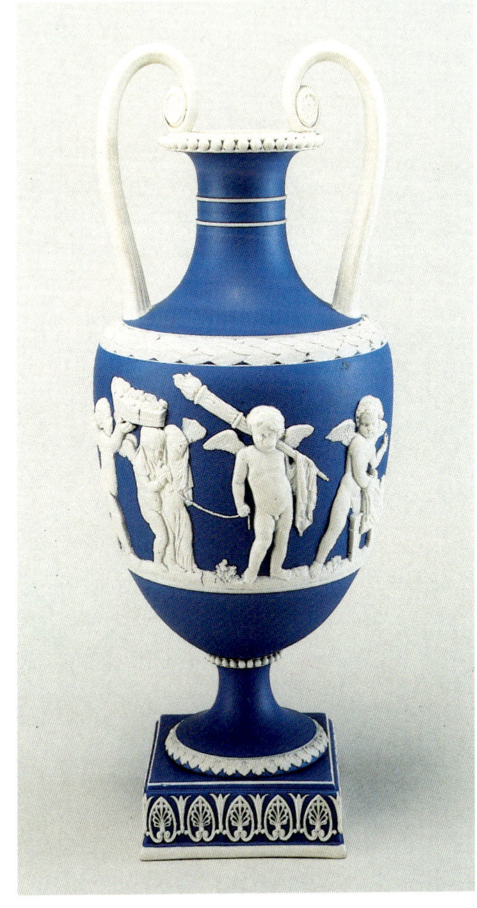

Color plate 74 *Vase,* Marriage of Cupid and Psyche, *ca. 1800, jasper, solid white ground with dark blue wash and white relief, 14 1/2" x 3 3/4" (cat. 616).*

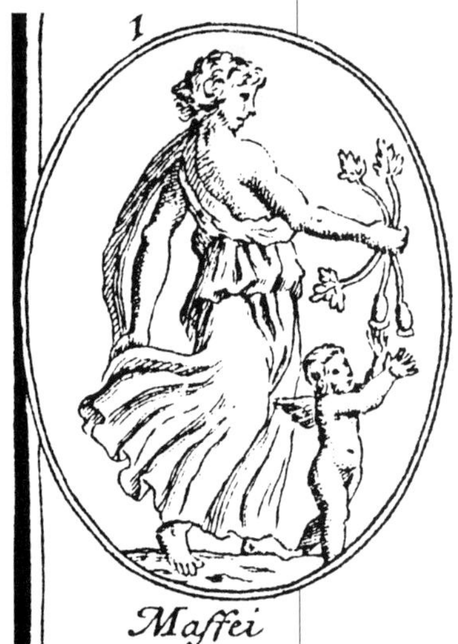

Fig. 24 *Montfaucon,* L'Antiquité expliquée, *vol. 1, pt. 1, p. 104, pl. 54, fig. 1.* Venus and Cupid with Poppies.

include Cupid seated on a stump, Cupid as a butterfly, and Venus and Cupid (cats. 907, 908, 939, pls. 75, 76). All have the "Wedgwood and Bentley" mark and a blue jasper wash over the solid gray-blue ground with multiple firing holes in the back. The same Venus and Cupid are also seen on a porphyry vase and a basalt vase in the collection (cats. 85, 108, pl. 76). The design source for the Venus and Cupid from the Maffei collection, is found in Montfaucon (fig. 24).[51] The same two figures of a woman and a child are also known as *Night Shedding Poppies* and *Ceres and Triptolemus*.

Two very finely detailed plaques were made by Wedgwood in commemoration of Solomon Gessner (1730-88), a Swiss poet, painter, and writer (cats. 810, 812, pl. 77). A monument in his honor was designed by Michel-Vincent Brandoin (1735-1807) and erected in Zurich,[52] and on January 23, 1790, Wedgwood wrote to Brandoin: "Mr Marindens partner at Birmingham had sent me . . . a copy of your beautiful design for a monument to Gessner. . . . I have likewise begun upon the monument also & shall when it is finished do myself the honour of begging your acceptance of one of the first copies of each piece."[53] Wedgwood's monument depicts the muses of painting and poetry mourning over an altar that displays a tiny portrait of Gessner; the accompanying medallion, with its angelic figure of Fame, has its possible design source in Montfaucon (fig. 25).[54] Similar medallions were issued to honor Elizabeth, a niece of Emperor Joseph II, and the recovery of the health of George III in 1789.

Several other blue-and-white and black-and-white jasper medallions in the Beeson collection are early examples, all being marked "Wedgwood & Bentley" in upper- and lowercase letters. The subjects are Alexander, Apollo, the Three Graces, a warrior, and Achilles (cats. 829, 830, 930, 956, 961, pl. 78). They all date to between 1775 and 1780 and are listed under various headings in the 1779 *Ornamental Catalogue*. Their contemporary frames are stamped, gilt-metal ormolu and are attributed to the workshop of Matthew Boulton and James Watt. In May 23, 1767, upon first meeting Boulton, Wedgwood wrote to Bentley: "He is I believe the first—or most complete manufacturer in England, in metal. He is very ingenious, Philosophical, & Agreeable."[55] Boulton and Wedgwood exchanged their ideas and information on technical skills, factory organization, personnel management and welfare, worldwide marketing, advertisement, and expansion of product lines. Even the Etruria factory was inspired by Boulton's Soho Factory in Birmingham. Because one made ceramics and the other metalware, Wedgwood and Boulton were not in direct competition with one another and therefore often joined forces in this manner.

Besides his representation on one of the medallions framed by Boulton,

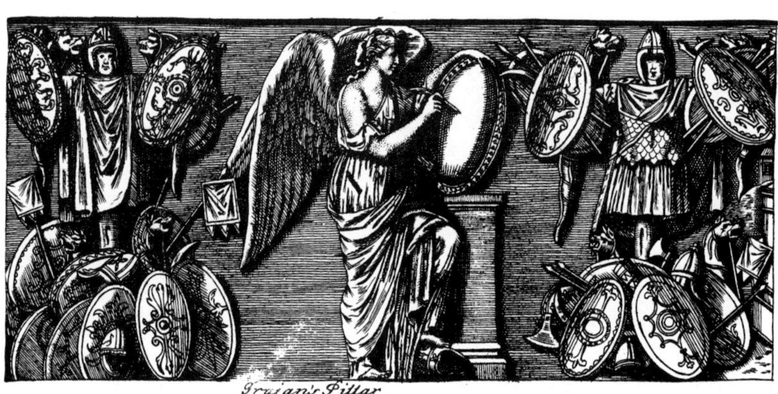

Fig. 25 *Montfaucon,* L'Antiquité expliquée, *vol. 4, pt. 1, p. 93, pl. 31, fig. 1.* Fame Writing upon a Shield.

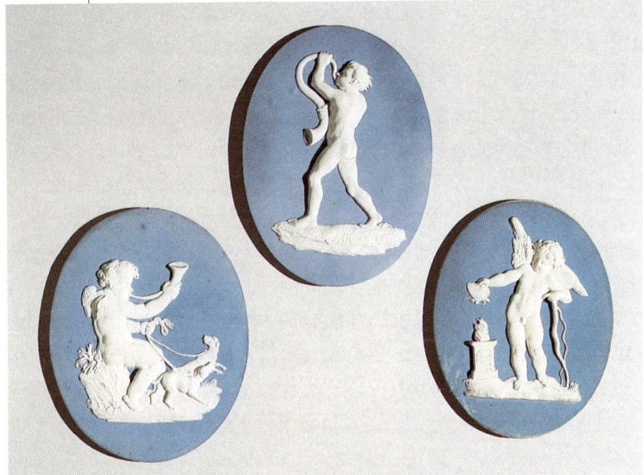

Color plate 75 Left, *Plaque,* Cupid Seated on a Stump, *1775-80, jasper, solid blue ground with dark blue wash on front and white relief, 5 7/16" x 4 3/8" (cat. 907);* center, *Plaque,* Bacchanalian Figure, *1775-80, jasper, solid blue ground with dark blue wash on front and white relief, 5 7/8" x 4 3/8" (cat. 909);* right, *Plaque,* Cupid as a Butterfly, *ca. 1780, jasper, solid blue ground with medium blue wash on front and white relief, 5 1/8" x 4" (cat. 908).*

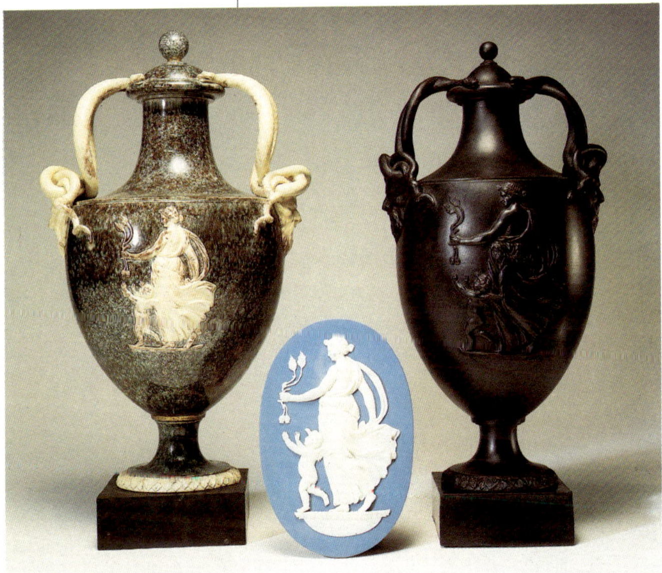

Color plate 76 Left, *Vase,* Venus and Cupid, *ca. 1775, white terra-cotta stoneware with imitation porphyry color underglaze, basalt base, and gilding, 15" x 4 1/4" (cat. 85);* center, *Plaque,* Venus and Cupid, *jasper, solid blue ground with dark blue wash on front and white relief, 6 3/8" x 4 1/4" (cat. 939);* right, *Vase,* Venus and Cupid, *ca. 1775, basalt, 12 15/16" x 3 11/16" (cat. 108).*

Color plate 77 Left, *Plaque,* Fame Writing upon a Shield, *ca. 1790, jasper, solid white ground with dark blue wash on front and back with white relief, 4 3/4" x 3 1/2" (cat. 810);* right, *Plaque,* Monument to Solomon Gessner, *ca. 1790, Michel-Vincent Brandoin (1735-1807), designer, jasper, solid white ground with dark blue wash on front and back and black and white relief, 4 5/8" x 3 3/8" (cat. 812).*

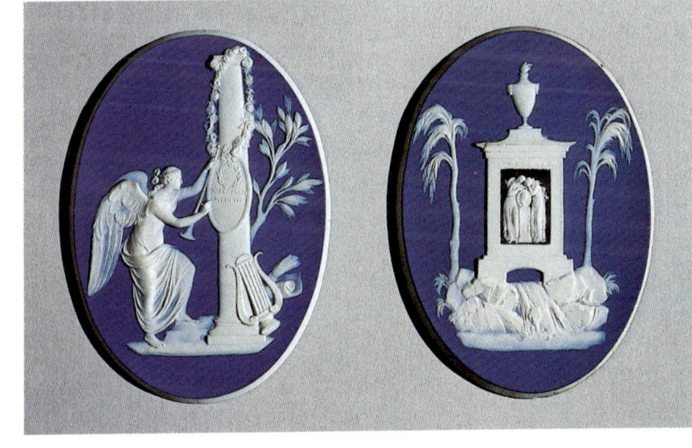

Color plate 78 Clockwise from top: *Medallion,* Apollo Musagettes, *1775-80, jasper, solid white ground with dark blue wash on front and white relief, ormolu frame, 2 1/16" x 1 11/16" (cat. 856); Medallion,* The Three Graces, *1775-80, jasper, variegated blue-and-white ground with dark blue wash on front and white relief, lapidary-polishing, ormolu frame, 2 1/16" x 1 11/16" (cat. 930); Medallion,* Achilles in His Tent, *ca. 1780, jasper, solid white ground with black wash on front and white relief, ormolu frame, 1 1/4" x 1" (cat. 830); Medallion,* A Seated Warrior, *ca. 1780, jasper, solid white ground with black wash on front and white relief, ormolu frame, 1 1/4" x 1" (Cat. 829); Portrait Medallion,* Alexander the Great, *1775-80, jasper, solid blue ground with white relief, ormolu frame, 2 1/16" x 1 13/16" (cat. 961).*

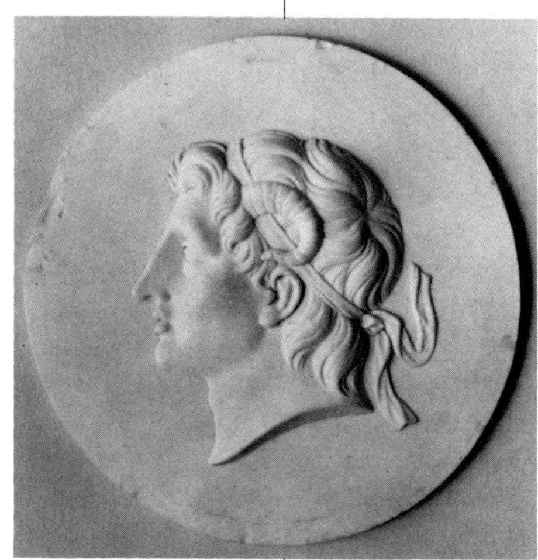

Fig. 26 *Portrait Medallion,* Alexander the Great, *1775-80, white ware, 3 11/16" (cat. 933).*

Alexander is represented two other times in the collection (cats. 932, 933, fig. 26). One is a small, self-framed version on which Alexander has, not a helmet, but a ram's horn upon his head. It is made of glass paste and was produced by James Tassie in 1779. Wedgwood and Bentley's copy of this example was first listed in the 1779 *Ornamental Catalogue*.[56] The second example, a larger version of the Tassie, is made of unglazed white ware, has ten firing holes, and is marked "Wedgwood & Bentley" in upper- and lowercase letters.

One of the largest classical medallions in the collection is of the Roman emperor Vespasian (cat. 843). In class 6 of the 1779 *Ornamental Catalogue*, Vespasian is listed as number 10. Under this heading is written, "The Caesars are from the best Antiques and highly finished." This medallion has a light blue ground with a dark blue wash and white relief. It has on the back the many firing holes that are typical of the Wedgwood and Bentley pieces and thus dates to about 1778.

Portrait Medallions

In the eighteenth century, the practice of having one's countenance immortalized in some media of portraiture gained a new popularity with the rise of such artists as Joshua Reynolds (1723-92), George Romney (1734-1802), Thomas Lawrence (1769-1830), and Henry Raeburn (1756-1823). For those interested in history, knowing exactly what someone now dead looked like when alive became important, for one's character, be it heroic or evil, was thought to be reflected in one's likeness. Prints, oils on canvas, as well as medallions and medals of the heroes of the century's many wars became desirable. For most people, however, canvases were unaffordable, and small portrait medallions in ivory, wax, plaster, or precious metals proved too fragile and quite expensive. With the introduction of cream ware, basalt, and jasper ware, Wedgwood commanded three media in which he could produce small, affordable portrait medallions with speed and in quantities sufficient to meet the growing demand. In 1776, Wedgwood wrote, on the subject of "Historical Cabinets": "The Heads you have mention'd are very few. We shall be able soon to add the Ks. of England, the same size as the Greeks. The whole will fill but about half a dozn. Drawers, especially if you mean to have the suit of Mythological Gems in a seperate Cabinet—Wod. not the English Poets make a pretty drawer in the Cabinet."[57] Portrait medallions remained in vogue into the early nineteenth century; by midcentury, the development of photography resulted in their eventual obsolescence.

The production of each medallion involved several steps. The first was to make a relief model from which an intaglio mold was taken. A master cast in plaster was then made from the intaglio mold, which was afterward sharpened and refinished. A working intaglio mold was then taken from the master cast. When compared to their jasper counterparts, these smear-glaze medallions are slightly larger because they are in the second fired state, whereas the jasper medallions have shrunk again during their third firing. Wedgwood described the method in a letter of May 23, 1777:

> In order to render our moulds everlasting, & allways sharp they should be made of clay burnt. For this purpose when we have a mould given to us, as in the case of the Muse, we are under the necessity of taking a press in clay out of the mould, & burning it. This is one diminishing of the size.—From this burnt impression we take a clay mould & burn that, which is a second lessening of the bassrelief, & from this mould we make the figures &c for sale which in our fine Jasper lessens the size very considerably.[58]

In the 1779 *Ornamental Catalogue* Wedgwood and Bentley offered for the first time a listing of 177 portraits of "Illustrious Moderns" (class 10), which included the following: "English Poets; Painters; Philosophers and Physicians; Divines, Artists, Antiquaries, Poets &c.; and Princes and Statesmen." They were made of either basalt or blue-and-white jasper and ranged in size from 2 by 1 3/4 inches to 17 by 4 inches. Most of the subjects were modeled in profile, but three-quarter or even full-face examples exist as well.[59] Of the 130 or so portrait medallions in the Beeson collection, about 40 have the "Wedgwood and Bentley" mark. Given this large number, only a few, the rarest and most relevant, can be discussed here.

The Beeson collection contains six of the twenty-four English poets in basalt (marked "Wedgwood & Bentley" in upper- and lowercase letters), with Chaucer, Gower, Lansdowne, Rochester, Shakespeare, and Waller represented (cats. 799, 800, 801, 802, 803, 805). Wedgwood and Bentley's basalt examples of the painters include Le Sueur and Maratti and, from the philosophers, Keder (cats. 794, 795, 804). All are listed in the 1779 *Ornamental Catalogue* and most in the catalog of 1773.

In the letter of February 1776 cited above, Wedgwood went on to suggest: "Suppose we were to sweep our Cabinet of the Black, & fill then with White, Blue, & other color'd Seals. . . . I think you may sell the color'd Seals at Tassies prices, but the Black ones should be lower'd, or rather Vanish when these appear."[60] In blue-and-white jasper, with the "Wedgwood & Bentley" mark, are the painters Annibale Carracci, Leonardo da Vinci, and Titian (cats. 791, 792, 793). In the philosopher section, also in blue-and-white jasper marked "WEDGWOOD & BENTLEY," is a medallion of Carolus Linnaeus (cat. 715). Listed in the section entitled "Divines" in the *Ornamental Catalogue* are two early jasper medallions, one of Hugo Grotius, with lapidary-polished edges, and the other of Jan Van Olden Barneveld (cats. 771, 774). In solid blue with a dark blue wash, the jasper medallion of Miguel de Cervantes Saavedra, listed as available only in intaglio form in the 1779 *Ornamental Catalogue*, also exists in the Beeson collection (cat. 775). Of this intaglio Wedgwood wrote on August 24, 1778, "Cervantes is come to hand & shall have all due respect paid to him."[61]

Wedgwood was pleased with the success that his portrait medallions enjoyed, and he soon invited his customers to have likenesses of their own families and friends made in wax from which he could reproduce medallions in stoneware. In the *Ornamental Catalogue* of 1773 he wrote:

> If the Nobility and Gentry of Great Britain should please to encourage this Design, they will not only procure to themselves everlasting Portraits, but have Pleasure of giving Life and Vigour to the Arts of Modelling and Engraving. The Art of making durable Copies, at a small Expence, will thus promote the Art of making Originals, and future Ages may view the Productions of the Age of George III with the same Veneration that we now gaze upon those of Alexander and Augustus.

Indeed, Wedgwood's portrait medallions have become important links to seventeenth- and eighteenth-century personalities. We owe these connections to past figures to Wedgwood's astute observations on human vanity. As he wrote to Bentley on July 2, 1776: "For inlaying in Snuff boxes our Kings & Queens will be very good things for England. We can make other Kings & Queens, & eminent Heads for other Countries & such subjects will be the most likely to go in quantities, for People will give more for their own Heads, or the Heads in fashion, than for any other subjects, & buy abundantly more of them."[62]

Wedgwood's main competitor in the field of portrait medallions was James Tassie, who produced glass-paste medallions in enormous quantities; his catalog of 1775, for example, lists over three thousand subjects. As mentioned earlier,

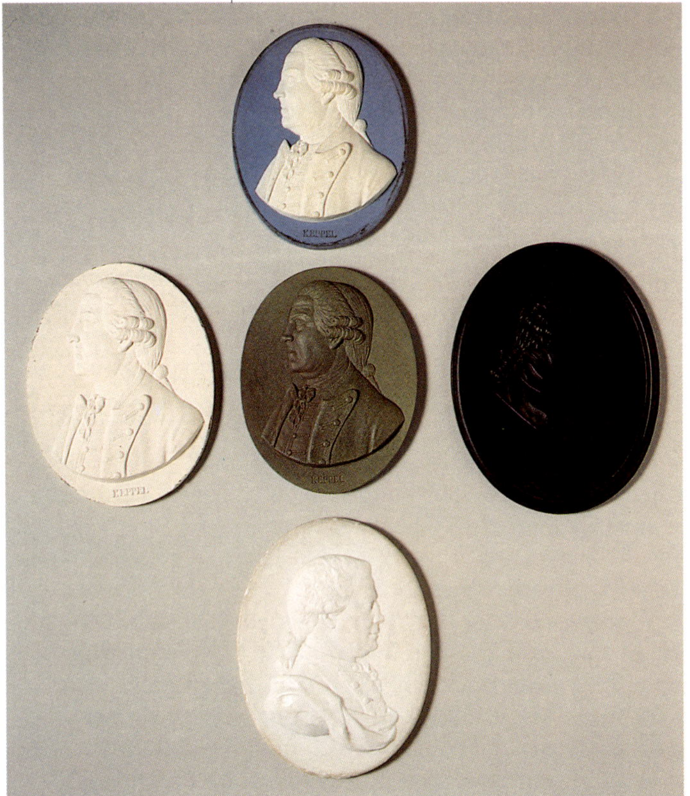

Color plate 79
Portrait Medallions, top, Admiral Keppel, *ca. 1780, jasper, solid blue ground with dark blue wash on front and white relief, 3 7/8" x 3 1/8" (cat. 736);* left, Admiral Keppel, *ca. 1780, white terra-cotta stoneware, 4" x 3 1/8" (cat. 733);* center, Admiral Keppel, *ca. 1780, jasper, solid blue ground with green wash on front, 3 7/8" x 3" (cat. 734);* right, Admiral Keppel, *ca. 1780, basalt, self-framed, 4 5/8" x 3 5/8" (cat. 732);* bottom, Admiral Keppel, *ca. 1780, James Tassie (1735-99), maker, Scotland, enamel paste, 4 3/8" x 3 3/8" (cat. 731).*

Wedgwood's relations with Tassie were cordial, and Tassie occasionaly provided Wedgwood with previously used molds from which Wedgwood would then produce his own portrait medallions. There are several examples of this duplication in the Beeson collection (cats. 731, 932).

Once he was provided with a design source, Wedgwood could produce these portrait medallions quickly and efficiently. This ease of production enabled him to take advantage of the notoriety of infamous and newly famous personages and sell their medallions when public interest in them was highest, as seen by the following letters on the medallion of Admiral Augustus Keppel (1725-86).

In the Beeson collection are five medallions of Keppel which aid our understanding of Wedgwood's marketing skills and the production of his portrait medallions (cats. 731, 732, 733, 734, 736, pl. 79). The first three depict Keppel as a young man. All have the "Wedgwood and Bentley" mark and date to about 1779, but they are in three different types of ware: white ware, blue-and-white jasper ware, and a light blue jasper-ware body with a bronzy green wash on the front. These were probably modeled by William Hackwood.[63] Wedgwood wrote to Bentley on February 25, 1779: "But why do you not send me his [Keppel's] head when it is advertised every day in shade—etching & wax, by Mrs. Harrington. Pray send me one of each by the first coach; we should have had it a month since, and advertis'd it for pictures, bracelets, ring seals, &c."[64] Just a few days later, on March 1, 1779, Wedgwood wrote: "He [Mr. Byerley] is stripped of all his Garricks & Shakespears fram'd in black, & says he could sell <u>thousands</u> of Keppels at any price. Oh Keppel Keppel—Why will not you send me a Keppel. I am perswaded if we had had our wits about us as we ought to have had 2 or 3 months since we might have sold £1000 worth of this gentlemans heads in various ways."[65] Twelve days later, the oven book indicates, this portrait was in production. The two remaining examples of Keppel are slightly larger in size, with Keppel in profile and facing the opposite direction; he also looks older. One is a self-framed basalt piece marked "Wedgwood and Bentley," and the other is a glass-paste example by James Tassie.

Wedgwood's design sources for posthumous subjects included ivory carvings, waxes, coins, bronze medallions, sculptures, paintings, and engravings. For living persons, such modelers as Joachim Smith, John Charles Lochée, Matthew Gosset and Isaac Gosset, Edward Burch, Charles Peart, Eley George Mountstephen, and William Hackwood made wax models. William Hackwood is today probably the most well known of the modelers of Wedgwood's tablets and portrait medallions, and he even signed some on their truncations. Wedgwood expressed his displeasure about this practice to Bentley in a letter dated December 22, 1777:

> You will see by looking under the shoulder of each that these heads are modelled by <u>Wm. Hackwood</u>, but I shall prevent his exposing himself again now that I have found out. I am not certain that he will not be offended if he is refus'd the

liberty of puting his name to the models which he makes quite new, & I shall be glad to have your opinion upon the subject. Mine is against any name being upon our articles besides W & B.[66]

Despite Wedgwood's reservations on this point, Hackwood was employed by Wedgwood for sixty-three years, and he produced many of the important portraits, including one of Wedgwood himself. Current opinion is that Wedgwood allowed Hackwood to sign his original work, but not other artists' portraits that he remodeled.[67] Wedgwood may have allowed Hackwood this compromise because he recognized the artist's consummate skill; as he wrote, on November 4, 1778, of Hackwood's work on a group of tablets: "Some of the tablets lately sent are finish'd very high by Hackwood at a considerable expence. I may perhaps name them to you in a P S, but if I should not you will easily perceive the difference in the hair, faces, fingers &c, & more palpably by all the parts capable of it being undercut which gives them the appearance, & nearly the reality of models."[68]

Wedgwood was eager to tap the portrait market represented by royalty and the circles that gathered around them. On September 7, 1771, he wrote to Bentley concerning an audience Bentley had recently had with King George and Queen Charlotte.

Their Majestys are very good indeed! I hope we shall not lose their favour, & may promise ourselves the greatest advantages from such Royal Patronage. . . . It was a good hint you gave them respecting their Portraits. I hope it will work . . . & am fully perswaded a good deal may be done in that way with many of their Majestys subjects, but we sho[d.] if possible do in this as we have done in other things—begin at the Head first, & then proceed to the inferior members.[69]

This audience eventually led to Wedgwood's making a series of coins of the rulers of England, from King Alfred in 1066 through King George III. The Beeson collection is fortunate to have a complete set of these portrait medallions in basalt, with the heads of the rulers on one side and their tombs on the reverse (cat. 756, pl. 80). Most are marked "I. Dassier," for Jean Dassier (1676-1763), a Swiss medalist and engraver who is also credited as the designer for the series of popes by Wedgwood and some of Wedgwood's portraits of figures from Roman history.[70] Others are unmarked, and one is marked "Kirk F." None, however, is impressed with a mark, but they were probably made during the Wedgwood and Bentley period. The portraits were supplied by Thomas Astle (1735-1803) from his collection of manuscripts now in the British Library. Many are thought to have been modeled by John Flaxman.[71]

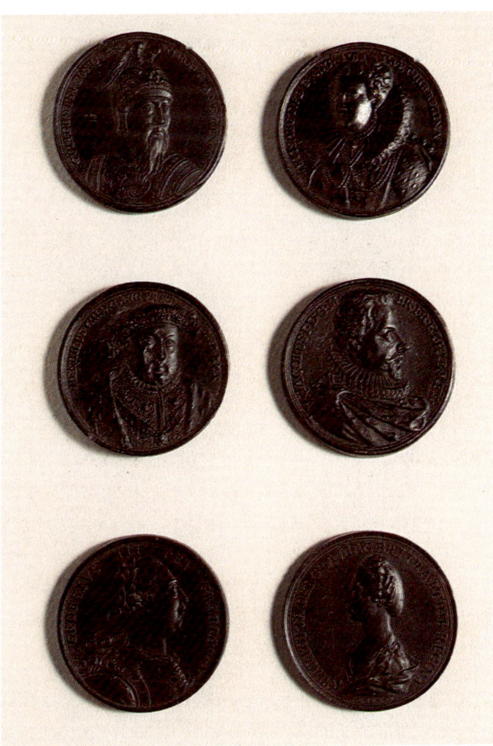

Color plate 80
Double Medallion Set of the Thirty-six Rulers of England from William the Conqueror through George III; ca. 1780; Jean Dassier (1676-1763), medalist and engraver, Switzerland; Kirk, engraver; basalt, 1 13/16" (cat. 756).

Wedgwood and Bentley produced several different models for portrait medallions of George III and Queen Charlotte. Two different portraits of each exist in the collection as well as one double portrait (cats. 743–49,

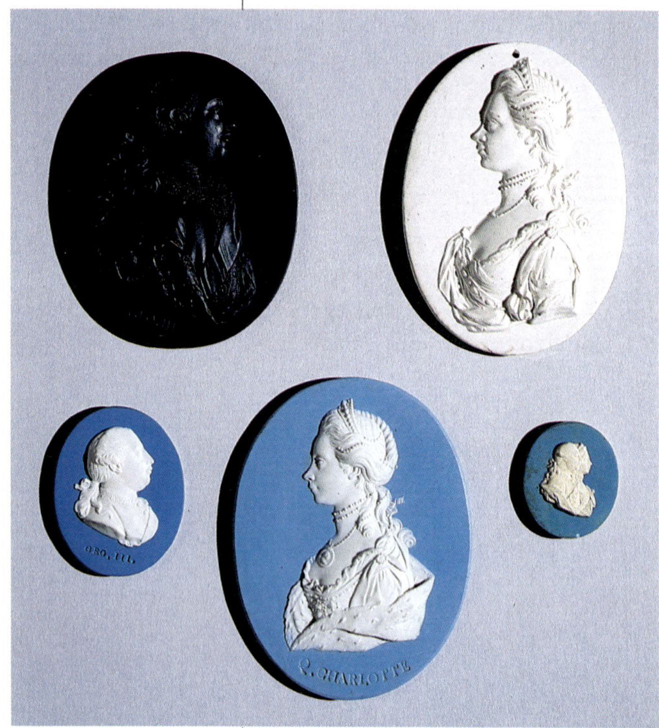

Color plate 81 *Portrait Medallions,* top left, George III, *ca. 1775, William Hackwood, modeler, after portrait by Isaac Gosset (1713-99), basalt, 3 1/4" x 2 5/8" (cat. 743);* top right, Queen Charlotte, *ca. 1775, cream ware, 3 7/16" x 2 1/2" (cat. 748);* bottom left, George III, *ca. 1800, jasper, solid blue ground with white relief, 3 15/16" x 3 1/16" (cat. 744);* bottom center, Queen Charlotte, *ca. 1780, jasper, solid blue ground with white relief, 3 1/2" x 2 11/16" (cat. 749);* bottom right, George III and Charlotte, *ca. 1780, jasper, solid white ground with blue wash on front and white relief, 1 1/4" x 1 1/16" (cat. 746).*

pl. 81). Of Charlotte there is a cream-ware example marked "WEDGWOOD" in uppercase letters. A second Charlotte has a solid blue ground and white jasper relief with one large and one small firing hole on the back, also marked "WEDGWOOD." Both were modeled by Hackwood, but the cream-ware example represents the first format, thus dating it to before 1776. Wedgwood wrote to Bentley on June 6, 1776: "We have now finished another edition of their Majesties. You will find a very considerable alteration in the Queen and I hope for the better. Indeed it is quite a new model both in the Portrait & Dress, & has that delicacy in the features which the other wanted."[72] The two medallions of George III in basalt and later in jasper also represent Hackwood's modeling before 1775. Both are marked "Wedgwood & Bentley" in upper- and lowercase letters and also bear the initials "W. H.," for William Hackwood, at the truncation on the basalt example. All were originally adapted from wax portraits by Isaac Gosset. The double portrait of King George and Queen Charlotte is blue-and-white jasper and is marked "Wedgwood & Bentley." It is also thought to have been modeled by Hackwood.

Wedgwood produced many separate medallions of the earlier monarchs of England. One of the finer examples in the collection is of Queen Elizabeth I, who reigned from 1558 to 1603 (cat. 741, pl. 82). The medallion has a light blue jasper ground with a dark blue wash on the front. The relief shows the queen in full-face view with elaborate detail for her costume, jewelry, hair, and face. The medallion is marked "Q. ELIZABETH" on the front and "WEDGWOOD & BENTLEY" on the back. It appeared first in the oven book of April 17, 1779, and subsequently in the 1779 *Ornamental Catalogue*. The design was probably adapted from the Armada medal.[73]

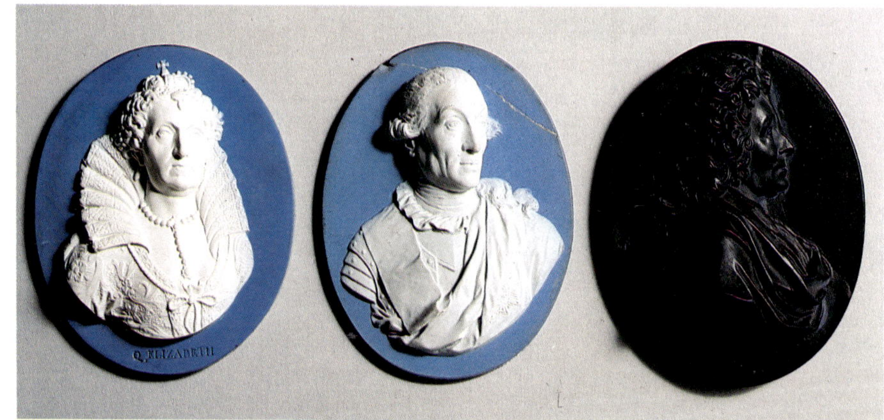

Color plate 82 *Portrait Medallions,* left, Queen Elizabeth I, *ca. 1780, jasper, solid blue ground with dark blue wash on front with white relief, 4" x 3 1/4" (cat. 741);* center, Sir Eyre Coote, *ca. 1788, Eley George Mountstephen (w. 1781-91), modeler, jasper, solid blue ground with white relief, 4 1/16" x 3 1/8" (cat. 763);* right, Sir Christopher Wren, *ca. 1785, David Le Marchand (1674-1726), modeler, basalt, 4 3/16" x 3 3/16" (cat. 711).*

Among the most unusual of the portrait medallions is another full-face view of Sir Eyre Coote (1726-83) in solid blue-and-white jasper (cat. 763, pl. 82). Coote became England's commander-in-chief in India in 1777. This medallion was modeled by Eley George Mountstephen in 1788 from a bust sculpted by Joseph Nollekens in 1779. It has one large firing hole and one thumbhole on the back and is impressed, in uppercase letters, "WEDGWOOD."

A basalt medallion of a commoner, Edward Bourne, who was a bricklayer at Etruria in the 1770s, is unlike most of the other portrait medallions that Wedgwood made in that Bourne was not at all famous (cat. 706). It seems that Bourne maintained the kilns and brick buildings for the factory, and Wedgwood honored him with this medallion, which was modeled by William Hackwood in 1779 (as it says in script on the truncation) and is incised, in script on the back, "Mr. Byrne Bricklayer 1779 Etruria." Wedgwood wrote to Bentley concerning the medallion on November 21, 1778: "Old Bournes is the man himself with every wrinkle, crink & cranny in the whole visage."[74] This medallion appears with the usual trowel on the front and is impressed "Wedgwood" in uppercase letters.

Foreign Subjects

As previously mentioned, Wedgwood was acutely aware of the market for portrait medallions of important British subjects both contemporary and historical. But he also recognized the same potential market for foreign subjects and commemoratives of foreign revolutions and events. His attempts toward exploiting this market are the subject of the following paragraphs, which describe the medallions that Wedgwood made of certain illustrious Americans, Frenchmen, Germans, and Italians.

Wedgwood was an ardent supporter of the American Revolution. He even predicted the war in a letter dated May 20, 1767: "Mr. Greenville & his party seem determin'd to Conquer England in America I believe. If the Americans do not comply with their demands respecting the quartering of Soldiers, the alternative, I am told, is to be, The suspension of the Legislative power in America. I tell them the Americans will then make Laws for themselves, & if we continue our Policy—for us too in a very short time. . . . If we must all be driven to America, you & I shall do very well amongst the Cherokees."[75]

The American trade was important to Wedgwood, for he sold a great deal of his ware abroad. As he wrote to Sir William Meredith on March 2, 1765:

> The bulk of our particular Manufacture you know is exported to foreign markets, for our home consumption is very trifleing in comparison to what are sent abroad, & the principal of these markets are the Continent & islands of N. America. To the Continent we send an amazing qu^{ty}. of white stone ware & some of the finer kinds, but for the Islands we cannot make anything too rich & costly, this trade to our Colonies we are apprehensive of loseing in a few years as they have set on foot some Potwork there already, and have at this time an agent amongst us hireing a number of our hands for establishing new Pottworks in South Carolina, having got one of our insolvent Master Potters there to conduct them.[76]

Among his known American correspondents was Benjamin Franklin (1706-90). And in his typically entrepreneurial fashion, Wedgwood developed several different portrait medallions of Franklin, three of which are in the Beeson collection (cats. 723, 722, pl. 83). First is a blue-and-white jasper example portraying Franklin, from the neck upward, as a Roman soldier in profile. Marked "Franklin" on the front, this Wedgwood and Bentley medallion dates to about 1775 and was modeled by William Hackwood. The second medallion, which is less than one inch in height, is an oval jasper piece and is set in a carved and inlaid snuffbox (cat. 522, pl. 128, p. 135); here

Franklin is portrayed as an old man. This medallion is marked "Wedgwood & Bentley" in upper- and lowercase letters, and the medallion itself is white with a medium blue wash on the ground back and front. The third is a twentieth-century medallion of Franklin dressed as an old man in eighteenth-century garb (cat. 722). Franklin was listed in the Wedgwood *Ornamental Catalogue* of 1779 under "Philosophers and Physicians" as "Dr. Benjamin Franklin, A.B.C."

A companion to the Franklin medallion was a similar medallion of George Washington (cat. 788, pl. 83), which also depicted this eighteenth-century man as a Roman soldier. The Beeson collection has this blue-and-white jasper medallion and a second of Washington in the same profile in basalt (cat. 789). The design was taken from a medal of Voltaire that was struck in Paris in 1777. On July 19, 1777, Wedgwood received the medal at Etruria to copy, and he wrote to Bentley, saying: "My objection to striking the medals from the Bronze you sent me rather increase. It would be doing no service to the cause of Liberty in general, at least so it appears to me, & might hurt us very much individually. Nay the personage is himself at this time more absolute than any Despot in Europe, how then can he be celebrated, in such circumstances as the Patron of Liberty? "[77] Wedgwood must have changed his mind, because in November 1777 an issue of medallions was described as the "Grand Duke of Muscovy," a pseudonym for Washington. In 1778 Washington's name was impressed on the front of these medallions.[78] Both Beeson medallions are finely detailed, are marked "Wedgwood & Bentley," and date to about 1778.

Indeed, if one considers the medallions in isolation from his other works, Wedgwood's thoughts seem to be never far from events in America. In relationship to the Franklin medallion, Wedgwood produced in 1787 a medallion of a bonded slave, a work inspired at least in part by a poem by Thomas Day (1748-89). The poem, written in 1773 and entitled *The Dying Negro*, contains the phrase "Am I not a Man and a Brother? " which Wedgwood impressed around the circumference of the medallion. Wedgwood adapted the design from a seal that belonged to the Society for the Abolition of the Slave Trade in England, of which he was an active member, and he sent four hundred of these medallions to Benjamin Franklin in Philadelphia in 1787. Franklin wrote in thanks on May 15, 1788, saying:

> Sir, I received the letter you did me the honour of writing on the 29th February past, with your valuable present of Cameos, which I am distributing among my friends; in whose countenances I have seen such marks of being affected by contemplating the figure of the Suppliant (which is admirably executed) that I am persuaded it may have an Effect equal to That of the best written Pamphlet in procuring Favour to these oppressed People. Please do accept my hearty thanks.[79]

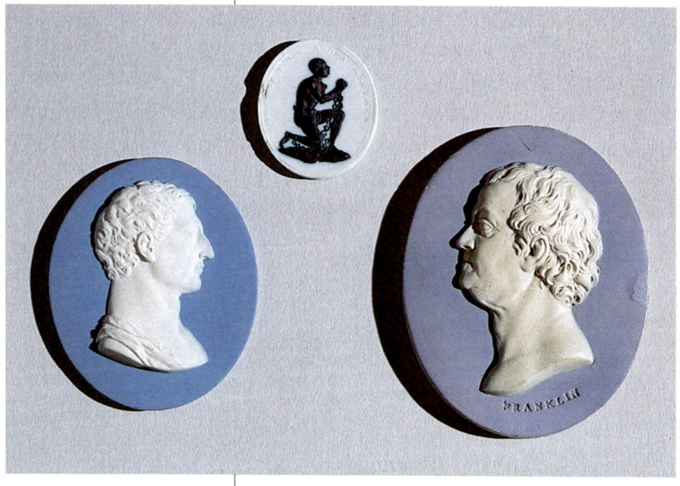

Color plate 83
Left, *Portrait Medallion,* George Washington, *ca. 1780, jasper, solid blue ground with blue wash on front and white relief, 2 1/8" x 1 3/4" (cat. 788);* center, *Medallion,* Slave, *ca. 1787, jasper, solid white ground with black relief, 1 3/16" x 1 1/16" (cat. 724);* right, *Portrait Medallion,* Benjamin Franklin, *ca. 1775, jasper, solid white ground with blue wash on front and white relief, 2 3/4" x 2 3/16" (cat. 723).*

The slave medallions were worn by both gentlemen and ladies and were very fashionable in the late eighteenth century. This black-and-white jasper medallion was designed by Henry Webber and modeled by William Hackwood. Two are in the Beeson collection, one from the eighteenth century and one from the twentieth (cats. 724, 725, pl. 83).

Another rare portrait medallion is of the American George Roupell (1726-94), a relatively obscure postmaster general for the southern department of North America and

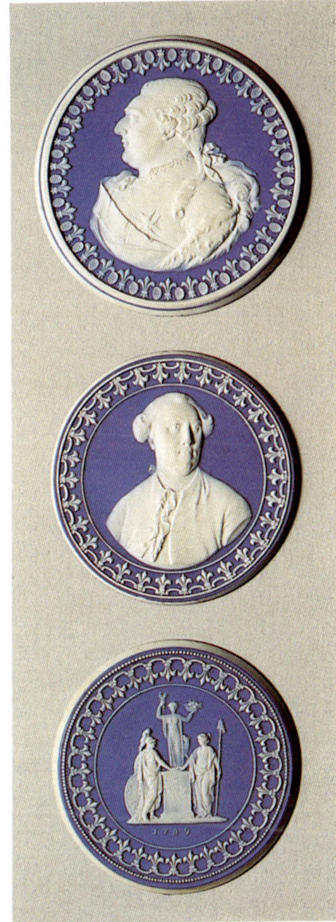

Color plate 84
Top, *Portrait Medallion,* Louis XVI of France, *ca. 1790, jasper, solid white ground with dark blue wash on front and back and white relief, 2 5/16" (cat. 780);* center, *Portrait Medallion,* Jacques Necker, *ca. 1790, jasper, solid white ground with blue wash on front and back and white relief, 2 3/8" (cat. 779);* bottom, *Medallion,* France and Liberty Joining Hands before a Statue of Plenty, *ca. 1789, jasper, solid white ground with dark blue wash on front and back and white relief, 2 5/16" (cat. 782).*

a customs officer at the port of Charleston (cat. 705). He owned a plantation called Ruplemonde in South Carolina. It is thought that his portrait was made because he helped with the search for china clay in the Carolinas and aided in its exportation to Wedgwood in England, although to date there is no evidence of this. A mold identifying the subject exists at the Wedgwood factory today.[80] A letter of November 8, 1778, from Wedgwood to Bentley states: "We sent a box by the coach last night containing 12 heads of Roupell which I understand were wanted."[81] The medallion thus dates to about 1778 and is marked "Wedgwood & Bentley."

Also in the Beeson collection is a portrait medallion of the American hero John Paul Jones (1747-92), along with a bronze medal, its design source (cat. 790). The medal was authorized by Congress in 1787 and was modeled by Augustin Dupré in Paris. (The die for the medal is now in the museum at the United States Naval Academy in Annapolis, Maryland.) The Wedgwood medallion is an exact copy of the medal, with the profile bust of Jones (taken from a bust by Houdon) on the obverse and, impressed around the edge, the tag "JOANNI PAULO JONES CLASSIS PRAEFECTO, COMITIA AMERICANA." The reverse shows the sea battle between Jones's ship, the *Bon Homme Richard,* and the British ship, the *Serapis,* during which, when asked to surrender, Jones spoke the famous words, "Sir, I have not yet begun to fight." He went on to win the battle. The inscription around the edge of the reverse reads: "HOSTIUM NAVIBUS CAPTIS AUT FUGATIS AD ORAM SCOTIAE XXIII SEPT. / MDCCLXXVIIII." It is now thought that this medallion was made in the twentieth century, because no record of it has been found in the oven books of 1787 and 1788. Two molds of different sizes, however, were located at the Wedgwood factory; they are dated July 9, 1906. On the rim of the jasper medallion is impressed "WEDGWOOD" and the letter "O"; this is the potter's mark of Bert Bentley, who was working for Wedgwood in the early twentieth century.[82]

Wedgwood produced his first commemorative medallions in 1787; the occasion was a commercial treaty between England and France. Due to their popularity, additional medallions were created, including those that commemorated the fall of the Bastille and the French Revolution. Three companion medallions and one smaller medallion in the Beeson collection relate to the French Revolution: a medallion depicting Louis XVI, king of France from 1774 until 1792; one of Jacques Necker, minister of finance to Louis XVI; an allegorical medallion commemorative of the revolution, with "France and Liberty Joining Hands before a Statue of Plenty;" and one showing a "Caduceus of Peace" (cats. 770, 780, 781, 782, pl. 84). Louis dismissed Necker in July 1789, an act triggering the attack on the Bastille on July 14 and consequently the French Revolution. Josiah II wrote to his father about the allegorical medallion on July 28, 1789: "Do you choose to have anything modelled of the same size which should relate to the late revolution in France & to the support given to public credit by the national assembly? What do you think of a figure of Public faith on an altar & France embracing Liberty in the front?"[83] All four medallions are wafer-thin, with a dark blue jasper wash, front and back, on a white ground. The edges are beveled and lapidary-polished, and the allegorical scene is dated 1789. The medallion of Louis XVI was adapted from a medal in about 1785.[84] There are also two other medallions of Louis XVI in the collection: a Wedgwood-and-Bentley, solid blue jasper example and a self-framed, basalt example that uses another design of Louis from a medal by Duvivier of 1782 (cats. 783, 784).[85]

For the German market, Wedgwood initiated in 1790 a series of at least eight medallions to commemorate the coronation of Leopold II as holy Roman emperor, all with a white ground and a dark blue jasper wash with white relief. The image used was a previously developed figure of Minerva, who represents Germany.[86] An example in the Beeson collection depicts Minerva with a shield at her feet on which is emblazoned the German eagle (rather than the head of Medusa), and she faces three figures standing to her left—Art, Labor, and Peace (cat. 824). The medallion is marked "Wedgwood" in uppercase letters and has lapidary-polished edges. The design of this medallion is associated with the Sydney Cove medallion, which was made from clay sent by Captain Arthur Phillip in Australia to Sir Joseph Banks, president of the Royal Society of London in 1789, who then gave some to Josiah Wedgwood (cat. 822).[87]

The last example in the Beeson collection that must be mentioned is yet another extremely rare medallion, that of Ferdinand IV (1751-1825), who had established the Kingdom of the Two Sicilies (Naples and Sicily) in 1816 (cat. 776). It has a solid blue ground with a dark blue jasper wash and white relief and is unmarked. As indicated by an extant invoice, John Flaxman modeled the piece in 1781.[88]

Tablets

Within the scope of this book, tablets are defined as flat, rectangular objects ornamented with bas-relief. Wedgwood seems to have hit upon the idea of making these objects in 1768; on November 6 of that year, he wrote: "I have lately had a Vision by night of some new Vases, Tablets, &c. with w^{ch}: Articles we shall certainly serve the whole World!"[89] His first tablets were made of basalt and molded in one piece, but in 1772 Wedgwood changed this method of production by sprigging the figures onto the black basalt slabs. Yet the stark black against the pale colors of even the Etruscan-decorated rooms proved too harsh. Wedgwood wrote to Bentley on September 7, 1771: "We will try some Tablets of other colours immediately, but I think there is more danger of the Pott appearance from brown China ones, or Ivory than from Black. But you shall see them & then decide in favour of those you like best."[90] Thus with the perfection of jasper ware, Wedgwood began to experiment with making sprigged tablets. The task was formidable, and Wedgwood struggled with the manufacture of the jasper tablets, particularly the large ones. He wrote to Bentley on May 29, 1776, "You will receive a few good things by the Diligence Amongst them a tablet; the only which has stood free of cracking in cooling out of four."[91] But by 1788 he seems to have conquered the cracking problem, because he sent to Bentley in London twelve large tablets, all of jasper ware, the first to be seen there. Wedgwood and Bentley had hoped that these larger tablets in particular would open up a new market with the architectural community, for the tablets were indeed appropriate for the Adam-style interiors then in vogue. He wrote to Bentley on August 9, 1778:

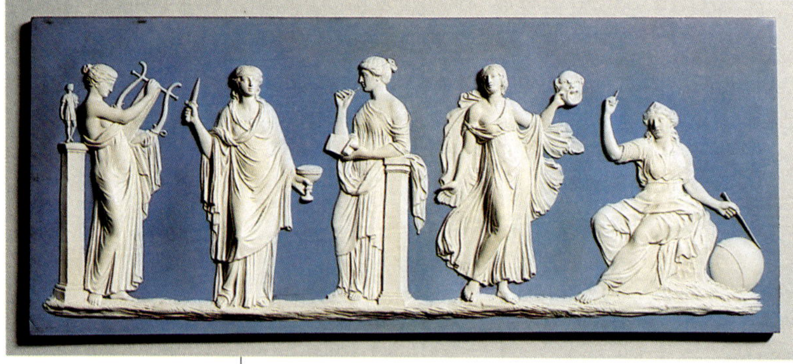

Color plate 85
Tablet, The Five Muses of Melpomene, Calliope, Thalia, Urania, Terpsichore, *ca. 1780, jasper, solid blue ground with dark blue wash on front and white relief, 15 1/4" x 6 1/4" (cat. 252).*

> You shall have a most glorious assortment for the opening of the next season, of Tablets, frises & blocks to go together in the composition of a chimney piece. . . . We can make the frises of any length & very true & even . . . & when we have completed our present suit of tablets & their accompaniments for chimney pieces we will make another attack on the architects & hope to conquer.[92]

These magnificent and unique tablets, however, were not promoted by the architects until the turn of the century. On June 19, 1779, well before the advent of this success, Wedgwood expressed his disappointment to Bentley: "We are really unfortunate in the introduction of our jasper into public notice, that we could not prevail upon the architects to be godfathers to our child. Instead of taking it by the hand, . . . they have cursed the poor infant."[93] Prominent architects of the day, such as Horace Walpole (1717-97) and William Chambers (1723-96), architect to George III, were stern critics of the Adam style and were therefore of little aid to Wedgwood and Bentley. Consequently, and despite Wedgwood and Bentley's best efforts, the tablets never sold well until after Bentley's death. Today, over 115 suites of tablets and plaques are known to have been produced, indicating that they later became as popular as Wedgwood and Bentley had hoped.[94]

Color plate 86
Bulb Pot, Apollo and the Nine Muses, *ca. 1790, jasper, solid blue ground with white relief and granulated body, 8 3/4" x 4 1/2" (cat. 371).*

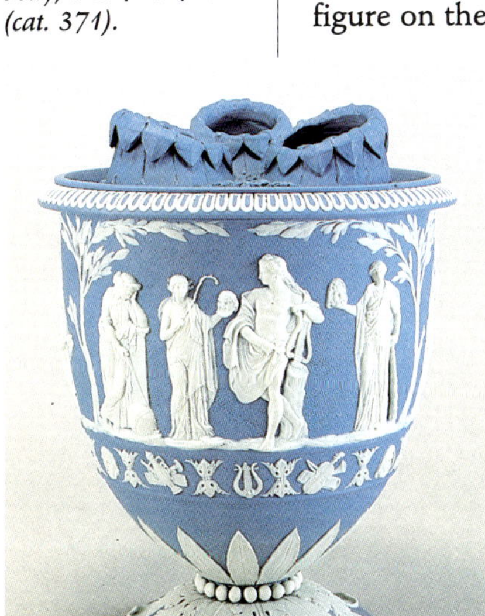

One of the most outstanding tablets in the Beeson collection is of five muses (cat. 252, pl. 85). The tablet has a light blue ground with a dark blue wash and white, sharply cut figures in bas-relief on the front and multiple firing holes behind each figure on the back; it is impressed "WEDGWOOD & BENTLEY" and dates to about 1780. Represented are the figures of Terpsichore, the muse of dance and choral song; Melpomene, the muse of tragedy; Calliope, the chief muse and the muse of epic poetry; Thalia, the muse of comedy and idyllic poetry; and Urania, the muse of astronomy. A bill from John Flaxman, Sr., dated January 3, 1775, invoices the modeling of figures of Terpsichore, Melpomene, Thalia, and Euterpe, but they are possibly some of the earliest works of the younger John Flaxman.[95] The original design for Terpsichore was a tablet in an antique yellow paste and was signed in Greek letters by Onesas. The figure of Thalia was derived from a Pompeian wall painting now in the Louvre.[96] Other Wedgwood correspondence of October 27, 1777, indicates that Flaxman was commissioned to model the remaining muses, but Wedgwood later asked Bentley to cancel the order if possible.[97] Yet, due to the sophistication of the modeling, the figures are generally accepted to be the work of one of the Flaxmans.

On a bulb pot and other vases in the Beeson collection is a different set of figures for the muses, who are accompanied by Apollo (cats. 307, 371, 388, pls. 86, 87, 88). These figures are possibly the work of Giuseppe Angelini (1742-1811) and were

Color plate 87
Left and right, *Pair of Vases,* Apollo and the Muses, *ca. 1790, jasper, solid ground with black and white relief, 11 3/4" x 3 5/16" (cat. 307);* center, *Ewer,* Muses, *ca. 1795, jasper, solid white ground with black wash and white relief, 11 1/4" x 2 5/8" (cat. 309).*

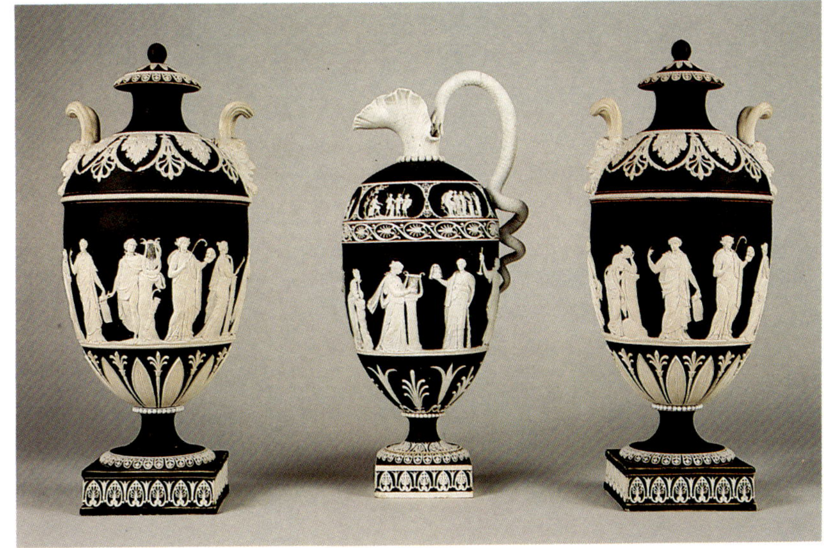

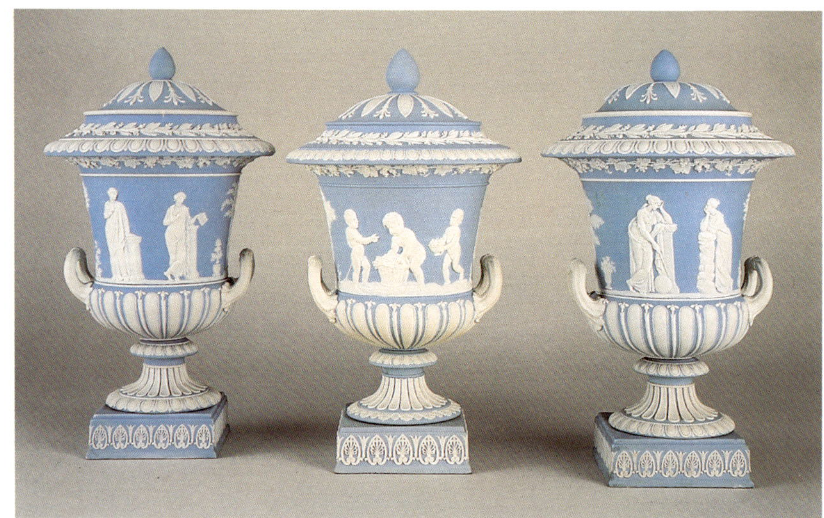

Color plate 88
Left and right, *Pair of Vases,* Apollo and the Nine Muses, *ca. 1880, jasper, solid white ground with blue wash and white relief, 12 5/8" x 4" (cat. 311);* center, *Vase,* Bacchanalian Boys at Play, *ca. 1880, jasper, solid blue ground with white relief, 12 1/4" x 4" (cat. 621).*

taken from the sarcophagus of the Muses now in the Salle des Caryatides of the Louvre.[98] Indeed, Angelini was paid by Wedgwood for a set of nine muses in 1789.[99] From Wedgwood's correspondence concerning Flaxman and Flaxman's invoice, it is difficult to determine which figures on these pieces were modeled by Flaxman and which were modeled by Angelini. The tablet described in the previous paragraph, however, being marked "WEDGWOOD & BENTLEY," rules out the possibility of Angelini being the modeler.

Two very fine tablets in the collection depict scenes of sacrifice (cats. 251, 253, pls. 64 [p. 89], 89). First appearing in the 1779 *Ornamental Catalogue,* the two are similar in composition and show a sacrificial bull being guided to an altar. *The Sacrifice to Eros* is the finest of these two tablets and, indeed, the finest tablet in the Beeson collection; it is attributed to Flaxman and dates to about 1778. It was also

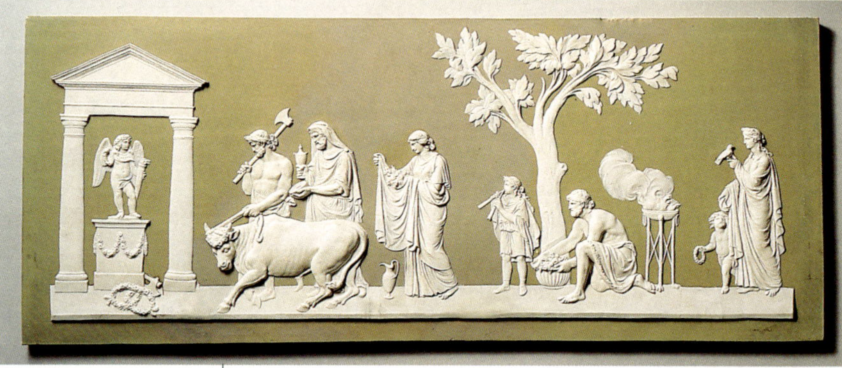

Color plate 89
Tablet, Sacrifice to Love, *ca. 1800, jasper, solid white ground with green wash on front and white relief, 24 7/8" x 9 3/4" (cat. 253).*

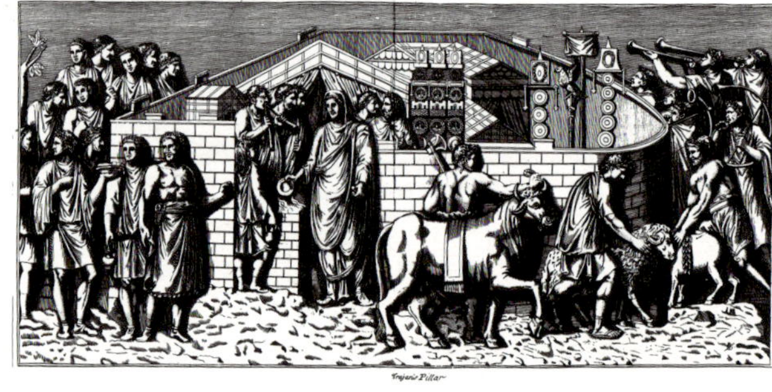

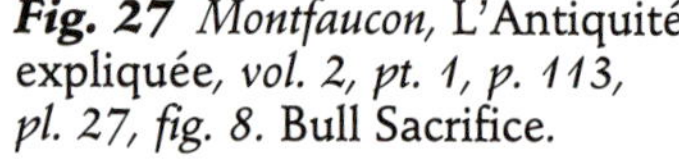

Fig. 27 *Montfaucon,* L'Antiquité expliquée, *vol. 2, pt. 1, p. 113, pl. 27, fig. 8.* Bull Sacrifice.

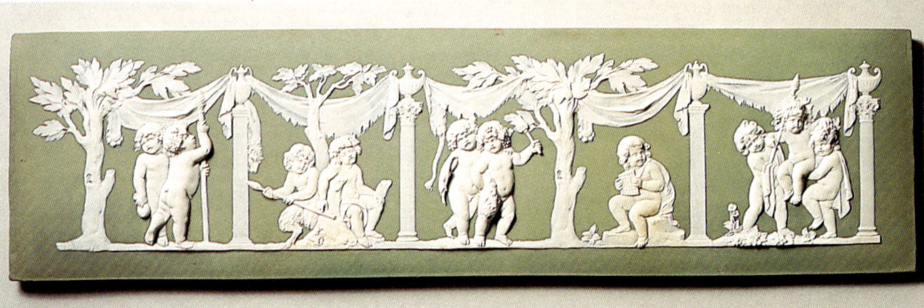

Color plate 90 *Tablet,* Boys with Panther Skins, *ca. 1880, jasper, solid white ground with green wash on front and white relief, 24" x 6 1/2" (cat. 277).*

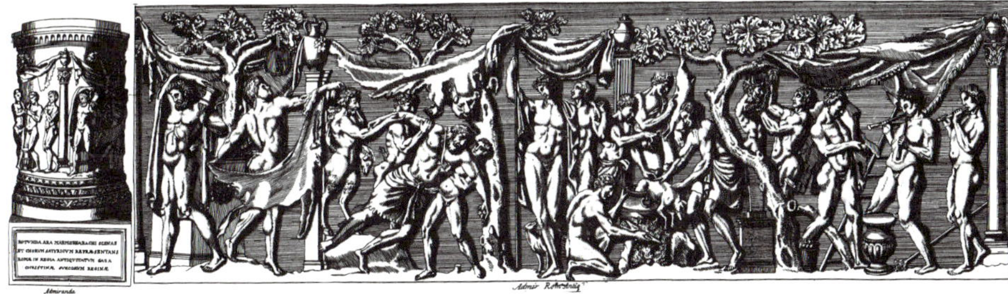

Fig. 28 *Montfaucon,* L'Antiquité expliquée, *vol. 2, pt. 1, p. 121, pl. 29, fig. 1.* Bacchanalian Ceremonies and Sacrifices.

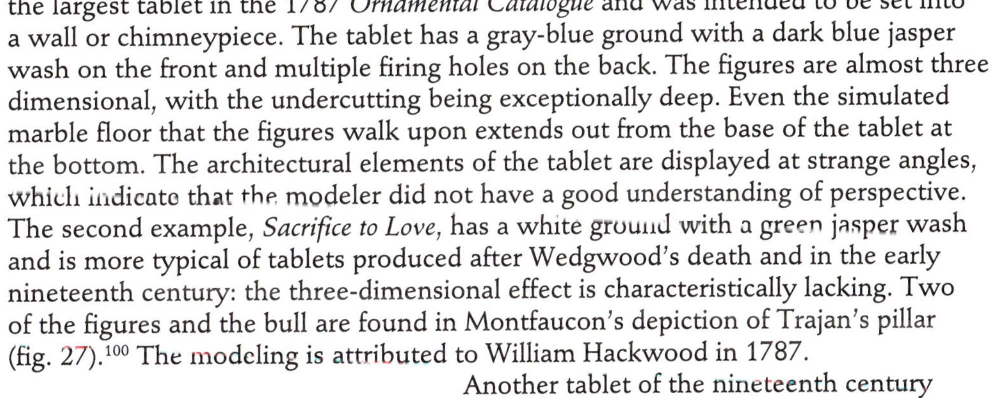

the largest tablet in the 1787 *Ornamental Catalogue* and was intended to be set into a wall or chimneypiece. The tablet has a gray-blue ground with a dark blue jasper wash on the front and multiple firing holes on the back. The figures are almost three-dimensional, with the undercutting being exceptionally deep. Even the simulated marble floor that the figures walk upon extends out from the base of the tablet at the bottom. The architectural elements of the tablet are displayed at strange angles, which indicate that the modeler did not have a good understanding of perspective. The second example, *Sacrifice to Love,* has a white ground with a green jasper wash and is more typical of tablets produced after Wedgwood's death and in the early nineteenth century: the three-dimensional effect is characteristically lacking. Two of the figures and the bull are found in Montfaucon's depiction of Trajan's pillar (fig. 27).[100] The modeling is attributed to William Hackwood in 1787.

Color plate 91 *Roundel,* Marsyas and Young Olympus, *ca. 1795, jasper, solid blue ground with blue wash on front and white relief, 11 1/4" (cat. 243).*

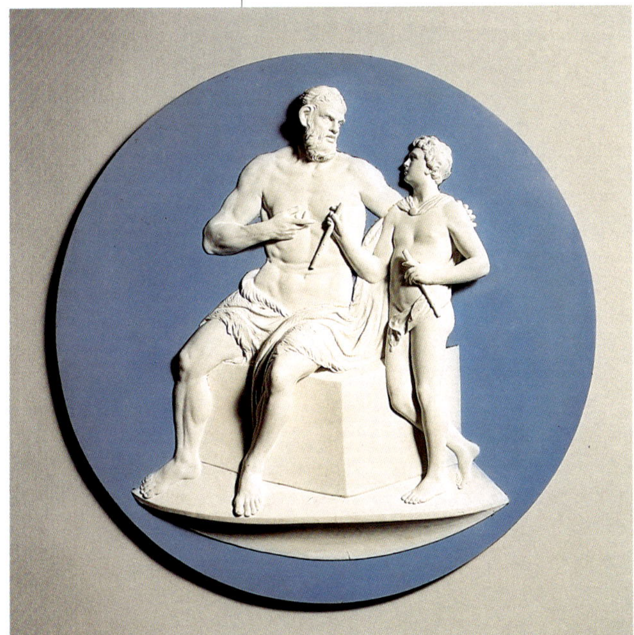

Another tablet of the nineteenth century depicts ten putti and fawns, figures designed by Lady Diana Beauclerk (1724-1808), an amateur artist who, from 1785 to 1789, supplied Wedgwood with sentimental scenes (cat. 277, pl. 90). These figures were also made in separate groupings for smaller tablets. This example, with its solid white ground and green jasper wash, is found as class 2, number 244, in Wedgwood's 1787 *Ornamental Catalogue*. Background swags of panther skins, columns with urns, and trees are taken from a design by Montfaucon (the figures in the original source are drunken adults) (fig. 28).[101] The tablet is impressed "Wedgwood" in uppercase letters and dates to about 1880.

The Herculaneum figure of Marsyas and the young Olympus is in a roundel format in the Beeson collection (cat. 243, pl. 91); it is listed in the French *Ornamental Catalogue* of 1788 (no. 61). This circular tablet is a late-eighteenth-century example in high, white relief against a medium-blue wash

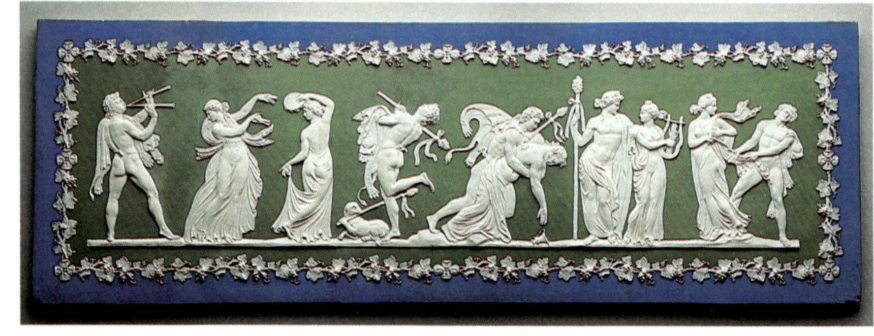

Color plate 92 *Tablet,* Bacchanalian Triumph, *ca. 1880, jasper, solid white ground with green-and-blue wash on front and white relief, 27" x 9" (cat. 260).*

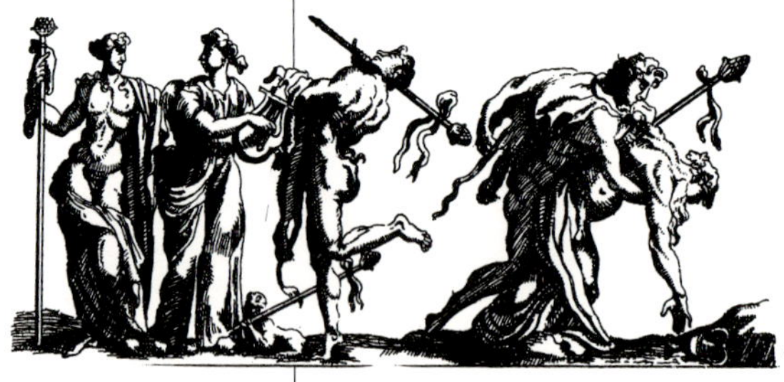

Fig. 29 *Montfaucon,* L'Antiquité expliquée, *vol. 2, pt. 1, p. 123, pl. 30, fig. 1.* Bacchus and Silenus.

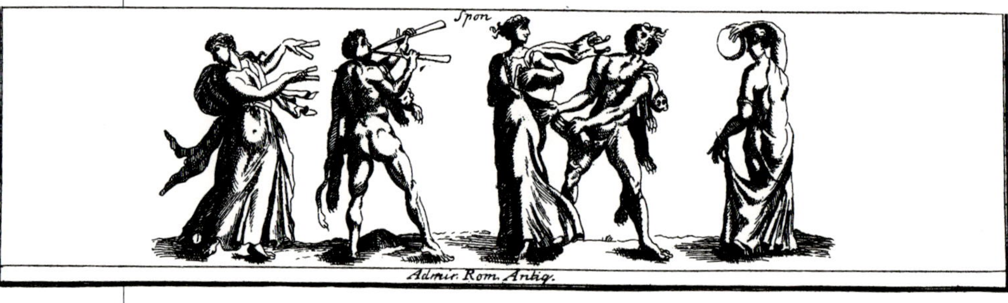

Fig. 30 *Montfaucon,* L'Antiquité expliquée, *vol. 2, pt. 1, p. 123, pl. 30, fig. 2.* Bacchanalian Dance.

on the front over a blue ground. The back has twenty-five firing holes and is marked "WEDGWOOD" in uppercase letters.

A final tablet from the nineteenth century shows a Bacchanalian triumph, with figures from the Borghese vase, now located at the Louvre. The design source is in Montfaucon (figs. 29, 30).[102] Five of the figures were modeled by either a Mrs. Landré or John Flaxman in 1777 and then remodeled by John De Vaere (w. 1785-1818) while he was working in Rome for Wedgwood. The tablet is covered with a blue and a green jasper wash on a white-jasper or white-stoneware ground (cat. 260, pl. 92). This use of color and the busy grapevine-border bas-relief around the figures are indicative of late-nineteenth-century decoration.

Frieze Room

At the Birmingham Museum of Art in Birmingham, Alabama, in the center of the gallery where the Beeson Wedgwood collection is located, is an Adamesque room constructed in 1977 to show a set of fifty-two jasper-ware tablets of various mythological themes (cats. 563–615, pls. 93, 94). Solid blue with white bas-relief, they are all impressed "WEDGWOOD" in uppercase letters plus various combinations of a letter and a number. Believed to date from the early nineteenth century, they have no firing holes on the back. Although suites of Wedgwood tablets are known to have been plentiful in the eighteenth century (see p. 109), a frieze extending the entire perimeter of a room is rare today.

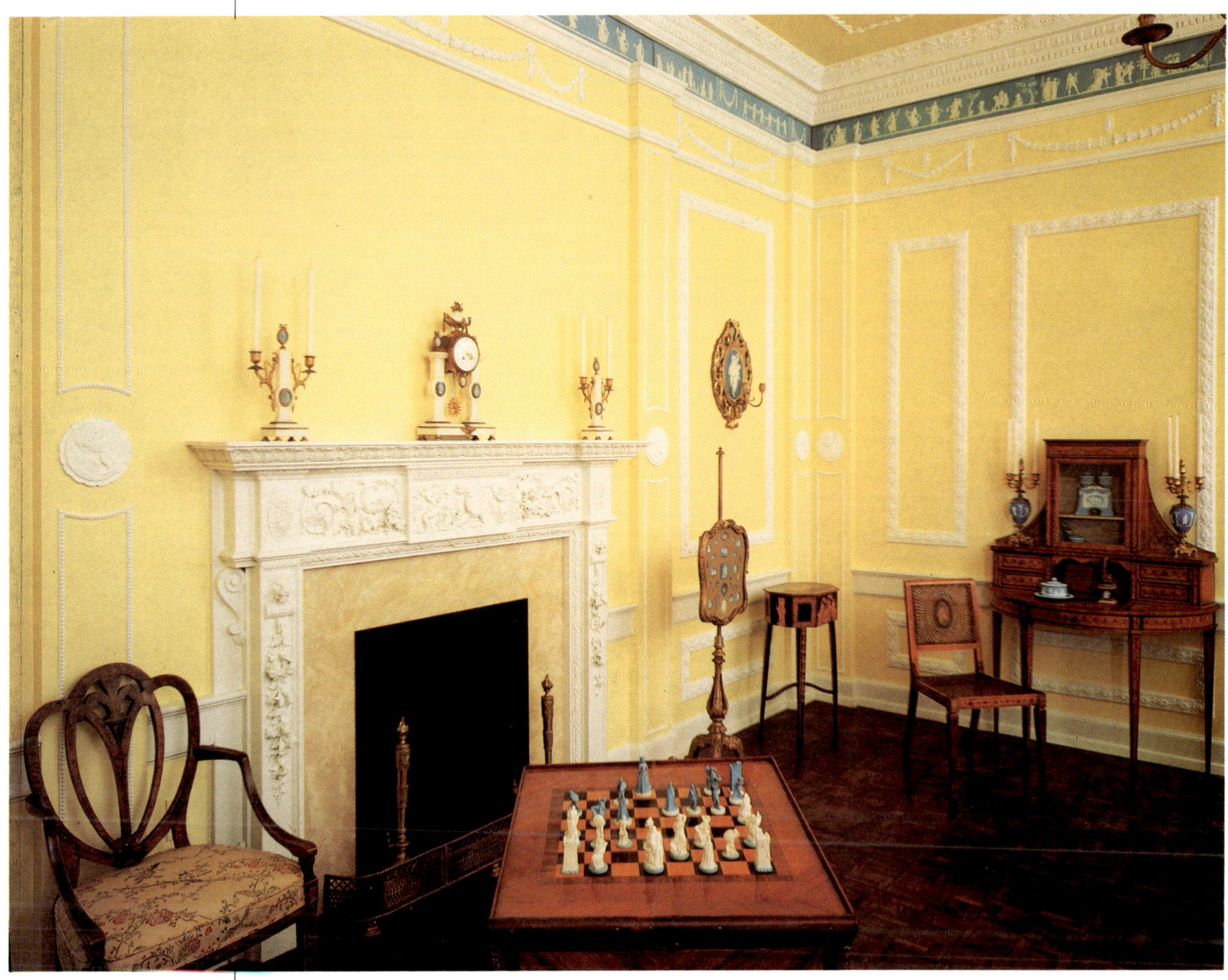

Color plate 93 *(For descriptions of Friezes, Chessmen, Mantel Garniture, and Firescreen, please see page 115.)* Above, *Firescreen, one of a Pair of Sconces,* Herculaneum Figures, *1775-80, jasper, solid blue ground with blue wash on front and white relief, Florentine mirrored frame, plaque: 10 1/8" x 7" (cat. 630).* Objects on desk, left and right, *Pair of Candelabra,* The Muses, *19th century, jasper, solid white ground with dark blue wash and white relief, set in gilded metal, 17" (cat. 626);* top shelf of desk, *Inkstand,* Marriage of Cupid and Psyche *and* Trophies of Love and Harmony, *ca. 1795, jasper, solid blue ground with white relief, 8 3/4" x 6 1/2" (cat. 627);* second shelf from top, *Inkwell, ca. 1785, jasper, solid blue ground with white relief and engine-turning, 1 7/8" x 2 1/2" (cat. 622);* bottom shelf left, *Covered Cosmetic Box and Under Dish,* Boys at Play, *ca. 1790, jasper, solid blue ground and white relief, box: 3 7/8" x 4 1/2", dish: 6 7/8" (cat. 624);* bottom shelf right, *Obelisk with Medallion, ca. 1800, jasper, solid white ground with dark blue wash and white relief, Derbyshire spar, 1 3/8" x 1 1/16" (cat. 623).*

The subjects of the tablets that compose the frieze in the Birmingham Museum of Art are the Dancing Hours, the marriage of Cupid and Psyche, the sacrifice to Hymen, Bacchanalian boys, the Bacchanalian triumph, the death of Hector, the birth of Achilles, Achilles handed to Chiron, all accented by numerous swags and paterae. Wedgwood wrote of this combination in August of 1778: "The tablets of dancing hours in this inv^{o}., are intended as frises to the marr[iag]e of Cupid &c which with two of the seasons for blocks will make a very complete chimney piece."[103]

Before the Beeson acquisition of this frieze, it was owned by the P. J. Dearden family in England and is believed to have been packed away as found during the late

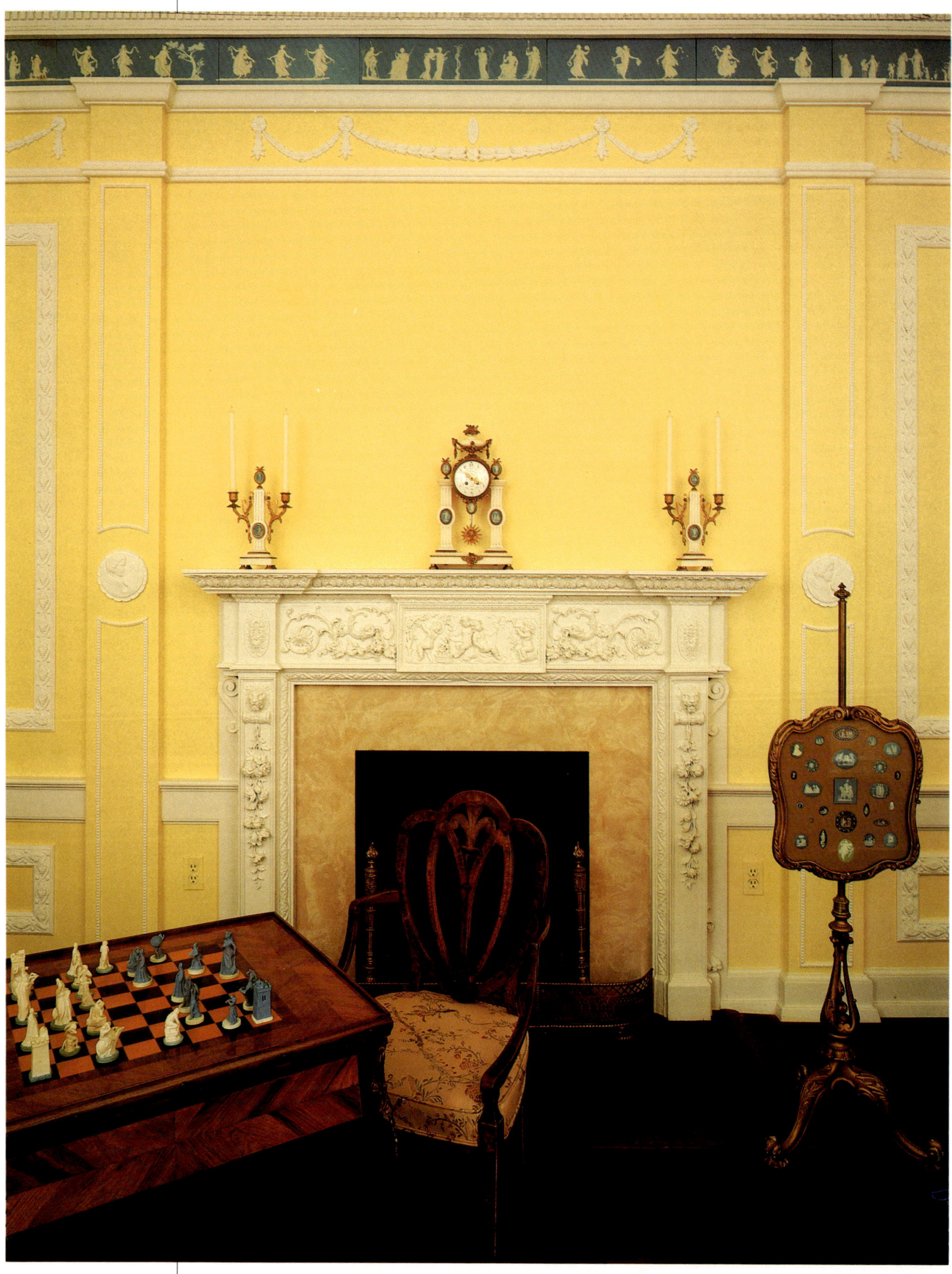

Color plate 94 *(p. 114) Frieze Room, Birmingham Museum of Art, Beeson Wedgwood Collection. The room is a re-creation of a neoclassical interior.* Along upper wall, *Fifty Frieze Tablets, nineteenth century, solid blue ground with white jasper relief (cats. 563–615);* lower left, *Twenty-six Chessmen, ca. 1790, John Flaxman (1755-1826), designer, jasper, solid white and solid blue, 3 5/16" (greatest height) (cat. 628);* center, *Mantel Garniture of Clock and Candlesticks, nineteenth century, jasper, solid light blue with white relief, marble, ormolu, and porcelain, five medallions: 1 5/16" x 1 1/32", four medallions: 1 5/8" x 1 5/16" (cat. 625);* right, *Firescreen, nineteenth century, twenty-four jasperware medallions, largest: 2 3/4" x 1 1/2", smallest: 7/8" x 5/8" (cats. 633–56).*

nineteenth century or perhaps earlier. It reappeared in 1968, after Dearden died and his grandchildren sold much of the estate. A shadow that ringed the edge of each tablet before it was recently cleaned showed that the frieze had been installed in a house or other structure whose location has yet to be discovered.

Experimental Teaware

Wedgwood's memorandum of 1777 suggests that small, experimental teacups and possibly other teaware were being produced, yet no teaware impressed with the mark of Wedgwood and Bentley is known. In the Beeson collection there are some small and delicate pieces of teaware, some made of solidly colored jasper and others of the washed jasper (pl. 95). They show a translucency similar to that possessed by porcelain and are finely potted. Many have an almost speckled effect within their coloring, as if the pigment were not consistently ground and mixed with the clay. These examples are early in the development of jasper ware, for they are often marked "Wedgwood" in both all uppercase and upper- and lowercase letters and have an "O" or a "3" or both. Although no definitive document about these marks has been located, they are generally found on this finely crafted teaware and may designate pieces of early production or special quality.[104]

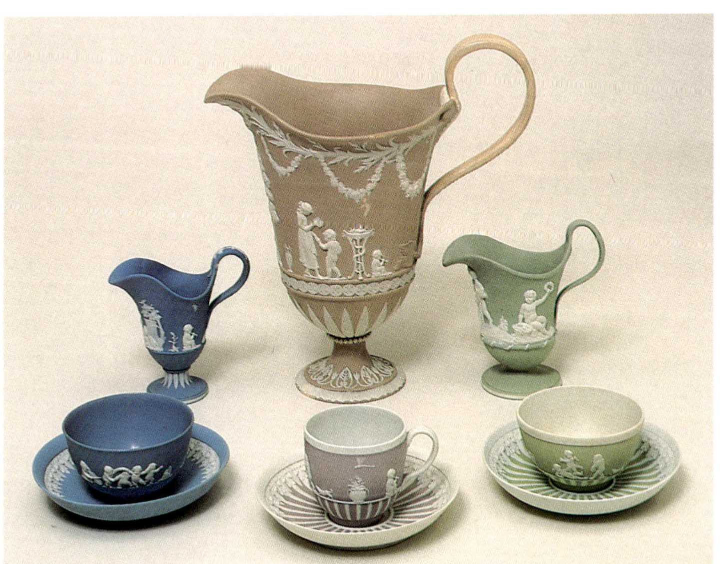

Color plate 95 Front row left, *Cup and Saucer, ca. 1785, jasper, solid blue ground with white relief, cup has engine-turning and lapidary-polishing, cup: 2 1/16" x 1 1/2", saucer: 5 1/16" (cat. 320);* center, *Cup and Saucer,* Cupids at Play, *ca. 1790, jasper, solid white ground with lilac wash, white relief, and engine-turning, cup has lapidary polishing, cup: 2 3/8" x 1 5/16" (cat. 335);* right, *Cup and Saucer,* Cupids at Play, *ca. 1785, jasper, solid white ground with green wash and white relief, cup has engine-turning and lapidary-polishing, cup: 1 7/8" x 1 1/2", saucer: 5 1/2" (cat. 334);* top row left, *Cream Pitcher from Five-piece Dejeuner Set, ca. 1790, jasper, solid blue ground with white relief and engine-turning, 4 5/16" x 1 3/4" (cat. 318);* center, *Pitcher,* Domestic Employment, *ca. 1790, jasper, solid lilac ground with white relief, 10" x 3 1/4" (cat. 329);* right, *Cream Pitcher,* Boys at Play, *ca. 1785, jasper, solid green ground with white relief, 4 13/16" x 2 3/8" (cat. 330).*

The Jasper-Ware Dilemma

One question that plagues researchers of jasper ware is exactly when Wedgwood began producing jasper hollowware. Jasper hollowware is almost never marked "Wedgwood & Bentley," the only exception being a small pedestal made to support a figure of Venus (cat. 287, pl. 96). At least four of these pedestals are known to exist: one in the Beeson collection, two in the British Museum, and one, which has a figure of Venus sitting on top, in a private collection.[105] All are marked "Wedgwood & Bentley" and are decorated with four cupids that symbolize the four seasons. The cupids were designed by John Flaxman, Sr., as an invoice of April 11, 1775, records ("Four Basso Relievos of the Seasons"). The shape was probably derived from Montfaucon, where it is described as "F. Bonanni has given us . . . a Tripod, and which we have here given after him: Each Face or Side exhibits a Genius, one of which carries an Oar upon his Neck; which seems to denote it an Altar of Neptune" (fig. 31).[106] The following letter of November 3, 1777, undoubtedly refers to these pedestals: "I am glad you liked the pedestal for the Venus. I though it well match'd—Love is ever in season, & pretty enough."[107] As with much of the early jasper ware by Wedgwood, the pedestal has a light blue ground, as seen in the interior, with a dark blue wash on the exterior and tiny firing holes—in this case, nine at the interior corners. The cupids' and the rams' heads are in relatively high relief and are quite detailed in their finishing. The mark is impressed "Wedgwood & Bentley" in upper- and lowercase letters, thus dating the piece to between 1777 and 1780.

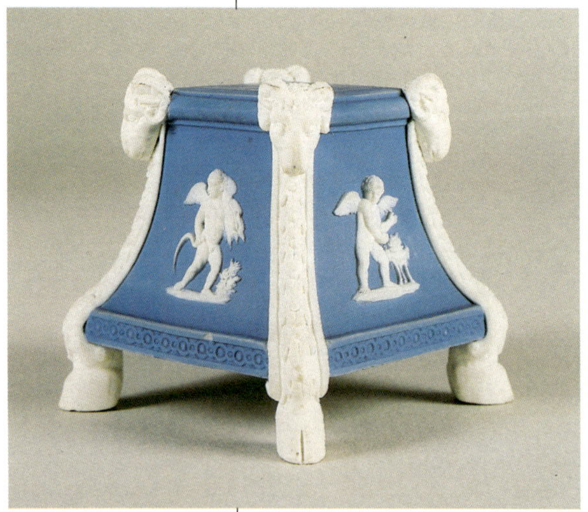

Color plate 96 *Pedestal,* The Four Seasons, *ca. 1775, jasper, solid blue ground with dark blue wash and white relief, 3 5/16" x 3 1/2" (cat. 287).*

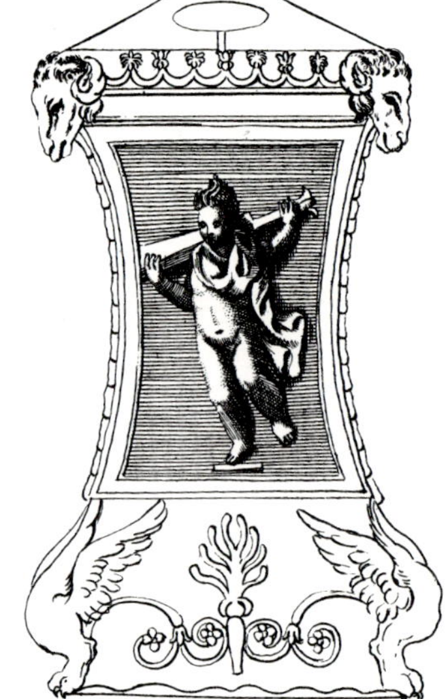

Fig. 31 *Montfaucon,* L'Antiquité expliquée, *vol. 2, pt. 1, p. 83, pl. 17, fig. 4.*

The physical evidence suggests that only this pedestal and possibly some teaware were produced prior to Bentley's death. On November 12, 1780, two weeks before Thomas Bentley died, Wedgwood wrote to him, saying, "I am contriving some vases for bodies, and bodies for vases."[108] Upon this letter and the existing teaware and pedestals rests the theory that Wedgwood was producing jasper-ware hollowware prior to 1781 but that he refrained from introducing it to the public because of his constant battle to balance the need "to stay ahead of his rivals against the need to sell existing stock. The over-hasty introduction of jasper vases might have made much of his stock of basalt and variegated vases at least temporarily unsaleable."[109] Wedgwood therefore waited until after the auction of the holdings of the Wedgwood and Bentley partnership on December 17, 1781, to introduce jasper hollowware in general and the vases in particular.

Vases

Wedgwood's early jasper-ware vases—that is, the jasper vases he produced in the eighteenth century—have certain identifying characteristics. Initially, Wedgwood fashioned his jasper vases by rearranging and reusing bas-reliefs and shapes from vases he had previously made in other media; he did, however, introduce new shapes as well as new colors. In general, the body of the typical vase from this period has a very smooth, almost glasslike finish. The clay frequently yields darker specks of color over the vase's entire surface. The bas-relief decoration is restrained, yet very detailed in its finishing. There is frequently a small bulbous form, called a sump cover, over the junction of the screw and nut at the bottom of the interior of the vase (fig. 32). And on many eighteenth-century and some early-nineteenth-century examples, the plinth was first formed of solid clay but with a routed-out hole in the center, producing a sump into which a screw was placed in order to attach the plinth to the body. The screw and hole were then covered with a plasterlike substance thought to be a mixture of pine resin and plaster-of-paris or gypsum, which was poured at boiling point into the sump of the warmed vase (fig. 33).[110] On some examples the plaster has been lost and the screwlike routing can be seen around the sides of the sump. Most have plinths of the same color as the body, as white plinths had become obsolete sometime after September 10, 1786, when John Wedgwood wrote to his father: "Every lady calles for plinths of the same colour as the Vase with the ornaments white. . . . It will be done for the next Vases."[111] By comparison, on late-nineteenth-century pieces, the plinth is hollow, with a hole in the center of a flanged, mold-made bottom, and there is no visible evidence of plaster fill. A screw penetrates from the plinth into the bottom of the vase, holding the two together (fig. 34).

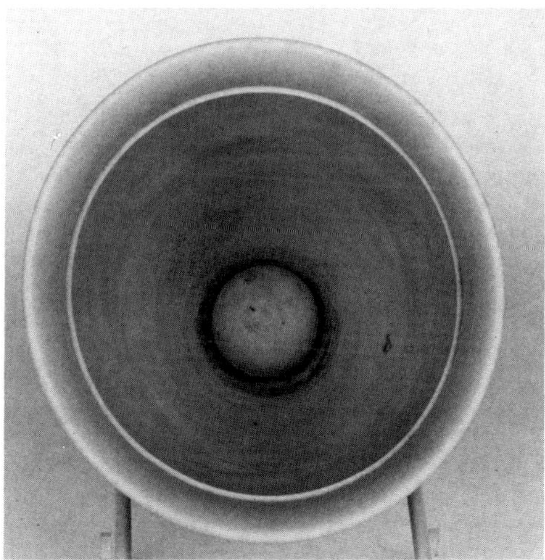

Fig. 32 *This view of an eighteenth-century vase shows the bulbous covering that is often referred to as a sump cover. It was used in most eighteenth-century vases.*

Fig. 33 *This view of the bottom of an eighteenth-century vase shows where the originally solid plinth was routed out in the interior in order for the screw and bolt to connect the vase and plinth. A plaster fill can be seen, as well as circular marks made by a router used to dig out the clay. Several firing holes are also visible.*

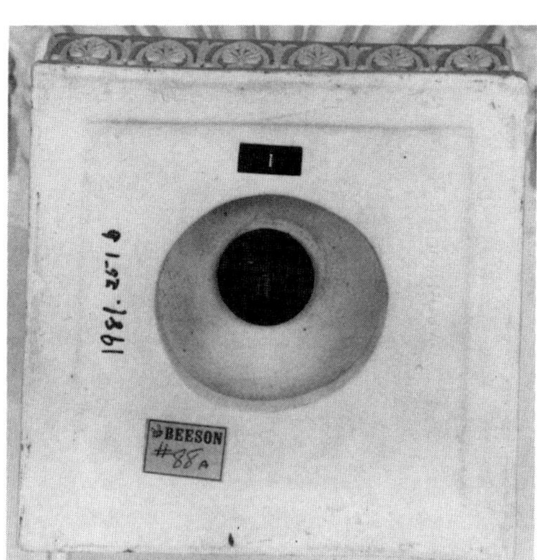

Fig. 34 *This view of the bottom of a nineteenth-century vase shows the plinth with a flanged interior where the screw and bolt connect. There is no plaster fill or firing hole.*

One of the most well known and celebrated jasper-ware vases is the Pegasus vase, or *Apotheosis of Homer*, as Wedgwood may have called it. Its prototype was made in Greece; William Hamilton acquired the original in Italy and sold it to the British Museum in 1763. Prior to its sale, however, Hamilton allowed Wedgwood to copy the vase, and in payment for the use of the design, Wedgwood sent him a copy of the figures in tablet format. In the Beeson collection is one of these early tablets, in basalt (cat. 124, pl. 35; see also

Color plate 97
Vase, Apotheosis of Virgil, *ca. 1875-85, jasper, solid white ground with black wash and white relief, 23 3/4" x 10 1/4" (cat. 310).*

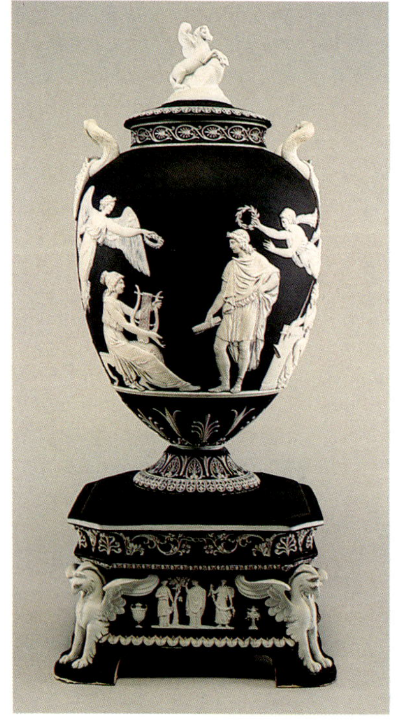

p. 56). Upon receiving the tablet in 1779, Hamilton wrote to Wedgwood: "[It] astonishes all the artists here, it is more pure & in a truer antique Taste than any of their performances tho' they have so many fine models before them."[112] The complete design, however, proved too detailed to be reproduced in vase form, so Wedgwood commissioned John Flaxman, Jr., to adapt the scene so that it could be accommodated by the surface of the vase. On June 24, 1786, Wedgwood presented to the British Museum his adaptation of the vase, which Wedgwood described to Hamilton as "the finest & most perfect I have ever made."[113]

Wedgwood's sixth edition of his *Ornamental Catalogue* of 1787 lists a second vase, entitled *Apotheosis of Virgil,* as a companion to the Homer (class 2, no. 266). This companion vase was modeled by Flaxman in about 1785. An oven book of the following year records a number of firings. Wedgwood appears to have produced only blue-and-white jasper examples of the Homer vase, whereas examples of its sister vase exist in blue, gray, and black.[114]

Color plates 98 & 99 *Vase,* left, Venus Drawn by Swans, *and* right, Cupids Attending Swans, *ca. 1786, Charles Le Brun (1629-90), designer, jasper, solid blue ground with white relief, 16" x 4" (cat. 281).*

In the Beeson collection is a black-and-white *Apotheosis of Virgil* (cat. 310, pl. 97), which was made in the late nineteenth century, as described in pottery memos at the factory: "Large black & white vases Pegasus with Griffin pedestals fired on 7 December 1875 were very good."[115] On the obverse of the vase is a figure of Minerva based on the Minerva Giustiniani in the Vatican Museum. Heads of Medusa appear at the handle terminals on this vase as well as on those of another vase in the collection (cat. 305. pl. 104, p. 121). The heads of Medusa on the latter vase were most likely copied from an illustration of a sandal in Montfaucon.[116] Design sources for the rest of the elements on the vase remain unknown.[117] (There are also two other Beeson objects with the Virgil theme: a roundel of about 1850 and another vase dating to between 1795 and 1820 [cats. 270, 310].)

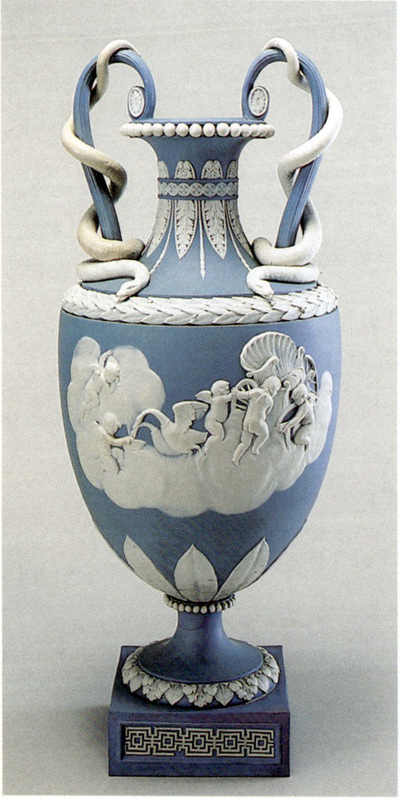

One of the most outstanding jasper-ware vases in the Beeson collection depicts, on one side, Venus in a chariot being drawn by swans and, on the other, Cupid attending the

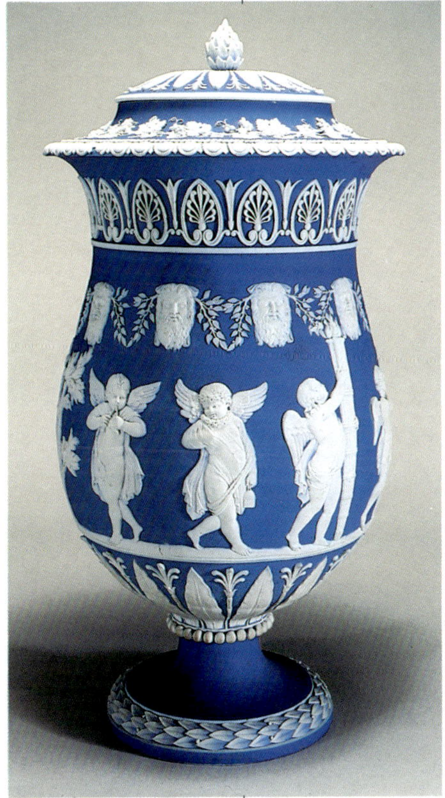

Color plate 100
Covered Vase,
Several Geniuses Representing the Pleasures of the Elysian Fields,
ca. 1795, Giuseppe Angelini, modeler, jasper, solid white ground with dark blue wash and white relief, 15" x 5 1/16" (cat. 282).

swans, subjects also found on plaques by Wedgwood (cat. 281, pls. 98, 99). The original design is attributed to Charles Le Brun (1619-90), the principal French decorative artist of the reign of Louis XIV. The design of the snake handles is probably based on late-sixteenth-century Italian majolica, which Wedgwood could have seen in several sources. Wedgwood's jasper vase, of a gray-blue ground with light blue wash and white relief, is superbly modeled. The vase dates to about 1786; the subject is listed as number 245 in the bas-relief class of Wedgwood's *Ornamental Catalogue* of 1787. The decoration portrays a rare combination of baroque figures among neoclassical ornaments. This vase and another in Frederick Rathbone's *Wedgwood* are impressed "WEDGWOOD" and "H," which Rathbone suggests may signify that Hackwood was the modeler.[118]

Another elaborately decorated jasper vase depicts a border of nine bearded men, below which are nine cupids carrying a garland of laurel branches (cat. 282; pl. 100). Beautiful foliage with berries cover the finial. In the sixth edition of the 1787 *Ornamental Catalogue,* in the category of bas-reliefs, design number 259, Henry Webber is listed as the artist. The vase is often titled *Sacrifice to Hymen,* taken from a cinerary urn that belonged to D. Lucellus Felix and is now in the Capitoline Museum.[119] The scene on the urn was intended to represent the hope of life after death: thus it might better be titled *Several Geniuses Representing the Pleasures of the Elysian Fields,* which was modeled by Giuseppe Angelini in 1787.[120] This vase has a dark blue jasper wash on a white ground with some bleeding into the figures and a sump cover on the interior. The vase dates to between 1790 and 1795.

In the Beeson collection is also a very fine lamp, often referred to as the Michelangelo lamp, made of solid blue and solid white jasper ware and dating to about 1785 (cat. 302, pl. 101). This lamp has lost its original top, but other similar pieces were made as incense burners. The metalsmiths Matthew Boulton and John Fothergill are known to have made an ormolu clock with the same three figures in 1772.[121] The source of the figures comes from a silver-gilt crucifix made by Antonio Gentile da Faenza in 1582; the crucifix, now at the treasury of Saint Peter's in Rome, was illustrated in William Chambers's *Treatise on Civil Architecture* under the title "Persians and Caryatides," drawn by Cipriani and engraved by Charles Grignion.[122] The reference to Michelangelo is explained by Chambers, for he notes that the figures were "copied from candelbres [*sic*], in Saint Peter's of the Vatican. They were cast from models of Michael Angelo Buonaroti." John Flaxman, Sr., modeled the figures for Wedgwood. The bowl above the figures is copied from Hellenistic bronze lamps of around 400 B.C.[123] which

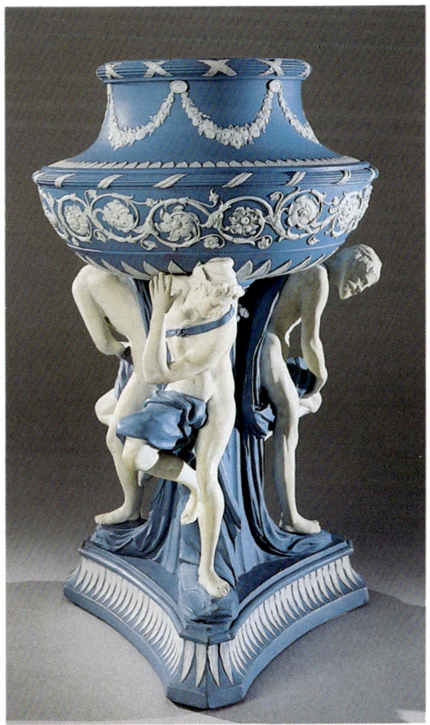

Color plate 101
Lamp, ca. 1785, jasper, solid blue ground with solid white figures and white relief, 11 1/8" x 7 1/2" (cat. 302).

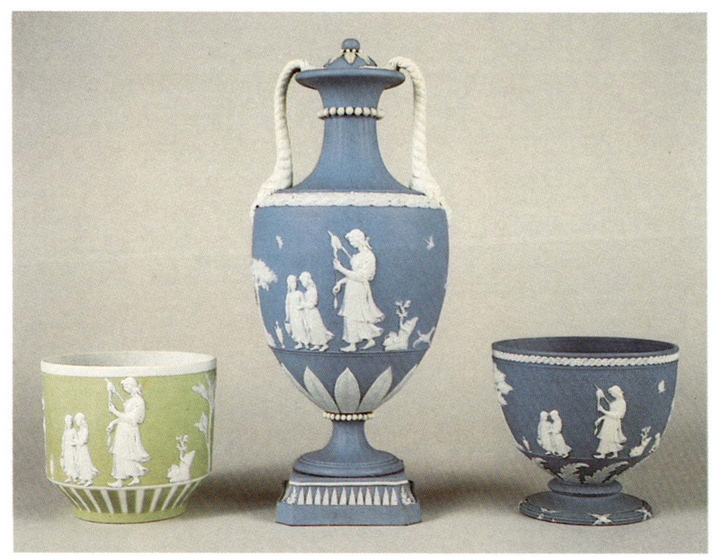

Color plate 102
Left, *Bowl,* Domestic Employment, *ca. 1790, jasper, solid white ground with green wash and white relief, engine-turning, 3 7/16" x 2 9/16" (cat. 328);* center, *Covered Vase,* Domestic Employment, *ca. 1785, jasper, solid blue ground with white relief, 10 5/8" x 3 1/4" (cat. 315);* right, *Bowl,* Domestic Employment, *ca. 1790, jasper, solid blue ground with white relief, granulated body, 3 3/4" x 3" (cat. 314).*

Color plate 103
Left, *Teapot,* Charlotte Mourning at the Tomb of Werther *and* Maid and Cupid at Play, *ca. 1790, jasper, solid blue ground with white relief and stippled body, 7 7/8" x 3 13/16" (cat. 325);* right, *Kettle and Stand, ca. 1790, jasper, solid blue ground with blue wash and white relief, engine-turning, handle: silver and wood, kettle: 5 3/4" x 7 5/16", stand: 6 15/16" (cat. 327).*

Wedgwood used frequently in his tripod vases.

In this collection, a number of jasper-ware vases and other objects from the late eighteenth century display domestic scenes designed by Lady Elizabeth Templetown (1747-1823), one of the amateur artists who designed numerous scenes for Wedgwood from 1783 to 1789. Toward the beginning of their association, on June 27, 1783, Wedgwood wrote to Lady Templetown:

> Mr. W. presents his most respectful comp[ts]. to Lady Templeton [*sic*] & is very happy to learn by his nephew Mr. Byerley that his attempt to copy in bas relief the charming groups of little figures her ladyship was so obliging as to lend him has met with that approbation which he durst not flatter himself with, & is sensible he owes much to Lady Templetons politeness on this occasion.[124]

Wedgwood's flattery may or may not have been sincere, but he must have thought the designs would please his buyers. These delicate, sentimental scenes often depict mothers and their children surrounded by flowers, flying insects, and decorative implements. William Hackwood is credited with transferring most of Templetown's designs from cut Indian paper to clay, an arrangement documented in a bill of April 30, 1785.[125] Templetown's scenes are incorporated with various other forms of decoration on jasper ware, including engine-turning, a granulated or stippled body, garlands, leaves, and lions' heads. In the Beeson collection are jasper-ware bowls, a pitcher, a tea caddy, a rum kettle, a teapot, and two vases with the various titles of *Domestic Employment, Family School, Maternal Affection, Poor Maria,* and *Charlotte Mourning at the Tomb of Werther* (pls. 102, 103). The last title refers to a group of objects depicting the character Charlotte from Goethe's romantic novel *The Sorrows of Young Werther* (1774): she kneels at the tomb of her lover, who has committed suicide for her sake. The subject was designed by Lady Templetown in 1787 and modeled by Hackwood in 1790.

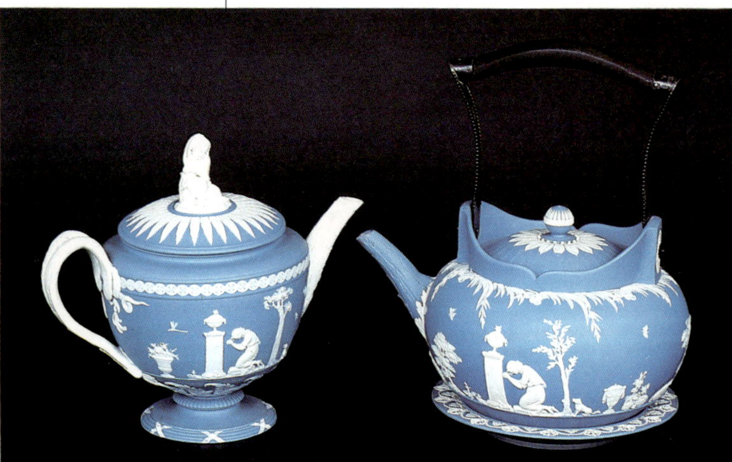

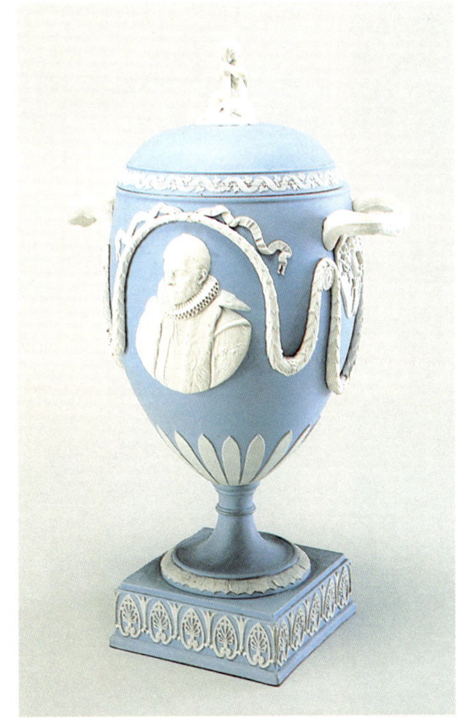

Color plate 104
Vase, Oliver Cromwell, William I (prince of Orange)*, and* Medusa*, ca. 1800, jasper, solid blue ground with white relief, 13" x 4 1/16" (cat. 305).*

Another jasper vase in the Beeson collection is considered rare because it displays an unusual combination of portrait medallions: those of Oliver Cromwell (1599-1658), on one side, and William I, of the Netherlands (1533-84), on the other (cat. 305, pl. 104). A basalt intaglio in the collection also depicts Cromwell, but he is accompanied by William III of England (1650-1702) (cat. 1008). The relationship of the two Williams and Cromwell was their promotion of Protestantism; the vase consequently may have been a commissioned piece. The vase has handles identical to those found on the vase entitled *Apotheosis of Virgil* in the Beeson collection (cat. 310, pl. 97, p. 118). This vase dates to about 1800 and was later produced by Wedgwood in majolica, along with other portrait and mythological medallions.

The contemporary fashionable interest in the excavations of Pompeii and Herculaneum is evidenced by engravings of ruins by Piranesi and garden ornaments such as the ruined arch in Kew Gardens, designed by William Chambers. Wedgwood responded by also producing a number of jasperware items that imitated and, indeed, appeared to be ancient objects weathered by time. (Views of ruins are particularly prominent on Wedgwood's Catherine the Great service as well as on his transfer-printed cream ware.) In the Beeson collection is a most rare "ruined" vase of a solid white body with a blue jasper wash: its rectangular base is decorated with classical figures and simulated lichen and corrosion (cat. 303, pl. 105). Another example is a vase composed of three "ruined" columns made of solid blue and solid white jasper (cat. 299, pl. 106). Both pieces have been attributed to the modeler William Keeling, but this attribution has not been documented. The broken column as a thematic decoration is also found in the collection on a vase and an inkstand (cat. 365, pl. 105; cat. 375). Another unusual representation

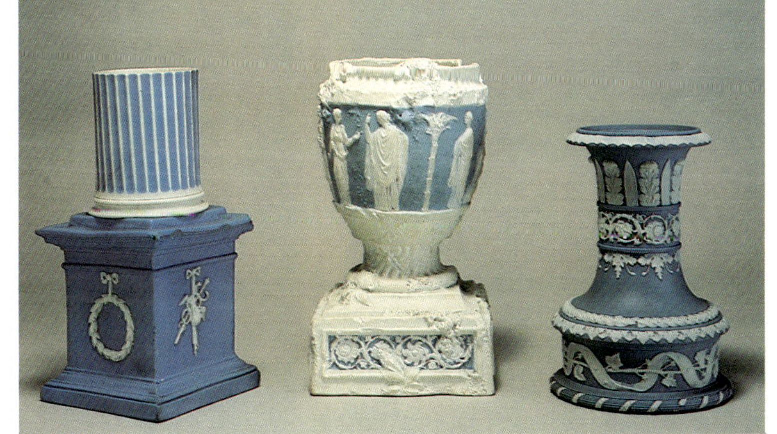

Color plate 105
Left, *Vase, ca. 1790, jasper, solid blue ground with white relief, 5" x 3 9/16" (cat. 369);* center, *Ruined Vase, ca. 1790, jasper, solid white ground with light blue wash, 6 3/8" x 3 5/8" (cat. 299);* right, *Vase, ca. 1795, jasper, solid blue ground with white relief on base, solid white ground with blue wash on column, 6 3/16" x 3" (cat. 365).*

Color plate 106 *Vase,* Ruined Columns*, ca. 1790, jasper, solid blue and solid white grounds, 9" x 4 7/16" x 12 1/3" (cat. 303).*

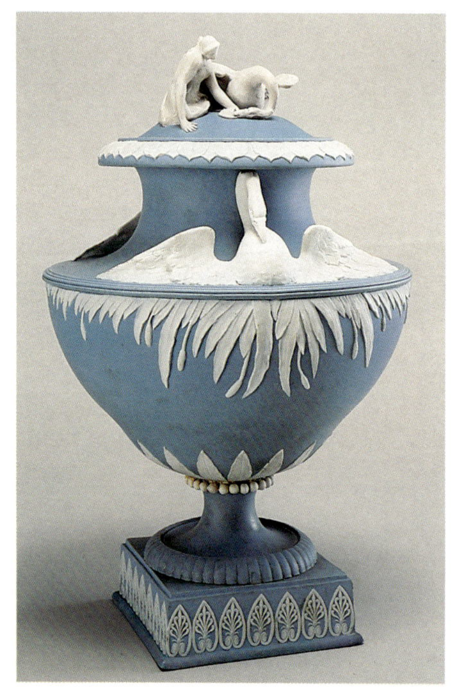

Color plate 107
Covered Vase, Leda and the Swan, *ca. 1795, jasper, solid blue ground with white relief, 10 7/8" x 4 13/16" (cat. 306).*

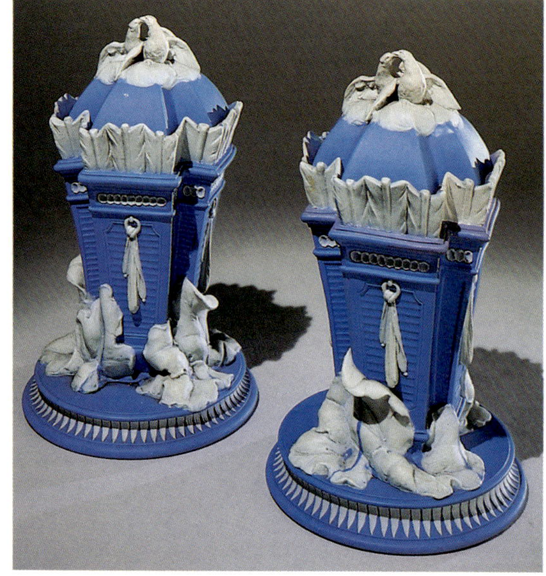

Color plate 108 *Pair of Quiver Vases, ca. 1795, jasper, solid blue ground with white relief, 8 3/4" x 5 1/2" (cat. 304).*

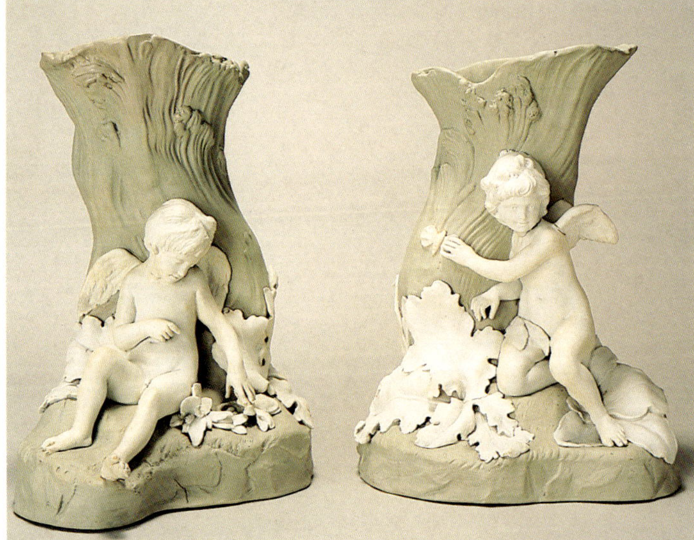

Color plate 109
Pair of Vases, Cupid with a Bird's Nest *and* Cupid with a Butterfly, *ca. 1785, jasper, solid green ground with solid white figures, 8 1/2" x 4 3/4" (cat. 360).*

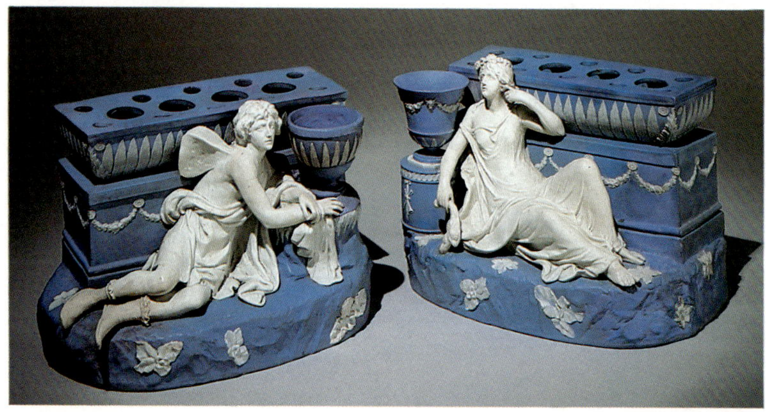

Color plate 110
Pair of Bulb Pots, Figures of Cupid and Psyche, *ca. 1790, jasper, solid blue ground with white relief and solid white figures, 5 1/2" x 4 3/4" (cat. 288).*

of an ancient object is seen in a jasper-ware inkstand shaped like a sarcophagus, with two urns on top functioning as inkwells (cat. 627, pl. 73, p. 97).

Another favorite theme among artists of the late eighteenth century was the story of Leda and the swan. Leda was the wife of Tyndareus, king of Sparta. Zeus came to her in the form of a swan, and soon thereafter she laid two eggs, one producing Castor and Pollux and the other Helen of Troy. In the Beeson collection, a solid blue jasper vase with white relief depicts this theme (cat. 306, pl. 107). It is dated about 1795 and is a beautiful example of the continuing quality of Wedgwood's ornamental ware even after the death of Bentley. Leda and the swan are both seen in three-dimensional form as the finial of the vase; the figures of swans are also used as the handles for the vase.

Another outstanding pair of vases in the collection is known as the quiver vases, so called because of the projecting, feathered arrow shafts at the top of each vase (cat. 304; pl. 108). They are covered with lids that have pairs of white jasper doves as the finials. Each of these vases has a solid blue body with a slightly darker blue wash and white relief and is marked "O" in addition to the uppercase "WEDGWOOD" mark, which is thought to be characteristic of the early pieces.

A pair of rare trumpet vases depicts cupid in three-dimensional form, one with a bird's nest and the other with a butterfly (cat. 360, pl. 109). Thought to date to about 1785, the vases are solid gray-green jasper with solid white figures.

Color plate 111 *Pair of Bulb Pots,* The Four Seasons, *ca. 1785, jasper, solid blue ground with white relief, 6 7/16" x 5" (cat. 285).*

Bough Pots

Wedgwood fashioned white terra-cotta stoneware, basalt, and jasperware bough pots in various shapes for holding flower arrangements and forced bulbs. Vases were primarily used for flowers in the eighteenth century, and flower and bulb pots were displayed on and under tables and on the hearth in the summer. Wedgwood wrote that flower arranging was "the Art of disposing the most beautiful production of Nature, in the most agreeable, picturesque, and strikeing manner."[126] Of particular note in the Beeson collection is a pair of bulb pots depicting Cupid and Psyche (cat. 288, pl. 110). Dating to about 1790, both figures lounge against a casket, and a small vase is at their side. The figures are three-dimensional, and their facial features and drapery are finely detailed. They rest on a rough blue ground, and sprays of flowers are scattered at varied intervals.

A second set of bough pots, square in form, has reliefs of cupids representing the four seasons (cat. 285, pl. 111). The shapes of the vessel and the palmlike trees that arch over each figure at the corners were probably derived from Montfaucon from the Saint Genevieve collection (fig. 35).[127] The cupids are adaptations from Flaxman's Marlborough gem, probably produced in 1782, when Flaxman recorded working on "Psyche for a flower pot."[128] These pots date to about 1785.

Fig. 35 *Montfaucon,* L'Antiquité expliquée, *vol. 5, pt. 1, p. 52, pl. 14, fig. 2.* Cabinet of S. Genevieve.

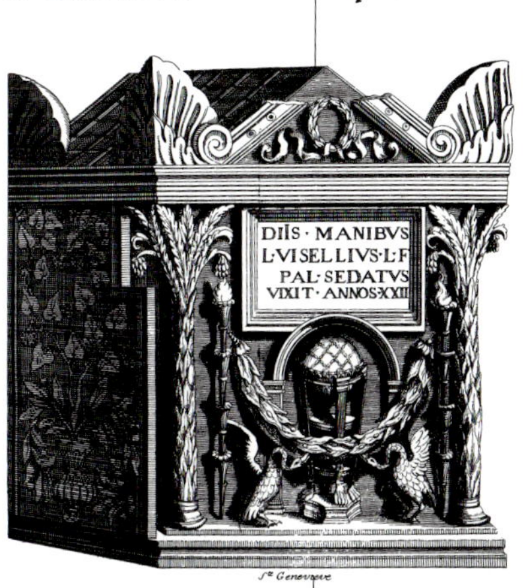

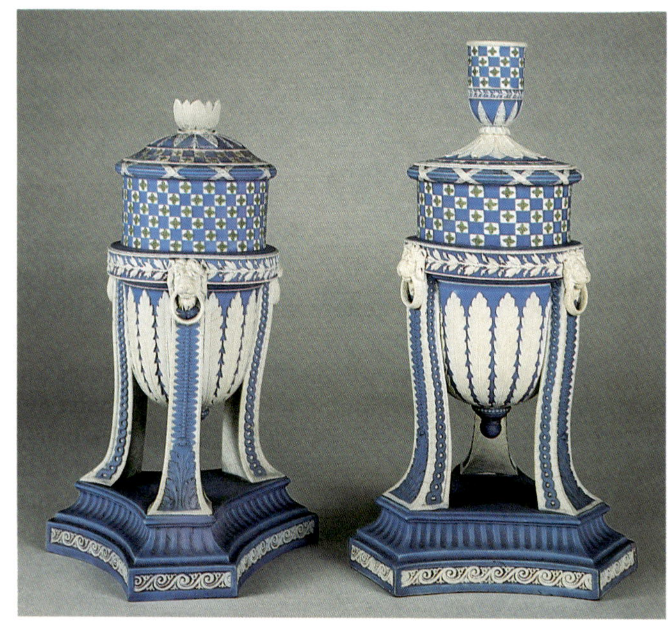

Color plate 112
Pair of Tripod Candle Urns, ca. 1795, jasper, solid white ground with blue wash and green-and-white relief, base solid blue ground with dark blue wash and white relief, 10 13/16" x 4 13/16" (cat. 414).

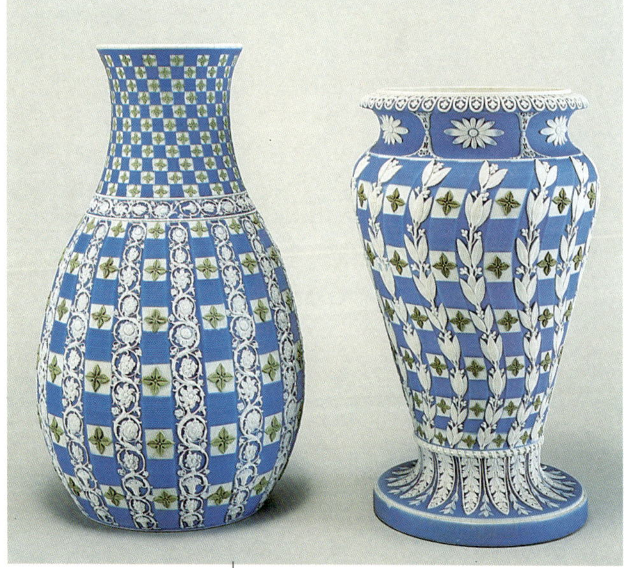

Color plate 113 Left, *Diced Vase, ca. 1785, jasper, solid white ground with blue wash and green-and-white relief, 9 1/2" x 4" (cat. 415);* right, *Vase, ca. 1795, jasper, solid white ground with blue wash and green-and-white relief, 8 1/2" x 4 7/16" (cat. 416).*

Color plate 114 Strapwork, left, *Potpourri Vase, ca. 1795, jasper, solid white ground with blue wash and green-and-white relief, 6 15/16" x 3 3/8" (cat. 412);* center, *Basket and Stand, ca. 1800, jasper, basket: solid white ground with dark blue wash and yellow, green, and white relief, stand: solid blue ground with dark blue wash and yellow, green, and white relief, basket: 4 3/4" x 5 1/4", stand: 8 9/16" (cat. 411);* right, *Potpourri Vase, ca. 1795, jasper, solid white ground with lilac wash and green-and-white relief, 6 11/16" x 3 7/8" (cat. 404).*

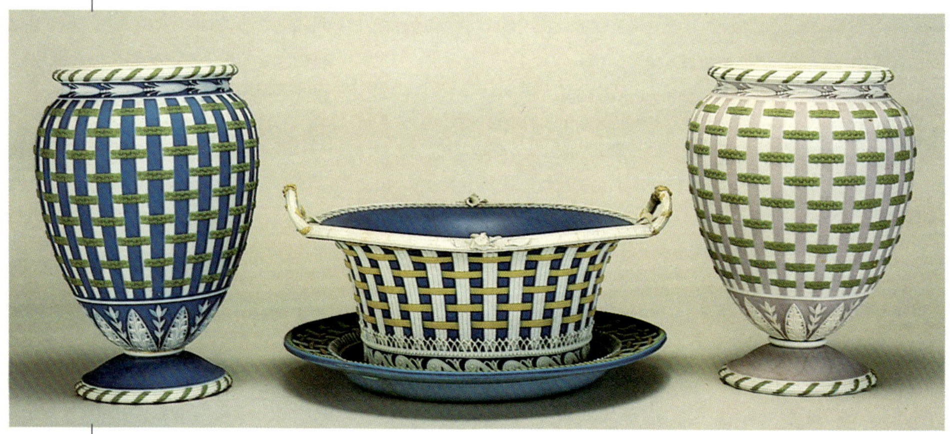

Diced Ware

Use of the potting technique of washing the coarse jasper body with a fine jasper slip enabled Wedgwood to produce a new type of decoration called diced ware (pl. 112). Initiated in 1786, the ware combined two, three, and four colors of jasper on small cabinet pieces. Originally, the "dice," or small squares, and accompanying quatrefoils were individually placed on the ware. This proved much too time-consuming and expensive, but, after the advent of the engine-turning lathe, Wedgwood regularly made diced ware and strapwork in the late eighteenth century. Solid white jasper pieces were washed in one color of jasper, then turned on the lathe. With a series of weights and pulleys and a cutting tool, the engine lathe could pare away a small portion of the outer wash at regular intervals, producing a checkered design of alternating squares of white and color. After this process was complete, jasper bas-relief ornaments, primarily quatrefoils in white or a third color, were applied to the piece. The Beeson collection is fortunate to have many examples of diced ware, in blue, lilac, green, and black, considered to be among the finest pieces of the end of Wedgwood's career. Two examples of eighteenth-century quality are a large vase and a flower holder; both have a dark blue jasper wash on a white ground with applied, green quatrefoils (cats. 415, 416, pl. 113).

Strapwork

A second form of decoration was a simple strapwork initially produced by the same method used to produce diced ware—that is, by cutting away the layer of the jasper wash with the engine lathe. Individual pieces of strapwork were then added to the body to form an intertwined pattern, a method that required of the artisan great skill. The Beeson collection has a small number of these pieces, but of particular interest is a flower vase of lilac wash with green strapwork (cat. 404, pl. 114) White bellflowers ring the upper rim, while foliage decorates the base of the body. A white reed and green ribbon border the foot and neck. The piece is not marked, but the crackled appearance on the base and the sump cover inside are both characteristic of eighteenth-century jasper ware.

Jewelry

Toward the end of the eighteenth century, England overshadowed France as the fashion capital of the world. Small accessories for dressing became extremely popular, and, as invoices of the period show, Wedgwood medallions mounted as jewelry were in constant and great demand. Produced from 1775 onward in the various jasper colors but chiefly in blue and white, the medallions used in jewelry were made of solid-colored jasper and jasper wash, often with beveled and lapidary-polished edges. Some double-sided examples were made which entailed the fusing of two medallions back to back, leaving a groove around the edges to accommodate the metal mount. The mounts were readily available, made by the over two hundred mounters known to have been working in Staffordshire and London. The metalsmith Matthew Boulton was known to have worked with Wedgwood and is frequently credited as the maker of his cut-steel mounts for jasper-ware medallions. Wedgwood wrote to Boulton on June 14, 1786: "I have left a few sets of my cameo buttons to be mounted, & shall be glad to increase our connection in this way, as well in selling you cameos for your trade, as in having them mounted by you for mine, both in gilt metal & steel, or in any other better way which your inventive genius may strike out."[129] More durable than marcasite mounts, which were also produced during this period, the steel was cut, chiselled, and filed into facets that, when polished, looked like diamonds. Wedgwood is known to have supplied Boulton with jasper medallions for shoe buckles, bracelets, brooches, buttons, chatelaines, necklaces, and watch fobs for silver and cut-steel mounts.

In the Beeson collection are a number of notable pieces of eighteenth-century cut-steel, mounted jewelry. One chatelaine or man's watch fob has multiple drops with three medallions and one intaglio seal (cat. 535). The longest drop ends in a medallion of Diomedes and the Palladium on a swivel on one side and a polished intaglio of Apollo and Marsyas on the other side. All are surrounded by cut-steel beads and frames.

A woman's chatelaine, which has a clasp so that it could be worn over the belt, has four drops of cut-steel loops and beads (cat. 536). The top medallion is of a nymph with a mirror. A separate gilt book with ivory pages is an unusual addition to the piece.

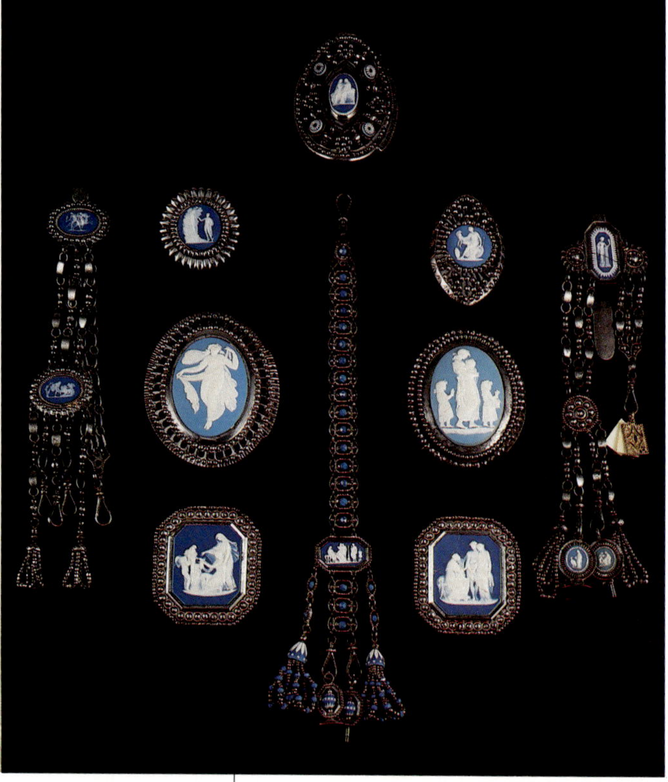

Color plate 115 *Selection of jasper-ware jewelry with steel cut mounts, eighteenth and nineteenth century (cats. 528, 529, 530, 531, 533, 534, 540, 541, 543).*

An oval woman's belt buckle has applied cut-steel beads on steel and four small, round, jasper medallions flowers as a part of an open-work frame (cat. 540, pl. 115). The frame supports a medallion of two classical figures. One side of this buckle is perforated so that it could be sewn to a belt or girdle.

A bracelet-and-brooch set has basalt intaglios framed by a row of round, silver gilt beads (cats. 538, 562). The bracelet has nine intaglios of graduated sizes; each intaglio bears the visage of a different pope and is marked "W&B" or "Wedgwood & Bentley," and most have an identification number. The largest intaglio is an extremely rare piece with a white wash of jasper or white terra-cotta stoneware on the back of a basalt front. A seal also attached to the bracelet has an intaglio of a nude female figure. The brooch is a portrait of a gentleman set in silver gilt beads with a convex back. The back is marked "Wedgwood & Bentley 237." Number 237 in the 1787 *Ornamental Catalogue* refers to Pope Leo XI. The ensemble probably dates to about 1775.

Another notable set of nineteenth-century jewelry features earrings of dark blue wash on white ground jasper and a bracelet with white, mythological reliefs (cats. 545, 561). Each tapered drop earring is suspended from a round jasper medallion with a flower that has a jargoon at its center. The bracelet has five double-faced medallions alternating with four flower medallions with jargoons matching the earrings. The set is mounted in gold and linked by gold chains.

George Stubbs is credited with the design for a series of nineteen horse studies for jasper-ware coat buttons which were modeled by Edward Burch in about 1788 or 1789. Having been copied by Bert Bentley, an early-twentieth-century jasper plaque of all nineteen examples, marked "Horse Studies," by G. Stubbs, R.A., exists at the Wedgwood Museum in Barlaston. The Beeson collection has three of these horses (although not set in jewelry mounts), two in solid blue-and-white jasper and the other in dark blue jasper wash (cats. 937, 938). The two solid examples have lapidary-polished edges; they are marked "WEDGWOOD" in uppercase letters and date to about 1790.

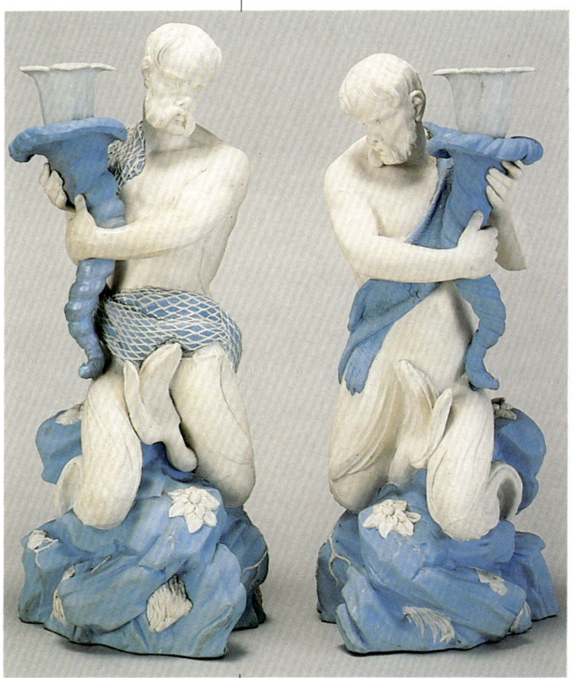

Color plate 116
Pair of Candlesticks, Triton, *ca. 1790, jasper, solid blue ground and solid white figures with white relief, 11 1/8" (cat. 297).*

Figures

Figures in basalt were commonly made by Wedgwood in the eighteenth century and particularly in the nineteenth century. A limited number were made in jasper, as cited by Robin Reilly, and some were listed in the *Ornamental Catalogue* of 1787.[130] Extant examples include statues of Mars, Venus, and Jupiter, made in about 1785. With one major exception, the jasper figures in the Beeson collection are represented in the chess set or are part of ewers, vases, or candlesticks. A most unusual pair of candlesticks displays the mythological figure of Triton, whose human torso ends in a fish tail (cat. 297, pl. 116). Triton was the son of Poseidon and Amphitrite, and in these candlesticks he holds a type of conch shell that he is often seen blowing in other artistic representations; in this example, the conch shell was designed to hold the candle. In the archives at the Wedgwood Museum are manuscripts dated September 25, 1769, and belonging to modelers Hoskins and Grant; they note "a mould of Triton from the bronze" which they were most likely producing for Wedgwood. This bronze Triton may have been the one which William Chambers acquired during his travels to Rome in the 1750s; he is known to have lent a Triton to both Wedgwood and Matthew Boulton in the 1770s.[131] This Triton was later paired with its mirror image by sculptor John Bacon.[132] Wedgwood first listed the figures in the 1773 *Ornamental Catalogue* as being after Michelangelo, but the design was probably inspired by Giovanni Lorenzo Bernini, for Wedgwood's candlesticks resemble a composite of various statues designed by Bernini from three different fountains in Rome.[133] The Wedgwood examples are thought to have possibly been modeled by Flaxman or Keeling, but Thomas Boot is recorded as having also made Tritons. A biscuit model of the Triton exists in the Wedgwood Museum in Barlaston, Stoke-on-Trent. Such candlesticks are seen by Wedgwood in basalt, caneware, and majolica as well as jasper ware.

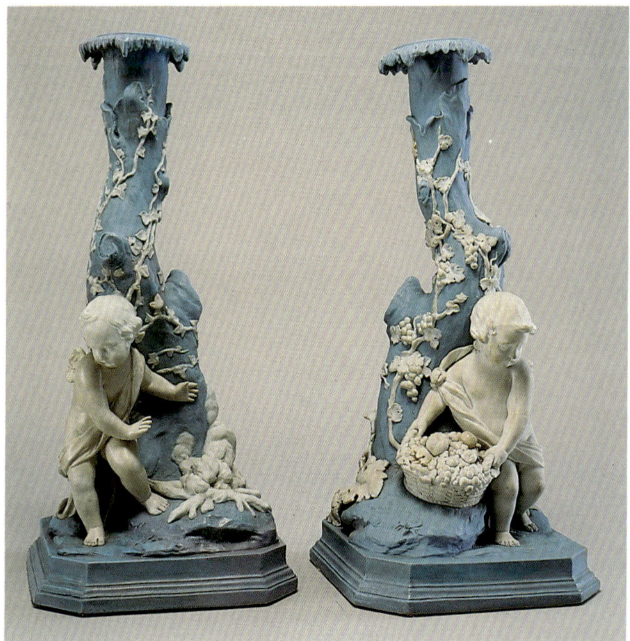

Color plate 117
Pair of Candlesticks, Autumn *and* Winter, *ca. 1785, jasper, solid blue ground and solid white figures with white relief, 10 3/8" (cat. 286).*

Another pair of jasperware, solid-blue-and-solid-white candlesticks in the collection is accented with figures of cherubs representing autumn and winter (cat. 286, pl. 117). Between 1726 and 1730, Thomson published a series of books entitled *The Four Seasons,*[134] which may have been the design source or inspiration for Wedgwood's piece. The candlesticks display a cupid at the base of a tree trunk acting as the candle holder. The scene of autumn depicts the cupid with a basket full of the fruits from the harvest; the winter candlestick has a cupid warming himself by a small fire. Both Hackwood and Flaxman have been credited as the modelers of these candlesticks, which were produced between 1785 and 1790.

Between 1783 and 1785, John Flaxman designed for Wedgwood a set of chessmen, the drawing for which is still in the Wedgwood Museum in Barlaston, England (pl. 118).[135] Chess was a popular pastime in the eighteenth century, and Wedgwood made approximately one hundred sets between 1785 and 1795; the figures were reissued in about 1865. On February 20, 1784, Wedgwood wrote to Flaxman, "We are getting foreward with the Chessmen, & hope soon to send a complete set to Greek street."[136] In the Beeson collection are twenty-six of Wedgwood's original thirty-two figures in solid blue-and-white jasper ware (cat. 628, pl. 119). Ten pieces in this set are thought to be eighteenth century, because they have small round bases with a groove around the top of the base, a hole in the center bottom, and show crazing or shrinkage marks on the body.[137] The king and queen are thought to be portraits of John Philip Kemble and Sarah Siddons, a well-known sister-brother team of English actors famous for their Shakespearean roles. The sets appeared in various colors—light blue, lilac, brown, white, gray-green, and green. The figures are medieval in style, in contrast with the classical forms and themes of the rest of Wedgwood's ware of this time.

As previously stated, there is one exception to the jasper figures in the Beeson collection as being represented in the chess set or as part of ewers, vases, or candlesticks. The exception, however, is an exceedingly important figure: *Britannia Triumphant* (cat. 279, pls. 120, 121). Made of solid white jasper with a white jasper wash and solid blue jasper with a blue jasper wash, the figure is also decorated with a small amount of green relief. The base has thirteen firing holes.

Britannia Triumphant was undoubtedly produced to glorify the British naval victories over France between 1798 and 1809. This female figure holds the portrait

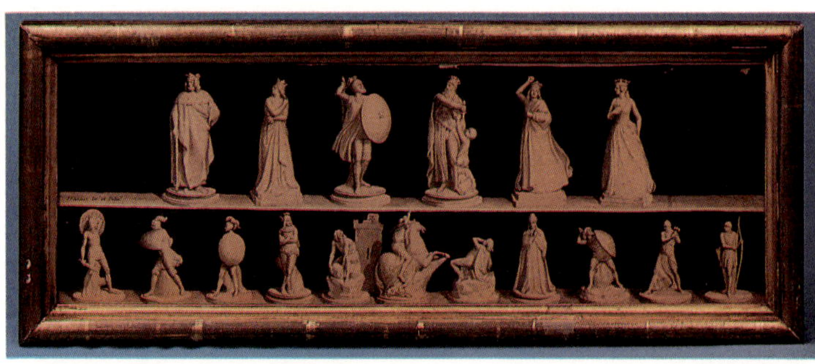

Color plate 118
John Flaxman, Jr., Drawing for a Chess Set, ca. 1785, pen, ink, and wash, signed: J Flaxman Invt et Delint, *6 7/8" x 20 3/8". Courtesy of the Trustees of the Wedgwood Museum, Barlaston, Stoke-on-Trent, England.*

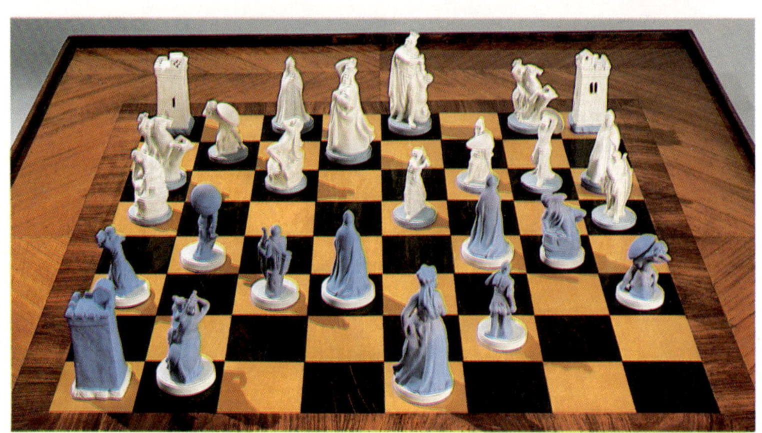

Color plate 119
Twenty-six Chessmen, ca. 1790 and nineteenth century, John Flaxman (1755-1826), designer, jasper, solid white and solid blue, 3 5/16" (greatest height) (cat. 628).

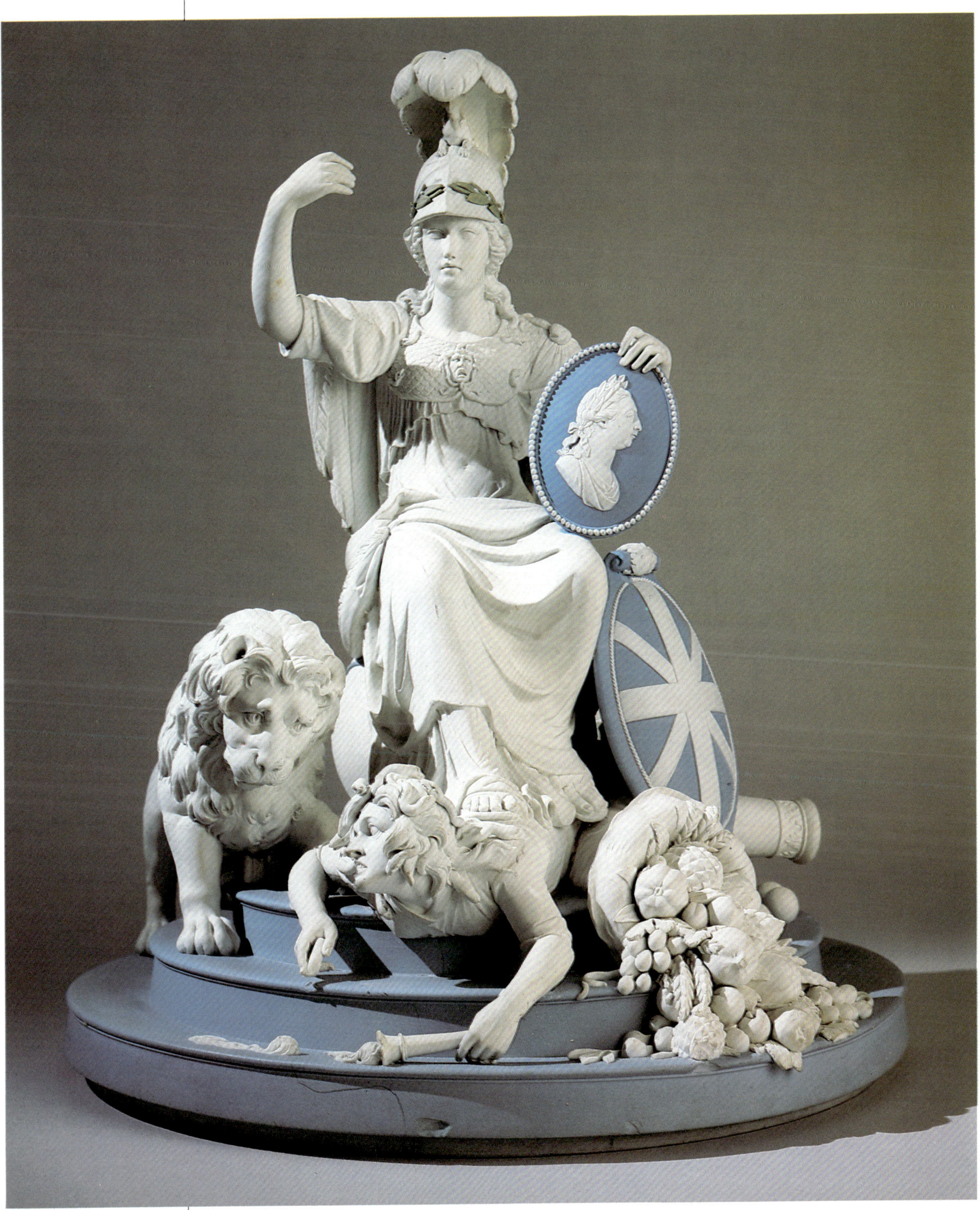

Color plate 120 *Figure,* Britannia Triumphant, *1798-1809, attributed to John Flaxman, Jr., modeler, jasper, solid blue with blue wash, and solid white with white wash and green relief, 13" x 11 7/16" (cat. 279).*

medallion of George III in her left hand and originally held a trident in her right hand. By her side sits the British lion.[138] At her feet and closely watched by the lion lies a fallen female figure representing France. A shield ornamented with the British flag, a cannon and balls, a ship's prow, and an overturned cornucopia surround Britannia.

Britannia was pictured in a hand-colored aquatint attributed to Wedgwood and Byerley, York Street, Saint James Square, in the February 1809 edition of Rudolph Ackermann's *Repository of the Arts* (fig. 36).[139] The original watercolor was painted by Thomas Hosmer Shepherd (1793-1864) when he was fifteen years old. Britannia is depicted in the center of the showroom underneath a domed temple on a large barrel pedestal. In the mold storage room at the Wedgwood Museum in Barlaston, England, molds for the barrel pedestal are dated April 26, 1800, and molds for the temple are marked "Theed's temple / March 1801."[140] William Theed (1764-1817) was a modeler who worked for Wedgwood from 1798 until 1804, when he left to design for the London silversmiths Rundell, Bridge, and Rundell. A wooden simulation of the temple now surrounds the figure at the Birmingham Museum of Art. Also at the Wedgwood Museum in Barlaston are two false-brick, barrel pedestals made originally to accommodate Britannia. The pedestals are ornamented with four portrait medallions of the great admirals: Admiral Lord Horatio Nelson (1758-1805), Admiral Viscount Adam Duncan (1731-1804), Admiral Richard Howe (1726-99), and Admiral John Jervis St. Vincent (1735-1823). The Nelson medallion was modeled by John De Vaere on November 9, 1798 (receipt I-22); the last three medallions were invoiced on December 24, 1798, by De Vaere (receipt I-23). These medallions are set in pairs between applied arched niches possibly intended for figures.

Henry Webber has been identified as the modeler of Britannia. Webber supposedly adaptated his Britannia from his earlier figure of Minerva, a statue he had, in turn, copied from a life-size statue of Britannia modeled by his teacher, John Bacon, Sr., for the tomb of the earl of Chatham, William Pitt the elder (1708-78), in Westminster Abbey. Robin Reilly calls into question this attribution to Webber: no documentation to support it has been found, and it is doubtful that he could have created such a sophisticated work when he had been employed at the factory only six months when the Minerva was first fired (as recorded in the oven books from December 8 through December 21 of 1782).[141] It seems more reasonable to attribute the modeling of the Minerva (still with the earl of Chatham's tomb as a possible design source) and the later Britannia to John Flaxman sometime between 1798, when the portrait medallions for Britannia's base were made, and 1809, when the Britannia was pictured in the York Street showroom print. (Even though Josiah Wedgwood I was deceased by this time, continuing market-

Color plate 121
Detail, Britannia Triumphant.

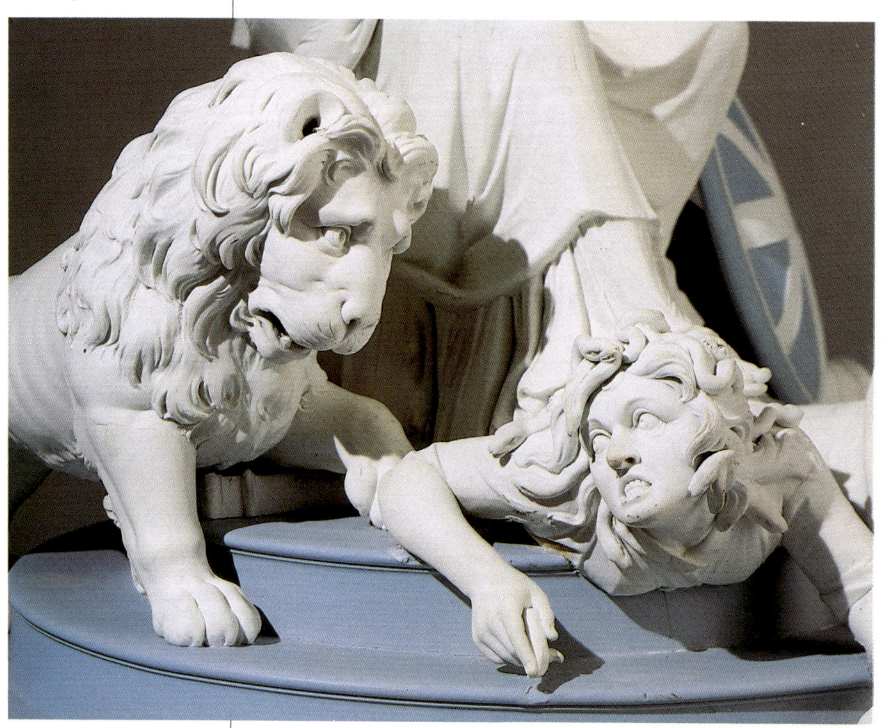

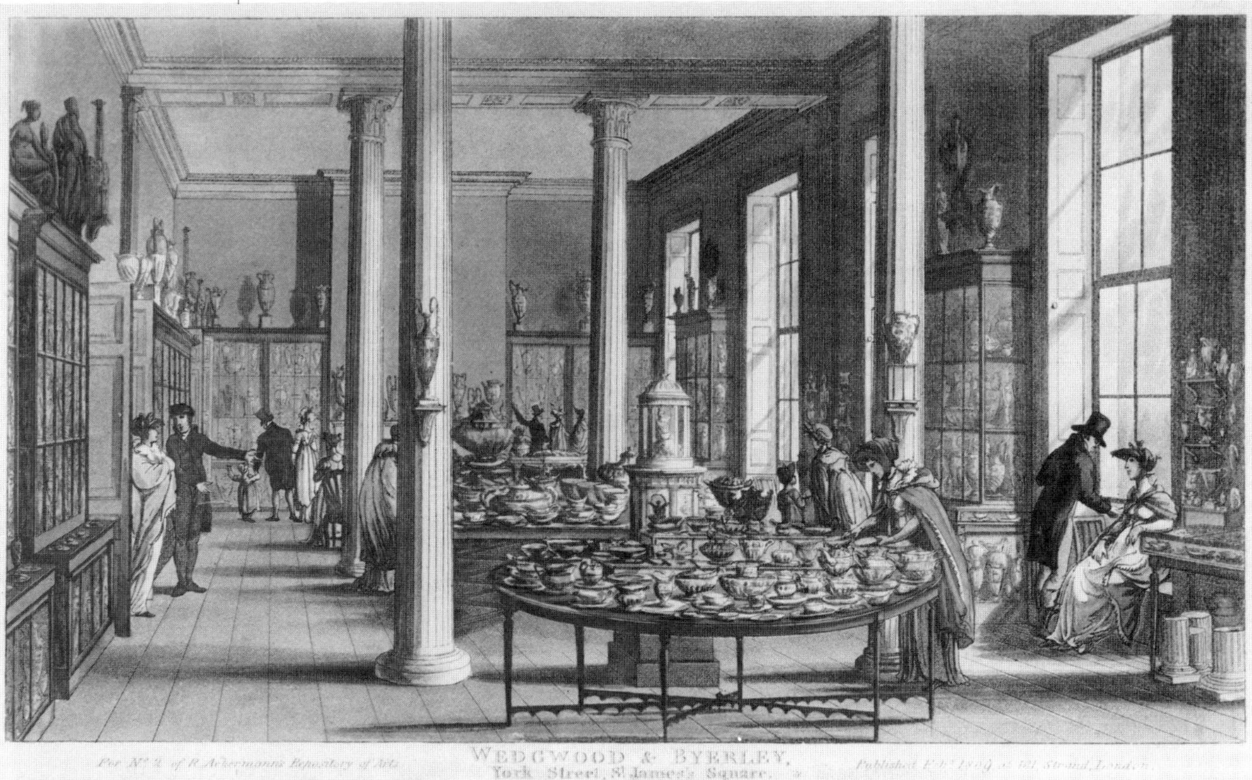

Fig. 36 *Wedgwood and Byerley, York Street, Saint James Square, showroom as depicted in hand-colored aquatint in Rudolph Ackermann's* Repository of the Arts, *February 1809, pl. 2. The original watercolor was drawn by Thomas Hosmer Shepherd (1793-1864) when he was fifteen years old. After the death of Josiah Wedgwood I, his son, Josiah Wedgwood II, and his nephew, Thomas Byerley, purchased the new showroom.*

ing schemes suggest that the introduction of the Britannia coincided with or followed close upon the publication of the pictorial rendition.)

Other circumstances substantiate the attribution to John Flaxman. He created figures similar to those manufactured by Wedgwood, and he frequently used the two allegorical figures of Minerva and Britannia, considered interchangeable on war monuments. In 1784, for example, Flaxman drew for Wedgwood a design for *The Manufacturers' Arms,* which included a seated figure of Britannia at the top. In 1799, Flaxman drew two more Britannias, these for a Napoleonic memorial competition: the first depicted a triumphal arch surmounted by a seated Britannia, the lion, and ship's prows (fig. 37); the second depicted a "Colossal Statue of Britannia for Greenwich Hill." This statue Flaxman actually modeled and exhibited at the Royal Academy in 1801 (now in the Soane Museum); it was justified with a pamphlet written by Flaxman himself.[142] (Neither drawing was ever commissioned.) Three years later, in 1802, the Treasury Committee of National Monuments commissioned Flaxman, along with four other sculptors, to create a series of individual memorials for the heroes of the Napoleonic Wars to be located in Saint Paul's Cathedral in London. Flaxman's memorial sculpture to Admiral Richard Howe depicts a life-sized, seated Britannia, with trident, atop the prow of the galley *Queen Charlotte*; the face of this Britannia is remarkably like that of the

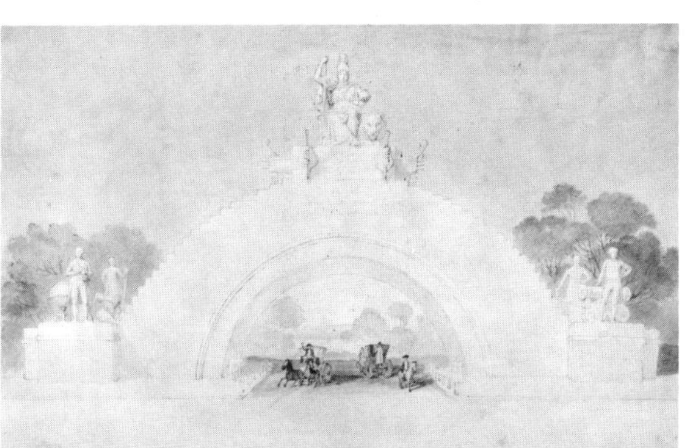

Fig. 37 *John Flaxman, Jr.,* Triumphal Arch Surmounted by Britannia, *1799, pen and ink, and pencil, 11 3/4" x 19", The Art Museum, Princeton University.*

Wedgwood example. The British lion rests peacefully on a second level below her feet. In 1807 Flaxman created yet another similar monument, this time to honor Lord Nelson, and he again utilized the figure of Britannia, this time called Minerva, accompanied by the British lion. In relation to the Wedgwood Britannia, this Minerva has the detail of the feathered helmet with sphinx, but even more similar is the decorative breastplate of the Medusa on both examples.[143]

In conclusion, there is little documentary evidence that John Flaxman did much more work for Wedgwood after 1787, when he went to study in Rome, although correspondence does exist between the two in 1790, and Flaxman was obviously still in some favor with the factory, as he was commissioned to design Wedgwood's tomb in 1795. Wedgwood's jasper figures and busts of the 1780s, of which there are few, have yet to be attributed to a specific modeler. Yet in the Mayer collection of the Liverpool City Museums is a circa-1802 jasper clock case of a female figure, symbolizing "Peace Destroying the Implements of War," which is quite similar in design and modeling to the figure of Britannia. In 1786 Josiah Wedgwood referred to a design of this character in a letter to John Flaxman, stating, "The burning of the implements of war and the figure of peace, then must form another group."[144] Although inconclusive, this statement gives additional credence to the belief that Flaxman was the designer of this small group of large figures.[145] If Flaxman did indeed design and model the Minerva of 1782, the figure could have been reused and he could have altered it for Britannia between 1798 and 1809, when he was so actively utilizing Britannia and Minerva for his tomb designs. It is hoped that future research will affirm or disaffirm Flaxman's involvement.

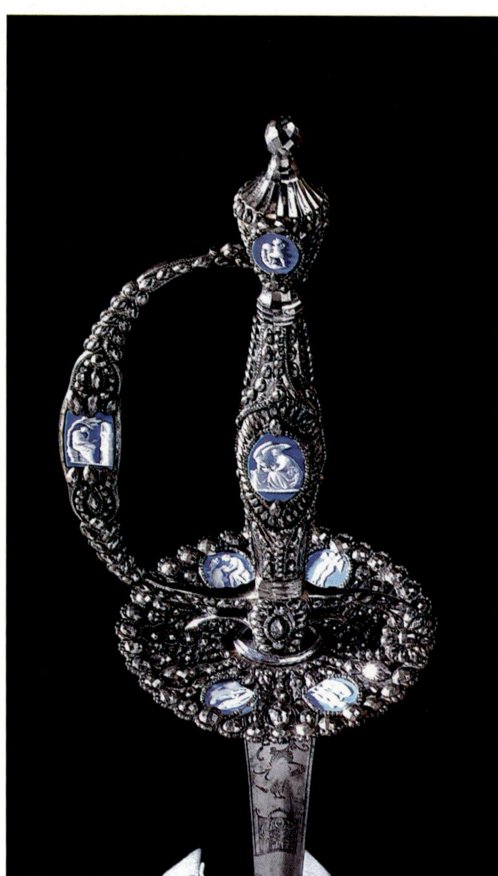

Color plate 122
Detail, Small-sword (color plate 123), inlaid with ten medallions.

Oddities

In his effort to accommodate the desires of the eighteenth-century market, Wedgwood produced a number of objects considered by many to be oddities, a few of which are found in the Beeson collection. A rare and outstanding example is a small-sword of about 1790, ornamented with ten blue-and-white jasper medallions set into a hilt faceted with steel-cut studs and beads (cat. 403, pls. 122, 123). The sword has a vase-shaped pommel first used on swords around 1780 due to the influence of Hamilton's *Antiquités*. These faceted swords, encrusted with neoclassical motifs, were standard for civilian court dress in Great Britain from the late eighteenth century to the present. Examples with Wedgwood medallions exist in a number of collections.[146] A few of the manufacturers of these swords include Thomas Gray, Sackville Street, London; the firm of Grancher in Paris; and Matthew Boulton, John Fothergill, and James Watt of Birmingham. In the Boulton pattern

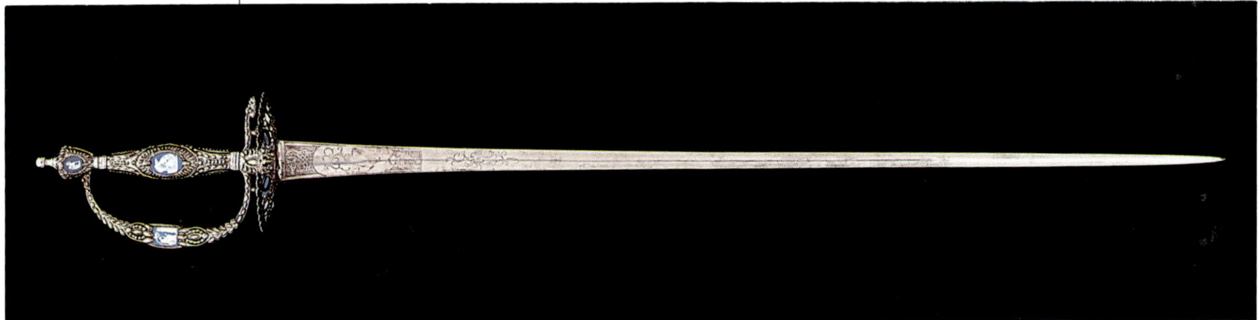

Color plate 123
Small-sword, ca. 1790, Jasper, solid white ground with dark blue wash, white relief, steel, and cut-steel mounts, 34" (cat. 403).

book in Birmingham, England, are hilts drawn with blank settings accompanied by the label "I Wd Cameos," which must refer to Wedgwood cameo and medallions.[147] Unless the sword is marked, however, the manufacturer is almost impossible to prove.[148] The sword in the Beeson collection dates from about 1790.

Another "oddity," scent flasks in a wide variety of shapes, were manufactured by most of the porcelain factories in the eighteenth century and were used by both men and women. Wedgwood's small jasper medallions of both classical and public figures lent themselves well to adorning scent flasks; their metallic fittings, which included small stoppers and chains attached to the necks of the scent flasks, were possibly the work of Boulton and Fothergill. Wedgwood wrote to his son Josiah on April 16, 1788:

> I think I wrote you before that some smelling bottles with Henry IV of France on one side, & his minister Sully on the other, would be very acceptable. The heads are too large I know for this purpose, but they will easily be made less, by shrinking & taking away part of the shoulder. . . . I shall send you some other heads for these purposes very soon.[149]

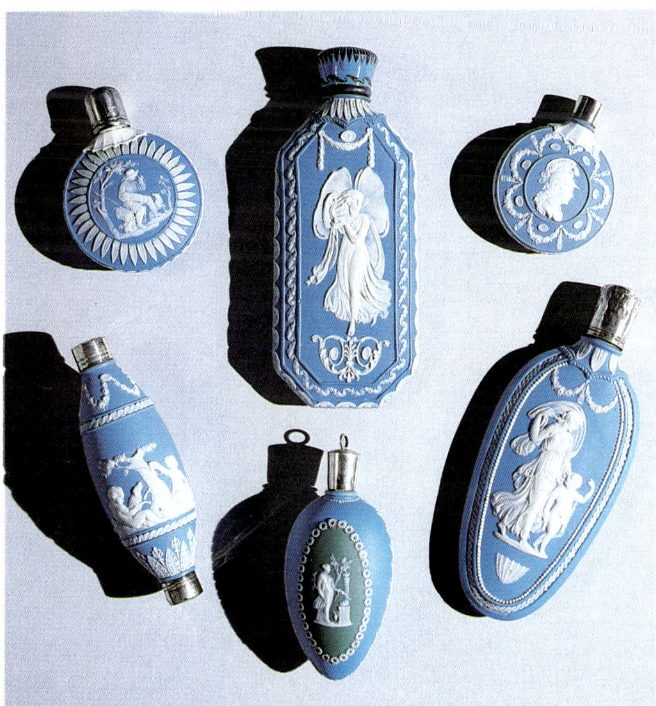

Color plate 124
Selection of jasperware scent bottles with silver stoppers, eighteenth and nineteenth century (cats. 492-500).

The Beeson collection is fortunate to have nine such flasks (cats. 492-500, pl. 124), two of which are double-sided scent flasks used for storing two different types of perfume, or for smelling salts. Each has a blue granulated surface with playful cupids in white relief. They are unmarked, but probably date to between 1785 and 1790.

Yet another oddity that Wedgwood produced was an oval paint box that he listed in his 1779 *Ornamental Catalogue*: "The Paint-Chests contain Sets of large and small Vessels, and neat Palats [*sic*] for the Use of those who paint in Water colours." The jasper box of solid blue ground with white relief in the Beeson collection dates

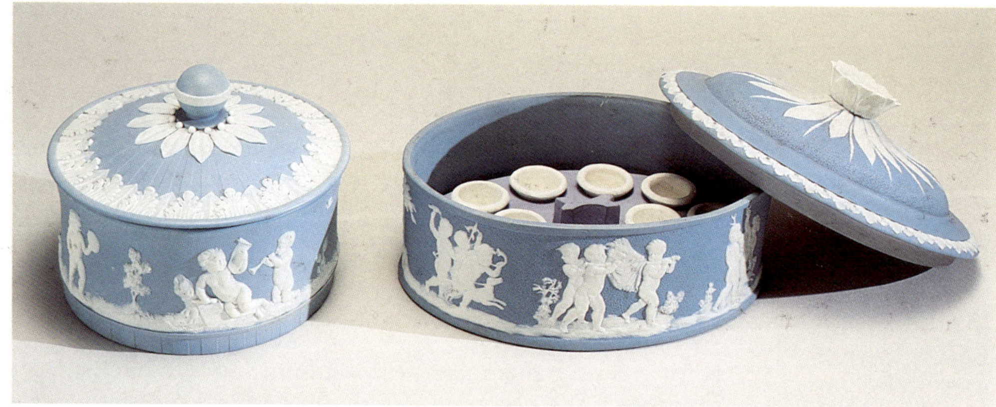

Color plate 125
Left, *Covered Cosmetic Box,* Boys at Play, *ca. 1790, jasper, solid blue ground and white relief, 3 7/8" x 4 1/2" (cat. 624);* right, *Paint Box,* Cupids Bringing Home the Game, *ca. 1785, jasper, solid blue granulated ground with white relief, 3 5/8" x 6" (cat. 373).*

to about 1785 and is elaborate in its decoration, with figures of cupid bringing home the game and playing music (cat. 373, pl. 125). The ground is granulated on the box's sides as well as on its top, which has a finial in the shape of a lotus blossom surrounded by leaves. The paint box contains two palettes and twelve small cups in a holder for the different paint colors. A second box, dating to between 1785 and 1795, is round, with a cover and underdish, and was intended for holding cosmetics (cat. 624, pl. 125). It is also solid blue jasper with white relief and marked "WEDGWOOD," with uppercase letters set separately. The cover and bowl have engine-turning; the cover is decorated with bas-relief of leafage. The figures of seven boys at play on the side of the box may have been designed by Lady Diana Beauclerk.

Trophy Plates

In the Beeson collection are five trophy plates from the late nineteenth century (cats. 337, 346, 347, 348, 350, pl. 126). Elaborately decorated with up to 170 separately applied reliefs, these plates have at least six different borders, which include quatrefoils, tiny mythological scenes, and ram's heads with garlands. Typical interior bas-relief subjects include the muses grooming Pegasus, Aurora in her chariot, the muses watering Pegasus (originally designed by Flaxman in 1775), and Bellerophon watering Pegasus. The color range encompasses Wedgwood's entire palette in jasper ware. A green-and-white example in the collection is marked faintly on the back "H. G. S. & F. C. S. / Winchester or Manchester, January 8th, 1880," an inscription that indicates it may have been intended as an anniversary gift (cat. 337). The name "trophy" plate was used in reference to ancient examples that depicted trophies of war and peace. These plates continue to be produced today and may have been the antecedent of the commemorative plates of the twentieth century.

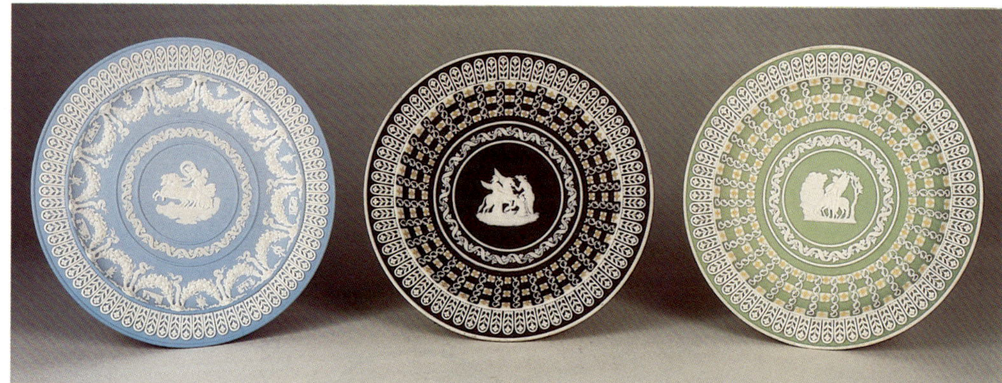

Color plate 126
Trophy Plates, left, Aurora in Her Chariot, *nineteenth century, jasper, solid blue ground with white relief, l8 13/16" (cat. 348);* center, Muses Grooming Pegasus, *nineteenth century, jasper, solid white ground with black wash and yellow-and-white relief, 8 3/4" (cat. 350);* right, Bellerophon Watering Pegasus, *nineteenth century, jasper, solid white ground with green wash and yellow-and-white relief, 8 9/16" (cat. 337).*

Summary

The quantity and diversity of jasper-ware objects grew throughout the eighteenth and nineteenth centuries. The intaglios alone numbered more than seventeen hundred, and there were also vases, tablets, medallions, flower holders, ewers, punch kettles, monteiths, and bowls (cat. 367, pl. 127), with the variety of designs ever increasing. Small items, such as snuffboxes, patch boxes, opera glasses, scent bottles, and jewelry, were also quite popular (cats. 520-26, pl. 128). The quality of all the eighteenth-century pieces is quite high: the white figures have great detail

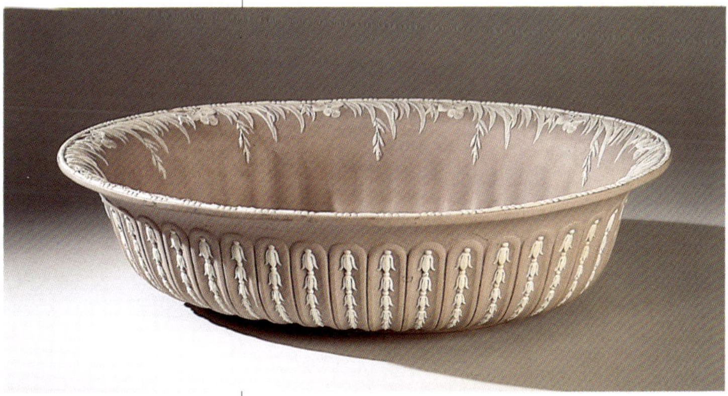

Color plate 127 *Bowl, ca. 1785, jasper, solid lilac ground with white relief, 3 1/4" x 13" (cat. 367). This oval bowl is a rare example of solid lilac jasper. The bas-relief ornamentation shows the use of the aquatic plants plus the classical motifs of the bead and reel edge and bellflowers. The rippled interior reveals the use of a mold for forming the body of the bowl.*

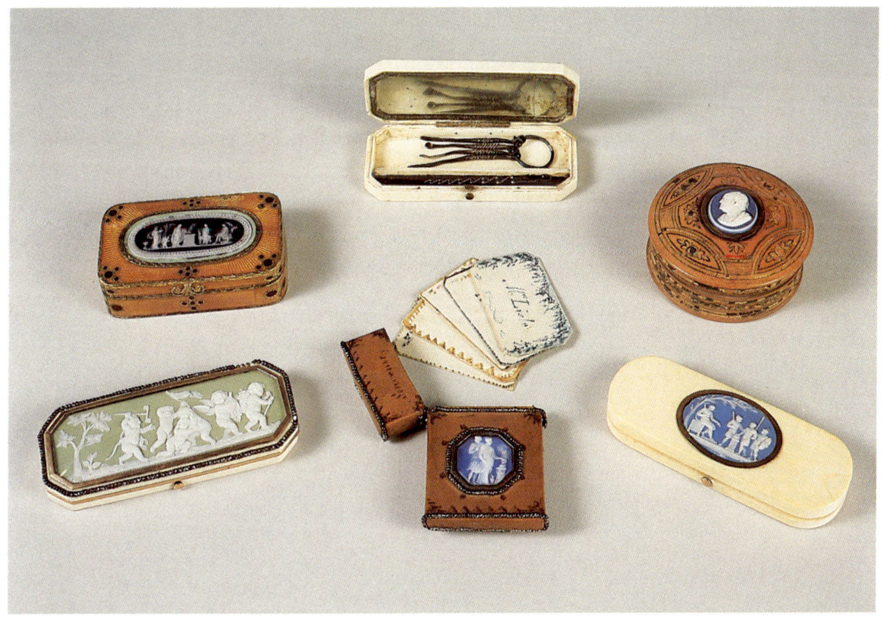

Color plate 128 Clockwise from top, *Patch Box with Toilet Implements,* Six Classical Figures, *ca. 1800, ivory box with jasper medallion in blue ground with white relief set in gold and fitted with steel toilet implements, medallion: 2 3/4" x 1", box: 3 5/8" x 1 1/2" (cat. 523); Snuff Box,* Portrait of Benjamin Franklin, *ca. 1780, wooden box with jasper medallion in solid white ground with dark blue laminate front and back and white relief, cameo: 7/8" x 3/4", box: 2 1/2" (cat. 522); Patch Box,* Mucius Scaevola before Lars Porsena, *ca. 1800, ivory box with jasper medallion in solid blue ground with white relief set in gold, plaquette: 1 7/16" x 1 1/8", box: 3 5/8" x 1 3/8" (cat. 526); Card Case,* Souvenir Danube, *ca. 1800, wooden case with two jasper medallions in solid white ground with blue wash and white relief, beeds, plaquette: 7/8", case: 2 5/8" x 1 3/4" (cat. 524); Patch Box, ca. 1800, ivory box with jasper medallion in solid green ground with white relief set in gold, plaquette: 3 7/16" (cat. 521); Patch Box, ca. 1800, gold and enamel box with jasper medallion in solid white ground with black-and-green wash and white relief, plaquette: 2 1/8" x 1 1/8", box: 2 7/8" x 1 7/8" (cat 520).*

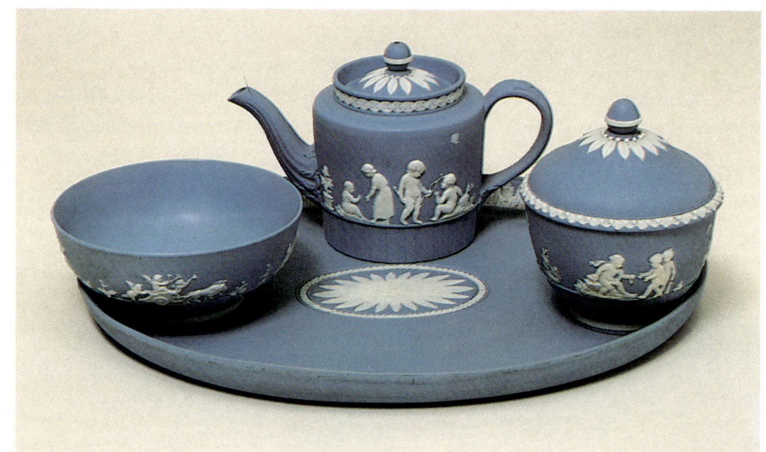

Color plate 129 Left, *Bowl,* Boys at Play, *ca. 1790, jasper, solid blue ground with white relief and engine-turning, 2 1/8" x 1 1/2" (cat. 317); Partial Dejeuner Set, ca. 1790, jasper, solid blue ground with white relief and engine-turning on teapot and sugar, pot: 4 1/4" x 3 1/4", sugar: 4 1/4" x 1 7/8", tray, 12 5/8" x 10 1/8" (cats. 318, 319). Note the fine quality of the relief on the eighteenth-century Dejeuner Set versus that on the nineteenth-century example (color plate 130). Further is the profusion of decoration, the shapes of the vessels, particularly the size of the cups, and the lack of engine-turning on objects made during the nineteenth century.*

and are almost translucent in their application, and the overall design of these objects seems to be closer to the original classical examples (pl. 129). In nineteenth-century examples, the reliefs are chalky, with less attention having been paid to application and detail; these same reliefs are often cracked during the vitrification (pl. 130).

From its invention until around 1820, jasper ware was readily made in three ways: a colored jasper slip over a white body, a colored slip over a colored body, and a solidly colored body. After about 1810 there began to be a decline in production of the number of larger pieces, and, after about 1820, only small, insignificant items were made.[150] At about that time it seems that the formula was lost, and the production of jasper ware ceased. It was replaced by the white stoneware (white porcelain) covered with a jasper wash. Josiah Bateman II wrote: "Very large pieces of ware were formerly made of jasper, but there was always much difficulty in it, the body for these purposes was coarsely ground. . . . There is considerable loss in making bisque ware [porcelain] with jasper bas reliefs."[151] This "porcelain" ware, as it was called at Etruria, replaced solid jasper until Francis Wedgwood reintroduced solid jasper in colors of pale blue, green, and lilac in 1860 (pl. 131). In 1866 he wrote:

> We have made a good deal of jasper since we began making solid Jasper again—it is not so good as the old has not such a waxy surface & is not so sharp

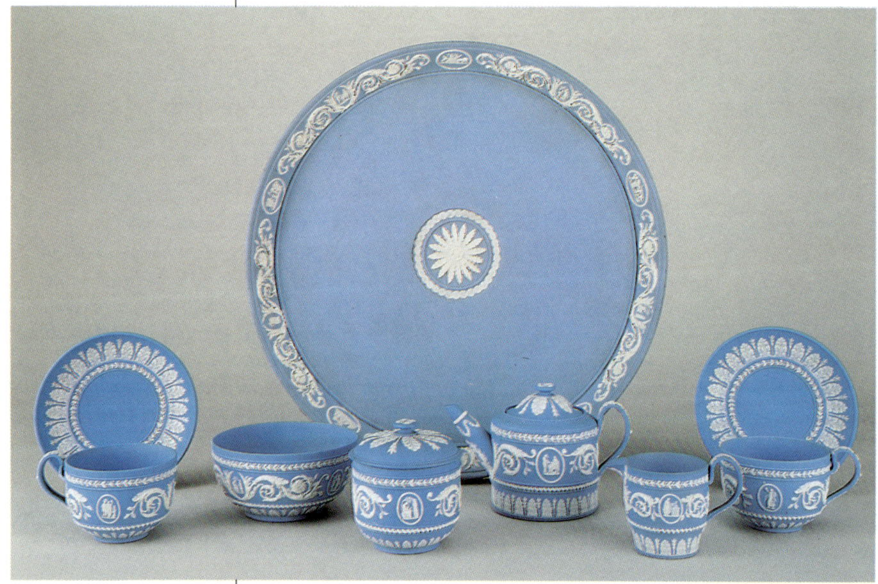

Color plate 130 *Seven-Piece Dejeuner Set, nineteenth century, jasper, solid blue ground with white relief, tray: 15 1/4", sugar: 3 9/16" x 2", creamer: 2 1/2" x 1 7/8", cups: 2 3/8" x 1 5/6", saucer: 5 7/16", waster: 2 5/16" x 1 1/2" (cat. 349).*

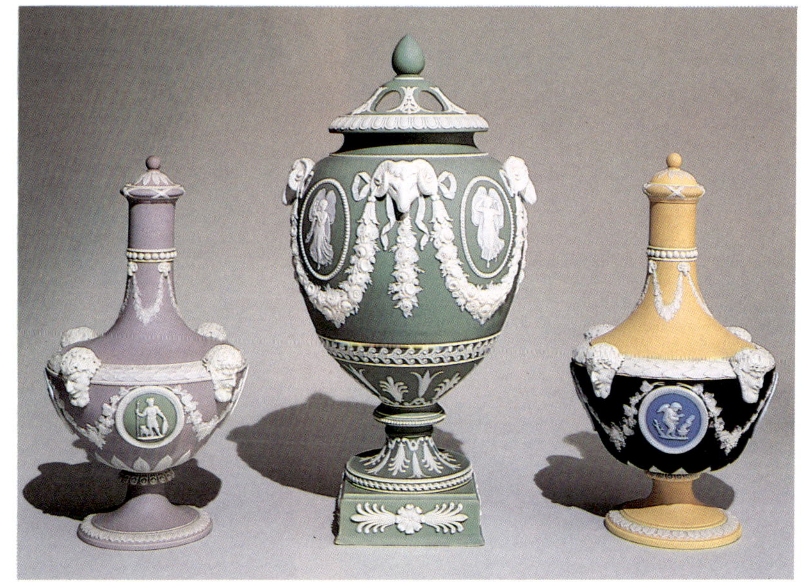

Color plate 131
Left, *One of a Pair of Barber Bottles, 1867, jasper, solid white ground with lilac-and-green wash and white relief, 10 1/16" x 3 3/4" (cat. 391);* center, *Potpourri Vase,* Horae, *nineteenth century, jasper, solid white ground with green wash and white relief, 13 1/7" x 4 1/16" (cat. 617);* right, *Barber Bottle, nineteenth century, jasper, solid white ground with brown, yellow, and blue wash and white relief, 10 9/16" x 3 7/8" (cat. 392).*

> & yet dryer so that it soils & when the soiling is well rubbed in a nailbrush & soap will not get it out it seems that the surface is full of little broken bubbles which hold the dirt. An old piece I had which had a very nice waxy feel had the same dirty specks but much smaller.[152]

By the 1870s jasper was produced in quantity in both solid colored and washed examples. Jasper was again discontinued during the Second World War and for the years immediately following until new jasper kilns were put into operation at the new Barlaston factory in 1949. By then, however, the heyday of English jasper ware had long been over. In the history of ceramics, Wedgwood's eighteenth-century invention of jasper ware was the greatest event since the discovery of porcelain, despite the fact that many of the shapes and ornaments of Wedgwood's jasper ware were not original. As Josiah Wedgwood himself explained to Erasmus Darwin: "I only pretend to have attempted to copy the fine antique forms, but not with absolute servility. I have endeavoured to preserve the stile and Sp^{t} or if you please the elegant simplicity of the antique forms."[153] In what he set out to do, Wedgwood succeeded supremely well. Because the jasper ware produced after Wedgwood's death was frequently neither elegant nor simple, the true greatness of Wedgwood's work is wonderfully represented in the collection of Dwight Moody and Lucille Stewart Beeson, the majority of whose jasper ware was made during Josiah Wedgwood's lifetime.

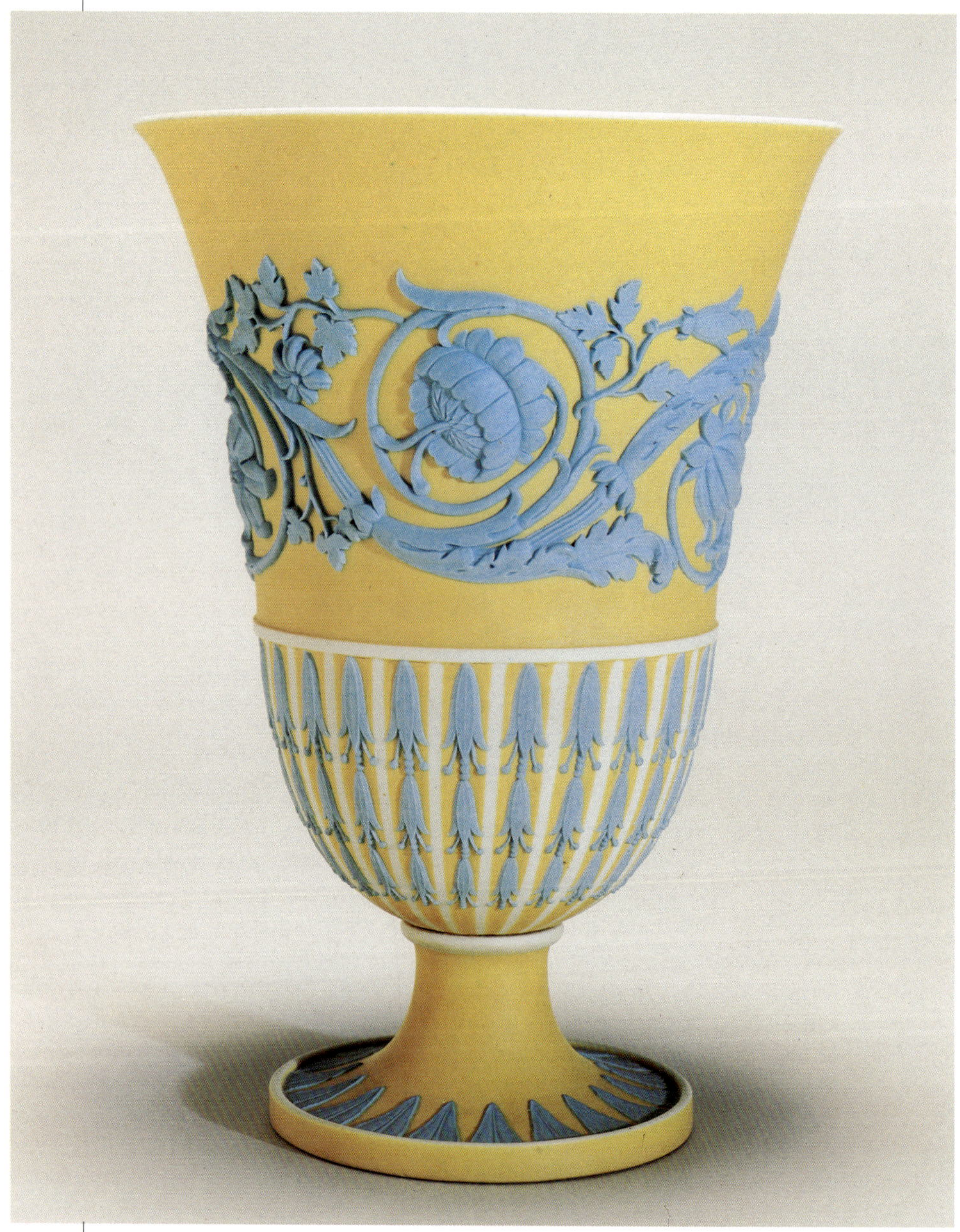

Color plate 132
Goblet Vase, ca. 1815, white stoneware with canary yellow jasper wash and blue jasper relief, 6 13/16" x 3" (cat. 658).

11
White Stoneware

At the Wedgwood factories, a "white porcelain" ware largely replaced jasper ware during the early years of the nineteenth century, when, as a result of the loss or misunderstanding of the formula, solid jasper began to explode in the kiln firing.[1] A further development of white terra-cotta stoneware, white porcelain or stoneware was more translucent than its predecessor—thus the name "white porcelain." Various colored jasper washes and reliefs were used for decoration on the ware, as Josiah Wedgwood II wrote: "Our Stone body has lately been used washed over with jasper slip & with jasper reliefs which seem to agree very well."[2] White stoneware continued to be manufactured until 1941, but, unlike jasper, it was not reintroduced after World War II.[3]

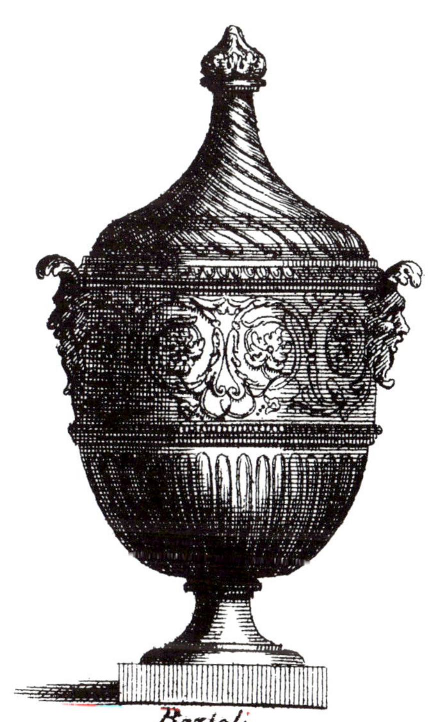

***Fig. 38** Montfaucon,* L'Antiquité expliquée, *vol. 5, pt. 1, p. 36, pl. 6, fig. 4.* Vase.

In the Beeson collection is a vase (cat. 658, pl. 132) that dates to about 1815 and represents the early use of white porcelain with tricolored jasper decoration. The body is covered in a canary-yellow jasper wash with light blue jasper reliefs of a Roman scroll and flowers outlined in white. A notation in

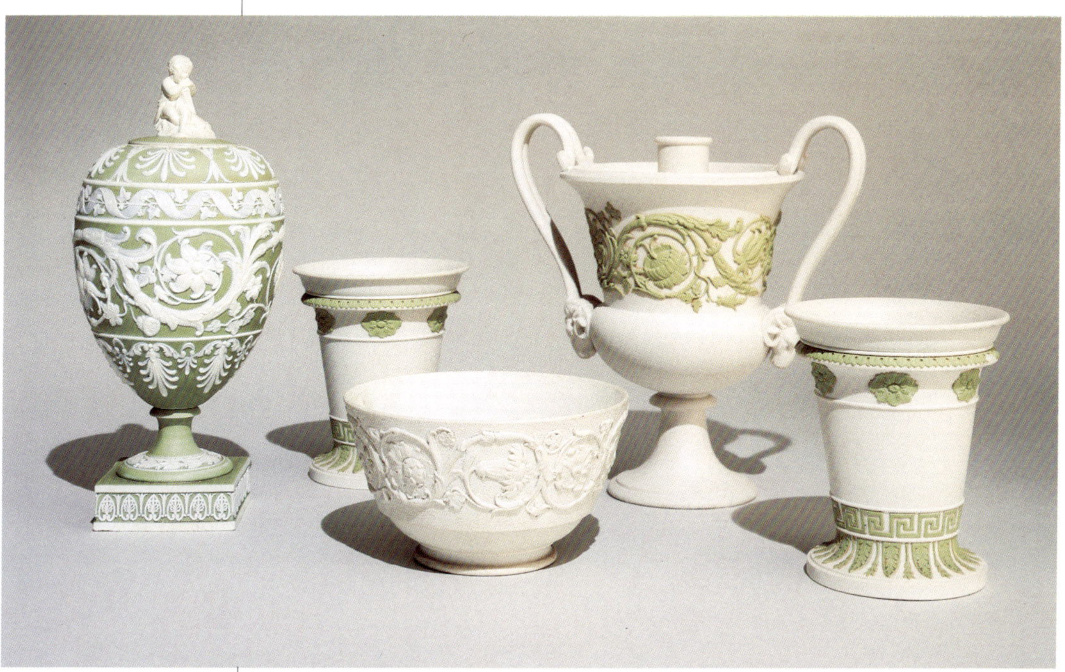

***Color plate 133** Other examples of white stoneware.* Left, *Covered Vase, ca. 1795, jasper or white stoneware, solid white ground with green wash and white relief, 8 3/8" x 1 1/2" (cat. 362);* center front, *Bowl, ca. 1815, white stoneware with white relief and granulated surface, 2 11/16" x 2 3/8" (cat. 657);* back and right, *Three-Piece Garniture, ca. 1815, white stoneware with green jasper relief,* center piece: *6 1/2" x 2 15/16",* left and right: *4 1/8" x 2 15/16" (cat. 659).*

a showroom order book of June 18, 1811, suggests the first use of this color combination: "Mr. Wedgwood says the Yellow Jasper with blue ornaments of which you sent a can as pattn will do very well."[4] The design of the bas-relief is possibly an adaptation from Montfaucon (fig. 38).[5] When held to the light, the vase is transparent, an indication of the medium of its body. Inside the bowl at the bottom is a sump cover, making the vase waterproof. This vase and the slate blue copy of the Portland vase (cat. 292, pl. 134, p. 143) were the Beesons' most cherished pieces.

12
The Portland Vase

The Portland vase, a delicately carved, cameo-glass vessel of Roman origin, has long been an object greatly admired by lovers of antiquity. The vase may have belonged to Emperor Augustus and has recently been attributed to the Roman sculptor Dioskourides, who produced the original between 30 and 20 B.C.[1] The body of the vase appears to be black with white relief, but it is actually cobalt blue. It was produced by inserting a gathering of free-blown blue glass on a blowpipe into a cup of white enamel, after which both were blown together into the vase shape. The handles were attached at the neck and drawn down to the shoulder, then wheel-cut, polished, and hand-carved in painstaking detail. Measuring nine and three-fourths inches in height, it measures seven inches at its widest point.

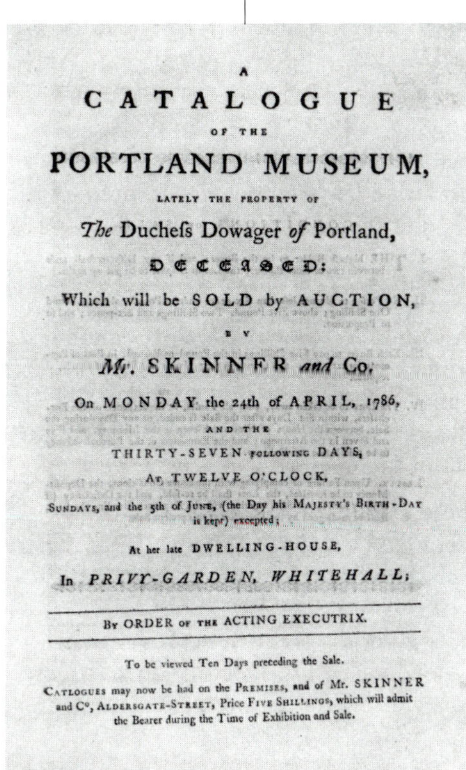

A

CATALOGUE

OF THE

PORTLAND MUSEUM,

LATELY THE PROPERTY OF

The Duchefs Dowager *of* Portland,

DECEASED:

Which will be SOLD by AUCTION,

BY

Mr. SKINNER *and* Co.

On MONDAY the 24th of APRIL, 1786,

AND THE

THIRTY-SEVEN FOLLOWING DAYS,

AT TWELVE O'CLOCK,

SUNDAYS, and the 5th of JUNE, (the Day his MAJESTY'S BIRTH-DAY is kept) excepted;

At her late DWELLING-HOUSE,

In *PRIVY-GARDEN, WHITEHALL;*

BY ORDER OF THE ACTING EXECUTRIX.

To be viewed Ten Days preceding the Sale.

CATLOGUES may now be had on the PREMISES, and of Mr. SKINNER and C°, ALDERSGATE-STREET, Price FIVE SHILLINGS, which will admit the Bearer during the Time of Exhibition and Sale.

Fig. 39 *Title page to the sale catalog for the auction by Skinner and Company of the Duchess of Portland's collection, April 24-June 7, 1786.*

The vase first became known to historians in the winter of 1600-1601 as a part of the collection of Cardinal Francesco Maria Borbone del Monte (1549-1627). The vase was seen at his Palazzo Madama by the Provençal scholar Nicolas-Claude Fabri de Peiresc (1580-1637). Cardinal Francesco Barberini acquired the vase in 1626 from the estate of Cardinal del Monte, and it remained in the Barberini family until about 1780, when it was sold to Scottish antiquarian James Byres (1733-1817). Before 1782, Sir William Hamilton, envoy to the court of Naples, purchased the vase from Byres, even though, as he wrote to Wedgwood in a letter of July 24, 1786, "God knows it was not very convenient for me at that moment." He went on to say of the vase: "Except the Apollo Belvedere, the Niobes, and two or three others of the first class marbles, I do not believe that there are any monuments of antiquity existing that were executed by so great an artist."[2]

Hamilton brought his treasure back to England, arriving on May 24, 1783. John Flaxman brought the vase to Wedgwood's attention on February 5, 1784, when he wrote to Wedgwood and urged him to come to London "to see Wm Hamilton's Vase; it is the finest production of Art that has been brought to England and seems to be the very apex of perfection to which you are endeavouring to bring your bisque and jasper."[3] Before September 8, 1784, Hamilton secretly sold the vase to the dowager duchess of Portland, who was described by Horace Walpole as "a simple woman but perfectly sober, and intoxicated only by empty vases."[4] It was to be displayed in her Portland Museum in London as the prize item among other natural and artificial curiosities, but she died on July 17, 1785, before she was able to place the vase on view. An estate auction that began on April 24, 1786, lasted for thirty-nine days, during which time some 4,263 lots from the collection were dispersed (fig. 39). The vase was purchased by the dowager's son, the third duke of Portland, who lent it to Wedgwood to copy on June 10, 1786. Two weeks later, Wedgwood wrote to Sir William Hamilton: "You will be pleased, I am sure, to hear what a treasure is just now put into my hands, I mean the exquisite Barberini vase with which you enriched this island, and which, now that we may call it the Portland vase, I hope will never depart from it. His Grace the Duke of Portland being the purchaser, at the sale of his late mother's museum, has generously lent it to me to copy, and permitted me to carry it down to this place."[5] In 1810, the fourth duke of Portland put the vase on loan to the British Museum. Unfortunately, in February 1845, a mad Irish painter smashed it into around two hundred pieces. The vase has been repaired three times since the accident.[6] In 1945 it was purchased from the seventh duke of Portland by the British Museum, where it is still on view today.

Even during its ancient life the Portland vase was broken and repaired, as evidenced by its new, or "married," glass base (now displayed separately from the vase). The existence of this base, which bears the figure of Paris, was first documented in a letter of August 16, 1635, from the artist Peter Paul Rubens (1577-1640) to de Peiresc. A repair from antiquity, the new base was cut down from a plaque made in the first half of the first century A.D., perhaps in Rome. It is believed to have portrayed the judgment of Paris and included Paris and the goddesses Hera, Athena, and Aphrodite; now, only a relief of the bust of Paris remains. Experts today disagree about the original Portland vase: some claim that it had a flat ring base, while others conclude that it had an amphora shape. Whatever the case, they agree that the vase must have been commissioned to commemorate a special occasion, possibly as a cinerary urn or as a wedding present.

The Beeson collection and the Wedgwood Museum in England each possess a plaster cast made by Josiah Wedgwood from the original vase in order to prepare his block molds for the bas-relief figures (cat. 293). A letter from Francis H. Wedgwood, dated 1910, presents the Beeson copy to a Mr. Gee, stating:

> We are indeed with pleasure to present to you a cast from the mould taken from the Original Portland vase from which Josiah Wedgwood, F. R. S. made his famous original reproductions. The cast in question is a fellow to the one in the Etruria Museum and shows the exact markings from the original mould which had to be removed in these pieces from the Duke of Portland's Vase, and it is precisely these markings which prove its chief interest in the eyes of a "Potter."[7]

Plaster-of-paris replicas of the Portland vase were also made by James Tassie from a mold made by Giovanni Pichler and commissioned between 1780 and 1782, when James Byres owned the vase. Sixty of these replicas were sold; one of them is now in the British Museum.

The Portland vase is considered one of Wedgwood's greatest achievements and became the first limited-edition and subscribed vase in the history of ceramics. Already highly regarded in the eighteenth century, the vase daunted even the confident Wedgwood. As he wrote to Hamilton on June 24, 1786:

> When I first engaged in this work, and had Montfaucon only to copy, I proceeded with spirit, and sufficient assurance that I should be able to equal, or excell if permitted, that copy of the vase; but now that I can indulge myself with full and repeated examinations of the original work itself, my crest is much fallen, and I should scarcely muster sufficient resolution to proceed if I had not, too precipitately perhaps, pledged myself to many of my friends to attempt it in the best manner I am able.[8]

Procuring the vase from the duke of Portland just three days after the auction in 1786, Wedgwood spent the next four years experimenting with the clay and working with modelers—Henry Webber, William Wood, William Hackwood, and his son Josiah—toward a perfect copy.[9] On June 24, 1786, Wedgwood pointed out to Hamilton that "a bas relief with all the figures of one uniform white color upon a dark ground, will be a very faint resemblance of what this artist has had the address to produce, by calling in the aid of colour to assist his relief."[10] Indeed, the original bodies produced by Wedgwood were of jasper colored with a "mixture of blue & black, & then dipped

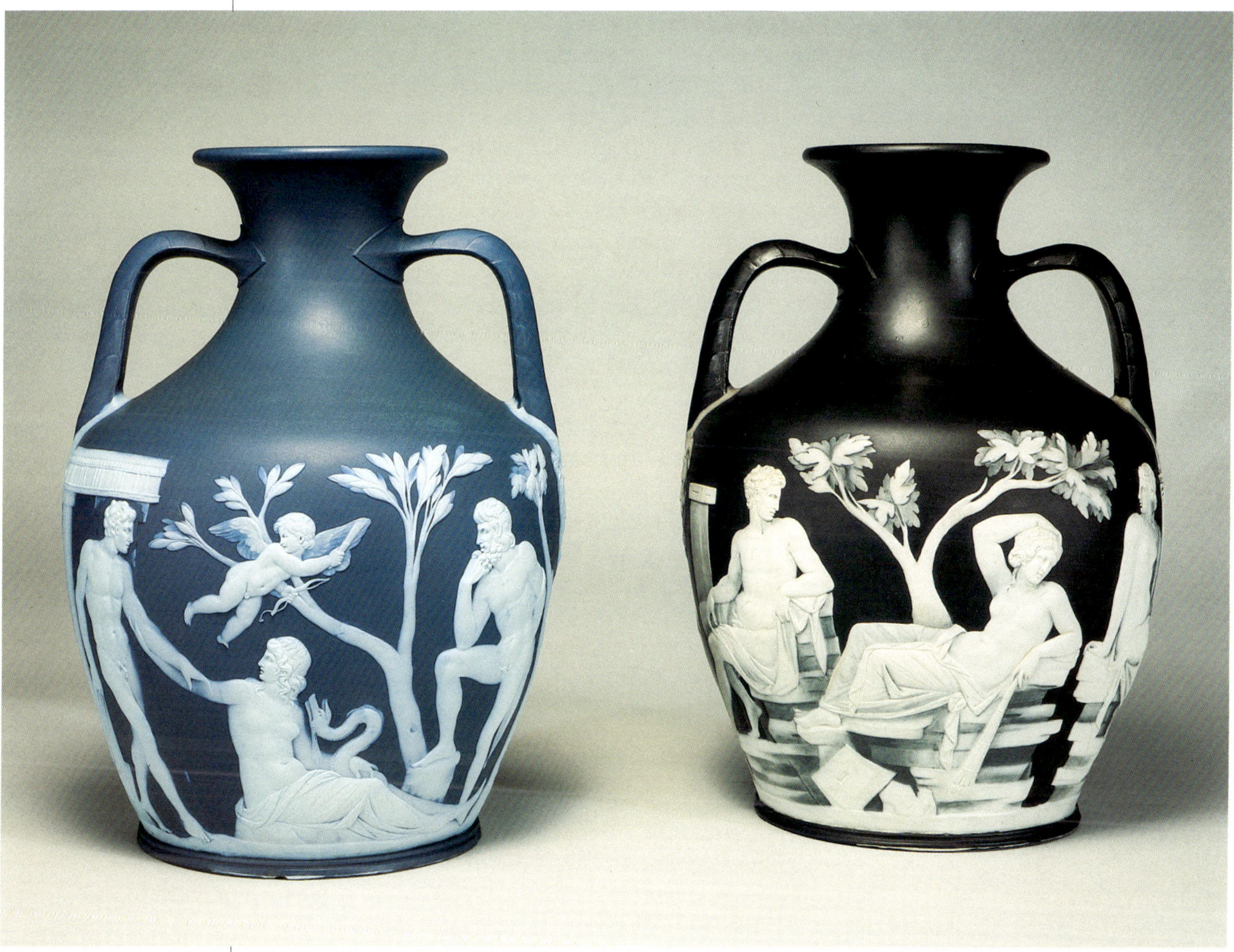

Color plate 134
Left, *Slate Blue Portland Vase Copy, ca. 1791, jasper, solid slate blue ground with blue wash and white relief, 9 3/4" x 4 15/16" (cat. 292);* right, *Darwin Portland Vase Copy, 1790-92, jasper, solid black ground with black wash and white relief and addition of local color, 10" x 5 1/16" (cat. 291).*

in black [slip]."[11] The coarser clay body could withstand the high firing temperature, and the finer slip was added for an attractive appearance.

In September of 1789, Wedgwood gave the first satisfactory copy of the Portland vase to his personal physician and friend, Dr. Erasmus Darwin. On May 1 of the following year, he showed another finished copy to Queen Charlotte.[12] Other examples were exhibited at Wedgwood's Greek Street showroom in Soho, with viewing by special admission only. Sir Joshua Reynolds certified on June 15, 1790: "I have compared the copy of the Portland vase with the original. I can venture to declare it to be a correct and faithful imitation."[13] Forty-three of the first-edition replicas—that is, those potted during the lifetime of Josiah Wedgwood I and fired between May 27, 1791, and December 1796—were recorded in the oven book, the record of kiln firings (although eleven of them were blistered and crackled). Some of them were made by Dan Hollinshead and finished by Hackwood.[14] Yet records indicate that Wedgwood did not sell many Portland vases, and for all of his efforts he was never compensated for development and production costs. At present, twenty-five of these originals are known to exist.

The Beeson collection has two first-edition copies (cat. 292, pl. 134). The first copy has a slate blue ground and is one of five known examples with slate blue coloring.[15] Another slate blue example was presented to the British Museum by John Wedgwood, Josiah's eldest son, in 1802. All five are thought to have been made in 1791 during a clay shortage of "Barberini black," when "some blue ones" were made.[16] Auction records show the Beeson vase to have been owned by Dr. John Lumsden Propert, who sold the piece through Christie, Manson, and Woods (June 11, 12, and 13, 1902). The purchaser, Frederick Rathbone, sold it almost immediately, on June 21, 1902, to a Mrs. Spranger, whose son, R. J. M. Spranger, inherited the vase. Upon his death, it was sold again by Christie, Manson, and Woods on November 30, 1964, this time to the Beesons. A note under the description of the vase for the Propert catalog sale states, "Given by Josiah Wedgwood to Apsley Pellatt, Esq." Recent research indicates that this reference is to Josiah II, not Josiah I, as "there is no evidence that Josiah I gave away any Portland vases in 1789 except the first perfect copy to Erasmus Darwin."[17] It is more likely, however, that Apsley Pellatt II (1791-1863), with other investors, bought the vase in 1829, when Wedgwood's York Street showroom was closed and almost all of the inventory was sold.[18]

Compared with the color of the British Museum copy, the blue ground of the Beeson vase is darker, possibly because the vase was passed through the kiln several times, thus giving the opaque jasper a vitreous, semitransparent condition similar to that of porcelain and producing the darker ground color. Alternatively, it may have been fired at a different time and at a higher temperature than the other vases, or the exterior jasper wash it was given may have been darker.

The second first-edition copy in the Beeson collection is known as the Darwin Portland vase, with the more traditional black ground and yellow-white relief (cat. 291, pl. 134). A black slip has been applied to the thinner parts of the white relief, to suggest a greater transparency between the body and the bas-relief. As with others of this first-edition set, a number was scripted in manganese and fired on the inside slip of the vase, but none are marked "Wedgwood." The number 12 appears on this vase, possibly indicating that it was the twelfth copy that Wedgwood produced. On September 24, 1965, the Beesons purchased the vase directly from Sir Robin Darwin. The vase was at that time on loan to the Victoria and Albert Museum.

Although unsupported by documentary evidence, Sir Robin claimed that, before the vase came into his possession, it was given to Dr. Erasmus Darwin by Wedgwood and descended to Dr. Robert Darwin, CharlesDarwin, Sir Francis Darwin, and Bernard Darwin indicating that it was the first perfect copy that Wedgwood is known to have presented to Dr. Erasmus Darwin in 1789.[19] There is now some question as to whether it was actually the first good copy, as this is also claimed about the Wedgwood Portland vase belonging to the Fitzwilliam Museum in Cambridge, England. Physical and documentary evidence traces the ownership of the vase at the Fitzwilliam in the Darwin family back to 1818, just sixteen years after the death of Erasmus. Given that first-edition-quality Portland copies with the manganese numbers 1, 3, 4, 6, 7, 8, and 9 are known to exist, at least one having been made after 1790, it is unclear why number 12 would have been given to Darwin and identified as the first good copy. Complicating the issue further are the numerous marriages of Wedgwoods and Darwins and the known purchase of a Portland vase in 1793 by Robert Waring Darwin (this vase is now in the Victoria and Albert Museum). The Wedgwood Museum in Barlaston has yet another "Darwin" vase, one that was owned by Ralph Vaughan Williams, who was a direct descendant of Erasmus Darwin and Josiah Wedgwood. Thus there are four existing Wedgwood Portland vases with connections to the Darwin family. The evidence does not necessarily prove, however, that the Beeson Portland vase was not owned by Erasmus Darwin, for he was a great admirer of Wedgwood and may have purchased a vase himself. Until more is known and the provenance further proved or disproved, the Beeson vase should be considered to be from the Darwin family.[20]

Over the years much has been written about the iconography of the Portland vase, including an account of the Barberini, now Portland, vase compiled and printed by Wedgwood himself, which he intended to accompany each Portland vase that he sold.[21] A dubious story from the Barberini family had it that the vase had been excavated between 1623 and 1644 from the supposed sepulcher of the Roman emperor Alexander Severus and his mother, Julia Mammaea, which was located beneath the Monte del Grano, outside Rome. This led to the theory that the figures on the vase are linked to Emperor Augustus and his family. Another popular theory came from Erasmus Darwin, who saw in the figures of the vase details of the Eleusinian mysteries, as he described in his long poem "The Botanic Garden" of 1789 and 1791. Wedgwood himself wrote that the "first groupe, therefore, would represent the solemn scene of death separating a great man from his family and his empire. The other side of the vase appears to be a separate picture, in continuation of the same subject, and flattering to the memory of the deceased; representing his entrance, under the figure of a beautiful young man, into Elysium."[22]

Of the twenty or so interpretations that have been offered, the theory currently accepted is that the figures on one side represent the birth of Augustus, who, as one who became master of the Roman world and ushered in the golden age of Rome, is shown emerging from an intact building; on the other side is the birth of Paris, who, as one who was instrumental in the events that led to the destruction of Troy, is shown surrounded by ruined architecture. This latest interpretation relates the iconography on the vase to the Augustan propaganda found in the *Aeneid*, which Virgil was writing at precisely the same time that Dioskourides was carving the vase. More specifically, as shown in the illustration of the Portland vase presented here (fig. 40), figure C is Atia, the mother of Augustus. According to mythology, Augustus was fathered by Apollo, who visited Atia in the form of a draco (snake like animal), which also appears on the vase. Cupid, figure B, indicates the sexual nature of the encounter between figure C and the draco. Figure A is thought to be Augustus, and figure D (as suggested in the past) is Neptune, whose intervention was partly responsible for the victory of Augustus at the Battle of Actium. On the other side is a scene that is a direct consequence of the opposing scene. Figure F may represent Hecuba, who dreamed that she gave birth to a torch and set fire to a great city. The child she bore was Paris, whose abduction of Helen led to the Trojan War and the destruction of Troy; figure E, therefore, is Paris. Figure G (again, an old attribution) is Venus, who promised Paris the most beautiful mortal woman if he would choose her as the most beautiful goddess. In essence, then, without the judgment of Paris, the Trojan War would never have taken place; without the Trojan War, Aeneas and his followers would never have founded Rome; without the founding of Rome, the golden age of Augustus would never have happened.[23]

Fig. 40 *Montfaucon,* L'Antiquité expliquée, *vol. 5, pt. 1, p. 36, pl. 6, fig. 1.* Portland Vase.

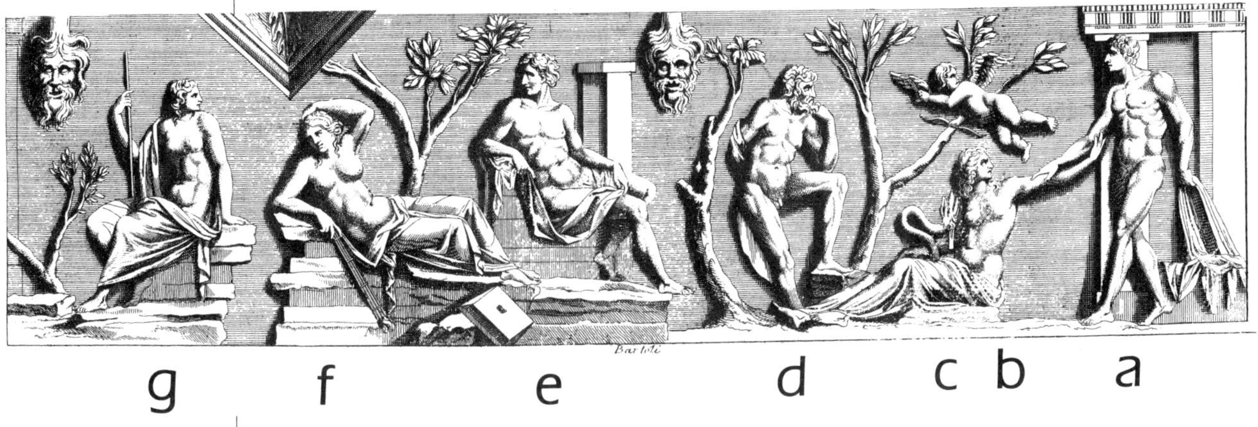

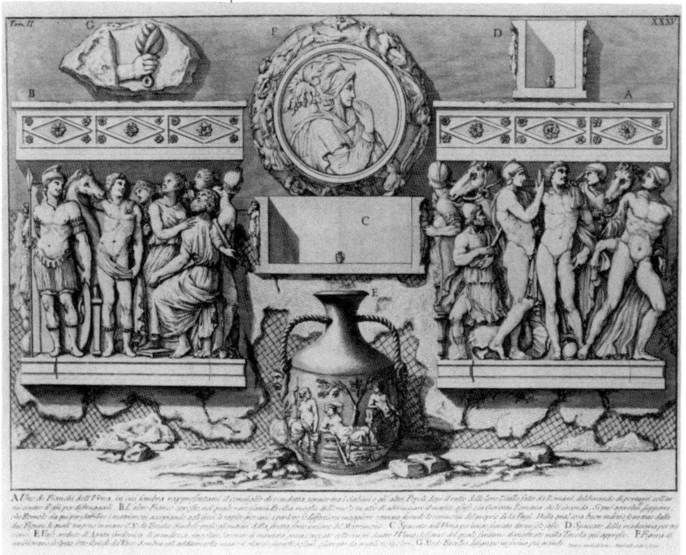

Fig. 41 Sarcophagus with Portland Vase, Battista Piranesi (1720-78). Engraving from Le Antichita romane, *bk. 2, pl. 35, published 1750-85.*

The Wedgwood company has subsequently issued several editions of the Portland vase in the nineteenth and twentith centuries.[24] In the Beeson collection is another example of the Portland vase, one made by Thomas Lovatt (1850-1915) (cat. 296). He was a chief ornamentor employed at Wedgwood from the mid-1800s into the early twentieth century who made fine reproductions of eighteenth-century plaques, complete with firing holes, and who also specialized in the Portland vase. Lovatt produced an unknown number of them in about 1880. This vase is incised "TL" at the base of the tree in the "ground." It is made of solid black jasper ware with white bas-relief but has no undercutting of the relief or "color" added to it.

The mystery and popularity of the Portland vase inspired various related items. In the Beeson collection, for example, is an engraving by Giovanni Battista Piranesi (1720-78) from *Le Antichita romane* (fig. 41). The print shows the vase and the supposed sarcophagus of Severus, in which it was found. Wedgwood produced in jasper ware two tablets that depict, in relief, both sides of the sarcophagus. One is in solid blue jasper with white and dates to about 1800. It has been erroneously titled *The Sacrifice of Iphigenia* by previous authors, but the scene is actually of *Achilles at Scyros* and was modeled by Camillo Pacetti in Rome in about 1788 (cat. 272, fig. 42).[25] The second tablet, entitled *Priam Begging the Body of Hector from Achilles*, has a solid white ground (probably white stoneware) with a green jasper wash on the front and white relief and also dates to around 1800 (cat. 273, fig. 43).

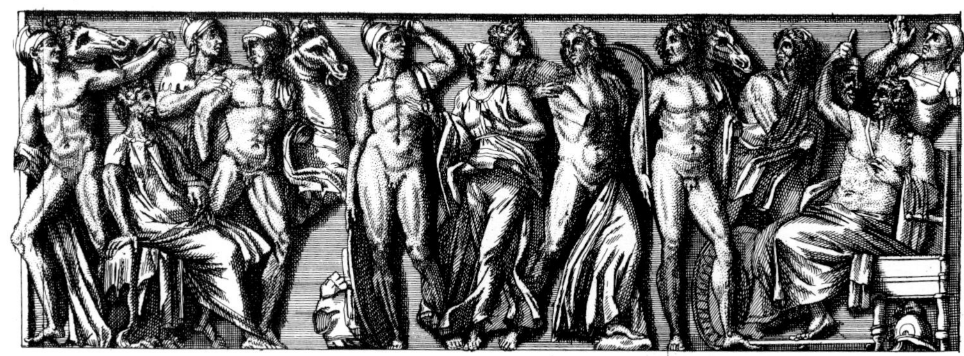

Fig. 42 Montfaucon, L'Antiquité expliquée, *vol. 5, pt. 1, p. 67, pl. 23, fig. 2.* Funeral Sport.

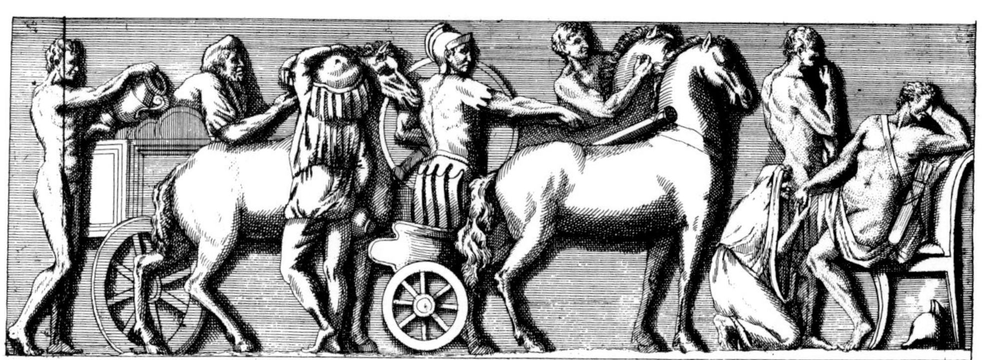

Fig. 43 Montfaucon, L'Antiquité expliquée, *vol. 5, pt. 1, p. 67, pl. 23, fig. 3.* Mourners.

13
Caneware

Caneware is an unglazed stoneware body of a local, buff-colored marl. Its fine-grained texture is highly malleable, making it an ideal medium for molding detail, and it is fusible at moderate temperatures. Josiah Wedgwood began experiments on the ware in the early 1770s, finally perfecting it about 1776. Wedgwood, however, first announced its availability in the *Ornamental Catalogue* of 1787, calling it "bamboo or cane-coloured bisque porcelain, . . . both plain, and enriched with Grecian and Etruscan ornaments." Conforming to this description, Wedgwood's first products in this ware were molded to look like bamboo canes. Made in both useful and ornamental ware, the pieces were decorated with bas-reliefs, enameling, and encaustic painting.

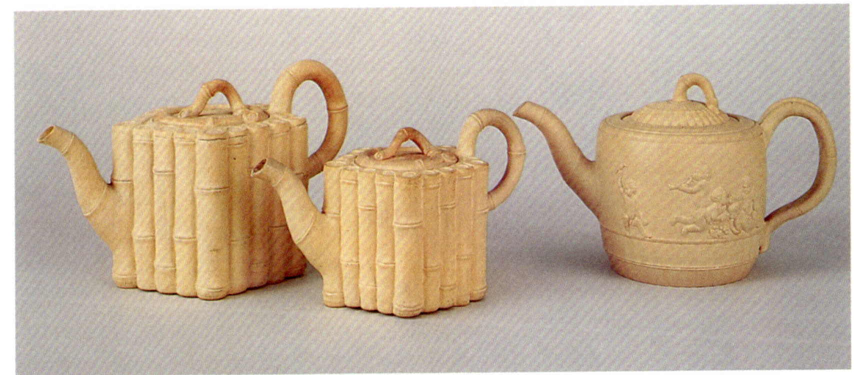

Color plate 135
Left, *Teapot,* Bamboo, *ca. 1780, caneware with glazed interior, 5" x 4 3/8" (cat. 425);* center, *Teapot,* Bamboo, *ca. 1780, caneware with glazed interior, 3 3/4" x 3 5/8" (cat. 426);* right, *Teapot,* Boys at Play, *ca. 1790, caneware with glazed interior, 4 5/8" x 3 3/8" (cat. 438).*

In the Beeson collection are two rare caneware teapots marked "Wedgwood & Bentley" (cats. 425, 426, pl. 135). Only slightly different in size, the teapots have tops, handles, and spouts formed of bamboo shoots in a light cane-color clay. Both of the interiors are glazed. On November 9, 1776, Wedgwood wrote to Bentley: "I am glad the Bamboo T.Pots are likely to sell. They may be afforded at the prices charg'd very well."[1] This form is also known to have been made in basalt.

A set of specialty pieces of caneware that first appeared in 1786 was created by Wedgwood at the suggestion of Richard Lovell Edgeworth: "I think oval baking dishes for meat pies in the shape of raised paste pies, with bunches of grapes, &c. &c., on their outsides, made of cane-coloured ware, not glazed, but nearly as possible the colour of the baked paste, would be a saleable article."[2] The first trials may have been unsuccessful, for Wedgwood's invoices reveal no caneware "pastry" pieces until about 1795. Shortages of and a high tax on flour during the revolutionary and Napoleonic wars prohibited the use of flour for pastry even in the royal household (rice was used instead). "The distillers left off malting, hackney coach fares were raised 25 percent, and Wedgwood made dishes to represent piecrust."[3] Four pieces in the Beeson collection were modeled and colored to resemble the piecrusts for a game pie, vegetable pie, and decorative pie and tart (cats. 428, 429, 430, 443, pl. 136). The unglazed exterior of each gives the

Color plate 136
Left, *Pastry Dish with Cherry Finial, ca. 1800, caneware with glazed interior, 1 15/16" x 8 1/2" (cat. 443);* center, *Pastry Dish, ca. 1795, caneware with glazed interior, 4 3/16" x 14 3/16" (cat. 428);* right, *Pastry Dish with Cauliflower Finial, ca. 1815, caneware with glazed interior, 5 1/4" x 8 5/8" (cat. 430).*

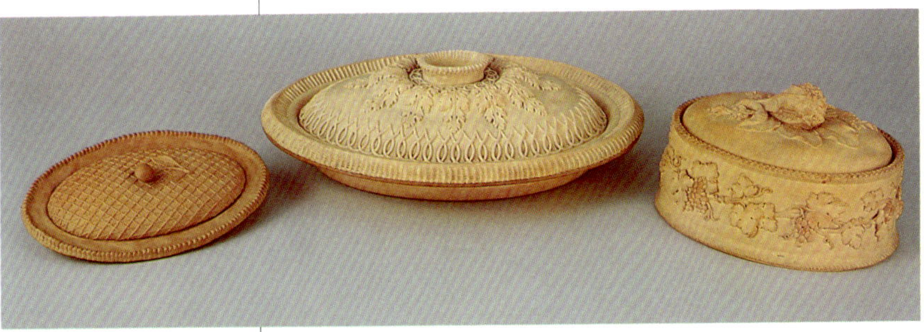

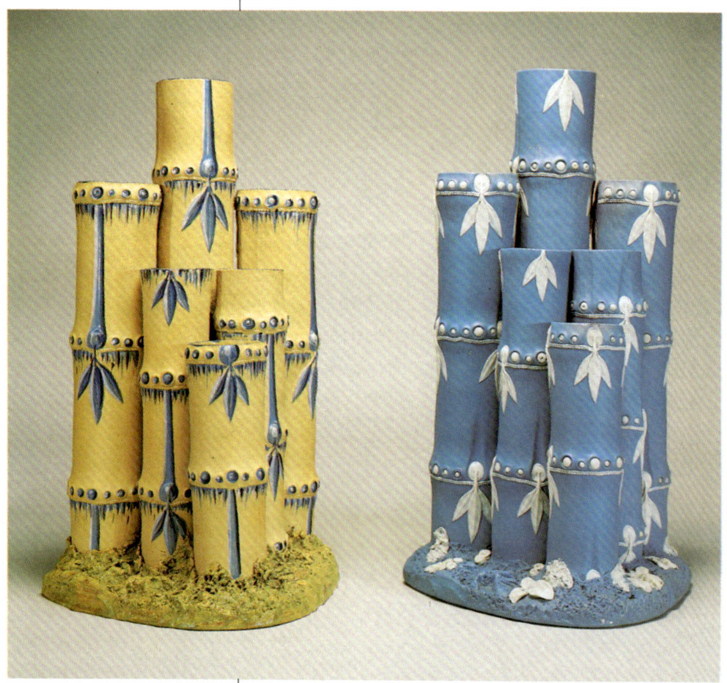

Color plate 137
Left, *Vase,* Bamboo, *ca. 1790, caneware with blue-and-white enamel decoration, 12 15/16" x 7 3/4" (cat. 431);* right, *Vase,* Bamboo, *ca. 1790, jasper with solid blue ground and white relief, 13 3/8" x 7 11/16" (cat. 283).*

appearance of a flour-based pastry, while the interior is glazed to prevent the filling from staining it. In the eighteenth century, bas-relief decoration of vegetables, fruit, and/or game was sprigged onto the ware, but thereafter it was molded.

A rare example of a pastry cake or conceit in the Beeson collection has white relief and is made of either caneware or "white porcelain bisque," as described in the 1787 catalog (cat. 442). Placed in the middle of the table, this piece gave the illusion of a grand pastry dessert decorated with lady fingers and white icing. A decorative bas-relief gallery, now missing, accented the outer edge of the top. The piece dates to about 1800.

Blue, white, and green enamel decoration were the colors commonly used to decorate caneware. Three examples in the Beeson collection have this decoration. Of particular note is a flower holder, in the shape of six bamboo columns of various heights, made around 1790 (cat. 431, pl. 137). Blue enameling accents the joints of the bamboo columns, which have small leaves, also in blue. The base is painted green and sprig-molded to look like moss. Produced with three to nine stalks and glazed inside to enable them to hold water, these vases were made in caneware, basalt, and several colors of jasper ware (cat. 283, pl. 137; another example in blue-and-white jasper is also in the Beeson collection).

Like Wedgwood's basalt, caneware is sometimes decorated with Etruscan motifs. A tea set, consisting of a tray, a creamer, and a cup and saucer, is accented with enamel colors of blue, green, red, black, beige, and gold (cat. 432, pl. 138). Triangular in shape, the tray has small, decorative, Etruscan vases and theatrical accessories painted over its surface. The cup and saucer and the creamer are ribbed to emulate cane or bamboo and have painted leaf borders at their tops.

More typical of the caneware is a tea service that includes a teapot, creamer,

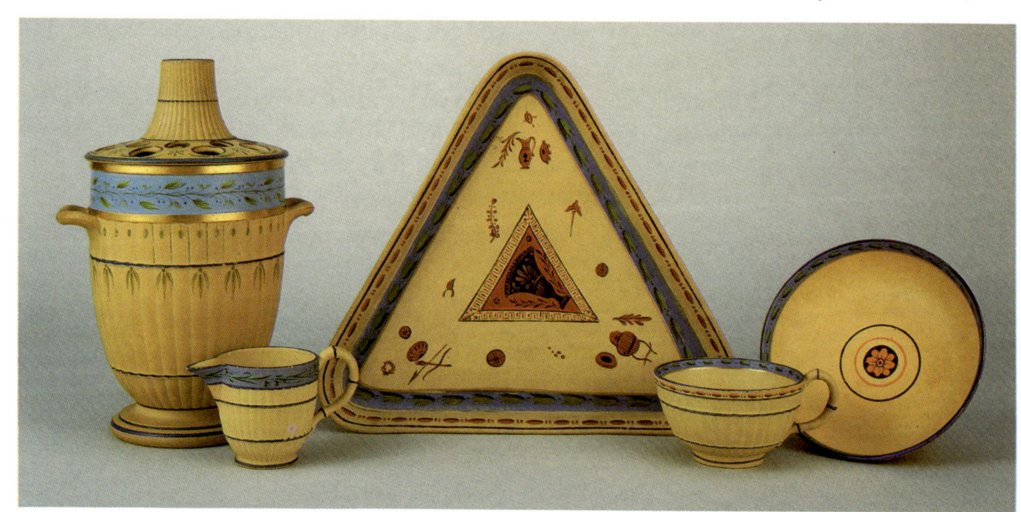

Color plate 138
Left, *Potpourri Vase, ca. 1790, caneware with blue, green, and gold enamel decoration, 8 3/8" x 3 9/16" (cat. 434);* right, *Dejeuner Set, ca. 1790, caneware with encaustic decoration and unglazed interiors, tray: 8 7/8", creamer: 2 3/16" x 1 3/8", cup: 1 5/16" x 1 1/2", saucer: 5 1/8" (cat 432).*

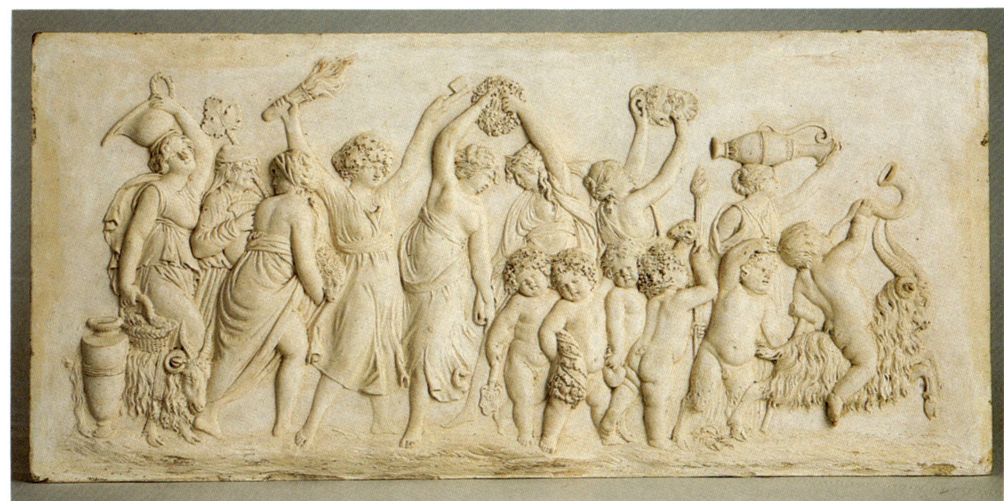

Color plate 139
Tablet, Bacchanalian Triumph, *1786, artificial stone, 21 1/4" x 9 1/2" (cat. 424).*

sugar, cup and saucer, and bowl (cats. 439, 440, 441). The pieces are light buff in color, and all but the teapot are unglazed inside. They are decorated with reliefs of drab or chocolate-colored ferns (polypody and blechnum), which are delicately undercut and tooled. The set, often called the "Darwin" series, dates from the 1830s.

A tablet entitled *Bacchanalian Triumph* also exists in the Beeson collection (cat. 424, pl. 139). In previous publications, the beautifully crafted tablet has been described as being made of caneware or white terra-cotta. The piece is unmarked but has the number 1786 incised on the back. This number as a date, however, is most confounding, for the use of terra-cotta by Wedgwood as late as 1786 would be extremely rare. (He introduced white terra-cotta stoneware for vases and tablets toward the end of 1772.) Recent analysis has determined that the tablet is not terra-cotta and, indeed, not by Wedgwood at all; instead, it is now attributed to the factory of Eleanor Coade.[4] Her ware was a form of stoneware called artificial stone, which is similar to but much finer than our modern cement. There were a number of manufacturers of this stone in the mid-eighteenth century, but the most prominent was Mrs. Coade's. In operation from 1769 to 1836, Coade's Artificial Stone Works in Lambeth was managed by Mrs. Coade and other members of her family. She employed many of the modelers who worked for Wedgwood, including Flaxman, De Vaere, Rossi, and Voyez. Competition between the two firms was keen, particularly in the sale of their chimneypiece ornaments, which were similar in appearance but not in price, with the less costly ones being made in Coade stone. Indeed, Mrs. Coade's catalog of 1784 carried over seven hundred different designs and was extremely successful. To this day, her architectural elements, which are remarkably impervious to pollution, appear on building exteriors and interiors throughout England.[5]

Color plate 140
Left and right, *Pair of Portrait Medallions,* Antony and Cleopatra, *ca. 1780, jasper, solid blue ground with blue wash on front and white relief, ormolu frame, 3 3/8" x 2 3/4" each (cat. 948);* center, *Canopic Vase,* Egyptian Symbols and Signs of the Zodiac, *ca. 1865-75, jasper, solid white ground with blue wash and white relief, 10" x 3" (cat. 374).*

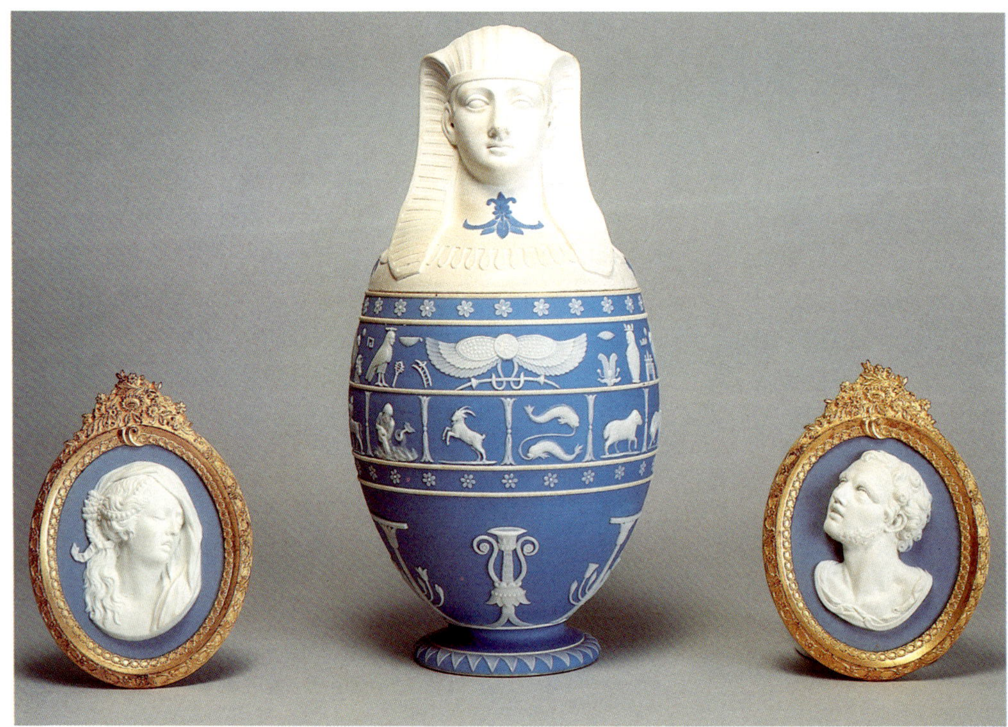

14
Wedgwood and the Egyptian Revival

A diversion to the prevailing taste for the neoclassic style was the attention Europeans paid to the exotic art of Egypt. This fascination grew during Napolean's Egyptian campaign in 1798 with the final victory of Viscount Horatio Nelson (Lord Nelson), the popular British naval commander, over Napoleon Bonaparte's fleet at the Battle of the Nile. Egypt, after centuries of seclusion, was reopened to Europeans, and soon Egyptian history and archaeology became immensely popular. To honor Lord Nelson, Josiah Wedgwood II issued on July 22, 1798, a semipolished basalt bust sculpted by Robert Shout of Holborn. Ten days later, on August 1, at the Battle of the Nile, Lord Nelson successfully destroyed the French fleet in Abukir Bay in Egypt, leaving Napoleon and his army stranded on the shore. Thus the word "Nile" was added to the medallion on Nelson's chest on the busts just issued at the Etruria workshop. A most interesting likeness of the commander, the bust shows his folded sleeve, as Nelson had lost his arm in a previous battle in 1797. A nineteenth-century example of this bust and a blue-and-white jasper portrait medallion of Nelson are in the Beeson collection (cats. 167, 765).

In the Beeson collection, and designed under the direction of Josiah Wedgwood I, are two fine portrait medallions of Egyptians Marc Antony (82–0 B.C.) and Cleopatra (69–30 B.C.) (cat. 948, pl. 140).[1] The plaster molds were probably supplied by Hoskins and Grant, and the modeling and finishing are attributed to William Hackwood in 1775. Created in blue-and-white jasper ware, the portraits depict the famous Egyptian lovers at the moment of death, with dramatic and agonized expressions. Wedgwood wrote to Bentley on November 5, 1775, that he was sending "some Antonies & Cleopatras, very fine & a few Bass reliefs. . . . The blue grounds are out of the last Kiln, & the Cleopatras, both of which are the finest things imaginable. It really hurts me to think of parting with these Gems, the fruit of twenty years toil, for the trifle I fear we must do, to make a business worth our notice of it."[2] The portraits are Egyptian in subject, but the costumes are Greco-Roman in design, revealing the prevalent eighteenth-century misconception of Antony and Cleopatra as classical figures. Even Wedgwood and Bentley list them as "Illustrious Romans" in the portrait-medallion section of their 1779 *Ornamental Catalogue*.

In 1802 two events led to a greater fascination with Egyptian designs. First was the publication of *A Journey to Upper and Lower Egypt*, by Baron Vivant Denon, a member of Lord Nelson's entourage. Second was the arrival in England of the Rosetta stone, the discovery of which caused great excitement and was surely one of the major factors instigating the use of Egyptian hieroglyphics as decoration. It took fifteen more years, however, for Jean-François Champollion (1790-1832) to decipher the Rosetta stone. Thus the Egyptian motifs that were used were purely decorative, inaccurate, Greco-Roman interpretations that were derived from printed sources available to Wedgwood in the eighteenth century.

To accommodate the Egyptian fashion, Josiah Wedgwood I and Josiah Wedgwood II produced various Egyptian-style candle holders, bookends, and mantel ornaments in basalt, jasper, and rosso-antico ware that were relatively simple in design. The Egyptian motif of the sphinx head, which dates to about 800 B.C. in Corinth, appears on many of these sculptural objects by Wedgwood and Bentley from around 1770. Wedgwood and Thomas Boot are attributed as modelers of these early pieces. In a letter to Bentley dated September 20, 1769, Wedgwood noted that Boot was "making Tritons & Sphinx's & does them very well better

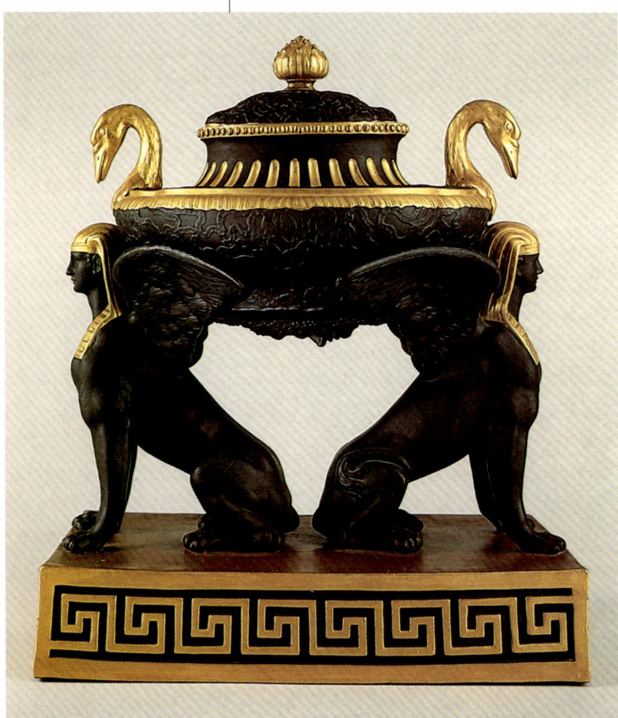

Color plate 141 *Sphinx Supporting Covered Bowl, ca. 1875, basalt, gilt decoration, 14 1/8" x 12 1/8" (cat. 161).*

than I expected."[3] Wedgwood made two types of sphinxes, one Egyptian and the other Greek, in a variety of media. His Egyptian sphinx combined the body of a couchant lion with a man's head wearing the Egyptian royal headdress; the Greek counterpart was a lioness with the breasts and head of a woman and the wings of an eagle.

The Beeson collection contains several nineteenth-century objects with the Egyptian sphinx. A basalt pair of Egyptian-style, couchant sphinxes is made with candle sockets, a form that was also made as paperweights in two sizes (cat. 159). The Egyptian sphinx appears again on a basalt tripod urn or incense burner (cat. 173, pl. 149, page 163); in this case the sphinxes have bodies in the shape of mummies with a single hairy paw, or monopodia, for the foot. The urn is decorated with the lotus flower—actually, an Egyptian crown—which Wedgwood and Bentley had used on an earlier intaglio. The design source for this urn is found in Montfaucon.[4] Josiah Wedgwood II took the same urn form and added hieroglyphic decoration in the nineteenth century.

Two Egyptian sphinxes with heavy gilding support a basalt, bipod bowl, under which is a head of Bacchus surrounded by grapes and leaves (cat. 161, pl. 141). This example dates from about 1875 but was produced until at least 1913. The shape is found in the Wedgwood shape book, which suggests that its first production was in about 1774; however, no eighteenth-century examples are known.[5] Another single sphinx of the same type in the Beeson

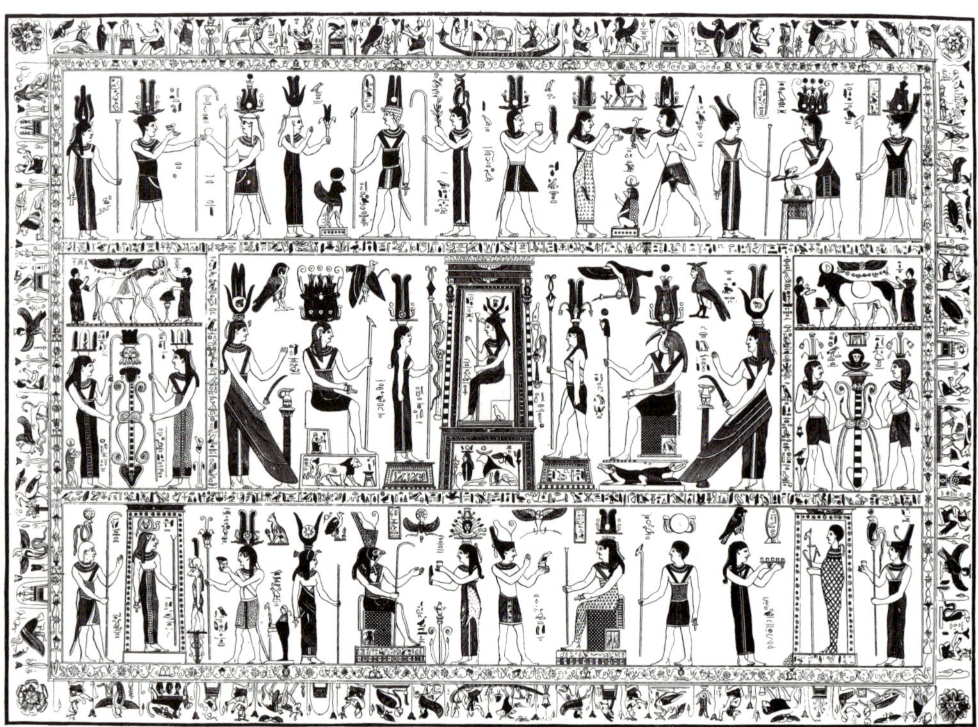

Fig. 44 *Montfaucon,* L'Antiquité expliquée, *vol. 2, pt. 2, p. 210, pl. 45, fig. 1.* Table of Isis.

collection was made of red stoneware and was lustered in platinum or silver (cat. 467). This rare piece is thought to date to about 1810.

Among the Greek sphinxes in the Beeson collection is a pair of basalt bookends that Wedgwood called his "large Modern Sphynx" (cat. 162). He first made them in 1770 and published them in his *Ornamental Catalogue* (1773). The faces are said to be portraits of two beautiful actresses of the time, Peg Woffington and Kitty Clive. The figures are thought to have been adapted from examples in the garden of the palace of Philip V of Spain at La Granja de San Ildefonso, near Segovia; these sphinxes were sculpted by René Fremin (1672-1744) between 1728 and 1740 (during his stay in Spain as first sculptor to the king). The same sphinxes, which were also popular in bronze and gold, appear in various gardens throughout Europe, and the English porcelain factories at Chelsea and Bow are known to have made this type of sphinx as well. The Wedgwood examples were possibly inspired by two plates in Montfaucon.[6]

A second distinct group of Egyptian objects was manufactured by Josiah Wedgwood II beginning in 1805: useful and ornamental ware with Egyptian "hieroglyphics"either as borders or as designs covering the entire piece. Most of the motifs were copied from two plates in Montfaucon (fig. 44).[7]

The Beeson collection contains four examples of his teaware that are ornamented with these hieroglyphics and with crocodile finials. The shapes for the pieces were adapted from an undecorated tea set that was issued earlier by Wedgwood and Bentley and was known even then as "Egyptian." One is a rare teapot of "rosy" or rosso-antico ware with white relief (cat. 463, pl. 143, p. 155). It is glazed on the interior and impressed "WEDGWOOD" in uppercase letters with the word "Niew" in script, thought to be a misspelling for "new."

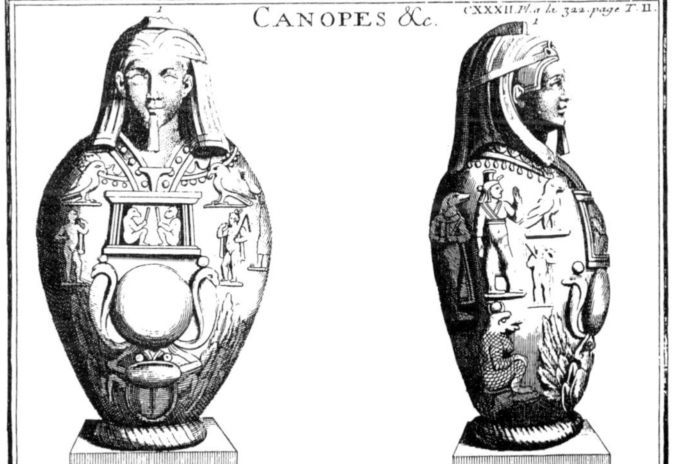

Fig. 45 *Montfaucon,* L'Antiquité expliquée, *vol. 2, pt. 2, p. 322, pl. 132, fig. 1.* Canopes etc.

Second is a tea set that represents a marriage of pieces from different sets, including a creamer, sugar bowl, and teapot in rosso antico with black relief (cats. 463–66; pl. 143, p. 155). They all date from about 1820 and are marked "WEDGWOOD" in uppercase letters. Only the creamer is glazed on the interior.

Josiah Wedgwood II used the term "canopic" to describe his highly decorated, human-headed, mummy-shaped vases of the nineteenth century. The design source for these vases is an illustration from Montfaucon (fig. 45).[8] Egyptian burial jars were undecorated and came in sets of four; the Egyptians preserved in them the viscera of the deceased and placed them in the tombs with the mummies. The jars made at Canopus, however, were figural forms, with men's heads, rounded feet, and relief decorations. Early archaeologists mistakenly used the name "Canopic," thinking they resembled Canopus, pilot of King Menelaus, when the jars were actually decorated in honor of Osiris, the god of the dead.

The Beeson collection includes a blue-and-white, jasper-ware canopic jar with a sphinx's head and shoulders that form the cover (cat. 374, pl. 140). On the body are five bands of purely decorative ornament containing rosettes, Egyptian symbols and hieroglyphics, signs of the zodiac, and papyrus and lotus plants. Interestingly, the line of rosettes that surrounds the vase is not an Egyptian design but was taken from a plate in Montfaucon that depicts an incorrectly restored monument. The piece dates to between 1865 and 1875 and is impressed "WEDGWOOD" in uppercase letters.

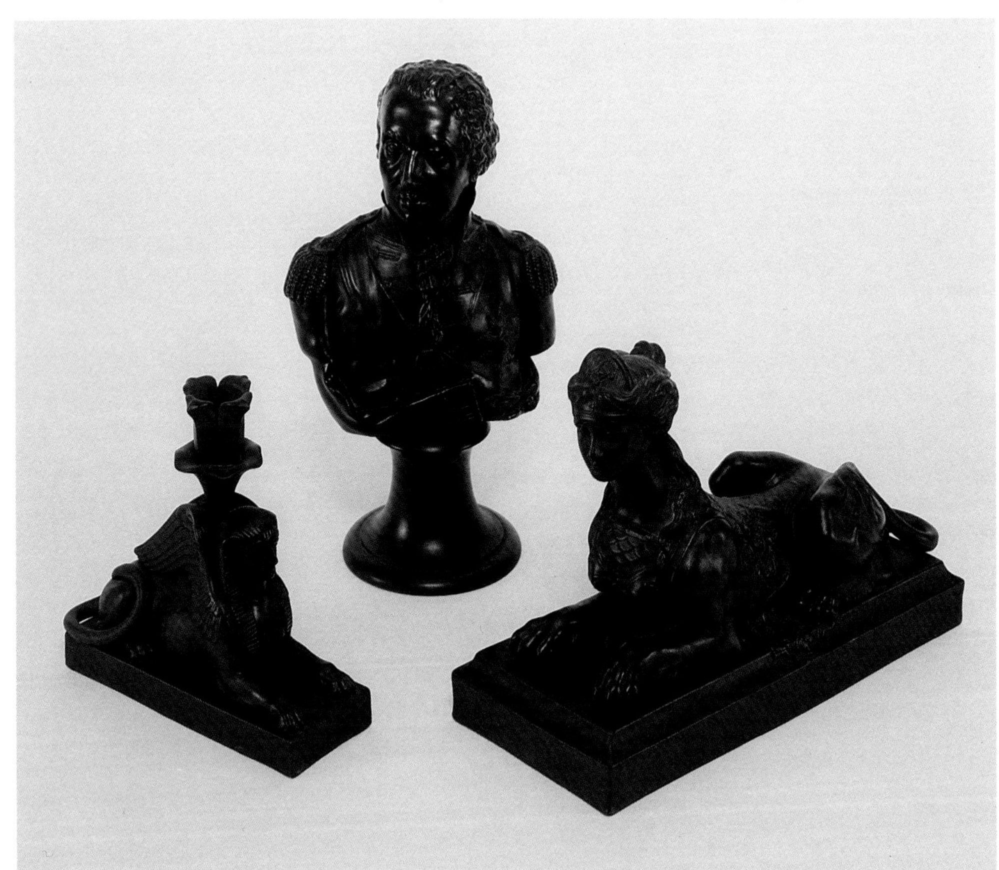

Color plate 142
Left, *One of a Pair of Sphinxes, nineteenth century, basalt, 4 3/8" x 6 11/16" x 2 3/8" (cat. 159);* center, *Bust,* Viscount Horatio Nelson (1758-1805), *nineteenth century, basalt, 11 1/2" x 4 1/4" (cat. 167);* right, *One of a Pair of Sphinxes, nineteenth century, 7 3/4" x 10 3/4" x 4 9/16" (cat. 162).*

15
Rosso-Antico Ware

"Rosso antico," meaning antique red, was the name that Wedgwood gave to an unglazed red stoneware with sprigged decoration that he began making in 1776. He had previously produced red stoneware in the style of the Elers brothers in the 1760s (see p. 17). Simple classical shapes were used and ornamented with applied reliefs in basalt or white stoneware. Having seen Roman redware, Bentley evidently insisted on its development. On March 10, 1776, Wedgwood wrote to Bentley, "I will try to imitate the Antico Rosso from your description but when I have done my best, I am afraid where one spectator thinks of Antico Rosso a hundred will be put in mind of a Red Teapot."[1] Wedgwood's unglazed red body ranged in color from red to a deep chocolate, depending on the firing temperature. It remained for Josiah Wedgwood II to promote the ware effectively in the early nineteenth century.

Examples of rosso antico in the Beeson collection reflect the manufacture of pottery under the guidance of Josiah Wedgwood II. They include the familiar classical motifs, Chinese designs, and Egyptian hieroglyphics (see pp. 153-54).

A pair of classical-style, red-stoneware vases with black basalt relief are beautiful examples of the rosso antico (cat. 458). Depicted on the body of one vase are two scenes: Cybele in a horse-drawn chariot, and the triumph of Cybele.[2] On the second vase are the figures of a classical man and woman attended by cupids, and attributed to Claude Michel Clodion. A small, blue-and-white jasper-ware medallion in the collection has the same subject (cat. 811).

A chocolate teapot and creamer exemplify the use of Chinese motifs on this ware (cats. 451, 452). The decoration is prunus blossoms and bamboo leaves in white jasper bas-relief. A stem of the plant acts as the handle on the teapot. The exterior of both pieces is dry-bodied, and the interior is glazed.

A second class of red stoneware that appeared in about 1805 was called simply terra-cotta, or "brown porcelain." Two covered potpourri vases in the Beeson

Color plate 143
Left, *Teapot,* Egyptian, *ca. 1820, rosso antico with basalt relief, 4 1/2" x 3 1/4" (cat 466);* center, *Sugar Bowl,* Egyptian, *ca. 1820, rosso antico with basalt relief, 3 1/2" x 2 1/2" (cat. 464);* right, *Teapot,* Egyptian, *ca. 1810, rosso antico with white stoneware relief, 3 3/4" x 2 1/2" (cat. 463).*

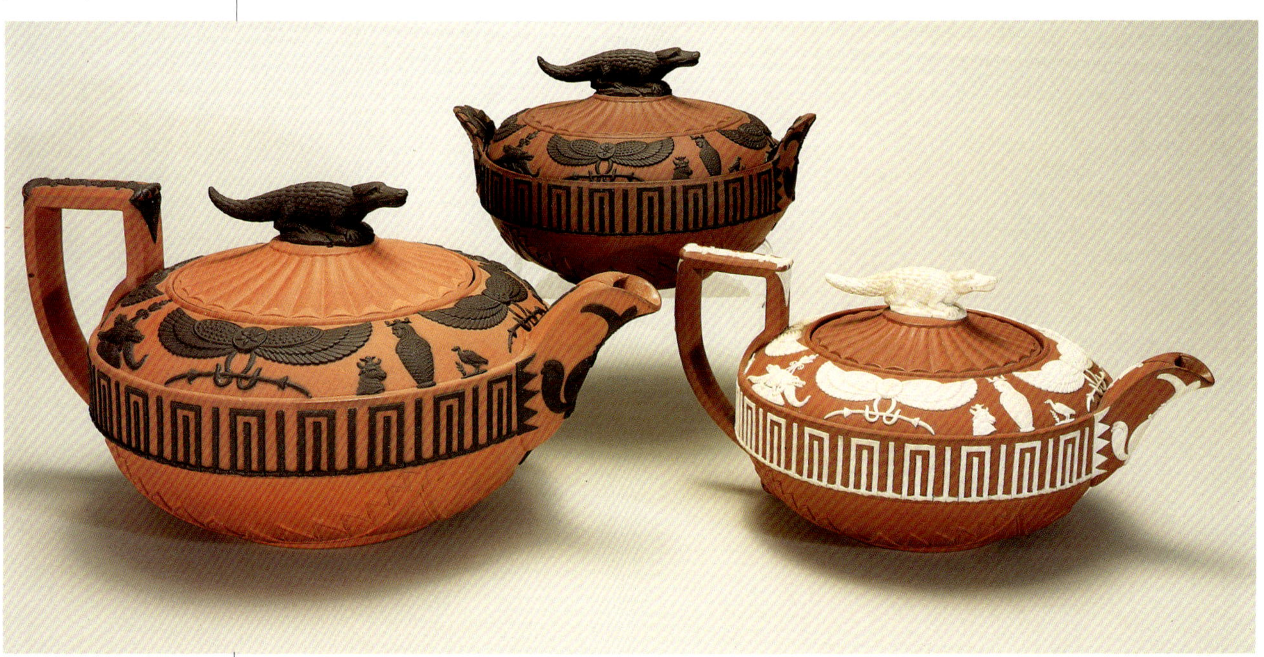

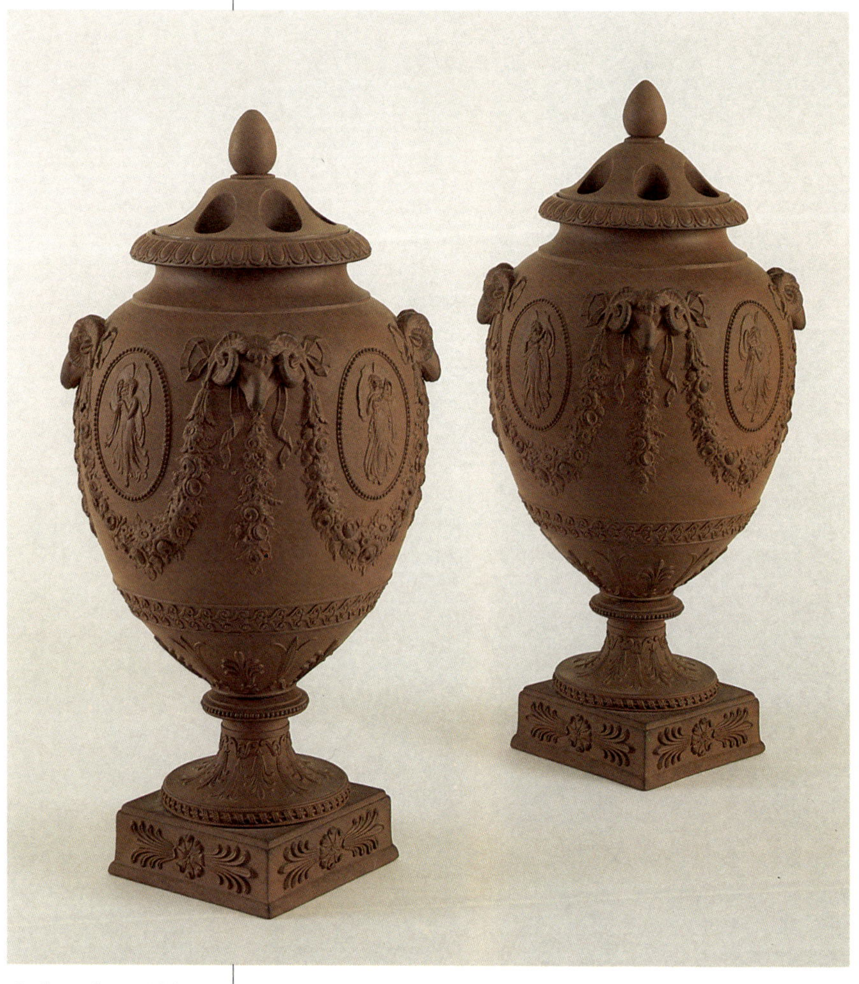

Color plate 144
Pair of Covered Potpourri Vases, Horae, *ca. 1820, stoneware, solid brown with replacement lids, 11 3/4" x 3 15/16" x 3 15/16" (cat. 454).*

collection are made completely of brown porcelain and are decorated with rams' heads' handles, swags, and medallions with the four Horae, the Greek goddesses of the seasons (cat. 454, pl. 144). These vases date to about 1820 and are identical to a green-and-white jasper-ware vase, also in the Beeson collection (cat. 617).

16
Drabware

Introduced by the Wedgwood factory around 1820, drabware remained in production until about 1863.[1] The body was a white stone or "porcelain" colored in varying shades of coffee to olive with reliefs in blue, white, cane, lilac, or chocolate, usually with a smear glaze. The drab color was obtained through a mixture of manganese and niter with the addition of a blue-stained glaze. The name "drab" was, unfortunately, well chosen, as the ware was never very popular. The ware is found as both useful and ornamental pieces. Examples in the Beeson collection date from the early to middle nineteenth century (cats. 668–73, pl. 145). The forms are typical of the period and resemble jasper ware in decoration.

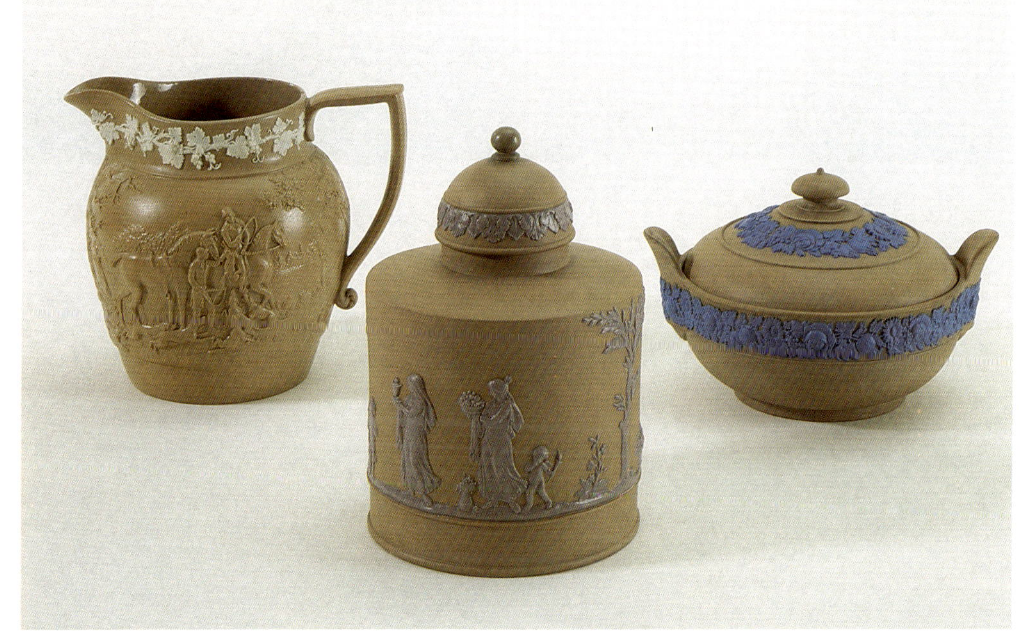

Color plate 145
Left, *Pitcher,* Hunting Scene, *nineteenth century, drabware with white relief and glazed interior, 5 1/4" x 3 1/4" (cat. 671);* center, *Tea Canister,* Domestic Employment, *ca. 1825, drabware with lilac relief, 6 1/4" x 4 1/2" (cat. 669);* right, *Sugar Bowl, nineteenth century, drabware with cobalt blue relief, 4" x 3 1/4" (cat. 670).*

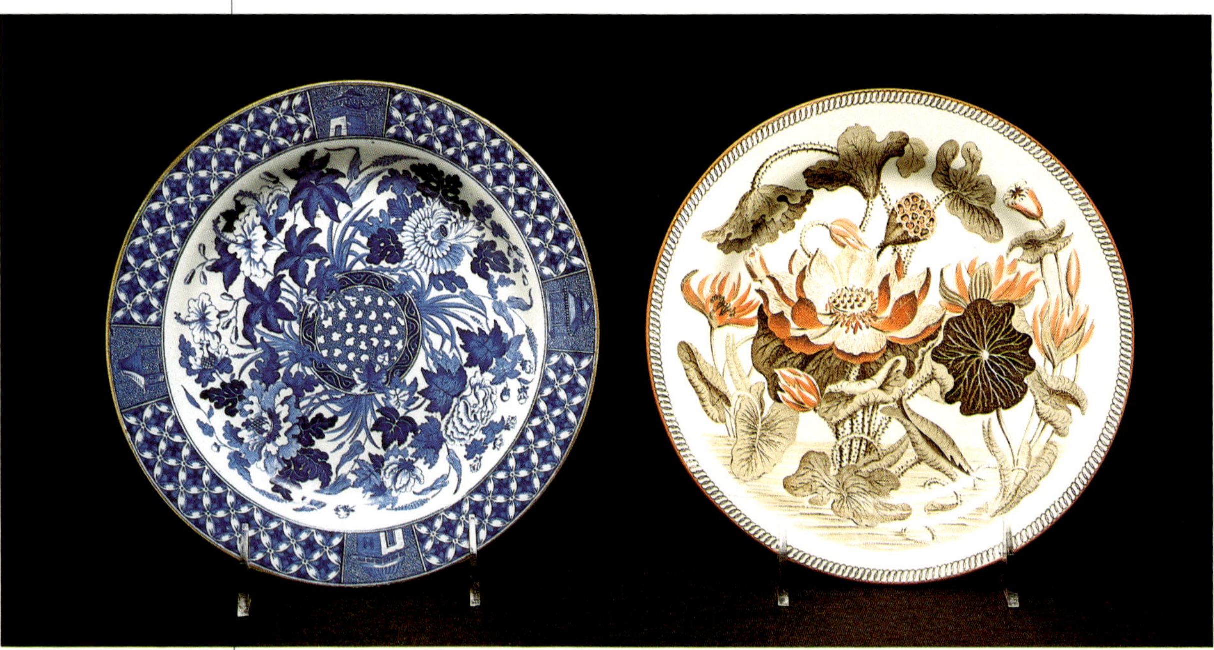

Color plate 146
Left, *Plate,* Hibiscus Pattern, *ca. 1810, pearl ware, transfer print with blue underglaze decoration and gilding, 8" (cat. 484);* right, *One of a Pair of Plates,* Water Lily, *ca. 1810, pearl ware, transfer print with orange underglaze decoration and gilding, 8 1/16" (cat. 478).*

17
Pearl Ware

In 1779 Wedgwood introduced "pearl white" to compete with a similar body that the Staffordshire potters called "China Glaze," produced as early as 1772 to accommodate the demand for blue-and-white porcelain.[1] Because cream ware had proven unsatisfactory for allover blue decoration and seemed to be losing favor, Thomas Bentley requested the new body early in the partnership. After many trials, Wedgwood achieved the goal and wrote to Bentley:

> I cannot make any great improvement in my present body but it will be china though I have endeavour'd all in my power to prevent it. However to give the brat a name you may set a cream-colour plate & one of the best blue & white ones before you, & suppose the one you are to name another degree whiter and finer still, but not transparent, & consequently not china.[2]

Bentley chose the name "pearl white," judging from a letter sent to him by Wedgwood on August 6, 1779:

> You know what Lady Dartmouth told us, that she, & her friends were tired of creamcolor, & so they would of Angels if they were shewn for sale in every chandlers shop through the town. The pearl white must be considered as a change rather than an improvement, & I must have something ready to succeed it when the public eye is pall'd, or it comes upon the town.[3]

The body, which we now call pearl ware, is whiter than cream ware as the result of a large portion of white clay and small quantities of flint and cobalt oxide added to the glaze and body.

Underglaze Blue Printing

As potters capitalized on the demand for oriental items in the late eighteenth century, underglaze blue printing became popular. While Josiah Wedgwood I had certainly been aware of this market and was capable of such production, he chose to promote jasper ware, perhaps because of his strong interest in neoclassicism. The demand became so great, however, that the Wedgwood factory was reduced to satisfying orders for blue wares by buying from competitors. In 1805, therefore, John Wedgwood, who was then in charge of Etruria, introduced underglaze blue printing in an effort to restore the leadership of the Wedgwood firm in the earthenware pottery business. Designs were pressed onto pearl, white, or cream biscuit ware by means of flat-press printing (versus glue-bat printing). Blue was the most common color used for decoration, because it could withstand most successfully the high-temperature firing essential for the transparent lead glaze.

Flat-press printing requires, first, that a sheet of wet, soapy pottery tissue be placed on a heated, etched plate colored with cobalt in a thick boiled oil. The paper is then cut, trimmed, and placed on the biscuit ware and rubbed with a rolled flannel or wooden boss. When the ware is immersed in water, the paper washes off; the color is unaffected, being mixed with oil. Prior to glazing it is necessary to remove the oil, which is accomplished by baking the piece in a hardening kiln. This procedure prevents the print from rejecting the water-based glaze. Before glazing, the ware is fired a second time to remove all moisture. A third firing is required in the glost oven at a very high temperature.[4]

John Wedgwood

John Wedgwood (1766-1844) was a man of varied interests and tastes. He was the founding treasurer of what later became the Royal Horticultural Society in 1804, and he was almost certainly the promoter of the new flower patterns of the period, which were produced chiefly in blue and white. The excellence of these printed wares, which were first offered for sale in 1807, is exemplified by the bold floral design of the "Hibiscus" pearl-ware plate in the Beeson collection (cat. 484, pl. 146).

John Wedgwood also introduced the "Water Lily" pattern, first printed in brown in 1808. Two plates in the Beeson collection with this design were transfer-printed and painted under the glaze on a cream-ware or pearl-ware body with overglaze gilt veining (cat. 478, pl. 146). The "Water Lily" was engraved by Semei Bourne in 1806 and re-engraved by John Robinson and William Hales between 1807 and 1809,[5] all three plants being from identifiable sources.[6] The brown design was supplanted eventually by the blue one made by Wedgwood in 1810. On May 2, 1811, Josiah Wedgwood II wrote a note to the London showroom, saying, "If you have any Brown Lily in the rooms, turn it all out that you may not take orders for it which we cannot execute but at a loss—we will print some in blue."[7]

The "Water Lily" pieces have often been erroneously called "Darwin" plates, because they were thought to have been made by Josiah I for Erasmus Darwin. Because they were not introduced until 1808, they may have been for Wedgwood's daughter Susannah, wife of Robert Darwin and mother of Charles Darwin. A letter of August 25, 1807, from Susannah to her brother Josiah II supports this theory: "We are very much obliged by your kind intention respecting the dinner service, which we are in no kind haste for, as it is not the custom of this town to give dinners in summer—I am therefore well inclined to follow your advice, and wait for the very handsome pattern."[8]

Between 1808 and 1809 another successful pattern—"Botanical Flowers"—was introduced, with forty-seven different flowers or groups of flowers depicted in blue on largely pearl-ware dinner services (cats. 480–83, pl. 147). Engraved by John Robinson and Thomas Longmore, each flower originally had a small number near the foot for identification.[9] Various sources were used for the flower designs, including *Botanical Magazine*, James Sowerby's *English Botany*, and Richard Salisbury's *Paradisus Londinenesis*.[10] On July 10, 1811, a memorandum from the London show-

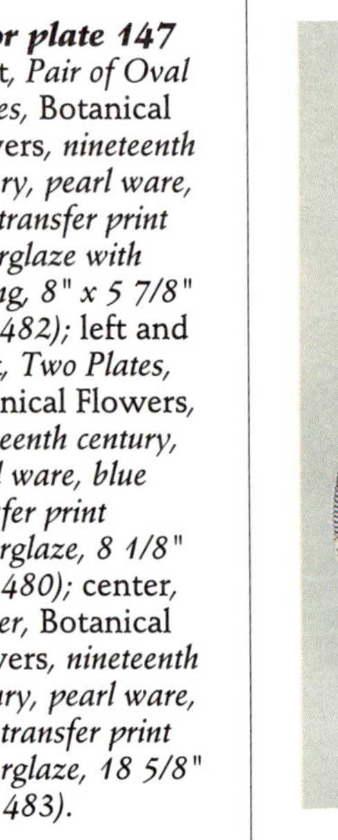

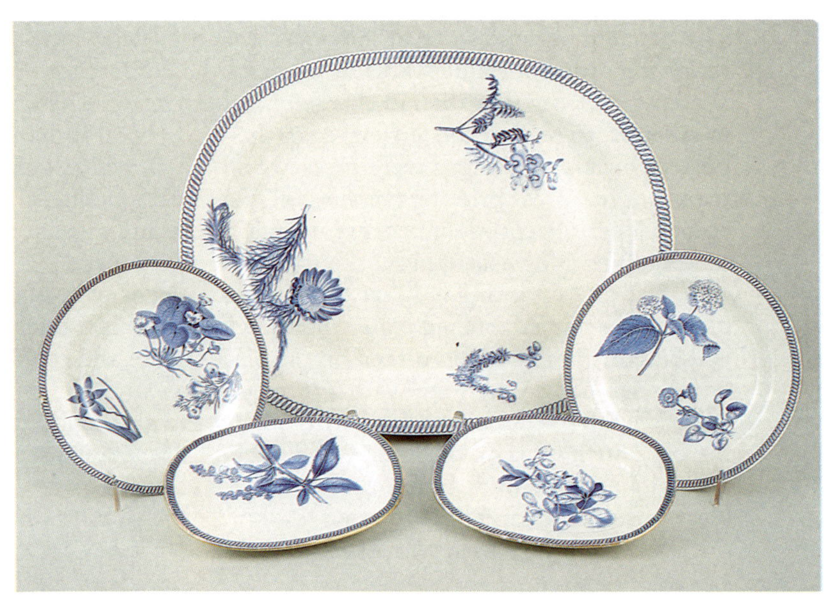

Color plate 147
Front, *Pair of Oval Dishes,* Botanical Flowers, *nineteenth century, pearl ware, blue transfer print underglaze with gilding, 8" x 5 7/8" (cat. 482);* left and right, *Two Plates,* Botanical Flowers, *nineteenth century, pearl ware, blue transfer print underglaze, 8 1/8" (cat. 480);* center, *Platter,* Botanical Flowers, *nineteenth century, pearl ware, blue transfer print underglaze, 18 5/8" (cat. 483).*

room to Etruria stated: "The flowers of which you send me the drawings and names I cannot make the use of I expected, & as I find that the flowers on the ware have not all got the nos. to them, perhaps it may be found worthwhile to re-engrave the Nos. which I suppose are worn out from the copper plate, but however that would probably be more trouble than the thing requires."[11] The reply stated: "If you think that numbers being put to the Flowers in 'Blue Flowers' pattern is desireable the trouble will be nothing."[12] Evidently this was not important, for the Beeson collection has a partial dinner service of sixteen pieces of the "Botanical Flowers" in underglaze blue without the numbers.

The "Nautilus" Service

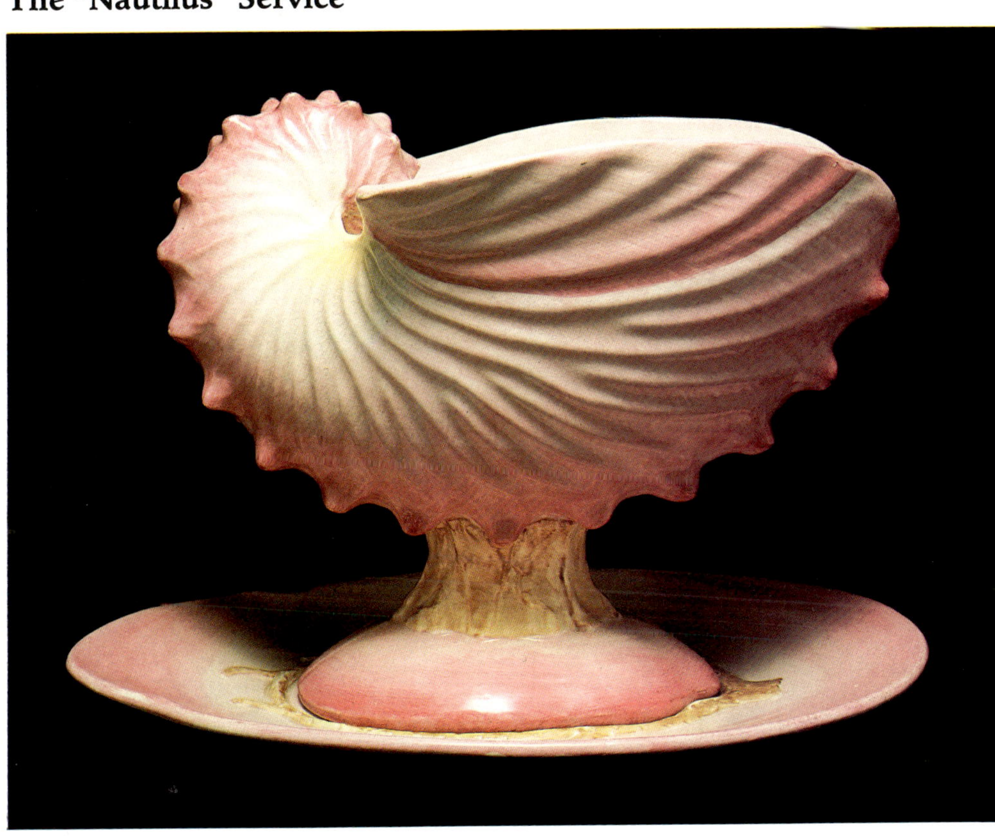

Color plate 148
Nautilus-Shaped Dessert Compote and Stand, ca. 1815, white ware with pink, yellow, orange, and pale brown underglaze decoration, centerpiece: 8" x 10 1/2", under-dish: 12 3/8" x 8" (cat. 471).

An amateur conchologist, Josiah Wedgwood I confessed in a letter to Bentley on September 15, 1778:

> I have got my face over a shell drawer, & find my self in imminent danger of becoming a connoisseur. You can scarcely conceive the progress I have made in a month or two in the deep & very elaborate science of shell fancying. Having arranged my whole collection in the most systematic manner, & studied them with the nicest attention, I can tell you, at sight, . . . distinctions which you, . . . would not understand, & might therefore under value. But this study, alass, like every other extention of the human mind, as it multiplies the avenues to our enjoyments discloses new sources of wants & anxieties, & at this present writing . . . a fine addition . . . would make me the happiest of chonchiologists.[13]

The first pieces of Wedgwood's "Nautilus" service appeared in about 1790, and a copy of his original drawing for a tureen and stand and eight plates, the designs of

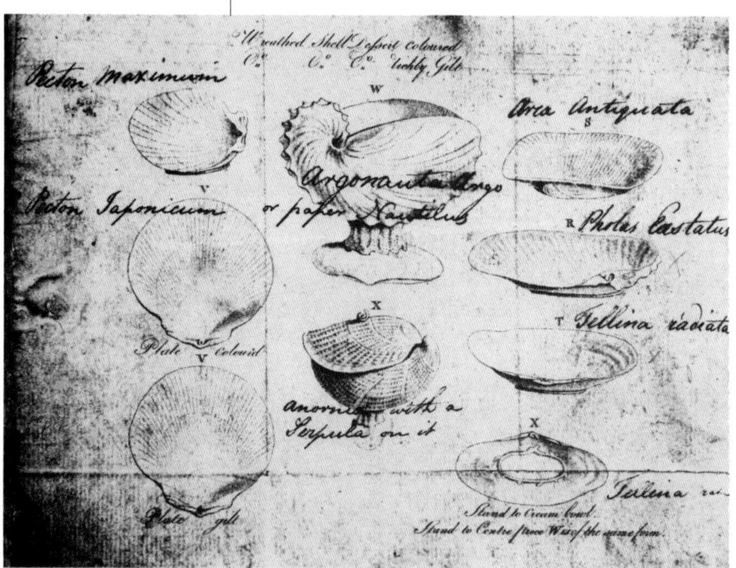

Fig. 46 *Wreathed Shell Dessert from the 1802 shape drawing book. Courtesy of the Trustees of the Wedgwood Museum, Barlaston, Stoke-on-Trent, England.*

which are correctly identified according to the terms used in conchology and titled "Wreathed Shell Dessert Coloured," is to be found in Wedgwood's pattern book and bears an 1802 watermark (fig. 46). The "Nautilus" dessert service in the Beeson collection is made of pearl ware or white ware with pink, yellow, orange, and brown decoration under the glaze (cats. 470, 471). The exact body of the tureen and stand are questionable (pl. 148), because the pearl ware manufactured after 1840, sometimes marked with the impressed "P" or "PEARL," has a glaze containing no cobalt blue staining, which often gives the body a white appearance very like that of white ware. The "Paper Nautilus" shell tureen is faithfully reproduced, although several times larger than the shell's natural size. The shell was first described by Carolus Linnaeus in 1758 and is actually the egg case for an octopod called *Argonauta argo*. An atellina, or "sunrise tellin," shell is the prototype for the tureen's stand. The eight accompanying plates copy the pecten japonicum shell. Most of these plates are marked "P" for pearl ware and "AEM" for April 1884.

18
Luster Decoration

The first reference to luster decoration in relation to the work of Josiah Wedgwood dates to 1776, when Thomas Bentley spoke of "gold coloured glazing on Earthen ware by fumegation . . . [which produced a] true copper glaze, looking like that metal, or betwixt that and Gold."[1] What Bentley was describing was a process by which a thin film of metal was deposited on the surface of a glazed body by a reducing kiln.[2] Yet for reasons unspecified, Wedgwood chose at that time not to pursue the experiments further.

Another method of achieving luster decoration was in use at Etruria by February of 1805. Gold-and-pink metallic luster was then produced by mixing gold or platinum in an oily resin and washing it over a fired glaze. The resin was burned

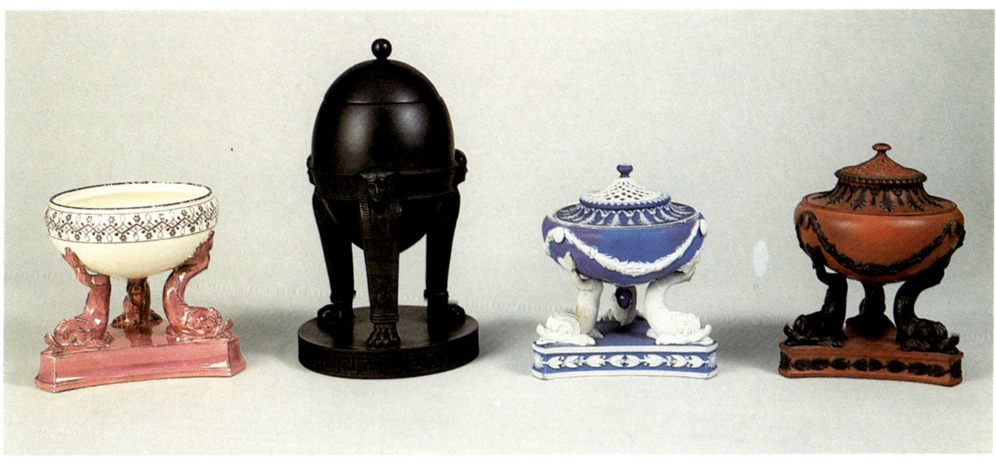

Color plate 149 Left, *Pastille Burner or Cassolette, ca. 1820, cream ware with rose luster and red-and-black enamel decoration, 4 3/8" x 4 1/8" (cat. 473);* second from left, *Pastille Burner or Cassolette, ca. 1805, basalt, 6 5/8" x 4 3/4" (cat. 173);* second from right, *Pastille Burner or Cassolette, ca. 1805, jasper, solid white ground with dark blue wash and white relief, 5 1/8" x 3 7/8" (cat. 396);* right, *Pastille Burner or Cassolette, ca. 1805, rosso antico with basalt relief, 5 1/2" x 3 9 16" (cat. 456).*

away through oxidation in an enameling kiln, leaving the metal compound on the surface.[3] In the Beeson collection, a rare redware sphinx decorated with platinum luster is thought to be an experimental piece from the early nineteenth century (cat. 467).[4]

Platinum and gold lusters, when first made, were used principally for tea and coffee ware as well as tripod pastille cassolettes.[5] A tripod cassolette in the Beeson collection also has luster decoration; in this case, purple-rose was painted on a dolphin base that supports a cream-ware bowl with transfer-printed motifs (cat. 473, pl. 149). There are in the Beeson collection four other examples of cassolettes in different wares, including jasper, basalt, and rosso antico, with four of the five having the mysterious notation "Josiah Wedgwood 2d February 1805" (cats. 173, 396, 456, pl. 149, fig. 47). While the significance of the date remains unknown, recent conjecture holds that it relates to a trial kiln firing inspired by the use of luster decoration.[6]

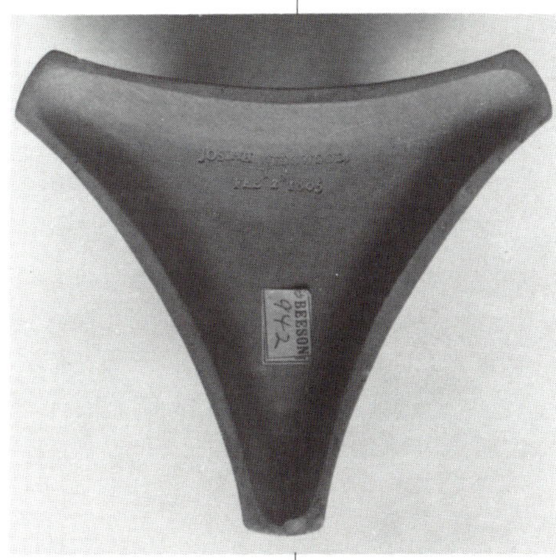

Fig. 47 *Detail of mark, Pastille Burner or Cassolette, ca. 1805, redware with basalt relief, 5 1/2" x 3 9/16" (cat. 456). (See far right above.)*

About 1809 a variegated luster was introduced by Wedgwood, as evidenced by a memorandum mentioning a "solution of gold with a little tin mixed with sweet wort & laid on with a feather."[7] The different colors, which were applied with a feather, were achieved by mixing gold (which fired the color pink), platinum (which fired gray), and iron (which fired orange).

By 1810 Josiah Wedgwood II was using this newly popular pink or purple variegated luster on cream ware, pearl ware, and especially white ware. Also known as "moonlight" luster, it was popular for only a short time, and the quantity was comparatively limited.

An example of variegated luster in the Beeson collection may be seen on a Krater, or tazza, vase made of white ware from about 1820 (cat. 474, pl. 150). The form is a copy of a Greek campana shape with two fitments, one solid and the other pierced to hold potpourri. The Spode shape book of 1820 described it as a "Pot-Pourri Bowpot on Square Plinth."[8]

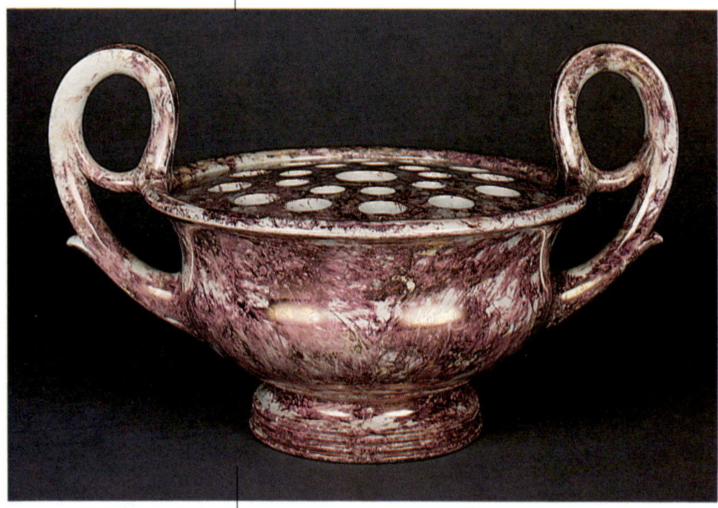

Color plate 150
Krater Vase with Two Fitments, ca. 1820, white ware with variegated luster decoration, 6 7/8" x 5" (cat. 474).

19
Émile-Aubert Lessore

A student of Jean-Auguste-Dominique Ingres, Émile-Aubert Lessore (1805-76) had his first success with the publication of fifty sketches he had completed during a tour of northern Africa in 1835; this was followed, in 1837, by the publication *Album Venitien*. A year after he joined the Sèvres factory in 1852, a pair of his vases was exhibited at the Paris Exposition and was later purchased by the emperor of Russia. Lessore left Sèvres in 1858, following disputes with fellow artists, and went to England. He worked briefly at the Minton factory in Staffordshire before moving to the Wedgwood factory in the spring of 1860. Delighted with the artistic freedom he finally had obtained, Lessore wrote, "I shut myself up at Etruria as in a tomb, without seeing the sun more than six times a year. I am racked with rheumatism, but my heart is full of joy. I am my own master, and my benefactors are satisfied with me."[1] The affiliation was a success for Wedgwood as well. Lessore worked with speed and enthusiasm, producing 136 pieces in just a few months. His work sold so rapidly that the Wedgwood firm offered him a permanent contract of four hundred pounds a year, a sum that probably made Lessore the firm's highest paid employee.

A multifaceted artist working in both watercolors and oils, Lessore was also an accomplished engraver and ceramic artist. Clement F. Wedgwood once described, in fascinating detail, Lessore's methods of ceramic production:

> He chooses CC (creamcolour) ware and has it dip't in Rockingham without stain so that it is very soft and of a very warm tint. In all small subjects such as trays, small vases, etc. the outline is printed for him in chocolate from drawings etched by himself on copper plates. These subjects are generally small Watteau scenes in a pastoral landscape, or cupids, or little german figures.
>
> The ornamentation of the piece is done at the same time as the printing. It generally consists in colouring the handles and feet and a few lines round the mouth. Celeste green and orange yellow being the colours most used. They are then fired in the Enamel Kiln.
>
> After the first fire Mr. Lessore takes them in hand and puts the colouring into the picture, when they are again fired and if not finished enough are again touched up and fired. In the case of larger pieces the subjects are first taken from the original on tissue paper, and then traced off on the vase with tracing paper, then drawn in pensil [*sic*] and finally the chocolate outline painted on, when they are fired like the rest. The colouring is then put on in one or more fires.[2]

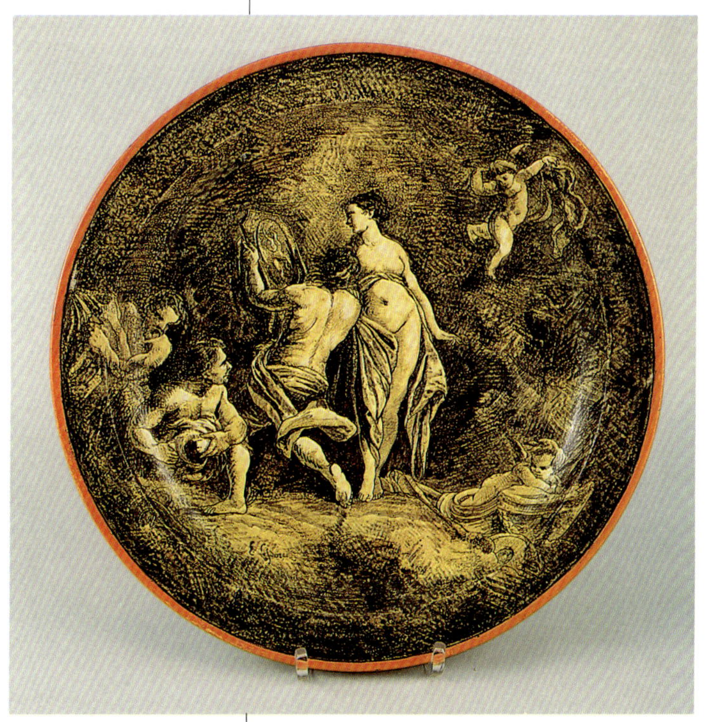

Color plate 151
Platter, Perseus and Andromeda, *ca. 1865, Émile Lessore (1805-76), artist, cream ware with green and orange underglaze decoration, 19 1/2" (cat. 487).*

In the Beeson collection are seven cream-ware pieces that were decorated by Lessore for Wedgwood in the late nineteenth century (cats. 485–91). A large round platter of about 1868 is of particular interest (cat. 487, pl. 151). Depicting the mythological scene of Perseus and Andromeda, this portrayal is thought to be an adaptation of two scenes of the same subject by Peter Paul Rubens.[3]

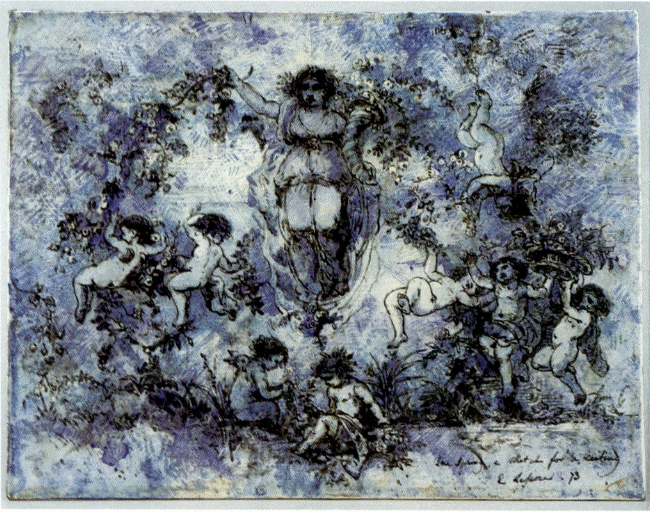

Color plate 152
Plaque, The Spring, A Sketch for a Ceiling, *1873, Émile Lessore (1805-76), artist, cream ware with blue-and-black underglaze decoration, 12" x 16" (cat. 486).*

Lessore achieved a great reputation as a painter at Wedgwood. His work was exhibited by the firm at the London International Exhibition of 1862 (for which he received wide acclaim), the Paris Exposition Universelle of 1867, and the Vienna Exposition of 1873. The severity of the English climate, which aggravated Lessore's rheumatism, prompted him to make an agreement with the Wedgwood firm in 1862 that he would live in Paris in the winter and London in the summer, provided that he stay at Etruria for ten days each month during the warm weather.[4] This agreement was later altered, and thereafter Lessore worked only in Marlotte, France.[5] Popular interest in Lessore's pieces began to wane after 1867, but he continued to supply Wedgwood with varying amounts of painted ware until his death in 1876. His talents were recognized during his lifetime, and his work was prized by Victorian collectors as an investment. After Lessore died, the remaining Lessore stock at Wedgwood was put on exhibition and dispersed at a very successful sale managed by John Mortlock, a London dealer.

A gift to the Beeson collection by Mrs. Byron A. Born, in memory of her husband, is a cream-ware plaque by Lessore, possibly one of the last pieces he painted for Wedgwood (cat. 486, pl. 152). The plaque depicts Rubenesque cupids surrounding a full-figured female who holds a horn of plenty; it is certainly one of Lessore's finest works and shows Lessore's free and masterly style. Written in the corner under the glaze is the inscription "The Spring, a sketch for a ceiling / E. Lessore 73." To date we do not know if this sketch was ever executed on a ceiling, but it is thought to be from a series of seasonal renderings.

Color plate 153
Three-Piece Jardiniere, 1867, Émile Lessore (1805-76), artist, Hugues Protât (fl. 1835-71), designer and modeler, pearl ware with polychrome enamel overglaze decoration, 22" x 24" (cat. 485).

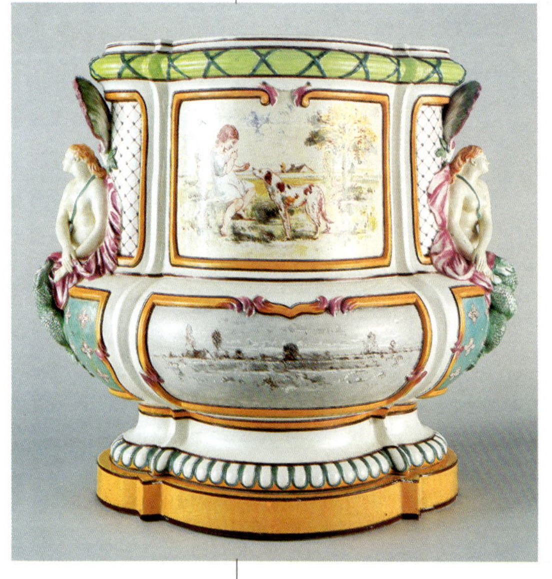

Another outstanding example decorated by Lessore is a signed pearl-ware jardiniere, which is marked "WEDGWOOD" and "OMV" for October 1867 (cat. 485, pl. 153). Because of its size and presence, this piece may have been exhibited at the Paris Exposition of 1871. The modeler is thought to be Hugues Protât, a French sculptor who worked for Wedgwood from 1858 until 1871 and whose work was often decorated by Lessore. The jardiniere is in three parts, with two separate stands connected to the main bowl with three long metal screws and bolts; large, sculpted mermaids and shells act as handles. Two different scenes—one of reapers, which is signed by Lessore, and one of a child and dog—are depicted in a large cartouche on either side, and two landscapes are depicted in separate cartouches below. The piece is outlined in a burnt yellow with red and green accents, colors that are typical of Lessore's palette during this period.

Notes

1. The Pottery Industry in Eighteenth-Century England

1. Haggar, Mountford, and Thomas, *Staffordshire Pottery Industry*, 11.
2. Wills, *English Pottery and Porcelain*, 117.
3. Quoted in Church, *Josiah Wedgwood*, 15-16.
4. McKendrick, *The Birth of a Consumer Society*, 9.
5. Josiah Wedgwood to Richard L. Edgeworth, February 13, 1786, E3-2485.
6. E25-18392.
7. E25-18232.
8. Hamilton and d'Hancarville, *Antiquités.*
9. William Hamilton to Josiah Wedgwood, May 23, 1786, uncataloged.
10. E26-18898.
11. E25-18147.
12. June 1, 1767, E25-18149.
13. Ibid.
14. E25-18261.
15. E25-18240.
16. E25-18341.
17. E25-18234.
18. Oven book, June 5 and 12, 1784: "2 dz & 3 dz blue & white lybols inlado by J. Wedgwood FRS" (E53-30015).
19. E25-18315.
20. E25-18252.

2. Staffordshire Pottery

1. E25-18772.
2. Dawson, *Masterpieces of Wedgwood*, 13.
3. Reilly, *Wedgwood* 1:33.
4. Barker, *William Greatbatch*, 14.
5. Ibid.
6. This attribution came from David Barker, assistant keeper of archaeology at the City Museum and Art Gallery at Hanley, Stoke-on-Trent, England. During the Wedgwood International Seminar at the Birmingham Museum of Art in May 1990, he applied rubbings of shards found at Fenton Vivian to this teapot.
7. Wedgwood Experiment Book 1, E26-19117.
8. Ibid.
9. The preceding information on William Greatbatch and his wares was generously supplied by David Barker in a letter dated July 11, 1988.
10. Barker, *William Greatbatch*, 49-50.
11. December 15, 1764, WM 22391-30.
12. Shaw, *History of the Staffordshire Potteries*, 190.
13. Shards of similar wares have been excavated by David Barker at the pottery sites of Whieldon, Greatbatch, and Warburton.

3. Josiah Wedgwood

1. Meteyard, *Life of Josiah Wedgwood* 1: 222-23, n. 1.
2. For a detailed account of the Wedgwood and Wedgwood partnership, see Niblett, "A Useful Partner."
3. Undated, E25-18183.
4. E25-18070.
5. E25-18071.
6. E25-18324.
7. E25-18152.
8. E25-18161.
9. W/M 1826.
10. Undated, E25-12336.
11. E25-18049.

12. Undated, E25-18252.
13. E25-18324.
14. Uncataloged.
15. February 3, 1770, E25-18287.
16. E25-18248.
17. December 17, 1767, E25-18177.
18. December 1, 1769, E25-18788.
19. McKendrick, "Factory Discipline," 33.
20. Ibid.
21. E26-19114.
22. E25-18269.
23. McKendrick, "Factory Discipline," 37.
24. Josiah Wedgwood Commonplace Book 1, 180, E39-28408.
25. McKendrick, "Cost Accounting."
26. E54-30023.
27. E25-18392.
28. Ibid.
29. Ibid.
30. The Price Book of Workmanship, E54-30023, 1-62.
31. Barlaston 31201. The list, dated August 10, 1770, is reproduced in Chellis, "Wedgwood and Bentley Source Books," 60.
32. E26-18950.
33. Received March 7, 1774, E25-18521.
34. July 3, 1779, E26-18905.
35. June 13, 1779, LHP.
36. LHP. This fact is proven even in an estate inventory in Jefferson County, Alabama, of 1840; "1 Wedgewood [*sic*] mortar" is listed (Jefferson County Courthouse, Birmingham, Alabama, Orphan Court Records, 1841-44, October 24, 1840, Estate Inventory of N. F. Randolph, who also owned an "apothecary table").
37. "Obituary of Josiah Wedgwood," *Gentleman's Magazine* 65, no. 85, (1795).
38. The Lunar Society (1766-1809) was a group of philosophic industrialists and scientists from the Midlands who met on the evening of the full moon to discuss their recent scientific experiments. The membership included Matthew Boulton, Erasmus Darwin, William Small, John Whitehurst, Richard Lovell Edgeworth, Thomas Day, James Keir, James Watt, William Withering, Joseph Priestley, Samuel Galton, Jr., Jonathan Stoke, and the Reverend Robert Augustus Johnson. The men were "scientific philosophers struggling to get their ideas to work, inventors struggling to get their discoveries applied, entrepreneurs struggling to match their output to demand" (McKendrick, "Role of Science," 276). Their desire for the unification of industry, commerce, and experiment has proven to be the basis for much of scientific discovery today.
39. E25-18166.
40. December 20, 1777, E25-18804.
41. E25-18320.

4. Cream Ware

1. Haggar, Mountford, and Thomas, *Staffordshire Pottery Industry*, 3-4.
2. *Selected Letters of Josiah Wedgwood*, 7.
3. LHP 388-3.
4. Wedgwood Experiment Book I, 257, E26-19117.
5. E25-18123.
6. July 9, 1771, LHP; November 15, 1772, E25-17420.
7. Wills, *English Pottery and Porcelain*, 118.
8. E25-18080.
9. The Aris's *Birmingham Gazette* noted on June 9, 1766, "Mr. Josiah Wedgwood, of Burslem, has had the Honour of being appointed Potter to Her Majesty" (Reilly, *Wedgwood* 1:201).
10. E25-18167.
11. Barnard, *Chats on Wedgwood Ware*, 93.
12. Reilly, *Wedgwood* 1:209.
13. Lockett and Halfpenny, *Creamware and Pearlware*, 22.
14. Drakard and Holdway, *Spode Printed Ware*, 40.
15. Quoted in ibid., 11.

16. Ibid., 11-13.

17. Reilly, *Wedgwood* 1:210, 245.

18. See ibid., 209-49, for a complete history of Wedgwood's negotiations with Sadler and Green.

19. April 3, 1765, E25-18072.

20. E25-18299.

21. E25-18161.

22. The design appears on porcelain, cream ware, and one tin-glazed earthenware example and was taken from an engraving after Louis-Pierre Boitard dated 1751.

23. The design source was engraved by Jan Both after Andries Both. Even more explicit is the tile for the sense of smell, showing the wiping of a baby's bottom. See Watney, "Some Liverpool Printed Tiles."

24. Hawes, "Longfellow, the Poet, and Sadler, the Tile Printer," 154.

25. Stretton, "Wedgwood Transfer-Printed Creamware."

26. W/M 1431.

27. E25-18726.

28. Towner, *English Cream-Coloured Earthenware,* 39.

29. Other known enamelers were located in Liverpool, Leeds, Yorkshire, and Staffordshire. See Lockett and Halfpenny, *Creamware and Pearlware,* 18.

30. E30-22341.

31. There are no known signed pieces by Rhodes or the "Rhodes school," so the pieces attributed to Rhodes are thus designated by virtue of his association with Wedgwood and related documentary evidence. For a complete discussion of the Rhodes school and their work, see Reilly, *Wedgwood* 1:250-66.

32. E25-18196.

33. Quoted in Reilly, *Wedgwood* 1:298.

34. The plate is entitled *A Vow to Castor* (Hamilton, *Antiquités,* vol. 1, pl. 55).

35. E25-18138.

36. Reilly, *Wedgwood* 1:186.

37. E25-18087.

38. The shell spout and the double-strap handles are thought to have been modeled by William Greatbatch (Reilly, *Wedgwood* 1:191).

39. E25-18356.

40. LHP, uncataloged letter.

41. LHP, uncataloged letter.

42. Reilly, *Wedgwood* 2:690.

43. The Artemisia medallion in the Beeson collection (cat. 698) is marked "C 111 S 1," which stands for class 3, section 1, of the Wedgwood and Bentley *Ornamental Catalogue* of 1779, in which Artemisia, queen of Caria, is listed as number 10. This medallion is different from the rest in that a blue enamel was painted over the glaze on the front. The face and neck of the subject were colored in a skin tone, while a brown enamel appears on the pupils of the eyes and outlines the hair and garment. This medallion is also self-framed.

5. The Frog Service of Catherine the Great of Russia

1. Lancelot "Capability" Brown (1715-1803) was a British architect and landscape designer. He designed the gardens at Kew and Blenheim in England. Josiah Wedgwood writes of meeting him on May 23, 1767 (E25-18147).

2. E25-18450.

3. E25-18452.

4. Thomas Bentley's catalog for the Frog Service was written in 1774 and published in French. It is translated into English in Williamson, *Imperial Russian Dinner Service,* 59-63.

5. March 23, 1773, E25-18450.

6. Reilly, *Wedgwood* 1:274.

7. November 14, 1773, E25-18498.

8. E25-18540.

9. A letter of May 3, 1984, to Lucille Beeson from Michael Raeburn gave the origin of the design source; this letter is located in the object file, accession number 1983.7, at the Birmingham Museum of Art, Birmingham, Alabama.

10. Buck and Buck, *Antiquities, vol.* 8, pl. 6.

11. This plate was one of a dozen that were sold in 1909 by Stoner and Evans in London and that may have originally belonged to Alexander Baxter. The original invoice from this sale is located in the object file, accession number 1986.638, at the Birmingham Museum of Art, Birmingham, Alabama.

12. The printed source for this view is Grose, *Antiquities of England and Wales,* vol. 3, unnumbered plate, engraved by S. Sparrow (dated July 10, 1774) from a drawing by Edward Eyre, Jr.

6. White Terra-cotta Stoneware

1. E25-181215.
2. E25-18271.
3. Quoted in Reilly, *Wedgwood* 1:367.
4. Ibid., 1:347.
5. Second Experiment Book, no. 1211.
6. Reilly, *Wedgwood* 1:366.
7. E25-18240.
8. February 14, 1769, E25-18229.
9. October 1, 1769, E25-18264.
10. LHP.
11. September 3, 1770, E25-18324.
12. E25-18319.
13. Similar handles occur on a French faience pot and cover in the Victoria and Albert Museum.
14. Clifford, "English Ceramic Vases," 164, pl. 71.
15. Ibid., 170, 171, pl. 82.
16. E25-18389.
17. Reilly, *Wedgwood* 1:380.
18. Commonplace Book 39-28498, 234. See also Roberts, "English Country House," 106.

7. Basalt

1. For more detailed information on the invention of basalt, see Dawson, *Masterpieces*, 35.
2. Commonplace Book recipes dated 1777 and July 1787, W/M 39-28410, pp. 236, 327.
3. E25-18208.
4. E25-18337.
5. August 11, 1770, E25-18316.
6. 1773 *Ornamental Catalogue*.
7. E25-18521.
8. E25-18316.
9. E96-17667.
10. Undated (probably February 14-20, 1769), E25-18232.
11. Hamilton, *Antiquités*, vol. 3, pl. 31. This plate depicts a painted earthenware kalyx Krater vase bought by the British Museum in 1772 from Sir William Hamilton. The only deviation from the Krater vase design is that the seated female figure was given a stool to sit on, versus being suspended in midair, and she holds a spear behind her instead of in front. (Dawson, 102-11).
12. Letter from Thomas Bentley to Sir William Hamilton, formerly in the possession of Mrs. Robert D. Chellis, Boston, Mass., now at the Birmingham Museum of Art.
13. E32-5365.
14. This document is now lost. See Mankowitz, *The Portland Vase*, 29-30.
15. Montfaucon, *L'Antiquité expliquée*, vol. 1, pt. 1, pl. 41.
16. Kelly, *Decorative Wedgwood*, 25.
17. Wedgwood Ms. 2-30951, Hoskins and Oliver invoice, December 31, 1770.
18. Dawson, *Masterpieces*, 110-12.
19. Clodion is thought to have copied the tablet from a bronze version inscribed to Cardinal Rohan in 1787. The original model is yet to be discovered, but was probably made of red terra-cotta.
20. Montfaucon, *L'Antiquité expliquée*, vol. 5, pl. 1, pg. 4, fig. 2. For additional discussion of one other figure, see Macht, *Classical Wedgwood Designs*, 83-84.
21. For a detailed discussion of this tablet, see Reilly, *Wedgwood* 1:487-89.
22. Macht, *Classical Wedgwood Designs*, 110-12.
23. E25-18264.
24. E25-18252.
25. E25-18552.
26. LHP.
27. E25-18558.
28. Reilly and Savage provide a list of subjects molded by Hoskins and Oliver in *Dictionary*, 192.
29. E25-18258.
30. E26-18859.

31. Reilly and Savage provide a list of subjects modeled by William Hackwood in *Dictionary*, 181.

32. May 28, 1770, E25-18304.

33. Invoice from Flaxman to Wedgwood, Wedgwood MS. I-205.

34. E25-18167.

35. Reilly and Savage, *Dictionary*, 353. A marble copy of a similar ancient figure by Coysevox is in the gardens of Versailles, and a later copy was made in bronze by sixteenth-century sculptor Giovanni da Bologna.

36. Chambers, *Treatise on Civil Architecture*, pl. 91; Dawson, *Masterpieces*, 55, 57.

37. E25-18673.

38. Stella, *Livre de vases*, pl. 2; Robin Reilly very kindly provided this information. See also Clifford, "English Ceramic Vases," 165, 175. An identical vase exists in the Fogg Art Museum of Harvard University in Cambridge, Mass. The modeler has not been determined.

39. Stefano della Bella, *Raccolta di vasi diversi . . .*, pl. 6; Clifford, "English Ceramic Vases," 166, 179.

40. Quoted in Clifford, "English Ceramic Vases," 162.

41. See the Beeson Frieze Room, p. 115, for an additional version of Dancing Hours.

42. Sir Laurence Dundas, a patron of Wedgwood, brought the frieze to Moor Park in Hertfordshire, England, in the 1760s (Kelly, *Decorative Wedgwood*, 62-63).

43. Reilly, *Wedgwood* 1:585–86.

44. T. Byerley to P. Swift, January 2, 1782, MS. 13-12452.

45. E25-18197.

46. E25-18237.

47. E25-18263.

48. *Ornamental Catalogue* of 1779.

49. E25-18474.

50. E25-18430.

51. E25-18701.

52. Reilly, *Wedgwood* 1:427–29.

53. Ibid., 631.

54. E25-18231

55. E25-18236.

56. E25-18787.

8. Etruscan Ware

1. E25-18183.

2. For more information on Hamilton as an antiquary, see Ramage, "Sir William Hamilton as Collector, Exporter, and Dealer."

3. E25-18258. Often confusing is the fact that Wedgwood also called his plain basalt ware "Etruscan" until 1773, when he began to use the term "Basaltes."

4. Noble, *Techniques of Painted Attic Pottery*.

5. Undated, E25-18257.

6. February 19, 1770, E25-18290.

7. January 21, 1771, LHP.

8. LHP.

9. June 13, 1771, LHP.

10. Wedgwood had had his leg amputated in May 1768 after a riding accident that injured his already frail leg.

11. E25-18269.

12. Hamilton and d'Hancarville, *Antiquités*, vol. 1, pl. 129.

13. Reilly, *Wedgwood* 1:436-38.

14. E25-18426.

15. Reilly, *Wedgwood* 1:440.

16. Haskell, *Past and Present*, 30-45, devotes a chapter to D'Hancarville and his relationship with Hamilton as well as to eighteenth-century philosophy.

17. Ramage, "Hamilton's Collection of Antiquities."

18. Dawson, *Masterpieces*, 91 and figs. 71, 72.

19. Montfaucon, *L'Antiquité expliquée*, vol. 1, pt. 2, pl. 18, fig. 1, from the Maffei collection. The author wishes to thank Aileen Dawson at the British Museum for her help with the research on this ewer, per a letter of October 4, 1988.

20. Josiah Wedgwood to Thomas Wedgwood, uncataloged letter of 1790.

9. Neoclassicisim

1. Quoted in Crook, *Greek Revival*, 2.

2. Ibid., 17.

3. Details about the wall paintings were first published in *Antiquities of Herculaneum* (*Le Antichitâ di Ercolano*) in an eight-volume series between 1757 and 1792. Under the patronage of Charles V, king of Naples, the work was not for sale and was made available only as a gift of the king.

4. The temples that were excavated included that of Ceres at Eleusis, of Juno at Samos, of Apollo near Miletus, of Diana at Magnesia, and of Nemesis at Rhamnos .

5. Quoted in Honour, *Age of Neoclassicism*, 4.

6. Adam and Adam, *Works in Architecture* 1:4-5.

10. Jasper Ware

1. September 17, 1769, E25-18255.

2. Reilly, *Wedgwood* 1:517-21.

3. January 23, 1790, E26-18991.

4. E25-18555.

5. E25-18556.

6. November 6, 1774, E25-18562.

7. E25-18557.

8. E25-18609.

9. E25-18614.

10. Reilly, *Wedgwood* 1:524.

11. E25-18578.

12. January 15, 1775, E25-18584.

13. E25-18642.

14. E25-18626.

15. E26-18976.

16. W/M 1455; later, dated copy handwritten by Alexander Chisholm.

17. E25-18746.

18. E25-18790.

19. W/M 1455.

20. See Evans, "Wedgwood, Windmills, and Water-power."

21. E25-18670.

22. E25-18673.

23. Reilly and Savage, *Wedgwood: The Portrait Medallions*, 81.

24. E26-18919.

25. Reilly, *Wedgwood* 1:533.

26. E31201. For an in-depth discussion of these books, see Johnson, "Books Belonging to Wedgwood and Bentley," and "Further Research."

The following is a complete list of Wedgwood and Bentley's library on August 10, 1770:

L'Antiquité expliquée par Montfaucon 15 Vol^S^ 1772
Hambleton's Etruscan Antiquities 2 Vol^S^
Museum Etruscum Gorii ___ 3 Vol^S^
Museum Romanum, de la Chausse 2 V^S^
Gemmae Antiquae Museum Florentinum 1st Vol
Turnbulls Painting of the Antients
Stosch's Gems by Picart fine Copy
Antiquities of Herculaneum. 6 Vol^S^ (Sheets)
Recueil de trois Cent Tetes et Sujets de Composition Gravés par Mr le Comte de Caÿlus 4°
Antiquities of Venice 2 Vol^S^ folio
Caylus's Antiquities 7 Vol^S^ 4°
Stella's Vases of the Louvre Folio
Plates for Ovids Metamorphosis 4 p^ts^
Recueil d'antiquités Romaines 4°, chiefly Vases
Verrerie par Kunkell et les Autres 4°
Montamy 12°
Bardon de peinture et La Sculpture 12°
Dictionaire d'Antiquité 16°
Lives of ye Saints ten Vol^S^ 4°
Rossi's Statues at Etruria
Temple of the Muses. d°
Potts Chymical works 4 Volumes
Hambletons Etruscan Antiquities 1 Vol S^r^ WWW
Cherron's Gems Folio
Stewarts Athens d°

Iconologie Historique par de la Fosse
Hogarths Analysis
Perriers Statues
Ficoroni's Gems
Middletons Antiquites.
British and Irish Peerage 3 Vol[s]

27. Quoted in Macht, *Classical Wedgwood Designs,* xv.
28. Ibid., xv.
29. Anonymous, *Le Antichita di Ercolano Esposte,* vol. 1 (Naples, 1757).
30. E25-18820.
31. Reilly and Savage, *Dictionary,* 205.
32. Macht, *Classical Wedgwood Designs,* 119.
33. Walker, *William Blake,* 43.
34. Montfaucon, *L'Antiquité expliquée,* 1:89.
35. Reilly and Savage, *Dictionary,* 235.
36. Montfaucon, *L'Antiquité expliquée,* 1:89.
37. Delhom, "James Tassie and Josiah Wedgwood," 112–13.
38. Stuart and Revett, *Antiquities of Athens,* vol. 1; Hamilton, *Antiquités* 2:57.
39. Reilly and Savage, *Dictionary,* 211, 126–27, 317.
40. Montfaucon, *L'Antiquité expliquée,* vol. 1, pt. 2, pl. 62, fig. 11.
41. Ibid., vol. 2, pt. 2, pl. 66, fig. 2.
42. E25-18641.
43. E25-18788.
44. Montfaucon, *L'Antiquité expliquée,* vol. 1, pt. 2, pl. 86, fig. 12.
45. Macht, *Classical Wedgwood Designs,* 32-34.
46. Montfaucon, *L'Antiquité expliquée,* vol. 1, pt. 2, pl. 61, fig. 3.
47. Macht, *Classical Wedgwood Designs,* 54-55.
48. Stosch, *Pierres antiques gravées,* pl. 70; Dawson, *Masterpieces,* 49; Reilly, *Wedgwood* 1:587.
49. Reilly, *Dictionary,* 232.
50. Bindman, *John Flaxman,* 53.
51. Montfaucon, *L'Antiquité expliquée,* vol. 1, pl. 54, fig. 1.
52. Reilly, *Wedgwood* 1:616.
53. E26-18991.
54. Montfaucon, *L'Antiquité expliquée,* vol. 1, pt. 1, pl. 31, fig. 1.
55. E25-18147.
56. Reilly and Savage, *Dictionary,* 17.
57. February 24, 1776, E25-18657.
58. E25-18760.
59. For a discussion of the age of portrait medallions, see Reilly and Savage, *Wedgwood: The Portrait Medallions,* 33-36.
60. E25-18657.
61. E25-18846.
62. E25-18679.
63. Reilly, *Wedgwood* 1:555.
64. E26-18878.
65. E26-18880.
66. E25-18805.
67. Reilly, *Wedgwood* 1:559.
68. E26-18859.
69. Uncataloged letter, LHP.
70. Reilly and Savage, *Dictionary,* 118.
71. Ibid., 26.
72. E25-18673.
73. Reilly and Savage, *Wedgwood: The Portrait Medallions,* 130.
74. E26-18862.
75. E25-18146.
76. E25-18067. "One of our insolvent Master Potters" may be a reference to Andrew Duche of Savannah and Charleston; see Rauschenberg, "Andrew Duche".
77. E25-18772.

78. Tattersall, *Wedgwood Portraits*, 94.

79. Benjamin Franklin to Josiah Wedgwood, May 15, 1788, Yale University Library.

80. Reilly and Savage, *Wedgwood: The Portrait Medallions*, 292.

81. E26-18860.

82. See Born, "John Paul Jones and the Wedgwood Medallions."

83. Uncataloged letter, Josiah Wedgwood, Jr., to Josiah Wedgwood, Sr., July 28, 1789.

84. Reilly and Savage, *Wedgwood: The Portrait Medallions*, 223.

85. Ibid., 222.

86. Buten, *Eighteenth-Century Wedgwood*, 152; Reilly and Savage, *Dictionary*, 215.

87. For an in-depth discussion of the Leopold medallions and their relationship to the Sydney Cove medallion, see Reilly, *Wedgwood* 1: 614–15.

88. Reilly, *Wedgwood* 2: 716.

89. E25-18213.

90. LHP.

91. E25-18671.

92. E25-18844.

93. E26-18898.

94. Kelly, *Decorative Wedgwood*, 12, 76–77.

95. Bindman, *Flaxman*, 52.

96. Macht, *Classical Wedgwood Designs*, 86-93.

97. E25-18788; Reilly, *Wedgwood* 1: 589.

98. Llewellyn, "Salesrooms, Early English Ceramics," 282. For another possible design source, see Montfaucon, *L'Antiquité expliquée*, vol. 1, pt. 1, pl. 30, fig. 1.

99. Reilly, *Wedgwood* 1:589.

100. Montfaucon, *L'Antiquité expliquée*, vol. 2, pt. 3, pl. 27.

101. Ibid., vol. 2, pt. 1, pl. 29, fig. 1.

102. Ibid., vol. 2, pt. 1, pl. 30, figs. 1, 2.

103. E25-18847.

104. Reilly, *Wedgwood* 1: 631.

105. Buten, *Eighteenth-Century Wedgwood*, 98.

106. Montfaucon, *L'Antiquité expliquée*, vol. 2, pt. 1, pl. 17, fig. 4.

107. E25-18790.

108. LHP.

109. Reilly, *Wedgwood* 1: 642-43.

110. I would like to thank Raymond Lane of Art Trading Ltd. in New York for this information.

111. W/M 6.

112. June 22, 1779, E32-5365.

113. E26-18976.

114. Mankowitz, *Wedgwood*, 108.

115. Pottery memos, 60-32834.

116. Montfaucon, *L'Antiquité expliquée*, vol. 3, pt. 1, pl. 34.

117. For an excellent study of the Homeric vase at the British Museum, see Dawson, *Masterpieces*, 102-11.

118. Rathbone, *Wedgwood*, 145.

119. Macht, *Classical Wedgwood Designs*, 61.

120. "Account of the Letters from and to Mr Angelo Dalmazzoni at Rome," 1788-90, W/M 1526; Reilly, *Wedgwood* 1: 627.

121. See Goodison, "Boulton's Geographical Clock."

122. Chambers, *Treatise on Civil Architecture*, 36.

123. Reilly and Savage, *Dictionary*, 239; Reilly, *Wedgwood* 1: 472.

124. E26-18958.

125. April 30, 1785, W/M 1755.

126. August 5, 1771, E25-18384.

127. Montfaucon, *L'Antiquité expliquée*, vol. 5, pt. 1, pl. 14, fig. 2.

128. Bindman, *John Flaxman*, 53.

129. Quoted in Norman, *Rapier and Small-Sword*, 390.

130. Reilly, *Wedgwood* 1:631–36; 2:754–57.

131. *Christie's Auction Catalog*, October 12, 1991, New York, Lot 11.

132. Clifford, "John Bacon and the Manufacturers," 294.

133. The fountains are: the Triton Fountain (1642–43) in the Piazza Barberini; the Fountain of the Moor (1653-5) in the Piazza Navona; and a fountain in the Palazzo Estense at Sassuolo. For more information on the relationship of these fountains to the tritons, see *Christie's Catalogue* (London, December 11, 1990), Lot 89. Also see Weese-Wehen, "Baroque Bronzes Intrigue West Coast Collectors." Candlesticks of the same figure were produced by Boulton and Fothergill, as seen in Goodison, *Ormolu: The Work of Matthew Boulton*, pp. 102–3, figs. 12 and 13, pl. 162g.

134. Thomson, *The Four Seasons*, 5.

135. Dawson, *Masterpieces*, 54.

136. E2-30189.

137. Liddell, *"Counterfeit Flaxman Chessmen."* For the most current discussion of the chess figures, including Flaxman's drawing and the bases of the figures, see Reichner, "Wedgwood Chessmen," 24-28.

138. The figure of Britannia used as a finial and the same lion and a unicorn also appear on a covered vase commemorating the coming of age of George, prince of Wales, in March of 1783. This sculpture is in the Felix Joseph Collection at the Borough Museum, The Castle Museum, Nottingham, England; Reilly, *Wedgwood* 1:651.

139. Ackermann, *Repository of the Arts*, February 1809, pl. 7.

140. I am grateful to Gaye Blake Roberts, Curator, Wedgwood Museum, Barlaston, Stoke-on-Trent, England, for this information.

141. Reilly, *Wedgwood* 1:640

142. Irwin, *John Flaxman*, 151–61.

143. Ibid., 163–65.

144. Reilly, *Dictionary*, 267.

145. Burman, *Joseph Mayer's Wedgwood Collection*, 204–7.

146. Similar swords exist in the Victoria and Albert Museum; the Museum of London; the Musée des Arts Decoratifs, Paris; the Castle Museum, Nottingham, England; the Lady Lever Art Gallery, Port Sunlight, England; and the Metropolitan Museum of Art, New York.

147. Letter to the author from Anthony North, Research Assistant, Metalwork Collection, Victoria and Albert Museum, October 18, 1991, in file 1991.788 at the Birmingham Museum of Art, Birmingham, Alabama.

148. Norman, *Rapier and Small-Sword*, 390–92.

149. E26-18979.

150. For a more complete analysis of the decline of jasper ware, see Reilly, *Wedgwood* 2.505 18.

151. Josiah Bateman to Josiah Wedgwood II, April 7, 1813, 18-16299.

152. Pottery memos, April 30, 1866, 60-32828.

153. Wedgwood to Darwin, June 28, 1789, E26-29002.

11. White Stoneware

1. March 24, 1810, 18-16167.
2. Pottery memos 1817, 60-32817.
3. Reilly, *Wedgwood* 2: 543-44.
4. Wedgwood Order Book 1801-1812.
5. Monfaucon, *L'Antiquité expliquée,* vol. 5, pl. 17, det. of fig. 3.

12. The Portland Vase

1. Letter to the author from David B. Whitehouse, Deputy Director, Corning Museum of Glass, Corning, New York, February 10, 1989. For additional information see Whitehouse, ed., *Journal of Glass Studies* 32, which is devoted entirely to new research on the original Portland vase.

2. Fothergill, *Sir William Hamilton, Envoy Extraordinary*, 192–93.

3. E2-30188.

4. Horace Walpole to the Countess of Upper Ossory, August 19, 1785, in Toynbee, *Letters of Horace Walpole*, 13:308.

5. June 24, 1786, E26-18976.

6. Shenker, "Celebrated Roman Vase."

7. This letter is in the Beeson collection, file 1986.224.

8. E26-18976. The Montfaucon reference is to *L'Antiquité expliquée*, vol. 5, pl. 6, figs. 1, 2.

9. Reilly, *Wedgwood* 1:197.

10. E26-18976.

11. Josiah Wedgwood I to Josiah Wedgwood II, May 9, 1790, E26-18993.

12. E82-14607.

13. This certificate was originally reproduced on p. v of Josiah Wedgwood's account book of 1790, but it is now lost.

14. Reilly, *Wedgwood* 1:678–79.

15. Dawson, *Masterpieces*, 150.

16. Reilly, *Wedgwood* 1:678; Josiah Wedgwood I to Josiah Wedgwood II, April 15, 1791, W/M 1460.

17. Letter from Robin Reilly to the author at Birmingham Museum of Art, Birmingham, Alabama, July 5, 1990, file 1983.25.

18. Reilly, *Wedgwood* 1:679; 2:41.

19. Ibid., 1:673.

20. Letter from Miss J. E. Poole, Assistant Keeper of Applied Art, Fitzwilliam Museum, Cambridge, England, August 30, 1988; letter from Mr. Robin Reilly, June 28, 1989; Dawson, "Appendix: Early Copies of the Portland vase," in *Masterpieces*, 149–50.

21. Wedgwood, Account of the Barberini, now Portland, vase; with the Various Explications of its Bas Reliefs that have been Given by Different Authors. A copy of this account, which was never published, is in the Beeson Wedgwood collection at the Birmingham Museum of Art, Birmingham, Alabama.

22. Wedgwood, "Abstract of Mr. Wedgwood's Conjectures on the Bas Reliefs of the Portland Vase," Description of the Portland vase, Beeson Wedgwood Collection, Birmingham Museum of Art, Birmingham, Alabama.

23. Letter to the author from David B. Whitehouse, Deputy Director, Corning Museum of Glass, Corning, New York, February 10, 1989. Note, further, that Aeneas actually founded Alba Longa and that mythology credits Romulus and Remus with founding Rome.

24. 60-32825, Pottery Memos, March-October 1845. For further discussion of these vases, see Reilly, *Wedgwood* 2:562.

25. Reilly, *Wedgwood* 1:601.

13. Caneware

1. E25-28714.

2. Meteyard, *Wedgwood Handbook*, 316.

3. Reilly, *Dictionary*, 163; quoted from Captain William Jesse, *The Life of George Brummell, Esq., Commonly Called Beau Brummell* (London: Saunders and Otley, 1844).

4. Letter to the author from Robin Reilly, July 1, 1988; letter to the author from Alison Kelly, June 3, 1991. Ms. Kelly also noted that a similar or duplicate tablet exists in the mantel at The Octagon in Washington, D.C. I am most grateful to Robin Reilly, Alison Kelly, and Raymond Lane for aiding in the research on this tablet.

5. Kelly, *Mrs, Coade's Stone*; Kelly, "Mrs. Coade's Stone"; Bimson, "Some Recent Research on Coade Stone"; Valpy and Kelly, "Advertisements for Artificial Stone in the *Daily Advertiser.*"

14. Wedgwood and the Egyptian Revival

1. Cleopatra was the eldest daughter of Ptolemy Auletes. She and her brother, Ptolemy, were to marry and assume the Egyptian royal throne. She was expelled by her brother, but, through the aid of Julius Caesar, she regained control. After Caesar's death, she fell in love with Marc Antony and accompanied him to the Battle of Actium in 31 B.C. She withdrew her fleet, causing Antony's defeat and spreading rumors of her death. Upon hearing this, Antony stabbed himself, and Cleopatra subsequently poisoned herself with the bite of an asp.

2. E25-18623.

3. E25-18258.

4. Montfaucon, *L'Antiquité expliquée*, vol. 2, pt. 1, pl. 18, fig. 8.

5. Shape Book, no. 140; Reilly, *Wedgwood* 2:111.

6. Montfaucon, *L'Antiquité expliquée*, vol. 2, pt. 2, pls. 129, 130.

7. Ibid., vol. 2, pt. 2, pls. 138, 139.

8. Ibid., pl. 132.

15. Rosso-Antico Ware

1. E25-18660.

2. Cybele was the Greek goddess of caverns. She personified the earth in its primitive and savage state, and her domain also included wild beasts. Thus she is appropriately depicted in a chariot drawn by lions, with the reverse scene showing the chariot with booty.

16. Drabware

1. Reilly, *Wedgwood* 2:552.

17. Pearl Ware

1. Miller, "Origins of Josiah Wedgwood's Pearlware," 174.

2. March 8, 1779, E26-18882.

3. E26-18914.

4. Drakard and Holdway, *Spode Printed Ware,* 22.

5. Reilly, *Wedgwood* 2:329

6. The star water lily (*Nymphaea stellata*) is from *Botanist's Repository*, October 1803, pl. 330. The lotus of Buddha (*Nelumbium speciosum*) derives from *Botanical Magazine*, February 1806, pl. 303. The lotus of Egypt (*Nymphaea lotus*) is from *Botanical Magazine*, December 1804, pl. 797.

7. Memorandum of Josiah Wedgwood II to York Street, London, showroom, 13-11684.

8. The Wedgwood Museum, Pamphlet, *The Wedgwoods and the Darwins: An Exhibition to Mark the Centenary of the Death of Charles Darwin* (1809-82), not paginated.

9. Reilly, *Wedgwood* 2:329.

10. Ibid., 333.

11. Josiah Byerley to Josiah Wedgwood II, July 10, 1811, 13-11712.

12. 13-12788.

13. E26-188851.

18. Luster Decoration

1. London Experiment Book, p. 53, 22-19122.

2. This was achieved by using an oxide or sulphide of some metal in a reducing kiln, in which the oxygen was removed, thus "reducing" the metal oxide to free, or liquid, form covering the body and causing the stained glaze with a reflecting film. The technique was not a new one, having been recorded in the thirteenth century in Persia and in the sixteenth century in Italy before its revival in the nineteenth century.

3. Reilly, *Wedgwood* 2:572.

4. See above, "Wedgwood and the Egyptian Revival," pp. 151–54.

5. The "cassolette," a French word meaning a small brazier in which aromatic pastilles may be burned or liquid perfumes evaporated, first appeared in England after 1657. The cassolette was usually shaped like a vase, but in the late eighteenth century the tripod shape, which was produced in imitation of Roman examples, became fashionable. Pastilles were cone-shaped mixtures of powdered, willow wood charcoal blended with fragrant oils and gum arabic that were burned in both the eighteenth and nineteenth centuries to cover up household odors. Those imported from the Orient contained a base of cow dung, powdered cinnamon, and cloves.

6. Reilly, *Wedgwood* 2:658–59.

7. November 9, 1809, W/M 1602; pottery memos, 60-32819.1828.

8. 1820 Spode shape book, fig. 71. See also Whiter, *Spode*, 94-95.

19. Émile-Aubert Lessore

1. Quoted in Buten and Pelehach, *Émile Lessore*, 17-18.

2. Clement F. Wedgwood, pottery memos, 1862.

3. According to the myth, anyone who looked upon Medusa directly would turn to stone. Perseus saved Andromeda from the fearful Medusa by cutting off the monster's head, a feat he accomplished by looking at its reflection in a mirror. In this depiction, the victorious Perseus shows Andromeda the snaky head of Medusa, which she appreciates through the safety of the mirror's reflection.

4. Memorandum of Arrangement between Messrs J. Wedgwood & Sons and Mr Lessore, June 2, 1862, 44-28943.

5. Buten and Pelehach, *Émile Lessore*, 50-51.

Catalog of the Works

The order of the items listed in this catalog section follows the arrangement of the objects in the Beeson Wedgwood gallery at the Birmingham Museum of Art, Birmingham, Alabama. It is also chronological according to Wedgwood's development of the different ware, and in some cases is further differentiated by the type of object (such as tea caddy spoons and jewelry). To locate a specific title, type of object, or type of ware, see the detailed index provided at the back of the book.

English Pottery

1. Teapot: ca. 1775
Agate ware
5 1/8 x 4 1/2 in (13 x 11.4 cm)
Mark: none
Provenance: Wolf Mankowitz, London; Dr. Francis Jennings Vurpillat, South Bend, Ind.
1979.203 a and b
Color plate 6

2. Teapot: ca. 1750-60
Cream ware, multicolored metallic oxides under clear glaze and applied decoration
4 5/8 x 4 1/4 in (11.7 x 10.7 cm)
Mark: none
Provenance: Dr. Francis Jennings Vurpillat, South Bend, Ind.
1979.20 a and b
Color plate 6

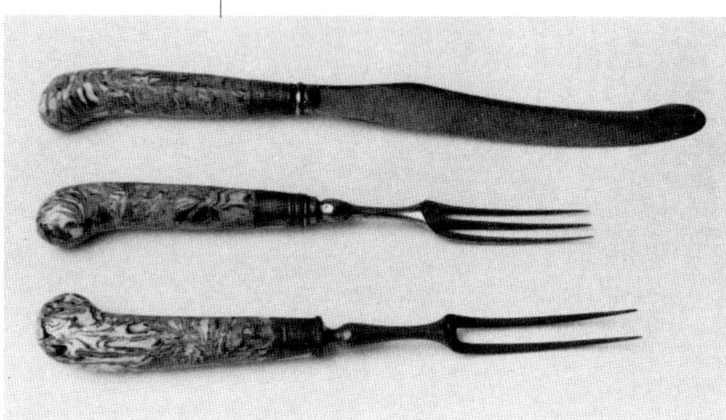

3. Two Forks and Knife: ca. 1760
Agate ware, steel
Knife: 8 13/16 in (22.3 cm); fork: 6 15/16 in (17.6 cm)
Mark: none
Provenance: Ann Brodkiewicz, Chicago
1980.177 a and b; 1980.178

4. Teapot: *Lion and Unicorn*, ca. 1740-50
Stoneware with salt glaze
5 1/4 x 3 3/8 x 2 5/8 in (13.3 x 8.5 x 6.7 cm)
Mark: none
Provenance: Fred J. Tongue, Santa Monica, Calif.
1979.166 a and b
Color plate 3

5. Teapot: *Prince Charles Stuart, the Young Pretender*, ca. 1760
Stoneware with salt glaze and overglaze polychrome enamels
4 3/4 x 3 3/4 x 4 in (12 x 9.5 x 10.1 cm)
Mark: none
Provenance: Ann Brodkiewicz, Chicago
1979.162 a and b
Color plate 3

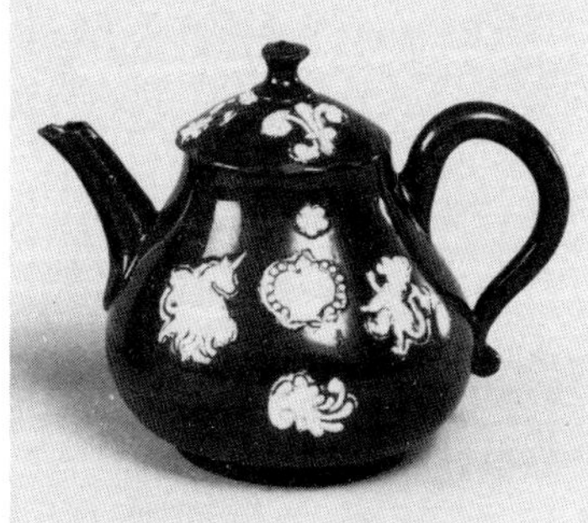

6. Teapot: *Lion and Unicorn*, ca. 1780
Red earthenware with interior and exterior clear glaze and applied cream-ware decoration
5 1/4 x 2 1/4 in (13.3 x 5.7 cm)
Mark: none
Provenance: Shreve, Crump, and Low Co., Boston; Dr. Francis Jennings Vurpillat, South Bend, Ind.
1976.165 a and b
Color plate 2

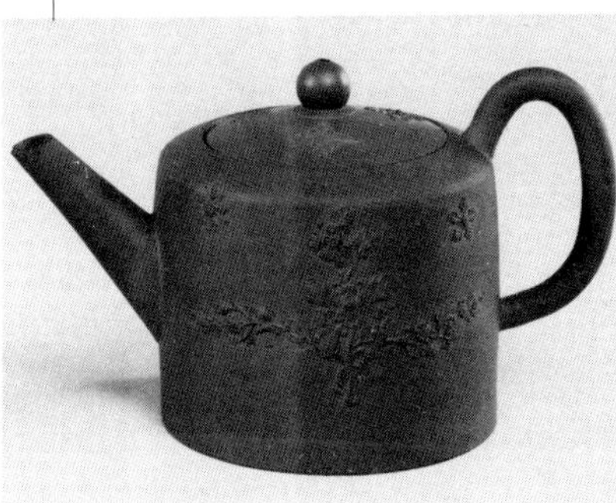

7. Teapot: ca. 1790
Red stoneware with applied decoration
4 3/8 x 4 1/8 in (11.1 x 10.4 cm)
Mark: square with pseudo-Chinese characters
Provenance: Dr. Francis Jennings Vurpillat, South Bend, Ind.
1979.162 a and b

8. Sugar Bowl: ca. 1770-80
Red stoneware with applied decoration
3 7/16 x 3 1/8 in (8.7 x 7.9 cm)
Mark: none
Provenance: Dr. Francis Jennings Vurpillat, South Bend, Ind.
1979.169
Color plate 4

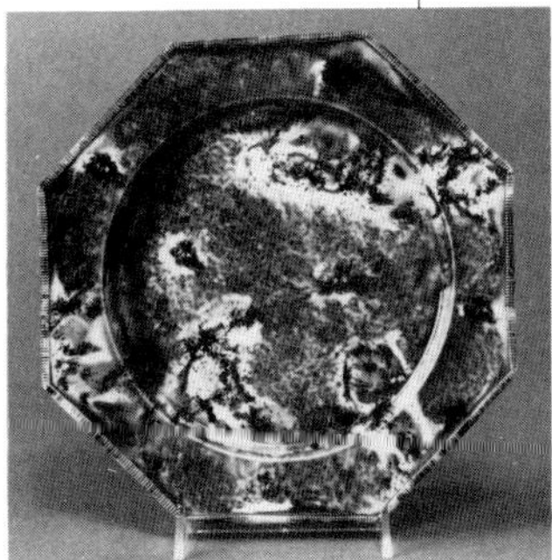

9. Plate: *Tortoiseshell*, ca. 1770
Staffordshire, England
Cream ware with multicolored metallic oxides under clear glaze
8 3/4 x 8 3/4 in (22.2 x 22.2 cm)
Mark: none
Provenance: M. Mellanay Delhom, Chicago; Fred J. Tongue, Santa Monica, Calif.
1979.204
Color plate 6

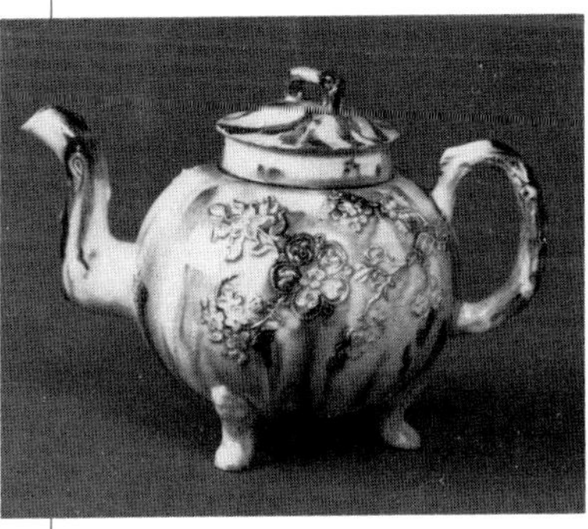

10. Teapot: ca. 1750-60
Staffordshire, England
Cream ware with multicolored metallic oxides under clear glaze and applied decoration, replacement lid
5 x 5 1/2 in (12.7 x 13.9 cm)
Mark: none
Provenance: Dr. Francis Jennings Vurpillat, South Bend, Ind.
1979.201 a and b

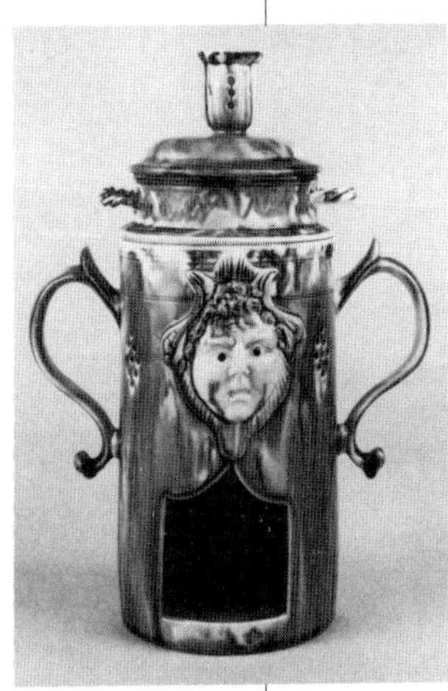

11. Veilleuse: ca. 1760
Cream ware with multicolored metallic oxides under clear glaze
11 x 4 1/2 in (27.5 x 11.4 cm)
Mark: none
Provenance: Art Trading Ltd., New York
1989.27.1-.3
Color plate 5

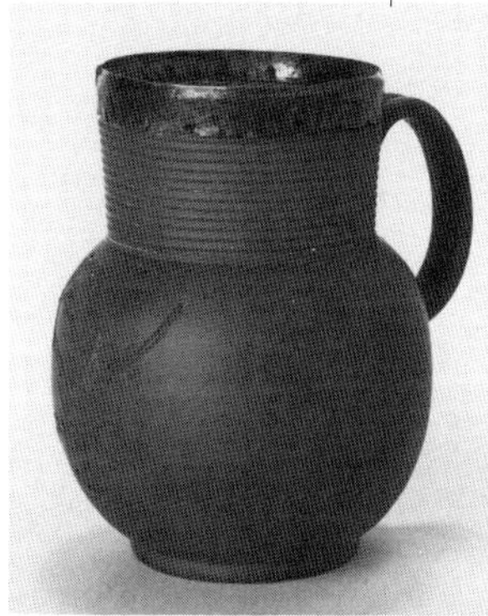

12. Mug: ca. 1690
Attributed to John Philip Elers and David Elers (w. 1688-1710)
Staffordshire, England
Red stoneware with applied decoration with silver rim
4 1/2 x 2 in (11.4 x 5 cm)
Mark: none
Provenance: Dr. Francis Jennings Vurpillat, South Bend, Ind.
1979.172
Color plate 1

13. Sugar Bowl: ca. 1760-70
Attributed to Josiah Wedgwood
Red stoneware with engine-turning
3 5/8 x 2 3/16 in (9.2 x 5.5 cm)
Mark: pseudo-Chinese characters, including a "w" on base and inside lid
Provenance: Dr. Francis Jennings Vurpillat, South Bend, Ind.
1979.171
Color plate 1

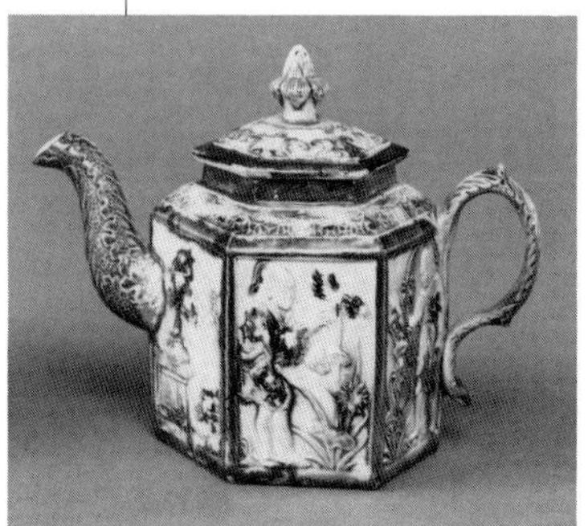

14. Teapot: *Chinese*, ca. 1760-70
Cream ware with multicolored metallic oxides under clear glaze
5 1/4 x 3 1/2 x 3 7/8 in (13.3 x 8.8 x 9.8 cm)
Mark: none
Provenance: Ann Brodkiewicz, Chicago
1979.182 a and b
Color plate 8

15. Teapot: ca. 1770-80
Attributed to William Greatbatch (1735-1813)
Staffordshire, England
Cream ware with multicolored metallic oxides under clear glaze and molded body
4 1/2 x 3 in (11.4 x 7.6 cm)
Mark: none
Provenance: Ann Brodkiewicz, Chicago
1979.159
Color plate 8

16. Teapot: ca. 1765-75
Attributed to William Greatbatch (1735-1813)
Staffordshire, England
Cream ware with green glaze and molded body
5 x 3 5/16 in (12.7 x 8.4 cm)
Mark: none
Provenance: Ann Brodkiewicz, Chicago
1979.180 a and b
Color plate 8

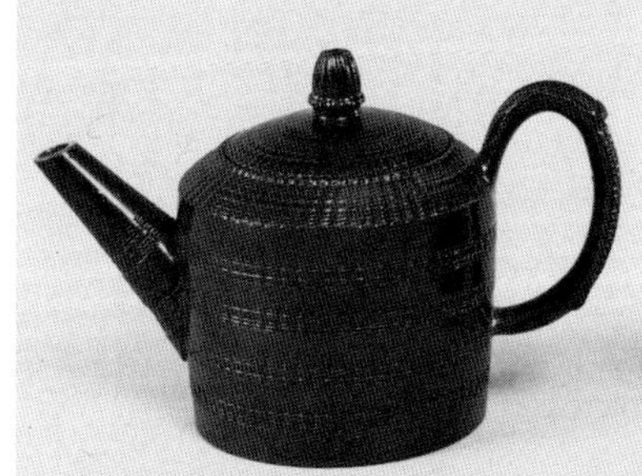

17. Teapot: ca. 1780
Red earthenware with interior and exterior clear glaze and engine-turning
4 x 3 1/4 in (10.1 x 8.2 cm)
Mark: none
Provenance: Dr. Francis Jennings Vurpillat, South Bend, Ind.
1979.168

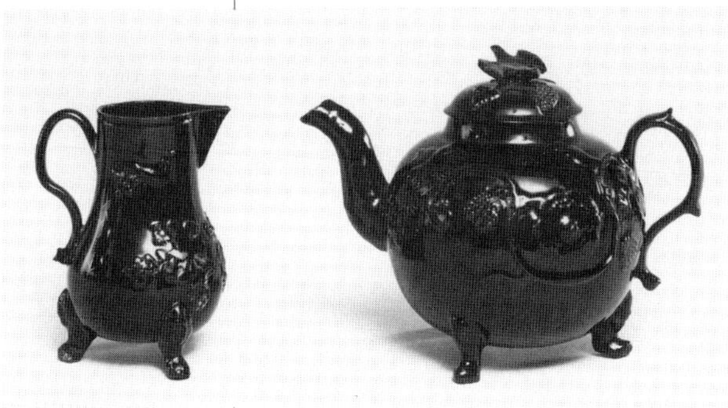

18. Cream Pitcher: ***Jackfield,*** **ca. 1755-60**
Attributed to Humphrey Palmer (1720-86)
Staffordshire, England
Red stoneware colored with manganese and iron oxides, covered with clear glaze, and applied decoration with overglaze gilding
4 3/8 x 2 3/4 in (11.1 x 6.9 cm)
Mark: none
Provenance: Ann Brodkiewicz, Chicago
1979.199
Color plate 2

19. Teapot: ***Jackfield,*** **ca. 1755-60**
Red stoneware colored with manganese and iron oxides, covered with clear glaze, and applied decoration with gilding
5 1/2 x 4 3/4 in (13.9 x 12 cm)
Mark: none
Provenance: Dr. Francis Jennings Vurpillat, South Bend, Ind.
1979.198 a and b
Color plate 2

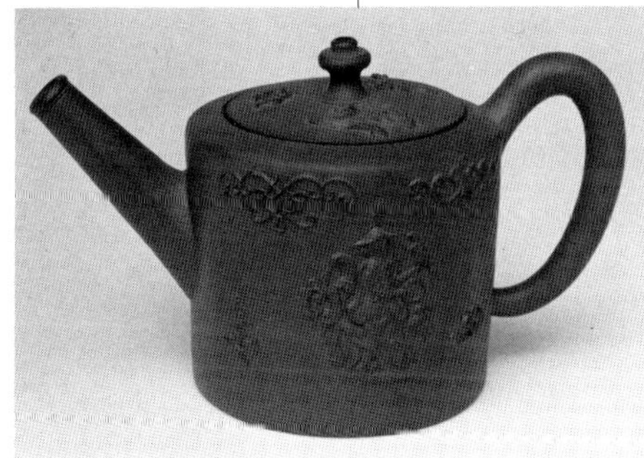

20. Miniature Teapot: ***Oriental Figures,*** **ca. 1760**
Red stoneware with applied decoration
2 7/8 x 2 7/16 in (7.3 x 6.1 cm)
Mark: none
Provenance: Bokhara E. Hailstone, England; Ann Brodkiewicz, Chicago
1980.162 a and b

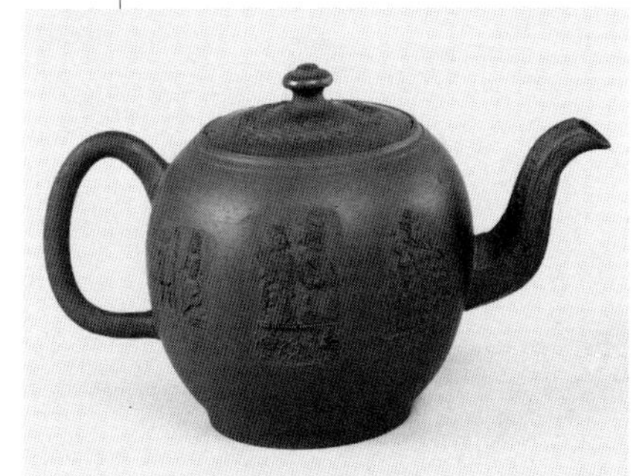

21. Teapot: ***Oriental Figures,*** **ca. 1780**
Red stoneware with applied decoration
4 1/4 x 2 3/8 in (10.7 x 6 cm)
Mark: none
Provenance: Dr. Francis Jennings Vurpillat, South Bend, Ind.
1979.167 a and b
Color plate 4

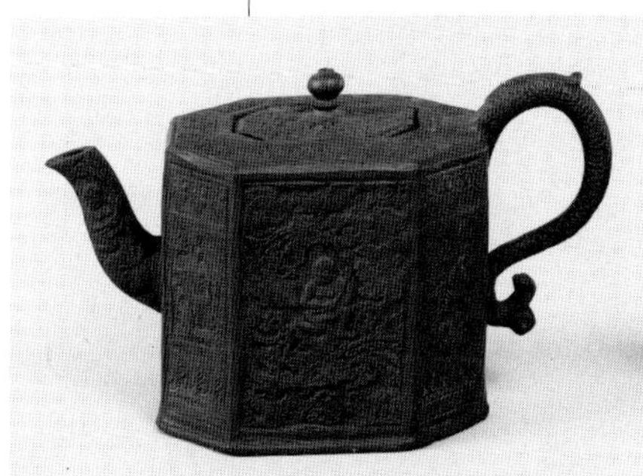

22. Teapot: ***Oriental Figures,*** **ca. 1760-70**
Attributed to Thomas Whieldon (1719-93)
Staffordshire, England
Red stoneware with applied decoration
3 7/8 x 3 1/4 x 3 5/8 in (9.8 x 8.2 x 9.2 cm)
Mark: none
Provenance: Dr. Francis Jennings Vurpillat, South Bend, Ind.
1979.173 a and b
Color plate 4

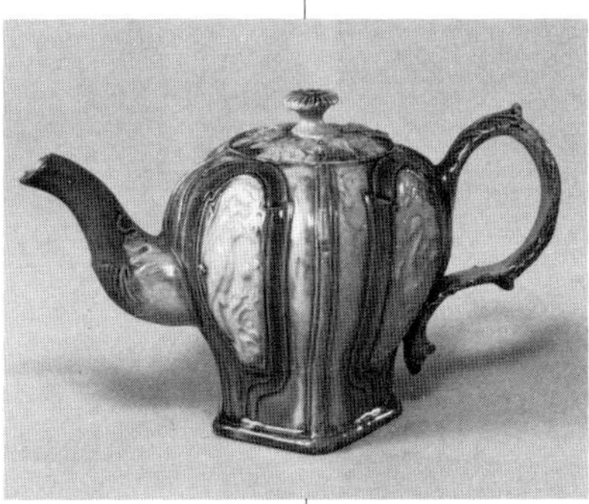

23. Teapot: *Oriental Birds*, ca. 1760-70
Cream ware with underglaze green decoration
4 1/4 x 2 1/2 x 2 1/2 in (10.7 x 6.2 x 6.2 cm)
Mark: none
Provenance: T. Murray Ragg, England; Fred J. Tongue, Santa Monica, Calif.; Dr. Francis Jennings Vurpillat, South Bend, Ind.
1979.163 a and b

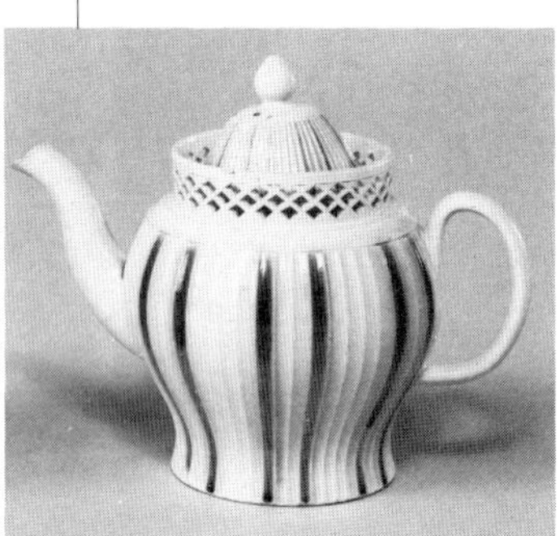

24. Teapot: ca. 1760-70
Cream ware with underglaze green decoration
5 1/2 x 3 in (13.9 x 7.6 cm)
Mark: none
Provenance: Dr. Francis Jennings Vurpillat, South Bend, Ind.
1979.161 a and b

25. Tea Canister: *Cauliflower*, ca. 1760-70
Attributed to William Greatbatch (1735-1813)
Staffordshire, England
Cream ware with green glaze, replacement lid
4 x 3 x 3 in (10.1 x 7.6 x 7.6 cm)
Mark: none
Provenance: Ann Brodkiewicz, Chicago
1979.175

26. Cream Pitcher: *Cauliflower*, ca. 1760-70
Attributed to William Greatbatch (1735-1813)
Staffordshire, England
Cream ware with green glaze
4 1/2 x 2 in (11.4 x 5 cm)
Mark: none
Provenance: Ann Brodkiewicz, Chicago
1979.179
Color plate 7

27. Sugar Bowl: *Cauliflower*, ca. 1760-70
Staffordshire, England
Cream ware with green glaze
4 1/2 x 2 3/8 x 2 1/2 in (11.4 x 6 x 6.2 cm)
Mark: none
Provenance: Ann Brodkiewicz, Chicago
1979.176

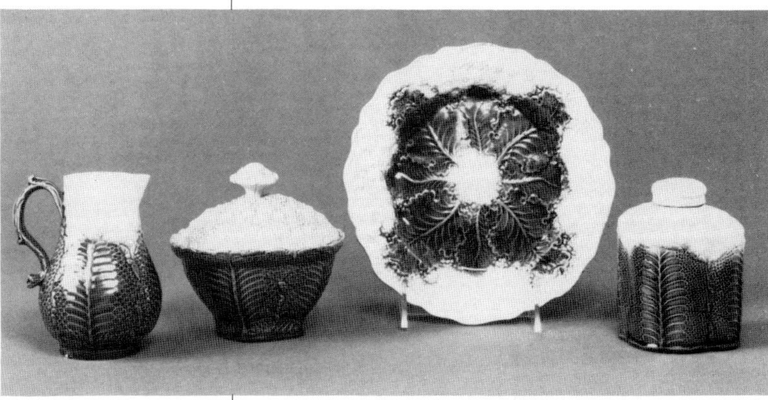

28. Plate: *Cauliflower*, ca. 1760-70
Staffordshire, England
Cream ware with green glaze
7 3/4 in (19.6 cm)
Mark: none
Provenance: Ann Brodkiewicz, Chicago
1979.177

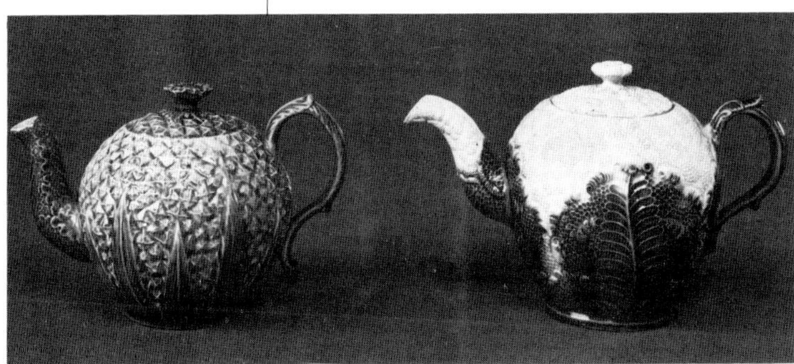

29. Teapot: *Cauliflower*, ca. 1760-70
Attributed to William Greatbatch (1735-1813)
Staffordshire, England
Cream ware with green glaze
4 1/2 x 2 3/8 in (11.4 x 6 cm)
Mark: none
Provenance: Ann Brodkiewicz, Chicago
1979.178
Color plate 7

30. Teapot: *Pineapple*, ca. 1760-70
Staffordshire, England
Cream ware with green-and-yellow-brown glaze
4 x 2 1/8 in (10.1 x 5.3 cm)
Mark: "C" within a circle
Provenance: Ann Brodkiewicz, Chicago
1979.181 a and b
Color plate 7

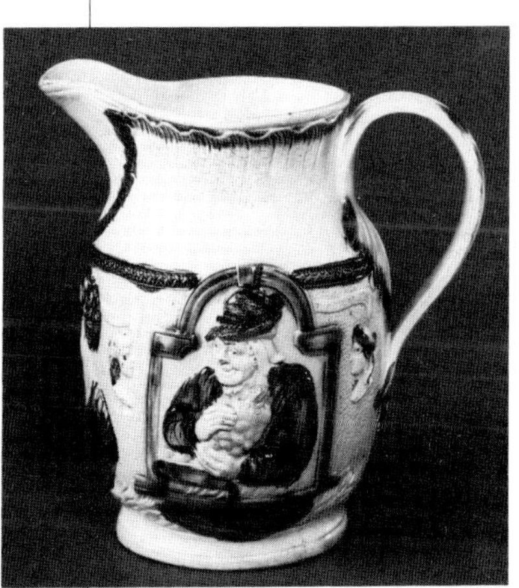

31. Pitcher: *The Spendthrift, the Miser, and Shakespeare*, ca. 1790
Attributed to Jean Voyez (1735-1800), modeler
Staffordshire, England
Cream ware with polychrome underglaze decoration
8 3/16 x 4 1/8 in (20.7 x 10.4 cm)
Mark: none
Provenance: Ann Brodkiewicz, Chicago
1979.183
Color plate 23

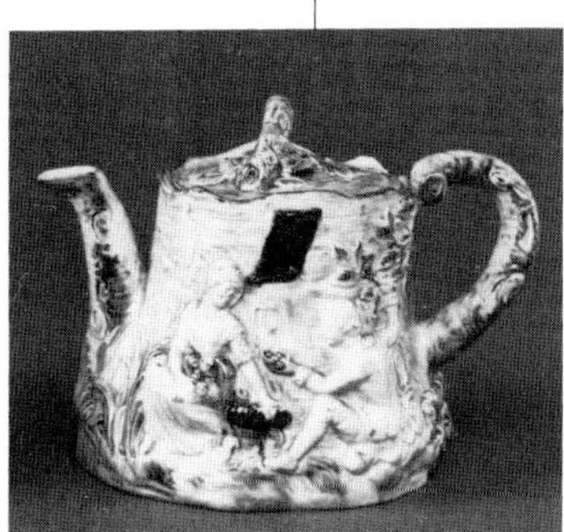

32. Teapot: *Fair Hebe*, ca. 1790
Attributed to Jean Voyez (1735-1800), modeler
Staffordshire, England
Cream ware with underglaze polychrome decoration and molded body
6 1/4 x 5 1/4 x 6 1/4 in (15.8 x 13.3 x 15.8 cm)
Mark: none
Provenance: Dr. Francis Jennings Vurpillat, South Bend, Ind.
1979.157
Color plate 23

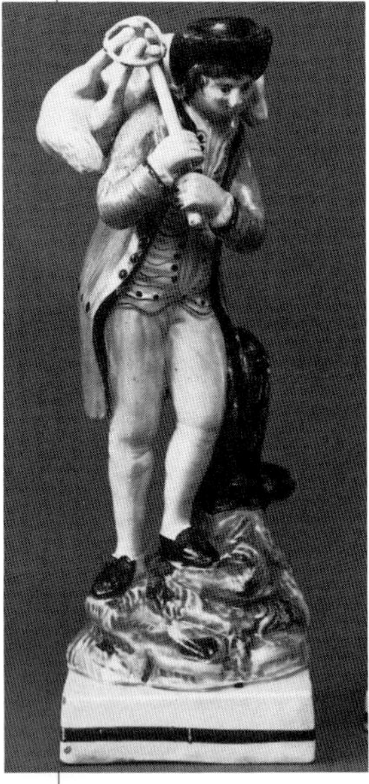

33. Shepherd Figure: *The Lost Sheep*, ca. 1795
Attributed to Ralph Wedgwood (1766-1837)
Staffordshire, England
Pearl ware with polychrome underglaze decoration
8 9/16 x 3 x 2 3/4 in (21.7 x 7.6 x 6.9 cm)
Mark: "WEDGWOOD"
Provenance: Ann Brodkiewicz, Chicago
1979.156

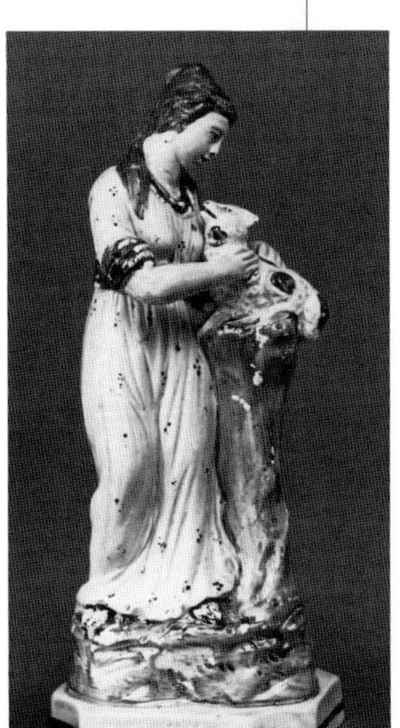

34. Female Figure: ca. 1795
Staffordshire, England
Pearl ware with polychrome underglaze decoration
7 7/16 x 2 1/2 x 3 1/4 in (18.8 x 6.2 x 8.2 cm)
Mark: none
Provenance: Ann Brodkiewicz, Chicago
1979.158

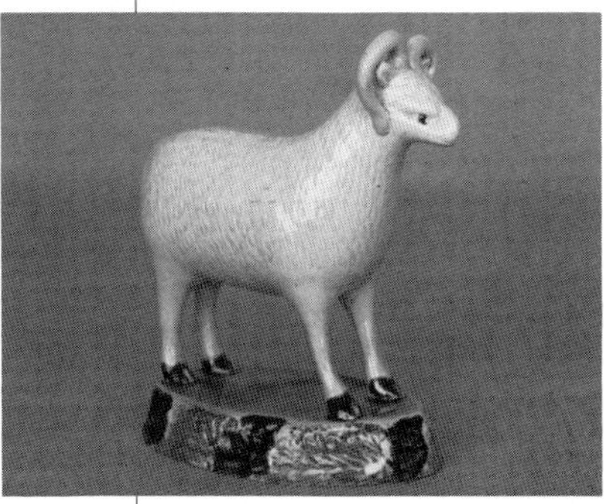

35. Figure: *Sheep*, ca. 1790
Cream ware with multicolored metallic oxides underglaze
6 3/16 x 3 1/4 x 5 in (15.7 x 8.2 x 12.7 cm)
Mark: none
Provenance: Ann Brodkiewicz, Chicago
1979.200

Cream Ware, Pearl Ware, and Mortar Ware

36. Catherine the Great of Russia Dinner Platter: *Ditchley Park, Oxfordshire,* 1773-74
Cream ware with overglaze mulberry-and-green enamel decoration
19 3/8 x 14 7/8 in (49.2 x 37.7 cm)
Mark: "WEDGWOOD" "434" on back in mulberry overglaze
Provenance: Sotheby's, London, December 18, 1968
1983.7
Color plate 25

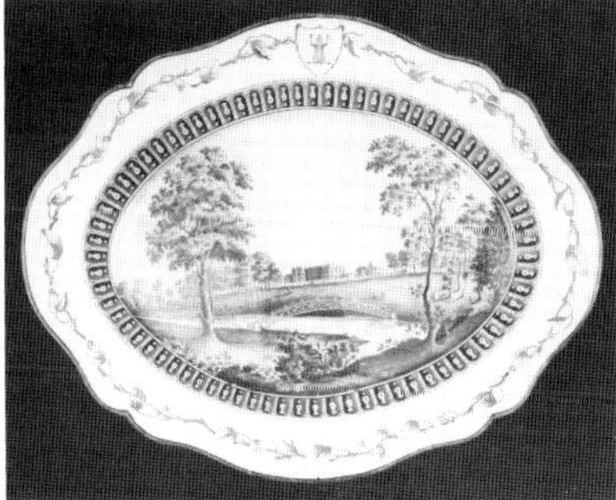

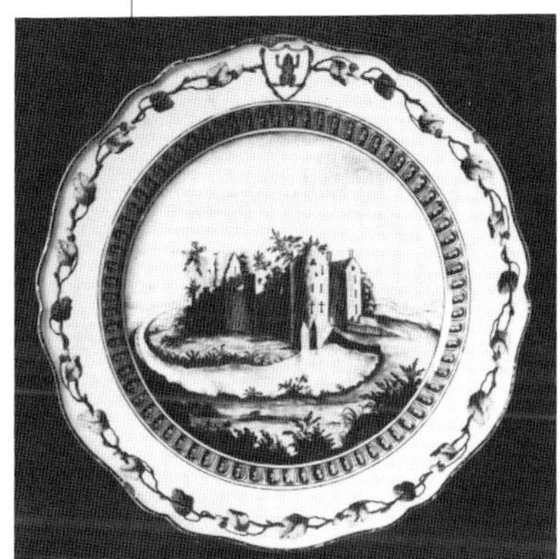

37. Catherine the Great Dinner Plate: *Saint Brivals Castle, Gloucestershire,* 1773-74
Cream ware with overglaze mulberry-and-green enamel decoration
9 7/8 in (25 cm)
Mark: "30" on back in mulberry overglaze
Provenance: Gift of Mrs. Byron A. Born in memory of her husband, Ho-ho-kus, N.J.
1986.638
Color plate 26

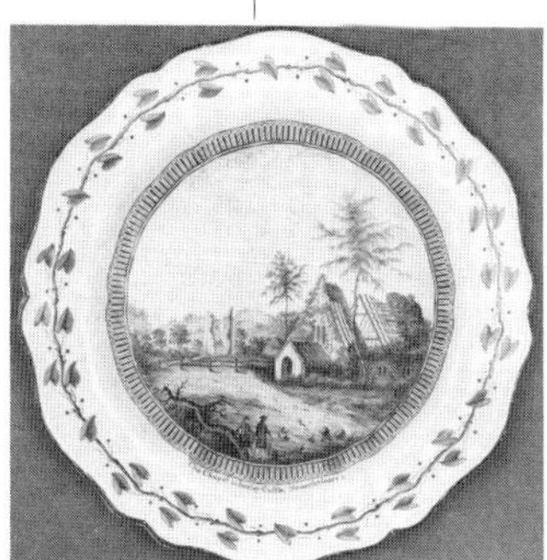

38. Catherine the Great of Russia Dessert Plate: *The Chapel in Fairley Castle, Somersetshire,* 1773-74
Cream ware with overglaze polychrome enamel decoration
8 15/16 in (22.7 cm)
Mark: none
Provenance: J. Brook, Bradford, England
1983.6
Color plate 26

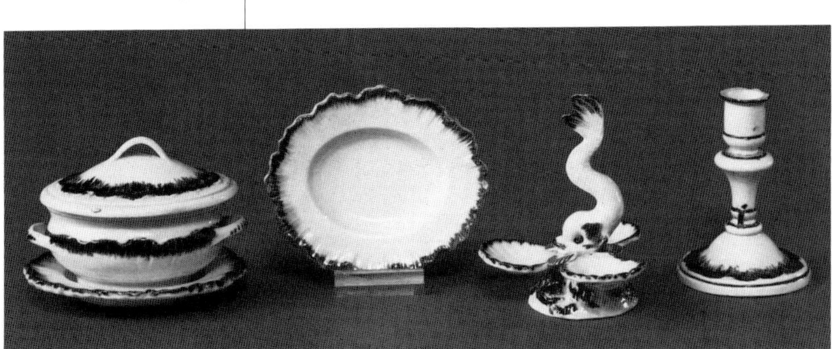

39. Sixty-One-Piece Miniature Dinner Set: ca. 1785
Cream ware with blue decoration under pearl glaze
Largest piece: 5 1/4 in (13.3 cm); smallest piece: 3 in (7.6 cm)
Marks: "WEDGWOOD" and "Wedgwood" with various letters and tool marks
Provenance: Ann Brodkiewicz, Chicago
1978.157.1-.61
Color plate 22

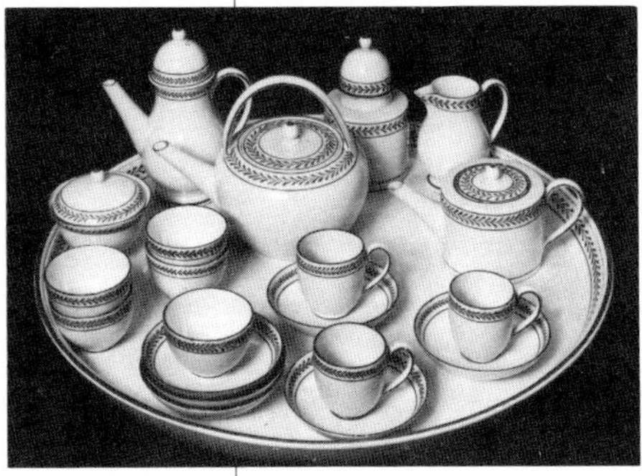

40. Twenty-One-Piece Miniature Coffee and Tea Set with Tray: ca. 1790
Cream ware with overglaze orange-and-brown enamel decoration
Largest piece: 14 3/8 in (37.3 cm); smallest piece: 1/2 x 1 in (1.2 cm)
Mark: "WEDGWOOD" impressed; cups and saucers no mark
Provenance: Art Trading Ltd., New York
1990.268.1-.11

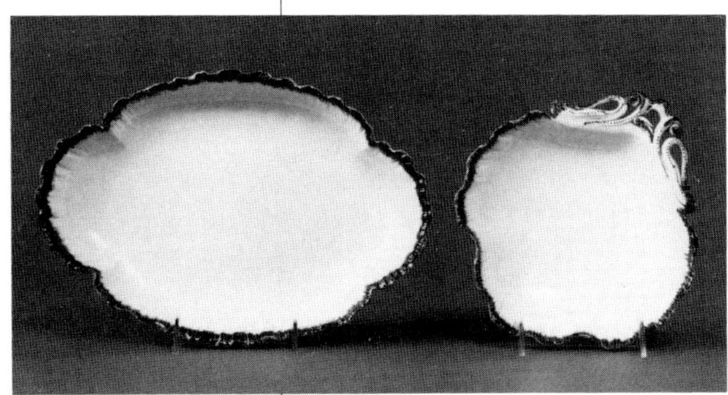

41. Dish: ca. 1780
Cream ware with blue underglaze decoration and gilding
8 1/2 x 12 9/16 in (21.5 x 31.9 cm)
Mark: "WEDGWOOD" "C" underglaze
Provenance: Fred J. Tongue, Santa Monica, Calif.
1978.156

42. Dish: ca. 1780
Cream ware with blue underglaze decoration and gilding
8 3/4 x 8 in (22.2 x 20.3 cm)
Mark: "WEDGWOOD" "B"
Provenance: Dr. Harold L. Klawans, Chicago
1978.155

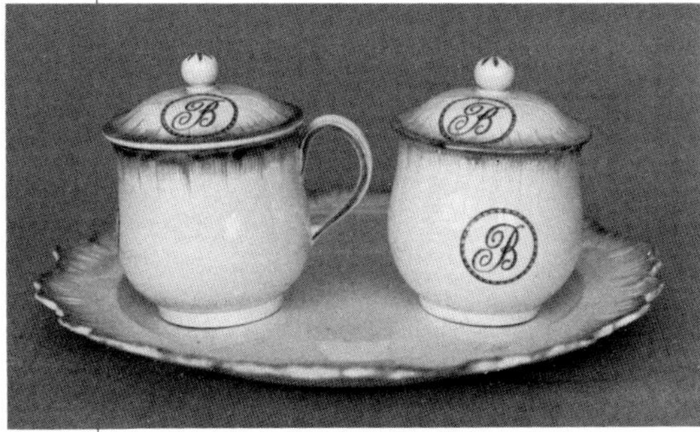

43. Pair of Plates with Covered Custard Cups: ca.1795
Cream ware with overglaze green enamel and underglaze transfer decoration
Plates: 7 7/8 in (20 cm); cups: 3 1/4 x 1 1/2 in (8.2 x 3.9 cm)
Mark: Plates: "WEDGWOOD" with tool marks; cups: tool marks
Provenance: M. Mellanay Delhom, Chicago; Ann Brodkiewicz, Chicago
1979.195 a and b, 1979.196 a, b, c, and d

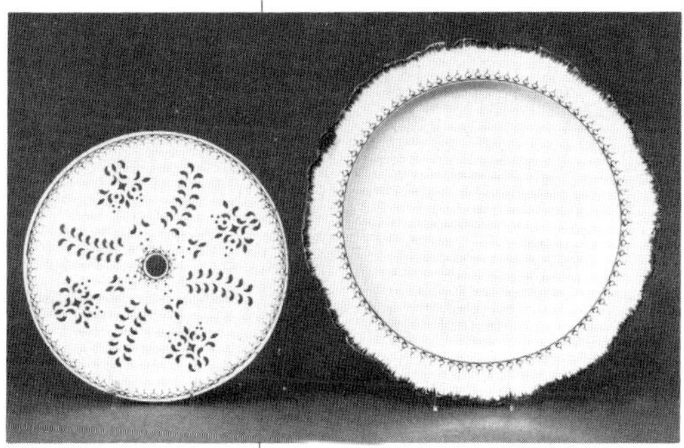

44. Platter and Pierced Drainer: ***Mared Pattern*****, ca. 1790**
Pearl ware with blue underglaze decoration
Dish: 17 1/2 in (44.4 cm); drainer: 12 1/2 in (31.7 cm)
Mark: dish: "WEDGWOOD";
drainer: "WEDGWOOD" "S" "17"
Provenance: Dr. Harold L. Klawans, Chicago
1978.169 a and b

45. Teapot: ca. 1780
Cream ware with gilding
6 1/2 x 3 in (16.5 x 7.6 cm)
Mark: "WEDGWOOD" with tool marks
Provenance: Byron A. Born, Ho-ho-kus, N.J.; Art Trading Ltd., New York
1989.15.1
Color plate 17

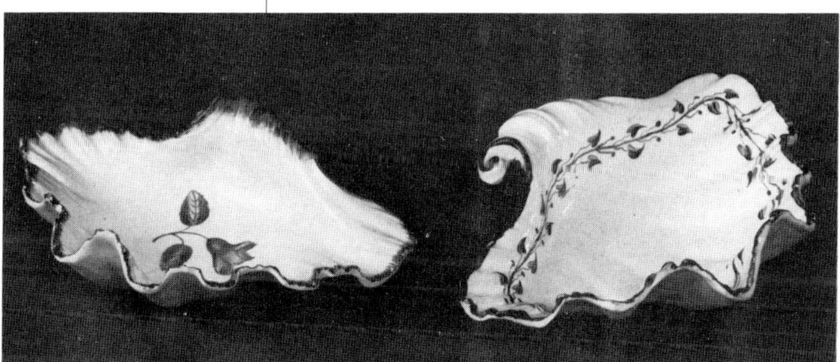

46. Sweetmeat Dish: ca. 1770
Cream ware with overglaze blue enamel decoration
1 3/4 x 7 5/8 x 5 3/8 in (4.4 x 19.3 x 13.6 cm)
Mark: "WEDGWOOD" "B"
Provenance: Dr. Harold L. Klawans, Chicago
1979.191

47. Sweetmeat Dish: ca. 1770
Cream ware with overglaze lilac enamel decoration
1 3/4 x 7 1/16 x 4 3/4 in (4.4 x 17.9 x 12 cm)
Mark: none
Provenance: Gift of Fred and Mary Tongue, Santa Monica, Calif.
1979.192

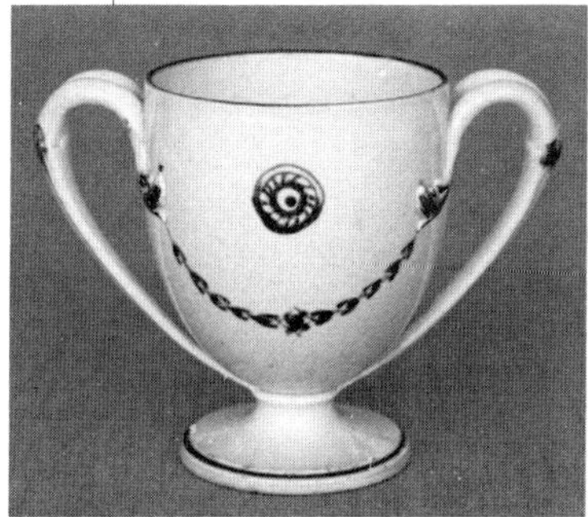

48. Loving Cup: ca. 1790
Cream ware with blue underglaze decoration
3 15/16 x 2 3/8 in (10 x 6 cm)
Mark: "wedgwood" "11" incised
Provenance: Ann Brodkiewicz, Chicago
1979.193

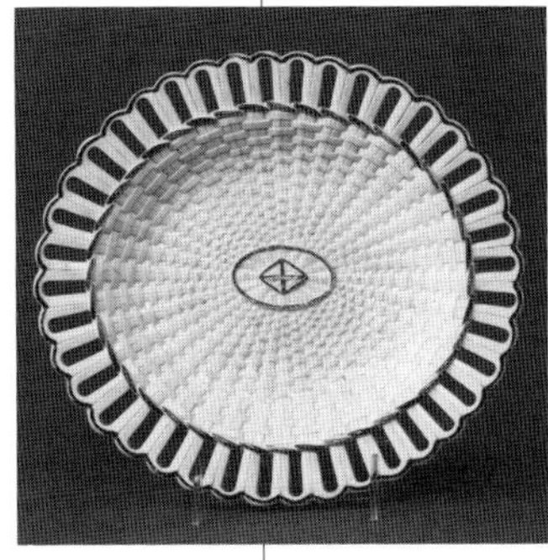

49. Stand for Fruit Basket: ca. 1800
Cream ware with overglaze black-and-red enamel decoration
10 3/8 x 9 1/4 in (26.3 x 23.4)
Mark: "WEDGWOOD"
Provenance: Dr. Harold L. Klawans, Chicago
1978.161

50. Fruit Basket and Stand: ca. 1790
Cream ware with overglaze brown-and-yellow enamel decoration
Basket: 8 7/8 x 7 3/4 in (22.5 x 19.6); dish: 9 5/8 x 8 1/4 in (24.4 x 20.9 cm)
Mark: "WEDGWOOD" with tool marks
Provenance: Fred J. Tongue, Santa Monica, Calif.
1979.189 a and b

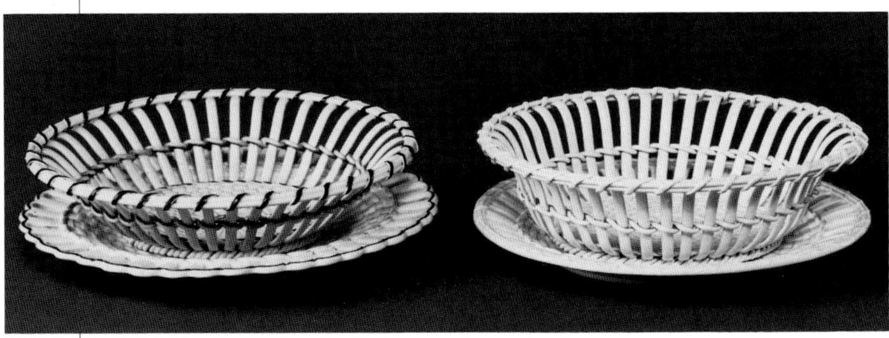

51. Fruit Basket and Stand: ca. 1780
Cream ware
Basket: 8 1/2 x 7 3/8 in (21.5 x 18.7 cm); dish: 10 9/16 x 9 7/16 in (26.8 x 23.9 cm)
Mark: "Wedgwood"
Provenance: Dr. Francis Jennings Vurpillat, South Bend, Ind.
1979.190 a and b

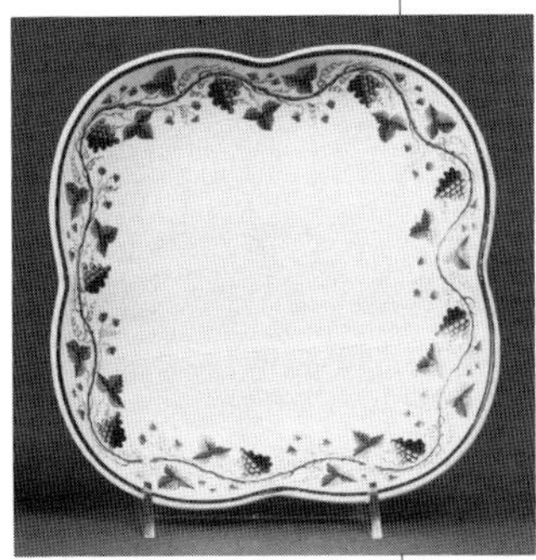

52. Dish: *Purple Vine Pattern*, ca. 1800
Pearl ware with overglaze enamel decoration
7 3/8 x 7 3/8 in (18.7 x 18.7 cm)
Mark: "WEDGWOOD" with tool marks
Provenance: Dr. Harold L. Klawans, Chicago
1978.159

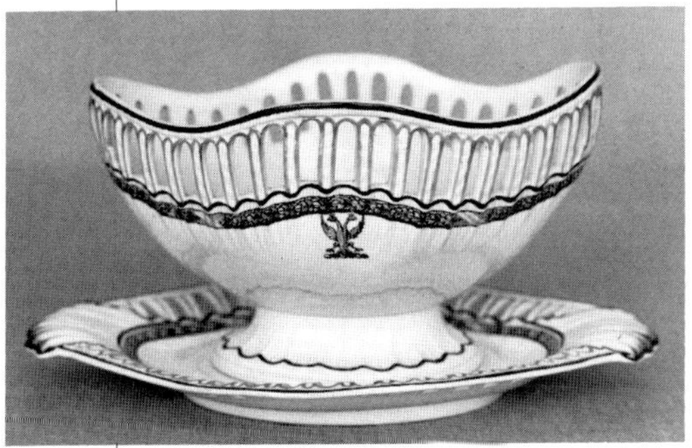

53. Armorial Footed Bowl and Underdish: ca. 1825
Crest of Bouverie Family
Engraved by J. Tilston
Cream ware with overglaze enamel decoration and crest
Bowl: 5 x 4 3/4 x 8 1/2 in (12.7 x 12 x 21.5 cm); dish: 11 x 8 in (27.9 x 20.3 cm)
Mark: "WEDGWOOD"
Provenance: A. J. Ostheimer, Hawaii; Fred J. Tongue, Santa Monica, Calif.
1979.184 a and b

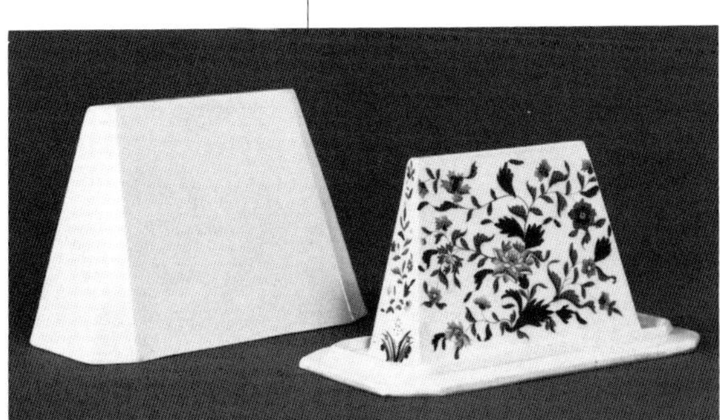

54. Jelly Mold Core and Undecorated Cover: ca. 1790
Cream ware with polychrome underglaze and overglaze enamel decoration
Cover: 6 3/8 x 6 1/2 x 9 in (16.1 x 16.5 x 22.8 cm); core: 5 x 5 1/4 x 9 9/16 in (12.7 x 13.3 x 24.2cm)
Mark: core: "WEDGWOOD"; mold: none
Provenance: M. Mellanay Delhom, Chicago; A. J. Ostheimer, Hawaii; Fred J. Tongue, Santa Monica, Calif.
1979.188 a and b
Color plate 18

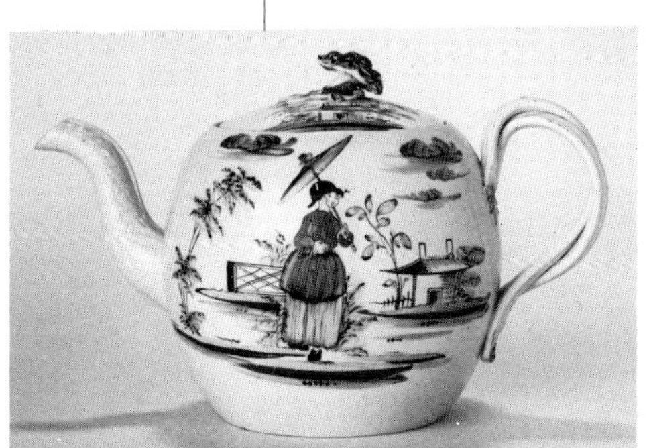

55. Teapot: ca. 1775
Cream ware with overglaze polychrome enamel decoration
5 5/16 x 3 3/8 in (13.4 x 8.5 cm)
Mark: "WEDGWOOD" "L" with tool marks
Provenance: M. Mellanay Delhom, Chicago; Dr. Francis Jennings Vurpillat, South Bend, Ind.
1979.160 a and b
Color plate 17

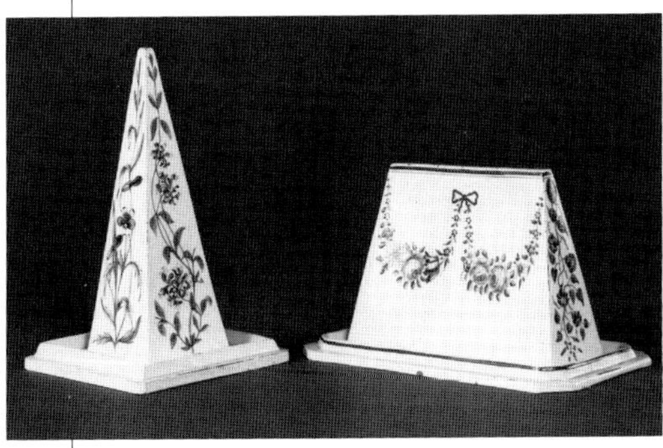

56. Jelly Mold Core: ca. 1790
Cream ware with overglaze polychrome enamel decoration
8 1/2 x 5 1/16 x 5 1/16 in (21.5 x 12.7 x 12.7 cm)
Mark: "WEDGWOOD" "LL"
Provenance: David Davis, Chicago; Ann Brodkiewicz, Chicago
1979.186
Color plate 18

57. Jelly Mold Core: ca. 1790
Cream ware with overglaze polychrome enamel decoration
4 7/8 x 4 3/8 x 8 1/2 in (12.2 x 9.8 x 21.5 cm)
Mark: none
Provenance: Fred J. Tongue, Santa Monica, Calif.
1979.187
Color plate 18

58. Teapot: *Grecian Bust*, ca. 1775
Cream ware with overglaze polychrome enamel decoration
5 3/4 x 2 1/8 in (14.6 x 5.3 cm)
Mark: "Wedgwood" with tool marks
Provenance: Byron A. Born, Ho-ho-kus, N.J.; Art Trading Ltd., New York
1989.14.1
Color plate 17

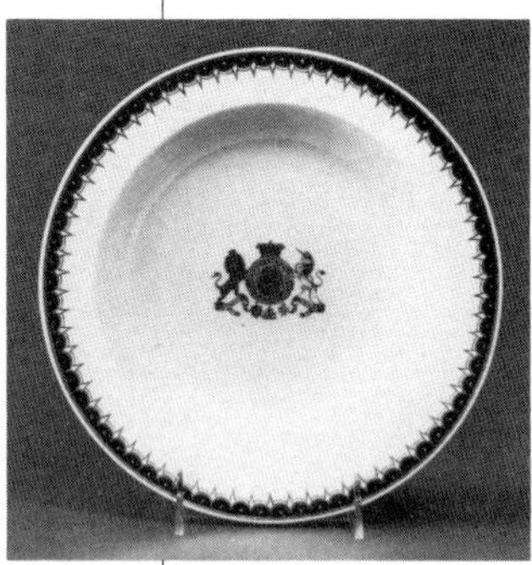

59. Armorial Soup Plate: ca. 1820
Cream ware with blue underglaze and overglaze polychrome enamel decoration, gilding, and crest
9 3/4 in (24.7 cm)
Mark: "WEDGWOOD" "B"
Provenance: Gift of Mr. and Mrs. Byron A. Born, Ho-ho-kus, N.J.
1976.3
The crest is of H. R. H., the Duke of Clarence, subsequently H. M. King William IV, 1830-37.

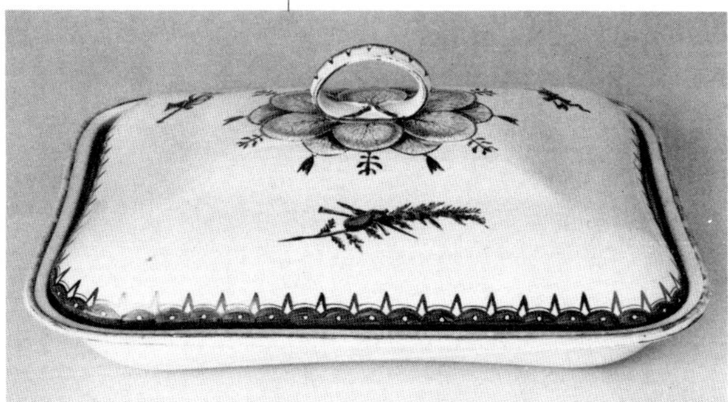

60. Covered Dish: ca. 1800
Cream ware with overglaze pink enamel decoration and gilding
4 1/4 x 9 x 10 3/4 in (10.7 x 22.7 x 27.3 cm)
Mark: "WEDGWOOD" "2"
Provenance: Dr. Harold L. Klawans, Chicago
1979.185 a and b

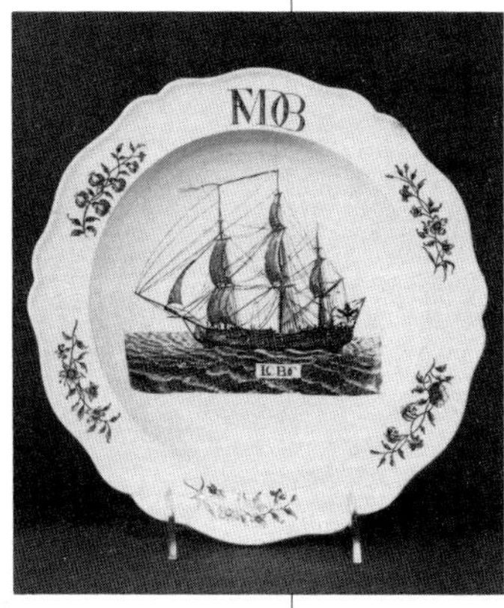

61. Deep Dish: *Russian Ship*, ca. 1780
Cream ware with transfer decoration and overglaze yellow enamel decoration
9 1/2 in (24.1 cm)
Mark: "WEDGWOOD" "2042" painted in purple-black enamel with tool mark
Provenance: Ann Brodkiewicz, Chicago
1978.164
This dish was made for the Baltic trade.

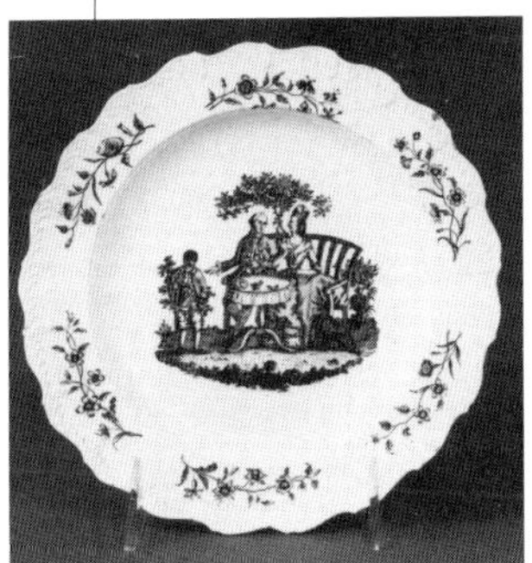

62. Plate: *The Tea Party*, ca. 1770
Cream ware with transfer decoration
7 5/8 in (19.3 cm)
Mark: "WEDGWOOD"
Provenance: Ann Brodkiewicz, Chicago
1978.166
Color plate 15

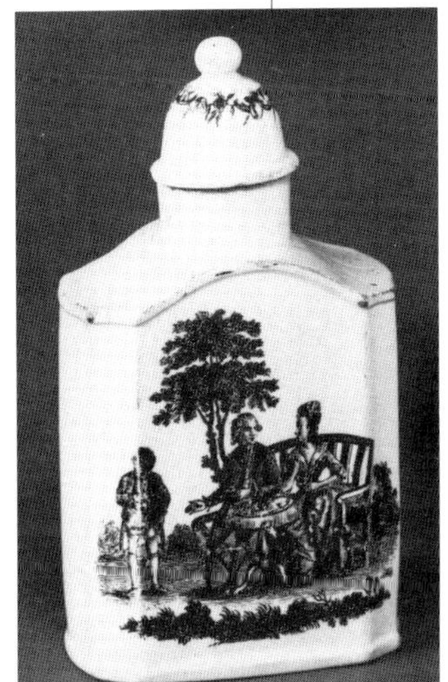

63. Tea Canister: *The Tea Party and The Good Shepherd*, ca. 1775
Cream ware with transfer decoration
5 9/16 x 2 1/4 x 3 3/16 in (14.1 x 5.7 x 8 cm)
Mark: "WEDGWOOD" "C"
Provenance: Ann Brodkiewicz, Chicago
1978.167 a and b
Color plate 15

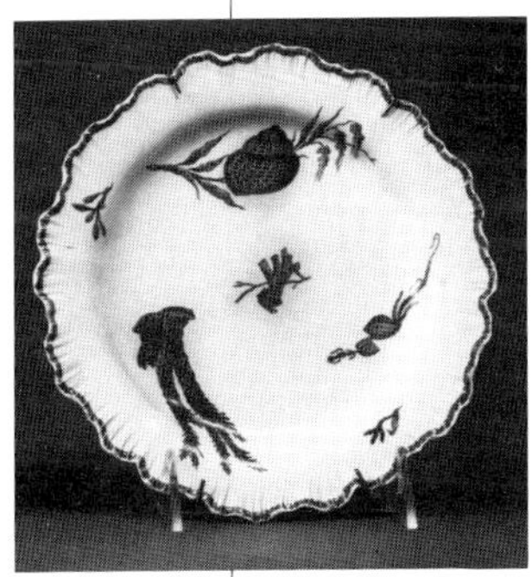

64. Plate: *Seashells*, ca. 1777
Cream ware with transfer and overglaze green enamel decoration
7 1/2 in (19 cm)
Mark: "WEDGWOOD"
Provenance: Ann Brodkiewicz, Chicago
1978.163

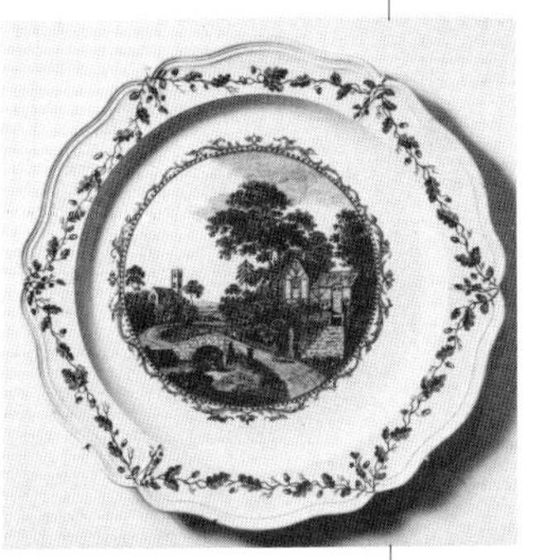

65. Platter: *English Landscape*, ca. 1790
Cream ware with transfer decoration
16 in (30 cm)
Mark: "WEDGWOOD"
Provenance: Art Trading Ltd., New York; Museum purchase in honor of Lucille Stewart Beeson with funds from Bromberg's, Inc., and the *New Yorker* magazine
1990.27
Color plate 21

66. Tile: *The Tithe Pig*, ca. 1775
Tin-glazed earthenware with transfer decoration
5 x 5 in (12.7 x 12.7 cm)
Mark: none
Provenance: unknown
1976.182

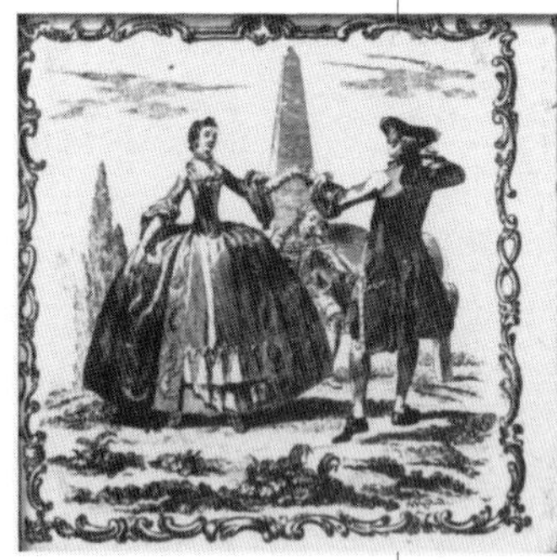

68

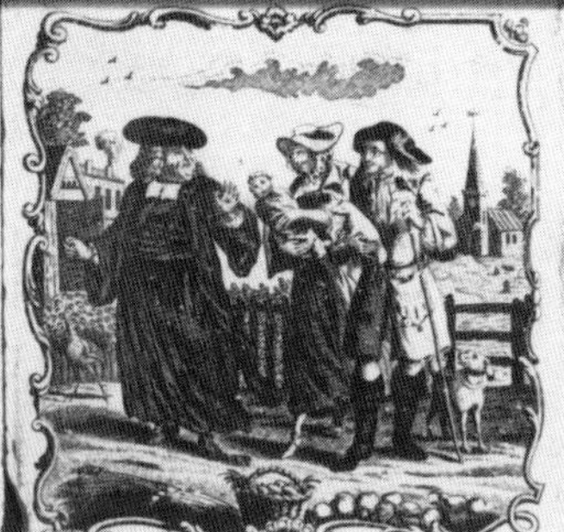

66

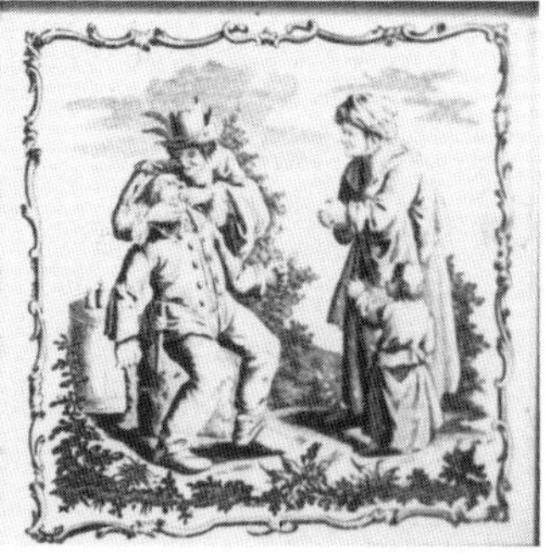

67

67. Tile: *Sense of Touch*, ca. 1775
Tin-glazed earthenware with transfer decoration
5 x 5 in (12.7 x 12.7 cm)
Mark: none
Provenance: unknown
1976.183

68. Tile: ca. 1775
Tin-glazed earthenware with transfer decoration
5 x 5 in (12.7 x 12.7 cm)
Mark: none
Provenance: unknown
1976.181

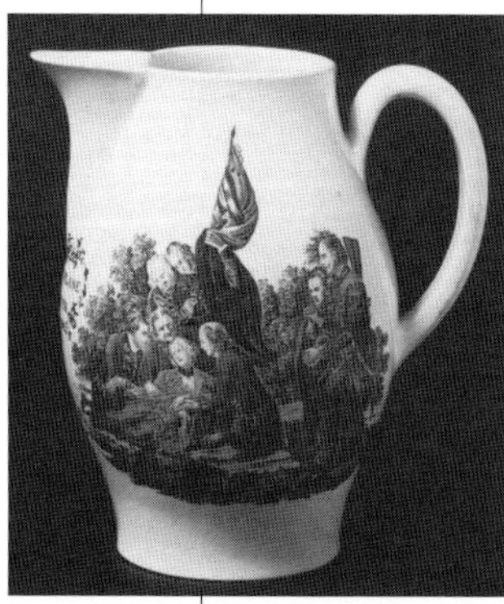

69. Pitcher: *Death of Wolfe and Taking the Enemy's Wind*, ca. 1780
Cream ware with transfer decoration
9 5/8 x 4 1/2 in (24.4 x 11.4 cm)
Mark: "WEDGWOOD" with tool marks; "EDWARD PLANE / FALMOUTH" in transfer decoration under spout
Provenance: Edward Plane Williams, England; Charles Smith, Philadelphia, Pa.
1976.244
Design source: *The Death of Wolfe* was taken from Benjamin West's painting of 1771 and engraved by William Wollett in 1776.

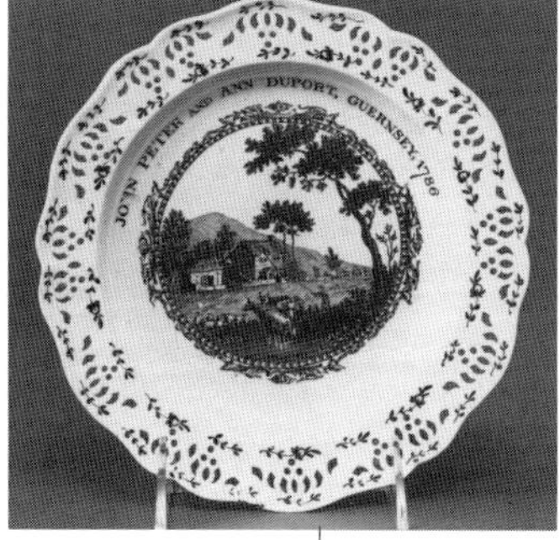

70. Plate: *Farm Scene*, ca. 1786
Cream ware with transfer decoration
7 3/4 in (19.6 cm)
Mark: "WEDGWOOD & Co"; "JOHN PETER AND ANN DUPORT, GUERNSEY, 1786" painted overglaze on front
Provenance: Otto Wasserman, New York
1978.165

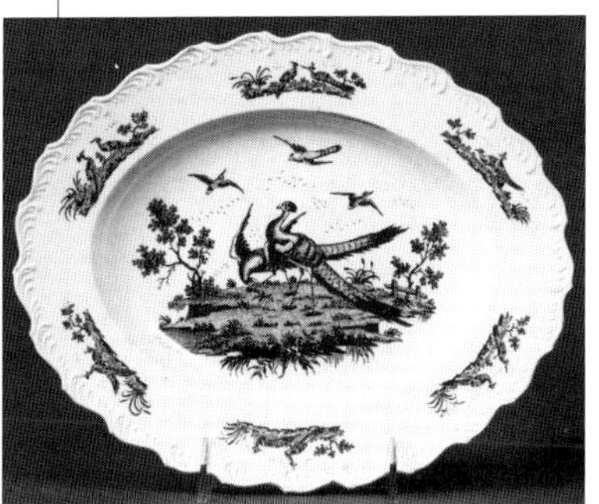

71. Platter: *Exotic Birds,* ca. 1780
Cream ware with red transfer decoration
11 1/8 x 9 in (28.2 x 22.8 cm)
Mark: "WEDGWOOD"
Provenance: Ann Brodkiewicz, Chicago
1978.160
Color plate 16

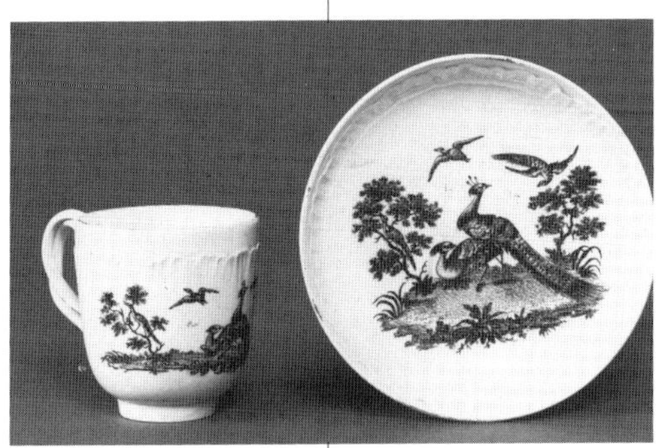

72. Cup and Saucer: *Exotic Birds,* ca. 1770
Cream ware with transfer decoration
Cup: 2 7/8 x 1 3/8 in (7.3 x 3.4 cm); saucer: 5 1/8 in (13 cm)
Mark: "WEDGWOOD" with tool marks
Provenance: Ann Brodkiewicz, Chicago
1978.168 a and b
Color plate 16

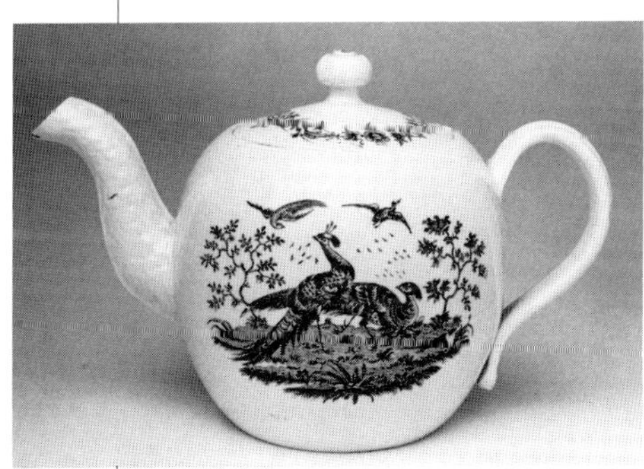

73. Teapot: *Exotic Birds,* ca. 1780
Cream ware with red transfer decoration
3 7/8 x 2 1/6 in (9.89 x 5.2 cm)
Mark: "Wedgwood" with tool marks
Provenance: Ann Brodkiewicz, Chicago
1980.180 a and b
Color plate 16

74. Veilleuse: ca. 1790
Cream ware
13 3/8 x 6 1/16 in (33.9 x 15.4 cm)
Mark: "WEDGWOOD" with tool mark
Provenance: Otto Wasserman, New York
1976.245
Color plate 13

75. Mortar and Pestle: ca. 1780
Stoneware
Mortar: 1 7/8 x 2 1/4 in (4.7 x 5.7 cm); pestle: 6 in (15.2 cm)
Mark: mortar: "Wedgwood & Bentley" "3"; pestle: none
Provenance: David Newbon, London
1976.248
Color plate 13

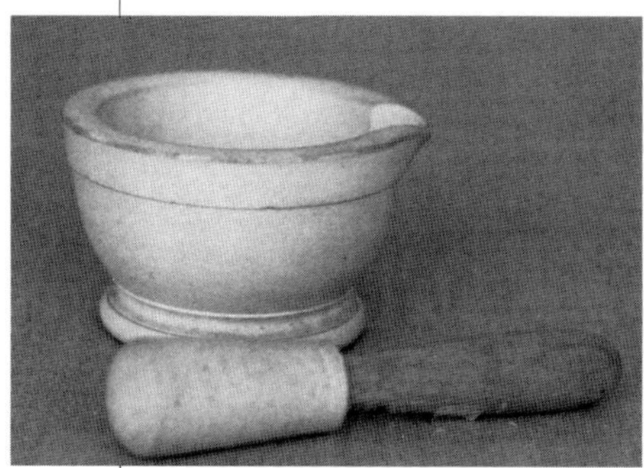

76. Mortar and Pestle: 19th century
Stoneware
Mortar: 2 7/16 x 3 1/16 in (6.1 x 7.7 cm);
pestle: 2 5/16 in (5.8 cm)
Mark: Mortar: tool mark; pestle: "WEDGWOOD" "3"
Provenance: Ann Brodkiewicz, Chicago
1985.437 a and b

77. Mortar and Pestle: ca. 1914-18
Stoneware
Mortar: 3 15/16 x 4 3/4 in (10 x 12 cm); pestle: 7 1/4 in (18.4 cm)
Mark: "WEDGWOOD / BEST COMPOSITION" "4" on mortar
with tool mark; "OOOO" impressed on pestle
Provenance: The Cinderella Antique Shoppe, Birmingham, Ala.
1976.247
Color plate 13

78. Cream Cullier: ca. 1780
Cream ware with pearl glaze
21 1/4 x 7 1/4 in (53.9 x 18.4 cm)
Mark: "Wedgwood / & Bentley"
Provenance: Gift of Mrs. Byron A. Born in
honor of Mr. Byron A. Born, Ho-ho-kus, N.J.
1986.637
Color plate 24

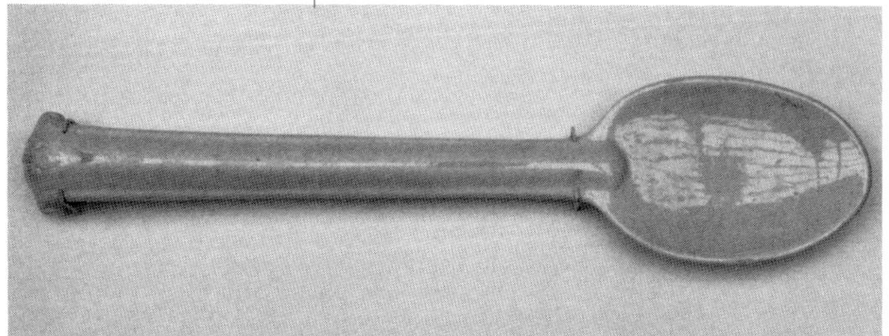

79. Dairy Spoon: ca. 1795
Cream ware
14 5/8 in (37.1 cm)
Mark: "WEDGWOOD" "U"
Provenance: Gift of Fred and Mary Tongue,
Santa Monica, Calif.
1976.246

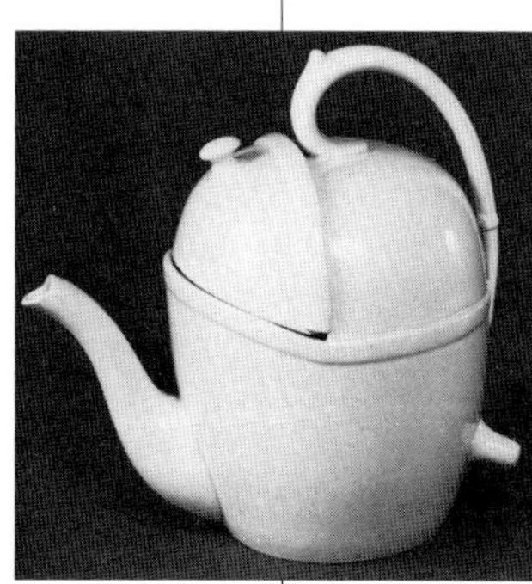

80. Teapot: *Simple yet Perfect,* ca. 1907
Cream ware
8 1/2 x 4 1/4 in (21.5 x 10.7 cm)
Mark: "PATENT / S.Y.P / WEDGWOOD" "3 V J" "T"
Provenance: Fred J. Tongue, Santa Monica, Calif.
1976.243

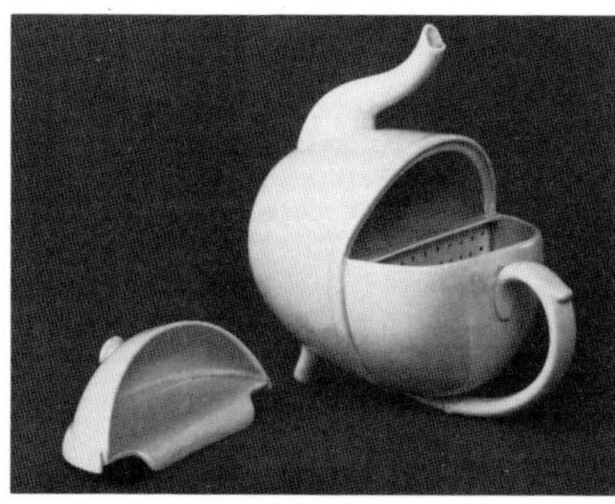

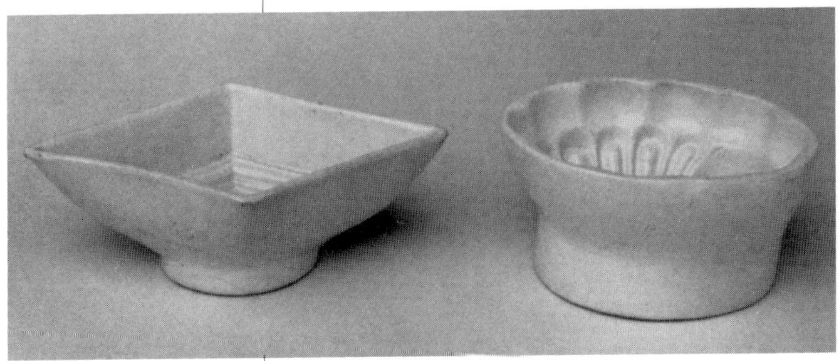

81. Footed Mold: ca. 1790
Cream ware
1 1/2 x 4 7/16 x 2 13/16 in
(3.9 x 11.2 x 7.1 cm)
Mark: "WEDGWOOD" "422" "C"
Provenance: Ann Brodkiewicz, Chicago
1980.161

82. Footed Mold: ca. 1795
Cream ware
1 11/16 x 3 1/16 x 2 7/16 in (2.3 x 7.7 x 6.1 cm)
Mark: "WEDGWOOD" "12"
Provenance: Ann Brodkiewicz, Chicago
1980.160

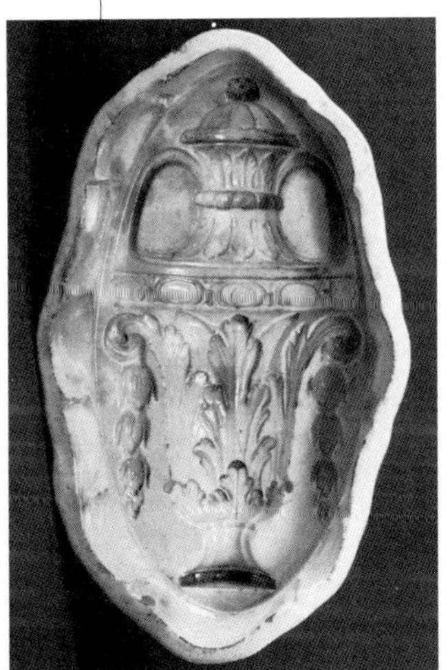

83. Mold: ca. 1790
Cream ware
2 x 7 x 4 1/2 in (5 x 17.7 x 11.4 cm)
Mark: "WEDGWOOD" "R"
Provenance: Ann Brodkiewicz, Chicago
1976.300
This mold was used to make blancmange, a flavored and sweetened milk pudding thickened with cornstarch. The French words *blanc mange* mean "white food." The mold depicts a classical urn with bellflowers, leaves, and decorative motifs typical of the Adamesque style.

White Terra-cotta Stoneware

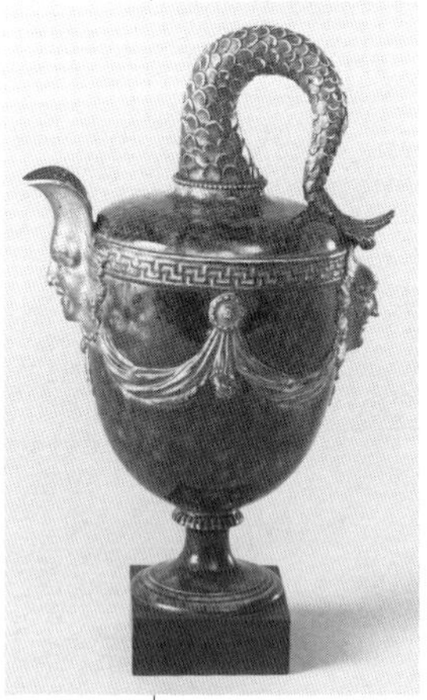

84. Stella Ewer: ca. 1775
White terra-cotta stoneware with sponged color underglaze, basalt base, and gilding
12 1/8 x 3 1/8 x 3 1/8 in (30.7 x 7.9 x 7.9 cm)
Mark: "WEDGWOOD AND BENTLEY ETRURIA" in circle around bolt
Provenance: Fred Schafer; Fred J. Tongue, Santa Monica, Calif.
1983.16
Color plate 28

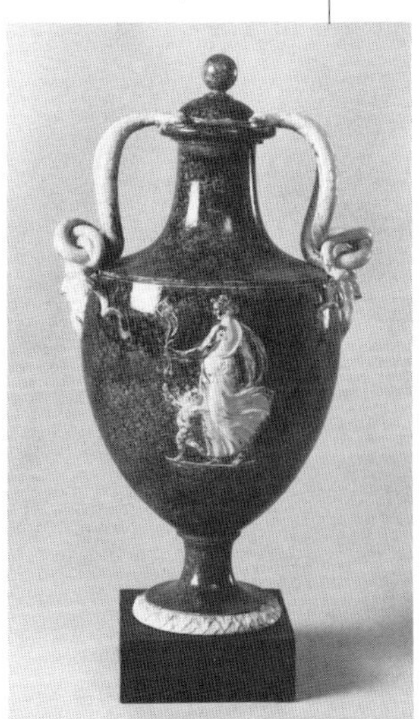

85. Covered Vase: *Venus and Cupid*, ca. 1775
White terra-cotta stoneware with imitation porphyry underglaze, basalt base, and gilding
15 x 4 1/4 x 4 1/4 in (38.1 x 10.7 x 10.7)
Mark: "WEDGWOOD & BENTLEY ETRURIA" in circle around bolt
Provenance: Viscount Esher, England; Sotheby's, London, 1965
1983.15 a and b
Color plate 76

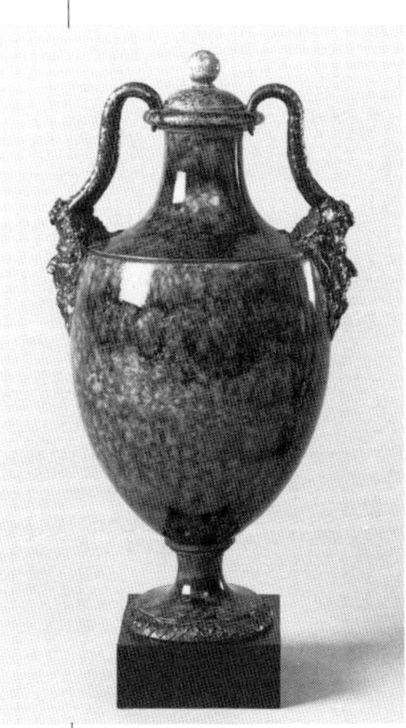

86. Covered Vase: ca. 1770
White terra-cotta stoneware with imitation porphyry underglaze, basalt base, and gilding
14 1/4 x 3 3/8 x 3 3/8 in (36.1 x 8.5 x 8.5 cm)
Mark: "WEDGWOOD & BENTLEY ETRURIA" in circle around bolt
Provenance: Otto Wasserman, New York
1983.22 a and b

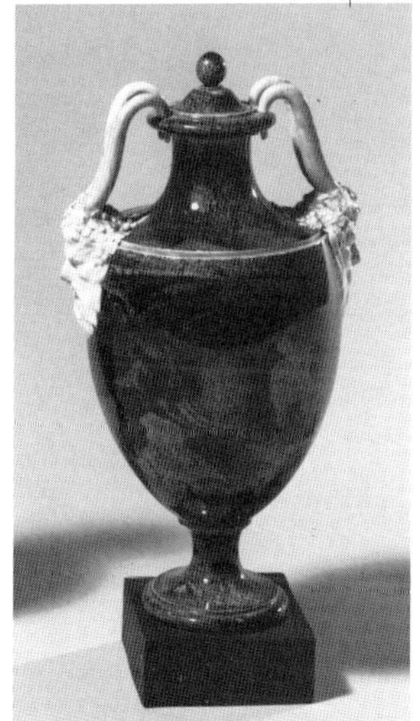

87. Covered Vase: ca. 1770
White terra-cotta stoneware with sponged color underglaze and basalt base
9 1/8 x 2 11/16 x 2 11/16 in (23.1 x 6.8 x 6.8 cm)
Mark: "WEDGWOOD AND BENTLEY ETRURIA" in circle around bolt
Provenance: David Davis, Chicago; Dr. Harold L. Klawans, Chicago
1983.9
Color plate 29

88. Covered Vase: ca. 1770
White terra-cotta stoneware with sponged color underglaze and basalt base
9 7/8 x 2 15/16 x 3 in (25 x 7.4 x 7.6 cm)
Mark: "WEDGWOOD AND BENTLEY ETRURIA" in circle around bolt
Provenance: Dr. Francis Jennings Vurpillat, South Bend, Ind.
1983.8
Color plate 29

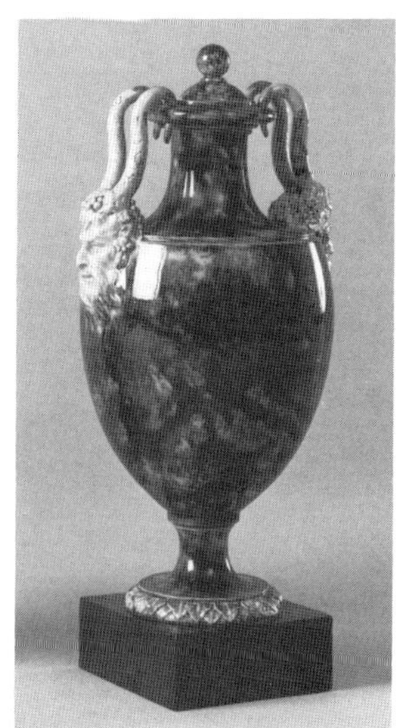

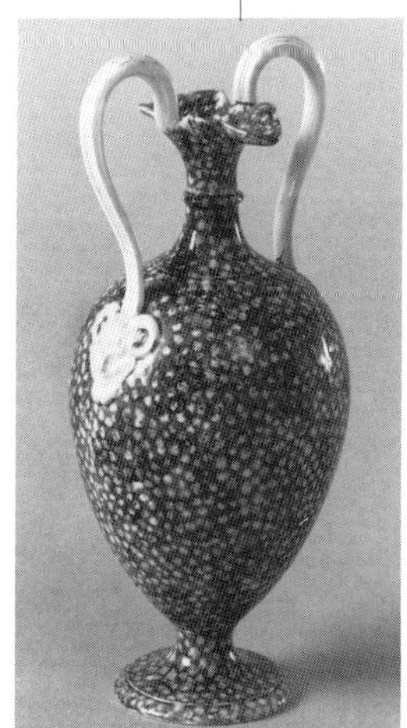

89. Vase: ca. 1776
White terra-cotta stoneware with *oeil de perdrix* effect underglaze
7 3/8 x 2 1/16 in (18.7 x 5.2 cm)
Mark: "950" incised
Provenance: Dr. Francis Jennings Vurpillat, South Bend, Ind.
1983.12

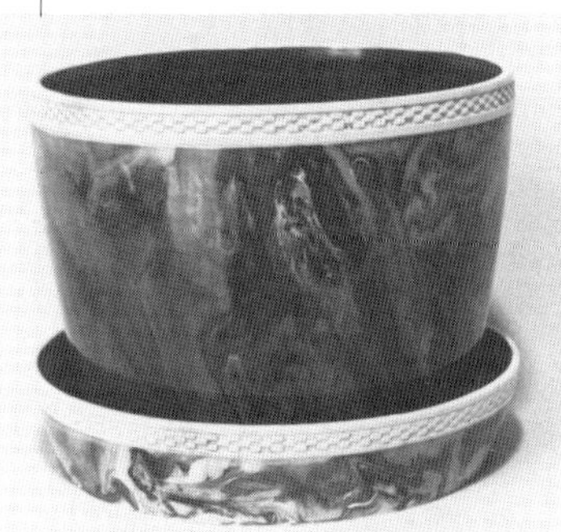

90. Bulb Pot and Underdish: ca. 1770
Cream ware or white terra-cotta stoneware with agate slip underglaze and glazed interior
Pot: 5 3/8 x 5 3/8 in (13.6 x 13.6 cm); dish: 1 9/16 x 6 1/2 in (4 x 16.5 cm)
Mark: "Wedgwood & Bentley"
Provenance: Ann Brodkiewicz, Chicago
1983.21 a and b

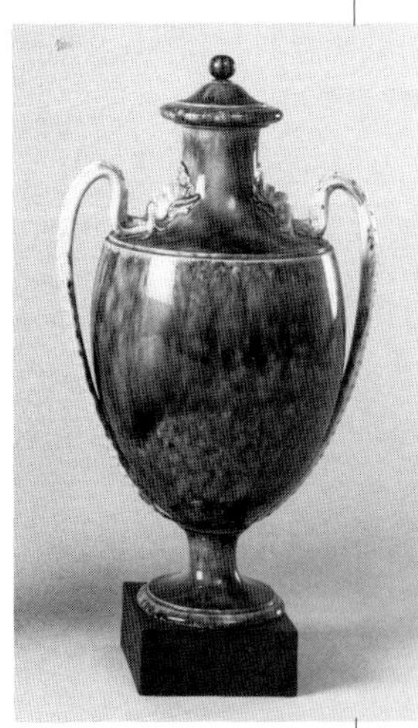

91. Pair of Bulb Pots: ca. 1770
Cream ware or white terra-cotta stoneware with agate slip underglaze, gilded border, and glazed interior
3 3/4 x 4 1/16 in (9.5 x 10.3 cm)
Mark: "Wedgwood & Bentley" "B 343", Grant's number in white enamel
Provenance: Maurice Harold Grant, England; Otto Wasserman, New York
1983.18 a and b, 1983.19 a and b
Color plate 27

92. Covered Vase: ca. 1770
White terra-cotta stoneware with sponged color underglaze and basalt base, replacement lid
12 1/2 x 3 3/16 x 3 3/16 in (31.7 x 8 x 8 cm)
Mark: "WEDGWOOD & BENTLEY ETRURIA" in circle around bolt
Provenance: David Davis, Chicago; Dr. Harold L. Klawans, Chicago
1983.13 a and b
Color plate 29

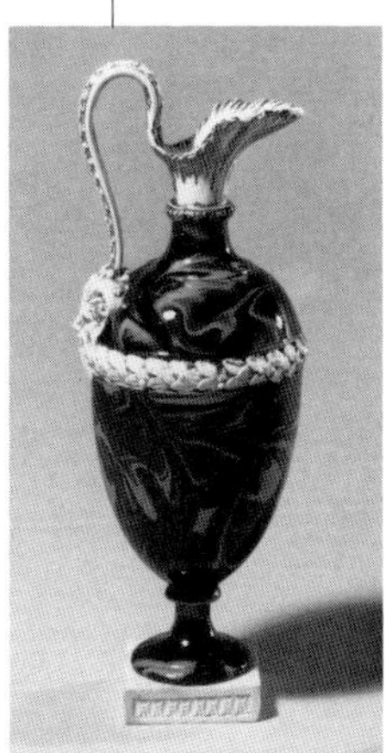

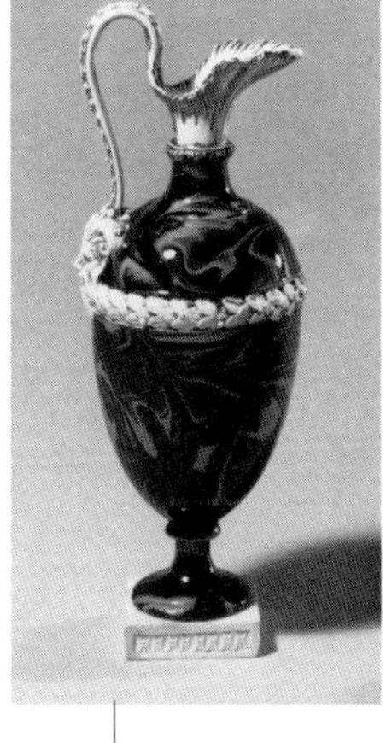

93. Ewer: ca. 1770
White terra-cotta stoneware with agate slip underglaze, white terra-cotta stoneware base, and gilding
8 15/16 x 1 7/8 x 1 7/8 in (22.7 x 4.7 x 4.7 cm)
Mark: "Wedgwood & Bentley"
Provenance: David Zeitlin, Merion, Penn.
1983.11
Color plate 27

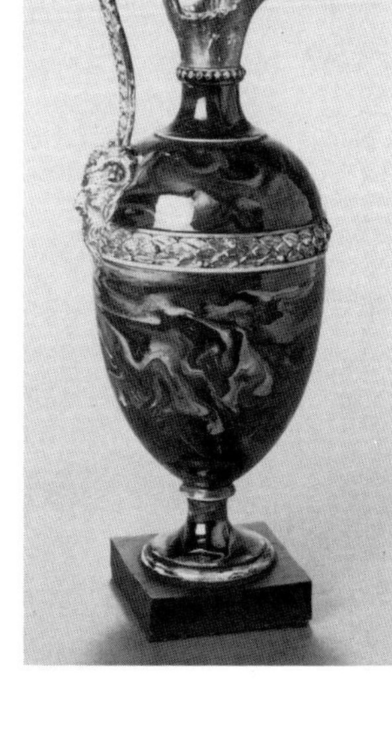

94. Ewer: ca. 1775
White terra-cotta stoneware with agate slip underglaze, basalt base, and gilding
11 1/8 x 2 11/16 x 2 11/16 in (28.2 x 6.8 x 6.8 cm)
Mark: "WEDGWOOD AND BENTLEY ETRURIA" in circle around bolt
Provenance: Shreve, Crump, and Low Co., Boston
1983.10

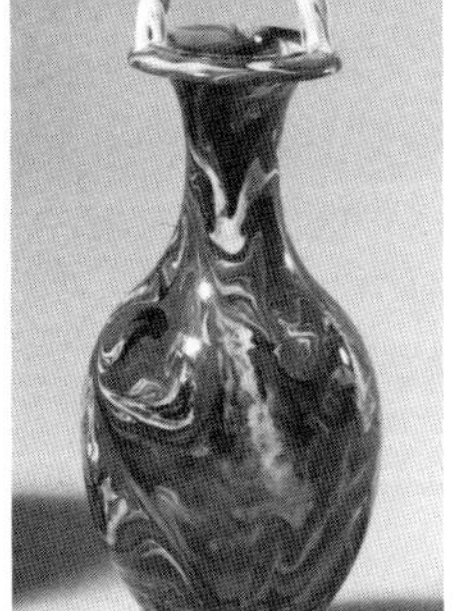

95. Vase: ca. 1775
White terra-cotta stoneware with agate slip underglaze and white terra-cotta stoneware base
8 7/8 x 2 3/16 x 2 3/16 in (22.5 x 5.5 x 5.5 cm)
Mark: "Wedgwood & Bentley"
Provenance: Dr. Francis Jennings Vurpillat, South Bend, Ind.
1983.20
Color plate 27

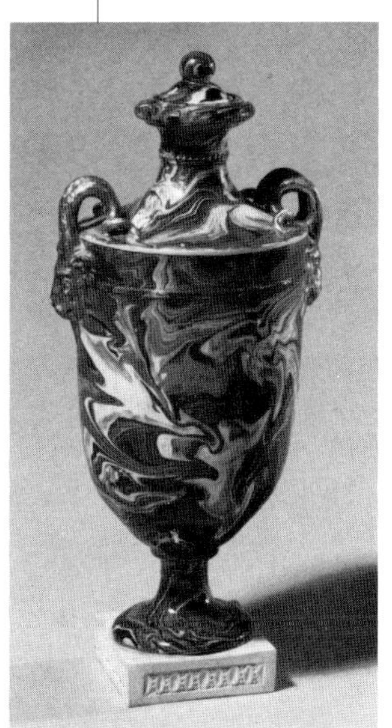

96. Covered Vase: ca. 1770
White terra-cotta stoneware with agate slip underglaze, white terra-cotta stoneware base, and gilding
8 3/4 x 2 1/4 x 2 1/4 in (22.2 x 5.7 x 5.7 cm)
Mark: "Wedgwood & Bentley"
Provenance: Otto Wasserman, New York
1983.17
Color plate 27

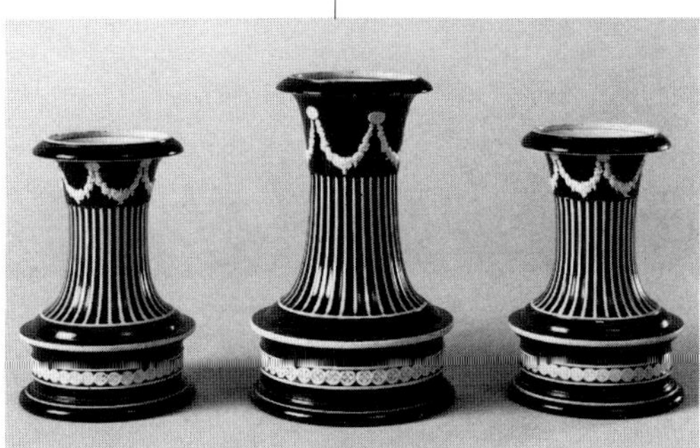

97. Pair of Vases: ca. 1790
White terra-cotta stoneware with slip decoration under pearl glaze
6 11/16 x 4 7/16 in (16.9 x 11.2 cm)
Mark: "WEDGWOOD"
Provenance: Ann Brodkiewicz, Chicago; Fred J. Tongue, Santa Monica, Calif.
1979.206 a and b
Color plate 31

98. Garniture Vase: ca. 1790
White terra-cotta stoneware with slip decoration under pearl glaze
8 1/16 x 5 1/4 in (20.4 x 13.3 cm)
Mark: "WEDGWOOD"
Provenance: Ann Brodkiewicz, Chicago
1979.207

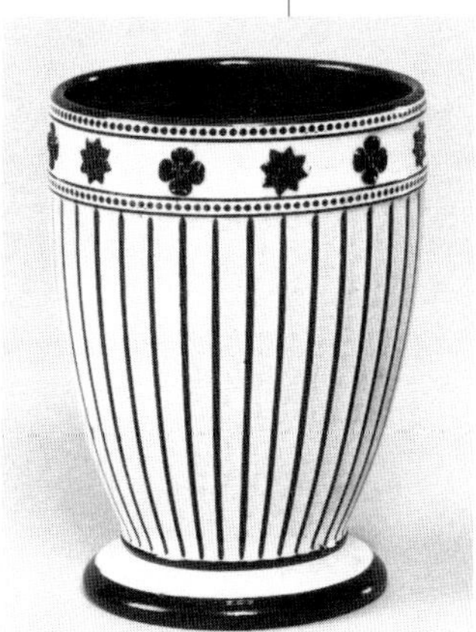

99. Vase: ca. 1800
White terra-cotta stoneware with slip decoration under clear glaze
4 1/2 x 2 13/16 in (11.4 x 7.1 cm)
Mark: "WEDGWOOD" with tool marks
Provenance: Ann Brodkiewicz, Chicago
1979.208

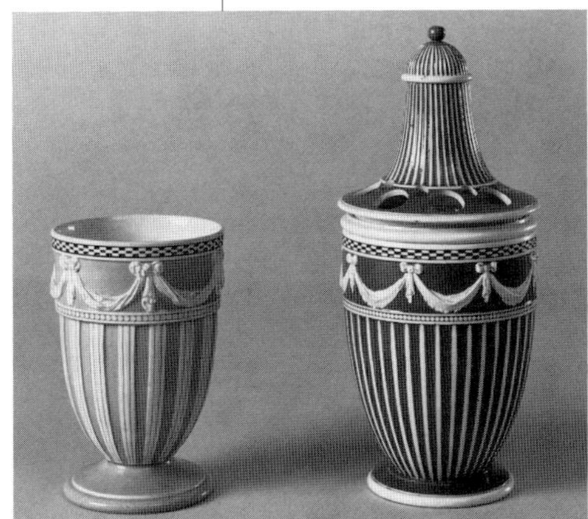

100. Vase: ca. 1780
White terra-cotta stoneware with slip decoration under clear glaze
5 7/16 x 3 3/8 in (13.8 x 8.5 cm)
Mark: "Wedgwood / & Bentley"
Provenance: Ann Brodkiewicz, Chicago
1979.210
Color plate 32

101. Bulb Pot: ca. 1785
Cream ware or white terra-cotta stoneware with slip decoration under pearl glaze, replacement lid
9 7/16 x 3 1/16 in (23.9 x 7.7 cm)
Mark: "WEDGWOOD" "K"
Provenance: Dr. Francis Jennings Vurpillat, South Bend, Ind.
1979.209 a-c
Color plate 32

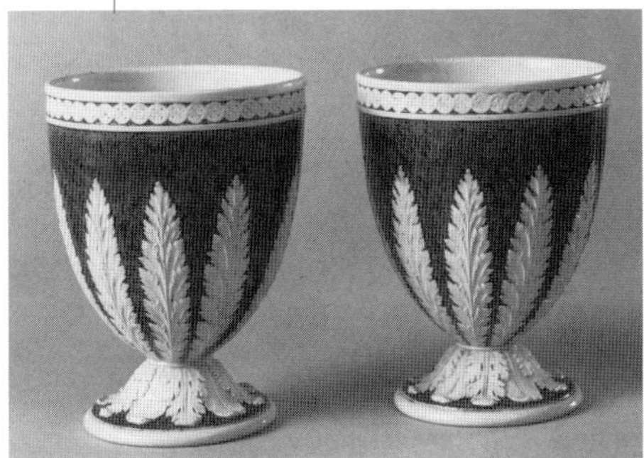

102. Pair of Vases: ca. 1770
White terra-cotta stoneware with imitation porphyry under pearl glaze
6 13/16 x 4 in (17.3 x 10.1 cm)
Mark: "WEDGWOOD" with tool marks
Provenance: Ann Brodkiewicz, Chicago
1979.211 a and b
Color plate 30

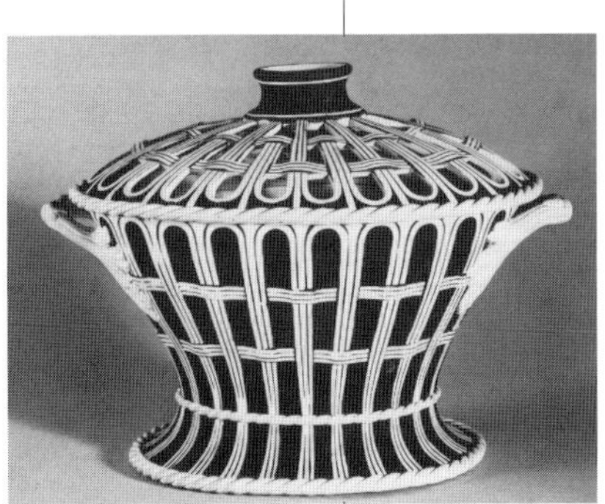

103. Bouquetière: ca. 1785
White terra-cotta stoneware with mat black slip decoration and glazed interior
8 1/4 x 6 1/4 x 7 3/4 in (20.9 x 15.7 x 19.6 cm)
Mark: "WEDGWOOD"
Provenance: Fred J. Tongue, Santa Monica, Calif.
1979.220 a and b
Color plate 33

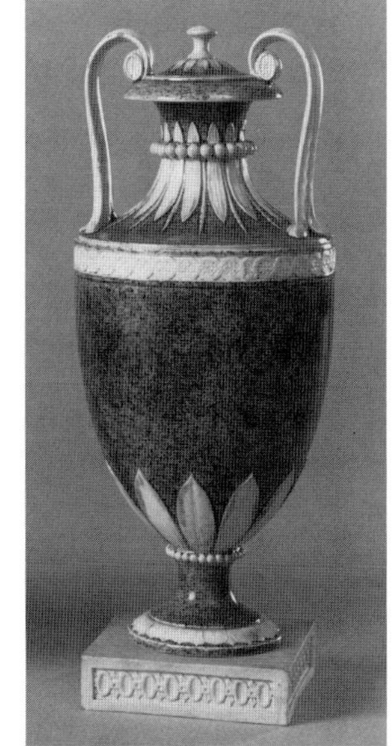

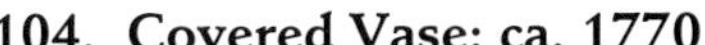

104. Covered Vase: ca. 1770
White terra-cotta stoneware with imitation porphyry under pearl glaze and white terra-cotta stoneware base
10 7/8 x 3 3/8 x 3 3/8 in (27.6 x 8.5 x 8.5 cm)
Mark: "WEDGWOOD" impressed separately
Provenance: Ann Brodkiewicz, Chicago
1979.212 a and b
Vase has sump cover.
Color plate 30

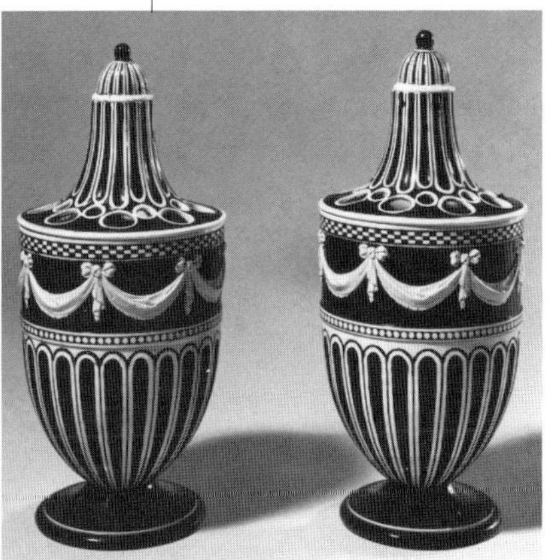

105. Pair of Potpourri Vases: ca. 1785
Cream ware or white terra-cotta stoneware with slip decoration under pearl glaze
10 15/16 x 3 7/8 in (27.7 x 9.8 cm)
Mark: a: "WEDGWOOD" "4"; b: "WEDGWOOD" "4 / N.o"
Provenance: Dr. Harold L. Klawans, Chicago
1979.215 a and b
Color plate 32

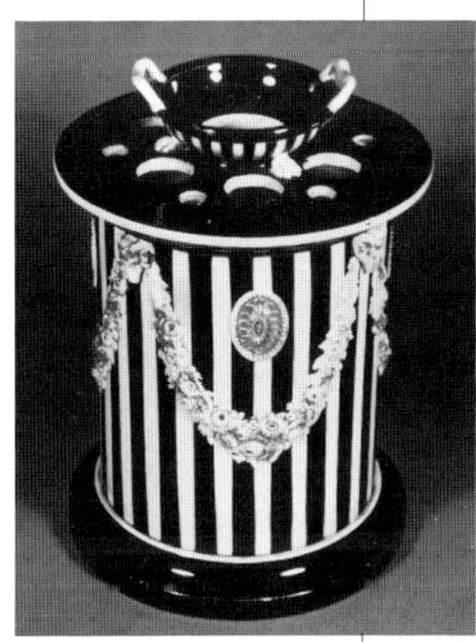

106. Potpourri Vase: ca. 1790
White terra-cotta stoneware with slip decoration under pearl glaze and gilt
8 15/16 x 6 1/4 in (22.7 x 15.8 cm)
Mark: "WEDGWOOD"
Provenance: Dr. Francis Jennings Vurpillat, South Bend, Ind.
1979.216
Color plate 31

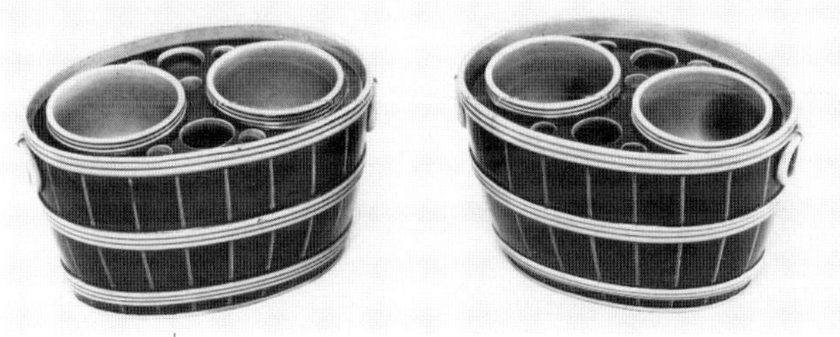

107. Pair of Bulb Pots: ca. 1790
Cream ware or white terra-cotta stoneware with slip decoration under clear glaze
3 11/16 x 2 3/4 x 4 1/2 in (9.3 x 6.9 x 11.4 cm)
Mark: "WEDGWOOD"
Provenance: unknown
1979.213 a and b, 1979.214 a and b

Basalt

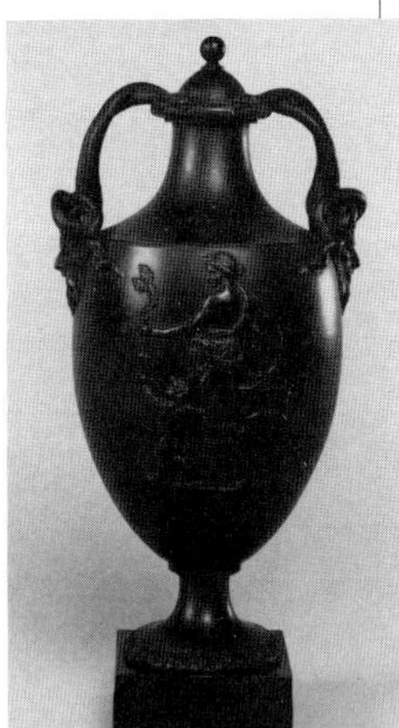

108. Vase: *Venus and Cupid,* ca. 1775
Basalt, replacement lid
12 15/16 x 3 11/16 x 3 11/16 in (32.8 x 9.3 x 9.3 cm)
Mark: "WEDGWOOD & BENTLEY ETRURIA" in circle around bolt
Provenance: Dr. Harold L. Klawans, Chicago
1979.252 a and b
Design source: Montfaucon, *L'Antiquité expliquée,* vol. 1, pl. 54, fig. 1
Color plate 76

109. Covered Vase: *Bacchanalian Boys,* ca. 1790
Basalt
19 5/16 x 5 1/2 in (49 x 13.9 cm)
Mark: "WEDGWOOD," "159" Grant's number in white enamel
Provenance: Richard Tangye and George Tangye, England; Maurice Harold Grant, England
1982.187 a and b
Color plate 44

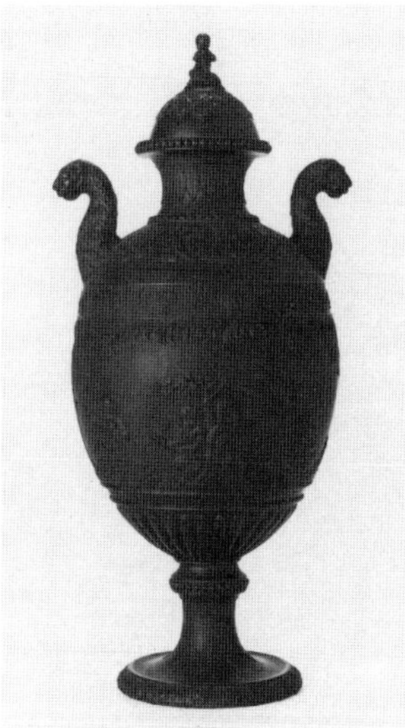

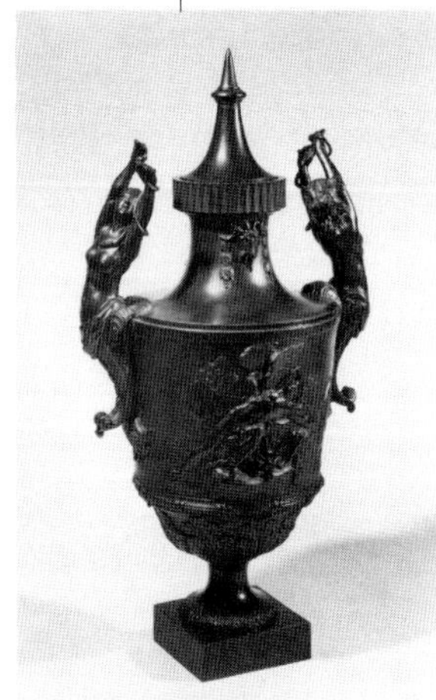

110. Vase: *Prometheus Bound,* ca. 1769
Jean Voyez (1735-1800), modeler
Basalt
20 1/4 x 4 x 4 in (51.4 x 10.1 x 10.1 cm)
Mark: "J. Voyez Sculp.t / 1769" in script beneath relief on both sides of vase
Provenance: Calland Collection, England; Dr. Francis Jennings Vurpillat, South Bend, Ind.
1979.227
Base is hollow with deep threaded cavity.
Color plate 48

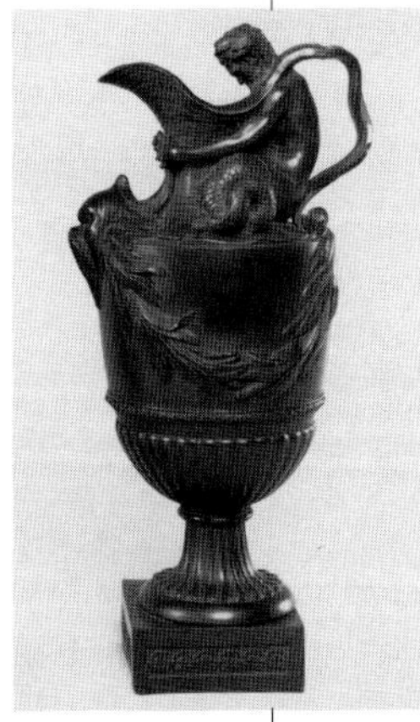

111. Wine Ewer: *Sacred to Bacchus,* ca. 1790
Basalt
16 1/4 x 4 3/16 x 4 3/16 in (41.2 x 10.6 x 10.6 cm)
Mark: "WEDGWOOD"
Provenance: Dr. Francis Jennings Vurpillat, South Bend, Ind.
1979.263

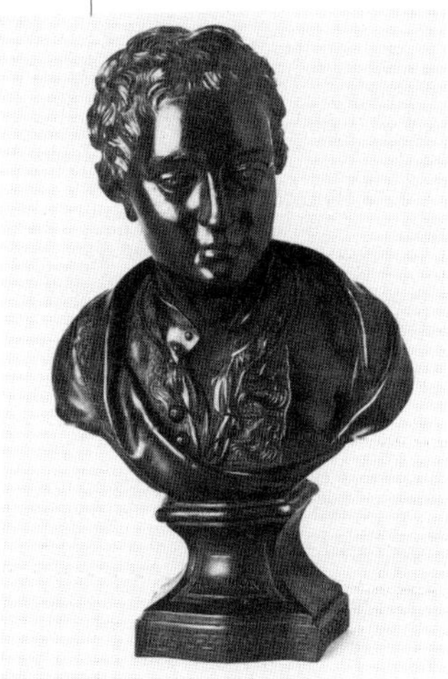

112. Roundel: ***Minerva*****, ca. 1780**
Basalt with gilt decoration, self-framed
7 3/4 x 6 3/4 in (19.6 x 17.1 cm)
Mark: none
Provenance: Art Trading Ltd., New York
1989.26.2
Color plate 36

113. Bust: ***Joseph Addison (1672-1719)*****, ca. 1780**
Basalt
14 1/4 x 3 3/4 x 5 in (36.1 x 9.5 x 12.7 cm)
Mark: "Wedgwood & Bentley" on rear;
"ADDISON" on front of base
Provenance: Ann Brodkiewicz, Chicago
1979.249
Color plate 40

114. Bust: ***Zingara*****, ca. 1775**
Basalt
8 x 3 1/8 in (20.3 x 7.9 cm)
Mark: "Wedgwood & Bentley" on back of bust
and interior of base; "ZINGARA" on back of bust
Provenance: Dr. Francis Jennings Vurpillat,
South Bend, Ind.
1980.124
Bust has eight firing holes.
Color plate 40

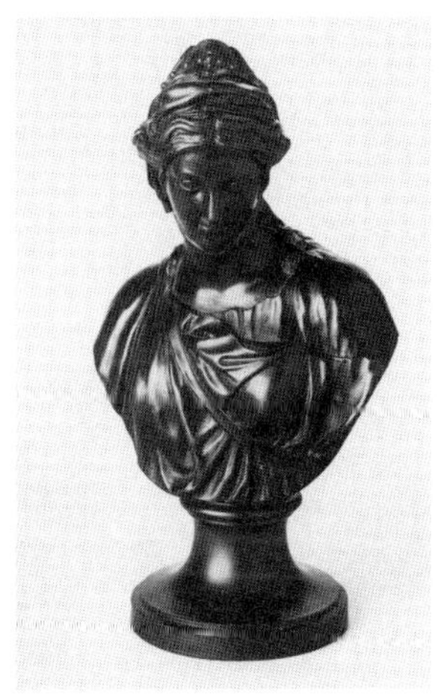

115. Covered Vase: ***Three Graces*****, ca. 1770**
Basalt, replacement lid
10 5/8 x 3 1/2 x 3 1/2 in (26.9 x 8.8 x 8.8 cm)
Mark: "WEDGWOOD & BENTLEY ETRURIA" in circle around bolt
Provenance: Dr. Harold L. Klawans, Chicago
1980.105 a and b

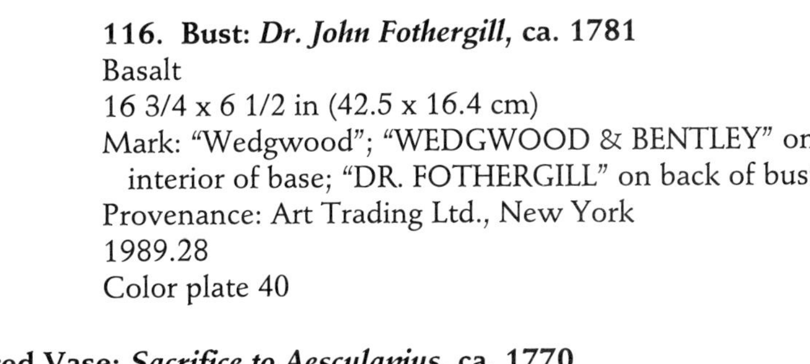

116. Bust: ***Dr. John Fothergill*****, ca. 1781**
Basalt
16 3/4 x 6 1/2 in (42.5 x 16.4 cm)
Mark: "Wedgwood"; "WEDGWOOD & BENTLEY" on
interior of base; "DR. FOTHERGILL" on back of bust
Provenance: Art Trading Ltd., New York
1989.28
Color plate 40

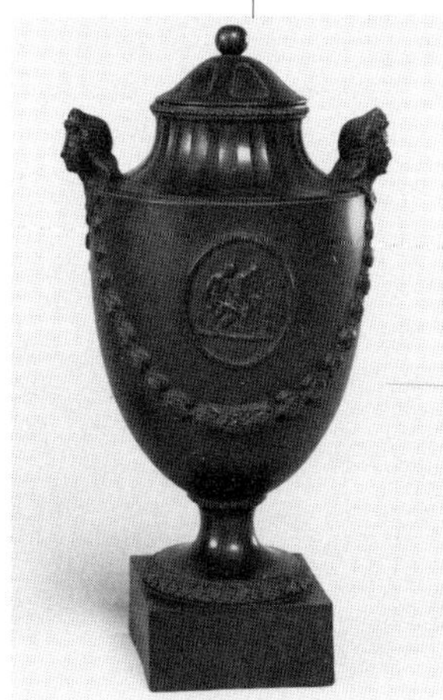

117. Covered Vase: ***Sacrifice to Aesculapius*****, ca. 1770**
Basalt, replacement lid
10 3/8 x 3 3/8 x 3 3/8 in (26.3 x 8.5 x 8.5 cm)
Mark: "WEDGWOOD & BENTLEY ETRURIA" in circle around bolt
Provenance: Dr. Harold L. Klawans, Chicago
1980.106 a and b

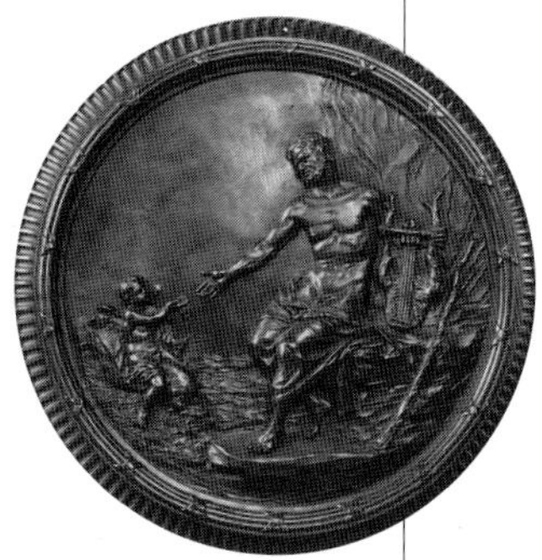

118. Roundel: *Letter to Polyphemus*, ca. 1775
Basalt, self-framed
15 in (38.1 cm)
Mark: none
Provenance: M. Mellanay Delhom, Chicago; Fred J. Tongue, Santa Monica, Calif.
1980.125
Color plate 37

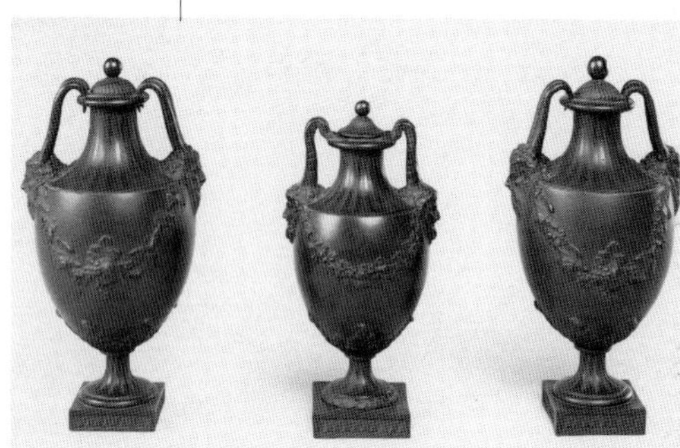

119. Pair of Covered Vases: ca. 1775
Basalt with engine-turning
8 13/16 x 2 1/8 x 2 1/8 in (22.3 x 5.3 x 5.3 cm)
Mark: "Wedgwood & Bentley"
Provenance: Ann Brodkiewicz, Chicago
1980.129 a and b
Color plate 41

120. Covered Vase: ca. 1775
Basalt with engine-turning
7 7/8 x 2 3/8 x 2 3/8 in (20 x 6 x 6 cm)
Mark: "Wedgwood & Bentley"
Provenance: Otto Wasserman, New York
1980.130 a and b
Vase has four firing holes.
Color plate 41

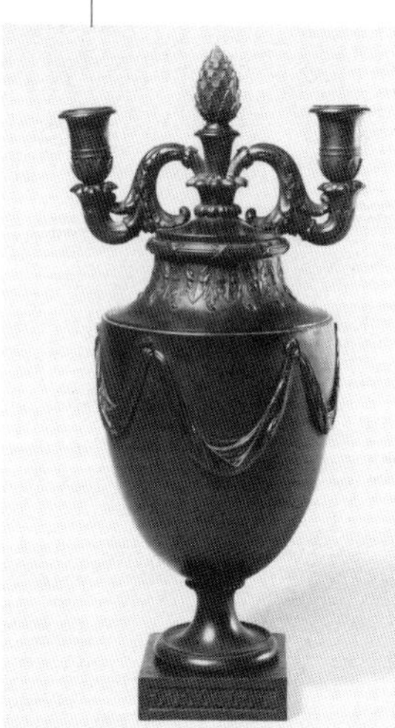

121. Vase with Candelabra: ca. 1780
Basalt
16 3/4 x 3 3/4 x 3 3/4 in (42.5 x 9.5 x 9.5 cm)
Mark: "WEDGWOOD & BENTLEY ETRURIA" in circle around bolt
Provenance: Ann Brodkiewicz, Chicago
1980.107 a and b
Vase has sump cover and a hollow base with four firing holes.
Color plate 34

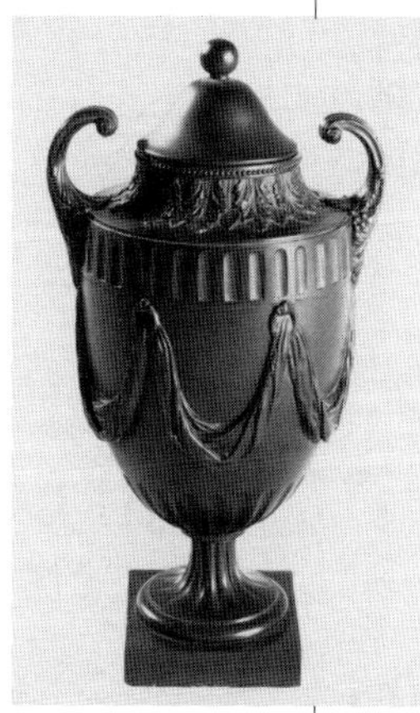

122. Covered Vase: ca. 1775
Basalt with engine-turning, replacement lid
8 7/8 x 2 15/16 x 2 15/16 in (22.5 x 7.4 x 7.4 cm)
Mark: "WEDGWOOD & BENTLEY ETRURIA" in circle around bolt
Provenance: Dr. Harold L. Klawans, Chicago
1980.139

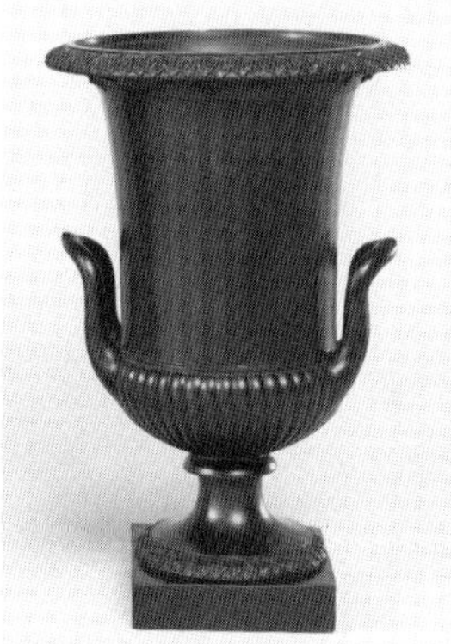

123. Vase: ca. 1775
Basalt with engine-turning
10 1/2 x 3 11/16 x 3 11/16 in (26.6 x 9.3 x 9.3 cm)
Mark: "WEDGWOOD & BENTLEY ETRURIA" in circle around bolt
Provenance: David Davis, Chicago; Dr. Francis Jennings Vurpillat, South Bend, Ind.
1979.257
Color plate 42

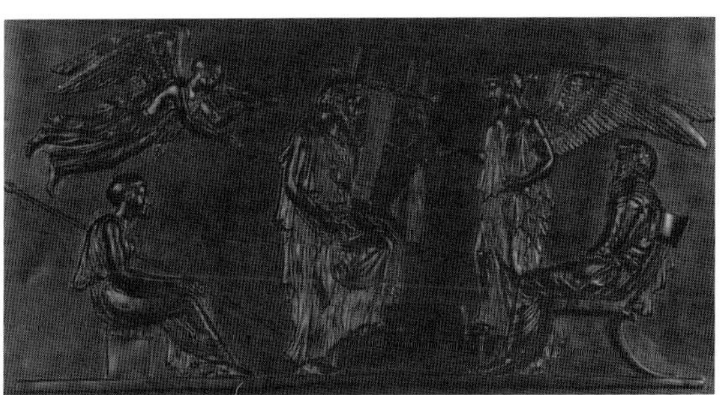

124. Tablet: *Apotheosis of Homer,* ca. 1775-80
Basalt, bronzing
7 3/4 x 14 3/4 in (19.6 x 37.4 cm)
Mark: "WEDGWOOD & BENTLEY" twice
Provenance: Art Trading Ltd., New York
1989.26.1
Design source: D'Hancarville, *Antiquités,* vol. 3, pl. 31
Color plate 35

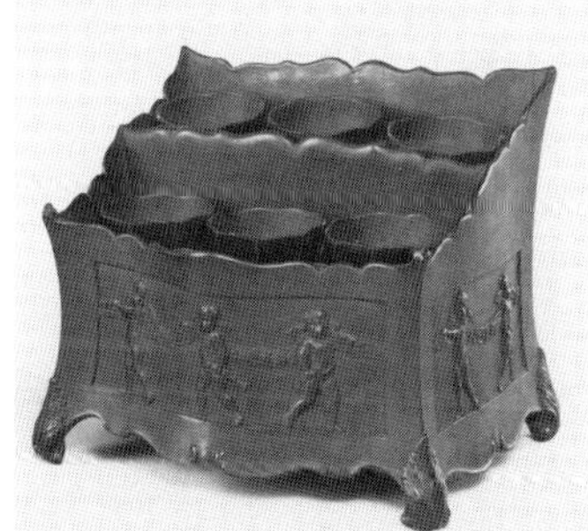

125. Bulb Pot: *Procession of Little Boys,* ca. 1775
Basalt, bulb holders removable with glazed interior
7 1/8 x 8 5/8 x 7 15/16 in (18 x 21.9 x 20.1 cm)
Mark: "Wedgwood & Bentley," "72" Grant's number in white enamel
Provenance: Maurice Harold Grant, England; Ann Brodkiewicz, Chicago
1980.123 a, b, and c
Color plate 43

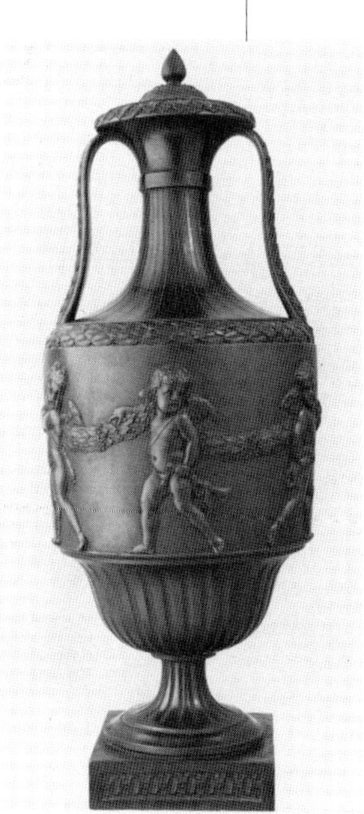

126. Covered Vase: *Procession of Little Boys,* ca. 1775
Basalt with engine-turning
21 5/8 x 3 13/16 x 3 13/16 in (54.9 x 9.6 x 9.6 cm)
Mark: "Wedgwood & Bentley"
Provenance: Christie's, London, May 16, 1966
1982.188
Vase has hollow base and one firing hole.
Color plate 43

127. Covered Vase: ca. 1775
Basalt, replacement lid
7 1/2 x 3 x 3 in (19 x 7.6 x 7.6 cm)
Mark: "WEDGWOOD & BENTLEY ETRURIA" in circle around bolt
Provenance: M. Mellanay Delhom, Chicago; Ann Brodkiewicz, Chicago
1980.132 a and b

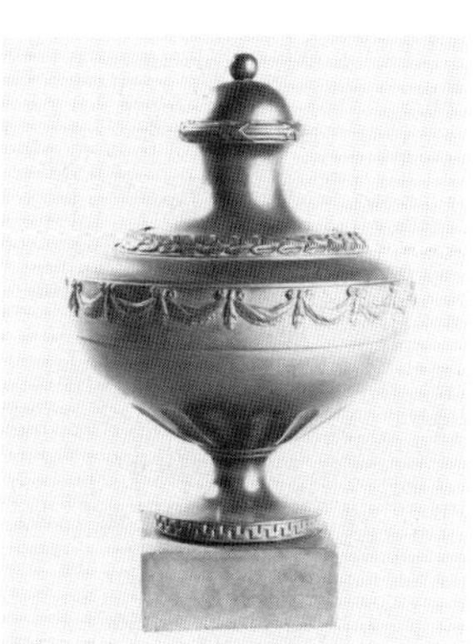

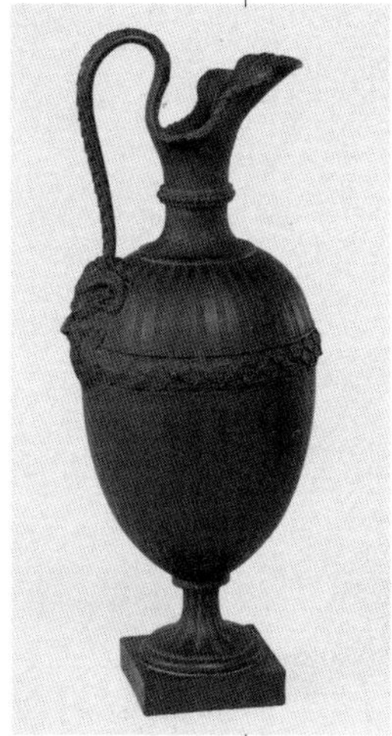

128. Ewer, ca. 1778
Basalt with engine-turning
9 1/2 x 1 15/16 x 1 15/16 in (24.1 x 4.9 x 4.9 cm)
Mark: "WEDGWOOD & BENTLEY ETRURIA" in circle around bolt
Provenance: M. Mellanay Delhom, Chicago; Ann Brodkiewicz, Chicago
1979.256
Color plate 42

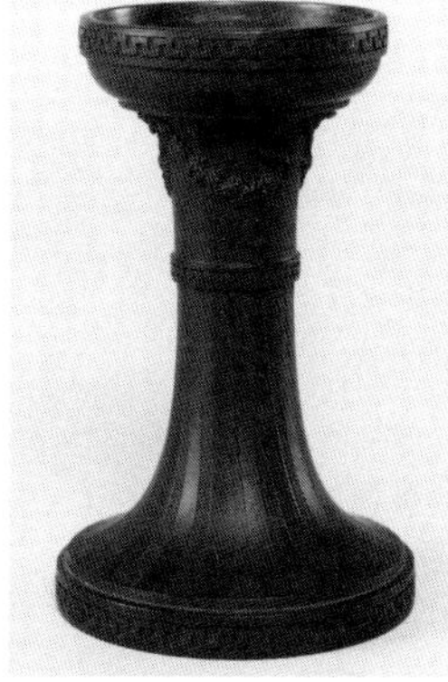

129. Vase: ca. 1775
Basalt with engine-turning
6 x 3 3/4 in (15.2 x 9.5 cm)
Mark: "Wedgwood / & Bentley" "14"
Provenance: M. Mellanay Delhom, Chicago;
Ann Brodkiewicz, Chicago
1980.131
Color plate 42

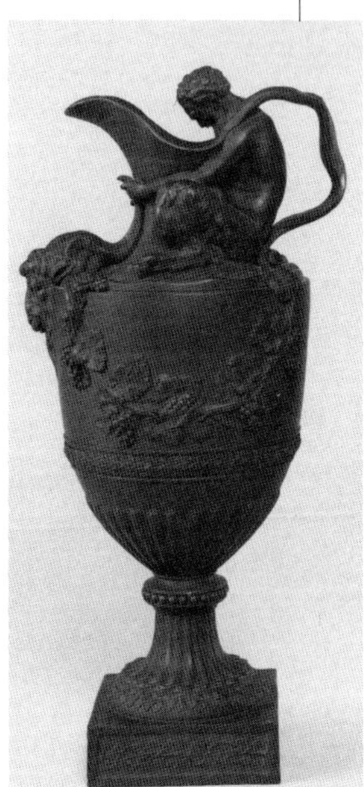

130. Water Ewer: *Sacred to Neptune*, ca. 1780
Basalt
15 1/4 x 4 x 4 in (38.7 x 10.1 x 10.1 cm)
Mark: "WEDGWOOD & BENTLEY ETRURIA" in circle around bolt
Provenance: Ann Brodkiewicz, Chicago
1979.262
Color plate 46

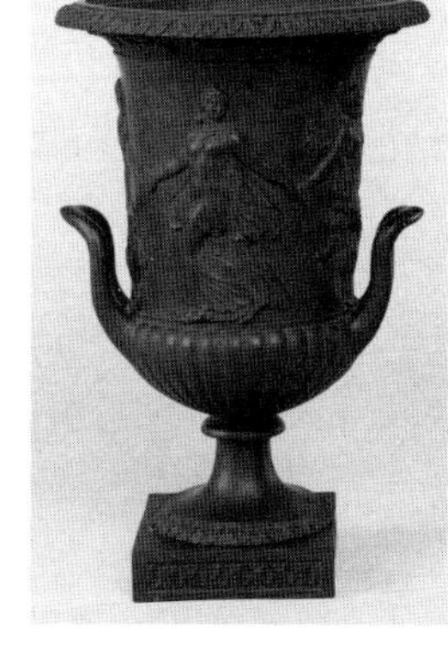

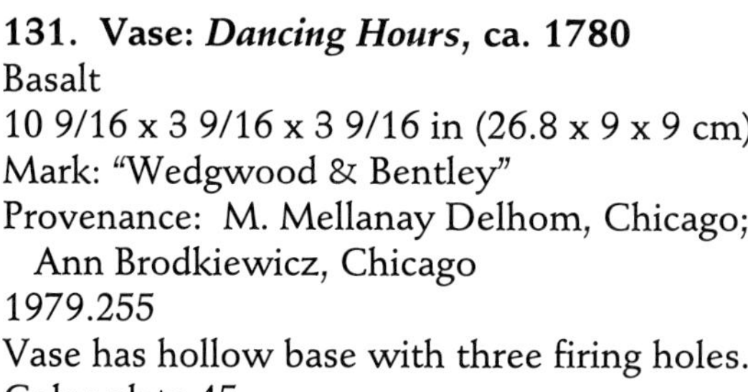

131. Vase: *Dancing Hours*, ca. 1780
Basalt
10 9/16 x 3 9/16 x 3 9/16 in (26.8 x 9 x 9 cm)
Mark: "Wedgwood & Bentley"
Provenance: M. Mellanay Delhom, Chicago;
Ann Brodkiewicz, Chicago
1979.255
Vase has hollow base with three firing holes.
Color plate 45

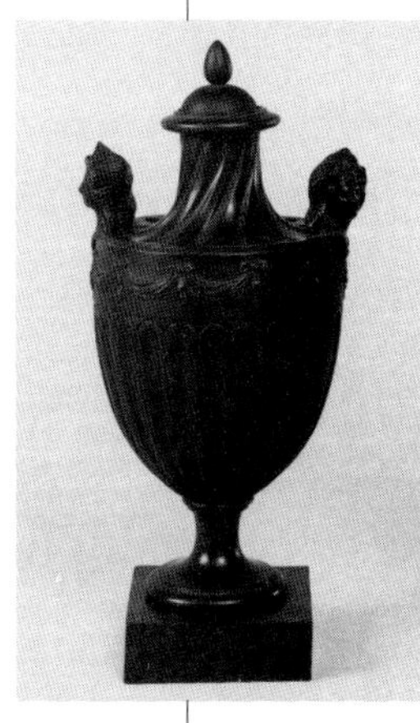

132. Covered Vase: ca. 1775
Basalt, replacement lid
10 x 3 3/8 x 3 3/8 in (25.4 x 8.5 x 8.5 cm)
Mark: "WEDGWOOD & BENTLEY ETRURIA" in circle on side of base
Provenance: Dr. Harold L. Klawans, Chicago
1979.250 a and b

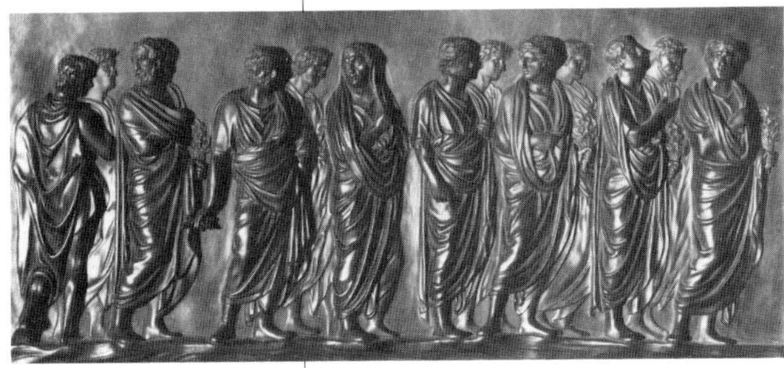

133. Tablet: *Roman Procession*, or *Procession of Senators*, ca. 1790
Basalt
20 1/4 x 10 in (51.4 x 25.4 cm)
Mark: "WEDGWOOD"
Provenance: Dr. Harold L. Klawans, Chicago
1979.254
Tablet was pressed into a mold, then eight figures were applied and finished by modeler. Each figure is supported from the back by three basalt "buttons."
Color plate 39

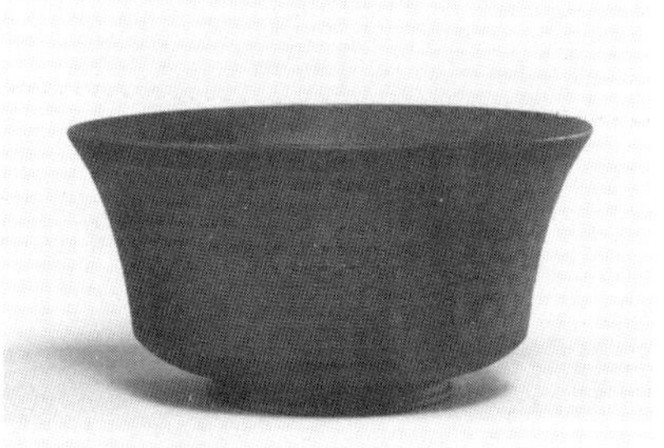

134. Basket-Weave Bowl: ca. 1800
Basalt with engine-turning
3 11/16 x 3 7/16 in (9.3 x 8.7 cm)
Mark: "WEDGWOOD" with tool marks
Provenance: Davidson's, Atlanta, Ga.
1979.226

135. Water Kettle: ca. 1775-80
Basalt with glazed interior
7 1/4 x 4 3/4 in (18.3 x 12 cm)
Mark: "Wedgwood & Bentley"
Provenance: Dr. Francis Jennings Vurpillat, South Bend, Ind.
1979.259
Color plate 50

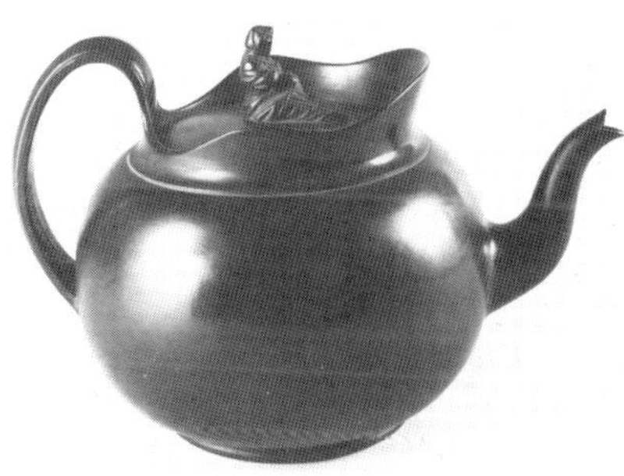

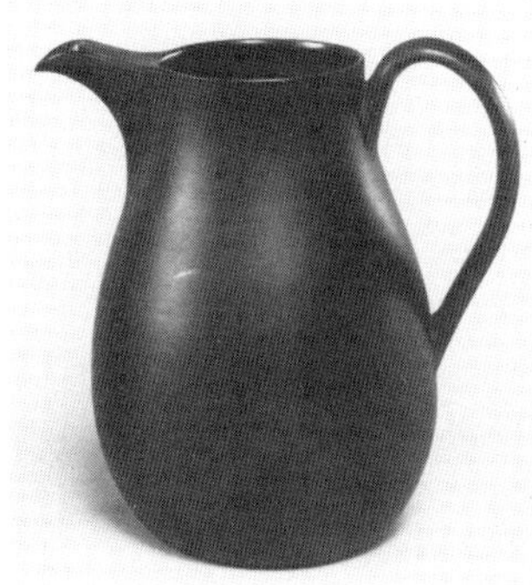

136. Pitcher: ca. 1775
Basalt with glazed interior
6 7/8 x 3 in (17.4 x 7.6 cm)
Mark: "Wedgwood & Bentley"
Provenance: Charles Smith, Philadelphia, Pa.
1979.261
Color plate 50

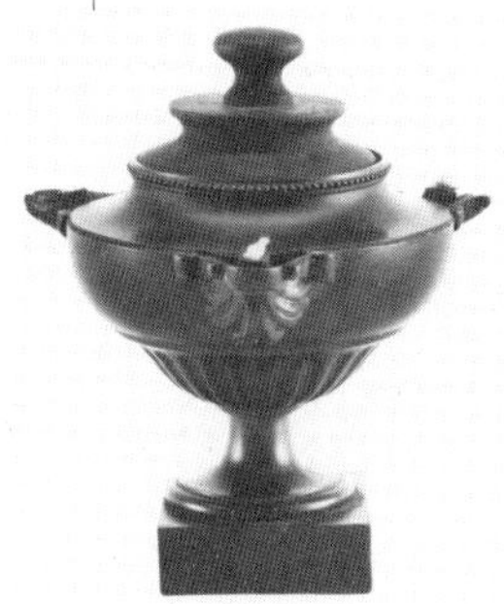

137. Hand Lamp: ca. 1780
Basalt with glazed interior, replacement lid
4 5/16 x 2 1/8 x 2 1/8 in (10.9 x 5.3 x 5.3 cm)
Mark: "WEDGWOOD & BENTLEY ETRURIA" in circle around bolt
Provenance: Dr. Francis Jennings Vurpillat, South Bend, Ind.
1985.438

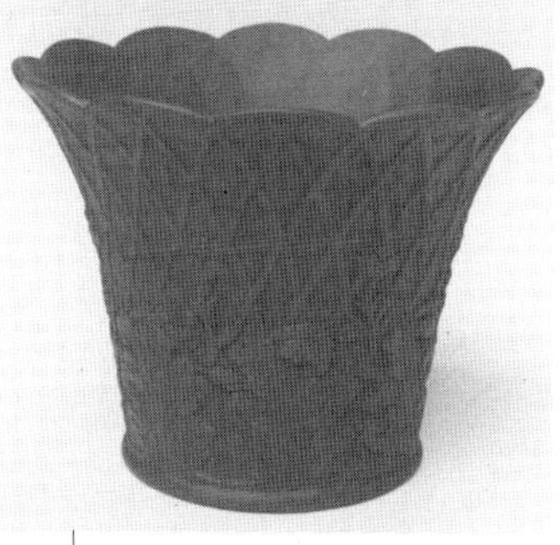

138. Vase: 19th century
Basalt
3 x 2 1/4 in (7.6 x 5.7 cm)
Mark: "WEDGWOOD" with tool mark
Provenance: Ann Brodkiewicz, Chicago
1980.155

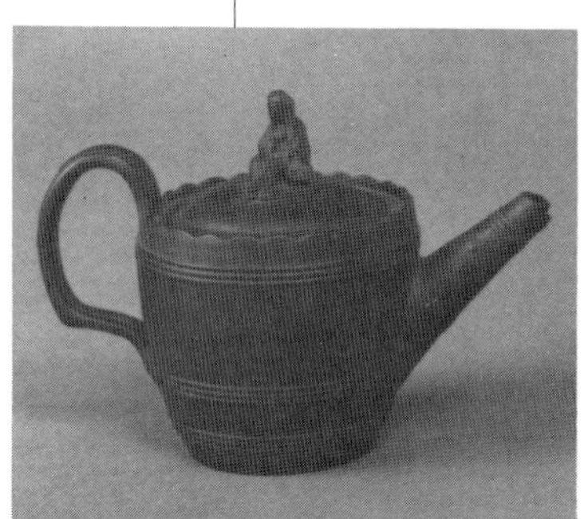

139. Teapot: ca. 1790
Basalt
3 13/16 x 2 in (9.6 x 5 cm)
Mark: "Wedgwood"
Provenance: Dr. Harold L. Klawans, Chicago
1980.111

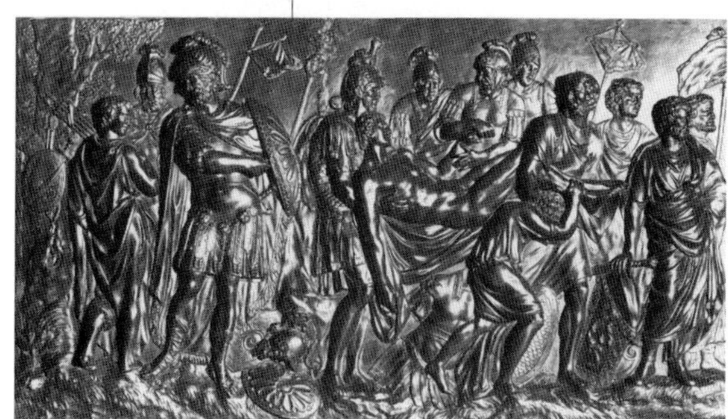

140. Tablet: *Death of Meleager*, ca. 1782
Basalt
19 3/4 x 11 1/8 in (50 x 28.2 cm)
Mark: none
Provenance: Dr. Francis Jennings Vurpillat,
South Bend, Ind.
1980.122
Color plate 38

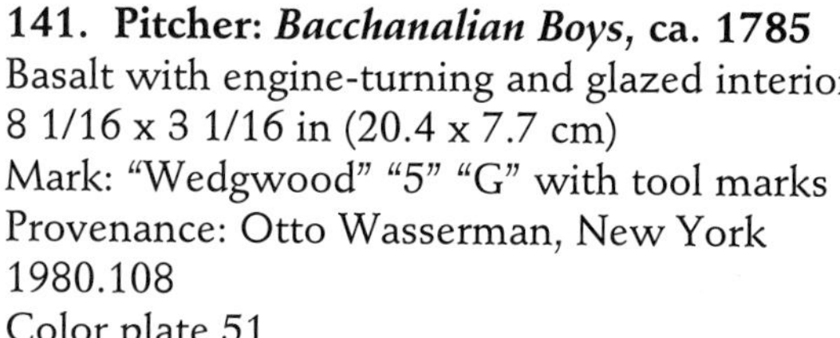

141. Pitcher: *Bacchanalian Boys*, ca. 1785
Basalt with engine-turning and glazed interior
8 1/16 x 3 1/16 in (20.4 x 7.7 cm)
Mark: "Wedgwood" "5" "G" with tool marks
Provenance: Otto Wasserman, New York
1980.108
Color plate 51

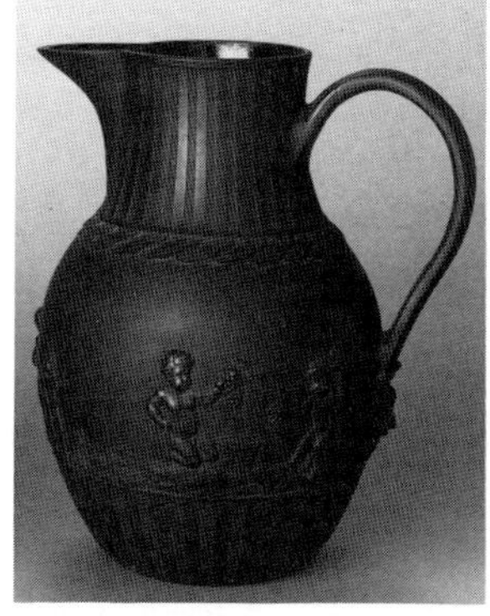

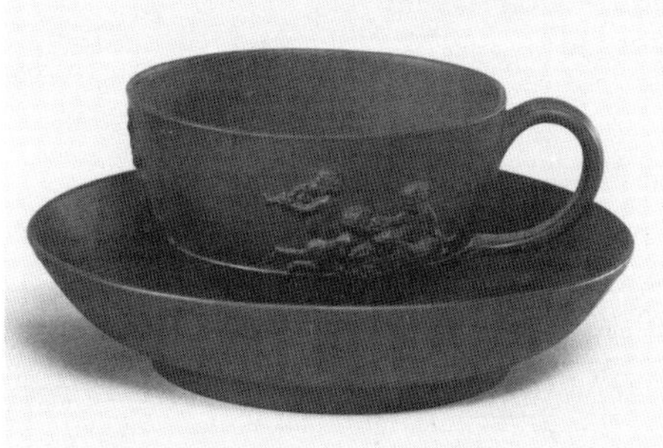

142. Cup and Saucer: *Bacchanalian Boys*, ca. 1780
Basalt with engine-turning
Cup: 1 7/8 x 1 3/8 in (4.7 x 3.4 cm); saucer: 5 in (12.7 cm)
Mark: cup: "WEDGWOOD" "3"; saucer: "WEDGWOOD" "2"
Provenance: Ann Brodkiewicz, Chicago
1980.114 a and b
Color plate 51

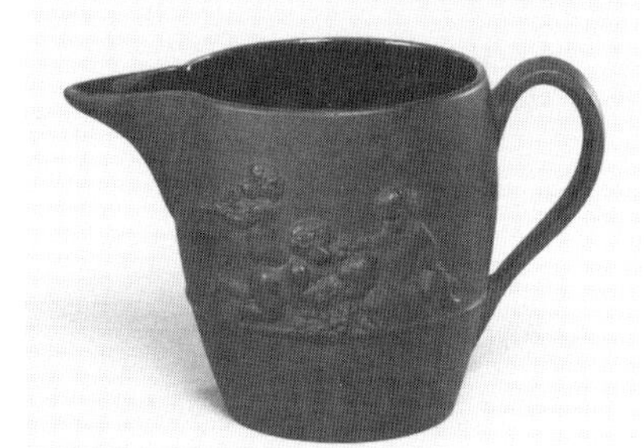

143. Cream Pitcher: *Bacchanalian Boys*, ca. 1785
Basalt with engine-turning and glazed interior
2 9/16 x 1 1/2 in (6.5 x 3.8 cm)
Mark: "Wedgwood" "1" "0"
Provenance: Dr. Francis Jennings Vurpillat, South Bend, Ind.
1980.112
Color plate 51

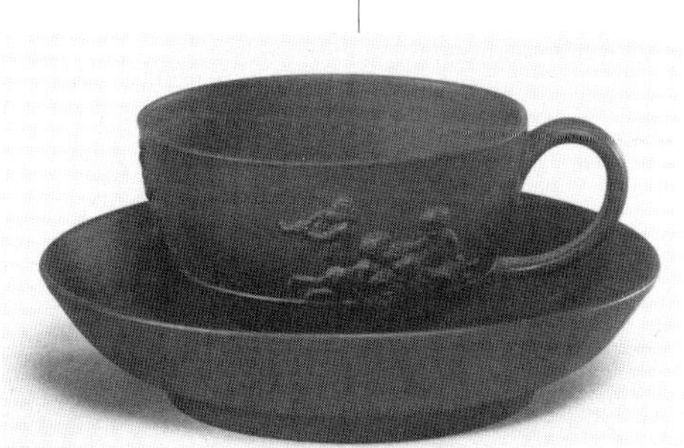

144. Cup and Saucer: *Bacchanalian Boys*, ca. 1780
Basalt with engine-turning
Cup: 1 7/8 x 1 3/8 in (4.7 x 3.4 cm); saucer: 5 1/16 in (12.8 cm)
Mark: cup: "WEDGWOOD" "3"; saucer: "WEDGWOOD" "2"
Provenance: M. Mellanay Delhom, Chicago; Ann Brodkiewicz, Chicago
1980.113 a and b

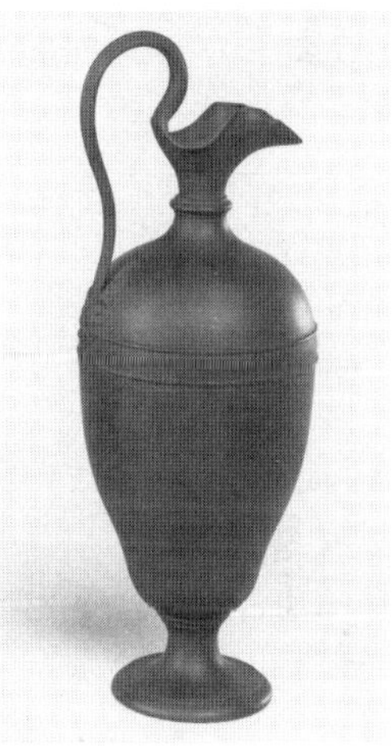

145. Ewer: ca. 1800
Basalt
7 11/16 x 1 7/8 in (19.5 x 4.7 cm)
Mark: "WEDGWOOD"
Provenance: Ann Brodkiewicz, Chicago
1979.260

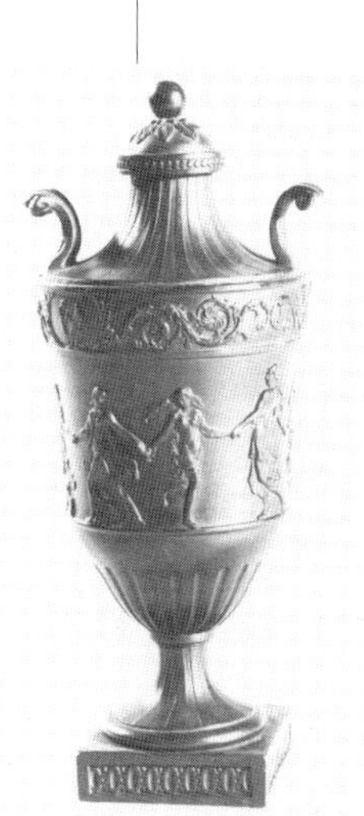

146. Covered Vase: *Dancing Hours*, ca. 1790
Basalt with engin-turning, replacement lid
6 3/8 x 1 15/16 x 1 15/16 in (16.1 x 4.9 x 4.9 cm)
Mark: "Wedgwood"
Provenance: Dr. Harold L. Klawans, Chicago
1980.133 a and b
Vase has flanged base and sump cover. Shoulder section and cover are removable.

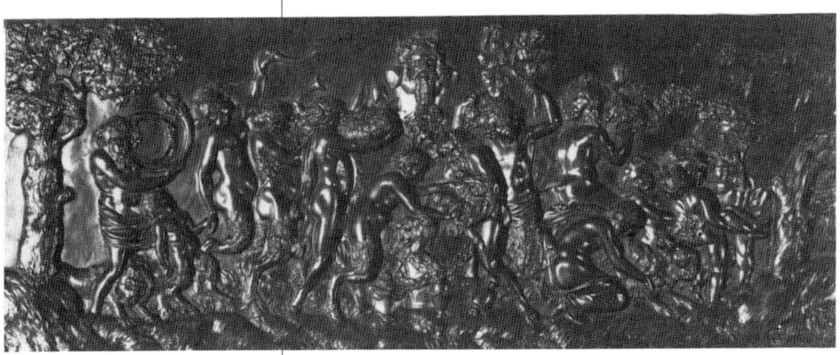

147. Tablet: *Bacchanalian Sacrifice*, ca. 1790
Basalt
20 1/2 x 9 in (52 x 22.8 cm)
Mark: "WEDGWOOD"
Provenance: Dr. Harold L. Klawans, Chicago
1980.104

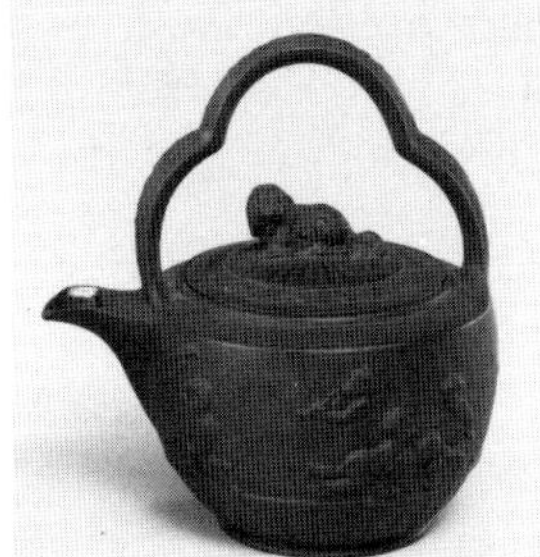

148. Rum Kettle: *Bacchanalian Boys*, ca. 1785
Basalt with engine-turning with glazed interior
5 1/4 x 2 1/4 in (13.3 x 5.7 cm)
Mark: "Wedgwood" with tool mark
Provenance: Ann Brodkiewicz, Chicago
1980.110 a and b

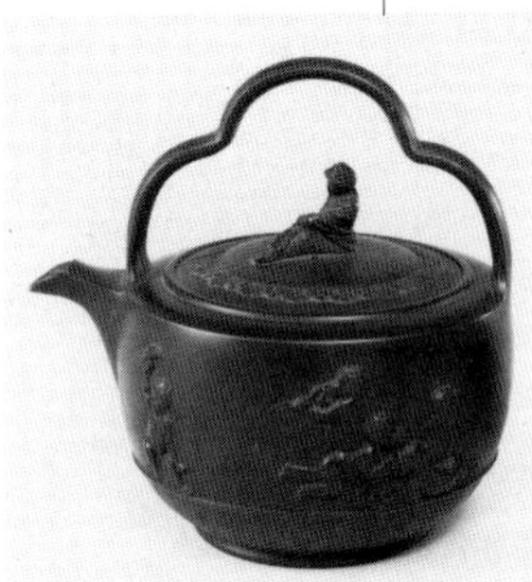

149. Rum Kettle: *Boys at Play*, ca. 1775-80
Basalt with engine-turning with glazed interior
7 1/4 x 3 3/4 in (18.4 x 12 cm)
Mark: "Wedgwood & Bentley"
Provenance: M. Mellanay Delhom, Chicago; Ann Brodkiewicz, Chicago
1980.109 a and b
Color plate 51

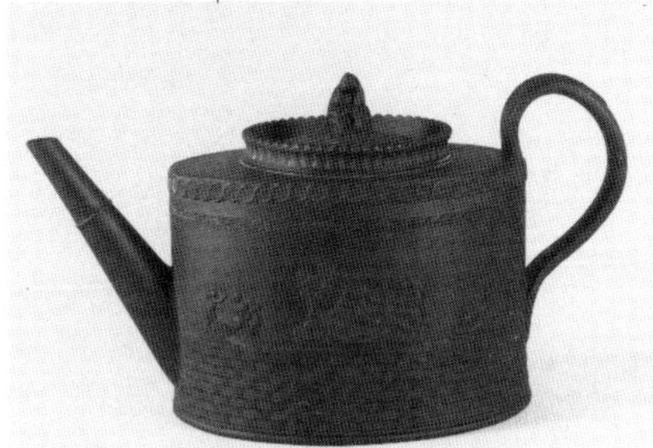

150. Teapot: ca. 1800
Elijah Mayer (w. 1784-1803), potter
Staffordshire, England
Basalt
5 5/8 x 4 5/8 x 6 3/16 in (14.2 x 11.7 x 15.7 cm)
Mark: "E. MAYER"
Provenance: Dr. Francis Jennings Vurpillat, South Bend, Ind.
1979.224 a and b

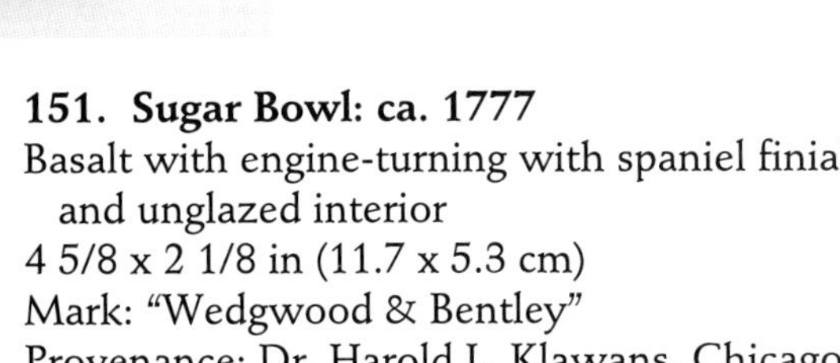

151. Sugar Bowl: ca. 1777
Basalt with engine-turning with spaniel finial and unglazed interior
4 5/8 x 2 1/8 in (11.7 x 5.3 cm)
Mark: "Wedgwood & Bentley"
Provenance: Dr. Harold L. Klawans, Chicago
1980.140 a and b
Color plate 52

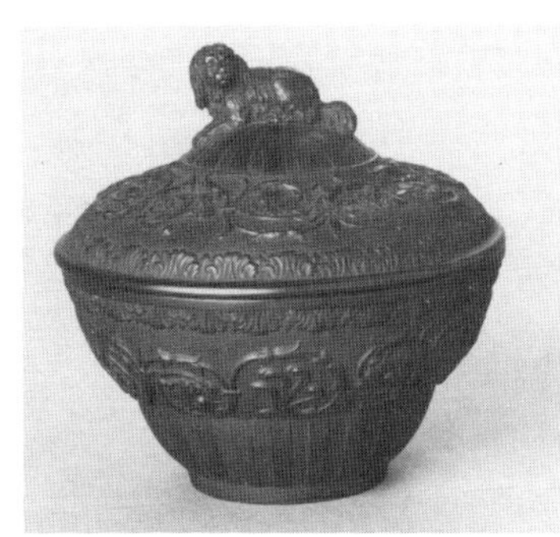

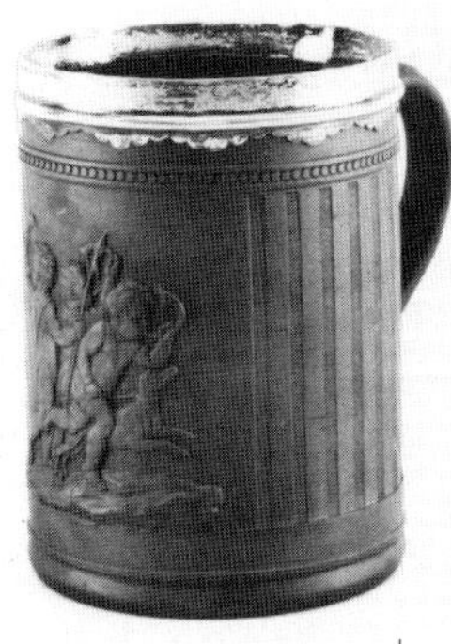

152. Mug: *Cupids Bringing Home the Game*, ca. 1780
Basalt with engine-turning with glazed interior, silver rim
3 11/16 x 2 3/4 in (9.3 x 6.9 cm)
Mark: "Wedgwood" "5"
Provenance: Ann Brodkiewicz, Chicago
1980.9

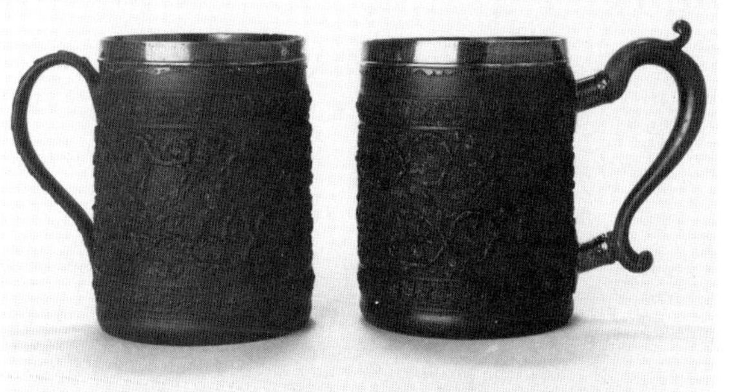

153. Cider Mug: ca. 1778
Peter Freeman (w. 1773-?) London silversmith
Basalt with glazed interior, silver rim, and fruitwood handle
5 3/4 x 4 1/4 in (14.6 x 10.7 cm)
Mark: "Wedgwood & Bentley" "P" "F"
Provenance: Tulk Collection, England; Dr. Harold L. Klawans, Chicago
1979.264
Color plate 52

154. Cider Mug: ca. 1778
Basalt with glazed interior, silver rim
5 13/16 x 4 5/16 in (14.7 x 10.9 cm)
Mark: "Wedgwood & Bentley"
Provenance: Christie's, London
1980.8
Color plate 52

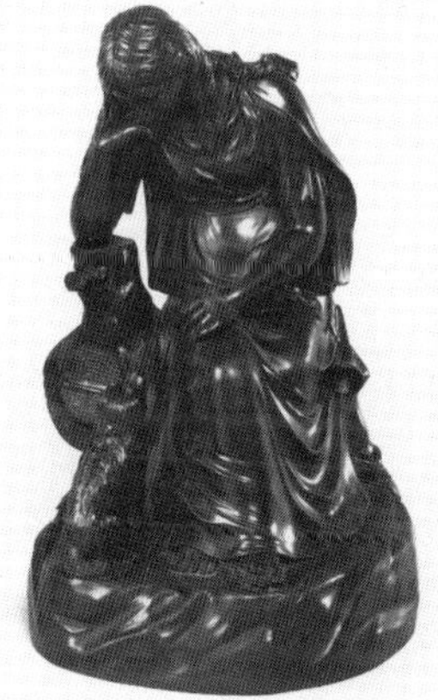

155. Figure: *Poor Maria*, 19th century
Lady Elizabeth Templetown (1747-1823), designer
Basalt
12 x 6 3/4 x 7 3/8 in (30.4 x 22.1 x 18.7 cm)
Mark: "WEDGWOOD" "S" "STERNES / POOR MARIA"
Provenance: Manheim's Gallery, New Orleans
1980.119

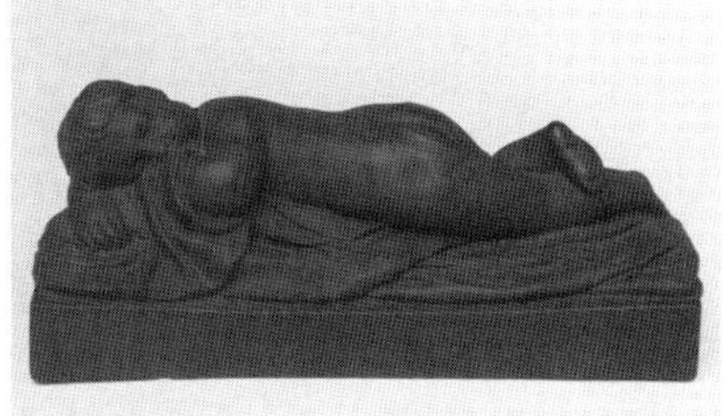

156. Figure: *Somnos*, 19th century
Basalt
1 3/4 x 4 7/16 x 2 1/16 in (4.4 x 11.2 x 5.2 cm)
Mark: "WEDGWOOD" "V"
Provenance: Wolf Mankowitz, London
1980.152

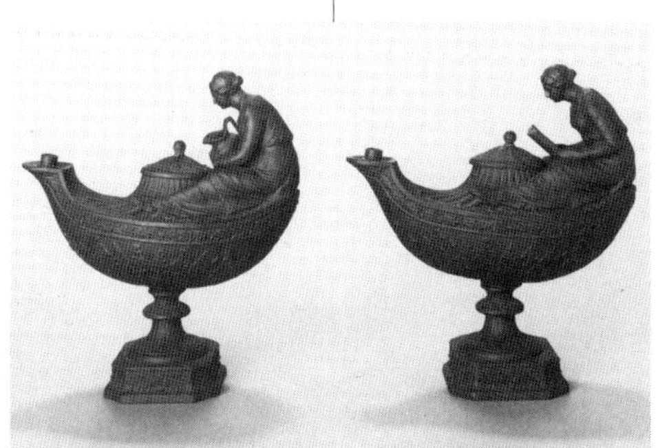

157. Pair of Vestal Reading Lamps: 19th century
Basalt
8 3/8 x 3 3/16 x 3 3/16 in (21.2 x 8 x 8 cm)
Mark: "WEDGWOOD" "W"
Provenance: Ann Brodkiewicz, Chicago
1980.115 a and b

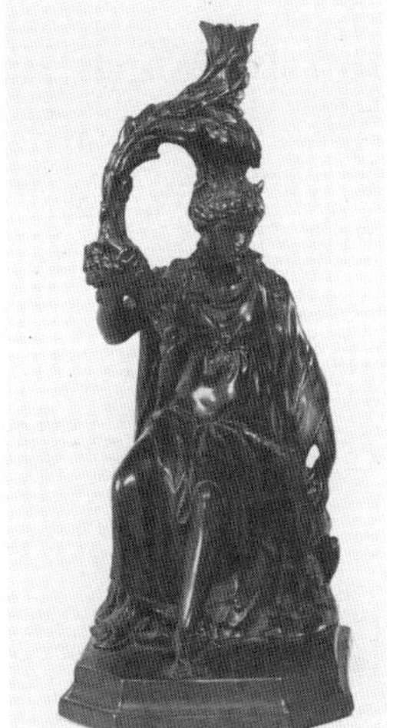

158. Candlestick: *Diana as Huntress*, 19th century
Basalt
11 1/8 x 6 5/8 x 4 3/4 in (28.2 x 16.8 x 12 cm)
Mark: "WEDGWOOD" "C" "DIANA"
Provenance: Fred J. Tongue, Santa Monica, Calif.
1980.136

159. Pair of Sphinxes: 19th century
Basalt
4 3/8 x 6 11/16 x 2 3/8 in (11.1 x 16.9 x 6 cm)
Mark: "WEDGWOOD"
Provenance: Dr. Harold L. Klawans, Chicago
1980.127 a and b
Color plate 142

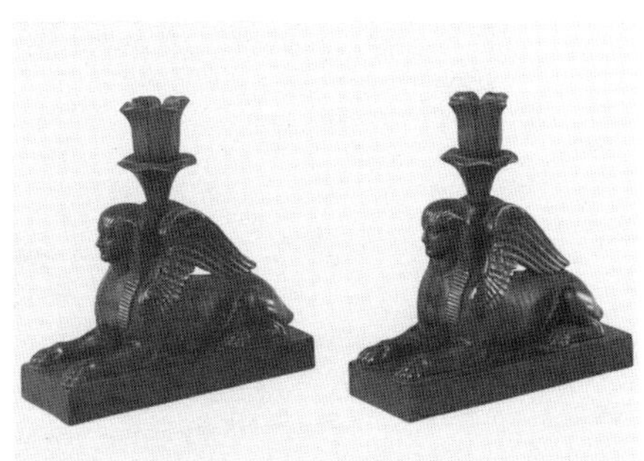

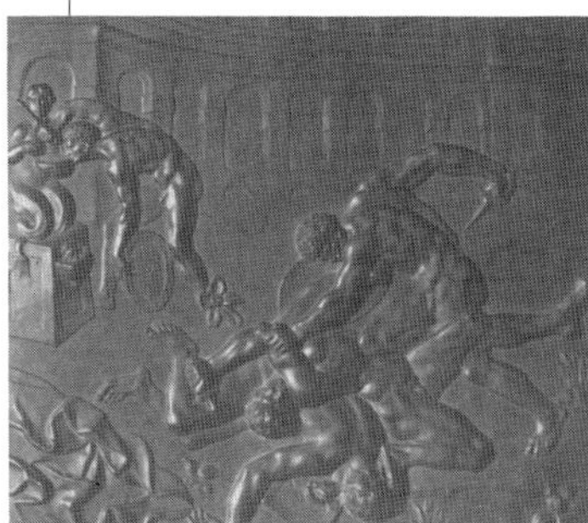

160. Plaque: *Gladiators in the Arena*, 19th century
Basalt
12 1/16 x 10 3/4 in (30.6 x 27.3 cm)
Mark: "WEDGWOOD" "C"
Provenance: Dr. Francis Jennings Vurpillat, South Bend, Ind.
1980.128

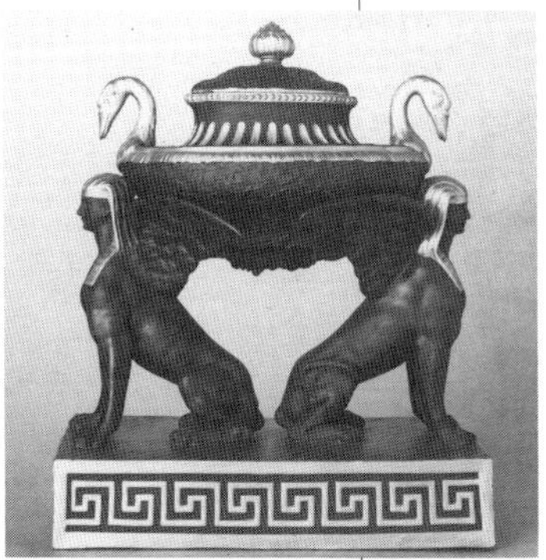

161. Sphinx Supporting Covered Bowl: ca. 1875
Basalt with gilt decoration
14 1/8 x 12 1/8 x 6 1/2 in (35.8 x 30.7 x 16.5 cm)
Mark: "WEDGWOOD"
Provenance: Fred J. Tongue, Santa Monica, Calif.
1980.120
Color plate 141

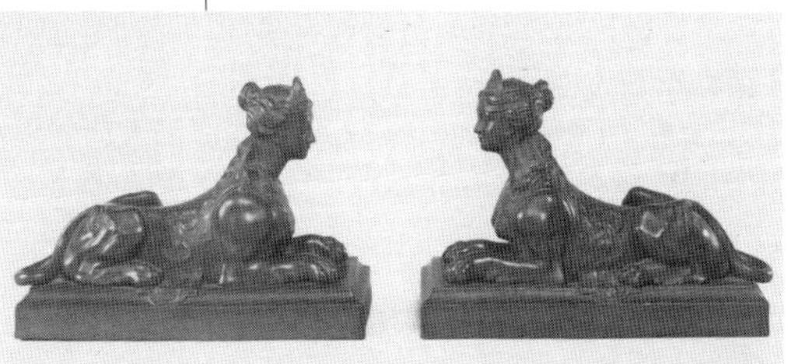

162. Pair of Sphinxes: 19th century
Basalt
7 3/4 x 10 3/4 x 4 9/16 in (19.6 x 27.3 x 11.5 cm)
Mark: "WEDGWOOD"
Provenance: Ann Brodkiewicz, Chicago
1980.126 a and b
Color plate 142

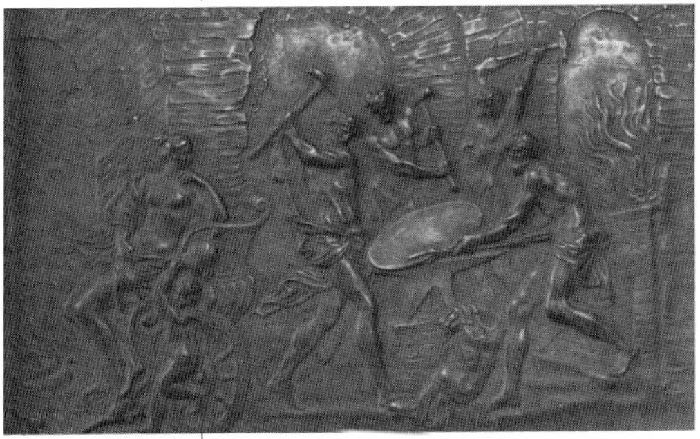

163. Plaque: *Vulcan at the Forge Watched by Venus in Her Chariot*, 19th century
Basalt
10 1/8 x 6 3/8 in (25.7 x 16.1 cm)
Mark: "WEDGWOOD" "D"
Provenance: Fred J. Tongue, Santa Monica, Calif.
1979.221

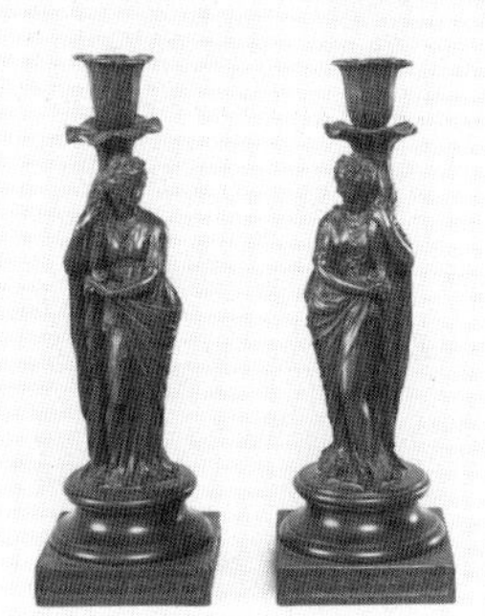

164. Pair of Candlesticks: *Female Figures*, 19th century
Basalt
a: 10 5/8 x 3 1/2 x 3 1/2 in (26.9 x 8.8 x 8.8 cm);
b: 10 1/2 x 3 1/2 x 3 1/2 in (26.6 x 8.8 x 8.8 cm)
Mark: "WEDGWOOD" with tool marks
Provenance: Fred J. Tongue, Santa Monica, Calif.
1980.137 a and b

165. Figure: *Crouching Venus*, 19th century
Basalt with metal base
14 1/2 x 6 1/2 x 9 in (36.8 x 16.5 x 22.8 cm)
Mark: "WEDGWOOD"
Provenance: Ann Brodkiewicz, Chicago
1979.258

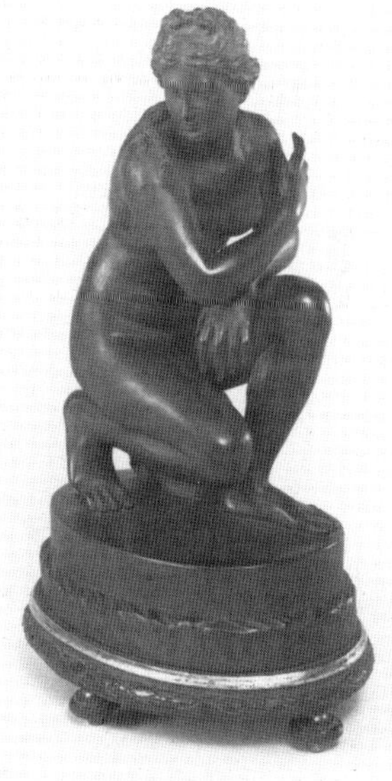

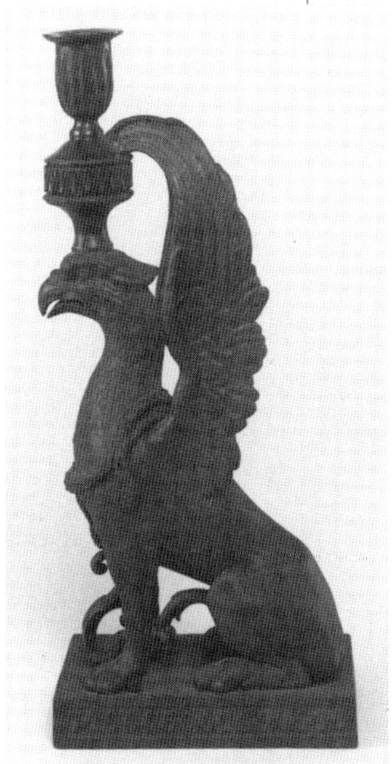

166. Candlestick: *Griffin*, 19th century
Basalt
11 1/8 x 3 1/4 x 5 9/16 in (28.2 x 8.2 x 14.1 cm)
Mark: "WEDGWOOD"
Provenance: Dr. Harold L. Klawans, Chicago
1980.134

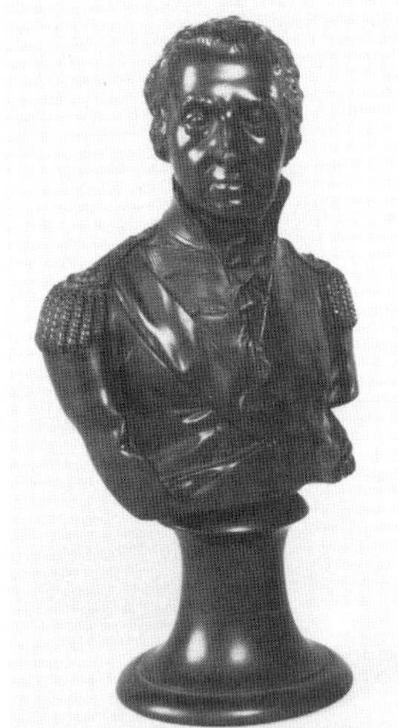

167. Bust: *Viscount Horatio Nelson (1758-1805)*, 19th century
Basalt
11 1/2 x 4 1/4 in (29.2 x 10.7 cm)
Mark: "WEDGWOOD" twice;
"Pubd. July 22nd / 1798 / R. Shout Scp / Holborn" in script on back of bust
Provenance: Ann Brodkiewicz, Chicago
1980.117
Color plate 142

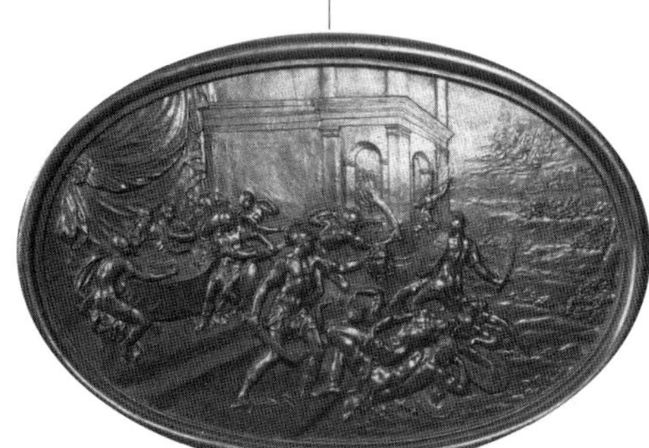

168. Plaque: *Marriage Supper of Perseus and Andromeda*, 19th century
Basalt
9 x 6 1/8 in (22.8 x 15.6 cm)
Mark: "WEDGWOOD"
Provenance: Fred J. Tongue, Santa Monica, Calif.
1979.217

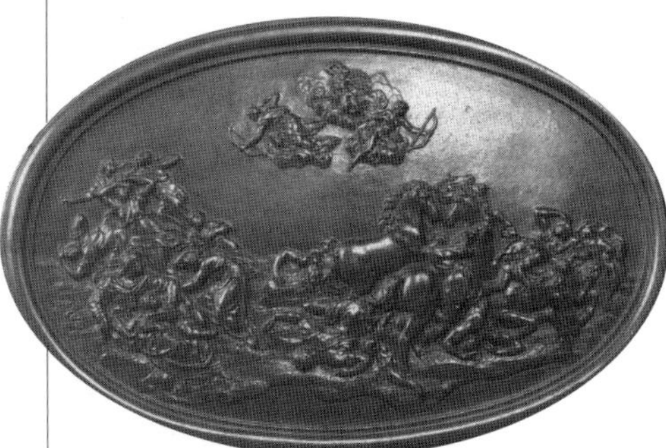

169. Plaque: *The Destruction of Niobe's Children*, 19th century
Basalt
9 1/8 x 5 7/8 in (23.1 x 14.9 cm)
Mark: "WEDGWOOD"
Provenance: Fred J. Tongue, Santa Monica, Calif.
1979.218

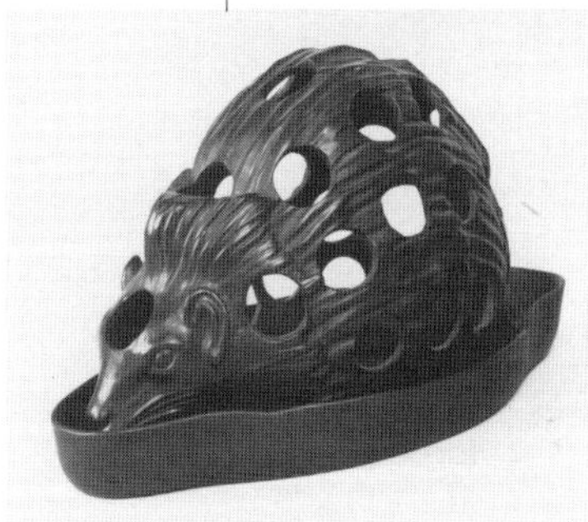

170. Porcupine Bulb Pot and Underdish: 19th century
Basalt
Bulb pot: 5 1/2 x 5 x 9 in (13.9 x 12.7 x 22.8 cm);
underdish: 9 15/16 x 5 7/8 in (25.2 x 14.9 cm)
Mark: "WEDGWOOD" "W"
Provenance: Sir George Duff-Dunbar, Scotland; Ann Brodkiewicz, Chicago
1980.138 a and b

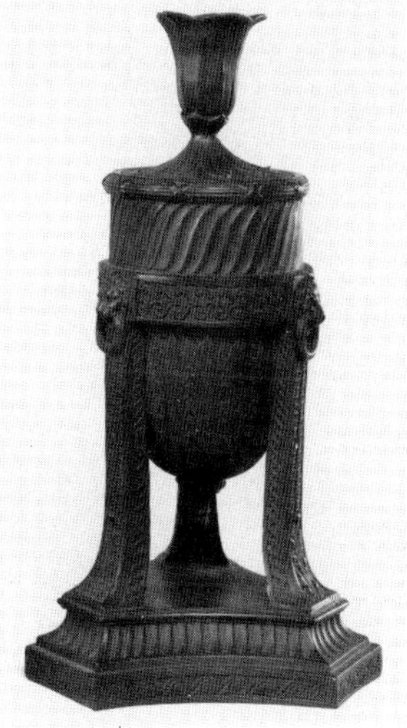

171. Tripod Candle Urn: 19th century
Basalt, top reverses to hold candle
11 x 4 3/4 x 4 3/4 in (27.9 x 12 x 12 cm)
Mark: "WEDGWOOD" "K"
Provenance: Fred J. Tongue, Santa Monica, Calif.
1979.253 a and b

172. Flower Holder: *Egret on Rock*, ca. 1918
Ernest W. Light, modeler
Basalt
7 1/2 x 3 x 3 5/8 in (19 x 7.6 x 9.2 cm)
Mark: "WEDGWOOD" "W"
Provenance: Isabelle del Correll, New Orleans
1980.135

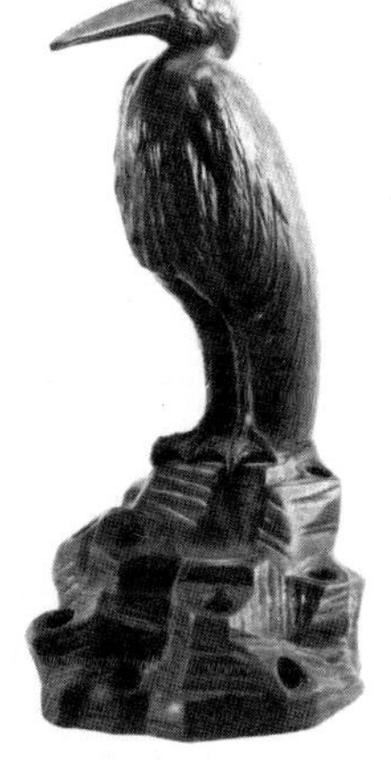

173. Pastille Burner, or Cassolette: ca. 1805
Basalt
4 3/4 x 6 5/8 in (excluding replacement lid) (16.8 x 12 cm)
Mark: "JOSIAH WEDGWOOD" "Feb Y2D 1085"
Provenance: Dr. Francis Jennings Vurpillat, South Bend, Ind.
1980.116 a and b
Color plate 149

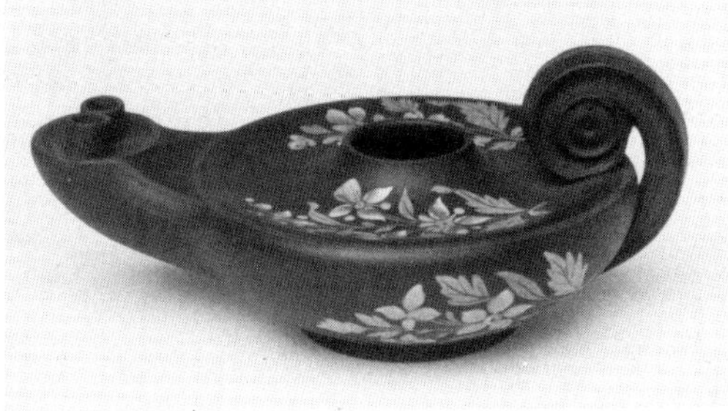

174. Hand Lamp: *Peony Pattern*, ca. 1820
Basalt with polychrome enamel decoration
2 x 3 1/8 x 5 1/4 in (5 x 7.9 x 13.3 cm)
Mark: "WEDGWOOD" with tool marks
Provenance: Dr. Harold L. Klawans, Chicago
1980.500

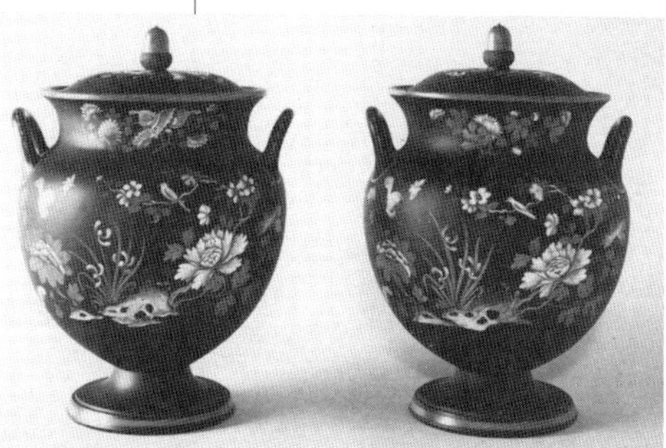

175. Pair of Potpourri Vases: *Peony Pattern*, ca. 1820
Basalt with polychrome enamel decoration
12 1/2 x 5 1/2 in (31.7 x 13.9 cm)
Mark: "WEDGWOOD" with tool marks
Provenance: Otto Wasserman, New York
1979.222 a and b; 1979.223 a and b
Color plate 47

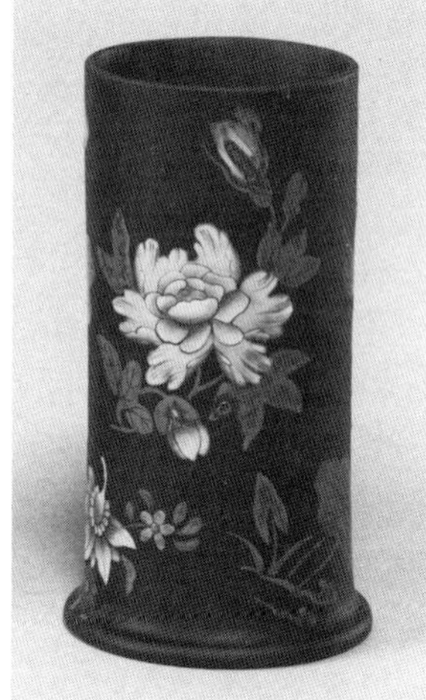

176. Vase: *Peony Pattern*, ca. 1820
Basalt with polychrome enamel decoration
4 1/8 x 2 1/4 in (10.4 x 5.7 cm)
Mark: "WEDGWOOD" "P" in gold
Provenance: Dr. Harold L. Klawans, Chicago
1979.219

177. Inkwell: ca. 1780
Basalt with engine-turning
2 x 3 in (5 x 7.6 cm)
Mark: "WEDGWOOD" "D" "63" Grant's number in white enamel
Provenance: Maurice Harold Grant, England; Dr. Harold L. Klawans, Chicago
1980.156

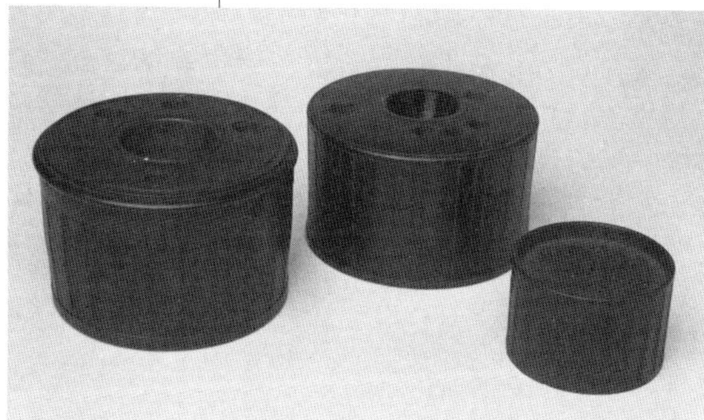

178. Sander: ca. 1790
Basalt with engine-turning
1 1/4 x 1 15/16 in (3.1 x 4.9 cm)
Mark: "WEDGWOOD" three times
Provenance: Dr. Harold L. Klawans, Chicago
1980.15

179. Inkwell: ca. 1775
Basalt with engine-turning
1 3/16 x 3 1/4 in (3 x 8.2 cm)
Mark: "Wedgwood & Bentley" "20" "126" Grant's number in white enamel
Provenance: Maurice Harold Grant, England; Dr. Francis Jennings Vurpillat, South Bend, Ind.
1980.158

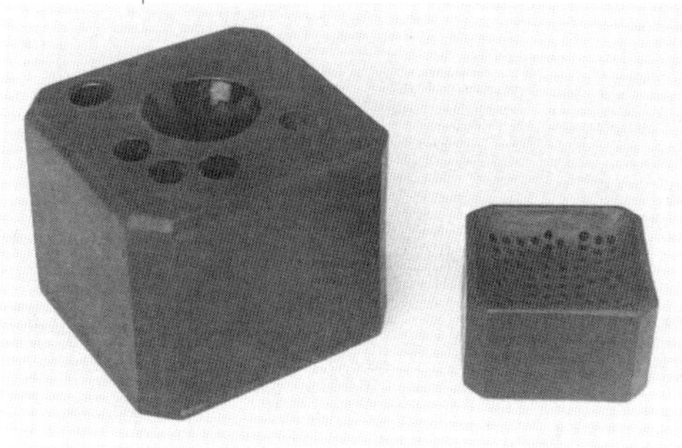

180. Inkwell, ca. 1775
Basalt
1 3/4 x 2 3/16 x 2 3/16 in (4.4 x 5.5 x 5.5 cm)
Mark: "Wedgwood & Bentley" "32"
Provenance: unknown
1980.153

181. Sander: ca. 1785
Basalt
13/16 x 1 3/8 x 1 3/8 in (2 x 3.4 x 3.4 cm)
Mark: "Wedgwood & Bentley"
Provenance: Ann Brodkiewicz, Chicago
1980.154

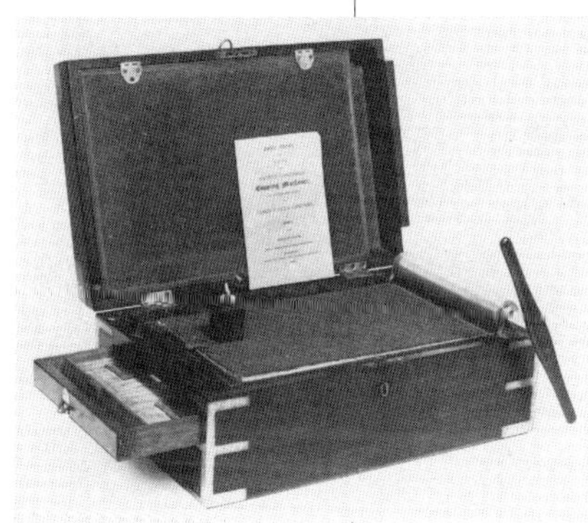

182. Copier with Inkwell: ca. 1780
James Watt, Birmingham, England (1739-1819)
Mahogany and brass box; basalt inkwell
Box: 6 7/8 x 17 3/4 x 11 1/2 in (17.4 x 45 x 29.2 cm);
inkwell: 1 1/2 x 1 1/4 x 1 1/4 in (3.8 x 3.1 x 3.1 cm)
Mark: box: "J. WATT & Co. / PATENTED"; inkwell: "WEDGWOOD" "K"
Provenance: Ann Brodkiewicz, Chicago
1989.131.1
Figure 11

Etruscan Ware

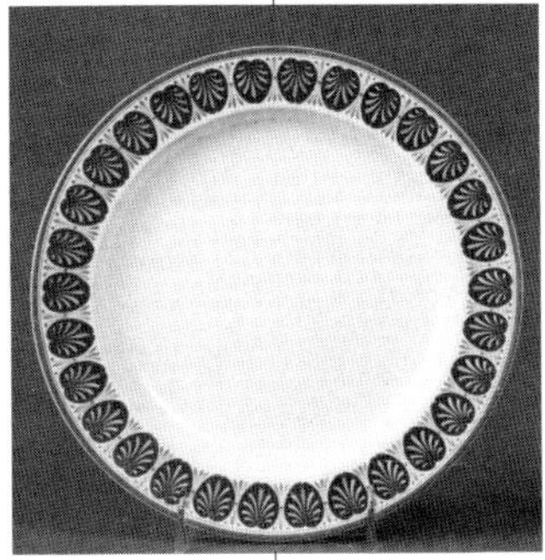

183. Plate: *Etruscan*, ca. 1790
Cream ware with red printed and black enamel overglaze decoration
9 3/4 in (24.7 cm)
Mark: "WEDGWOOD" "9" "D"; "42" in black enamel overglaze
Provenance: Fred J. Tongue, Santa Monica, Calif.
1978.153
Color plate 20

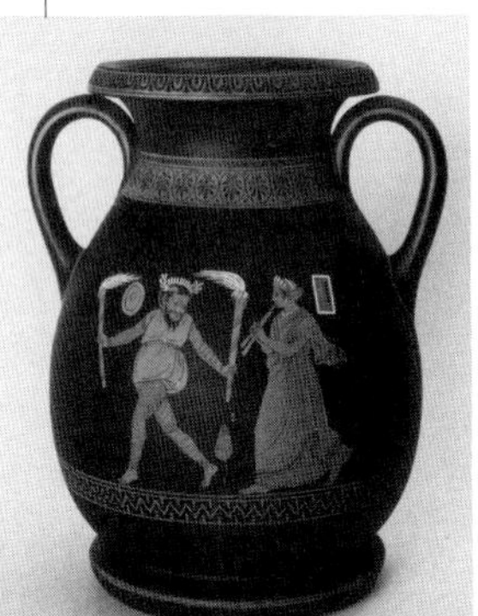

184. Vase: *Scene of a Theatre*, ca. 1815
Basalt with encaustic decoration
11 1/4 x 9 in (28.5 x 22.8 cm)
Mark: "WEDGWOOD" with tool marks
Provenance: D. M. and P. Manheim, New York
1982.180
Design source: Hamilton, *Antiquités*, vol. 1, pl. 43
Color plate 53

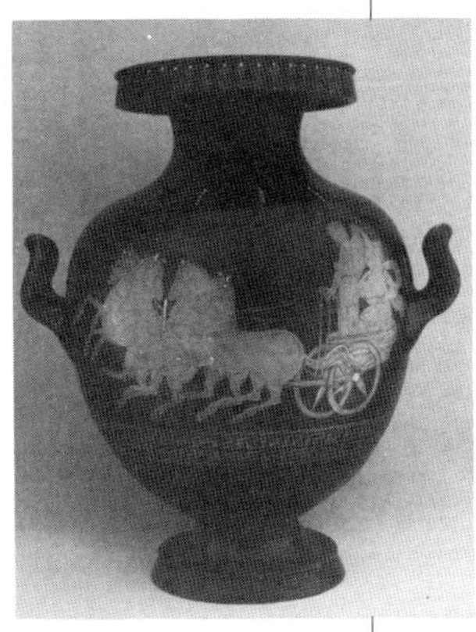

185. Pair of Vases: *Diomedes Casting His Spear against Mars, The Race of Atalanta and Hippomenes*, ca. 1790
Basalt with encaustic decoration
11 7/8 x 4 5/8 in (30.1 x 11.7 cm)
Mark: "WEDGWOOD" "943"
Provenance: Dr. Harold L. Klawans, Chicago
1982.172 a and b
Design source: a: Hamilton, *Antiquités*, vol. 1, pl. 130; b: vol. 2, pl. 22
Color plate 58

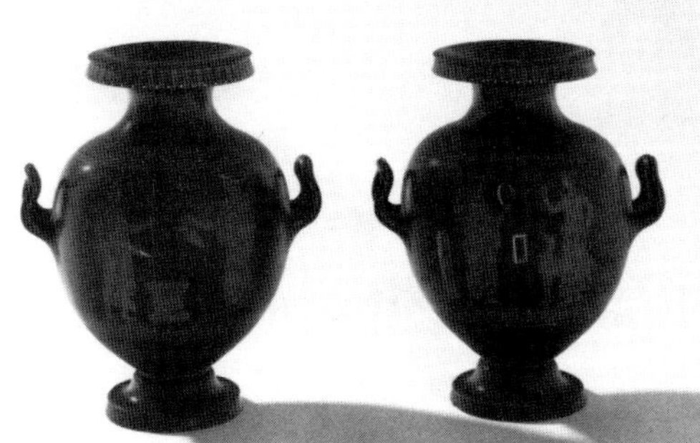

186. Pair of Vases: *A Sacrifice*, ca. 1785
Basalt with encaustic decoration
a: 9 x 3 1/2 in (22.8 x 8.8 cm);
b: 8 15/16 x 3 1/2 in (22.7 x 8.8 cm)
Mark: a: "WEDGWOOD" "No 943" incised;
b: "WEDGWOOD" "943" incised with tool marks
Provenance: Dr. Francis Jennings Vurpillat, South Bend, Ind.
1982.178 a and b
Design source: a: Hamilton, *Antiquités*, vol. 1, pl. 122; b: vol. 1, pl. 109
Color plate 57

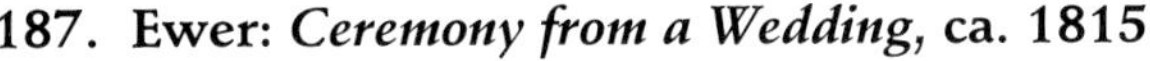

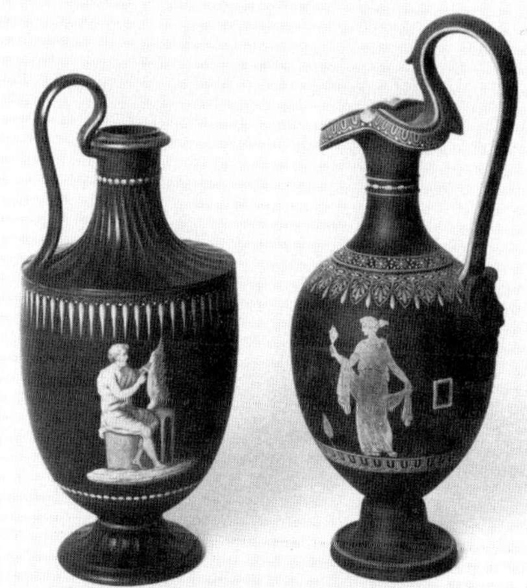

187. Ewer: *Ceremony from a Wedding*, ca. 1815
Basalt with encaustic decoration
10 1/2 x 2 7/16 in (26.6 x 6.1 cm)
Mark: "WEDGWOOD"
Provenance: Ann Brodkiewicz, Chicago
1982.175
Design source: adaptation of Hamilton, *Antiquités*, vol. 2, pl. 45
Color plate 56

188. Ewer: *Daedalus Building His Wings*, ca. 1775-80
Basalt with engine-turning and encaustic decoration
9 1/4 x 2 11/16 in (23.4 x 6.8 cm)
Mark: none
Provenance: Dr. Francis Jennings Vurpillat, South Bend, Ind.
1982.174
Design source: Montfaucon, *L'Antiquité expliquée*, vol. 1, pl. 18, fig. 1
Color plate 56

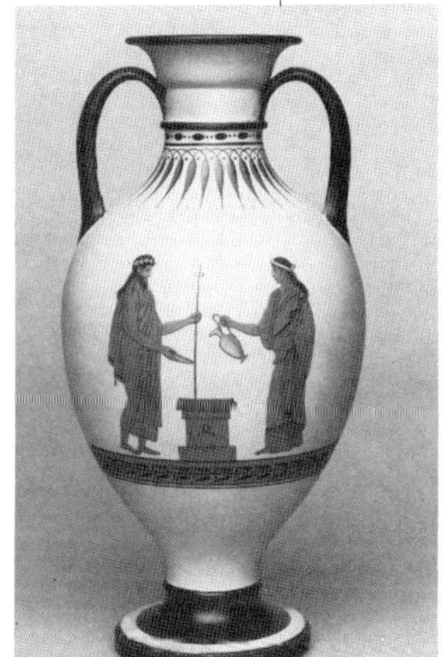

189. Vase: *A Sacrifice*, ca. 1790
Caneware with encaustic decoration
8 3/4 x 2 3/4 in (22.2 x 6.9 cm)
Mark: "WEDGWOOD" "167"
Provenance: Fred J. Tongue, Santa Monica, Calif.
1976.259
Design source: Hamilton, *Antiquités*, vol. 1, pl. 122
Color plate 57

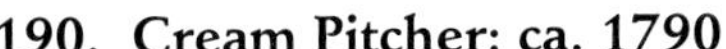

190. Cream Pitcher: ca. 1790
Basalt with encaustic decoration
2 5/16 x 2 1/4 in (5.8 x 5.7 cm)
Mark: none
Provenance: Dr. Francis Jennings Vurpillat, South Bend, Ind.
1982.183

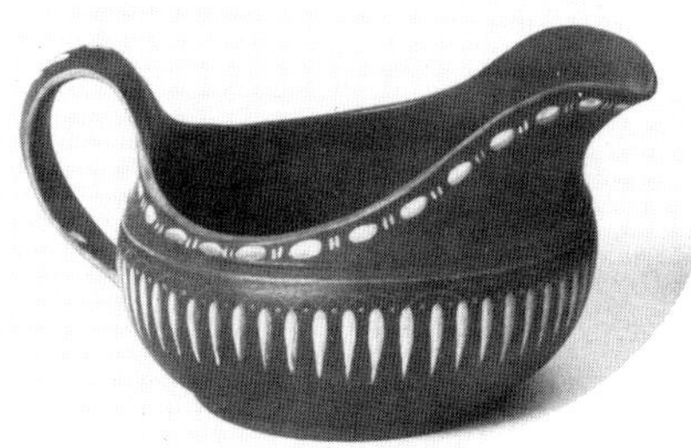

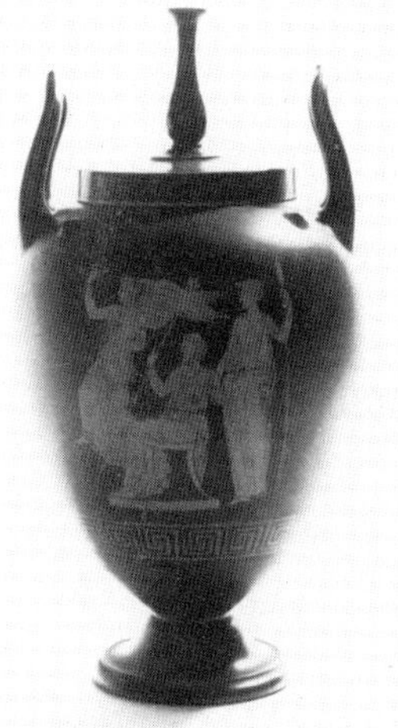

191. Covered Vase: *Three Classical Figures*, ca. 1790
Basalt with encaustic decoration
13 3/4 x 4 1/4 in (34.9 x 10.7 cm)
Mark: "WEDGWOOD" "93" incised with tool marks
Provenance: Fred J. Tongue, Santa Monica, Calif.
1982.173 a and b
Design source: Hamilton, *Antiquités*, vol. 2, pl. 37

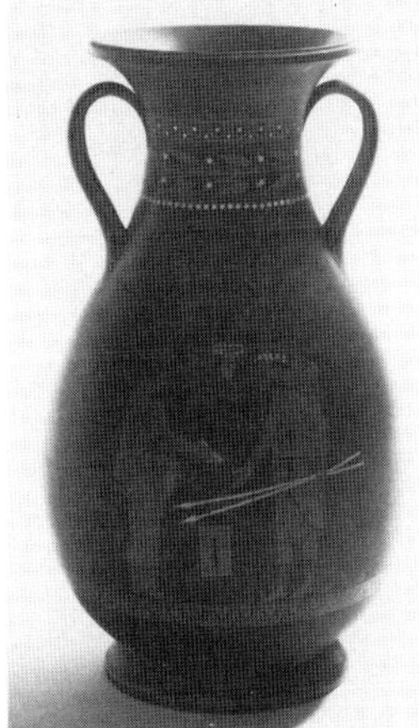

192. Vase: *A Sacrifice*, ca. 1815
Basalt with encaustic decoration
8 7/8 x 3 1/2 in (22.5 x 8.8 cm)
Mark: "WEDGWOOD"
Provenance: Ann Brodkiewicz, Chicago
1982.171
Design source: adaptation of Hamilton, *Antiquités*, vol. 2, pl. 61

193. Plaque: *Amore e Leone*, ca. 1770
Basalt with encaustic decoration
9 1/4 x 6 1/16 in (23.4 x 15.4 cm)
Mark: none
Provenance: Irving J. Newman, England; Fred J. Tongue, Santa Monica, Calif.
1982.169
Design source: Philipp Stosch, *Pierres antiques gravées*, pl. 53
Color plate 59

194. Plaque: *Athlete Oiling Himself*, ca. 1770
Basalt with encaustic decoration
5 1/2 x 7 1/2 in (13.9 x 19 cm)
Mark: none
Provenance: David Davis, Chicago; Dr. Francis Jennings Vurpillat, South Bend, Ind.
1982.176
Color plate 59

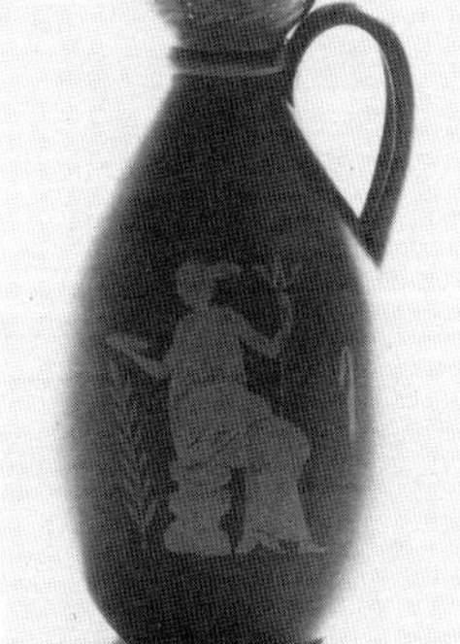

195. Vase: *Classical Figure*, ca. 1815
Basalt with encaustic decoration
5 3/4 x 1 15/16 in (14.6 x 4.9 cm)
Mark: "WEDGWOOD" "171" incised with tool marks
Provenance: Dr. Harold L. Klawans, Chicago
1982.170
Design source: adaptation of Hamilton, *Antiquités*, vol. 3, pl. 47, and vol. 2, pl. 45

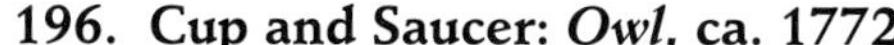

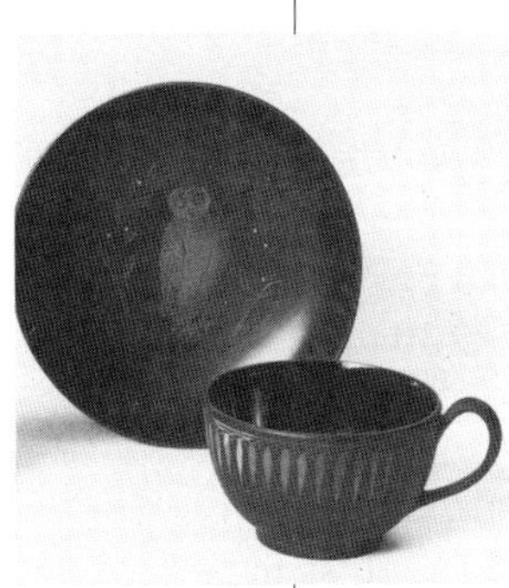

196. Cup and Saucer: *Owl*, ca. 1772
Basalt with encaustic decoration; cup has glazed interior
Cup: 1 3/4 x 1 1/2 in (4.4 x 3.8 cm); saucer: 5 3/16 in (13.1 cm)
Mark: "XXXIX" Grant's number in white enamel
Provenance: Maurice Harold Grant, England; Marshall Field and Co., Chicago; Dr. Francis Jennings Vurpillat, South Bend, Ind.
1982.179 a and b
Design source: Hamilton, *Antiquités*, vol. 1, pl. 41; Wedgwood Pattern Book, 1770, no. 58
Color plate 60

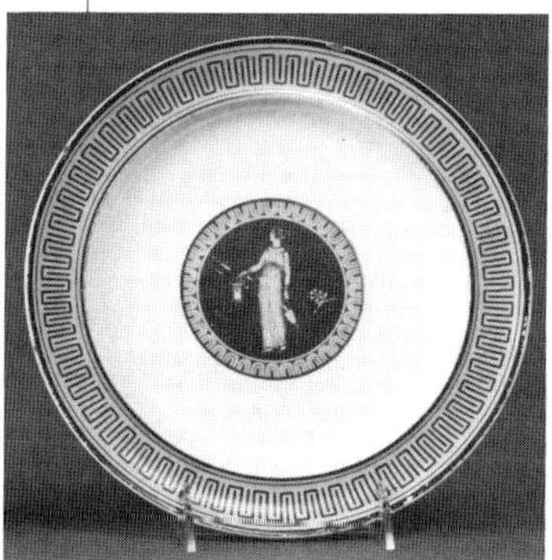

197. Plate: *Etruscan*, ca. 1790
Cream ware with red printed and black enamel underglaze decoration
9 11/16 in (24.6 cm)
Mark: "WEDGWOOD" with tool marks
Provenance: Fred J. Tongue, Santa Monica, Calif.
1978.152
Color plate 20

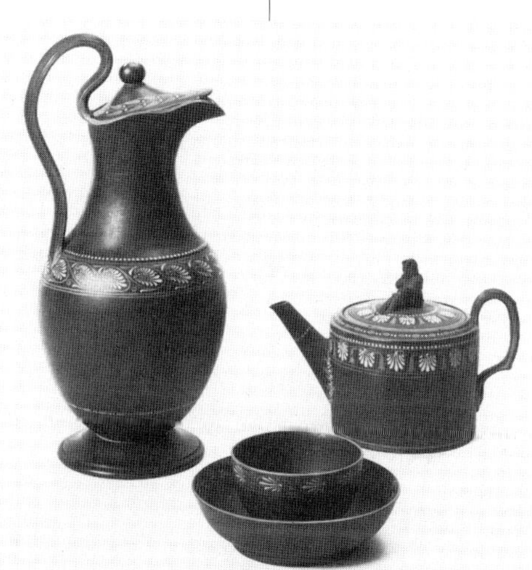

198. Teapot: ca. 1780
Basalt with encaustic decoration
4 1/4 x 3 1/8 in (10.7 x 7.9 cm)
Mark: "Wedgwood"
Provenance: D. M. and P. Manheim, New York;
Dr. Francis Jennings Vurpillat, South Bend, Ind.
1982.184 a and b
Design source: Wedgwood Pattern Book, 1770, no. 71
Color plate 60

199. Cup and Saucer: ca. 1785
Basalt with encaustic decoration
Cup: 1 11/16 x 1 3/8 in (4.2 x 3.4 cm); saucer: 4 5/16 in (10.9 cm)
Mark: cup: none; saucer: "Wedgwood" "1"
Provenance: Dr. Francis Jennings Vurpillat, South Bend, Ind.
1982.181 a and b
Color plate 60

200. Covered Chocolate Pot: ca. 1780
Basalt with encaustic decoration and glazed interior
10 x 3 1/2 in (25.4 x 8.8 cm)
Mark: "Wedgwood & Bentley" "247" in white enamel on base and inside cover
Provenance: Richard Tangye and George Tangye, England; David Davis, Chicago; Dr. Harold L. Klawans, Chicago
1982.182 a and b
Color plate 60

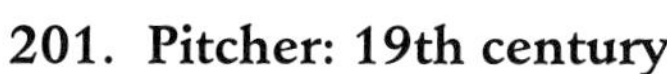

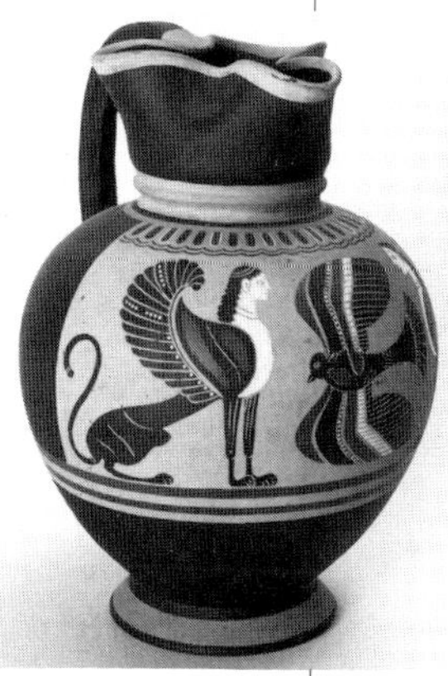

201. Pitcher: 19th century
Basalt with encaustic decoration
8 1/2 x 3 7/16 in (21.5 x 8.7 cm)
Mark: "WEDGWOOD" "N"
Provenance: Dr. Francis Jennings Vurpillat, South Bend, Ind.
1982.185
Design source: adaptation from "Collection of Engravings", *Ancient Vases of Sir William Hamilton*, published by William Tischbein, 1795, vol. 3, pl. 59

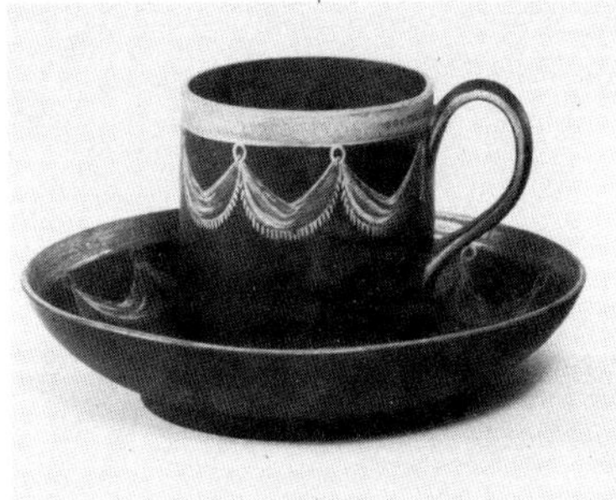

202. Cup and Saucer: ca. 1800
Basalt with encaustic decoration
Cup: 2 7/16 x 2 1/4 in (6.1 x 5.7 cm); saucer: 5 1/16 in (12.8 cm)
Mark: "WEDGWOOD" "2"
Provenance: Spranger Collection, England; Ann Brodkiewicz, Chicago
1980.118 a and b

Seals

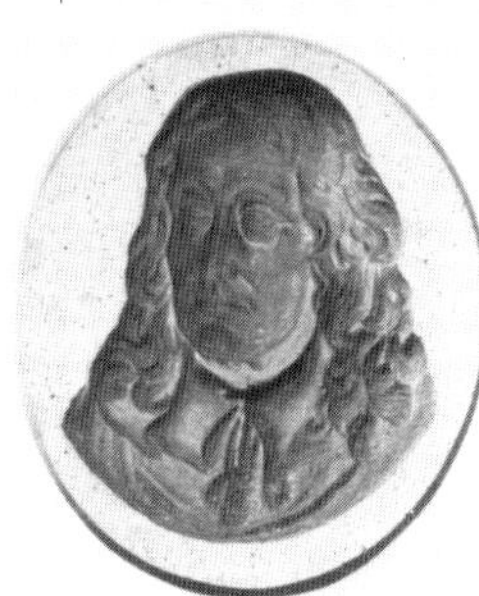

203. Seal: *Henry IV*, ca. 1790
Basalt
7/8 x 3/4 in (2.2 x 1.9 cm)
Mark: none
Provenance: Dr. Harold L. Klawans, Chicago
1980.102

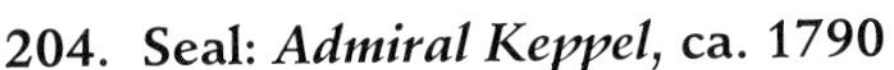

204. Seal: *Admiral Keppel*, ca. 1790
Basalt
7/8 x 3/4 in (2.2 x 1.9 cm)
Mark: none
Provenance: Dr. Harold L. Klawans, Chicago
1980.91

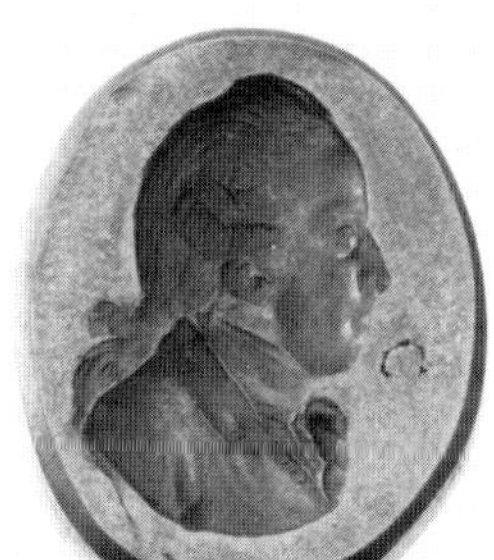

205. Seal: *Male Head*, ca. 1790
Basalt
13/16 x 11/16 in (2 x 1.7 cm)
Mark: none
Provenance: Dr. Harold L. Klawans, Chicago
1980.94

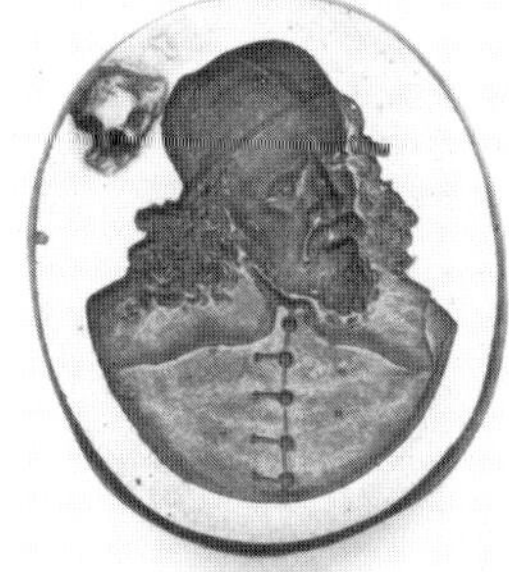

206. Seal: *Cardinal Richelieu*, ca. 1790
Basalt
3/4 x 5/8 in (1.9 x 1.5 cm)
Mark: none
Provenance: Dr. Harold L. Klawans, Chicago
1980.88

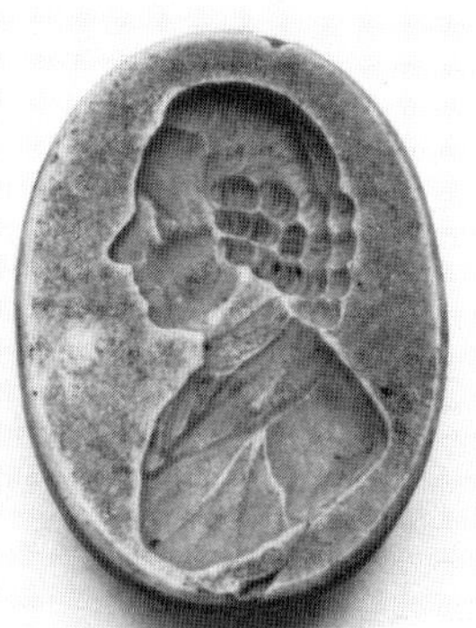

207. Seal: *Dr. Joseph Priestley*, ca. 1780
Agate ware
7/8 x 3/4 in (2.2 x 1.9 cm)
Mark: none
Provenance: Dr. Harold L. Klawans, Chicago
1980.82

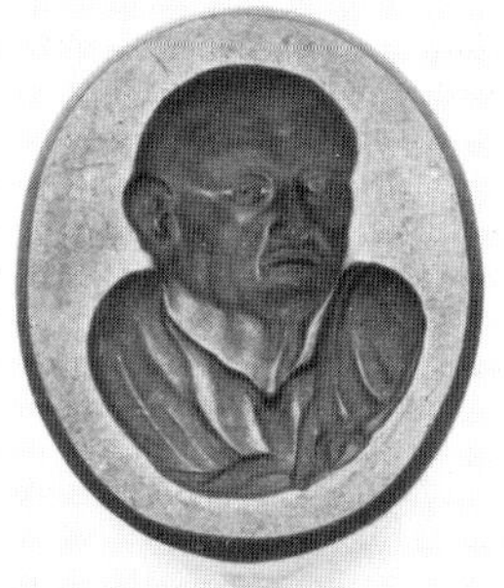

208. Seal: *Classical Male Head*, ca. 1790
Basalt
13/16 x 5/8 in (2 x 1.5 cm)
Mark: none
Provenance: Dr. Harold L. Klawans, Chicago
1980.92

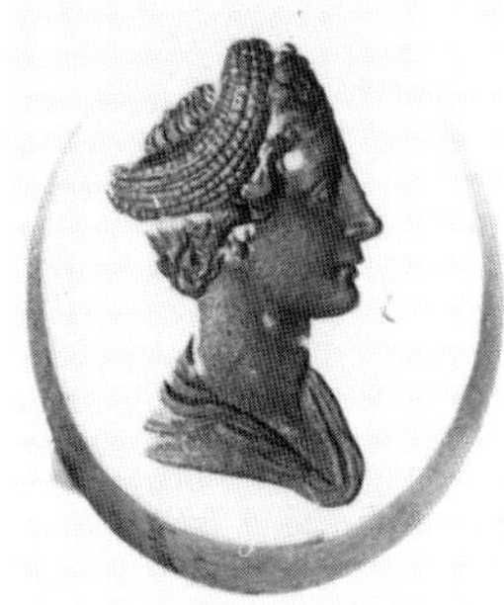

209. Seal: *Classical Female Head,* ca. 1790
Basalt
3/4 x 5/8 in (1.9 x 1.5 cm)
Mark: none
Provenance: Dr. Harold L. Klawans, Chicago
1980.77

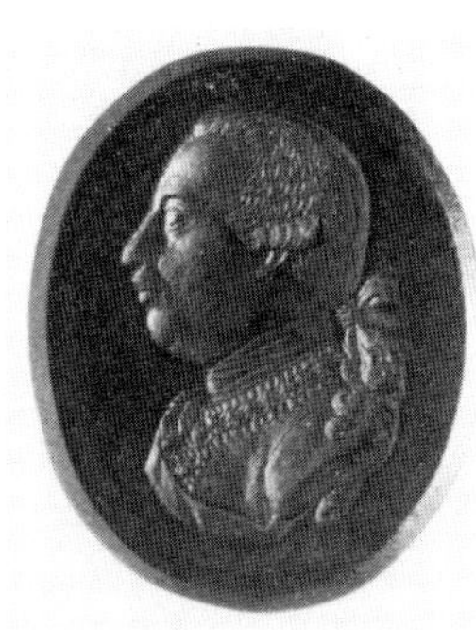

210. Seal: *George III,* ca. 1790
Basalt
11/16 x 9/16 in (1.7 x 1.4 cm)
Mark: none
Provenance: Dr. Harold L. Klawans, Chicago
1980.71

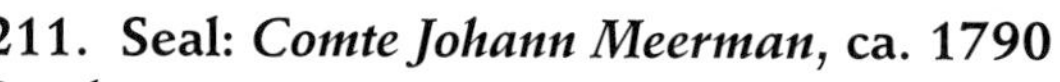

211. Seal: *Comte Johann Meerman,* ca. 1790
Basalt
5/8 x 1/2 in (1.5 x 1.2 cm)
Mark: none
Provenance: Dr. Harold L. Klawans, Chicago
1980.68

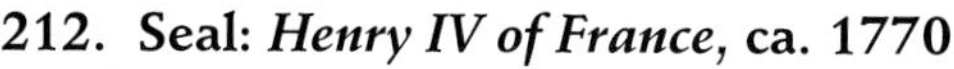

212. Seal: *Henry IV of France,* ca. 1770
Basalt
7/8 x 11/16 in (2.2 x 1.7 cm)
Mark: none
Provenance: Dr. Harold L. Klawans, Chicago
1980.66

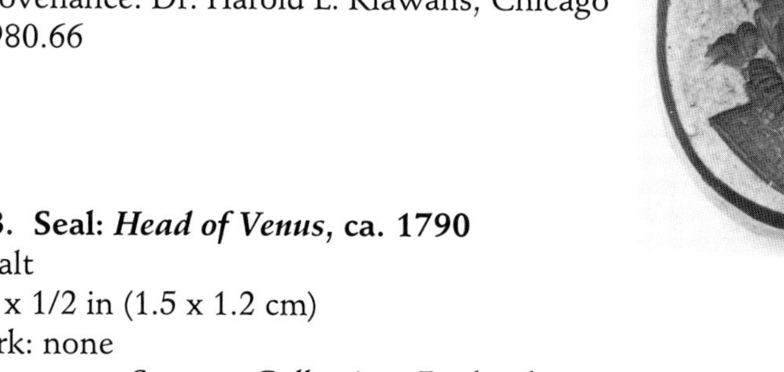

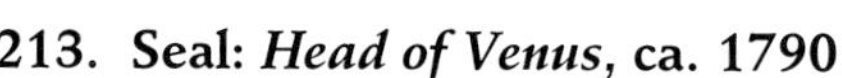

213. Seal: *Head of Venus,* ca. 1790
Basalt
5/8 x 1/2 in (1.5 x 1.2 cm)
Mark: none
Provenance: Symons Collection, England; Dr. Harold L. Klawans, Chicago
1980.101

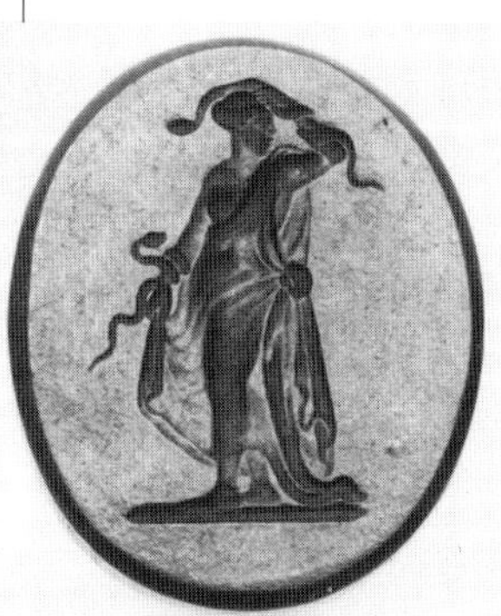

214. Seal: *Classical Female Figure,* ca. 1790
Basalt
7/8 x 3/4 in (2.2 x 1.9 cm)
Mark: none
Provenance: Dr. Harold L. Klawans, Chicago
1980.99

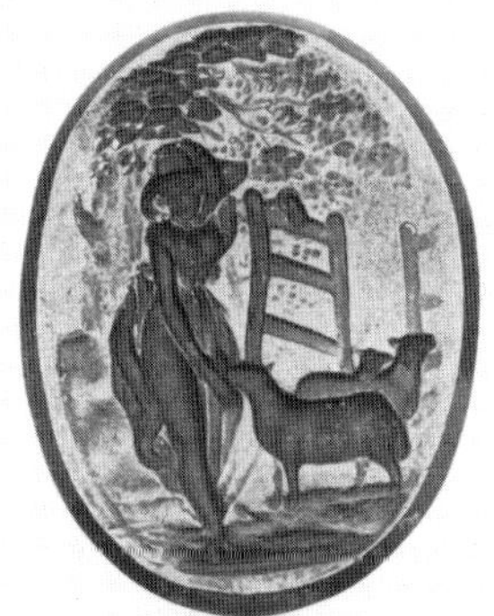

215. Seal: *A Shepherdess and Sheep*, ca. 1790
Basalt
31/32 x 3/4 in (2.4 x 1.9 cm)
Mark: none
Provenance: Dr. Harold L. Klawans, Chicago
1980.96

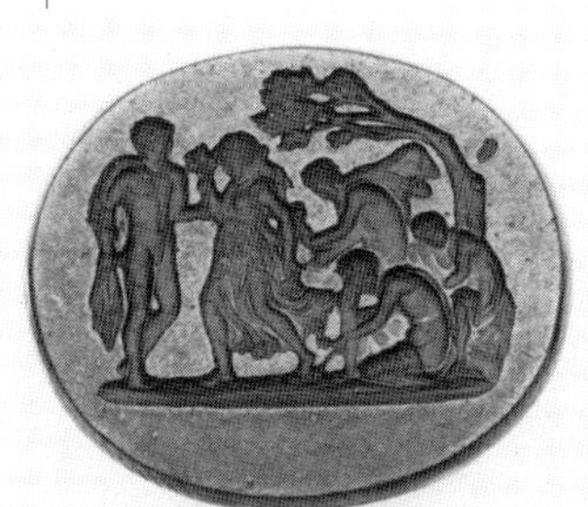

216. Seal: *Choice of Hercules*, ca. 1790
Basalt
7/8 x 3/4 in (2.2 x 1.9 cm)
Mark: none
Provenance: Dr. Harold L. Klawans, Chicago
1980.90

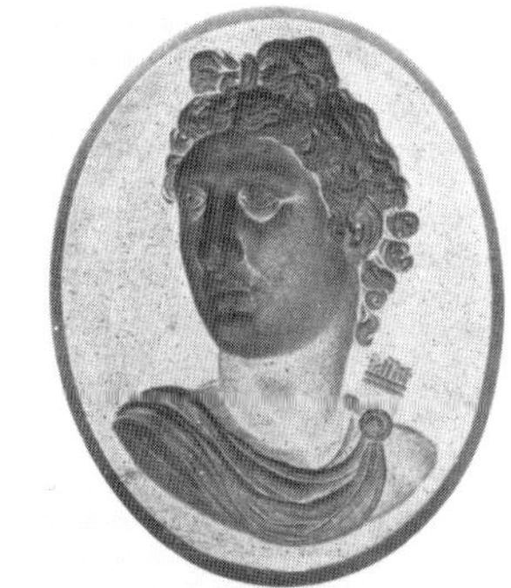

217. Seal: *Head of Apollo*, ca. 1790
Basalt
7/8 x 3/4 in (2.2 x 1.9 cm)
Mark: none
Provenance: Dr. Harold L. Klawans, Chicago
1980.85

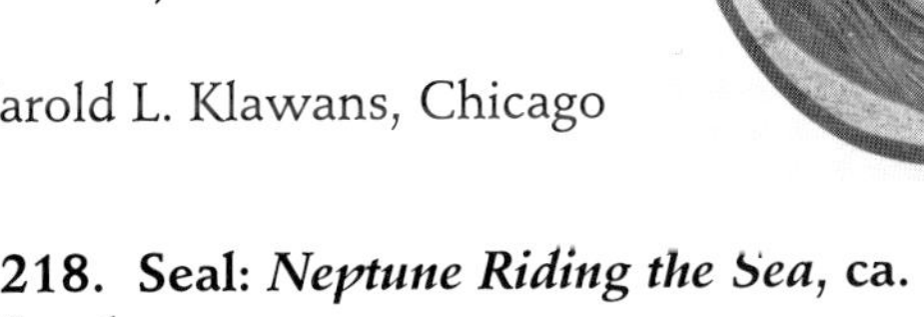

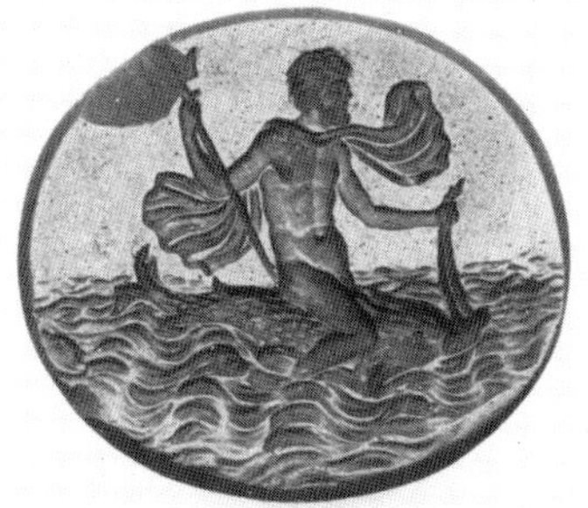

218. Seal: *Neptune Riding the Sea*, ca. 1790
Basalt
7/8 x 13/16 in (2.2 x 2 cm)
Mark: none
Provenance: Dr. Harold L. Klawans, Chicago
1980.75

219. Seal: *Alphabetic Cypher*, ca. 1790
Basalt
11/16 x 9/16 in (1.7 x 1.4 cm)
Mark: none
Provenance: Dr. Harold L. Klawans, Chicago
1980.98

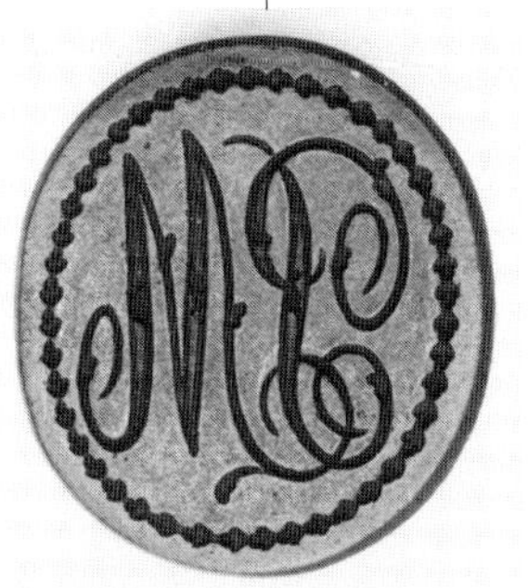

220. Seal: *Alphabetic Cypher*, ca. 1790
Basalt
3/4 x 5/8 in (1.9 x 1.5 cm)
Mark: none
Provenance: Dr. Harold L. Klawans, Chicago
1980.103

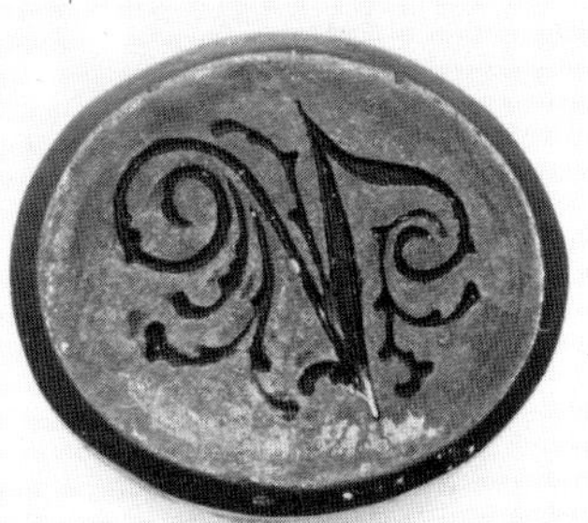

221. Seal: *Alphabetic Cypher*, ca. 1780
Basalt
7/8 x 3/4 in (2.2 x 1.9 cm)
Mark: none
Provenance: Dr. Francis Jennings Vurpillat, South Bend, Ind.
1977.122.27

222. Seal: *Alphabetic Cypher*, ca. 1790
Jasper, solid dark blue
7/8 x 3/4 in (2.2 x 1.9 cm)
Mark: none
Provenance: Dr. Harold L. Klawans, Chicago
1980.80

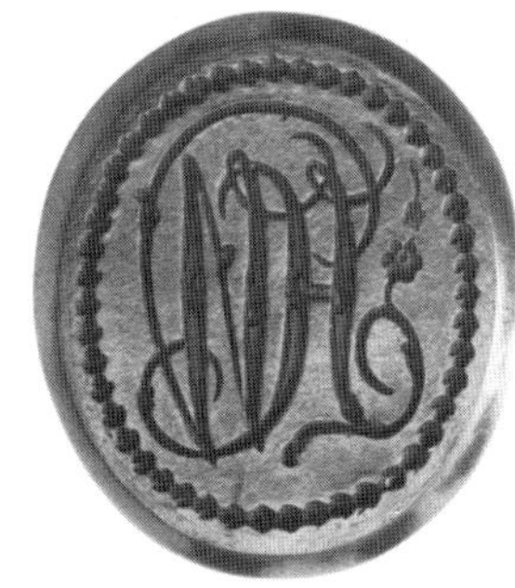

223. Seal: *Alphabetic Cypher*, ca. 1790
Basalt
7/8 x 3/4 in (2.2 x 1.9 cm)
Mark: none
Provenance: Dr. Harold L. Klawans, Chicago
1980.69

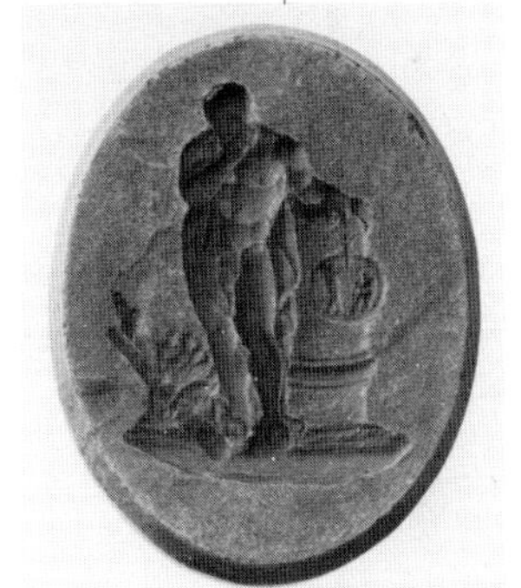

224. Seal: *Hercules*, ca. 1790
Jasper, solid dark blue
1 1/8 x 7/8 in (2.8 x 2.2 cm)
Mark: none
Provenance: Dr. Harold L. Klawans, Chicago
1980.81

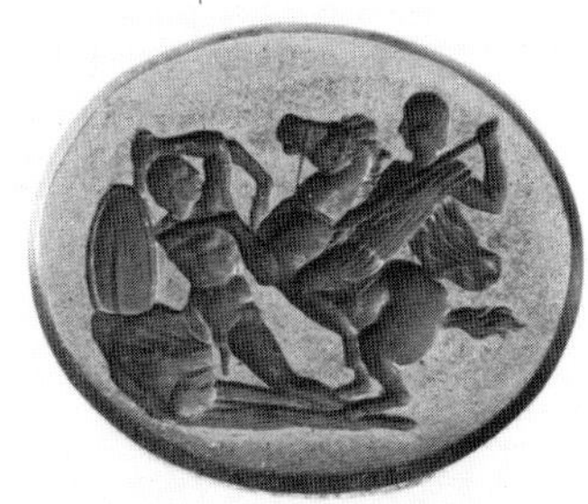

225. Seal: *Mounted Warrior Attacking*, ca. 1790
Basalt
7/8 x 1 in (2.2 x 2.5 cm)
Mark: none
Provenance: Dr. Harold L. Klawans, Chicago
1980.87

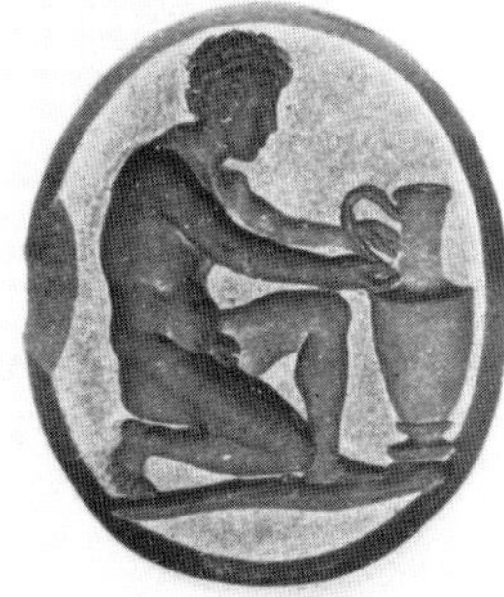

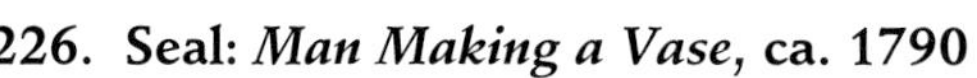

226. Seal: *Man Making a Vase*, ca. 1790
Basalt
5/8 x 1/2 in (1.5 x 1.2 cm)
Mark: none
Provenance: Dr. Harold L. Klawans, Chicago
1980.79

227. Seal: *Two Mounted Warriors Confronting,* ca. 1790
Basalt
7/16 x 9/16 in (1.1 x 1.4 cm)
Mark: none
Provenance: Dr. Harold L. Klawans, Chicago
1980.95

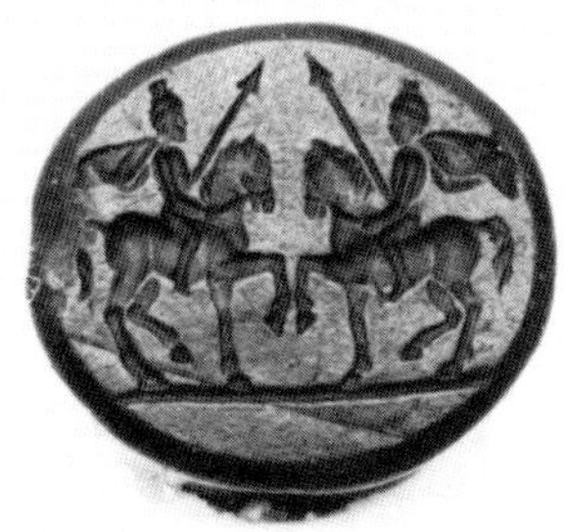

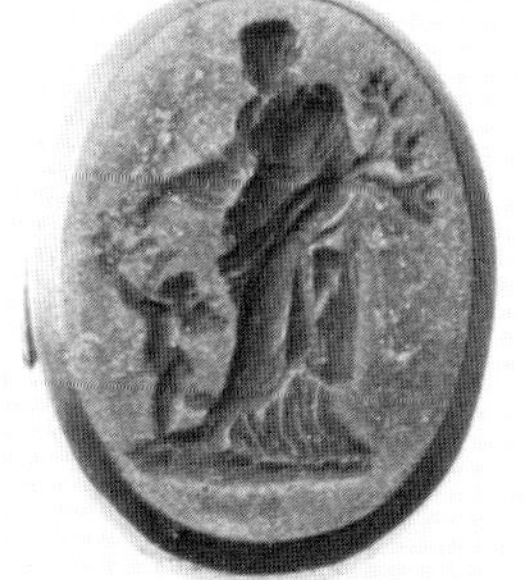

228. Seal: *Venus and Cupid,* ca. 1790
Basalt
9/16 x 7/16 in (1.4 x 1.1 cm)
Mark: none
Provenance: Dr. Harold L. Klawans, Chicago
1980.97

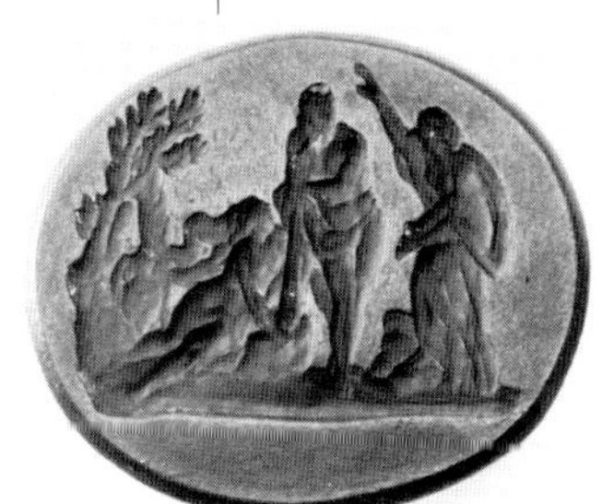

229. Seal: *Peace,* ca. 1790
Basalt
7/8 x 3/4 in (2.2 x 1.9 cm)
Mark: none
Provenance: Dr. Harold L. Klawans, Chicago
1980.83

230. Seal: *Hope with Anchor,* ca. 1790
Basalt
15/16 x 3/4 in (2.3 x 1.9 cm)
Mark: none
Provenance: Dr. Harold L. Klawans, Chicago
1980.93

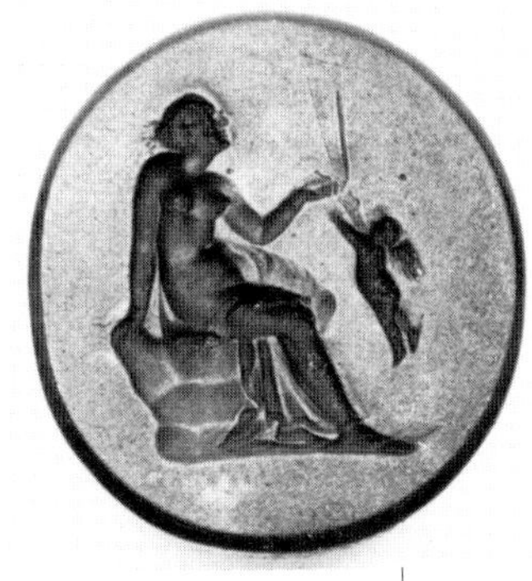

231. Seal: *Venus and Cupid,* ca. 1790
Basalt
1 3/16 x 3/4 in (3 x 1.9 cm)
Mark: none
Provenance: Dr. Harold L. Klawans, Chicago
1980.89

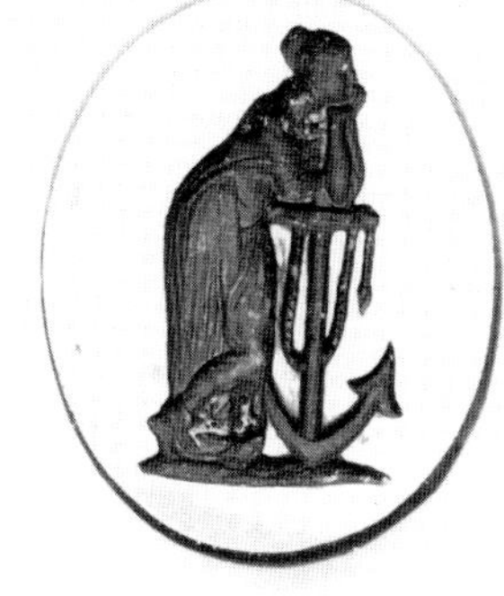

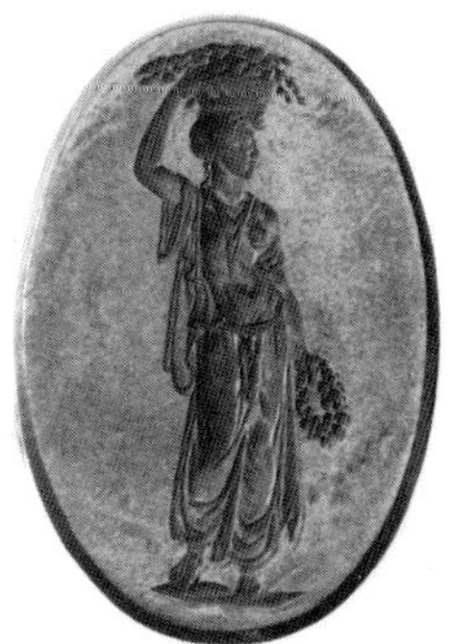

232. Seal: *Flora,* ca. 1790
Basalt
1 1/4 x 7/8 in (3.1 2.2 cm)
Mark: none
Provenance: Dr. Harold L. Klawans, Chicago
1980.84

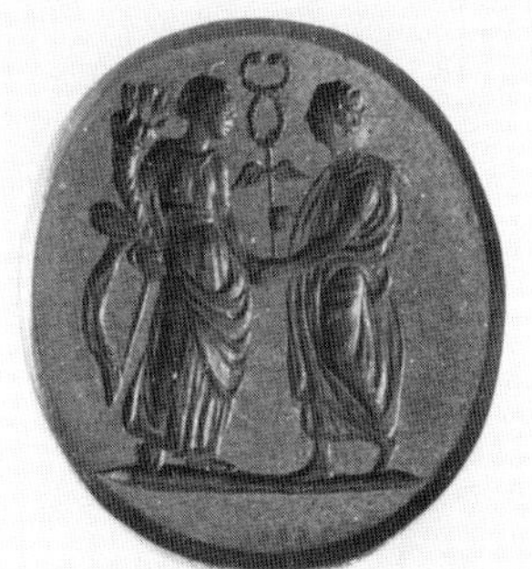

233. Seal: *A Roman Wedding*, ca. 1790
Basalt
3/4 x 5/8 in (1.9 x 1.5 cm)
Mark: none
Provenance: Dr. Harold L. Klawans, Chicago
1980.78

234. Seal: *Mercury Sitting upon Aries*, ca. 1790
Basalt
3/4 x 5/8 in (1.9 x 1.5 cm)
Mark: none
Provenance: Dr. Harold L. Klawans, Chicago
1980.100

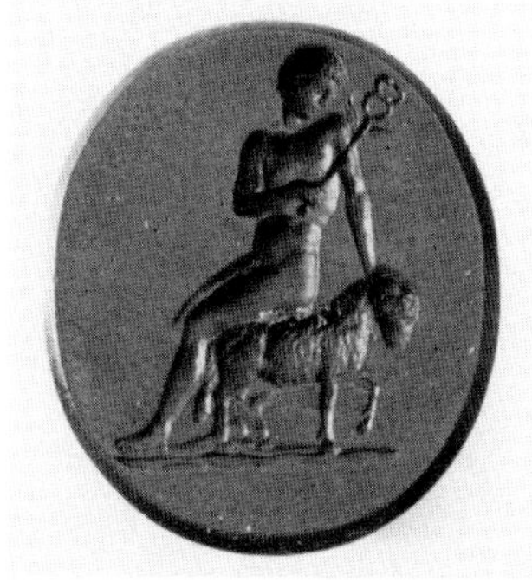

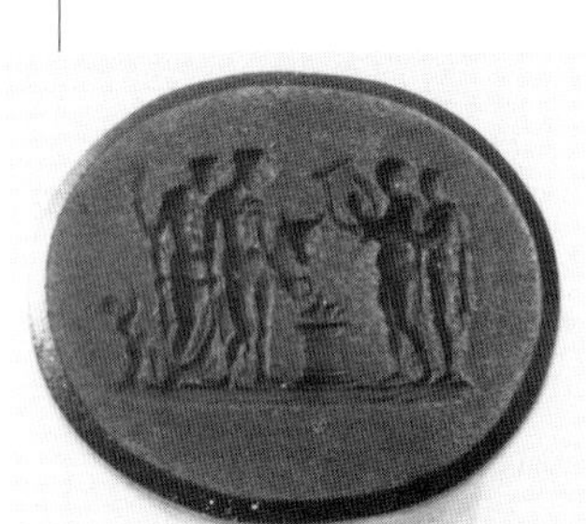

235. Seal: *A Sacrifice*, ca. 1790
Basalt
5/8 x 1/2 in (1.5 x 1.2 cm)
Mark: none
Provenance: Dr. Harold L. Klawans, Chicago
1980.86

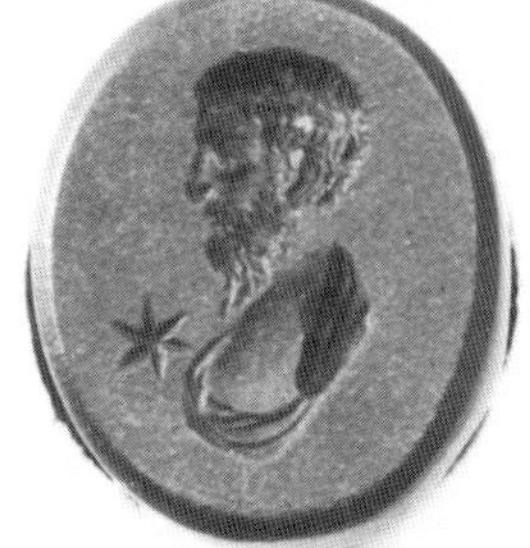

236. Seal: *Pythagoras*, ca. 1790
Basalt
1/2 x 3/8 in (1.2 x .9 cm)
Mark: none
Provenance: Symons Collection, England; Dr. Harold L. Klawans, Chicago
1980.74

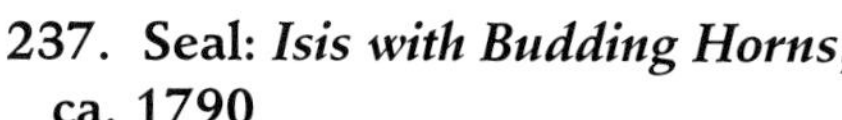

237. Seal: *Isis with Budding Horns*, ca. 1790
Basalt
1/2 x 3/8 in (1.2 x .9 cm)
Mark: none
Provenance: Symons Collection, England; Dr. Harold L. Klawans, Chicago
1980.73

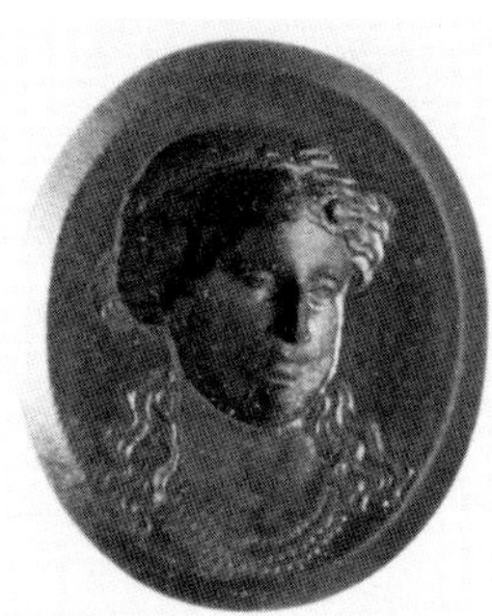

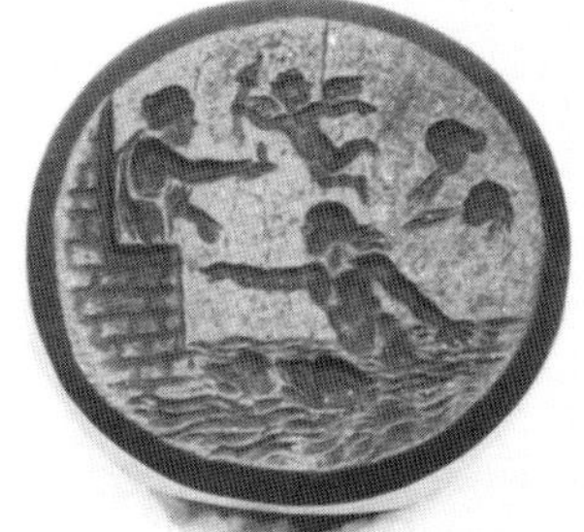

238. Seal: *Hero and Leander*, ca. 1790
Basalt
1/2 x 7/16 in (1.2 x 1.1 cm)
Mark: none
Provenance: Dr. Harold L. Klawans, Chicago
1980.76

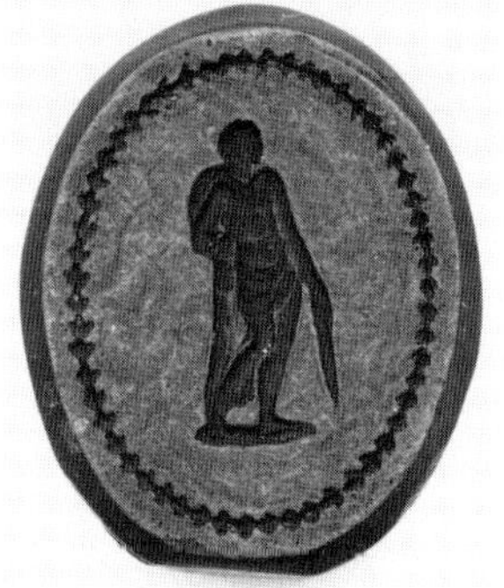

239. Seal: ***Classical Figure*****, ca. 1790**
Basalt
7/8 x 3/4 in (2.2 x 1.9 cm)
Mark: none
Provenance: Dr. Harold L. Klawans, Chicago
1980.70

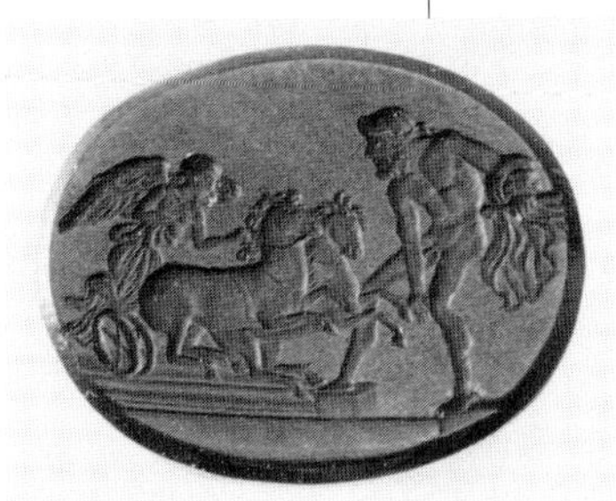

240. Seal: ***Hercules Staying the Chariot of Victory*****, ca. 1790**
Basalt
7/8 x 11/16 in (2.2 x 1.7 cm)
Mark: none
Provenance: Dr. Harold L. Klawans, Chicago
1980.72

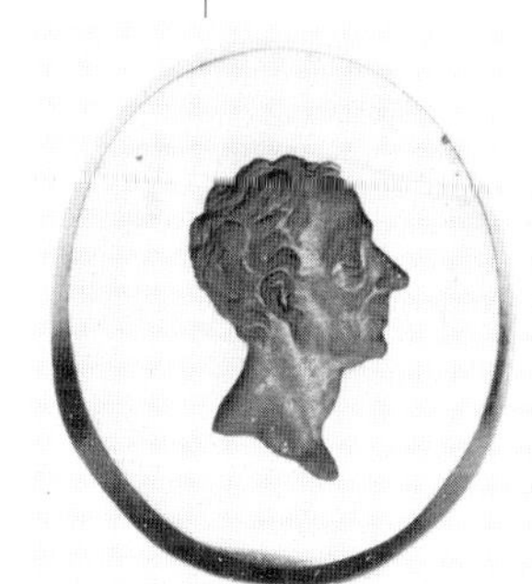

241. Seal: ***Head of Laocoön*****, ca. 1790**
Basalt
3/4 x 5/8 in (1.9 x 1.5 cm)
Mark: none
Provenance: Dr. Harold L. Klawans, Chicago
1980.67

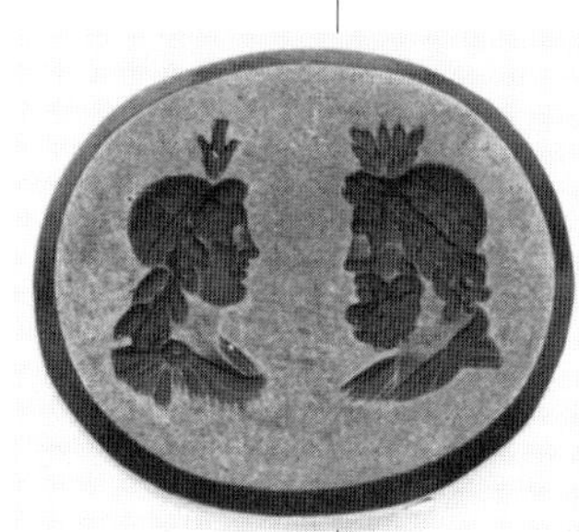

242. Seal: ***Man and Woman*****, ca. 1770**
Basalt
3/4 x 5/8 in (1.9 x 1.5 cm)
Mark: none
Provenance: Dr. Harold L. Klawans, Chicago
1980.65

Jasper-Ware Tablets, Plaques, and Roundels

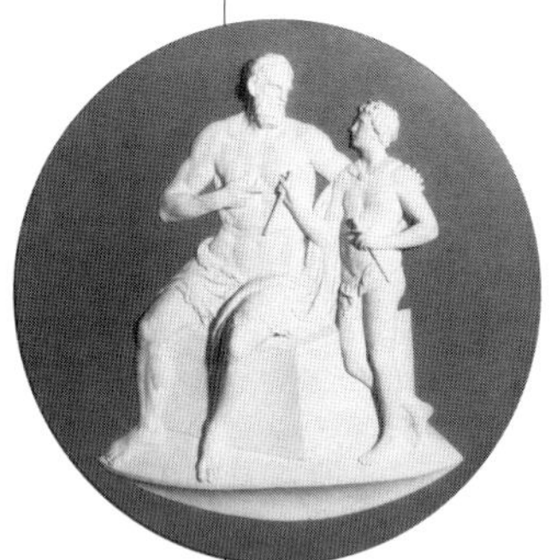

243. Roundel: ***Marsyas and Young Olympus*****, ca. 1795**
Jasper, solid blue ground with blue wash on front and white relief
11 1/4 in (28.5 cm)
Mark: "WEDGWOOD"
Provenance: Dr. Francis Jennings Vurpillat, South Bend, Ind.
1981.237
Back has 25 firing holes.
Color plate 91

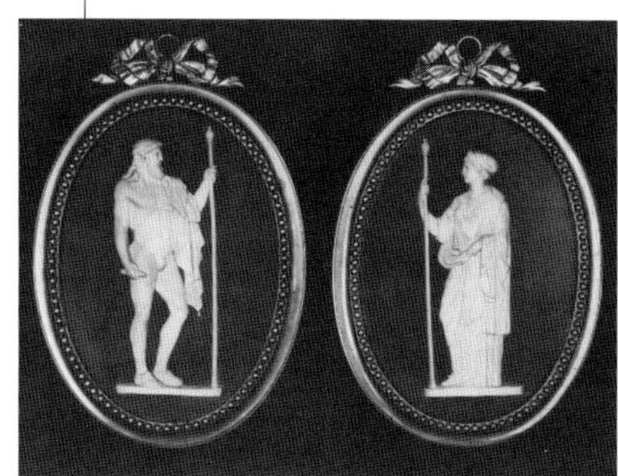

244. Plaque: ***Jupiter*****, 1775-80**
Jasper, solid blue ground with blue wash on front and white relief
7 7/16 x 5 1/2 in (18.8 x 13.9 cm)
Mark: "WEDGWOOD & BENTLEY"
Provenance: Eustace Hand, England; Fred J. Tongue, Santa Monica, Calif.; Dr. Francis Jennings Vurpillat, South Bend, Ind.
1981.229
Design source: Montfaucon, *L'Antiquité expliquée,* vol. 1, pt. 1, pl. 7, fig. 12
Color plate 69

245. Plaque: ***Juno*****, 1775-80**
Jasper, solid blue ground with blue wash on front and white relief
7 3/8 x 5 1/2 in (18.7 x 13.9 cm)
Mark: "WEDGWOOD & BENTLEY"
Provenance: Eustace Hand, England; Fred J. Tongue, Santa Monica, Calif.; Dr. Francis Jennings Vurpillat, South Bend, Ind.
1981.230
Color plate 69

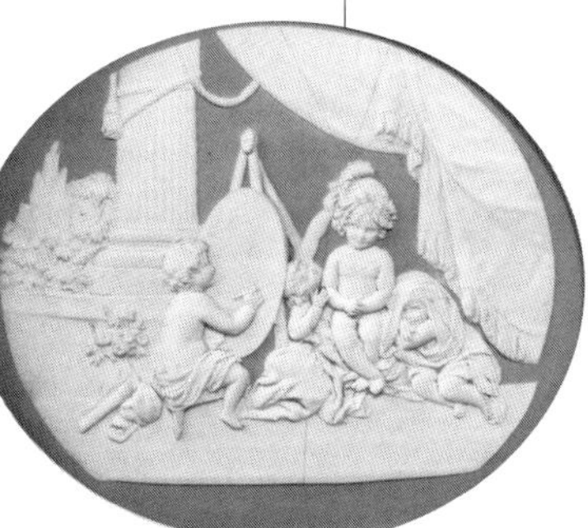

246. Plaque: ***Infant Academy*****, ca. 1790**
Jasper, solid blue ground with white relief
7 1/8 x 6 1/8 in (18 x 15.5 cm)
Mark: "WEDGWOOD"
Provenance: Fred J. Tongue, Santa Monica, Calif.
1982.32

247. Plaque: *Bacchanalian Boys at Play,* ca. 1775-80
Jasper, solid blue ground with blue wash on front and white relief
7 7/16 x 5 9/16 in (18.8 x 14.1 cm)
Mark: "WEDGWOOD & BENTLEY"
Provenance: Eustace Hand, England; Fred J. Tongue, Santa Monica, Calif.; Dr. Francis Jennings, Vurpillat, South Bend, Ind.
1985.426

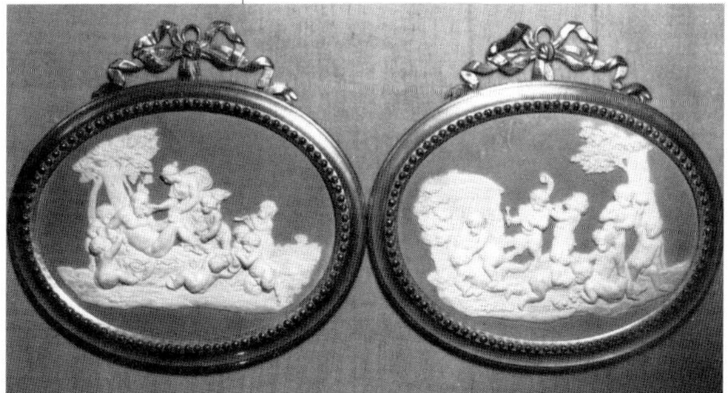

248. Plaque: *The Drunken Silenus,* ca. 1775-80
Jasper, solid blue ground with blue wash on front and white relief
7 5/16 x 5 9/16 in (18.5 x 14.1 cm)
Mark: "WEDGWOOD & BENTLEY"
Provenance: Eustace Hand, England; Fred J. Tongue, Santa Monica, Calif.; Dr. Francis Jennings Vurpillat, South Bend, Ind.
1976.134

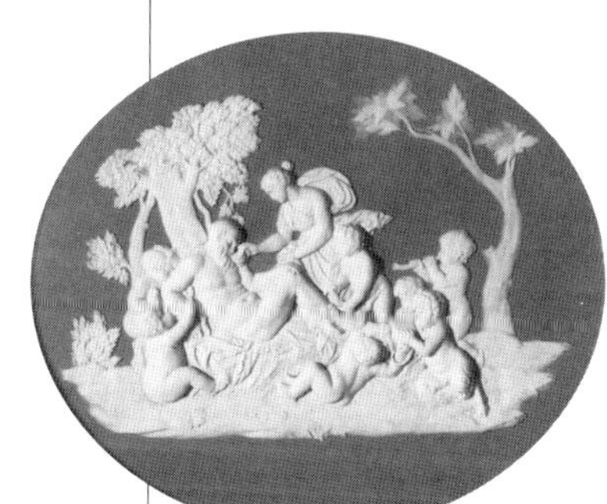

249. Plaque: *The Drunken Silenus,* ca. 1790
Jasper, solid blue ground with white relief
8 3/8 x 7 in (21.2 x 17.7 cm)
Mark: "WEDGWOOD"
Provenance: David Davis, Chicago; Dr. Harold L. Klawans, Chicago
1976.174
Back has six firing holes.

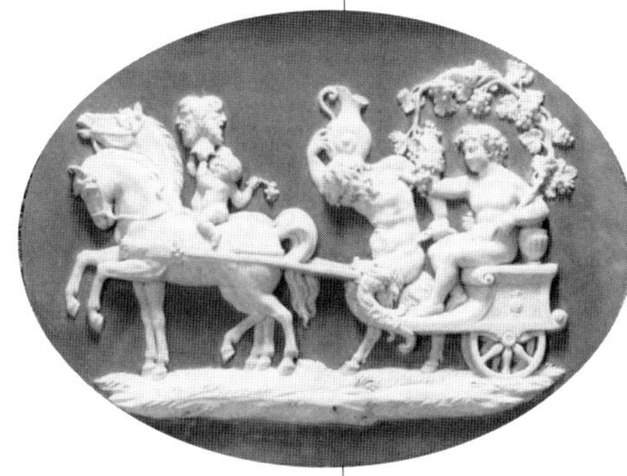

250. Plaque: *Triumph of Bacchus,* ca. 1775-80
Jasper, solid blue ground with blue wash on front and white relief
9 5/8 x 7 1/8 in (24.4 x 1.8 cm)
Mark: "WEDGWOOD & BENTLEY"
Provenance: Lord Wantage, England; Dr. Francis Jennings Vurpillat, South Bend, Ind.
1985.427

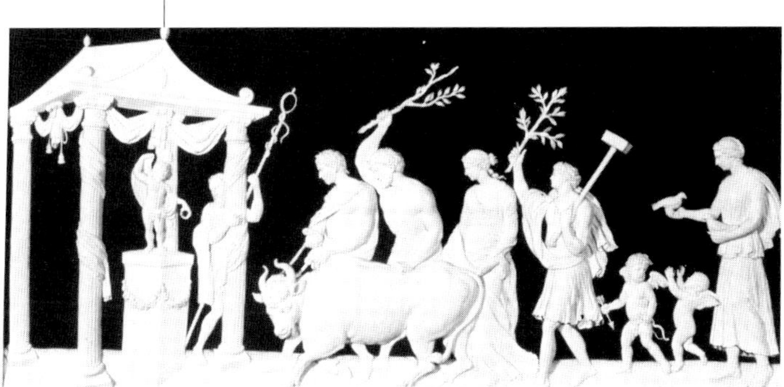

251. Tablet: *Sacrifice to Eros,* ca. 1780
Jasper, solid blue ground with dark blue wash on front and white relief
22 1/8 x 10 5/8 in (56.1 x 26.9 cm)
Mark: "WEDGWOOD"
Provenance: Dr. Francis Jennings Vurpillat, South Bend, Ind.
1983.1
Back has 64 firing holes.
Color plates 64 and 65

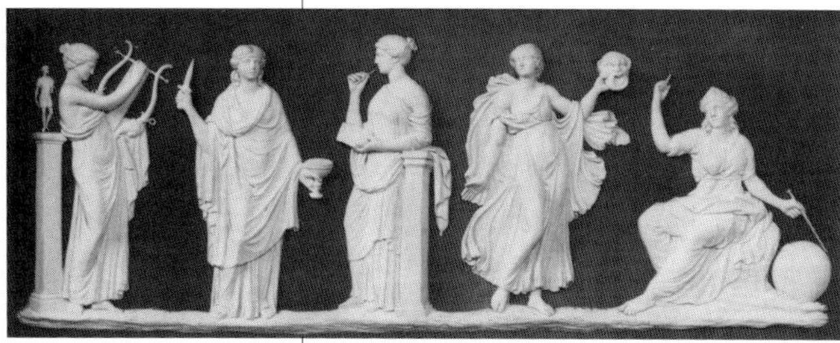

252. Tablet: *The Five Muses of Melpomene, Calliope, Thalia, Urana, Terpsichore,* ca. 1780
Jasper, solid blue ground with dark blue wash on front and white relief
15 1/4 x 6 1/4 in (38.7 x 15.8 cm)
Mark: "WEDGWOOD & BENTLEY" "2"
Provenance: Dr. Francis Jennings Vurpillat, South Bend, Ind.
1981.228
Back has 28 firing holes.
Color plate 85

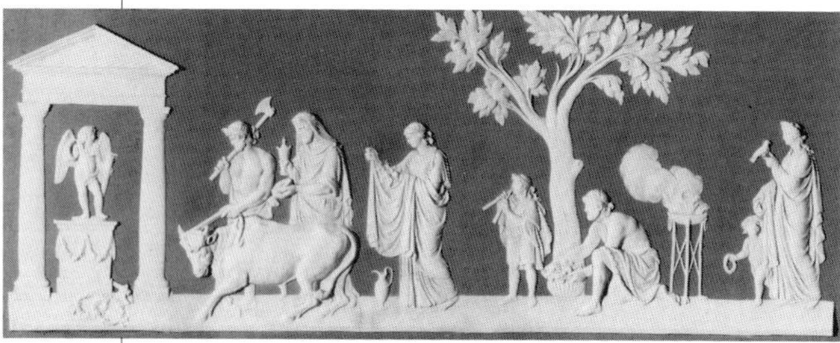

253. Tablet: *Sacrifice to Love,* ca. 1800
Jasper, solid white ground with green wash on front and white relief
24 7/8 x 9 3/4 in (63.1 x 24.7 cm)
Mark: "WEDGWOOD"
Provenance: Dr. Francis Jennings Vurpillat, South Bend, Ind.
1980.317
Color plate 89

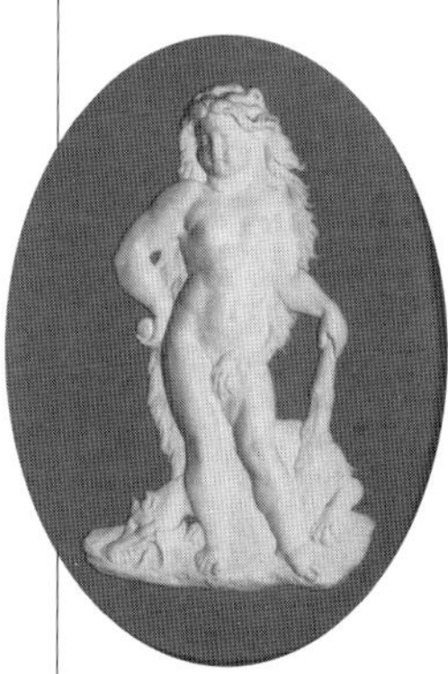

254. Plaque: *Young Hercules,* ca. 1775-80
Jasper, solid blue ground with blue wash on front and white relief
6 1/4 x 5 in (15.8 x 12.7 cm)
Mark: "WEDGWOOD & BENTLEY"
Provenance: David Davis, Chicago; Dr. Harold L. Klawans, Chicago
1982.25
Back has seven firing holes.
Color plate 71

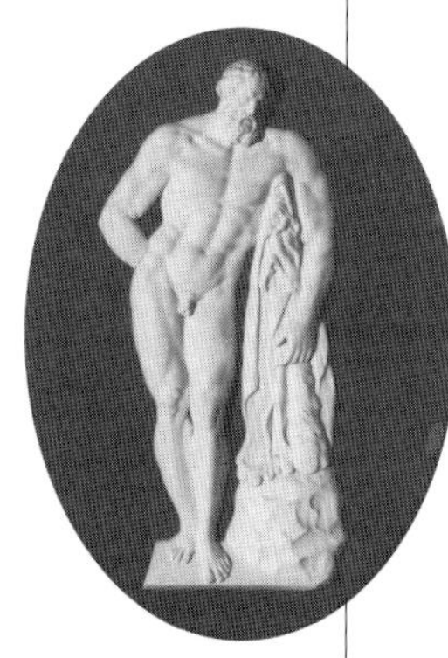

255. Plaque: *The Farnese Hercules,* ca. 1775-80
Jasper, solid blue ground with dark blue wash on front and white relief
7 1/2 x 5 1/2 in (19 x 13.9 cm)
Mark: "WEDGWOOD & BENTLEY"
Provenance: David Davis, Chicago; Dr. Harold L. Klawans, Chicago
1982.24
Back has 10 firing holes.
Design source: Montfaucon, *L' Antiquité expliquée,* vol. 1, pt. 2, pl. 62, fig. 11
Color plate 71

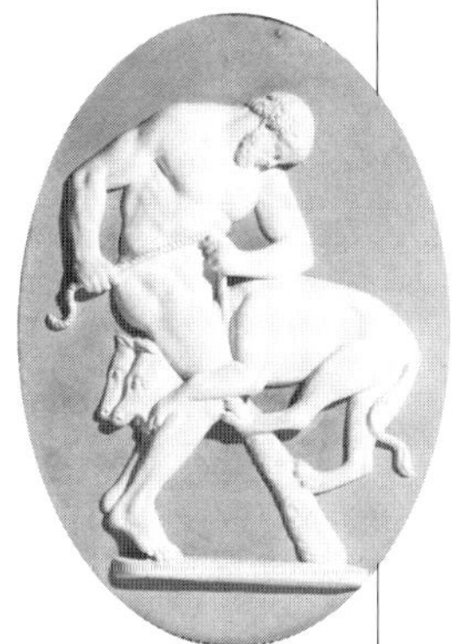

256. Plaque: *Hercules Binding Cerberus,* ca. 1775-80
Jasper, solid blue ground with white relief
7 3/8 x 5 9/16 in (18.7 x 14.1 cm)
Mark: "WEDGWOOD & BENTLEY"
Provenance: M. Mellanay Delhom, Chicago; Ann Brodkiewicz, Chicago
1982.29
Back has four firing holes.
Design source: Montfaucon, *L' Antiquité expliquée,* vol. 1, pt. 2, pl. 66, fig. 3
Color plate 71

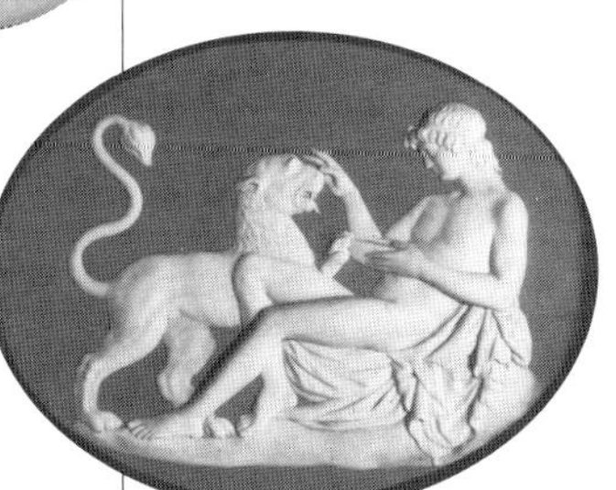

257. Plaque: *Bacchus and the Panther,* ca. 1800
Jasper, solid blue ground with white relief
9 x 6 15/16 in (22.8 x 17.6 cm)
Mark: "WEDGWOOD"
Provenance: William Erasmus Darwin, England; Dr. Harold L. Klawans, Chicago
1982.2

258. Roundel: *Herculaneum Figure,* 19th century
Jasper, solid white ground with blue wash on front with white relief
12 in (30.4 cm)
Mark: "WEDGWOOD"
Provenance: Fred J. Tongue, Santa Monica, Calif.
1982.17
Back has nine firing holes.

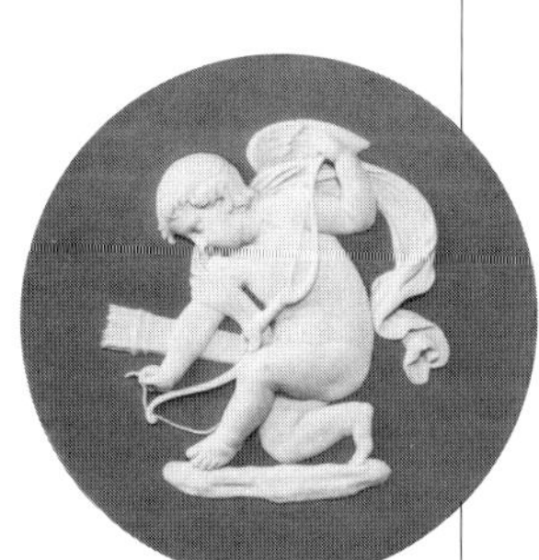

259. Plaque: *Cupid Stringing His Bow,* ca. 1800
Jasper, solid white ground with green wash on front and white relief
6 3/16 in (15.7 cm)
Mark: "WEDGWOOD"
Provenance: Dr. Francis Jennings Vurpillat, South Bend, Ind.
1980.341

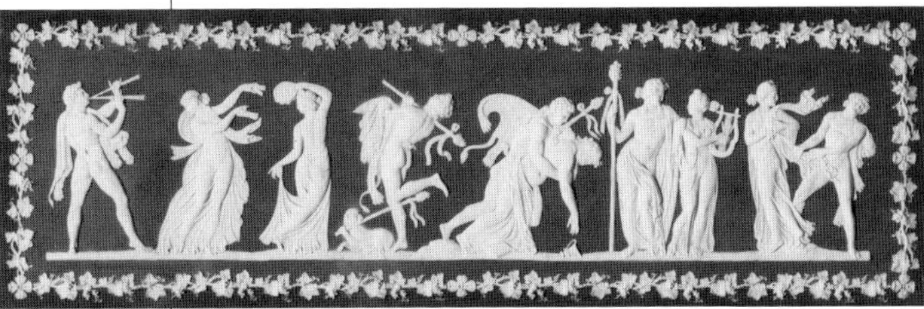

260. Tablet: *Bacchanalian Triumph,* ca. 1800
Jasper, solid white ground with green-and-blue wash on front and white relief
27 x 9 in (68.5 x 22.8 cm)
Mark: "WEDGWOOD"
Provenance: Andrews Collection, Cardiff, Wales; W. Russell Button Gallery, Chicago; Dr. Francis Jennings Vurpillat, South Bend, Ind.
1982.7
Design source: Montfaucon, *L' Antiquité expliquée,* vol. 2, pt. 2, pl. 30, figs. 1, 2
Color plate 92

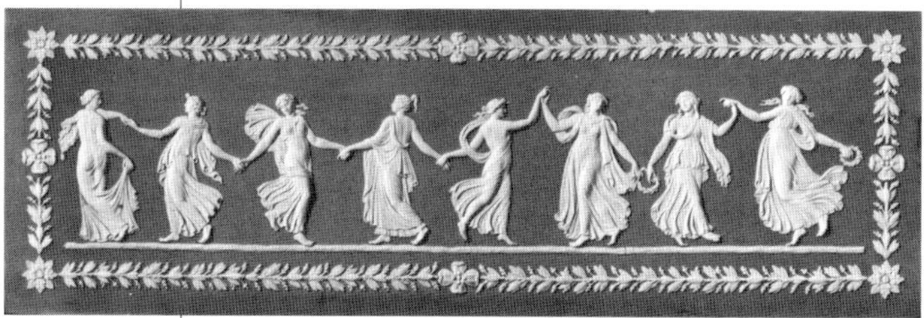

261. Tablet: *Dancing Hours,* 19th century
Jasper, solid white ground with green-and-blue wash on front and white relief
18 1/2 x 6 1/4 in (46.9 x 15.8 cm)
Mark: "WEDGWOOD"
Provenance: Toby House, New York
1985.431

262. Tablet: *Dancing Hours,* 19th century
Jasper, solid white ground with lilac-and-green wash on front and white relief
10 5/8 x 3 7/8 in (26.9 x 9.8 cm)
Mark: "WEDGWOOD" "J"
Provenance: Davidson's, Atlanta, Ga.
1985.419

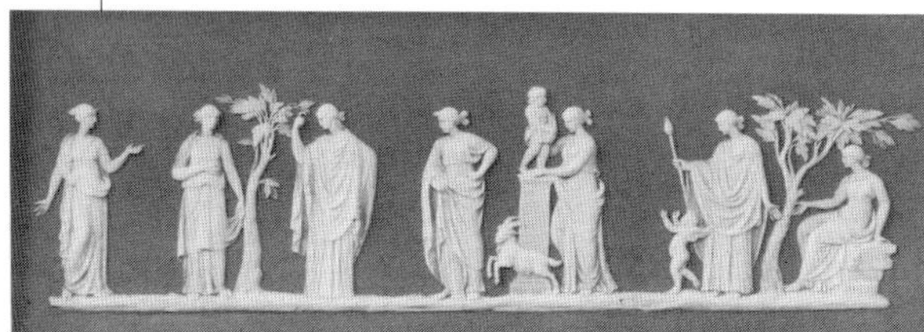

263. Tablet: *A Sacrifice,* 19th century
Jasper, solid white ground with green wash on front and white relief
10 3/4 x 5 in (27.3 x 12.7 cm)
Mark: "WEDGWOOD"
Provenance: Toby House, New York
1980.339

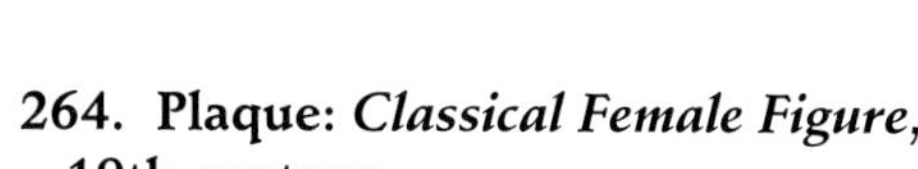

264. Plaque: *Classical Female Figure,* 19th century
Jasper, solid white ground with green wash on front and white relief
9 1/4 x 5 1/2 in (23.4 x 13.9 cm)
Mark: "WEDGWOOD"
Provenance: Purchased in New Orleans
1976.178

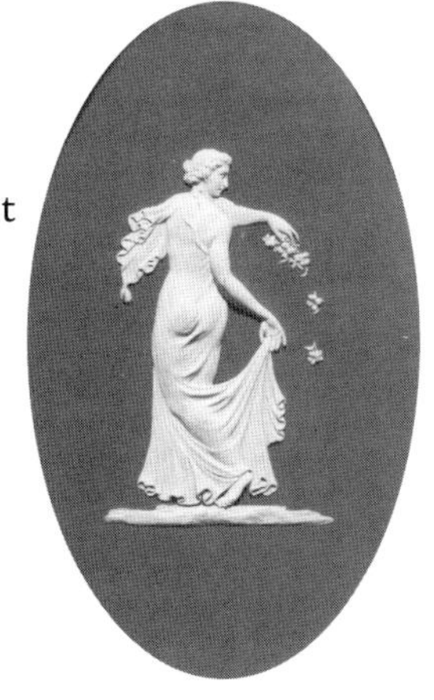

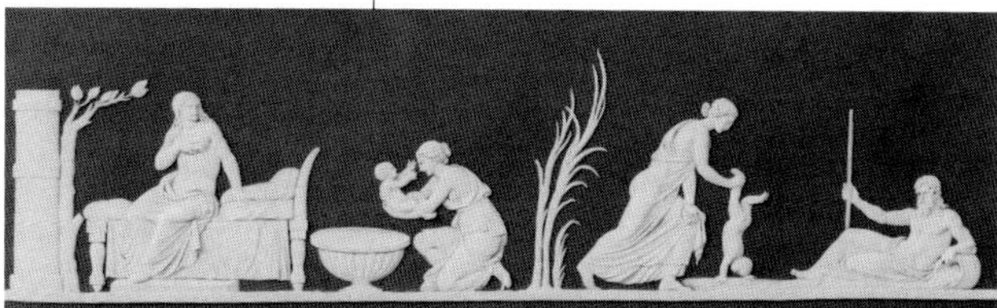

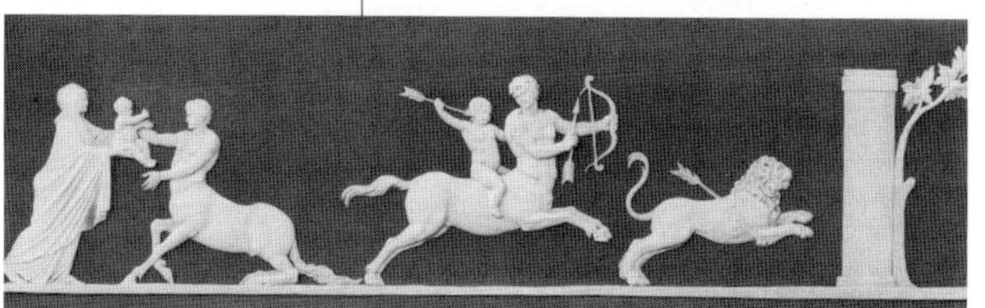

265. Pair of Tablets: *Birth and Dipping of Achilles* and *Achilles Delivered to Chiron, the Centaur, by Thetis,* ca. 1890
Jasper, solid white ground with green wash on front and white relief
18 x 6 1/8 in (45.7 x 15.5 cm)
Mark: a: "WEDGWOOD";
b: "WEDGWOOD / ENGLAND"
Provenance: The Edwardian Shop, Chicago
1980.309 and 1980.310

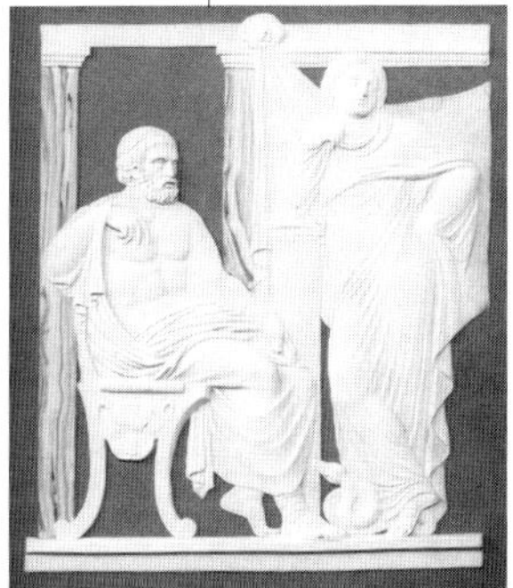

266. Tablet: *Aesculapius and Hygeia,* 19th century
Jasper, solid blue ground with white relief; local color added to columns
9 1/2 x 8 5/16 in (24.1 x 21.1 cm)
Mark: "WEDGWOOD" "O"
Provenance: Seal Simons, Philadelphia, Pa.
1977.129

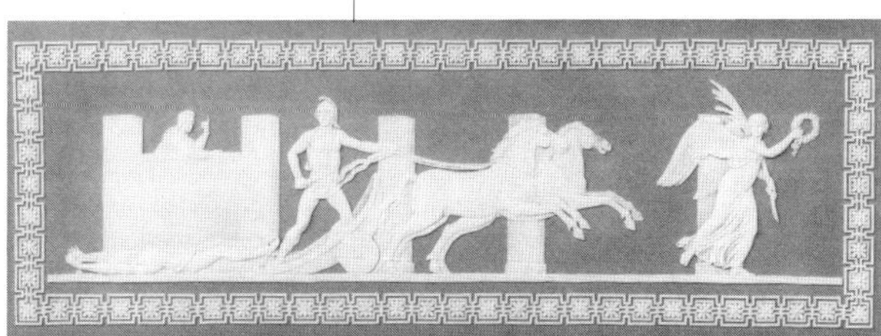

267. Tablet: *Achilles Dragging Hector around the Walls of Troy,* 19th century
Jasper, solid blue ground with white relief
9 1/2 x 7 7/16 in (49.5 x 18.8 cm)
Mark: "WEDGWOOD" "O"; "Achilles Dragging Hector around the Walls of Troy" incised
Provenance: Dr. Francis Jennings Vurpillat, South Bend, Ind.
1981.269

268. Plaque: *Herculaneum Figure,* 19th century
Jasper, solid blue ground with white relief
8 5/8 x 7 1/2 in (21.9 x 19 cm)
Mark: "WEDGWOOD"
Provenance: Manheim's Gallery, New Orleans
1976.179

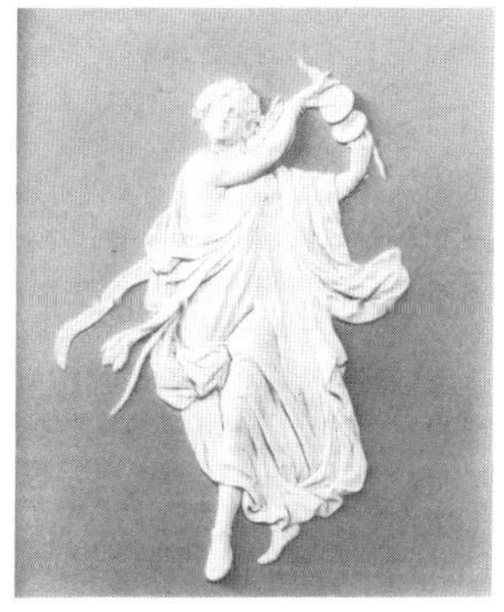

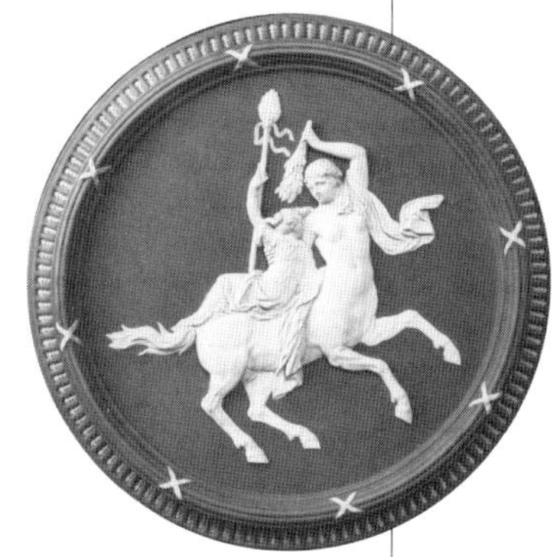

269. Roundel: *Centaur and Bacchante;* or, *Nessus and Dejaira,* ca. 1870
Attributed to Thomas Lovatt (1850-1915), modeler
Jasper, solid white ground with green wash on front and white relief, self-framed
15 7/8 in (40.3 cm)
Mark: "WEDGWOOD" "1" "T.L."
Provenance: Dr. Francis Jennings Vurpillat, South Bend, Ind.
1980.308
Back has 14 firing holes.

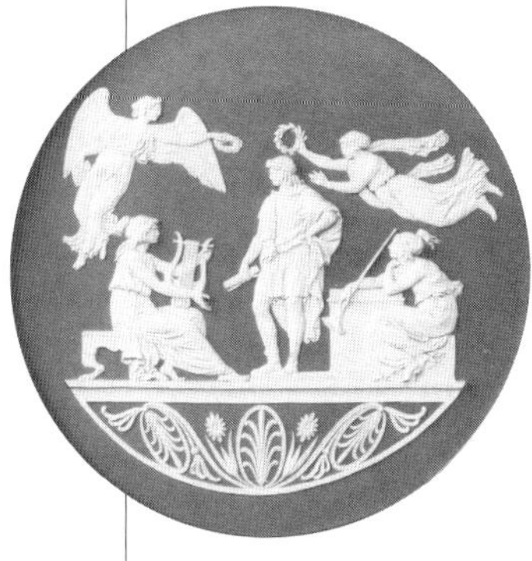

270. Roundel: *Apotheosis of Virgil,* 19th century
Jasper, solid white ground with blue wash on front and back and white relief
15 3/8 in (39 cm)
Mark: "WEDGWOOD"
Provenance: Fred J. Tongue, Santa Monica, Calif.
1981.255

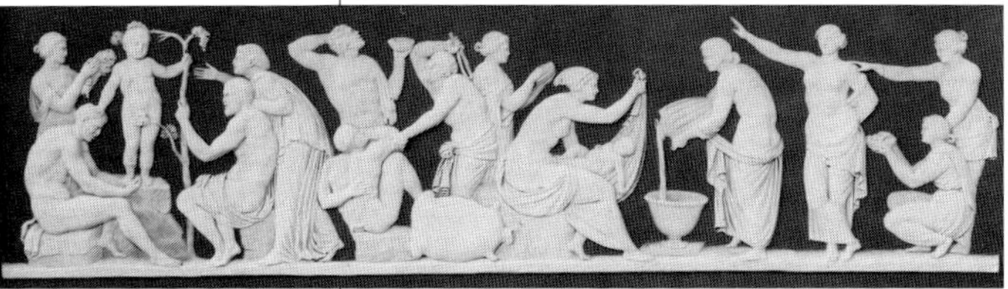

271. Tablet: *The Education of Bacchus,* ca. 1800
Jasper, solid blue ground with blue wash on front and white relief
22 7/8 x 7 in (58.1 x 17.7 cm)
Mark: "WEDGWOOD"
Provenance: Dr. Francis Jennings Vurpillat, South Bend, Ind.
1981.244

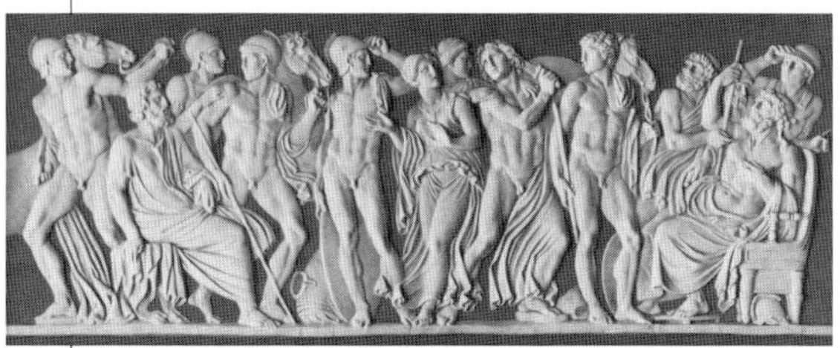

272. Tablet: *Achilles at Scyros,* ca. 1800
Jasper, solid blue ground with white relief
15 1/2 x 6 1/2 in (39.3 x 16.5 cm)
Mark: "WEDGWOOD" twice
Provenance: Dr. Francis Jennings Vurpillat, South Bend, Ind.
1981.220
Design source: Montfaucon, *L'Antiquité expliquée,* vol. 5, pt. 2, pl. 23, fig. 2

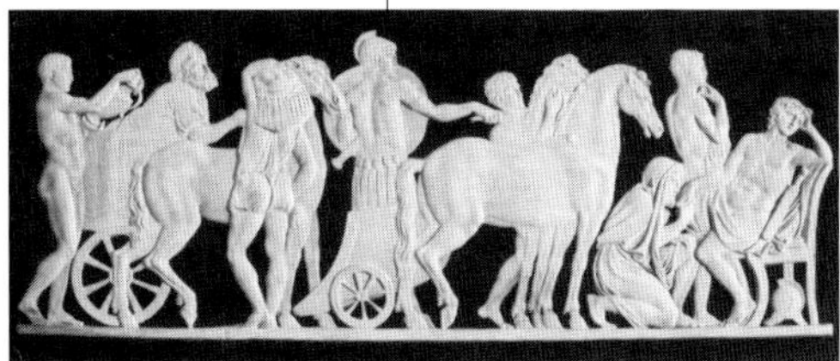

273. Tablet: *Priam Begging the Body of Hector from Achilles,* ca. 1800
Jasper, solid white ground with green wash on front and white relief
16 1/4 x 7 1/16 in (41.2 x 17.9 cm)
Mark: "WEDGWOOD"
Provenance: Fred J. Tongue, Santa Monica, Calif.
1985.432
Design source: Montfaucon, *L'Antiquité expliquée,* vol. 5, pt. 2, pl. 23, fig. 3

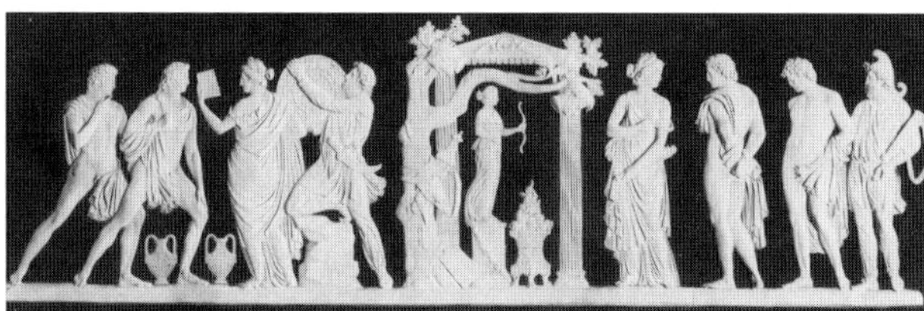

274. Tablet: *Orestes and Pylades at the Temple of Diana,* ca. 1800
John De Vaere (w. 1790-1810), modeler
Jasper, solid white ground with black wash on front and white relief
7 1/2 x 22 5/8 in (57.4 x 19 cm)
Mark: "WEDGWOOD"
Provenance: Abbott Collection, England; Dr. Francis Jennings Vurpillat, South Bend, Ind.
1980.181
Design source: Sarcophagus, originally in Palazzo Accoramboni and now in Munich.

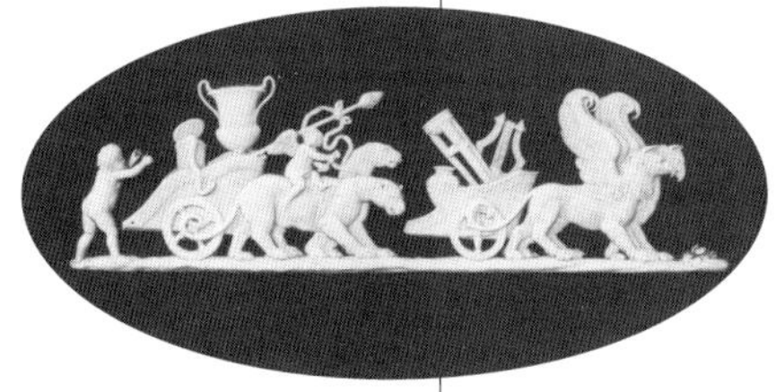

275. Plaque: *Cupid and the Infant Mercury*, 19th century
Jasper, solid white ground with black wash on front and white relief
14 3/8 x 7 3/16 in (36.5 x 18.2 cm)
Mark: "WEDGWOOD"
Provenance: Samuel Oster Collection, England; Sotheby's, London, 1972
1980.184

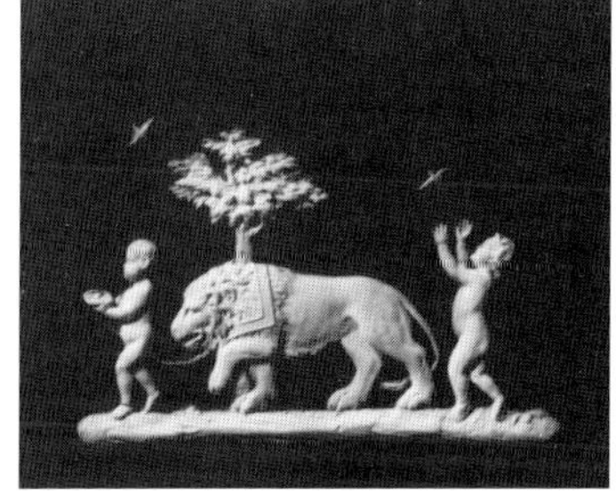

276. Plaque: *Power of Love*, ca. 1800
Jasper, solid white ground with black ground inlaid in center and white relief
6 5/8 x 5 5/8 in (16.8 x 14.2 cm)
Mark: "WEDGWOOD"
Provenance: W. Russell Button Gallery, Chicago
1980.182

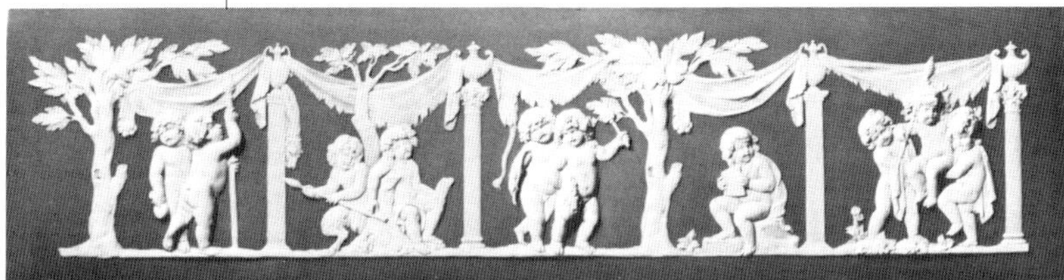

277. Tablet: *Boys with Panther Skins*, ca. 1880
Jasper, solid white ground with green wash on front and white relief
6 1/2 x 24 in (60.9 x 16.5 cm)
Mark: "WEDGWOOD" "O" "A 11"
Provenance: Fred J. Tongue, Santa Monica, Calif.
1980.328
Design source: Montfaucon, *L' Antiquité expliquée,* vol. 2, pt. 2, pl. 29, fig. 1
Color plate 90

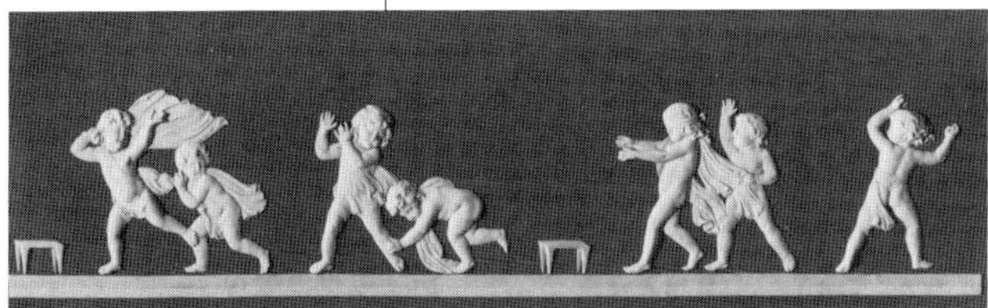

278. Tablet: *Blind Man's Bluff*, 19th century
Jasper, solid white ground with green wash on front and white relief
6 1/4 x 18 in (45.7 x 15.8 cm)
Mark: "WEDGWOOD"
Provenance: W. Russell Button Gallery, Chicago
1980.329

Jasper Ware

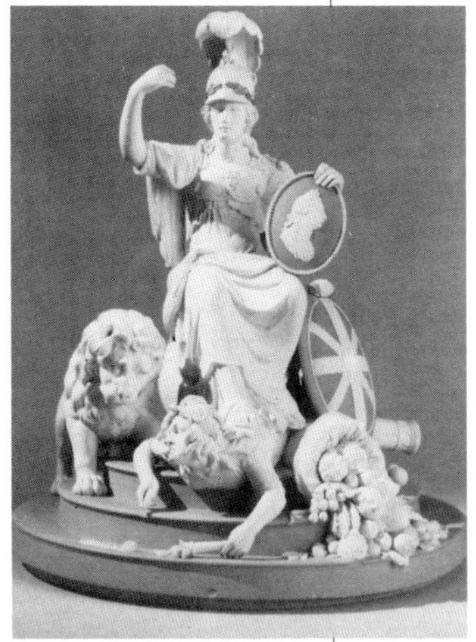

279. Figure: *Britannia Triumphant,* ca. 1798-1809
Attributed to John Flaxman, Jr., modeler
Jasper, solid blue with blue wash; solid white ground with white wash and green relief
13 x 11 7/16 in (33 x 29 cm)
Mark: none
Provenance: Dr. James R. Ricks, New Orleans; Art Trading Ltd., New York
1990.1
Figure has 13 firing holes in the base.
Color plates 120 and 121

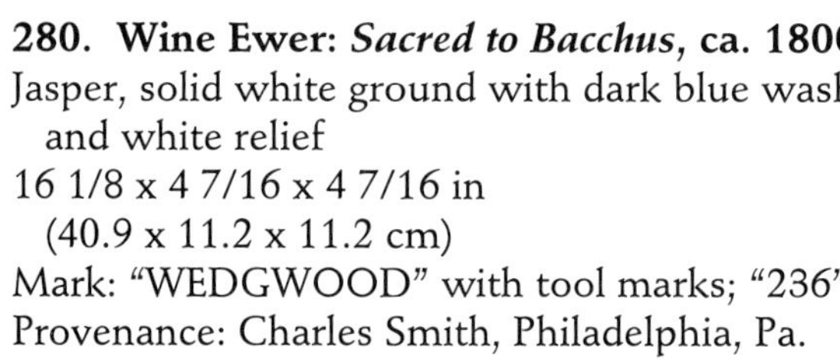

280. Wine Ewer: *Sacred to Bacchus,* ca. 1800
Jasper, solid white ground with dark blue wash and white relief
16 1/8 x 4 7/16 x 4 7/16 in (40.9 x 11.2 x 11.2 cm)
Mark: "WEDGWOOD" with tool marks; "236"
Provenance: Charles Smith, Philadelphia, Pa.
1982.14
Ewer has sump cover.
Color plate 46

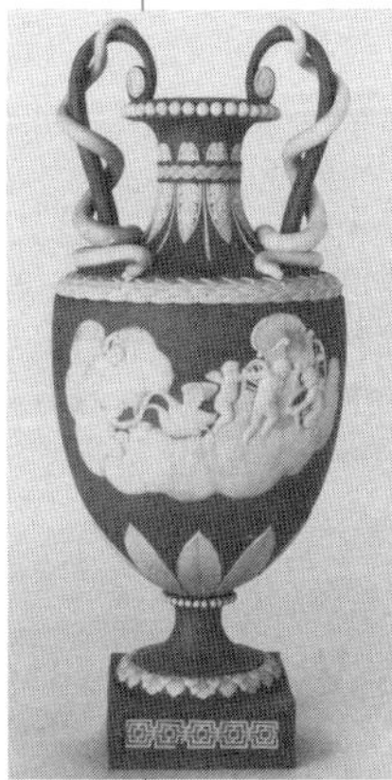

281. Vase: *Venus Drawn by Swans* and *Cupids Attending Swans,* ca. 1786
Charles Le Brun (1619-90), designer
Jasper, solid blue ground with light blue wash and white relief
16 x 4 x 4 in (40.6 x 10.1 x 10.1 cm)
Mark: "WEDGWOOD" "H"
Provenance: M. Mellanay Delhom, Chicago; Dr. Francis Jennings Vurpillat, South Bend, Ind.
1982.191
Vase has sump cover. Base has threaded cavity partially filled with plaster around bolt with eight firing holes.
Color plates 98 and 99

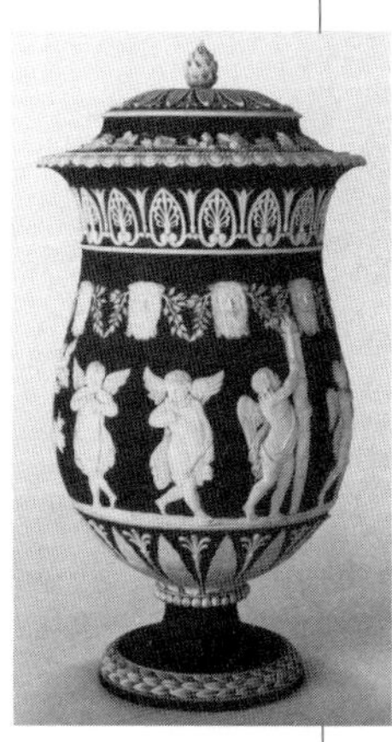

282. Covered Vase: *Several Geniuses Representing the Pleasures of the Elysian Fields,* ca. 1795
Giuseppe Angelini (1709-98), modeler
Jasper, solid white ground with dark blue wash and white relief
15 x 5 1/16 in (38.1 x 12.8 cm)
Mark: "WEDGWOOD" twice
Provenance: Mottahedeh, New York
1982.186 a and b
Vase has sump cover.
Color plate 100

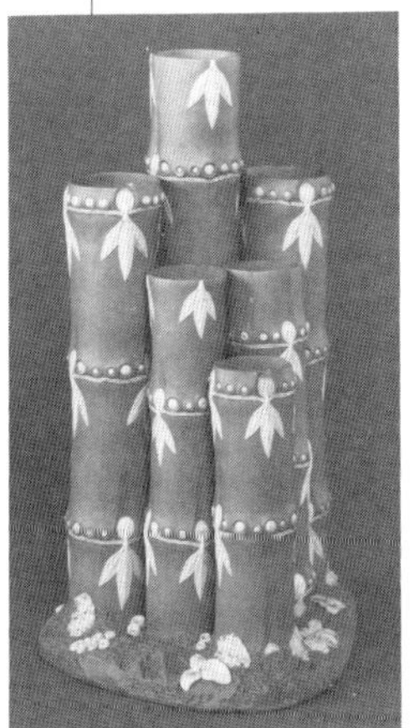

283. Vase: *Bamboo*, ca. 1790
Jasper, solid blue ground with white relief
13 3/8 x 7 11/16 x 7 1/4 in (33.9 x 19.5 x 18.4 cm)
Mark: "WEDGWOOD" "S"
Provenance: Dr. Harold L. Klawans, Chicago
1982.30
Color plate 137

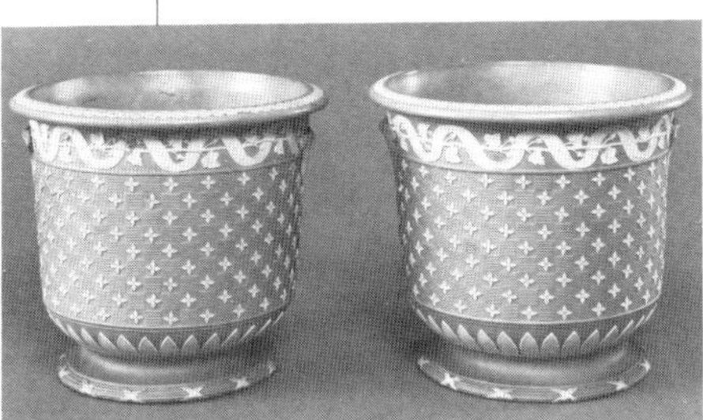

284. Pair of Vases: ca. 1800
Jasper, solid blue ground with white relief and engine-turning
6 3/8 x 5 1/4 in (16.1 x 13.3 cm)
Mark: "WEDGWOOD" with tool mark
Provenance: Harold L. Klawans, Chicago
1981.270 a and b
Interiors are lapidary-polished.

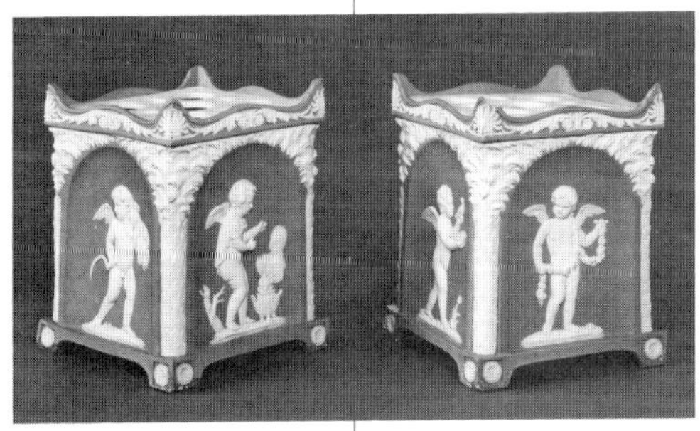

285. Pair of Bulb Pots: *The Four Seasons*, ca. 1785
Jasper, solid blue ground with white relief
6 7/16 x 5 x 5 in (16.3 x 12.7 x 12.7 cm)
Mark: "WEDGWOOD"
Provenance: The Earl of Caurdor, England; Dr. Francis Jennings Vurpillat, South Bend, Ind.
1981.271 a and b; 1981.272 a and b
Design source: Montfaucon, *L' Antiquité expliquée,* vol. 5, pt. 2, pl. 14, fig. 2
Color plate 111

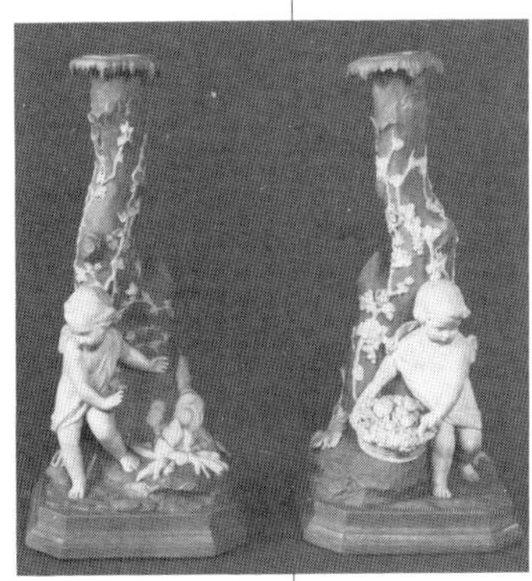

286. Pair of Candlesticks: *Autumn and Winter*, ca. 1785
Jasper, solid blue ground and solid white figures with white relief
10 3/8 x 5 x 5 in (26.3 x 12.7 x 12.7 cm)
Mark: "WEDGWOOD"
Provenance: Dr. Francis Jennings Vurpillat, South Bend, Ind.
1983.2 a and b
Color plate 117

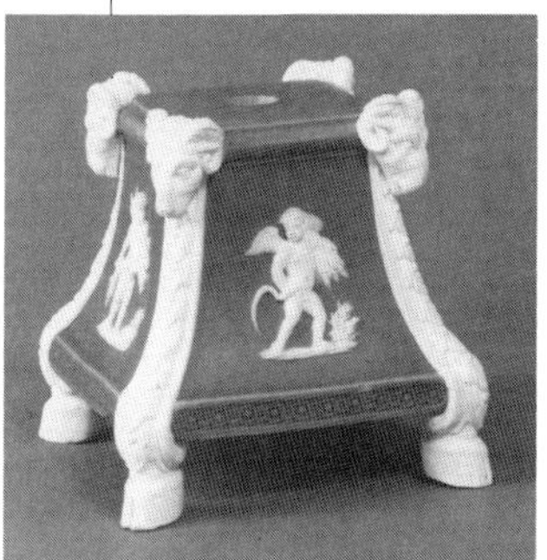

287. Pedestal: *The Four Seasons*, ca. 1775
Jasper, solid blue ground with dark blue wash and white relief
3 5/16 x 3 1/2 in (8.4 x 8.8 cm)
Mark: "Wedgwood & Bentley"
Provenance: Dr. Francis Jennings Vurpillat, South Bend, Ind.
1982.10
Design source: Montfaucon, *L' Antiquité expliquée,* vol. 2, pt. 1, p. 82, pl. 17, fig. 4
Color plate 96

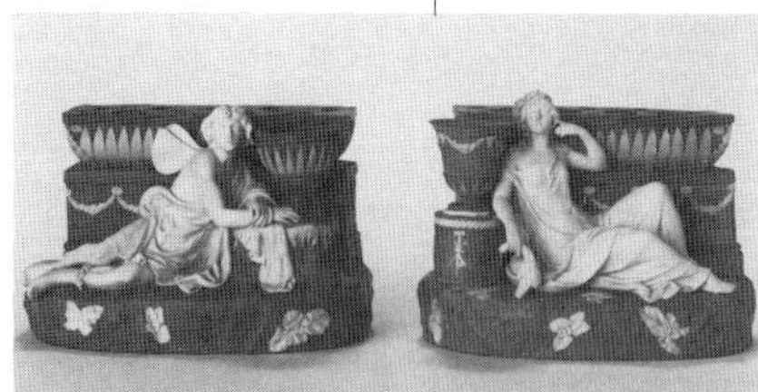

288. Pair of Bulb Pots: *Figures of Cupid and Psyche*, ca. 1790
Jasper, solid blue ground with white relief and solid white figures
5 1/2 x 4 3/4 in (13.9 x 12 cm)
Mark: "WEDGWOOD"
Provenance: a: Dr. Francis Jennings Vurpillat, South Bend, Ind.; b: Ann Brodkiewicz, Chicago
1981.241-.242
Color plate 110

289. Portland Vase Copy: ca. 1860
Stoneware, solid white ground with bright blue wash
6 7/8 x 3 3/8 in (17.4 x 8.5 cm)
Mark: "WEDGWOOD"; "V" with incised tool mark
Provenance: Rich's, Birmingham, Ala.
1985.614

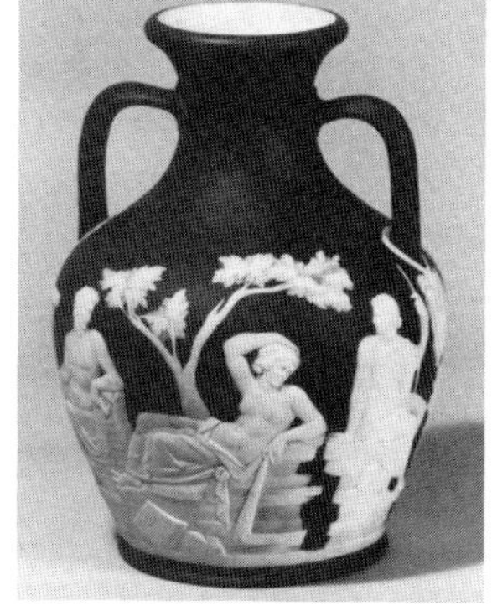

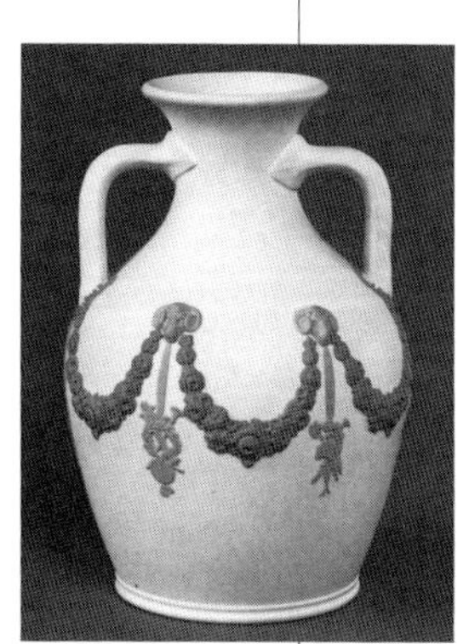

290. Miniature Portland Vase Copy: ca. 1860
Jasper, solid white ground with green-and-lilac relief
6 1/8 x 3 in (15.5 x 7.6 cm)
Mark: "WEDGWOOD"; "6" with tool marks
Provenance: Charles Smith, Philadelphia, Pa.
1981.223

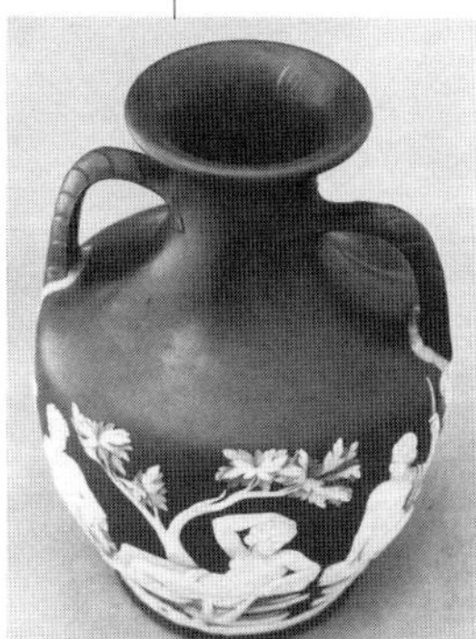

291. Darwin Portland Vase Copy: ca. 1790-92
Jasper, solid black ground with black wash and white relief and addition of local color
10 x 5 1/16 in (25.4 x 12.8 cm)
Mark: "12" written in manganese pencil on neck interior
Provenance: Sir Robin Darwin, England
1983.26
Color plate 134

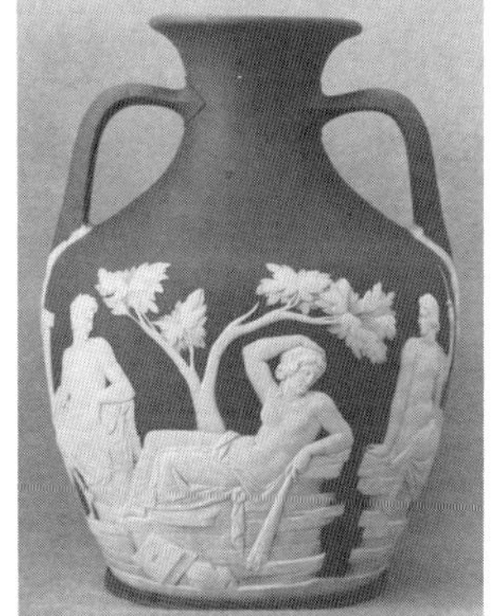

292. Slate Blue Portland Vase Copy: ca. 1791
Jasper, solid slate blue ground with blue wash and white relief
9 3/4 x 4 15/16 in (24.7 x 12.5 cm)
Mark: none
Provenance: Presented by Josiah Wedgwood to Apsley Pellatt, England; Dr. J. Lumsden-Propert, England; Mrs. Spranger, England; R. J. M. Spranger, England; Christie's, London, November 30, 1964
1983.25
Color plate 134

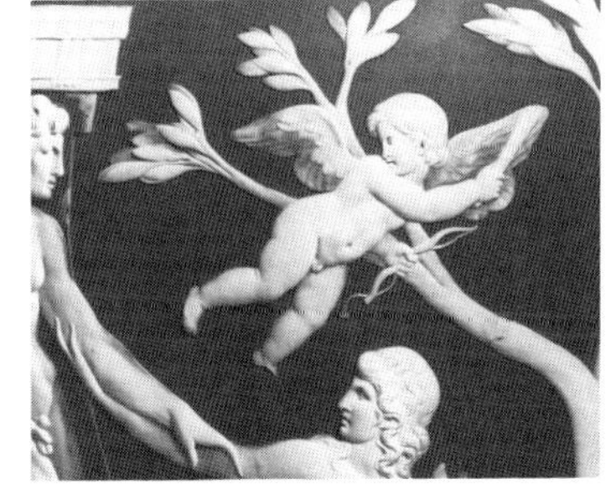

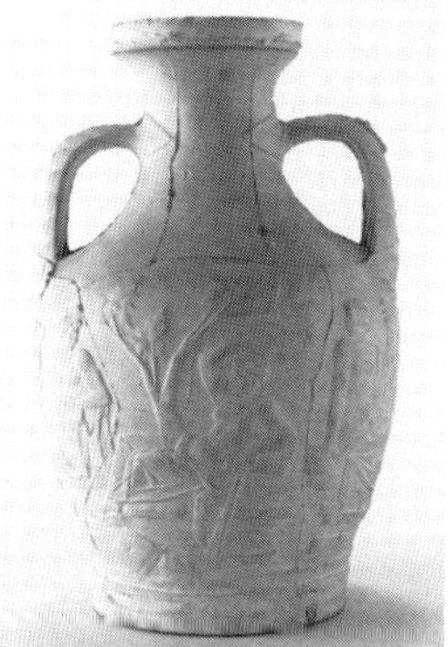

293. Plaster Cast of the Portland Vase: ca. 1790
White plaster made from original Portland vase
9 1/16 x 4 5/8 in (23 x 11.7 cm)
Mark: none
Provenance: David Zeitlin, Merion, Pa.
1981.224

294. Miniature Portland Vase Copy: 1971-72
Basalt
3/4 in (2 cm)
Mark: none
Provenance: Gift of Harry Sheldon, Crewe, England
1981.226

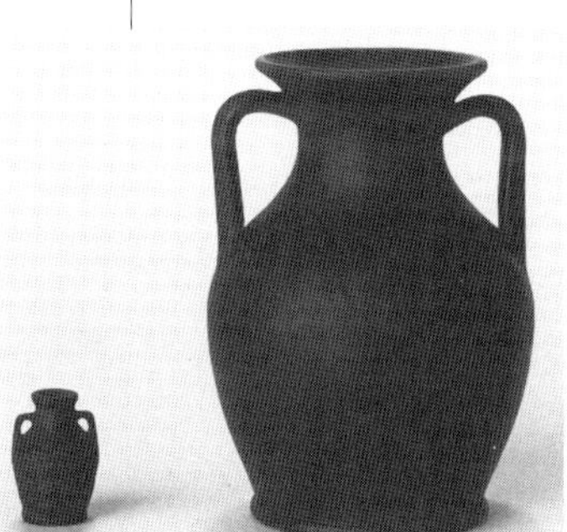

295. Miniature Portland Vase Copy: 20th century
Basalt
3 x 1 9/16 in (7.5 x 3.9 cm)
Mark: "WEDGWOOD" with incised tool mark
Provenance: Otto Wasserman, New York
1981.222

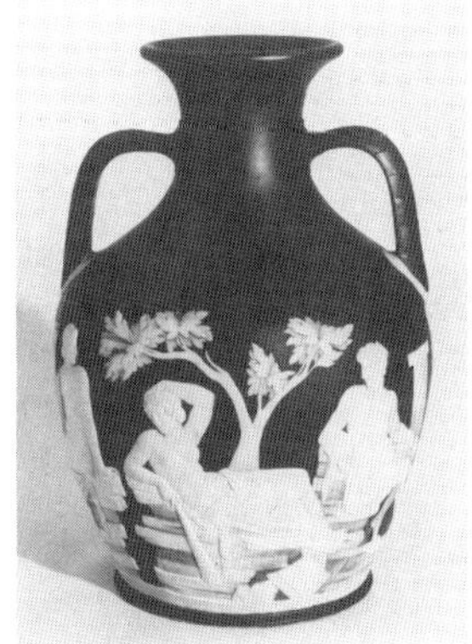

296. Portland Vase Copy: ca. 1880
Thomas Lovatt (1850-1915), modeler
Jasper, solid black ground with white relief
10 7/16 x 5 1/8 in (26.5 x 13 cm)
Mark: "WEDGWOOD" twice on base rim; "TL" incised above Wedgwood mark
Provenance: Wolf Mankowitz, London
1985.436

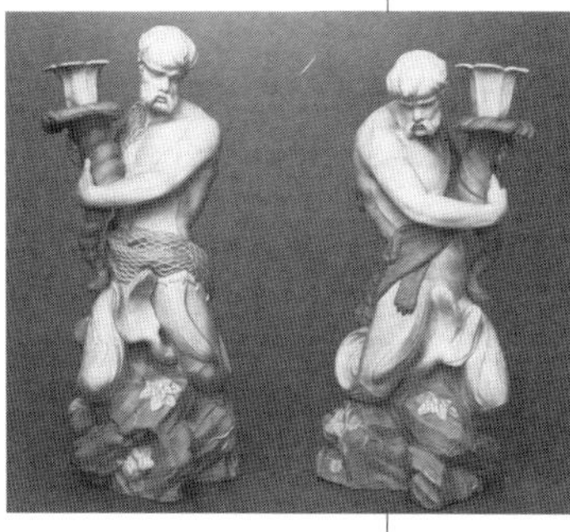

297. Pair of Candlesticks: *Triton*, ca. 1790
Jasper, solid blue ground and solid white figures with white relief
11 1/8 in (28.2 cm)
Mark: "WEDGWOOD"
Provenance: Tulk Collection, England; Dr. Francis Jennings Vurpillat, South Bend, Ind.
1983.4 a and b
Color plate 116

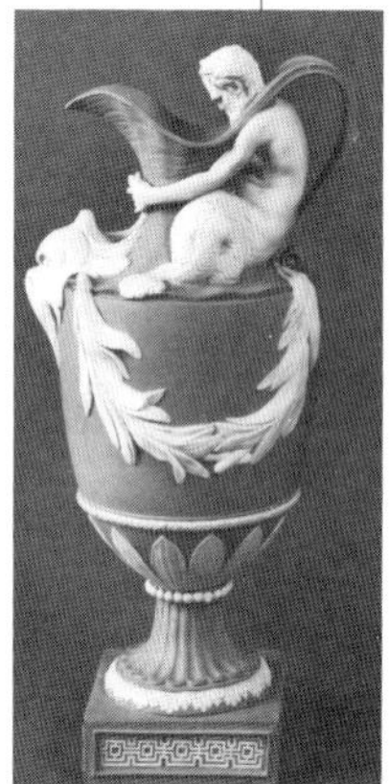

298. Pair of Water Ewers: *Sacred to Neptune*, ca. 1800
Jasper, solid blue ground with white relief
15 3/8 x 4 3/16 in (39 x 10.6 cm)
Mark: "WEDGWOOD" "K"
Provenance: M. Mellanay Delhom, Chicago; Dr. Francis Jennings Vurpillat, South Bend, Ind.
1982.22
Ewers have sump covers.
Color plate 46

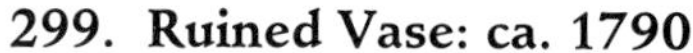

299. Ruined Vase: ca. 1790
Jasper, solid white ground with light blue wash
6 3/8 x 3 5/8 x 3 5/8 in (16.1 x 9.2 x 9.2 cm)
Mark: "WEDGWOOD"
Provenance: M. Close Collection, England; Dr. Francis Jennings Vurpillat, South Bend, Ind.
1983.5
Color plate 105

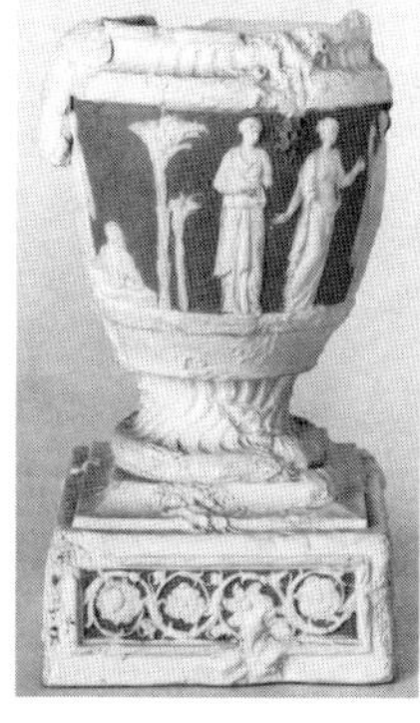

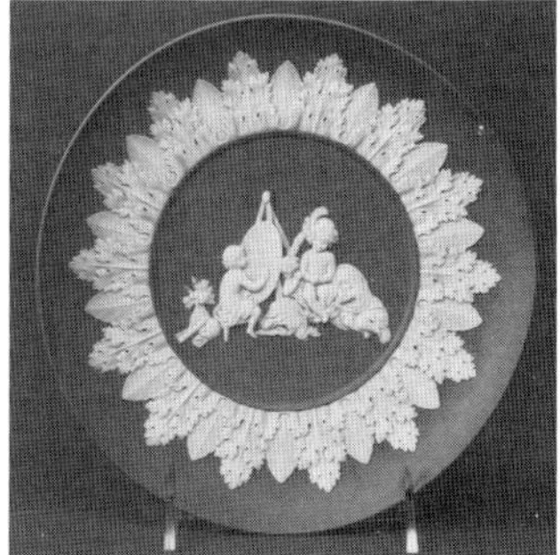

300. Plate: *Infant Academy*, ca. 1790
William Hackwood (ca. 1757-1839), modeler after a painting by Sir Joshua Reynolds (1723-92)
Jasper, solid blue ground with white relief and engine-turning
7 13/16 in (19.8 cm)
Mark: "WEDGWOOD"
Provenance: Ann Brodkiewicz, Chicago
1982.31

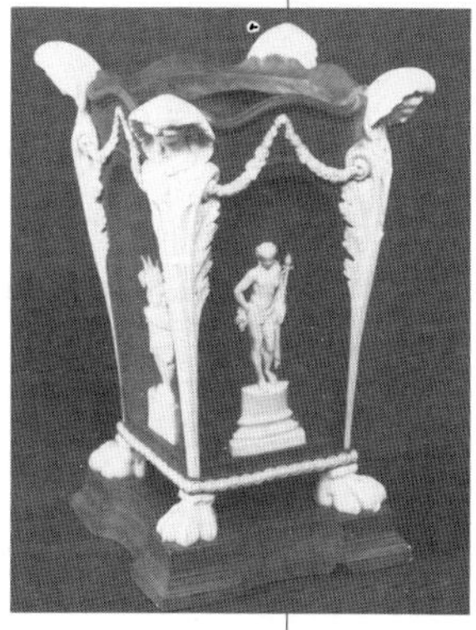

301. Vase: ca. 1800
Jasper, solid blue ground with white relief
8 3/8 x 4 3/4 x 4 3/4 in (21.2 x 12 x 12 cm)
Mark: "WEDGWOOD"
Provenance: Charles Smith, Philadelphia, Pa.
1981.260

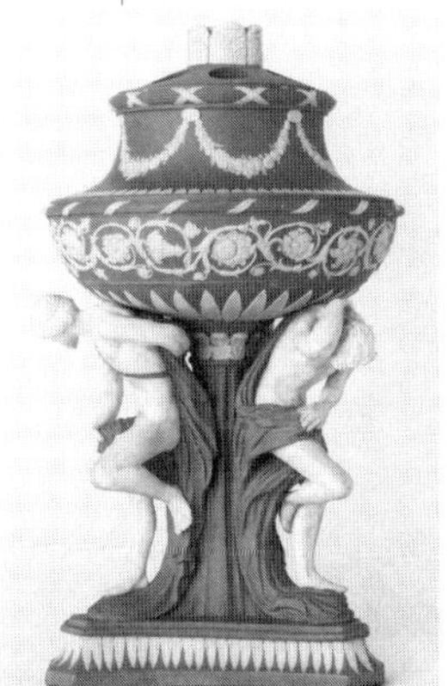

302. Lamp: ca. 1785
Jasper, solid blue ground with solid white figures and white relief, replacement lid
11 1/8 x 7 1/2 x 7 1/2 in (28.2 x 19 x 19 cm)
Mark: "WEDGWOOD"
Provenance: Dr. Francis Jennings Vurpillat, South Bend, Ind.
1982.190 a and b
Base has four firing holes.
Color plate 101

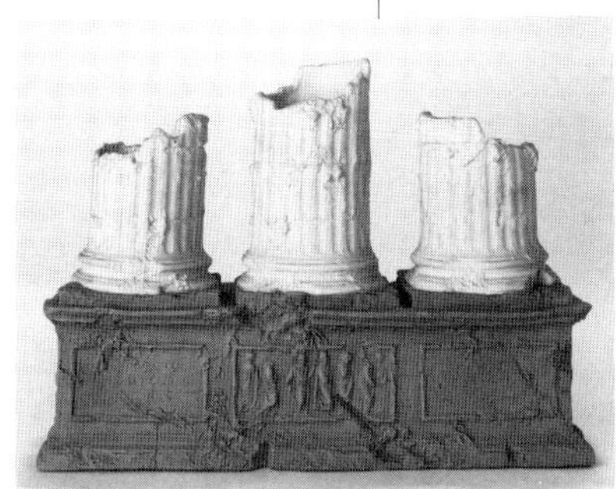

303. Vase: *Ruined Columns*, ca. 1790
Jasper, solid blue and solid white grounds
9 x 4 7/16 x 12 1/3 in (22.8 x 11.2 x 31.4 cm)
Mark: "WEDGWOOD" with tool mark
Provenance: Frederick Rathbone, London; Dr. Francis Jennings Vurpillat, South Bend, Ind.
1983.3
Color plate 106

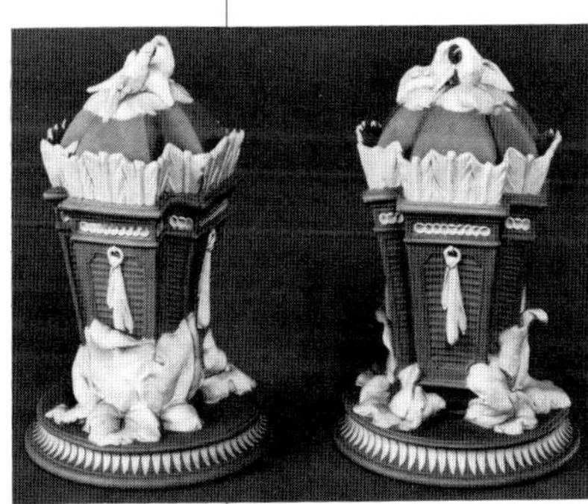
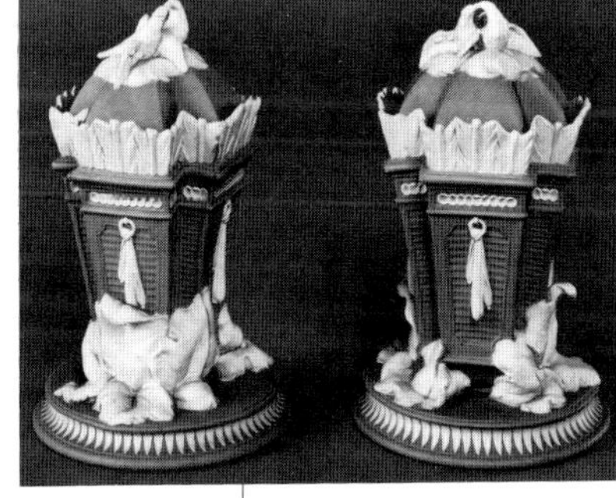

304. Pair of Quiver Vases: ca. 1795
Jasper, solid blue ground with dark blue wash and white relief
8 3/4 x 5 1/2 in (22.2 x 13.9 cm)
Mark: "WEDGWOOD" "O"
Provenance: Dr. Harold L. Klawans, Chicago
1981.256 a and b; 1981.257 a and b
Color plate 108

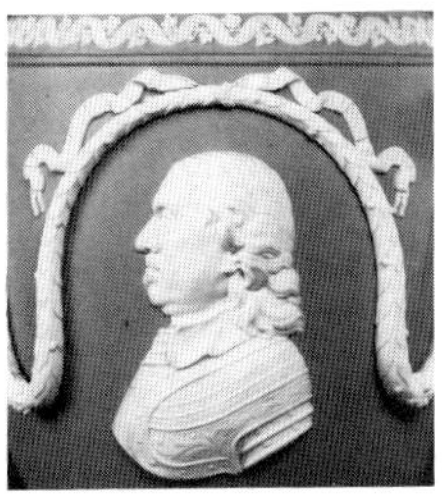
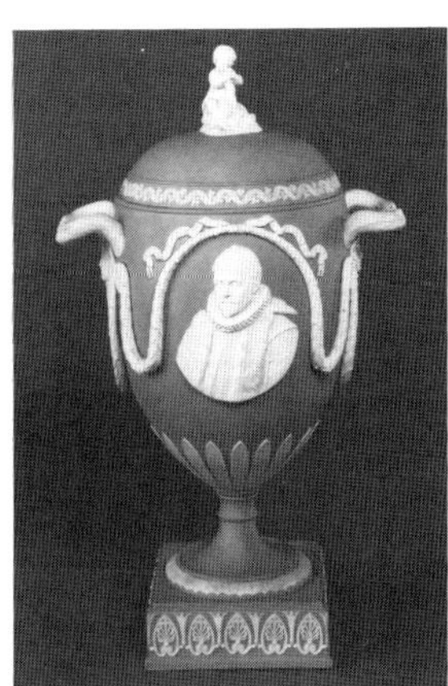

305. Covered Vase: *Oliver Cromwell* and *William I, Prince of Orange,* and *Medusa*, ca. 1800
Jasper, solid blue ground with white relief
13 x 4 1/16 x 4 1/16 in (33 x 10.3 x 10.3 cm)
Mark: "WEDGWOOD" "505" incised with tool mark
Provenance: Dr. Harold L. Klawans, Chicago
1982.192
Base has cavity around bolt.
Color plate 104

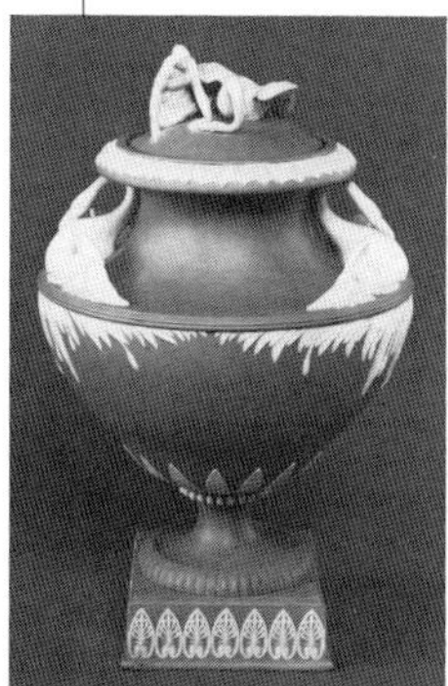

306. Covered Vase: *Leda and the Swan*, ca. 1795
Jasper, solid blue ground with white relief
10 7/8 x 4 13/16 x 4 13/16 in (27.6 x 12.2 x 12.2 cm)
Mark: "WEDGWOOD" "V" incised
Provenance: Dr. Francis Jennings Vurpillat, South Bend, Ind.
1981.266 a and b
Vase has sump cover. Base has threaded cavity around bolt filled with plaster and one firing hole.
Color plate 107

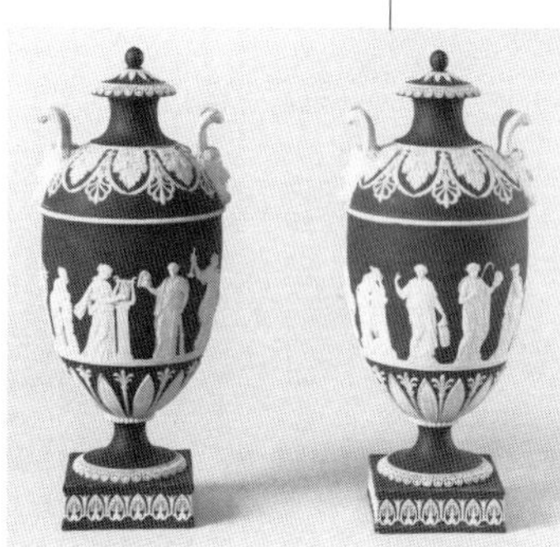

307. Pair of Vases: *Apollo and the Muses*, ca. 1790
Jasper, solid white ground with black wash and white relief
11 3/4 x 3 5/16 x 3 5/16 in (29.8 x 8.4 x 8.4 cm)
Mark: "WEDGWOOD"
Provenance: Otto Wasserman, New York
1982.68 a and b
Each vase has sump cover. Each base has cavity around bolt filled with plaster and eight firing holes.
Color plate 87

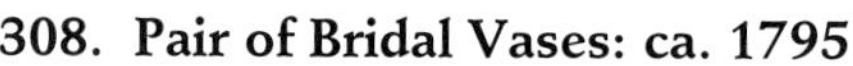

308. Pair of Bridal Vases: ca. 1795
Jasper, solid white ground with black wash and green-and-white relief, engine-turning
7 1/8 x 3 3/4 in (18 x 9.5 cm)
Mark: "WEDGWOOD"
Provenance: Dr. Harold L. Klawans, Chicago
1982.64 a and b

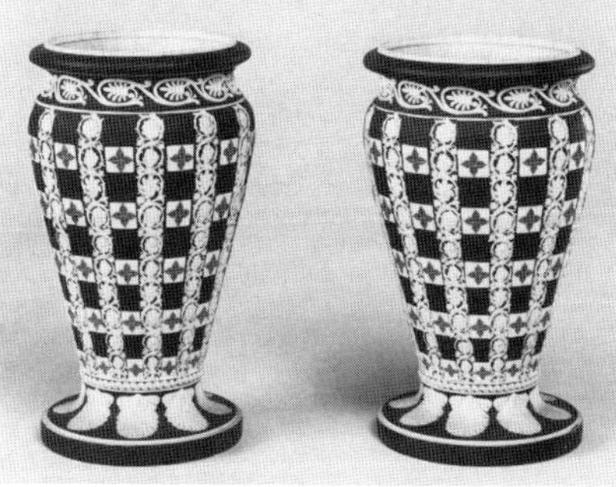

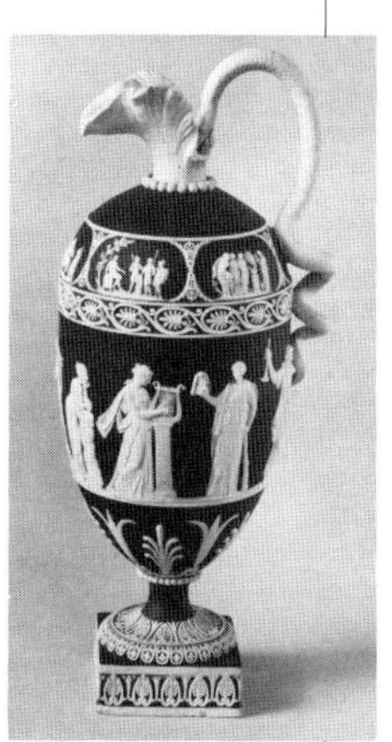

309. Ewer: *Apollo and the Muses*, ca. 1795
Jasper, solid white ground with black wash and white relief
11 1/4 x 2 5/8 x 2 5/8 in (28.5 x 6.6 x 6.6 cm)
Mark: "WEDGWOOD" "H"
Provenance: Dr. Francis Jennings Vurpillat, South Bend, Ind.
1982.69
Base has cavity filled with plaster and eight firing holes.
Color plate 87

310. Covered Vase: *Apotheosis of Virgil*, ca. 1875-85
Jasper, solid white ground with black wash and white relief
23 3/4 x 10 1/4 x 10 1/4 in (60.3 x 26 x 26 cm)
Mark: "WEDGWOOD"
Provenance: Dr. Francis Jennings Vurpillat, South Bend, Ind.
1980.185
Base has four firing holes.
Color plate 97

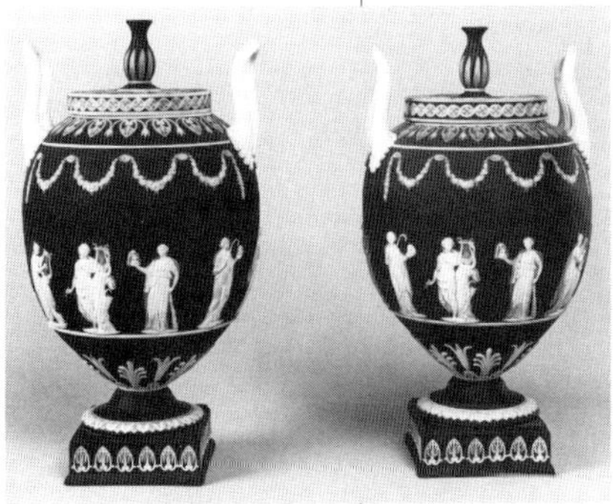

311. Pair of Covered Vases: *Apollo and the Nine Muses*, ca. 1880
Jasper, solid white ground with black wash and white relief
a: 12 x 3 5/8 x 3 5/8 in (30.4 x 9.2 x 9.2 cm);
b: 11 3/4 x 3 5/8 x 3 5/8 in (29.8 x 9.2 x 9.2 cm)
Mark: "WEDGWOOD" "W" twice
Provenance: Purchased in New Orleans
1980.183 a and b
Each base has cavity around bolt and four firing holes.
Color plate 88

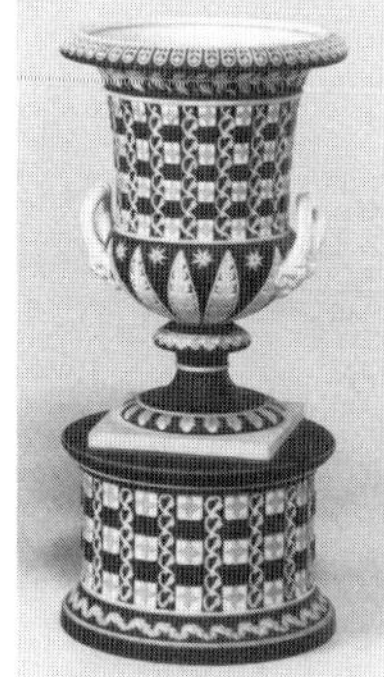

312. Vase on Pedestal, ca. 1800
Jasper, solid white ground with black wash and yellow-and-white relief
6 7/8 x 3 1/4 in (17.4 x 8.2 cm)
Mark: "WEDGWOOD" "O"
Provenance: Knight Collection, Birmingham, Ala.
1982.61

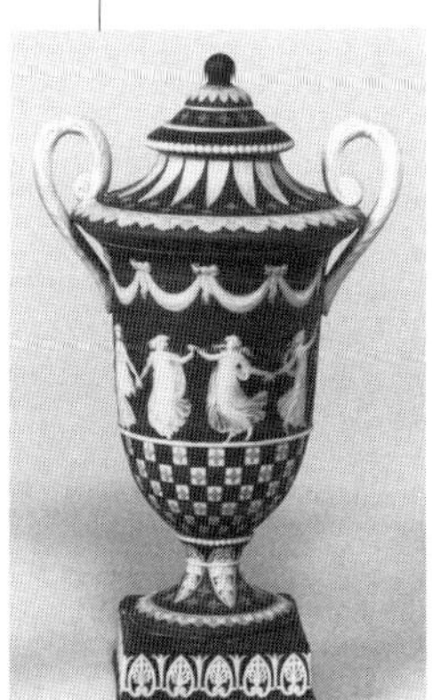

313. Covered Vase: *Dancing Hours*, ca. 1875
Jasper, solid white ground with black wash and yellow-and-white relief
8 3/4 x 2 1/8 x 2 1/8 in (53.2 x 5.3 x 5.3 cm)
Mark: "WEDGWOOD"
Provenance: Dr. Francis Jennings Vurpillat, South Bend, Ind.
1982.63

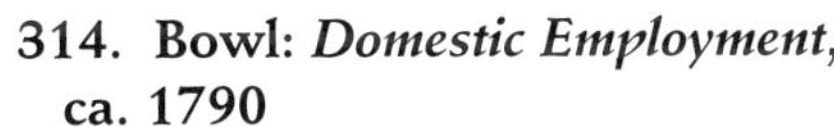

314. Bowl: *Domestic Employment*, ca. 1790
Jasper, solid blue ground with white relief, granulated body
3 3/4 x 3 in (9.5 x 7.6 cm)
Mark: none
Provenance: David Zeitlin, Merion, Pa.
1981.259
Color plate 102

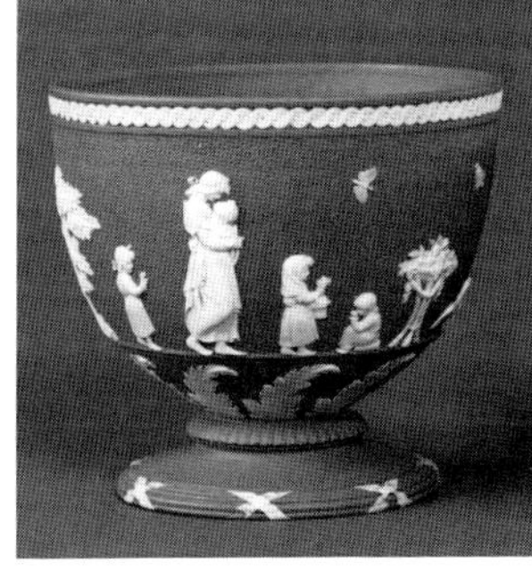

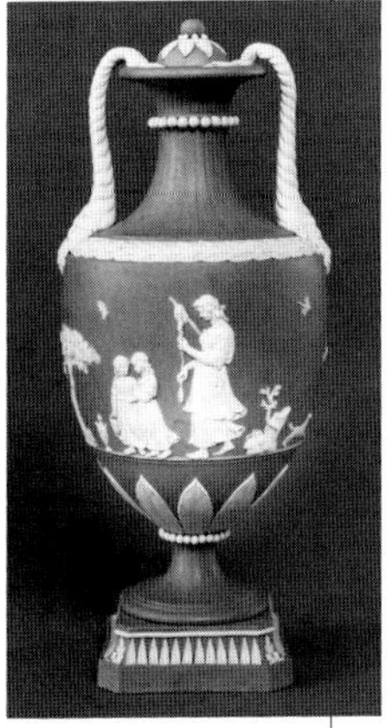

315. Covered Vase: *Domestic Employment*, ca. 1785
Jasper, solid blue ground with white relief, replacement lid
10 5/8 x 3 1/4 x 3 1/4 in (26.9 x 8.2 x 8.2 cm)
Mark: "WEDGWOOD" with tool mark
Provenance: Dr. Francis Jennings Vurpillat, South Bend, Ind.
1982.189
Vase has sump cover. Base has cavity filled with plaster around bolt with one firing hole.
Color plate 102

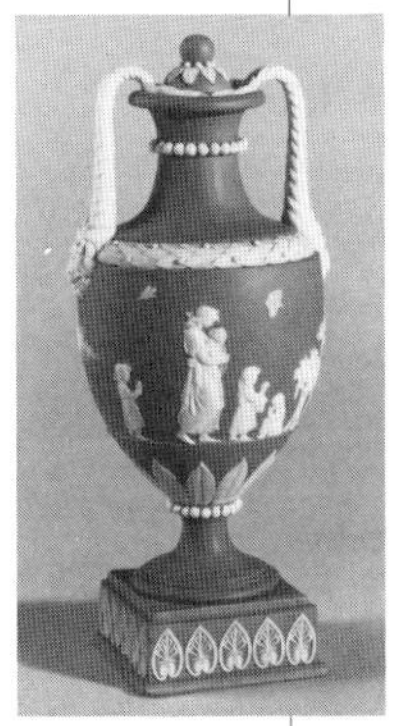

316. Covered Vase: *Domestic Employment*, ca. 1785
Jasper, solid blue ground with white relief, replacement lid
6 15/16 x 2 7/8 x 2 7/8 in (17.6 x 7.3 x 7.3 cm)
Mark: "WEDGWOOD" "T"
Provenance: M. Mellanay Delhom, Chicago; Ann Brodkiewicz, Chicago
1981.258 a and b
Vase has sump cover. Base has cavity around bolt filled with plaster and four firing holes.

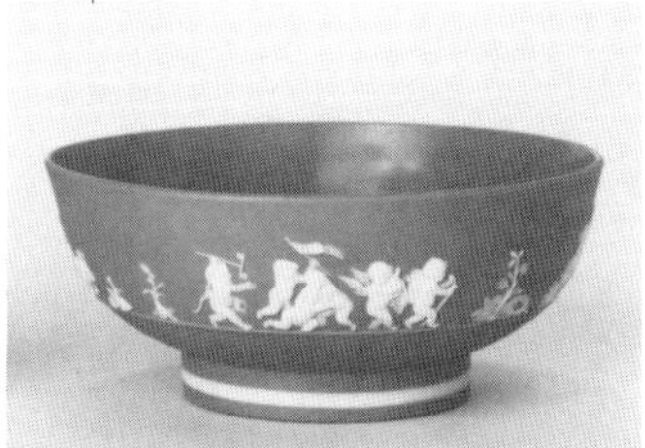

317. Bowl: *Boys at Play*, ca. 1790
Jasper, solid blue ground with white relief and engine-turning
2 1/8 x 2 1/2 in (5.3 x 6.3 cm)
Mark: "Wedgwood" "H" "Z"
Provenance: Dr. Francis Jennings Vurpillat, South Bend, Ind.
1981.234.3
Color plate 129

318. Five-Piece Dejeuner Set: ca. 1790
Jasper, solid blue ground with white relief and engine-turning
Teapot: 4 1/4 x 3 1/4 in (10.7 x 8.2 cm); sugar bowl: 4 1/4 x 1 7/8 in (10.7 x 4.7 cm); pair of cups: 2 x 1 7/16 in (5 x 3.6 cm); creamer: 4 5/16 x 1 3/4 in (10.9 x 4.4 cm); pair of saucers: 5 1/8 in (13 cm)
Mark: "WEDGWOOD" "3" on all pieces
Provenance: Ann Brodkiewicz, Chicago
1981.234.4-.8
Color plates 95 and 129

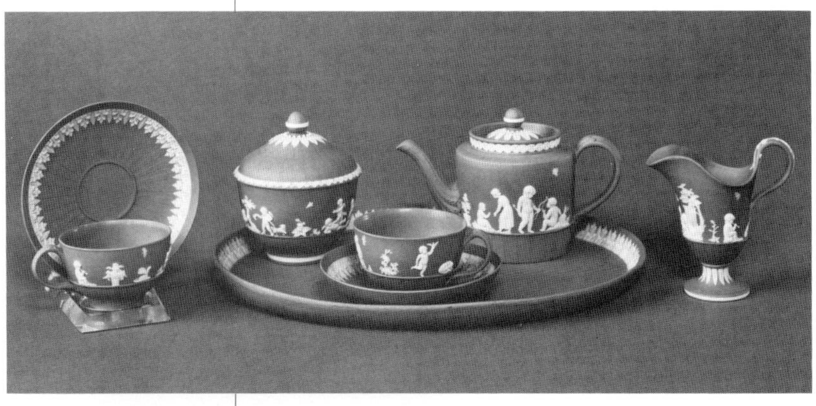

319. Tray for Dejeuner Set: ca. 1790
Jasper, solid blue ground with white relief
1 3/8 x 12 5/8 x 10 1/8 in (3.4 x 32 x 25.7 cm)
Mark: "WEDGWOOD" "W"
Provenance: David Davis, Chicago; Dr. Harold L. Klawans, Chicago
1981.234.1
Color plate 129

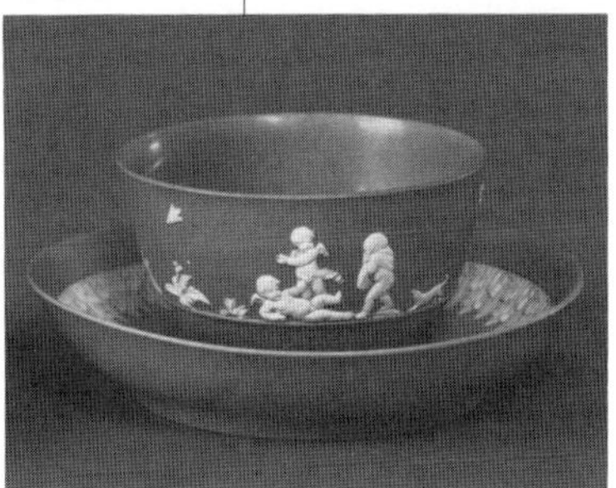

320. Cup and Saucer: ca. 1785
Jasper, solid blue ground with white relief; cup has engine-turning and lapidary-polishing
Cup: 2 1/16 x 1 1/2 in (5.2 x 3.8 cm); saucer: 5 1/16 in (12.8 cm)
Mark: cup: "WEDGWOOD" "3" "X"; saucer: "Wedgwood" "3" "S"
Provenance: Dr. Francis Jennings Vurpillat, South Bend, Ind.
1981.264
Color plate 95

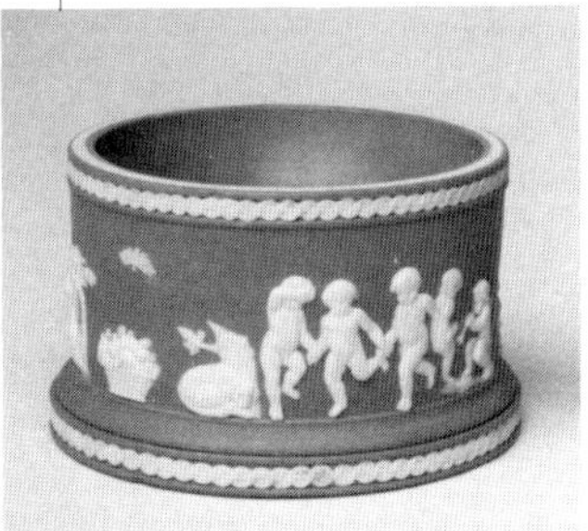

321. Salt Cellar: *Cupids at Play*, ca. 1785
Jasper, solid blue ground with white relief, interior lapidary-polishing
1 15/16 x 3 1/4 in (4.9 x 8.2 cm)
Mark: "WEDGWOOD" "3" "S" incised
Provenance: Dr. Francis Jennings Vurpillat, South Bend, Ind.
1980.147

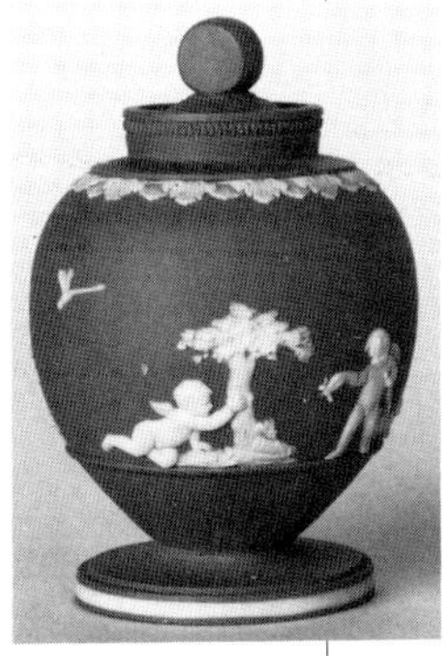

322. Covered Tea Canister: *Cupids at Play*, ca. 1790
Jasper, solid blue with blue wash, white relief, and engine-turning
4 1/2 x 2 3/8 in (11.4 x 6 cm)
Mark: "Wedgwood"
Provenance: Ann Brodkiewicz, Chicago
1981.234.2

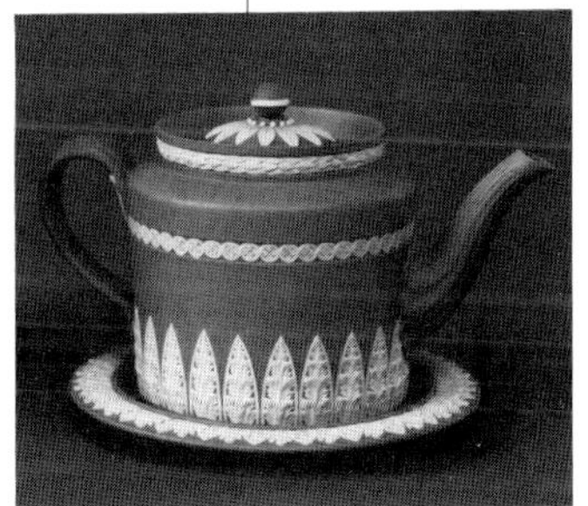

323. Teapot and Stand: *Acanthus*, ca. 1795
Jasper, solid blue ground with white relief
Teapot: 5 1/4 x 4 3/8 in (13.3 x 11.1 cm); stand: 6 7/8 in (17.4 cm)
Mark: "WEDGWOOD" "3" "O"
Provenance: David Davis, Chicago; M. Mellanay Delhom, Chicago; Ann Brodkiewicz, Chicago
1982.23 a, b, and c

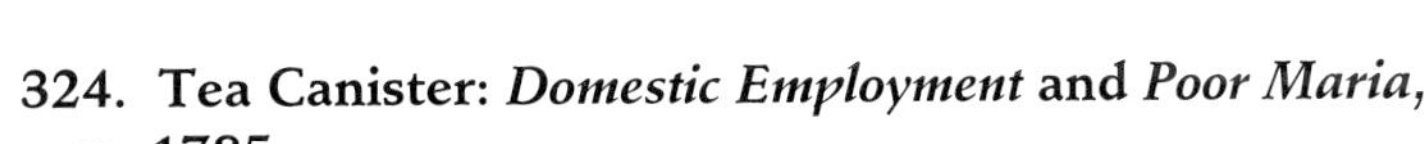

324. Tea Canister: *Domestic Employment* and *Poor Maria*, ca. 1785
Jasper, solid blue ground with white relief and engine-turning
5 1/2 x 2 9/16 in (13.9 x 6.1 cm)
Mark: "WEDGWOOD" "3" "O"
Provenance: M. Mellanay Delhom, Chicago; Dr. Francis Jennings Vurpillat, South Bend, Ind.
1981.261 a and b

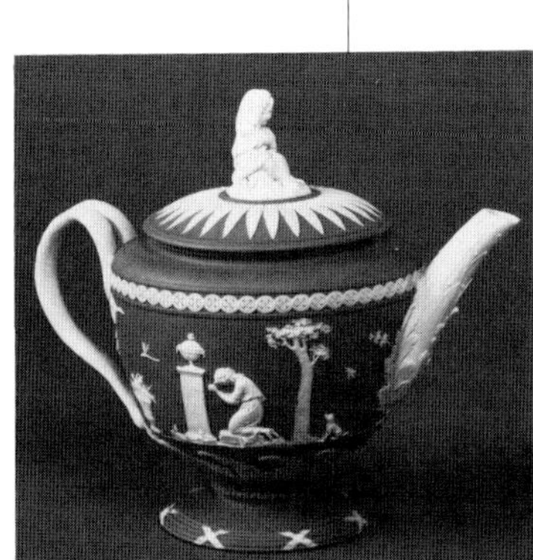

325. Teapot and Stand: *Charlotte Mourning at the Tomb of Werther* and *Maid and Cupid at Play*, ca. 1790
Jasper, solid blue ground with white relief and stippled body
Teapot: 7 7/8 x 3 13/16 in (20 x 9.6 cm); stand: 6 15/16 in (17.6 cm)
Mark: "WEDGWOOD"
Provenance: David Davis, Chicago; Dr. Francis Jennings Vurpillat, South Bend, Ind.
1982.19 a and b
Color plate 103

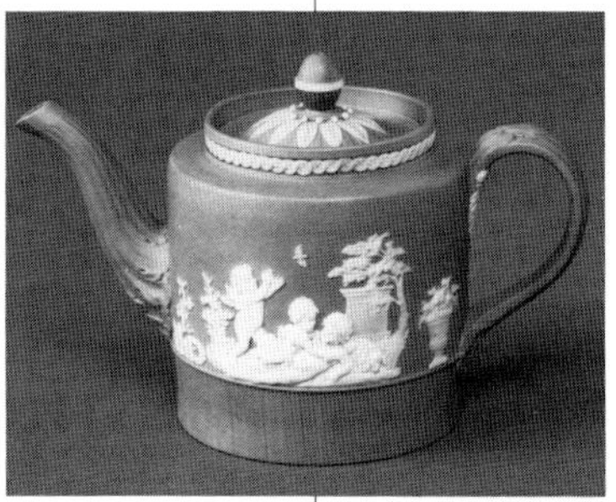

326. Teapot: *Cupids at Play*, ca. 1785
Jasper, solid blue ground with white relief and engine-turning
4 1/4 x 3 5/16 in (10.7 x 8.3 cm)
Mark: "Wedgwood" "Z"
Provenance: Dr. Francis Jennings Vurpillat, South Bend, Ind.
1981.267 a and b

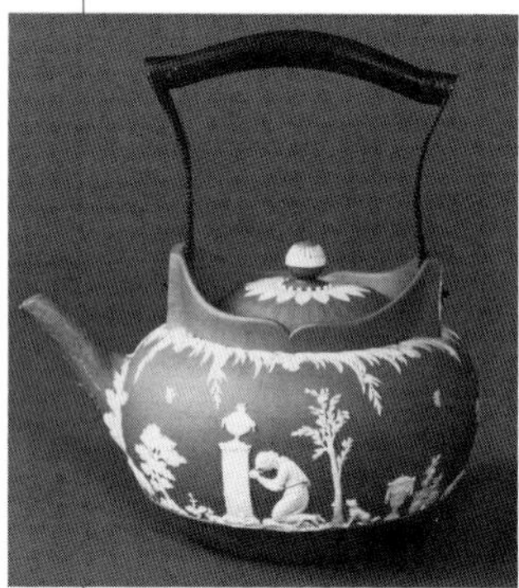

327. Kettle: *Charlotte Mourning at the Tomb of Werther*, ca. 1795
Jasper, solid blue ground with blue wash and white relief, engine-turning; handle: silver and wood
5 3/4 x 7 5/16 in (14.6 x 18.5 cm)
Mark: "WEDGWOOD" with tool marks
Provenance: Ann Brodkiewicz, Chicago
1982.21 a and b
Color plate 103

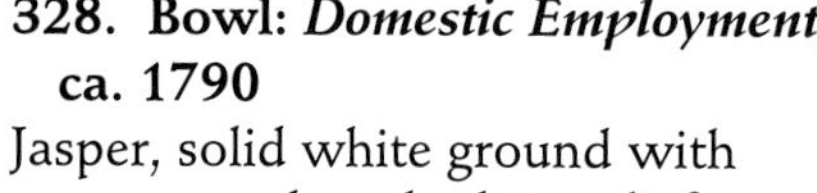

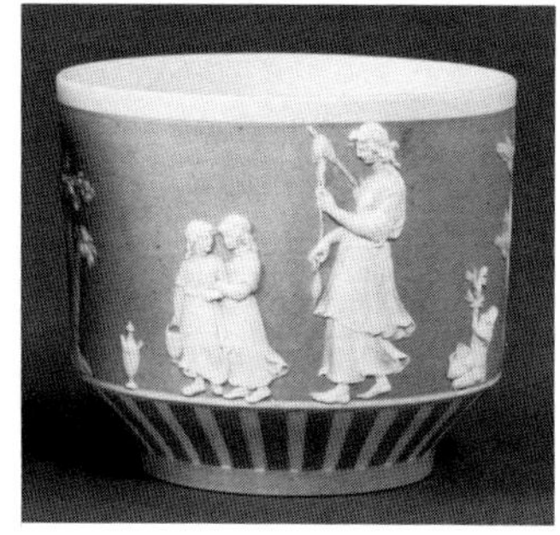

328. Bowl: *Domestic Employment*, ca. 1790
Jasper, solid white ground with green wash and white relief, engine-turning
3 7/16 x 2 9/16 in (8.7 x 6.5 cm)
Mark: "WEDGWOOD" "A"
Provenance: Dr. Francis Jennings Vurpillat, South Bend, Ind.
1980.323
Color plate 102

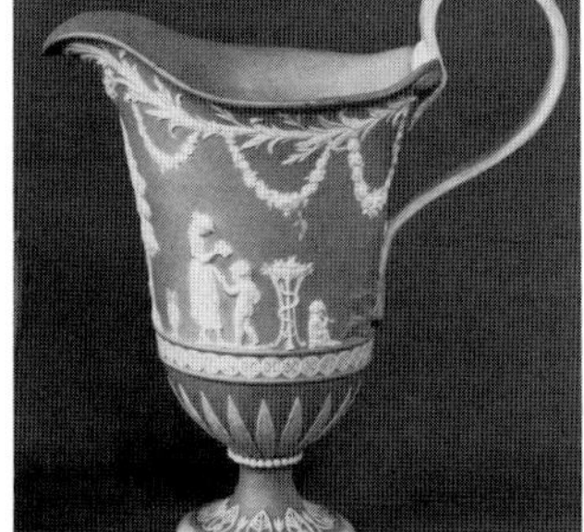

329. Pitcher: *Domestic Employment*, ca. 1790
Jasper, solid lilac ground with white relief
10 x 3 1/4 in (25.4 x 8.2 cm)
Mark: "WEDGWOOD"
Provenance: Dr. Francis Jennings Vurpillat, South Bend, Ind.
1980.298
Color plate 95

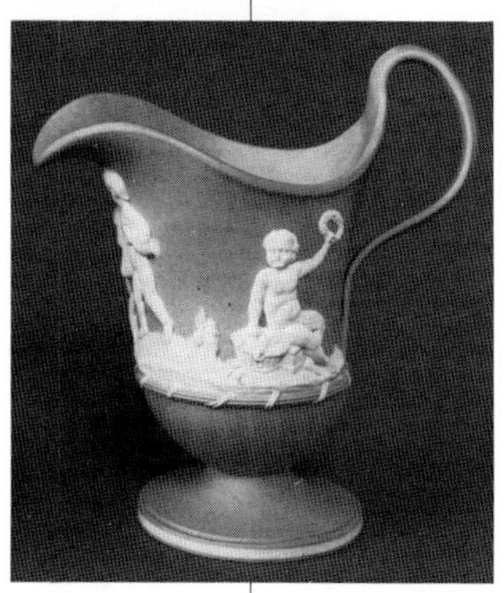

330. Cream Pitcher: *Boys at Play*, ca. 1785
Jasper, solid green ground with white relief
4 13/16 x 2 3/8 in (12.2 x 6 cm)
Mark: "Wedgwood"
Provenance: Dr. Francis Jennings Vurpillat, South Bend, Ind.
1980.322
Color plate 95

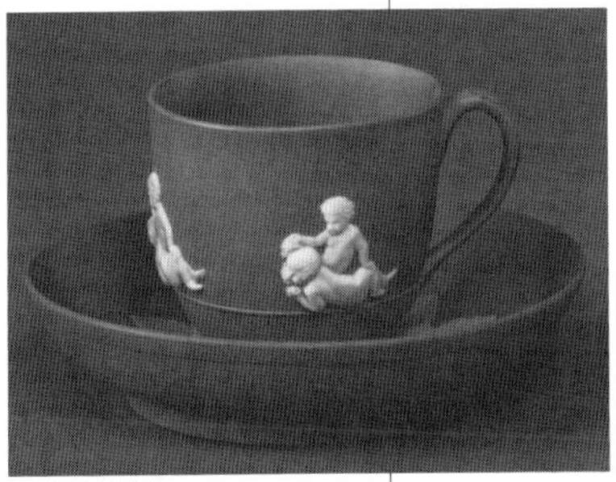

331. Cup and Saucer: *Boys at Play*, ca. 1795
Jasper, solid lilac ground with white relief and engine-turning
Cup: 2 1/2 x 1 3/8 in (6.3 x 3.4 cm); saucer: 5 1/8 in (13 cm)
Mark: cup: "Wedgwood"; saucer: "WEDGWOOD"
Provenance: D. M. and P. Manheim, New York; Dr. Francis Jennings Vurpillat, South Bend, Ind.
1980.300 a and b

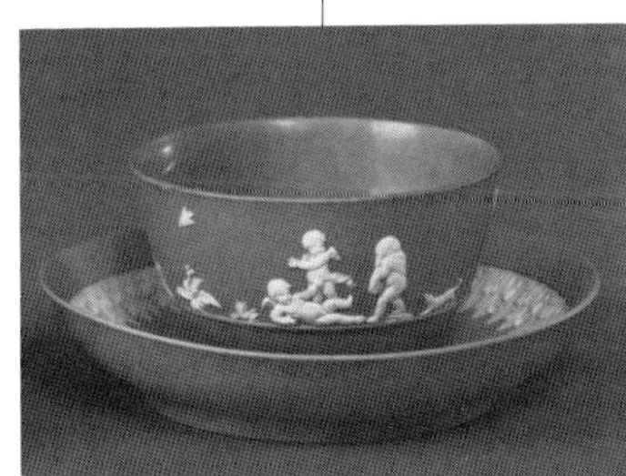

332. Cup and Saucer: *Cupids at Play*, ca. 1790
Jasper, solid blue ground with white relief and engine-turning; cup has interior lapidary-polishing
Cup: 1 5/8 x 1 1/2 in (4.1 x 3.8 cm); saucer: 5 1/16 in (12.8 cm)
Mark: "Wedgwood"
Provenance: Sir George Duff-Dunbar, Scotland; Ann Brodkiewicz, Chicago
1981.265 a and b

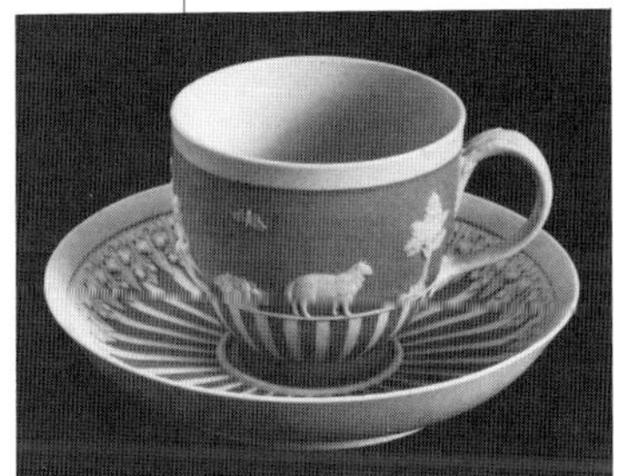

333. Cup and Saucer: *Domestic Employment*, ca. 1790
Jasper, solid white ground with lilac wash, white relief, and engine-turning; cup has interior lapidary-polishing
Cup: 2 1/2 x 1 3/8 in (6.3 x 3.4 cm); saucer: 5 in (12.7 cm)
Provenance: David Davis, Chicago; Ann Brodkiewicz, Chicago
1980.302 a and b

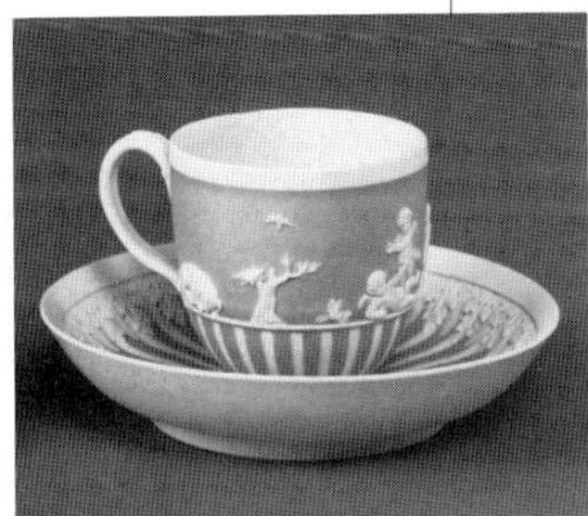

334. Cup and Saucer: *Cupids at Play*, ca. 1785
Jasper, solid white ground with green wash and white relief, cup has engine-turning and interior lapidary-polishing
Cup: 1 7/8 x 1 1/2 in (4.7 x 3.8 cm); saucer: 5 1/2 in (13.9 cm)
Mark: "Wedgwood"
Provenance: M. Mellanay Delhom, Chicago; Ann Brodkiewicz, Chicago
1980.326 a and b
Color plate 95

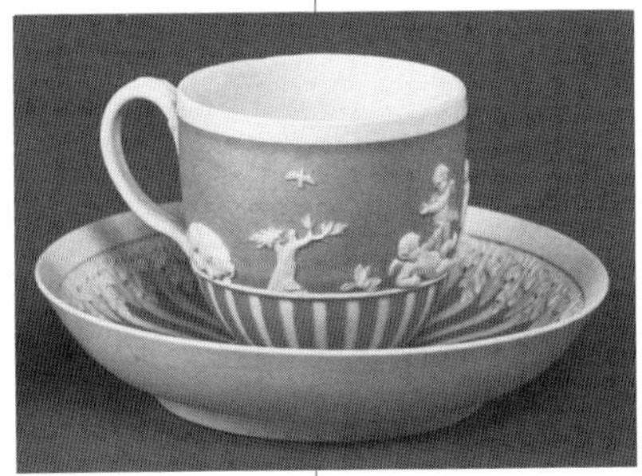

335. Cup and Saucer: *Cupids at Play*, ca. 1790
Jasper, solid white ground with lilac wash, white relief, and engine-turning; cup has interior lapidary-polishing
Cup: 2 3/8 x 1 5/16 in (6 x 3.3 cm); saucer: 5 in (12.7 cm)
Mark: cup: "WEDGWOOD" "3" "O"; saucer: "WEDGWOOD" "3" "S"
Provenance: Otto Wasserman, New York
1980.301 a and b
Color plate 95

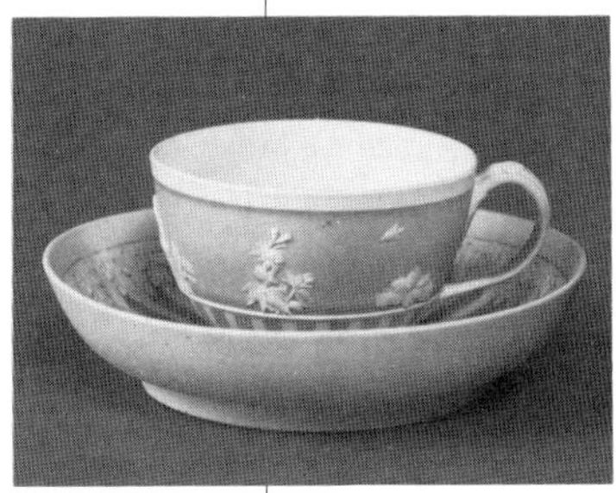

336. Cup and Saucer: *Domestic Employment*, ca. 1785
Jasper, solid white ground with green wash and white relief; cup has interior lapidary-polishing
Cup: 2 1/4 x 1 3/8 in (5.7 x 3.4 cm); saucer: 5 1/8 in (13 cm)
Mark: "WEDGWOOD" "3"
Provenance: Allman Collection, England; Dr. Francis Jennings Vurpillat, South Bend, Ind.
1980.327 a and b

337. Trophy Plate with Quatrefoil: *Bellerophon Watering Pegasus*, ca. 1880
Jasper, solid white ground with green wash and yellow-and-white relief
8 9/16 in (21.7 cm)
Mark: "WEDGWOOD" with tool marks
Provenance: Dr. Francis Jennings Vurpillat, South Bend, Ind.
1982.67
Color plate 126

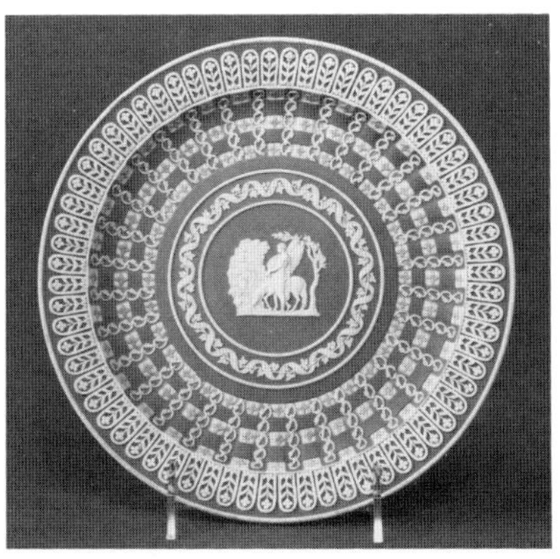

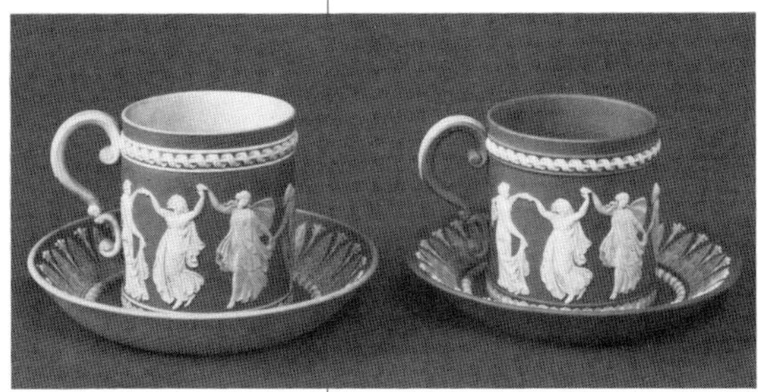

338. Cup and Saucer: *Dancing Hours*, 19th century
Jasper, solid white ground with green wash and white relief
Cup: 3 x 2 in (7.6 x 5 cm); saucer: 5 in (12.7 cm)
Mark: cup: "WEDGWOOD" "C" with tool mark; saucer: none
Provenance: Dr. Francis Jennings Vurpillat, South Bend, Ind.
1980.314 a and b

339. Cup and Saucer: *Dancing Hours*, 19th century
Jasper, solid blue ground with white relief
Cup: 2 9/16 x 2 9/16 in (6.5 x 6.5 cm); saucer: 5 1/16 in (12.8 cm)
Mark: "WEDGWOOD" with tool marks
Provenance: Otto Wasserman, New York
1982.4 a and b

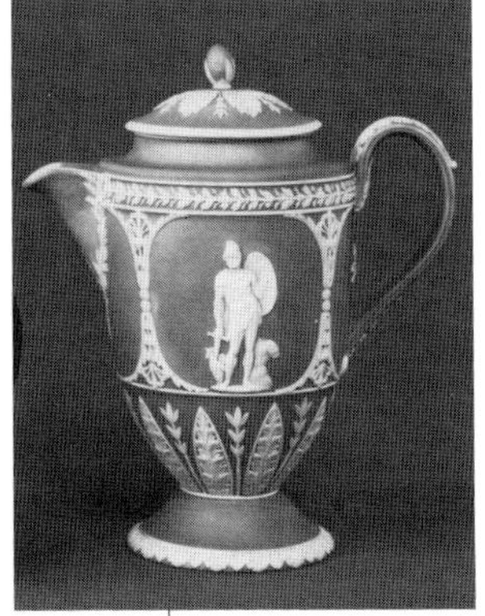

340. Coffeepot: *Hope and Warrior*, 19th century
Jasper, solid white ground with green wash and white relief
8 1/4 x 3 3/8 in (20.9 x 8.5 cm)
Mark: "WEDGWOOD" "Z"
Provenance: Sir George Duff-Dunbar, Scotland; M. Mellanay Delhom, Chicago; Dr. Francis Jennings Vurpillat, South Bend, Ind.
1980.337 a and b

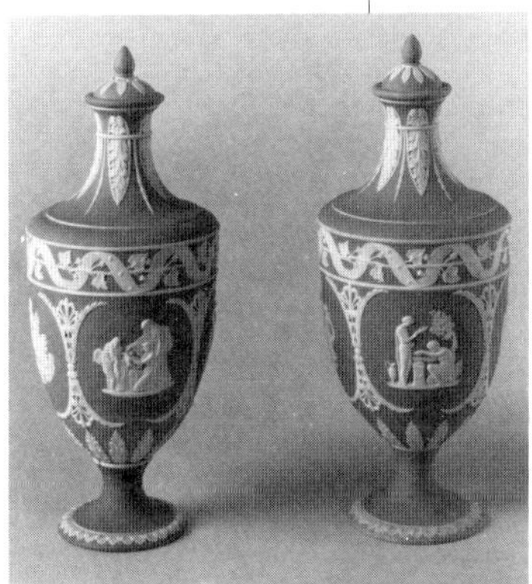

341. Pair of Covered Vases: *Classical Figures*, 19th century
Jasper, solid white ground with green wash and white relief
a: 9 13/16 x 2 7/8 in (23.3 x 7.3 cm); b: 9 11/16 x 2 7/8 in (24.6 x 7.3 cm)
Mark: a: "WEDGWOOD" "B"; b: "WEDGWOOD" "A 10"
Provenance: Purchased in New York
1980.315 a and b; 1980.316 a and b

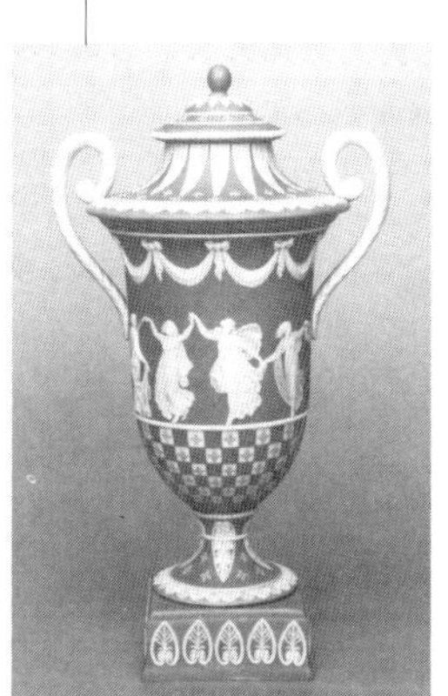

342. Covered Vase: *Dancing Hours*, ca. 1800
Jasper, solid white ground with green wash and blue-and-white relief
8 3/4 x 2 7/16 x 2 7/16 in (22.2 x 6.1 x 6.1 cm)
Mark: "WEDGWOOD"
Provenance: Ann Brodkiewicz, Chicago
1980.235
Base has cavity around bolt and two firing holes.

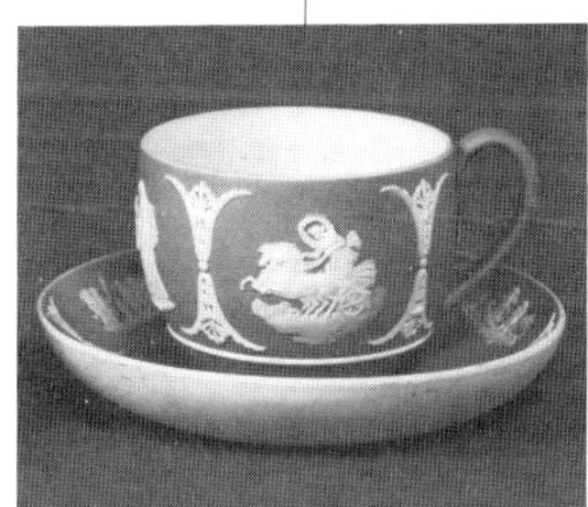
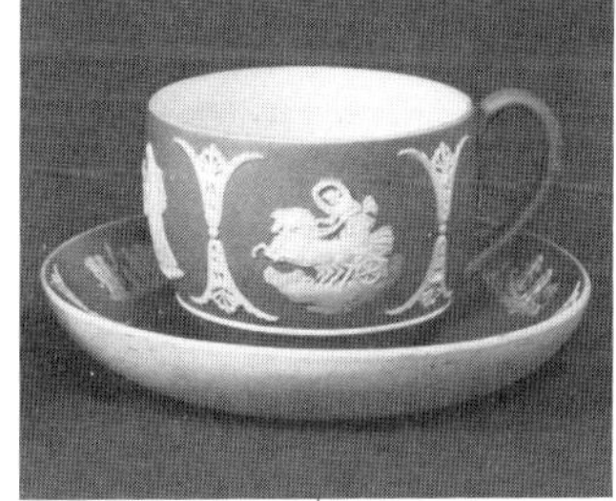

343. Cup and Saucer: *Classical Figures*, 19th century
Jasper, solid white ground with lilac wash and white relief, cup has interior glaze
Cup: 2 3/8 x 2 in (6 x 5 cm); saucer: 5 5/8 in (14.2 cm)
Mark: "WEDGWOOD" "C" "N"
Provenance: David Davis, Chicago
1978.120 a and b

344. Teapot: *Acanthus*, ca. 1790
Jasper, solid white ground with lilac wash and white relief
4 3/8 x 4 3/16 in (11.1 x 10.6 cm)
Mark: "WEDGWOOD"
Provenance: Sir George Duff-Dunbar, Scotland; Dr. Francis Jennings Vurpillat, South Bend, Ind.
1978.130 a and b

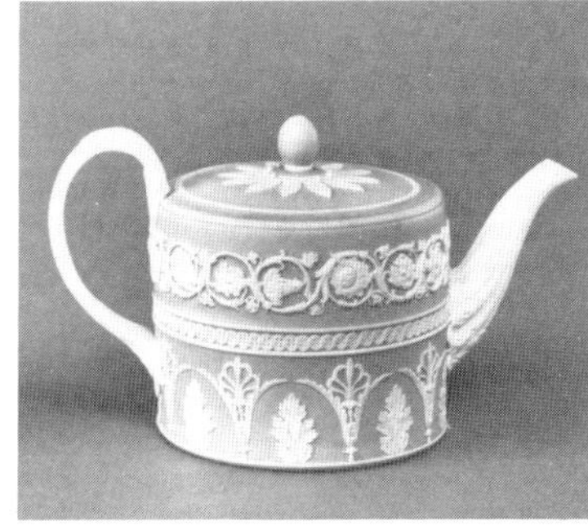

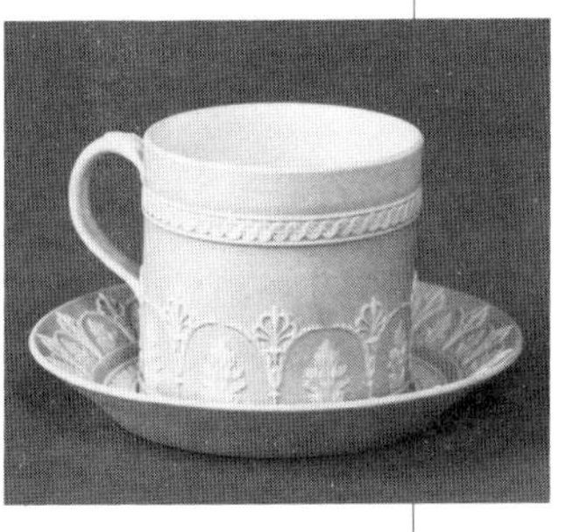

345. Cup and Saucer: *Acanthus*, ca. 1800
Jasper, solid white ground with lilac wash and white relief; cup has interior lapidary-polishing.
Cup: 2 1/2 x 2 11/16 in (6.3 x 6.8 cm); saucer: 4 3/4 in (12 cm)
Mark: cup: "WEDGWOOD" "3" "H"; saucer: "WEDGWOOD" "3"
Provenance: Dr. Francis Jennings Vurpillat, South Bend, Ind.
1978.125 a and b

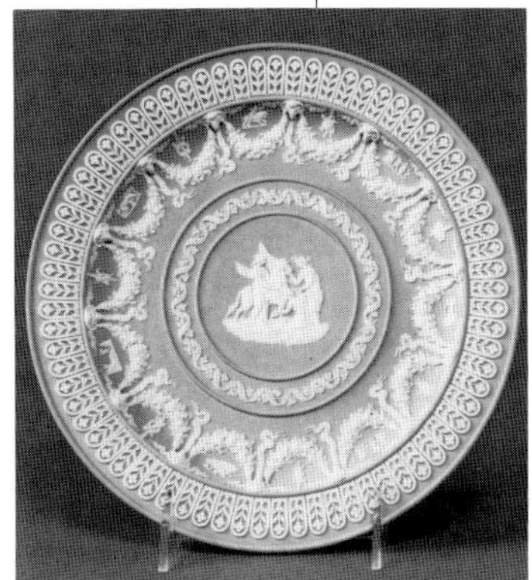

346. Trophy Plate: ***Muses Grooming Pegasus*****, ca. 1880**
Jasper, solid blue ground with white relief
8 13/16 in (22.3 cm)
Mark: "WEDGWOOD" "H" with tool marks
Provenance: D. M. and P. Manheim, New York
1981.262

347. Trophy Plate with Quatrefoil: ***Bellerophon Watering Pegasus*****, ca. 1880**
Jasper, solid white ground with black wash and white relief
8 3/8 in (21.2 cm)
Mark: "WEDGWOOD" with tool mark
Provenance: M. Close Collection, England; Dr. Harold L. Klawans, Chicago
1982.66

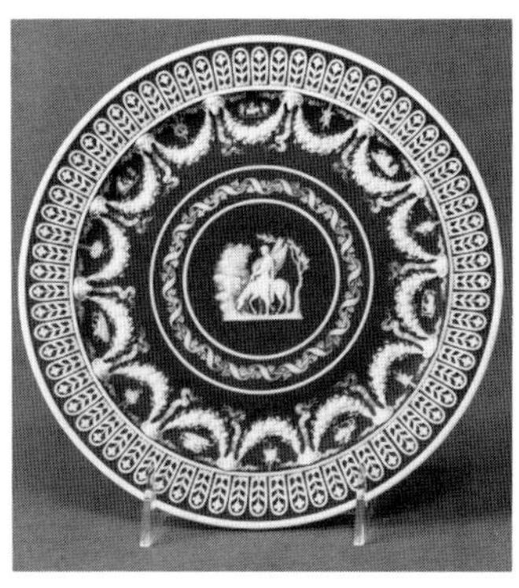

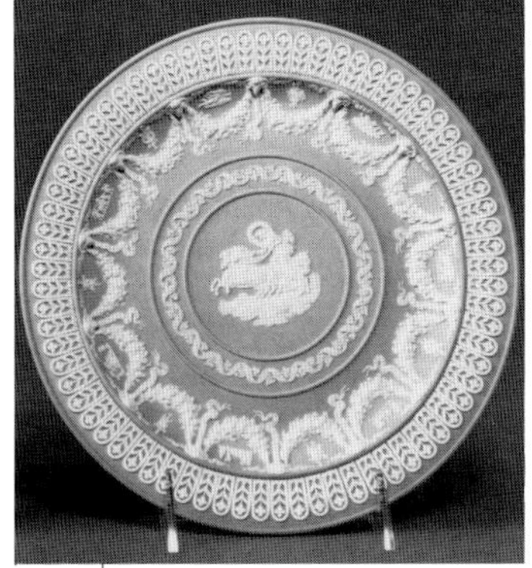

348. Trophy Plate: ***Aurora in Her Chariot*****, ca. 1880**
Jasper, solid blue ground with white relief
8 13/16 in (22.3 cm)
Mark: "WEDGWOOD" "H" with tool marks
Provenance: D. M. and P. Manheim, New York
1981.263
Color plate 126

349. Seven-Piece Dejeuner Set: 19th century
Jasper, solid blue ground with white relief
Tray: 15 1/4 in (38.7 cm);
sugar bowl: 3 9/16 x 2 in (9 x 5 cm);
creamer: 2 1/2 x 1 7/8 in (6.3 x 4.7 cm);
pair of cups: 2 3/8 x 1 5/8 in (6 x 4.1 cm);
pair of saucers: 5 7/16 in (13.8 cm);
waster: 2 5/16 x 1 1/2 in (5.8 x 3.8 cm)
Mark: tray: "WEDGWOOD" "L";
sugar bowl: "WEDGWOOD" "YZX";
creamer: "WEDGWOOD" "YZX" "N";
teapot: "WEDGWOOD" "YZX";
cups: "WEDGWOOD";
saucers: "WEDGWOOD" "V";
waster: "WEDGWOOD" "L" "V"
Provenance: Tray, sugar bowl, creamer: Dr. Francis Jennings Vurpillat, South Bend, Ind.; teapot, waster, cups, and saucers: Purchased in Oslo, Norway
1985.444.1-.7
Color plate 130

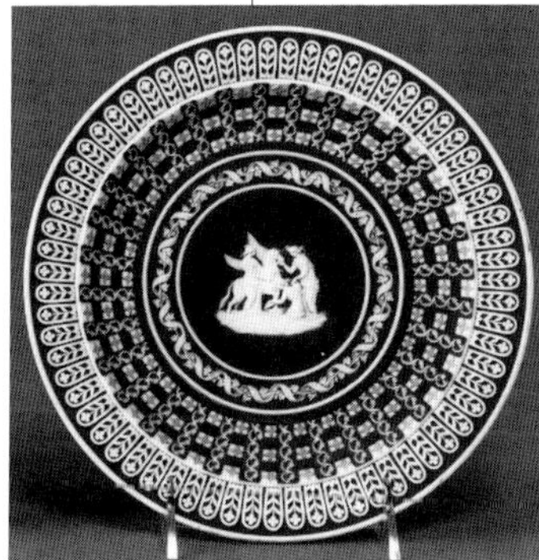

350. Trophy Plate with Quatrefoil: ***Muses Grooming Pegasus,*** **ca. 1880**
Jasper, solid white ground with black wash and yellow-and-white relief
8 3/4 in (22.2 cm)
Mark: "WEDGWOOD" with tool marks
Provenance: Knight Collection, Birmingham, Ala.
1980.338
Color plate 126

351. Cup and Saucer: ***Classical Figures and Swags,*** **ca. 1860**
Jasper, solid blue ground with lilac-and-white relief
Cup: 2 9/16 x 2 1/2 in (6.5 x 6.3 cm); saucer: 5 1/4 in (13.3 cm)
Mark: cup: "WEDGWOOD" with tool marks; saucer: "WEDGWOOD" with tool marks
Provenance: Henry Stern's, New Orleans
1981.236 a and b

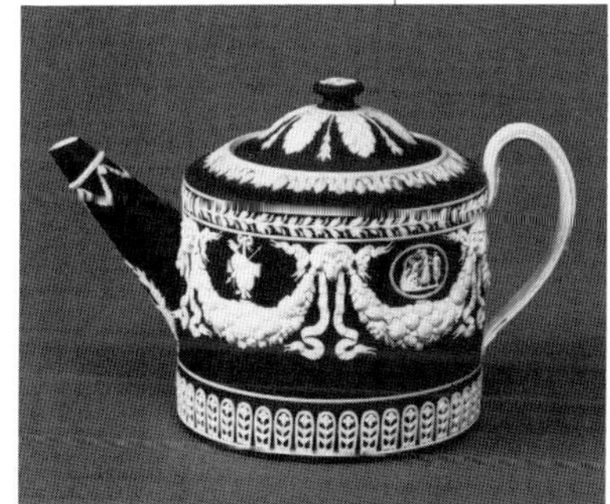

352. Teapot: ***Classical Figures and Swags,*** **ca. 1810**
Jasper, solid white ground with black wash and white relief
5 1/2 x 5 1/8 in (13.9 x 13 cm)
Mark: "WEDGWOOD" with tool mark
Provenance: unknown
1982.62 a and b

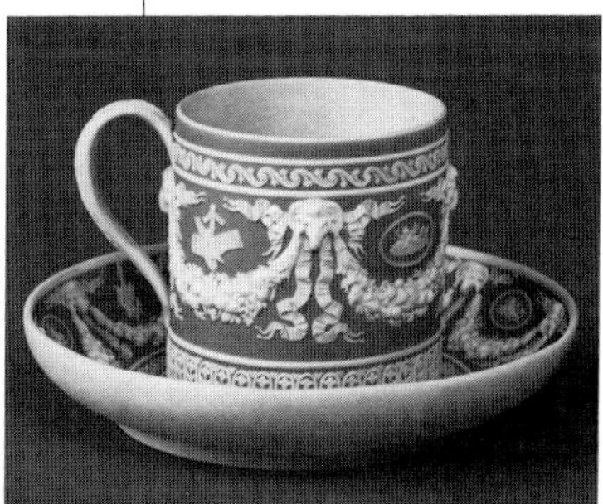

353. Cup and Saucer: ***Classical Figures and Swags,*** **ca. 1860**
Jasper, solid white ground with green wash and lilac relief
Cup: 2 3/4 x 2 1/2 in (6.9 x 6.3 cm); saucer: 5 1/4 in (11.5 cm)
Mark: "WEDGWOOD"
Provenance: Dr. Francis Jennings Vurpillat, South Bend, Ind.
1980.318 a and b

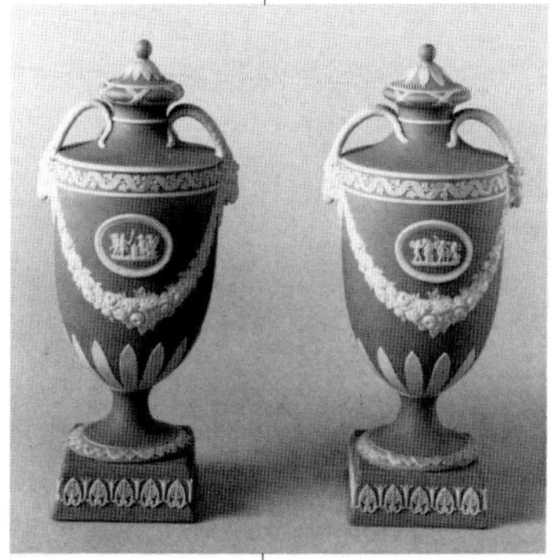

354. Pair of Covered Vases: ***Marriage of Cupid and Psyche*** **and** ***Sacrifice to Hymen,*** **19th century**
Jasper, solid white ground with green wash and lilac-and-white relief
a: 10 1/4 x 3 3/16 x 3 3/16 in (26 x 8 x 8 cm); b: 10 3/8 x 3 3/16 x 3 3/16 in (26.3 x 8 x 8 cm)
Mark: "WEDGWOOD"
Provenance: Toby House, New York
1980.332 a and b
Each vase has cavity around bolt and two firing holes.

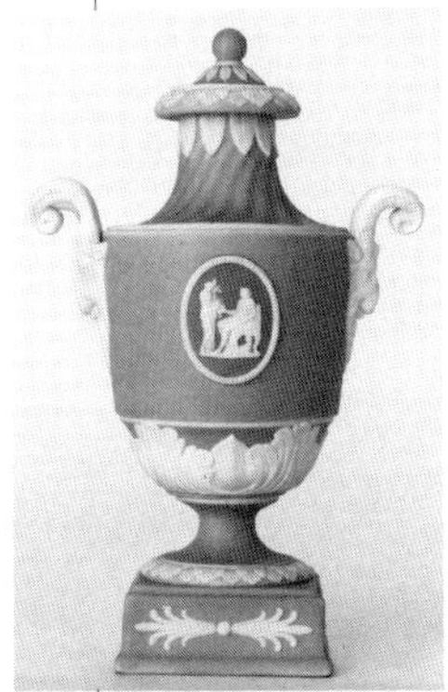

355. Covered Vase: *Aesculapius and Hygeia,* ca. 1800
Jasper, solid white ground with lilac wash and green-and-white relief
5 3/4 x 1 15/16 x 1 15/16 in (14.6 x 4.9 x 4.9 cm)
Mark: "WEDGWOOD"
Provenance: Dr. Francis Jennings Vurpillat, South Bend, Ind.
1978.121 a and b
Base is hollow.

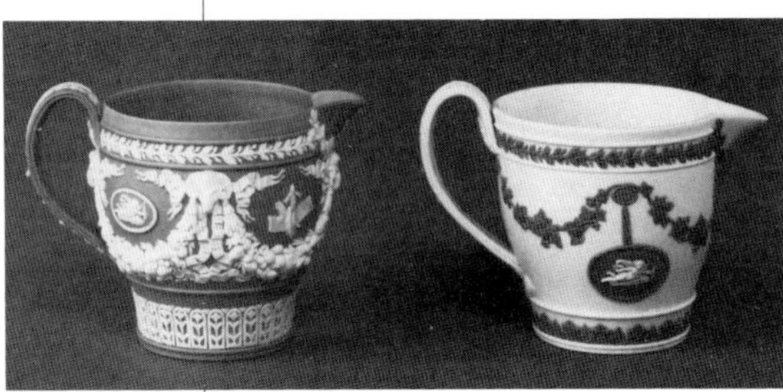

356. Cream Pitcher: *Classical Figures and Swags,* ca. 1860
Jasper, solid blue ground with lilac-and-white relief
2 5/8 x 1 3/4 in (6.6 x 4.4 cm)
Mark: "WEDGWOOD" "O" with tool marks
Provenance: Dr. Harold L. Klawans, Chicago
1981.235

357. Cream Pitcher: *Classical Figures and Swags,* ca. 1880
Jasper, solid white ground with green-and-lilac relief
2 1/2 x 1 3/4 in (6.3 x 4.4 cm)
Mark: "WEDGWOOD"
Provenance: Dr. Harold L. Klawans, Chicago
1980.335

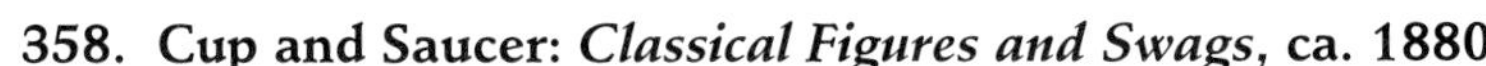

358. Cup and Saucer: *Classical Figures and Swags,* ca. 1880
Jasper, solid white ground with green-and-lilac relief
Cup: 2 1/2 x 2 3/8 in (6.3 x 6 cm); saucer: 5 3/8 in (13.6 cm)
Mark: cup: "WEDGWOOD" "DFV"; saucer: "WEDGWOOD"
Provenance: M. Close Collection, England; Dr. Harold L. Klawans, Chicago
1980.334 a and b

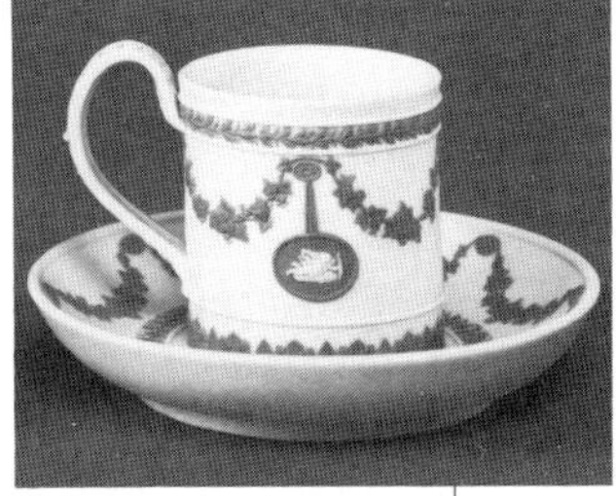

359. Cup and Saucer: *Classical Figures and Swags,* ca. 1880
Jasper, solid white ground with green-and-lilac relief
Cup: 2 13/16 x 2 7/16 in (7.1 x 6.1 cm); saucer: 5 5/16 in (13.4 cm)
Mark: cup: "WEDGWOOD"; saucer: "WEDGWOOD"
Provenance: Dr. Francis Jennings Vurpillat, South Bend, Ind.
1980.336 a and b

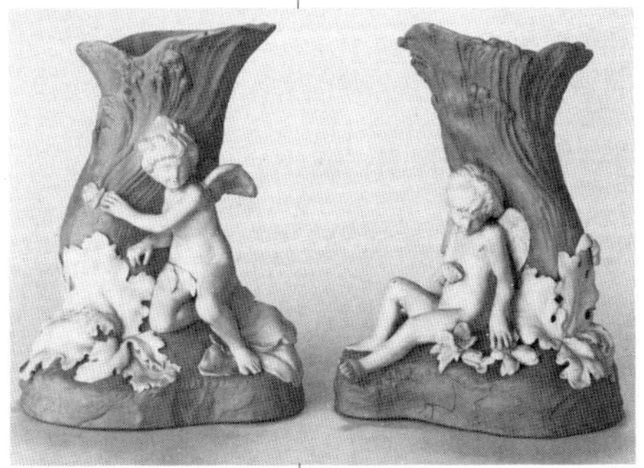

360. Pair of Vases: *Cupid with a Butterfly* and *Cupid with a Bird's Nest,* ca. 1785
Jasper, solid green ground with solid white figures
8 1/2 x 4 3/4 x 6 3/8 in (21.5 x 12 x 16.2 cm)
Mark: "WEDGWOOD"
Provenance: J. Tulk Collection, England; Dr. Francis Jennings Vurpillat, South Bend, Ind.
1980.321 a and b
Color plate 109

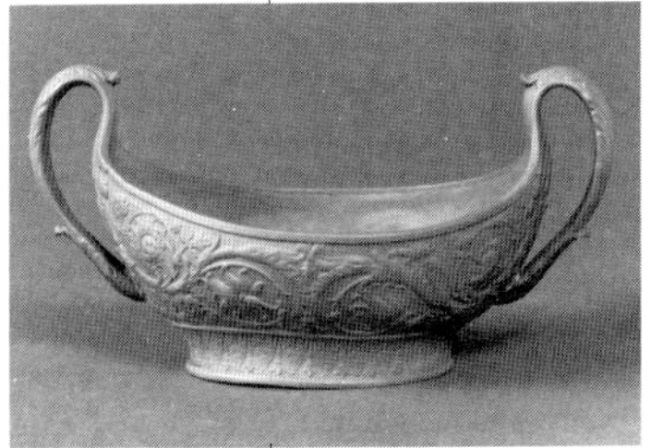

361. Bowl: *Roman Scroll and Flowers*, 19th century
Jasper, solid green ground with granulated surface
3 7/8 x 7 7/16 x 3 3/4 in (9.8 x 18.8 x 9.5 cm)
Mark: "WEDGWOOD"
Provenance: Dr. Francis Jennings Vurpillat, South Bend, Ind.
1980.312

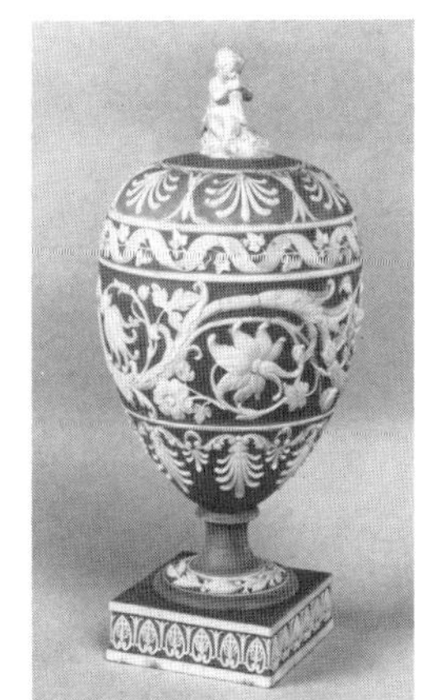

362. Covered Vase: Roman Scroll and Flowers, ca. 1795
Jasper or white stoneware, solid white ground with green wash and white relief
8 3/8 x 2 1/2 x 2 1/2 in (21.2 x 6.3 x 6.3 cm)
Mark: "WEDGWOOD" "H"
Provenance: Fred J. Tongue, Santa Monica, Calif.; Dr. Francis Jennings Vurpillat, South Bend, Ind.
1980.331
Vase has sump cover. Base has cavity around bolt filled with plaster and four firing holes.
Color plate 133

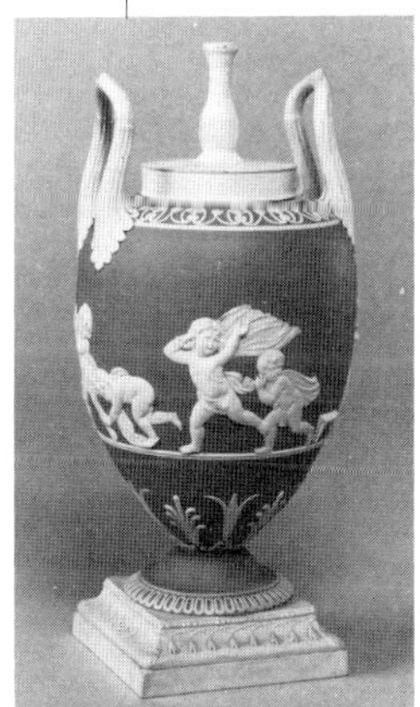

363. Covered Vase: *Blind Man's Bluff*, ca. 1790
Jasper, solid white ground with green wash and white relief, replacement lid
10 3/4 x 4 x 4 in (27.3 x 10.1 x 10.1 cm)
Mark: "WEDGWOOD"
Provenance: David Davis, Chicago; Dr. Francis Jennings Vurpillat, South Bend, Ind.
1980.324
Vase has sump cover. Base has cavity around bolt filled with plaster and one firing hole.

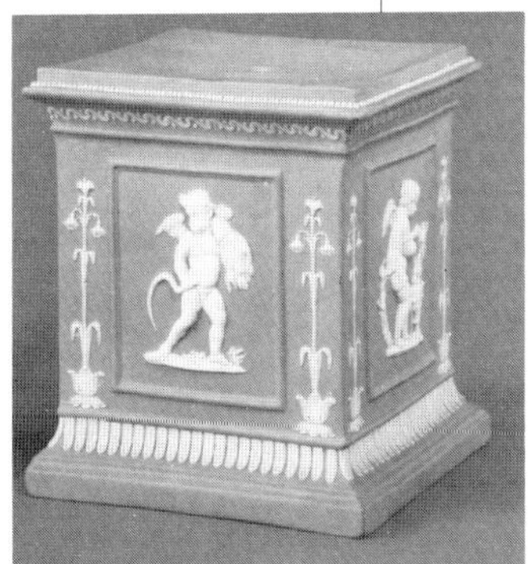

364. Pedestal: ca. 1785
Jasper, solid blue ground with blue wash and white relief
6 x 5 5/16 x 5 5/16 in (15.2 x 13.4 x 13.4 cm)
Mark: "WEDGWOOD"
Provenance: Dr. Harold L. Klawans, Chicago
1981.250

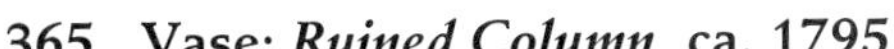

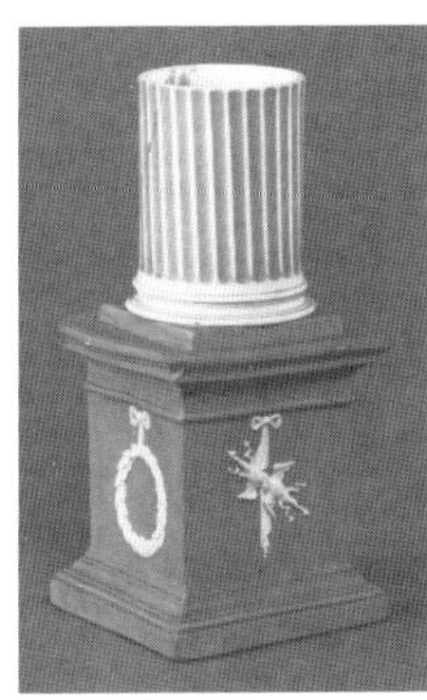

365. Vase: *Ruined Column*, ca. 1795
Jasper, solid blue ground with white relief on base; solid white ground with blue wash on column
6 3/16 x 3 x 3 in (15.7 x 7.6 x 7.6 cm)
Mark: "WEDGWOOD" "V"
Provenance: Dr. Harold L. Klawans, Chicago
1981.276
Color plate 105

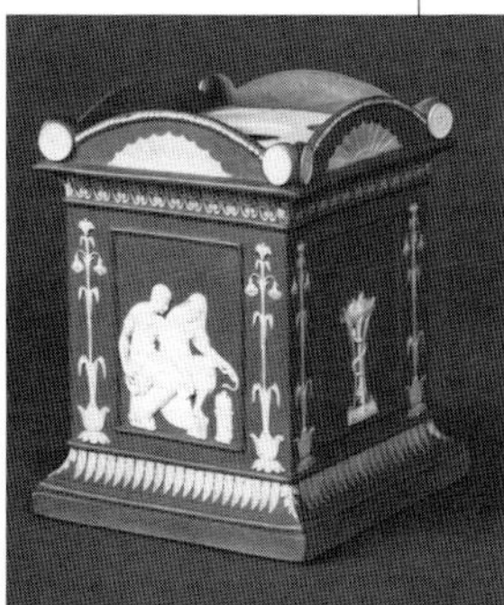

366. Bulb Pot: *Nemesis, Aesculapius, and Diomedes,* ca. 1790
Jasper, solid blue ground with white relief, solid white fitments
6 x 4 3/4 x 4 3/4 in (15.2 x 12 x 12 cm)
Mark: "WEDGWOOD" "M"
Provenance: Ann Brodkiewicz, Chicago
1981.273 a and b

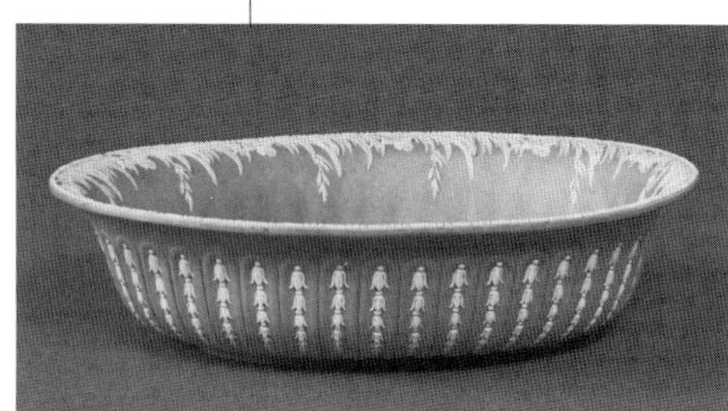

367. Bowl: *Bellflowers and Aquatic Plants,* ca. 1785
Jasper, solid lilac ground with white relief
3 1/4 x 13 x 10 5/16 in (8.2 x 33 x 27 cm)
Mark: "WEDGWOOD"
Provenance: D. M. and P. Manheim, New York; Dr. Francis Jennings Vurpillat, South Bend, Ind.
1980.305
Color plate 127

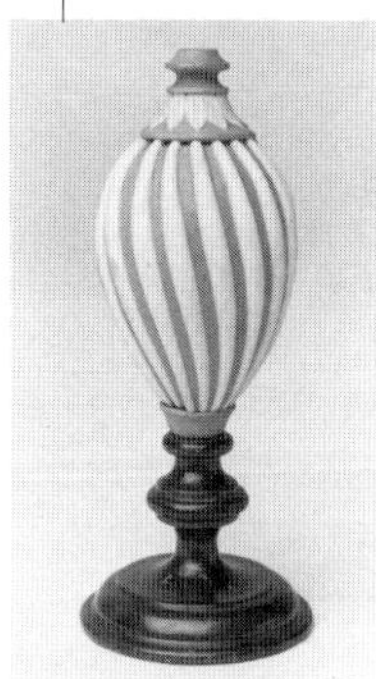

368. Bellpull: ca. 1780
Jasper, solid blue ground with white relief
2 1/2 x 1 1/4 in (6.3 x 3.1 cm)
Mark: none
Provenance: M. Close Collection, England; Dr. Harold L. Klawans, Chicago
1980.170

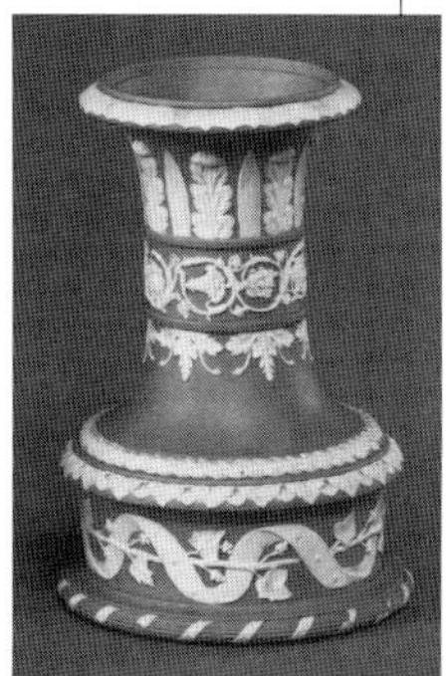

369. Vase: *Acanthus, Roman Scroll and Flowers, and Ribbons and Ivy,* ca. 1790
Jasper, solid blue ground with white relief
5 x 3 9/16 in (12.7 x 9 cm)
Mark: "WEDGWOOD" "3"
Provenance: Dr. Francis Jennings Vurpillat, South Bend, Ind.
1981.275
Color plate 105

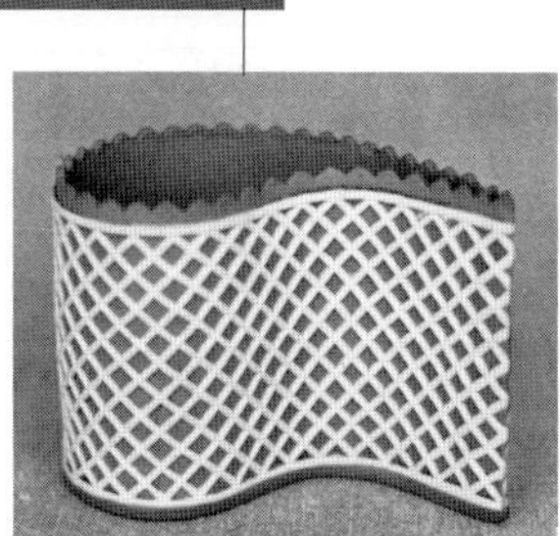

370. Custard Cup: ca. 1785
Jasper, solid blue ground with white relief
1 7/8 x 1 1/2 x 3 in (4.7 x 3.8 x 7.6 cm)
Mark: "WEDGWOOD" "H"
Provenance: Dr. Francis Jennings Vurpillat, South Bend, Ind.
1980.164

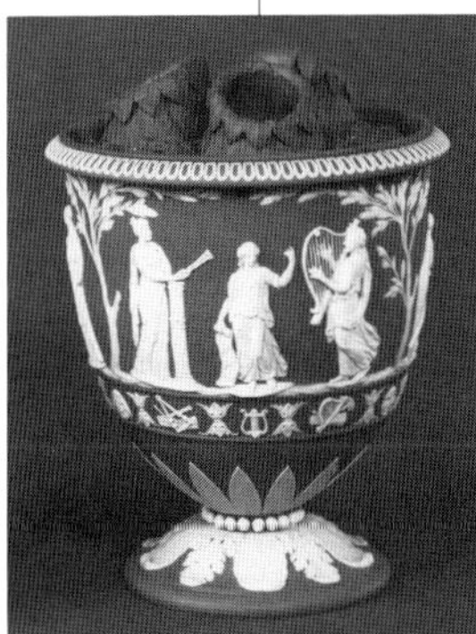

371. Bulb Pot: *Apollo and the Nine Muses*, ca. 1790
Jasper, solid blue ground with white relief, granulated body
8 3/4 x 4 1/2 in (22.2 x 11.4 cm)
Mark: "WEDGWOOD" "V"
Provenance: Seal Simons, Philadelphia, Pa.
1981.232 a and b
Pot has sump cover.
Design source: Montfaucon, *L' Antiquité expliquée,* vol. 1, pt. 2, pl. 30, fig. 1
Color plate 86

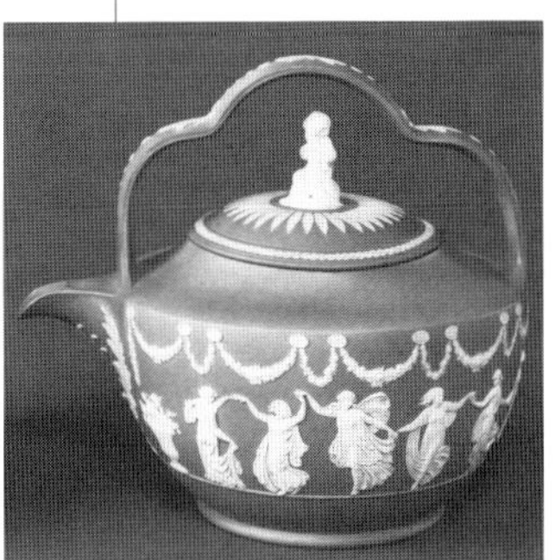

372. Kettle: *Dancing Hours*, ca. 1795
Jasper, solid blue ground with white relief and engine-turning
8 1/4 x 4 5/16 in (20.9 x 10.9 cm)
Mark: "WEDGWOOD" "M"
Provenance: David Davis, Chicago; Dr. Francis Jennings Vurpillat, South Bend, Ind.
1982.6

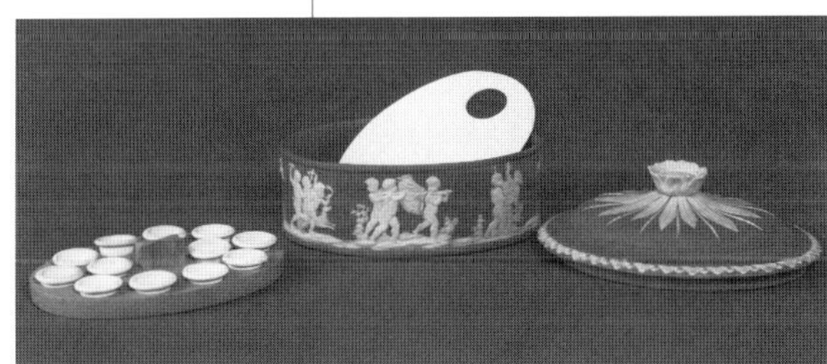

373. Paint Box: *Cupids Setting Out for the Hunt*, ca. 1785
Jasper, solid blue ground with white relief
3 5/8 x 4 1/2 x 6 in (9.2 x 11.4 x 15.2 cm)
Mark: "WEDGWOOD" "V"
Provenance: M. Mellanay Delhom, Chicago; Dr. Francis Jennings Vurpillat, South Bend, Ind.
1981.279.1-.16
Color plate 125

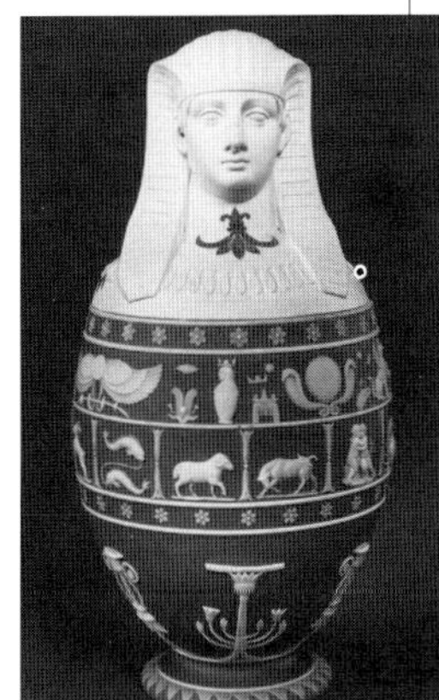

374. Canopic Vase: *Egyptian Symbols and Signs of the Zodiac*, ca. 1865-75
Jasper, solid white ground with blue wash and white relief
10 x 3 in (25.4 x 7.6 cm)
Mark: "WEDGWOOD"
Provenance: Otto Wasserman, New York
1982.193 a and b
Color plate 140

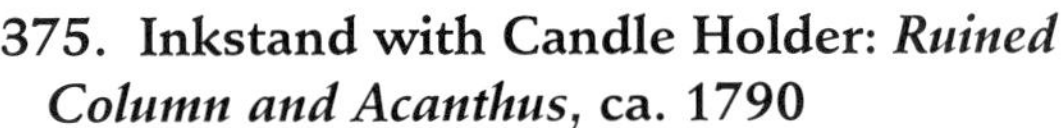

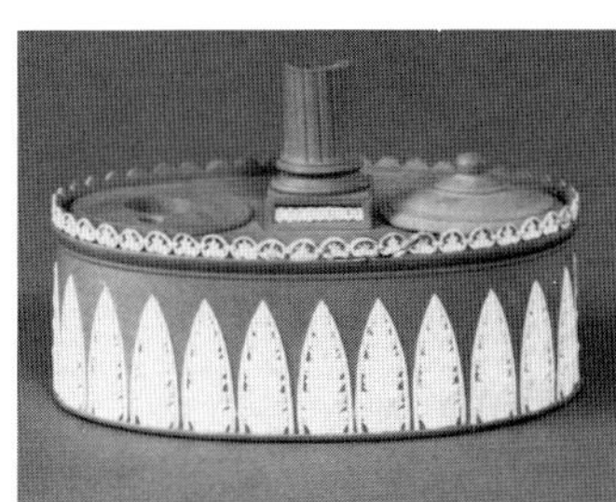

375. Inkstand with Candle Holder: *Ruined Column and Acanthus*, ca. 1790
Jasper, solid blue ground with white relief
3 3/4 x 4 1/2 x 6 1/16 in (9.5 x 11.4 x 15.4 cm)
Mark: "WEDGWOOD" "G"
Provenance: M. Mellanay Delhom, Chicago; Dr. Francis Jennings Vurpillat, South Bend, Ind.
1981.277
Base has three firing holes.

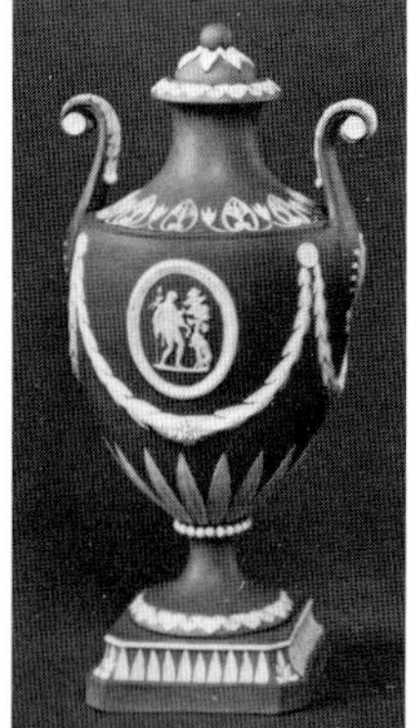

376. Covered Vase: *Classical Figures*, ca. 1790
Jasper, solid blue ground with white relief, replacement lid
7 13/16 x 2 15/16 x 2 15/16 in (19.8 x 7.4 x 7.4 cm)
Mark: "WEDGWOOD"
Provenance: Dr. Francis Jennings Vurpillat, South Bend, Ind.
1981.238 a and b
Vase has sump cover. Base has cavity around bolt filled with plaster and one firing hole.

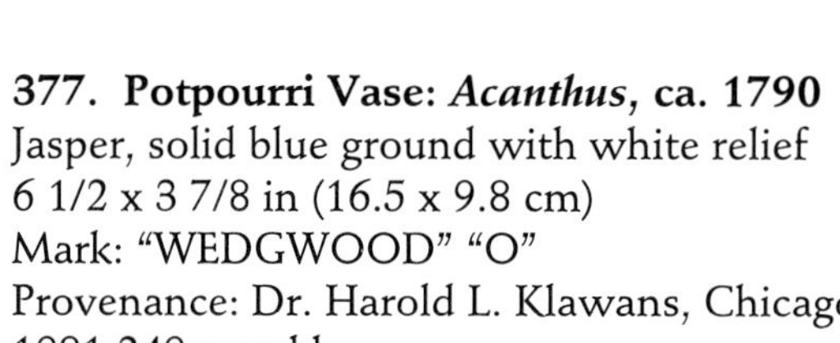

377. Potpourri Vase: *Acanthus*, ca. 1790
Jasper, solid blue ground with white relief
6 1/2 x 3 7/8 in (16.5 x 9.8 cm)
Mark: "WEDGWOOD" "O"
Provenance: Dr. Harold L. Klawans, Chicago
1981.249 a and b

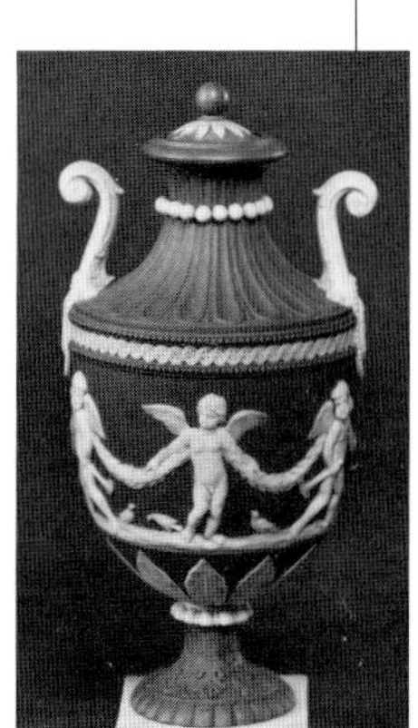

378. Covered Vase: *Procession of Cupids*, ca. 1785
Jasper, solid blue ground with white terra-cotta stoneware base, replacement lid
8 1/8 x 2 5/16 x 2 5/16 in (20.6 x 5.8 x 5.8 cm)
Mark: "Wedgwood"
Provenance: David Davis, Chicago; Dr. Francis Jennings Vurpillat, South Bend, Ind.
1981.240 a and b
Vase has sump cover.

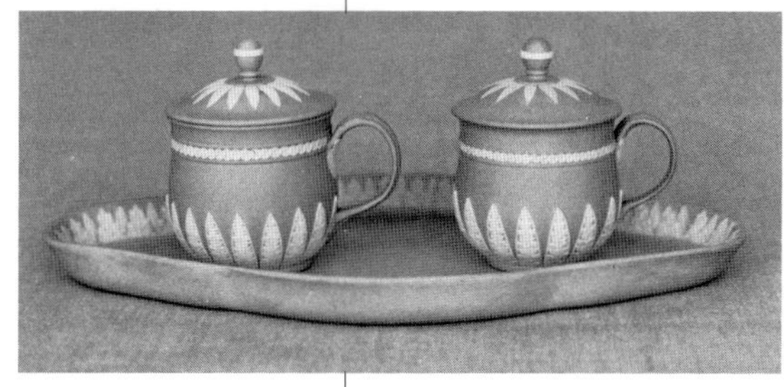

379. Pair of Covered Custard Cups with Tray: *Acanthus*, ca. 1795
Jasper, solid blue ground with white relief and lapidary-polishing
Cups: 3 3/8 x 1 5/8 in (8.5 x 4.1 cm); tray: 11/16 x 10 3/16 x 5 3/4 in (1.7 x 25.8 x 14.6 cm)
Mark: "WEDGWOOD"
Provenance: Dr. Francis Jennings Vurpillat, South Bend, Ind.
1981.268.1-.5

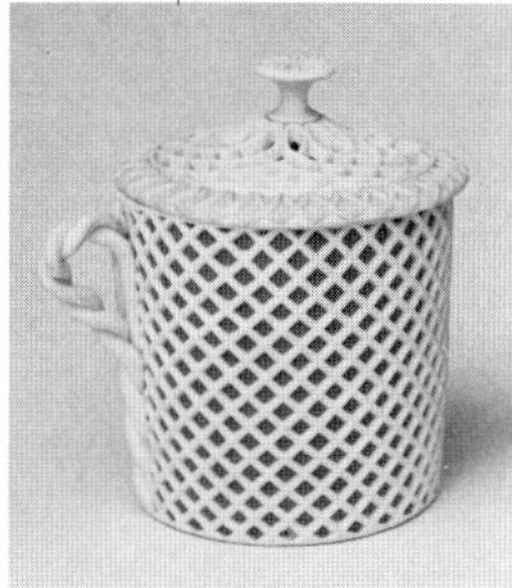

380. Custard Cup and Cover: ca. 1780
Jasper, solid white ground with blue wash and white relief
2 1/4 x 1 7/8 in (5.7 x 4.7 cm)
Mark: "WEDGWOOD"
Provenance: M. Close Collection, England; Dr. Harold L. Klawans, Chicago
1980.163 a and b

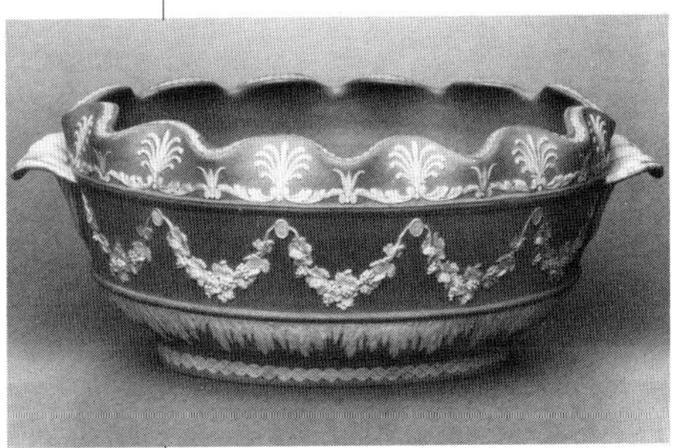

381. Monteith: ca. 1790
Jasper, solid blue ground with white relief
5 3/8 x 8 1/2 x 11 9/16 in (13.6 x 21.5 x 29.3 cm)
Mark: "WEDGWOOD" "V"
Provenance: Tulk Collection, England; Dr. Francis Jennings Vurpillat, South Bend, Ind.
1981.243

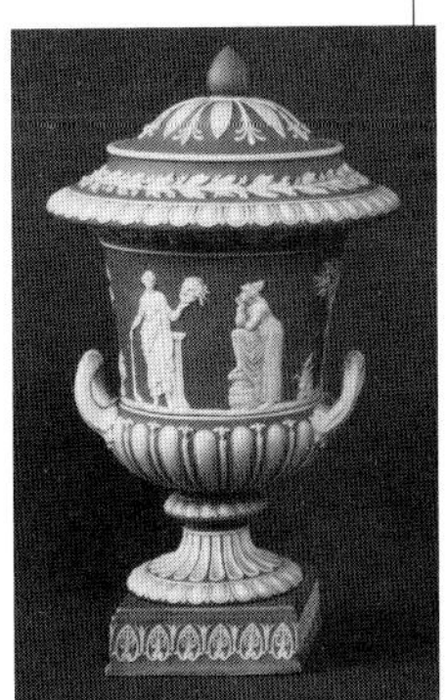

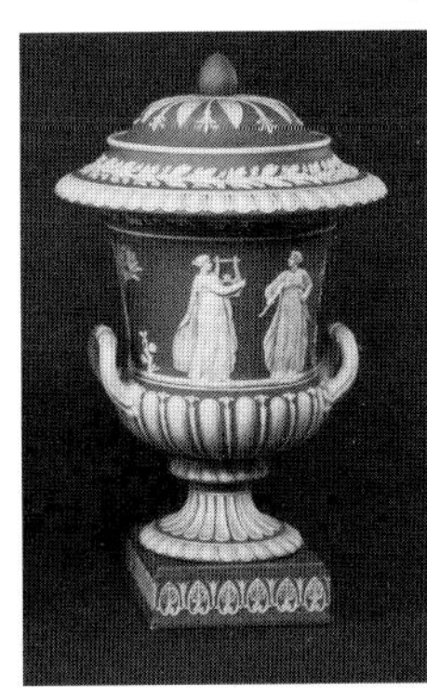

382. Pair of Vases: *The Nine Muses*, ca. 1880
Jasper, solid white ground with blue wash and white relief
12 5/8 x 4 x 4 in (32 x 10.1 x 10.1 cm)
Mark: "WEDGWOOD" with tool mark
Provenance: Toby House, New York
1981.251 a and b; 1981.252 a and b
Base is hollow.
Design source: Montfaucon, *L' Antiquité expliquée,* vol. 1, pt. 1, pl. 30, fig. 1

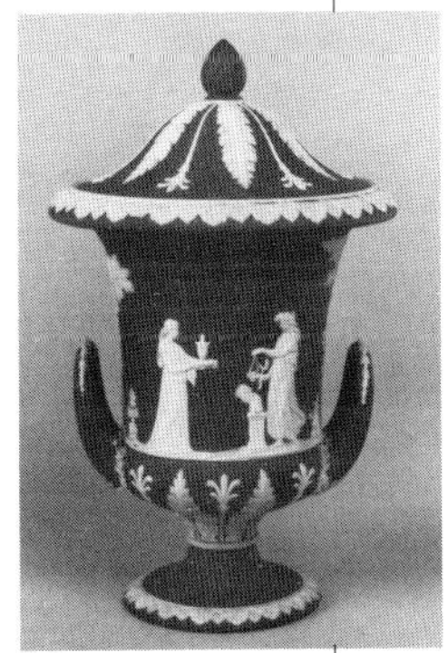

383. Covered Vase: *A Sacrifice*, ca. 1930
Jasper, solid white ground with mulberry wash and white relief
11 x 4 in (27.9 x 10.1cm)
Mark: "WEDGWOOD / ENGLAND" "5" with tool mark
Provenance: Fred J. Tongue, Santa Monica, Calif.
1976.218

384. Pair of Vases: *Monopodia, Swags, and Classical Figures*, ca. 1875-85
Jasper, solid blue ground with white relief
7 x 4 1/8 in (17.7 x 10.4 cm)
Mark: "WEDGWOOD" "H" "7" with tool mark
Provenance: Otto Wasserman, New York
1981.274 a and b

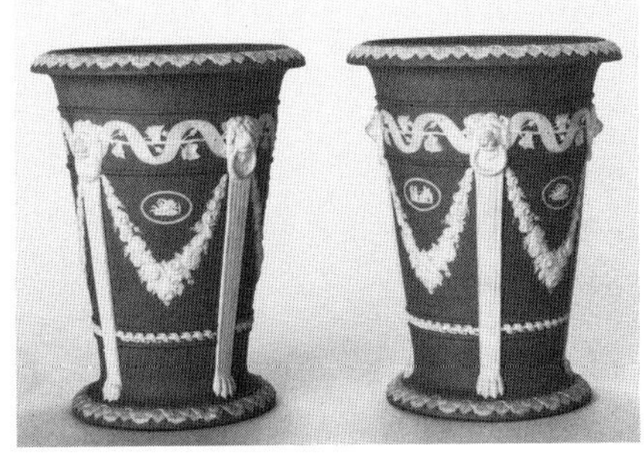

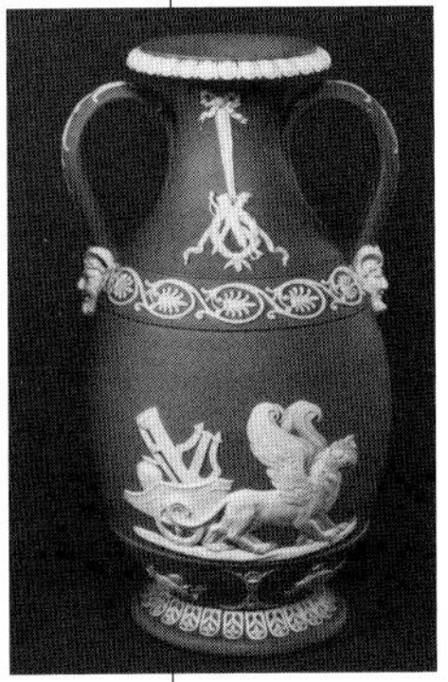

385. Vase: *Triumph of Cybele*, 19th century
Jasper, solid blue ground with white relief
9 5/8 x 3 3/4 in (24.4 x 9.5 cm)
Mark: "WEDGWOOD"
Provenance: Dr. Francis Jennings Vurpillat, South Bend, Ind.
1982.20

386. Candlestick: *Juno*, ca. 1810
Jasper, solid white ground with blue wash and white relief; figure, solid white ground
9 1/2 x 3 3/4 x 3 3/4 in (24.1 x 9.5 x 9.5 cm)
Mark: "WEDGWOOD" "C"
Provenance: Dr. Harold L. Klawans, Chicago
1981.239
Figure and base are hollow.

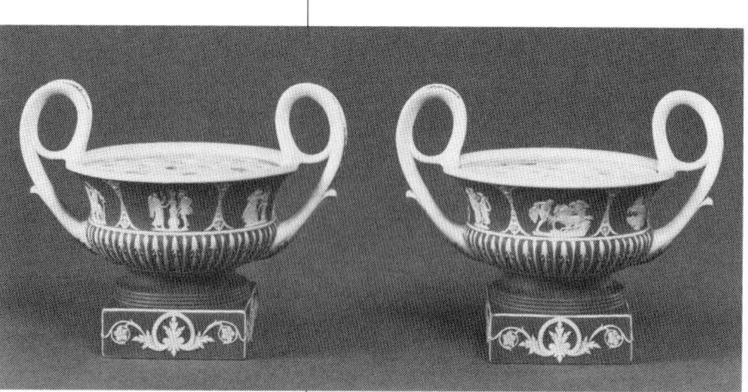

387. Pair of Bulb Pots: *Classical Figures*, ca. 1820
Jasper, solid white ground with dark blue wash and white relief
6 5/8 x 3 5/8 x 3 5/8 in (16.8 x 9.2 x 9.2 cm)
Mark: "WEDGWOOD" with tool mark
Provenance: Charles Smith, Philadelphia, Pa.
1982.8 a and b; 1982.9 a and b
Bases are hollow, with four firing holes each; interiors are glazed.

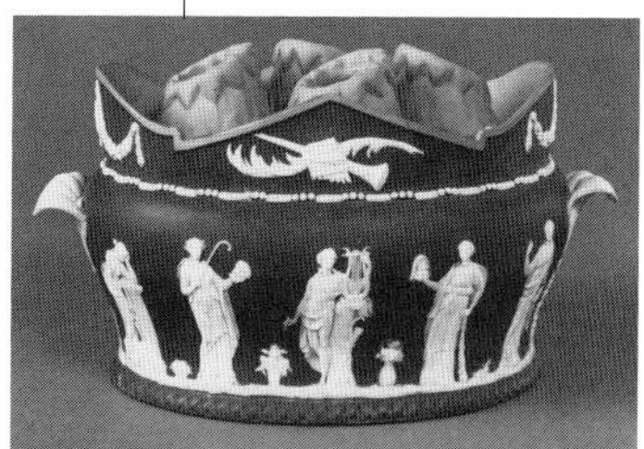

388. Bulb Pot: *Apollo and the Nine Muses*, ca. 1795
Jasper, solid blue ground with dark blue wash on front and white relief
5 1/2 x 5 x 7 9/16 in (13.9 x 12.7 x 19.2 cm)
Mark: "WEDGWOOD"
Provenance: Dr. Francis Jennings Vurpillat, South Bend, Ind.
1982.13 a and b
Design source: Montfaucon, *L'Antiquité expliquée,* vol. 1, pt. 1, pl. 30, fig. 1

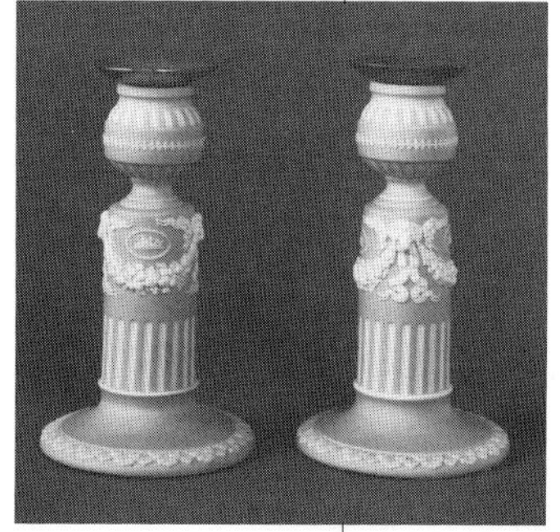

389. Pair of Candlesticks: *Classical Figures and Swags*, ca. 1930
Jasper, solid white ground with yellow wash and white relief, brass sockets
5 3/4 x 3 3/4 in (14.6 x 9.5 cm)
Mark: "WEDGWOOD" "A" with tool marks
Provenance: Dr. Francis Jennings Vurpillat, South Bend, Ind.
1982.29 a and b

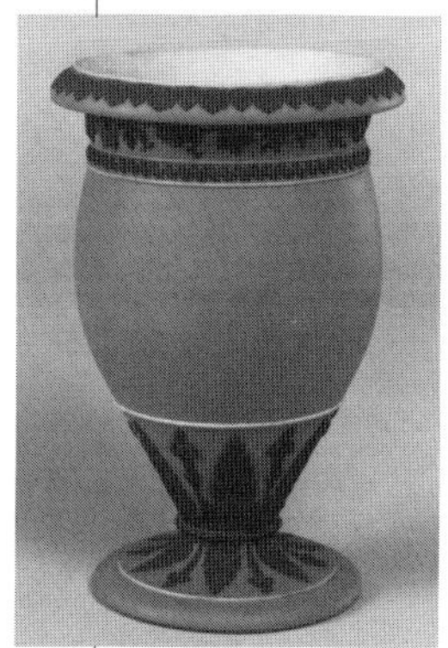

390. Vase: ca. 1930
Jasper, solid white ground with mustard wash and brown relief
7 15/16 x 4 3/16 in (20.1 x 10.6 cm)
Mark: "WEDGWOOD" "A"
Provenance: Dr. Francis Jennings Vurpillat, South Bend, Ind.
1982.27

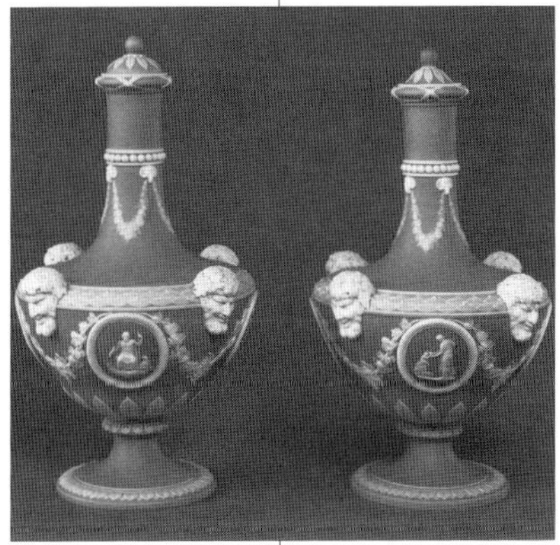

391. Pair of Barber Bottles: *Classical Figures and Swag,* 1867
Jasper, solid white ground with lilac-and-green wash and white relief
10 1/16 x 3 3/4 in (25.5 x 9.5 cm)
Mark: "WEDGWOOD" "Y" "HKV"
Provenance: Atlanta, Ga.
1980.303 a and b
Color plate 131

392. Barber Bottle: *Classical Figures and Swag,* 19th century
Jasper, solid white ground with brown, yellow, and blue wash and white relief
10 9/16 x 3 7/8 in (26.8 x 9.8 cm)
Mark: "WEDGWOOD" with tool marks
Provenance: Dr. Francis Jennings Vurpillat, South Bend, Ind.
1982.28
Color plate 131

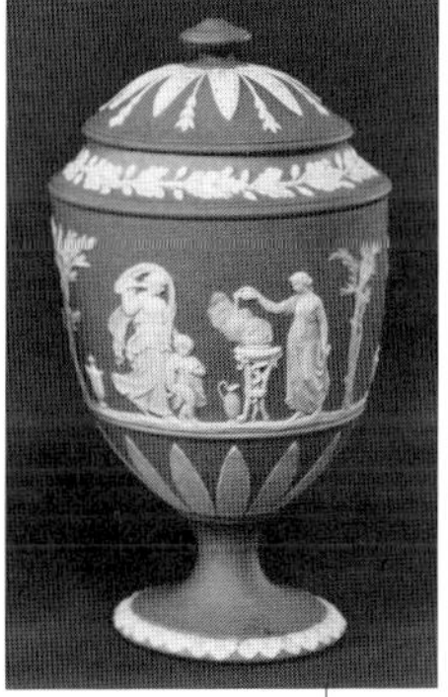

393. Covered Vase: *A Sacrifice,* ca. 1800
Jasper, solid blue ground with white relief
7 1/2 x 2 1/2 in (19 x 6.3 cm)
Mark: "WEDGWOOD"
Provenance: Charles Smith, Philadelphia, Pa.
1981.247 a and b

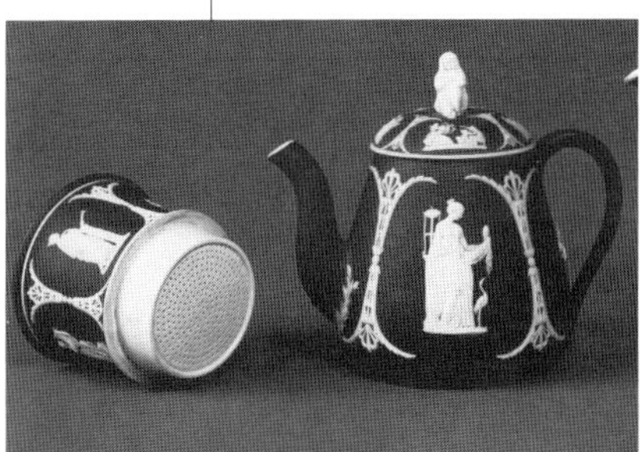

394. Coffee Biggin: *Classical Figures,* 1886
Jasper, solid white ground with dark blue wash and white relief
9 1/4 x 4 in (23.4 x 10.1 cm)
Mark: "WEDGWOOD" "DGO" "159"
Provenance: Dr. Harold L. Klawans, Chicago
1982.11 a, b, and c

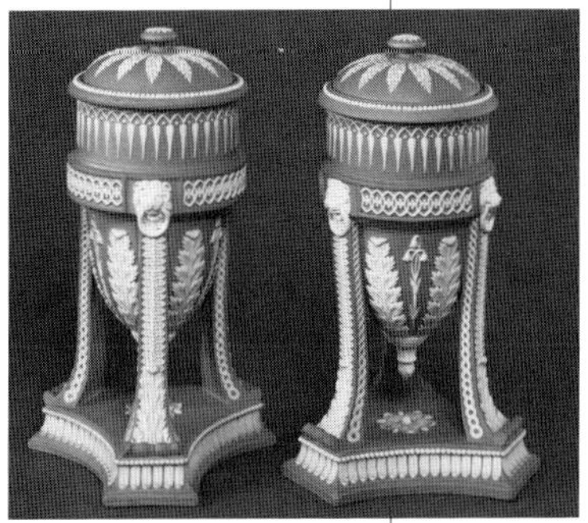

395. Pair of Tripod Candle Urns: 19th century
Jasper, solid blue ground with white relief
8 x 3 7/8 x 3 7/8 in (20.3 x 9.8 x 9.8 cm)
Mark: "WEDGWOOD" "J"
Provenance: W. Russell Button Gallery, Chicago
1981.254 a and b; 1981.246 a and b

Miscellaneous Jasper Ware

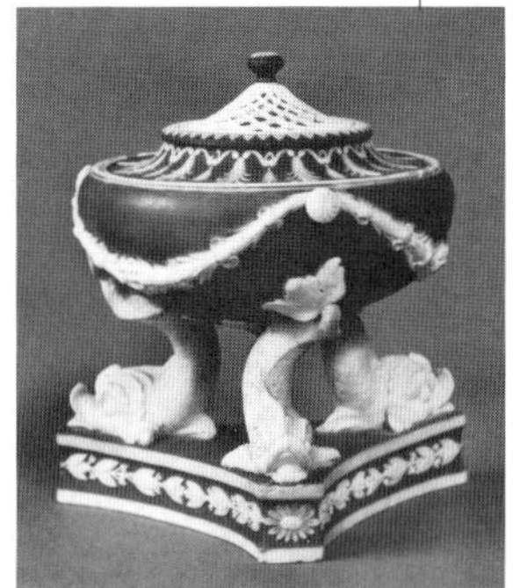

396. Pastille Burner, or Cassolette: ca. 1805
Jasper, solid white ground with dark blue wash and white relief
5 1/8 x 3 7/8 x 4 1/2 in (13 x 9.8 x 11.4 cm)
Mark: "JOSIAH WEDGWOOD / FEB Y2D 1805"
Provenance: Dr. Francis Jennings Vurpillat, South Bend, Ind.
1982.15 a and b
Color plate 149

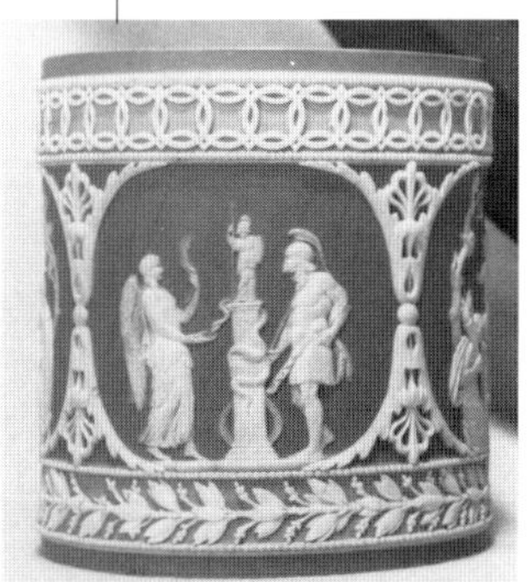

397. Drum for Chandelier: *Classical Figures*, 19th century
Jasper, solid white ground with dark-blue-and-lilac wash and white relief
3 1/8 x 2 7/8 in (7.9 x 7.3 cm)
Mark: "WEDGWOOD" "3" incised
Provenance: Dr. Harold L. Klawans, Chicago
1982.12

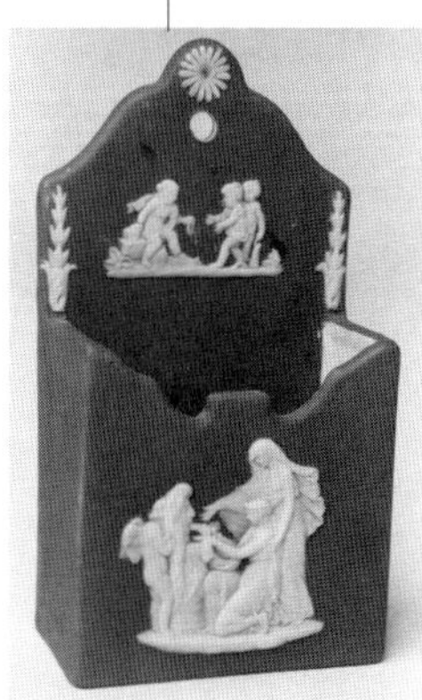

398. Matchbox: *Cupid*, 20th century
Jasper, solid white ground with dark blue wash and white relief
4 1/2 x 2 1/2 x 1 3/8 in (11.4 x 6.3 x 3.4 cm)
Mark: "WEDGWOOD" "ETRURIA / ENGLAND"
Provenance: Col. Earl W. Camp, New Smyrna Beach, Fla.
1980.173

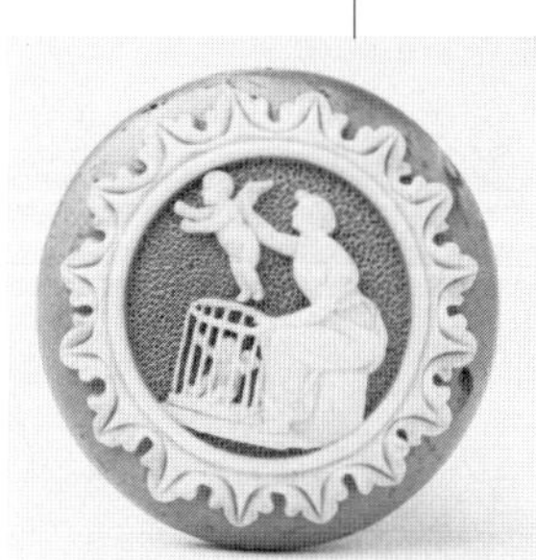

399. Umbrella or Cane Handle: *Cupid Market*, 19th century
Jasper, solid blue ground with white relief
2 3/4 x 1 1/2 in (6.9 x 3.8 cm)
Mark: none
Provenance: Dr. Harold L. Klawans, Chicago
1980.175

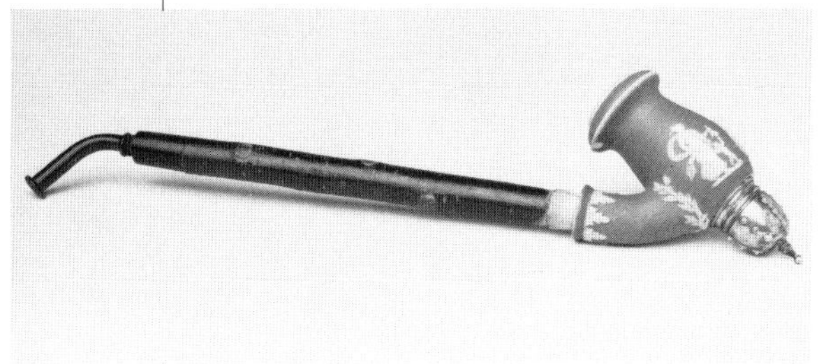

400. Pipe: ca. 1850
William Edwards Staite
Jasper, solid white ground with dark blue wash and white relief
2 5/8 x 1 in (top diameter) (6.6 x 2.5 cm)
Mark: "STAITES PATENT / WEDGWOOD"
Provenance: Dr. Francis Jennings Vurpillat, South Bend, Ind.
1980.171

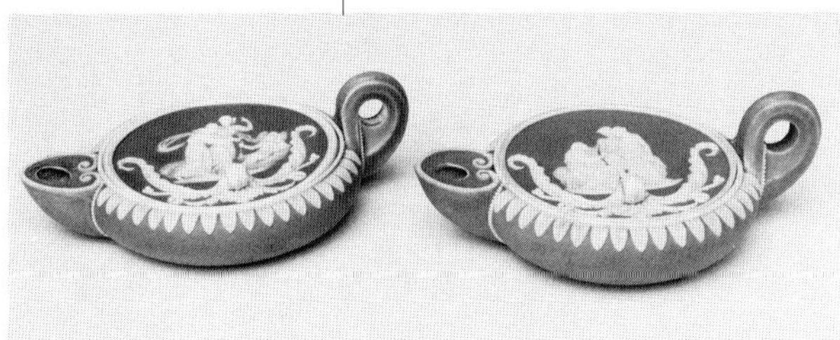

401. Hand Lamp: *Coriolanus with Wife and Mother*, ca. 1800
Jasper, solid white ground with dark blue wash with white relief
3 5/16 x 2 3/4 in (8.4 x 6.9 cm)
Mark: "WEDGWOOD"
Provenance: Dr. Harold L. Klawans, Chicago
1980.165 a and b

402. Hand Lamp: ca. 1800
Jasper, solid white ground with dark blue wash with white relief
3 3/8 x 2 3/4 in (8.5 x 6.9 cm)
Mark: "WEDGWOOD" "Z"
Provenance: M. Mellanay Delhom, Chicago; Dr. Francis Jennings Vurpillat, South Bend, Ind.
1980.166

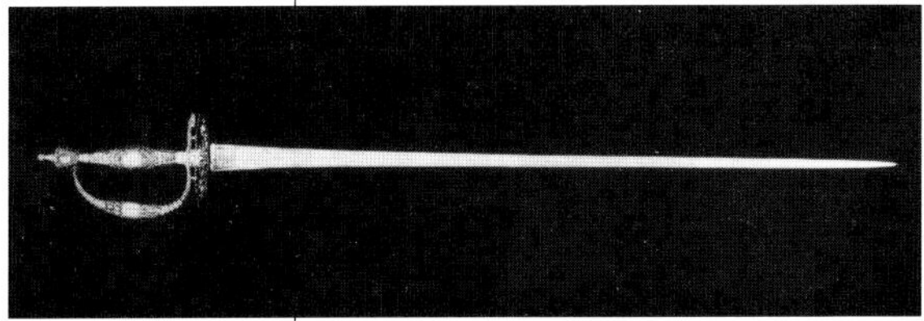

403. Small-sword: ca. 1790
Jasper, solid white ground with dark blue wash and white relief, steel and cut-steel mounts
34 in (84.6 cm)
Mark: undetermined
Provenance: Byron A. Born, Ho-ho-kus, N. J.; Art Trading Ltd., New York
1991.788
Color plates 122 and 123

Diced Ware and Strapware

404. Potpourri Vase: *Strapware*, ca. 1795
Jasper, solid white ground with lilac wash and green-and-white relief
6 11/16 x 3 7/8 in (16.9 x 9.8 cm)
Mark: none
Provenance: David Davis, Chicago; Dr. Francis Jennings Vurpillat, South Bend, Ind.
1978.119
Vase has sump cover.
Color plate 114

405. Bulb Pot: *Strapware*, ca. 1800
Jasper, solid white ground with lilac wash and green relief
3 7/16 x 3 5/16 in (8.7 x 8.4 cm)
Mark: "WEDGWOOD" "Z"
Provenance: Dr. Harold L. Klawans, Chicago
1978.123

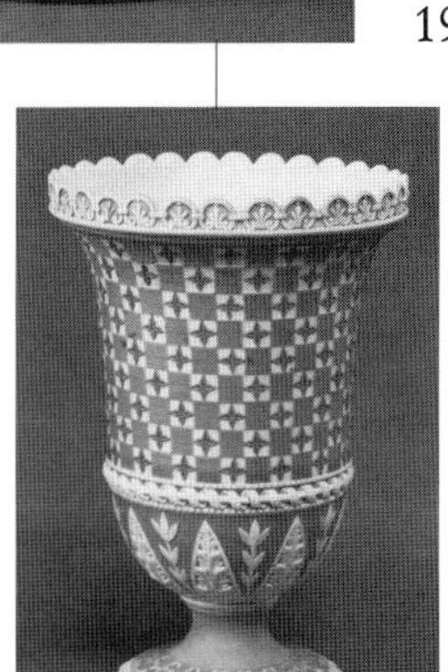

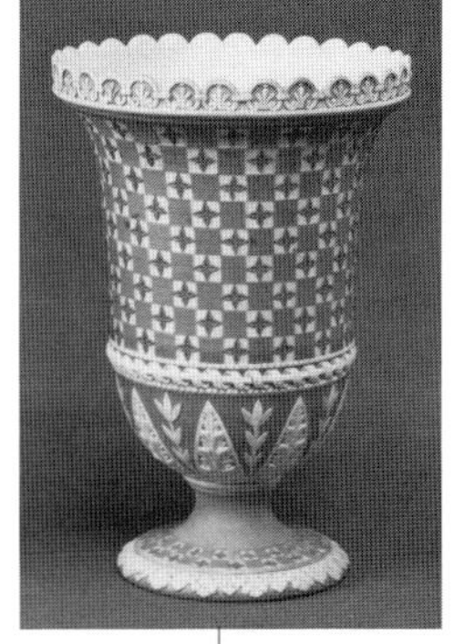

406. Vase: *Diced Ware*, ca. 1800
Jasper, solid white ground with lilac wash and green-and-white relief
6 x 2 3/4 in (15.2 x 6.9 cm)
Mark: "WEDGWOOD" "O" "3"
Provenance: Sir George Duff-Dunbar, Scotland; M. Mellanay Delhom, Chicago; Dr. Francis Jennings Vurpillat, South Bend, Ind.
1978.122

407. Teapot: *Diced Ware*, ca. 1785
Jasper, solid white ground with lilac wash and green-and-white relief
4 1/2 x 4 1/2 in (11.4 x 11.4 cm)
Mark: "WEDGWOOD"
Provenance: Dr. Francis Jennings Vurpillat, South Bend, Ind.
1978.129 a and b

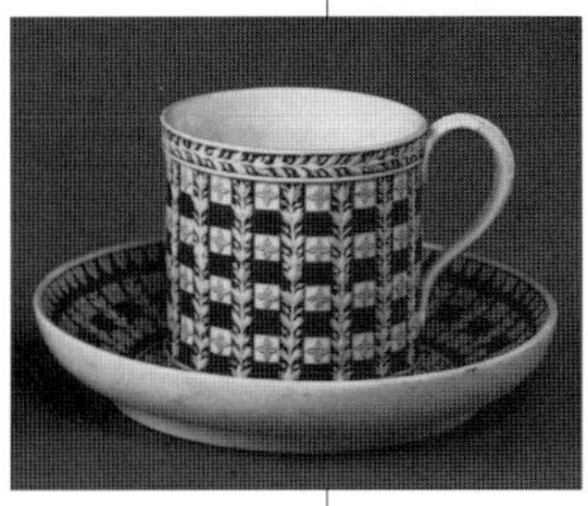

408. Cup and Saucer: *Diced Ware*, ca. 1790
Jasper, solid white ground with lilac wash and green-and-white relief
Cup: 2 1/2 x 2 in (6.3 x 5 cm); saucer: 4 9/16 in (11.5 cm)
Mark: cup: "WEDGWOOD" "3" "H"; saucer: "WEDGWOOD" "Z"
Provenance: Frederick Rathbone, London
1978.128 a and b

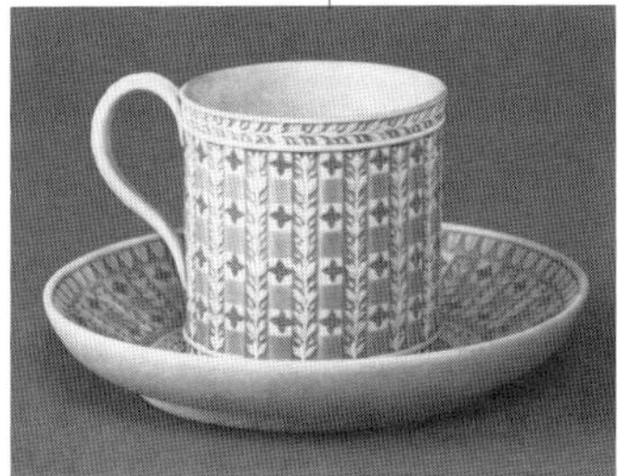

409. Cup and Saucer: *Diced Ware*, ca. 1790
Jasper, solid white ground with lilac wash and green-and-white relief
Cup: 2 9/16 x 2 9/16 in (6.5 x 6.5 cm); saucer: 5 3/8 in (13.6 cm)
Mark: cup: "WEDGWOOD"; saucer: "WEDGWOOD" "212" in black enamel
Provenance: Frederick Rathbone, London; Dr. Harold L. Klawans, Chicago
1978.127 a and b

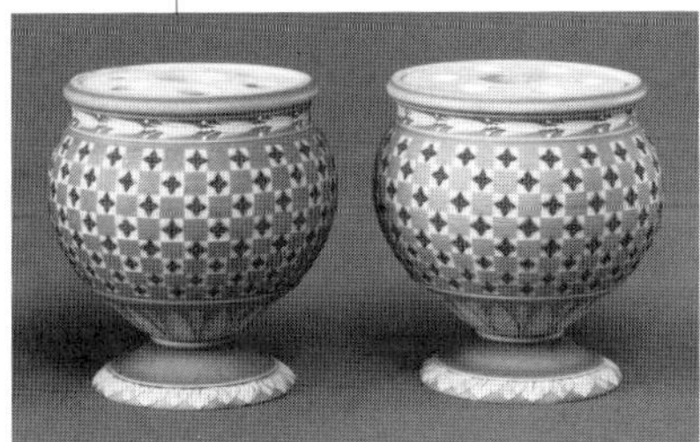

410. Pair of Potpourri Vases: *Diced Ware*, ca. 1800
Jasper, solid white ground with lilac wash and green-and-white relief
4 1/16 x 2 3/4 in (10.3 x 6.9 cm)
Mark: none
Provenance: Otto Wasserman, New York
1978.126 a and b
Vases have sunk pots.

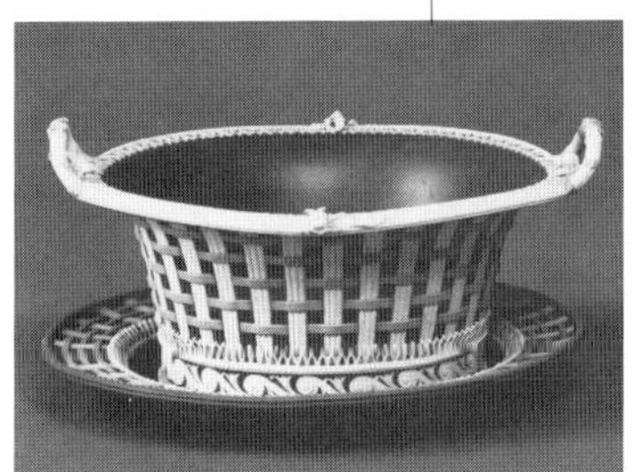

411. Basket and Stand: *Strapware*, ca. 1800
Basket: jasper, solid white ground with dark blue wash and yellow, green, and white relief; stand: jasper, solid blue ground with dark blue wash and yellow, green, and white relief
Basket: 4 3/4 x 5 1/4 in (12 x 13.3 cm); stand: 8 9/16 in (21.7 cm)
Mark: "WEDGWOOD" "Z" (bowl)
Provenance: Dr. Francis Jennings Vurpillat, South Bend, Ind.
1978.132 a and b
Color plate 114

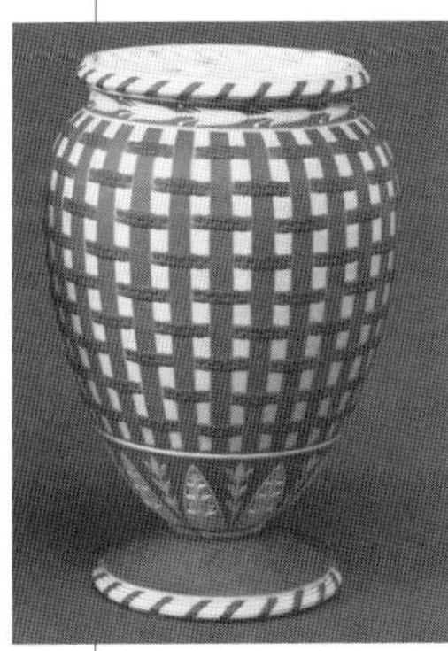

412. Potpourri Vase: *Strapware*, ca. 1795
Jasper, solid white ground with blue wash and green-and-white relief
6 15/16 x 3 3/8 in (17.6 x 8.5 cm)
Mark: "WEDGWOOD" "Z" "H"
Provenance: David Davis, Chicago; Dr. Francis Jennings Vurpillat, South Bend, Ind.
1978.133
Vase has sump cover.
Color plate 114

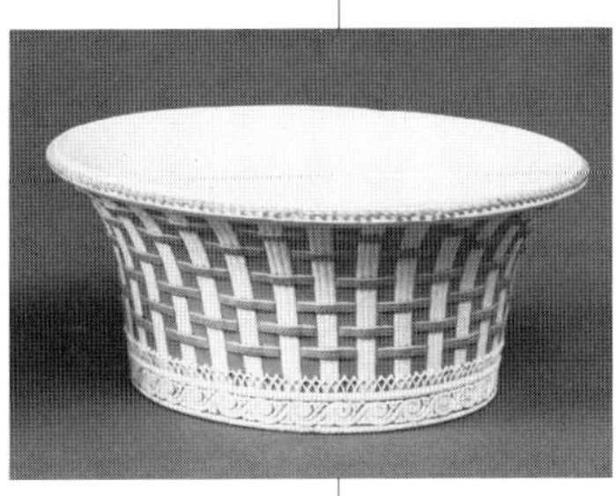

413. Bowl: *Strapware*, ca. 1800
Jasper, solid white ground with green wash and yellow-and-white relief
8 3/16 x 5 1/2 in (20.7 x 13.9 cm)
Mark: "WEDGWOOD"
Provenance: Ann Brodkiewicz, Chicago
1980.319

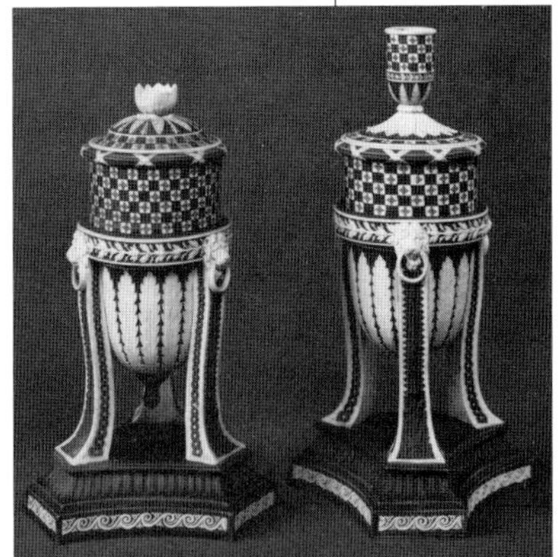

414. Pair of Tripod Candle Urns: *Diced Ware,* ca. 1795
Jasper, solid white ground with blue wash and green-and-white relief; base solid blue ground with dark blue wash and white relief
10 13/16 x 4 13/16 x 4 13/16 in (27.4 x 12.2 x 12.2 cm)
Mark: "WEDGWOOD"
Provenance: a: Dr. Francis Jennings Vurpillat, South Bend, Ind.; b: Dr. Harold L. Klawans, Chicago
1978.138.1-.2
Each base has three firing holes.
Color plate 112

415. Vase: *Diced Ware,* ca. 1785
Jasper, solid white ground with blue wash and green-and-white relief
9 1/2 x 4 in (24.1 x 10.1 cm)
Mark: "WEDGWOOD"
Provenance: Wolf Mankowitz, London
1981.233
Color plate 113

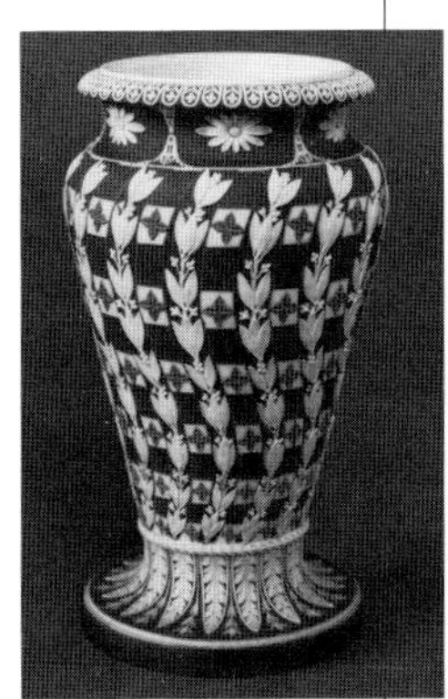

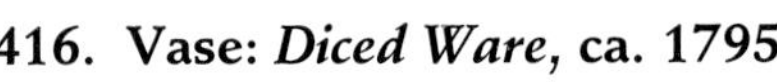

416. Vase: *Diced Ware,* ca. 1795
Jasper, solid white ground with blue wash and green-and-white relief
8 1/2 x 4 7/16 in (21.5 x 11.2 cm)
Mark: "WEDGWOOD"
Provenance: Dr. Francis Jennings Vurpillat, South Bend, Ind.
1978.131
Color plate 113

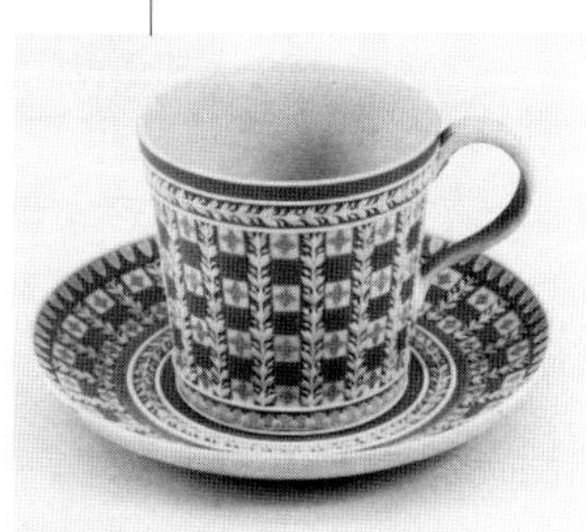

417. Cup and Saucer: *Diced Ware,* ca. 1790
Jasper, solid white ground with dark blue wash and yellow-and-white relief
Cup: 2 9/16 x 2 9/16 in (6.5 x 6.5 cm); saucer: 5 3/16 in (14.7 cm)
Mark: "WEDGWOOD" with tool marks
Provenance: Ann Brodkiewicz, Chicago
1980.135 a and b

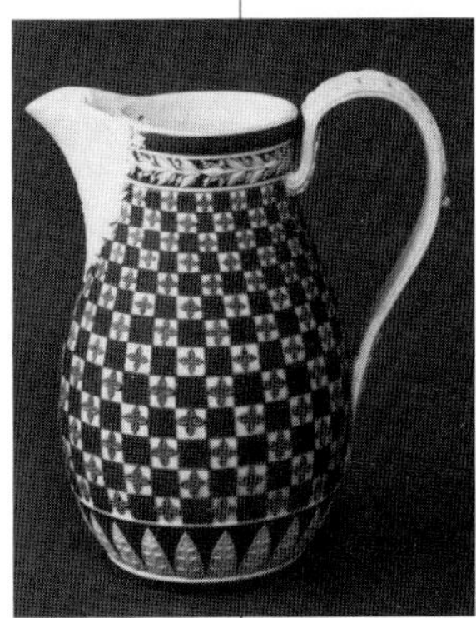

418. Cream Pitcher: *Diced Ware,* ca. 1785
Jasper, solid white ground with blue wash and green-and-white relief
4 7/16 x 1 11/16 in (11.2 x 4.2 cm)
Mark: "WEDGWOOD" "H" "H"
Provenance: Dr. Francis Jennings Vurpillat, South Bend, Ind.
1978.136

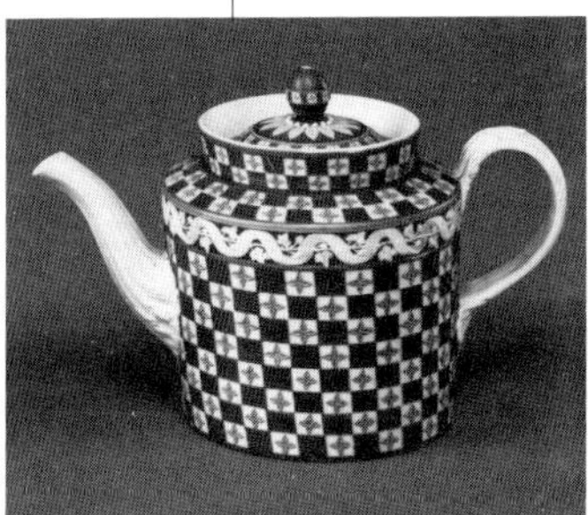

419. Teapot: *Diced Ware*, ca. 1785
Jasper, solid white ground with blue wash and green-and-white relief
4 1/2 x 3 1/4 in (11.4 x 8.2 cm)
Mark: "WEDGWOOD" "3" "3"
Provenance: Dr. Francis Jennings Vurpillat, South Bend, Ind.
1978.137 a and b

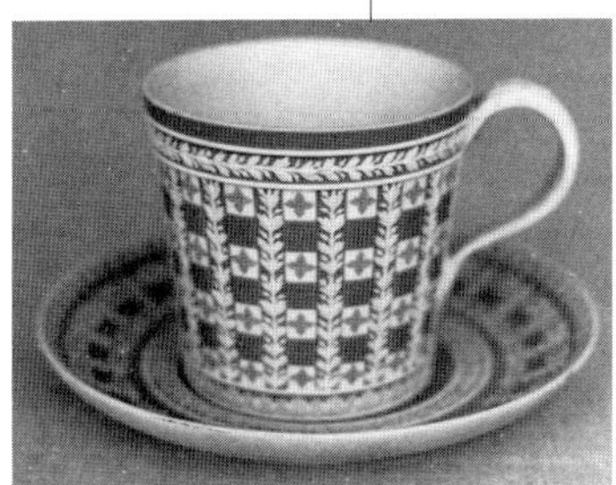

420. Cup and Saucer: *Diced Ware*, ca. 1790
Jasper, solid white ground with green wash and yellow-and-white relief
Cup: 2 7/8 x 2 3/8 in (7.3 x 6 cm); saucer: 5 3/8 in (13.6 cm)
Mark: "WEDGWOOD" with tool marks
Provenance: Dr. Francis Jennings Vurpillat, South Bend, Ind.
1980.320 a and b

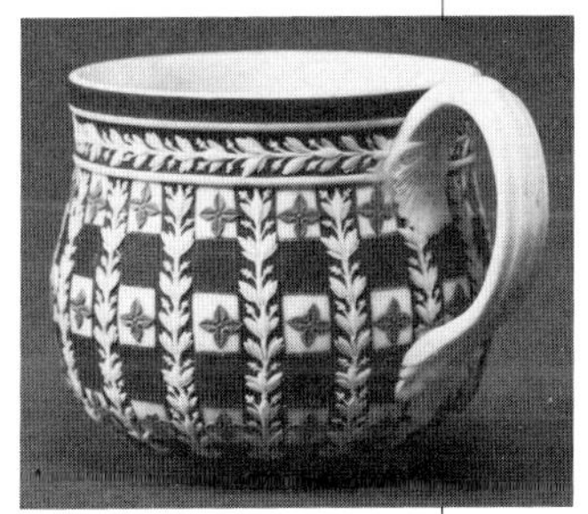

421. Custard Cup: *Diced Ware*, ca. 1790
Jasper, solid white ground with dark blue wash and green-and-white relief
2 5/16 x 1 5/8 in (5.8 x 4.1 cm)
Mark: "WEDGWOOD" "Z"
Provenance: Dr. Francis Jennings Vurpillat, South Bend, Ind.
1978.139

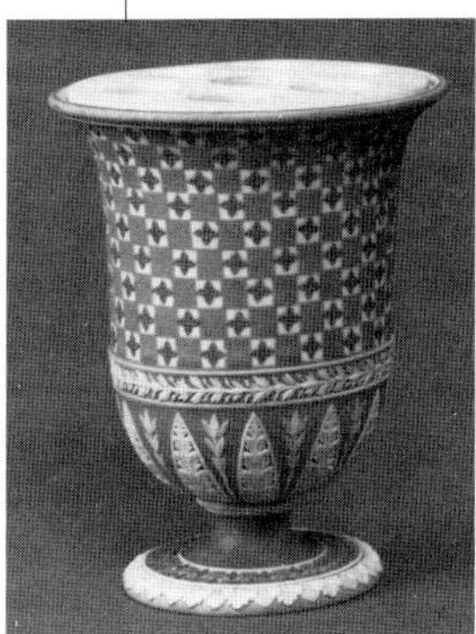

422. Potpourri Vase: *Diced Ware*, ca. 1795
Jasper, solid white ground with blue wash and dark-blue-and-white relief
5 3/8 x 2 13/16 in (13.6 x 7.1 cm)
Mark: "WEDGWOOD"
Provenance: Dr. Francis Jennings Vurpillat, South Bend, Ind.
1978.134
Vase has sump cover.

Caneware

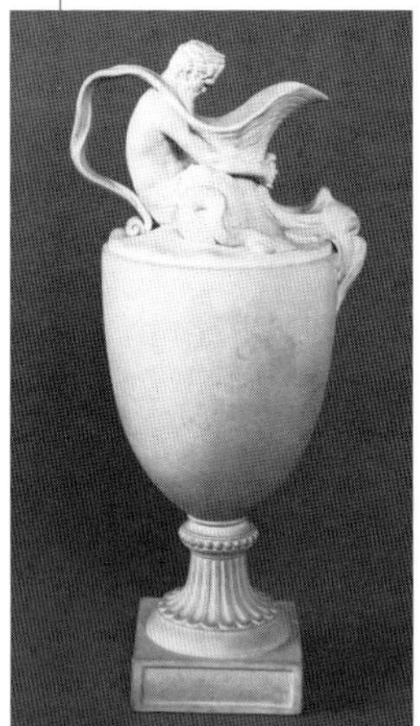

423. Water Ewer: *Sacred to Neptune*, 19th century
Caneware, tracings for exterior decoration
17 1/4 x 4 1/2 x 4 1/2 in (43.8 x 11.4 x 11.4 cm)
Mark: "WEDGWOOD"
Provenance: Dr. Francis Jennings Vurpillat, South Bend, Ind.
1976.286
Color plate 46

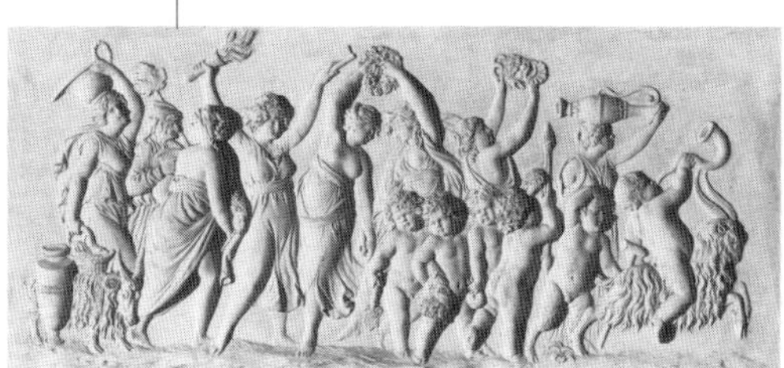

424. Tablet: *Bacchanalian Triumph*, 1786
Artificial stone
21 1/4 x 9 1/2 in (53.9 x 24.1 cm)
Mark: "1786"
Provenance: Shadford-Walker Collection, England; Frederick Rathbone, London; Ann Brodkiewicz, Chicago
1976.268
Design source: Clodion (Claude Michel, 1738-1814)
Color plate 139

425. Teapot: *Bamboo*, ca. 1780
Caneware, glazed interior
5 x 4 3/8 x 4 1/2 in (12.7 x 9.8 x 11.4 cm)
Mark: "Wedgwood & Bentley"
Provenance: M. Mellanay Delhom, Chicago; Dr. Francis Jennings Vurpillat, South Bend, Ind.
1976.262
Color plate 135

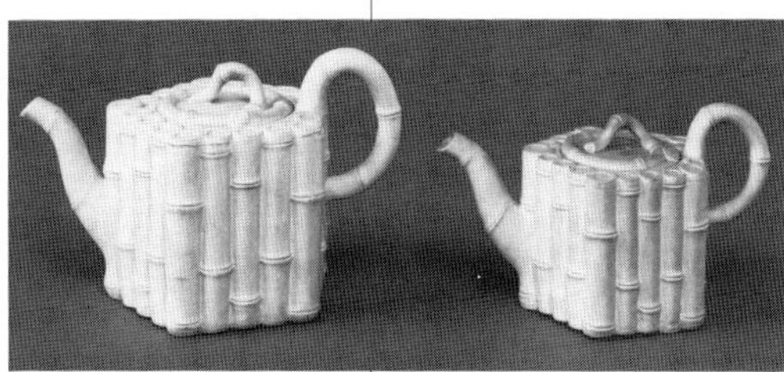

426. Teapot: *Bamboo*, ca. 1780
Caneware, glazed interior
3 3/4 x 3 1/2 x 3 5/8 in (9.5 x 8.8 x 8.5 cm)
Mark: "Wedgwood & Bentley"
Provenance: Dr. Harold L. Klawans, Chicago
1976.264
Color plate 135

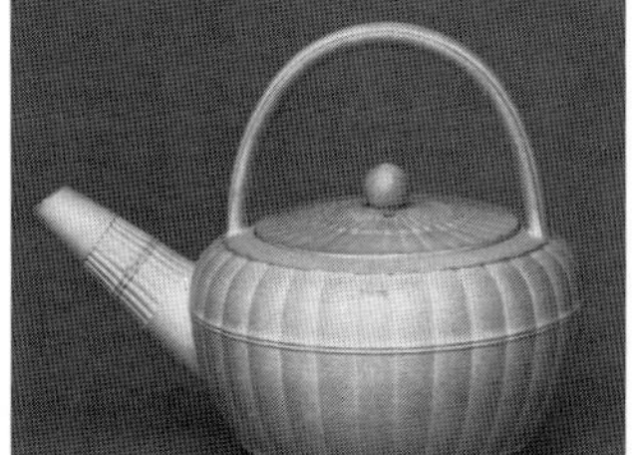

427. Miniature Tea or Punch Pot: ca. 1790
Caneware, glazed interior
3 3/4 x 2 1/16 in (9.5 x 5.2 cm)
Mark: "WEDGWOOD" "X"
Provenance: Ann Brodkiewicz, Chicago
1976.263

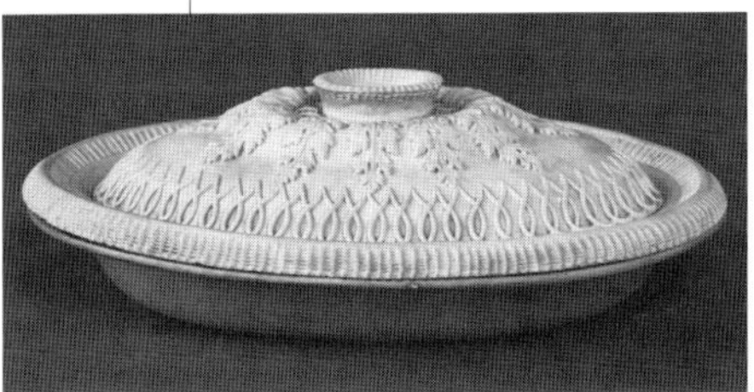

428. Pastry Dish: ca. 1795
Caneware, glazed interior
4 3/16 x 10 1/2 x 14 3/16 in (10.6 x 26.6 x 36 cm)
Mark: "WEDGWOOD" "3" with tool mark
Provenance: Dr. Francis Jennings Vurpillat, South Bend, Ind.
1976.276
Color plate 136

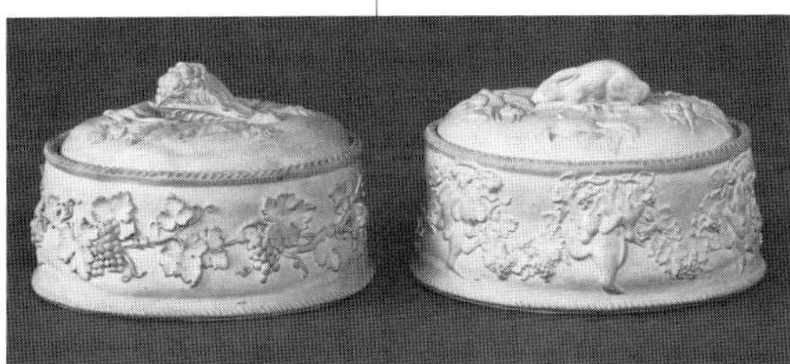

429. Pastry Dish with Rabbit Finial: 19th century
Caneware, glazed interior
5 1/8 x 8 13/16 x 6 7/16 in (13 x 22.3 x 16.3 cm)
Mark: "WEDGWOOD" "W" "8" "BTP"
Provenance: Isabelle del Correll, New Orleans
1976.277

430. Pastry Dish with Cauliflower Finial: ca. 1815
Caneware, glazed interior
5 1/4 x 8 5/8 x 6 1/4 in (13.3 x 21.9 x 25.9 cm)
Mark: "WEDGWOOD" "O"
Provenance: Dr. Harold L. Klawans, Chicago
1976.275 a and b
Color plate 136

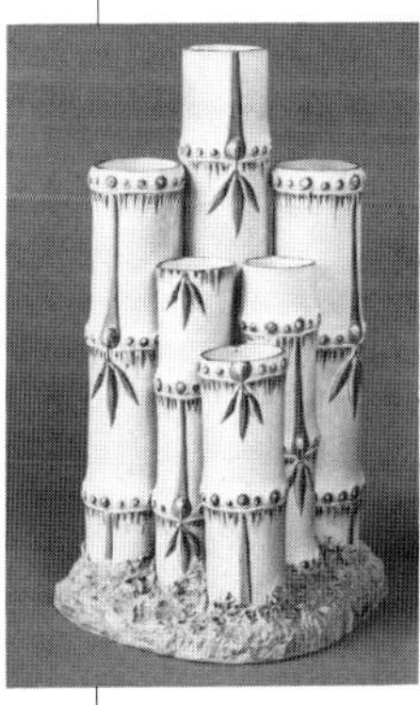

431. Vase: *Bamboo*, ca. 1790
Caneware with blue-and-white enamel decoration
12 15/16 x 7 3/4 x 7 1/4 in (32.8 x 19.6 x 18.4 cm)
Mark: "WEDGWOOD"
Provenance: Dr. Francis Jennings Vurpillat, South Bend, Ind.
1976.266
Color plate 137

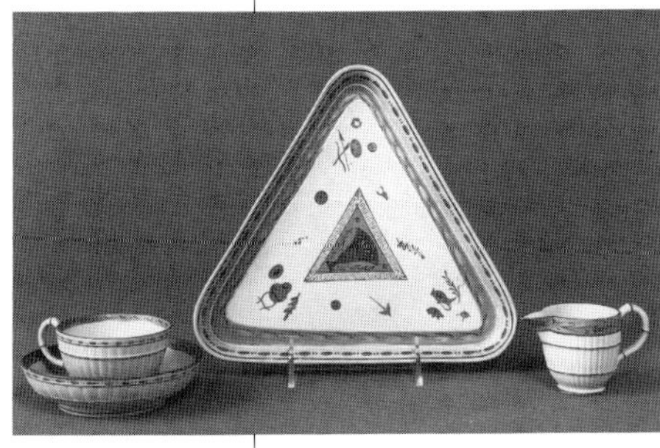

432. Dejeuner Set: ca. 1790
Caneware with encaustic decoration, unglazed interiors
Tray: 11/16 x 8 9/16 x 8 5/8 x 8 7/8 in (1.7 x 21.7 x 21.8 x 22.5 cm); creamer: 2 3/16 x 1 3/8 in (5.5 x 3.4 cm); cup: 1 5/16 x 1 1/2 in (3.3 x 3.8 cm); saucer: 5 1/8 in (13 cm)
Mark: tray: "WEDGWOOD" "V" incised; creamer: "Wedgwood" "S"; cup: "WEDGWOOD" "2"; saucer: "Wedgwood" "2"
Provenance: Dr. Harold L. Klawans, Chicago
1976.281 a and b; 1976.282; 1976.283
Color plate 138

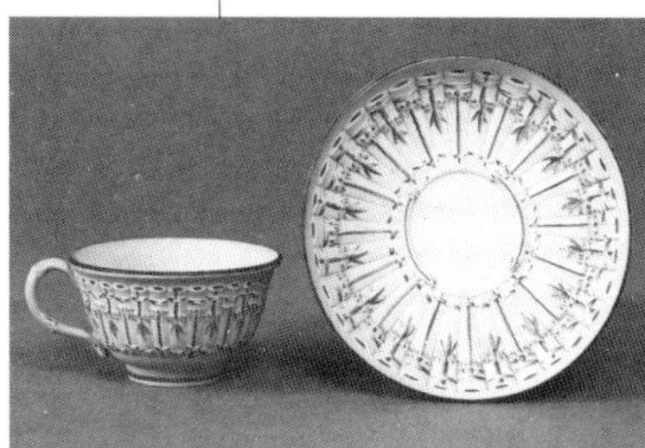

433. Cup and Saucer: *Bamboo*, ca. 1790
Caneware with blue-and-white enamel decoration, unglazed interior
Cup: 2 x 1 1/2 in (5 x 3.8 cm); saucer: 5 1/4 in (13.3 cm)
Mark: cup: "Wedgwood" "11" in blue enamel; saucer: "Wedgwood" "4"
Provenance: Dr. Francis Jennings Vurpillat, South Bend, Ind.
1976.267 a and b

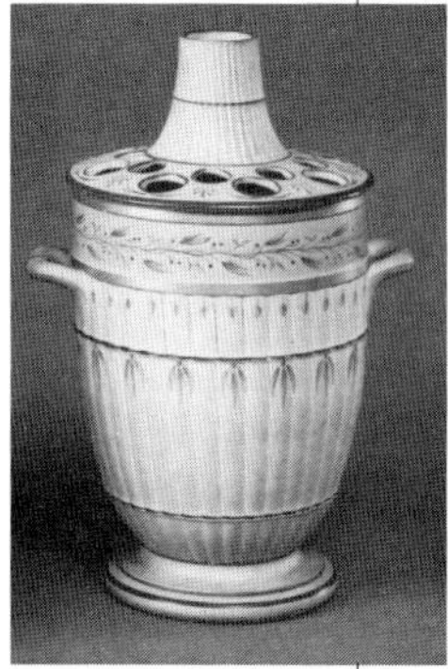

434. Potpourri Vase: ca. 1790
Caneware with blue, green, and gold enamel decoration
8 3/8 x 3 9/16 in (21.2 x 9 cm)
Mark: "Wedgwood" "O"
Provenance: Dr. Francis Jennings Vurpillat, South Bend, Ind.
1976.280 a and b
Color plate 138

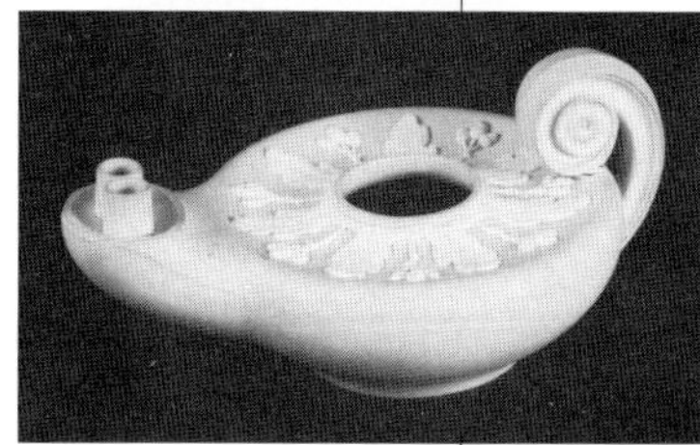

435. Hand Lamp: ca. 1800
Caneware with white relief, glazed interior
1 5/16 x 3 in (3.3 x 7.6 cm)
Mark: "WEDGWOOD"
Provenance: Dr. Francis Jennings Vurpillat, South Bend, Ind.
1976.287

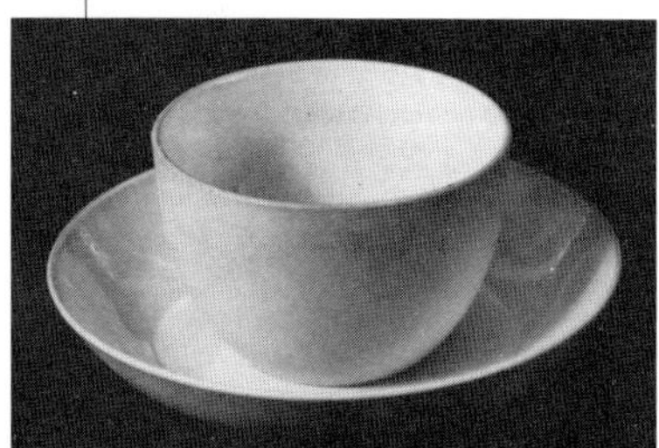

436. Cup and Saucer: ca. 1800
Caneware with glazed pearl slip interior
Cup: 2 3/16 x 1 13/16 in (5.5 x 4.6 cm); saucer: 5 3/8 in (13.6 cm)
Mark: "WEDGWOOD" with tool marks
Provenance: Dr. Francis Jennings Vurpillat, South Bend, Ind.
1976.260

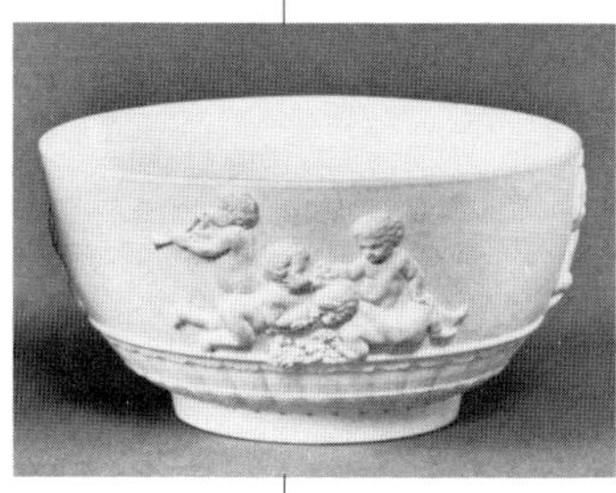

437. Waste Bowl: *Bacchanalian Boys*, ca. 1790
Caneware with glazed pearl slip interior
2 5/16 x 2 3/8 in (5.8 x 6 cm)
Mark: "Wedgwood"
Provenance: Dr. Harold L. Klawans, Chicago
1976.279

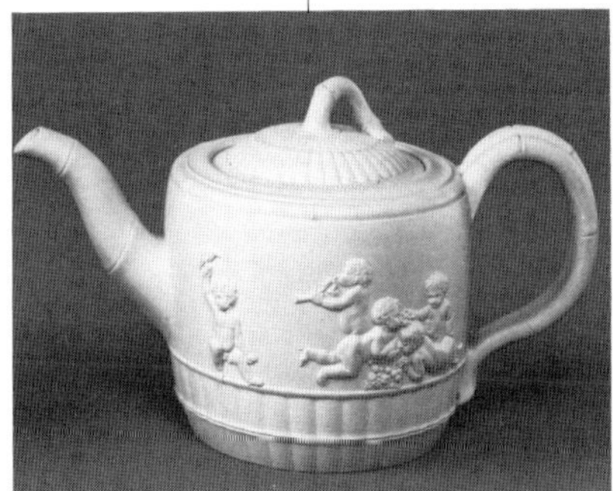

438. Teapot: *Boys at Play,* ca. 1790
Caneware, unglazed interior
4 5/8 x 3 3/8 in (11.7 x 8.5 cm)
Mark: "Wedgwood" "S" with tool marks
Provenance: David Davis, Chicago; Ann Brodkiewicz, Chicago
1976.278 a and b
Color plate 135

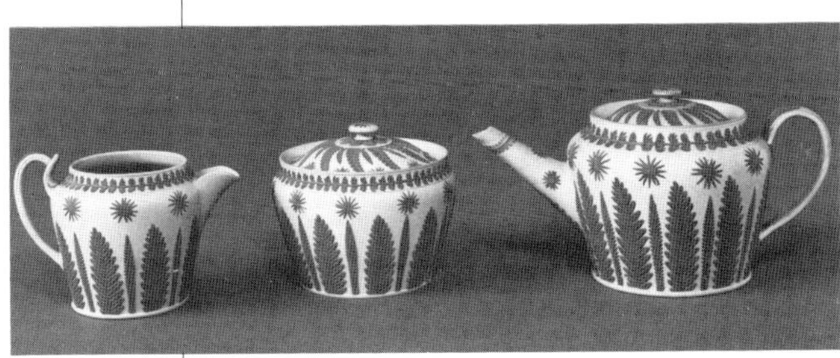

439. Teapot, Cream Pitcher, Sugar Bowl: *Darwin Pattern,* ca. 1830
Caneware with dark green relief; teapot, glazed interior
Teapot: 3 7/8 x 3 7/16 in (9.8 x 8.7 cm); creamer: 2 7/8 x 2 7/16 in (7.3 x 6.1 cm); sugar bowl: 3 1/4 x 2 15/16 in (8.2 x 7.4 cm)
Mark: "WEDGWOOD" with tool marks
Provenance: Ann Brodkiewicz, Chicago
1976.269; 1976.270; 1976.271 a and b

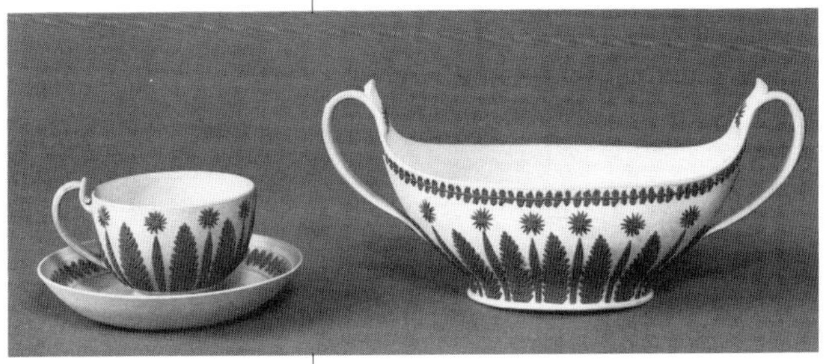

440. Cup and Saucer: *Darwin Pattern,* ca. 1830
Caneware with dark green relief, unglazed interior
Cup: 3 1/8 x 1 9/16 in (7.9 x 3.9 cm); saucer: 5 in (12.7 cm)
Mark: cup: "WEDGWOOD" with tool marks; saucer: "WEDGWOOD" "69"
Provenance: Byron A. Born, Ho-ho-kus, N.J.
1976.272

441. Bowl: *Darwin Pattern,* ca. 1830
Caneware with dark green relief, unglazed interior
4 1/4 x 3 5/8 x 2 15/16 in (10.7 x 9.2 x 7.4 cm)
Mark: "WEDGWOOD"
Provenance: Dr. Francis Jennings Vurpillat, South Bend, Ind.
1976.273

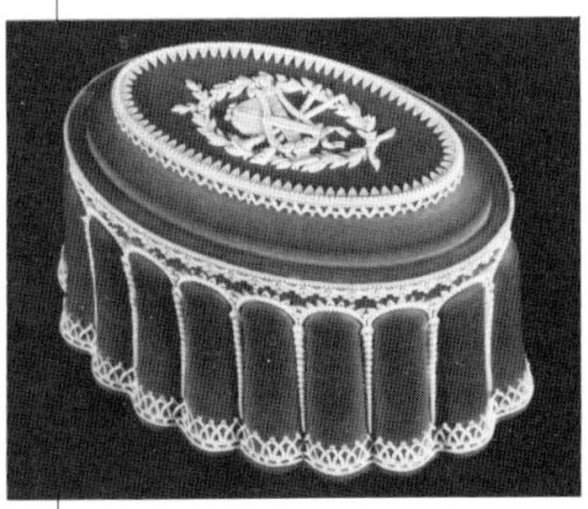

442. Conceit: ca. 1800
Caneware
5 1/2 x 8 x 5 1/8 in (13.9 x 20.3 x 13 cm)
Mark: "WEDGWOOD / G"
Provenance: Art Trading Ltd., New York
1990.267

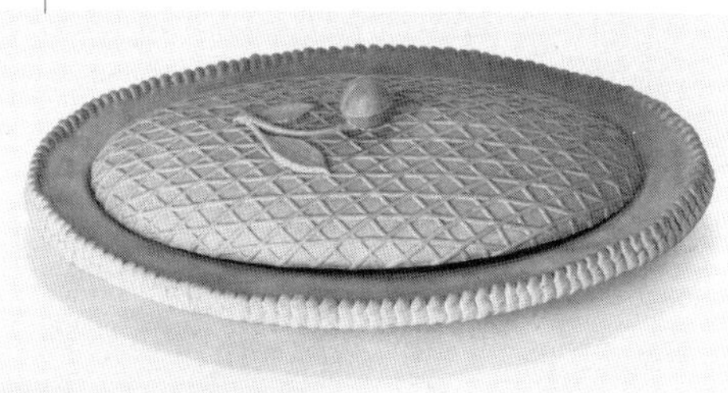

443. Pastry Dish with Cherry Finial: ca. 1800
Caneware, glazed interior
1 15/16 x 8 1/2 x 5 1/2 in (4.9 x 21.5 x 13.9 cm)
Mark: "WEDGWOOD" "G"
Provenance: Fred J. Tongue, Santa Monica, Calif.
1976.274 a and b
Color plate 136

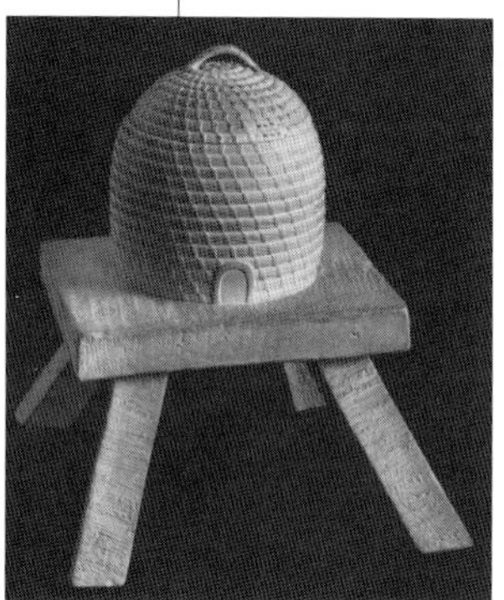

444. Honey Pot and Cover: *Beehive Bench*, ca. 1820
Caneware, glazed interior
6 1/2 x 6 in (16.5 x 15.2 cm)
Mark: "WEDGWOOD" "V" incised
Provenance: Art Trading Ltd., New York
1991.800

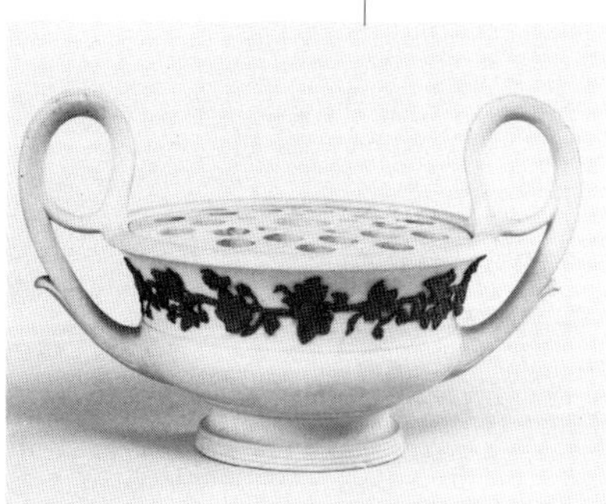

445. Potpourri Vase: ca. 1815
Caneware with brown relief
6 1/4 x 3 3/4 in (15.8 x 9.5 cm)
Mark: "WEDGWOOD" "A"
Provenance: Dr. Harold L. Klawans, Chicago
1976.285

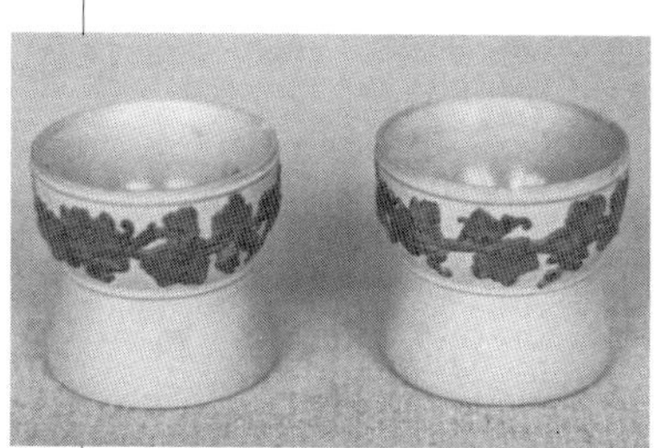

446. Pair of Egg Stands: 19th century
Caneware with dark green relief
1 19/32 x 1 5/8 in (4 x 4.1 cm)
Mark: none
Provenance: Dr. Francis Jennings Vurpillat, South Bend, Ind.
1976.284

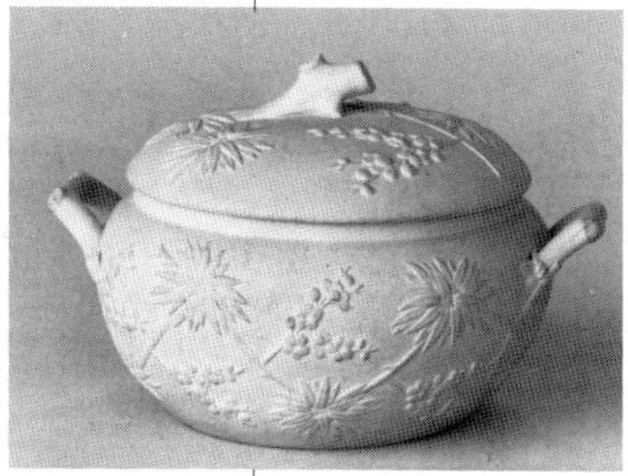

447. Sugar Bowl: *Prunus*, ca. 1800
Caneware, unglazed interior
3 1/2 x 2 5/8 in (8.8 x 6.6 cm)
Mark: "WEDGWOOD" "W"
Provenance: Ann Brodkiewicz, Chicago
1976.261

Rosso Antico

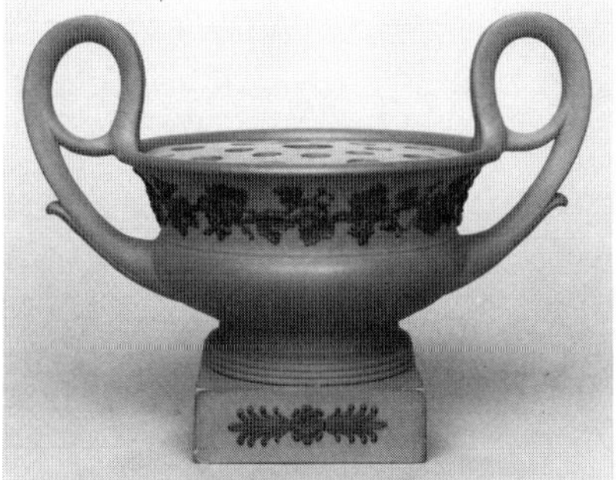

448. Potpourri Vase: ca. 1815
Rosso antico with black relief
8 1/4 x 4 1/4 x 4 1/4 in (20.9 x 10.7 x 10.7 cm)
Mark: "WEDGWOOD" "RK"
Provenance: Dr. Francis Jennings Vurpillat, South Bend, Ind.
1976.229
Base has four firing holes.

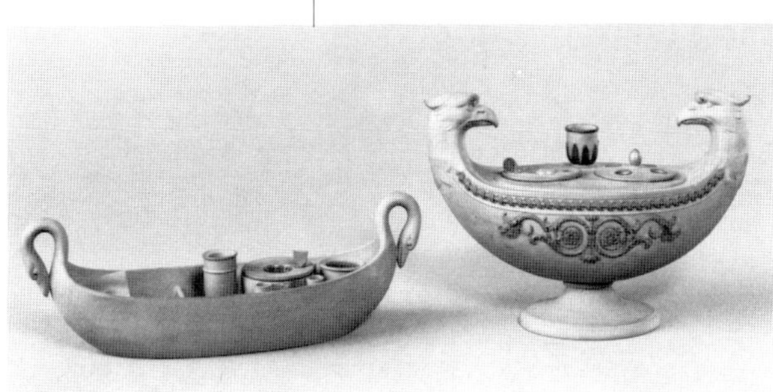

449. Inkstand: ca. 1815
Rosso antico with black relief and removable fitments
6 x 4 x 8 3/8 in (15.2 x 10.1 x 21.2 cm)
Mark: "WEDGWOOD"
Provenance: Dr. Francis Jennings Vurpillat, South Bend, Ind.
1976.226

450. Inkstand: ca. 1815
Rosso antico with removable fitments
3 1/2 x 3 1/16 x 10 in (8.8 x 7.7 x 25.4 cm)
Mark: "WEDGWOOD" "W"
Provenance: Dr. Harold L. Klawans, Chicago
1976.227

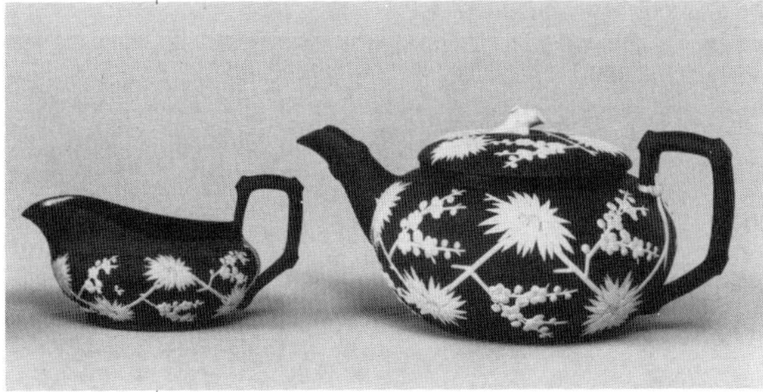

451. Teapot: *Prunus*, ca. 1810
Stoneware with white relief and glazed interior
4 1/16 x 3 3/8 in (10.3 x 8.5 cm)
Mark: "WEDGWOOD"
Provenance: Dr. Francis Jennings Vurpillat, South Bend, Ind.
1976.251

452. Cream Pitcher: *Prunus*, ca. 1810
Stoneware with white relief and glazed interior
2 13/16 x 2 1/8 x 2 5/8 in (7.1 x 5.3 x 6.6 cm)
Mark: "WEDGWOOD"
Provenance: Ann Brodkiewicz, Chicago
1976.252

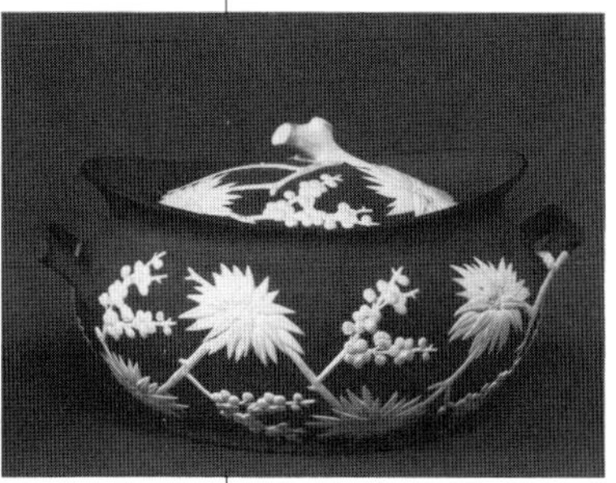

453. Sugar Bowl: *Prunus*, ca. 1810
Rosso antico with white stoneware relief
3 1/4 x 2 3/4 x 3 3/8 in (8.2 x 6.9 x 8.5 cm)
Mark: "WEDGWOOD"
Provenance: Ann Brodkiewicz, Chicago
1976.249

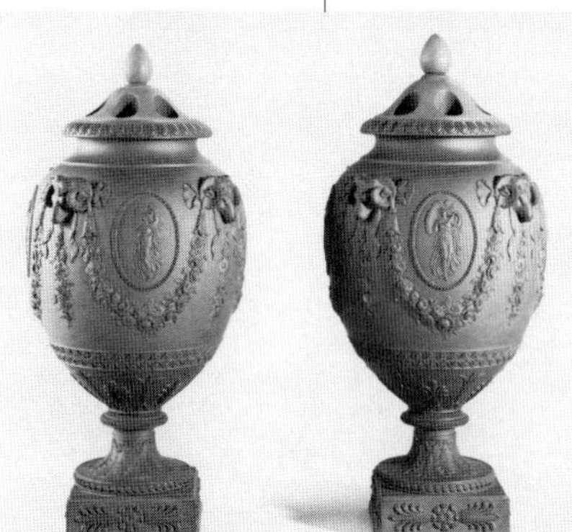

454. Pair of Covered Potpourri Vases: *Horae*, ca. 1820
Stoneware, solid brown with replacement lids
a: 11 5/8 x 3 15/16 x 3 15/16 in (29.5 x 10 x 10 cm);
b: 11 3/4 x 3 15/16 x 3 15/16 in (29.8 x 10 x 10 cm)
Mark: "WEDGWOOD" "J"
Provenance: Dr. Francis Jennings Vurpillat, South Bend, Ind.
1976.228 a and b
Base has cavity around bolt and four firing holes.
Color plate 144

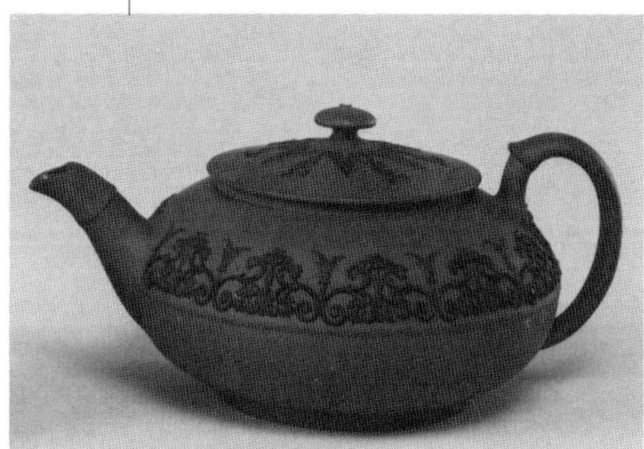

455. Teapot: ca. 1830
Rosso antico with basalt relief and glazed interior
4 3/4 x 4 1/4 in (12 x 10.7 cm)
Mark: "WEDGWOOD" "11"
Provenance: Harold L. Klawans, Chicago
1976.225

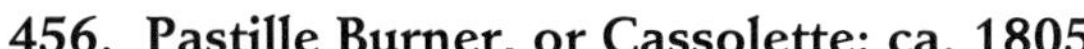

456. Pastille Burner, or Cassolette: ca. 1805
Rosso antico with basalt relief
5 1/2 x 3 9/16 x 4 1/2 in (13.9 x 9 x 11.4 cm)
Mark: "JOSIAH WEDGWOOD / Feb 2 1805"
Provenance: Fred J. Tongue, Santa Monica, Calif.
1976.231 a and b
Color plate 149

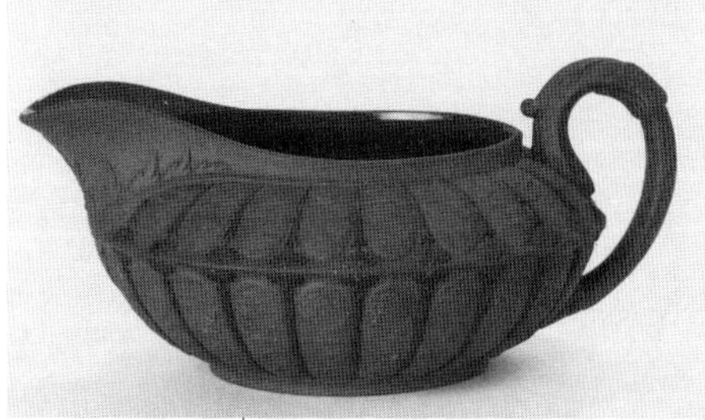

457. Cream Pitcher: ca. 1830
Rosso antico with basalt relief and glazed interior
2 3/4 x 2 1/8 x 2 7/8 in (6.9 x 5.3 x 7.3 cm)
Mark: "WEDGWOOD"
Provenance: Ann Brodkiewicz, Chicago
1976.222

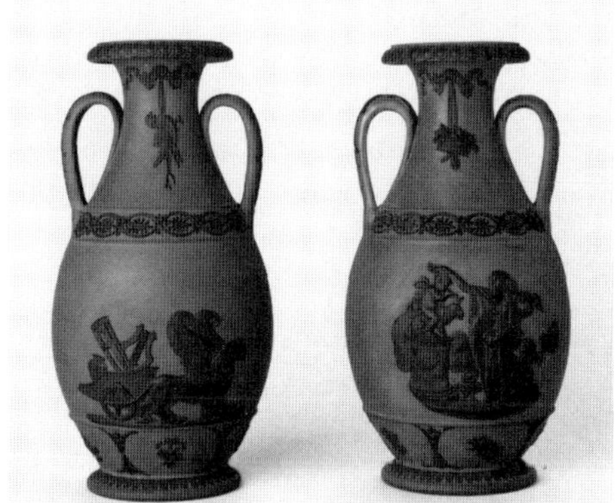

458. Pair of Vases: *Cybele in Chariot Drawn by Lions* and *Triumph of Cybele*, ca. 1810
Rosso antico with basalt relief
10 x 3 5/8 in (25.4 x 9.2 cm)
Mark: "WEDGWOOD" "440" with tool marks
Provenance: M. Mellanay Delhom, Chicago; Ann Brodkiewicz, Chicago
1976.221

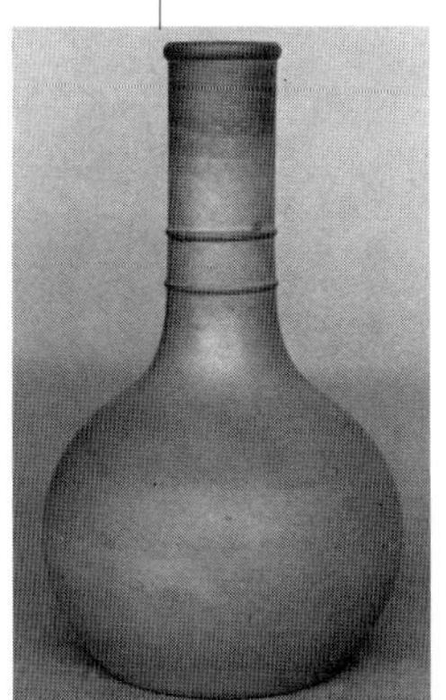

459. Carafe: 19th century
Terra-cotta stoneware
9 7/8 x 4 1/16 in (25 x 10.3 cm)
Mark: "WEDGWOOD" "T" with tool mark
Provenance: Isabelle del Correll, New Orleans
1976.220

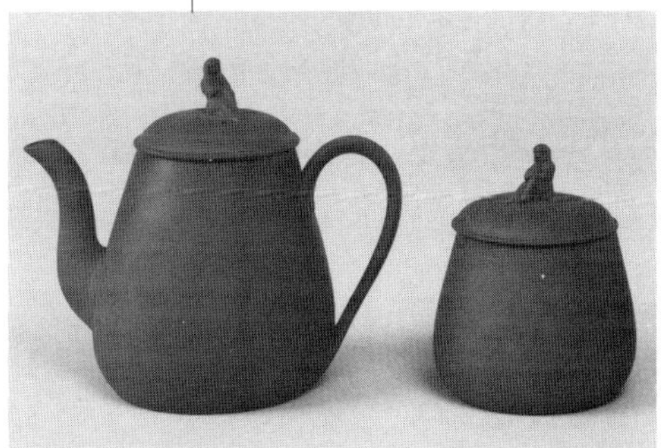

460. Sugar Bowl: ca. 1825
Rosso antico with glazed interior
4 1/2 x 3 in (11.4 x 7.6 cm)
Mark: "WEDGWOOD" "30" with tool mark
Provenance: Dr. Harold L. Klawans, Chicago
1976.224

461. Coffeepot: ca. 1825
Rosso antico with glazed interior
6 x 3 15/16 in (15.2 x 10 cm)
Mark: "WEDGWOOD" "24" "5" with tool mark
Provenance: Dr. Harold L. Klawans, Chicago
1976.223

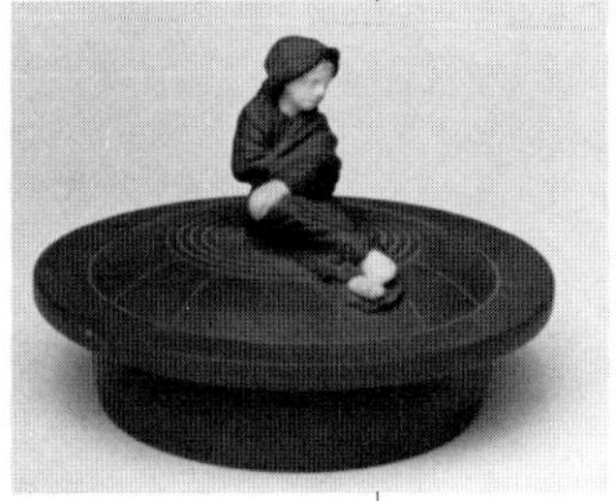

462. Top for Teapot: ca. 1825
Rosso antico with white stoneware
1 3/4 in (4.4 cm)
Mark: none
Provenance: Dr. Harold L. Klawans, Chicago
1980. 168

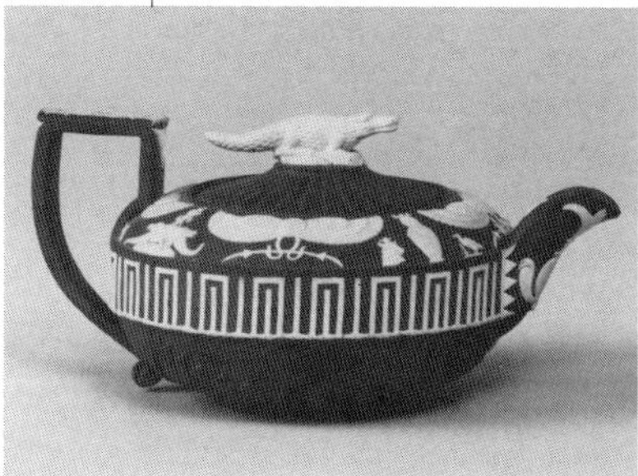

463. Teapot: *Egyptian*, ca. 1810
Rosso antico with white stoneware relief
3 3/4 x 2 1/2 in (9.5 x 6.2 cm)
Mark: "WEDGWOOD" "N I E W" incised
Provenance: Dr. Francis Jennings Vurpillat, South Bend, Ind.
1976.250
Color plate 143

464. Sugar Bowl: *Egyptian*, ca. 1820
Rosso antico with basalt relief
3 1/2 x 2 1/2 in (8.8 x 6.3 cm)
Mark: "WEDGWOOD"
Provenance: Dr. Harold L. Klawans, Chicago
1976.234
Color plate 143

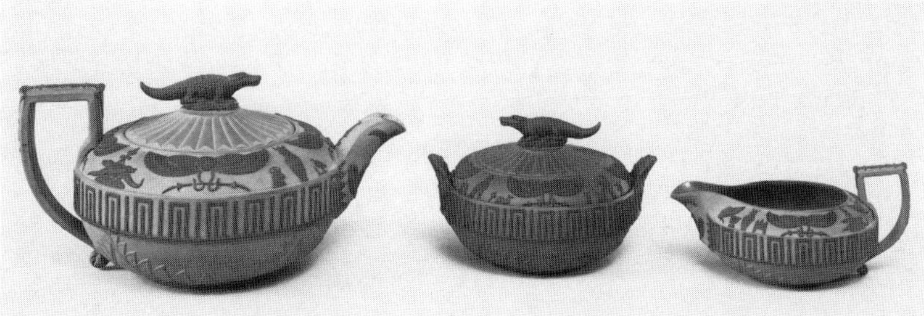

465. Cream Pitcher: *Egyptian*, ca. 1820
Rosso antico with basalt relief
1 7/8 x 2 in (4.7 x 5 cm)
Mark: "WEDGWOOD" "W"
Provenance: David Newbon, London
1976.233

466. Teapot: *Egyptian*, ca. 1820
Rosso antico with basalt relief
4 1/2 x 3 1/4 in (11.4 x 8.2 cm)
Mark: "WEDGWOOD" "I"
Provenance: Otto Wasserman, New York
1976.232
Color plate 143

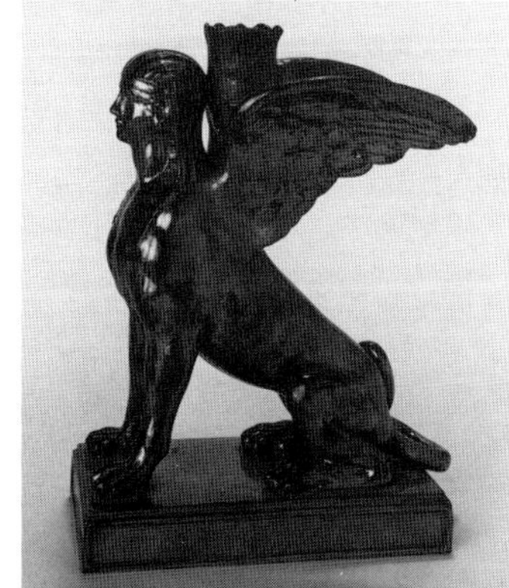

467. Sphinx Candle Holder: ca. 1810
Red earthenware with silver luster
10 1/16 x 4 1/8 x 7 5/16 in (25.5 x 10.4 x 18.5 cm)
Mark: "WEDGWOOD"
Provenance: Fred J. Tongue, Santa Monica, Calif.
1980.121
Base has eight firing holes.

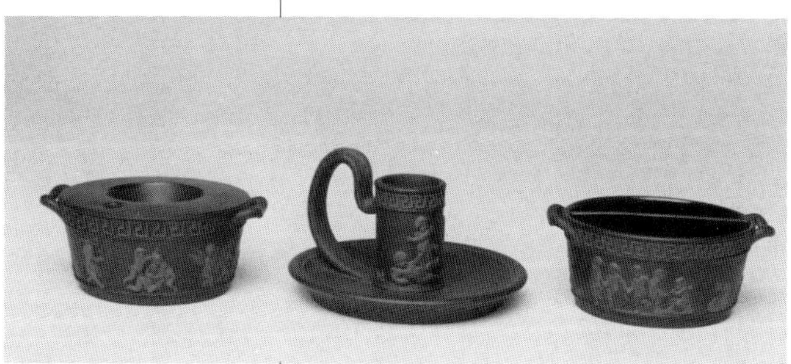

468. Three-Piece Desk Set: *Boys at Play*, ca. 1810
Rosso Antico
Inkwell: 1 7/16 x 2 1/2 in (3.6 x 6.3 cm); candle holder: 2 1/4 x 3 3/4 in (5.7 x 9.5 cm); sand and wax box: 1 7/16 x 2 1/2 in (3.6 x 6.3 cm)
Mark: inkwell: none; candle holder: "WEDGWOOD" "Z"; box: "WEDGWOOD" "Z"
Provenance: Dr. Francis Jennings Vurpillat, South Bend, Ind.
1980.159 a, b, and c

Nineteenth-Century Pearl Ware and White Ware

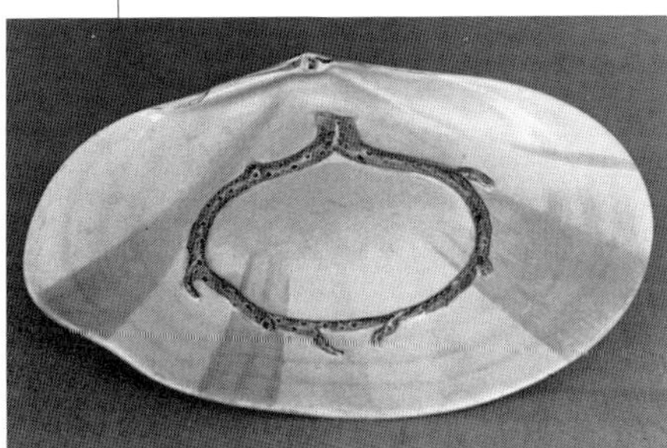

469. Nautilus Stand: ca. 1815
White ware, pink, yellow, orange, and pale brown underglaze decoration
9 x 5 7/8 in (22.8 x 14.9 cm)
Mark: "WEDGWOOD" "X"
Provenance: Dr. Harold L. Klawans, Chicago
1976.298

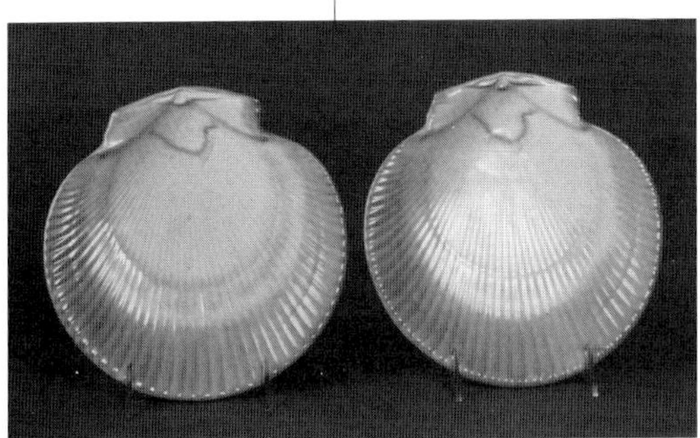

470. Eight Shell-Shaped Plates: 19th century
Pearl ware and white ware, pink-and-yellow underglaze decoration
8 5/8 x 8 1/4 in (21.9 x 20.8 cm)
Mark: "WEDGWOOD" with various tool marks, some with "P" with various date letters
Provenance: Purchased in Birmingham, Ala.
1976.290-.297

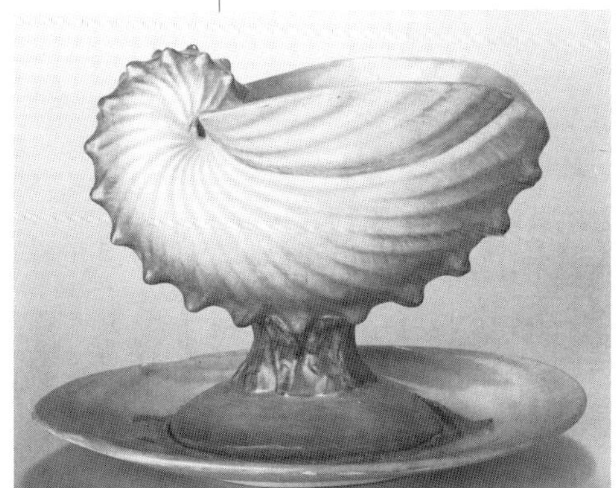

471. Nautilus Dessert Compote and Stand: ca. 1815
White ware, pink, yellow, orange, and pale brown underglaze decoration
Stand: 12 3/8 x 8 in (31.4 x 20.3 cm); compote: 8 x 10 1/2 x 6 5/8 in (20.3 x 26.6 x 16.8 cm)
Mark: "WEDGWOOD"
Provenance: Fred J. Tongue, Santa Monica, Calif.
1976.288 a and b
Color plate 148, fig. 46

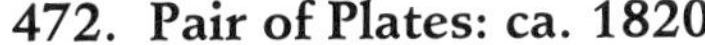

472. Pair of Plates: ca. 1820
White ware with variegated luster decoration
8 in (20.3 cm)
Mark: a: "WEDGWOOD" "H" "H"; b: "WEDGWOOD" "1" "1"
Provenance: Ann Brodkiewicz, Chicago
1976.165 a and b

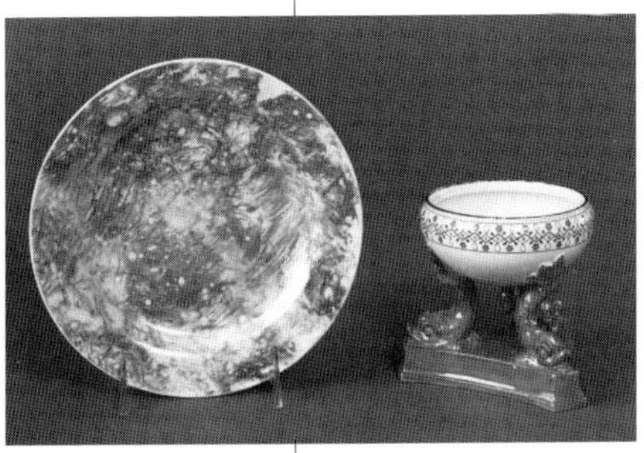

473. Pastille Burner, or Cassolette: ca. 1815
Cream ware with rose luster, red-and-black enamel overglaze decoration
4 3/8 x 4 1/8 x 5 1/4 in (11.1 x 10.4 x 13.3 cm)
Mark: "WEDGWOOD"
Provenance: Ann Brodkiewicz, Chicago
1976.169
Color plate 149

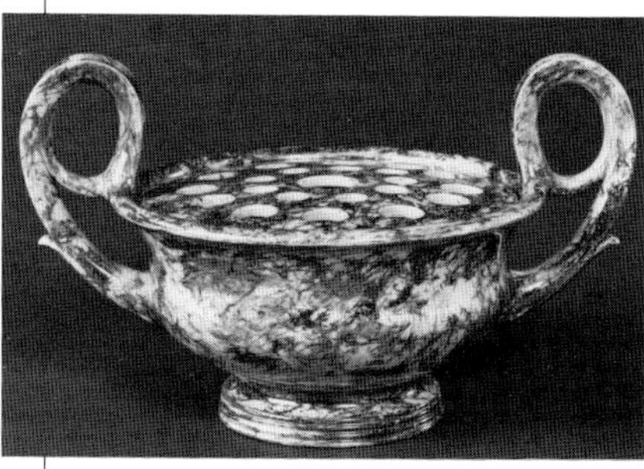

474. Krater Vase with Two Fitments: ca. 1820
White ware with variegated luster decoration
6 7/8 x 5 in (17.4 x 12.7 cm)
Mark: "WEDGWOOD"
Provenance: Sir George Duff-Dunbar, Scotland; M. Mellanay Delhom, Chicago; Ann Brodkiewicz, Chicago
1976.166
Color plate 150

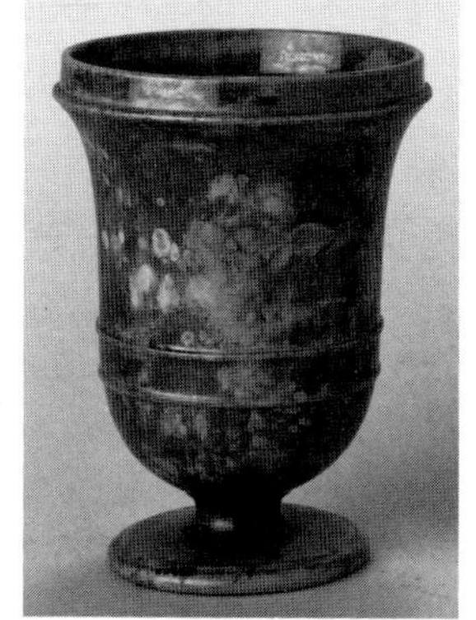

475. Vase: ca. 1820
Cream ware with variegated luster decoration
4 1/8 x 2 1/8 in (10.4 x 5.3 cm)
Mark: "WEDGWOOD" with tool marks
Provenance: Ann Brodkiewicz, Chicago
1976.167

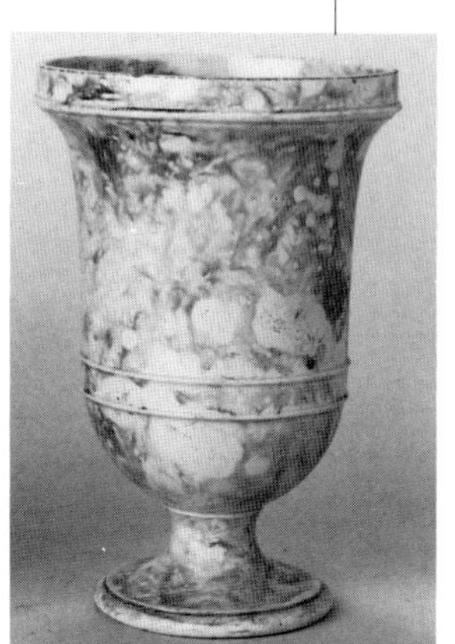

476. Vase: ca. 1820
Pearl ware with variegated luster decoration
5 1/2 x 2 1/2 in (13.9 x 6.3 cm)
Mark: "WEDGWOOD" with tool marks
Provenance: Sir George Duff-Dunbar, Scotland; Dr. Francis Jennings Vurpillat, South Bend, Ind.
1976.168

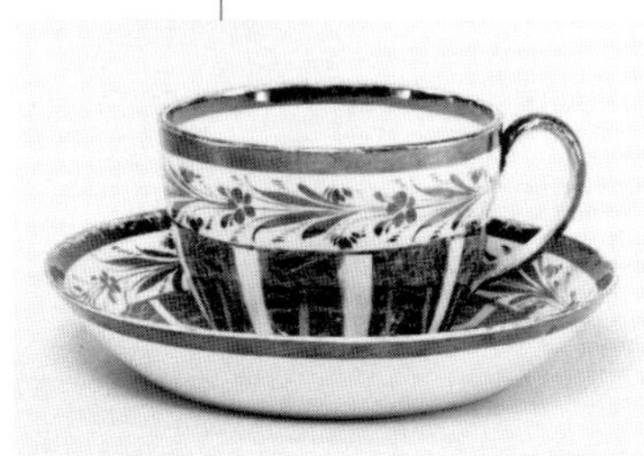

477. Cup and Saucer: 19th century
Pearl ware with luster decoration
Cup: 2 1/16 x 1 3/4 in (5.2 x 4.4 cm); saucer: 5 1/8 in (13 cm)
Mark: cup: none; saucer: "WEDGWOOD" with tool mark
Provenance: Fred J. Tongue, Santa Monica, Calif.
1976.170 a and b

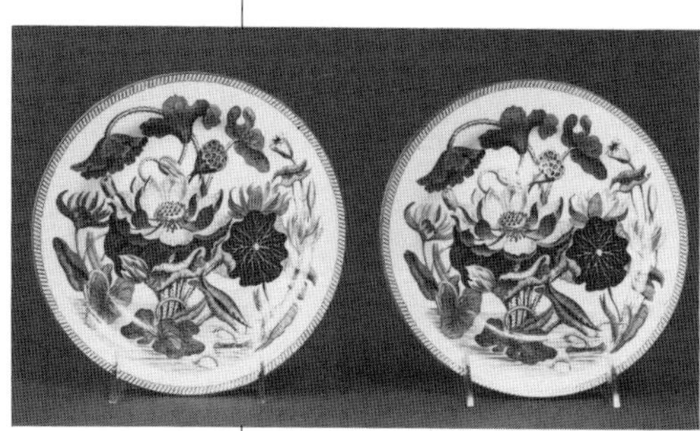

478. Pair of Plates: *Water Lily*, ca. 1810
Pearl ware, transfer print with orange underglaze decoration and overglaze gilding
8 1/16 in (20.4 cm)
Mark: "WEDGWOOD" with tool marks
Provenance: Ann Brodkiewicz, Chicago
1979.205 a and b
Color plate 146

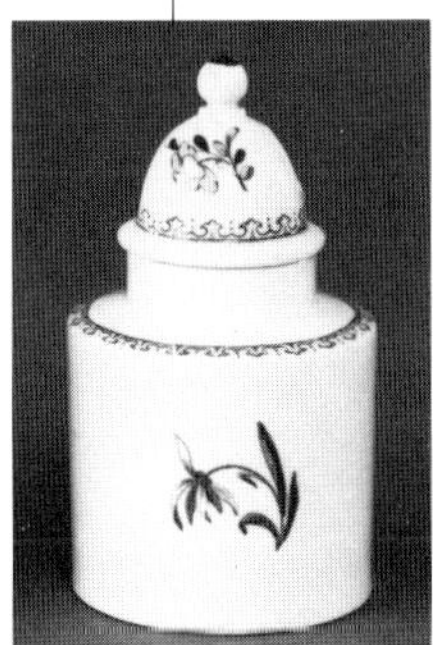

479. Tea Canister: ca. 1815
White ware, blue transfer print underglaze
4 1/2 x 2 9/16 in (11.4 x 6.5 cm)
Mark: "WEDGWOOD" in underglaze blue
Provenance: Dr. Harold L. Klawans, Chicago
1979.194 a and b

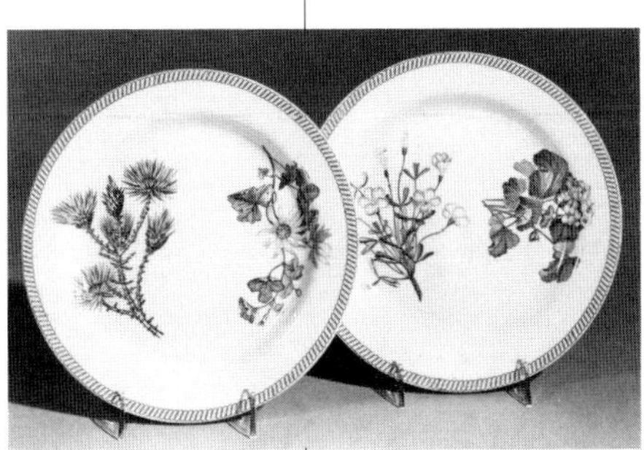

480. Four Plates: *Botanical Flowers*, 19th century
Pearl ware, blue transfer print underglaze
8 1/8 in (20.6 cm)
Mark: a: "WEDGWOOD" "33"; b: "WEDGWOOD" "33"; "11" blue underglaze; c: "WEDGWOOD" "5" "5" "W/W" in blue underglaze; d: "WEDGWOOD" "1" "1"
Provenance: Frankie Engel Antiques Co., Birmingham, Ala.
1976.150-.153
Color plate 147

481. Ten Plates: *Botanical Flowers*, 19th century
Pearl ware, blue transfer print underglaze
9 13/16 in (24.9 cm)
Mark: "WEDGWOOD" with tool marks
Provenance: Frankie Engel Antiques Co., Birmingham, Ala.
1976.154-.163

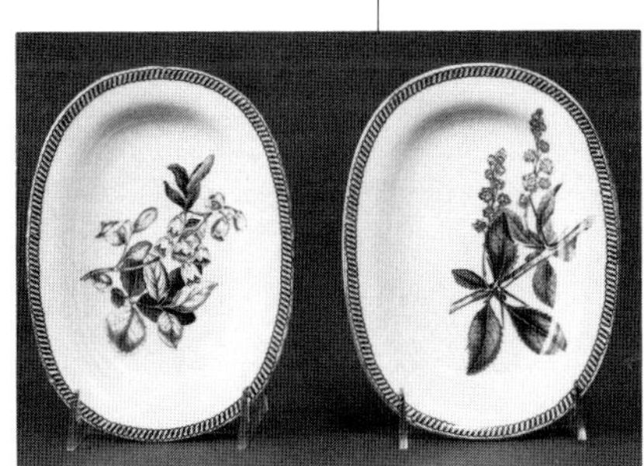

482. Pair of Oval Dishes: *Botanical Flowers*, 19th century
Pearl ware, blue transfer print underglaze
8 x 5 7/8 in (20.3 x 14.9 cm)
Mark: "WEDGWOOD"
Provenance: Ann Brodkiewicz, Chicago
1976.149 a and b
Color plate 147

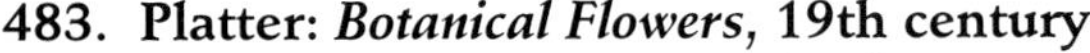

483. Platter: *Botanical Flowers*, 19th century
Pearl ware, blue transfer print underglaze
18 5/8 x 14 in (47.3 x 35.5 cm)
Mark: "WEDGWOOD" with tool marks blue underglaze
Provenance: Frankie Engel Antiques Co., Birmingham, Ala.
1976.164
Color plate 147

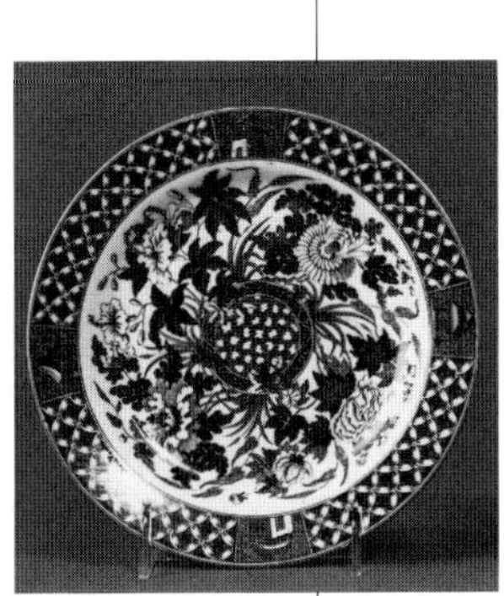

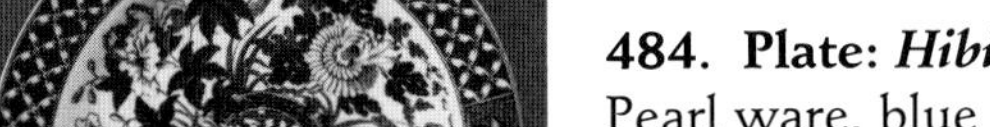

484. Plate: *Hibiscus Pattern*, ca. 1810
Pearl ware, blue transfer print underglaze and gilding
8 in (20.3 cm)
Mark: "WEDGWOOD" "4" "4"
Provenance: Dr. Harold L. Klawans, Chicago
1978.154
Color plate 146

The Work of Émile-Aubert Lessore

485. Three-Piece Jardiniere: 1867
Émile-Aubert Lessore (1805-76), artist
Hugues Protat (fl. 1835-71), designer and modeler
Pearl ware, polychrome enamel overglaze decoration
22 x 24 x 16 in (55.8 x 60.9 x 40.6 cm)
Mark: container: "E. Lessore" in script on front;
two bases: "WEDGWOOD" "OMV" "PEARL" "M" "F"
Provenance: Byron A. Born, Ho-ho-kus, N.J.; Art Trading Ltd., New York
1989.14
Color plate 153

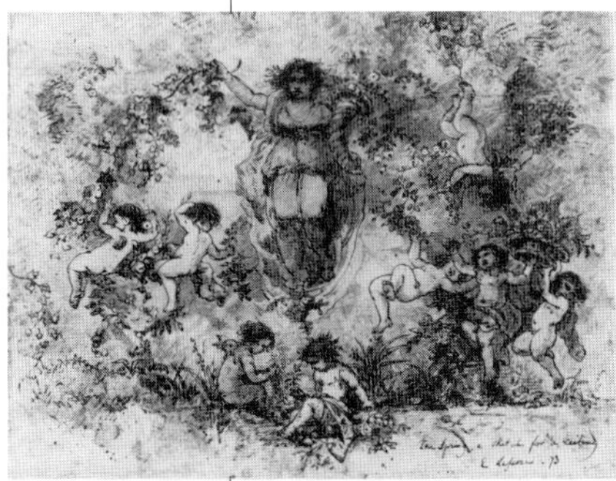

486. Plaque: *The Spring, a Sketch for a Ceiling,* 1873
Émile-Aubert Lessore (1805-76), artist
Cream ware with blue-and-black underglaze decoration
12 x 16 in (30.4 x 40.6 cm)
Mark: "The Spring, a sketch for a ceiling / E. Lessore. 73" in script on front
Provenance: Gift of Mrs. Byron A. Born in memory of her husband, Ho-ho-kus, N.J.
1987.190
Color plate 152

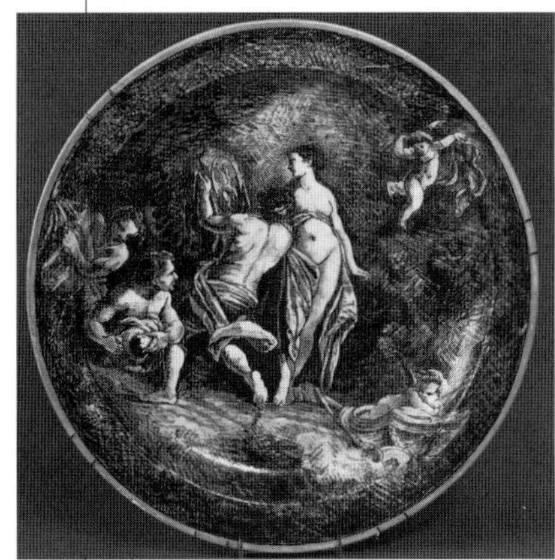

487. Platter: *Perseus and Andromeda,* ca. 1865
Émile-Aubert Lessore (1805-76), artist
Cream ware, green-and-orange underglaze decoration
19 1/2 in (49.5 cm)
Mark: "WEDGWOOD" "E. Lessore" in script on front
Provenance: Otto Wasserman, New York
1976.144
Color plate 151

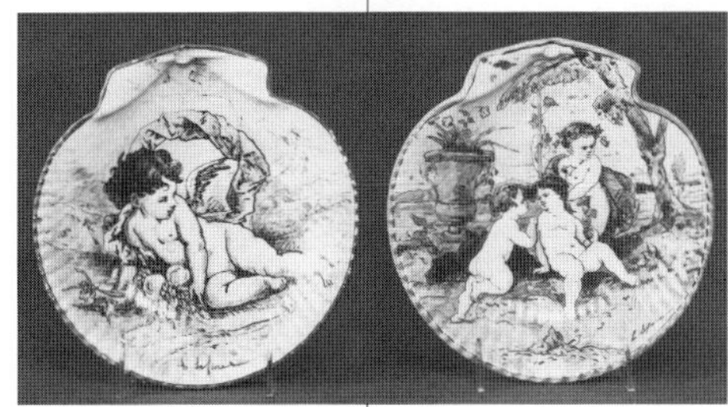

488. Pair of Shell Plates: *Cupid and Bacchanalian Boys,* 1860 or 1867
Émile-Aubert Lessore (1805-76), artist
a: pearl ware, polychrome underglaze decoration;
b: cream ware, polychrome underglaze decoration
a: 8 3/8 x 8 1/4 in (26.3 x 20.9 cm);
b: 8 1/2 x 8 3/8 in (21.5 x 26.3 cm)
Mark: a: "WEDGWOOD / PEARL" "R" "V" "E. Lessore" in script on front; b: "WEDGWOOD" "AVO" or "OAV" "E. Lessore" in script on front
Provenance: M. Mellanay Delhom, Chicago; Ann Brodkiewicz, Chicago
1976.146 a and b

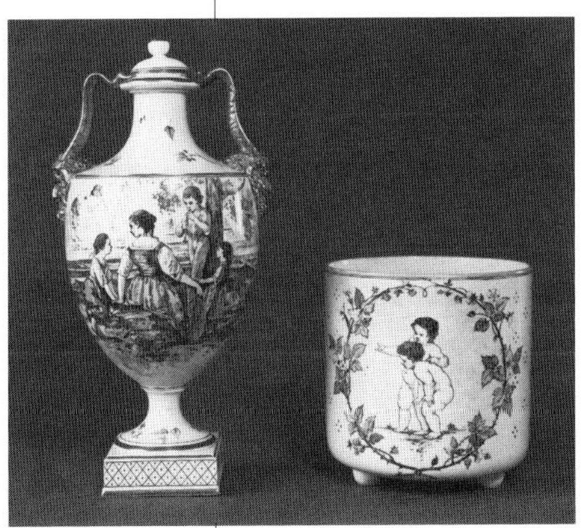

489. Covered Vase: *Children in the Woods,* ca. 1869
Émile-Aubert Lessore (1805-76), artist
Cream ware, polychrome underglaze decoration and gilding
14 1/4 x 4 x 4 in (36.1 x 10.1 x 10.1 cm)
Mark: "WEDGWOOD" "JOX" "E. Lessore" in script on front
Provenance: M. Mellanay Delhom, Chicago;
Ann Brodkiewicz, Chicago
1976.145
Base is hollow.

490. Jardiniere: *Mother and Child and Putti,* ca. 1865
Émile-Aubert Lessore (1805-76), artist
Cream ware, polychrome underglaze decoration
7 1/2 x 7 1/4 in (19 x 18.4 cm)
Mark: "WEDGWOOD" "T" "E. Lessore" in script on front
Provenance: Dr. Francis Jennings Vurpillat, South Bend, Ind.
1976.147

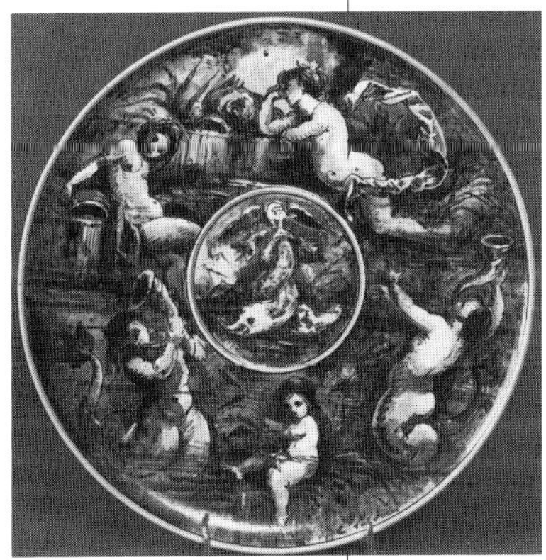

491. Plate: *Putti and Sea Creatures,* ca. 1862
Émile-Aubert Lessore (1805-76), artist
Cream ware with gray-and-orange underglaze decoration
12 in (30.4 cm)
Mark: "WEDGWOOD" "AVQ" with tool mark; "E. Lessore" in script on front
Provenance: M. Mellanay Delhom, Chicago; Fred J. Tongue, Santa Monica, Calif.
1976.148

Scent Flasks

492. Scent Flask: *Nymphs,* ca. 1790
Jasper, solid blue ground with white relief and silver-and-enamel stopper
4 7/8 x 2 in (12.3 x 5 cm)
Mark: none
Provenance: Ann Brodkiewicz, Chicago
1977.73
Color plate 124

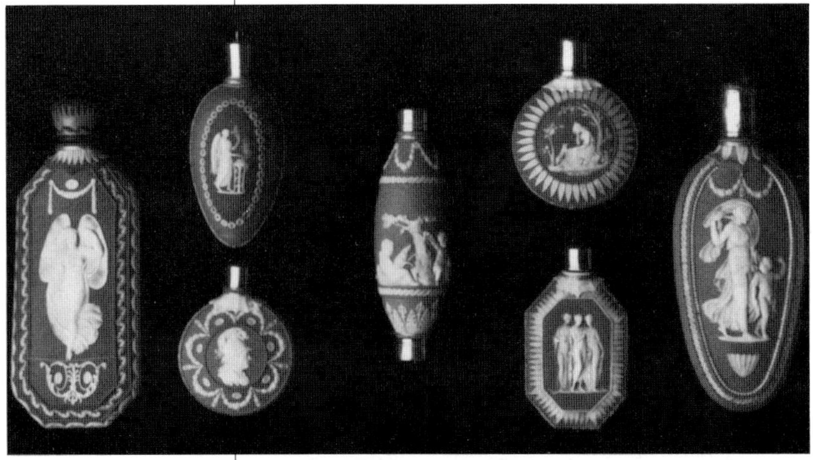

492 493, 494 495 496, 497 498

493. Scent Flask: *A Sacrifice,* ca. 1790
Jasper, solid blue ground with green-and-white relief and silver stopper
3 1/4 x 1 3/8 in (8.2 x 3.4 cm)
Mark: none
Provenance: M. Mellanay Delhom, Chicago
1977.74
Color plate 124

494. Scent Flask: *Catherine the Great as Minerva,* ca. 1790
Jasper, solid blue ground with white relief and silver stopper
2 in (5 cm)
Mark: none
Provenance: Ann Brodkiewicz, Chicago
1977.75
Color plate 124

495. Double Scent Flask: *Boys at Play,* ca. 1790
Jasper, solid blue granulated ground with white relief and silver stoppers
3 in (7.6 cm)
Mark: none
Provenance: Dr. Harold L. Klawans, Chicago
1977.69
Color plate 124

496. Scent Flask: *Poor Maria,* ca. 1785
Jasper, solid blue ground with white relief and silver stopper
2 1/4 x 1 3/4 in (5.7 x 4.4 cm)
Mark: none
Provenance: Godfrey W. Ford, England; Dr. Harold L. Klawans, Chicago
1977.70
Color plate 124

497. Scent Flask: *Three Graces and a Sacrifice,* ca. 1790
Jasper, solid blue ground with white relief and silver stopper
2 5/8 x 1 1/2 in (8.2 x 4.4 cm)
Mark: none
Provenance: Godfrey W. Ford, England; Dr. Harold L. Klawans, Chicago
1977.71
Color plate 124

498. Scent Flask: *Venus and Cupid,* ca. 1795
Jasper, solid blue ground with white relief and silver stopper
5 x 2 in (12.7 x 5 cm)
Mark: none
Provenance: Godfrey W. Ford, England; Dr. Harold L. Klawans, Chicago
1977.72
Color plate 124

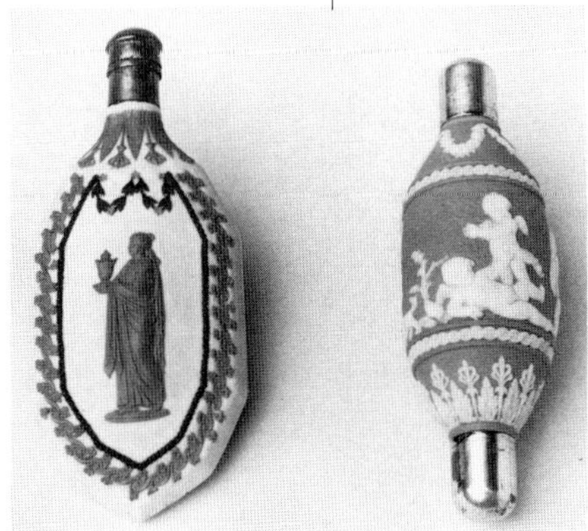

499. Scent Flask: *Female Classical Figure,* ca. 1790
John Turner (1738-86), potter
Jasper, solid white ground with blue-and-black relief and silver stopper
3 1/4 x 1 3/4 in (8.2 x 4.4 cm)
Mark: "TURNER" "17"
Provenance: M. Mellanay Delhom, Chicago; Ann Brodkiewicz, Chicago
1980.150

500. Double Scent Flask: *Blind Man's Bluff,* ca. 1790
Jasper, solid blue granulated ground with white relief and silver stoppers
3 5/16 in (8.1 cm)
Mark: none
Provenance: Dr. Francis Jennings Vurpillat, South Bend, Ind.
1980.176

Tea-Caddy Spoons

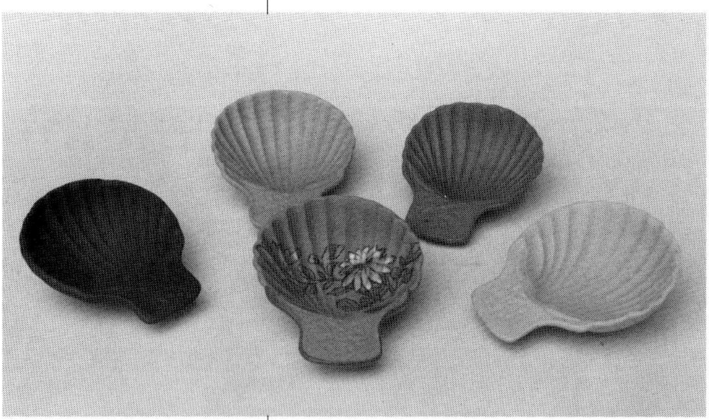

501. Shell-Shaped Tea-Caddy Spoon: ca. 1815-28
Basalt
2 3/16 x 1 3/4 in (5.5 x 4.4 cm)
Mark: "WEDGWOOD"
Provenance: Ann Brodkiewicz, Chicago
1980.141.4

502. Shell-Shaped Tea-Caddy Spoon: ca. 1815-28
Jasper, solid aqua ground
2 1/4 x 1 7/8 in (5.7 x 4.7 cm)
Mark: "WEDGWOOD"
Provenance: Ann Brodkiewicz, Chicago
1980.141.3

503. Shell-Shaped Tea-Caddy Spoon: ca. 1815-28
Jasper, solid green ground with polychrome enamel decoration
2 5/16 x 1 7/8 in (5.8 x 4.7 cm)
Mark: "WEDGWOOD"
Provenance: Ann Brodkiewicz, Chicago
1980.141.2

504. Shell-Shaped Tea-Caddy Spoon: ca. 1815-28
Jasper, solid dark blue ground
2 3/16 x 1 3/4 in (5.5 x 4.4 cm)
Mark: "WEDGWOOD"
Provenance: Ann Brodkiewicz, Chicago
1980.141.1

505. Shell-Shaped Tea-Caddy Spoon: ca. 1815-28
Jasper, solid lilac ground
2 3/16 x 1 3/4 in (5.5 x 4.4 cm)
Mark: "WEDGWOOD"
Provenance: Sir George Duff-Dunbar, Scotland; Dr. Francis Jennings Vurpillat, South Bend, Ind.
1980.141.5

Classical Medallions Produced for Insertion into Boxes

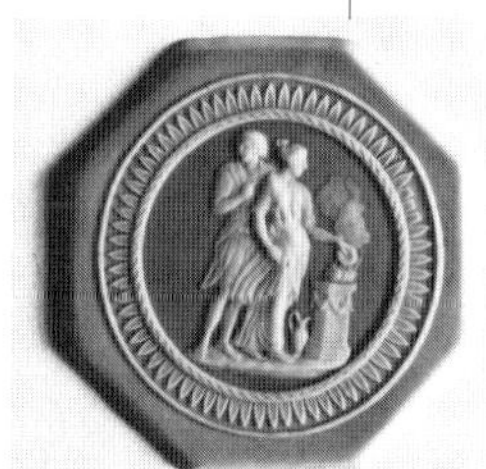

506. Medallion: ***A Sacrifice,*** **ca. 1800**
Jasper, solid white ground with blue-and-yellow wash on front and white relief
1 3/4 x 1 3/4 in (4.4 x 4.4 cm)
Mark: "WEDGWOOD" "I" incised
Provenance: Dr. Francis Jennings Vurpillat, South Bend, Ind.
1977.122.35

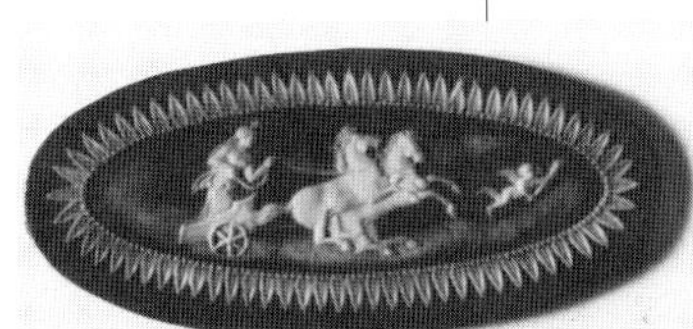

507. Medallion: ***Eros in His Chariot,*** **ca. 1800**
Jasper, solid white ground with black wash and white relief
2 1/4 x 1 1/32 in (5.7 x 2.6 cm)
Mark: "WEDGWOOD" "W" incised
Provenance: Otto Wasserman, New York
1977.87

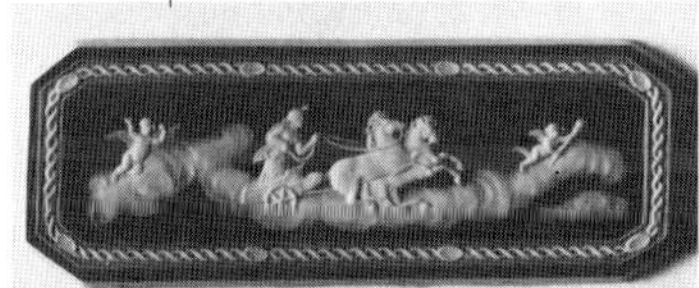

508. Medallion: ***Eros in His Chariot,*** **ca. 1800**
Jasper, solid white ground with black wash on front and green-and-white relief
1 x 2 11/16 in (2.5 x 6.8 cm)
Mark: "WEDGWOOD"
Provenance: Dr. Harold L. Klawans, Chicago
1977.67.10

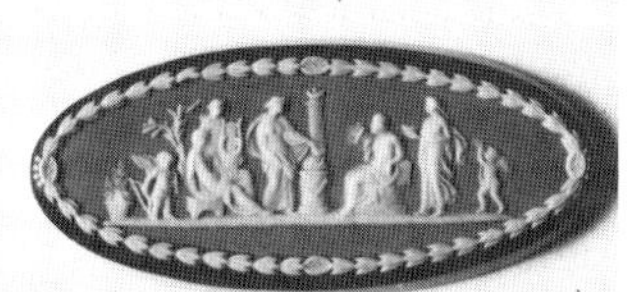

509. Medallion: ***A Group of Classical Figures,*** **ca. 1800**
Jasper, solid white ground with green-and-black wash on front and white relief with polished edges
13/16 x 1 13/16 in (2 x 4.6 cm)
Mark: "WEDGWOOD"
Provenance: Dr. Francis Jennings Vurpillat, South Bend, Ind.
1977.122.38

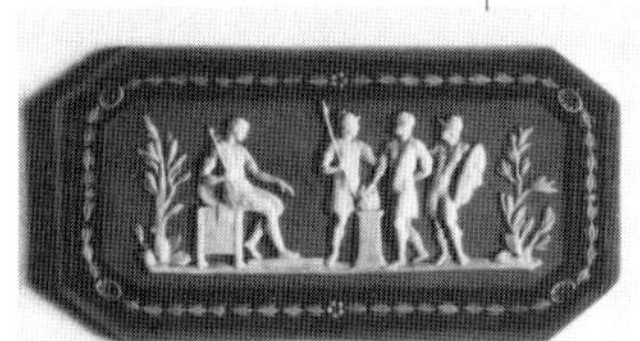

510. Medallion: ***A Group of Classical Figures,*** **ca. 1800**
Jasper, solid white ground with lilac and dark blue wash on front and white relief
1 1/4 x 2 1/2 in (3.1 x 6.3 cm)
Mark: "WEDGWOOD" "I" incised
Provenance: Dr. Francis Jennings Vurpillat, South Bend, Ind.
1977.122.36

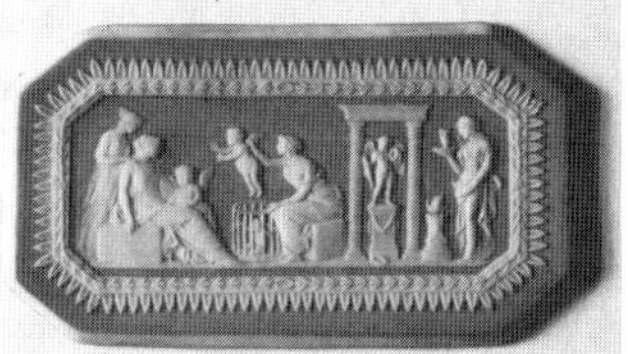

511. Medallion: ***Cupid Market,*** **ca. 1800**
Jasper, solid white ground with lilac-and-blue wash and white relief
2 5/8 x 1 1/2 in (6.6 x 3.8 cm)
Mark: "WEDGWOOD" "F" incised
Provenance: Otto Wasserman, New York
1977.88

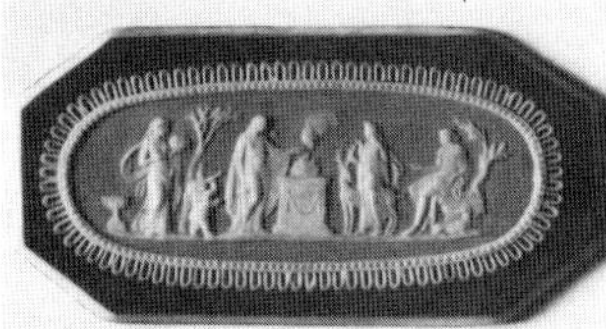

512. Medallion: *A Sacrifice*, ca. 1800
Jasper, solid white ground with lilac-and-dark-blue wash and white relief
2 3/16 x 1 1/16 in (5.5 x 2.7 cm)
Mark: "WEDGWOOD" "L"
Provenance: Otto Wasserman, New York
1977.91

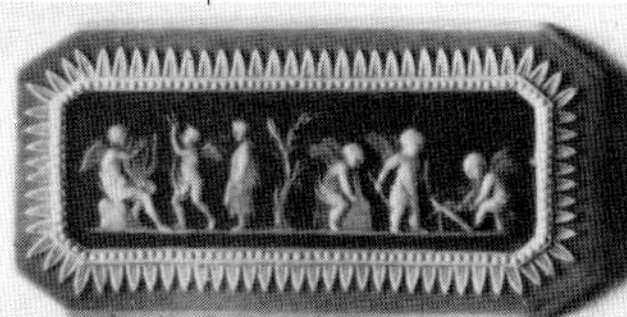

513. Medallion: *A Group of Cupids*, ca. 1800
Jasper, solid white ground with lilac-and-dark-blue wash on front and white relief with polished edges
13/16 x 1 5/8 in (2 x 4.1 cm)
Mark: "WEDGWOOD" "3" incised
Provenance: Dr. Francis Jennings Vurpillat, South Bend, Ind.
1977.122.37

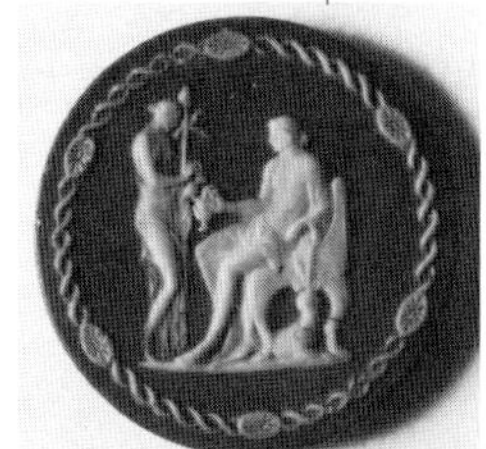

514. Medallion: *Two Classical Figures*, ca. 1800
Jasper, solid white ground with dark blue wash on front with white relief
15/16 in (2.3 cm)
Mark: none
Provenance: Dr. Harold L. Klawans, Chicago
1977.67.9

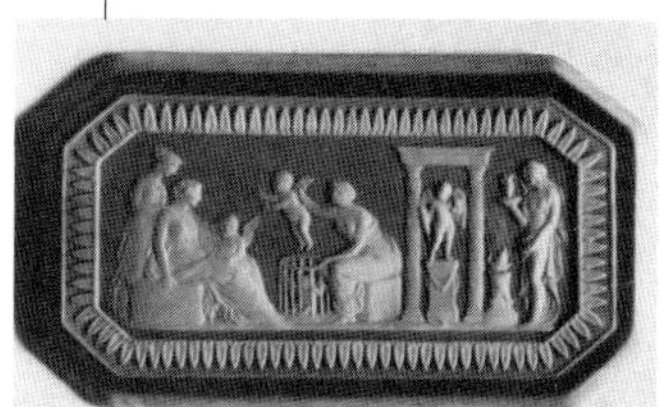

515. Medallion: *Cupid's Market*, ca. 1800
Jasper, solid white ground with green-and-dark-blue wash on front and white relief
2 5/8 x 1 1/2 in (6.6 x 3.8 cm)
Mark: "WEDGWOOD"
Provenance: Purchased in New Orleans
1977.92

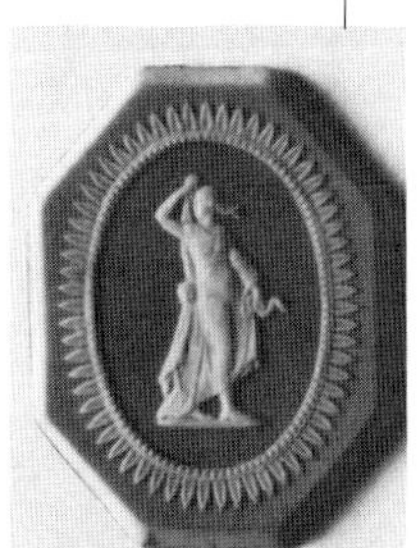

516. Medallion: *A Priestess with a Serpent*, ca. 1800
Jasper, solid white ground with green-and-blue wash and white relief
1 1/2 x 1 1/4 in (3.8 x 3.1 cm)
Mark: "WEDGWOOD"
Provenance: Otto Wasserman, New York
1977.90

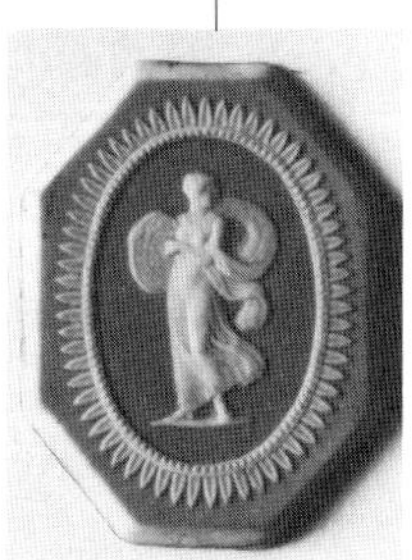

517. Medallion: *Nymph Playing Cymbals*, ca. 1800
Jasper, solid white ground with green-and-blue wash and white relief
1 1/2 x 1 1/4 in (3.8 x 3.1 cm)
Mark: "WEDGWOOD" "R" incised
Provenance: Otto Wasserman, New York
1977.89
Design source: Montfaucon, *L' Antiquité expliquée,* vol. 3, pt. 2, pl. 61, fig. 9

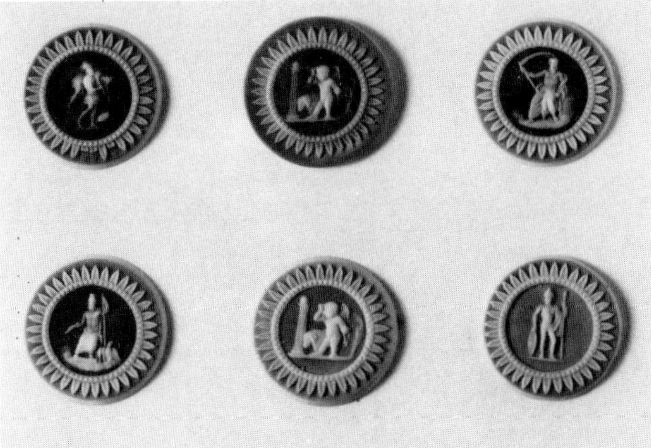

518. Six Medallions: ***Classical Figures and Cupids,*** **ca. 1800**
Jasper, solid white ground with lilac, green, blue, and dark blue wash on front and white relief with polished edges
3/4 in (1.9 cm)
Mark: "WEDGWOOD"
Provenance: Dr. Francis Jennings Vurpillat, South Bend, Ind.
1977.122.39-.44

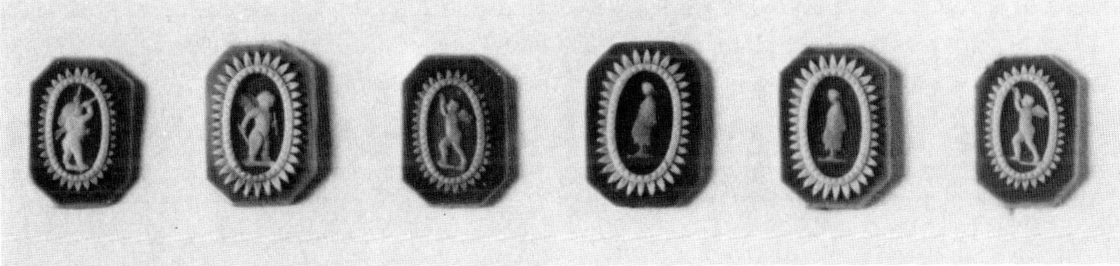

519. Six Medallions: ***Classical Figures and Cupids,*** **ca. 1800**
Jasper, solid white ground with lilac, green, and dark blue wash on front and white relief with polished edges on all but one
7/16 x 9/16 in (1.1 x 1.4 cm)
Mark: "WEDGWOOD" on all but one
Provenance: Dr. Francis Jennings Vurpillat, South Bend, Ind.
1977.122.45-.50

Boxes with Classical Medallion Insertions

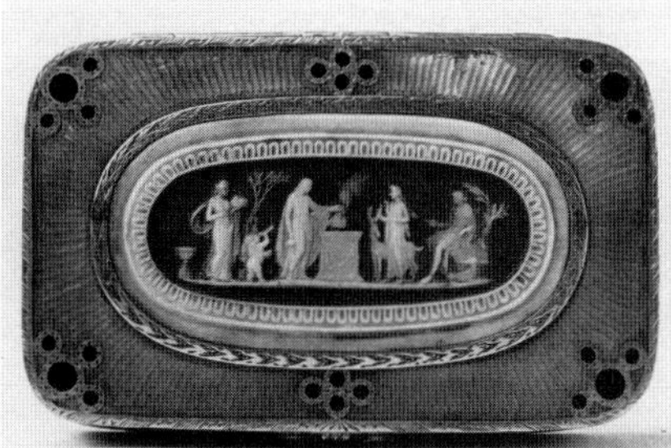

520. Patch Box: ca. 1800
Gold and enamel box with jasper medallion in solid white ground with black-and-green wash and white relief
Box: 2 7/8 x 1 7/8 in (7.3 x 4.7 cm); medallion: 2 1/8 x 1 1/8 in (5.3 x 2.8 cm)
Mark: "WEDGWOOD" "L"
Provenance: Ann Brodkiewicz, Chicago
1980.151
Color plate 128

521. Patch Box: ca. 1800
Ivory box with jasper medallion in solid green ground with white relief, set in gold
Box: 3 5/8 x 1 7/16 in (9.2 x 3.6 cm); medallion: 3 7/16 x 1 3/8 in (8.7 x 3.6 cm)
Mark: none
Provenance: Ann Brodkiewicz, Chicago
1980.144
Color plate 128

522. Snuffbox: *Portrait of Benjamin Franklin*, ca. 1780
Wooden box with jasper medallion in solid white ground with dark blue laminate front and back and white relief
Box: 2 1/2 in (6.3 cm); medallion: 7 13/16 x 3 3/8 in (2.2 x 1.9 cm)
Mark: "Wedgwood & Bentley"
Provenance: Dr. Harold L. Klawans, Chicago
1980.148
Color plate 128

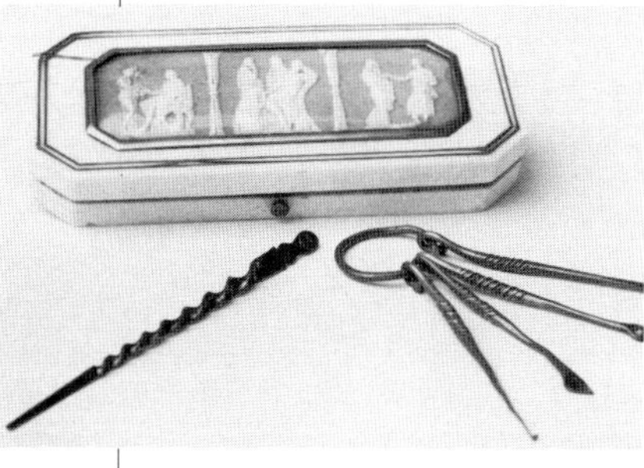

523. Patch Box with Toilette Articles: *Six Classical Figures*, ca. 1800
Ivory box with jasper medallion, blue ground with white relief, set in gold and fitted with steel toilette articles
Box: 3 5/8 x 1 1/2 in (9.2 x 3.8 cm); medallion: 2 3/4 x 1 in (6.9 x 2.5 cm)
Mark: none
Provenance: Dr. Harold L. Klawans, Chicago
1980.142
Color plate 128

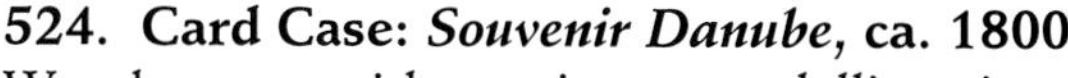

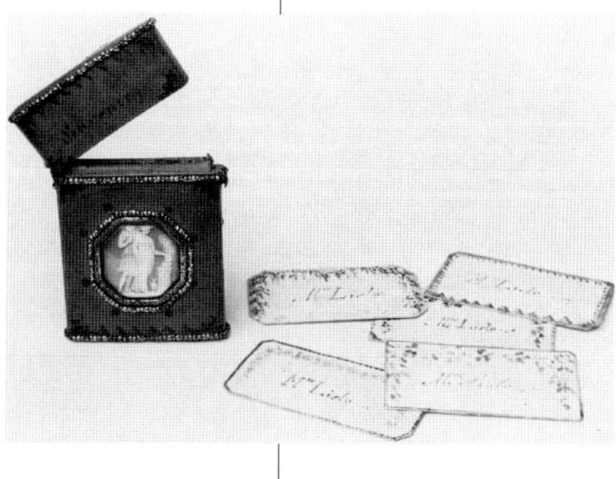

524. Card Case: *Souvenir Danube*, ca. 1800
Wooden case with two jasper medallions in solid white ground with blue wash and white relief, cut-steel beads
Case: 2 5/8 x 1 3/4 in (6.6 x 4.4 cm); medallion: 7/8 in (2.2 cm)
Mark: none
Provenance: Ann Brodkiewicz, Chicago
1980.179
Case has five hand-painted cards bearing the name "Mrs. Lisle."
Color plate 128

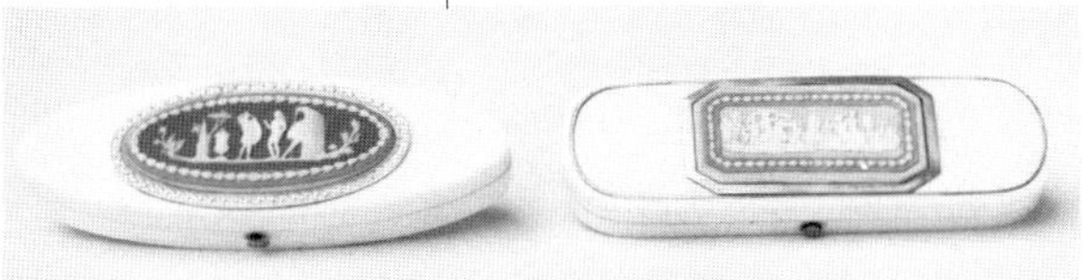

525. Patch Box: ca. 1800
Ivory box with jasper medallion in solid white ground with green, lilac, and white relief, set in gold
Box: 3 1/4 x 1 in (8.2 x 2.5 cm); medallion: 1 1/2 x 3/4 in (3.8 x 1.9 cm)
Mark: none
Provenance: David Davis, Chicago; Miss Frances Oliver, Birmingham, Ala.
1980.145

526. Patch Box: *Mucius Scaevola before Lars Porsena*, ca. 1800
Ivory box with jasper medallion, solid blue ground with white relief, set in gold
Box: 3 5/8 x 1 3/8 in (8.7 x 3.6 cm); medallion: 1 7/16 x 1 1/8 in (3.6 x 3.4 cm)
Mark: "WEDGWOOD"
Provenance: Godfrey W. Ford, England; Dr. Harold L. Klawans, Chicago
1980.143
Color plate 128

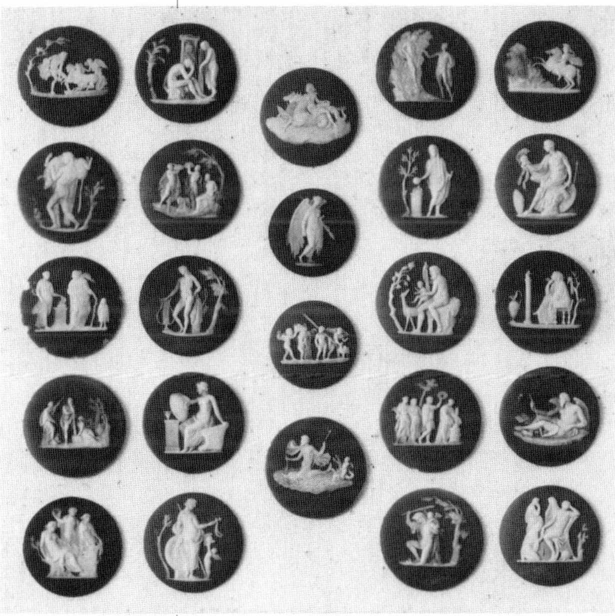

527. Twenty-Four Medallions in a Case: ca. 1800
Jasper, solid white ground with dark blue wash on front and white relief; jasper, solid blue with white relief (7 and 16 only)
1 in (2.5 cm)
Mark: "WEDGWOOD"
Provenance: Dr. Francis Jennings Vurpillat, South Bend, Ind.
1977.123.1-.24

1. *Ulysses Stopping the Chariot of Victory*
2. *Hercules Killing a Bull*
3. *Sacrifice to Hygeia*
4. *Judgment of Hercules*
5. *Aesculapius and Hygeia*
6. *Soldier Bringing the News of the Death of Patroclus to Achilles*
7. *The Corybantes Striking Their Buckles to Prevent the Cries of the Infant Jupiter from Being Heard by Saturn*
8. *Apollo*
9. *Minerva*
10. *Venus and Cupid*
11. *A Hereid, or a Sea Horse*
12. *Winged Figure with a Spear*
13. *Marriage of Cupid and Psyche*
14. *Neptune Riding the Sea*
15. *Perseus and Andromeda*
16. *A Sacrifice*
17. *Hercules with His Son*
18. *Priest Sacrificing*
19. *Hercules Overcome by Love*
20. *Marcus Curtius*
21. *A Warrior*
22. *A Roman Matron*
23. *Saturn*
24. *Volumnia and Coriolanus*

Jewelry

528. Medallion Chatelaine: *Classical Group*, ca. 1800
Jasper, solid white ground with blue wash and white relief and cut-steel mount
Medallion: 1/2 x 1 in (1.2 x 2.5 cm)
Mark: not visible
Provenance: Shadford-Walker Collection, England; Dr. Harold L. Klawans, Chicago
1977.163.4
Color plate 115

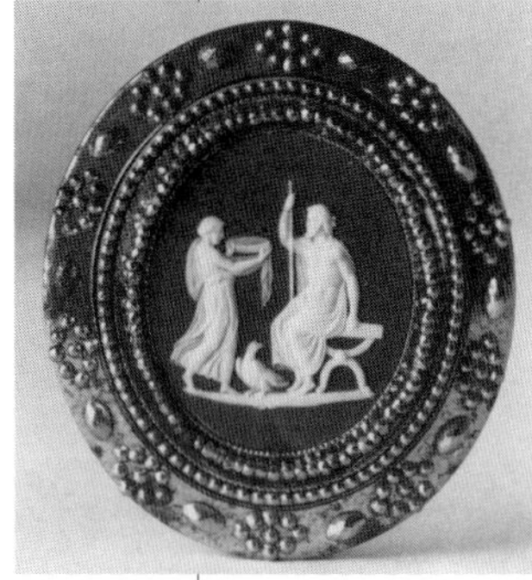

529. Medallion Brooch: *An Offering to Jupiter*, ca. 1800
Jasper, solid white ground with dark blue wash and white relief, set in cut-steel mount
Medallion: 2 9/16 x 2 3/8 in (6.5 x 6 cm)
Mark: none visible
Provenance: Godfrey W. Ford Collection, England; Dr. Harold L. Klawans, Chicago
1977.166
Color plate 115

530. Medallion Button: *Mercury and Venus*, ca. 1800
Jasper, solid white ground with blue wash and white relief with cut-steel mount
Medallion: 1 in (2.5 cm)
Mark: not visible
Provenance: Shadford-Walker Collection, England; Dr. Harold L. Klawans, Chicago
1977.163.2
Color plate 115

531. Medallion Brooch: *Cupid Dressing in a Mask*, ca. 1800
Jasper, solid blue ground with dark blue wash and white relief and cut-steel mount
Medallion: 1 5/8 x 1 3/8 in (4.1 x 3.4 cm)
Mark: not visible
Provenance: Shadford-Walker Collection, England; Dr. Harold L. Klawans, Chicago
1977.163.7
Color plate 115

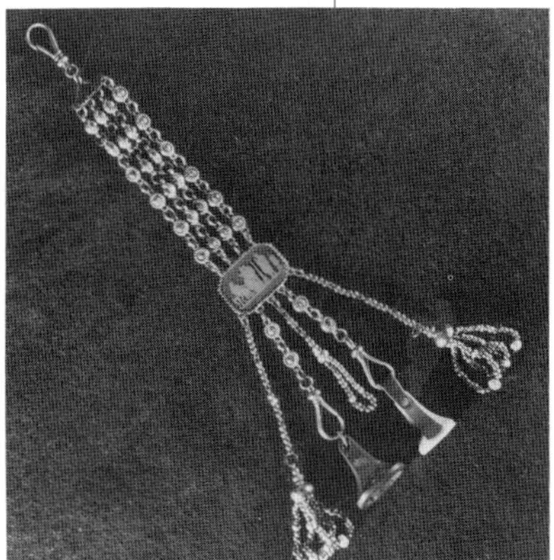

532. Double-Medallion Chatelaine: *Priam Begging the Body of Hector* and *The Choice of Hercules*, and two seals, ca. 1800
Jasper, solid white ground with dark blue wash and white relief set in cut-steel mount; seals: jasper and basalt
Chatelaine: 8 in (20.3 cm) long; medallion: 1 x 5/8 in (2.5 x 1.5 cm)
Mark: none visible
Provenance: Godfrey W. Ford, England; Dr. Harold L. Klawans, Chicago
1977.159

533. Medallion Brooch: *Coriolanus with Wife and Mother*, ca. 1800
Jasper, solid blue ground with dark blue wash and white relief and cut-steel mount
Medallion: 1 5/8 x 1 3/8 in (4.1 x 3.4 cm)
Mark: "WEDGWOOD"
Provenance: Shadford-Walker Collection, England; Dr. Harold L. Klawans, Chicago
1977.163.8
Color plate 115

534. Medallion Brooch: ***Achilles in His Tent*, ca. 1800**
Jasper, solid white ground with blue wash and white relief with cut-steel mount
Medallion: 1 in (2.5 cm)
Mark: not visible
Provenance: Shadford-Walker Collection, England; Dr. Harold L. Klawans, Chicago
1977.163.3
Color plate 115

535. Triple-Medallion Chatelaine: ***Aurora and Biga and Seated Woman*; *Seated Women with Bow and Nymph*; *Diomedes and the Palladium*; and intaglio of *Apollo and Marsyas*; and seal; ca. 1800**
a, b: jasper, solid white ground with blue wash and white relief;
c: jasper, solid blue ground with white relief; d: basalt, all in cut-steel mount
Chatelaine: 13 1/2 in (length) (34.2 cm); medallion: 1 x 3/4 in (2.5 x 1.9 cm); intaglio/medallion: 1 3/8 x 1 in (3.4 x 2.5 cm); seal: 1 in (2.5 cm)
Mark: none visible
Provenance: Dr. Harold L. Klawans, Chicago
1977.162

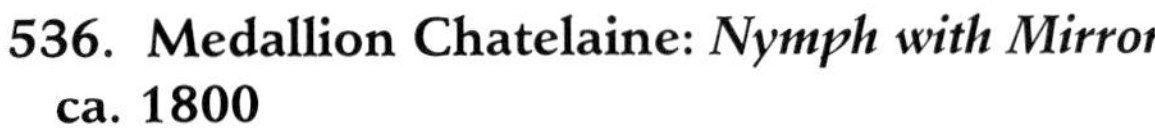

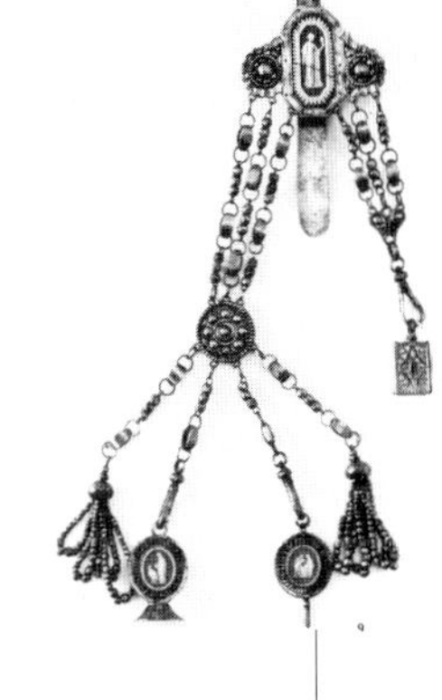

536. Medallion Chatelaine: ***Nymph with Mirror*, ca. 1800**
Jasper, solid blue ground with dark blue wash and white relief and cut-steel mount
Medallion: 1 1/4 x 5/8 in (3.1 x 1.5 cm)
Mark: "WEDGWOOD"
Provenance: Shadford-Walker Collection, England; Dr. Harold L. Klawans, Chicago
1977.163.9

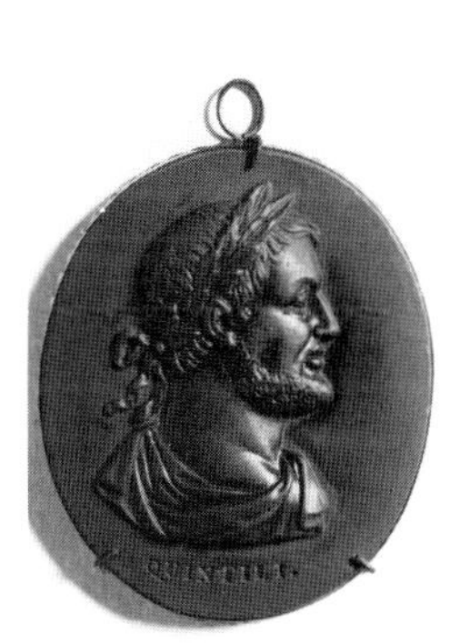

537. Medallion Brooch: ***Quintili*, ca. 1785**
Basalt, set in silver mount
Medallion: 2 1/16 x 1 1/4 in (5.2 x 3.1 cm)
Mark: "Wedgwood"
Provenance: Dr. Harold L. Klawans, Chicago
1977.150

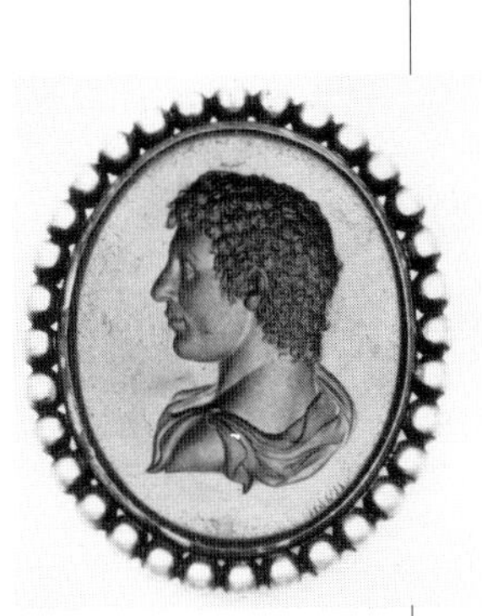

538. Intaglio Brooch: ca. 1775
Basalt, silver gilt mount with gold chain
Intaglio: 1 7/16 x 1 1/4 in (3.6 x 3.1 cm)
Mark: "Wedgwood & Bentley" "237"
Provenance: Dr. Harold L. Klawans, Chicago
1977.145

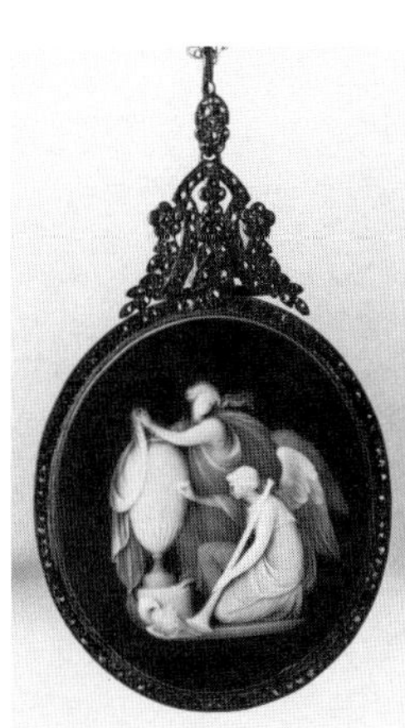

539. Medallion Brooch: ***Mourners at Urn of Ashes of Elizabeth, Sister of Louis XVI*, ca. 1800**
Jasper, solid white ground with black wash on front and white relief, set in silver mount with marcasites
Medallion: 2 1/6 x 1 3/4 in (5.1 x 4.4 cm)
Mark: none visible
Provenance: M. Mellanay Delhom, Chicago; Sir George Duff-Dunbar, Scotland; Ann Brodkiewicz, Chicago
1977.176

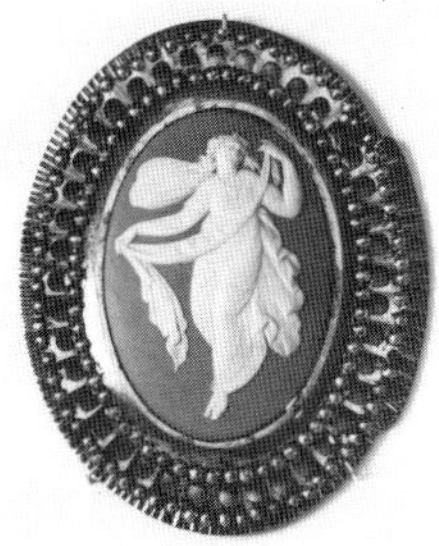

540. Medallion Belt Buckle: *Psyche*, ca. 1800
Jasper, solid blue ground with white relief and cut-steel mount
Medallion: 2 x 1 3/4 in (5 x 4.4 cm)
Mark: not visible
Provenance: Shadford-Walker Collection, England; Dr. Harold L. Klawans, Chicago
1977.163.5
Color plate 115

541. Medallion Belt Buckle: *Domestic Employment*, ca. 1800
Jasper, solid blue ground with white relief and cut-steel mount
Medallion: 2 x 1 3/4 in (5 x 4.4 cm)
Mark: not visible
Provenance: Shadford-Walker Collection, England; Dr. Harold L. Klawans, Chicago
1977.163.6
Color plate 115

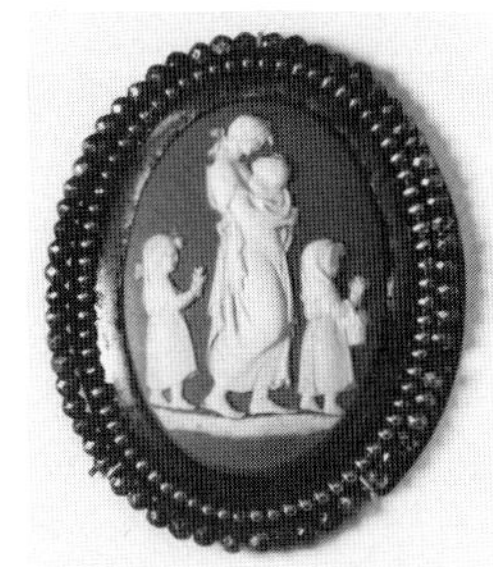

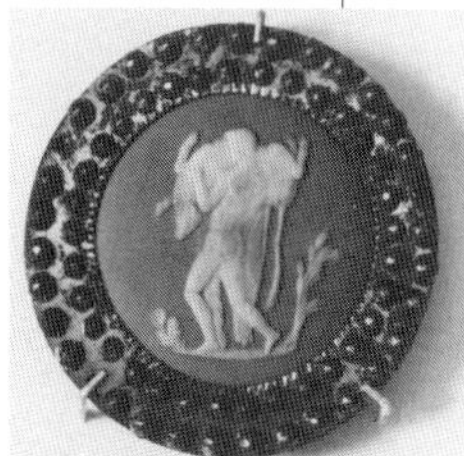

542. Medallion Button: *Hercules and Boar*, ca. 1790
Jasper, solid blue ground with white relief, steel-cut mount
Medallion: 1 in (2.5 cm)
Mark: none
Provenance: Dr. Francis Jennings Vurpillat, South Bend, Ind.
1977.165

543. Medallion Belt Buckle: *Two Classical Female Figures*, ca. 1800
Jasper, solid white ground with blue wash and white relief with cut-steel buckle
Medallion: 1 x 5/8 in (2.5 x 1.5 cm)
Mark: none visible
Provenance: Shadford-Walker Collection, England; Dr. Harold L. Klawans, Chicago
1977.163.1
Color plate 115

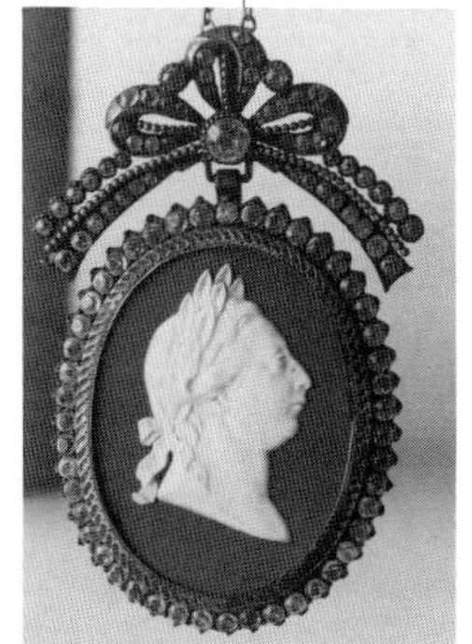

544. Medallion Brooch: *George III as a Roman Emperor*, ca. 1800
Jasper, solid white ground with dark blue wash and white relief; set in silver mount with jargoons and gold liner
Medallion: 1 13/16 x 1 7/16 in (4.6 x 3.6 cm)
Mark: none visible
Provenance: M. Close Collection, England; Dr. Harold L. Klawans, Chicago
1977.175

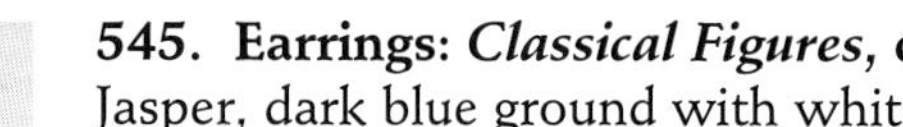

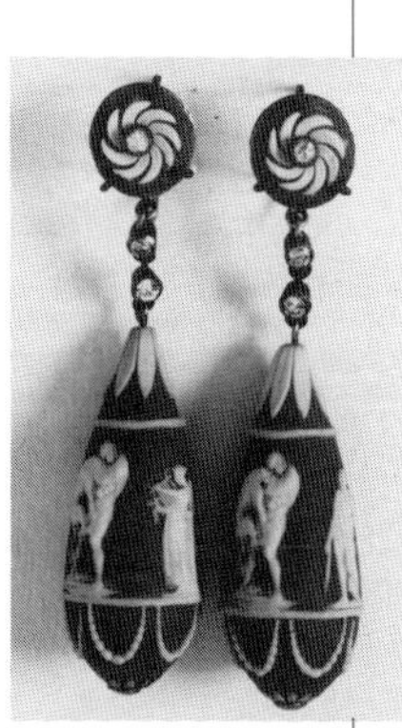

545. Earrings: *Classical Figures*, ca. 1800
Jasper, dark blue ground with white relief, set in gold mount with jargoons
Earrings: 2 1/2 in (6.3 cm) long
Mark: none visible
Provenance: Sir George Duff-Dunbar, Scotland; M. Mellanay Delhom, Chicago
1977.148.1-.2

546. Medallion Chatelaine: *Hercules and Omphale* and *Hercules Staying the Chariot of Victory*, ca. 1800
Jasper, solid blue ground with dark blue wash and white relief and cut-steel mount
Medallion: 1 5/8 x 1 3/8 in (4.1 x 3.4 cm)
Mark: "WEDGWOOD"
Provenance: Shadford-Walker Collection, England; Dr. Harold L. Klawans, Chicago
1977.163.8

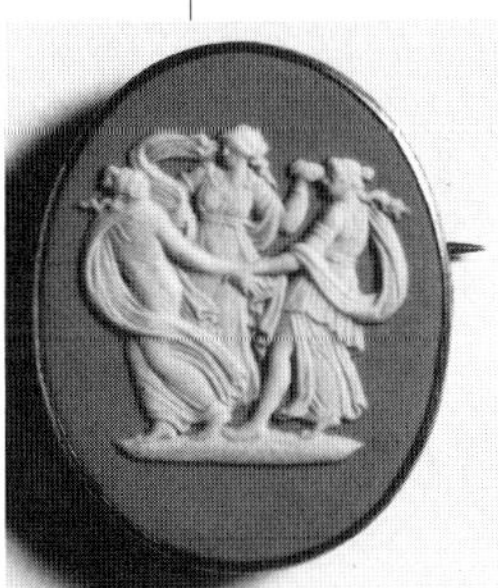

547. Medallion Brooch: *The Three Graces*, ca. 1800
Jasper, solid blue ground with white relief, set in silver mount
Medallion: 2 5/8 x 1 3/8 in (6.6 x 3.1 cm)
Mark: "WEDGWOOD" "27" incised
Provenance: Dr. Harold L. Klawans, Chicago
1977.149

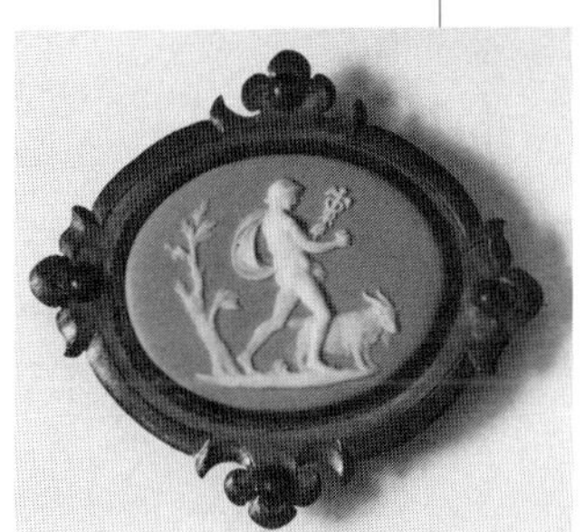

548. Medallion Brooch: *Mercury Holding the Head of Aries*, ca. 1800
Jasper, solid blue ground with white relief, set in brass mount
1 9/16 x 1 1/4 in (3.9 x 3.1 cm)
Mark: "WEDGWOOD" "234" incised
Provenance: Dr. Harold L. Klawans, Chicago
1990.4

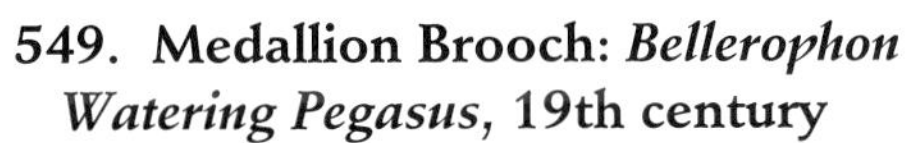

549. Medallion Brooch: *Bellerophon Watering Pegasus*, 19th century
Jasper, solid blue ground with white relief, set in silver mount
Medallion: 1 7/8 x 1 3/8 in (4.7 x 3.4 cm)
Mark: "WEDGWOOD" with tool mark
Provenance: Gift of Mrs. Charles O. Caddis
1980.396

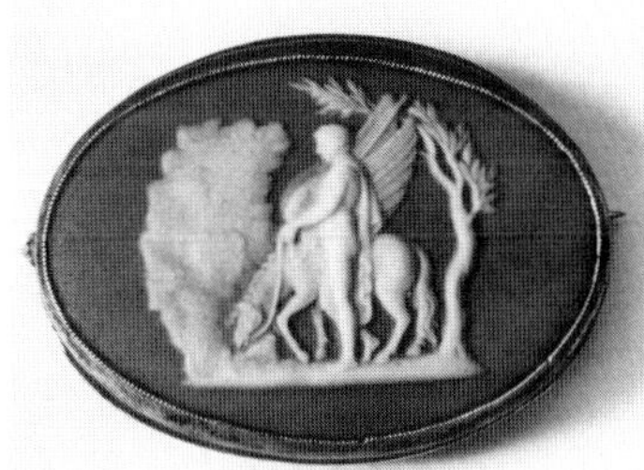

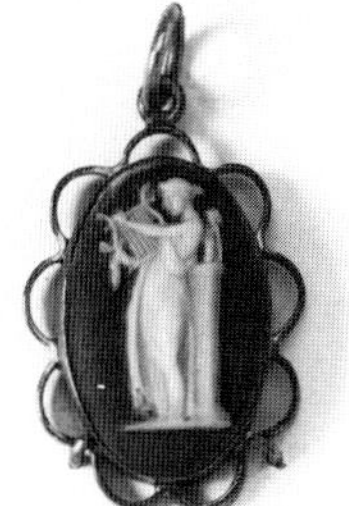

550. Medallion Brooch: *Classical Figure with Lyre*, ca. 1800
Jasper, solid dark blue ground with white relief, set in gold mount
Medallion: 11/16 x 1/2 in (1.7 x 1.1 cm)
Mark: "WEDGWOOD" with tool mark
Provenance: Purchased in Malta, September 1961
1977.137

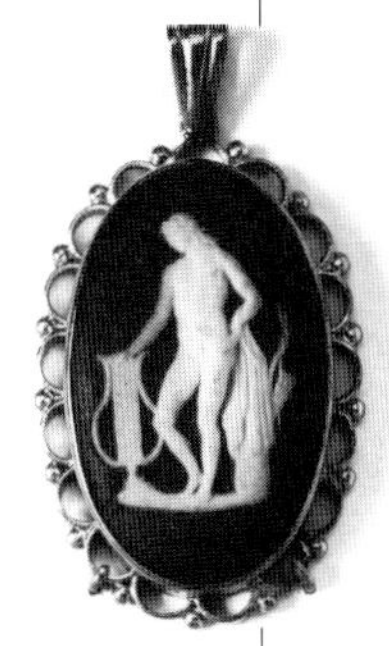

551. Medallion Brooch: *Apollo*, ca. 1800
Jasper, solid white ground with dark blue wash and white relief, set in gold mount
Medallion: 1 1/8 x 7/16 in (2.8 x 1 cm)
Mark: "WEDGWOOD" with tool mark
Provenance: Silver Vaults, London
1977.138

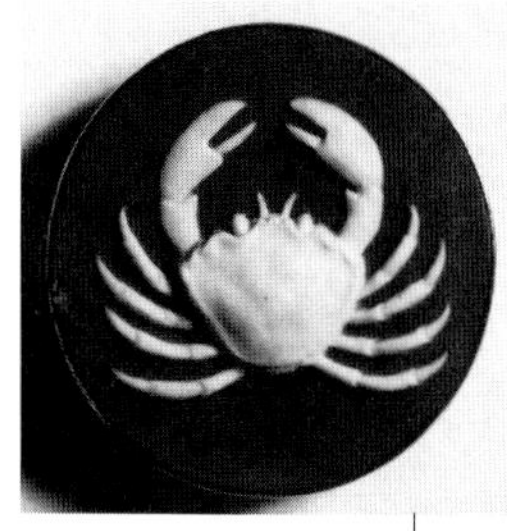

552. Medallion Brooch: *Crab*, ca. 1800
Jasper, solid white ground with blue wash and white relief, set in silver mount
Medallion: 1 1/2 in (3.8 cm)
Mark: none visible
Provenance: Dr. Harold L. Klawans, Chicago
1977.146

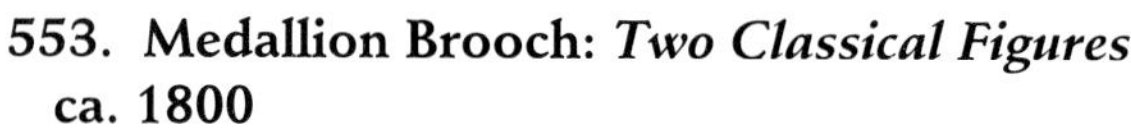

553. Medallion Brooch: *Two Classical Figures*, ca. 1800
Jasper, solid white ground with dark blue wash on front and back with white relief, lapidary-polishing, set in silver mount
Medallion: 1 1/16 x 3/4 in (2.7 x 1.9 cm)
Mark: "WEDGWOOD"
Provenance: Dr. Harold L. Klawans, Chicago
1977.151

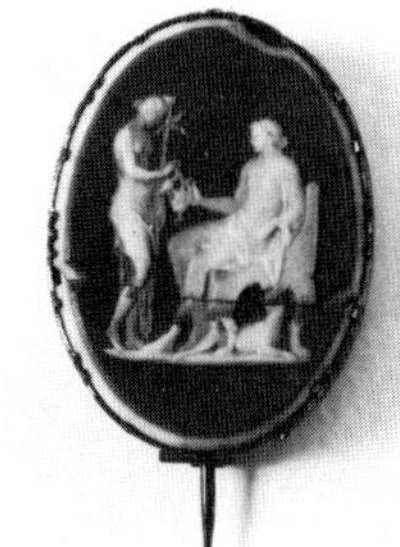

554. Medallion Stick Pin: *Hope*, ca. 1800
Jasper, solid blue ground with white relief, lapidary-polished edge, gold mount
Medallion: 5/8 in (1.5 cm)
Mark: none
Provenance: Dr. Harold L. Klawans, Chicago
1977.174

555. Medallion Hat Pin: *Classical Figure with Lyre*, 19th century
Jasper, solid white ground with dark blue wash and white relief
Medallion: 7/8 in (2.2 cm)
Mark: "WEDGWOOD" "R"
Provenance: unknown
1977.157

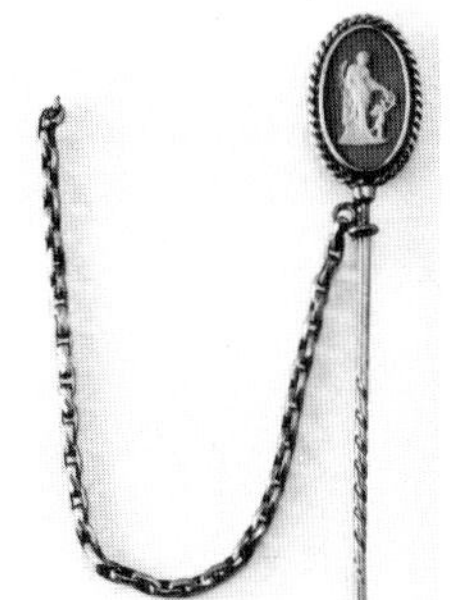

556. Double-Medallion Scarf Pin: *Jupiter* and *Venus and Cupid*, ca. 1800
Jasper, light blue ground with white relief, set in gilt mount
Medallion: 5/8 x 1/2 in (1.5 x 1.2 cm)
Mark: none
Provenance: Dr. Harold L. Klawans, Chicago
1977.164

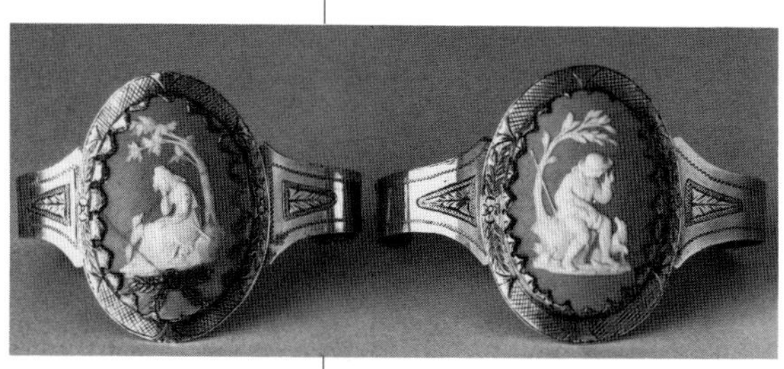

557. Pair of Medallion Bracelets: *Poor Maria* and *Bourbonnais Shepherd*, ca. 1800
Jasper, solid white ground with green wash with white relief, set in steel mounts
Medallion: 2 1/16 x 1 5/8 in (5.2 x 4.1 cm)
Mark: none visible
Provenance: Dr. Francis Jennings Vurpillat, South Bend, Ind.
1977.172 and 1977.173

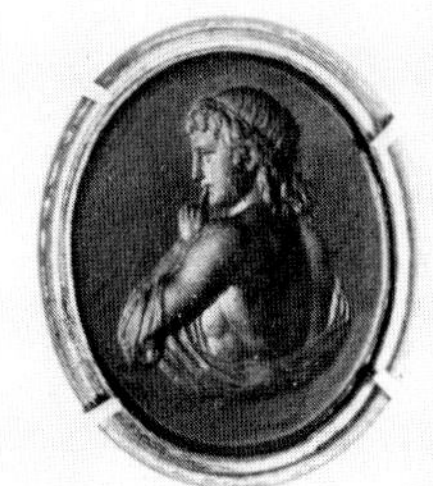

558. Intaglio/Seal: ***Silence,*** **ca. 1790**
Basalt with gilt mount
13/16 x 3/4 in (2.1 x 1.9 cm)
Mark: "Wedgwood" "347"
Provenance: unknown
1977.14.10

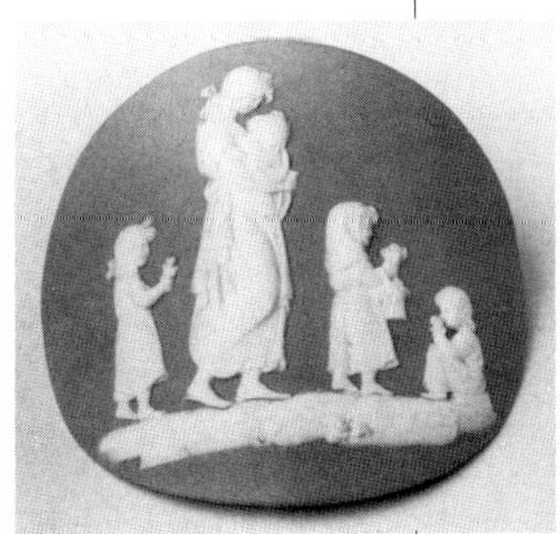

559. Medallion Shoe Buckle: ***Domestic Employment,*** **ca. 1800**
Jasper, solid blue ground with white relief, convex
Medallion: 2 3/8 x 3 3/16 in (6 x 8 cm)
Mark: none
Provenance: David Davis, Chicago; Ann Brodkiewicz, Chicago
1980.169

560. Medallions: ***Zodiac Signs,*** **ca. 1800**
Jasper, solid white ground with blue wash on front and back with white relief
1 x 9/16 in (2.5 x 1.4 cm)
Mark: none
Provenance: Dr. Francis Jennings Vurpillat, South Bend, Ind.
1977.122.17-.26

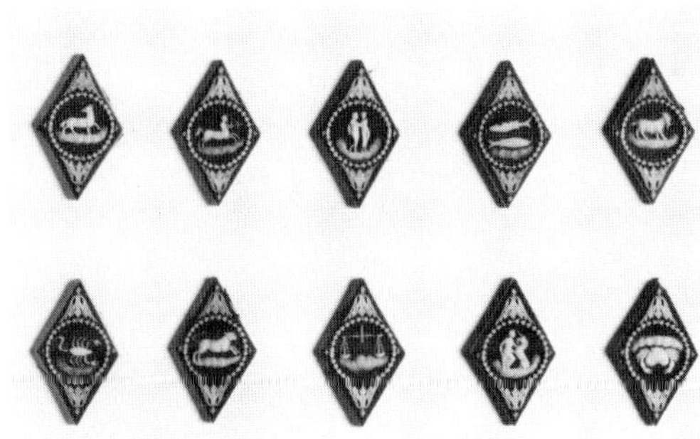

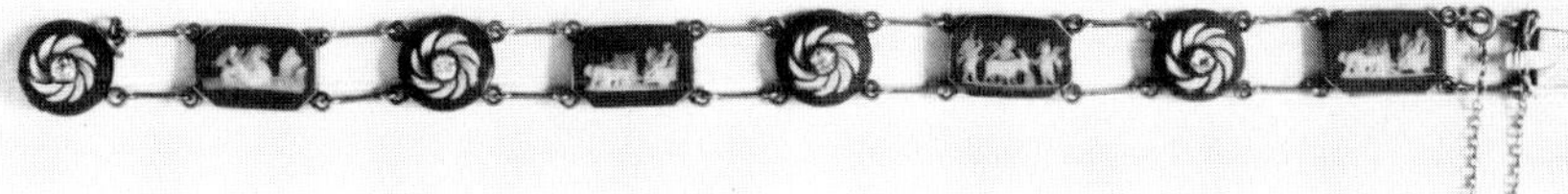

561. Bracelet: ***Classical Figures,*** **ca. 1800**
Jasper, dark blue ground with white relief, set in gold mount with jargoons
Bracelet: 7 1/2 in (19 cm)
Mark: none visible
Provenance: Sir George Duff-Dunbar, Scotland; M. Mellanay Delhom, Chicago
1977.148.2

562. Bracelet with Nine Intaglios and One Seal: ***Socrates, Head*****;** ***Hermes Trismegistus, Head*****;** ***A Furious Fawn, Figure*****;** ***Thalia, Muse of Comedy, Figure*****;** ***Diana, Huntress, Figure*****;** ***Bacchante, Figure*****;** ***Polyhymnia, Muse of Rhetoric, Head*****;** ***Lucius Verus, Head,*** **ca. 1775**
Basalt, eight intaglios in silver gilt mounts, one white stoneware back and basalt front center of bracelet, basalt intaglio seal
Smallest intaglio: 1/2 x 3/4 in (1.2 x 1.9 cm); largest intaglio: 7/8 x 11/16 in (2.2 x 1.7 cm)
Seal: 1 in (2.5 cm)
Mark: all either "W&B" or "Wedgwood / & Bentley" "236," "234," "143," "156," "161," "124," "61," "113"; center intaglio has no number; seal: none
Provenance: Dr. Harold L. Klawans, Chicago
1977.144.1-.9

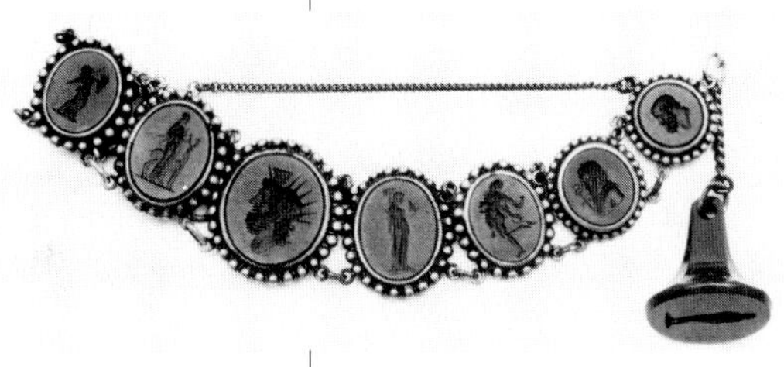

The Jasper-Ware Frieze

Catalogue numbers 563 through 615 are color plates 93 and 94, on pages 113-14.

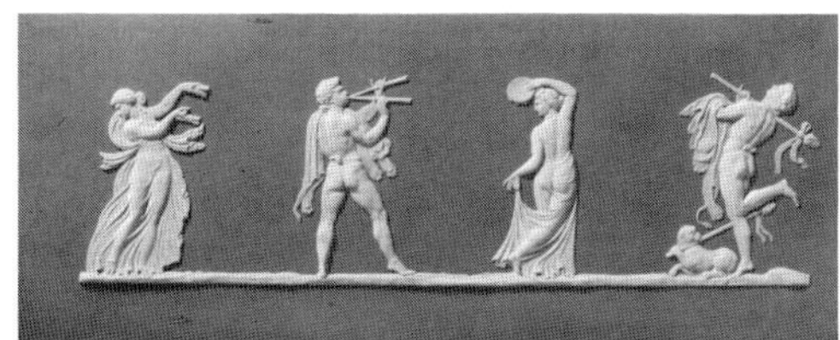

563. Frieze: *Bacchantes*, ca. 1820
Jasper, solid blue ground with white relief
18 3/4 x 7 9/16 in (47.6 x 19.2 cm)
Mark: "WEDGWOOD" "O" "F2"
Provenance: P. J. Dearden, England; Sotheby's, London, February 27, 1968
1976.102

564. Frieze: *Swag and Medallions*, ca. 1820
Jasper, solid blue ground with white relief
10 3/8 x 7 1/2 in (26.3 x 19 cm)
Mark: "WEDGWOOD" "O" "B-5"; "O" incised on bottom edge
Provenance: P. J. Dearden, England; Sotheby's, London, February 27, 1968
1976.94

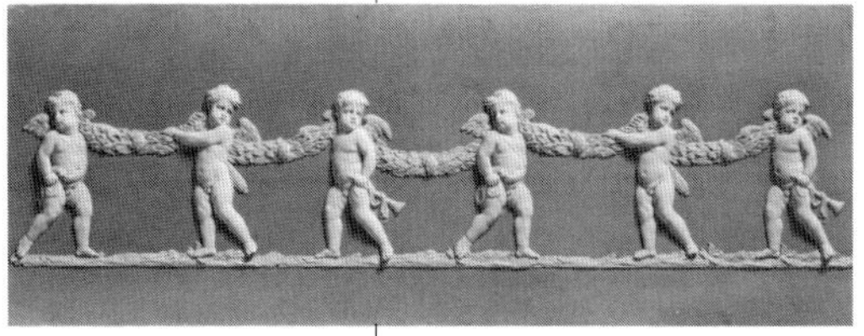

565. Frieze: *Procession of Cupids*, ca. 1820
Jasper, solid blue ground with white relief
20 x 7 5/8 in (50.8 x 19.3 cm)
Mark: "WEDGWOOD" "O" "G1"; "O" incised on bottom edge
Provenance: P. J. Dearden, England; Sotheby's, London, February 27, 1968
1976.104

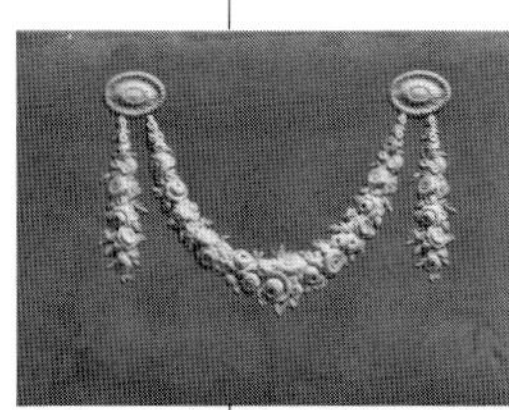

566. Frieze: *Swag and Medallions*, ca. 1820
Jasper, solid blue ground with white relief
10 1/8 x 7 1/2 in (25.7 x 19 cm)
Mark: "WEDGWOOD" "O" "G2"; "O" incised on top edge
Provenance: P. J. Dearden, England; Sotheby's, London, February 27, 1968
1976.95

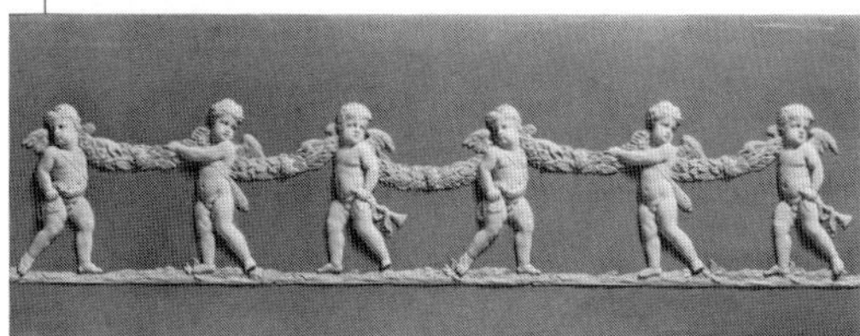

567. Frieze: *Procession of Cupids*, ca. 1820
Jasper, solid blue ground with white relief
19 15/16 x 7 5/8 in (50.6 x 19.3 cm)
Mark: "WEDGWOOD" "O" "5"; "O" incised on bottom edge
Provenance: P. J. Dearden, England; Sotheby's, London, February 27, 1968
1976.140

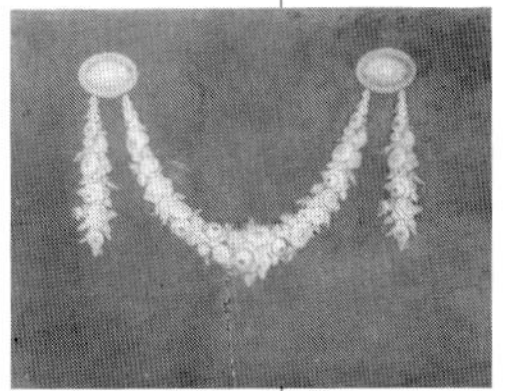

568. Frieze: *Swag and Medallions*, ca. 1820
Jasper, solid blue ground with white relief
10 1/8 x 7 1/2 in (25.7 x 19 cm)
Mark: "WEDGWOOD" "O" "G-4"; "O" incised on bottom edge
Provenance: P. J. Dearden, England; Sotheby's, London, February 27, 1968
1976.96

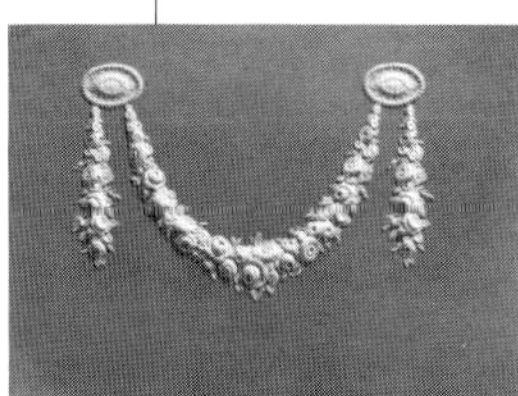

569. Frieze: *Swag and Medallions*, ca. 1820
Jasper, solid blue ground with white relief
10 x 7 1/2 in (25.4 x 19 cm)
Mark: "WEDGWOOD" "O" "B7"; "O" "O" incised on bottom edge
Provenance: P. J. Dearden, England; Sotheby's, London, February 27, 1968
1976.97

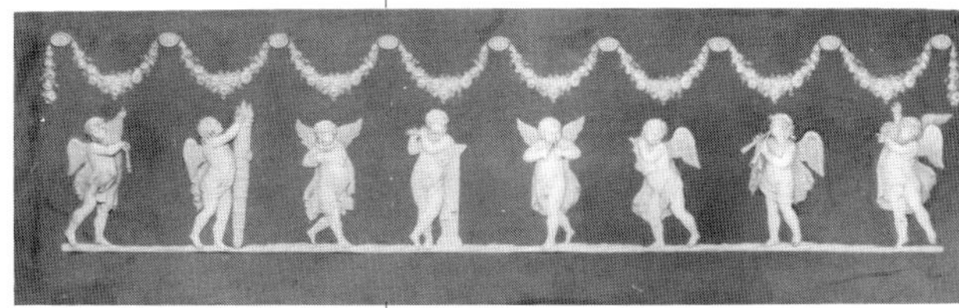

570. Frieze: *Sacrifice to Hymen*, ca. 1820
Jasper, solid blue ground with white relief
25 x 7 5/8 in (63.5 x 19.3 cm)
Mark: "WEDGWOOD" "O"; "O" "O" incised on bottom edge
Provenance: P. J. Dearden, England; Sotheby's, London, February 27, 1968
1976.103

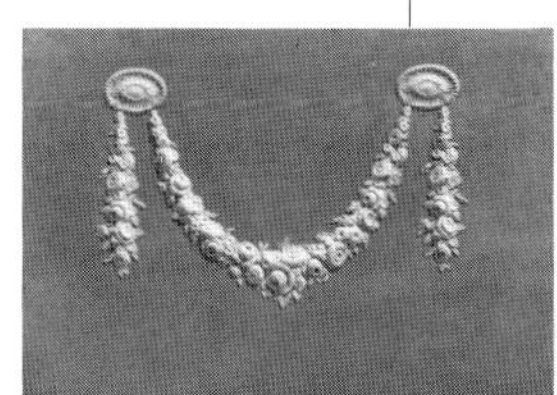

571. Frieze: *Swag and Medallions*, ca. 1820
Jasper, solid blue ground with white relief
10 1/4 x 7 1/2 in (26 x 19 cm)
Mark: "WEDGWOOD" "O" "BX1"; "O" "O" incised on bottom edge
Provenance: P. J. Dearden, England; Sotheby's, London, February 27, 1968
1976.98

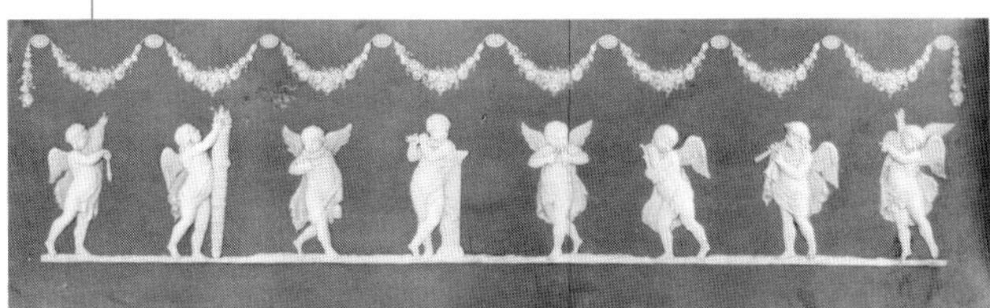

572. Frieze: *Sacrifice to Hymen*, ca. 1820
Jasper, solid blue ground with white relief
25 1/8 x 7 5/8 in (63.8 x 19.3 cm)
Mark: "WEDGWOOD" "O"; "O" incised on bottom edge
Provenance: P. J. Dearden, England; Sotheby's, London, February 27, 1968
1976.141

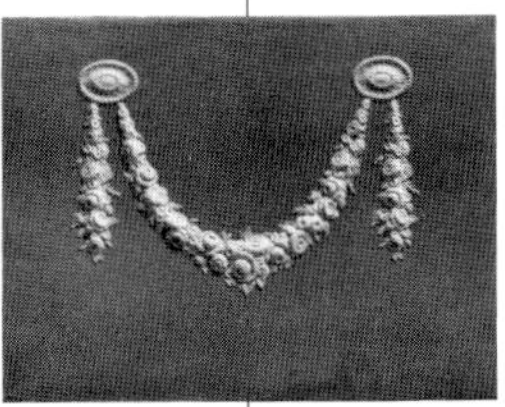

573. Frieze: *Swag and Medallions,* ca. 1820
Jasper, solid blue ground with white relief
9 1/2 x 7 5/8 in (24.1 x 19.3 cm)
Mark: "WEDGWOOD" "O" "E 4"; "O" incised on bottom edge
Provenance: P. J. Dearden, England; Sotheby's, London, February 27, 1968
1976.99

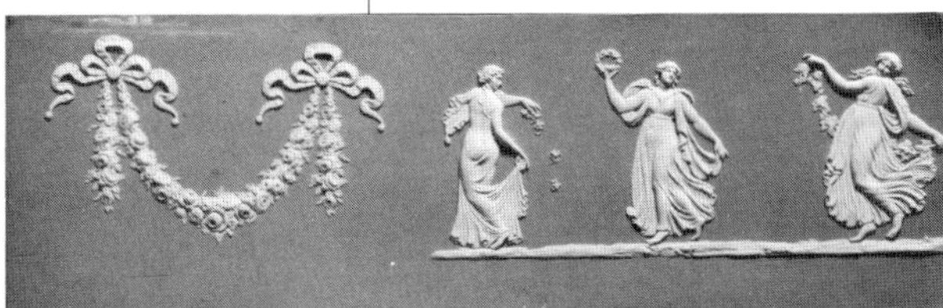

574. Frieze: *Dancing Hours and Swag,* ca. 1820
Jasper, solid blue ground with white relief
23 5/8 x 7 1/2 in (65 x 19 cm)
Mark: "WEDGWOOD" "O"; "O" "O" "O" incised on bottom edge
Provenance: P. J. Dearden, England; Sotheby's, London, February 27, 1968
1976.105

575. Frieze: *Dancing Hours,* ca. 1820
Jasper, solid blue ground with white relief
23 1/2 x 7 1/2 in (59.6 x 19 cm)
Mark: "WEDGWOOD" "O"; "O" "O" "O" incised on bottom edge
Provenance: P. J. Dearden, England; Sotheby's, London, February 27, 1968
1976.106

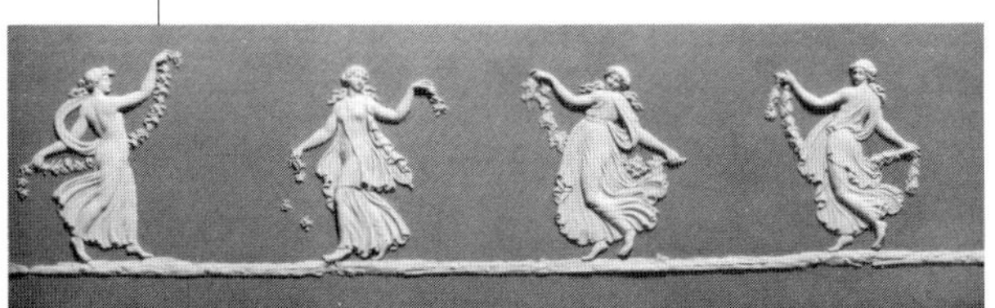

576. Frieze: *Dancing Hours,* ca. 1820
Jasper, solid blue ground with white relief
23 5/8 x 7 1/2 in (60 x 19 cm)
Mark: "WEDGWOOD" "O"; "O" "O" incised on bottom edge
Provenance: P. J. Dearden, England; Sotheby's, London, February 27, 1968
1976.107

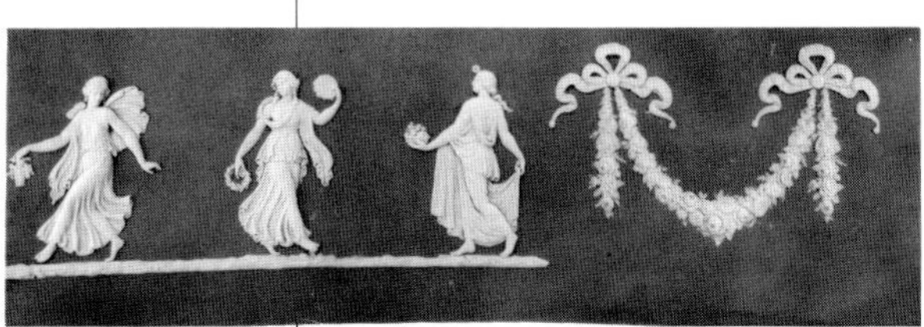

577. Frieze: *Dancing Hours and Swag,* ca. 1820
Jasper, solid blue ground with white relief
23 3/4 x 7 5/8 in (60.3 x 19.3 cm)
Mark: "WEDGWOOD" "O"; "O" "O" "O" incised on bottom edge
Provenance: P. J. Dearden, England; Sotheby's, London, February 27, 1968
1985.433a

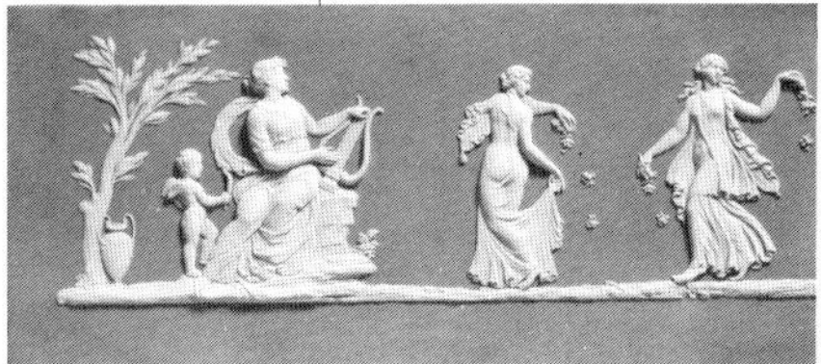

578. Frieze: *Cupid, Terpsichore, Dancing Hours*, ca. 1820
Jasper, solid blue ground with white relief
16 5/16 x 7 3/8 in (41.4 x 18.7 cm)
Mark: "WEDGWOOD" "O" "D I"; "O" incised on top edge
Provenance: P. J. Dearden, England; Sotheby's, London, February 27, 1968
1976.108

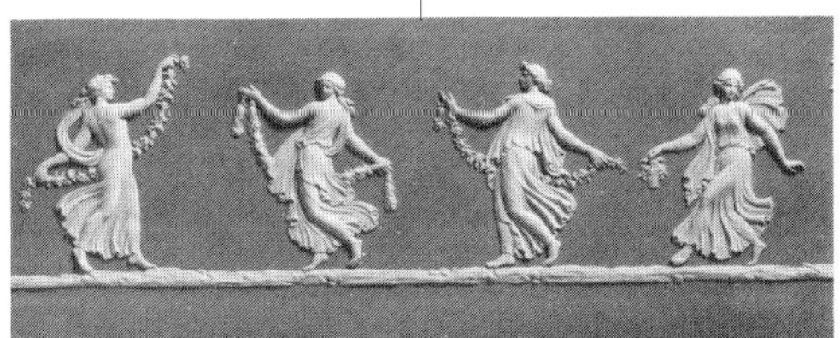

579. Frieze: *Dancing Hours*, ca. 1820
Jasper, solid blue ground with white relief
18 7/8 x 7 5/8 in (47.9 x 19.3 cm)
Mark: "WEDGWOOD" "O" "D 2"; "O" incised on bottom edge
Provenance: P. J. Dearden, England; Sotheby's, London, February 27, 1968
1976.109

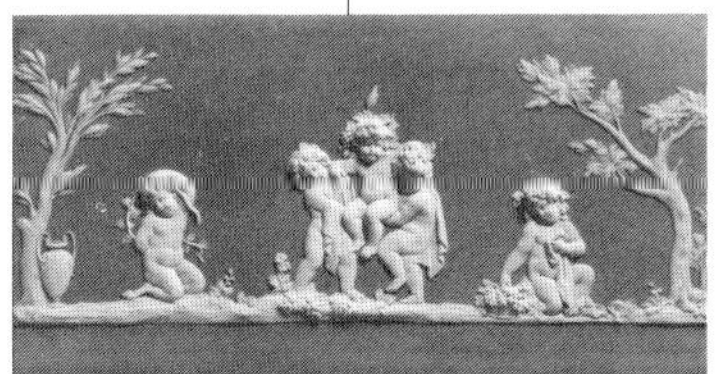

580. Frieze: *Bacchanalian Boys*, ca. 1820
Jasper, solid blue ground with white relief
13 1/2 x 7 1/2 in (34.2 x 19 cm)
Mark: "WEDGWOOD" "O" "D 3"; "O" incised on bottom edge
Provenance: P. J. Dearden, England; Sotheby's, London, February 27, 1968
1976.110

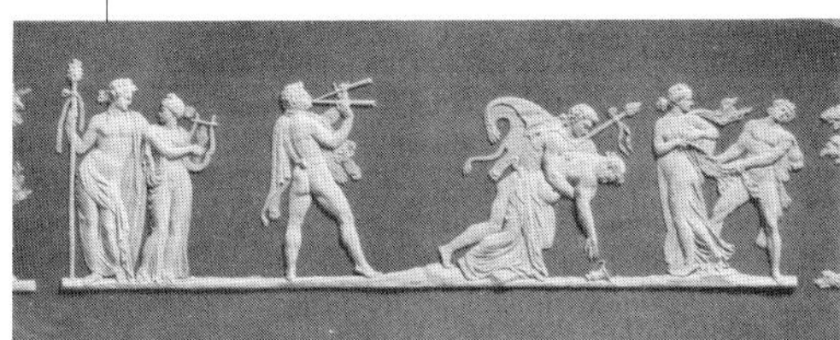

581. Frieze: *Bacchanalian Triumph*, ca. 1820
Jasper, solid blue ground with white relief
18 3/4 x 7 1/2 in (47.6 x 19 cm)
Mark: "WEDGWOOD" "O" "D 4"; "O" incised on bottom edge
Provenance: P. J. Dearden, England; Sotheby's, London, February 27, 1968
1976.111

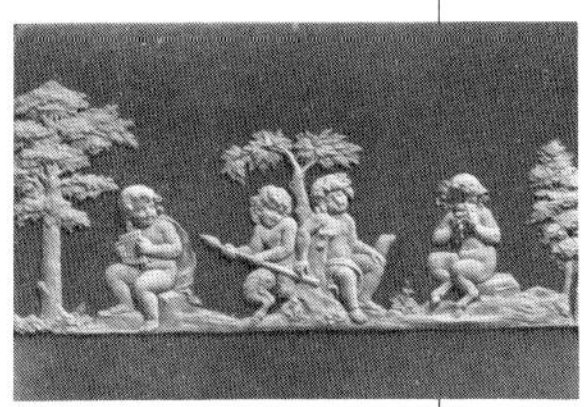

582. Frieze: *Bacchanalian Boys*, ca. 1820
Jasper, solid blue ground with white relief
11 1/4 x 7 1/2 in (28.5 x 19 cm)
Mark: "WEDGWOOD" "O" "D 5"; "O" incised on bottom edge
Provenance: P. J. Dearden, England; Sotheby's, London, February 27, 1968
1976.112

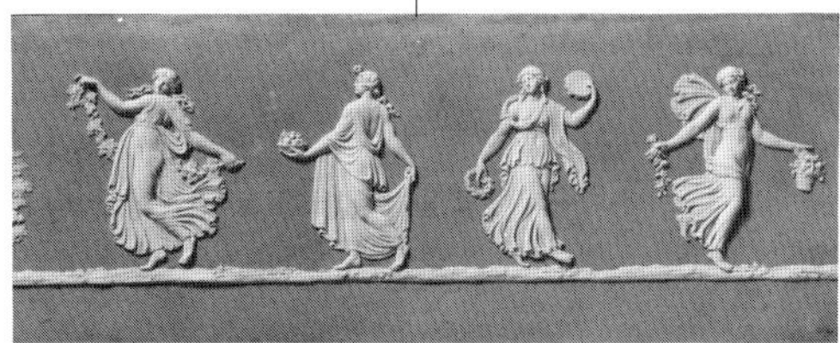

583. Frieze: *Dancing Hours*, ca. 1820
Jasper, solid blue ground with white relief
19 x 7 5/8 in (48.2 x 19.3 cm)
Mark: "WEDGWOOD" "O" "D 6"; "O" incised on bottom edge
Provenance: P. J. Dearden, England; Sotheby's, London, February 27, 1968
1976.113

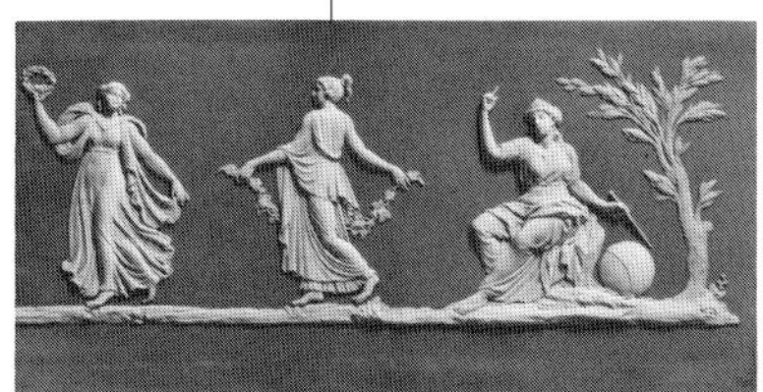

584. Frieze: *Dancing Hours and Muse*, ca. 1820
Jasper, solid blue ground with white relief
15 x 7 9/16 in (38.1 x 19.2 cm)
Mark: "WEDGWOOD" "O" "D 7"; "O" incised on bottom edge
Provenance: P. J. Dearden, England; Sotheby's, London, February 27, 1968
1976.114

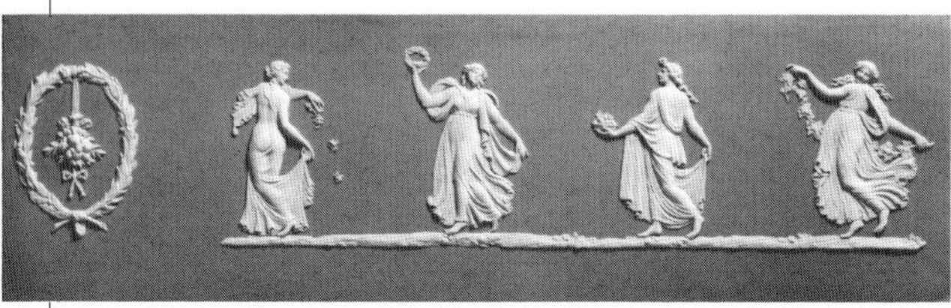

585. Frieze: *Dancing Hours*, ca. 1820
Jasper, solid blue ground with white relief
25 1/8 x 7 5/8 in (63.8 x 19.3 cm)
Mark: "WEDGWOOD" "O" "B 10"; "O" "O" incised on bottom edge
Provenance: P. J. Dearden, England; Sotheby's, London, February 27, 1968
1976.115

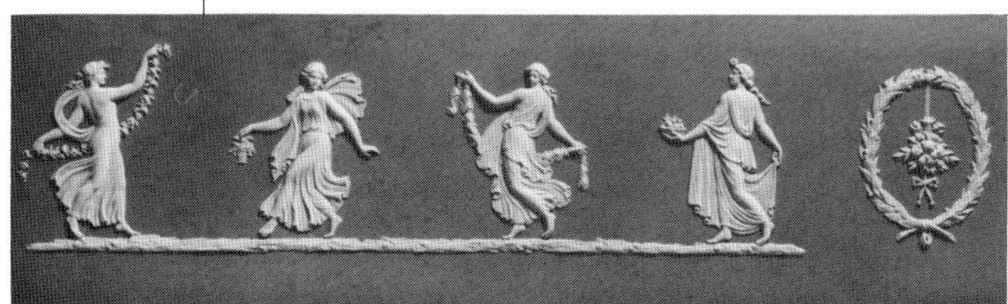

586. Frieze: *Dancing Hours*, ca. 1820
Jasper, solid blue ground with white relief
25 1/2 x 7 1/2 in (64.7 x 19 cm)
Mark: "WEDGWOOD" "O" "B 8"; "O" "O" incised on bottom edge
Provenance: P. J. Dearden, England; Sotheby's, London, February 27, 1968
1976.116

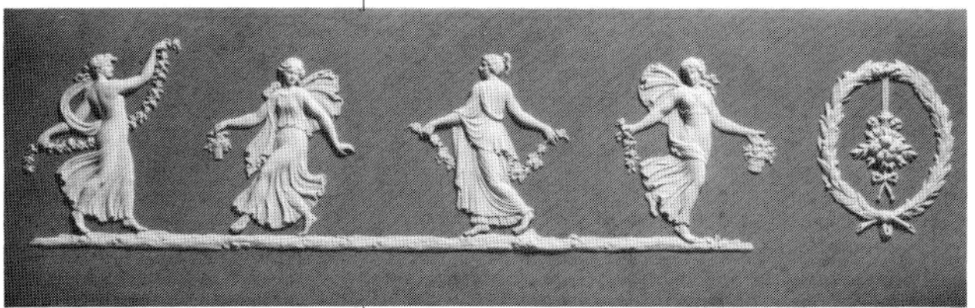

587. Frieze: *Dancing Hours*, ca. 1820
Jasper, solid blue ground with white relief
24 3/4 x 7 1/2 in (62.8 x 19 cm)
Mark: "WEDGWOOD" "O" "B 2"; "O" incised on bottom edge
Provenance: P. J. Dearden, England; Sotheby's, London, February 27, 1968
1976.117

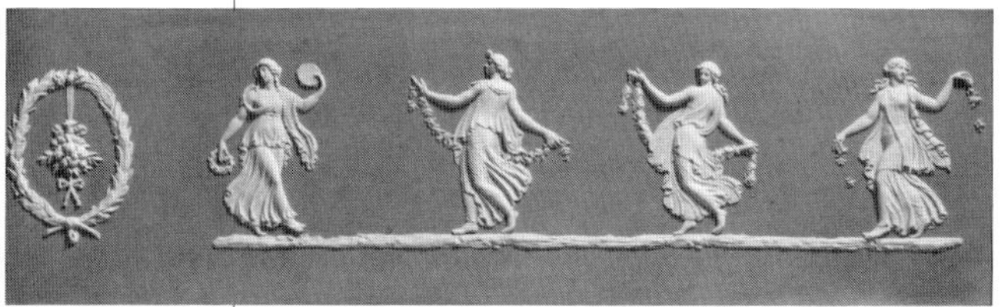

588. Frieze: *Dancing Hours,* ca. 1820
Jasper, solid blue ground with white relief
25 3/8 x 7 1/2 in (64.4 x 19 cm)
Mark: "WEDGWOOD" "O" "B 4"; "O" "O" incised on bottom edge
Provenance: P. J. Dearden, England; Sotheby's, London, February 27, 1968
1976.118

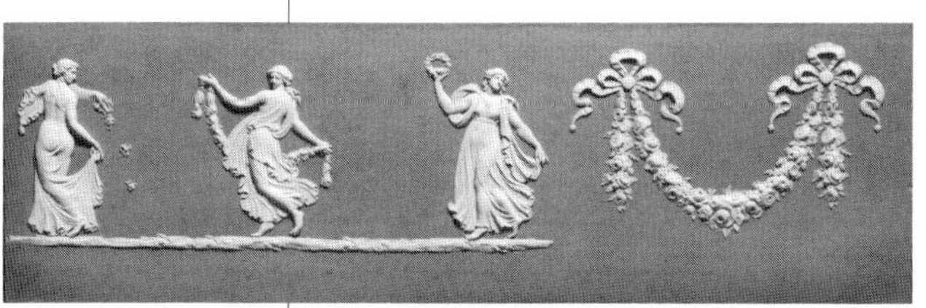

589. Frieze: *Dancing Hours and Swag,* ca. 1820
Jasper, solid blue ground with white relief
23 1/2 x 7 1/2 in (59.6 x 19 cm)
Mark: "WEDGWOOD" "O"; "O" incised on bottom edge
Provenance: P. J. Dearden, England; Sotheby's, London, February 27, 1968
1976.119

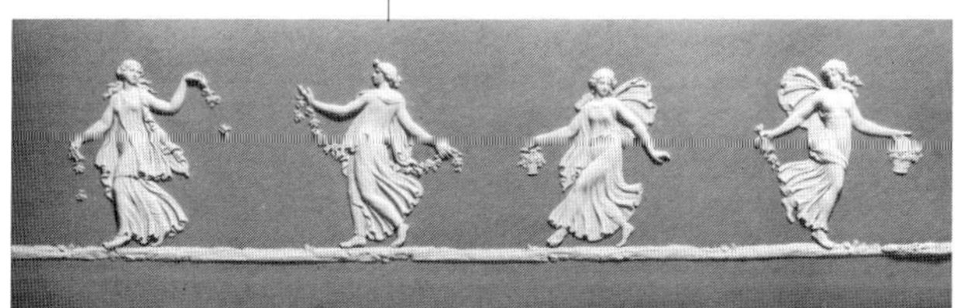

590. Frieze: *Dancing Hours,* ca. 1820
Jasper, solid blue ground with white relief
23 1/2 x 7 1/2 in (59.6 x 19 cm)
Mark: "WEDGWOOD" "O"; "O" "O" incised on bottom edge
Provenance: P. J. Dearden, England; Sotheby's, London, February 27, 1968
1976.120

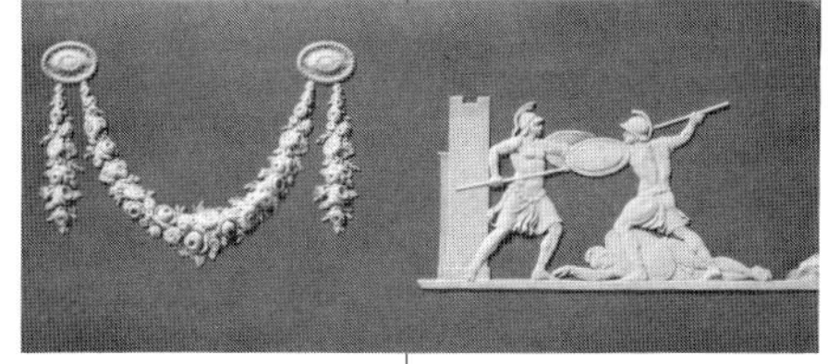

591. Frieze: *Death of Hector and Swag,* ca. 1820
Jasper, solid blue ground with white relief
17 x 7 5/8 in (43.1 x 19.3 cm)
Mark: "WEDGWOOD" "O" "A 7"; "O" incised on bottom edge
Provenance: P. J. Dearden, England; Sotheby's, London, February 27, 1968
1976.121

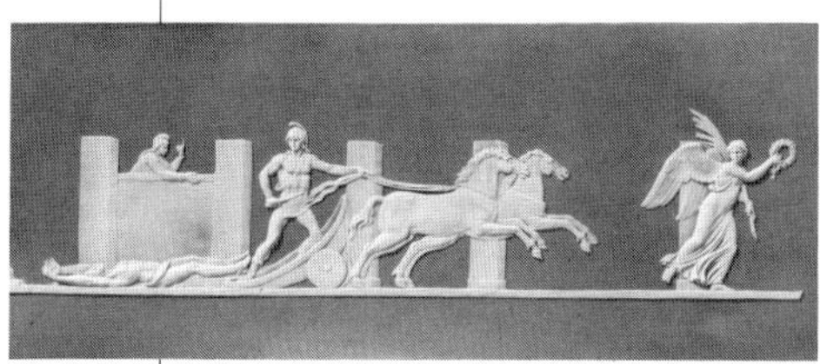

592. Frieze: *Achilles Dragging Hector around the Walls of Troy,* ca. 1820
Jasper, solid blue ground with white relief
18 3/8 x 7 1/2 in (46.6 x 19 cm)
Mark: "WEDGWOOD" "O" "A 6"; "O" incised on bottom edge
Provenance: P. J. Dearden, England; Sotheby's, London, February 27, 1968
1976.122

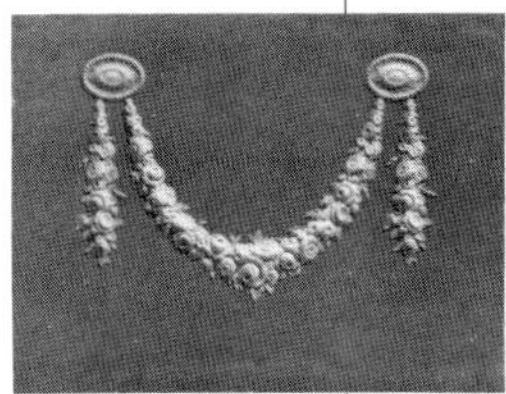

593. Frieze: *Swags and Medallions*, ca. 1820
Jasper, solid blue ground with white relief
9 5/8 x 7 1/2 in (24.4 x 19 cm)
Mark: "WEDGWOOD" "E 2"; "O" incised on bottom edge
Provenance: P. J. Dearden, England; Sotheby's, London, February 27, 1968
1976.100

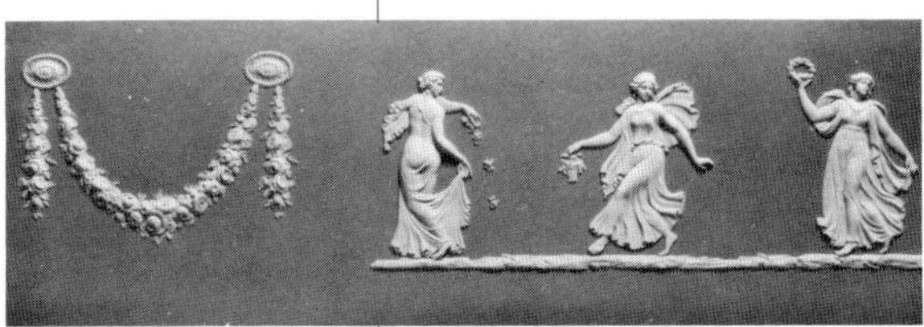

594. Frieze: *Swags, Medallions, and Dancing Hours*, ca. 1820
Jasper, solid blue ground with white relief
22 3/4 x 7 5/8 in (57.7 x 19.3 cm)
Mark: "WEDGWOOD" "O" "A 5"; "O" incised on bottom edge
Provenance: P. J. Dearden, England; Sotheby's, London, February 27, 1968
1976.123

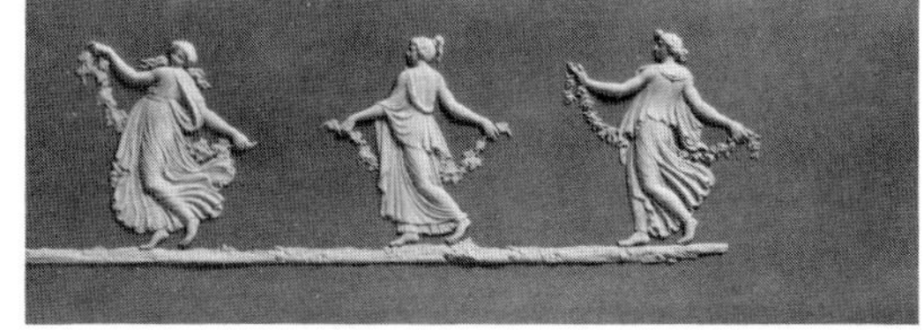

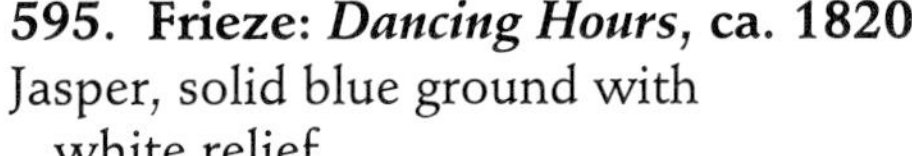

595. Frieze: *Dancing Hours*, ca. 1820
Jasper, solid blue ground with white relief
19 1/2 x 7 5/8 in (49.5 x 19.3 cm)
Mark: "WEDGWOOD" "O" "A-1"; "O" incised on bottom edge
Provenance: P. J. Dearden, England; Sotheby's, London, February 27, 1968
1976.124

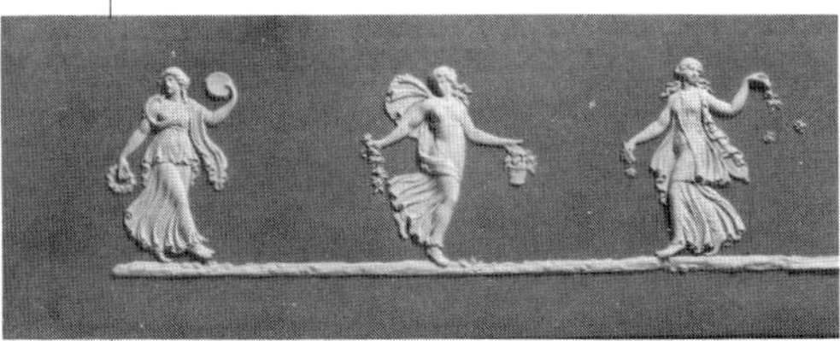

596. Frieze: *Dancing Hours*, ca. 1820
Jasper, solid blue ground with white relief
20 5/16 x 7 5/8 in (51.5 x 19.3 cm)
Mark: "WEDGWOOD" "O" "G 1"; "O" "O" incised on bottom edge
Provenance: P. J. Dearden, England; Sotheby's, London, February 27, 1968
1976.125

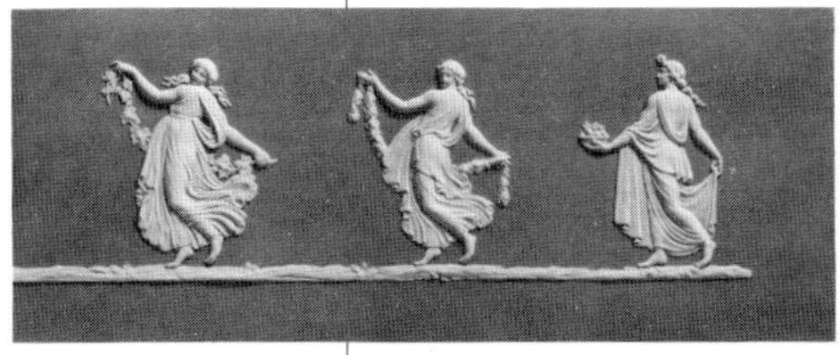

597. Frieze: *Dancing Hours*, ca. 1820
Jasper, solid blue ground with white relief
18 3/8 x 7 1/2 in (46.6 x 19 cm)
Mark: "WEDGWOOD" "O" "8 A"; "O" incised on bottom edge
Provenance: P. J. Dearden, England; Sotheby's, London, February 27, 1968
1976.126

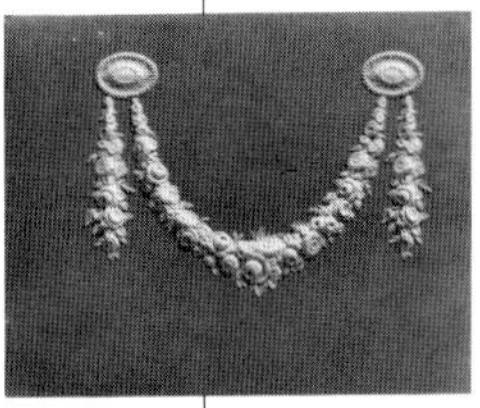

598. Frieze: *Medallions and Swag,* ca. 1820
Jasper, solid blue ground with white relief
9 1/2 x 7 5/8 in (24.1 x 19.3 cm)
Mark: "WEDGWOOD" "O" "B 1"; "O" incised on bottom edge
Provenance: P. J. Dearden, England; Sotheby's, London, February 27, 1968
1976.101

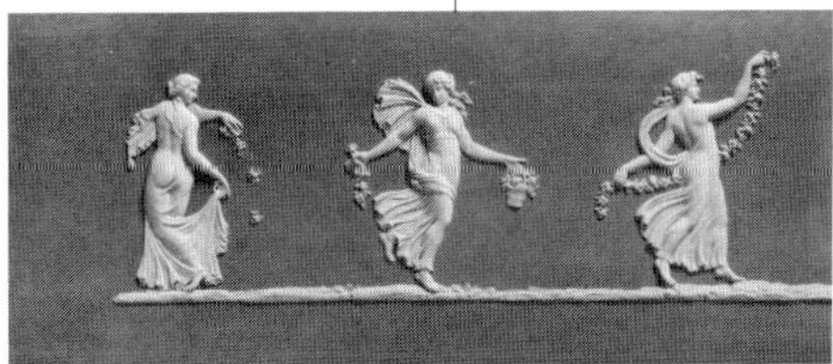

599. Frieze: *Dancing Hours,* ca. 1820
Jasper, solid blue ground with white relief
17 x 7 1/2 in (43.1 x 19 cm)
Mark: "WEDGWOOD" "O" "12 A"
Provenance: P. J. Dearden, England; Sotheby's, London, February 27, 1968
1976.127

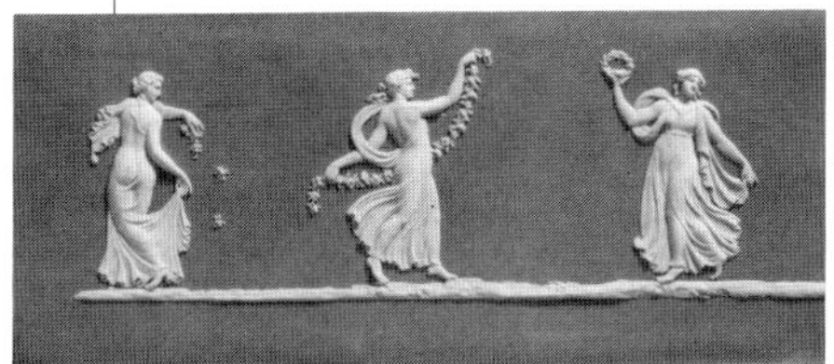

600. Frieze: *Dancing Hours,* ca. 1820
Jasper, solid blue ground with white relief
16 7/8 x 7 1/2 in (42.8 x 19 cm)
Mark: "WEDGWOOD" "O" "67"
Provenance: P. J. Dearden, England; Sotheby's, London, February 27, 1968
1976.128

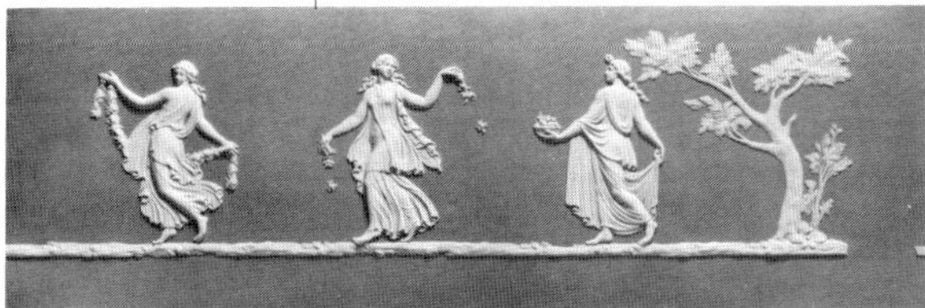

601. Frieze: *Dancing Hours,* ca. 1820
Jasper, solid blue ground with white relief
22 3/4 x 7 5/8 in (57.7 x 19.3 cm)
Mark: "WEDGWOOD" "O" "A-4"
Provenance: P. J. Dearden, England; Sotheby's, London, February 27, 1968
1976.129

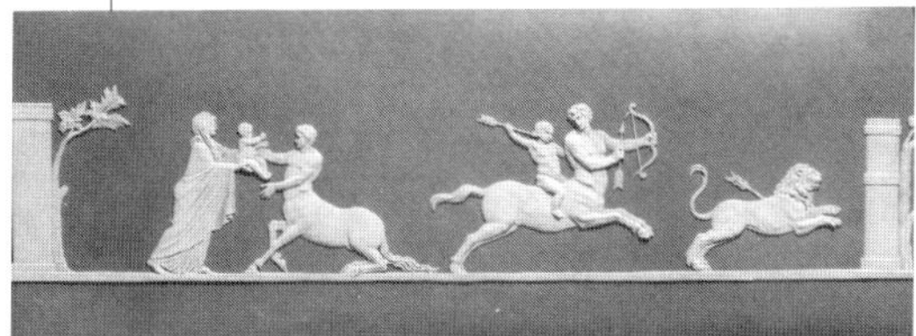

602. Frieze: *Achilles Handed to Chiron by His Mother,* ca. 1820
Jasper, solid blue ground with white relief
20 1/8 x 7 5/8 in (51.1 x 19.3 cm)
Mark: "WEDGWOOD" "O" "A 3"
Provenance: P. J. Dearden, England; Sotheby's, London, February 27, 1968
1976.130

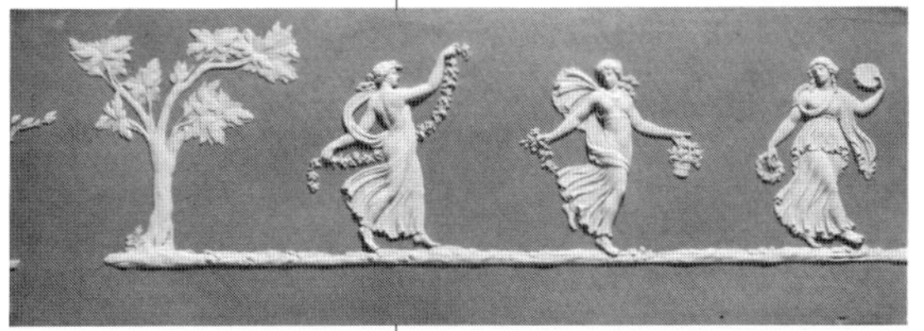

603. Frieze: *Dancing Hours,* ca. 1820
Jasper, solid blue ground with white relief
21 1/8 x 7 1/2 in (53.6 x 19 cm)
Mark: "WEDGWOOD" "O" "A 2"
Provenance: P. J. Dearden, England; Sotheby's, London, February 27, 1968
1976.131

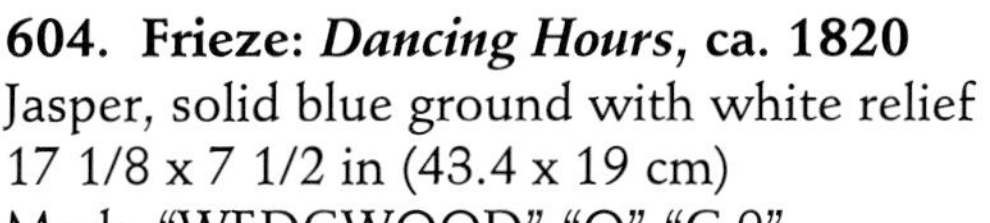

604. Frieze: *Dancing Hours,* ca. 1820
Jasper, solid blue ground with white relief
17 1/8 x 7 1/2 in (43.4 x 19 cm)
Mark: "WEDGWOOD" "O" "C 9"
Provenance: P. J. Dearden, England; Sotheby's, London, February 27, 1968
1976.132

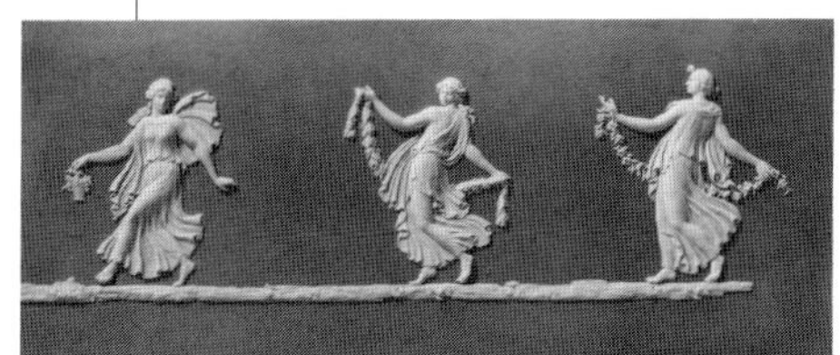

605. Frieze: *Dancing Hours,* ca. 1820
Jasper, solid blue ground with white relief
17 3/4 x 7 1/2 in (45 x 19 cm)
Mark: "WEDGWOOD" "O" "C 3"
Provenance: P. J. Dearden, England; Sotheby's, London, February 27, 1968
1976.133

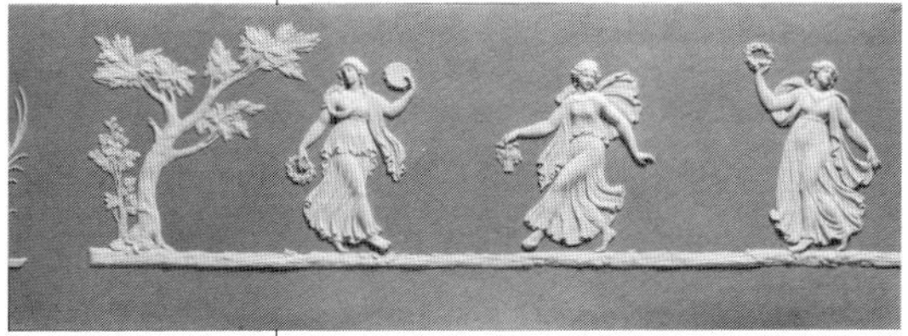

606. Frieze: *Dancing Hours,* ca. 1820
Jasper, solid blue ground with white relief
21 x 7 5/8 in (53.3 x 19.3 cm)
Mark: "WEDGWOOD" "O" "9 A"
Provenance: P. J. Dearden, England; Sotheby's, London, February 27, 1968
1976.134

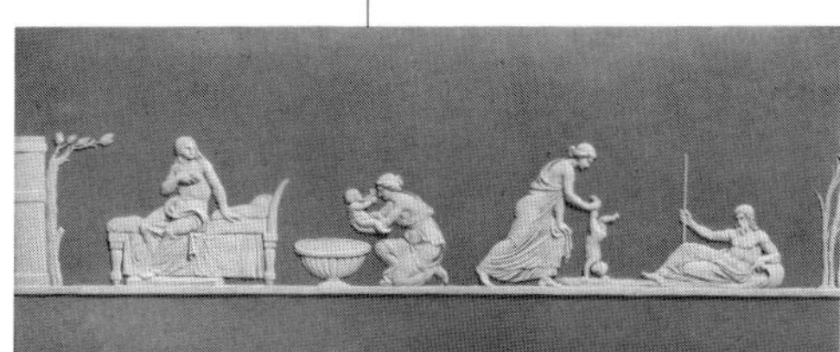

607. Frieze: *Birth and Dipping of Achilles,* ca. 1820
Jasper, solid blue ground with white relief
18 3/4 x 7 5/8 in (47.6 x 19.3 cm)
Mark: "WEDGWOOD" "O" "1O A"
Provenance: P. J. Dearden, England; Sotheby's, London, February 27, 1968
1976.135

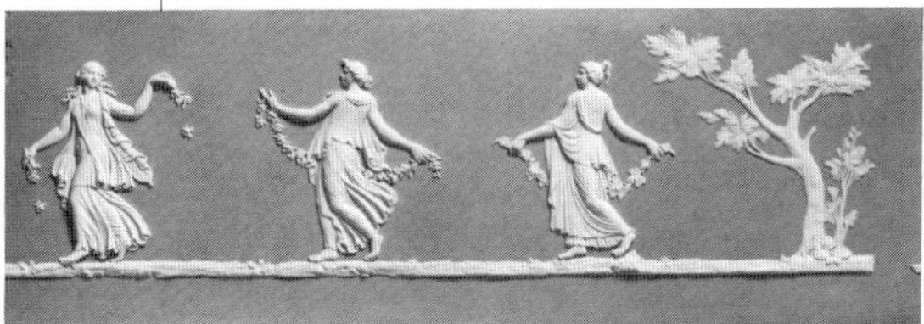

608. Frieze: *Dancing Hours,* ca. 1820
Jasper, solid blue ground with white relief
21 1/4 x 7 5/8 in (53.9 x 19.3 cm)
Mark: "WEDGWOOD" "O" "11A"
Provenance: P. J. Dearden, England; Sotheby's, London, February 27, 1968
1976.136

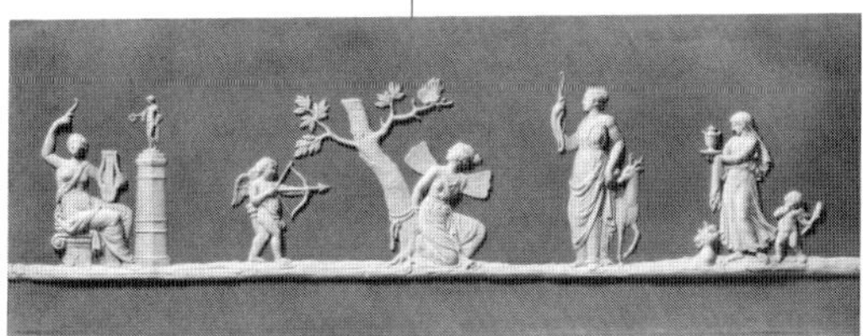

609. Frieze: *Psyche Bound to a Tree,* ca. 1820
Jasper, solid blue ground with white relief
19 1/2 x 7 1/2 in (49.5 x 19 cm)
Mark: "WEDGWOOD" "O" "C 2"
Provenance: P. J. Dearden, England; Sotheby's, London, February 27, 1968
1976.137

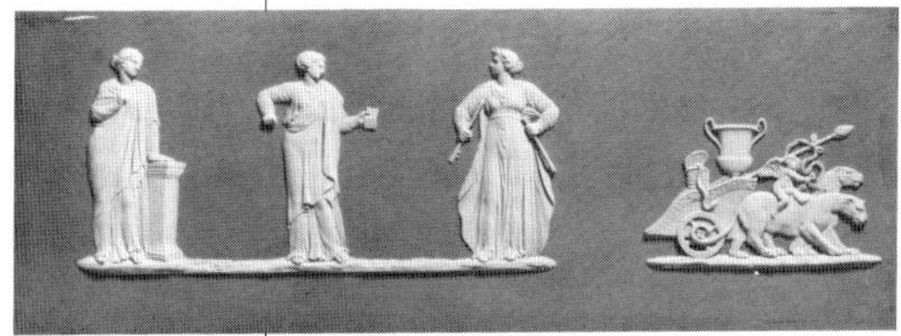

610. Frieze: *Three Muses and Cupid in a Chariot,* ca. 1820
Jasper, solid blue ground with white relief
20 3/4 x 7 5/8 in (52.7 x 19.3 cm)
Mark: "WEDGWOOD" "O" "C2"
Provenance: P. J. Dearden, England; Sotheby's, London, February 27, 1968
1976.138

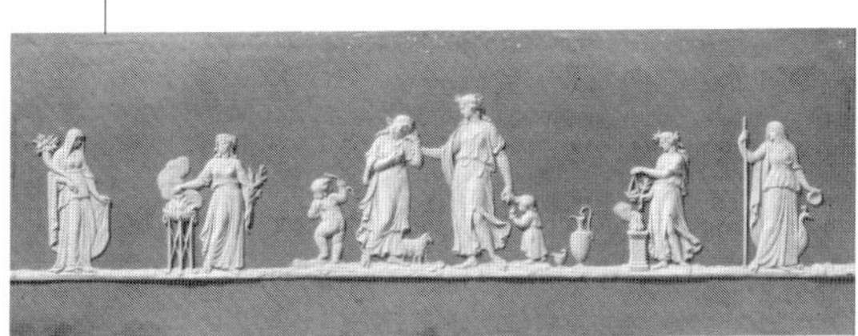

611. Frieze: *Offering to Peace,* ca. 1820
Jasper, solid blue ground with white relief
20 7/8 x 7 5/8 in (53 x 19.3 cm)
Mark: "WEDGWOOD" "O" "C 8"
Provenance: P. J. Dearden, England; Sotheby's, London, February 27, 1968
1976.139

612. Frieze: *Vitruvian Scroll,* ca. 1820
Jasper, solid blue ground with white relief
24 3/8 x 7 5/8 in (61.9 x 19.3 cm)
Mark: "WEDGWOOD", "O" "O" incised on bottom edge
Provenance: P. J. Dearden, England; Sotheby's, London, February 27, 1968
1985.434

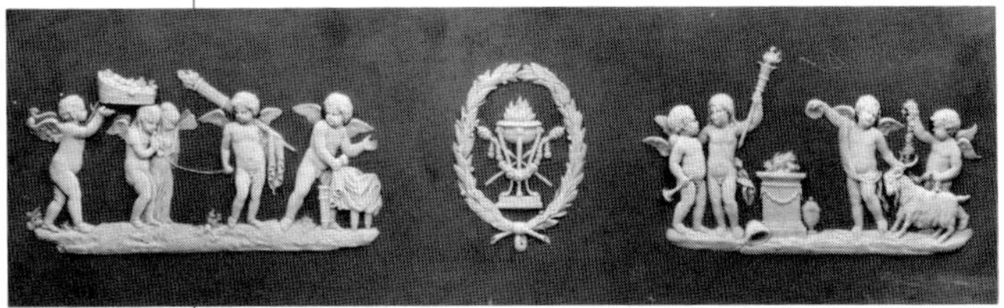

613. Frieze: *Marriage of Cupid and Psyche* and *Sacrifice to Hymen*, ca. 1820
Jasper, solid blue ground with white relief
25 3/8 x 7 9/16 in (64.4 x 19.2 cm)
Mark: "WEDGWOOD" "O" "E 3"; "O" incised on bottom edge
Provenance: P. J. Dearden, England; Sotheby's, London, February 27, 1968
1985.435

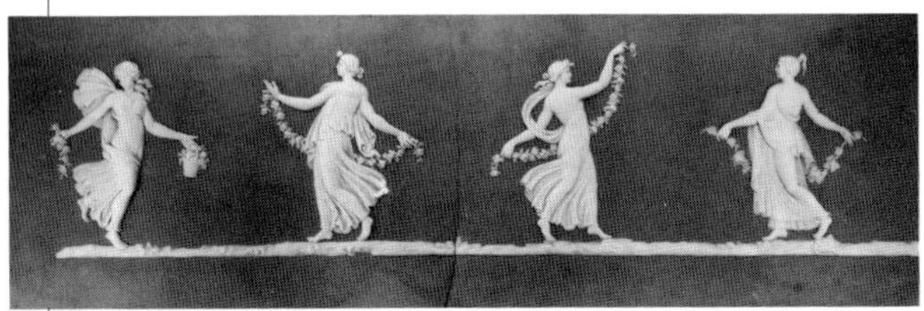

614. Frieze: *Dancing Hours*, ca. 1820
Jasper, solid blue ground with white relief
23 3/8 x 7 5/8 in (59.2 x 19.3 cm)
Mark: "WEDGWOOD" "O"; "O" "O" incised on bottom edge
Provenance: P. J. Dearden, England; Sotheby's, London, February 27, 1968
1985.433b

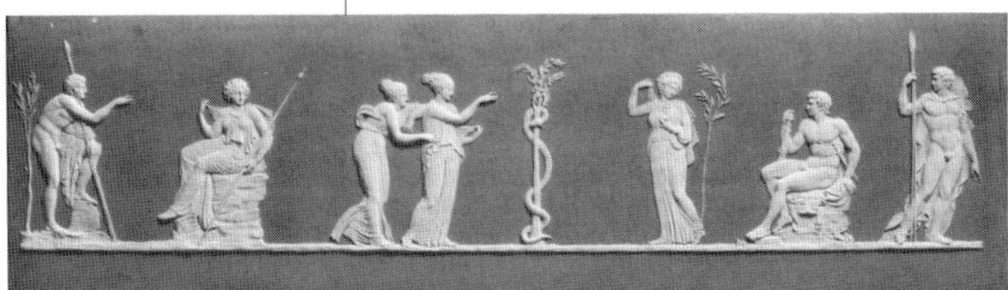

615. Frieze: *Hercules in the Garden of the Hesperides*, ca. 1820
Jasper, solid blue ground with white relief
25 7/8 x 7 1/2 in (65.5 x 19 cm)
Mark: "WEDGWOOD" "O" "B6"
Provenance: P. J. Dearden, England; Sotheby's, London, February 27, 1968
1976.351

Other Objects in the Frieze Room

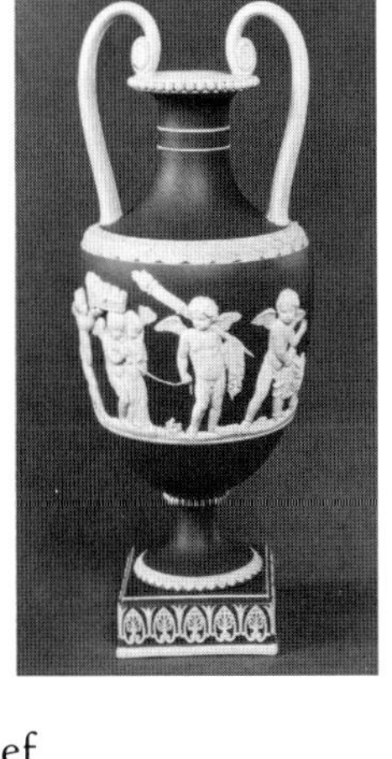

616. Vase: ***Marriage of Cupid and Psyche,* ca. 1800**
Jasper, solid white ground with dark blue wash and white relief
14 1/2 x 3 3/4 in (36.8 x 9.5 cm)
Mark: "WEDGWOOD"
Provenance: Dr. Francis Jennings Vurpillat, South Bend, Ind.
1982.16
Vase has sump cover; base is hollow with four firing holes.
Color plate 74

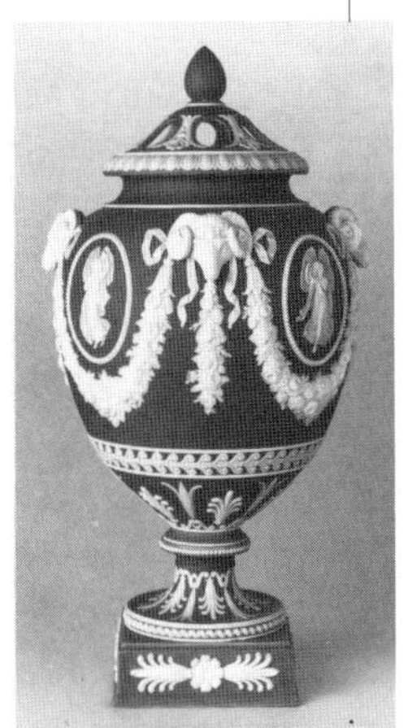

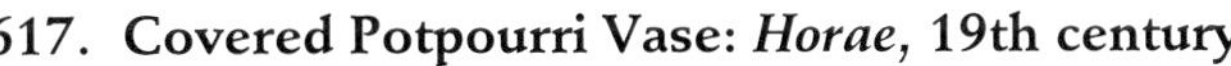

617. Covered Potpourri Vase: ***Horae,* 19th century**
Jasper, solid white ground with green wash and white relief
13 7/8 x 4 1/16 in (35.2 x 10.3 cm)
Mark: "WEDGWOOD" "2"
Provenance: Manheim's Gallery, New Orleans
198.313
Base has cavity around bolt with four small firing holes.
Color plate 131

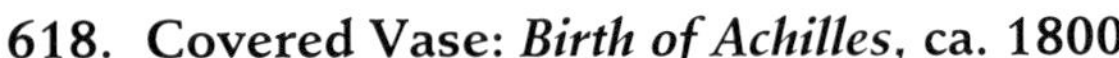

618. Covered Vase: ***Birth of Achilles,* ca. 1800**
Jasper, solid white ground with lilac wash and white relief
12 7/8 x 4 in (32.7 x 10.1 cm)
Mark: "WEDGWOOD"
Provenance: Abbott Collection, England; Dr. Francis Jennings Vurpillat, South Bend, Ind.
1980.304 a and b
Base is hollow.

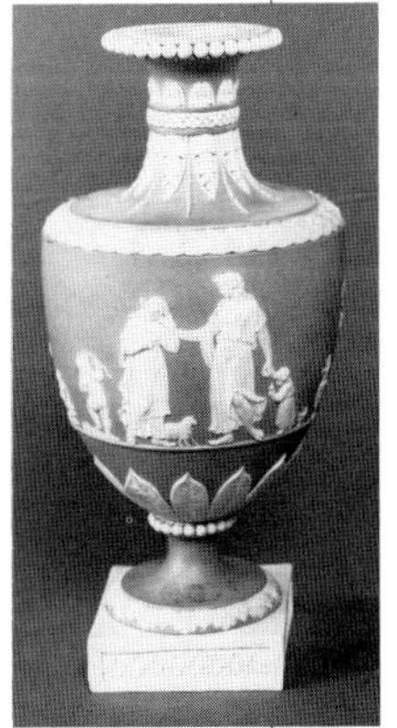

619. Vase: ***Domestic Employment,* ca. 1790**
Jasper, solid blue ground with white relief and white terra-cotta stoneware base
11 5/16 x 3 9/16 in (28.7 x 9 cm)
Mark: "WEDGWOOD"
Provenance: Dr. Francis Jennings Vurpillat, South Bend, Ind.
1982.18
Vase has sump cover.

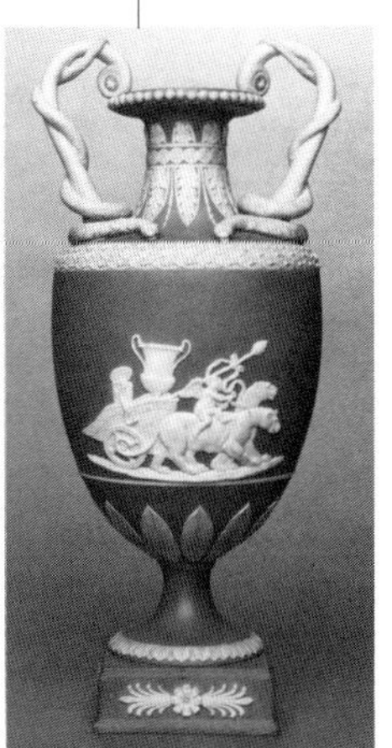

620. Vase: ***Cupid Drawn by Lions,* 19th century**
Jasper, solid white ground with lilac wash and white relief
13 3/4 x 3 11/16 in (34.9 x 9.3 cm)
Mark: "WEDGWOOD"
Provenance: Dr. Francis Jennings Vurpillat, South Bend, Ind.
1980.307
Base is hollow.

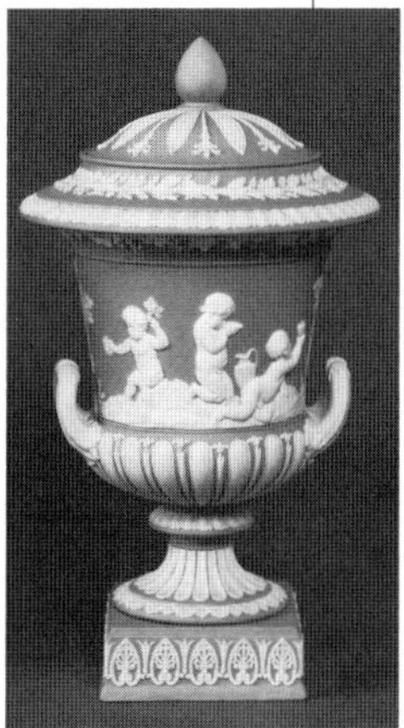

621. Vase: *Bacchanalian Boys at Play,* ca. 1880
Jasper, solid blue ground with white relief
12 1/4 x 4 in (31.1 x 10.1 cm)
Mark: "WEDGWOOD"
Provenance: Manheim Galleries, New Orleans
1981.253 a and b
Base has cavity around bolt and four firing holes.
Color plate 88

622. Inkwell: ca. 1785
Jasper, solid blue ground with white relief and engine-turning
1 7/8 x 2 1/2 in (4.7 x 6.3 cm)
Mark: "Wedgwood"
Provenance: David Davis, Chicago; Dr. Harold L. Klawans, Chicago
1980.149
Color plate 93

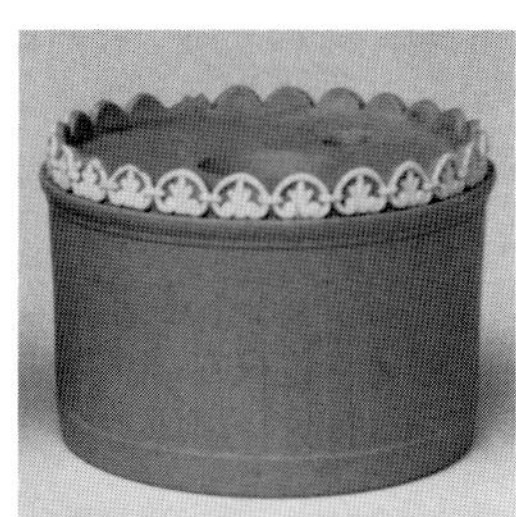

623. Obelisk with Medallion: ca. 1800
Jasper, solid white ground with dark blue wash and white relief, Derbyshire spar
1 3/8 x 1 1/16 in (3.4 x 2.7 cm)
Mark: none
Provenance: Ann Brodkiewicz, Chicago
1983.14
Color plate 93

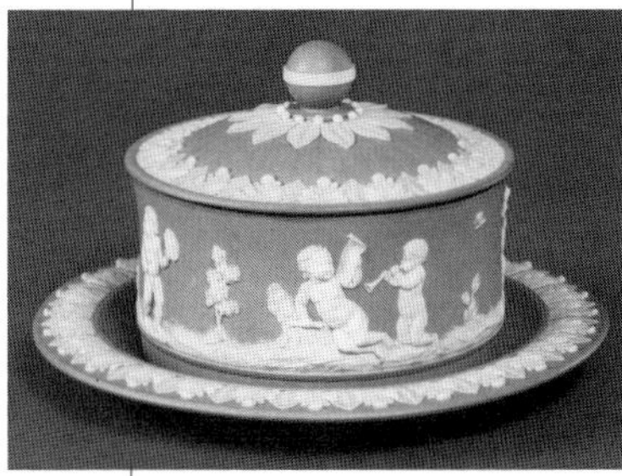

624. Covered Cosmetic Box and Underdish: *Boys at Play,* ca. 1790
Jasper, solid blue ground and white relief
Box: 3 7/8 x 4 1/2 in (9.8 x 11.4 cm); dish: 6 7/8 in (17.4 cm)
Mark: "WEDGWOOD"
Provenance: Otto Wasserman, New York
1981.254 a, b, and c
Color plates 93 and 125

625. Mantel Garniture of Clock and Candlesticks: 19th century
Jasper, solid light blue with white relief, marble, ormolu, porcelain
Five medallions: 1 5/16 x 1 1/32 in (3.3 x 2.6 cm); four medallions: 1 5/8 x 1 5/16 in (4.1 x 3.3 cm)
Mark: "WEDGWOOD" "O"; "MAISON ENGERRAN L. MAEGHT / AMIENS" on clock face
Provenance: Manheim's Gallery, New Orleans
1985.439.1-.3
Color plate 934

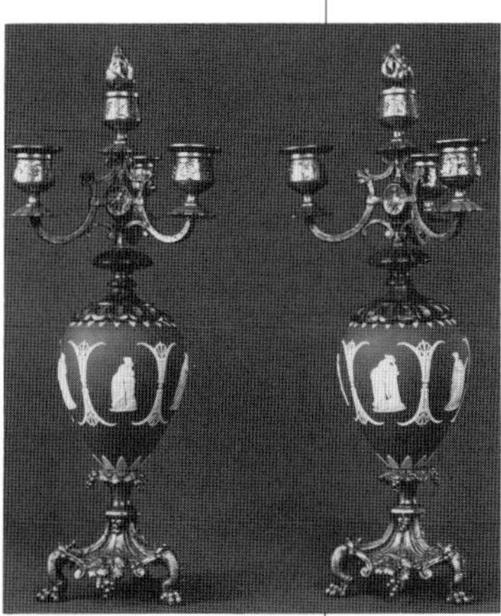

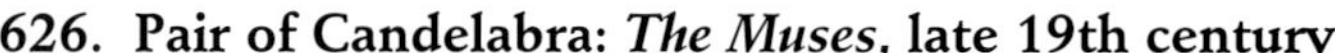

626. Pair of Candelabra: *The Muses,* late 19th century
Jasper, solid white ground with dark blue wash and white relief, set in gilded metal
Candelabra: 17 in (43.1 cm); drum: 5 x 3 in (12.7 x 7.6 cm)
Mark: none visible
Provenance: Purchased in New Orleans
1977.119 and 1977.120
Color plate 93

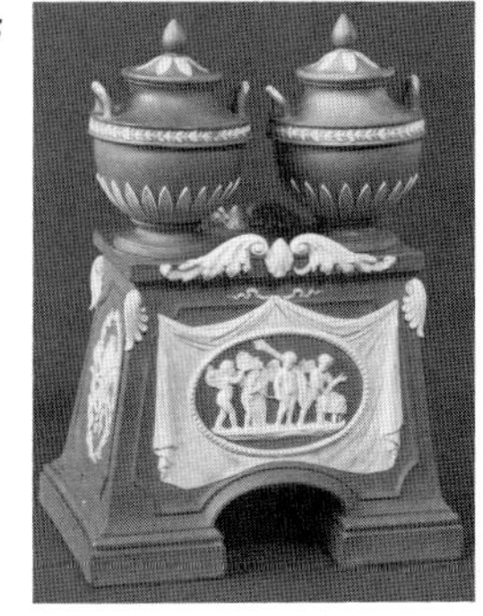

627. Inkstand: ***Marriage of Cupid and Psyche*** **and** ***Trophies of Love and Harmony*****, ca. 1795**
Jasper, solid blue ground with white relief
8 3/4 x 6 1/2 in (22.2 x 16.5)
Mark: "WEDGWOOD"
Provenance: Dr. Francis Jennings Vurpillat, South Bend, Ind.
1981.248
Color plates 73 and 93

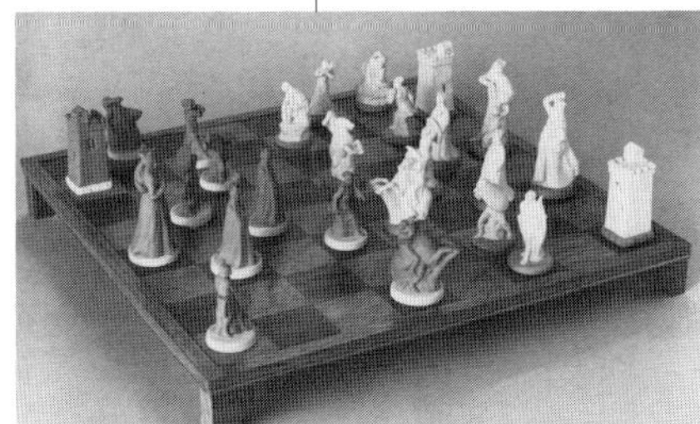

628. Twenty-six Chessmen: ca. 1790
John Flaxman (1755-1826), designer
Jasper, solid white and solid blue
3 5/16 in (greatest height) (7.9 cm)
Mark: none
Provenance: Fred J. Tongue, Santa Monica, Calif.
1981.278.1-.26
Color plates 94 and 119

629. Reproduction Chandelier with 18th-Century Drum: ***Swag and Medallion*****, ca. 1790**
Jasper, solid blue ground with white relief
Drum: 3 3/8 x 3 1/2 in (8.5 x 8.8 cm)
Mark: "WEDGWOOD"
Provenance: Ann Brodkiewicz, Chicago
1976.142

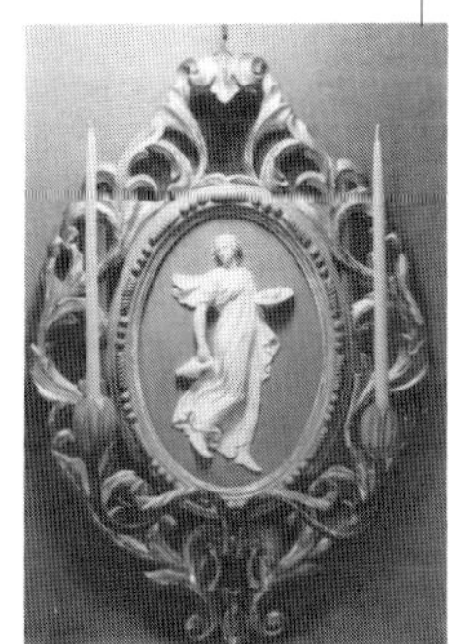

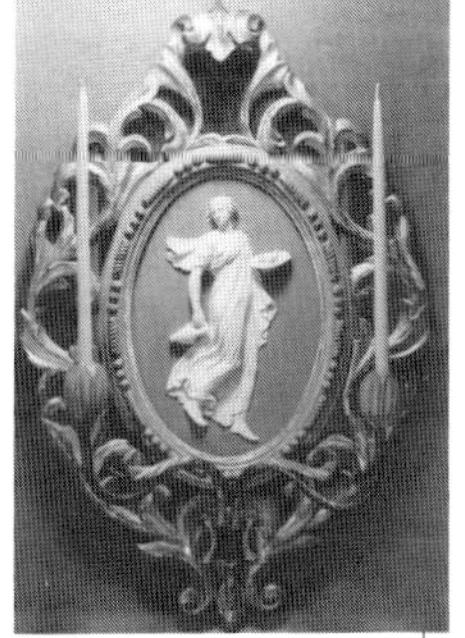

630. Pair of Sconces: ***Herculaneum Figures*****, 1775-80**
Jasper, solid blue ground with blue wash on front and white relief; Florentine mirrored frame
Plaque: 10 1/8 x 7 in (25.7 x 17.7 cm)
Mark: "WEDGWOOD & BENTLEY"
Provenance: Dr. Francis Jennings Vurpillat, South Bend, Ind.; Fred J. Tongue, Santa Monica, Calif.
1985.422 a and b
Backs have 16 and 19 firing holes, respectively.
Color plates 67, 68, and 93

631. Pair of Chandeliers: ***The Muses*****, 19th century**
Jasper, solid white ground with blue wash and white relief, set in gilded metal
17 1/2 in (44.4 cm); drum: 5 1/2 x 4 in (13.9 x 10.1 cm)
Mark: none visible
Provenance: Manheim's Gallery, New Orleans
1976.143

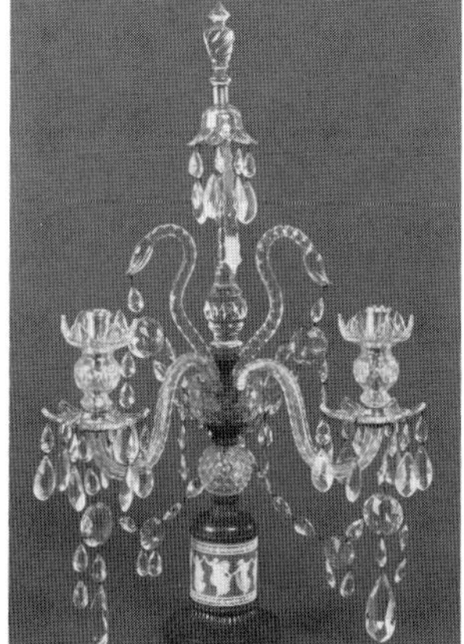

632. Pair of Candelabra: ***The Dancing Hours*****, ca. 1800**
Jasper, solid white ground with blue wash with white relief, burnished gilt metal base, Waterford crystal
23 3/4 in (60.3 cm)
Drum: 2 1/2 x 2 in (6.2 x 5 cm)
Mark: "WEDGWOOD"
Provenance: Fred J. Tongue, Santa Monica, Calif.
1982.3 a and b

Fire Screen with Medallions

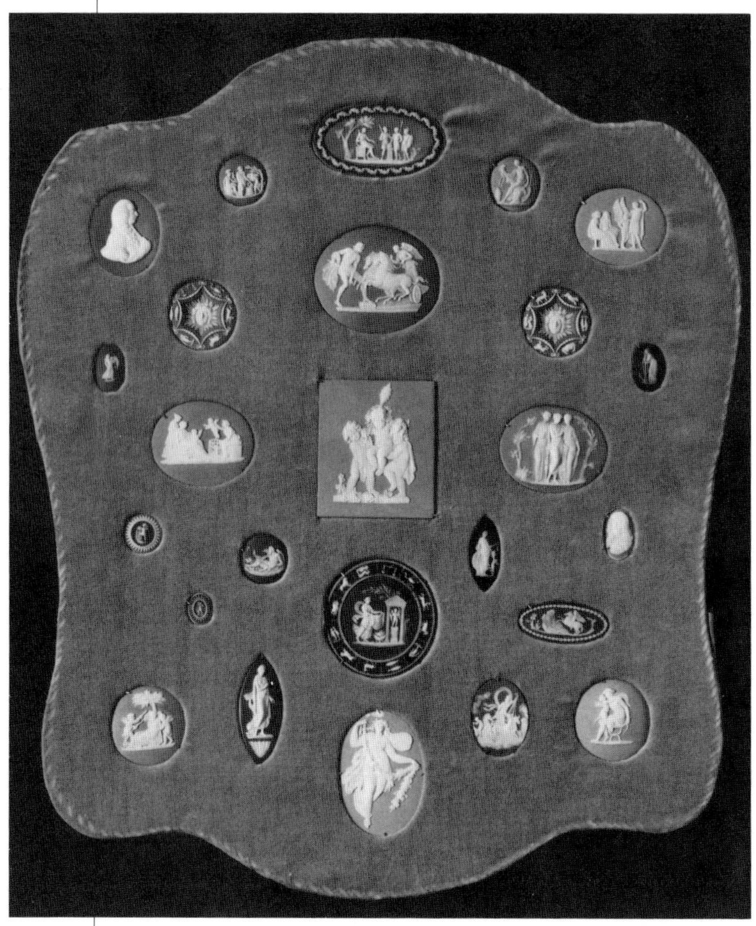

633. Medallion: ***Mucius Scaevola,*** **ca. 1800**
Jasper, solid white ground with lilac wash and blue-and-white relief
2 3/4 x 1 1/2 in (6.9 x 3.8 cm)
Mark: "WEDGWOOD" "H"
Provenance: Dr. Harold L. Klawans, Chicago
1977.95

634. Medallion: ***Sacrifice to Hymen,*** **ca. 1800**
Jasper, solid white ground with lilac-and-blue wash and white relief
2 5/8 in (6.6 cm)
Mark: "WEDGWOOD"
Provenance: Dr. Harold L. Klawans, Chicago
1977.96

635. Medallion: ***Achilles in His Tent,*** **19th century**
Jasper, solid blue ground with white relief
1 1/16 in (2.7 cm)
Mark: "WEDGWOOD" "6" incised
Provenance: Dr. Harold L. Klawans, Chicago
1977.111

636. Medallion: *Portrait of Lord Camden*, ca. 1790
Jasper, solid blue ground with blue wash and white relief
1 5/8 x 1 3/8 in (4.1 x 3.4 cm)
Mark: "4 V 1" in script
Provenance: Lady Mount Stephen, London; Dr. Harold L. Klawans, Chicago
1977.106

637. Medallion: *Classical Figures with Angel*, ca. 1800
Jasper, solid blue ground with white relief
1 11/16 x 1 1/2 in (4.2 x 3.8 cm)
Mark: "WEDGWOOD" "137" incised
Provenance: Dr. Harold L. Klawans, Chicago
1977.109

638. Pair of Medallions: *Phoebus Surrounded by the Zodiac*, ca. 1790
Jasper, solid blue ground with white relief
1 3/8 in (3.4 cm)
Mark: none
Provenance: Dr. Harold L. Klawans, Chicago
1977.100 a and b

639. Medallion: *Achilles Staying the Chariot of Victory*, 19th century
Jasper, solid blue ground with white relief
2 1/2 x 2 in (6.3 x 5 cm)
Mark: "WEDGWOOD" "94" incised
Provenance: Dr. Harold L. Klawans, Chicago
1977.107

640. Medallion: *Classical Female Figure with Veil*, 19th century
Jasper, solid dark blue ground with white relief
7/8 x 9/16 in (2.2 x 1.4 cm)
Mark: none
Provenance: Dr. Harold L. Klawans, Chicago
1977.113

641. Medallion: *Hope*, 19th century
Jasper, solid white ground with black wash and white relief
7/8 x 5/8 in (2.2 x 1.5 cm)
Mark: "WEDGWOOD"
Provenance: Dr. Harold L. Klawans, Chicago
1977.114

642. Medallion: *The Cupid Market*, 19th century
Jasper, solid blue ground with white relief
2 x 1 9/16 in (5 x 3.9 cm)
Mark: "WEDGWOOD"
Provenance: Dr. Harold L. Klawans, Chicago
1977.117

643. Medallion: *Bacchanalian Boys*, ca. 1790
Jasper, solid blue ground with white relief
2 9/16 x 2 5/16 in (6.5 x 5.8 cm)
Mark: none
Provenance: Dr. Harold L. Klawans, Chicago
1977.108

644. Medallion: *The Three Graces*, ca. 1800
Jasper, solid blue ground with white relief
2 1/8 x 1 5/8 in (5.3 x 4.1 cm)
Mark: "WEDGWOOD"
Provenance: Dr. Harold L. Klawans, Chicago
1977.110

645. Medallion: *Roman Warrior*, ca. 1800
Jasper, solid white ground with lilac-and-blue wash and white relief
13/16 in (2 cm)
Mark: "WEDGWOOD"
Provenance: Dr. Harold L. Klawans, Chicago
1977.102

646. Medallion: *Father Time*, ca. 1800
Jasper, solid white ground with dark blue wash and white relief
1 in (2.5 cm)
Mark: none
Provenance: Dr. Harold L. Klawans, Chicago
1977.99

647. Medallion: *Minerva and Cupid*, 19th century
Jasper, solid white ground with black wash and white relief
1 3/8 x 5/8 in (3.4 x 1.5 cm)
Mark: "WEDGWOOD" "J"
Provenance: Dr. Harold L. Klawans, Chicago
1977.67.5

648. Medallion: *George Frideric Handel*, ca. 1790
Jasper, solid white ground with lilac wash and white relief
1 x 11/16 in (2.5 x 1.7 cm)
Mark: "WEDGWOOD"
Provenance: David Davis, Chicago; Dr. Harold L. Klawans, Chicago
1977.97

649. Medallion: *Cupid*, ca. 1800
Jasper, solid white ground with lilac-and-green wash and white relief
11/16 x 1/2 in (1.7 x 1.2 cm)
Mark: "WEDGWOOD"
Provenance: Dr. Harold L. Klawans, Chicago
1977.101

650. Medallion: *A Sacrifice and the Zodiac*, ca. 1800
Jasper, solid white ground with lilac-and-blue wash and white relief
2 1/4 in (5.5 cm)
Mark: "WEDGWOOD"
Provenance: Dr. Harold L. Klawans, Chicago
1977.98

651. Medallion: *Mounted Warrior*, ca. 1800
Jasper, solid white ground with lilac-and-blue wash and white relief
1 11/16 x 11/16 in (4.2 x 1.7 cm)
Mark: "WEDGWOOD"
Provenance: Dr. Harold L. Klawans, Chicago
1977.103

652. Medallion: *Venus Bound by Cupid*, 19th century
Jasper, solid blue ground with white relief
1 1/2 in (3.8 cm)
Mark: "WEDGWOOD"
Provenance: Dr. Harold L. Klawans, Chicago
1977.115

653. Medallion: *Nymph with Dolphin*, ca. 1790
Jasper, solid blue ground with dark blue wash and white relief
2 1/16 x 7/8 in (5.2 x 2.2 cm)
Mark: "WEDGWOOD & CO"
Provenance: Dr. Harold L. Klawans, Chicago
1977.116

654. Medallion: *Herculaneum Nymph with Garland*, ca. 1800
Jasper, solid white ground with green wash and white relief
2 3/8 x 1 3/4 in (6 x 4.4 cm)
Mark: "WEDGWOOD"
Provenance: Dr. Harold L. Klawans, Chicago
1977.105

655. Medallion: *Neptune*, ca. 1800
Jasper, solid white ground with dark blue wash back and front with white relief
1 3/8 x 1 1/8 in (3.4 x 2.8 cm)
Mark: none
Provenance: Godfrey W. Ford, England; Dr. Harold L. Klawans, Chicago
1977.118

656. Medallion: *Venus and Cupid*, 19th century
Jasper, solid blue ground with white relief
1 1/2 in (3.8 cm)
Mark: "WEDGWOOD" "37"
Provenance: Dr. Harold L. Klawans, Chicago
1977.104

Miscellaneous Wares

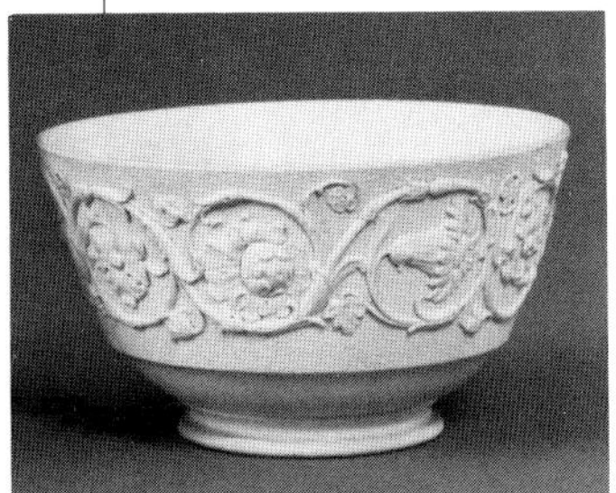

657. Bowl: *Roman Scroll and Flowers,* ca. 1815
White stoneware with white relief and granulated surface
2 11/16 x 2 3/8 in (6.8 x 6 cm)
Mark: "WEDGWOOD" "X"
Provenance: Dr. Harold L. Klawans, Chicago
1976.237
Color plate 133

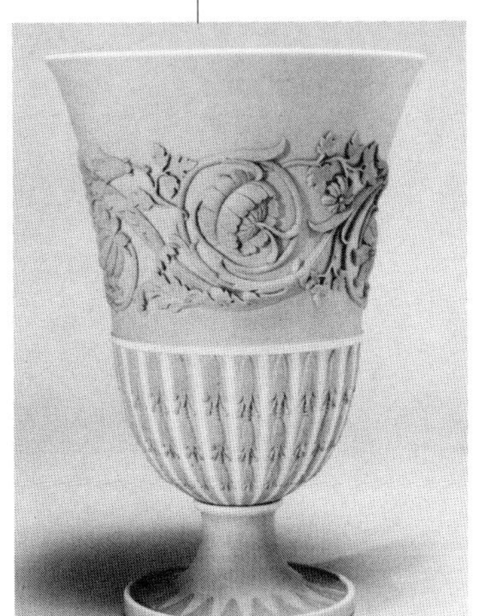

658. Goblet Vase: *Roman Scroll and Flowers,* ca. 1815
White stoneware with canary yellow jasper wash and blue jasper relief and engine-turning
6 13/16 x 3 in (17.3 x 7.6 cm)
Mark: "WEDGWOOD" "A"
Provenance: Toby House, New York
1981.227
Vase has sump cover.
Design source: Montfaucon, *L'Antiquité expliquée,* vol. 5, pt. 1, pl. 6, fig. 4
Color plate 132

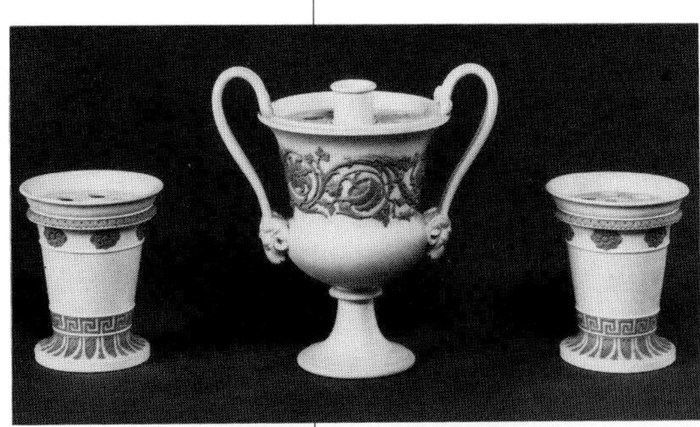

659. Three-Piece Vase Garniture: *Roman Scroll and Flowers,* ca. 1815
White stoneware with green jasper relief and glazed interior
a: 6 1/2 x 2 15/16 in (16.5 x 7.4 cm);
b and c: 4 1/8 x 2 15/16 in (10.4 x 7.4 cm)
Mark: a, b, and c: "WEDGWOOD" with tool marks; a: "RK"
Provenance: D. M. and P. Manheim, New York
1980.330 a, b, and c
Color plate 133

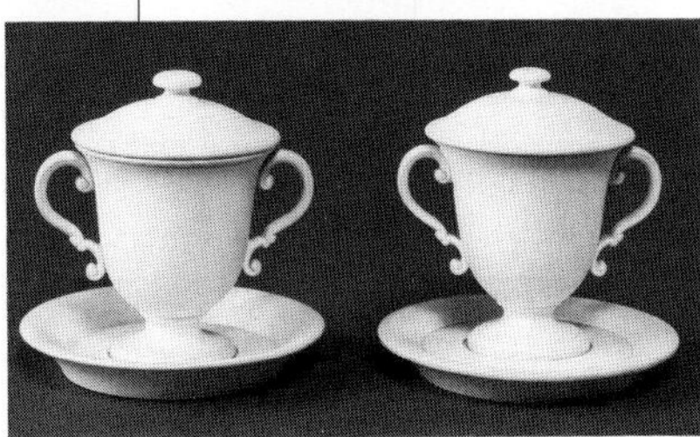

660. Pair of Covered Chocolate Cups and Saucers: ca. 1820
White stoneware, cup and cover have glazed interior
Cup: 3 x 2 in (7.6 x 5 cm); saucer: 4 5/16 in (10.9 cm)
Mark: "WEDGWOOD" with tool marks
Provenance: a: Dr. Harold L. Klawans, Chicago;
b: Dr. Francis Jennings Vurpillat, South Bend, Ind.
1976.235.1 a and b

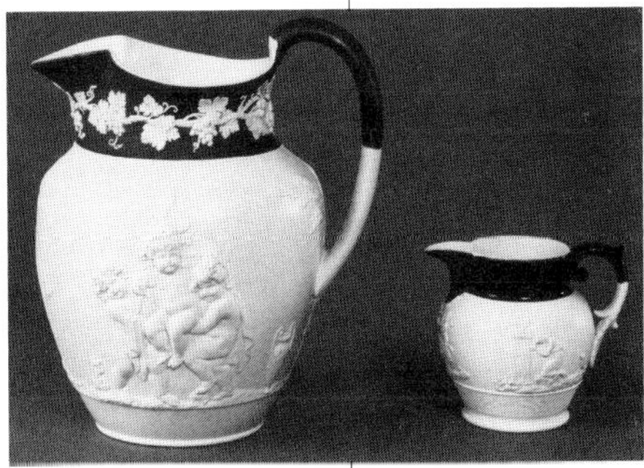

661. Cream Pitcher: *Charlotte at the Tomb of Werther* and *Bourbonnais Shepherd*, ca. 1820
White stoneware, smear glaze with blue decoration
3 1/16 x 1 15/16 in (7.7 x 4.9 cm)
Mark: none
Provenance: Gift to the collection from M. O. Wiser and Gary Cheval, The Toby House, Stamford, Conn.
1976.299

662. Pitcher: *Bacchanalian Boys*, ca. 1820
White stoneware, smear glaze and cobalt decoration
7 1/8 x 3 in (18 x 7.6 cm)
Mark: "WEDGWOOD" "O"
Provenance: Dr. Francis Jennings Vurpillat, South Bend, Ind.
1976.241

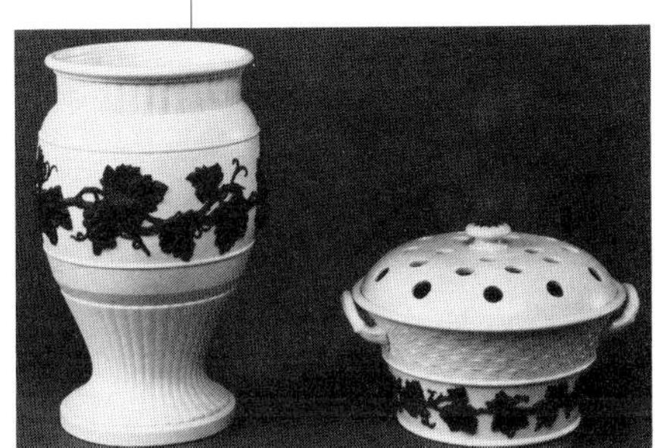

663. Vase: *Grapevine*, ca. 1820
White stoneware, smear glaze and brown relief
6 5/8 x 3 1/4 in (16.8 x 8.2 cm)
Mark: "WEDGWOOD" with tool marks
Provenance: Charles Smith, Philadelphia Penn.
1976.236

664. Covered Basket: *Grapevine*, ca. 1825
White stoneware, smear glaze and cobalt blue relief
3 1/2 x 3 3/8 in (8.8 x 8.5 cm)
Mark: "WEDGWOOD" with tool marks
Provenance: Dr. Francis Jennings Vurpillat, South Bend, Ind.
1976.240

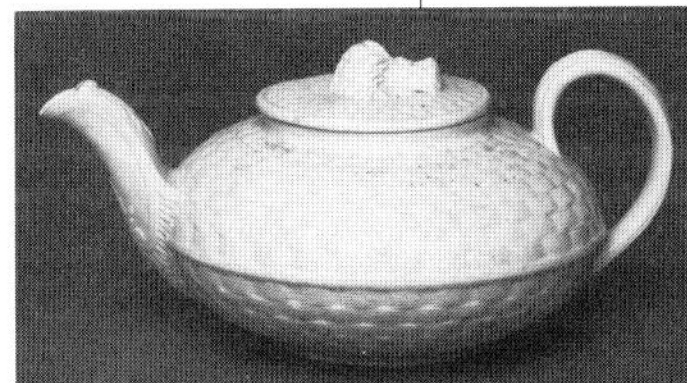

665. Teapot: *Basket-Weave Pattern*, ca. 1830
White stoneware with smear glaze
3 1/4 x 2 1/2 in (8.2 x 6.3 cm)
Mark: "WEDGWOOD" "O" incised with tool marks
Provenance: Dr. Francis Jennings Vurpillat, South Bend, Ind.
1976.242 a and b

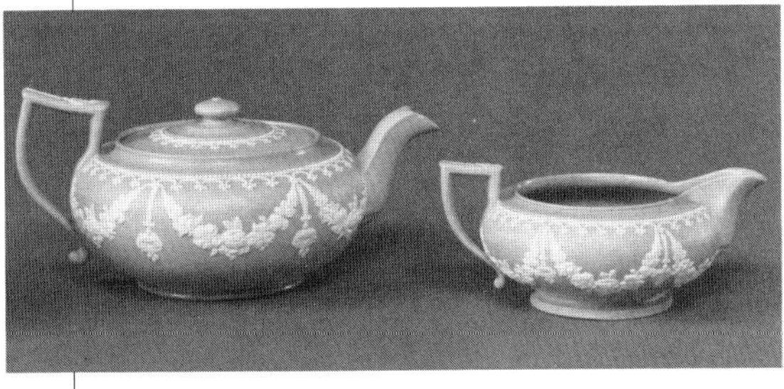

666. Teapot: *Flower Swags*, 19th century
Stoneware
3 1/2 x 3 1/16 in (8.8 x 7.7 cm)
Mark: "WEDGEWOOD" [*sic*]
Provenance: Charles Smith, Philadelphia, Pa.
1976.238

667. Cream Pitcher: *Flower Swags*, 19th century
Stoneware
2 1/2 x 2 1/2 in (6.3 x 6.3 cm)
Mark: "WEDGEWOOD" [*sic*]
Provenance: Charles Smith, Philadelphia, Pa.
1976.239

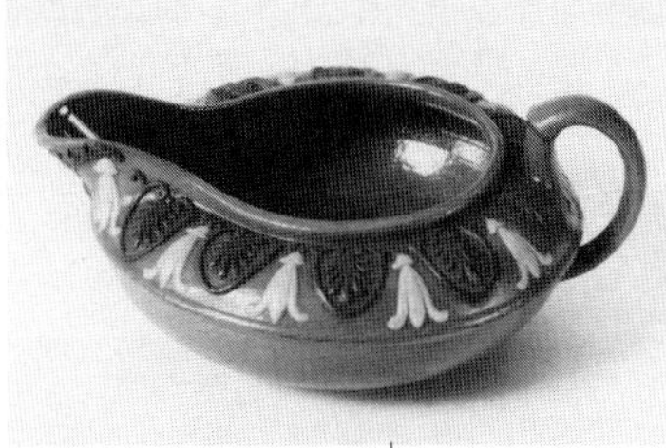

668. Cream Pitcher: *Acanthus*, ca. 1828
Drabware with blue-and-white relief
1 7/8 x 1 3/4 in (4.7 x 4.4 cm)
Mark: illegible
Provenance: Dr. Francis Jennings Vurpillat, South Bend, Ind.
1976.258

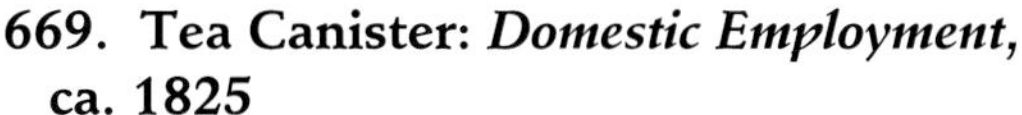

669. Tea Canister: *Domestic Employment*, ca. 1825
Drabware with lilac relief
6 1/4 x 4 1/2 in (15.8 x 11.4 cm)
Mark: "WEDGWOOD" "O"
Provenance: Dr. Francis Jennings Vurpillat, South Bend, Ind.
1976.255
Color plate 145

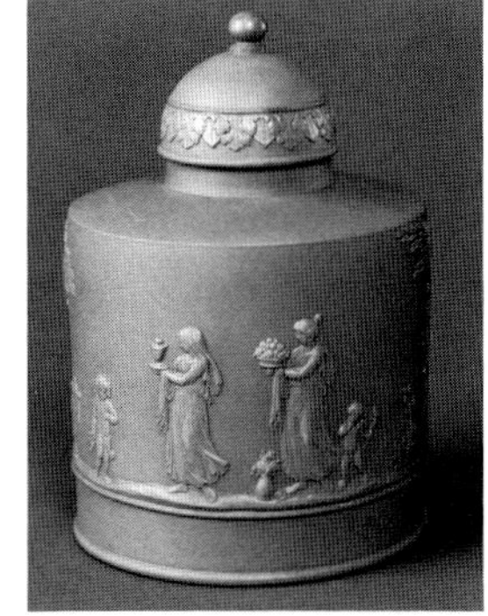

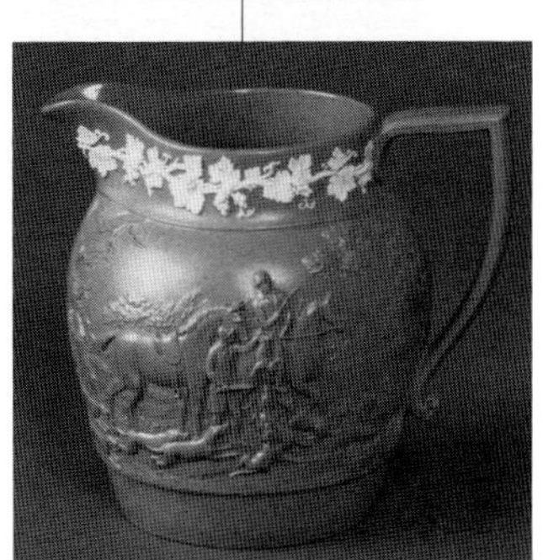

670. Sugar Bowl: 19th century
Drabware with cobalt blue relief
4 x 3 1/4 in (10.1 x 8.2 cm)
Mark: "WEDGWOOD" "O" with tool marks
Provenance: Dr. Francis Jennings Vurpillat, South Bend, Ind.
1976.256
Color plate 145

671. Pitcher: *Hunting Scene*, 19th century
Drabware, white relief, glazed interior
5 1/4 x 3 1/4 in (13.3 x 8.2 cm)
Mark: "WEDGWOOD" with tool marks
Provenance: Dr. Francis Jennings Vurpillat, South Bend, Ind.
1976.254
Color plate 145

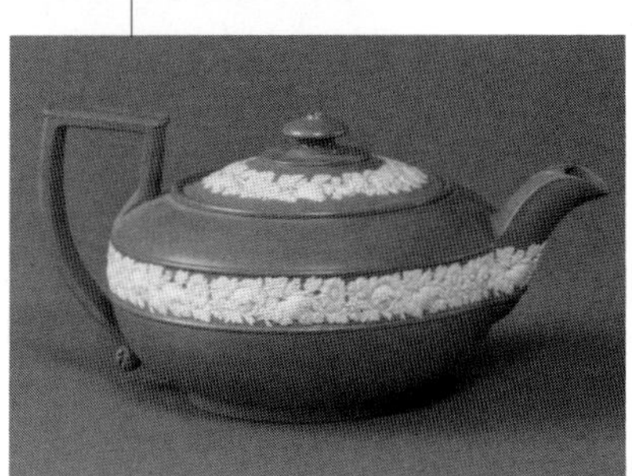

672. Teapot: ca. 1825
Drabware, white relief
3 1/2 x 8 1/8 in (8.8 x 20.6 cm)
Mark: "WEDGWOOD" "O"
Provenance: Purchased in Saint Petersburg, Fla.
1976.253

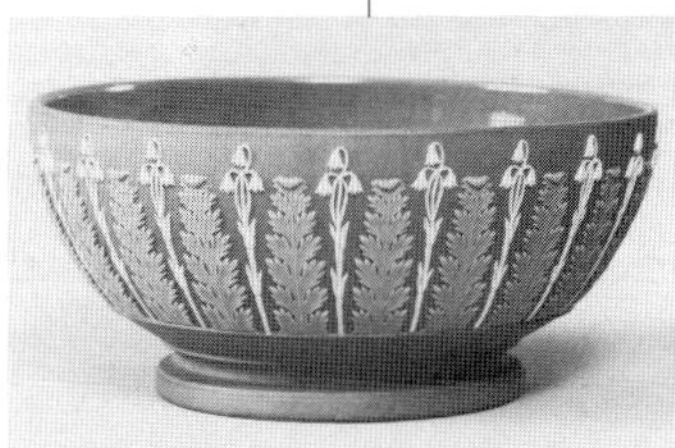

673. Bowl: 19th century
Drabware, lilac-and-white relief, glazed interior
3 3/16 x 4 1/4 in (8 x 10.7 cm)
Mark: "WEDGWOOD" with tool marks
Provenance: Dr. Francis Jennings Vurpillat, South Bend, Ind.
1976.257

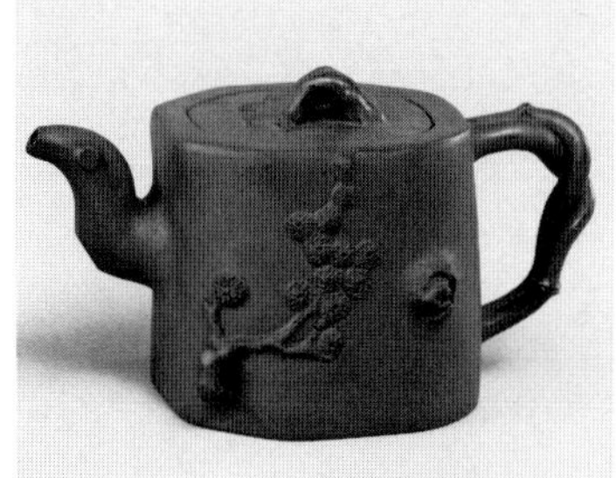

674. Teapot: *Xixing Ware*, 20th century
China
Red stoneware, applied decoration
3 5/8 x 3 5/8 in (9.2 x 9.2 cm)
Mark: Chinese characters
Provenance: Dr. Francis Jennings Vurpillat, South Bend, Ind.
1979.170 a and b

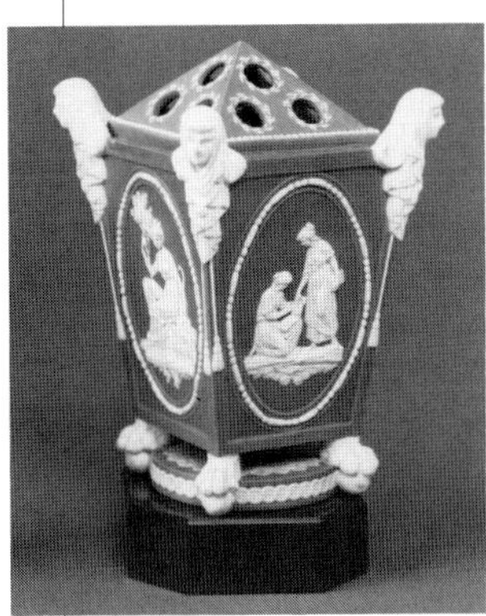

675. Vase: ca. 1790
John Turner (1738-86), potter
Jasper, solid blue ground with blue wash and white relief
8 x 3 3/4 in (20.3 x 9.5 cm)
Mark: "TURNER" "1"
Provenance: Dr. Francis Jennings Vurpillat, South Bend, Ind.
1979.225

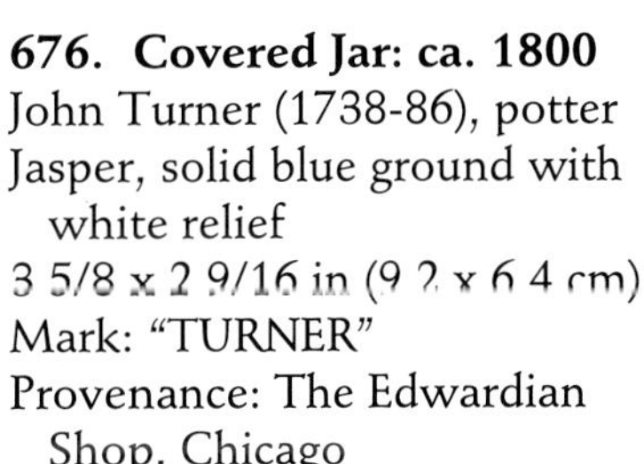

676. Covered Jar: ca. 1800
John Turner (1738-86), potter
Jasper, solid blue ground with white relief
3 5/8 x 2 9/16 in (9.2 x 6.4 cm)
Mark: "TURNER"
Provenance: The Edwardian Shop, Chicago
1979.236 a and b

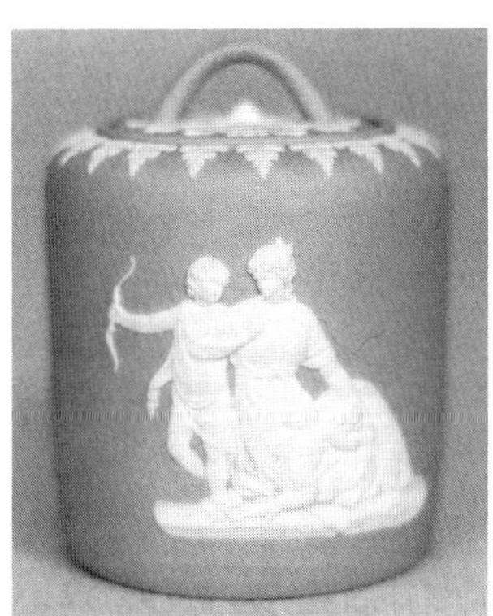

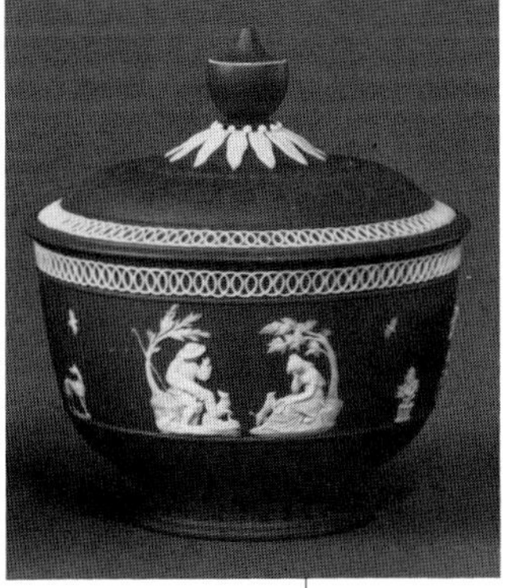

677. Sugar Bowl: *Poor Maria* and *Bourbonnais Shepherd*, ca. 1790
William Adams (1746-1805), potter
Tunstall, England
Jasper, solid dark blue ground with white relief
4 3/4 x 2 7/16 in (12 x 6 cm)
Provenance: Dr. Francis Jennings Vurpillat, South Bend, Ind.
1979.235 a and b

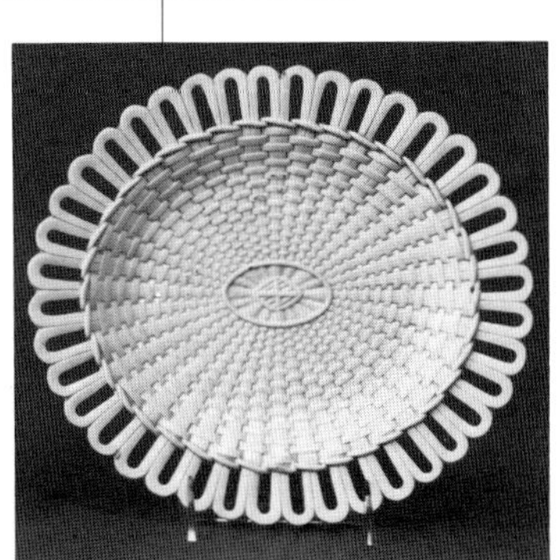

678. Stand for Fruit Basket: ca. 1790
Cream ware
8 7/8 x 7 3/8 in (22.5 x 18.7 cm)
Mark: "W***"
Provenance: Dr. Francis Jennings Vurpillat, South Bend, Ind.
1978.162

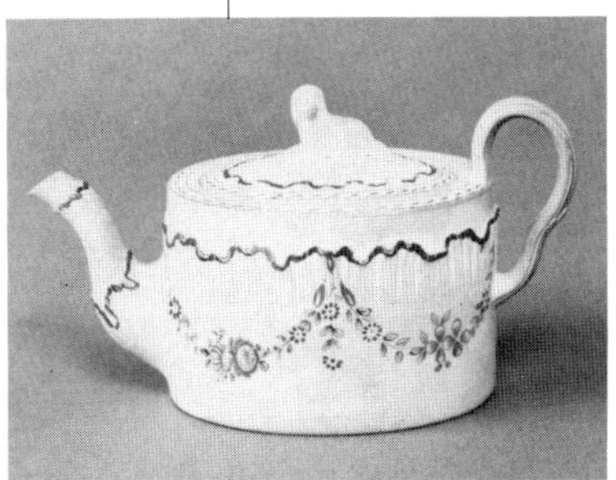

679. Teapot: 1780-85
Caneware with polychrome enamel decoration and glazed interior
4 3/8 x 4 3/4 in (11.1 x 12 cm)
Mark: none
Provenance: Ann Brodkiewicz, Chicago
1979.164 a and b

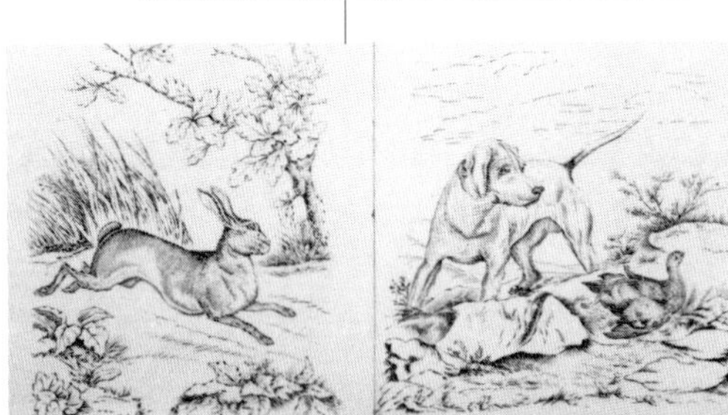

680. Tiles: *Sporting Scenes*, ca. 1880
Col. Henry Hope Crealock (1831-91), artist
Earthenware, photographic print
8 1/8 in (20.6 cm)
Mark: "JOSIAH / WEDGWOOD & SONS / ETRURIA" raised letters; "T" "H" painted on back
Provenance: Col. Earl W. Camp, New Smyrna Beach, Fla.
1976.180 a and b

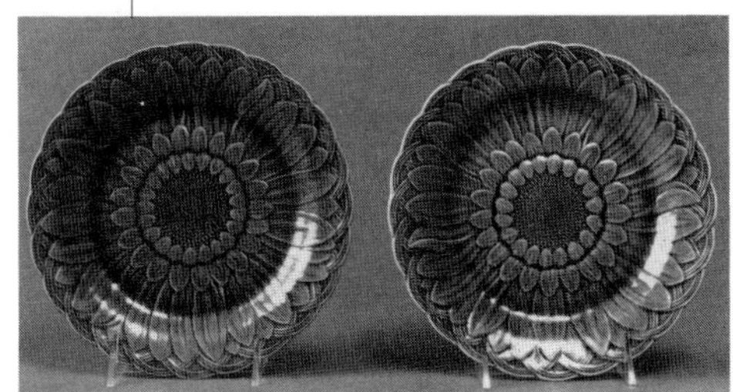

681. Three Plates: *Sunflower*, ca. 1880
Earthenware, green glaze over molded design
8 1/2 in (21.5 cm)
Mark: "WEDGWOOD" "F"
Provenance: Purchased in Malta
1976.171-.173

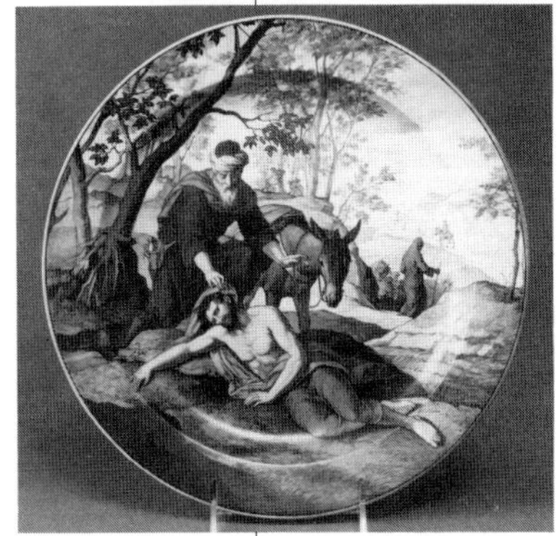

682. Plate: *The Good Samaritan*, 1864
George Eyre, modeler
Cream ware with polychrome overglaze decoration
12 15/16 in (32.8 cm)
Mark: "WEDGWOOD" "D" "DNS" "Le Bon Samaritan" in blue enamel overglaze; "Eyg" in enamel on proper left front of plate; "BARNICOT & BANFIELD / CRYSTAL PALACE / Sydenham" on green round sticker
Provenance: Ann Brodkiewicz, Chicago
1976.219

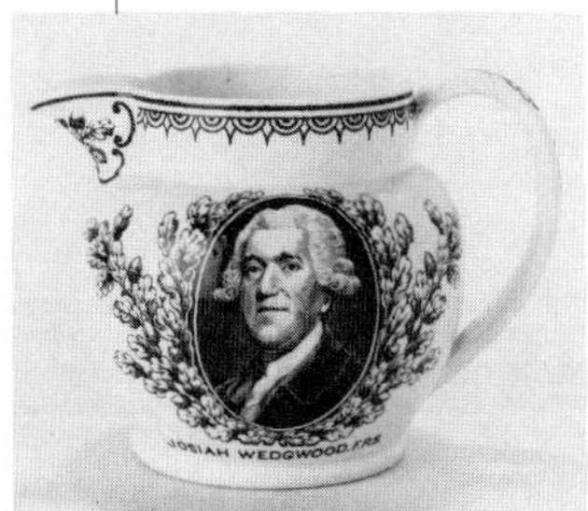

683. Commemorative Pitcher: *Josiah Wedgwood*, ca. 1930
Cream ware with transfer decoration
3 3/4 x 2 13/16 in (9.5 x 7.14 cm)
Mark: "WEDGWOOD" "W" "MADE IN ENGLAND"; "WEDGWOOD BICENTENARY 1730-1930" printed in black in a circle
Provenance: Biloxi, Miss.
1978.146

Experimental Medallions

Catalog numbers 684 through 699 are color plate 61 on page 84.

684. Medallion: *Venus Hiding Cupid on a Dolphin*, ca. 1775
Jasper, solid white ground
1 x 13/16 in (2.5 x 2 cm)
Mark: none
Provenance: Dr. Francis Jennings Vurpillat, South Bend, Ind.
1977.122.1

685. Medallion: *Venus Hiding Cupid on a Dolphin*, ca. 1775
Jasper, solid white ground with lilac enamel on front and lilac wash on back
1 x 13/16 in (2.5 x 2 cm)
Mark: none
Provenance: Dr. Francis Jennings Vurpillat, South Bend, Ind.
1977.122.2

686. Medallion: *Three Graces*, ca. 1775
Jasper, solid white ground with lilac enamel on front and lilac wash on back
1 x 13/16 in (2.5 x 2 cm)
Mark: none
Provenance: Dr. Francis Jennings Vurpillat, South Bend, Ind.
1977.122.3

687. Medallion: *Achilles Staying the Chariot of Victory*, ca. 1775
Jasper, solid white ground with lilac enamel on front and lilac wash on back
13/16 x 1 in (2 x 2.5 cm)
Mark: none
Provenance: Dr. Francis Jennings Vurpillat, South Bend, Ind.
1977.122.4

688. Medallion: *Corybantes Striking Their Bucklers to Cries of the Infant Jupiter from Being Heard by Saturn*, ca. 1775
Jasper, solid white ground with lilac enamel on front and lilac wash on back
13/16 x 1 in (2 x 2.5 cm)
Mark: none
Provenance: Dr. Francis Jennings Vurpillat, South Bend, Ind.
1977.122.5

689. Medallion: *Harpocrates*, ca. 1775
Jasper, solid white ground with yellow enamel on front and black wash on back
3/4 x 9/16 in (1.9 x 1.4 cm)
Mark: none
Provenance: Dr. Francis Jennings Vurpillat, South Bend, Ind.
1977.122.10

690. Medallion: *Bacchus and Ariadne Riding a Tiger*, ca. 1775
Jasper, solid white ground with yellow enamel on front and black wash on back
3/4 x 9/16 in (1.9 x 1.4 cm)
Mark: none
Provenance: Dr. Francis Jennings Vurpillat, South Bend, Ind.
1977.122.9

691. Medallion: *Hercules Holding the World,* ca. 1775
Jasper, solid white ground with lilac enamel on front and black wash on back
3/4 x 11/16 in (1.9 x 1.7 cm)
Mark: none
Provenance: Dr. Francis Jennings Vurpillat, South Bend, Ind.
1977.122.6

692. Medallion: *Hercules Binding Cerberus,* ca. 1775
Jasper, solid white ground with gray enamel on front and black wash on back
7/8 x 5/8 in (2.2 x 1.5 cm)
Mark: none
Provenance: Dr. Francis Jennings Vurpillat, South Bend, Ind.
1977.122.7

693. Medallion: *Head of Woman,* ca. 1775
Jasper, solid white ground with lilac wash on front with white relief
13/16 x 3/4 in (2 x 1.9 cm)
Mark: none
Provenance: Dr. Francis Jennings Vurpillat, South Bend, Ind.
1977.122.8

694. Medallion: *Cato,* ca. 1780
Jasper, solid white ground with lilac wash on front with white relief
3/4 x 5/8 in (1.9 x 1.5 cm)
Mark: "1122"
Provenance: Dr. Francis Jennings Vurpillat, South Bend, Ind.
1977.122.16

695. Medallion: *Male Head,* ca. 1795
Jasper, solid light brown ground with white glass-paste relief
7/8 x 5/8 in (2.2 x 1.5 cm)
Mark: "EDGWOOD"
Provenance: M. Mellanay Delhom, Chicago; Ann Brodkiewicz, Chicago
1982.46
The relief was made by James Tassie and applied to a Wedgwood ground.

696. Medallion: *Female Head,* ca. 1790
Jasper, solid brown ground with white relief
3/4 x 9/16 in (1.9 x 1.4 cm)
Mark: "Wedgwood"
Provenance: M. Mellanay Delhom, Chicago; Ann Brodkiewicz, Chicago
1982.40

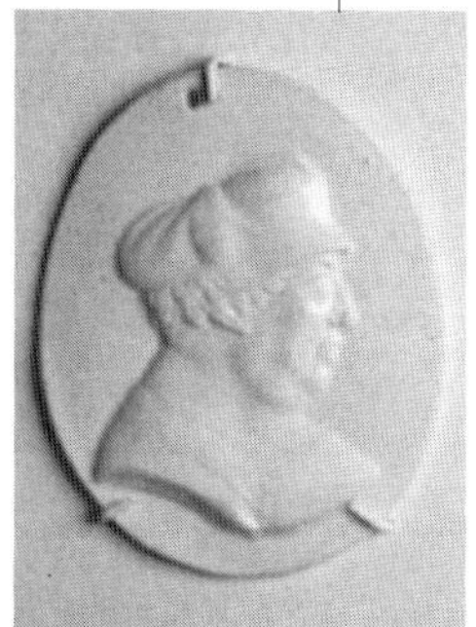

697. Portrait Medallion: *Bust of Male Figure,* ca. 1780
White terra-cotta stoneware or cream ware with clear glaze
2 1/8 x 1 13/16 in (5.3 x 4.6 cm)
Mark: "WEDGWOOD"
Provenance: Dr. Francis Jennings Vurpillat, South Bend, Ind.
1977.122.33
Color plate 61

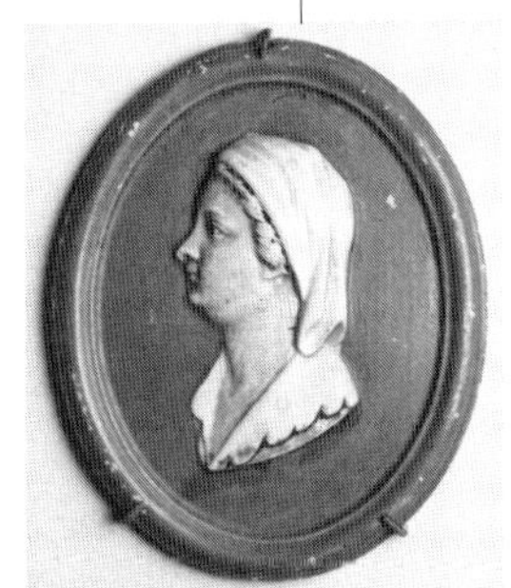

698. Portrait Medallion: *Artemisia*, 19th century
Cream ware with enamel decoration
3 x 2 7/16 in (7.6 x 6.1 cm)
Mark: "WEDGWOOD" "Artemisia" "C 111 S 1" incised
Provenance: Dr. Francis Jennings Vurpillat, South Bend, Ind.
1977.122.32
Color plate 61

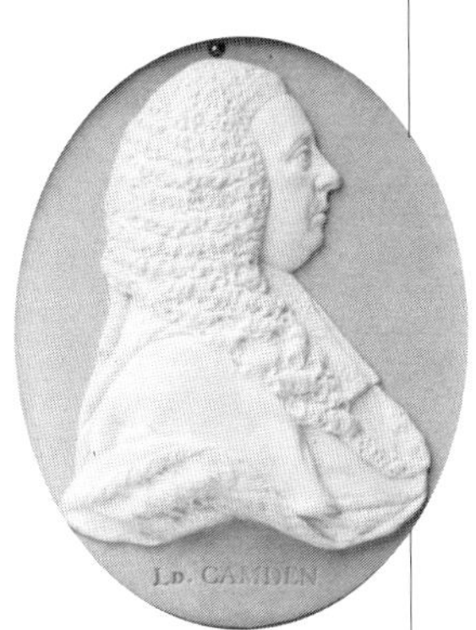

699. Portrait Medallion: *Lord Charles Pratt Camden*, ca. 1778
Jasper, solid blue ground with light blue wash and white relief
3 1/4 x 2 11/16 in (8.2 x 6.8 cm)
Mark: "Wedgwood & Bentley"; "I [impressed] of wind [incised] M / & I [impressed] of water mill [incised]" on back; "LD. CAMDEN" impressed on front
Provenance: Henry Stern, New Orleans
1979.95
Back has four firing holes.
Color plate 61

700. Medallion: *Senators Killing Caesar*, ca. 1780
Jasper, solid white ground with blue wash on front and white relief
2 3/4 x 1 29/32 in (6.9 x 4.8 cm)
Mark: "Wedgwood & Bentley"
Provenance: Ann Brodkiewicz, Chicago
1982.34

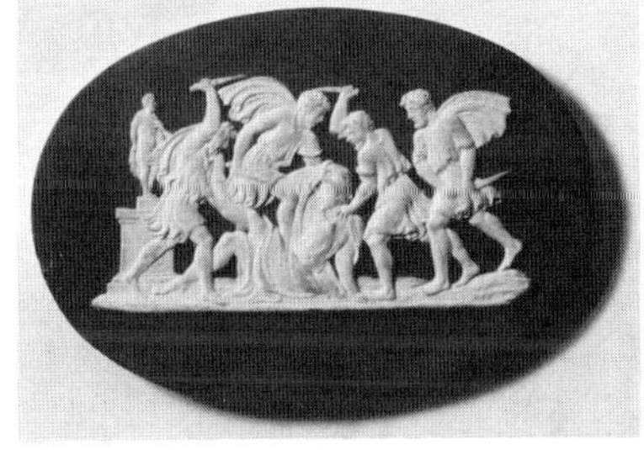

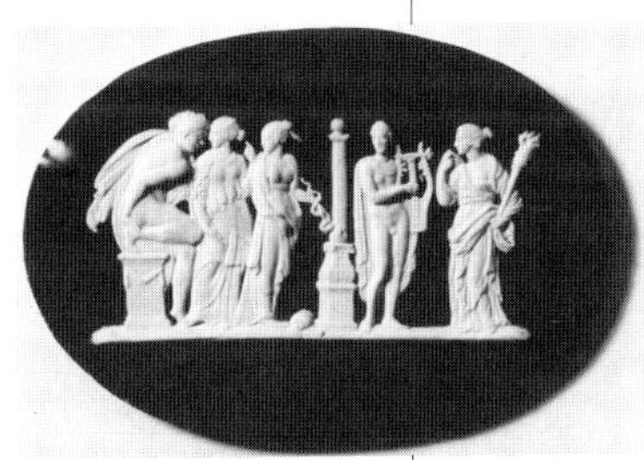

701. Medallion: *A Sacrifice*, ca. 1780
Jasper, solid white ground with dark blue wash on front and white relief
1 15/16 x 2 3/4 in (4.9 x 6.9 cm)
Mark: "Wedgwood & Bentley"
Provenance: Sir George Duff-Dunbar, Scotland; M. Mellanay Delhom, Chicago
1982.56

702. Medallion: *Daedalus Fixing the Wings of Icarus*, ca. 1780
Jasper, solid blue ground with dark-blue-and-brown wash and white relief
1 11/16 x 1 5/16 in (4.2 x 3.3 cm)
Mark: "Wedgwood & Bentley"
Provenance: Ann Brodkiewicz, Chicago
1982.35
Color plate 66

703. Medallion: *Daedalus Fixing the Wings of Icarus*, ca. 1780
Jasper, marbled blue-and-white ground with dark wash on front and white relief
1 3/8 x 1 3/4 in (3.4 x 4.4 cm)
Mark: "Wedgwood & Bentley"
Provenance: Sir George Duff-Dunbar, Scotland; M. Mellanay Delhom, Chicago
1982.60
Color plate 66

Portrait Medallions: Illustrious Moderns

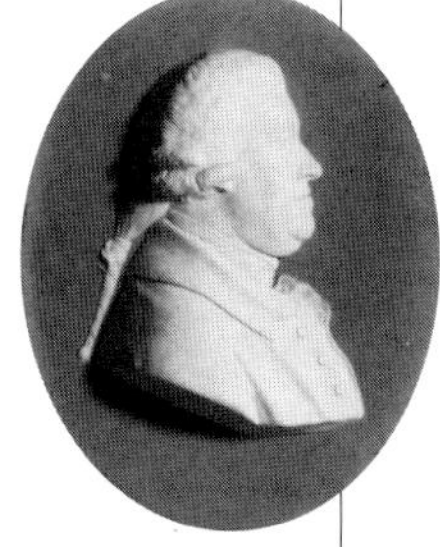

704. Portrait Medallion: *Samuel More*, ca. 1790
Jasper, solid white ground with green wash front and back with white relief
3 7/8 x 3 1/8 in (9.8 x 7.9 cm)
Mark: "WEDGWOOD"
Provenance: Ann Brodkiewicz, Chicago
1978.172

705. Portrait Medallion: *George Roupell*, ca. 1780
Jasper, solid blue ground with dark blue wash and white relief
3 7/8 x 3 3/16 in (9.8 x 8 cm)
Mark: "Wedgwood & Bentley"
Provenance: Ann Brodkiewicz, Chicago
1979.132
Back has two firing holes.

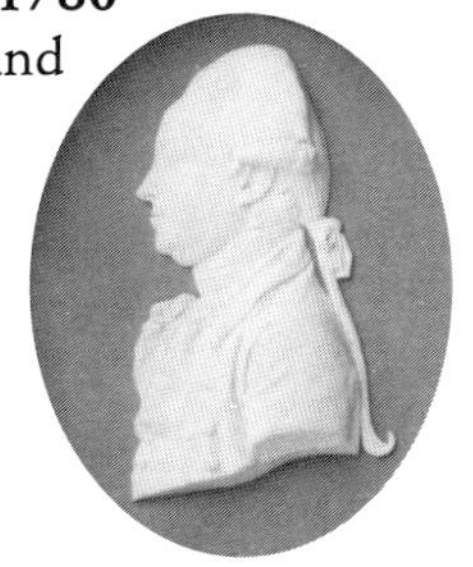

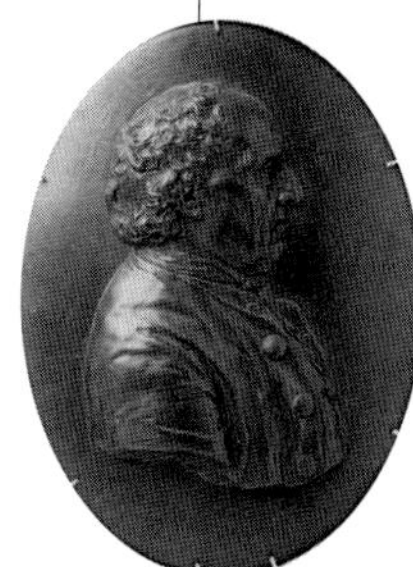

706. Portrait Medallion: *Edward Bourne*, 19th century
Basalt
4 1/4 x 3 1/16 in (10.7 x 7.7 cm)
Mark: "WEDGWOOD"; "Wm. Hackwood, 1779" incised on truncation; "Mr. Byrne / Bricklayer Etruria / 1779" incised on back
Provenance: Dr. Harold L. Klawans, Chicago
1979.140

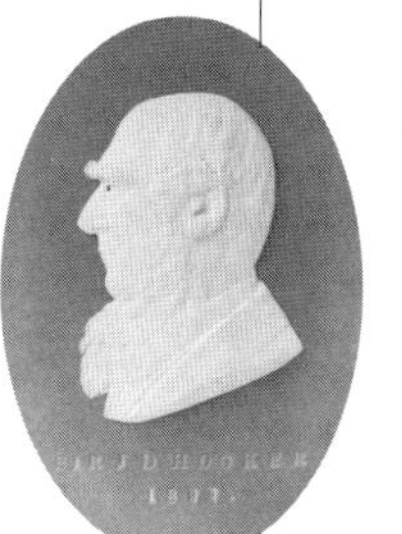

707. Portrait Medallion: *Sir Joseph Dalton Hooker*, ca. 1897
Jasper, solid white ground with olive green wash and white relief
4 1/16 x 2 7/8 in (10.3 x 7.3 cm)
Mark: "WEDGWOOD"; "SIR J D Hooker / 1897" impressed on front
Provenance: Dr. Harold L. Klawans, Chicago
1979.113

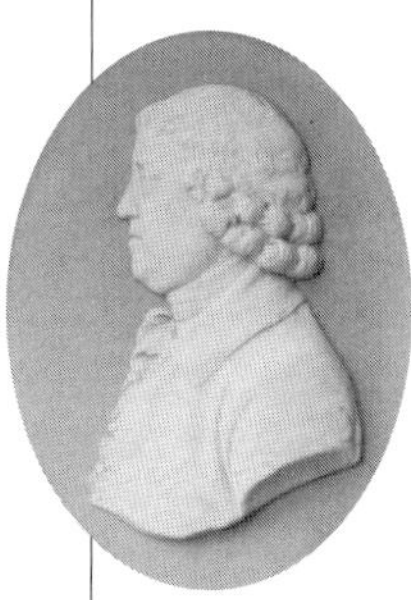

708. Portrait Medallion: *Josiah Wedgwood*, 19th century
Jasper, solid blue ground with white relief
4 3/16 x 3 1/4 in (10.6 x 8.2 cm)
Mark: "WEDGWOOD" twice
Provenance: D. M. and P. Manheim, New York
1978.145

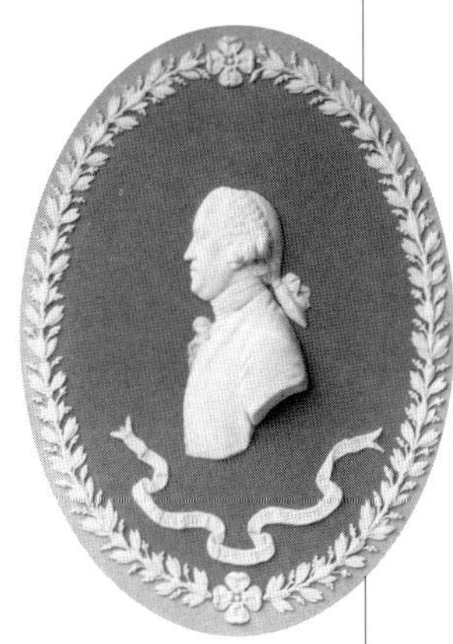

709. Portrait Medallion: *Josiah Wedgwood*, 19th century
Jasper, solid white ground with blue-and-green wash on front and white relief
9 5/16 x 7 7/16 in (23.6 x 18.8 cm)
Mark: "WEDGWOOD" "II"
Provenance: Dr. Francis Jennings Vurpillat, South Bend, Ind.
1978.141
Back has two firing holes.

710. Portrait Medallion: *Josiah Wedgwood*, ca. 1800
William Hackwood (d. 1839), designer and modeler
Jasper, solid white ground with dark blue wash front and back and white relief
4 x 3 3/16 in (10.1 x 8 cm)
Mark: "WEDGWOOD"; "W. H." incised on front at truncation of shoulder
Provenance: David Davis, Chicago; Ann Brodkiewicz, Chicago
1978.142
Color plate 9

711. Portrait Medallion: *Sir Christopher Wren*, ca. 1785
David LeMarchand (1674-1736), modeler
Basalt
4 3/16 x 3 3/16 in (10.6 x 8 cm)
Mark: "WEDGWOOD" "C 10 / S 4 / 4"
Provenance: Ann Brodkiewicz, Chicago
1979.145
Back has large thumbprint depression.
Color plate 82

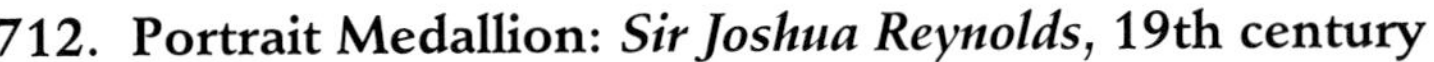

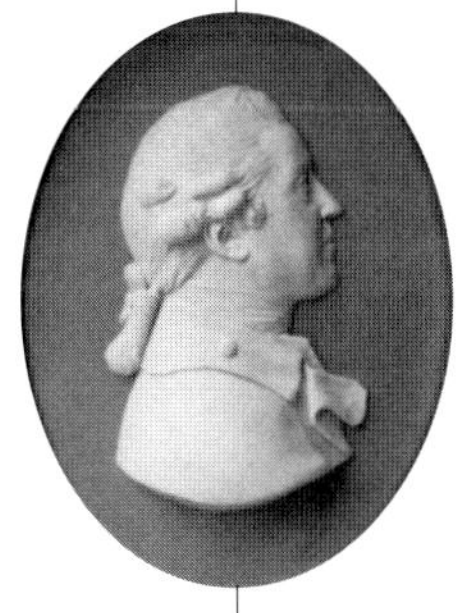

712. Portrait Medallion: *Sir Joshua Reynolds*, 19th century
Jasper, solid blue ground with white relief
4 3/8 x 3 3/16 in (11.1 x 8 cm)
Mark: "WEDGWOOD"; "Sir Joshua Reynolds" incised in script on back
Provenance: W. Russell Button Gallery, Chicago
1979.141

713. Portrait Medallion: *John Flaxman as a Boy*, 19th century
Jasper, solid blue ground with white relief
2 3/4 x 2 1/16 in (6.9 x 5.2 cm)
Mark: "WEDGWOOD" twice; "Flaxman when 14 years of age" in script on back
Provenance: Dr. Harold L. Klawans, Chicago
1979.118

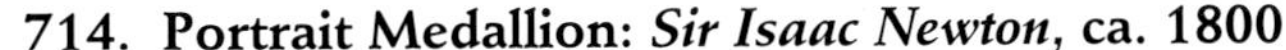

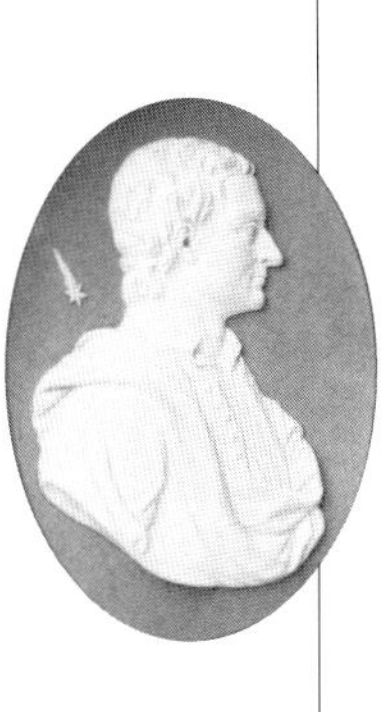

714. Portrait Medallion: *Sir Isaac Newton*, ca. 1800
Jasper, solid white ground with dark blue wash front and back with white relief
3 11/16 x 3 in (9.3 x 7.6 cm)
Mark: "WEDGWOOD"
Provenance: Ann Brodkiewicz, Chicago
1979.144
Back has two firing holes.

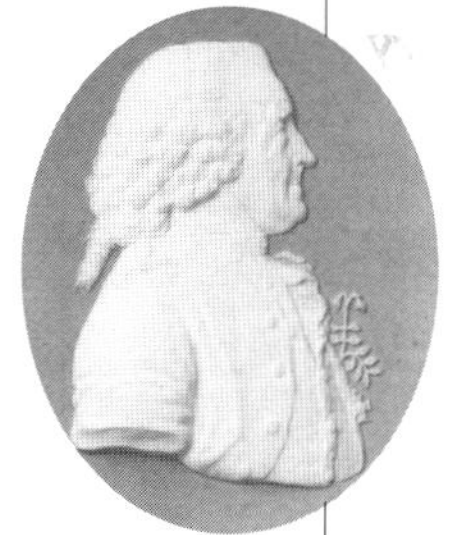

715. Portrait Medallion: *Carolus Linnaeus with Tea Flower*, ca. 1780
Jasper, solid blue ground with dark blue wash on front and white relief
3 1/4 x 2 3/4 in (8.2 x 6.9 cm)
Mark: "WEDGWOOD & BENTLEY"
Provenance: Ann Brodkiewicz, Chicago
1978.170
Back has one firing hole.

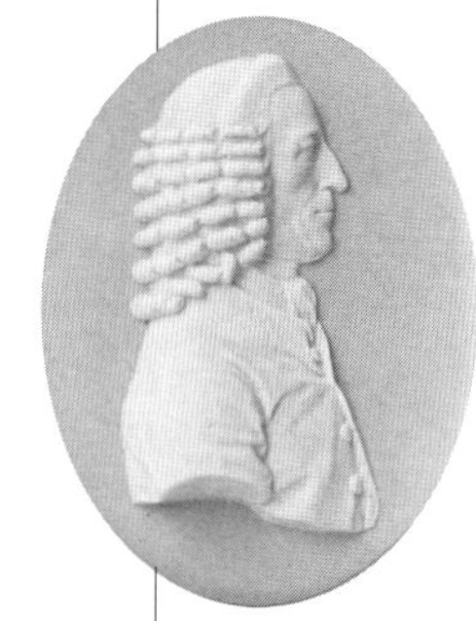

716. Portrait Medallion: *Dr. John Fothergill*, 19th century
Jasper, solid blue ground with white relief
4 1/2 x 3 9/16 in (11.4 x 9 cm)
Mark: "WEDGWOOD"; "DR FOTHERGILL" on back
Provenance: Schindler's Antique Shop, Charleston, S.C.
1979.131

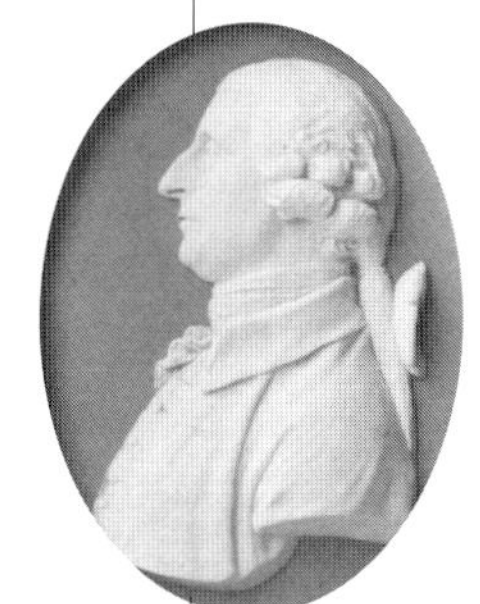

717. Portrait Medallion: *Dr. William Buchan*, ca. 1800
Jasper, solid white ground with blue wash with white relief
4 3/16 x 3 5/16 in (10.6 x 8.4 cm)
Mark: "WEDGWOOD"
Provenance: Ann Brodkiewicz, Chicago
1979.115
Back has two firing holes.

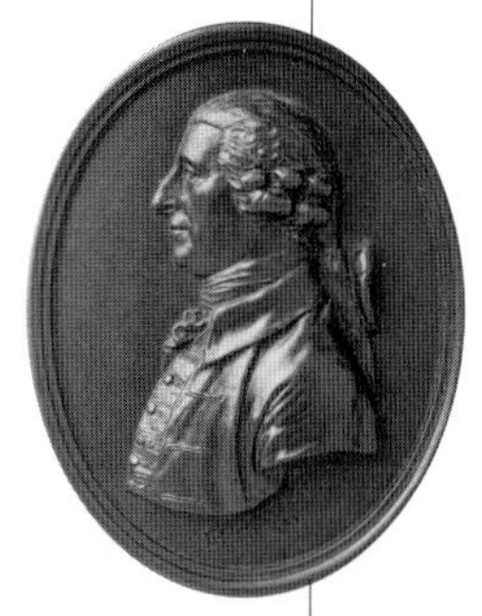

718. Portrait Medallion: *Dr. William Buchan*, ca. 1785
Basalt
4 7/32 x 3 3/8 in (10.7 x 8.5 cm)
Mark: "Wedgwood"; "BUCKAN" on front
Provenance: Godfrey W. Ford Collection, England;
Dr. Harold L. Klawans, Chicago
1979.116
There is a deep thumbprint on back to aid in the firing.

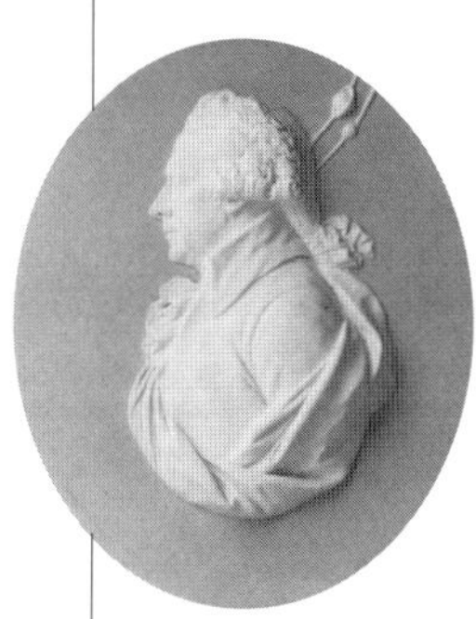

719. Portrait Medallion: *Sir William Herschel*, 19th century
Jasper, solid blue ground with white relief
4 5/16 x 3 1/2 in (10.9 x 8.8 cm)
Mark: "WEDGWOOD"; "HERSCHEL" on back
Provenance: unknown
1979.151

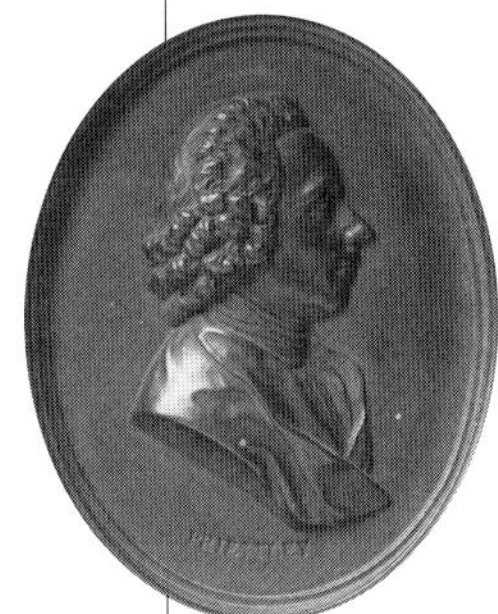

720. Portrait Medallion: ***Joseph Priestley*, ca. 1785**
Basalt
4 3/16 x 3 3/8 in (10.6 x 8.5 cm)
Mark: "Wedgwood"; "PRIESTLEY" impressed on front
Provenance: Ann Brodkiewicz, Chicago
1979.123
Back has thumbprint depression.

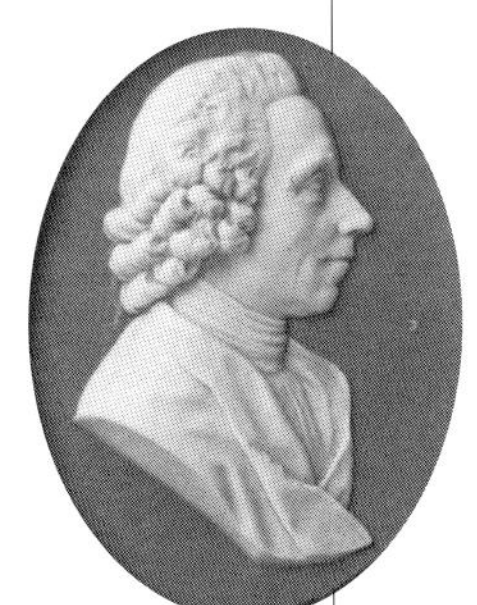

721. Portrait Medallion: ***Joseph Priestley*, ca. 1790**
Jasper, solid white ground with dark blue wash front and back with white relief
3 5/8 x 2 7/8 in (9.2 x 7.3 cm)
Mark: "WEDGWOOD" twice
Provenance: unknown
1979.119

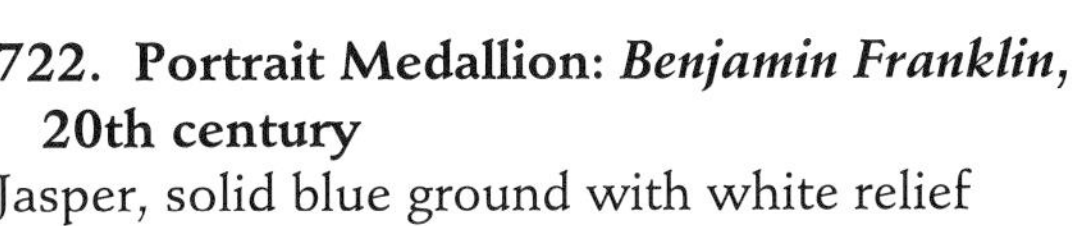

722. Portrait Medallion: ***Benjamin Franklin*, 20th century**
Jasper, solid blue ground with white relief
3 1/4 x 2 3/8 in (8.2 x 6 cm)
Mark: "WEDGWOOD"; "O" "Franklin" in script on back
Provenance: Toby House, New York
1979.93

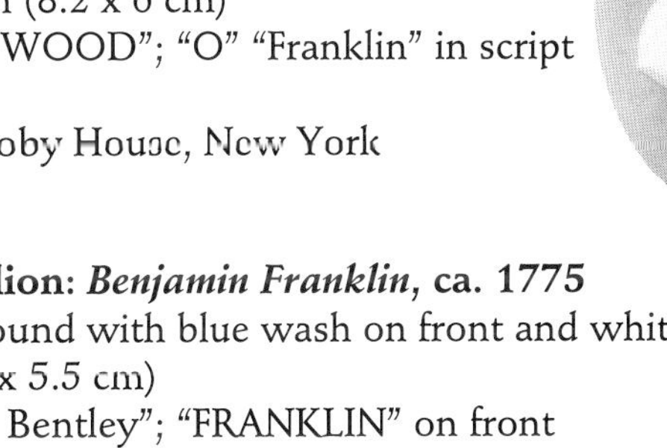

723. Portrait Medallion: ***Benjamin Franklin*, ca. 1775**
Jasper, solid white ground with blue wash on front and white relief
2 3/4 x 2 3/16 in (6.9 x 5.5 cm)
Mark: "Wedgwood & Bentley"; "FRANKLIN" on front
Provenance: Ann Brodkiewicz, Chicago
1979.138
Back has two firing holes.
Color plate 83

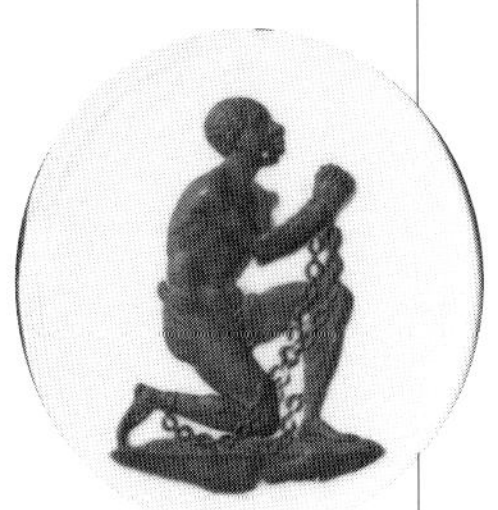

724. Medallion: ***Slave*, ca. 1787**
Jasper, solid white ground with black relief
1 3/16 x 1 1/16 in (3 x 2.7 cm)
Mark: "AM I NOT A MAN AND A BROTHER?" around border on front
Provenance: Ann Brodkiewicz, Chicago
1976.200
Color plate 83

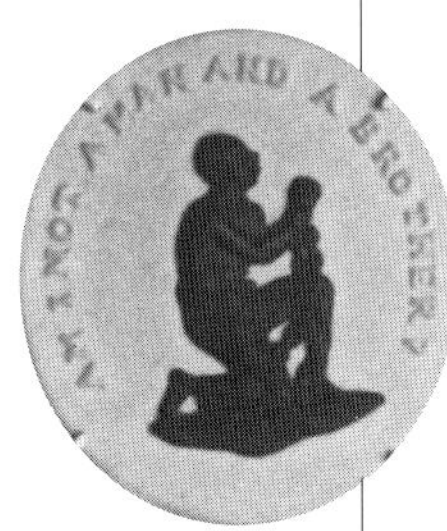

725. Medallion: ***Slave*, 1959**
Jasper, solid white ground with black relief
1 1/4 x 1 1/8 in (3.1 x 2.8 cm)
Mark: "WEDGWOOD / MADE IN / ENGLAND / 59 / EC"; "AM I NOT A MAN AND A BROTHER?" around border on front
Provenance: Dr. Harold L. Klawans, Chicago
1985.420

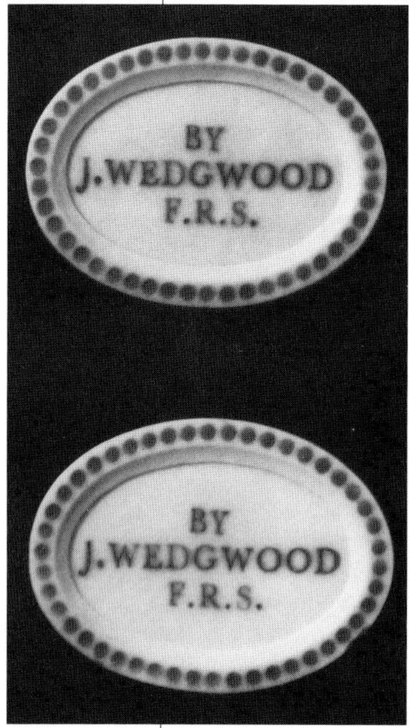

726. Medallion: *Josiah Wedgwood F. R. S.*, 1784
Jasper, solid white ground with blue inlay
1 7/8 x 1 3/8 in (4.7 x 3.4 cm)
Mark: "BY / J. WEDGWOOD / F. R. S." on front; "No 170" on back
Provenance: Dr. Francis Jennings Vurpillat, South Bend, Ind.
1977.122.30
Color plate 66

727. Medallion: *Josiah Wedgwood F. R. S.*, 1784
Jasper, solid white ground with blue inlay
1 7/8 x 1 3/8 in (4.7 x 3.4 cm)
Mark: "BY / J. WEDGWOOD / F. R. S." on front; "No 10" on back
Provenance: M. Mellanay Delhom, Chicago; Ann Brodkiewicz, Chicago
1982.49

728. Miniature Portrait: *Josiah Wedgwood*, 20th century
Wax
5 3/4 x 5 3/4 in (in frame) (14.6 x 14.6 cm)
Mark: "J. Flaxman" incised in script on truncation of shoulder
Provenance: Ann Brodkiewicz, Chicago
1978.144 a and b

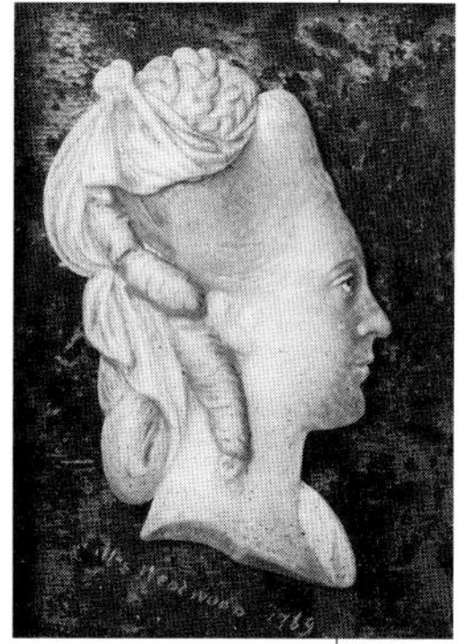

729. Miniature Portrait: *Sarah Wedgwood Wedgwood*, 20th century
Wax
9 x 7 3/4 in (in frame) (22.8 x 19.6 cm)
Mark: "I. F." incised on truncation of shoulder; "Mrs. WEDGWOOD. 1769" written below portrait on glass backing
Provenance: unknown
1978.143

730. Miniature Portrait: *Erasmus Darwin*, 20th century
Wax and oil paint
6 1/4 in (in frame) (15.8 cm)
Mark: none
Provenance: Ann Brodkiewicz, Chicago
1976.217
Copy of oil portrait by Joseph Wright of Derby painted in 1770.

731. Portrait Medallion: *Admiral Keppel*, ca. 1780
James Tassie (1735-99), Scotland, maker
Enamel paste
4 3/8 x 3 3/8 in (11.1 x 8.5 cm)
Mark: "T" under truncated shoulder
Provenance: Ann Brodkiewicz, Chicago
1979.86
Color plate 79

732. Portrait Medallion: *Admiral Keppel*, ca. 1780
Basalt
4 5/8 x 3 5/8 in (11.7 x 9.2 cm)
Mark: "Wedgwood / & Bentley"; "KEPPEL" impressed on front
Provenance: Ann Brodkiewicz, Chicago
1979.85
Back has thumbprint depression.
Color plate 79

733. Portrait Medallion: *Admiral Keppel*, ca. 1780
White terra-cotta stoneware
4 x 3 1/8 in (10.1 x 7.9 cm)
Mark: "Wedgwood & Bentley"; "KEPPEL" impressed on front
Provenance: Ann Brodkiewicz, Chicago
1979.89
Back has two firing holes.
Color plate 79

734. Portrait Medallion: *Admiral Keppel*, ca. 1780
Jasper, solid blue ground with green wash on front
3 7/8 x 3 in (9.8 x 7.6 cm)
Mark: "WEDGWOOD & BENTLEY" "2709"; "KEPPEL" impressed on front
Provenance: Ann Brodkiewicz, Chicago
1979.88
Back has three firing holes.
Color plate 79

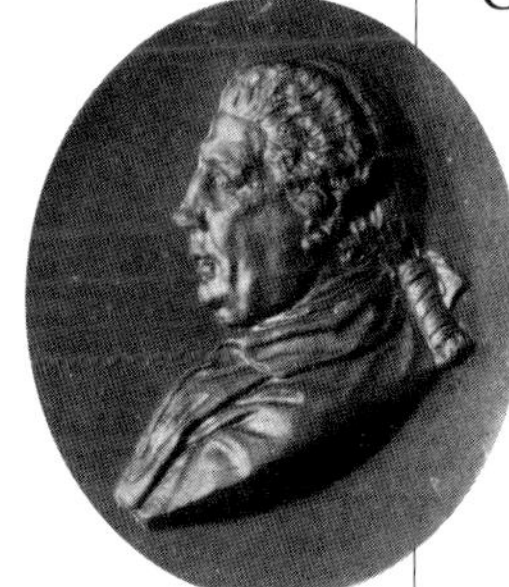

735. Intaglio: *Admiral Keppel*, ca. 1790
Basalt
7/8 x 3/4 in (2.2 x 1.9 cm)
Mark: "WEDGWOOD" "383"
Provenance: Dr. Harold L. Klawans, Chicago
1980.54

736. Portrait Medallion: *Admiral Keppel*, ca. 1780
Jasper, solid blue ground with dark blue wash on front and white relief
3 7/8 x 3 1/8 in (9.8 x 7.9 cm)
Mark: "WEDGWOOD & BENTLEY"; "KEPPEL" impressed on front
Provenance: Ann Brodkiewicz, Chicago
1979.87
Back has three firing holes.
Color plate 79

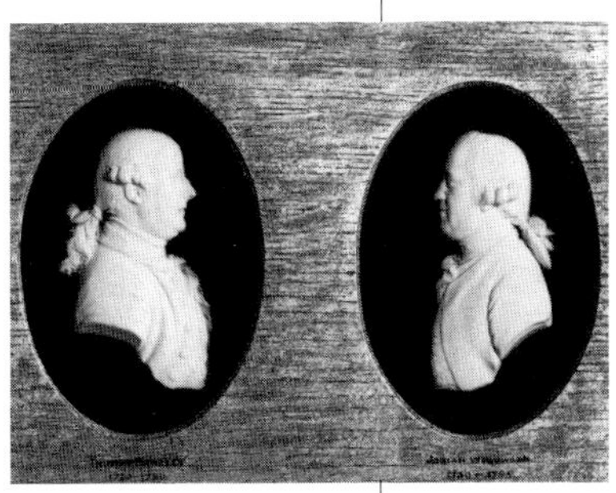

737. Pair of Portrait Medallions: *Josiah Wedgwood and Thomas Bentley*, 19th century
Jasper, solid white ground with black wash on front and white relief
4 13/16 x 3 5/16 in (12.2 x 8.4 cm)
Mark: "WEDGWOOD"; "Wedgwood" "Bentley" incised
Provenance: Ann Brodkiewicz, Chicago
1978.140 a and b

738. Portrait Medallion: ***Sir William Hamilton,*** **1772**
Basalt, encaustic decoration on front and back
6 3/16 x 4 7/16 in (15.7 x 11.2 cm)
Mark: Inscribed in ink on back: "Wedgwood & Bentley beg Sir William Hamilton will do them the honor to accept of an Etruscan Bas relief Portrait of himself, as a small testimony of Respect and gratitude to a Gentleman who has confirmed his obligations upon this Kingdom in-general and upon themselves in particular which may be the means, not only of improving and refining the Public Taste but of keeping alive that Sacred Fire, which his Collection of inestimable Models has happily Kindled in Great Britain, so long as burnt Earthe and Etruscan Painting shall endure. Great Newport Street, April 30, 1772."
Provenance: Hamilton Family, England; M. Mellanay Delhom, Chicago
1982.177
Medallion has large thumbprint depression on back.
Color plate 55

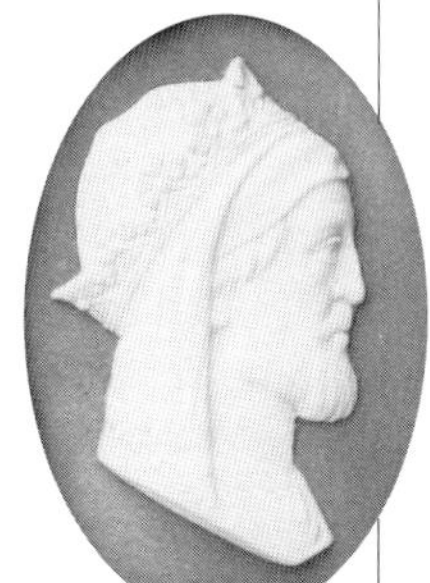

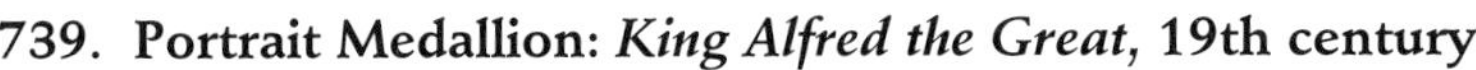

739. Portrait Medallion: ***King Alfred the Great,*** **19th century**
Jasper, solid white ground with dark blue wash on front and white relief, convex
2 1/2 x 1 3/4 in (6.3 x 9.6 cm)
Mark: "WEDGWOOD" "J"
Provenance: Henderson's, Birmingham, Ala.
1979.143

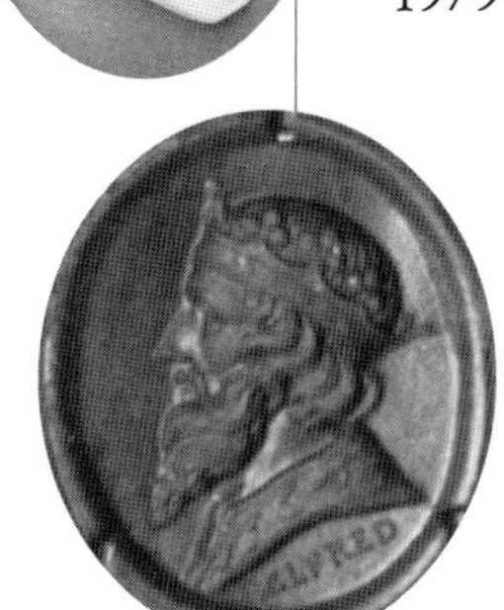

740. Intaglio: ***King Alfred the Great,*** **ca. 1790**
Basalt
1 x 7/8 in (2.5 x 2.2 cm)
Mark: "WEDGWOOD"; "ALFRED" in reverse on front of intaglio
Provenance: Dr. Harold L. Klawans, Chicago
1980.40

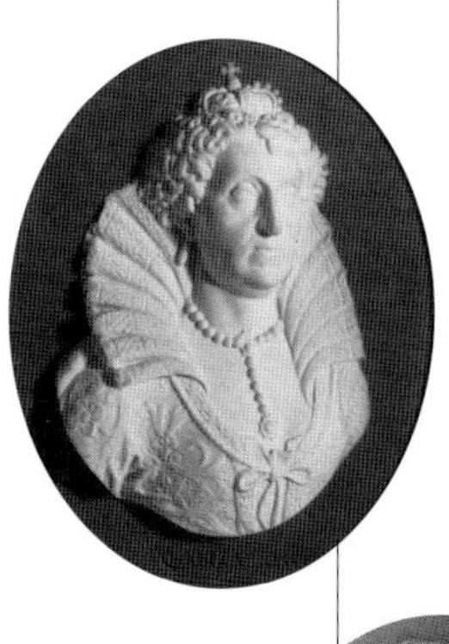

741. Portrait Medallion: ***Queen Elizabeth I,*** **ca. 1780**
Jasper, solid blue ground with dark blue wash on front with white relief
4 x 3 1/4 in (10.1 x 8.2 cm)
Mark: "WEDGWOOD & BENTLEY"; "Q. ELIZABETH" on front
Provenance: Dr. Francis Jennings Vurpillat, South Bend, Ind.
1982.38
Back has three firing holes.
Color plate 82

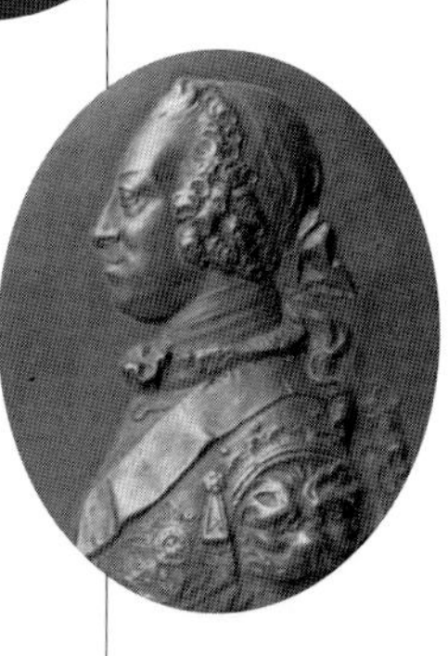

742. Portrait Medallion: ***George IV, Prince of Wales,*** **ca. 1780**
Basalt
3 3/16 x 2 5/8 in (8 x 6.6 cm)
Mark: "Wedgwood & Bentley"; "FR. PR. OF WALES" on back
Provenance: Ann Brodkiewicz, Chicago
1979.90

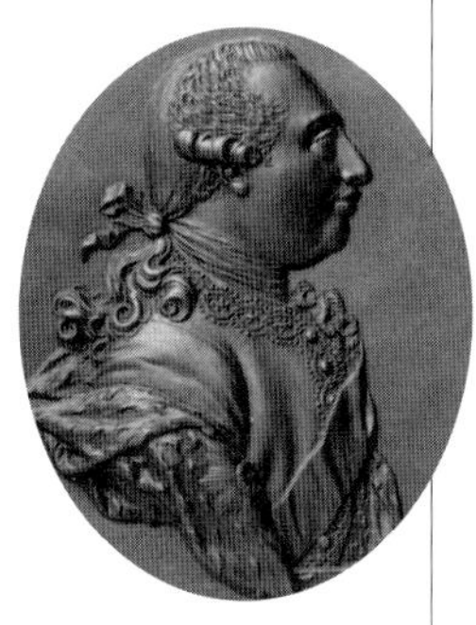

743. Portrait Medallion: *George III*, ca. 1775
Basalt
3 1/4 x 2 5/8 in (8.2 x 6.6 cm)
Mark: "Wedgwood & Bentley"; "W. H." raised under shoulder, "GEO. III" on front
Provenance: Ann Brodkiewicz, Chicago
1979.91
Back has thumbprint depression.
Color plate 81

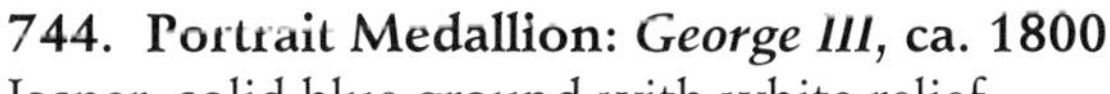

744. Portrait Medallion: *George III*, ca. 1800
Jasper, solid blue ground with white relief
3 15/16 x 3 1/16 in (10 x 7.7 cm)
Mark: "WEDGWOOD"; "George Third" in script on back
Provenance: Lady Mount Stephen, London; Dr. Harold L. Klawans, Chicago
1979.142
Color plate 81

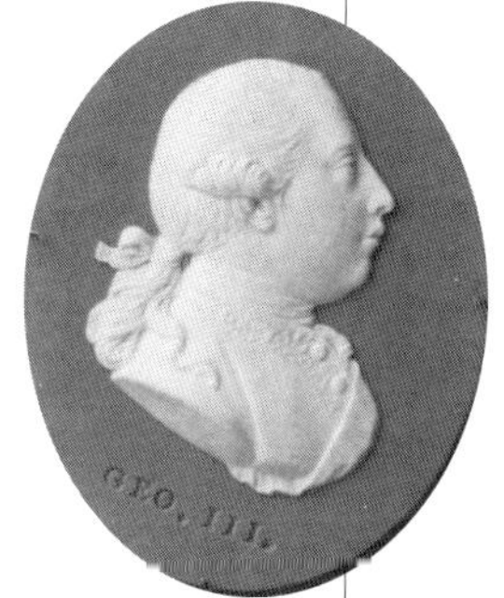

745. Portrait Medallion: *George III*, ca. 1775
Jasper, solid blue ground with blue wash on front and white relief
1 7/8 x 1 3/8 in (4.7 x 3.4 cm)
Mark: "Wedgwood & Bentley / GEO. III." impressed on front
Provenance: David Newbon, London
1979.133
Back has one firing hole.

746. Portrait Medallion: *George III and Charlotte*, ca. 1780
Jasper, solid white ground with blue wash on front and white relief
1 1/4 x 1 1/16 in (3.1 x 2.7 cm)
Mark: "Wedgwood & Bentley"
Provenance: M. Mellanay Delhom, Chicago; Ann Brodkiewicz, Chicago
1982.42
Color plate 81

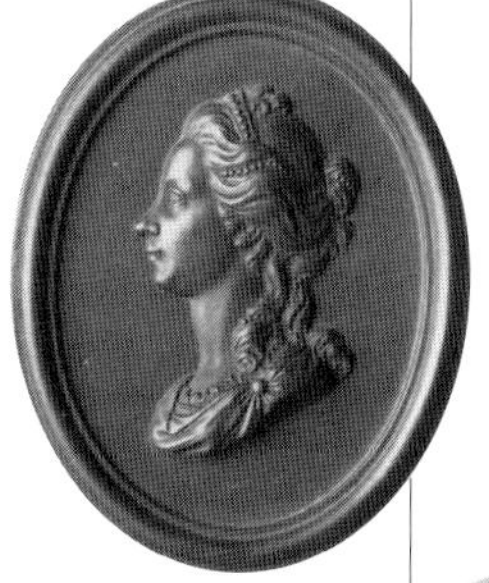

747. Portrait Medallion: *Queen Charlotte*, ca. 1790
Basalt
2 7/8 x 2 5/16 in (7.3 x 5.8 cm)
Mark: "Wedgwood" "36"
Provenance: Ann Brodkiewicz, Chicago
1977.132

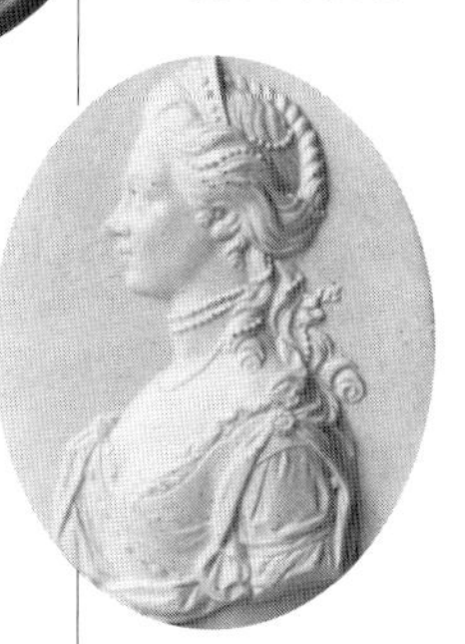

748. Portrait Medallion: *Queen Charlotte*, ca. 1775
Cream ware
3 7/16 x 2 1/2 in (8.7 x 6.3 cm)
Mark: "WEDGWOOD"; "Queen Caroline" incised on back
Provenance: Ann Brodkiewicz, Chicago
1979.134
Color plate 81

749. Portrait Medallion: ***Queen Charlotte*****, ca. 1780**
Jasper, solid blue ground with white relief
3 1/2 x 2 11/16 in (8.8 x 6.8 cm)
Mark: "WEDGWOOD"; "Q. CHARLOTTE" impressed on front
Provenance: Ann Brodkiewicz, Chicago
1979.135
Back has two firing holes.
Color plate 81

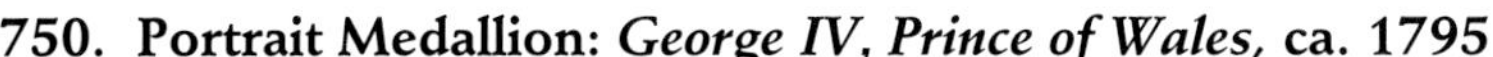

750. Portrait Medallion: ***George IV, Prince of Wales,*** **ca. 1795**
Jasper, solid white ground with dark blue wash on front and white relief
3 5/8 x 2 7/8 in (9.1 x 7.2 cm)
Mark: "WEDGWOOD"
Provenance: Ann Brodkiewicz, Chicago
1979.129
Back has two large firing holes.

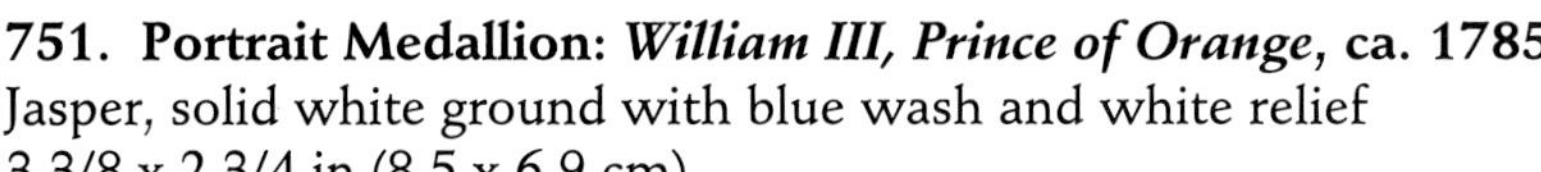

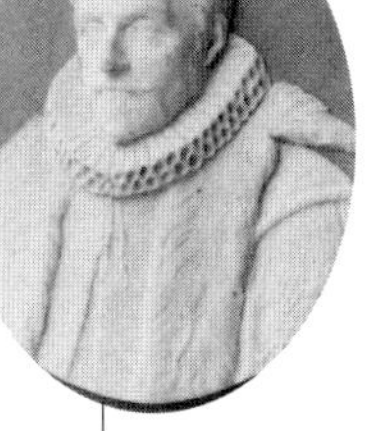

751. Portrait Medallion: ***William III, Prince of Orange*****, ca. 1785**
Jasper, solid white ground with blue wash and white relief
3 3/8 x 2 3/4 in (8.5 x 6.9 cm)
Mark: "WEDGWOOD" "William the first Prince of Orange" incised on back
Provenance: Ann Brodkiewicz, Chicago
1979.136
Back has three firing holes.

752. Portrait Medallion: ***Frederick Augustus, Duke of York and Albany*****, ca. 1785**
Jasper, solid white ground with dark blue wash on front and back with white relief
3 3/4 x 3 in (9.5 x 7.6 cm)
Mark: "WEDGWOOD"
Provenance: Ann Brodkiewicz, Chicago
1979.126
Back has two firing holes.

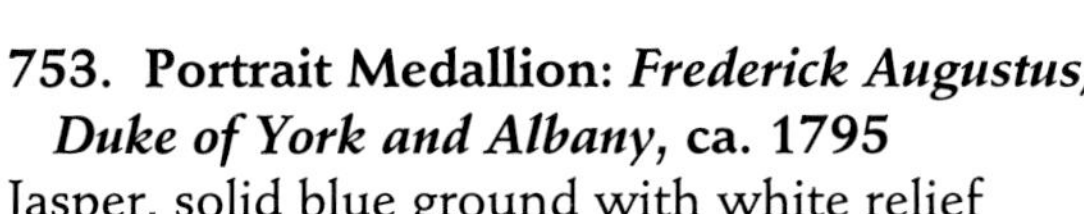

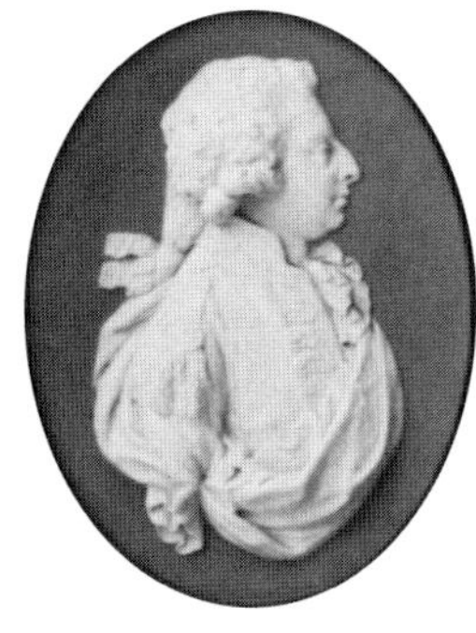

753. Portrait Medallion: ***Frederick Augustus, Duke of York and Albany*****, ca. 1795**
Jasper, solid blue ground with white relief
4 3/16 x 3 3/8 in (10.6 x 8.5 cm)
Mark: "WEDGWOOD"
Provenance: Ann Brodkiewicz, Chicago
1979.148

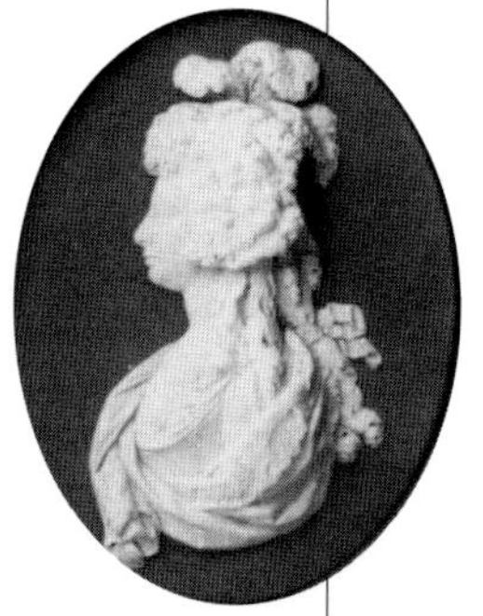

754. Portrait Medallion: ***Princess Charlotte Augusta Matilda*****, ca. 1785**
Jasper, solid blue ground with dark blue wash back and front with white relief
3 5/8 x 2 15/16 in (9.2 x 7.4 cm)
Mark: "WEDGWOOD"
Provenance: Ann Brodkiewicz, Chicago
1979.130
Back has two firing holes.

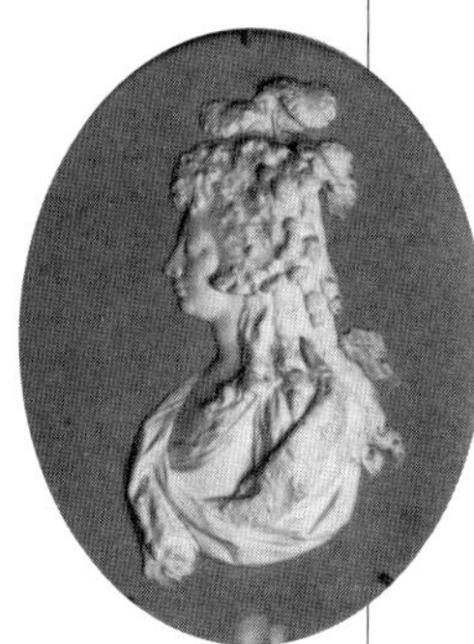

755. Portrait Medallion: *Princess Charlotte Augusta Matilda*, ca. 1800
Jasper, solid white ground with lilac wash front and back with white relief
3 7/8 x 3 1/8 in (9.8 x 7.9 cm)
Mark: "WEDGWOOD"
Provenance: Ann Brodkiewicz, Chicago
1980.299
Back has two firing holes.

756. Double-Medallion Set: *The Thirty-six Rulers of England from William the Conqueror through George III*, ca. 1780
Basalt
1 13/32 in (3.5 cm)
Mark: "J.D., I.D., I.D.F., L.P.F., KIRK F." or "J. Dassier"; each has Roman spelling of ruler's name, date, and tomb information.
Provenance: Fred J. Tongue, Santa Monica, Calif.
1977.93.1-.36
Color plate 80

757. Portrait Medallion: *Lord Camden*, ca. 1778
Jasper, solid blue ground with dark blue wash and white relief
1 11/16 x 1 7/16 in (4.2 x 3.6 cm)
Mark: "Wedgwood & Bentley"
Provenance: Ann Brodkiewicz, Chicago
1977.142
Back has two firing holes.
Color plate 63

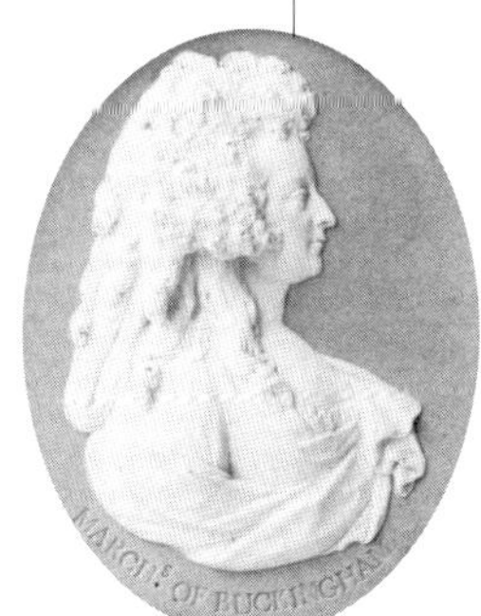

758. Portrait Medallion: *Marchioness of Buckingham*, ca. 1790
Jasper, solid blue ground with white relief
3 15/16 x 3 1/8 in (10 x 7.9 cm)
Mark: "WEDGWOOD"; "MARCH.s OF BUCKINGHAM" impressed on front
Provenance: Ann Brodkiewicz, Chicago
1979.120
Back has two firing holes.

759. Portrait Medallion: *Marquis of Buckingham*, ca. 1790
Jasper, solid white ground with blue wash and white relief
4 x 3 1/4 in (10.1 x 8.2 cm)
Mark: "WEDGWOOD"; "MARQUIS. OF BUCKINGHAM" impressed on front
Provenance: Ann Brodkiewicz, Chicago
1979.121
Back has two firing holes.

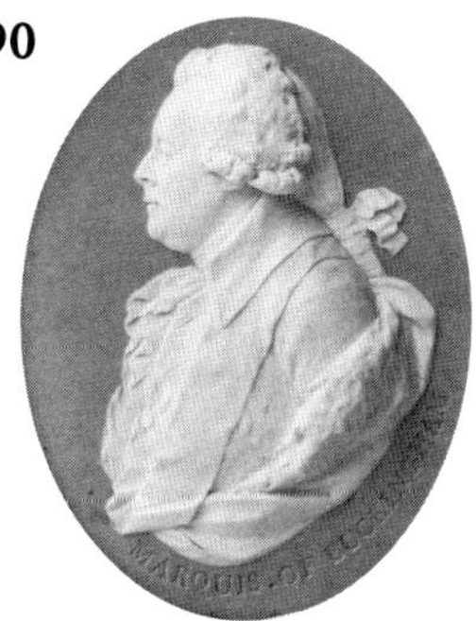

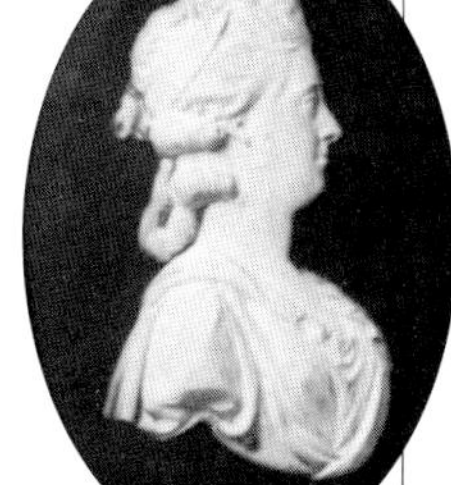

760. Portrait Medallion: *Lady Banks*, 19th century
Jasper, solid white ground with black wash on front and white relief
4 1/8 x 2 7/8 in (10.4 x 7.3 cm)
Mark: "WEDGWOOD"; "Lady Banks" incised on back
Provenance: Charles Smith, Philadelphia, Pa.
1979.83

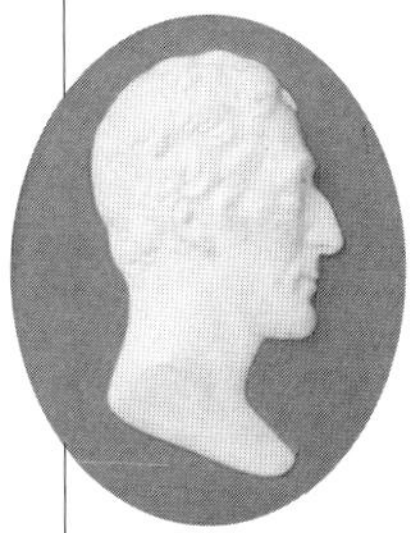

761. Portrait Medallion: *Arthur W. Wellington*, 19th century
Jasper, solid white ground with dark blue wash and white relief
2 15/16 x 2 3/8 in (7.4 x 6 cm)
Mark: "WEDGWOOD"
Provenance: Dr. Harold L. Klawans, Chicago
1979.98
Back has two firing holes.

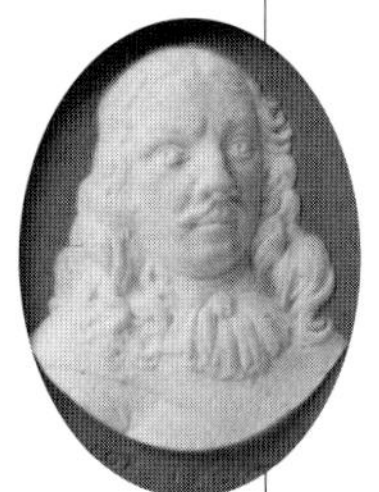

762. Portrait Medallion: *Cornelius Tromp*, ca. 1790
Jasper, solid blue ground with blue wash on front and white relief
2 1/4 x 1 11/16 in (5.7 x 4.2 cm)
Mark: "Wedgwood"; "COR. TROMP" impressed on front
Provenance: Otto Wasserman, New York
1979.92

763. Portrait Medallion: *Sir Eyre Coote*, ca. 1790
Jasper, solid blue ground with white relief
4 1/16 x 3 1/8 in (10.3 x 7.9 cm)
Mark: "WEDGWOOD"
Provenance: Dr. Harold L. Klawans, Chicago
1981.280
Back has one large firing hole and thumbhole.
Color plate 82

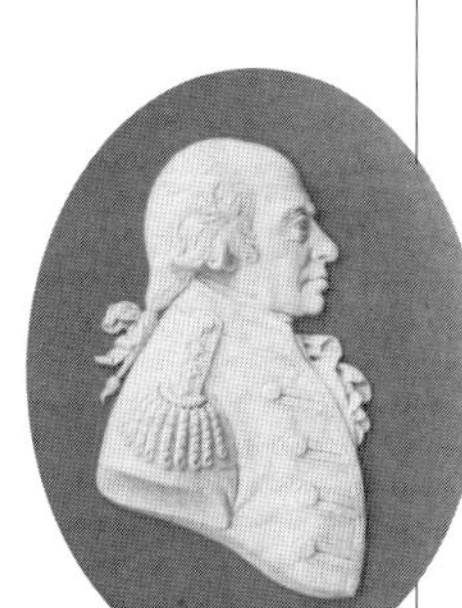

764. Portrait Medallion: *Admiral Richard Howe*, ca. 1798
Jasper, solid white ground with dark blue wash front and back with white relief
3 7/8 x 2 7/8 in (9.8 x 7.3 cm)
Mark: "WEDGWOOD"
Provenance: Ann Brodkiewicz, Chicago
1979.122
Back has two firing holes.

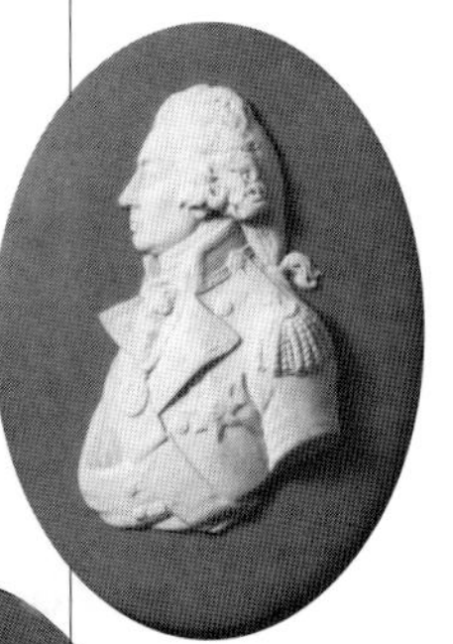

765. Portrait Medallion: *Lord Horatio Nelson*, 19th century
Jasper, solid blue ground with white relief
4 3/8 x 3 1/8 in (11.1 x 7.9 cm)
Mark: "WEDGWOOD"; "Nelson" in script
Provenance: W. Russell Button Gallery, Chicago
1979.152

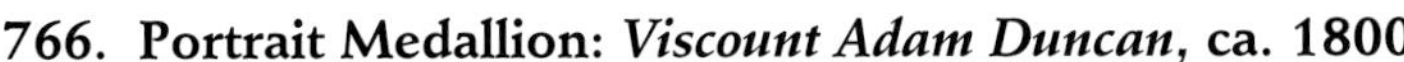

766. Portrait Medallion: *Viscount Adam Duncan*, ca. 1800
Jasper, solid white ground with green wash on back and front with white relief
3 7/8 x 3 1/8 in (9.8 x 7.9 cm)
Mark:
Provenance: Ann Brodkiewicz, Chicago
1978.171
Back has two firing holes.

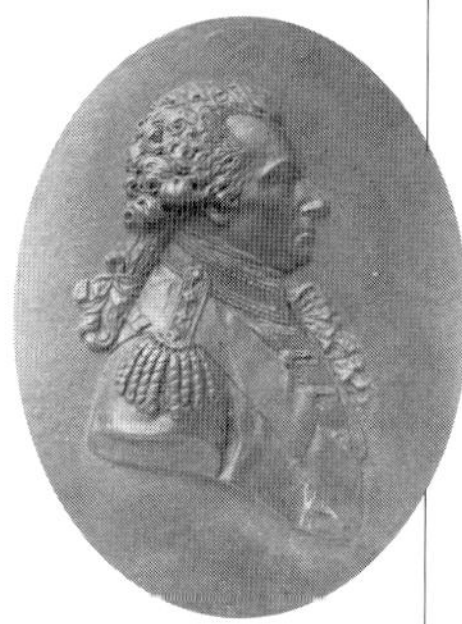

767. Portrait Medallion: ***Sir John Jervis, First Earl of St. Vincent*, ca. 1800**
Basalt
3 7/8 x 3 in (9.8 x 7.6 cm)
Mark: "WEDGWOOD"; "7" "L. St Vincent" incised in script on back
Provenance: Dr. Harold L. Klawans, Chicago
1979.110

768. Portrait Medallion: ***Captain James Cook*, 19th century**
Basalt
4 5/16 x 3 1/4 in (10.9 x 8.2 cm)
Mark: "WEDGWOOD"; "LAVATER" incised on back
Provenance: Dr. Harold L. Klawans, Chicago
1979.111

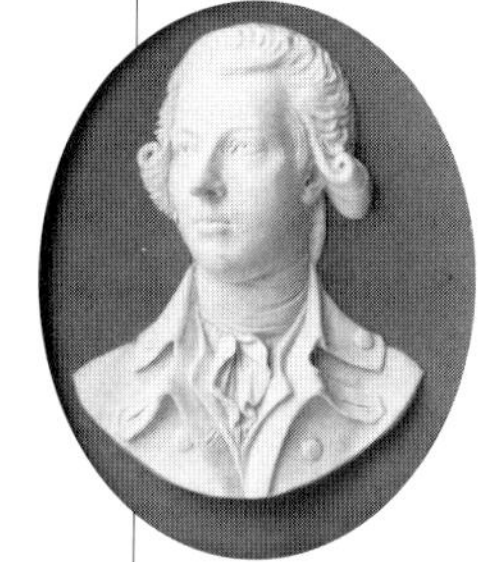

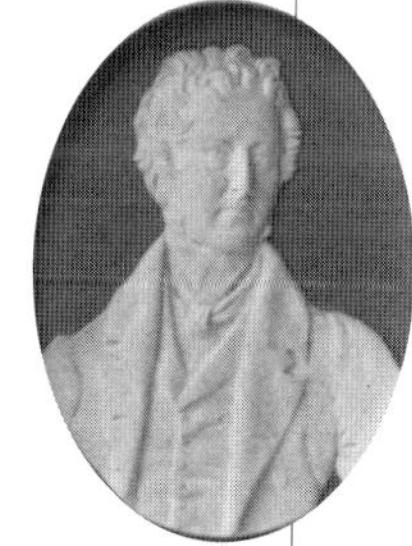

769. Portrait Medallion: ***William Pitt*, ca. 1795**
Jasper, solid blue ground with dark blue wash front and back with white relief
3 3/4 x 3 1/8 in (9.5 x 7.9 cm)
Mark: "WEDGWOOD"
Provenance: Ann Brodkiewicz, Chicago
1979.139
Back has two firing holes.

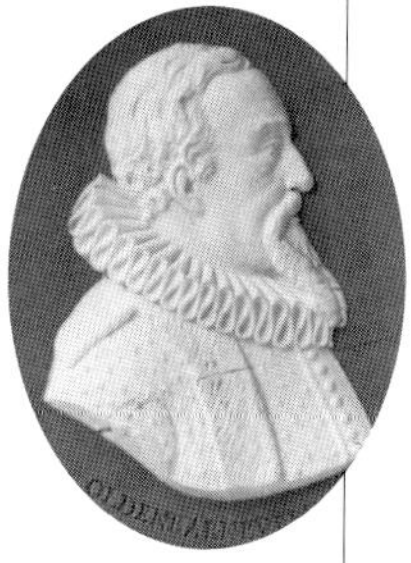

770. Portrait Medallion: ***Sir Robert Peel*, 19th century**
Jasper, solid white ground with dark blue wash front and back with white relief
3 5/16 x 3 1/16 in (8.4 x 7.7 cm)
Mark: "WEDGWOOD"
Provenance: Lady Mount Stephen, England; Dr. Harold L. Klawans, Chicago
1979.114
Back has eight firing holes.

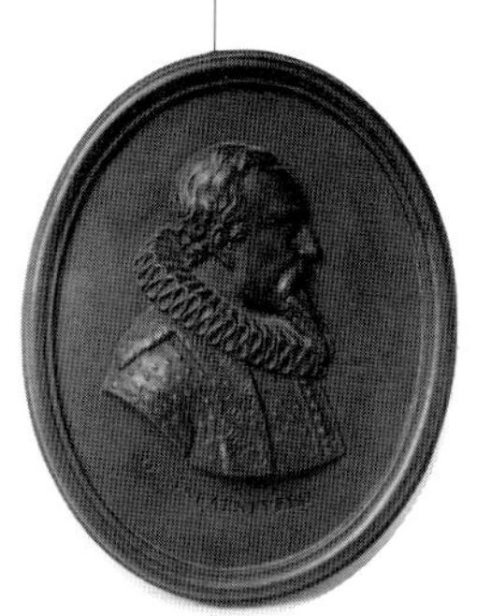

771. Portrait Medallion: ***Jan Van Olden Barneveld*, ca. 1780**
Jasper, solid blue ground with dark blue wash on front and white relief
3 7/16 x 2 11/16 in (8.7 x 6.8 cm)
Mark: "Wedgwood & Bentley"; "OLDENBARNEVELD" impressed on front
Provenance: Ann Brodkiewicz, Chicago
1979.265
Back has two firing holes.

772. Portrait Medallion: ***Jan Van Olden Barneveld*, ca. 1785**
Basalt
4 1/16 x 3 1/4 in (10.3 x 8.2 cm)
Mark: "Wedgwood"
Provenance: Ann Brodkiewicz, Chicago
1979.117
Back has thumbprint depression.

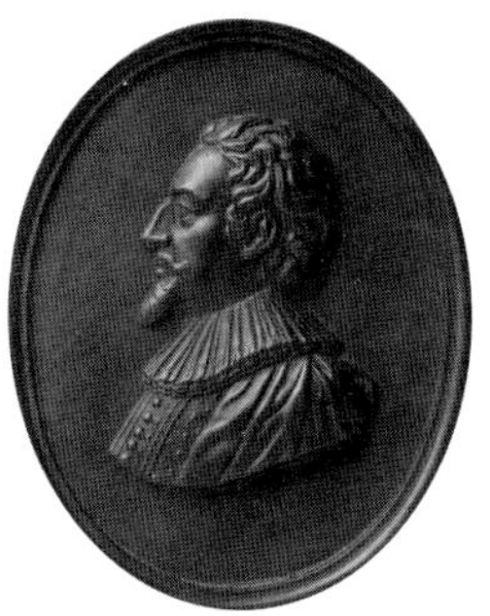

773. Portrait Medallion: *Hugo Grotius*, ca. 1785
Basalt
4 1/16 x 3 1/4 in (10.2 x 8.2 cm)
Mark: "Wedgwood"; "GROTIUS" impressed on front
Provenance: Ann Brodkiewicz, Chicago
1979.96
Back has thumbprint depression.

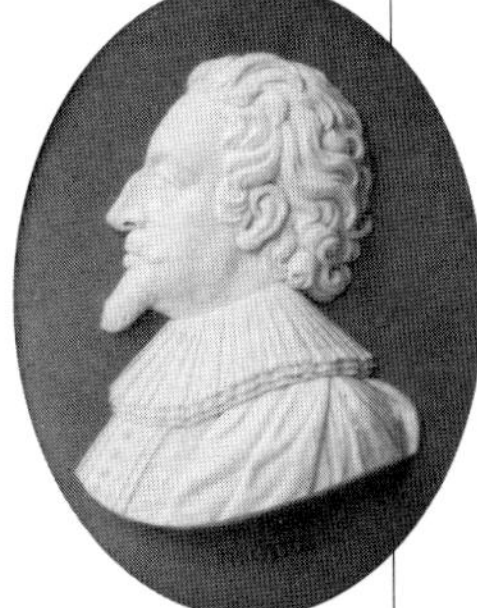

774. Portrait Medallion: *Hugo Grotius*, ca. 1780
Jasper, solid blue ground with dark blue wash and white relief
4 5/8 x 3 15/16 in (11.7 x 10 cm)
Mark: "WEDGWOOD & BENTLEY"; "GROTIUS" impressed on front
Provenance: Otto Wasserman, New York
1979.97
Back has two firing holes.

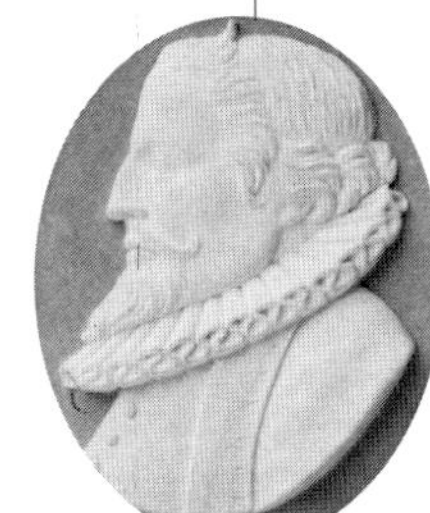

775. Portrait Medallion: *Miguel de Cervantes Saavedra*, ca. 1780
Jasper, solid blue ground with dark blue wash on front and white relief
2 3/16 x 1 3/4 in (5.5 x 4.4 cm)
Mark: "Wedgwood & Bentley" with dark ink wash on mark
Provenance: Otto Wasserman, New York
1979.94
Back has two firing holes.

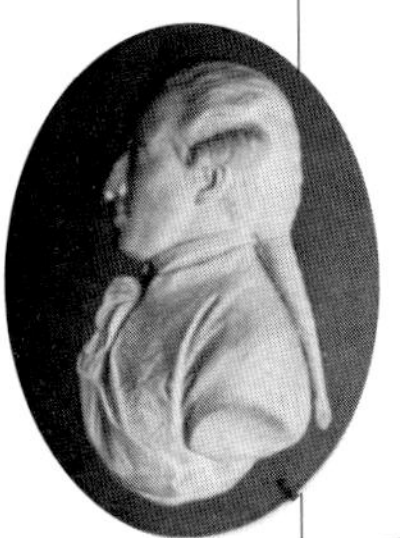

776. Portrait Medallion: *Ferdinand IV of Naples*, ca. 1800
Jasper, solid blue ground with dark blue wash and white relief
3 x 2 1/4 in (7.6 x 5.7 cm)
Mark: none
Provenance: Dr. Harold L. Klawans, Chicago
1979.146

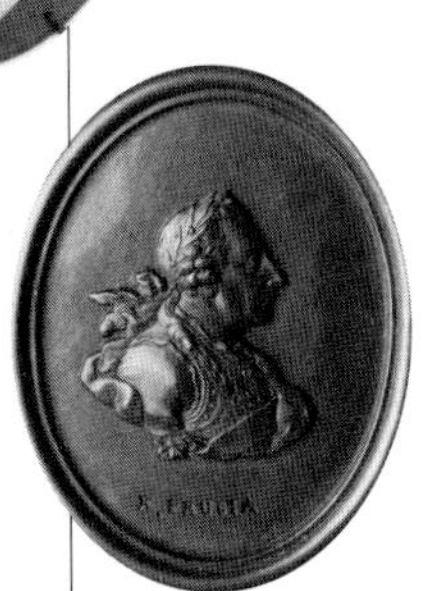

777. Portrait Medallion: *King Frederick of Prussia*, ca. 1780
Basalt
2 13/16 x 2 13/16 in (7.1 x 7.1 cm)
Mark: "Wedgwood & Bentley"; "K.PRUSSIA" impressed on front
Provenance: Ann Brodkiewicz, Chicago
1977.79

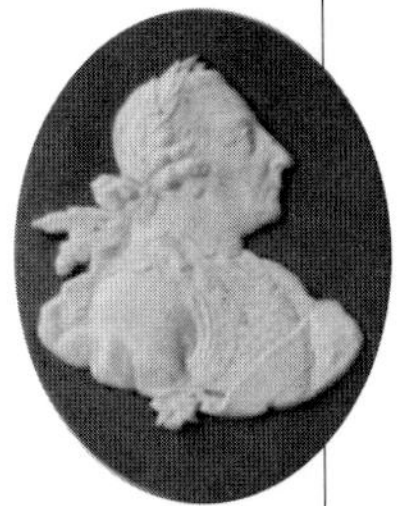

778. Portrait Medallion: *King Frederick of Prussia*, ca. 1780
Jasper, solid blue ground with dark blue wash on front and white relief
1 13/16 x 1 7/16 in (4.6 x 3.6 cm)
Mark: "Wedgwood & Bentley"
Provenance: Ann Brodkiewicz, Chicago
1979.128
Back has two firing holes.

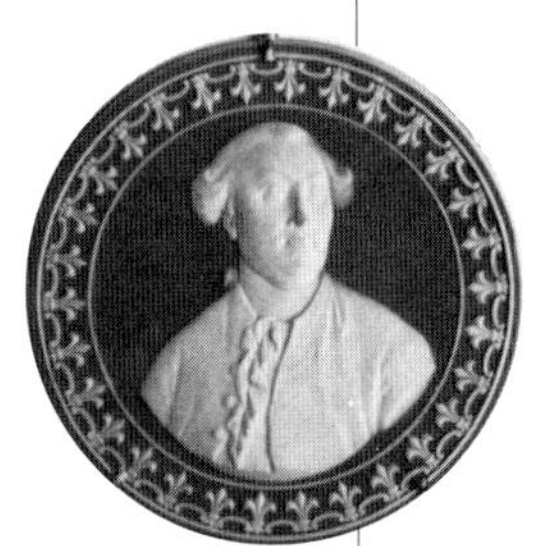

779. Portrait Medallion: ***Jacques Necker*****, ca. 1790**
Jasper, solid white ground with blue wash front and back and white relief
2 3/8 in (6 cm)
Mark: "WEDGWOOD" "I"
Provenance: Dr. Harold L. Klawans, Chicago
1979.154
Color plate 84

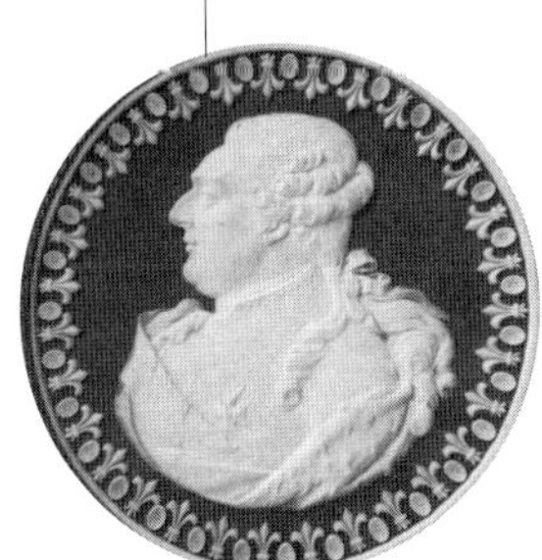

780. Portrait Medallion: ***Louis XVI of France*****, ca. 1790**
Jasper, solid white ground with dark blue wash front and back and white relief
2 5/16 in (5.8 cm)
Mark: "WEDGWOOD"
Provenance: Ann Brodkiewicz, Chicago
1979.149
Color plate 84

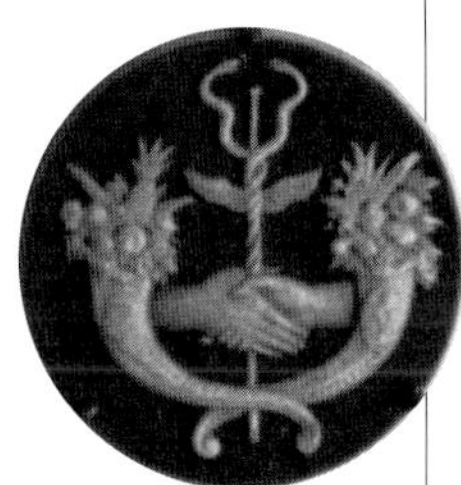

781. Medallion: ***Caduceus of Peace*****, ca. 1790**
Jasper, solid white ground with dark blue wash on front and back and white relief
1 in (2.5 cm)
Mark: "WEDGWOOD"
Provenance: Gift to Dwight and Lucille Beeson from Dr. Bob Jones of Bob Jones University, Louisville, Ky.
1990.5

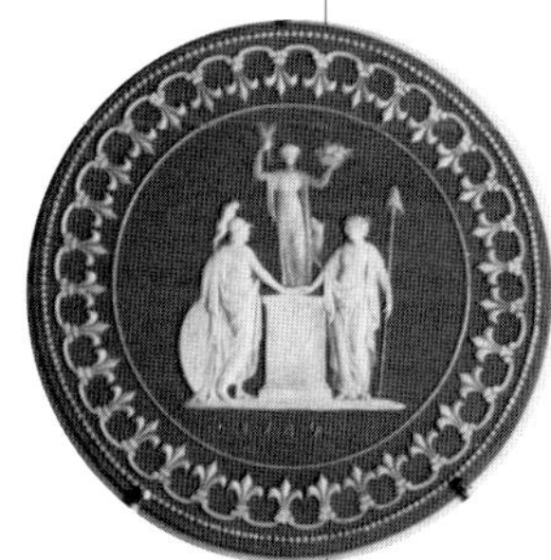

782. Medallion: ***France and Liberty Joining Hands before a Statue of Plenty*****, ca. 1789**
Jasper, solid white ground with dark blue wash on front and back and white relief
2 5/16 in (5.8 cm)
Mark: "WEDGWOOD"; "1789" on front
Provenance: Godfrey W. Ford, England; Dr. Harold L. Klawans, Chicago
1979.155
Color plate 84

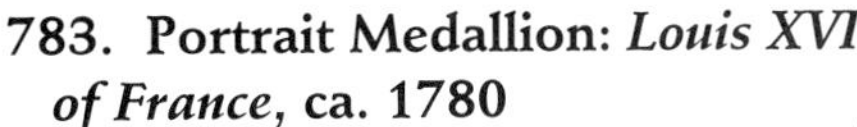

783. Portrait Medallion: ***Louis XVI of France*****, ca. 1780**
Basalt
7/8 x 3/4 in (2.2 x 1.9 cm)
Mark: "WEDGWOOD"
Provenance: Dr. Francis Jennings Vurpillat, South Bend, Ind.
1977.122.28

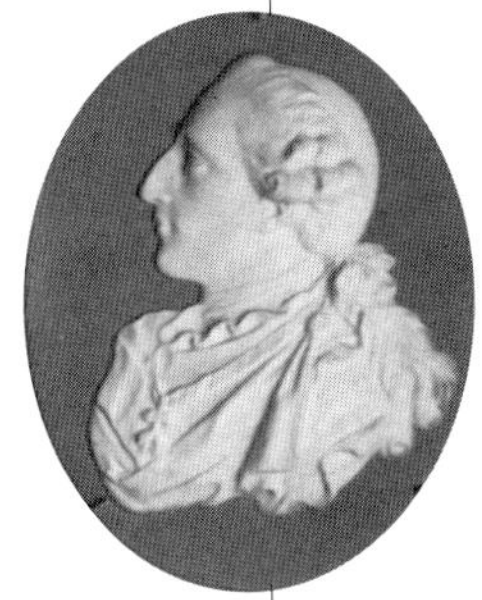

784. Portrait Medallion: ***Louis XVI of France*****, ca. 1780**
Jasper, solid blue ground with white relief
3 3/8 x 2 11/16 in (8.5 x 6.8 cm)
Mark: "WEDGWOOD & BENTLEY"
Provenance: M. Mellanay Delhom, Chicago
1985.442
Back has one firing hole.

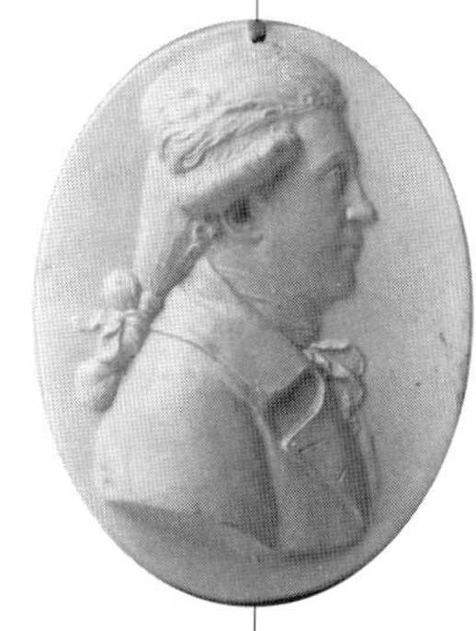

785. Portrait Medallion: *Prince Lambertini*, 19th century
Cream ware
4 x 3 1/16 in (10.1 x 7.7 cm)
Mark: "WEDGWOOD"; "Prince Lambertini" written in script on back
Provenance: Ann Brodkiewicz, Chicago
1979.153

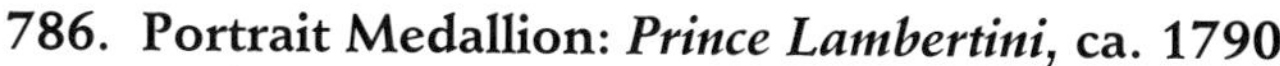

786. Portrait Medallion: *Prince Lambertini*, ca. 1790
Jasper, solid blue ground with white relief
4 1/8 x 3 3/16 in (10.4 x 8 cm)
Mark: "WEDGWOOD"
Provenance: Ann Brodkiewicz, Chicago
1979.150
Back has two firing holes.

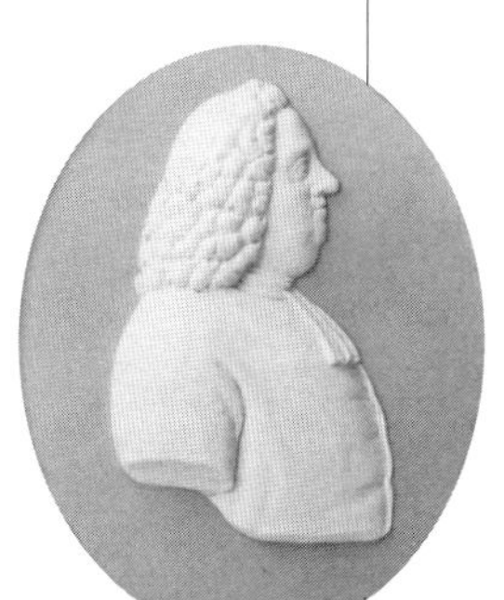

787. Portrait Medallion: *William Penn*, 19th century
Jasper, solid blue ground with white relief
4 3/8 x 3 1/2 in (11.1 x 8.8 cm)
Mark: "WEDGWOOD"; "W. Penn" in script
Provenance: unknown
1979.137

788. Portrait Medallion: *George Washington*, ca. 1780
Jasper, solid blue ground with blue wash on front and white relief
2 1/8 x 1 3/4 in (5.3 x 4.4 cm)
Mark: "Wedgwood & Bentley"
Provenance: unknown
1979.125
Color plate 83

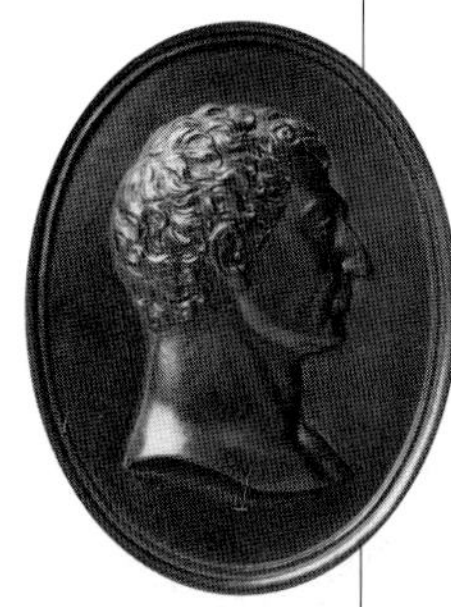

789. Portrait Medallion: *George Washington*, ca. 1780
Basalt
4 1/16 x 3 1/4 in (10.3 x 8.2 cm)
Mark: "Wedgwood & Bentley"
Provenance: Hoocker Collection, England; Dr. Francis Jennings Vurpillat, South Bend, Ind.
1979.124
Back has thumbprint depression.

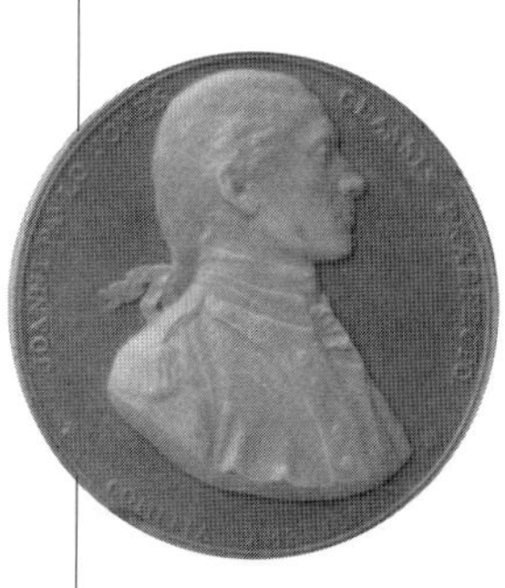

790. Portrait Medallion: *John Paul Jones*, 20th century
Jasper, solid blue ground with white relief, bronze medal companion
Medallion: 2 in (5 cm); medal: 2 1/4 in (5.7 cm)
Mark: "WEDGWOOD" "O"; "JOANNI PAVLO JONES / CLASSIS PRAEFECTO / COMITIA AMERICANA" in relief on front
Provenance: Dr. Harold L. Klawans, Chicago
1978.151 and 1978.174

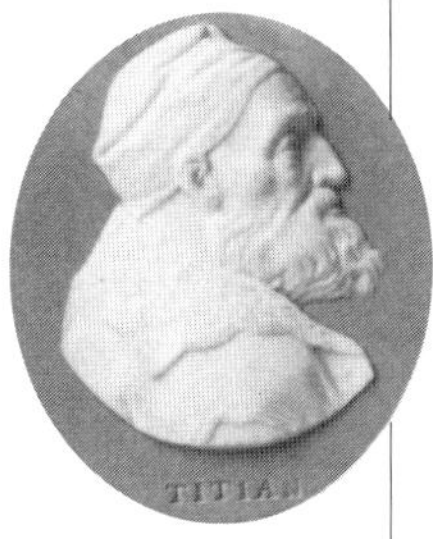

791. Portrait Medallion: *Titian*, ca. 1780
Jasper, solid blue ground with blue wash on front and white relief
2 1/8 x 1 3/4 in (5.3 x 4.4 cm)
Mark: "Wedgwood & Bentley"; "TITIAN" impressed on front
Provenance: David Davis, Chicago; M. Mellanay Delhom, Chicago; Ann Brodkiewicz, Chicago
1979.108
Back has two firing holes.

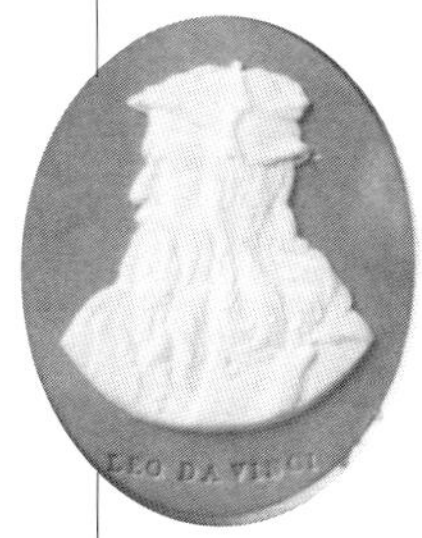

792. Portrait Medallion: *Leonardo da Vinci*, ca. 1780
Jasper, solid blue ground with blue wash on front and white relief
2 1/8 x 1 3/4 in (5.3 x 4.4 cm)
Mark: "Wedgwood & Bentley"; "LEO DA VINCI" impressed on front
Provenance: David Davis, Chicago; M. Mellanay Delhom, Chicago; Ann Brodkiewicz, Chicago
1979.109

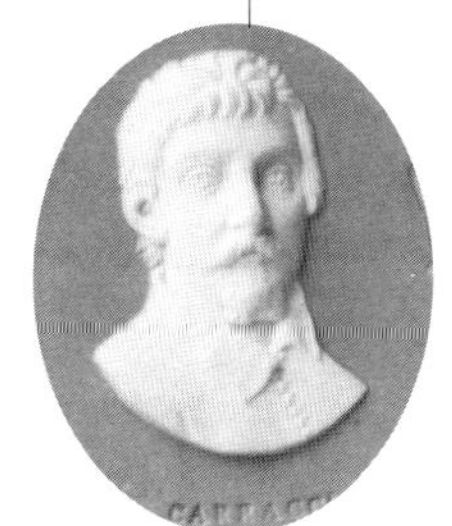

793. Portrait Medallion: *Annibale Carracci*, ca. 1778
Jasper, solid light blue ground with dark blue wash on front and white relief
2 1/8 x 1 3/4 in (5.3 x 4.4 cm)
Mark: "Wedgwood & Bentley"; "CARRACCI" impressed on front
Provenance: David Davis, Chicago; M. Mellanay Delhom, Chicago; Ann Brodkiewicz, Chicago
1979.107
Back has two firing holes.

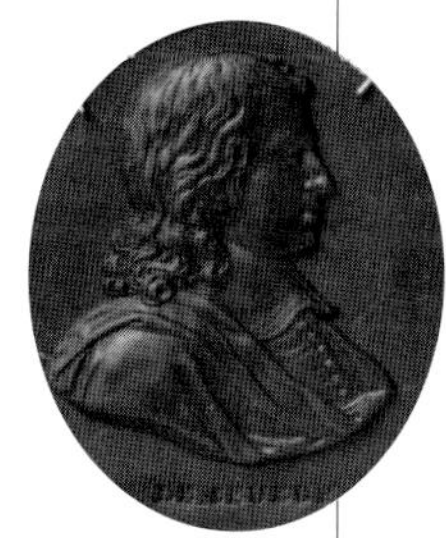

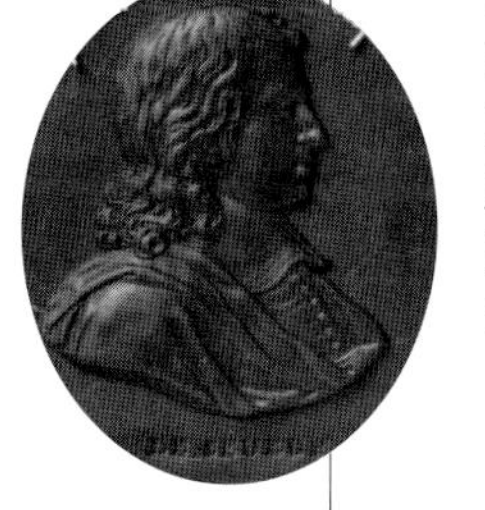

794. Portrait Medallion: *Eustache Le Sueur*, ca. 1775
Basalt
2 x 1 11/16 in (5 x 4.2 cm)
Mark: "Wedgwood & Bentley"; "LE SEUEUR" [*sic*] impressed on front
Provenance: M. Mellanay Delhom, Chicago; Ann Brodkiewicz, Chicago
1979.102

795. Portrait Medallion: *Carlo Maratti*, ca. 1775
Basalt
1 15/16 x 1 11/16 in (4.9 x 4.2 cm)
Mark: "Wedgwood & Bentley"; "C. MARATTI" impressed on front
Provenance: M. Mellanay Delhom, Chicago; Ann Brodkiewicz, Chicago
1979.101

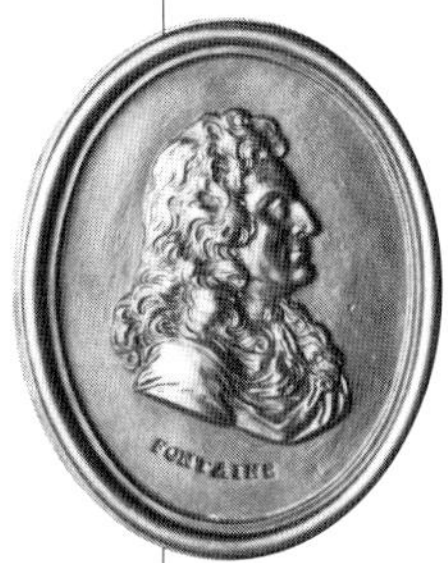

796. Portrait Medallion: *Jean de la Fontaine*, ca. 1780
Basalt
2 3/4 x 2 1/4 in (6.9 x 5.7 cm)
Mark: "Wedgwood & Bentley"; "FONTAINE" impressed on front
Provenance: M. Mellanay Delhom, Chicago; Ann Brodkiewicz, Chicago
1977.77

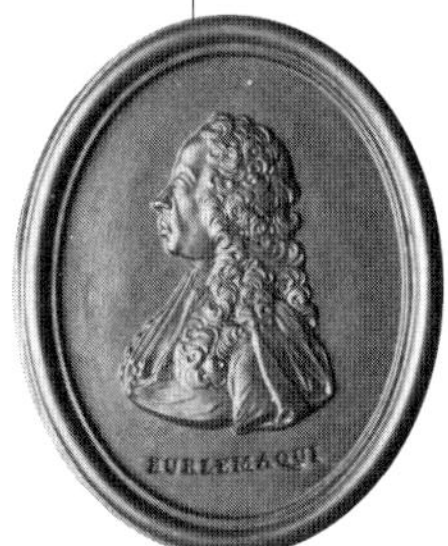

797. Portrait Medallion: *Jean Jacques Burlemaqui*, ca. 1780
Basalt
2 11/16 x 2 3/16 in (6.8 x 5.5 cm)
Mark: "WEDGWOOD"; "BURLEMAQUI" impressed on front
Provenance: Ann Brodkiewicz, Chicago
1977.76

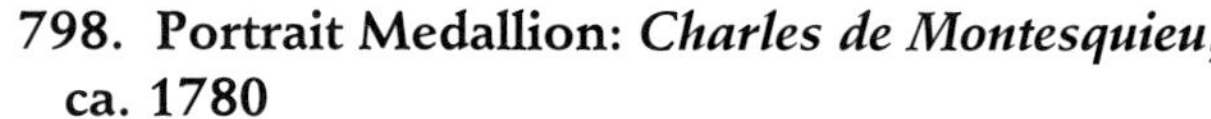

798. Portrait Medallion: *Charles de Montesquieu*, ca. 1780
Basalt
2 3/4 x 2 1/4 in (6.9 x 5.7 cm)
Mark: "Wedgwood / & Bentley"; "MONTESQ." impressed on front
Provenance: Ann Brodkiewicz, Chicago
1977.78

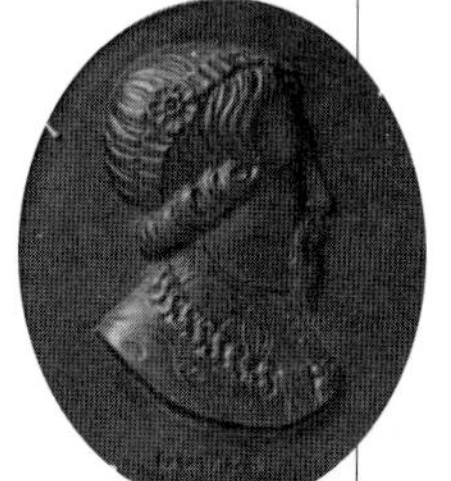

799. Portrait Medallion: *John Gower*, ca. 1775
Basalt
2 x 1 3/4 in (5 x 4.4 cm)
Mark: "Wedgwood & Bentley"; "GOWER" impressed on front
Provenance: M. Mellanay Delhom, Chicago; Ann Brodkiewicz, Chicago
1979.99

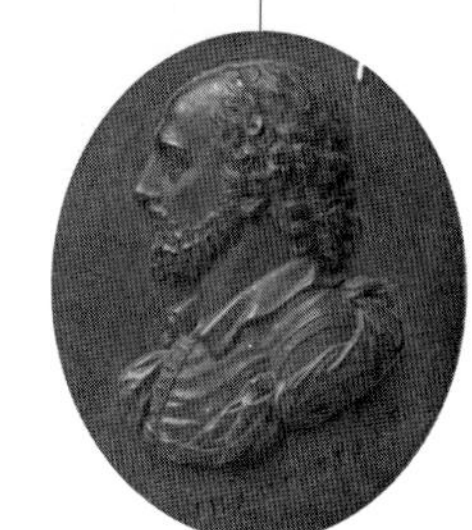

800. Portrait Medallion: *William Shakespeare*, ca. 1775
Basalt
2 x 1 5/8 in (5 x 4.1 cm)
Mark: "Wedgwood & Bentley"; "SHAKESPEARE" impressed on front
Provenance: Dr. Harold L. Klawans, Chicago
1979.105

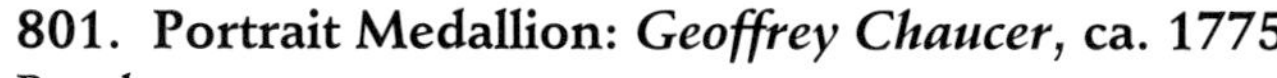

801. Portrait Medallion: *Geoffrey Chaucer*, ca. 1775
Basalt
2 1/16 x 1 11/16 in (5.2 x 4.2 cm)
Mark: "Wedgwood & Bentley"; "CHAUCER" impressed on front
Provenance: Dr. Harold L. Klawans, Chicago
1979.106

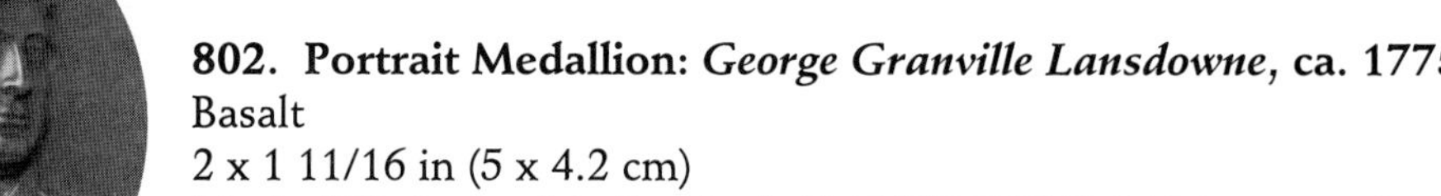

802. Portrait Medallion: *George Granville Lansdowne*, ca. 1775
Basalt
2 x 1 11/16 in (5 x 4.2 cm)
Mark: "Wedgwood & Bentley"; "LANSDOWN" [*sic*] impressed on front
Provenance: M. Mellanay Delhom, Chicago; Ann Brodkiewicz, Chicago
1979.100

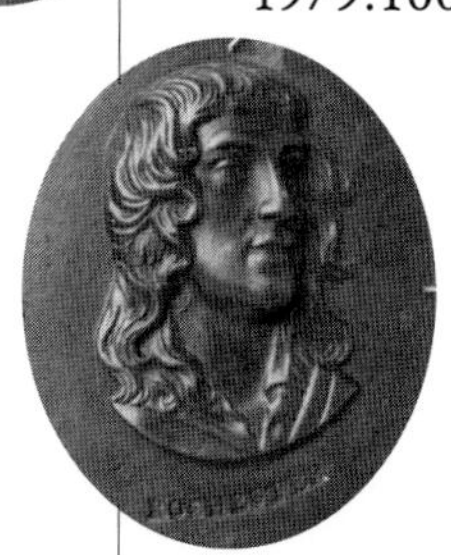

803. Portrait Medallion: *John W. Rochester*, ca. 1775
Basalt
2 x 1 11/16 in (5 x 4.2 cm)
Mark: "Wedgwood & Bentley"; "ROCHESTER" impressed on front
Provenance: M. Mellanay Delhom, Chicago; Ann Brodkiewicz, Chicago
1979.103

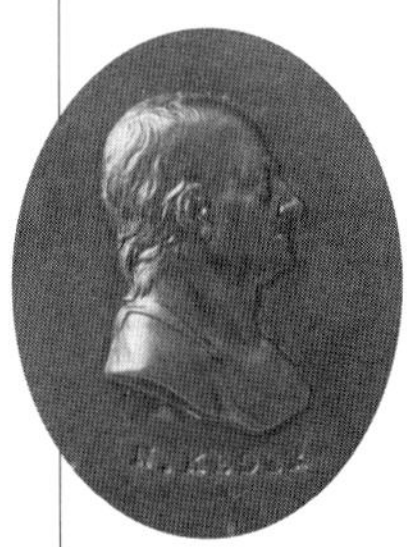

804. Portrait Medallion: ***Nicholas Keder*****, ca. 1775**
Basalt
1 3/4 x 1 7/16 in (4.4 x 3.6 cm)
Mark: "Wedgwood & Bentley"; "N. KEDER" impressed on front
Provenance: Ann Brodkiewicz, Chicago
1979.127

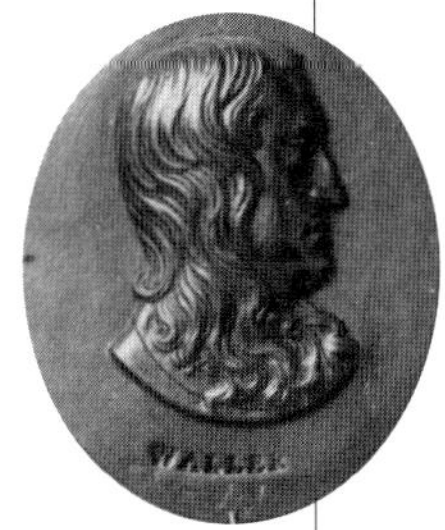

805. Portrait Medallion: ***Edmund Waller*****, ca. 1775**
Basalt
2 x 1 3/4 in (5 x 4.4 cm)
Mark: "Wedgwood & Bentley"; "WALLER" impressed on front
Provenance: M. Mellanay Delhom, Chicago; Ann Brodkiewicz, Chicago
1979.104

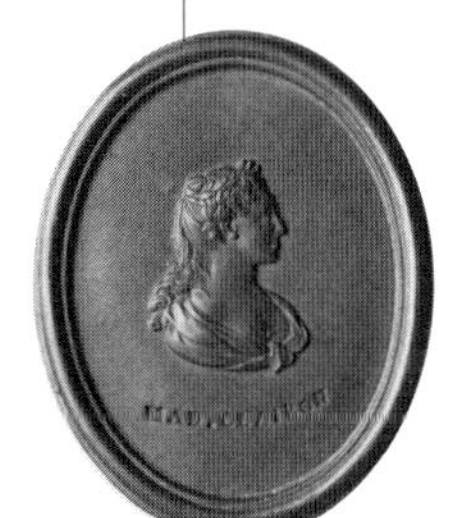

806. Portrait Medallion: ***Josepha Hippolyte Léres Clairon de la Tudi*****, ca. 1780**
Basalt
2 7/16 x 2 in (6.1 x 5 cm)
Mark: "Wedgwood & Bentley"; "MAD. CLAIRON" impressed on front
Provenance: M. Mellanay Delhom, Chicago; Ann Brodkiewicz, Chicago
1977.131

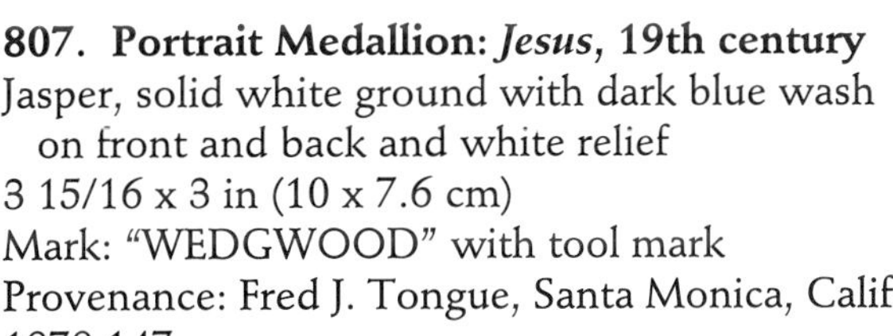

807. Portrait Medallion: ***Jesus*****, 19th century**
Jasper, solid white ground with dark blue wash on front and back and white relief
3 15/16 x 3 in (10 x 7.6 cm)
Mark: "WEDGWOOD" with tool mark
Provenance: Fred J. Tongue, Santa Monica, Calif.
1979.147

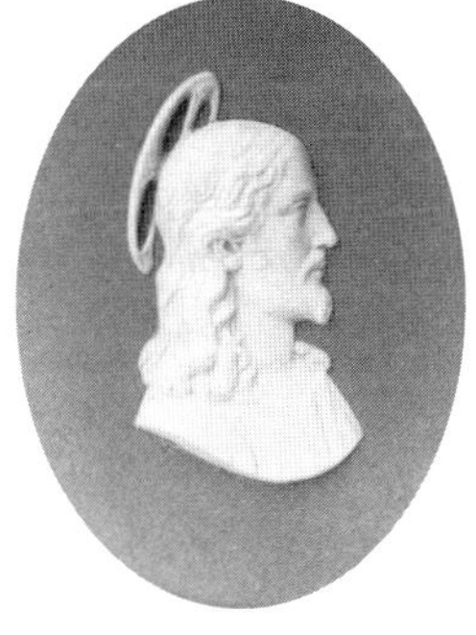

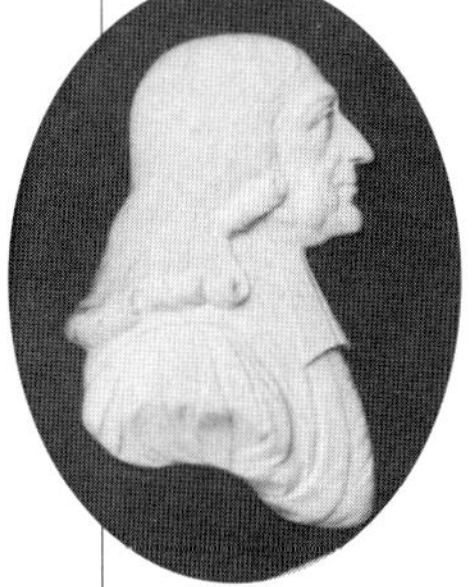

808. Portrait Medallion: ***John Wesley*****, 19th century**
Jasper, solid white ground with black wash and white relief
3 1/2 x 2 1/2 in (8.8 x 6.3 cm)
Mark: "WEDGWOOD" "I"
Provenance: Charles Smith, Philadelphia, Pa.
1978.173

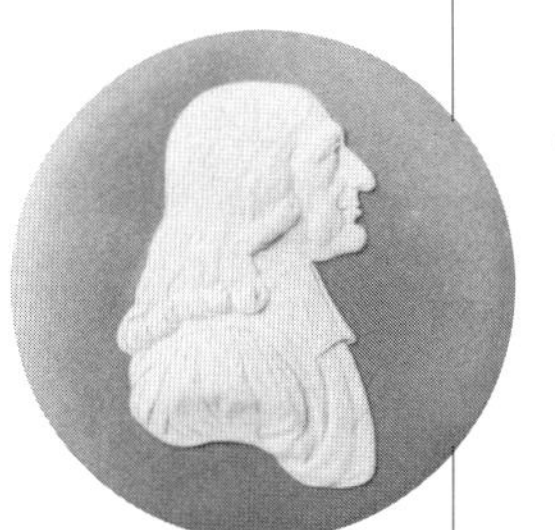

809. Portrait Medallion: ***John Wesley*****, 1965**
Jasper, solid green ground with white relief
2 9/16 in (6.5 cm)
Mark: "WEDGWOOD / MADE IN ENGLAND / N B / JOHN WESLEY"
Provenance: Wedgwood Factory
1979.84

Classical Medallions

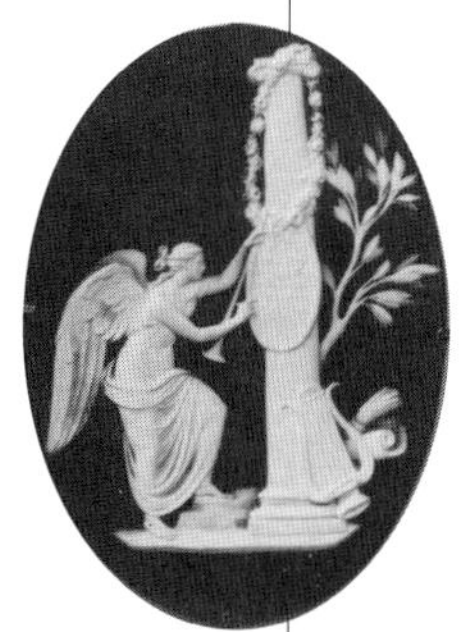

810. Medallion: *Fame Writing upon a Shield,* ca. 1790
Jasper, solid white ground with dark blue wash on front and back with white relief
4 3/4 x 3 1/2 in (12 x 8.8 cm)
Mark: "WEDGWOOD"; "QUAE SITAM / MERITIS" on front
Provenance: Christie's, London, June 14, 1965
1976.176
Design source: Montfaucon, *L'Antiquité expliquée,* vol. 1, pt. 2, 93, Fig. 25
Color plate 77

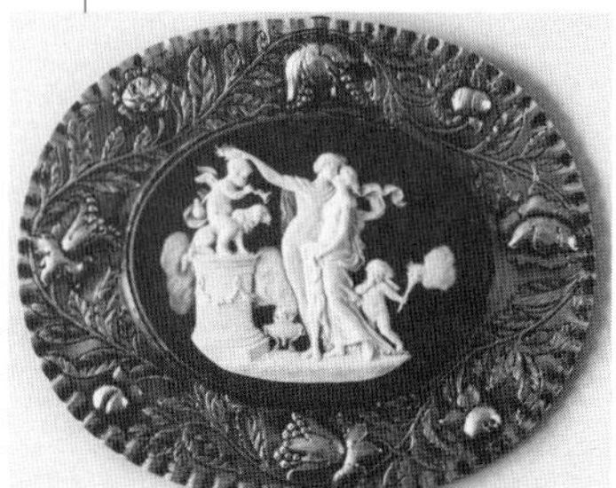

811. Medallion: *Classical Figures with Cupid,* ca. 1790
Jasper, solid blue ground with dark blue wash on front and back and white relief; lapidary-polishing on edges
4 1/16 x 3 3/16 in (10.3 x 8 cm)
Mark: "WEDGWOOD"
Provenance: Christie's, London, June 14, 1965
1985.425

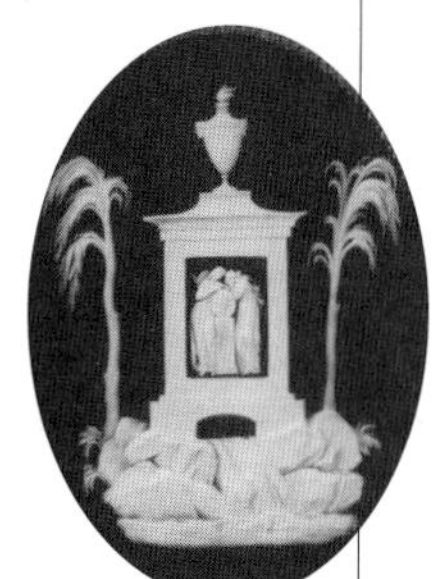

812. Medallion: *Monument to Solomon Gessner,* ca. 1790
Michel-Vincent Brandoin (1735-1807), designer
Jasper, solid white ground with dark blue wash on front and back and black-and-white relief
4 5/8 x 3 3/8 in (11.7 x 8.5 cm)
Mark: "WEDGWOOD"; "S. GESSNER" on front
Provenance: Dr. Harold L. Klawans, Chicago
1976.201
Color plate 77

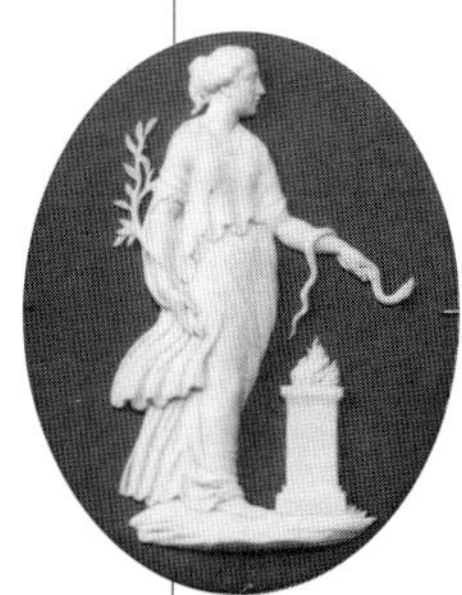

813. Medallion: *Hygeia,* 1775-80
Jasper, solid blue ground with white relief
3 5/16 x 2 5/8 in (8.4 x 6.6 cm)
Mark: "Hygeia-Goddess of Health" in ink on back
Provenance: Godfrey W. Ford, England; Dr. Harold L. Klawans, Chicago
1976.210
Color plate 72

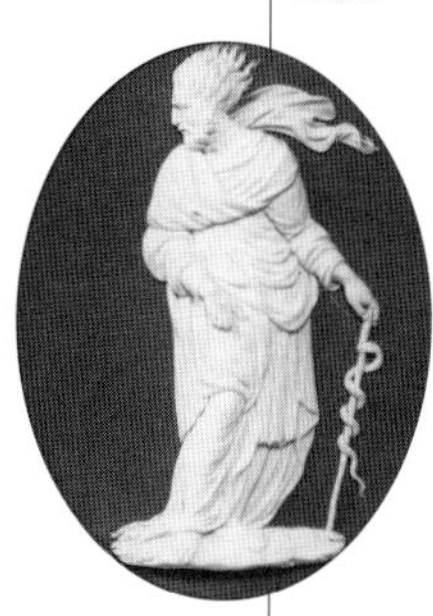

814. Medallion: *Aesculapius,* ca. 1780
Jasper, solid blue ground with white relief
3 1/4 x 2 9/16 in (8.2 x 6.5 cm)
Mark: "Wedgwood & Bentley"
Provenance: Godfrey W. Ford, England; Dr. Harold L. Klawans, Chicago
1976.209
Color plate 72

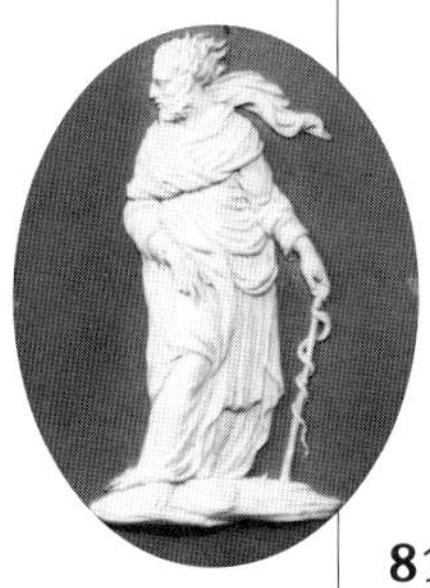

815. Medallion: *Aesculapius*, 1775-80
Jasper, solid blue ground with blue wash on front and white relief
3 5/16 x 2 3/4 in (8.4 x 6.9 cm)
Mark: "Wedgwood & Bentley"
Provenance: W. Bartlett, England; Dr. Harold L. Klawans, Chicago
1976.185
Back has two firing holes.

816. Medallion: *Aesculapius and Hygeia*, ca. 1780
Jasper, marbled blue-and-white ground with dark blue wash on front and white relief
1 3/4 x 1 3/8 in (4.4 x 3.4 cm)
Mark: "Wedgwood & Bentley"
Provenance: Sir George Duff-Dunbar, Scotland; M. Mellanay Delhom, Chicago
1982.53
Color plate 72

817. Medallion: *A Sacrifice to Aesculapius*, ca. 1780
Jasper, solid white ground with dark wash on front and white relief
1 7/8 x 2 3/4 in (4.7 x 6.9 cm)
Mark: "Wedgwood & Bentley"
Provenance: Sir George Duff-Dunbar, Scotland; M. Mellanay Delhom, Chicago
1982.57
Design source: Montfaucon, *L' Antiquité expliquée,* vol. 1, pt. 2, pl. 86
Color plate 72

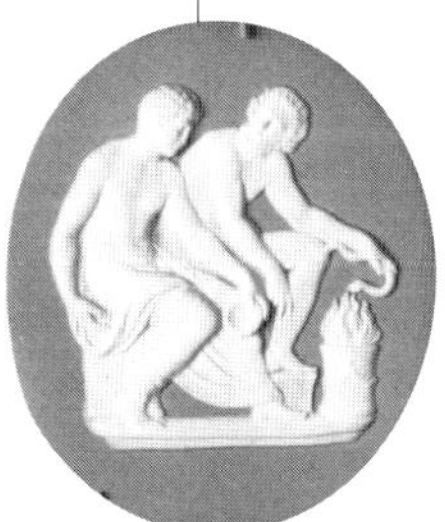

818. Medallion: *Aesculapius Treating a Youth*, ca. 1780
Jasper, solid blue ground with white relief
2 5/8 x 2 3/16 in (6.6 x 5.5 cm)
Mark: "Wedgwood & Bentley"
Provenance: M. Mellanay Delhom, Chicago; Ann Brodkiewicz, Chicago
1982.47

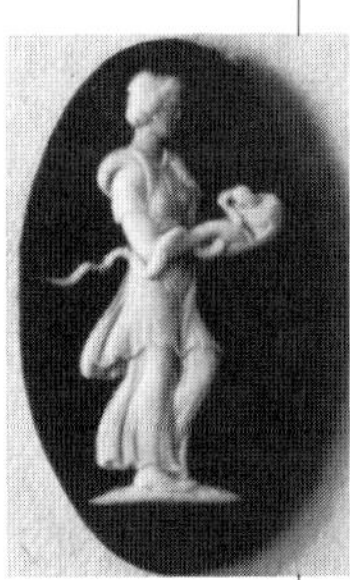

819. Medallion: *Classical Figure*, ca. 1780
Jasper, solid white ground with dark blue wash on front and light blue wash on back and white relief
1 x 5/8 in (2.5 x 1.5 cm)
Mark: none
Provenance: Dr. Francis Jennings Vurpillat, South Bend, Ind.
1977.122.90

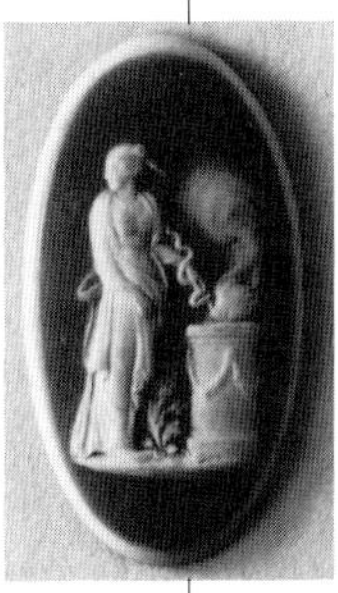

820. Medallion: *A Sacrifice to Hygeia*, ca. 1790
Jasper, solid white ground with blue wash front and back with white relief, lapidary-polishing
1 3/16 x 5/8 in (3 x 1.5 cm)
Mark: "WEDGWOOD" "H"
Provenance: M. Mellanay Delhom, Chicago; Ann Brodkiewicz, Chicago
1982.43

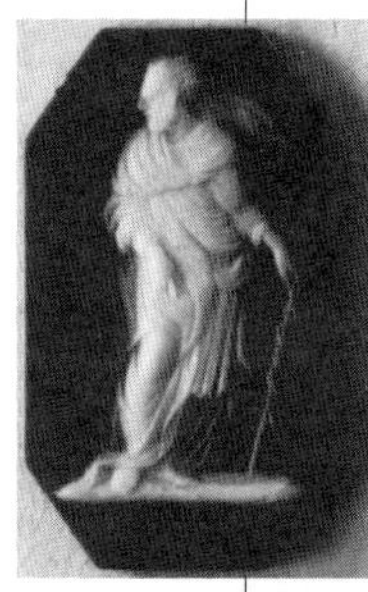

821. Medallion: *Aesculapius*, ca. 1790
Jasper, solid white ground with dark blue wash on front and blue wash on back and white relief
1 x 5/8 in (2.5 x 1.5 cm)
Mark: none
Provenance: Dr. Francis Jennings Vurpillat, South Bend, Ind.
1977.122.81

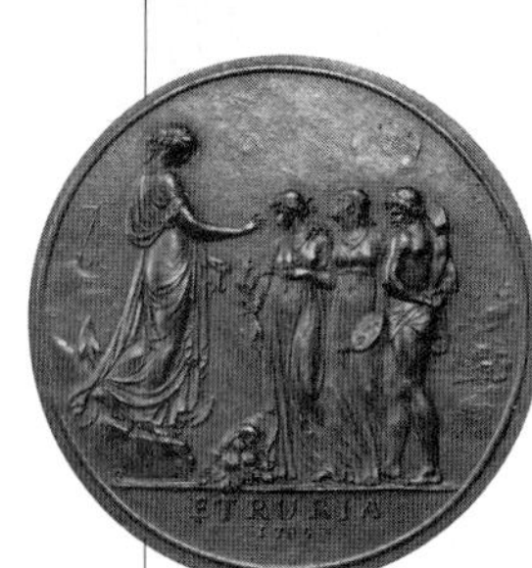

822. Medallion: *Sydney Cove*, 19th century
Basalt
2 7/16 in (6.1 cm)
Mark: "WEDGWOOD"; "ETRURIA / w1789" on face
Provenance: Ann Brodkiewicz, Chicago
1976.202

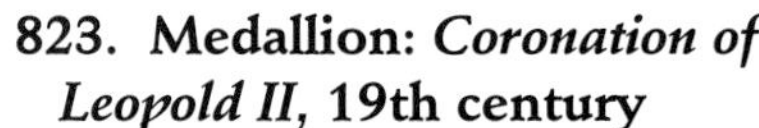

823. Medallion: *Coronation of Leopold II*, 19th century
Jasper, solid blue ground with white relief
2 15/16 x 2 1/16 in (7.4 x 5.2 cm)
Mark: "WEDGWOOD"
Provenance: Ann Brodkiewicz, Chicago
1976.177

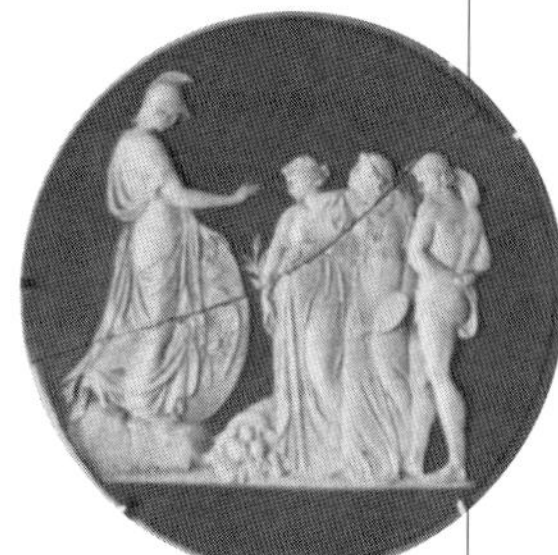

824. Medallion: *Germany Encouraging Art and Labour with Peace to Work for the Prosperity of the Empire*, ca. 1790
Jasper, solid white ground with blue wash on front and back and white relief, lapidary-polished edges
2 3/16 in (5.5 cm)
Mark: "WEDGWOOD"
Provenance: Dr. Francis Jennings Vurpillat, South Bend, Ind.
1977.122.84

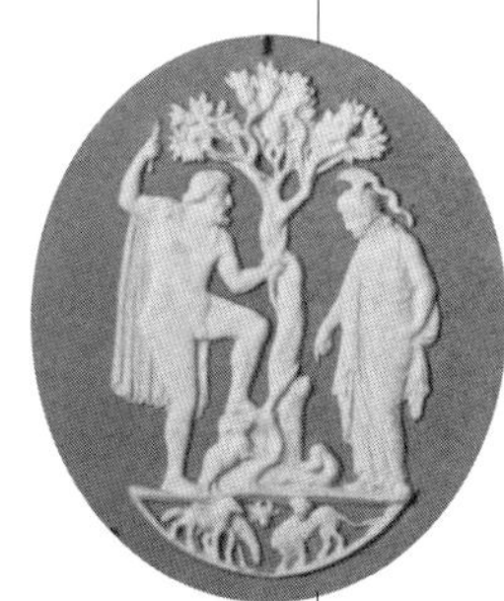

825. Medallion: *The Naming of Athens*, ca. 1790
Jasper, solid white ground with green wash on front and light blue on back and white relief
2 1/2 x 2 3/16 in (6.3 x 5.5 cm)
Mark: "Wedgwood"
Provenance: Ann Brodkiewicz, Chicago
1982.45

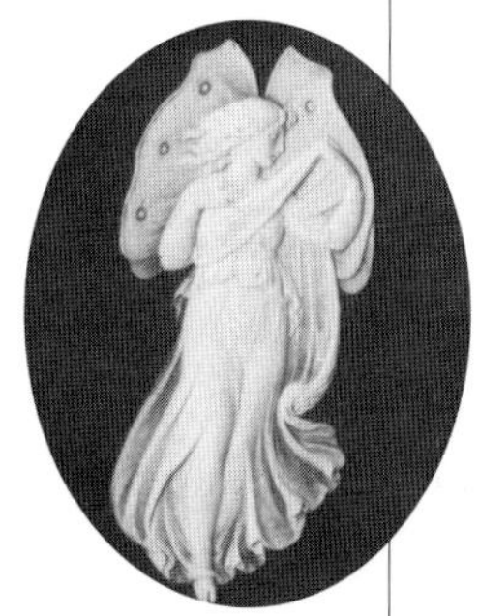

826. Medallion: *Zephyr*, ca. 1800
Jasper, solid white ground with dark blue wash on front and back and white relief
2 11/16 x 2 3/16 in (6.8 x 5.5. cm)
Mark: "WEDGWOOD"
Provenance: Church Collection, England; Godfrey W. Ford, England; Dr. Harold L. Klawans, Chicago
1976.193

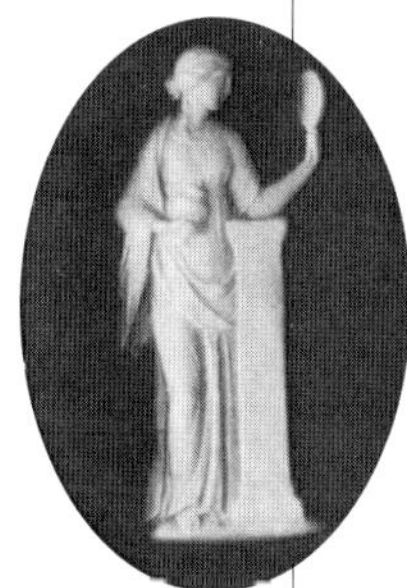

827. Medallion: *Woman Holding a Mirror*, 19th century
Jasper, solid white ground with dark blue on front and white relief
1 7/8 x 1 5/16 in (4.7 x 3.3 cm)
Mark: "WEDGWOOD"
Provenance: Purchased in New Orleans
1976.190

828. Medallion: *Signs of the Zodiac* and *Coriolanus with Wife and Mother*, ca. 1800
Jasper, solid white ground with lilac-and-dark-blue wash on front and white relief
2 7/16 in (6.1 cm)
Mark: "WEDGWOOD"; "D" incised
Provenance: Col. Earl W. Camp, New Smyrna Beach, Fla.
1976.187

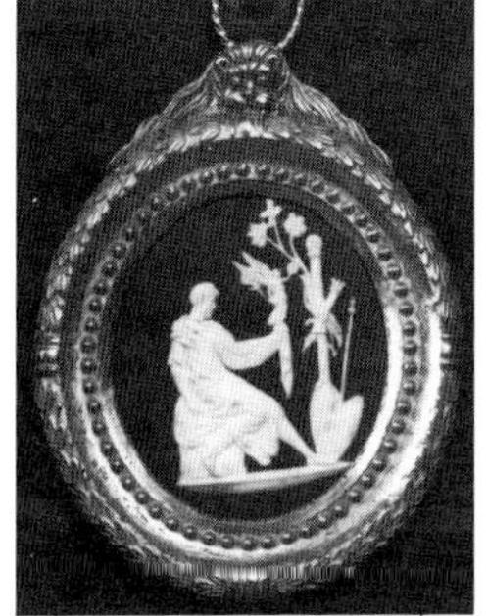

829. Medallion: *A Seated Warrior*, ca. 1780
Jasper, solid white ground with black wash on front and white relief, ormolu frame
1 1/4 x 1 in (3.1 x 2.5 cm)
Mark: "Wedgwood & Bentley"
Provenance: W. Bartlett, England; Dr. Harold L. Klawans, Chicago
1977.82
Color plate 78

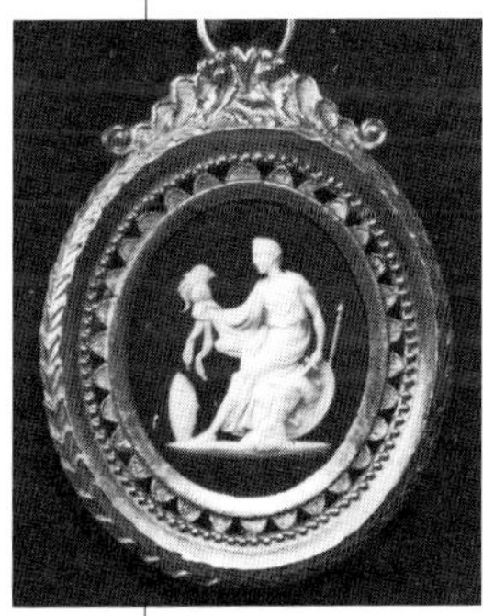

830. Medallion: *Achilles in His Tent*, ca. 1780
Jasper, solid white ground with black wash on front and white relief, ormolu frame
1 1/4 x 1 in (3.1 x 2.5 cm)
Mark: "Wedgwood & Bentley"
Provenance: W. Bartlett, England; Dr. Harold L. Klawans, Chicago
1977.81
Color plate 78

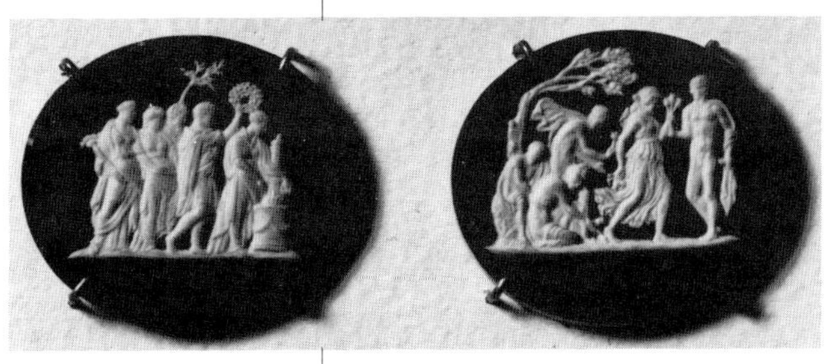

831. Medallion: *Classical Figures*, ca. 1780
Jasper, solid white ground with black wash and white relief
1 1/8 x 1 in (2.6 x 2.5 cm)
Mark: "Wedgwood & Bentley"
Provenance: Gift of Fred and Mary Tongue, Santa Monica, Calif.
1976.216

832. Medallion: *Classical Figures*, ca. 1780
Jasper, solid white ground with black wash on front and white relief
1 x 1 3/16 in (2.5 x 3 cm)
Mark: "Wedgwood & Bentley"
Provenance: D. M. and P. Manheim, New York
1977.130.1

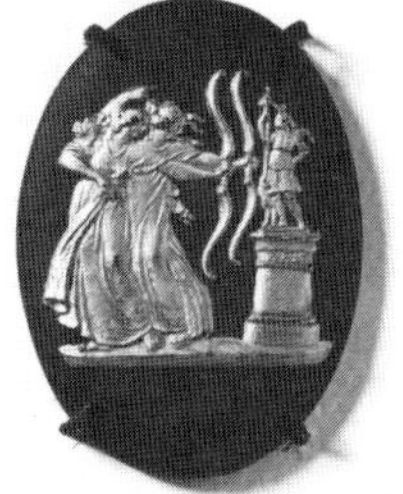
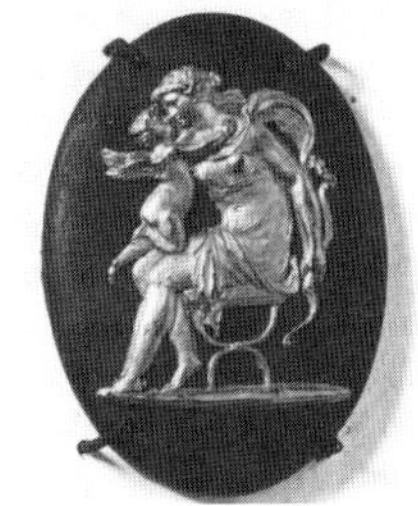

833. Pair of Medallions: *Venus and Cupid* and *Two Classical Figures*, 19th century
Basalt with gold relief
1 3/8 x 1 in (3.4 x 2.5 cm)
Mark: "WEDGWOOD"; "N 4144" painted in gold on back
Provenance: Dr. Francis Jennings Vurpillat, South Bend, Ind.
1977.122.34

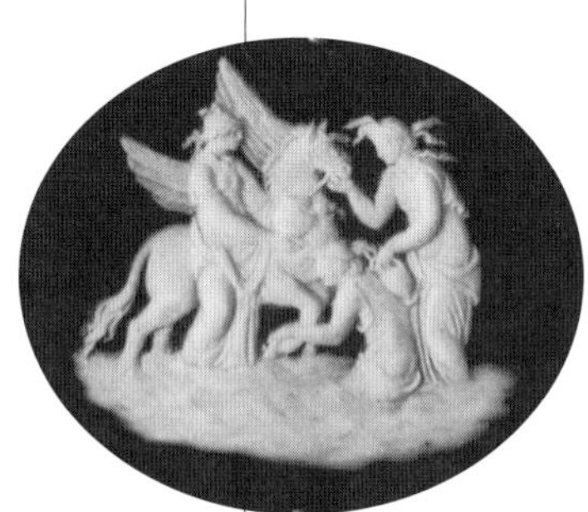

834. Medallion: *Muses Grooming Pegasus*, ca. 1800
Jasper, solid white ground with black wash on front and white relief
2 x 1 9/16 in (5 x 3.9 cm)
Mark: "WEDGWOOD"; "51" incised
Provenance: Dr. Harold L. Klawans, Chicago
1976.198

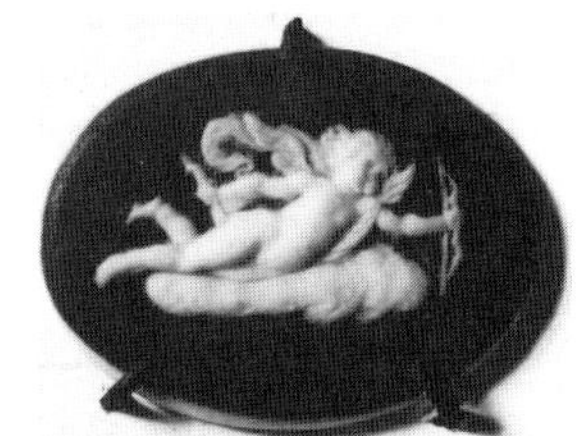

835. Medallion: *Cupid*, ca. 1800
Jasper, solid white ground with black wash on front and white relief
5/8 x 13/16 in (1.5 x 2 cm)
Mark: "WEDGWOOD"
Provenance: Dr. Francis Jennings Vurpillat, South Bend, Ind.
1977.122.102

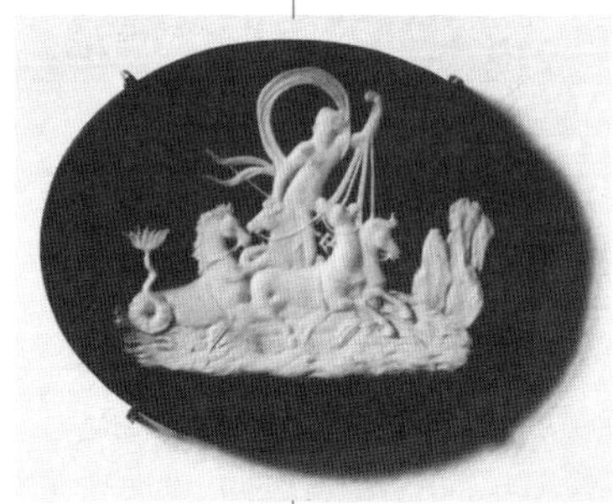

836. Medallion: *Neptune Riding the Sea*, ca. 1780
Jasper, solid white ground with black wash and white relief
1 7/8 x 1 1/2 in (4.7 x 3.8 cm)
Mark: "Wedgwood & Bentley"
Provenance: Ann Brodkiewicz, Chicago
1982.36
Design source: Montfaucon, *LÆ Antiquité expliquée,* vol.1, pt. 2, pl. 16, fig. 25

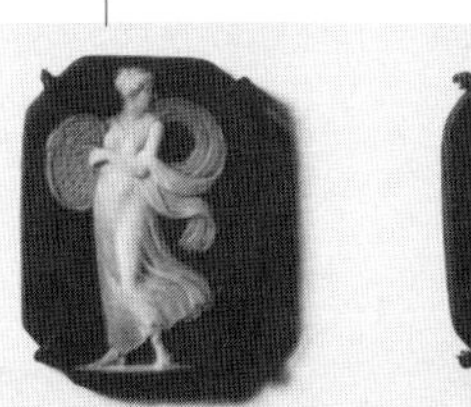
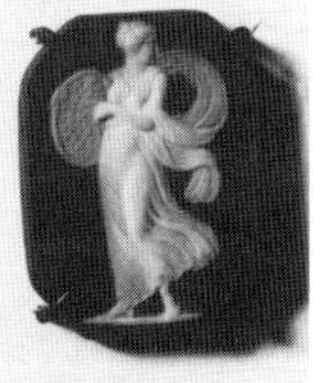

837. Pair of Medallions: *Classical Figures*, ca. 1790
Jasper, solid black ground with white relief
7/8 x 11/16 in (2.2 x 1.7 cm)
Mark: "WEDGWOOD"; "H" incised
Provenance: Dr. Francis Jennings Vurpillat, South Bend, Ind.
1977.122.74-.75

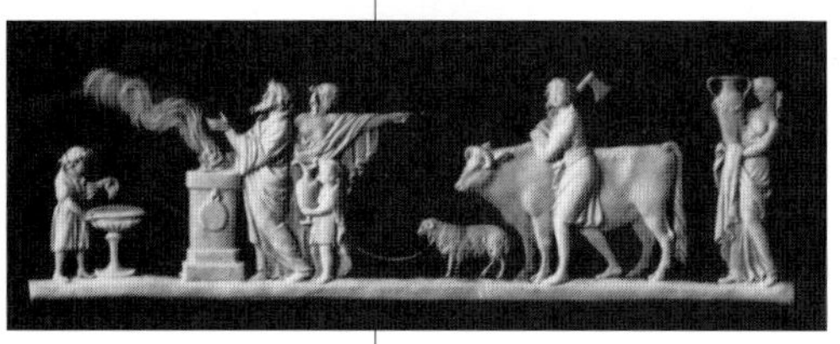

838. Medallion: *Sacrifice of Bullock and Sheep*, ca. 1800
Jasper, solid white ground with black wash on front with white relief
1 15/16 x 4 1/2 in (11.4 x 4.9 cm)
Mark: "WEDGWOOD"
Provenance: Godfrey W. Ford, England; Dr. Harold L. Klawans, Chicago
1982.65

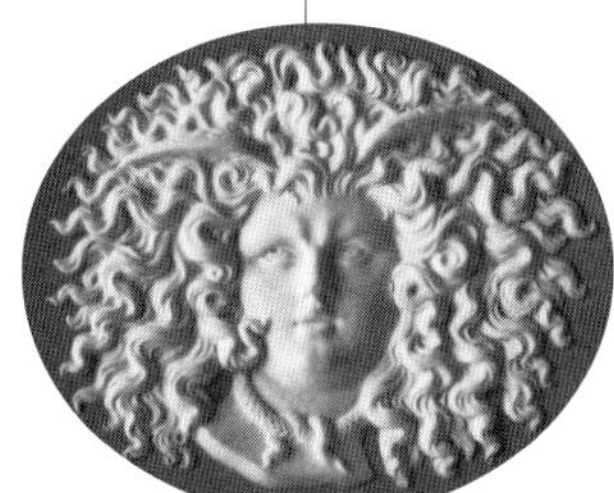

839. Medallion: *Medusa*, ca. 1775-80
Jasper, solid blue ground with blue wash on front and white relief
2 7/8 x 2 3/8 in (7.3 x 6 cm)
Mark: "Wedgwood & Bentley"
Provenance: Godfrey W. Ford, England; Dr. Harold L. Klawans, Chicago
1976.196
Color plate 70

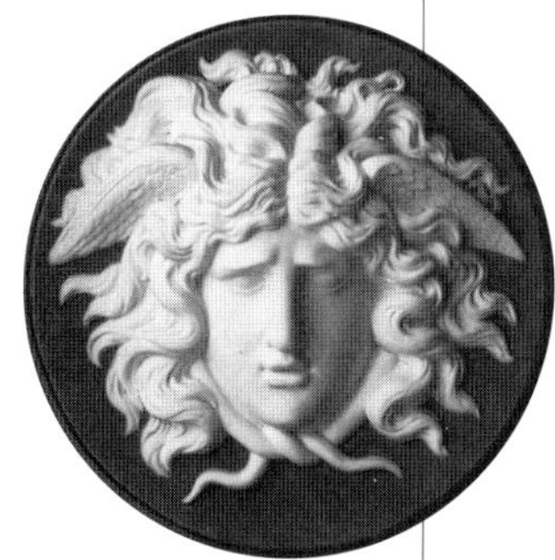

840. Medallion: *Medusa*, ca. 1775-80
Jasper, laminated in three layers, solid light blue, dark blue, and light blue, with white relief
5 1/8 in (13 cm)
Mark: "WEDGWOOD & BENTLEY"; "155 g Wash" incised
Provenance: Dr. Francis Jennings Vurpillat, South Bend, Ind.
1977.121
Back has 16 firing holes.
Color plate 70

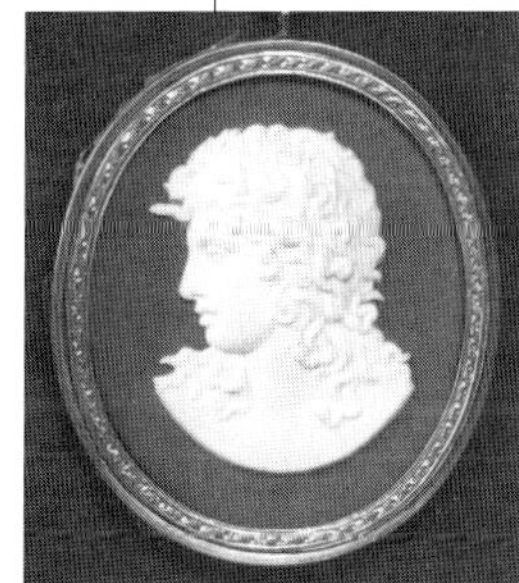

841. Medallion: *Strozzi Medusa in Profile*, ca. 1775-80
Jasper, solid blue ground with darker blue wash on front and white relief
2 1/8 x 1 13/16 in (5.3 x 4.6 cm)
Mark: "Wedgwood & Bentley"
Provenance: M. Mellanay Delhom, Chicago; Ann Brodkiewicz, Chicago
1977.84
Back has one firing hole.
Color plate 70

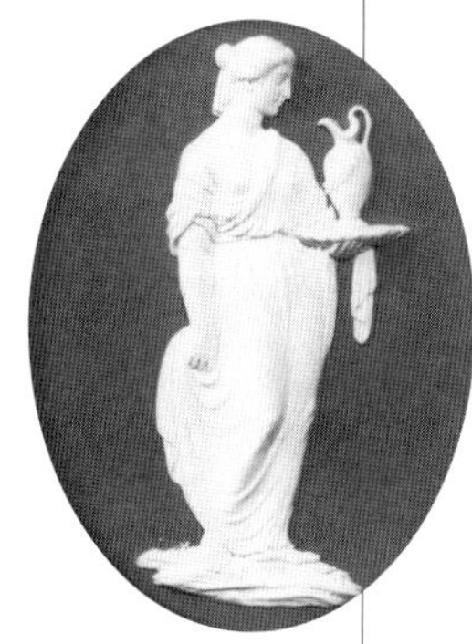

842. Medallion: *A Priestess*, ca. 1775-80
Jasper, solid blue ground with dark blue wash on front and white relief
6 13/16 x 5 1/8 in (17.3 x 13 cm)
Mark: "WEDGWOOD & BENTLEY"
Provenance: Ann Brodkiewicz, Chicago
1976.194
Back has nine firing holes.

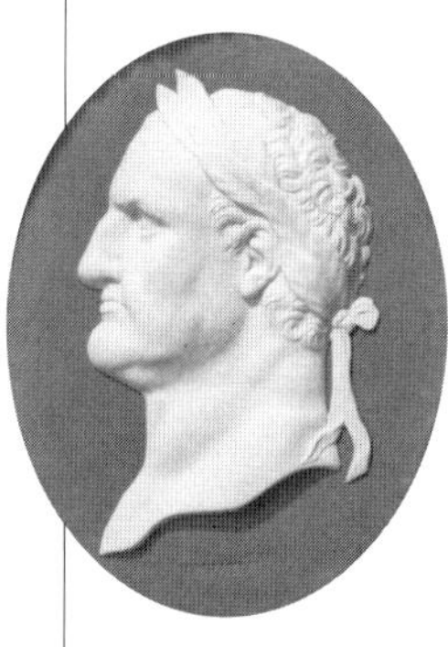

843. Portrait Medallion: *Vespasian*, ca. 1775-80
Jasper, solid blue ground with dark blue wash and white relief
5 3/8 x 4 7/16 in (13.6 x 11.2 cm)
Mark: "WEDGWOOD & BENTLEY"; "VESPATIAN" on front
Provenance: Ann Brodkiewicz, Chicago
1985.440
Back has 12 firing holes.

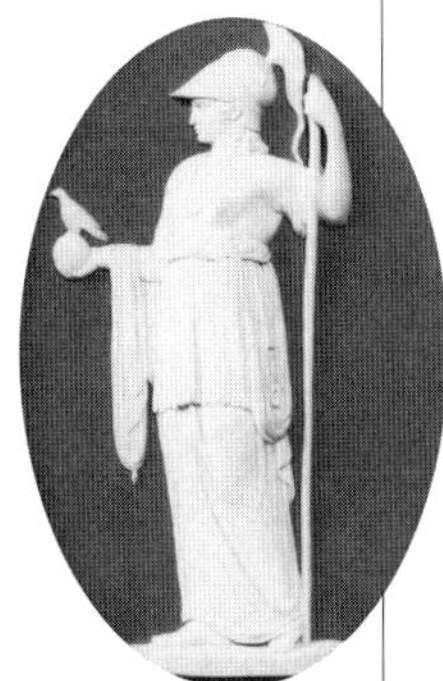

844. Medallion: *Minerva*, ca. 1775-80
Jasper, solid blue ground with dark blue wash on front and white relief
6 1/2 x 4 1/8 in (16.5 x 10.4 cm)
Mark: "WEDGWOOD & BENTLEY"
Provenance: M. Mellanay Delhom, Chicago; Ann Brodkiewicz, Chicago
1976.213
Back has eight firing holes.

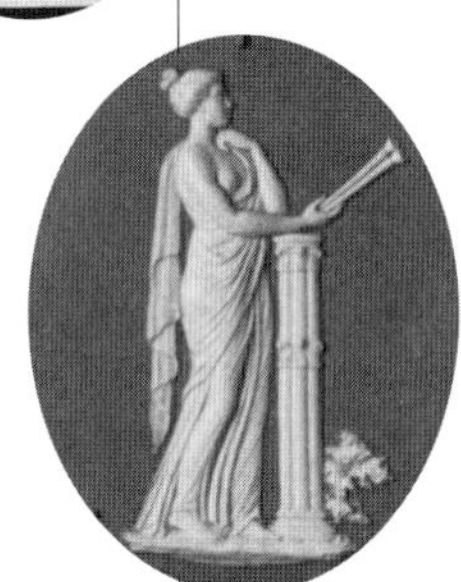

845. Medallion: *Euterpe*, ca. 1780
Jasper, solid blue ground with blue wash on front and white relief
3 1/4 x 2 5/8 in (8.2 x 6.6 cm)
Mark: "WEDGWOOD & BENTLEY"
Provenance: M. Mellanay Delhom, Chicago; Ann Brodkiewicz, Chicago
1982.48

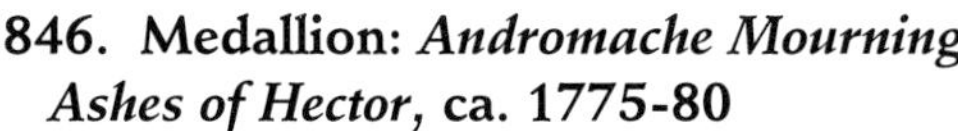

846. Medallion: *Andromache Mourning Ashes of Hector*, ca. 1775-80
Jasper, solid blue ground with white relief
3 1/16 x 2 9/16 in (7.7 x 6.5 cm)
Mark: "WEDGWOOD & BENTLEY"
Provenance: Christie's, London, June 14, 1965
1976.191

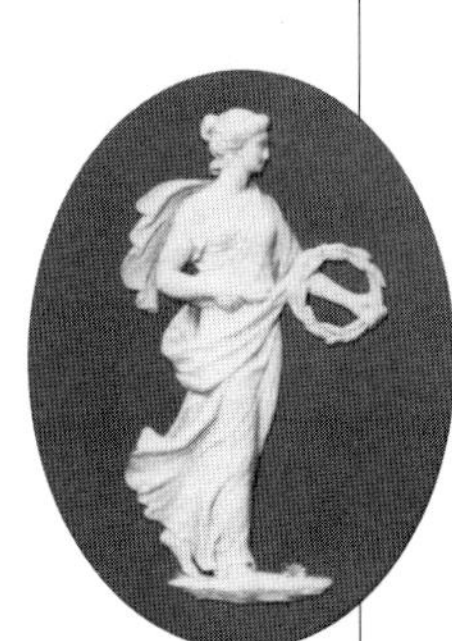

847. Medallion: *Ceres*, ca. 1775-80
Jasper, solid blue ground with dark blue wash on edge and front and white relief, lapidary-polishing
3 13/16 x 3 in (9.6 x 7.6 cm)
Mark: "WEDGWOOD & BENTLEY"
Provenance: M. Mellanay Delhom, Chicago; Ann Brodkiewicz, Chicago
1985.430
Back has four firing holes.

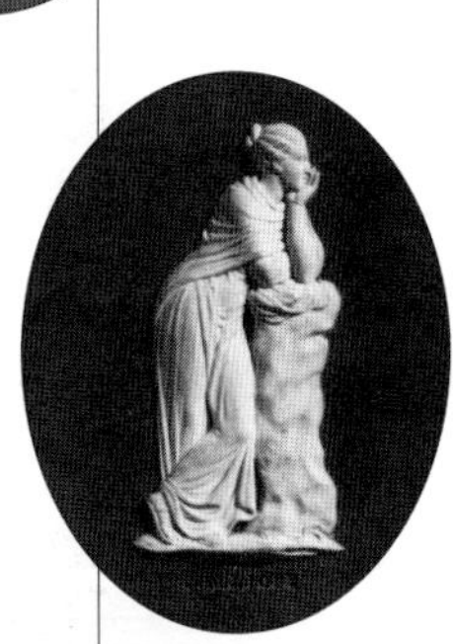

848. Medallion: *Calliope*, ca. 1775-80
Jasper, solid blue ground with dark blue wash on front and white relief
3 5/16 x 2 3/4 in (8.3 x 6.9 cm)
Mark: "Wedgwood & Bentley"; "CALLIOPE" on front
Provenance: Fred J. Tongue, Santa Monica, Calif.
1976.188
Back has five firing holes.

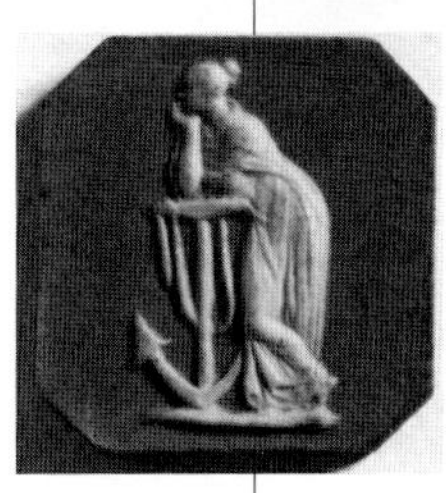

849. Medallion and Intaglio: *Hope* and *Three Classical Figures*, ca. 1790
Jasper, solid blue ground with white relief
3/4 x 3/4 in (1.9 x 1.9 cm)
Mark: none
Provenance: Dr. Harold L. Klawans, Chicago
1977.67.12

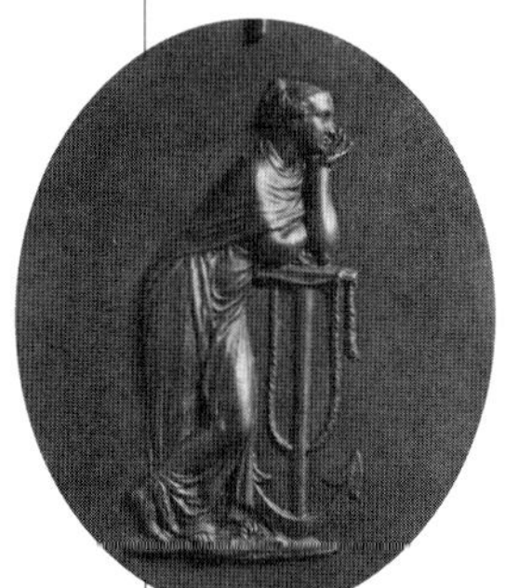

850. Medallion: *Hope,* ca. 1775-80
Basalt
2 15/16 x 2 7/16 in (7.3 x 6.1 cm)
Mark: "Wedgwood & Bentley"
Provenance: Ann Brodkiewicz, Chicago
1976.189
Design source: Montfaucon, *L' Antiquité expliquée,* vol. 1, pl. 30, fig. 1

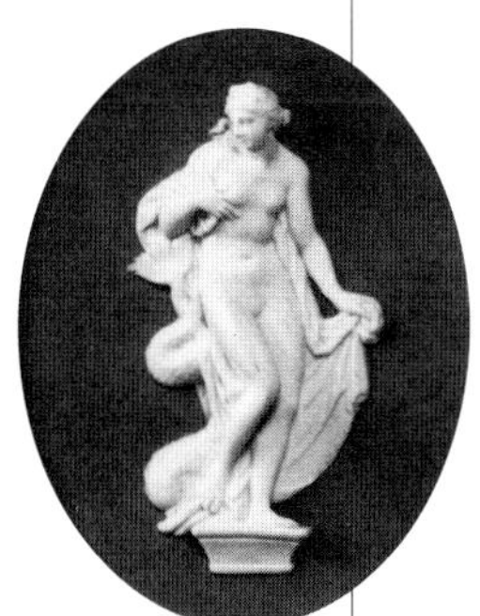

851. Medallion: *Venus Anadyomene* or *Venus of the Sea,* ca. 1785
Jasper, solid white ground with blue wash on front and white relief
3 3/8 x 2 5/8 in (8.5 x 6.6 cm)
Mark: "WEDGWOOD"
Provenance: Seal Simons, Philadelphia, Pa.
1976.208
Back has four firing holes.

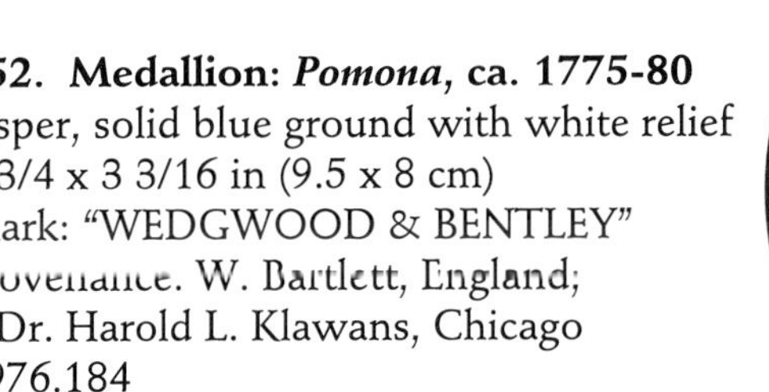

852. Medallion: *Pomona,* ca. 1775-80
Jasper, solid blue ground with white relief
3 3/4 x 3 3/16 in (9.5 x 8 cm)
Mark: "WEDGWOOD & BENTLEY"
Provenance: W. Bartlett, England;
Dr. Harold L. Klawans, Chicago
1976.184

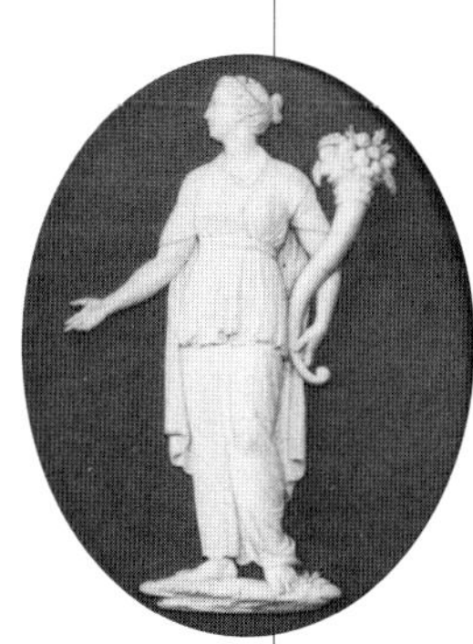
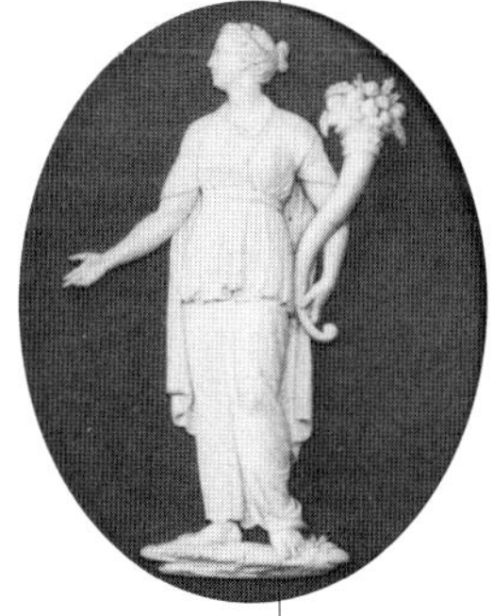

853. Medallion: *Abundantia,* ca. 1775-80
Jasper, solid blue ground with blue wash on front and white relief
3 1/4 x 2 9/16 in (8.2 x 6.5 cm)
Mark: "WEDGWOOD & BENTLEY"
Provenance: Fred J. Tongue, Santa Monica, Calif.
1976.186
Design source: Montfaucon, *L' Antiquité expliquée,* vol. 3, pl. 36, fig. 7

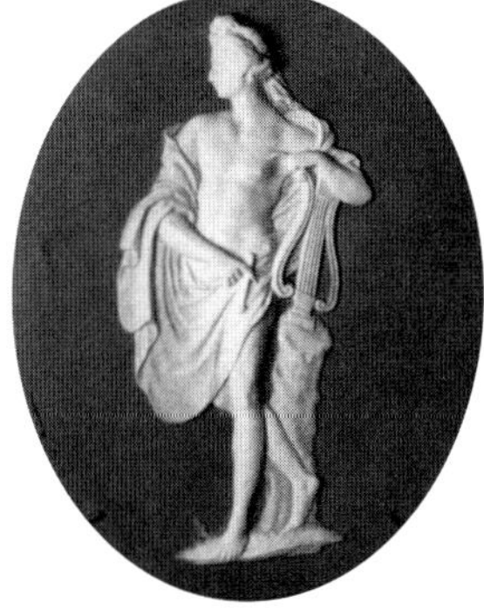

854. Medallion: *Apollo,* ca. 1780
Jasper, solid blue ground with blue wash on front and white relief
4 x 3 1/4 in (10.1 x 8.2 cm)
Mark: "WEDGWOOD & BENTLEY"
Provenance: M. Mellanay Delhom, Chicago;
Ann Brodkiewicz, Chicago
1982.51

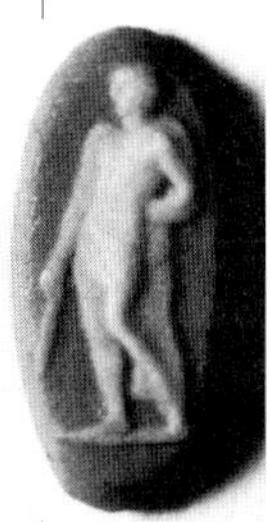

855. Medallion for Ring Setting: *Male Classical Figure,* 19th century
Jasper, solid blue ground with white relief
9/16 x 1/4 in (1.4 x .6 cm)
Mark: "WEDGWOOD"
Provenance: New Orleans
1980.172

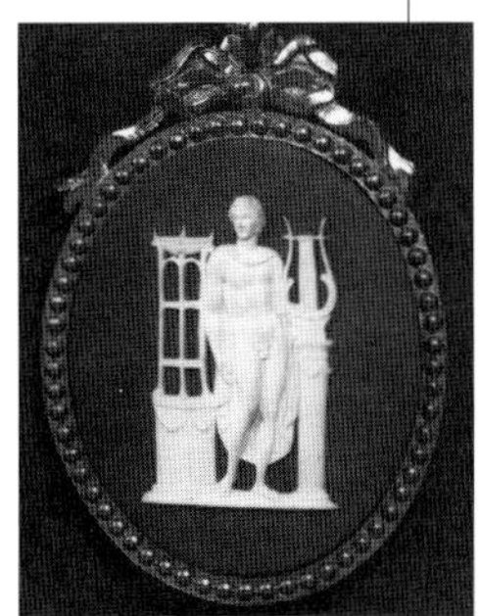

856. Medallion: *Apollo Musagettes*, ca. 1775-80
Jasper, solid white ground with dark blue wash on front and white relief, ormolu frame
2 1/16 x 1 11/16 in (5.2 x 4.2 cm)
Mark: "Wedgwood & Bentley"
Provenance: W. Bartlett, England; Dr. Harold L. Klawans, Chicago
1977.83
Design source: James Spence, *Polymetis* . . ., frontispiece
Color plate 78

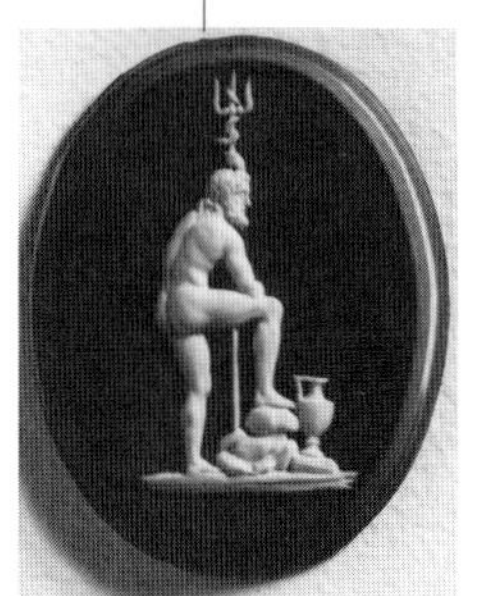

857. Medallion: *Neptune*, ca. 1780
Jasper, marbled blue-and-white ground with dark blue wash on front and white relief
1 1/2 x 1 1/4 in (3.8 x 3.1 cm)
Mark: "Wedgwood & Bentley"
Provenance: Sir George Duff-Dunbar, Scotland; M. Mellanay Delhom, Chicago
1982.54
Color plate 66

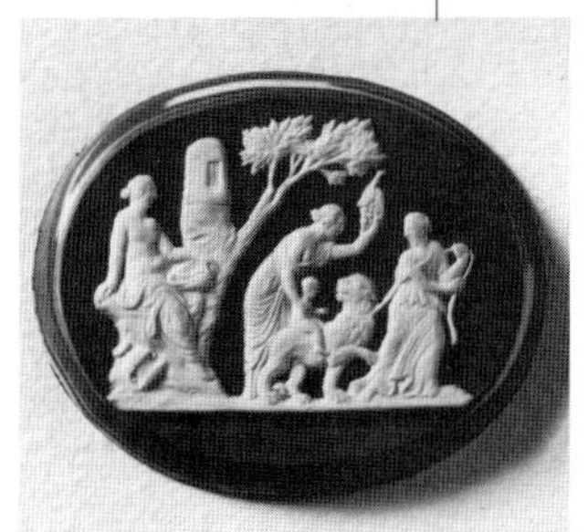

858. Medallion: *The Education of Bacchus*, ca. 1780
Jasper, marbled blue-and-white ground with dark wash on front and white relief
1 3/8 x 1 3/4 in (3.4 x 4.4 cm)
Mark: "Wedgwood & Bentley"
Provenance: Sir George Duff-Dunbar, Scotland; M. Mellanay Delhom, Chicago
1982.58
Color plate 66

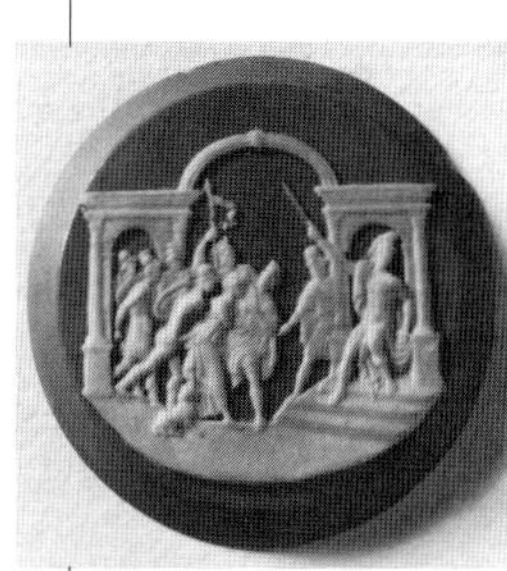

859. Medallion: *Roman Soldiers*, ca. 1790
Jasper, solid blue ground with white relief, lapidary-polishing
1 9/16 in (3.9 cm)
Mark: none
Provenance: D. M. and P. Manheim, New York
1977.130.8

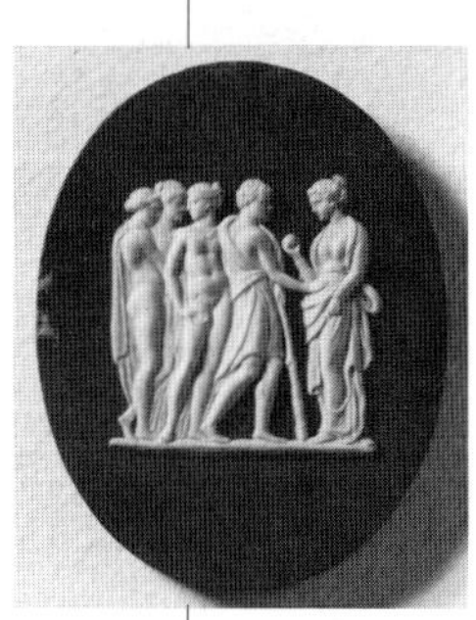

860. Medallion: *Hercules and the Golden Apples*, ca. 1780
Jasper, marbled blue-and-white ground with dark wash on front and white relief
1 11/16 x 1 3/8 in (4.2 x 3.4 cm)
Mark: "Wedgwood & Bentley"
Provenance: Sir George Duff-Dunbar, Scotland; M. Mellanay Delhom, Chicago
1982.55

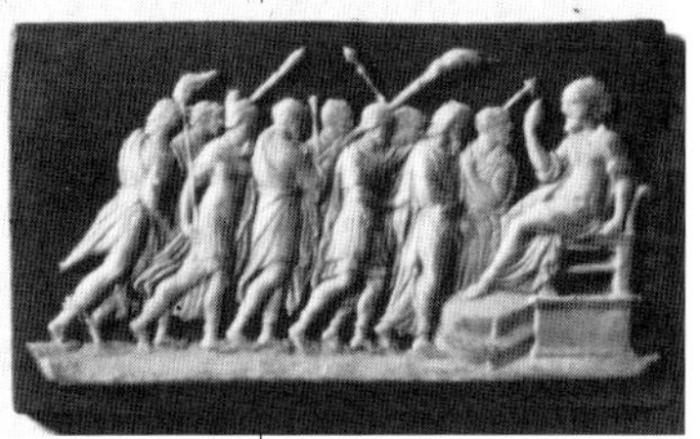

861. Medallion: *Classical Figures*, ca. 1800
Jasper, solid blue ground with white relief
15/16 x 1 5/8 in (2.3 x 4.1 cm)
Mark: none
Provenance: D. M. and P. Manheim, New York
1977.130.5

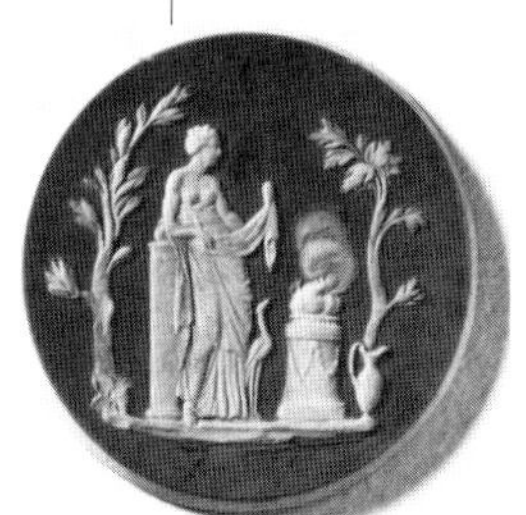

862. Medallion: *A Sacrifice*, ca. 1800
Jasper, solid white ground with blue wash on front and back with white relief
1 1/2 in (3.8 cm)
Mark: none
Provenance: Dr. Harold L. Klawans, Chicago
1977.67.11

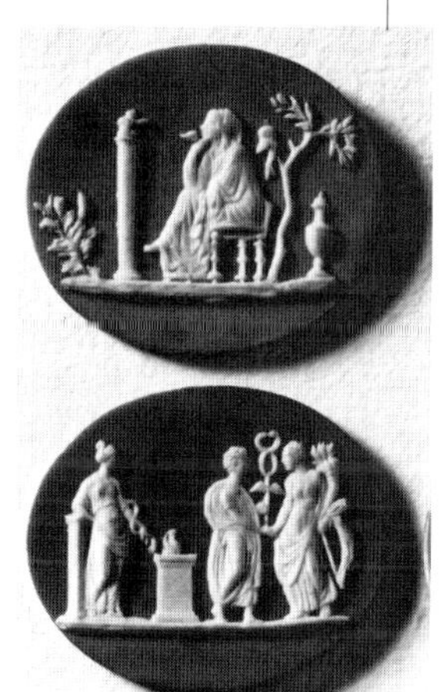

863. Medallion: *A Roman Woman*, ca. 1800
Jasper, solid white ground with green wash on front and white relief
1 x 1 1/4 in (2.5 x 3.1 cm)
Mark: none
Provenance: D. M. and P. Manheim, New York
1977.130.7

864. Medallion: *Classical Figures*, ca. 1800
Jasper, solid white ground with green wash front and back with white relief
1 x 1 1/4 in (2.5 x 3.1 cm)
Mark: none
Provenance: D. M. and P. Manheim, New York
1977.130.9

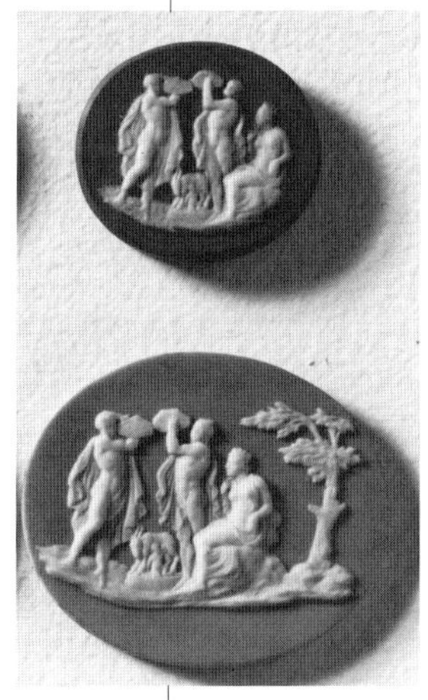

865. Medallion and Intaglio: *The Corybantes Striking Their Bucklers to Prevent the Cries of the Infant Jupiter from Being Heard by Saturn*, ca. 1780
Jasper, solid blue ground with white relief, lapidary-polishing on edges and intaglio
7/8 x 3/4 in (2.2 x 1.9 cm)
Mark: none
Provenance: Dr. Francis Jennings Vurpillat, South Bend, Ind.
1977.122.13

866. Medallion: *The Corybantes Striking Their Bucklers to Prevent the Cries of the Infant Jupiter from Being Heard by Saturn*, ca. 1790
Jasper, solid white ground with green wash on front and back with white relief
1 1/16 x 1 1/4 in (2.7 x 3.1 cm)
Mark: none
Provenance: D. M. and P. Manheim, New York
1977.130.13

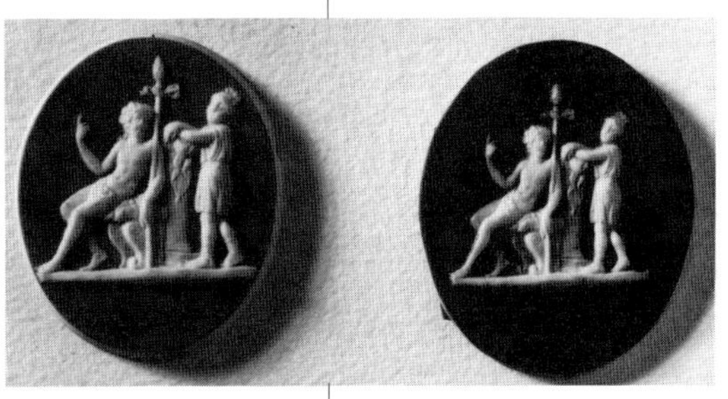

867. Medallion: *Classical Figures*, ca. 1780
Jasper, solid white ground with white relief and lapidary-polished edges
1 1/4 x 1 in (3.1 x 2.5 cm)
Mark: "NNo. green" in script
Provenance: Dr. Francis Jennings Vurpillat, South Bend, Ind.
1977.122.73

868. Medallion: *Classical Figures*, ca. 1800
Jasper, solid white ground with dark blue wash on front and back with white relief
1 1/4 x 1 in (3.1 x 2.5 cm)
Mark: "WEDGWOOD"
Provenance: D. M. and P. Manheim, New York
1977.130.16

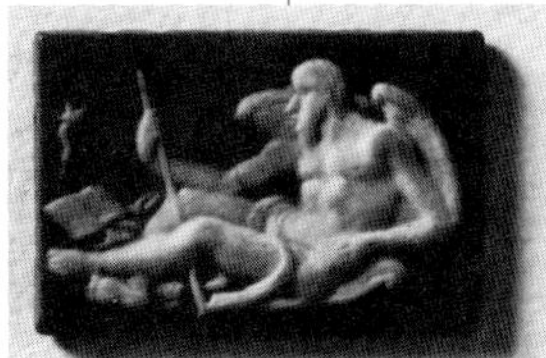

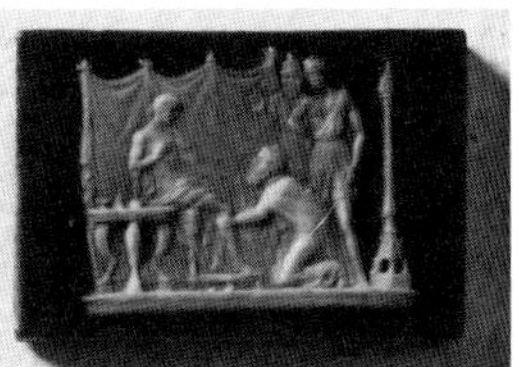

869. Medallion: *Saturn*, ca. 1790
Jasper, solid blue ground with dark blue wash on front and white relief
5/8 x 15/16 in (1.5 x 2.3 cm)
Mark: none
Provenance: D. M. and P. Manheim, New York
1977.130.12

870. Medallion: *Achilles in His Tent*, ca. 1800
Jasper, solid white ground with dark blue wash on front and light blue wash on back with white relief
5/8 x 15/16 in (1.5 x 3.4 cm)
Mark: none
Provenance: D. M. and P. Manheim, New York
1977.130.14

871. Medallion: *Classical Figures*, ca. 1800
Jasper, solid blue ground with white relief
1/2 x 11/16 in (1.2 x 1.7 cm)
Mark: none
Provenance: D. M. and P. Manheim, New York
1977.130.2

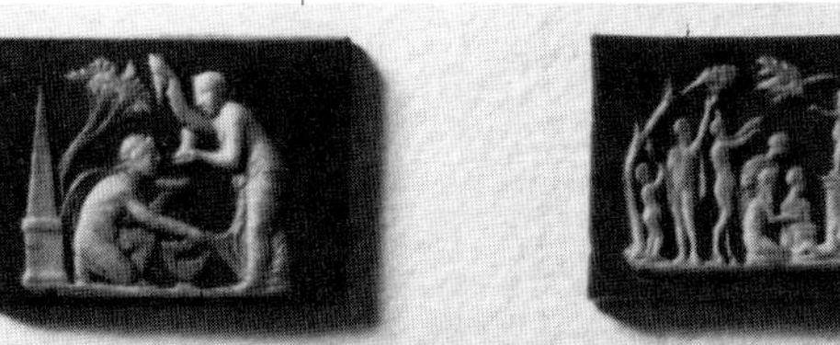

872. Medallion: *Classical Figures*, ca. 1800
Jasper, solid white ground with blue wash front and back with white relief
1/2 x 11/16 in (1.2 x 1.7 cm)
Mark: none
Provenance: D. M. and P. Manheim, New York
1977.130.3

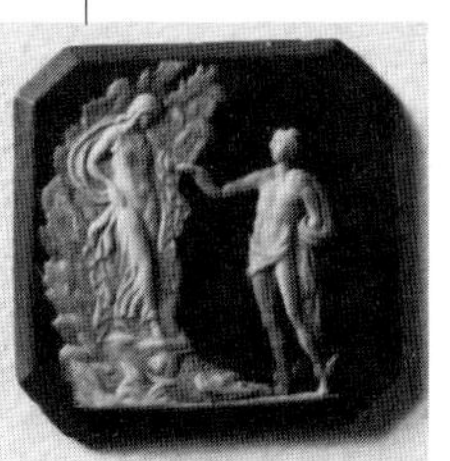

873. Medallion: *Perseus and Andromeda*, ca. 1780
Jasper, solid blue ground with dark blue wash on front and white relief, lapidary-polished edges
15/16 x 15/16 in (2.3 x 2.3 cm)
Mark: "WEDGWOOD"
Provenance: Dr. Francis Jennings Vurpillat, South Bend, Ind.
1977.122.85

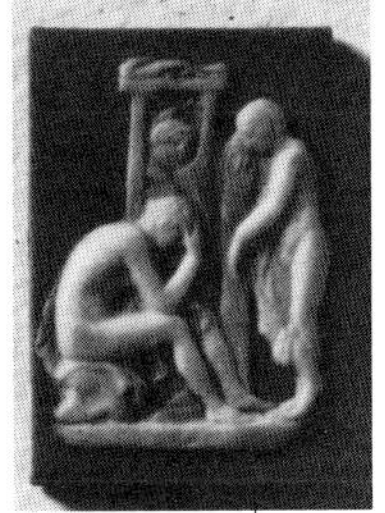

874. Medallion: *Soldier Bringing the News of the Death of Patroclus to Achilles,* ca. 1780
Jasper, solid blue ground with white relief
7/8 x 5/8 in (2.2 x 1.5 cm)
Mark: none
Provenance: Dr. Francis Jennings Vurpillat, South Bend, Ind.
1977.122.86

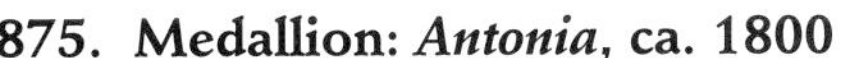

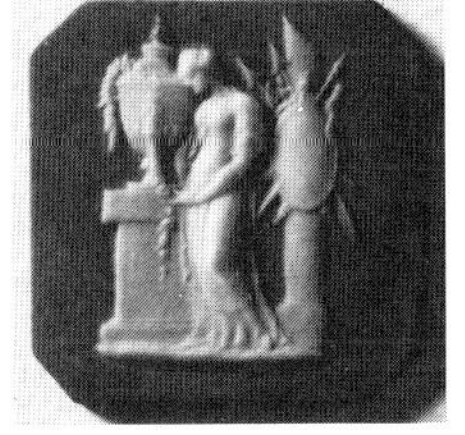

875. Medallion: *Antonia,* ca. 1800
Jasper, solid blue ground with white relief
15/16 x 15/16 in (2.3 x 2.3 cm)
Mark: none
Provenance: Dr. Harold L. Klawans, Chicago
1977.67.3

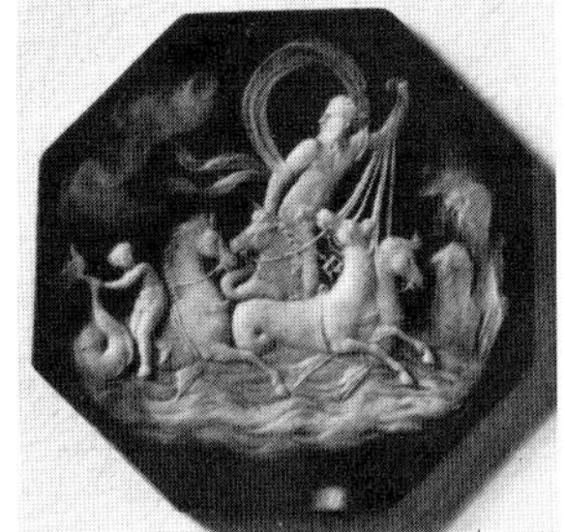

876. Medallion: *Neptune Riding the Sea,* ca. 1800
Jasper, solid white ground with dark blue wash on front and back with white relief
1 7/16 x 1 3/8 in (3.6 x 3.4 cm)
Mark: "WEDGWOOD"
Provenance: Dr. Harold L. Klawans, Chicago
1977.67.7

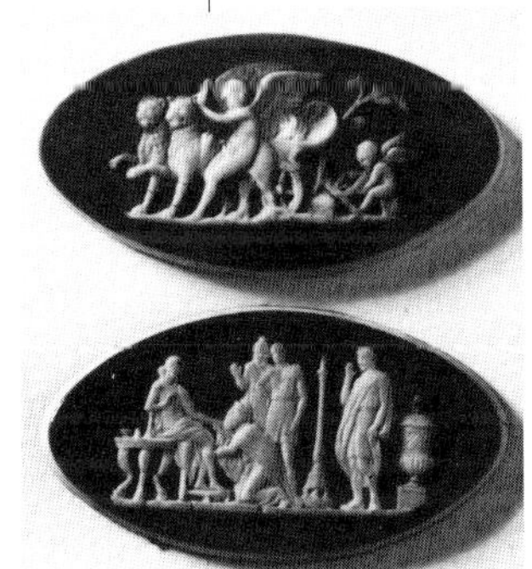

877. Medallion: *Cupids and Lions,* ca. 1800
Jasper, solid white ground with dark blue wash on front and white relief, lapidary-polishing
5/8 x 1 3/8 in (1.5 x 3.4 cm)
Mark: "WEDGWOOD"
Provenance: D. M. and P. Manheim, New York
1977.130.6

878. Medallion: *Classical Figures,* ca. 1800
Jasper, solid white ground with dark blue wash front and back with white relief, lapidary-polishing
3/4 x 1 3/8 in (1.9 x 3.4 cm)
Mark: "WEDGWOOD"
Provenance: D. M. and P. Manheim, New York
1977.130.4

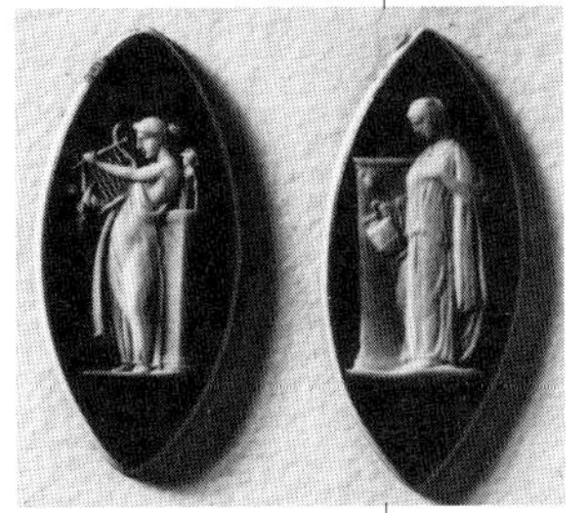

879. Pair of Medallions: *Classical Figures,* ca. 1790
Jasper, solid white ground with dark blue wash on front and back and white relief, lapidary-polished edges
1 3/16 x 1/2 in (3 x 1.2 cm)
Mark: "WEDGWOOD"
Provenance: Dr. Francis Jennings Vurpillat, South Bend, Ind.
1977.122.78-.79

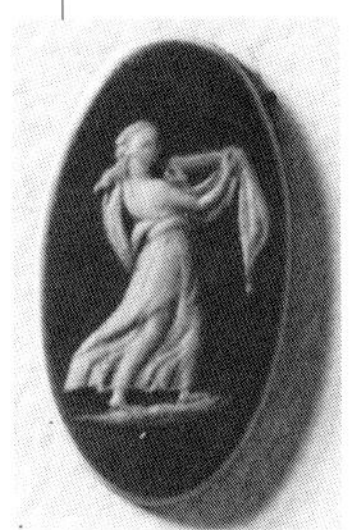

880. Medallion: *Classical Figure,* ca. 1780
Jasper, solid white ground with dark blue wash on front and back and white relief; lapidary-polished edges
7/8 x 7/16 in (2.2 x 1.1 cm)
Mark: "WEDGWOOD"
Provenance: Dr. Francis Jennings Vurpillat, South Bend, Ind.
1977.122.94

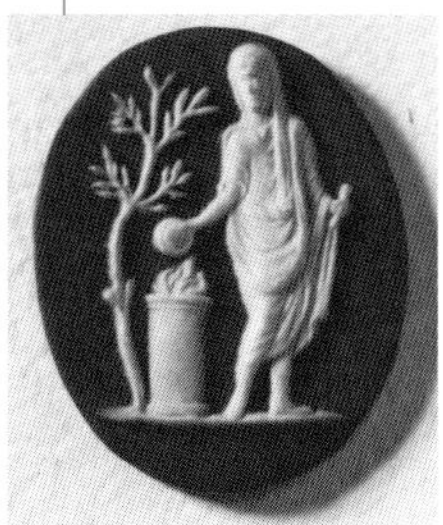

881. Medallion: *A Sacrifice,* ca. 1800
Jasper, solid white ground with dark blue wash on front and back with white relief
1 x 13/16 in (2.5 x 2 cm)
Mark: none
Provenance: D. M. and P. Manheim, New York
1977.130.17

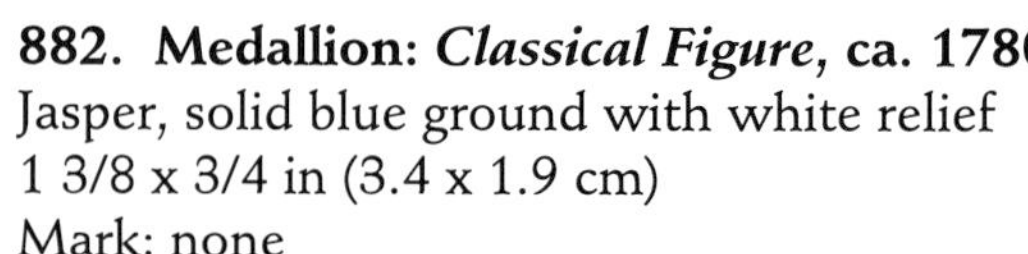

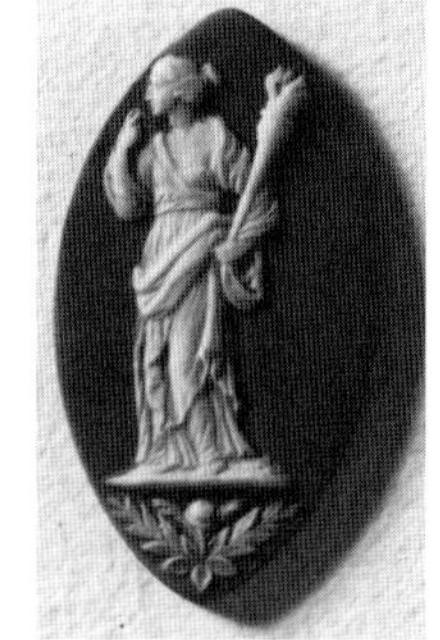

882. Medallion: *Classical Figure,* ca. 1780
Jasper, solid blue ground with white relief
1 3/8 x 3/4 in (3.4 x 1.9 cm)
Mark: none
Provenance: Dr. Francis Jennings Vurpillat, South Bend, Ind.
1977.122.87

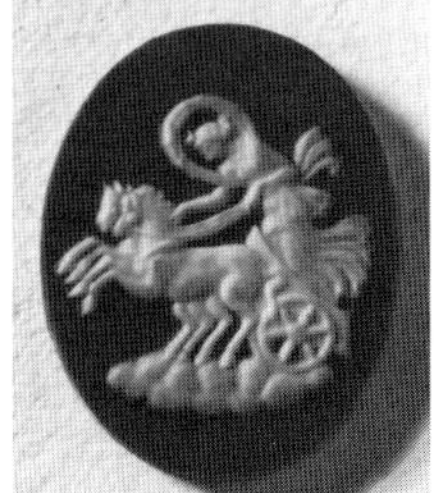

883. Medallion: *Aurora in Her Chariot,* ca. 1800
Jasper, solid white ground with dark blue wash on front and light blue wash on back with white relief
1 x 3/4 in (2.5 x 1.9 cm)
Mark: none
Provenance: D. M. and P. Manheim, New York
1977.130.15
Design source: Montfaucon, *L' Antiquité expliquée,* vol. 3, pt. 1, pl. 34

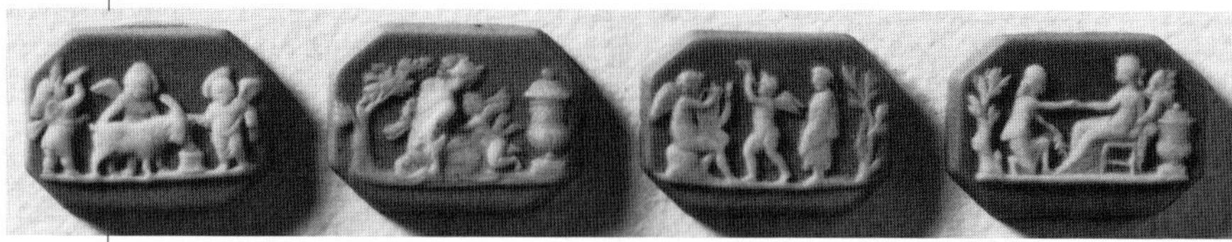

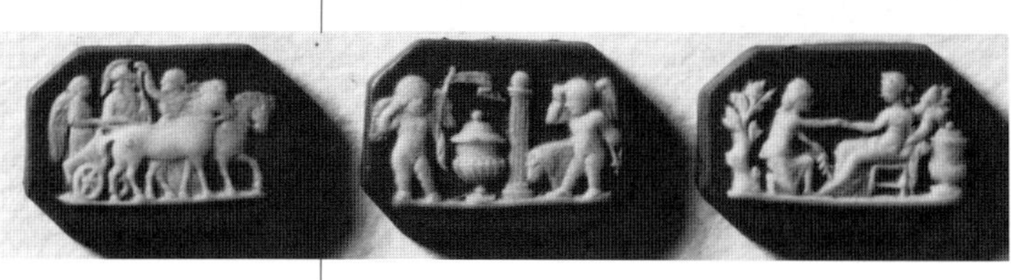

884. Seven Medallions: *Classical Figures and Cupids,* ca. 1780
Jasper, solid blue or green ground with white relief
1/2 x 11/16 in (1.2 x 1.7 cm)
Mark: "WEDGWOOD"; "&" on two only
Provenance: Dr. Francis Jennings Vurpillat, South Bend, Ind.
1977.122.66-.72

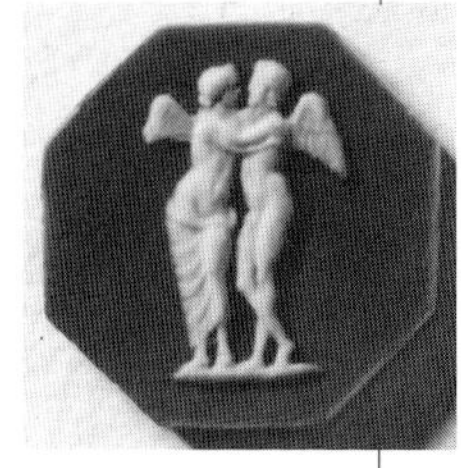

885. Double Medallion: *Classical Figures,* ca. 1780
Jasper, solid white ground with blue wash on front and back and white relief
5/8 x 5/8 in (1.5 x 1.5 cm)
Mark: none
Provenance: Dr. Francis Jennings Vurpillat, South Bend, Ind.
1977.122.93

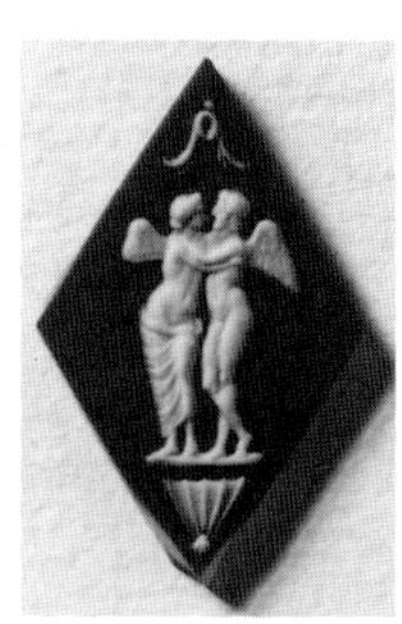

886. Medallion: *Classical Figures,* ca. 1780
Jasper, solid white ground with dark blue wash on front and light blue wash on back and white relief
1 x 5/8 in (2.5 x 1.5 cm)
Mark: none
Provenance: Dr. Francis Jennings Vurpillat, South Bend, Ind.
1977.122.88

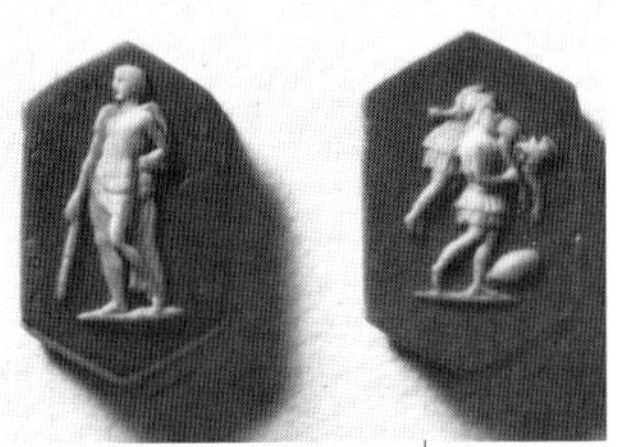

887. Pair of Double-Sided Medallions: *Classical Figures*, ca. 1800
Jasper, solid white ground with blue wash on front and back and white relief
9/16 x 3/8 in (1.4 x .9 cm)
Mark: none
Provenance: Dr. Francis Jennings Vurpillat, South Bend, Ind.
1977.122.82-.83

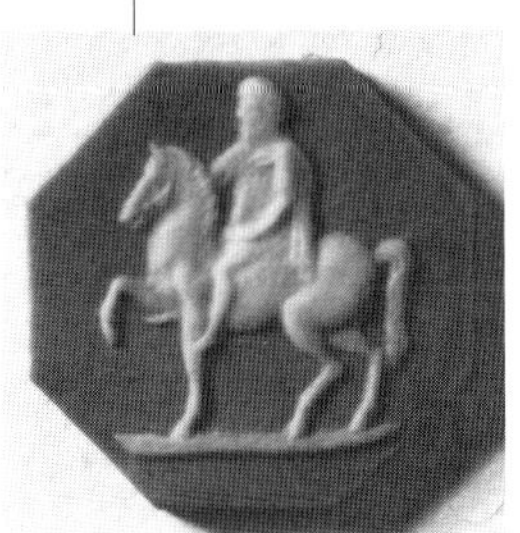

888. Medallion: *Classical Figure*, ca. 1780
Jasper, solid blue ground with white relief
9/16 x 9/16 in (1.4 x 1.4 cm)
Mark: none
Provenance: Dr. Francis Jennings Vurpillat, South Bend, Ind.
1977.122.95

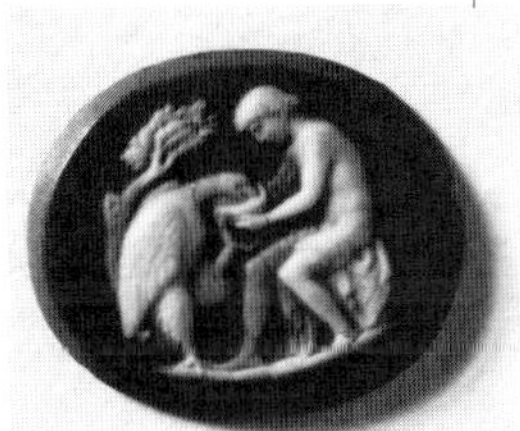

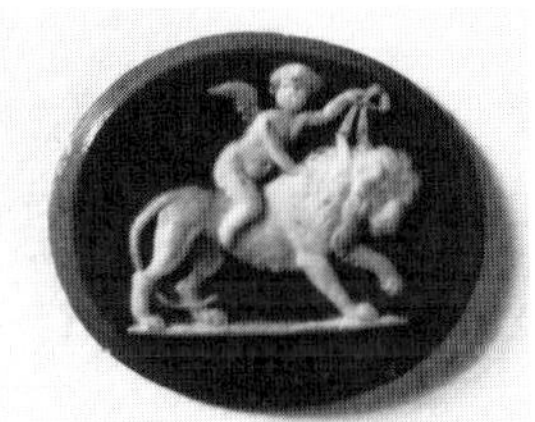

889. Medallion: *Ganymedes*, ca. 1790
Jasper, solid blue ground with dark blue wash on front and white relief, lapidary-polishing
5/8 x 3/4 in (1.5 x 1.9 cm)
Mark: none
Provenance: D. M. and P. Manheim, New York
1977.130.10
Design source: Montfaucon, *L' Antiquité expliquée,* vol. 1, pt. 1, pl. 11, fig. 13

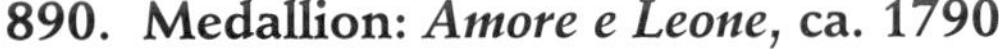

890. Medallion: *Amore e Leone*, ca. 1790
Jasper, solid blue ground with dark blue wash on front and white relief, lapidary-polishing
5/8 x 3/4 in (1.5 x 1.9 cm)
Mark: none
Provenance: D. M. and P. Manheim, New York
1977.130.11
Design source: Montfaucon, *L' Antiquitee expliquée,* vol. 1, pt. 1, pl. 58, fig. 6

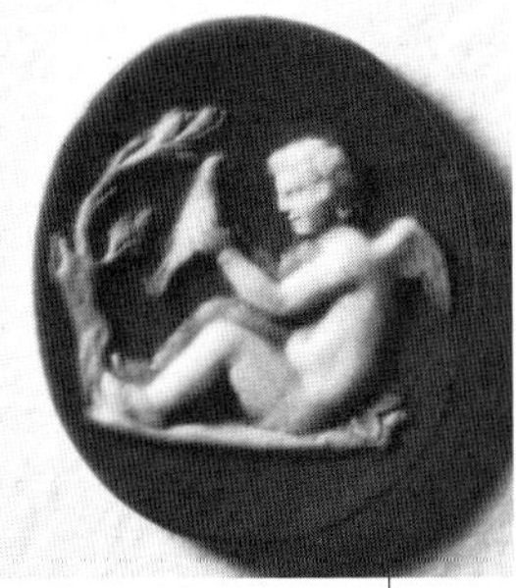

891. Medallion: *Cupid*, ca. 1780
Jasper, solid white ground with blue wash on front and white relief
3/4 x 5/8 in (1.9 x 1.5 cm)
Mark: none
Provenance: Dr. Francis Jennings Vurpillat, South Bend, Ind.
1977.122.92

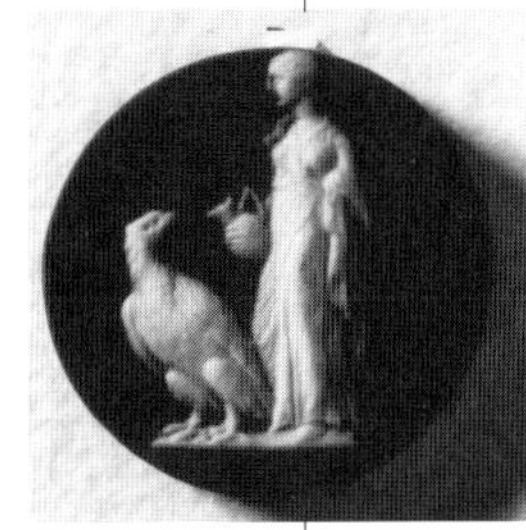

892. Double Medallion: *Classical Figures*, ca. 1780
Jasper, solid white ground with blue wash on front and back and white relief
5/8 in (1.5 cm)
Mark: none
Provenance: Dr. Francis Jennings Vurpillat, South Bend, Ind.
1977.122.96

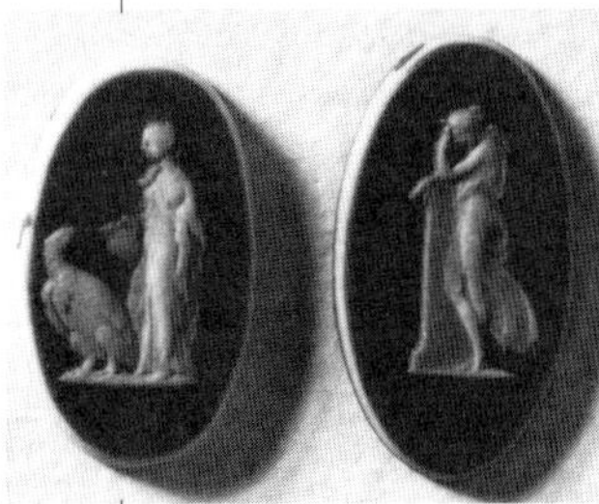

893. Medallion: ***Classical Figure,*** **ca. 1780**
Jasper, solid white ground with blue wash on front and white relief
5/8 x 3/8 in (1.5 x .9 cm)
Mark: "WEDGWOOD"
Provenance: Dr. Francis Jennings Vurpillat, South Bend, Ind.
1977.122.100

894. Medallion: ***Classical Figure,*** **ca. 1780**
Jasper, solid white ground with dark blue wash on front and back and white relief
11/16 x 3/8 in (1.7 x .9 cm)
Mark: "WEDGWOOD"
Provenance: Dr. Francis Jennings Vurpillat, South Bend, Ind.
1977.122.101

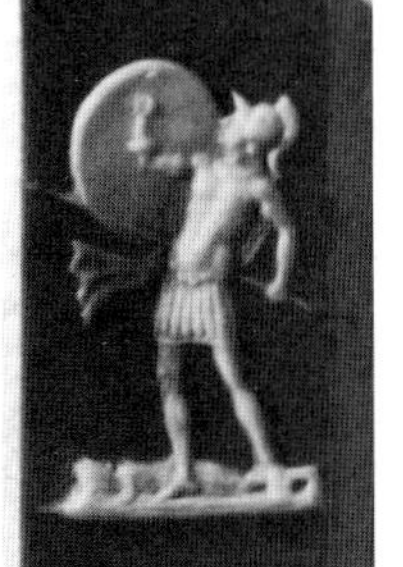

895. Medallion: ***Classical Figure,*** **ca. 1780**
Jasper, solid white ground with dark blue wash on front and light blue wash on back and white relief
15/16 x 1/2 in (2.3 x 1.2 cm)
Mark: none
Provenance: Dr. Francis Jennings Vurpillat, South Bend, Ind.
1977.122.89

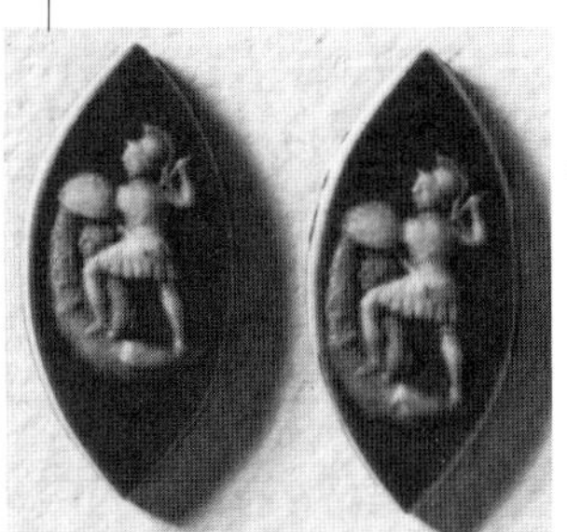

896. Pair of Medallions: ***Classical Figures,*** **ca. 1790**
Jasper, solid white ground with dark blue wash on front and back and white relief, lapidary-polished edges
3/4 x 3/8 in (1.9 x .9 cm)
Mark: "WEDGWOOD"
Provenance: Dr. Francis Jennings Vurpillat, South Bend, Ind.
1977.122.76-.77

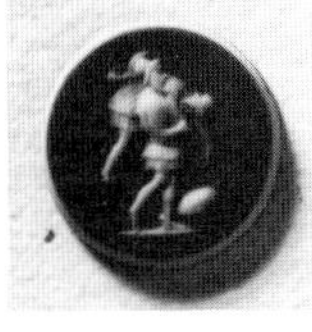
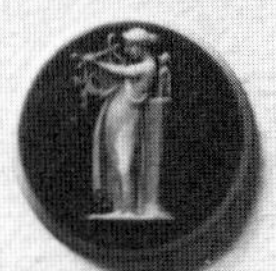
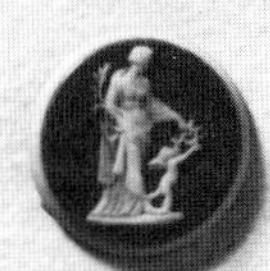
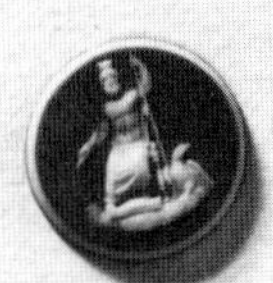
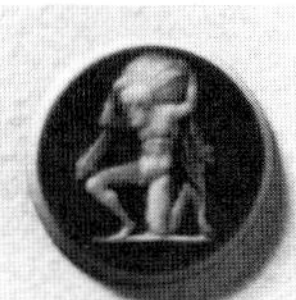

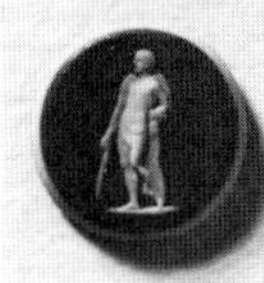
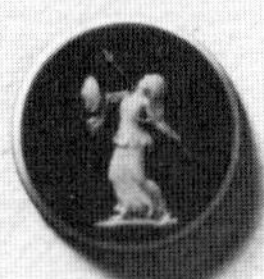
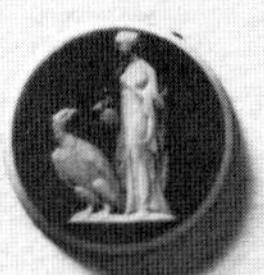
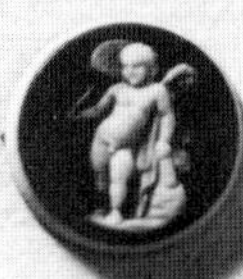

897. Nine Medallions: ***Classical Figures and Cupids,*** **ca. 1800**
Jasper, solid white ground with dark blue wash front and back and white relief and lapidary- polished edges
9/16 in (1.4 cm)
Mark: "WEDGWOOD" on one only
Provenance: Dr. Francis Jennings Vurpillat, South Bend, Ind.
1977.122.57-.65

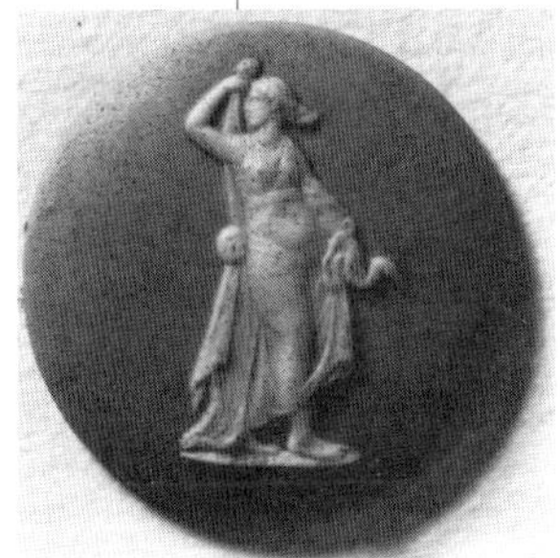

898. Medallion: *Priestess with Serpent,* 19th century
Jasper, solid blue ground with white relief
1 1/8 in (2.8 cm)
Mark: "WEDGWOOD"; "25" incised
Provenance: Dr. Harold L. Klawans, Chicago
1976.352

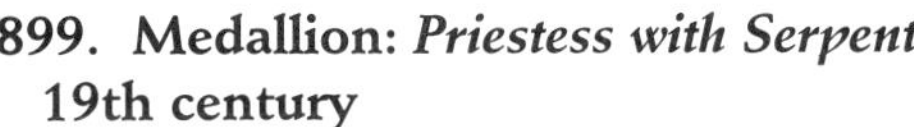

899. Medallion: *Priestess with Serpent,* 19th century
Jasper, solid gray-blue ground with white relief
7/8 x 7/16 in (2.2 x 1.1 cm)
Mark: none
Provenance: Dr. Francis Jennings Vurpillat, South Bend, Ind.
1977.122.42

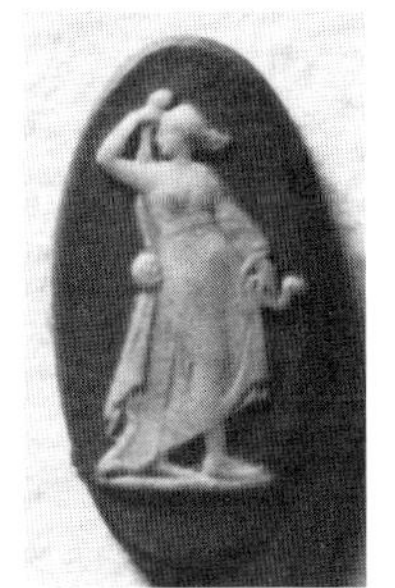

900. Six Medallions: *Classical Figures and Cupids,* ca. 1800
Jasper, solid blue ground with white relief
5/8 in (1.5 cm)
Mark: none
Provenance: Dr. Francis Jennings Vurpillat, South Bend, Ind.
1977.122.51-.56

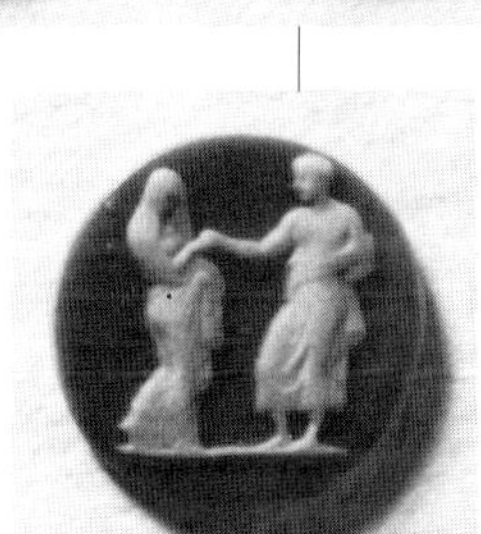

901. Medallion: *Classical Figures,* ca. 1780
Jasper, solid white ground with blue wash on front and white relief
1/2 in (1.2 cm)
Mark: none
Provenance: Dr. Francis Jennings Vurpillat, South Bend, Ind.
1977.122.97

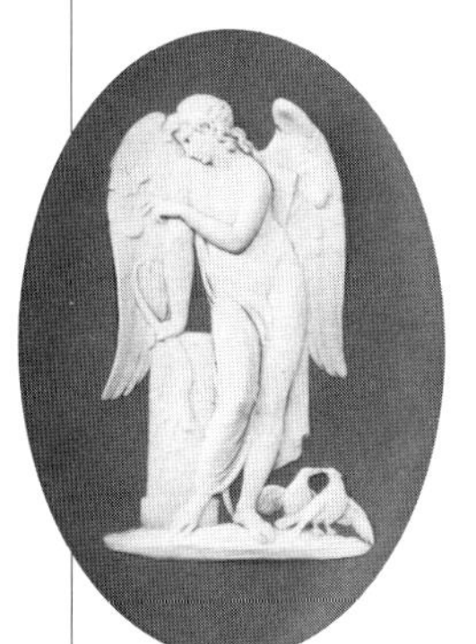

902. Medallion: *Boy Leaning on His Quiver with Doves,* ca. 1800
Jasper, solid blue ground with white relief
6 1/4 x 4 3/8 in (15.8 x 11.1 cm)
Mark: "WEDGWOOD"
Provenance: Dr. Francis Jennings Vurpillat, South Bend, Ind.
1976.175

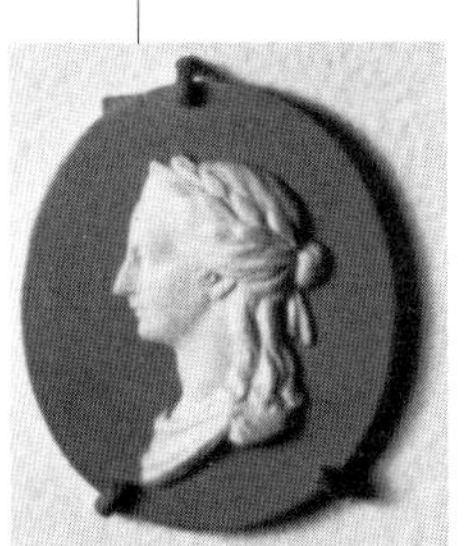

903. Medallion: *Classical Female Head,* ca. 1790
Jasper, solid white ground with lilac wash on front and white relief
1 3/8 x 1 1/8 in (3.4 x 2.8 cm)
Mark: "Wedgwood"
Provenance: M. Mellanay Delhom, Chicago; Ann Brodkiewicz, Chicago
1982.44

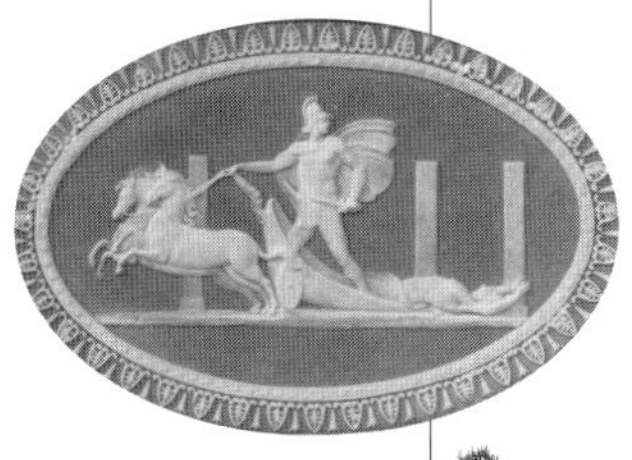

904. Medallion: *Achilles Dragging Hector around the Walls of Troy*, 19th century
Jasper, solid white ground with lilac-and-green wash on front and white relief
3 x 3 3/4 in (9.5 x 7.6 cm)
Mark: "WEDGWOOD" impressed
Provenance: Ann Brodkiewicz, Chicago
1978.124

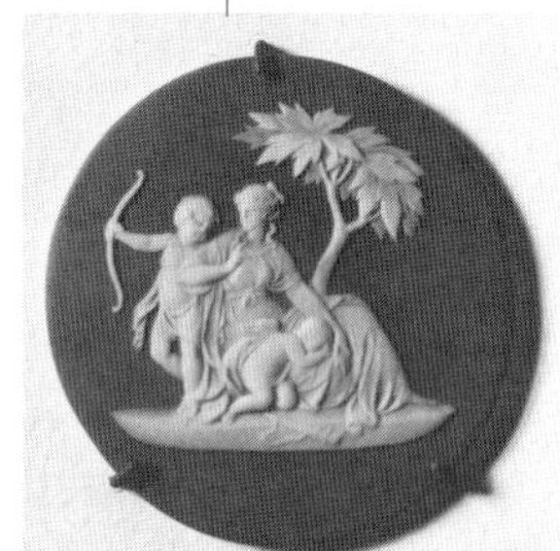

905. Medallion: *Psyche Bound to a Tree*, 19th century
Jasper, solid white ground with lilac wash on front and white relief
2 1/2 in (6.3 cm)
Mark: "WEDGWOOD"; "46" incised
Provenance: Dr. Francis Jennings Vurpillat, South Bend, Ind.
1977.122.29

906. Medallion: *Dancing Hour Figure*, 19th century
Jasper, solid blue ground with white relief
5 3/4 x 3 7/8 in (14.6 x 9.8 cm)
Mark: "WEDGWOOD"
Provenance: New Orleans
1976.177

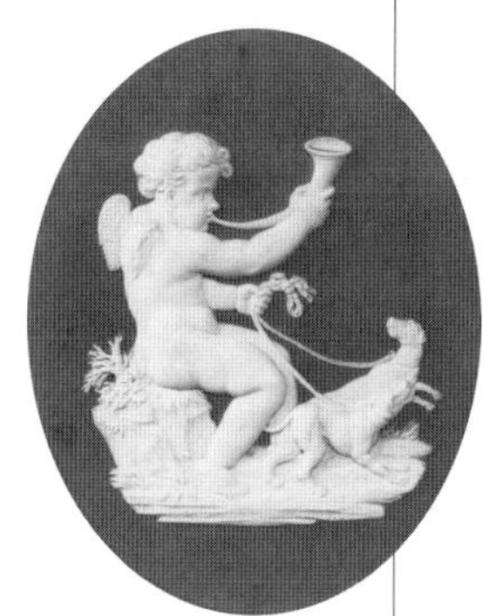

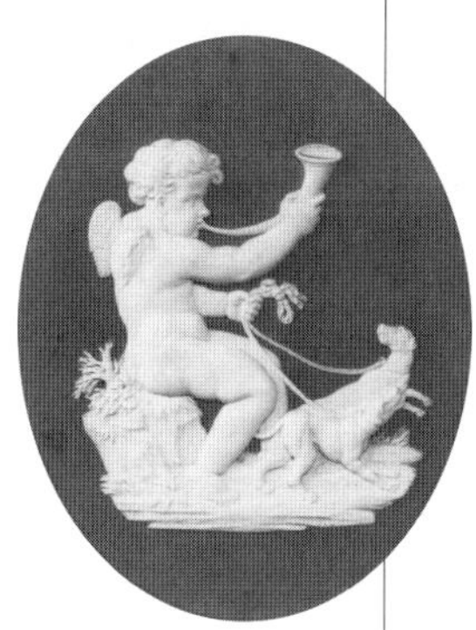

907. Medallion: *Cupid Seated on a Stump*, ca. 1775-80
Jasper, solid blue ground with dark blue wash on front and white relief
5 7/16 x 4 3/8 in (13.8 x 11.1 cm)
Mark: "WEDGWOOD & BENTLEY"
Provenance: Dr. Harold L. Klawans, Chicago
1976.215
Base has six firing holes.
Color plate 75

908. Medallion: *Cupid as a Butterfly*, ca. 1780
Jasper, solid blue ground with medium blue wash on front and white relief
5 1/8 x 4 in (13 x 10.1 cm)
Mark: "WEDGWOOD & BENTLEY"
Provenance: Fred J. Tongue, Santa Monica, Calif.
1976.204
Back has six firing holes.
Color plate 75

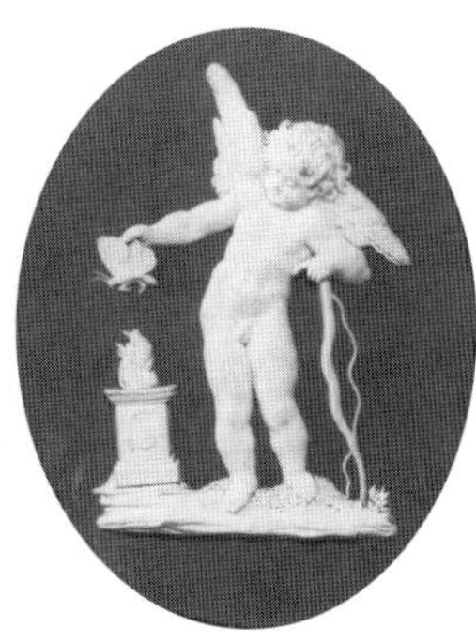

909. Medallion: *Bacchanalian Figure*, ca. 1775-80
Jasper, solid blue ground with dark blue wash on front and white relief
5 7/8 x 4 3/8 in (14.9 x 11.1 cm)
Mark: "WEDGWOOD & BENTLEY"
Provenance: David Davis, Chicago; Dr. Harold L. Klawans, Chicago
1978.213
Back has two firing holes.
Color plate 75

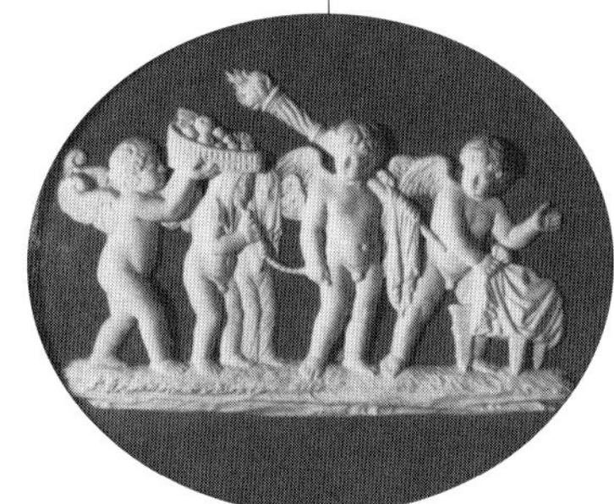

910. Medallion: ***Marriage of Cupid and Psyche,*** **ca. 1775-80**
Jasper, solid blue ground with dark blue wash on front and white relief
3 3/8 x 2 11/16 in (8.5 x 6.8 cm)
Mark: "Wedgwood & Bentley"
Provenance: Fred J. Tongue, Santa Monica, Calif.
1976.211
Back has six firing holes.
Color plate 73

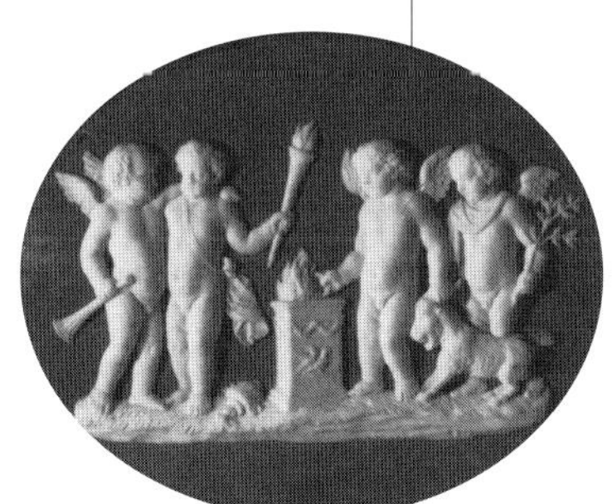

911. Medallion: ***Sacrifice to Hymen,*** **ca. 1775-80**
Jasper, solid blue ground with dark blue wash on front and white relief
3 1/2 x 2 7/8 in (8.8 x 7.3 cm)
Mark: "Wedgwood & Bentley"
Provenance: Dr. Francis Jennings Vurpillat, South Bend, Ind.
1976.212
Back has firing holes.
Color plate 73

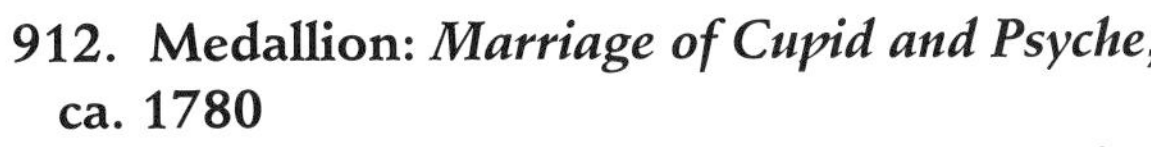

912. Medallion: ***Marriage of Cupid and Psyche,*** **ca. 1780**
Jasper, solid dark blue ground with white relief
2 5/8 x 3 1/4 in (8.2 x 6.6 cm)
Mark: "Wedgwood & Bentley"
Provenance: M. Mellanay Delhom, Chicago; Ann Brodkiewicz, Chicago
1982.41

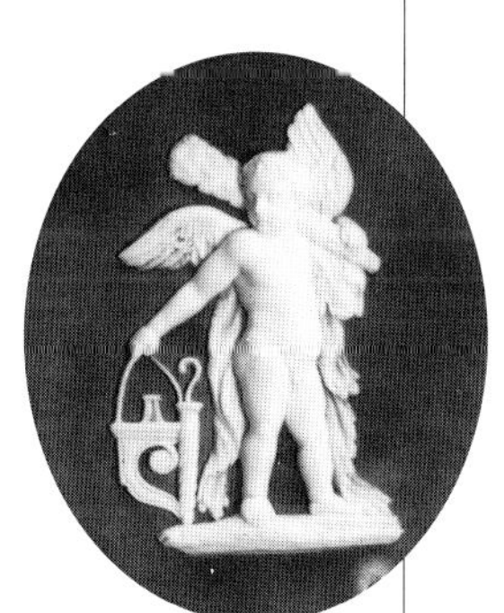

913. Medallion: ***Cupid with Club of Hercules,*** **ca. 1775**
Jasper, solid white ground with blue wash on front and white relief
2 1/4 x 1 7/8 in (5.7 x 4.7 cm)
Mark: "Wedgwood & Bentley"
Provenance: Godfrey W. Ford, England; Dr. Harold L. Klawans, Chicago
1976.216

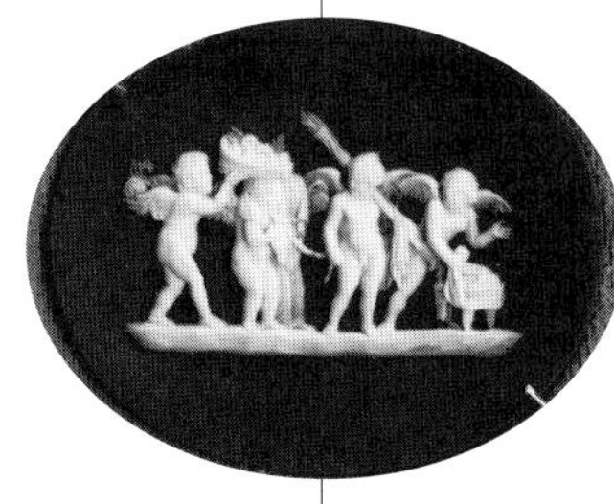

914. Medallion: ***The Marriage of Cupid and Psyche,*** **ca. 1775**
Jasper, solid blue ground with laminated white and blue above and white relief
1 5/8 x 1 3/8 in (4.1 x 3.4 cm)
Mark: "Wedgwood & Bentley"
Provenance: Godfrey W. Ford, England; Dr. Harold L. Klawans, Chicago
1976.216

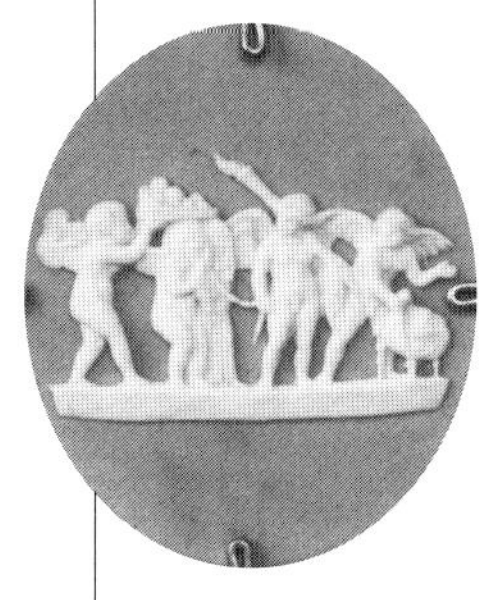

915. Medallion: ***The Marriage of Cupid and Psyche,*** **ca. 1800**
Jasper, solid white ground with green wash on front and back and white relief
1 3/4 x 1 1/2 in (4.4 x 3.8 cm)
Mark: "WEDGWOOD"
Provenance: Dr. Harold L. Klawans, Chicago
1976.199

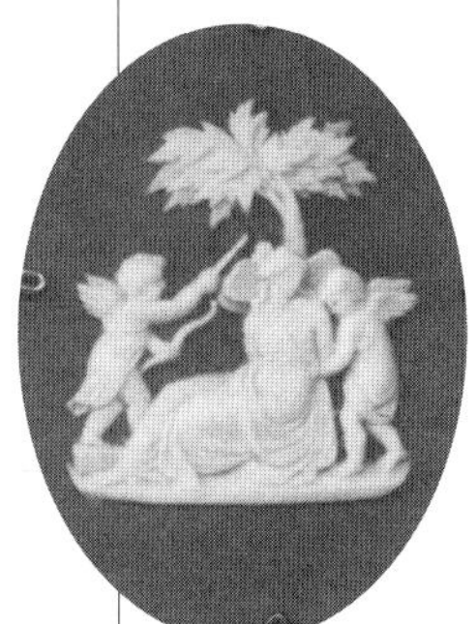

916. Medallion: *Psyche Wounded and Bound by Cupids*, ca. 1800
Jasper, solid white ground with lilac wash on front and white relief
2 x 1 1/2 in (5 x 3.8 cm)
Mark: "WEDGWOOD"
Provenance: Dr. Harold L. Klawans, Chicago
1976.197

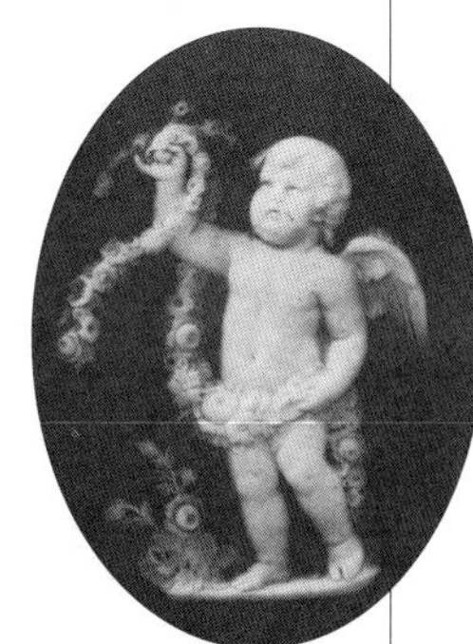

917. Medallion: *Cupid as Summer*, 19th century
Jasper, solid white ground with dark blue wash on front and back and white relief
2 3/8 x 1 13/16 in (6 x 4.6 cm)
Mark: "WEDGWOOD" "V"
Provenance: Godfrey W. Ford, England; Dr. Harold L. Klawans, Chicago
1976.203

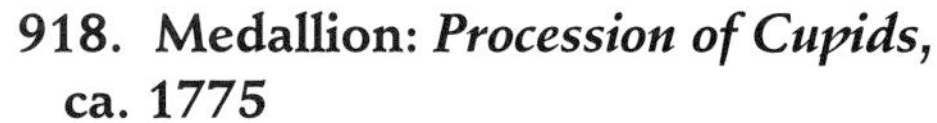

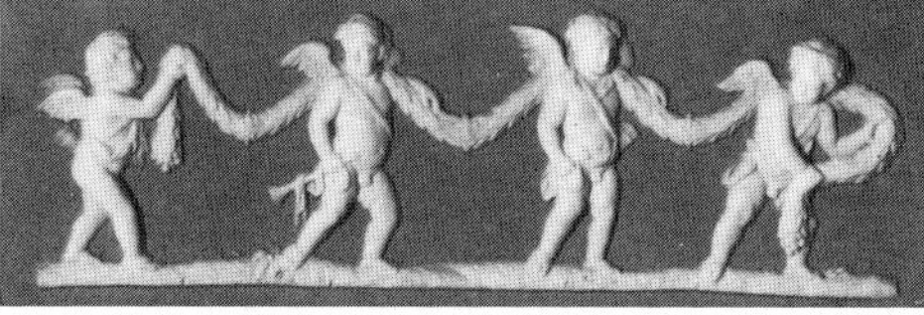

918. Medallion: *Procession of Cupids*, ca. 1775
Jasper, solid blue ground with white relief
1 5/8 x 4 1/16 in (4.1 x 10.2 cm)
Mark: "WEDGWOOD & BENTLEY"
Provenance: Godfrey W. Ford, England; Dr. Harold L. Klawans, Chicago
1977.143

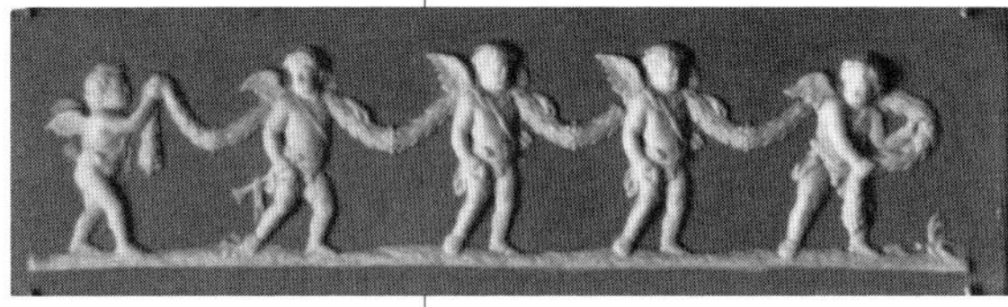

919. Medallion: *Procession of Cupids*, ca. 1800
Jasper, solid blue ground with white relief
1 11/16 x 6 in (4.2 x 15.2 cm)
Mark: "WEDGWOOD"
Provenance: Dr. Harold L. Klawans, Chicago
1977.67.4

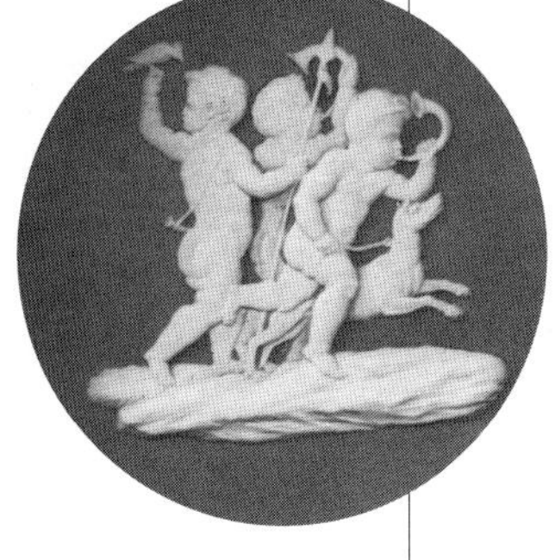

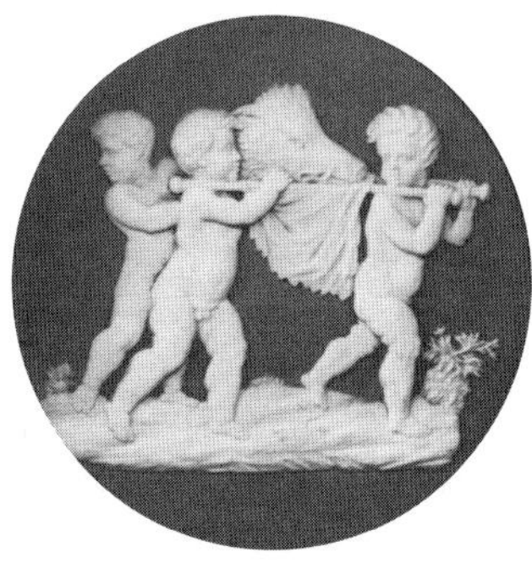

920. Pair of Medallions: *Cupids Setting Out on the Hunt* and *Bringing Home the Game*, 19th century
Jasper, solid blue ground with white relief, concave surface
5 in (12.7 cm)
Mark: a: "WEDGWOOD" "J"; b: none visible
Provenance: Otto Wasserman, New York
1976.195.1-.2

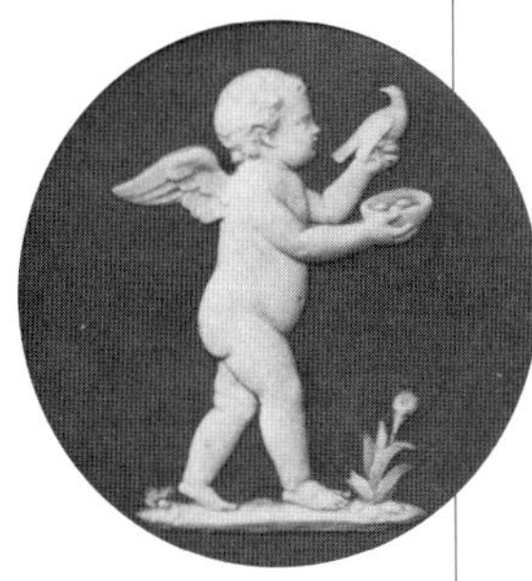

921. Medallion: *Spring*, 19th century
John Flaxman (1755-1826), designer
Jasper, solid white ground with green wash on front and white relief
4 1/4 in (10.7 cm)
Mark: "WEDGWOOD"
Provenance: Knight Collection, Birmingham, Ala.
1980.311

922. Medallion: *Omphale with Lion Skin and Club of Hercules*, ca. 1775-80
Jasper, solid white ground with dark blue wash on front and white relief
3 3/16 x 2 9/16 in (8 x 6.5 cm)
Mark: "WEDGWOOD & BENTLEY"
Provenance: Godfrey W. Ford, England;
Dr. Harold L. Klawans, Chicago
1976.207
Design source: Montfaucon, *L' Antiquité expliquée*,
vol. 1, pt. 2, pl. 68, fig. 9

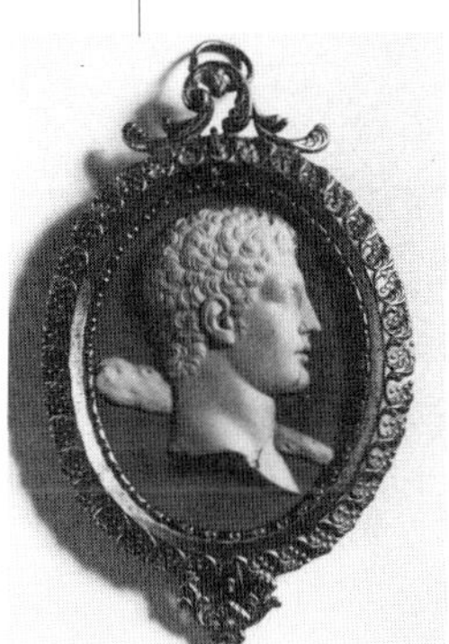

923. Medallion: *Hercules and His Club*, ca. 1775-80
Jasper, solid blue ground with white relief,
ormolu frame
2 1/8 x 1 11/16 in (5.3 x 4.2 cm)
Mark: "Wedgwood / & Bentley"
Provenance: Ann Brodkiewicz, Chicago
1977.169
Back has one firing hole.

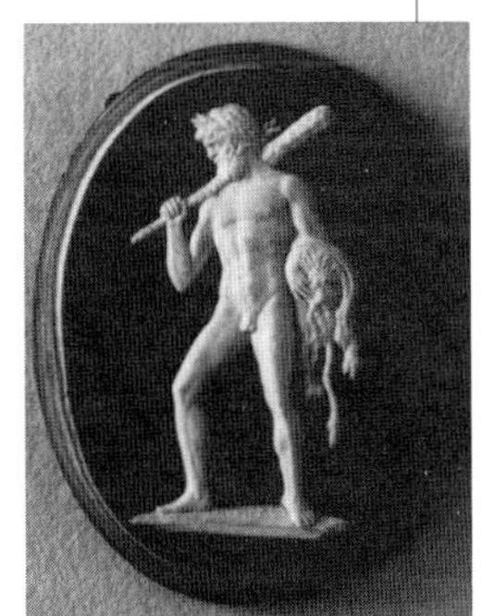
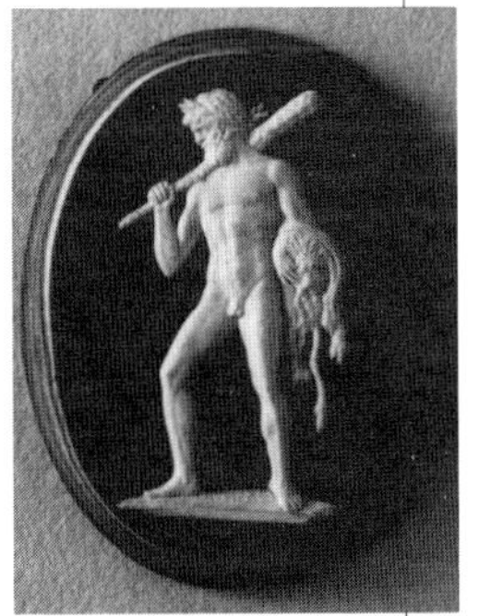

924. Medallion: *Hercules and His Club*, ca. 1780
Jasper, marbled blue-and-white ground with dark wash on front and white relief
1 9/16 x 1 1/4 in (3.9 x 3.1 cm)
Mark: "Wedgwood / & Bentley"
Provenance: Sir George Duff-Dunbar, Scotland; M. Mellanay Delhom, Chicago
1982.59

925. Medallion: *Hercules and the Boar*, ca. 1790
Jasper, solid white ground with dark blue wash on
front and blue wash on back and white relief
1 x 5/8 in (2.5 x 1.5 cm)
Mark: none
Provenance: Dr. Francis Jennings Vurpillat, South Bend, Ind.
1977.122.80

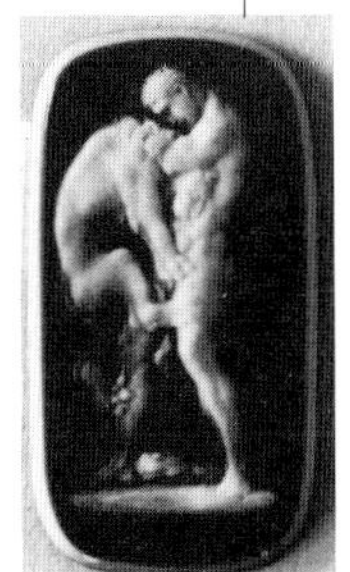

926. Medallion: *Hercules Binding Cerberus*, ca. 1780
Jasper, solid white ground with dark blue wash on front
and back and white relief; lapidary-polished edges
1 1/8 x 5/8 in (2.8 x 1.5 cm)
Mark: "WEDGWOOD"
Provenance: Dr. Francis Jennings Vurpillat, South Bend, Ind.
1977.122.91

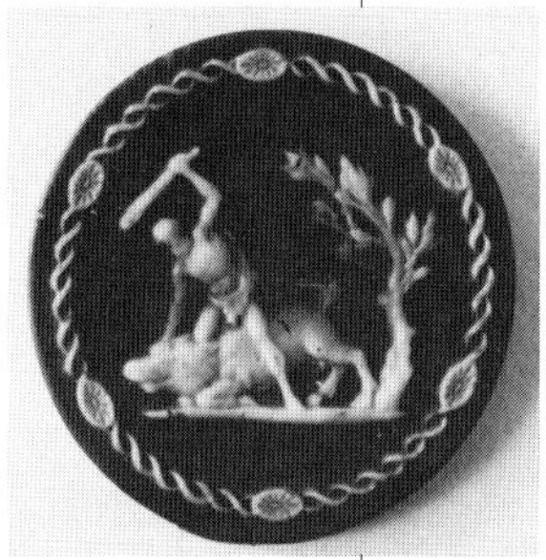

927. Medallion: *Hercules Killing the Cretan Bull,* ca. 1800
Jasper, solid white ground with dark blue wash on front with white relief
15/16 in (2.3 cm)
Mark: none
Provenance: Dr. Harold L. Klawans, Chicago
1977.67.8

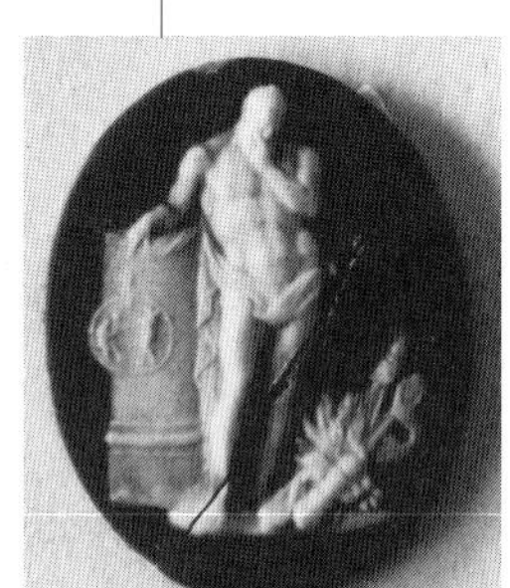

928. Medallion: *Hercules,* ca. 1780
Jasper, solid white ground with dark blue wash on front and light blue wash on back and white relief
15/16 x 3/4 in (2.3 x 1.9 cm)
Mark: none
Provenance: Dr. Francis Jennings Vurpillat, South Bend, Ind.
1977.122.98

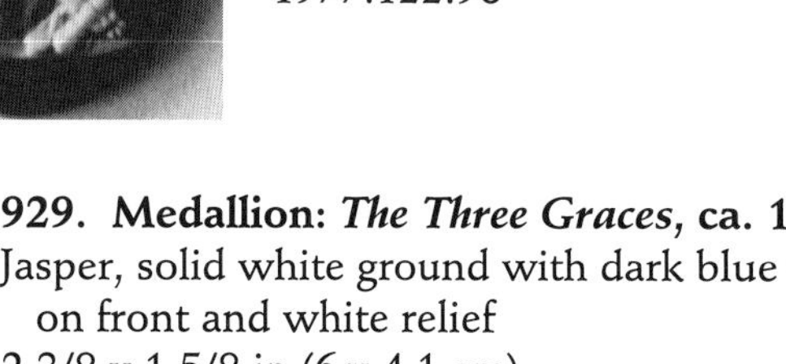

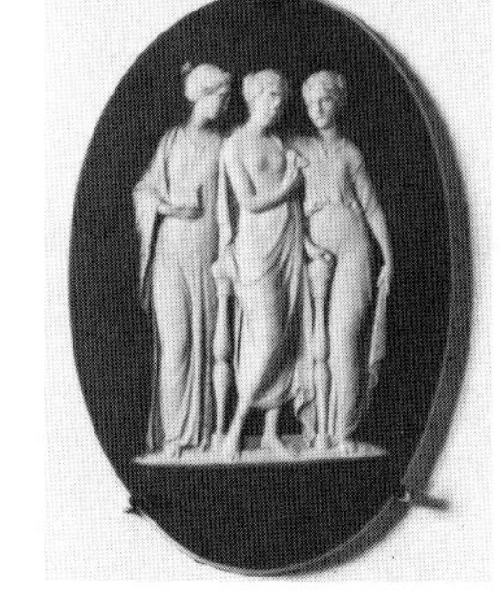

929. Medallion: *The Three Graces,* ca. 1800
Jasper, solid white ground with dark blue wash on front and white relief
2 3/8 x 1 5/8 in (6 x 4.1 cm)
Mark: "WEDGWOOD"
Provenance: Dr. Harold L. Klawans, Chicago
1977.67.6

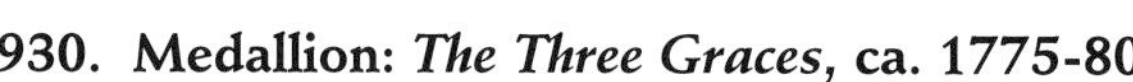

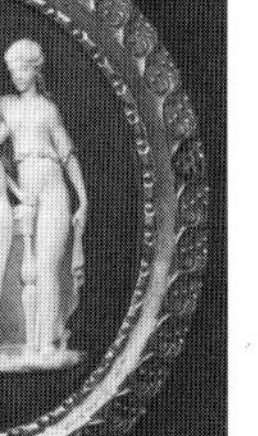

930. Medallion: *The Three Graces,* ca. 1775-80
Jasper, variegated blue-and-white ground with dark blue wash on front and white relief, lapidary-polishing, ormolu frame
2 1/16 x 1 11/16 in (5.2 x 4.2 cm)
Mark: "Wedgwood & Bentley"
Provenance: Christie's, London, June 14, 1965
1977.85
Color plate 78

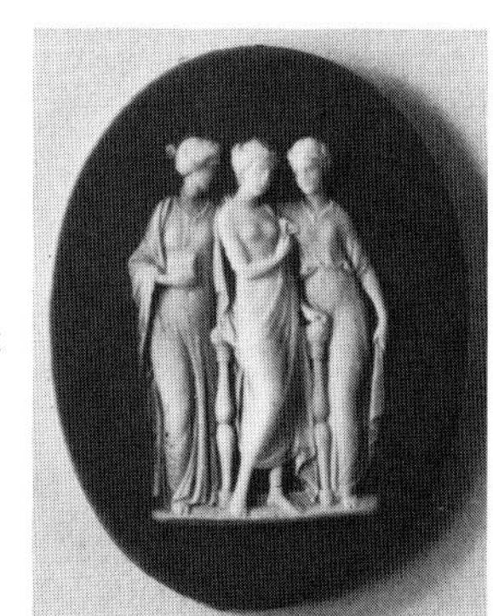

931. Medallion: *The Three Graces,* ca. 1800
Jasper, solid white ground with lilac wash on front and white relief
2 x 1 9/16 in (5 x 3.9 cm)
Mark: "WEDGWOOD"; "147" in script
Provenance: Dr. Harold L. Klawans, Chicago
1977.67.2

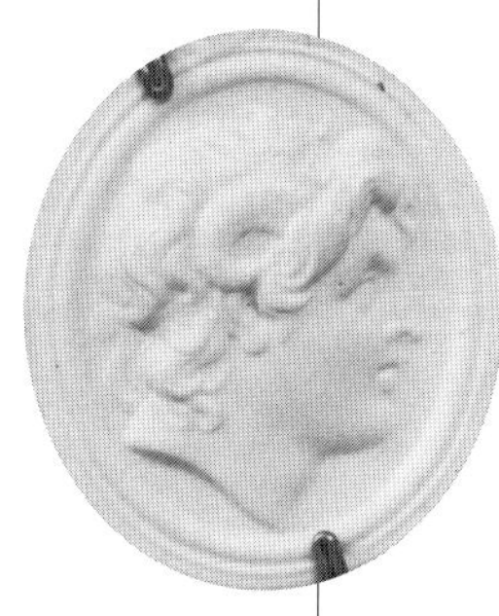

932. Medallion: *Alexander the Great,* ca. 1775
James Tassie (1735-99), Scotland, maker
Enamel paste
1 3/4 x 1 1/4 in (4.4 x 3.1 cm)
Mark: none
Provenance: M. Mellanay Delhom, Chicago; Ann Brodkiewicz, Chicago
1976.206

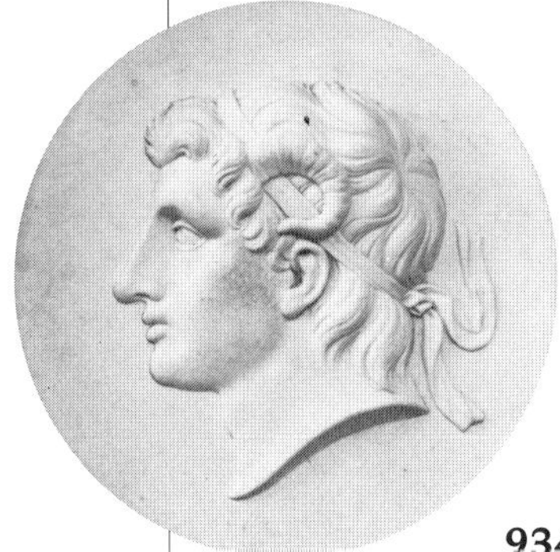

933. Medallion: *Alexander the Great*, ca. 1775-80
White terra-cotta stoneware
3 11/16 in (9.3 cm)
Mark: "Wedgwood & Bentley"
Provenance: Sir George Duff-Dunbar, Scotland; M. Mellanay Delhom, Chicago; Ann Brodkiewicz, Chicago
1977.168
Figure 26

934. Medallion: *Venus de' Medici*, ca. 1780
Jasper, solid lilac, white, and dark blue ground, laminated
1 x 11/16 in (2.5 x 1.7 cm)
Mark: "Wedgwood & Bentley"
Provenance: Gift of M. Mellanay Delhom, Chicago
1980.306
Design source: Joseph Spence, *Polymetis . . .*, pl. 5.

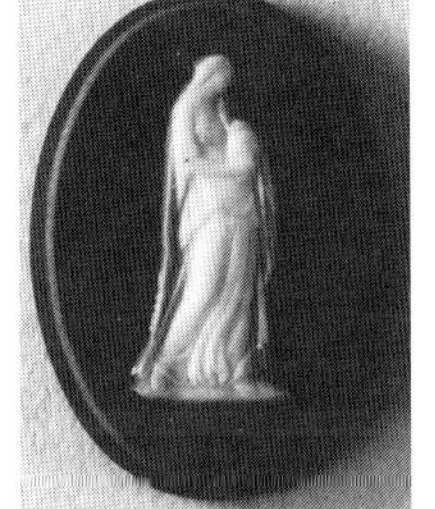

935. Medallion: *Classical Figure*, ca. 1780
Jasper, laminated dark blue, light blue, and gray ground with white relief, lapidary-polishing on edges
3/4 x 11/16 in (1.9 x 1.7 cm)
Mark: none
Provenance: Dr. Francis Jennings Vurpillat, South Bend, Ind.
1977.122.14

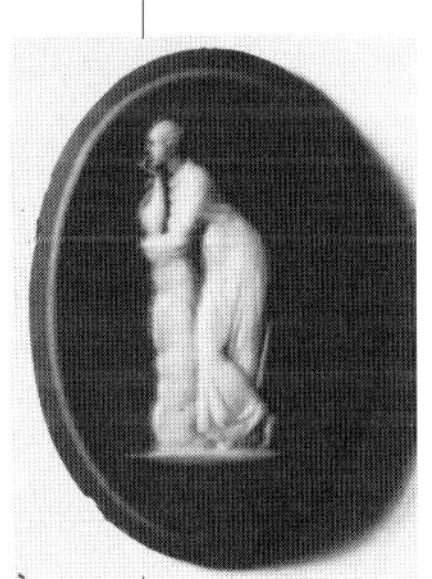

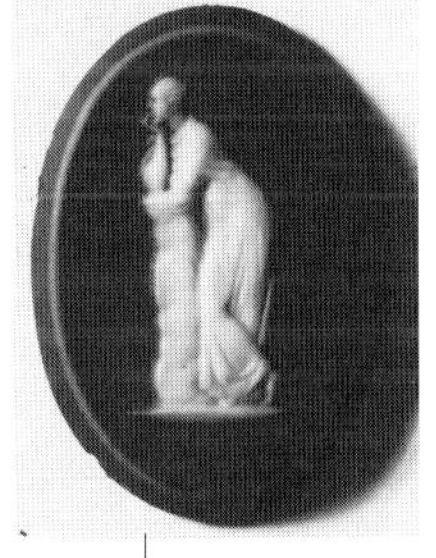

936. Medallion: *Calliope*, ca. 1780
Jasper, laminated dark blue, light blue, and gray ground with white relief, lapidary-polishing on edges
3/4 x 11/16 in (1.9 x 1.7 cm)
Mark: none
Provenance: Dr. Francis Jennings Vurpillat, South Bend, Ind.
1977.122.15

937. Pair of Medallions: *Horses*, ca. 1790
Edward Burch (1730-1814), modeler
Jasper, solid blue ground with white relief, lapidary-polishing
1 7/16 in (3.6 cm)
Mark: "WEDGWOOD"
Provenance: Ann Brodkiewicz, Chicago
1982.5 and 1982.1a

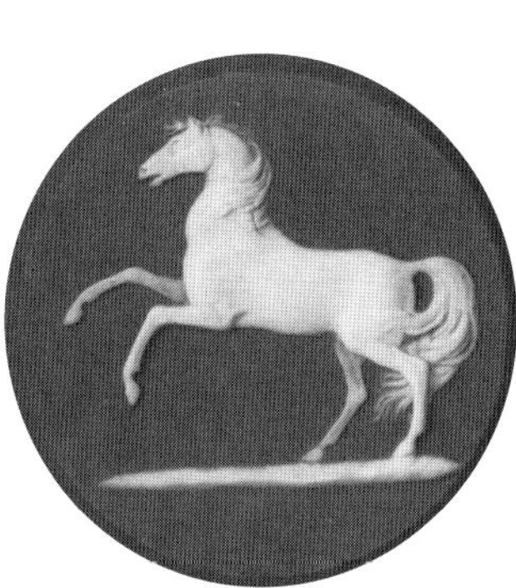

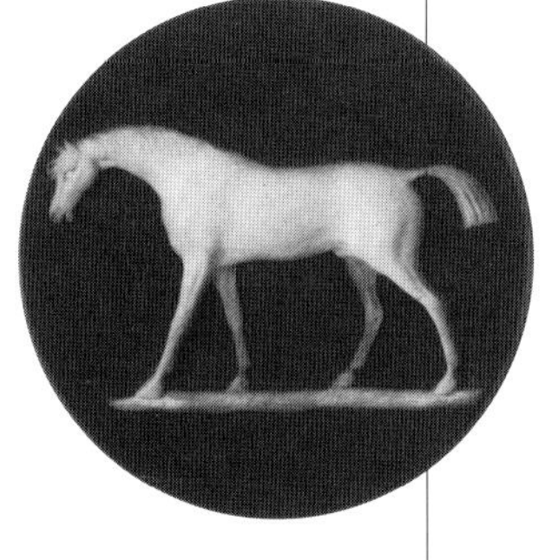

938. Medallion: *Horse*, ca. 1800
Jasper, solid white ground with dark blue wash on front and white relief, lapidary-polishing
1 5/16 in (3.3 cm)
Mark: "WEDGWOOD"
Provenance: Dr. Francis Jennings Vurpillat, South Bend, Ind.
1982.1b

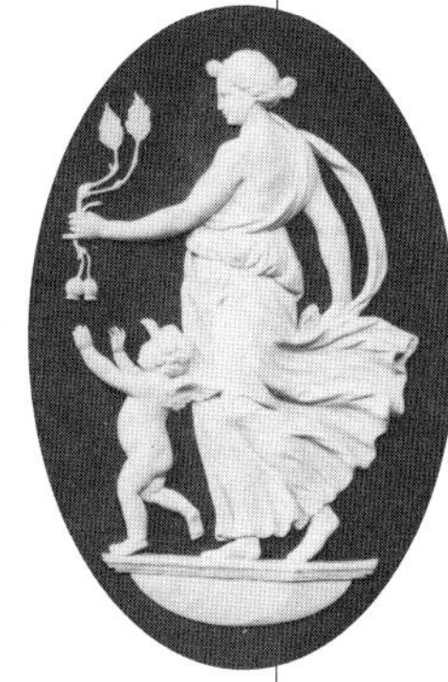

939. Medallion: *Venus and Cupid*, ca. 1775-80
Jasper, solid blue ground with dark blue wash on front and white relief
6 3/8 x 4 1/4 in (16.1 x 10.7 cm)
Mark: "WEDGWOOD & BENTLEY"
Provenance: M. Mellanay Delhom, Chicago; Ann Brodkiewicz, Chicago
1976.214
Back has 10 firing holes.
Design source: Montfaucon, *L' Antiquité expliquée,* vol. 1, pl. 54, fig. 1
Color plate 76

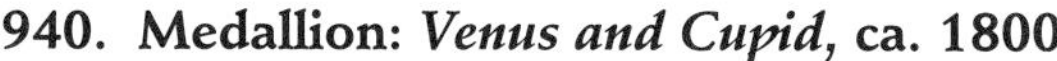

940. Medallion: *Venus and Cupid*, ca. 1800
Jasper, solid white ground with green wash on front and white relief
1 1/2 in (3.8 cm)
Mark: "WEDGWOOD"
Provenance: Dr. Harold L. Klawans, Chicago
1977.67.1

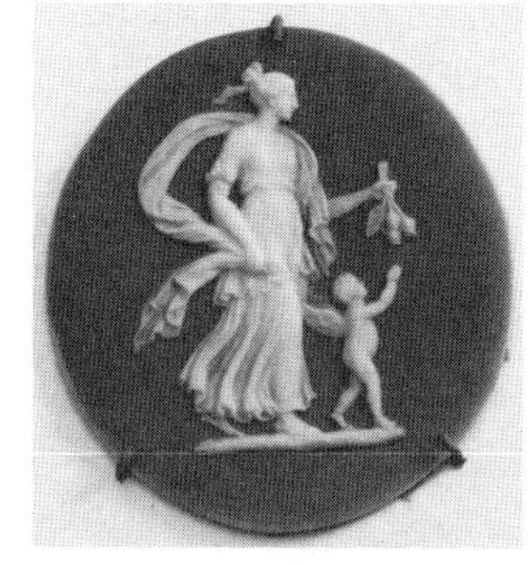

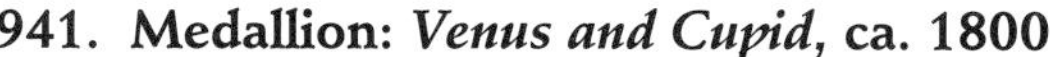

941. Medallion: *Venus and Cupid*, ca. 1800
Jasper, solid white ground with black wash on front and white relief
1 3/4 x 1 3/8 in (4.4 x 3.4 cm)
Mark: "WEDGWOOD"; "63" in script
Provenance: Dr. Harold L. Klawans, Chicago
1977.67.5

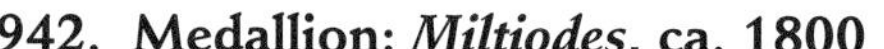

942. Medallion: *Miltiodes*, ca. 1800
Jasper, solid blue ground with darker blue wash on front and white relief
6 7/8 x 4 3/4 in (17.4 x 12 cm)
Mark: "WEDGWOOD"; "MILTIODES" incised on back
Provenance: Fred J. Tongue, Santa Monica, Calif.
1977.171

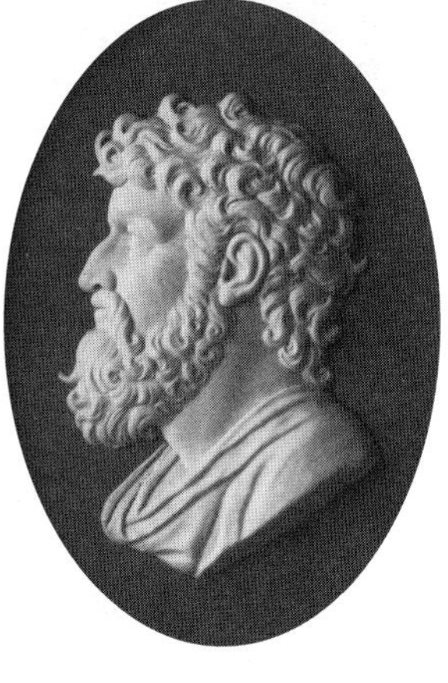

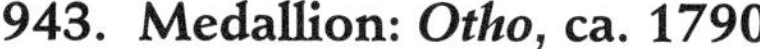

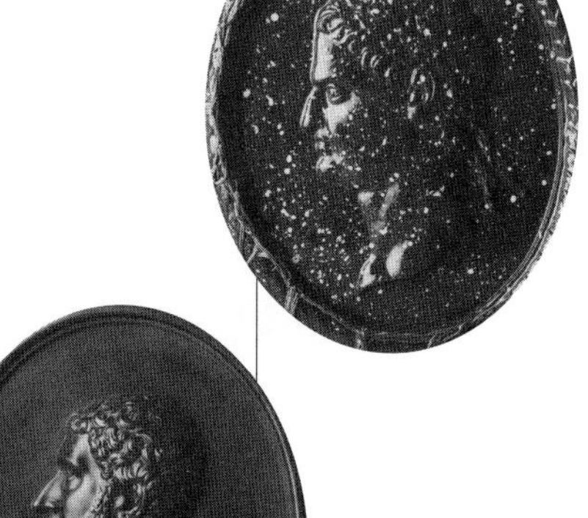

943. Medallion: *Otho*, ca. 1790
Earthenware, speckled brown glaze to imitate natural stone
4 x 3 1/4 in (10.1 x 8.2 cm)
Mark: "WEDGWOOD / OTHO" on back
Provenance: Dr. Harold L. Klawans, Chicago
1977.141

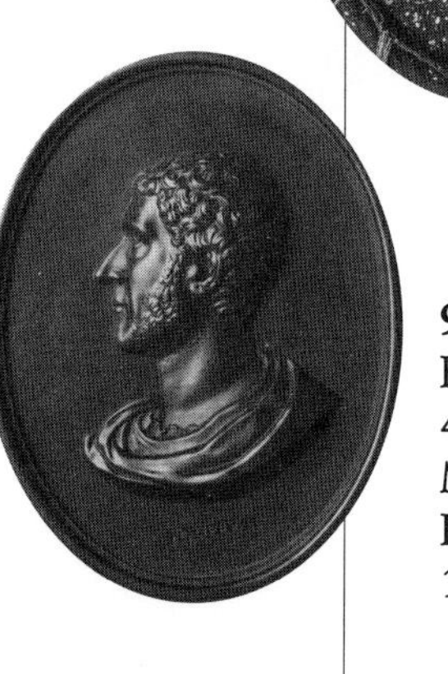

944. Medallion: *Pompey*, ca. 1770-80
Basalt
4 11/16 x 3 3/4 in (11.9 x 9.5 cm)
Mark: "Wedgwood"; "POMPEY M" on front
Provenance: Ann Brodkiewicz, Chicago
1977.135

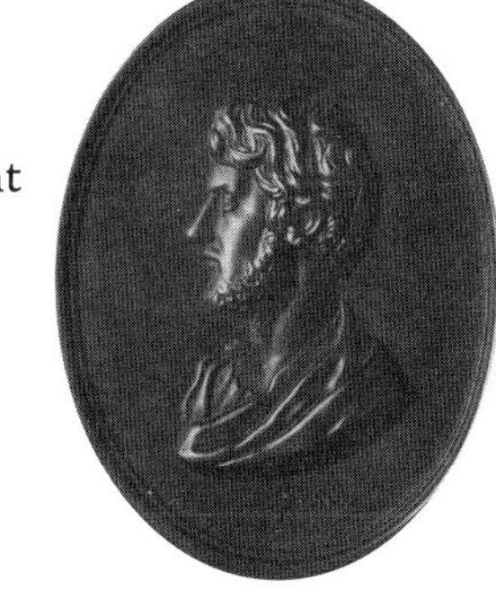

945. Medallion: *Brutus*, ca. 1775
Basalt
4 5/8 x 3 11/16 in (11.7 x 9.3 cm)
Mark: "Wedgwood & Bentley"; "BRUTUS" on front
Provenance: M. Mellanay Delhom, Chicago;
Ann Brodkiewicz, Chicago
1977.136

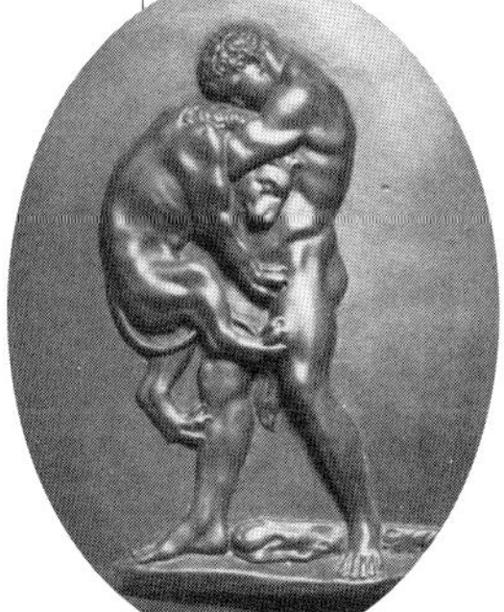

946. Medallion: *Hercules Strangling the Nemean Lion*, 19th century
Basalt
7 1/16 x 5 3/8 in (17.9 x 13.6 cm)
Mark: "WEDGWOOD" "J"
Provenance: W. Russell Button Gallery, Chicago
1985.423

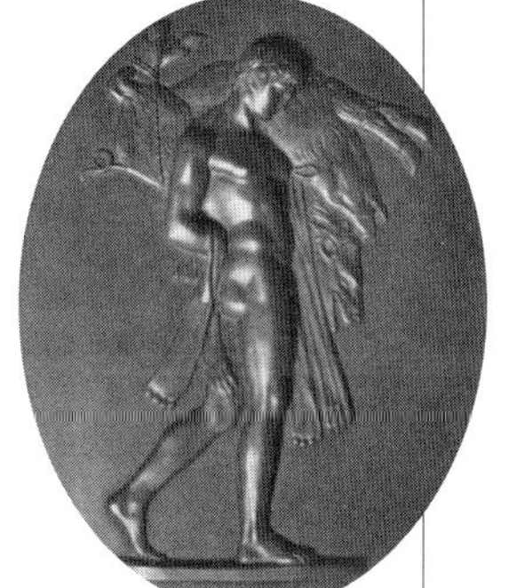

947. Medallion: *Hercules and the Erymanthian Boar*, 19th century
Basalt
7 7/16 x 5 5/8 in (18.8 x 14.2 cm)
Mark: "WEDGWOOD"
Provenance: W. Russell Button Gallery, Chicago
1985.424

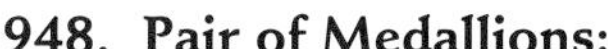

948. Pair of Medallions: *Antony and Cleopatra*, ca. 1780
Jasper, solid blue ground with blue wash on front and white relief
3 3/8 x 2 3/4 in (8.5 x 6.9 cm)
Mark: "WEDGWOOD & BENTLEY"
Provenance: Dr. Francis Jennings Vurpillat, South Bend, Ind.
1981.231 a and b
Color plate 140

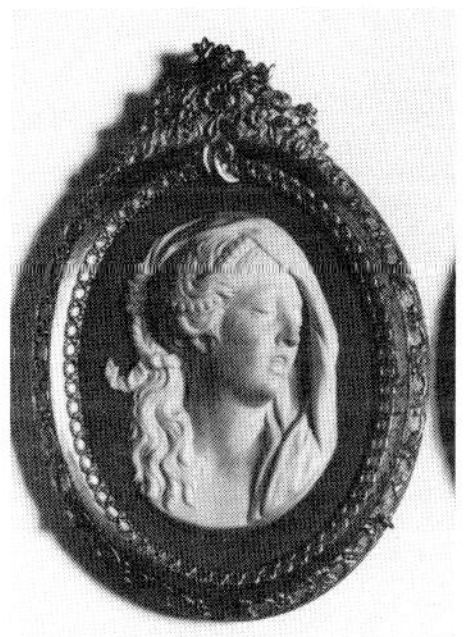

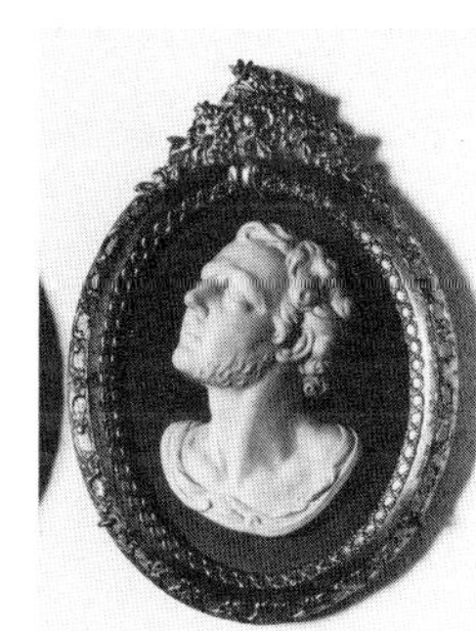

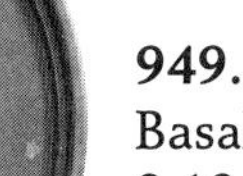

949. Medallion: *Julius Caesar*, ca. 1790
Basalt
2 13/16 x 2 5/16 in (7.1 x 5.8 cm)
Mark: "WEDGWOOD"
Provenance: Otto Wasserman, New York
1979.237

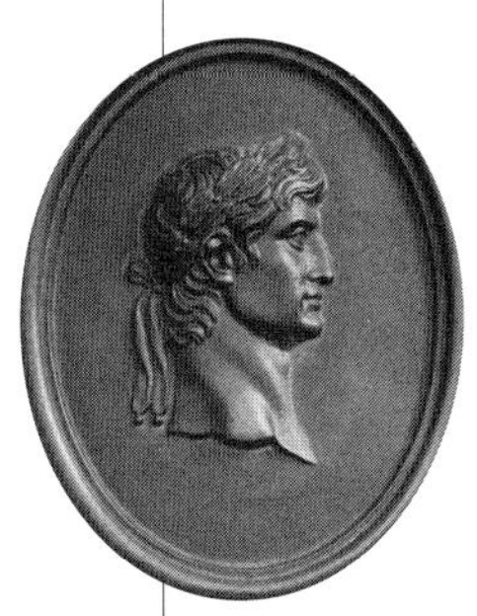

950. Medallion: *Augustus Caesar*, ca. 1790
Basalt
2 13/16 x 2 1/4 in (7.1 x 5.7 cm)
Mark: "WEDGWOOD"
Provenance: Otto Wasserman, New York
1979.238

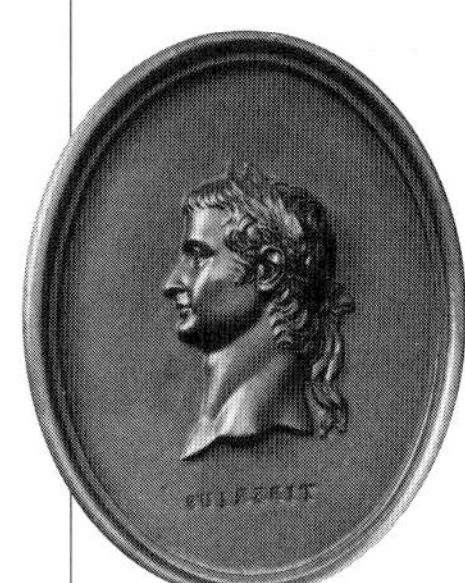

951. Medallion: *Tiberius*, ca. 1780
Basalt
2 3/4 x 2 1/4 in (6.9 x 5.7 cm)
Mark: "Wedgwood & Bentley" "3"; "TIBERIUS" impressed on front
Provenance: Otto Wasserman, New York
1979.247

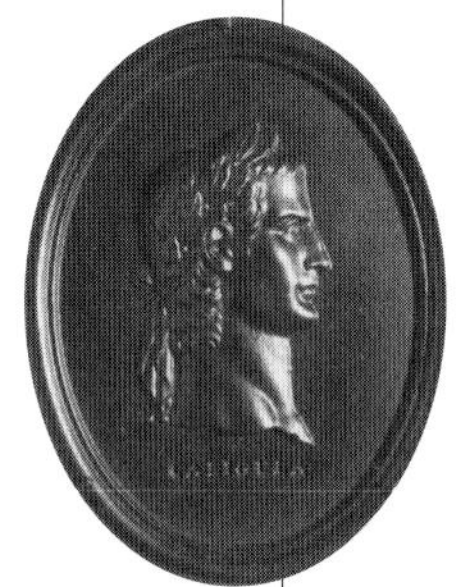

952. Medallion: *Caligula*, ca. 1790
Basalt
2 13/16 x 2 5/16 in (7.1 x 5.8 cm)
Mark: "Wedgwood"; "CALIGULA" impressed on front
Provenance: Otto Wasserman, New York
1979.248

953. Medallion: *Claudius*, ca. 1780
Basalt
2 3/4 x 2 1/4 in (6.9 x 5.7 cm)
Mark: "Wedgwood & Bentley";
"CLAUDIUS" impressed on front
Provenance: Otto Wasserman, New York
1979.239

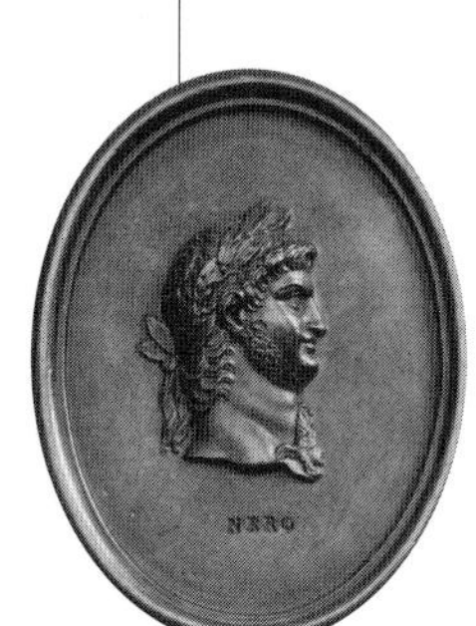

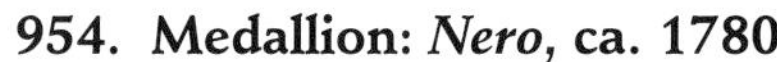

954. Medallion: *Nero*, ca. 1780
Basalt
2 3/4 x 2 1/4 in (6.9 x 5.7 cm)
Mark: "Wedgwood & Bentley" "6"; "NERO" impressed on front
Provenance: Dr. Harold L. Klawans, Chicago
1979.240

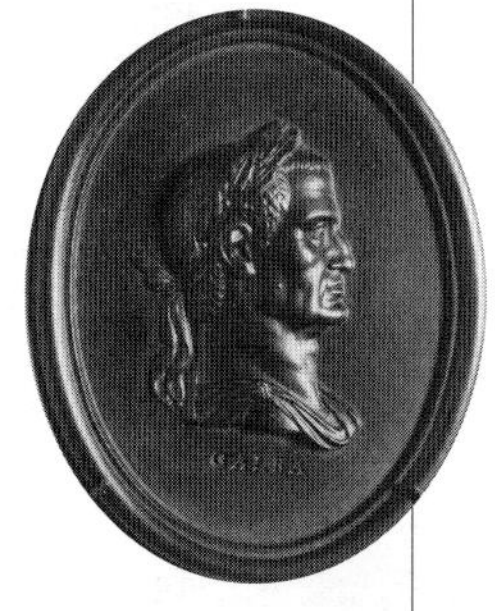

955. Medallion: *Galba*, ca. 1790
Basalt
2 3/4 x 2 5/16 in (6.9 x 5.8 cm)
Mark: "Wedgwood"; "GALBA" impressed on front
Provenance: Otto Wasserman, New York
1979.241

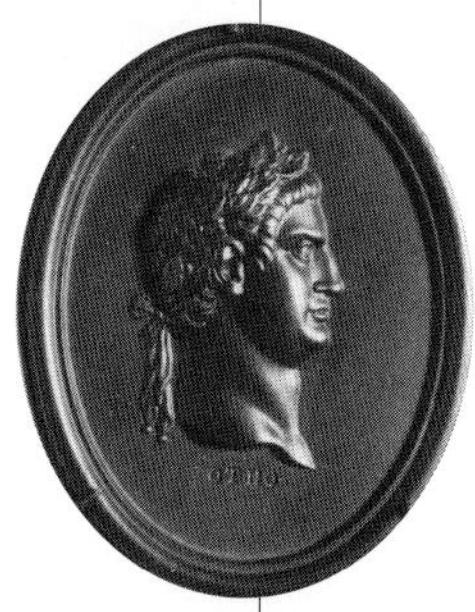

956. Medallion: *Otho*, ca. 1790
Basalt
2 3/4 x 2 5/16 in (6.9 x 5.8 cm)
Mark: "Wedgwood"; "OTHO" impressed on front
Provenance: Otto Wasserman, New York
1979.242

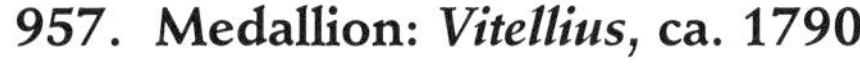

957. Medallion: *Vitellius*, ca. 1790
Basalt
2 3/4 x 2 1/4 in (6.9 x 5.7 cm)
Mark: "Wedgwood"; "VITELLIUS" impressed on front
Provenance: Otto Wasserman, New York
1979.243

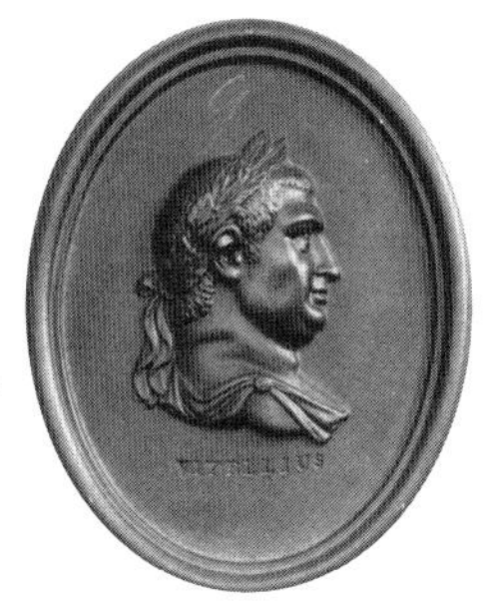

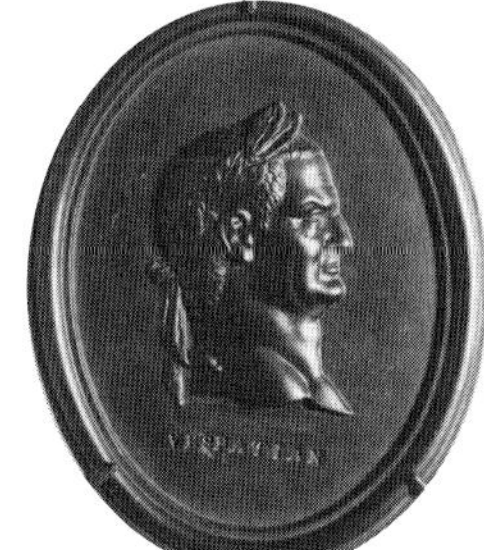

958. Medallion: *Vespasian*, ca. 1780
Basalt
2 3/4 x 2 1/4 in (6.9 x 5.7 cm)
Mark: "Wedgwood & Bentley"; "VESPATIAN" impressed on front
Provenance: Otto Wasserman, New York
1979.244

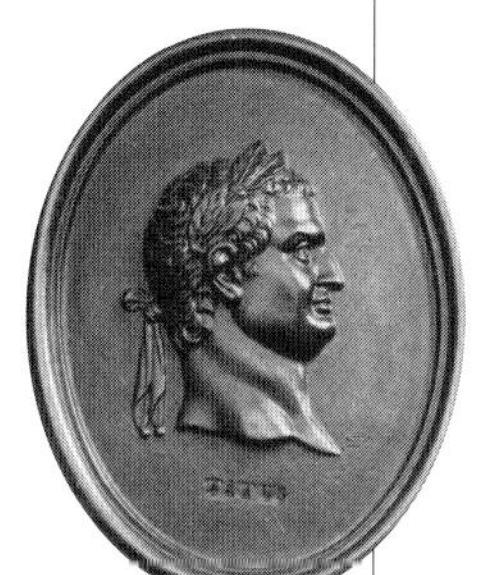

959. Medallion: *Titus*, ca. 1780
Basalt
2 3/4 x 2 1/4 in (6.9 x 5.7 cm)
Mark: "Wedgwood & Bentley" "II"; "TITUS" impressed on front
Provenance: Otto Wasserman, New York
1979.245

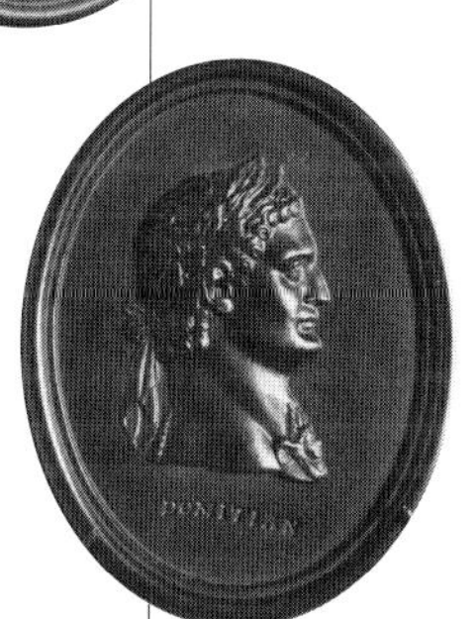

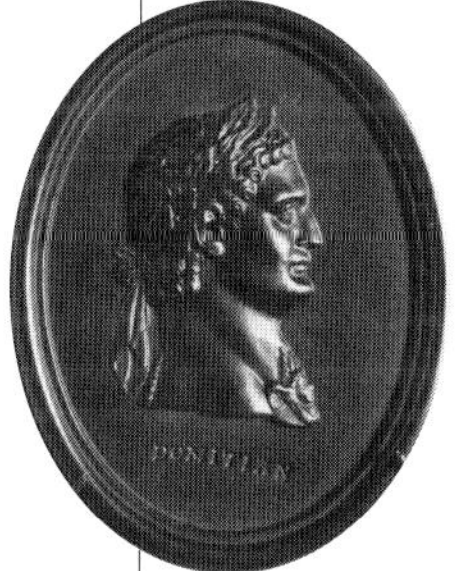

960. Medallion: *Domitian*, ca. 1780
Basalt
2 3/4 x 2 1/4 in (6.9 x 5.7 cm)
Mark: "Wedgwood & Bentley" "12"; "DOMITIAN" impressed on front
Provenance: Otto Wasserman, New York
1979.246

961. Medallion: *Alexander the Great*, ca. 1775-80
Jasper, solid blue ground with white relief, ormolu frame
2 1/16 x 1 13/16 in (5.2 x 4.6 cm)
Mark: "Wedgwood & Bentley"; "32" "ALEXANDER" on back
Provenance: Ann Brodkiewicz, Chicago
1977.168
Design source: Montfaucon, *L' Antiquité expliquée,* vol. 1, pt. 1, pl. 42, fig. 13.
Color plate 78

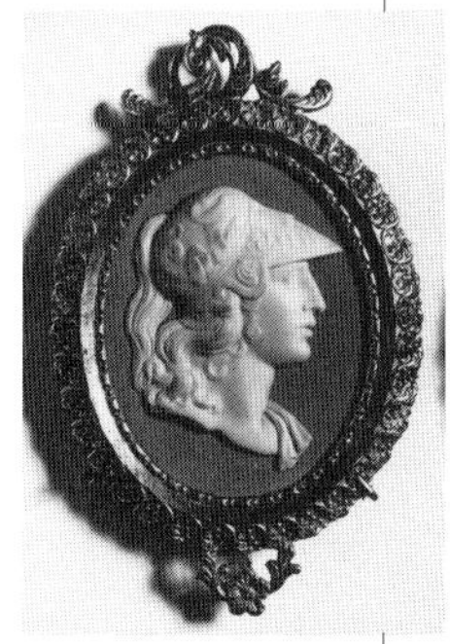

962. Medallion: *Aristophanes*, ca. 1775-80
Jasper, solid blue ground with white relief
2 1/16 x 1 13/16 in (5.2 x 4.6 cm)
Mark: "Wedgwood & Bentley"; "21" "ARISTOPHANES" on back
Provenance: Ann Brodkiewicz, Chicago
1977.167

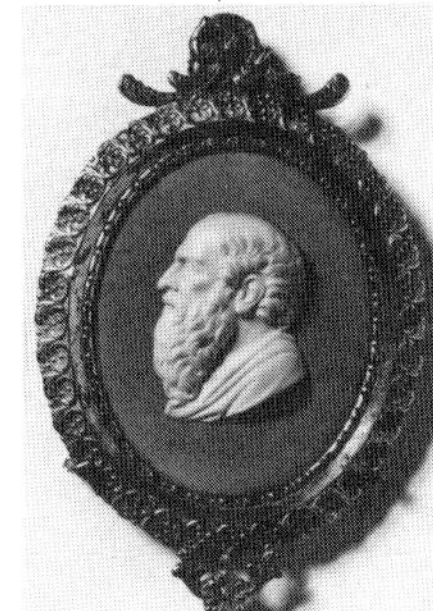

963. Medallion: *Diogenes*, ca. 1775-80
Jasper, solid blue ground with white relief
2 1/16 x 1 7/8 in (5.2 x 4.7 cm)
Mark: "Wedgwood & Bentley" "31" "DIOGENES"
Provenance: Ann Brodkiewicz, Chicago
1977.170

964. Medallion: *Homer*, ca. 1775-80
Jasper, solid blue ground with white relief
2 1/8 x 1 3/4 in (5.3 x 4.4 cm)
Mark: "Wedgwood & Bentley";
"2" "HOMER" on back
Provenance: Dr. Harold L. Klawans, Chicago
1977.124

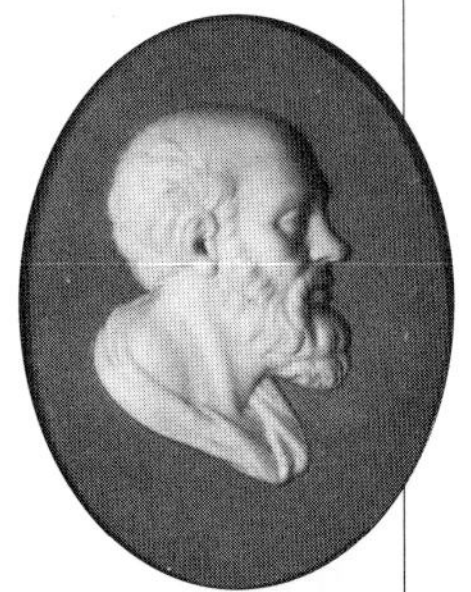

965. Medallion: *Epicurus*, ca. 1775-80
Jasper, solid blue ground with white relief
2 1/8 x 1 3/4 in (5.3 x 4.4 cm)
Mark: "Wedgwood & Bentley"; "35" "EPICURUS" on back
Provenance: Dr. Francis Jennings Vurpillat, South Bend, Ind.
1977.140

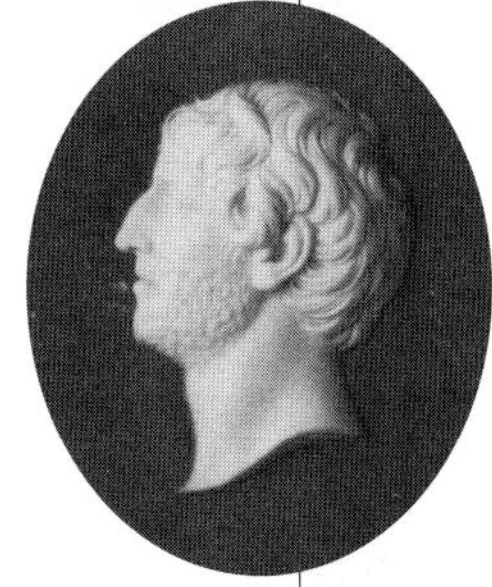

966. Medallion: *Pompey the Great*, ca. 1775-80
Jasper, solid blue ground with white relief
2 1/8 x 1 3/4 in (5.3 x 4.4 cm)
Mark: "Wedgwood & Bentley"; "POMPEY M" on back
Provenance: David Davis, Chicago; Dr. Harold L. Klawans, Chicago
1977.139
Back has one firing hole.

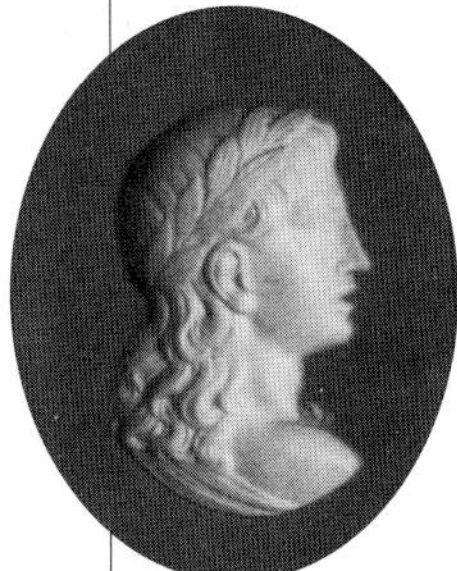

967. Medallion: *Virgil*, ca. 1775-80
Jasper, solid blue ground with white relief
2 1/8 x 1 3/4 in (5.3 x 4.4 cm)
Mark: "Wedgwood & Bentley"; "VIRGIL" on back
Provenance: Dr. Harold L. Klawans, Chicago
1977.128
Back has one firing hole.

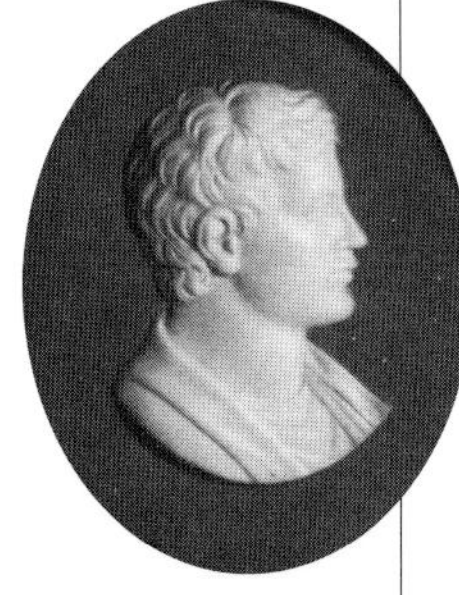

968. Medallion: *Horace*, ca. 1775-80
Jasper, solid blue ground with white relief
2 1/8 x 1 3/4 in (5.3 x 4.4 cm)
Mark: "Wedgwood & Bentley"; "HORACE" on back
Provenance: Dr. Harold L. Klawans, Chicago
1977.127
Back has one firing hole.

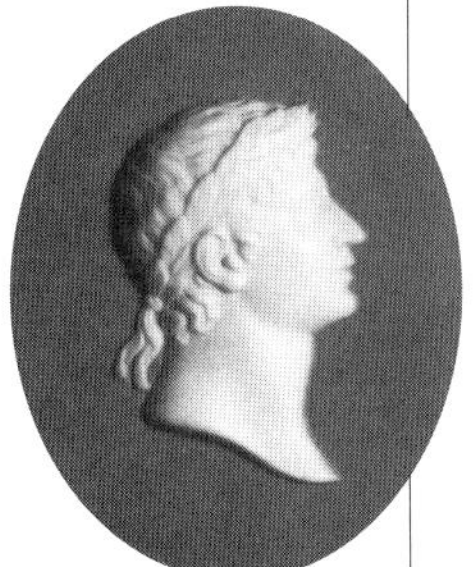

969. Medallion: *Ovid*, ca. 1775-80
Jasper, solid blue ground with white relief
2 1/8 x 1 3/4 in (5.3 x 4.4 cm)
Mark: "Wedgwood & Bentley"; "OVID" on back
Provenance: Dr. Harold L. Klawans, Chicago
1977.126
Back has one firing hole.

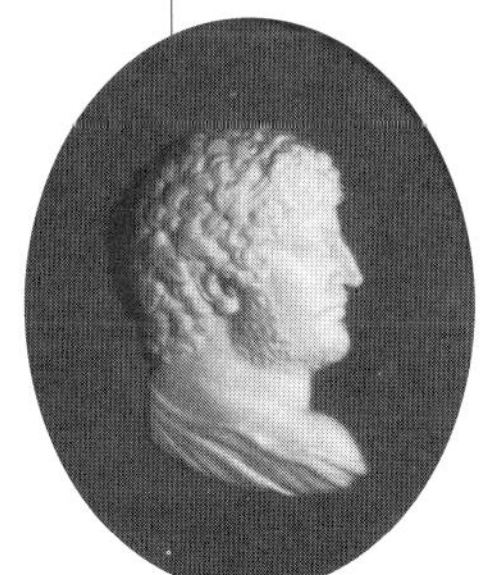

970. Medallion: *Perseus*, ca. 1775-80
Jasper, solid blue ground with white relief
2 1/8 x 1 3/4 in (5.3 x 4.4 cm)
Mark: "Wedgwood & Bentley"; "PERSEUS POET" on back
Provenance: Dr. Harold L. Klawans, Chicago
1977.125
Back has one firing hole.

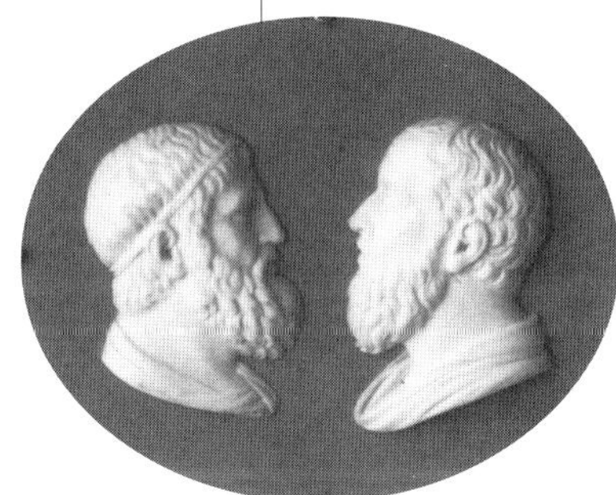

971. Medallion: *Cleanthus and Chrysippus*, ca. 1775-80
Jasper, solid blue ground with white relief
2 3/4 x 2 1/8 in (6.9 x 5.3 cm)
Mark: "Wedgwood & Bentley"
Provenance: David Davis, Chicago; Dr. Harold L. Klawans, Chicago
1977.155

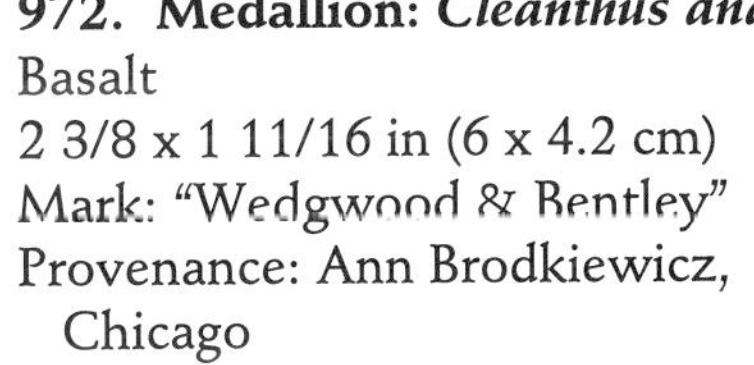

972. Medallion: *Cleanthus and Chrysippus*, ca. 1775
Basalt
2 3/8 x 1 11/16 in (6 x 4.2 cm)
Mark: "Wedgwood & Bentley"
Provenance: Ann Brodkiewicz, Chicago
1977.154

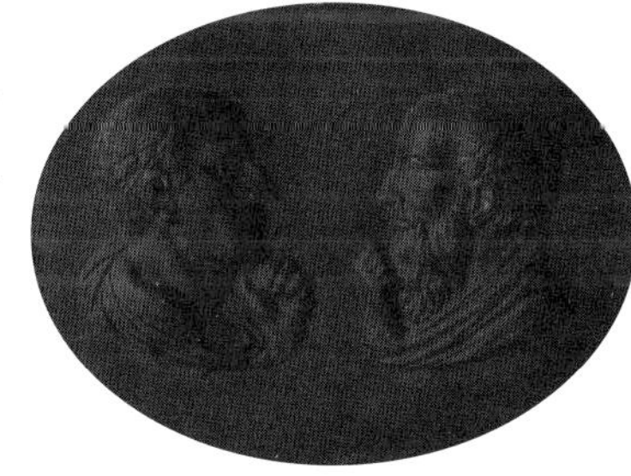

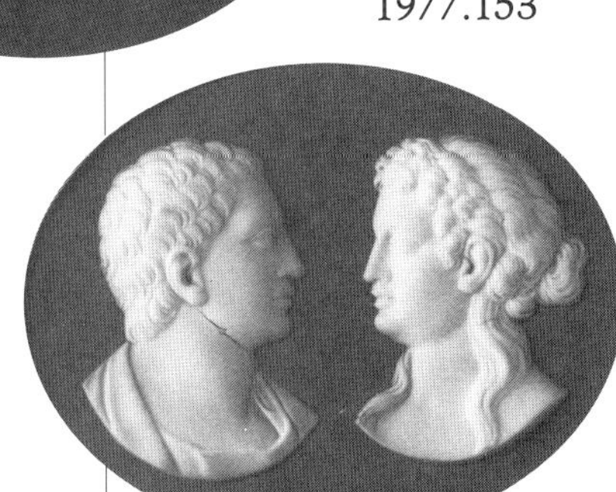

973. Medallion: *Plato and Pitticus*, ca. 1780
Jasper, solid blue with white relief
2 7/16 x 1 15/16 in (6.1 x 4.9 cm)
Mark: "Wedgwood & Bentley"
Provenance: David Davis, Chicago; Dr. Harold L. Klawans, Chicago
1977.153

974. Medallion: *Phthias and Sappho*, ca. 1780
Jasper, solid blue ground with white relief
2 11/16 x 2 1/8 in (6.8 x 5.3 cm)
Mark: "Wedgwood & Bentley"
Provenance: Ann Brodkiewicz, Chicago
1977.156

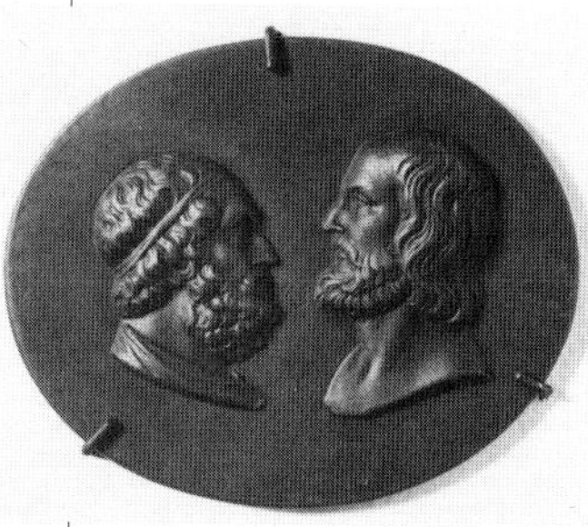

975. Medallion: *Confronting Heads*, ca. 1775
Basalt
2 7/16 x 1 15/16 in (6.1 x 4.9 cm)
Mark: “Wedgwood & Bentley”
Provenance: Ann Brodkiewicz, Chicago
1982.37

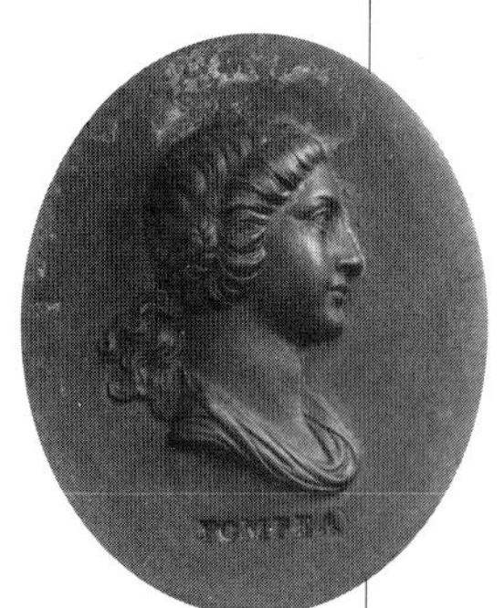

976. Medallion: *Pompea*, ca. 1790
Basalt
2 1/16 x 1 3/4 in (5.2 x 4.4 cm)
Mark: “Wedgwood”; “POMPEA” impressed on front
Provenance: M. Mellanay Delhom, Chicago; Ann Brodkiewicz, Chicago
1982.50

977. Medallion: *Otho*, ca. 1780
Basalt
1 1/8 x 1 5/8 in (2.8 x 4.1 cm)
Mark: “WEDGWOOD”
“OTHO” on back
Provenance: Dr. Harold L. Klawans, Chicago
1977.61

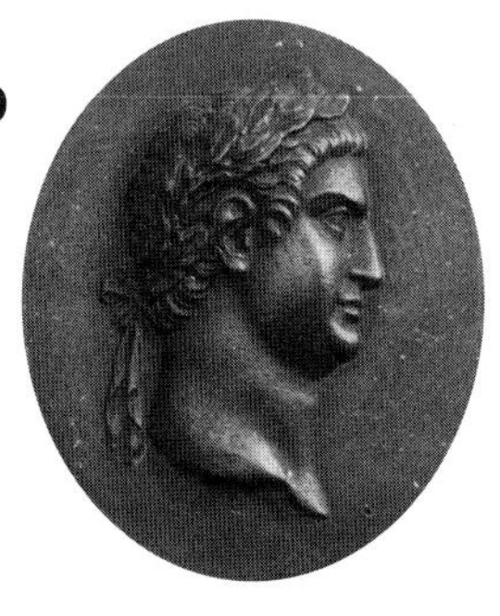

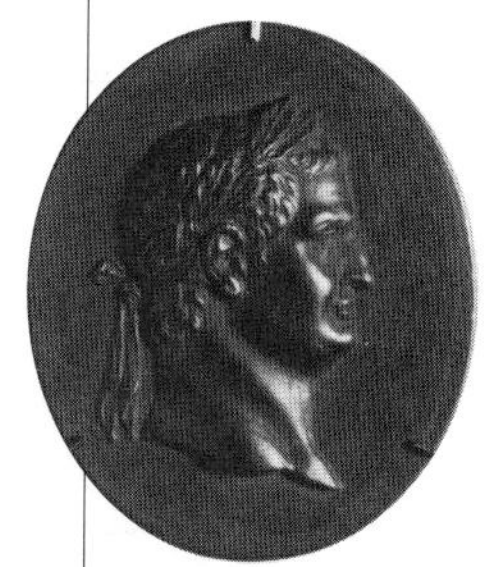

979. Medallion: Vitellius, ca. 1785
Basalt
1 7/8 x 1 5/8 in (4.7 x 4.1 cm)
Mark: “WEDGWOOD”; “VITELLIUS” on back
Provenance: Dr. Harold L. Klawans, Chicago
1977.66

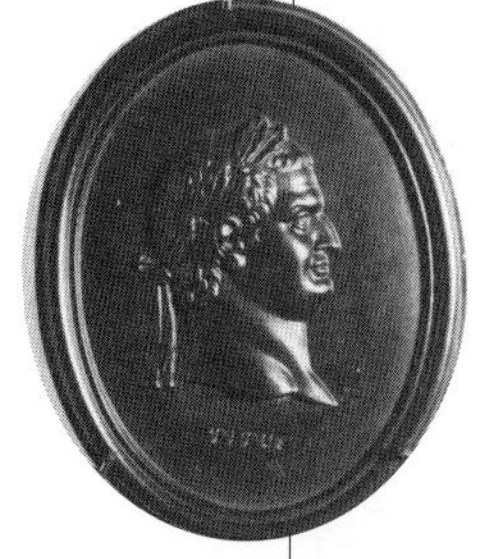

979. Medallion: *Titus*, ca. 1785
Basalt
1 15/16 x 1 5/8 in (4.9 x 4.1 cm)
Mark: “WEDGWOOD”; “TITUS” on back
Provenance: Dr. Harold L. Klawans, Chicago
1977.65

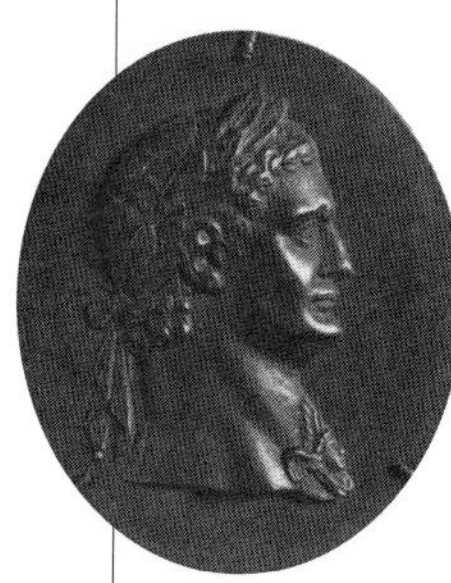

980. Medallion: *Domitian*, ca. 1785
Basalt
1 15/16 x 1 5/8 in (4.9 x 4.1 cm)
Mark: “WEDGWOOD”; “DOMITIAN” on front
Provenance: Dr. Harold L. Klawans, Chicago
1977.57

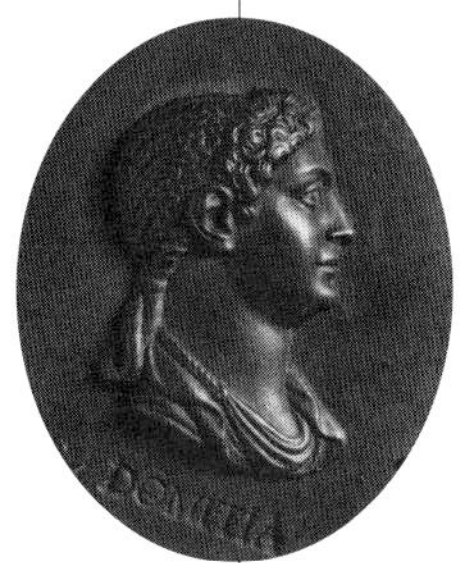

981. Medallion: *Domitia*, ca. 1785
Basalt
2 1/8 x 1 3/4 in (5.3 x 4.4 cm)
Mark: "WEDGWOOD"; "DOMITIA" on front
Provenance: Dr. Harold L. Klawans, Chicago
1977.56

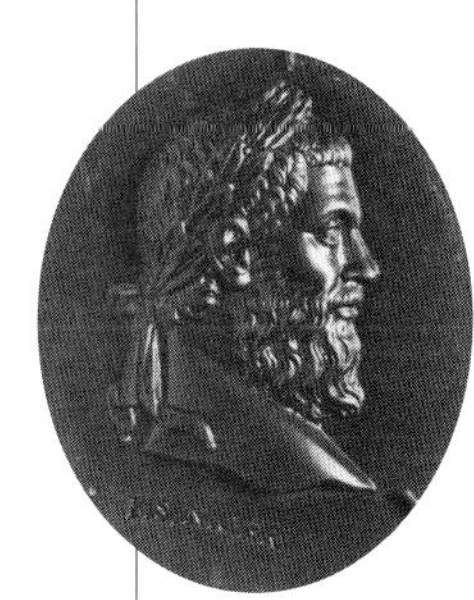

982. Medallion: *Pescennius Niger*, ca. 1770
Basalt
2 x 1 11/16 in (5 x 4.2 cm)
Mark: "Wedgwood & Bentley"; "PIS. NIGER" on front
Provenance: M. Mellanay Delhom, Chicago; Ann Brodkiewicz, Chicago
1977.62

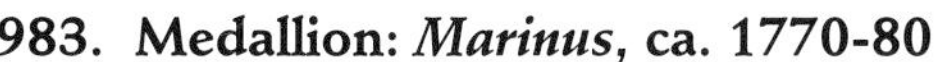

983. Medallion: *Marinus*, ca. 1770-80
Basalt
2 x 1 11/16 in (5 x 4.2 cm)
Mark: "Wedgwood & Bentley";
"MARRINUS" on front
Provenance: Dr. Harold L. Klawans
1977.60

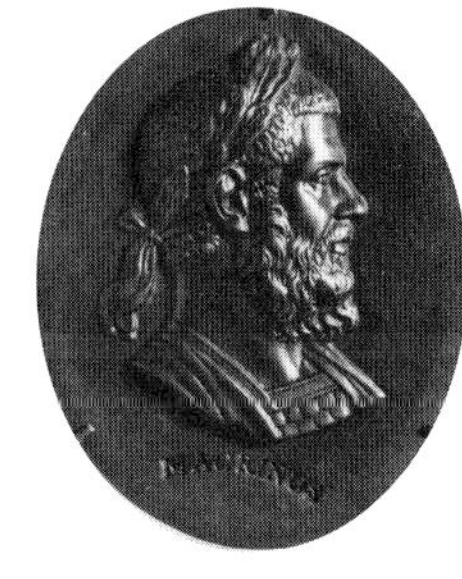

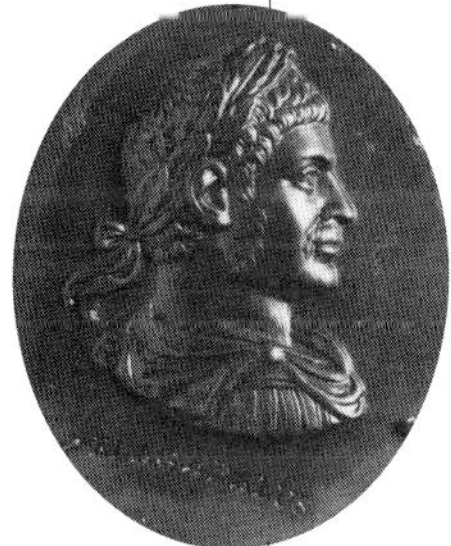

984. Medallion: *Elagabalus*, ca. 1775-80
Basalt
2 x 1 11/16 in (5 x 4.2 cm)
Mark: "Wedgwood & Bentley"; "ELAGABALUS" on front
Provenance: M. Mellanay Delhom, Chicago; Ann Brodkiewicz, Chicago
1977.58

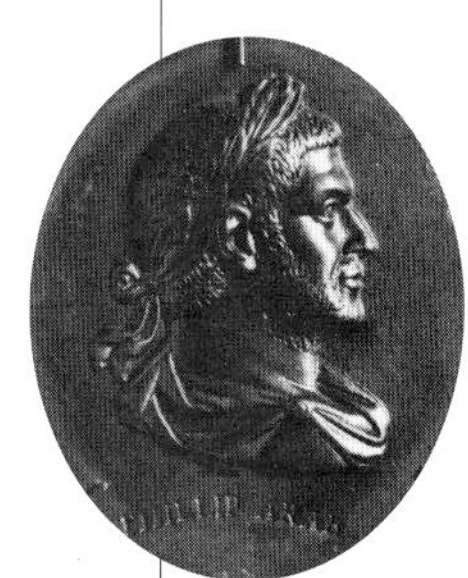

985. Medallion: *Phillip Arab*, ca. 1770
Basalt
2 x 1 11/16 in (5 x 4.2 cm)
Mark: "Wedgwood & Bentley"; "PHILLIP ARAB" on front
Provenance: M. Mellanay Delhom, Chicago; Ann Brodkiewicz, Chicago
1977.55

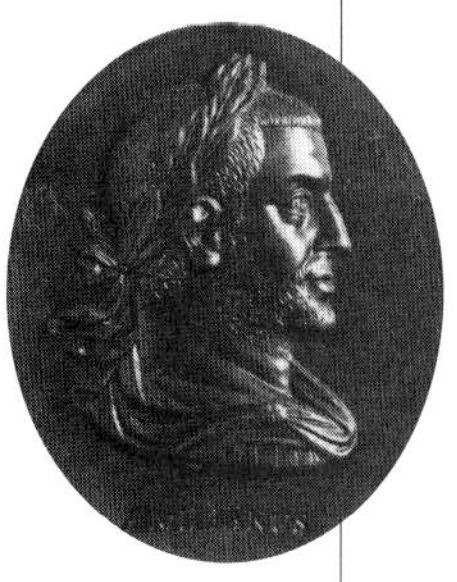

986. Medallion: *Aemilianus*, ca. 1770
Basalt
2 x 1 11/16 in (5 x 4.2 cm)
Mark: "Wedgwood & Bentley"; "AEMILIANUS" on front
Provenance: M. Mellanay Delhom, Chicago; Ann Brodkiewicz, Chicago
1977.53

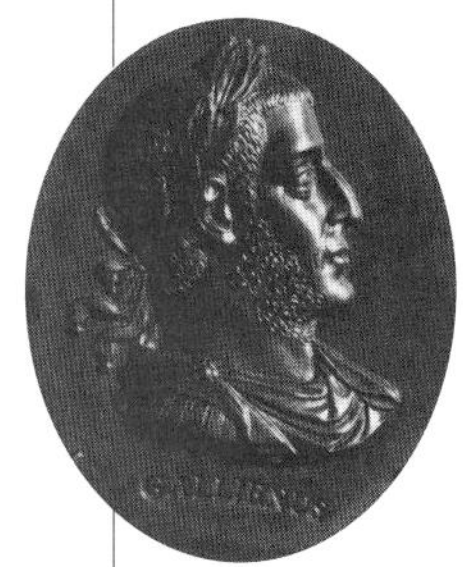

987. Medallion: *Gallienus*, ca. 1770-80
Basalt
2 x 1 11/16 in (5 x 4.2 cm)
Mark: "Wedgwood & Bentley"; "GALLIENUS" on front
Provenance: M. Mellanay Delhom, Chicago;
Ann Brodkiewicz, Chicago
1977.59

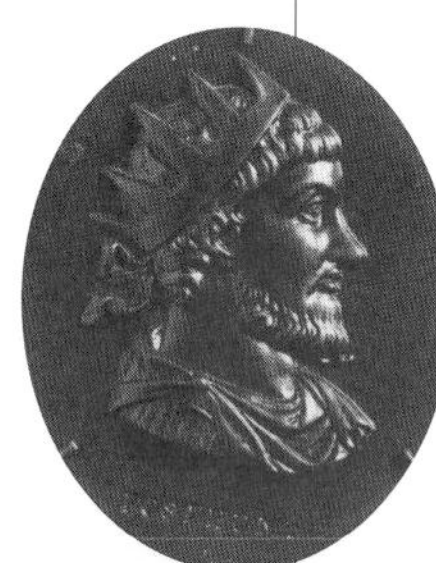

988. Medallion: *Posthum*, ca. 1770-80
Basalt
2 x 1 11/16 in (5 x 4.2 cm)
Mark: "Wedgwood & Bentley"; "POSTHUM" on front
Provenance: M. Mellanay Delhom, Chicago; Ann Brodkiewicz, Chicago
1977.63

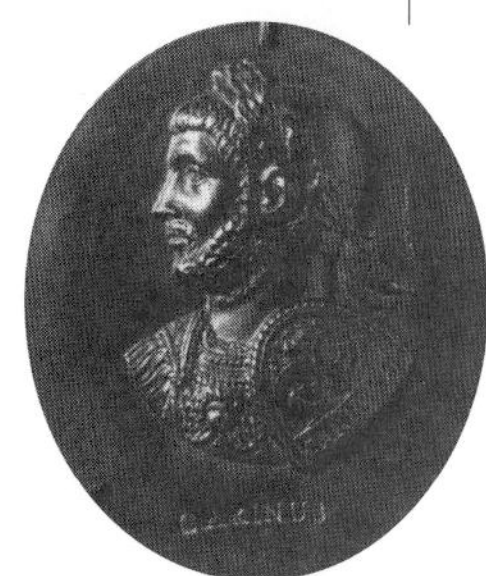

989. Medallion: *Carinus*, ca. 1780
Basalt
2 x 1 11/16 in (5 x 4.2 cm)
Mark: "Wedgwood & Bentley"; "CARINUS" on front
Provenance: M. Mellanay Delhom, Chicago; Ann Brodkiewicz, Chicago
1982.52

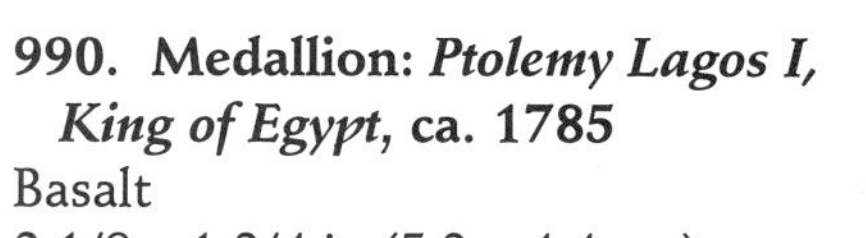

990. Medallion: *Ptolemy Lagos I, King of Egypt*, ca. 1785
Basalt
2 1/8 x 1 3/4 in (5.3 x 4.4 cm)
Mark: "WEDGWOOD"; "PTOL.LA" on front
Provenance: Dr. Harold L. Klawans, Chicago
1977.64

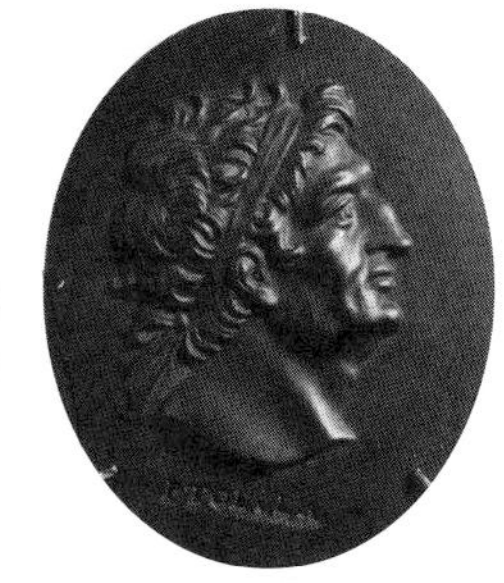

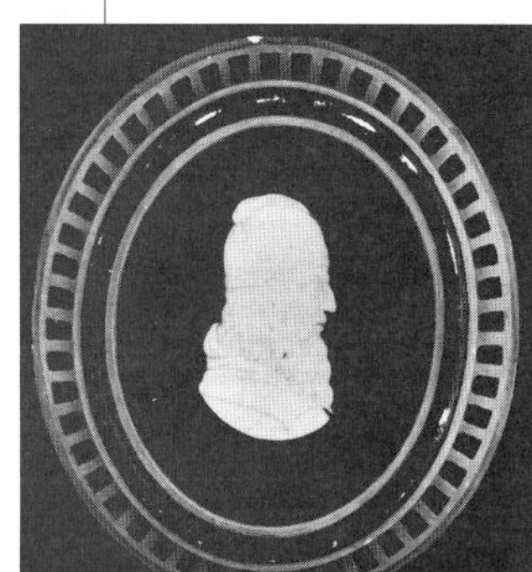

991. Medallion: *Antiochus Hierax*, ca. 1785
Basalt
2 3/16 x 1 13/16 in (5.5 x 4.6 cm)
Mark: "WEDGWOOD"; "ANTIOC.HI" on front
Provenance: Dr. Harold L. Klawans, Chicago
1977.54

992. Medallion: *Aristotle*, ca. 1775
White terra-cotta stoneware with encaustic decoration
3 3/4 x 3 7/16 in (8.8 x 8.5 cm)
Mark: "ARISTOTLE" impressed on front
Provenance: Art Trading Ltd., New York
1991.789

Intaglios

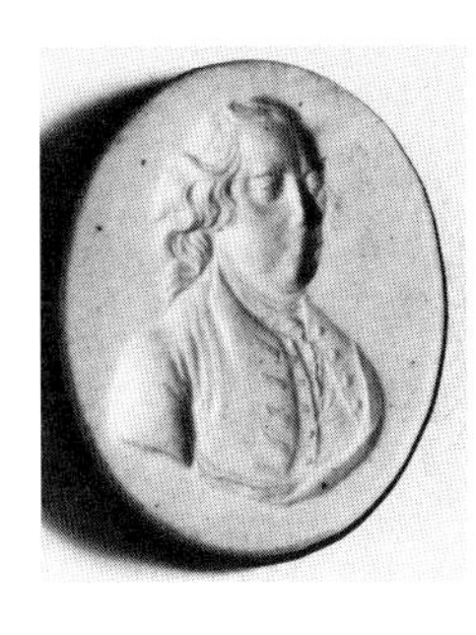

993. Intaglio: *Doctor Lucas*, ca. 1775
Jasper, brown ground with white layer on front
7/8 x 3/4 in (2.2 x 1.9 cm)
Mark: "Wedgwood & Bentley" "275"
Provenance: Dr. Harold L. Klawans, Chicago
1977.152.2
Color plate 49

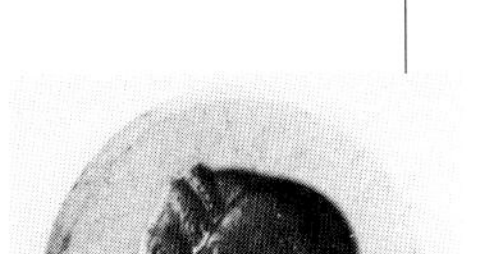

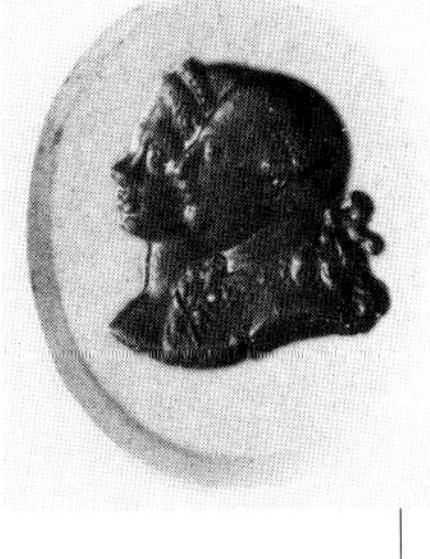

994. Intaglio: *George III and Charlotte*, ca. 1775
Basalt, blue jasper wash on front and back
13/16 x 11/16 in (2 x 1.7 cm)
Mark: none
Provenance: Dr. Harold L. Klawans, Chicago
1977.152.16

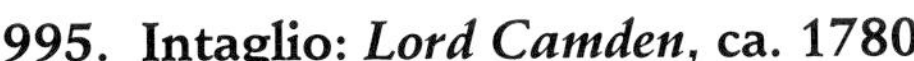

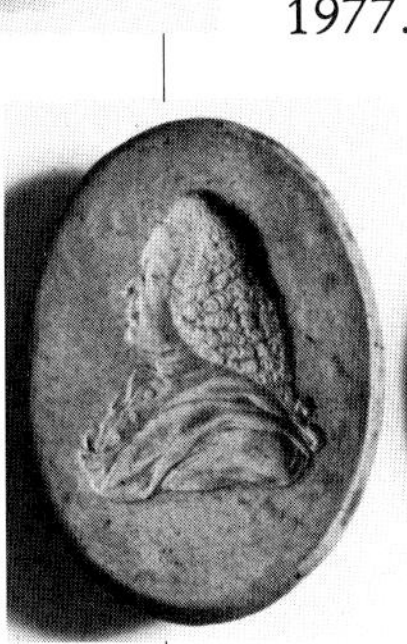

995. Intaglio: *Lord Camden*, ca. 1780
Caneware
15/16 x 11/16 in (2.3 x 1.7 cm)
Mark: none
Provenance: Dr. Harold L. Klawans, Chicago
1977.152.4
Color plate 496

995. Intaglio: *Lord Camden*, ca. 1790
Basalt
7/8 x 5/8 in (2.2 x 1.5 cm)
Mark: "WEDGWOOD" "14153"
Provenance: Dr. Harold L. Klawans, Chicago
1980.37
Color plate 63

997. Intaglio: *Bust of Man*, ca. 1780
Jasper, marbled blue-and-white ground
with blue wash on front
7/8 x 3/4 in (2.2 x 1.9 cm)
Mark: none
Provenance: Dr. Francis Jennings
Vurpillat, South Bend, Ind.
1977.122.11

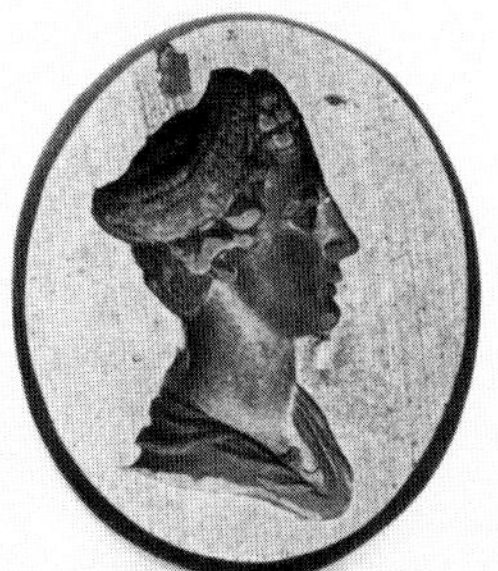

998. Intaglio: *Classical Female Head*, ca. 1775
Basalt, blue-jasper overlay on front
3/4 x 5/8 in (1.9 x 1.5 cm)
Mark: "Wedgwood & Bentley" impressed in circle around "1617"
Provenance: Ann Brodkiewicz, Chicago
1982.33

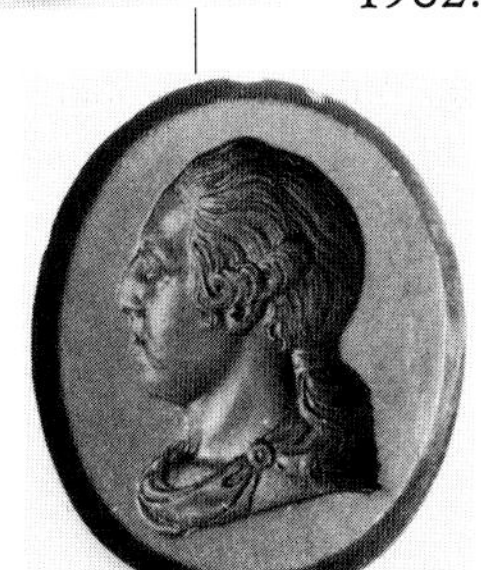

999. Intaglio: *H. R. H. Duke of Gloucester*, ca. 1780
Basalt
3/4 x 5/8 in (1.9 x 1.5 cm)
Mark: "Wedgwood & Bentley" "283"
Provenance: Dr. Harold L. Klawans, Chicago
1980.22

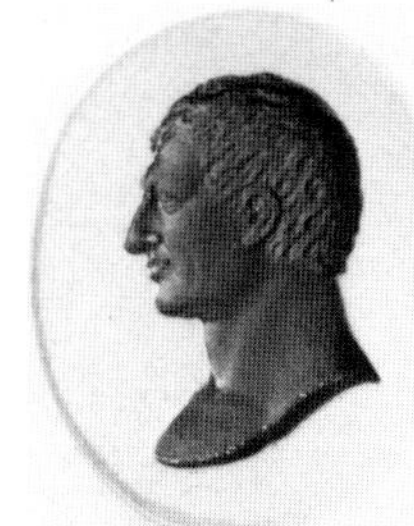

1000. Intaglio: *George Washington*, ca. 1780
Basalt, blue jasper wash front and back
7/8 x 3/4 in (2.2 x 1.9 cm)
Mark: none
Provenance: Dr. Harold L. Klawans, Chicago
1977.152.9

1001. Intaglio: *Miguel de Cervantes Saavedra*, ca. 1790
Basalt
3/4 x 5/8 in (1.9 x 1.5 cm)
Mark: "WEDGWOOD" "370"
Provenance: Dr. Harold L. Klawans, Chicago
1980.44

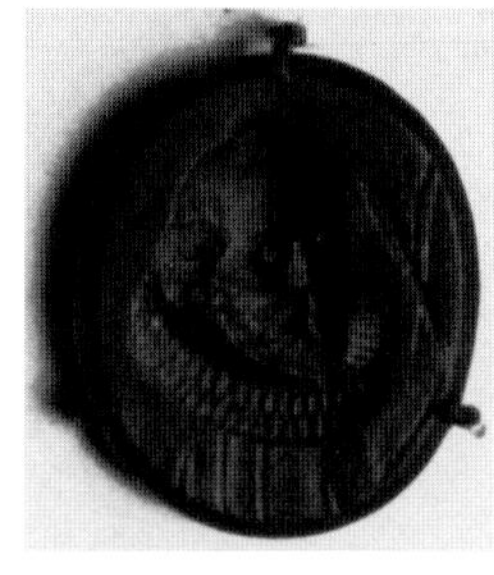

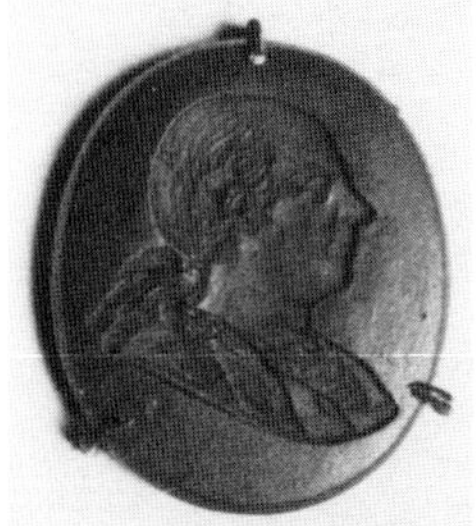

1002. Intaglio: *Prince of Prussia*, ca. 1790
Basalt
7/8 x 3/4 in (2.2 x 1.9 cm)
Mark: "WEDGWOOD" "385"
Provenance: Dr. Harold L. Klawans, Chicago
1980.56

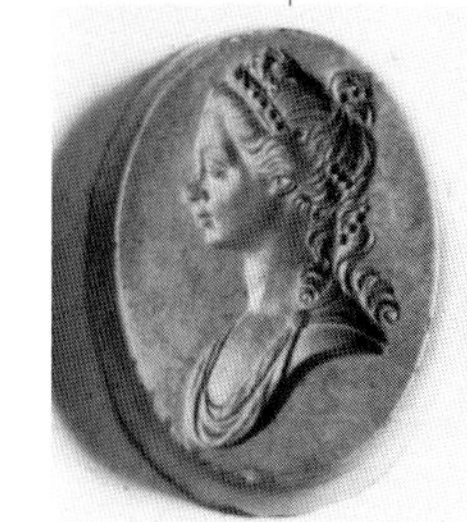

1003. Intaglio: *Queen Charlotte*, ca. 1780
Jasper, solid white ground with blue wash
1 x 3/4 in (2.5 x 1.9 cm)
Mark: none
Provenance: Dr. Harold L. Klawans, Chicago
1979.230

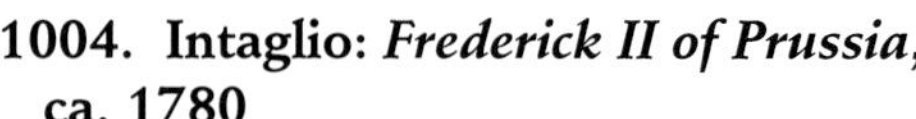

1004. Intaglio: *Frederick II of Prussia*, ca. 1780
Basalt, blue jasper wash front and back
7/8 x 3/4 in (2.2 x 1.9 cm)
Mark: none
Provenance: Dr. Harold L. Klawans, Chicago
1980.152.10

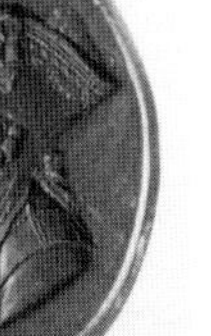

1005. Intaglio: *Frederick II of Prussia*, ca. 1790
Basalt
7/8 x 3/4 in (2.2 x 1.9 cm)
Mark: "WEDGWOOD" "411"
Provenance: Dr. Harold L. Klawans, Chicago
1980.45

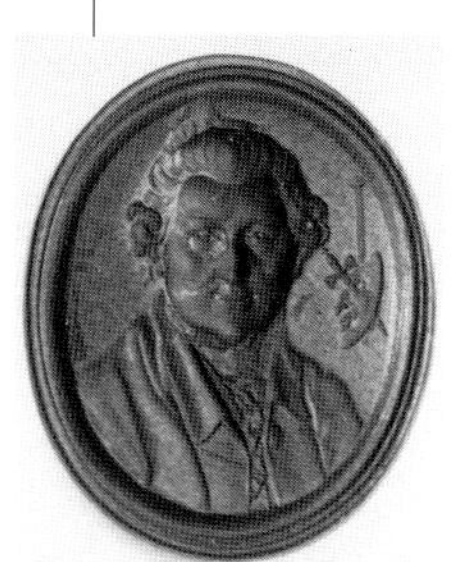

1006. Intaglio: *David Garrick*, ca. 1790
Basalt
15/16 x 13/16 in (2.3 x 2 cm)
Mark: "WEDGWOOD" "14195"; "BROWN" in reverse on front
Provenance: Dr. Harold L. Klawans, Chicago
1980.52

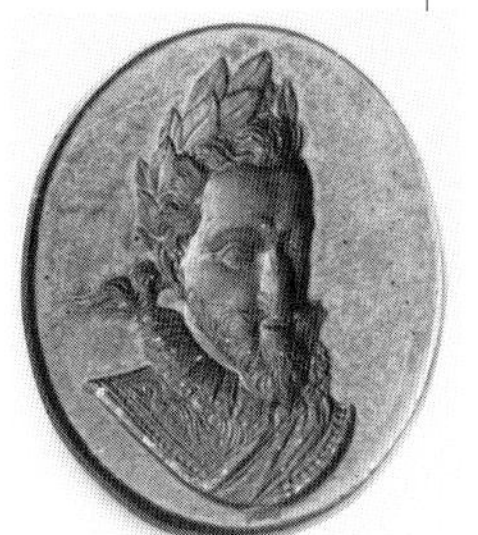

1007. Intaglio: ***Henry IV of France,*** **ca. 1790**
Basalt
1 x 3/4 in (2.5 x 1.9 cm)
Mark: "WEDGWOOD" "32"
Provenance: Dr. Harold L. Klawans, Chicago
1980.57

1008. Intaglio: ***Oliver Cromwell and William III,*** **ca. 1790**
Basalt
1 x 13/16 in (2.5 x 2 cm)
Mark: "WEDGWOOD" "15763"
Provenance: Dr. Harold L. Klawans, Chicago
1980.50

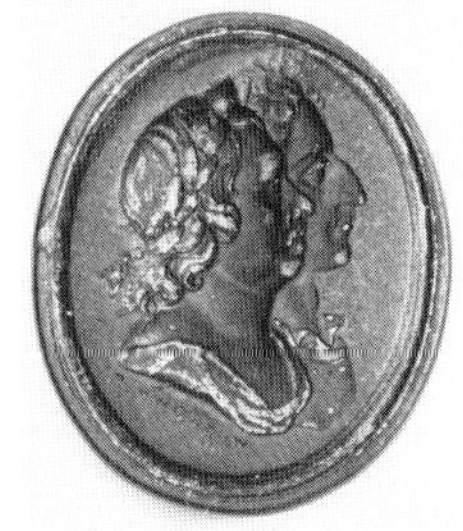

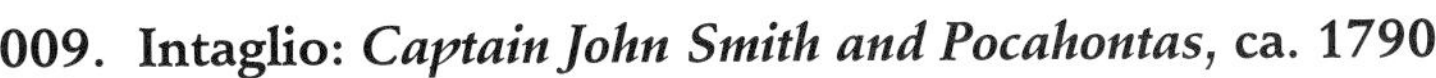

1009. Intaglio: ***Captain John Smith and Pocahontas,*** **ca. 1790**
Basalt
1 1/8 x 7/8 in (2.8 x 2.2 cm)
Mark: "WEDGWOOD"
Provenance: Dr. Harold L. Klawans, Chicago
1980.39

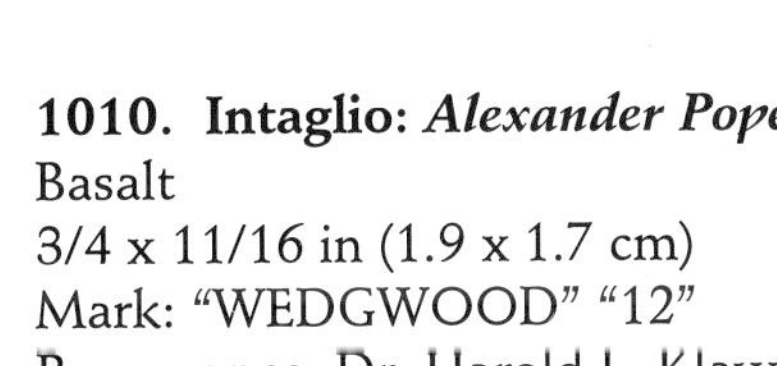

1010. Intaglio: ***Alexander Pope,*** **ca. 1790**
Basalt
3/4 x 11/16 in (1.9 x 1.7 cm)
Mark: "WEDGWOOD" "12"
Provenance: Dr. Harold L. Klawans, Chicago
1980.55

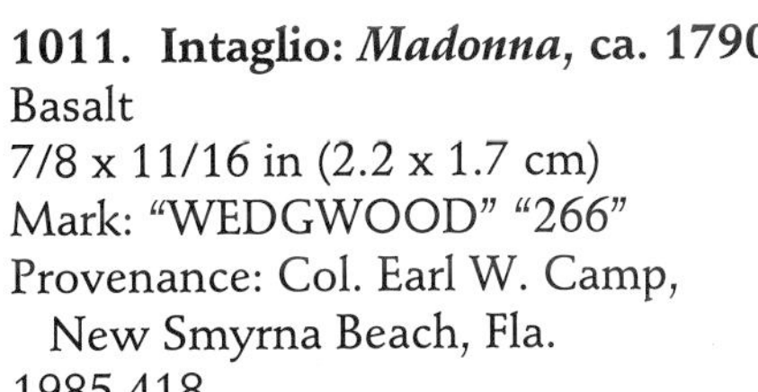

1011. Intaglio: ***Madonna,*** **ca. 1790**
Basalt
7/8 x 11/16 in (2.2 x 1.7 cm)
Mark: "WEDGWOOD" "266"
Provenance: Col. Earl W. Camp, New Smyrna Beach, Fla.
1985.418

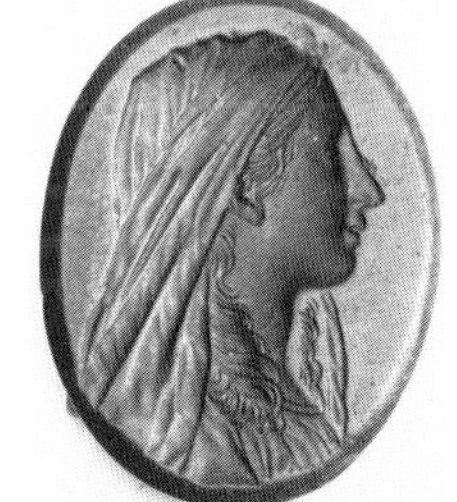

1012. Intaglio: ***Antonia with Urn,*** **ca. 1790**
Basalt
2 1/4 x 1 in (5.7 x 2.5 cm)
Mark: "WEDGWOOD"
Provenance: Godfrey W. Ford, England; Dr. Harold L. Klawans, Chicago
1980.64

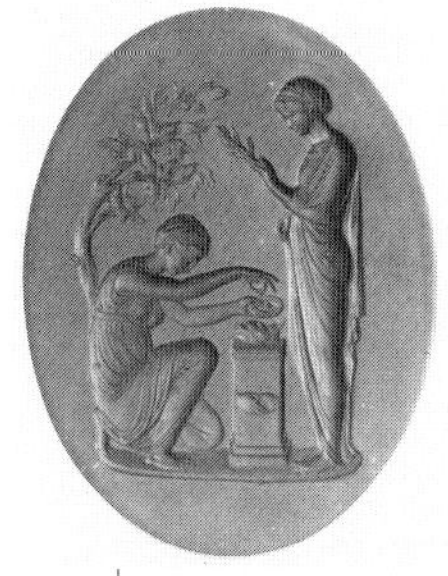

1013. Intaglio: ***Sacrifice to Peace,*** **ca. 1790**
Basalt
2 1/2 x 2 in (6.3 x 5 cm)
Mark: "WEDGWOOD"
Provenance: Dr. Harold L. Klawans, Chicago
1980.60
Color plate 49

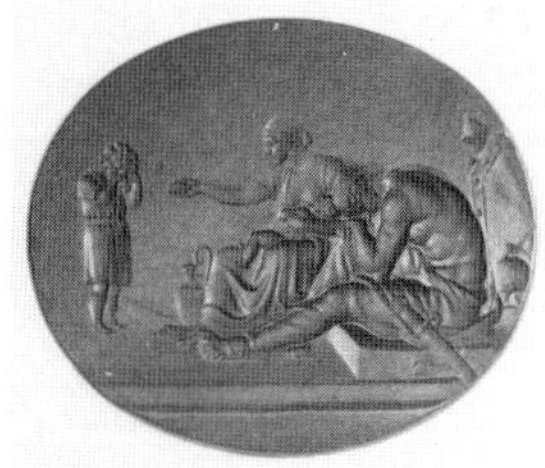

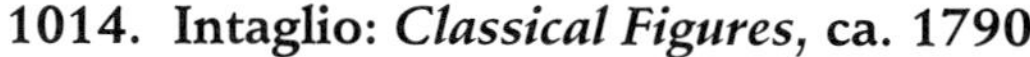

1014. Intaglio: *Classical Figures*, ca. 1790
Basalt
1 5/8 x 1 7/8 in (4.1 x 4.7 cm)
Mark: "WEDGWOOD"
Provenance: Dr. Harold L. Klawans, Chicago
1980.35

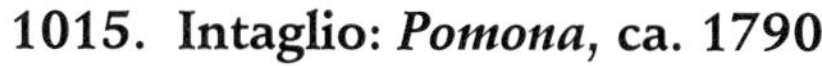

1015. Intaglio: *Pomona*, ca. 1790
Basalt
2 1/4 x 1 in (5.7 x 2.5 cm)
Mark: "WEDGWOOD"
Provenance: Dr. Harold L. Klawans, Chicago
1980.63

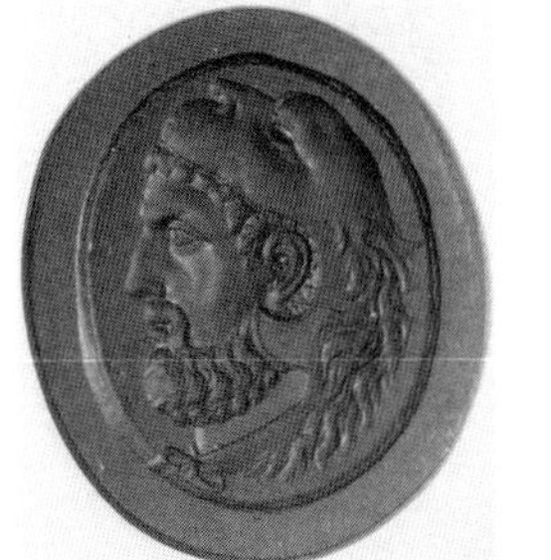

1016. Intaglio: *Bearded Hercules*, ca. 1790
Basalt
2 x 1 3/4 in (5 x 4.4 cm)
Mark: "WEDGWOOD"
Provenance: Dr. Harold L. Klawans, Chicago
1980.36

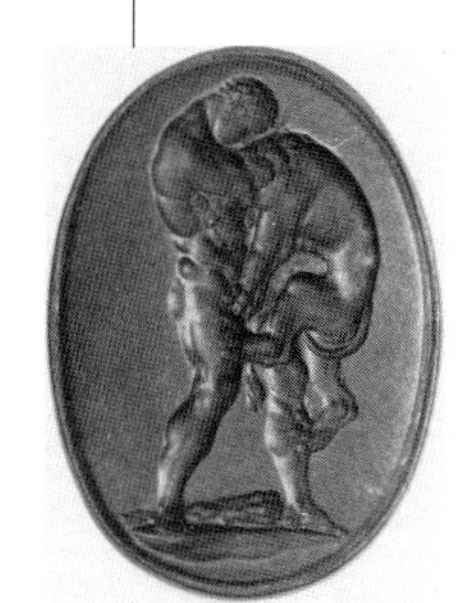

1017. Intaglio: *Hercules Strangling the Nemean Lion*, ca. 1790
Basalt
1 3/8 x 1 in (3.4 x 2.5 cm)
Mark: "WEDGWOOD"
Provenance: Dr. Harold L. Klawans, Chicago
1980.58

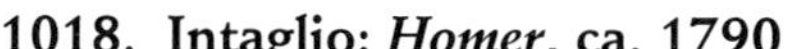

1018. Intaglio: *Homer*, ca. 1790
Basalt
1 1/4 x 1 in (3.1 x 2.5 cm)
Mark: "WEDGWOOD"
Provenance: Dr. Harold L. Klawans, Chicago
1980.61
Color plate 49

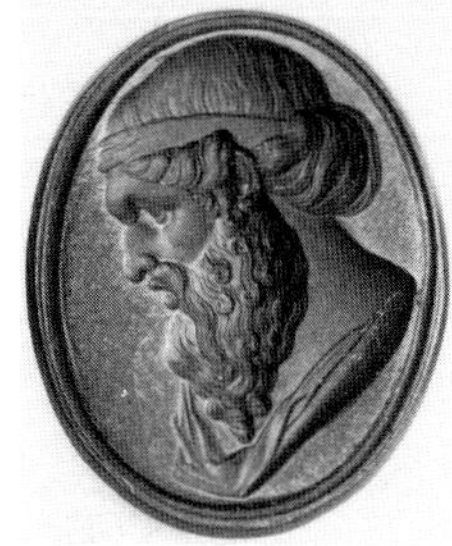

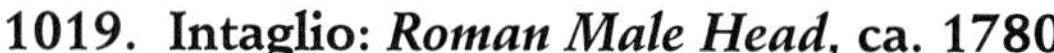

1019. Intaglio: *Roman Male Head*, ca. 1780
Basalt, blue jasper wash front and back
7/8 x 3/4 in (2.2 x 1.9 cm)
Mark: none
Provenance: Dr. Harold L. Klawans, Chicago
1977.152.7

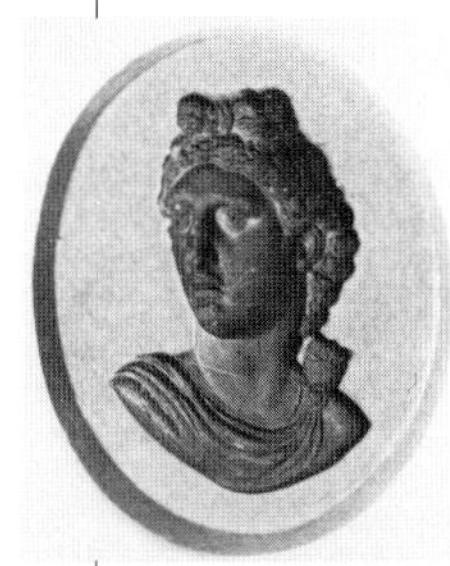

1020. Intaglio: *Apollo*, ca. 1780
Basalt, blue jasper wash front and back
1 x 7/8 in (2.5 x 2.2 cm)
Mark: none
Provenance: Dr. Harold L. Klawans, Chicago
1977.152.8
Color plate 49

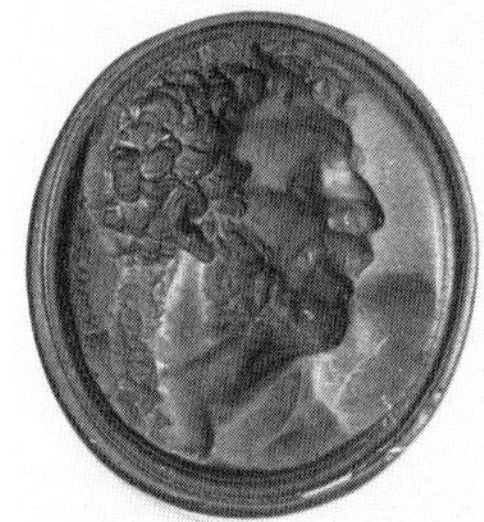

1021. Intaglio: *Classical Male Head,* ca. 1790
Basalt
1 x 7/8 in (2.5 x 2.2 cm)
Mark: "WEDGWOOD"; "BROWN" in reverse on front
Provenance: Dr. Harold L. Klawans, Chicago
1980.31
Color plate 49

1022. Intaglio: *Classical Male Head,* ca. 1790
Basalt
1 x 11/16 in (2.5 x 1.7 cm)
Mark: "WEDGWOOD"; "BROWN" in reverse on front
Provenance: Dr. Harold L. Klawans, Chicago
1980.47

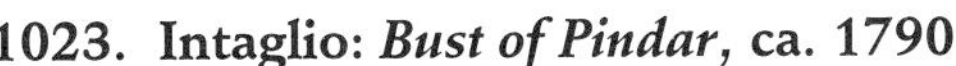

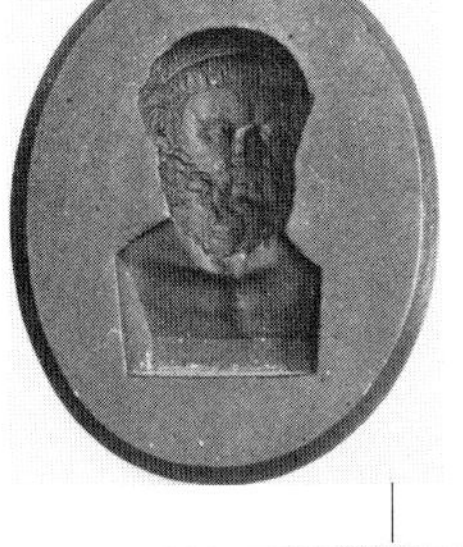

1023. Intaglio: *Bust of Pindar,* ca. 1790
Basalt
1 x 7/8 in (2.5 x 2.2 cm)
Mark: "WEDGWOOD" "329"
Provenance: Dr. Harold L. Klawans, Chicago
1980.46
Color plate 49

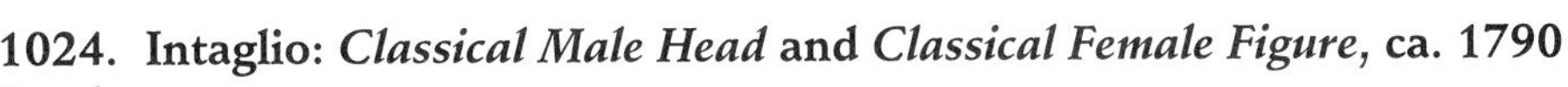

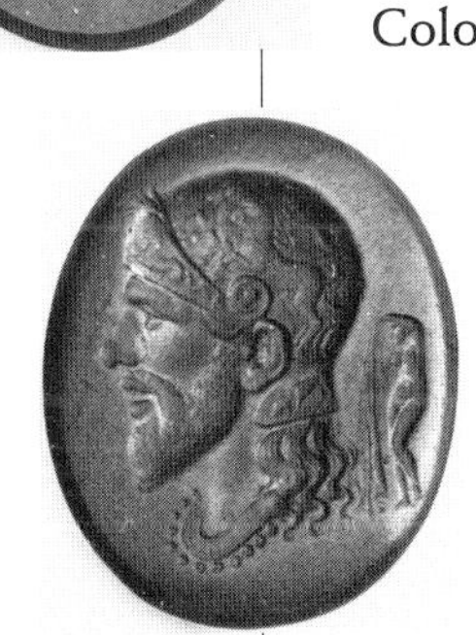

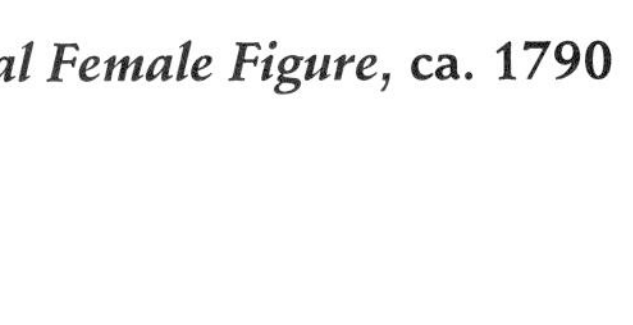

1024. Intaglio: *Classical Male Head* and *Classical Female Figure,* ca. 1790
Basalt
1 x 7/8 in (2.5 x 2.2 cm)
Mark: "WEDGWOOD"
Provenance: Dr. Harold L. Klawans, Chicago
1980.42

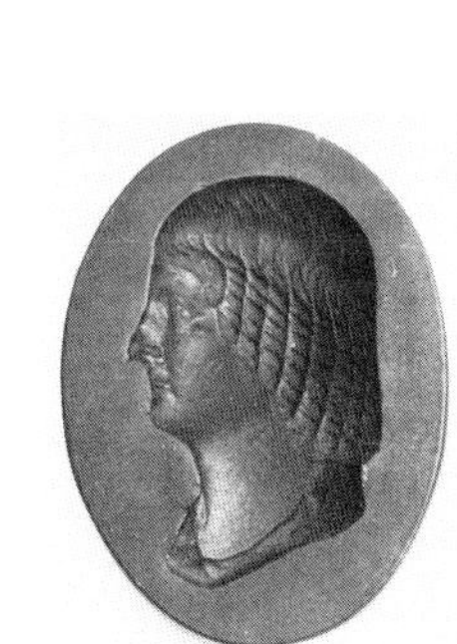

1025. Intaglio: *Classical Female Head,* ca. 1790
Basalt
1 1/8 x 7/8 in (2.8 x 2.2 cm)
Mark: "WEDGWOOD"
Provenance: Dr. Harold L. Klawans, Chicago
1980.38

1026. Intaglio: *Classical Male Head,* ca. 1790
Basalt
3/4 x 11/16 in (1.9 x 1.7 cm)
Mark: "WEDGWOOD"
Provenance: Col. Earl W. Camp, New Smyrna Beach, Fla.
1985.421.4

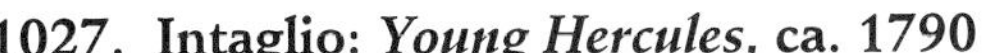

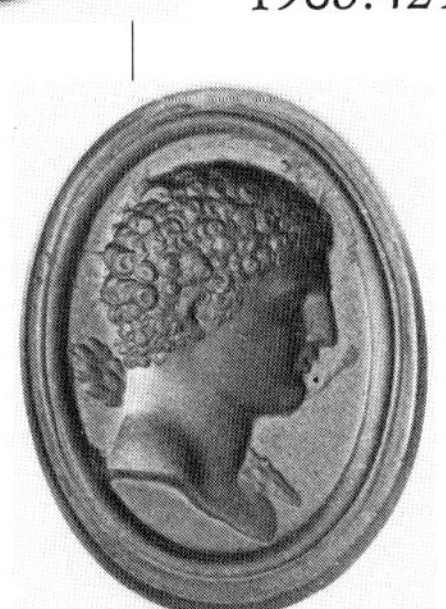

1027. Intaglio: *Young Hercules,* ca. 1790
Basalt
1 x 13/16 in (2.5 x 2 cm)
Mark: "WEDGWOOD" "5311"
Provenance: Col. Earl W. Camp, New Smyrna Beach, Fla.
1985.421.1

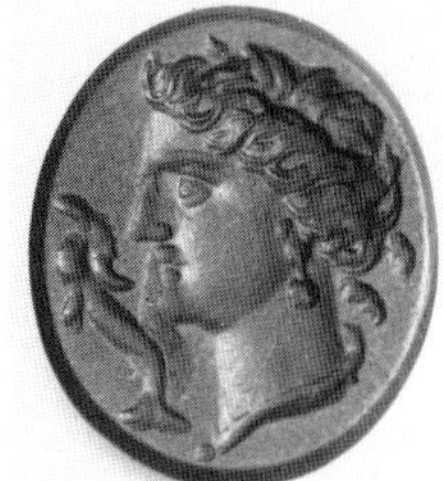

1028. Intaglio: *Amphitrite and Dolphin*, ca. 1790
Basalt
3/4 x 11/16 in (1.9 x 1.7 cm)
Mark: "WEDGWOOD" "2580"
Provenance: Dr. Harold L. Klawans, Chicago
1980.32

1029. Intaglio: *Classical Female Head*, ca. 1790
Basalt
15/16 x 11/16 in (2.3 x 1.7 cm)
Mark: "WEDGWOOD" "11538"
Provenance: Dr. Harold L. Klawans, Chicago
1980.33

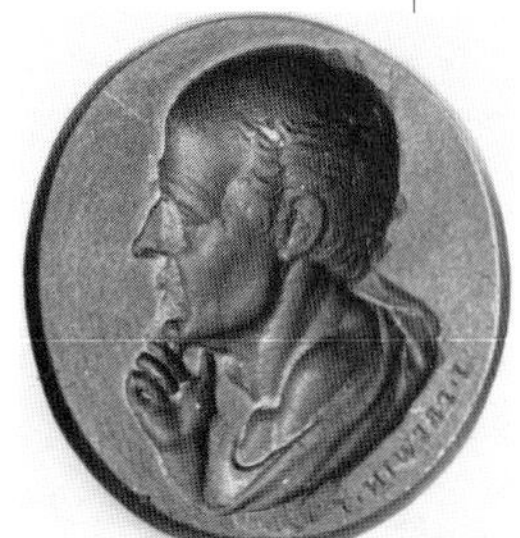

1030. Intaglio: *Head of Antisphenes*, ca. 1790
Basalt
7/8 x 3/4 in (2.2 x 1.9 cm)
Mark: "WEDGWOOD" "9936"; "I. PREWIN" in reverse on front
Provenance: Dr. Harold L. Klawans, Chicago
1980.48

1031. Intaglio: *Medusa*, ca. 1790
Basalt
1 1/8 x 15/16 in (2.8 x 2.3 cm)
Mark: "WEDGWOOD" "238"
Provenance: Dr. Harold L. Klawans, Chicago
1980.49
Color plate 70

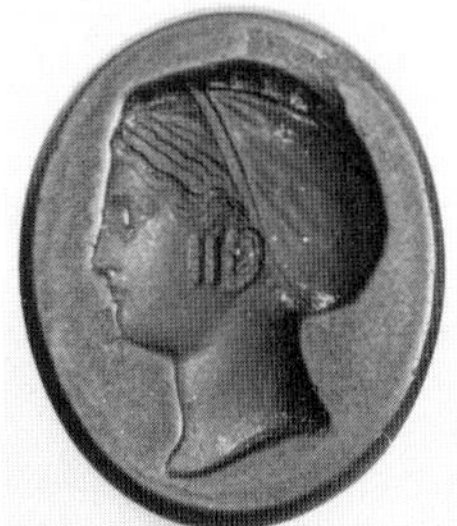

1032. Intaglio: *Sappho*, ca. 1790
Basalt
3/4 x 5/8 in (1.9 x 1.5 cm)
Mark: "WEDGWOOD" "10207"
Provenance: Col. Earl W. Camp, New Smyrna Beach, Fla.
1985.421.2

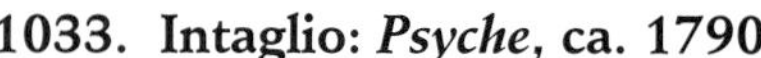

1033. Intaglio: *Psyche*, ca. 1790
Basalt
7/8 x 3/4 in (2.2 x 1.9 cm)
Mark: "WEDGWOOD" "7051"
Provenance: Col. Earl W. Camp, New Smyrna Beach, Fla.
1985.421.3

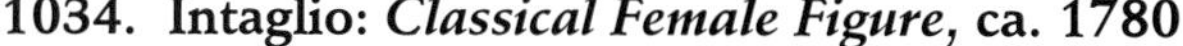

1034. Intaglio: *Classical Female Figure*, ca. 1780
Caneware
3/4 x 5/8 in (1.9 x 1.5 cm)
Mark: none
Provenance: Dr. Harold L. Klawans, Chicago
1979.232

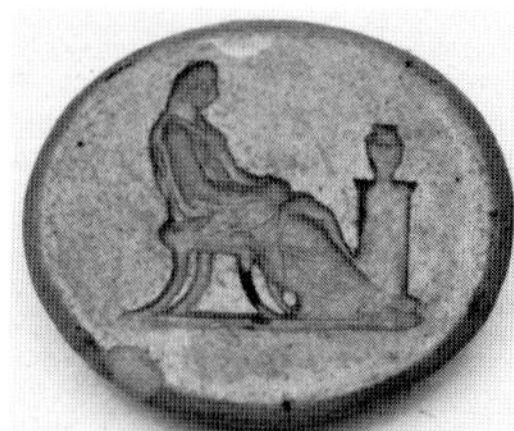

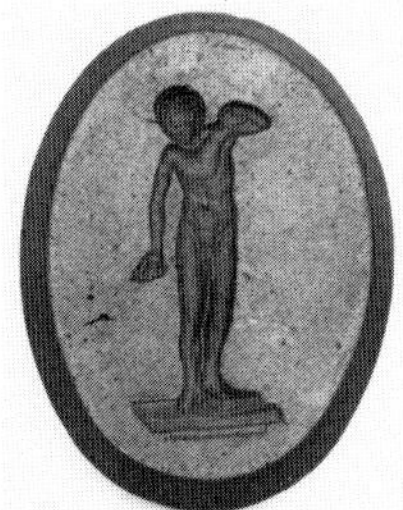

1035. Intaglio: *A Wrestler*, ca. 1800
Rosso antico
3/4 x 9/16 in (1.9 x 1.4 cm)
Mark: none
Provenance: Dr. Harold L. Klawans, Chicago
1979.231

1036. Intaglio: *Two Classical Figures*, ca. 1780
Basalt, blue jasper wash front and back
13/16 x 3/4 in (2 x 1.9 cm)
Mark: none
Provenance: Dr. Harold L. Klawans, Chicago
1977.152.12

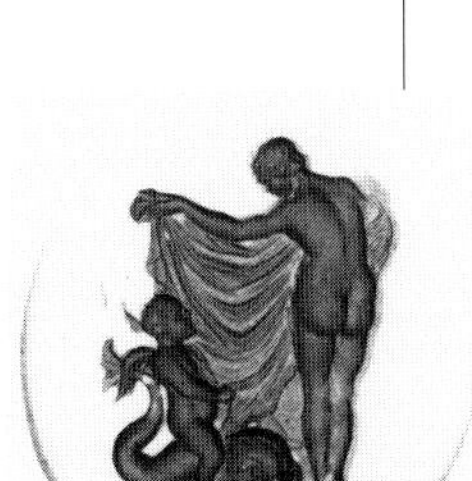

1037. Intaglio: *Venus Hiding Cupid on a Dolphin*, ca. 1775
Jasper, brown ground with white layer on front
3/4 in (1.9 cm)
Mark: "Wedgwood & Bentley" in circle
Provenance: Dr. Harold L. Klawans, Chicago
1977.152.1
Color plate 49

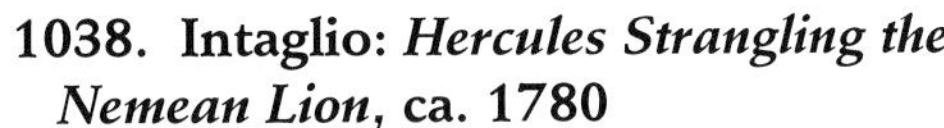

1038. Intaglio: *Hercules Strangling the Nemean Lion*, ca. 1780
Basalt, blue jasper wash on front
7/8 x 11/16 in (2.2 x 1.7 cm)
Mark: none
Provenance: Dr. Harold L. Klawans, Chicago
1977.152.13

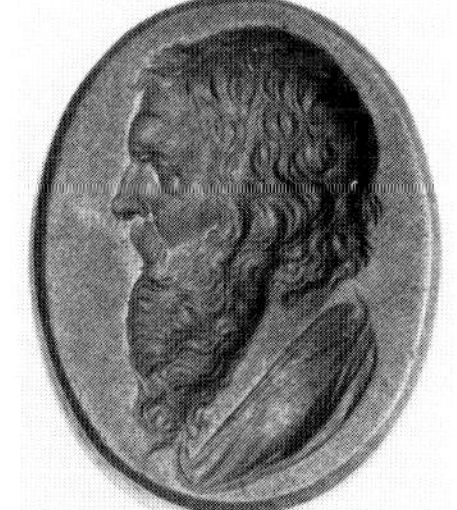

1039. Intaglio: *Aristophanes*, ca. 1780
Jasper, solid blue ground
7/8 x 11/16 in (2.2 x 1.7 cm)
Mark: none
Provenance: Dr. Harold L. Klawans, Chicago
1977.152.15

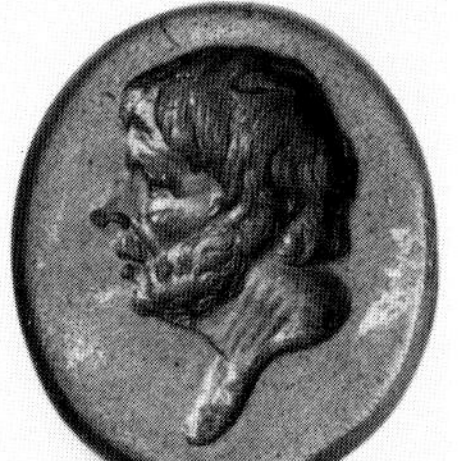

1040. Intaglio: *Seneca*, ca. 1775
Basalt
3/4 x 5/8 in (1.9 x 1.5 cm)
Mark: "Wedgwood & Bentley" "239"
Provenance: M. Mellanay Delhom, Chicago; Ann Brodkiewicz, Chicago
1982.39

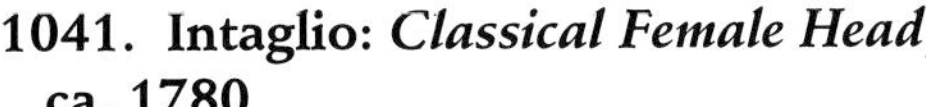

1041. Intaglio: *Classical Female Head*, ca. 1780
Jasper, solid dark blue
3/4 x 5/8 in (1.9 x 1.5 cm)
Mark: none
Provenance: Dr. Harold L. Klawans, Chicago
1979.234

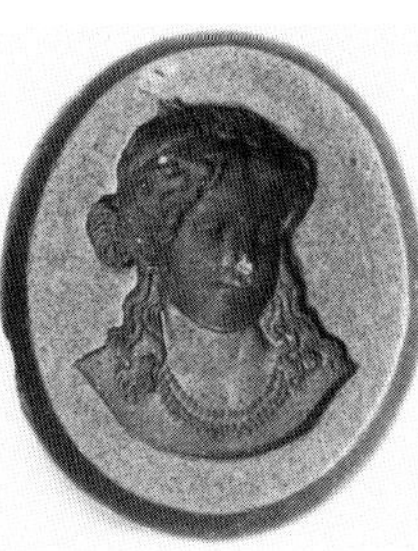

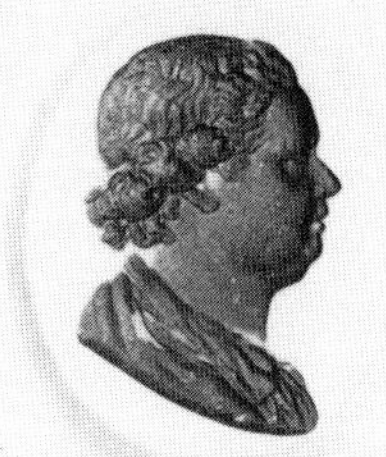

1042. Intaglio: *Roman Male Head,* ca. 1775
Basalt, gray jasper wash front and back
13/16 x 11/16 in (2 x 1.7 cm)
Mark: none
Provenance: Dr. Harold L. Klawans, Chicago
1977.152.3
Color plate 49

1043. Intaglio: *Roman Male Head,* ca. 1780
Basalt, blue jasper wash front and back
7/8 x 11/16 in (2.2 x 1.7 cm)
Mark: none
Provenance: Dr. Harold L. Klawans, Chicago
1977.152.6

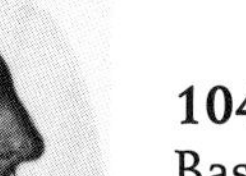

1044. Intaglio: *Classical Male Head,* ca. 1780
Basalt, blue jasper wash front and back
13/16 x 3/4 in (2 x 1.9 cm)
Mark: none
Provenance: Dr. Harold L. Klawans, Chicago
1977.152.11

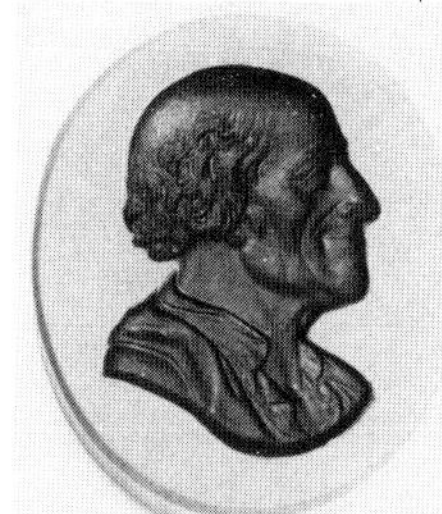

1045. Intaglio: *Voltaire,* ca. 1780
Basalt, blue jasper wash front and back
7/8 x 11/16 in (2.2 x 1.7 cm)
Mark: none
Provenance: Dr. Harold L. Klawans, Chicago
1977.152.5

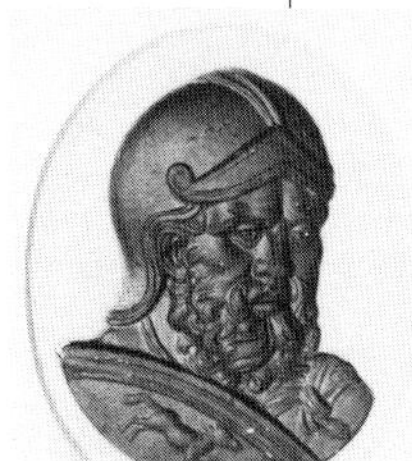

1046. Intaglio: *Roman Male Head,* ca. 1780
Basalt, blue jasper wash on front and back
1 x 3/4 in (2.5 x 1.9 cm)
Mark: none
Provenance: Dr. Harold L. Klawans, Chicago
1977.152.14

1047. Intaglio: *Classical Male Head,* ca. 1780
Cane ware
3/4 x 5/8 in (1.9 x 1.5 cm)
Mark: none
Provenance: Dr. Francis Jennings Vurpillat, South Bend, Ind.
1977.122.12

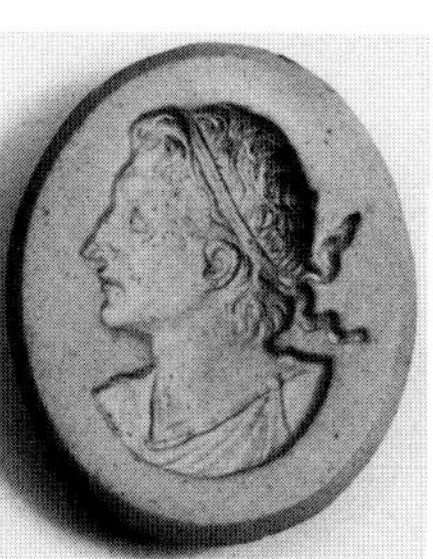

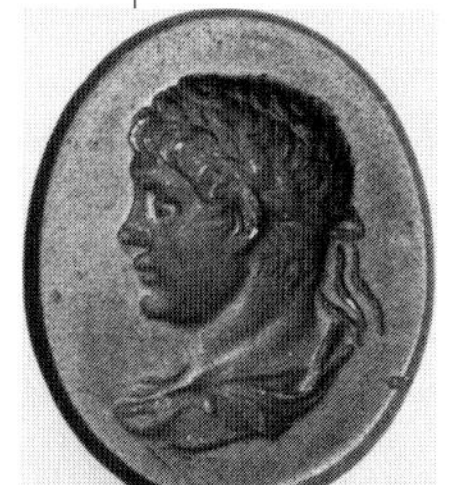

1048. Intaglio: *Classical Male Head,* ca. 1780
Humphrey Palmer (1720-86), potter
Basalt
5/8 x 1/2 in (1.5 x 1.2 cm)
Mark: "PALMER" "135"
Provenance: Dr. Harold L. Klawans, Chicago
1979.233

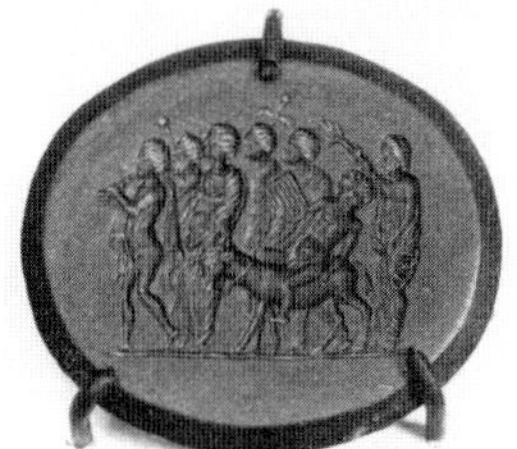

1049. Intaglio: *Bacchanalian Figures*, ca. 1780
Basalt
3/4 x 5/8 in (1.9 x 1.5 cm)
Mark: "Wedgwood & Bentley" "247"
Provenance: Dr. Harold L. Klawans, Chicago
1980.27

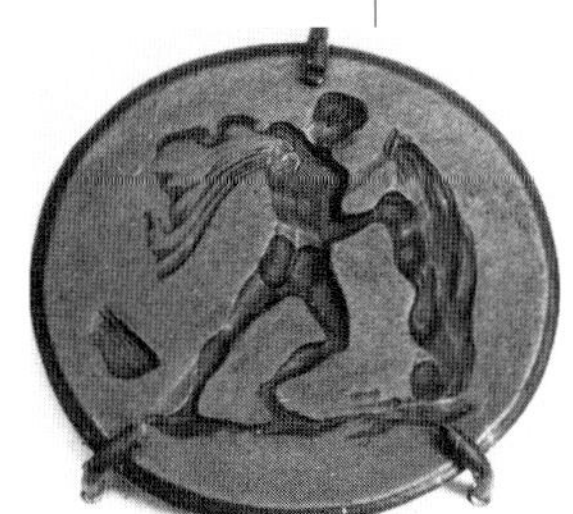

1050. Intaglio: *Theseus Raising a Stone*, ca. 1780
Basalt
13/16 x 11/16 in (2 x 1.7 cm)
Mark: "Wedgwood & Bentley" "94"
Provenance: Dr. Harold L. Klawans, Chicago
1980.21

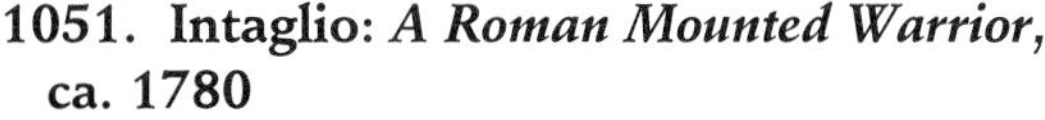

1051. Intaglio: *A Roman Mounted Warrior*, ca. 1780
Basalt
7/8 x 1 in (2.2 x 2.5 cm)
Mark: "Wedgwood & Bentley" "337"
Provenance: Dr. Harold L. Klawans, Chicago
1980.20

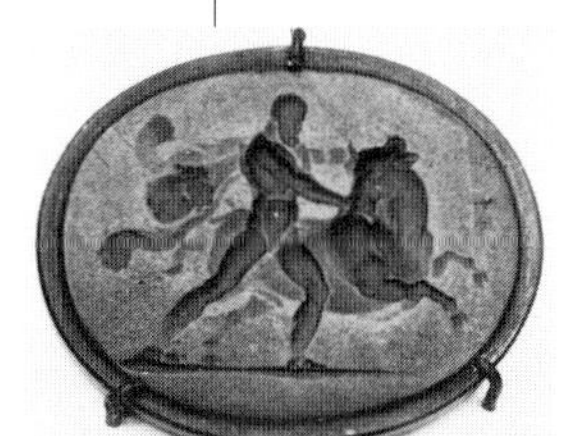

1052. Intaglio: *Hercules Killing the Cretan Bull*, ca. 1790
Basalt
3/16 x 1 in (3 x 2.5 cm)
Mark: "WEDGWOOD"
Provenance: Dr. Harold L. Klawans, Chicago
1980.53

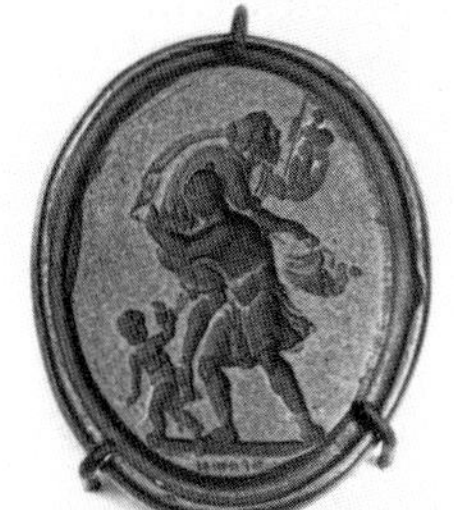

1053. Intaglio: *Aeneas Carrying Anchises*, ca. 1790
Basalt
1 x 7/8 in (2.5 x 2.2 cm)
Mark: "WEDGWOOD"; "BROWN" in reverse on front
Provenance: Dr. Harold L. Klawans, Chicago
1980.41

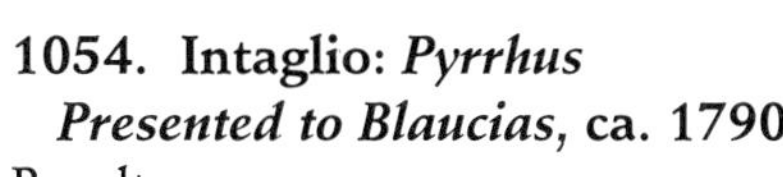

1054. Intaglio: *Pyrrhus Presented to Blaucias*, ca. 1790
Basalt
1 1/2 x 1 1/8 in (3.8 x 2.8 cm)
Mark: "WEDGWOOD"; "BROWN" in reverse on front
Provenance: Dr. Harold L. Klawans, Chicago
1980.51

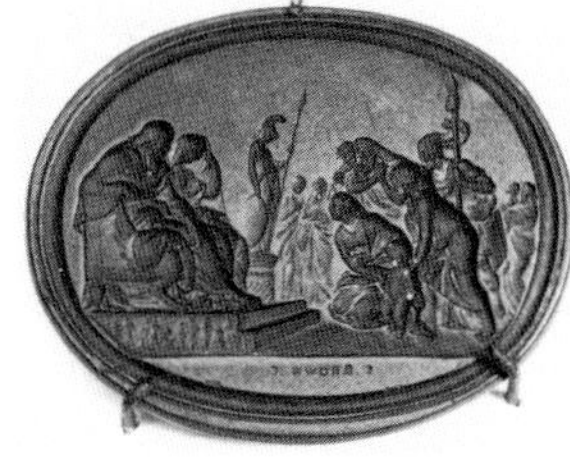

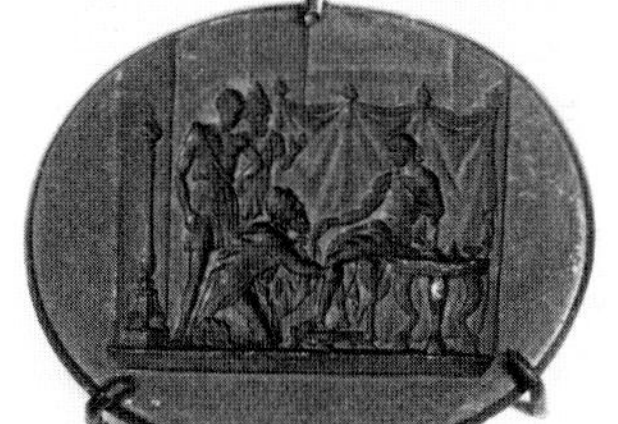

1055. Intaglio: *Priam Begging the Body of Hector from Achilles*, ca. 1790
Basalt
1 x 7/8 in (2.5 x 2.2 cm)
Mark: "WEDGWOOD" "308"
Provenance: Dr. Harold L. Klawans, Chicago
1980.34

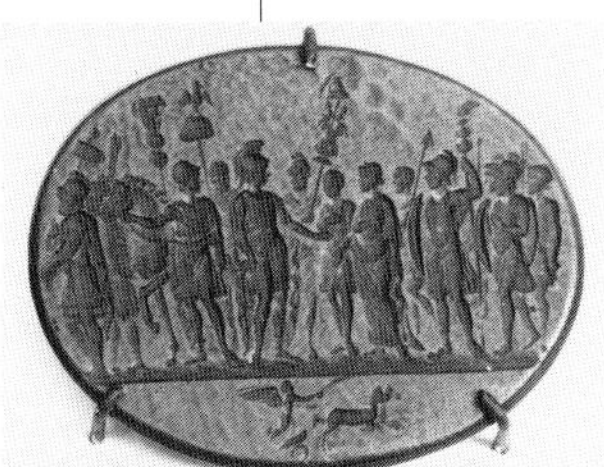

1056. Intaglio: *Roman Military Scene*, ca. 1790
Basalt
1 x 1 1/4 in (2.5 x 3.1 cm)
Mark: "WEDGWOOD"
Provenance: Dr. Harold L. Klawans, Chicago
1980.43

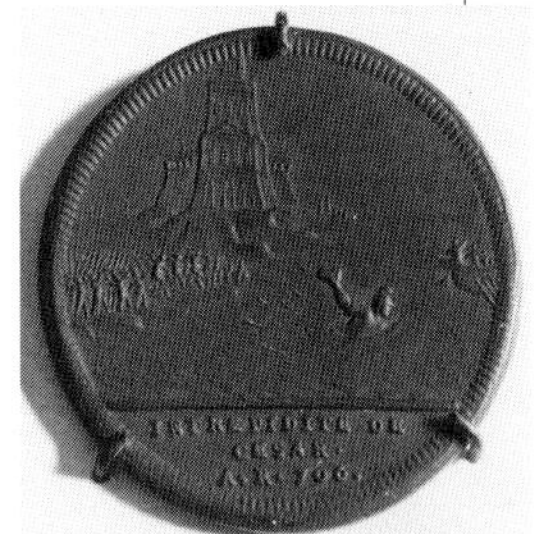

1057. Double-Sided Medallion: *Caesar and His Fortune* and *Intrepidity of Caesar*, ca. 1795
Basalt
1 1/16 in (2.7 cm)
Mark: "CESAT ET SA FORTUTE A.D. 706" "INTREPEDITE DE CESAR A.D. 706"
Provenance: Dr. Francis Jennings Vurpillat, South Bend, Ind.
1977.122.31

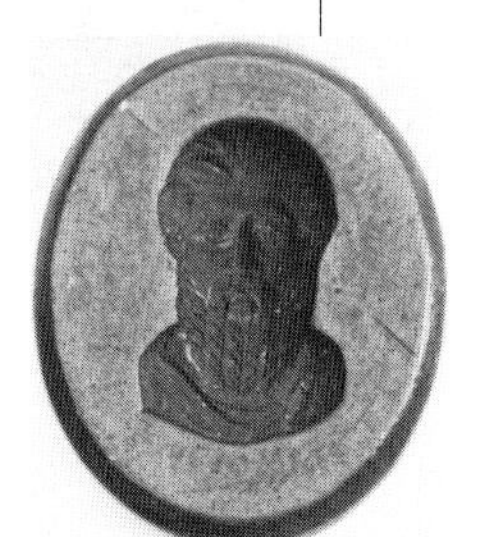

1058. Intaglio: *Classical Male Head*, ca. 1780
Basalt
5/8 x 1/2 in (1.5 x 1.2 cm)
Mark: "Wedgwood & Bentley"
Provenance: Dr. Harold L. Klawans, Chicago
1980.26

1059. Intaglio: *Mars*, ca. 1780
Basalt
11/16 x 1/2 in (1.7 x 1.2 cm)
Mark: "W & B" "246"
Provenance: Dr. Harold L. Klawans, Chicago
1980.17

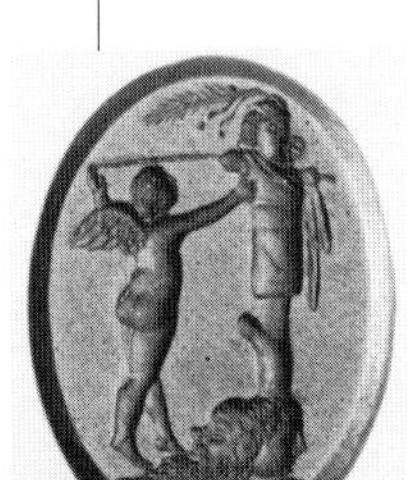

1060. Intaglio: *Cupid*, ca. 1780
Basalt
5/8 x 1/2 in (1.5 x 1.2 cm)
Mark: "Wedgwood & Bentley" "168"
Provenance: Dr. Harold L. Klawans, Chicago
1980.19

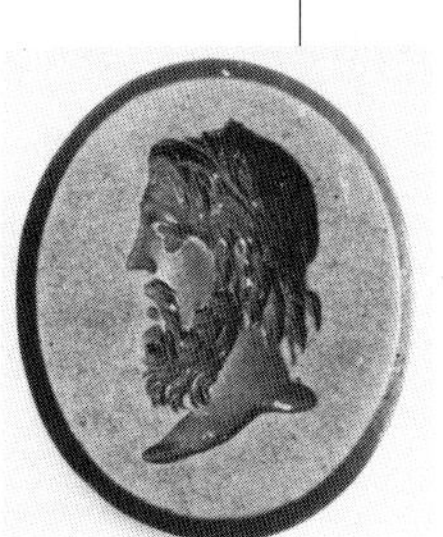

1061. Intaglio: *Theocritus, Poet*, ca. 1780
Basalt
5/8 x 1/2 in (1.5 x 1.2 cm)
Mark: "W & B" "234"
Provenance: Dr. Harold L. Klawans, Chicago
1980.29

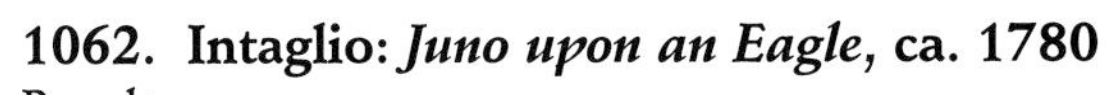

1062. Intaglio: *Juno upon an Eagle*, ca. 1780
Basalt
5/8 x 9/16 in (1.5 x 1.4 cm)
Mark: "Wedgwood & Bentley" "123"
Provenance: Dr. Harold L. Klawans, Chicago
1980.30

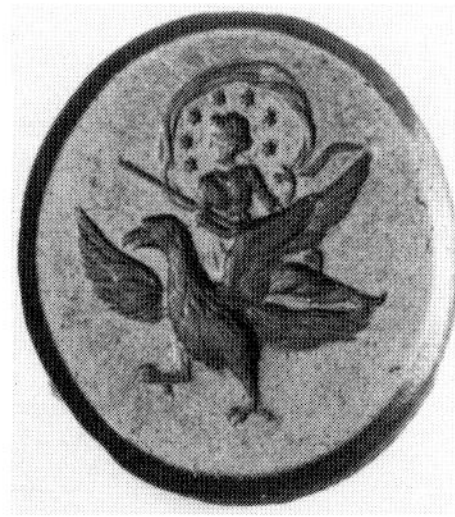

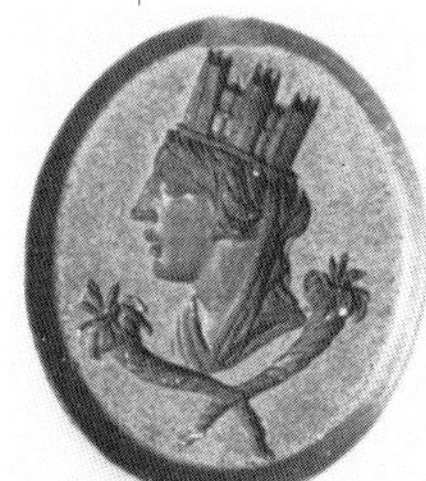

1063. Intaglio: *Cybele*, ca. 1780
Basalt
9/16 x 1/2 in (1.4 x 1.2 cm)
Mark: "W & B" "255"
Provenance: Dr. Harold L. Klawans, Chicago
1980.28

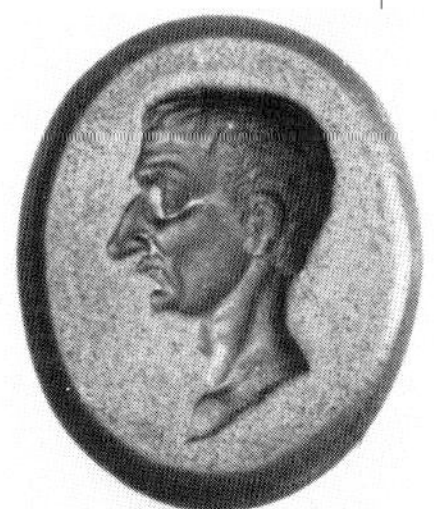

1064. Intaglio: *Livy*, ca. 1780
Basalt
5/8 x 1/2 in (1.5 x 1.2 cm)
Mark: "W & B" "189"
Provenance: Dr. Harold L. Klawans, Chicago
1980.16

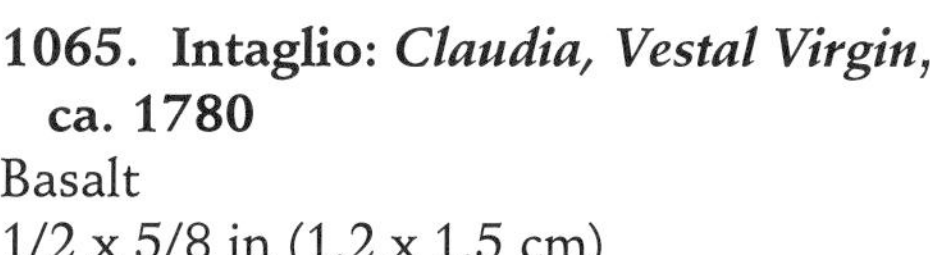

1065. Intaglio: *Claudia, Vestal Virgin*, ca. 1780
Basalt
1/2 x 5/8 in (1.2 x 1.5 cm)
Mark: "W & B" "176"
Provenance: Dr. Harold L. Klawans, Chicago
1980.15

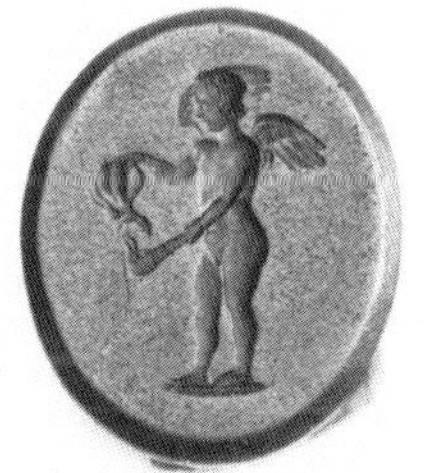

1066. Intaglio: *Cupid Inflaming the Mind*, ca. 1780
Basalt
1/2 x 7/16 in (1.2 x 1.1 cm)
Mark: "W & B" "88"
Provenance: Dr. Harold L. Klawans, Chicago
1980.18

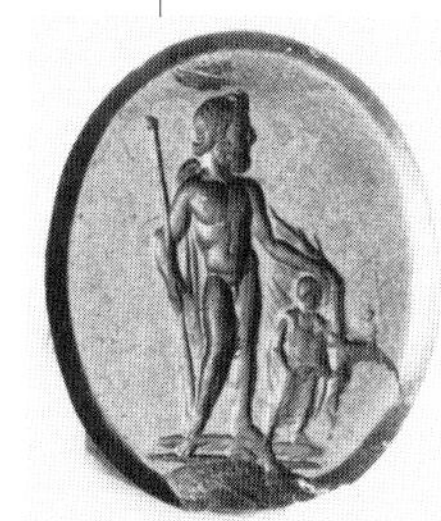

1067. Intaglio: *Jupiter Conservator*, ca. 1780
Basalt
5/8 x 1/2 in (1.5 x 1.2 cm)
Mark: "Wedgwood & Bentley" "139"
Provenance: Dr. Harold L. Klawans, Chicago
1980.12

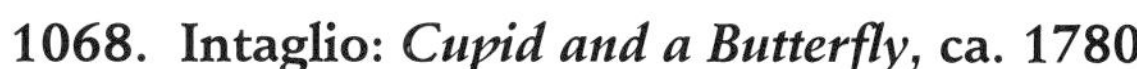

1068. Intaglio: *Cupid and a Butterfly*, ca. 1780
Basalt
9/16 x 1/2 in (1.4 x 1.2 cm)
Mark: "W & B" "351"
Provenance: Dr. Harold L. Klawans, Chicago
1980.24

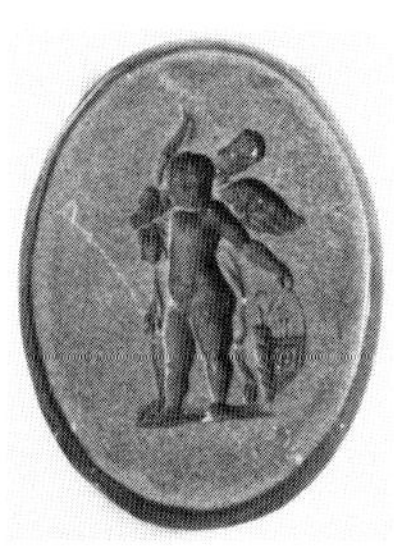

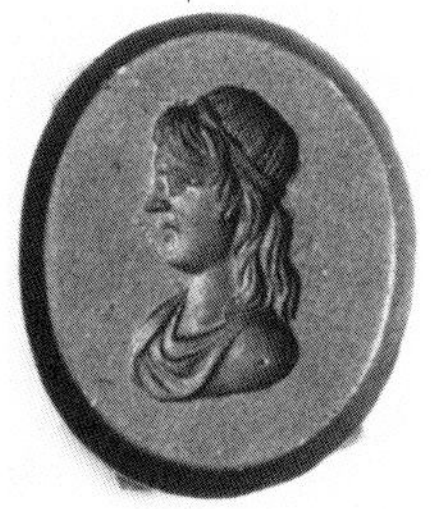

1069. Intaglio: *Lucius Apuleius*, ca. 1780
Basalt
1/2 x 7/16 in (1.2 x 1.1 cm)
Mark: "W & B" "231"
Provenance: Dr. Harold L. Klawans, Chicago
1980.13

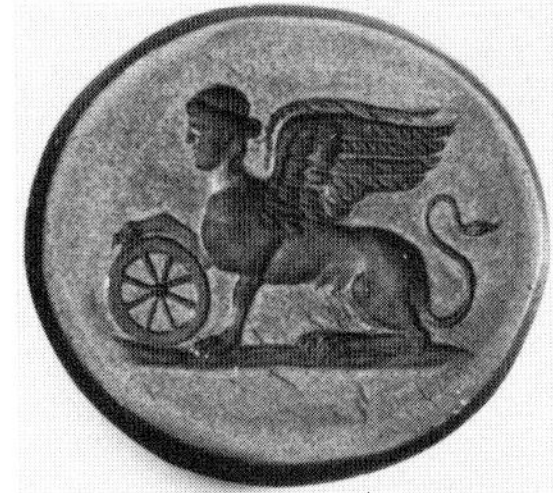

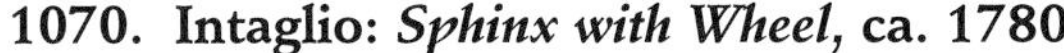

1070. Intaglio: *Sphinx with Wheel,* ca. 1780
Basalt
3/4 x 5/8 in (1.9 x 1.5 cm)
Mark: "Wedgwood & Bentley"
Provenance: Dr. Harold L. Klawans, Chicago
1980.25

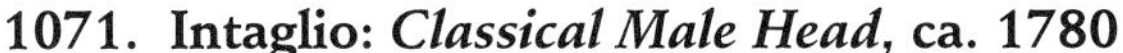

1071. Intaglio: *Classical Male Head,* ca. 1780
Basalt
5/8 x 1/2 in (1.5 x 1.2 cm)
Mark: "Wedgwood & Bentley"
Provenance: Dr. Harold L. Klawans, Chicago
1980.26

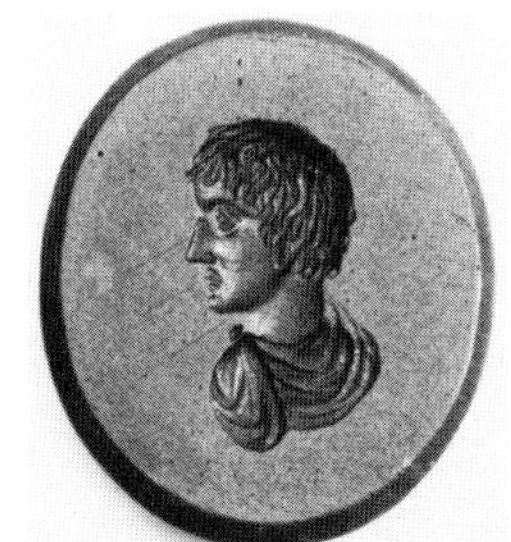

1072. Intaglio: *Alphabetic Cypher,* ca. 1780
Basalt
3/4 in (1.9 cm)
Mark: "Wedgwood & Bentley" in a circle
Provenance: Dr. Harold L. Klawans, Chicago
1980.23

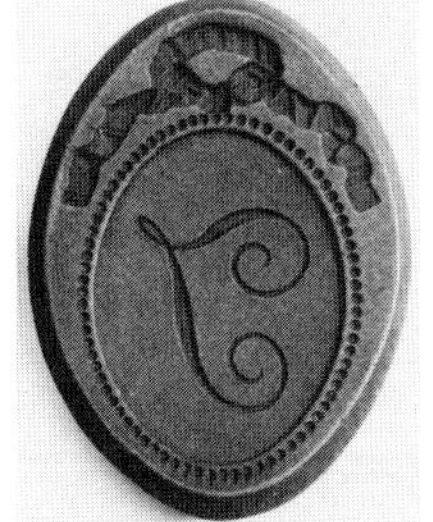

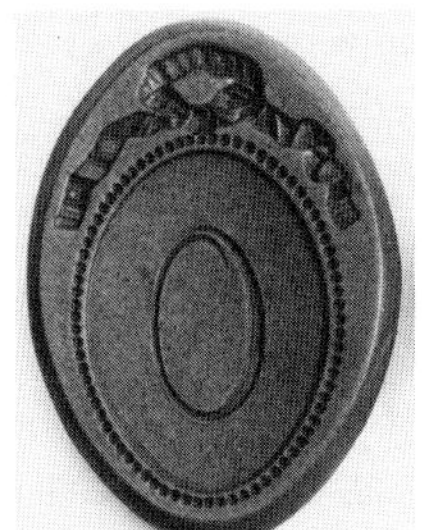

1073. Pair of Intaglios: *Alphabetic Cypher,* ca. 1790
Jasper, solid dark blue
1 x 3/4 in (2.5 x 1.9 cm)
Mark: "O" "L" as cypher on front
Provenance: Dr. Harold L. Klawans, Chicago
1979.229 a and b

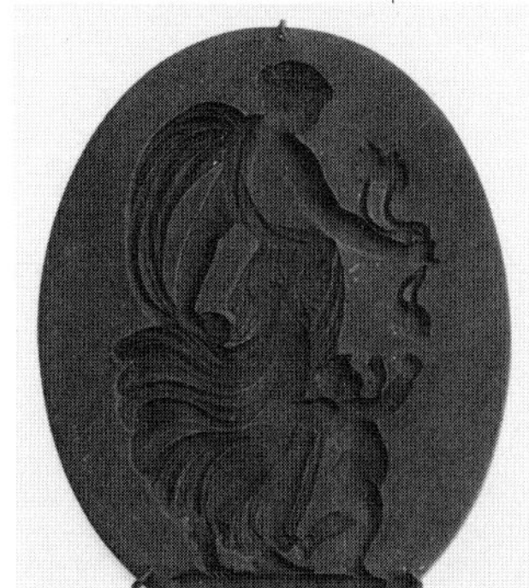

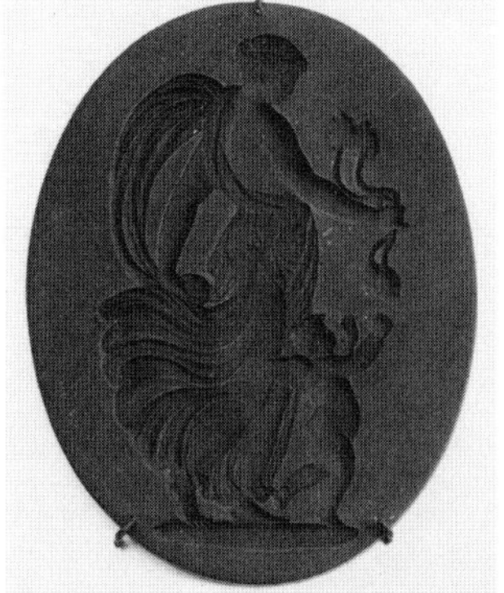

1074. Intaglio: *Venus and Cupid,* ca. 1790
Basalt
2 1/2 x 2 in (6.3 x 5 cm)
Mark: "WEDGWOOD"
Provenance: Dr. Harold L. Klawans, Chicago
1980.59

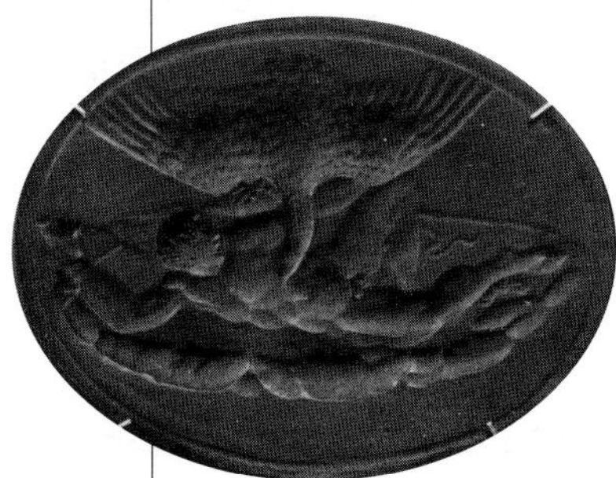

1075. Intaglio: *Prometheus and the Eagle,* ca. 1790
Basalt
2 1/2 x 3 3/8 in (8.5 x 6.3 cm)
Mark: "WEDGWOOD"
Provenance: Dr. Harold L. Klawans, Chicago
1980.62

Bibliography

Ackermann, Rudolph. *Repository of the Arts*. February 1809.

Adam, Robert, and James Adam. *The Works in Architecture*. 2 vols. London: 1773–79. A 3rd posthumous volume was published in 1822.

Andrews, Henry C. *The Botanist's Repository*. 10 vols. 1804.

Barker, David. *William Greatbatch: A Staffordshire Potter*. London: Jonathan Horne, 1991.

Barnard, Harry. *Chats on Wedgwood Ware*. London: T. Fisher Unwin, 1924.

Bartoli, Pietro Santi. *Admiranda Romanorum Antiquitatem*. Rome, 1693.

Bella, Stefano della. *Raccolta de vasi diversi . . . Paris*, ca. 1646.

Bimson, Mavis. "Some Recent Research on Coade Stone." *English Ceramic Circle Transactions* 12, pt. 3 (1986): 203–5.

Bindman, David, ed. *John Flaxman*. London: Thames and Hudson, 1979.

Born, Byron A. "John Paul Jones and the Wedgwood Medallions." *Wedgwood International Seminar Proceedings* 26 (1981): 195–203.

Buck, Nathaniel, and Samuel Buck. *Antiquities*. 8 vols. London: Robert Sayer, 1720-42.

Burman, Lionel A. *Joseph Mayer of Liverpool, 1803-1886*. Occasional Papers, n.s., 11. London: Society of Antiquaries of London, in Association with the National Museums and Galleries on Merseyside, 1988.

Buten, David. *Eighteenth-Century Wedgwood*. New York: Methuen, 1980.

_____. *Wedgwood and America: Wedgwood Bas-Relief Ware*. Monographs in Wedgwood Studies, nos. 1 and 2. Merion, Pa.: Buten Museum of Wedgwood, 1977.

Buten, David, and Patricia Pelehach. *Émile Lessore, 1805-1876: His Life and Work*. Monographs in Wedgwood Studies, no. 3. Merion, Pa.: Buten Museum of Wedgwood, 1979.

Cadbury, Paul S. *The Lunar Society of Birmingham*. London: University of London Press, 1966.

Caylus, Anne-Claude-Phillippe de Thubieres, Comte de. *Receuil d'antiquités egyptiennes, etrusques, grecques, et romaines*. 7 vols. Paris, 1752-67.

Chaldecott, John A. "Presidental Address: Josiah Wedgwood (1730-95), Scientist." *British Journal for the History of Science* 8 (1975): 1-16.

Chambers, William. *A Treatise on Civil Architecture*. London, 1759.

_____. *A Treatise on the Decorative Part of Civil Architecture*. 3rd ed. London: J. Smeeton, 1791.

Chellis, Mrs. Robert D. "Wedgwood and Bentley Source Books." *Wedgwood International Seminar Proceedings* 7 (1962): 60–64.

Church, A. H. *Josiah Wedgwood*. New York: Macmillan,1903.

Clifford, Timothy. "John Bacon and the Manufacturers." *Apollo* 75. (October 1985): 288-304.

_____. "Some English Ceramic Vases and Their Sources, Part 1." *English Ceramic Circle Transactions* 10, no. 3 (1978): 159–73.

Crook, J. Mordaunt. *The Greek Revival*. London: John Murray, 1972.

Dawson, Aileen. *Masterpieces of Wedgwood in the British Museum*. London: British Museum Publications, 1984.

Delhom, M. Mellanay. "James Tassie and Josiah Wedgwood: A Study in Parallels." *Wedgwood International Seminar Proceedings* 7 (1962): 111--20.

Denvir, Bernard. *Eighteenth-Century Art, Design, and Society, 1689-1789*. London: Longman Group, 1983.

Des Fontaines, J. K., with John Chaldecott and John Tindall. *Josiah Wedgwood: "The Arts and Sciences United."* Staffordshire: Josiah Wedgwood and Sons, 1978.

Drakard, David, and Paul Holdway. *Spode Printed Ware.* London: Longman Group, 1983.

Edwards, Diana. *Neale Pottery and Porcelain: Its Predecessors and Successors, 1763-1820.* London: Barrie and Jenkins, 1987.

Evans, Hilary. "Wedgwood, Windmills, and Water-power," *Wedgwood International Society Proceedings* 8 (1970): 243–51.

Flaxman, John. *The Iliad of Homer, engraved by T. Piroli from the Compositions of John Flaxman.* London: J Matthews, 1793.

Fothergill, Brian. *Sir William Hamilton, Envoy Extraordinary.* New York: Harcourt, Brace, and World, 1969.

Goodison, Nicholas. "Matthew Boulton's Geographical Clock." *Connoisseur* 166, no. 670 (December 1967): 213-21.

_____. *Ormolu: The Work of Matthew Boulton.* London: Phaidon Press, Ltd., 1974

Grose, Francis. *Antiquities of England and Wales.* 4 vols. London: S. Hooper, 1773-87.

Haggar, R. G., A. R. Mountford, and J. Thomas. *The Staffordshire Pottery Industry.* Rpt. Stafford: Staffordshire County Library, 1981.

Hamer, Frank, and Janet Hamer. *The Potter's Dictionary of Materials and Techniques.* London: A. and C. Black, 1986.

Hamilton, Sir William. *Collection of Engravings from Ancient Vases of Greek Workmanship.* 3 vols. Naples: Wilhelm Tischbein, 1791-95.

Hamilton, Sir William, and P. H. d'Hancarville. *Antiquités etrusques, grecques, et romaines.* 4 vols. Naples, 1766-77.

Haskell, Francis. *Past and Present in Art and Taste.* New Haven: Yale University Press, 1987.

Hawes, Lloyd E. "Longfellow, the Poet, and Sadler, the Tile Printer." *Wedgwood International Seminar Proceedings* 11 (1966): 149-59.

Honour, Hugh. *The Age of Neoclassicism: A Handlist to the Fourteenth Exhibition of the Council of Europe, the Royal Academy, and the Victoria and Albert Museum.* London and Harlow: Shenval Press, 1972.

Irwin, David. *John Flaxman, 1775-1826.* London: Studio Vista, 1979.

Johnson, Harwood A. "Books Belonging to Wedgwood and Bentley the 10th of Augt 1770," *Ars Ceramica* 7 (1990): 13-23.

_____. "Further Research: Books Belonging to Wedgwood and Bentley the 10th of Augt 1770," *Ars Ceramica* 8 (1991): 34.

Kelly, Alison. *Decorative Wedgwood in Architecture and Furniture.* London: Country Life, 1965.

_____. "Mrs. Coade's Stone." *English Ceramic Circle Transactions* 2, pt. 2 (1982): 102-8.

_____. *Mrs, Coade's Stone.* Worcester: Self-Publishing Assoc., 1990.

_____. *The Story of Wedgwood.* New York: Viking Press, 1962.

Le Antichità di Ercolano Esposte. 8 vols. Naples: Nella Regia Stamperia of Charles V, king of Naples, 1757-92.

Liddell, Donald M. "Counterfeit Flaxman Chessmen." *Antiques Magazine* 47, no. 5 (May 1945): 276–77.

Llewellyn, Briony. "Salesrooms, Early English Ceramics." *Connoisseur* 199, no. 802 (December 1978): 282.

Lockett, T. A., and P. A. Halfpenny, P. A., eds. *Creamware and Pearlware.* Stoke-on-Trent: City Museum and Art Gallery, 1986.

_____. *Stonewares and Stone Chinas of Northern England to 1851.* Stoke-on-Trent: City Museum and Art Gallery, 1982.

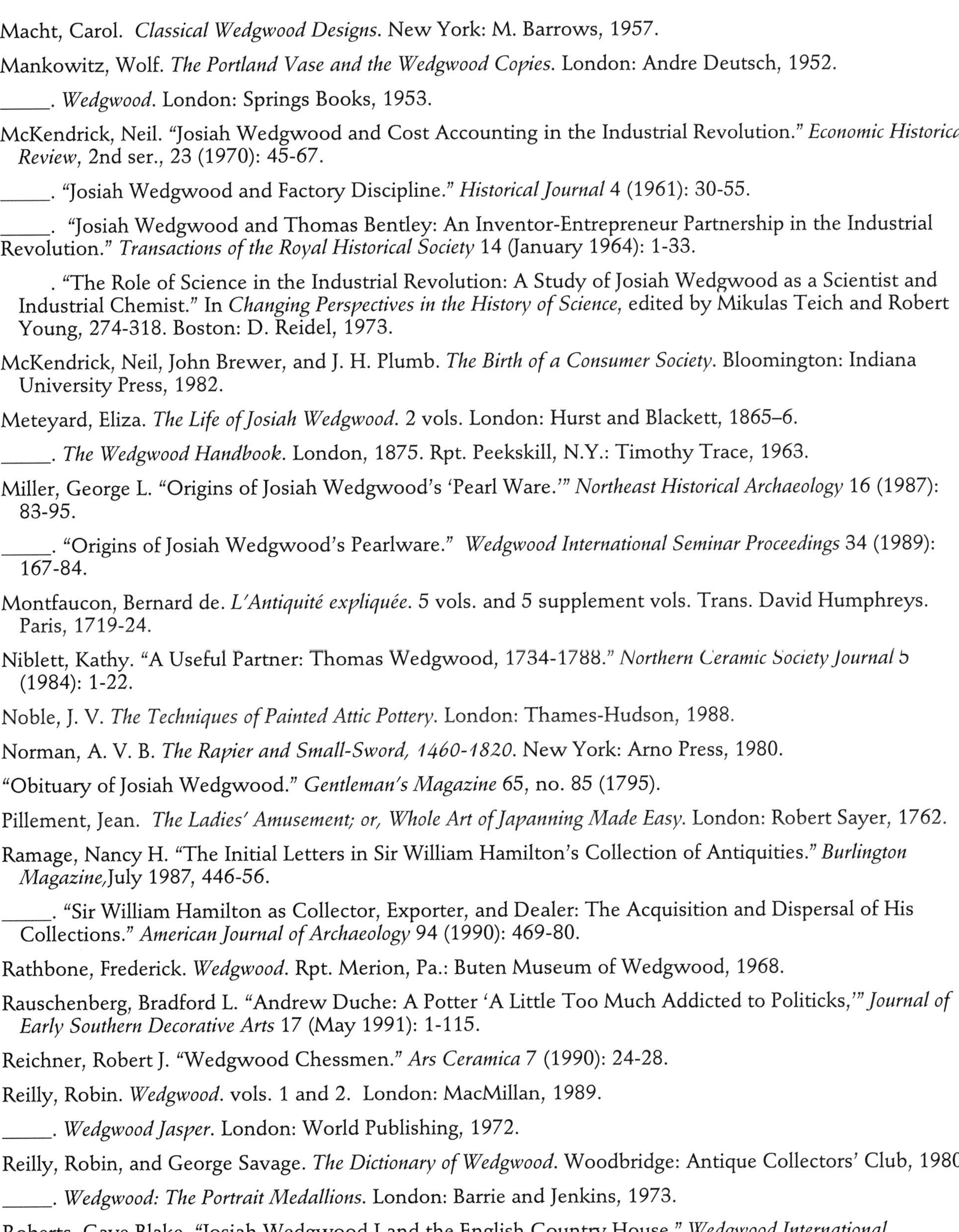

Macht, Carol. *Classical Wedgwood Designs.* New York: M. Barrows, 1957.

Mankowitz, Wolf. *The Portland Vase and the Wedgwood Copies.* London: Andre Deutsch, 1952.

_____. *Wedgwood.* London: Springs Books, 1953.

McKendrick, Neil. "Josiah Wedgwood and Cost Accounting in the Industrial Revolution." *Economic Historical Review,* 2nd ser., 23 (1970): 45-67.

_____. "Josiah Wedgwood and Factory Discipline." *Historical Journal* 4 (1961): 30-55.

_____. "Josiah Wedgwood and Thomas Bentley: An Inventor-Entrepreneur Partnership in the Industrial Revolution." *Transactions of the Royal Historical Society* 14 (January 1964): 1-33.

. "The Role of Science in the Industrial Revolution: A Study of Josiah Wedgwood as a Scientist and Industrial Chemist." In *Changing Perspectives in the History of Science,* edited by Mikulas Teich and Robert Young, 274-318. Boston: D. Reidel, 1973.

McKendrick, Neil, John Brewer, and J. H. Plumb. *The Birth of a Consumer Society.* Bloomington: Indiana University Press, 1982.

Meteyard, Eliza. *The Life of Josiah Wedgwood.* 2 vols. London: Hurst and Blackett, 1865–6.

_____. *The Wedgwood Handbook.* London, 1875. Rpt. Peekskill, N.Y.: Timothy Trace, 1963.

Miller, George L. "Origins of Josiah Wedgwood's 'Pearl Ware.'" *Northeast Historical Archaeology* 16 (1987): 83-95.

_____. "Origins of Josiah Wedgwood's Pearlware." *Wedgwood International Seminar Proceedings* 34 (1989): 167-84.

Montfaucon, Bernard de. *L'Antiquité expliquée.* 5 vols. and 5 supplement vols. Trans. David Humphreys. Paris, 1719-24.

Niblett, Kathy. "A Useful Partner: Thomas Wedgwood, 1734-1788." *Northern Ceramic Society Journal* 5 (1984): 1-22.

Noble, J. V. *The Techniques of Painted Attic Pottery.* London: Thames-Hudson, 1988.

Norman, A. V. B. *The Rapier and Small-Sword, 1460-1820.* New York: Arno Press, 1980.

"Obituary of Josiah Wedgwood." *Gentleman's Magazine* 65, no. 85 (1795).

Pillement, Jean. *The Ladies' Amusement; or, Whole Art of Japanning Made Easy.* London: Robert Sayer, 1762.

Ramage, Nancy H. "The Initial Letters in Sir William Hamilton's Collection of Antiquities." *Burlington Magazine,* July 1987, 446-56.

_____. "Sir William Hamilton as Collector, Exporter, and Dealer: The Acquisition and Dispersal of His Collections." *American Journal of Archaeology* 94 (1990): 469-80.

Rathbone, Frederick. *Wedgwood.* Rpt. Merion, Pa.: Buten Museum of Wedgwood, 1968.

Rauschenberg, Bradford L. "Andrew Duche: A Potter 'A Little Too Much Addicted to Politicks,'" *Journal of Early Southern Decorative Arts* 17 (May 1991): 1-115.

Reichner, Robert J. "Wedgwood Chessmen." *Ars Ceramica* 7 (1990): 24-28.

Reilly, Robin. *Wedgwood.* vols. 1 and 2. London: MacMillan, 1989.

_____. *Wedgwood Jasper.* London: World Publishing, 1972.

Reilly, Robin, and George Savage. *The Dictionary of Wedgwood.* Woodbridge: Antique Collectors' Club, 1980.

_____. *Wedgwood: The Portrait Medallions.* London: Barrie and Jenkins, 1973.

Roberts, Gaye Blake. "Josiah Wedgwood I and the English Country House." *Wedgwood International Seminar Proceedings* 27 (1982): 98-114.

Robinson, Eric. *An Exhibition to Commemorate the Bicentenary of the Lunar Society of Birmingham.* Birmingham, Eng.: Birmingham Museum and Art Gallery, 1966.

Shaw, Simeon. *History of the Staffordshire Potteries.* 1829. Rpt. New York: Praeger, 1970.

Shenker, Israel. "A Celebrated Roman Vase Has Become a Twentieth-Century Phoenix." *Smithsonian,* 20, no. 4, (July, 1989):53-63.

Spence, Reverend. *Mr. Polymetis; or, An Enquiry Concerning the Agreement between the Works of the Roman Poets and the Remains of the Antient Artists.* London: Prints for R. and J. Dodsley, 1755.

Stella, Jacques de. *Livres de vases aux Galeries de Louvre.* Paris, 1667.

Stillman, Damie. *English Neoclassical Architecture.* 2 vols. London: Zwemmer, 1988.

Stosch, Philipp, Baron von. *Pierres antiques gravées, sur lesquelles les graveurs ont mis leurs noms: Dessinées et gravées en cuivre sur les originaux ou d'aprés les empreintes, par Bernard Picart.* Amsterdam: Chez Bernard Picart, le Romain, 1724.

Stretton, Norman. "Some Sources for Designs on Wedgwood Transfer-Printed Creamware." *Magazine Antiques* 121 (June 1982): 1390-95.

Stuart, James, and Nicholas Revett. *The Antiquities of Athens.* 4 vols. London, 1762-1816.

Tassie, James. *A Descriptive Catalogue of a General Collection of Ancient and Modern Gems, Cameos, as Well as Intaglios.* 2 vols. R. E. Raspe, 1791.

Tattersall, Bruce. *Stubbs and Wedgwood.* London: Tate Gallery, 1974.

_____. *Wedgwood Portraits and the American Revolution.* Washington, D.C.: National Portrait Gallery, Smithsonian Institution, 1976.

Thomson, James. *The Four Seasons.* London, 1726–30.

Towner, Donald C. *English Cream-Coloured Earthenware.* London: Faber and Faber, 1978.

Toynbee, Mrs. Paget, ed. *Letters of Horace Walpole.* Oxford: Clarendon Press, 1903–25.

Valpy, Nancy, and Alison Kelly. "Advertisements for Artificial Stone in the *Daily Advertiser*" *English Ceramic Circle Transactions,* 12, pt. 3 (1986): 206-26.

Vien, Joseph Marie. *Suite de vases composée dans le gout de l'antique.* Paris, 1760.

Walker, Corlette R. *William Blake in the Art of His Time.* Santa Barbara: University Art Museum, University of California, 1976.

Watney, Bernard. "Some Liverpool Printed Tiles." *Burlington Magazine* 129, no. 1034 (May 1987): 316-21.

Weatherill, Lorna. *The Growth of the Pottery Industry in England, 1660-1815.* New York and London: Garland, 1986.

_____. *The Pottery Trade and North Staffordshire, 1660-1760.* Manchester: Manchester University Press, 1971.

Josiah Wedgwood. *Account of the Barberini, Now Portland Vase, with the Various Explications of Its Bas-Reliefs That Have Been Given by Different Authors.* 1790.

_____. *Catalogue of Cameos, Intaglios, Medals, Bas-reliefs, Busts, and Small Statues, with a general Account of Tablets, Vases, Escritoires, and Other Ornamental and Useful Articles . . .* 6th ed. Etruria, 1787. French translation, 1787.

_____. *Correspondence of Josiah Wedgwood, 1781-1795.* Edited by Katherine Eufemia Farrer. 1906. Rpt. Didsbury, Manchester: E. J. Morten, 1973.

_____. *Letters of Josiah Wedgwood, 1771-1780.* Edited by Katherine Eufemia Farrer. 2 vols. 1903. Rpt. Didsbury, Manchester: E. J. Morten, 1973.

_____. *The Selected Letters of Josiah Wedgwood.* Edited by Ann Finer and George Savage. New York: Born and Hawes, 1965.

Wedgwood, Josiah, and Thomas Bentley. *A Catalogue of Cameos, Intaglios, Medals and Bas-reliefs; with a general Account of Vases and Other Ornaments, after the Antique, made by Wedgwood and Bentley.* London, 1773. 60 pp.

_____. *A Catalogue of Cameos, Intaglios, Medals, Busts, Small Statues, and Bas-reliefs; with a General Account of Vases and Other Ornaments, after the Antique Made by Wedgwood and Bentley.* London, 1774. 2nd ed. French translation. 1774. 3rd ed. 1775 Reissue of the second edition with six additional pages and wood cut illustration of inkstand.; 4th ed. London, 1777. 4th ed. Dutch translation, Amsterdam, 1778; 5th ed. London, 1779; 5th ed. French translation, 1779; 5th ed. German translation, 1779.

_____. *A catalogue of different articles of Queen's ware, which may be either plain, gilt, or embellished with enamel paintings, manufactured by Josiah Wedgwood, potter to her Majesty.* 1774.

Wedgwood, Josiah and Sons. *1817 Queen's Ware Catalogue.* Three editions between ca. 1817 and 1849.

_____. *The Wedgwoods and The Darwins: An Exhibition to Mark the Centenary of the Death of Charles Darwin, 1809-1882.* Staffordshire, 1982.

Weese-Wehen, Joy De. "Baroque Bronzes Intrigue West Coast Collectors." *Antique Monthly* 10, no. 6 (June 1977): 5C.

Whitehouse, David B., ed. *Journal of Glass Studies* 32. Corning, N. Y.: Corning Museum of Glass, 1990.

Whiter, Leonard. *Spode.* New York: Praeger, 1970.

Williamson, G. C. *The Imperial Russian Dinner Service.* London: George Bell and Sons, 1909.

Williams-Wood, Cyril. *English Transfer-Printed Pottery and Porcelain.* London: Faber and Faber, 1981.

Wills, Geoffrey. *English Pottery and Porcelain.* New York: Doubleday, 1969.

Young, Arthur. *Six Month's Tour through the North of England.* 4 vols. London: W. Strahan, 1770–71.

Index

C

I

J

V

W